Kutuzov

Kutuzov

ALEXANDER
MIKABERIDZE

*A Life in War
and Peace*

OXFORD
UNIVERSITY PRESS

OXFORD
UNIVERSITY PRESS

Oxford University Press is a department of the University of Oxford. It furthers
the University's objective of excellence in research, scholarship, and education
by publishing worldwide. Oxford is a registered trade mark of Oxford University
Press in the UK and certain other countries.

Published in the United States of America by Oxford University Press
198 Madison Avenue, New York, NY 10016, United States of America.

Library of Congress Cataloging-in-Publication Data
Names: Mikaberidze, Alexander, author.
Title: Kutuzov : a life in war and peace / Alexander Mikaberidze.
Description: New York, NY : Oxford University Press, 2022. |
Includes bibliographical references and index. |
Identifiers: LCCN 2022003428 (print) | LCCN 2022003429 (ebook) |
ISBN 9780197546734 (hardback) | ISBN 9780197546741 |
ISBN 9780197546758 (epub) | ISBN 9780197546765
Subjects: LCSH: Kutuzov, Mikhail Illarionovich, svetleĭshiĭ kniaz'
Smolenskiĭ, 1745–1813. | Generals—Russia—Biography. |
Napoleonic Wars, 1800–1815—Campaigns—Russia.
Classification: LCC DK169.K8 M44 2022 (print) |
LCC DK169.K8 (ebook) |
DDC 355.3/310947—dc23/eng/20220228
LC record available at https://lccn.loc.gov/2022003428
LC ebook record available at https://lccn.loc.gov/2022003429

DOI: 10.1093/oso/9780197546734.001.0001

9 8 7 6 5 4 3 2 1

Printed by Integrated Books International, United States of America

For
Frederick C. Schneid
and
Kenneth G. Johnson

CONTENTS

LIST OF MAPS

ACKNOWLEDGMENTS

THIS BOOK WOULD NOT have been possible without the support, advice, and assistance of an extraordinarily generous group of people and institutions.

For institutional support I am indebted to the staff of the Boris Nikolayevich Yeltsin Presidential Library, the Institute of Russian Literature (Pushkinskii Dom) of the Russian Academy of Sciences, the Russian State Library, the National Digital Library of the Ministry of Culture of the Russian Federation, the Nekrasov Central Library of Moscow, and the Vernadsky National Library of Ukraine. Special thanks go to the staff of the Russian State Military Historical Archive and Lithuanian State Historical Archives for patiently accommodating my requests for remote research when the pandemic interrupted my travel plans. I have been privileged to hold the Ruth Herring Noel Endowed Chair at Louisiana State University–Shreveport and rely on support from the Louisiana Board of Regents Endowed Professor/Chair Program.

Many people read drafts of this book at various stages in its writing. Brian Smith was the first to examine the manuscript and I will be forever grateful to him for the many lovely discussions of Kutuzov's life. Michael V. Leggiere, John H. Gill, and Frederick C. Schneid kindly took time from their hectic research schedules to help me with mine, encouraging me when I felt despondent and sharing valuable advice on writing and interpretation. Alexander Martin, Lee Eysturlid, Jonathan North, Jonathan Abel, Natalia Griffon de Pleineville, Mark Gerges, Emir Yener, Cengiz Fedakar, Kenneth Johnson, Ernest Blakeney, and Braeden Harris have reviewed parts of the manuscript, provided ample feedback, and saved me from misinterpretations and embarrassing gaffes. Eugene Miakinkov kindly commented on the chapters exploring Kutuzov's place and role in the Russian Military Enlightenment. I am grateful to Lidia Ivchenko, the doyen of Kutuzovian studies in Russia, for offering feedback and research leads. Zurab Sulaberidze, my compatriot and an astute scholar of late eighteenth-century Russian foreign policy, shared his knowledge and scholarship with me. My heartfelt thanks go also to Dimitri Gorchkoff for his assistance with the documents related to the French occupation of Moscow.

I want to acknowledge Professor Donald D. Horward, who is the main reason I have become a historian. A friend, a mentor, a father figure, and a role model for me, he passed away the day I finished writing this manuscript. This will be the first book I have written that I won't be able to share with him. Still, I know that this book owes much to my conversations with him and to his loving support over the years.

This book would not have been possible without the unwavering support of the board members of the Noel Foundation: Shelby Smith, Delton Smith, the late Gilbert Shanley, Merritt B. Chastain Jr., Steven Walker, Stacy Williams, Richard Bremer, Richard D. Lamb, Claire Adkins Sevier, George Patton Fritze, and Oliver G. Jenkins. I have been also very fortunate to have exemplary colleagues—Cheryl White, Helen Wise, Gary Joiner, and Elisabeth Liebert—who have patiently borne one too many Napoleonic conversations with me.

Away from the halls of academia, Dmitry and Svitlana Ostanin and Mikhail and Nataly Khoretonenko bolstered my morale with ample libations and discussions of Russian history. I am grateful to Martha Lawler, Robert and Ann Leitz, Janie Richardson, Jerard R. Martin, and Sara Herrington for their support and encouragement.

Writing well is a skill not easily acquired, especially when dealing with a foreign language. But I was very fortunate to have an outstanding team at Oxford University Press. I owe a great debt of gratitude to my editor, Timothy Bent, whose meticulous and intelligent editing clarified my prose and helped me grow as a writer. Zara Cannon-Mohammed, Amy Whitmer, and the entire production team are the epitome of professionalism. Thanks also to my agent, Dan Green, who supported the idea of a military biography and helped the book get off the ground. It was a joy to collaborate with Richard Britton on the maps.

My deepest appreciation is reserved for my family. Writing a book is a solitary experience, and I have spent many an evening sitting at my computer and begging words to arrange themselves on a page. My wife and children stoically endured my absence, and their love, patience, and understanding made this book possible.

This book is dedicated to my dear friends and colleagues, Frederick C. Schneid and Kenneth G. Johnson, who possess all of Kutuzov's virtues and none of his vices.

Alexander Mikaberidze
Shreveport, Louisiana
April 28, 2022

RUSSIANS HAVE TRADITIONALLY BEEN given a first name and their father's name as patronymic; thus, Mikhail Illarionovich refers to Mikhail the son of Illarion. To make it easier for the reader, I omitted patronymic names and used Anglicized versions of names if they had been already established in the English-language historiography (i.e., Peter instead of Petr, Paul for Pavel, Catherine for Ekaterina); I do, however, use Nikolai and Mikhail, rather than Nicholas and Michael. Kutuzov's last name has been spelled in a myriad of different ways—Kutusow, Kutusoff, Koutousoff, Koutosoff, Koutouzow, Kutusov—but I chose Kutuzov since it the version widely used today.

Until 1917, Russia continued to employ the Julian Old Style calendar that was progressively falling behind the Gregorian New Style calendar used in the West; in the eighteenth century, it was eleven days behind, and in the nineteenth, twelve days. In the main text, I use the Gregorian calendar for all dates, but in references, both Old and New Style dates are shown.

Russia's main currency was the ruble, but estimating the income of officials remains complicated by diverse factors. It varied tremendously. One advertisement in 1800 offered an unmarried clerk an annual salary of 150 rubles plus accommodation (clothing and food). A decade later it cost almost 500 rubles a year to be a member of the third merchant guild, which put it beyond the means of almost all townspeople. Feeding a family of four would have cost about 250–750 rubles a year, and if we account for costs of rent and firewood, a small family required upward of 800 rubles per year to lead a decent life in a town. In the military, a soldier's annual pay was about 10 rubles, while a junior officer's, on average, was twenty-five to thirty times higher. During the Napoleonic Wars, majors earned about 500–600 rubles a year, lieutenant colonels 700–800, and colonels 1,000–1,200; general officers' pay was, of course, higher, 2,000–2,500 rubles for a major general and some

8,000–9,000 rubles for a field marshal. Officers holding a military command received an additional allowance: a regimental commander received 3,000 rubles per year, and a corps commander 10,000 rubles.

Throughout the book I variously refer to the Russian ruler as the czar, emperor, autocrat, and sovereign. The ruler's children held the titles of grand prince (*velikii knyaz*) and grand princess (*velikaya knyazhnya*), which are traditionally translated as grand duke and grand duchess.

The Russian sovereigns had a diverse set of orders and decorations with which to acknowledge and reward their loyal officials and military leaders. The highest of them was the Order of Apostle St. Andrew the First Called, established in 1698. Next in hierarchy came the Order of St. Alexander of Neva (1725), the Order of St. Vladimir (1782, four grades), the Order of St. Anna (created as a dynastic order in 1735 but declared an imperial order in 1797, four grades), and finally the Order of St. John of Jerusalem (the Maltese Cross), which was awarded only during the reign of Emperor Paul. As an exclusively military award, the Order of St. George (1769) was treated differently than other decorations. The fourth and third grades recognized military valor and were bestowed on junior officers. The higher grades, however, were reserved for senior officer corps only; as a rule, the second grade was granted to a commanding officer for a victorious combat, while the first grade, the rarest of the awards, recognized a triumph in a campaign. Thus, while there were thousands of recipients of the two lowest grades, only 125 earned the second grade and just 25 garnered the first grade during the entire Russian imperial era. Only four individuals ever earned the complete set of all four grades: Kutuzov, Mikhail Barclay de Tolly, Ivan Paskevich, and Ivan Diebitsch.

During the imperial era, Russian military ranks were similar to those in other European powers but were regulated by the Table of Ranks, a hierarchy of fourteen categories of positions and ranks that Peter the Great adopted as the foundation for a system of promotion based on personal ability and performance rather than on birth and genealogy. In addition to regular military ranks, the Russian army utilized administrative and staff ranks, such as adjutant general and flügel adjutant.

Russian Military Ranks

1st Grade	General Field Marshal
2nd Grade	Général-en-chef (1730–1796)
	General of the Infantry (1796–1917) General of the Cavalry General of the Artillery (1796–1917, replaced General Feldzeugmeister) Engineer-General General Provisionsmeister Quartermaster General

3rd Grade	General-Poruchik (1741–1796, though retained in artillery)
	Lieutenant General (1796–1917)
4th Grade	Major General
5th Grade	Brigadier (1722–1798)
6th Grade	Colonel
7th Grade	Lieutenant Colonel
8th Grade	Premier/First Major Second Major Major
9th Grade	Captain; Rittmeister (rotmistr) in cavalry; Captain Lieutenant in artillery
10th Grade	Staff Captain; Staff-Rittmeister
11th Grade	Lieutenant
12th Grade	Sub-lieutenant

A NY RUSSIAN WOULD IMMEDIATELY recognize him by his patronym alone. He was the general who led the victory over Napoleon's Grande Armée during the Patriotic War of 1812 and helped restore Russia's pride. More than its pride, its very sense of national purpose and identity. The triumph over Napoleonic France raised Russia's prestige to unprecedented heights, helping shape both its destiny and that of world history, and his role in it all, at least from the Russian perspective, is unquestioned. More than a national hero, he became a legend, achieving a stature few military leaders, in Russia or elsewhere, in any era, could rival.

For half a century Mikhail Illarionovich Golenischev-Kutuzov, or simply Kutuzov, as he is widely known, served in almost every major conflict in which Russia and its empresses and emperors engaged. He was a man of contrasts, inspiring and exasperating, of considerable personal charm and keen intellect, but calculating and artful; a loving father of five daughters who relished life with great enthusiasm and a strong sense of fun, but whom contemporaries castigated as a "one-eyed old satyr" and an inveterate womanizer. His mentality was cosmopolitan yet he was an unabashed proponent of the Russian imperialism who could not fully express with what "pleasure and gratitude" he received the news of the partitioning of the Polish-Lithuanian Commonwealth in 1793. He also handsomely profited from it, gaining vast tracts of lands in western Ukraine; it is not surprising, therefore, that with the outbreak of the Russo-Ukranian War in 2014, Kutuzov came to personify the Russian colonialism, leading to some of his monuments being dismantled in Ukraine. As a commander he was sometimes accused, particularly late in his military career, of being too cautious, even cowardly, yet over his lifetime he displayed great personal courage on the battlefield, where he was seriously wounded twice and not expected to survive. The scars on his face, along with sixteen medals, including the complete set of the Order of Saint George for gallantry and military prowess—the first ever to be garnered by an individual—testified to his heroism and daring. Yet he was equally a courtier, cunning and compliant, full of obsequious flattery and deference to those above his station. To many of his contemporaries, he was the embodiment of fading standards, a relic of a bygone era. In death, he was transformed from a flawed figure into a national monument.

Long celebrated in Russia, particularly during the Soviet era, when he was lionized, Kutuzov's life and career remain overlooked in the West, in part because he has not been well served by his biographers. Of the handful of English, French, or German biographies that exist, all show their age or lack scholarly rigor; most are translations of Soviet publications or entirely derived from them.[1] For example, Kutuzov's standard English biography—Roger Parkinson's *The Fox of the North*—is nearly fifty years old and suffers from shortcomings, including a good number of factual mistakes and uncritical acceptance of Soviet embellishments.[2] Though more even-handed, the most recent French biography, published in 1990, has become a bibliographic curiosity.[3] Western narratives of the Napoleonic Wars usually mention only Kutuzov's involvement in the battles at Austerlitz in 1805 and Borodino in 1812; both were major engagements, but they do not reflect the full extent of his accomplishments and importance. This is largely because of critical commentaries found in letters and memoirs of those who felt he had missed opportunities to defeat Napoleon in battle. Writing in October 1812, Sir Robert Wilson, the British commissioner to the Russian army, lamented that "Kutuzov affords a memorable instance of incapacity in a chief, of an absence of any quality that ought to distinguish a commander."[4] Kutuzov has received a more balanced, albeit cursory, treatment in recent studies of Russia during the Napoleonic Wars, most notably by British historian Dominic Lieven, who calls him a "charismatic leader who knew how to win his men's confidence and affection," a "sly and far-sighted politician and negotiator," and "a skillful, courageous, and experienced soldier." Lieven captures Kutuzov's contradictions when he adds (somewhat unjustly) that he was also a "lazy and inefficient administrator," with limitations as a tactician but mastery of "public relations."[5]

In my own publications, from a trilogy on Napoleon's invasion of Russia in 1812 to a recent book on the global nature of the Napoleonic Wars, I reconsidered the contributions of all the major Russian commanders, including Barclay de Tolly and Peter Bagration, colorful and significant figures. Yet Kutuzov was the one who stood out, if only because he lay at the heart of so much triumph and controversy. Curiosity motivates most historians. Years ago, looking at the magnificent bronze statue of Kutuzov in front of the Cathedral of Our Lady of Kazan in St. Petersburg, a monument to the Russian triumph over Napoleon, I felt the challenge of seeking what lay beneath that degree of adulation. More recently, I found myself no less curious about a figure both so exalted and so dismissed. The recent bicentennial celebration of the Napoleonic era produced a wave of new publications on the French, British, Prussian, Austrian, and Spanish political and military leaders. So many have been the subject of new works—Emperor Napoleon, Field Marshal Gebhard Leberecht von Blücher, Gerhard von Scharnhorst, and the Duke of Wellington, as well as French marshals Louis-Alexandre Berthier, Joachim Murat, and Auguste Viesse de Marmont, and even the "unfortunate" Austrian general Karl Mack von Leiberich—that enrich our understanding of their lives and contributions.[6] On the other hand, Russian figures (aside from Czar Alexander) are entirely overlooked, even though they played a crucial role in defeating Napoleon and shaping Europe's destiny.[7] Kutuzov's life provides a unique opportunity to reflect on and perhaps even rectify this.

What little the Western public knows about Kutuzov mainly is due to Tolstoy's *War and Peace*. Among its vast catalog of wisdom about the human condition, the novel reflects a vision of war that is anything but triumphant or monumental. War is, instead, chaotic, impenetrable, and unmanageable, minimizing the relevance of even the greatest military leaders in the face of forces over which they have no control. Tolstoy's portrait of Kutuzov—pensive and even existential, overweight, and morose—undermines credence in the science of war. In a famous scene, Kutuzov falls asleep in front of the allied commander at the council of war on the eve of Austerlitz; at Borodino, the novel's climax, Kutuzov indulges in eating a roasted chicken while carnage unfolds in front of him. Describing a meeting between Prince Andrei Bolkonskii and Kutuzov, Tolstoy writes that the more Prince Andrei "realized the absence of all personal motive in that old man—in whom there seemed to remain only the habit of passions, and in place of an intellect (grouping events and drawing conclusions) only the capacity calmly to contemplate the course of events—the more reassured he was that everything would be as it should." It is clear to Prince Andrei that Kutuzov "will not devise or undertake anything," but that he "will hear everything, remember everything, and put everything in its place." In Tolstoy's telling, Kutuzov recognizes that there are forces in the universe that are "stronger and more important than his own will."[8]

In passages like these, Tolstoy offers a great-man view of history, though a portrait radically different from that of Napoleon, a rational practitioner of war, a man who seeks to understand and control events. Kutuzov, by contrast, has a clear vision of the true nature of warfare, the impenetrable fog of it, and therefore suppresses his own will, eschews decision-making on the battlefield, and assumes the stance of a passive observer.[9]

The Tolstoyean view of Kutuzov, fascinating and haunting as it is, cast a shadow that endures to the present day. Many now remember Kutuzov mainly for napping on the eve of Austerlitz and little else. Few are aware of his diplomatic successes, his campaigns against the Ottomans, or his contributions to the Russian Military Enlightenment. It is time to lift him out of Tolstoy's novel—endlessly rich a universe though it is—and place him in the world he helped to shape.

If Western historical literature has dismissed Kutuzov, the reverse is true of the Russian publications. There Kutuzov retains his stature. This mythologizing started early. On the whole, his Russian contemporaries were critical of Kutuzov during most of his long career, but by the time of his death in the spring of 1813 there had been a change. He was not only held in high regard in Russian society at large but eulogized as *Спаситель Отечества*, "the Savior of the Nation," and buried in the imposing Cathedral of Our Lady of Kazan, the central memorial to the Russian triumph over Napoleon. The exaltation obscured less attractive traits of the man who rarely spoke his mind openly and was notorious for double-dealing. The mythmaking reached new heights starting in the mid-twentieth century, when the Soviet regime deliberately crafted an image of his greatness for the purposes of state consolidation amid a devastating war. Joseph Stalin's insistence that Kutuzov was the brilliant strategist who had routed Napoleon with a brilliantly exe- cuted master plan—ostensibly what Stalin himself did to the invading Nazi armies during World War II—was instrumental in the amplification of the Kutuzovian legend; it was no accident that during the Great Patriotic War, as World War II is known in Russia, the Order of Kutuzov was introduced as one of the highest military awards, recognizing the military prowess of a new generation of Soviet military commanders. Kutuzov was effectively enlisted into the Soviet government's propaganda campaign, and this, in turn, deter- mined the direction of Russian scholarship for decades to come.

The collapse of the Soviet Union and the turbulent decade that followed it left a deep scar on the Russian national psyche. Vladimir Putin's narrative of the era of national decline and humiliation set the stage for his mission to re- store Russia's greatness and strength. In forging a new national identity, the Russian government continues to employ history to mediate the complex re- lations between the state and the people. In this process, the Napoleonic-era events and personalities still play an important role, as showcased by the bi- centennial celebrations in 2012. Kutuzov holds a special place in the pantheon of Russian heroes. A survey conducted during the bicentennial celebrations in 2012 showed that almost two-thirds of people credited Kutuzov with saving Russia from the Napoleonic threat. In fact, in the Russian public's imagin- ation, he has eclipsed almost all his contemporaries. In 2000, a poll showed that the majority of the Russians considered Kutuzov as "the greatest figure of the 19th century," ahead of Pushkin, Tchaikovskii, Dmitry Mendeleyev, even Tolstoy.[10] In more recent surveys (2016–2021), Russian citizens de- pendably voted Kutuzov among the top three most distinguished Russian commanders (after Georgi Zhukov, the Soviet commander during World War II, and Alexander Suvorov, the last generalissimo of the Russian Empire) and, at number fifteen, in the top twenty of the world's most distinguished historical figures, slightly behind Napoleon (number fourteen) but ahead of Isaac Newton (number nineteen) and Mikhail Gorbachev (number twenty). Remarkably, some political observers even contend that in confronting the West, Putin has adopted Kutuzov's grand strategy of avoiding decisive confrontation with a stronger opponent and exhausting it through attrition and asymmetrical engagement.[11]

This book undertakes a thorough reassessment of Kutuzov, who deserves better than either disparaging dismissal or hero worship. I am determined not merely to offer a clear-eyed account of the life of this singular individual but also to show that his story embodies the saga of Russian military history and imperial endeavors at the onset of the modern era. This work thus intertwines three core components—an honest portrait of Kutuzov's life and career; a survey of those aspects of Russian history in which he was so central, including relations with Poland and the Ottoman Empire; and, finally, an attempt to understand how he was perceived, both by his contemporaries and by later generations. I hope the last will show how powerful the process of mythmaking can be, and how it can supplant historical truth.

Ultimately, this is a life, and like so many who have attempted to write a biography, I have tried to follow James Boswell's advice. The best biographies, he writes in his *Life of Samuel Johnson*, enable the reader to accompany the subject, "as it were to see him live, and to 'live o'er each scene' with him, as he actually advanced through the several stages of his life." Kutuzov left behind a considerable body of public and private correspondence, military orders, and other documents. I consulted the voluminous anthologies of his papers and was privileged to gain access to thousands of pages of documents from the Lithuanian, Russian, and French archives. These allowed me to reexamine Kutuzov's career in detail, based on original sources. But even when there is a wealth of information, there are always the pitfalls of interpretation. I have tried to be judicious, making allowance for Kutuzov's motives, while trying to express what he "might" have felt, thought, or done. A close examination of numerous diaries, letters, and memoirs of his contemporaries helped me glean insights into both his character and how it was interpreted even during the course of his life. In short, I have sought to look at him from as many perspectives as possible—those of friends and foes alike—adhering as closely as possible to the German historian Leopold von Ranke's dictum *wie es eigentlich gewesen*, "to show what actually happened."[12]

PART I

CHAPTER I | A Boy from Pskov Province, 1747–1762

O N SATURDAY, SEPTEMBER 16 (September 5 in the Julian calendar), 1747, a child was born into a Russian noble family, the Golenischev-Kutuzovs. He was named Mikhail after the holy day of the Commemoration of the Miracle of Archangel Michael at Colossae, which Orthodox Christians celebrate the following day. The archangel is seen by the Christians as the commander of the heavenly host, and his namesake would eventually become one of Russia's most distinguished military leaders.

The Golenischev-Kutuzovs were a junior (cadet) branch of the Kutuzovs, a family that could trace its origins back to the Middle Ages. The *General Armory of the Nobility of the Russian Empire*, the imperially approved authoritative record of the Russian noble households, notes that the family's founder was "a certain honest man by the name of Gavriil" who migrated from Prussia to the Novgorod region in the second half of the thirteenth century.[1] Nineteenth-century Russian historians argued that Gavriil belonged to the "Slaveno-Rus" population that resided west of the Vistula River.[2] Considering the complexities of identifying premodern Slavic identities, such claims are open to discussion.[3] But it is known that until the Middle Ages the indigenous population of Prussia was known by the name "Old Prussians" (German, "Prußen"; Polish, "Prusowie"; Russian, "Prussy") and traditionally had been identified with the Baltic peoples. In the thirteenth century, the State of the Teutonic Order, with papal blessing, embarked on the Northern Crusades, which targeted the Baltic, Finnic, and West Slavic peoples, many of whom they killed or forced to flee eastward.[4] Among the thousands fleeing the onslaught of the Teutonic knights was a certain Gatusha, who in 1263 migrated from Prussia to Novgorod, converted to Orthodox Christianity, and adopted the baptismal name of Gavriil. Some Russian historians embellished Kutuzov's family lineage by asserting that this Gavriil was a close companion

MAP 1 Western Provinces of the Russian Empire

of Prince Alexander Nevskii of Novgorod, who fought against the Swedish and Teutonic knights and distinguished himself in the great Novgorodian victory over the Swedish and Norwegian knights on the Neva River in July 1240. Such claims are unfounded.[5]

Gavriil proved adept at adjusting to his new homeland, and his off-spring—fourteen generations separate him from the field marshal—went on to achieve even greater success. They produced successive generations of officials and military commanders (*vojvodas*) who steadily increased the family's wealth and stature. They gained a last name as well. "The Russian folk express themselves forcefully," observed the novelist Nikolai Gogol. "If they endow somebody with a nickname, it applies to a person's kin and posterity, and that person will take it with him to his job, into retirement . . . and to the ends of the earth."[6] Nicknames were ubiquitous in medieval society, and the reasons for bestowing them were frequently ephemeral and whimsical. Some were given for character traits, others were applied sardonically or facetiously, and still others were bestowed by one's foul-mouthed neighbors. Gavriil's great-grandson Alexander must have earned quite a reputation, for he was given the nickname "Kutuz" (the hot-tempered one), which followed his descendants and turned into the family's surname.[7] Alexander's eldest son, Fedor Kutuz—or Kutuzov, if we add a surname possessive typical of many Russian last names—moved to Moscow and married into the boyar (old aristocracy) elite, a testament to the savvy, cleverness, and political acumen of these early Kutuzovs. Another son, Ananii Kutuz, stayed in Novgorod, where his son, Vasilii Kutuz, further elevated the family's fortunes when he was chosen as the *posadnik* (mayor) of Novgorod and earned the moniker "Golenische" (boot-shaft), thus creating the Golenischev-Kutuzov branch.[8]

Both the Kutuzovs and their Golenischev-Kutuzov cousins prospered through the years, serving as diplomats, palace officials, and military commanders, contributing to the rise of the Grand Duchy of Moscow and its transformation into the Czardom of Russia.[9] They weathered the turbulent and bloody reign of Ivan the Terrible and the subsequent Time of Troubles (1598–1613), a period of profound political crisis that followed the demise of Ivan's son and led to the establishment of the Romanov dynasty. The family fortunes revived with the success of Ivan Savinovich Golenischev-Kutuzov, who distinguished himself in several wars waged by the newly installed Romanov czars. They in turn rewarded him with estates in the Velikolutskii and Toropetskii districts of Pskov province (located in northwestern Russia); in fact, by 1699, two dozen members of the Golenischev-Kutuzov family owned estates. No less important for the social standing of the family was inclusion in the famed "Velvet Book," the official register of genealogies of Russia's most illustrious families.[10] Ivan Savinovich had four sons, one of whom, Ivan Ivanovich—Kutuzov's great-great-grandfather—served as a flügel-adjutant to Field Marshal General Count Boris Sheremetev during the Great Northern War (1700–1721), which marked the rise of Russia as an imperial power in northeastern Europe. Ivan Ivanovich's son, Matvei, followed the family tradition of military service, served in the Azovskii Infantry Regiment, and finished his career as a captain in the Velikolutskii Garrison Battalion at Smolensk. He married twice and before dying in July 1747 produced four children, of whom the eldest was son Illarion (Hilarion), the future field marshal's father.[11]

Illarion Matveevich Golenischev-Kutuzov had an illustrious career in the Russian military, though, contrary to numerous claims, he did not start his service under Peter the Great. Graduating from the military engineering school in St. Petersburg in early 1737 at the age of nineteen, he embarked on a career with the Corps of Engineers that spanned the reigns of five Russian monarchs.[12] One of the most talented and distinguished Russian engineers, he was a highly educated man for his time and was, in later years, nicknamed "Razumnaya Kniga" (The Wise Book) for his deep knowledge and experience. Illarion Matveevich was a workaholic who devoted himself to military service, taking only two short furloughs in over twenty years. Rising to the rank of engineer major general in 1763, he directed various construction projects at Kronstadt, Vyborg (Viipuri), Kexholm (Priozersk), and St. Petersburg, including the St. Petersburg Arsenal and the Ekaterininskii Canal (present-day Griboedov's Canal), which protected the imperial capital from flooding; Empress Catherine II herself gifted him a diamond-encrusted gold snuffbox for this achievement.[13]

Illarion Golenischev-Kutuzov saw action during the new Russo-Ottoman War (1768–1774), when he commanded engineer units. However, he seems to have suffered an accident that jeopardized his health and cut short his career; in April 1770, his letters mention a broken bone that did not properly heal and prevented him from returning to active service. He never fully recovered from this injury and, in November 1770, requested permission to leave the military on the grounds of "decrepitude and illness." His request was granted. In recognition of his long and distinguished service, Illarion Matveevich was allowed to retire with the rank of a lieutenant general and appointed to the Senate, a supreme legislative, judicial, and executive body of the Russian Empire. But he longed for a quiet life in his native Pskov province and by the late 1770s had settled in the village of Stupino, in Opochetskii district, where he spent the last few years of his life as the marshal of local nobility before passing away in 1784.[14]

By contrast, we know very little about Mikhail Kutuzov's mother. Even her name remains the subject of debate, with most claiming that she was from the Beklemishev family. However, already in 1813, one of the first biographies of Kutuzov noted that his father was married to a woman "from the Bedrinskii family."[15] More crucially, archival documents uncovered by Russian historians Yu. Yablochkin, L. Makeenko, and I. Tikhonov all point to Anna Illarionovna Bedrinskaya as the mother of the future field marshal.[16] Like the Golenischev-Kutuzovs, the Bedrinskiis were of middling status. Anna's father, Illarion Zakharovich Bedrinskii, served in the Velikolutskii Garrison Battalion (the same unit in which Kutuzov's paternal grandfather had served) and, after retiring as a captain of the Narvskii Garrison Regiment, married Praskovya Moiseevna Beshentsova, with whom he had a daughter in 1728. Anna Illarionovna would have been just sixteen years old when she was betrothed to the twenty-seven-year-old Illarion Golenishchev-Kutuzov. Considering contemporary mores and Illarion's frenzied work schedule, we can safely assume that the marriage was arranged, and that the couple hardly knew each other before the wedding. Their marriage probably took place in late 1745, almost certainly after the groom's return from a mission to Stockholm that spring.

—·—ΞΚ✦ΞΞ—·—

Considering his fame and celebrity, surprisingly little is known about Mikhail Kutuzov's early life. Even the year and place of his birth are subjects of major disagreement.[17] Births and deaths were traditionally documented in church records, but an entry for Kutuzov's birth has never been located. Furthermore, eighteenth-century Russian administrative records did not contain a column for date of birth and instead noted an individual's age, which in most cases represented a clerk's best estimate.[18] Kutuzov's contemporaries were themselves uncertain of the field marshal's exact age when he died. Some obituaries recorded that he had passed away at the age of sixty-eight, others at seventy.[19] Still, the contemporary consensus leaned toward 1745 as his birth year, and when Kutuzov's ashes were buried in the Cathedral of Our Lady of Kazan in St. Petersburg in June 1813, his tombstone was engraved with that date, and it remains so.[20] Subsequent generations of historians repeated this date in their works, even after evidence to the contrary had emerged.[21] Indeed, archival evidence points to 1747 as the birthdate. Kutuzov could not have been born in 1745 or 1746 because he had an elder sister, Anna, who was born in August 1746.[22] Furthermore, he himself believed that he had been born in 1747. When filling out his record of service (*formulyarnyi spisok*) in January 1791, he wrote in the age column, "I am forty-three years old," meaning he was born in 1747.[23] Of the more than thirty documents containing details of Kutuzov's age, only three indicate 1745 as his date of birth. The others point to 1747.[24]

It was also long alleged that Kutuzov had been born in the Russian imperial capital, St. Petersburg. Actually, in the mid-eighteenth century children of Russian nobles were, for the most part, born on rural estates. Kutuzov probably was no exception. In 1746–1747, his father was preoccupied with various construction projects, including the building of the Kronstadt Canal, and was constantly on the move. It is highly unlikely that he would have kept his pregnant wife and an infant daughter with him or left them unattended in St. Petersburg. Because his own parents were already dead, Illarion Matveevich probably would have left his wife in the care of his mother-in-law, who owned several estates in the Pskov region. The fact that no birth records have ever been found in church registers in St. Petersburg further reinforces this supposition.[25]

Then there is the matter of his mother's subsequent fate. Most of Kutuzov's biographies claim that she died while he was still an infant.[26] Yet Mikhail was not the couple's last child—he also had a younger brother, Semen (Simon), and sister, Darya.[27] The last of these children was born in 1755, by which time Mikhail would have been eight years old, hardly an infant; most probably Kutuzov's mother died after giving birth to Darya, which is indirectly confirmed by Illarion Matveevich's request for a month-long furlough that year, probably to organize his wife's funeral and make arrangements for his children. He never remarried and, instead, shouldered the burden of raising four children, one of whom, Semen, later showed signs of mental disability.[28]

Whenever it happened, Anna Illarionovna's death was a great tragedy for the family. It deprived Mikhail of the warmth and gentleness of his mother's affection during the formative stages of his life. The world as he knew it had ended. He now faced the reality of having no mother or paternal grandparents, and a habitually absent father. Studies have shown the profound impact the loss of parent can have on a child's emotional development, diminishing their capacity to form interpersonal and intimate relationships. But these studies also reveal the resilience of children's developmental processes and their ability to recover when surrounded with emotional support from other family members. For Mikhail, such succor came from his maternal grandmother, Praskovya Bedrinskaya, a "well-meaning woman," as one contemporary described her, who loved her grandchildren tenderly and who took on the responsibility of raising them while her son-in-law was gone on missions.[29]

For the first decade of his life, Mikhail's immediate world would have been his grandparents' estate in Pskov province, about 200 miles southwest of St. Petersburg. The countryside there is rich and beautiful, with streams flowing in small gullies amid rolling plains and forests—an exciting place for a child to wander and explore, especially a child of the aristocracy. The basis of the Russian nobles' power was the endurance of the land systems under their control, ranging from huge estates to the relatively smaller landed patrimonies. Before the great age of noble estate building, aristocratic life in the Russian province lacked the elegance and luxury with which it is usually associated. The provincial gentry led a modest existence, and the "nests of gentlefolk," to borrow Ivan Turgenev's memorable description, were mostly small wooden homes, often indistinguishable from peasant houses.[30] Andrei Bolotov, the Russian agriculturist and prolific memoirist, was born just nine years before Kutuzov and shared similar childhood experiences, growing up in the Tula region (south of Moscow). In his memoirs, Bolotov recalled the humble appearance of his family home, where rooms were furnished with simple tables and benches, and pictures of saints hung on the dark wooden walls. A Russian landowner who grew up in Smolensk province recalled that his family lived in a "modest hut" with small windows and three sparsely decorated rooms.[31]

Kutuzov spent his childhood in one of these homely houses, where, so far as we can tell, he had a happy childhood (even after his mother's untimely death) in the care of his loving and deeply religious grandmother, who did her best to instill in him traditional values and Orthodox beliefs. Growing up in this rural environment sculpted Kutuzov's character and worldview. Lev Engelhardt, whose memoirs offer insights into a patrician child's life in the eighteenth-century Russian countryside, described the relative simplicity of village life and recalled that "my education resembled the system advocated by {French philosopher Jean-Jacques} Rousseau himself—that of the Noble Savage."[32] Rousseau was not the first to claim that the original "man"—the indigene and outsider—was pure and innocent, not yet "corrupted" by civilization and therefore still possessing humanity's innate goodness. Decades before him, the English poet John Dryden proclaimed, "I am as free as nature first made man / Ere the base laws of servitude began / When wild in woods the noble savage ran."[33] Rousseau popularized this concept and connected it to education, which he envisaged as divided into distinct stages, stating with the infant's "age of nature."[34] Kutuzov enjoyed the relative simplicity of rural life, running around in a simple shirt, wandering through the woods in search of mushrooms or berries, and fishing in the nearby rivulets. Yet, perhaps because of his mother's absence, the boy matured quickly. According to Filip Sinel'nikov, who knew the field marshal and collected family stories of his childhood, Kutuzov stood out among other children for having "not the slightest inclination for playfulness," "always avoiding his peers and seeking the company of adults, whom he peppered with numerous questions." A pensive and precocious child, he was "so curious," wrote Sinel'nikov, "that he could spend an entire day asking questions and listening to adults responding to his queries."[35]

Living in the village, Mikhail would have interacted with common folk, imbibing their piety and superstition, as well as their love for folk tales, singing, and dancing. But the rhythm of life in the village—strictly patriarchal and traditional—would have also exposed him to the rigid dichotomy of a society divided between the powerful and powerless. A moral evil that some contemporary Russians already recognized, serfdom remained at the very heart of the Russian state and society until the second half of the nineteenth century. It was a system of tangled relations between the landlord, who possessed the land, and the peasants, who were bound to it. Its roots can be traced back to the reign of Czar Ivan the Terrible, but the process of "enserfment" was codified into law by the Council Code (Ulozhenie) of 1649, which permanently bound peasants to the land on which they toiled. The relations between landowners and serfs involved a complex variety of legal, economic, social, cultural, and sociopsychological issues. As a child, Kutuzov would have been cared for by serf nursemaids and servants who made the aristocratic life comfortable; they cleaned and tidied homes, kept the fires going, cooked daily meals, and catered to the landowner's whims. Despite his young age, Kutuzov, the *barchuk* (lord's son), exercised authority over those who served him. In the words of the Russian satirist Mikhail Saltykov-Schedrin, the noble child "grew up in the lap of serfdom, was fed on the milk of a serf woman, brought up by serf nurses . . . and witnessed the horrors of the bondage of serfdom in all their grimness."[36]

One of the principles underpinning Russian society was "the gentry serves, the state provides," as the axiom went, meaning that the monarchy rewarded service by the nobility to the state with populated estates and serfs, then allowed use in perpetuity. Thus, the social status of a noble was in many respects determined through his usefulness to the crown, while his wealth was measured in the size of the estate and the number of "souls" (Russian *dusha*, meaning both a "soul" in the spiritual sense and a "male serf" within serfdom) on it. Serfs were highly valuable assets, as they not only cultivated land, grew produce, and provided free labor but also could be used as collateral, against which many Russian nobles borrowed money. Nikolai Gogol exploited this peculiar practice, and its absurd implications, in *Dead Souls* (published in 1842), a work that narrates the adventures of the landless but ambitious civil servant who seeks to climb the social ladder by buying "dead souls"—the papers relating to serfs who have died since the last census but who remain on record—and mortgaging them to acquire funds to create his own vast estate.

The aristocracy expanded enormously during the eighteenth century, and as many as half a million men and women could claim noble pedigree by the end of the century.[37] Despite its small size, this privileged estate spanned the economic spectrum. Contrary to popular perceptions, very few noblemen possessed large estates and fabulous riches. "The Russian nobility is the poorest in the whole wide world," observed a visiting foreigner in 1803.[38] Indeed, the vast majority of nobles had little or no property and lived at subsistence level. Minister of Public Instruction Karl Lieven's remark that "the line of our noble estate extends so indiscernibly that one end touches the steps of the throne while the other is almost lost in the peasantry" suggests there was a wide variation in serf ownership among the landed gentry. Figures for Tambov province in the eighteenth century show that the largest holdings were those of L. Naryshkin, with 8,444 male serfs; D. Naryshkin, with 3,750; Count K. Razumovskii, with 5,750; and Batashov, who owned 2,905 "souls." But next to them were petty noblemen, with the four poorest ones owning but a few serfs.[39] "In some villages," wrote Nikolai Turgenev, "there are noblemen whom you cannot tell apart from peasants either by their appearance or by their way of life and work."[40] Surviving documentation for 1777 shows that 76 percent of the noble estates had fewer than 60 souls, while just 12 percent owned more than 150;[41] of the Russian officers who served under Kutuzov at the Battle of Borodino, 77 percent claimed neither to own estates nor to be heirs to estates.[42]

By this measure, the Golenischev-Kutuzovs were very prosperous. They belonged to that tiny group—no more than 2 percent—of nobles who owned more than 500 souls. This was a reflection of the meritorious service several generations of the Golenischev-Kutuzovs had rendered to the Russian crown. The royal decree of 1673 thus praised the family for its faithful service and involvement in the campaigns against the Crimean Khanate and the Polish-Lithuanian Commonwealth, granting it new estates and confirming lands that had already been given in 1633, 1659, 1663, and 1670. In the eighteenth century the family continued to excel, advancing through the ranks through their contribution to the monarchy, just as Peter the Great had envisioned. As the result, by the time Mikhail Kutuzov was born, his family had joined the ranks of affluent landowners in Russia, with surviving documents indicating that his grandfather and father lorded over 500 to 600 souls (the actual number of serfs would have been at least twice as high) residing in a dozen or so villages in Pskov province.[43]

We do not know what kind of landowners the Golenischev-Kutuzovs were in their seigniorial abodes. The law gave Russian nobles nearly unchecked authority over serfs, who were considered possessions of landlords. Landowners could determine every aspect of village life and acted as agents of the state, maintaining social order, collecting taxes, and raising recruits for the army; as one Russian nobleman observed, "There were only two classes in Russia: the governing and the governed, of whom the former could do everything and the latter nothing."[44] Some eighteenth-century landowners were notorious for abusing their serfs—Daria Saltykova, the infamous "man-eater" of Moscow, took a sadistic pleasure in torturing her serfs and, in 1768, was arrested for killing dozens of them. But she was the exception rather than the rule. Most owners adopted the role of patriarchs and took pride in their paternalistic care for their serfs.[45] The more enterprising landowners—and Kutuzov, in later years, was certainly among them—tried to improve their estates, introducing European crop systems and animal husbandry, and establishing and maintaining distilleries and factories.[46]

Peter the Great had sought to modernize the Russian state in the early eighteenth century, but not society.[47] Under his leadership Russia emerged as one of the largest empires in the world, with its territory stretching from the shores of the Baltic Sea to the wilderness of Kamchatka. Its society was still deeply rooted in early modern traditions, with a small class of nobles presiding over a highly hierarchical and complex social system that involved nearly 500 different ranks and statuses.[48] Though he never considered abolishing the institution of serfdom, Peter introduced extensive and transformative reforms, including the creation of the Table of Ranks (1722), which served as an instrument of social engineering. Peter envisioned it as a way to systematize military, civil, and court ranks, and to correlate status and seniority to state service. The Table of Ranks created a hierarchy of fourteen ranks that were achieved not through pedigree and heredity but through zealous and competent (albeit never-ending) service. It was not intended to be egalitarian, a point underscored by Henning Friedrich, Count von Bassewitz, a foreign observer: "What [Peter] had in mind was not the abasement of the noble estate. On the contrary, it all tended towards instilling in the nobility a desire to distinguish themselves from common folk by merit as well as by birth."[49] While much has been made of Peter's Westernizing reforms, they were limited to the upper echelons of Russian society, which were compelled to model themselves culturally on the European example. Much of the Russian population continued its traditional way of life in the provinces. Indeed, the Petrine reforms strengthened serfdom, autocratic governance, hierarchy, and universal state service. The casualties and beneficiaries of these reforms were noble families, who were now beholden to the state to earn and keep an estate and the "living wealth," as the serfs were occasionally called.[50]

One effect of this system was that there was virtually no respectable outlet for the Russian gentry's talents other than court or military service. This was especially true for the gentry living in provinces, where civil administration was still rudimentary. The arts were done in one's spare time and not as a professional undertaking; very few members of the gentry embarked on a clerical path; even fewer considered the law or other professions. "The gentry was almost entirely in state service, that is in the capitals or with the army somewhere in the borderlands," notes one Russian historian, adding that provincial towns were populated mostly by the half-literate lower middle classes (*meschanstvo*) and tradesmen. The town of Pskov, the administrative center of the province where Kutuzov grew up, had fewer than 500 citizens.[51] His father would have stood out among these provincial nobles. He was a cultivated man who understood the importance of edification and used cultural refinement—the study of history and foreign languages, as well as adoption of Western clothes and familiarity with European culture and art—as a means of distinguishing himself (and his family) and legitimizing his privileged status. This contrast between Westernized elite and the general population caused no confusion. Literate nobles such as Illarion Matveevich saw themselves as Russian precisely because they were educated and cultured, and their knowledge and practice of Western languages and rituals underscored their cultural attainment without also undermining their sense of identity.[52]

Contemporaries frequently lamented the nobility's indifference to general education. Most nobles wallowed in ignorance; "anyone who knows Russia also knows on what unsteady foundation our so-called aristocracy rested," scathingly noted one contemporary.[53] Kutuzov was fortunate to have been born into a family that valued education. Despite being frequently away from the family supervising various engineering projects, Illarion Matveevich still managed to ensure, personally and with the help of tutors, that his eldest son was properly instructed. This would have been a challenging task in the Russian countryside. Yakov Otroshenko, the future general who was born into the minor gentry in Kyiv province in 1779, lamented the fact that when he was growing up there were very few people around him who "understood that the knowledge of sciences was crucial for a young man's future." Instead, "I was kept at home and told fairy tales about the Little Russian [Ukrainian] witches, mermaids, and so on."[54] When Sergei Tuchkov, a future lieutenant-general and senator, was just five years old, his father hired a local priest and an officer to train him. "Both of them had not the slightest ability to make their scarce knowledge either relatable or interesting," reminisced Tuchkov. Nor was their replacement, a Dutch tutor, any better. He was "slightly mad," did not speak a word of Russian, and was a fanatical alchemist. "Since he had no knowledge of chemistry," observed Tuchkov facetiously, "all of his experiments were a total failure, but he never gave up."[55] Illarion Matveevich, as an engineer and a man of science, wanted a different kind of education for his son. Under his supervision, young Mikhail learned mathematics, geometry, history, and geography. He showed an aptitude for languages, learning German, French, and Latin. In later years he gained proficiency in Polish, Swedish, and Turkish, and all this served him well throughout his long career.[56]

From birth, Kutuzov was destined for a military career. The Golenischev-Kutuzovs prided themselves on a long history of military service, which was reflected in their coat of arms: an azure shield with a black eagle holding a sword in its claws.[57] Illarion Matveevich sought to ensure a bright future for his children, but that would be tied to state service. In many respects, young Mikhail had no alternative career options. Peter made it obligatory for every young nobleman to serve in the military, first as a private and then as a non-commissioned officer; only after completing this service in the lower ranks was he given an officer's commission. After the czar died in 1725, the aristocracy did exploit loopholes in the system, putting their children on the roster of some regiment almost as soon as they were born. While the "private" slept in his cradle or played in the yard, his years of service accrued, and promotion went on automatically until he was old enough to enter the service with an officer's commission. The case of Peter Dolgorukov, who would play an important role in Kutuzov's life in 1805, offers one example of such blatant manipulation of the system. He was listed on the rolls of the Life Guard Izmailovskii Regiment at the age of three months, started actual service as a captain at the age of fifteen, and earned a promotion to major general at the age of twenty-one.

Empress Elisabeth's decree of December 22, 1742, required all sons of nobles, upon reaching the age of seven, to appear at the Herald's College (Gerol'dmeisterskaya Kontora) to be registered and examined; upon completion of the exam, they were then allowed to return home on the promise to continue their studies and undergo a second examination five years later.[58] Kutuzov's turn to appear for registration was in 1754 (confirming once more his date of birth). His father was, as always, fully committed to his work and could not spare a moment to travel with his son, so it was his uncle Ivan Matveevich Golenischev-Kutuzov, a retired lieutenant of the Ladozhskii Infantry Regiment in St. Petersburg, who accompanied the young boy to the examination. The relevant record at the Herald's College shows that on July 30, 1754, "Titular Counsellor Ivan Matvei's son Golenischev-Kutuzov brought in a minor Mikhail [Il]larion's son Golenischev-Kutuzov, who is shown to be seven years old and currently studying Russian grammar."[59] The staff of the Herald's College interviewed the child, examined his genealogy and social standing—"his father owns 400 souls," they noted in the registration—and then sent him back home with instructions to continue his studies and return by the summer of 1760, when the boy would have turned twelve years old.[60]

Little is known about this period of Kutuzov's boyhood. His father served in Riga, and the boy might have occasionally visited him there; his early biographer does note that Illarion Matveevich did his best to prepare his son for the military career ahead and "personally tutored and queried" his son.[61] Young Mikhail probably spent part of the year on his family's estate in rural Pskov province and passed the other half—very likely the winter months—with his father in the city, occasionally also staying with his uncle Ivan Matveevich Golenischev-Kutuzov in St. Petersburg, where he would have encountered many family friends and relatives, not least of them Ivan Loginovich Golenischev-Kutuzov (1729–1802), the future admiral and general-intendant of the Russian fleet, who took a genuine interest in his distant cousin.[62]

Eventually it came time for the boy to go to a military school. Illarion Matveevich chose to enroll his son in the newly created Joint Artillery and Engineer Noble School (JAENS),[63] an institution that played an important role in Russia's efforts to modernize its military through a reformed educational system.[64] As with many other reforms, it was Peter the Great who laid the foundation for Russian military education, establishing dozens of military schools across the empire and making education compulsory for noblemen. His successors continued to sponsor and expand the military educational system. The eleven-year reign of Empress Elisabeth (1741–1762) witnessed a major reform of the military schools championed by General Feldzugmeister Prince Peter Shuvalov and Général-en-chef Abraham Hannibal (the poet Alexander Pushkin's Abyssinian great-grandfather), who pointed out existing problems within military schools and called for restructuring. In May 1758 Elisabeth approved the proposal, prepared by Hannibal and Shuvalov, to create an entirely new institution, the Joint Artillery and Engineer Noble School, by merging two existing specialist schools—the Artillery and Engineer Schools—that Peter had founded.[65]

With the help of Russian scholars, including Mikhail Lomonosov, perhaps the most famous academic of his age, General Feldzugmeister Shuvalov developed the new school's curriculum to focus on two ambitious goals. First, the school would seek to create a homogenous corps of well-trained disciplined professional officers who would live and breathe the same military ethos. Second, it was to mold these future officers through a rigorous curriculum that reflected not only the technical emphasis of European military schools but also the ideals of the Enlightenment with their emphasis on humanities. The main objective of this new educational approach was to contribute to the country's modernization and Westernization by creating a new type of Russian nobleman who would be "European-minded and modern and capable of actively serving a modern and power-directed state."[66] To achieve this, Shuvalov and his supporters believed that technical expertise alone was not sufficient. A mastery of foreign languages and deep understanding of historical, political, and economic processes were essential for aspiring officers. "History would lift the veil of antiquity and present great heroes and commanders," wrote Shuvalov, and "instill more virtues into the heart of a young man than most earnest moralizing and would be of incalculable benefit for a military man."[67] Little attention was paid to Russian literature or history. To the contrary, the very purpose of this education was to remove pupils from their traditional environments and shape them into what one Russian reformer called "a new type of people."

The JAENS was designed for 135 cadets whose education would be subsidized by the state, but children from affluent noble families could be also admitted as *svoekoshtnyi*, meaning that they would pay for their own expenses. The curriculum offered cadets a wide variety of subjects, including tactics, history, geography, arithmetic, algebra, geometry, hydraulics, physics, chemistry, civil architecture, artillery, and fortification, as well as foreign languages, fencing, and dancing. Drawing held a prominent place in the curriculum because the school administration reasoned that the cadets would one day need to sketch an enemy position or a battlefield. The school's facilities included a printing shop, a hospital, and a small library, where the cadets could peruse foreign publications. Shuvalov personally supervised the selection of the instructors, who included some of the best Russian specialist officers. The school would become one of the best military educational institutions in the Russian Empire.[68]

A number of historians claimed that twelve-year-old Mikhail was enrolled in the JAENS in 1757 and finished it just two years later, in 1759.[69] Actually,

Illarion Matveevich began the process of enrolling his son in the military school in the spring of 1759. On April 17, he asked Engineer Major General N. Muravyev, the acting military governor of Riga, to have his son tested in engineering and artillery sciences. The following day, an engineer officer examined young Mikhail and confirmed his proficiency in various military subjects. Encouraged by the results, the elder Kutuzov then petitioned Prince Shuvalov to accept his "eleven-year-old son Mikhail" into the JAENS to study artillery. In the letter, the father proudly noted that his offspring had studied "Russian grammar," had a good mastery of the German language, "could speak and translate from French (though not fluently)," and could translate from Latin as well. He also mentioned that the boy had passed an examination in Riga and excelled in history, geography, and "all those sciences that are related to artillery, namely arithmetic, geometry, and study of fortifications." This letter is also noteworthy for the elder Kutuzov's request to postpone his son's enrollment in the JAENS until he had completed his current studies at home.[70] Shuvalov not only accommodated this request but went beyond it. In August, he signed an order formally enrolling the eleven-year-old Kutuzov in the school, granted him the rank of a corporal, and gave him a deferral that allowed Mikhail to remain with his family and complete his studies before joining the school.[71] Why Shuvalov extended such benevolence is not clear. Nonetheless, Kutuzov obviously benefited from the privileged status that his family held, given that such a furlough was granted only to those applicants who were considered both capable and affluent enough to afford education at home.

The deferral turned out to be short. Illarion Matveevich was soon reassigned from Riga to St. Petersburg. He bought a house on Third Artillery Street and moved his children to the capital. Now that he was in St. Petersburg, Mikhail no longer needed a deferral, and on October 21, 1759, he began formally attending the JAENS, embarking on a military career that would span fifty-four years. He was indeed considered a *svoekoshtnyi* cadet, meaning that he was responsible for his own room and board; he continued to live at his father's home while attending courses at the JAENS.

Kutuzov thrived at the school. Just ten days after his enrollment he was already being praised for his "commitment to studying" and promoted to the noncommissioned officer rank of *kaptenarmus* (from French *capitaine d'armes*).[72] A month later, in December 1759, Count Shuvalov reviewed Kutuzov's file once more and had him again tested. The results showed that the young boy excelled in languages and mathematics and showed promise in engineering, which was hardly surprising, considering his father's background. Ober-Kriegskommissar Mikhailo Mordvinov, who directed the JAENS, informed Shuvalov that Kaptenarmus Kutuzov had demonstrated "considerable knowledge in languages and mathematics" and that because of his exceptional predisposition for these subjects he should be employed at school.

Thus, despite his tender age Kutuzov was chosen to instruct other cadets and spent the following year teaching arithmetic and geometry at the Combined Soldiers School. Impressed by the young boy's accomplishments, Shuvalov promoted him once more—this time to a cadet first class (*konduktor 1-go klassa*)—and recommended him for the engineering section, rather than artillery as Illarion Kutuzov initially wanted. Mikhail continued to study and teach in 1760–1761.[73]

Kutuzov was an exemplary cadet who not only taught fellow classmates but also excelled in his own courses, taught by some of the most capable officers in Russia, including Général-en-chef Abraham Hannibal (engineering), Captain Ivan Kartmazov (artillery), Pavel Florinskii (geometry and arithmetic), Yakov Kozel'skii (algebra and mechanics), and Ivan Vel'yashev-Volyntsev (artillery and geometry).[74] The JAENS curriculum was rather progressive for its time, with a focus on student-led and self-paced educational process guided, assessed, and enriched by knowledgeable and engaged teachers. The director developed a personalized curriculum for each cadet, one that gave them the time they needed to understand concepts fully and meet individualized learning goals.[75]

Kutuzov graduated from the JAENS in sixteen months, earning his promotion to officer in mid-March 1761. Normally cadets were expected to spend up to three years studying. He had grown physically and intellectually. His certificate of graduation testified that he had expanded beyond the "engineering and artillery sciences" and studied history, ethics, philosophy, literature, arts, and drawing.[76] Though only fourteen, he emerged from the military school more confident of himself, more proficient in sciences—"algebra, trigonometry, mechanics, fortification engineering and artillery," as listed on the certificate—and the humanities. He was now one of the youngest cadets to achieve an engineer officer's rank. Little wonder that he was asked to stay at the school for a bit longer.[77]

⊷⊶ ⚌✦⚌⚌ ⊷⊶

Kutuzov embarked on a military career during a turbulent period in European history. He was nine when the Seven Years' War erupted in 1756. The war, which involved all major European powers, was sparked by Austria's attempt to win back the fertile province of Silesia, wrested from it by Frederick II of Prussia eight years earlier. But the conflict also involved Britain and France's struggle for colonial control of North America and Asia. Global in scope, the war was waged from the Silesian plains to Bengal to Canada and the Caribbean islands, pitting an alliance of Prussia and Britain against France, Austria, Spain, and Russia. By the time Kutuzov graduated from the Joint Artillery and Engineer Noble School, Prussia was in dire straits. Beset by the Austrian and Russian armies, its economy was depleted and its armies worn out. Frederick believed that only luck could save him. It found him in January 1762 when Russian empress Elisabeth died and was replaced by Peter III, a Prussophile. The new czar made peace with Frederick and allied himself with Prussia for a joint action against his enemies, both decisions that proved highly unpopular with the Russian elites.

These changes influenced Kutuzov's career.[78] Just days before Mikhail graduated from the JAENS in February 1762, Peter III signed the Manifesto on the Freedom of the Nobility, putting an end to the compulsory nature of the nobility's state service and granting it wider freedoms.[79] For many contemporaries this came as a shock; the new sense of freedom felt disorienting. Yet the manifesto proclaimed reassuringly that "nobles may continue to serve as long as and wherever they wish, on a voluntary basis." Some left state and military service and returned to manage their estates. But for many noblemen the only acceptable career remained state service, which was the main source of income and security. Kutuzov chose what the manifesto described as a noble's "moral obligation"—to serve the state. In many respects, he had no other option. The Table of Ranks created a social hierarchy to which individual nobles attached considerable importance, given that their personal status was partly defined by their rank (chin), which was in turn earned through the military or civil service. Even after Peter III's proclamation, noblemen continued to serve the state. In addition to offering an honorable and stable source of income, service conferred an identity. Kutuzov's upbringing imbued in him a sense of obligation to which he would remain true for the duration of his long military career.[80]

In March 1762, merely days after graduating, Kutuzov learned that he was appointed as a flügel-adjutant to Prince Peter August Friedrich, Duke of Schleswig-Holstein-Sonderburg-Beck. The duke had started his career in Hesse-Kassel before moving to Russia, where he made a successful military career. Empress Elisabeth promoted him to général-en-chef and appointed him governor of Reval (modern-day Tallinn, Estonia). He was a "fair and decent commander, serves readily, and is a respectable soldier," as Field Marshal Burkhard Christoph von Münnich characterized him in 1739, before adding, "But he does not have any special talents . . . and, not knowing the Russian language, he struggles to command."[81] Peter III's accession to the throne was a windfall for the sixty-four-year-old duke. As the emperor's close relative, he was promoted to the rank of the field marshal general and allowed to recruit a larger staff. Among the officers selected to assist the new field marshal was Kutuzov.[82] Some of Kutuzov's biographers ascribed this decision to the influence of Empress Consort Catherine, who later became known for her partiality to young officers at her palace. During one of the military reviews, the story goes, Catherine had noticed Ensign Kutuzov, who had performed well during exercises, and recommended him to her husband, who in turn assigned him to the duke.[83] The story is most certainly apocryphal and the reality more prosaic. The duke selected Kutuzov because he was one of the top graduates from JAENS and proficient in foreign languages, which was particularly important considering the duke's lack of knowledge of Russian.

Whatever the case, this was an auspicious start for a military career. At the age of fifteen, Kutuzov went from newly graduated ensign to staff officer assigned to one of the most senior military commanders in the Russian army.[84] In his new capacity, Kutuzov was responsible for the duke's chancellery, and all of the field marshal's orders, reports, proposals, and any other documents would have passed through his hands. Kutuzov was a quick learner and took full advantage of this opportunity.

In July 1762, just as Kutuzov was starting the third month at his new job, Emperor Peter III was deposed in a coup led by his wife, Catherine, who moved to claim the imperial crown. It is impossible to say whether Kutuzov knew what was coming. However, in one historian's apt description, "the opposition to Peter III walked the streets in uniform."[85] While in St. Petersburg, young Kutuzov would have encountered disgruntled officers—or maybe overheard his own relatives or acquaintances—discussing their rising anger over Peter III's policies, be it the introduction of Prussian-style uniforms and drills or his decision to pull Russia out of the Seven Years' War just as the country was on the cusp of defeating Frederick the Great of Prussia. At dawn on July 9, while Peter III was away from St. Petersburg, the Imperial Guard regiments took over the imperial capital and proclaimed Catherine the new empress. The next morning they proceed to the imperial residence at Oranienbaum, outside the city. Peter III was forced to abdicate and then transported under guard to Ropsha, some distance from St. Petersburg. The conspirators could not make up their minds what to do with the fallen ruler—imprisonment in one of the fortresses and repatriation to Holstein were rejected as too risky. But fate—in the form of the ringleader Count Alexey Orlov—intervened. On July 17, Peter III was found dead of what was officially declared a severe attack of hemorrhoidal colic and an apoplectic stroke.

In the post-coup changes, the Duke of Schleswig-Holstein-Sonderburg-Beck was forced out of his position and his staff was downsized, with officers reassigned.[86] Kutuzov probably stayed in Reval through the summer of 1762. In September, he received news that he was being promoted to captain and given command of a company in the Astrakhanskii Infantry Regiment, one of the oldest and most distinguished regiments in the Russian army, stationed in St. Petersburg (not in Astrakhan, as some Kutuzov biographers had claimed).[87] Less than two weeks later, he learned the identity of his new regimental commander, one of the most extraordinary figures in Russian military history.

CHAPTER 2

The Masters and the Apprentice, 1763–1771

A SHORT AND WIRY man, and legendarily eccentric, Alexander Vasilievich Suvorov was an outstanding military theorist and practitioner, combining practical experience with enlightened intelligence, sarcastic wit, and an indomitable will. The son of a général-en-chef, he was born in November 1730 and suffered from a sickly constitution that dampened his father's hopes for a military career for him. But the boy demonstrated remarkable willpower and determination, overcoming his disabilities by developing a rigorous regimen of physical exercises and spartan lifestyle for which he would later become famous. More crucially, using his father's vast library, he educated himself in mathematics, literature, philosophy, geography, and history.[1]

In 1742, at the age of twelve, Suvorov met General Hannibal—whom two decades later Mikhail Kutuzov would encounter at the JAENS. Hannibal left a lasting impression on the sensitive boy and prompted him to pursue a military career. In 1748, Suvorov enlisted as a private in the Life Guard Semeyonovskii Regiment and went on to attend the Cadet Corps of Land Forces, the professional military education institution that Empress Anna established in 1731 to train a new generation of Russian officers. Quickly advancing through the ranks, Suvorov was already a major when he gained his first battle experience during the Seven Years' War. Distinguishing himself, Suvorov became a colonel at the age of thirty-two and was given command of the Astrakhanskii Infantry Regiment in September 1762. It was in this regiment that Suvorov and Kutuzov first met.

Suvorov returned home from the Seven Years' War with ideas on how to prepare soldiers for war. Putting into practice the lessons learned fighting Frederick the Great's Prussians on the rolling fields of Silesia, he insisted on progressive and realistic training that combined a grasp of the psychology of the Russian peasant soldiers with insights into the nature of warfare. He remained at the Astrakhanskii Infantry Regiment only several months, but he was already experimenting with methods that he would systematize in his *Regimental Regulations* (1764-1765) and then in the *Art of Victory* (1795), a work that had a significant influence on the Russian way of war.[2] Suvorov was among the first Russian commanders to devote attention to counteracting the general lack of literacy in the army. As early as the 1760s, he demonstrated an ability to communicate his thoughts in a way that was readily comprehensible; his orders of the day used aphorisms, idiomatic phrases, and even rhymes that the rank and file could understand and follow. He opposed ceremonial frills, mindless parade drills, and goose-stepping and was an ardent proponent of training under simulated battlefield conditions, including long marches and river crossings, live fire exercises, and bayonet attacks. "Train hard, fight easy," he advised. "Train easy and you will have hard fighting." Suvorov emphasized planning and strategy as well as speed and mobility, accuracy of gunfire, and the use of the bayonet; his guiding belief was in a maneuverable warfare that identified the enemy's weakest point and struck at it decisively.

The impact on the young Kutuzov was doubtless significant, though it led some Soviet historians to embellish the relationship between the colonel and his junior officer; some claimed that even as a company commander Kutuzov reflected Suvorov's style of command. Such claims seem farfetched and exaggerate the relationship between them. There was a difference in age, rank, and experience, not to mention of temperament; in later years, their approach to military affairs differed as well. More crucially, Suvorov and Kutuzov served together for merely eight months—in April 1763, Suvorov was given command of the Suzdalskii Infantry Regiment.[3] It seems unlikely that Kutuzov, a fifteen-year-old officer fresh out of military school, would have developed a close relationship with the veteran commander in such a short period of time.[4] Still, encountering a strong and innovative person like Suvorov left an imprint on the young man, and Suvorov's tireless interest in the welfare of his soldiers would have been undoubtedly impressed upon him. Suvorov, who was exacting of his officers, praised Kutuzov as a capable and hardworking junior officer who had shown due "diligence in fulfilling responsibilities of his rank." He noted that Kutuzov took care of his subordinates and trained them well in military drill, for which, in Suvorov's words, the young man had a "zeal." He also praised his company commander for "not reporting himself sick for the sake of indolence" and for behaving "in everything as it befits an honest officer." Kutuzov possessed "no character blemishes" and was worthy of promotion for his "assiduous service."[5]

Like all young officers, Kutuzov was eager to prove himself in action. He got his opportunity when political turmoil erupted in Poland-Lithuania in the wake of the death of Polish king Augustus III in October 1763. Empress Catherine threw her support behind her onetime lover Stanislaw August Poniatowski and committed financial and military resources to ensure his selection as the new king of Poland; in late 1764, as the Polish Sejm (assembly) met to elect a new king, Catherine dispatched Russian military to ensure that her candidate prevailed. Kutuzov was among those officers who volunteered for service in Poland and joined the troops that Major General Ivan (Hans Heinrich) von Weymarn led to Warsaw.[6]

Little is known about Kutuzov's actual service in Poland. The royal election was a quarrelsome affair that occasioned clashes between Poniatowski's supporters and opponents. Kutuzov was involved in some of the melees, and although none of them were large or significant, they marked his baptism by fire. His early biographies eulogized him for demonstrating, as one put it, "valor and fearlessness, repeatedly volunteering for missions that involved great difficulties and dangers."[7] Surviving evidence suggests that he first distinguished himself during fighting near Warsaw, where the troops of Prince Karol Stanisław Radziwiłł, one of the strongest of the Polish magnates, attacked a Russian detachment but were repelled and pursued; later Kutuzov was among those storming the entrenched Polish positions on the Ovruč River.[8] In September 1764, Catherine got what she wanted— the Sejm elected Poniatowski as the new king of Poland. Six months later, Kutuzov returned to his regiment in St. Petersburg. He took his first furlough (*domovoi otpusk*) in mid-September 1765, spending eight months at home before rejoining his regiment in May 1766.[9] It was probably during this restful period that he developed closer relations with his uncle Ivan Loginovich Golenischev-Kutuzov, who had played the part of an older friend and advisor. Ivan Loginovich had made a brilliant career in the Russian navy, becoming an intendant general of the Russian fleet and later the director of the Naval Cadet Corps.[10] Kutuzov would have learned much from this intelligent, sociable, and well-connected general. Kutuzov's own father was ordinarily preoccupied with exacting work. Thus, it is hardly surprising that Mikhail became close to Ivan Loginovich, later referring to him as "father" (*batyushka*) in his letters. His uncle's house on Bolshaya Morskaya Street in St. Petersburg had a vast personal library that would have been very useful to Mikhail. Here he read books of literature, philosophy, and geography, as well as works of ancient and modern military theory and practice. Mingling at his uncle's dinner parties, Kutuzov would have met influential members of St. Petersburg society, made valuable connections, and developed the social and diplomatic skills that would make him famous.

The Astrakhanskii Infantry Regiment was one of the units on garrison duty in the Russian imperial capital, and for the next three years Kutuzov performed garrison responsibilities in and around the imperial residencies.[11] This was an eventful period. Empress Catherine II sought to consolidate her authority and pursued a diverse set of policies to reform Russia's central and local government, legal system, public health, and education. In late 1766 she called the Legislative Commission, which was tasked with reviewing and codifying Russian laws. Although not intended as a parliament in the modern sense, the Legislative Commission was designed to continue the reforms that had begun with Peter the Great. The Russian legal system was an assortment of new and old laws that had not been fully reconciled. There was dire need for a legal overhaul, one that would examine all the laws, rescind those that had become obsolete, reconcile those that contradicted each other, and identify legal gaps and loopholes. Catherine wrote a lengthy *nakaz* (set of instructions) for the commission, outlining her vision of governance, which drew heavily upon the ideas of the Enlightenment philosophes (especially Charles de Montesquieu and Cesare Beccaria), though, as critics pointed out, the empress also ignored the Enlightenment's call for political reform.

The Legislative Commission, which had 564 delegates and was broken down into a number of special committees, began its deliberations in 1767. It required a large staff to support its work and drew upon a cadre of military officers. In the summer of 1767, young Captain Kutuzov thus became one of twenty-two officers assigned to the Legislative Commission, where they were tasked with clerical duties.[12] Most of these officers were from the elite guard regiments. Kutuzov was among just three regular army officers selected for this assignment, and the only one from the Astrakhanskii Infantry Regiment.[13] This selection was not the result of the empress's lascivious eye, as it is sometimes alleged, but a testament to Kutuzov's growing reputation as a capable and hardworking officer. He was indeed a physically fit and "handsome young man," combining a sharp mind with "pleasing manners and attention to detail," enthused Sinel'nikov, Kutuzov's contemporary and first biographer. "Pleasantness of his behavior and resourcefulness in conversations imbued everyone with love and respect for him."[14]

Kutuzov was assigned to the Justice Committee and was responsible for maintaining meeting notes, drafting agendas, copying laws, and preparing documents for the commission's approval. Some of these documents have survived in the Russian archives, including the daily and weekly journals of the commission that Kutuzov wrote in October and November 1767. This would have been a heady time in Kutuzov's young life, for he found himself at the epicenter of imperial reforms. He honed administrative skills that later played an important role in his career, preparing memos on a broad range of topics that expanded his intellectual horizons and range of contacts. After a year and a half of deliberating, however, the Legislative Commission became split along class lines, with the delegates of the gentry opposing initiatives by the merchant representatives and clashing with the representatives of the lower classes. Serf ownership, property rights, and privileges enjoyed by the nobility created fault lines along which the commission fractured—to the great alarm of the empress, who worried about civil war. In 1768, using worsening international circumstances as an excuse, Catherine disbanded the Legislative Commission and put an end to her ambitious initiative. Disappointed, Kutuzov returned to his regiment. He would soon have plenty to preoccupy him, for war loomed.

After the election of Stanisław Poniatowski, Catherine enjoyed considerable influence over the Polish throne. She had compelled the Sejm to grant full political rights to non-Catholics (which in practice meant Orthodox Christians), effectively bringing Poland under a Russian protectorate. In response, a group of Polish nobles and gentry (szlachta) gathered at the fortress of Bar to form a confederation to challenge King Stanisław and to demand Poland's independence from Russia. The Bar Confederation, as this association became known, faced an uphill struggle. Confronted by the royal Polish army (supported by the Russians), the confederates had to abandon Bar and flee to the Ukrainian provinces in the southeast; some Polish nobles sought shelter in the Ottoman Empire, beseeching the sultan to intervene.[15] With the Ottoman sultan duly threatening war unless Russia withdrew from Poland, Catherine II moved quickly to suppress the Bar Confederation and sent reinforcements under the command of Général-en-chef Peter Olitz to support King Stanisław's campaign in Ukraine. A newly created Russian corps of three carabineer units and four infantry regiments, under the command of Major General Hans Heinrich von Weymarn, entered Polish territory. Captain Kutuzov led one of the flying detachments that were tasked with securing the voivodeships (districts) of Kyiv and Bracław, the two southeastern provinces of the Polish-Lithuanian Commonwealth. Although the Russian forces prevailed over the confederates, they were unable to quell uprisings that broke out in support of the confederation in other parts of the Polish-Lithuanian Commonwealth.

Only vague information is available on Kutuzov's service during this war; stories recorded in early anthologies and in Filip Sinel'nikov's multivolume biography are impossible to verify. Nonetheless, the campaign in Poland contributed to Kutuzov's growing reputation as a brave and capable officer. He had shown tactical sense and decisiveness in the actions near Żwaniec and Okopy, where he led his men against the enemy's fortified positions, defeated them, and then undertook a vigorous pursuit.[16] And yet Kutuzov also seems to have become the victim of his own success, as his accomplishments aroused jealousy and resentment. "Rapid success, which Kutuzov gained in a rather short period of time," lamented one of his early biographers, "soon garnered him ill-wishers and envious people" who tried to undermine his career.[17] Kutuzov's official service record does contain an interesting annotation made in 1769 that suggests there was an attempt to delay the young officer's advancement because his promotion to a captain was considered premature and he was told to wait until "those holding seniority in the same rank are promoted above him."[18] We do not know who these ill-wishers were or what Kutuzov's reaction to such news was. Still, he seems to have seen it as a challenge to prove his naysayers wrong. The 1768 campaign was just the proving ground. Kutuzov later observed that serving in Poland allowed him to lead "a merry life," adding, "But I did not comprehend war then."[19] It was the Russo-Ottoman War, which the events in Poland had provoked, that offered Kutuzov a proper schooling in the art of war and a chance to distinguish himself.

In July 1768, after yet another loss against Russian forces in the Podolye region, a group of Bar Confederation troops fled south, seeking the safety of the Ottoman realm. The pro-Russian local irregulars, the *haidamaks*, pursued them all the way to Balta, a small but prosperous market town on the Kodyma River that marked the border with the Ottoman Empire. In the ensuing fighting the *haidamaks* plundered the town and massacred its Jewish residents. Exploiting this chaotic situation, the Turks from Galta, a small settlement on the Ottoman side of the Kodyma, crossed the river and ransacked the town once more, killing its Christian residents. Upon learning about this attack, the *haidamaks* returned to Balta, crossed the river in violation of the imperial border, and sacked the Ottoman village. Russia denied any culpability for the *haidamaks'* waywardness. Nonetheless, the incident enraged Sultan Mustafa III, who was already seriously alarmed by the recent events in Poland and the growth of the Russian influence in Wallachia, Montenegro, and Georgia and felt that it was imperative to make a stand. With the encouragement of his Polish confederates and the backing of the French embassy, the sultan issued an ultimatum, threatening Russia with war if it did not immediately stop its intervention in Poland and withdraw troops from the Polish territories. Upon receiving the Russian refusal, the Ottomans considered the Balta-Galta incident as the *casus belli* and took the Russian ambassador prisoner on October 6/17, 1768, thereby signaling the start of a new war against Russia.[20]

This was not the first conflict between Russia and the Ottoman Empire, which shared a long border and had been bitter rivals for over a century. At their greatest extent in the sixteenth century, the Ottomans claimed sovereignty over all of Asia Minor, the Balkan Peninsula, Hungary, the Black Sea littoral, south Caucasia, Syria-Palestine, and the coastal states of North Africa. Furthermore, in his capacity as caliph or spiritual leader of the world's Muslims, the sultan held nominal leadership over much of the Islamic world, stretching from the Atlantic coast of Africa to India. Yet the empire's heyday was long past. By the late eighteenth century, the Ottomans were grappling with a host of domestic and foreign challenges that contributed to internal turmoil and loss of provinces, weakened the empire's finances, and encouraged the predations of European powers. While the sultans maintained nominal claims to Algeria, Libya, and Egypt, actual power resided in the hands of local elites, who often defied the sultan's authority. In the Balkans and Caucasus, the Ottomans faced the resurgent aspirations of local peoples (Greeks, Serbs, Georgians, etc.) and the growing ambitions of the Russian and Austrian Empires, which showed interest in ever-larger parts of the Ottoman realm.

The first formal contact between Russia and the Ottoman Empire took place in the fifteenth century.[21] Early Russo-Ottoman relations were marked by a clear distinction in status between the powerful Ottoman Empire and the rising Russian principality; the sultans often relegated Russian affairs to their vassal khans of the Crimea, who conducted periodic raiding expeditions into the southern Russian regions. By the mid-sixteenth century, however, the Muscovite state had become strong enough to resist the sultan's proxies. In 1552–1556, Czar Ivan IV the Terrible conquered the Kazan and Astrakhan khanates, which were major Ottoman allies; he commemorated his triumph by building the iconic Cathedral of St. Basil, which still stands on Red Square in Moscow. The Russo-Ottoman struggles intensified as Russian rulers sought to extend their influence into Ukraine, then part of the great Polish-Lithuanian Commonwealth and neighbored the Crimean khanate. Thus, the Russian decision to support Ukrainian Cossacks against the Poles provoked a war not only against the Polish-Lithuanian Commonwealth but also against the Crimean khanate, which was supported by the Ottoman Empire. It was the first of many Russo-Ottoman wars.

The early Russo-Ottoman conflicts—those of 1676–1681, 1686–1700, 1711, and 1735–1739—highlighted the continued vitality of the Ottoman military and its ability to repel Russian and Austrian forces and defend the realm. Between 1745 and 1768, as Russia was preoccupied with events in Europe, the Ottoman Empire experienced a period of relative peace and moderate reforms, though it failed to resolve its economic problems and curb administrative mismanagement; neither did the Ottomans succeed in establishing a modernized standing army, one of the key assets of the contemporary European states. The mid-eighteenth-century wars—the War of the Austrian Succession (1740–1748) and the Seven Years' War (1756–1763)—served as the crucible that forged modern European armies. By remaining outside the battlefields of these wars, the Ottomans missed a generation of developments and struggled to close the gap in training, organization, and technology that increasingly separated them from European armies.[22] This failure proved to be consequential in 1768.

Upon receiving the news of the war with the Ottomans, Catherine gathered a council of war that deliberated on strategic and operational plans. It was agreed that three Russian armies would be committed to the southern theater. Général-en-chef Prince Alexander Golitsyn was appointed to lead the First Army, the main striking force, which was to advance from Kyiv toward the Ottoman frontiers. The Second Army was placed under command of Count Peter Rumyantsev, who received instructions to defend Russia's southern borderlands, from Ekaterinoslav to Bakhmut. The Third Army, under Général-en-chef Peter Olitz, was the smallest of the Russian armies and, after being deployed at Lutsk, was tasked with observing Polish affairs. In the spring of 1769 Golitsyn crossed into Ottoman territory and advanced to the upper Dniester, where he sought to capture Kamenets Podol'sk and Khotin in order to contain the Ottoman forces advancing through Moldavia into Poland. However, Golitsyn lacked zeal and proved himself a plodder as he supervised the siege of Khotin between April and September 1769. Irritated by such lackluster performance, the Council of War ordered Golitsyn recalled and replaced by Peter Rumyantsev. His arrival marked a dramatic turn in the war.[23]

The new commander in chief could not have been more different from Golitsyn in mindset and approach. Rumyantsev was a fastidious man, known for his biting wit, thorough understanding of military affairs, and prickly temperament. He "loved and respected no one in the world," observed Comte Alexandre Langeron, who had known him well, before adding that Rumyantsev was also "the most brilliant of all Russian generals."[24] The son of one of Peter the Great's closest advisors, Rumyantsev had a turbulent youth, at one point enlisting in the Prussian army. But he was brought back home, forgiven, and enrolled in the Land Cadet Corps (Sukhoputnyi Shliakhetskii Korpus), which had been founded in 1731 by Empress Anna to provide the basic education appropriate to a newly commissioned officer. He did not stay long, earning a reputation as a restless cadet with a penchant for pranks. Rumyantsev was given the rank of lieutenant and sent to a field army. His first fighting took place during the Russo-Swedish War of 1741–1743, though it was the Seven Years' War that made him a leader. Rumyantsev commanded a brigade at Gross-Jagersdorf (1757), where he led a timely charge that contributed to the Russian victory, and then commanded a division during a rout of the Prussian army at Kunersdorf (1759). Over the next two years he honed his skills fighting the Prussians while also emulating their military. "He fought against Frederick the Great," noted one Russian contemporary, "but he also admired his skill and genius . . . and could not speak of him without enthusiasm." Rumyantsev "had no great opinion of his fellow countrymen and invariably lived surrounded by Germans."[25]

Rumyantsev was a vocal critique of the long and drawn-out maneuver, of positional and "geometric" warfare, and especially of the Austrian "cordon system," which emphasized careful selection of positions and defensive deployment of forces. He instead asserted that the art of war lay in mobility and concentration of superior numbers at a decisive point, an idea that foreshadowed Napoleon's operational approach by a few decades. The general should have "one main point on the ground," Rumyantsev wrote, and must "drive for it with all his efforts, inasmuch as by taking it he will deny all others dependent on it." He championed the "marching separately, fighting together" principle that he would practice against the Turks with devastating efficiency. "At its fundamentals," he wrote a friend, "the art of war boils down to holding the main objective of the war constantly in view and to remaining aware of what proved useful or damaging in similar cases in past times, taking into account the lay of the land and the associated advantages and difficulties, and evaluating the intentions of the enemy by working out what we might do if we were in his place."[26]

Now in charge of the First Army, Rumyantsev began preparations for a new campaign. During the winter of 1770, he developed plans for the spring offensive. The most recent reports showed that the Ottoman army, under the command of Grand Vizier Yağlıkçızade Mehmet Emin Pasha, had gathered near Isaccea and intended to advance northward to Bender (south of present-day Chişinău), which the Ottomans expected would be the main target of the Russian efforts. With the arrival of the Anatolian and Rumelian levies and the army of the Crimean khan Qaplan II Giray, the grand vizier would muster some 70,000 soldiers.[27] Rumyantsev understood that to confront such a large enemy force, time and mobility would be key. He left the task of besieging the fortress of Bender to the Second Army while his own First Army focused its efforts on seeking and confronting Ottoman forces (and their Crimean Tatar auxiliaries) before they could unite. Rumyantsev thought that by destroying enemy field armies, he could accelerate the fall of the Ottoman fortresses and consolidate the Russian presence in Moldavia and parts of Wallachia. Furthermore, by moving along the eastern bank of the Prut River and shifting his forces south toward the Danube, he hoped to avoid the plague that was wreaking havoc in Moldavia.

Over the long winter months, Rumyantsev restructured the three Russian armies committed to war against the Ottoman Empire. The smallest of them, the Third Army, would support the First Army. Reinforcements started arriving in January 1770, though it took several months for Rumyantsev to bring his regiments up to full strength. To increase the army's mobility and effectiveness, Rumyantsev simplified regimental assignments, increasing the proportion of combatants to noncombatants, with most of the latter left behind for garrison duties or other assignments.[28] More crucially, he developed

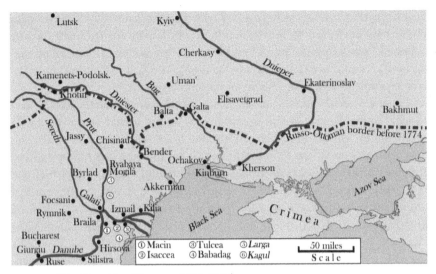

MAP 2 The Danubian Theater, 1770-1774

new training ordinances that distilled the lessons Rumiantsev had drawn from his experiences in the Seven Years' War.[29]

Among the reinforcements was the Smolenskii Infantry Regiment, in which twenty-two-year-old Captain Kutuzov was then serving.[30] To ensure a properly functioning staff, Rumyantsev made changes at headquarters and sought out capable officers for staff positions. Among them was Kutuzov, who in late spring 1770 was appointed to the general headquarters as the divisional quartermaster and placed under the command of Major General Friedrich Wilhelm Bauer, the First Army's quartermaster general. This was a prestigious appointment, one that Kutuzov owed both to his talents and to the fact that his father was serving at headquarters as an engineer major general in charge of engineer units.[31] As a special staff officer, the division quartermaster was responsible for conducting reconnaissance missions, assisting the commanding officer, and distributing the march orders to relevant subordinate officers. The quartermaster explored the field of operations, determined the lines of advance and retreat, chose proper points for bridges, examined fords, assigned quarters, and laid out camps. Kutuzov was in the thick of it.

The First Army left its quarters at Khotin in early June 1770 and marched southeast.[32] Despite the vast numerical superiority of the Ottoman army—an estimated 200,000 men against the First Army's 31,500 men—Rumyantsev was confident of success.[33] He believed that his men were better trained, disciplined, and organized. His confidence was shared by Empress Catherine, who knew that soldiers were inspired by great commanders.[34] The Russians might have been even more confident had they known the tribulations their opponent was experiencing. The Ottoman army suffered from many systemic and organizational problems, including difficulty in sustaining military expenditures and the collapse of its supply system.[35]

On the march, the Russian army was organized into three mobile divisional "corps."[36] After ten days of marching in hot weather over bad roads, the Russians learned that a large Ottoman force—some 15,000 Turks and 20,000 Tatars under the Crimean khan Qaplan II Giray and Abaza Pasha of Ruşçuk—was threatening the Russian corps under Nikolai Repnin, which had been recalled from Wallachia. Slowed down by his supply train, Rumyantsev knew that he could not march his main force fast enough to rescue Repnin near Ryabaya Mogila (present-day Stănileşti). Instead, he dispatched a detachment under Quartermaster General Bauer with instructions to make a forced march through the night and reach the enemy's rear in time to help Repnin.[37] Among the staff officers selected for this mission was Kutuzov.

On June 21, as Bauer was hurrying to his rescue, Repnin held his ground against the Turks near Ryabaya Mogila. Khan Qaplan Giray was informed of Bauer's approach and split his forces, leaving the Ottoman infantry to pin down Repnin and leading some 20,000 Crimean Tatars to destroy the isolated Russian detachment. Although outnumbered, Bauer chose to strike first, placing cavalry on flanks and leading infantry into a wood that offered good protection against the enemy horsemen. The fighting continued most of the afternoon, and by day's end the Tatars were forced to give up and retreat to a fortified camp a few miles from Ryabaya Mogila.[38] Kutuzov distinguished himself on this occasion, and Rumyantsev commended him for his sedulousness and diligence, remarking that he and his colleagues "feared neither dangers nor hardships and eagerly went to fight the enemy."[39]

Two days after the battle, the First Army pitched its camp about four miles from Repnin and Bauer's forces. The Ottomans remained at their fortified camp near Ryabaya Mogila, where they received additional reinforcements, increasing their total strength to 70,000 men. On June 27, Rumyantsev reconnoitered enemy positions that were atop a high hill overlooking the marshes of the Prut River. The Ottoman camp was well situated, with its the northern approaches protected by the Călmăţiu Creek, the marshes precluding any attack from the west, and a deep ravine protecting it from the south. Bauer recommended attacking the eastern side of the camp, but Rumyantsev chose a bolder course of action. The following morning, June 28, the Russian army formed three attack columns. Bauer was given command of the central column, whose objective was to assault the northern face of the enemy camp, while Repnin's columns was sent on a flanking maneuver on the right to get into the enemy's rear and cut its line of retreat. At dawn the Russians advanced under cover of heavy artillery fire. Bauer deployed his men in squares and launched an assault on the forward trench line of the enemy camp, which pinned down the Ottoman forces. As a result, Qaplan Giray was surprised by Repnin's troops appearing on his right flank. Unable to stem the Russian advance, he ordered the camp abandoned and pulled his forces southward.[40]

Encouraged by his victory at Ryabaya Mogila, Rumyantsev moved in pursuit of the Ottoman army, which was trying to regroup on the banks of the Larga River in anticipation of the arrival of fresh troops.[41] Bauer's corps, together with Repnin's troops, was moved forward as the vanguard of the army and supported by a detachment commanded by Gregory Potemkin, the talented and good-looking son of modest landowners who was destined to become Empress Catherine's favorite and Kutuzov's munificent patron.[42] As the quartermaster, Kutuzov spent the next few days surveying the enemy positions and identifying their strengths and weaknesses. He was involved in some combats since Bauer's forces skirmished with the Ottomans for several days. On July 16 the Tatar cavalry launched a major attack on Bauer's right flank, forcing him to dispatch twelve cavalry squadrons in counterattack. The Ottomans brought in reinforcements that pushed the Russian cavalrymen back. Although Kutuzov's involvement remains hazy—and some details were clearly embellished in later years—his official record of service does show him taking part in this battle. During the fighting Bauer reinforced his cavalry with infantry forces, including two companies of light infantrymen led by Kutuzov, who then spent much of that afternoon skirmishing with the enemy forces.[43]

The Ottoman main camp was set up near the confluence of the Prut, Larga, and Babikul Rivers, where the steep riverbank slopes and marshes offered additional protection. Reinforced with earthworks and fortifications, it housed some 30,000 troops, with another 50,000 men scattered in separate entrenchments around it. On July 16, Rumyantsev convened a council of war at which he discussed his plan of action with senior officers.[44] He was well aware of the large size of the Ottoman army and especially of the Ottoman cavalry, which, in the words of Gregory Potemkin, "advance like an overflowing torrent."[45] It took strict discipline to hold ground against an assault by thousands of these riders, who charged, as one war veteran put it, with "frightful howling, the cries of Allah Allah, encouraging Muslims and scaring the Christians."[46] Yet the mass of the Ottoman cavalry consisted of unpaid irregulars who individually were skilled horsemen but collectively formed an ill-disciplined force.[47] Never comfortable on the defensive, Rumyantsev was determined to go on the offensive even with his smaller army. He decided to deploy a battle array of infantry squares, a design intended to negate the overwhelming numbers of the Ottoman horsemen.

The council of war approved the plan, which called for secretly erecting bridges over the Larga River at night and then launching the main attack from the northeast, between the Larga and Babikul Rivers, on the enemy's right flank. To ensure the success of this assault, Rumyantsev committed most of his army to it while ordering a diversionary attack across the Larga against the enemy's central position. This was a risky plan whose success depended on timely completion of preparations and on close coordination of actions between the Russian units. Kutuzov and other quartermasters were tasked with leading, in darkness, thousands of Bauer's troops to the specially designated third bridge over the Larga and then ensuring the well-timed crossing of the remaining forces and artillery across the first and third bridges.[48] They accomplished this task; "the blackness of the night could neither delay nor stop our movement," extolled the army's official *Journal of Military Operations*.[49]

Shortly after midnight of July 17, the Russian vanguard crossed the river and dug in on the heights on the opposite riverbank. Over the next two hours, Kutuzov and his quartermaster colleagues guided thousands more soldiers across the river. By 4 a.m., the Russian army was ready for assault, which began at once.[50] The Ottomans remained oblivious to the Russian movements because, as one participant admitted, their sentries fell asleep and allowed the Russians to move within striking distance of the encampment.[51] As in the last battle, Rumyantsev ordered his men to form squares—Bauer's infantry on the left, Repnin's and Potemkin's men in two squares on the right, with cavalry in between. General Peter Melissino's seventeen guns took up a position on the heights between Repnin's and Potemkin's squares and began bombarding the enemy positions. Khan Qaplan II Giray tried to push the enemy back by counterattacking with most of his cavalry, but he could not accomplish much against the stubbornness of the Russian squares and the murderous fire of their muskets and cannon. The Russian attack unfolded so rapidly and efficiently that by late afternoon the battle was over. The Ottomans were forced to evacuate their main camp and flee, leaving behind more than 1,000 killed and wounded, eight banners, more than thirty cannon, and much of their supply train; the Russian losses amounted to 29 killed and 62 wounded.[52] Kutuzov's performance—both as a quartermaster and in terms of his personal gallantry in battle—was noticed. The day after the battle Rumyantsev issued an order promoting him to "the ober-quarter-master of premier major rank," skipping the rank of second major.[53]

Larga did not decide the outcome of the campaign, but it had a crucial and immediate impact on the operational level, ending joint operations between the Ottomans and the Crimean Tatars. Khan Qaplan Giray took his men across the Sal'cha River toward Ismail and Kiliia, while the Turks retreated toward their supply depots and the fast-approaching main army under Grand Vizier Ivazpashazade Halil Pasha, who crossed the Danube and marched up the Pruth to meet the fleeing troops from Larga. The Ottoman forces numbered some 150,000 men, with almost 80,000 Tatar auxiliaries expected to join them soon. However, these staggering numbers do not tell the whole story. Large as it was on paper, the Ottoman army's battle strength was far lower. Ahmed Resmi Efendi, the clear-eyed Ottoman statesman, lamented the woeful state of the Ottoman military. Many of the units were full on paper but half that strength in reality. The pashas "gathered around them a filthy horde of thieves and homeless who left nothing but destruction and ruin in their passage." The men of state, "in order to maintain the proper pomp and circumstance in the wilderness," were "accompanied by up to 1000 red-cloaked, showy, personal retainers who were good for nothing but decorating the roadway." The Ottoman diplomat bemoaned the presence of tens of thousands of camp followers—"tent-pitchers, servants, beggars and hucksters, parasites, perhaps Jews and infidels, and the riff-raff of Istanbul"— who burdened the army and hampered its operations.[54]

The grand vizier, on the other hand, was confident of his army as he rested at a camp near the village of Kagul (Cahul, Moldova), where Rumyantsev confronted him in early August. The ensuing battle was one of the most decisive victories in Russian military history.

On July 31, the victories of Ryabaya Mogila and Larga fresh in his mind, Rumyantsev approached Kagul with confidence and came across the Ottoman camp on the right side of the river.[55] Informed of the Russian approach, Halil Pasha surveyed Russian positions and made preparations for an attack later the following morning. Aware that the Crimean Tatars could arrive soon, Rumyantsev decided to attack that same night. Drawing upon his experiences at Ryabaya Mogila and Large, he again employed infantry squares. Each division was ordered to form an "oblong square in such a way that the lateral sides [corresponded] to half the front side," with artillery in the center and corners of the squares; light infantry (in battalion squares) and cavalry (two ranks deep) were dispersed between the squares to provide additional support. Rumyantsev's intention was to create an extended line of five infantry squares that could confront the enemy from different directions while still remaining close enough to lend mutual support. These squares would also sustain the impetus of the advancing infantry through close coordination with the fast-moving artillery and cavalry.[56]

Early in the morning of August 1, the Russian army quietly left its position and advanced toward the Ottoman camp. Although the Turks were busy making their own preparations for an attack, the Russian predawn attack surprised them and disrupted their plans. As the Russian infantry charged forward and artillery fire lit up the sky, Halil Pasha ordered his cavalry to counterattack across the entire length of the battle line. The haste of the attack had not allowed time for proper planning. The Ottoman charges were poorly coordinated, allowing the Russian squares, backed with artillery and cavalry, to repel them and inflict considerable losses. An Ottoman flanking maneuver had also failed, as Rumyantsev diverted his reserves to

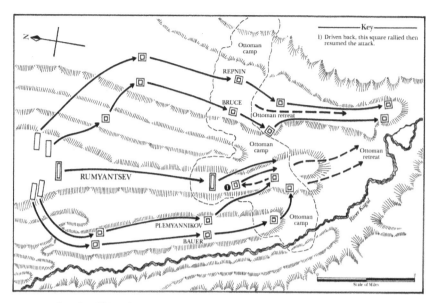

Key

1) Driven back, this square rallied then resumed the attack.

MAP 3 Battle of Kagul

confront it. Rumyantsev's men—Kutuzov's among them—soon reached
the Ottoman campsite, where fierce fighting ensued. The Ottomans focused their artillery fire on the squares of Général-en-chef Peter Olitz
and Lieutenant General Peter Plemyannikov, which suffered considerable
losses. As Bauer's and Plemyannikov's troops reached the first line of enemy
trenches, some 10,000 Janissaries, an elite corps of slave soldiers drawn from
the Ottoman Christians, attacked and managed to break Plemyannikov's
square, forcing the Russians to flee. Yet the timely arrival of Rumyantsev,
who personally rushed to halt the fleeing Russian soldiers, as well as the
massed fire of the Russian artillery commanded by General Peter Melissino,
rallied the Russian side; the men regrouped and resumed their advance with
the cry of "Vivat Ekaterina!" ("Long live Catherine!"). As at Larga, the intense fighting in the center diverted the grand vizier's attention from what
was happening on his left flank, where Bauer's men managed to fight their
way to the Ottoman trenches. Other Russian units attacked the enemy rear.
By late morning, the Crimean Tatar cavalry took flight, sparking desertion
in other Ottoman units and leaving the Janissaries to bear the brunt of the
battle. Having already suffered heavy losses and fearful of being encircled
inside the camp, they began to flee. Halil Pasha was unable to stem their
flight despite his best efforts.[57] The day ended with the Ottoman army in
full retreat, leaving behind as many as 20,000 of their dead and wounded
and more than 130 cannon. As before, the entire camp was left behind,
providing a bountiful prize for the victorious Russians, who lost fewer than
1,000 men.

Rumyantsev refused to let his now-staggering opponent slip away. He ordered Bauer's division to pursue the retreating enemy all the way to Kartal, where the Ottomans had to cross the Danube by boat to Isaccea. By the time Russians approached late in the evening, the Ottoman army was in full disarray. "There were no boats, and all the supplies and edibles remain in enemy hands," reported an Ottoman eyewitness. "There was nothing to eat: had there been, no one could have swallowed it. Everyone sat like a heron looking into the Danube. . . . Across from us was the [Danube flotilla] but neither clapping nor shouting reached them. The scoundrels would not send a boat to ask about our situation, ignoring even the Grand Vizier. [Some] 40,000 to 50,000 soldiers scattered every which way." Seeing the enemy's disorder, Bauer deployed his artillery on the hills overlooking the river and proceeded to assault the desperate enemy. Ahmed Resmi Efendi, who witnessed the mayhem in the Ottoman army, described how "those remaining at Kartal awaited the boats as if it were Judgment Day." Panic, exasperation, and desperation drove those still with some strength to throw themselves into the water, but most of them drowned.[58] By day's end, the Russians had captured hundreds of Ottoman prisoners and immense quantities of matériel, including twenty-six cannon, which the fleeing enemy had abandoned on the riverbank. The great Russian victory of Kagul was now complete. It earned Rumyantsev the rank of field marshal.

Rumyantsev followed up on his triumph by capturing the fortress of Izmail by the end of July, then those of Kilia, Akkerman, and Brăila in August and September. His main goal had been accomplished—he had driven most of the Ottoman forces in Bucak, Moldavia, and Wallachia back across the Danube and captured their key logistical hubs.[59] Knowing full well how weak his army now was, Rumyantsev thus chose to rest on his well-deserved laurels and call the campaign over. In late August, in his correspondence with the empress, he was already discussing moving the army to winter quarters, and in early fall he decided to assist Panin's Second Army in its efforts to capture the fortress of Bender, whose garrison was still resisting with intense determination.[60] On Rumyantsev's order, General Repnin was to lead his corps to reinforce the Second Army while Quartermaster General Bauer, who had performed so well during the summer campaign, was to assist Panin in the direction of the siege. Before departing, Bauer gathered a group of experienced and capable staff officers who volunteered to accompany him to Bender. Among them was Ober Quartermaster Kutuzov, whose decision to step forward on his own volition may have been an expression not only of the ambition typical of young officers but also of the desire to prove any remaining naysayers wrong. At any event, while his comrades rested at the winter quarters, Kutuzov fought with the Second Army at Bender, where the Ottoman garrison was reeling from a plague outbreak that claimed numerous lives, including senior military leaders.[61]

By the time Bauer and Kutuzov reached Bender, Panin had decided against the protracted siege and in favor of storming the fortress. Kutuzov volunteered to participate in the assault, which was scheduled for the night of September 27. Late in the evening the Russians set off huge mines that breached the fortress walls and allowed the attacking Russian columns to breach the fortress. In darkness, Kutuzov rushed with soldiers into the breach and spent all night fighting inside the town until the Ottoman garrison surrendered. By dawn, the Russian imperial flag waved above the fortress.[62]

Kutuzov had fully vindicated himself. Praised for his involvement in the assault, he returned to the headquarters of the First Army, where he remained until early November, when he asked for the transfer to a field unit. The fact that his reassignment took place "at his own request" has caused a debate among Kutuzov's biographers. Soviet historians argued that the request manifested Kutuzov's exasperation with "the dominant influence that German officers" held in the headquarters and "their mutual support of each other and unmerited rewarding and promotion."[63] Such claims ring hollow. In approving Kutuzov's request, the War College noted that with the army in winter quarters, the general headquarters had no vacancy for a quartermaster of the premier major rank. It is also evident, as some Russian historians have argued, that after the glorious summer campaign Kutuzov "felt within him a predisposition toward a field service rather than a staff one."[64] This may explain why he was often found in the thick of fighting in June and July and why he volunteered to take part in the assault at Bender. By nature active and ambitious, Kutuzov might have dreaded the prospect of repetitive staff work while in winter quarters and preferred being out with soldiers. In any case, his request was approved. On November 6, 1770, he was appointed a premier major in the Smolenskii Infantry Regiment and was then assigned to a grenadier company of the Starooskolskii Infantry Regiment.[65]

The winter months went by and both sides prepared for the next year's campaign. Despite the impressive and one-sided victories at Larga and Kagul, the war was not progressing as successfully as the Russian government had hoped. Counteracting success in Moldavia and south Ukraine were setbacks in the Mediterranean, where Russian invasions of the Morea and Lemnos had failed.[66] Catherine II needed a breakthrough to end a war that was already entering its third year. The Russian strategic plan for 1771 envisioned Rumyantsev's First Army remaining largely on the defensive and making occasional raids and diversionary strikes across the Danube while the Second Army took on a more offensive role, tasked with invading the khanate of the Crimean Tatars, a stalwart ally of the Ottomans. Even with new reinforcements, Rumyantsev still had fewer than 40,000 men to take on a much larger Ottoman force. The previous summer's victories had nonetheless made him confident of success.

The 1771 campaign in Moldavia and Wallachia turned out to be quite different. The new Ottoman grand vizier, Silahdar Mehmed Pasha, learned from
his predecessor's mistakes and chose not to invade Wallachia, avoiding the
kind of pitched battles that had turned out so badly for the Turks. Instead,
he remained on the defensive along the Danube River, where he concentrated
his resources and spent much time strengthening the remaining Ottoman
fortresses. This strategy frustrated Rumyantsev, who was forced to spend
months attacking Ottoman positions on the lower Danube. Control of the
river fortresses enabled the Ottomans to thwart the Russian advance and
conduct cross-river raids into Russian-controlled territory, which produced
some success. During this "war of posts," as one historian has described it,[67]
Rumyantsev spread his forces across a wide front, with the First Division
remaining in Moldavia, prepared to shift whichever way the Ottomans
threatened.[68] Kutuzov was not initially involved in these skirmishes because,
in the winter reshuffling, the Starooskolskii Infantry Regiment was assigned
to the reserve division.

The situation soon changed. Taking advantage of the fact that the Russian
forces were stretched over a wide front, the Ottomans concentrated their
forces near Rusçuk before crossing the river to attack the Russian-held fortress of Giurgiu. The small Russian garrison bravely resisted in the hope that
it would be relieved but was forced to surrender in mid-June. Emboldened by
this success, the Ottomans then conducted cross-river strikes at several other
points on the Danube River and sent some 10,000 men toward Bucharest,
though this latter attack was repelled by General Nikolai Repnin's contingent. In July Repnin, seriously ill, went on leave and turned command of the
Wallachian Corps over to Lieutenant General Reinholt Wilhelm von Essen,
who, aware of the Ottomans massing near Giurgiu and Turnu, requested
reinforcements, which included the reserve troops led by Major General
Peter Tekelli. Thus, by October 1771, Kutuzov found himself in Bucharest.

The strategic situation was seemingly turning to the Ottomans' favor.
The grand vizier had committed some 50,000 men, under Ahmed Pasha, to
the task of reclaiming Bucharest, where the Russians had fewer than 15,000
men. Much was at stake; the French ambassador to the Sublime Porte (as the
Ottoman Empire was colloquially called) believed that if Ahmed Pasha won,
it was "likely that all of Wallachia would be cleared of the Russians."[69] On
October 30, the Ottomans approached the Văcărești Monastery, just a few
miles from Bucharest.[70] Essen decided to anticipate the enemy attack and,
employing the Rumyantsevan tactic, advanced with his small corps deployed
into three infantry squares, with cavalry in the intervals. At the same time,
Tekelli's detachment had made a forced march through the night to get behind the enemy lines so that at dawn it struck the Ottomans from the rear,
just as Essen launched a frontal attack with his squares.[71] Caught between
two converging assaults, Ahmed Pasha tried to exploit his superiority in

cavalry to both assault the Russian squares and seek to turn the Russian flank to seize the road to Bucharest. Neither attempt succeeded. Essen successfully preempted a flanking maneuver by committing the Russian cavalry, which, though fewer in number, drove the Ottoman horsemen back. Nor was the Ottoman cavalry able to break any of the Russian squares, which met the enemy with deadly musket fire and canister.

By late afternoon Ahmed Pasha admitted defeat and retreated toward Giurgiu, with the Russians in hot pursuit. The Ottomans lost well over 2,000 men, more than a dozen cannon, and ten banners; Russian losses amounted to just 55 killed and 199 wounded.[72] Among the officers recognized for exceptional service during this battle was Kutuzov, whom Essen commended for gallantry and perseverance: "Not only was he sent more than once to different places to observe battle positions, and notwithstanding the great dangers brought back the most trustworthy reports to his superiors, but throughout that day, took upon himself to volunteer for all dangerous missions."[73] Several weeks later Kutuzov was promoted to lieutenant colonel.[74]

The battle near Bucharest was the last major engagement of the campaign. In November, Rumyantsev ordered his troops to winter quarters and Kutuzov's regiment moved to Moldavia. Thus ended one of the most memorable chapters of Kutuzov's military career. The battles of Ryabaya Mogila, Larga, and Kagul represented great victories for the Russian forces and were a testament to the skills of the Russian commander in chief. Time and again, Rumyantsev outsmarted and outfought his opponents, demonstrating a remarkable degree of operational and tactical flexibility that negated the Ottomans' numerical superiority. These battles featured innovative use of independent divisional squares, light mobile jäger battalions, and effective coordination during nighttime movements.

For Kutuzov, the war had provided a unique opportunity to learn the art of warfare by observing a master practitioner, one whose approach to war can be summarized in the following principles: audacity, speed and mobility, surprise, concentration, and flexibility. The young officer learned much simply by being at headquarters, observing generals at work, interacting with staff officers, and developing relationships. More crucially, he gained invaluable practical experience conducting reconnaissance, selecting battle positions, ensuring coordination between units, and participating in combat. It would be hard to find better practical training than this. And Kutuzov thrived with it. He arrived at the First Army as a captain and left as a lieutenant colonel. Serving under Rumyantsev had laid the foundation for Kutuzov's approach and practice of warfare, prompting him later to remark that before the campaign against the Turks he "did not comprehend the war" and that he had "gained a genuine understanding of the art of war only under the influence of the great hero of Larga and Kagul."[75]

CHAPTER 3 | At Death's Door, 1772–1785

TEN YEARS AFTER GRADUATING from military school, Kutuzov was already a senior officer and a veteran of several campaigns. His gregariousness, quick wit, generosity, and appetite for good living earned him a wide circle of friends, among whom he became known as a raconteur and impressionist.[1] Indeed, years before turning into the hoary and solemn man of public imagination, Kutuzov was an energetic young man with a flair for parody. Yet one night of boisterousness cost him dearly.

In the spring of 1772, after two exhausting campaigns, Russia and the Ottoman Empire turned to diplomatic negotiations that lasted through the rest of the year. The armies remained in their quarters, and officers and soldiers did their best to pass time as jovially as they could. One evening Kutuzov went with his comrades to one of the Bucharest haunts. Drinking and relaxing, these men sang, cheered, and reminisced about their brave deeds. When it was his turn to entertain, Kutuzov decided to tell a story that he embellished with various impersonations, including one of Rumyantsev himself. His imitation of the field marshal's strutting gait and manners elicited much laughter and delight among fellow officers that night. The following morning, however, brought devastating news. One of the officers—perhaps one of Kutuzov's earlier ill-wishers?—had reported this joke to his superior, who in turn informed Rumyantsev, a proud and vain man who took umbrage at being the butt of laughter among the officers. Kutuzov's punishment was swift and exacting. His unblemished fighting record saved him from getting thrown out of the army, but he was struck from the list of officers awaiting awards for service against the Ottomans and forced to leave the First Army. Disgraced and humiliated, he managed to get himself transferred to the Second Army in the Crimea.[2]

This incident had significant consequences for Kutuzov's life. A good-humored and outgoing man, he was stunned by such a betrayal from a fellow officer (whose identity remains unknown), whom he might have considered a comrade. He would find it hard to offer his trust again. It would have felt personal, even unreal: years of devoted service and hard work, distinction on the battlefield, and volunteering for perilous missions were effectively expunged by a puerile misstep. The transfer to the Crimea, a secondary theater of war, was clearly a demotion. His father, furious, made him promise to change his behavior. Kutuzov began gradually to become cautious and withdrawn, reserving his opinions and being more circumspect of people surrounding him. But the incident shaped Kutuzov's life in another way. It was while serving in the Crimea that Kutuzov had his first brush with death.

The situation in the Crimea remained tense. The new Crimean khan, Selim III Giray, who had recovered his throne after the death of Qaplan II Giray, struggled to contain the growth of Russian influence in the peninsula, especially after his predecessor fled to the Russian-controlled area and the Nogai tribesmen, seeing the Ottomans' power decline, defected to the Russian side. In 1771, the Second Army, under Général-en-chef Prince Vasilii Dolgorukov, invaded the Crimea; with the help of thousands of Nogai, the Russians defeated Selim in a series of engagements and forced him to surrender. With the fall of Bahçesaray, Perekop, Kerch, and Yenikale, the Crimean khanate found itself almost completely subjugated to Russian power.[3] Kutuzov came to the Crimea too late to take part in these battles. Nonetheless, General Dolgorukov empathized with the plight of this disgraced officer, whose talents and experience he quickly appreciated. He assigned him to Major General Ivan Kochius's detachment, which operated near the Kinburn peninsula (in the northwestern corner of the Crimean peninsula). Kutuzov remained there for almost two years. He was repeatedly commended for hard work and service. Tasked with reconnoitering the area, he "fulfilled the task with such success that far exceeded the expectations [of his superiors]," commented one contemporary, and ensured the success of the Russian military operations.[4] Praising his "zealous and assiduous fulfillment of all orders," Dolgorukov tasked Kutuzov with assisting Lieutenant General Ivan Jacobi in forming the units of the Moscow Legion (Moskovskii legion), a new joint arms corps comprising light infantry and irregular cavalry that would be well suited for the operations in the rugged Crimean terrain. Just five months after arriving, Kutuzov was commended for taking a grenadier battalion "formed of young and inexperienced recruits" and training them so well that the unit soon reached "prime condition and excellent understanding of the service" and performed well in skirmishes.[5]

The Ottomans were clearly upset at the Russian expansion in the Crimea, where the new khan had signed a formal agreement at Karasu Bazaar, establishing "an alliance and eternal friendship" between the Crimean khanate and the Russian Empire. Behind the rhetoric, however, lay the stark reality of the khanate falling under Russian sway. The numerous Tatar tribal and religious leaders who had fled the peninsula for the safety of Istanbul petitioned the Ottoman authorities to intervene in the Crimea. Their wishes seemed fulfilled when, in the summer of 1774, just as Russian and Ottoman diplomats were negotiating a peace treaty at the village of Küçük Kaynarca (today Kaynardzha, Bulgaria), a large Ottoman expedition—estimated at some 30,000 men—landed near Alushta, the onetime Genoese colony on the southeastern side of the Crimean peninsula.

Dolgorukov immediately diverted forces to confront the invasion.[6] Lieutenant General Valentin Musin-Pushkin took charge of a detachment of 2,750 men—including Kutuzov's grenadiers—and rushed to Alushta to prevent the Ottomans from establishing a foothold.[7] By the time he arrived at the southeastern coastline, the Ottomans had already set up their camps and sent an advance guard (about 8,000 men under Ismail Agha) to secure a fortified position near the villages of Shumy (present-day Kutuzovka) and Teterchi in a mountainous valley, about two miles inland. To reach this place, the Russians had to pass a canyon so steep and wooded that "just two persons could walk on a path running through the frightening narrows."[8] The ground was equally difficult beyond the narrows—the Ottoman positions at Shumy were on the high ground amidst "rocky hills" and "further strengthened with retrenchments" including a stone wall across the defile; two batteries were set up on the neighboring heights to protect the approaches.[9]

On August 4, unaware that the peace treaty ending the war had already been signed, Musin-Pushkin approached the Ottoman positions near Shumy and, unable to maneuver around them, decided to take them by assault.[10] Borrowing a page from Rumyantsev's tactical book, Musin-Pushkin deployed his infantry in squares in the valley and ordered them to attack the enemy's position, with the goal of driving the Ottomans back to the sea. "As soon as [our] troops launched the attack," the Russian commander reported, "they encountered ferocious artillery and musket fire." Taking advantage of the rugged environment, which hindered the Russian advance, reported the Russian commander, the Ottomans "fiercely resisted for two hours," and made the Russians "shed blood to gain every inch of the ground."[11] On the left wing, Kutuzov steadied his men as they slowly marched down "the steep mountain slopes" and toward a stone wall from where the enemy maintained steady musket fire.[12] Despite being fresh recruits, these soldiers demonstrated great discipline, composure, and gallantry under fire, and Kutuzov was later praised for having trained them to perform as well as veteran soldiers.[13]

The Russian advance was hindered by three rows of trenches that the Ottomans had dug in front of the stone wall, and which Kutuzov's men now had to cross under fire. Just as the grenadiers were climbing out of the middle ditch, Kutuzov, leading by example from the front, climbed onto a large rock on the edge of the ditch to rally his men.[14] As he urged his men forward, an Ottoman musket ball struck him between his eye and left temple, passing through his skull and coming out the other side.[15] Kutuzov fell from the rock into the ditch, landing on the bodies of dead and wounded men.[16] He was extremely lucky—the odds of surviving a half-inch lead projectile smashing the sphenoid (or temporal) bone, passing through the human cranium, and exiting on the other side are astronomically small.[17] He was also fortunate that as the troops pushed forward to secure victory, some grenadiers carried their unconscious and bleeding commander off the battlefield and to the care of the physicians, who rushed to tend to him as well as they could considering the circumstances and the critical nature of the injury.[18]

The odds of Kutuzov's survival seemed very slender. "Injuries of the head," observed British surgeon George James Guthrie, based on his experiences during the Napoleonic Wars, "are difficult of distinction, doubtful in their character, treacherous in their course, and for the most part fatal in their results."[19] As a rule, a gunshot wound to the head involves two types of injuries: the direct penetration of the cranium by a projectile and the damage caused by a pressure wave emanating from the fast-moving projectile traveling through the tissue; even if the bullet itself did not cause direct damage to the brain tissue, the pressure wave could easily cause both bleeding and brain swelling, which can lead to death. Patients with gunshot wounds of the cranium thus require prompt medical treatment to stop blood loss and prevent intracranial hematoma, which nearly always results in a fatal outcome. Furthermore, upon striking Kutuzov's temple, the musket ball would have punched out a hole and driven fragments of bone, hair, and tissue inside, thus introducing foreign bodies that could amplify the damage and cause infection and inflammation, often with lethal complications.

We do not know what treatment he received in those crucial first hours after the injury, when "life is not destroyed yet fluctuates on the verge of destruction," as Guthrie put it.[20] They would have almost certainly followed advice found in the contemporary medical treatises on head injuries and tried to "subdue inflammatory action."[21] Given the nature of Kutuzov's wound, there was no need to extract the projectile, a painful and risky exercise that involved inserting a probe (oftentimes a surgeon's own finger) into the wound. Instead, the physicians would have first cleaned the entrance and exit wounds and tried to clear all contaminating matter from them. They would have then bandaged Kutuzov's wound and conveyed him northward to receive proper medical care at a hospital. Traveling in a carriage on the rutted wooden-log tracks must have been an excruciating experience. Still, Kutuzov survived the arduous trip and continued his treatment in the Russian imperial capital.

There were a few promising signs. Kutuzov was young and in robust health, which made those around him express some hope for his recovery. As gruesome as the injury was, his brain was undamaged and, contrary to popular imagination, both of Kutuzov's eyes remained intact; the bullet did damage the muscles of the right eye, which thereafter was slightly crossed, but Kutuzov did not lose the eye and never resorted to an eye patch (as he is usually portrayed as wearing). His sight was impaired, however.

Kutuzov's life hung in the balance for the next several months. He managed to get through this agonizing period with the care and support of his father and the rest of the family. Years later, one of his students witnessed a scene that offers us a glimpse of what that first post-injury meeting between father and son might have been. Before graduating from the Land Noble Cadet Corps in December 1794, Sergei Glinka, who would become famous as a writer and memoirist, was required to pass an examination in Russian literature, which Kutuzov, as the then director of the Cadet Corps, attended. The theme for that year's examination essay was the meeting between a father and his wounded son returning from the battlefield. "When it was my turn," recalled Glinka, "I began to read my essay loudly and with great passion. Kutuzov listened to me attentively. His face gradually changed; his cheeks blushed as I read the following words, 'I am wounded, father, but my blood has been shed for my Fatherland and my wound has brought me laurels of glory! When your son returns home and you hold him in your embrace, only then the exuberant beating of your heart will whisper, 'This son has not betrayed his father's expectations!' Upon hearing these words, tears shimmered in Kutuzov's eyes; he approached and embraced me." For Kutuzov, Glinka's words must have touched a sensitive note and brought back the memories of that late summer day in 1774 when his father welcomed him back home.[22]

Many months of slow recovery followed, but by March 1775, Kutuzov felt well enough to submit a formal request for a furlough to complete his recovery. The War College must have been very surprised to hear from a man whom almost everyone considered to be at death's door. It conveyed the necessary documents to Empress Catherine II, who admired Kutuzov's heroism and seemingly miraculous survival. "We must look after our Kutuzov," the empress is said to have told her confidants. "He is destined to be my great general."[23] Whether or not she foresaw Kutuzov's future, the empress did extend considerable support to the injured officer. During the summer of 1775, she gifted him 1,000 gold rubles to cover expenses of his medical treatment.[24] She then awarded him the Order of St. George (fourth class), a recently created award designed to recognize gallantry in action,[25] and granted a year-long furlough, at full pay, so he could "seek treatment of his wound at the warm waters" in Europe.[26]

Kutuzov spent the next year and a half convalescing and undertaking a grand tour of Europe, visiting Prussia, Austria, the Dutch Republic, and parts of Italy. The news of his injury and miraculous survival spread widely, and he became something of a celebrity. In Berlin and Vienna, he was welcomed in high society, meeting the Prussian king, Frederick the Great, and dining with Austrian field marshals Ernst Gideon von Laudon and Franz Moritz von Lacy. It seems likely that Kutuzov spent some time at the University of Strasbourg, which had a sizable community of Russian students. Though no direct evidence of him formally attending the university has been uncovered yet, Kutuzov probably sat in on some courses.[27] He spent many weeks undergoing medical treatments in Leiden, then a great center of medical learning. According to Kutuzov's acquaintances and early biographers, medical scholars were astonished by the nature of Kutuzov's injury. Some refused to believe that he could have survived it. While in Leiden, Kutuzov heard that a local professor of surgery and anatomy was scheduled to give a talk to demonstrate that Kutuzov's injury was nothing but "a fable," believing that at the very least he would have lost his sight. As the professor completed his talk, Kutuzov stood up and said, "Dear professor, here I am, and I can see you without a problem."[28]

Kutuzov's physical scars healed, but the less visible wounds did not. Despite fully recovering his cognitive abilities, which is remarkable in itself, he suffered from headaches, dizziness, lethargy, and sensitivity to light for the rest of his life; in later years he frequently complained about drowsiness and weariness of his eyes and found writing letters a strenuous exercise.[29] Modern medical scholarship has shown the extent to which even slight damage to areas of the prefrontal cortex can cause subtle (in some cases even pronounced) changes in personality.[30] The incident with Rumyantsev had made Kutuzov more circumspect around people. The injury he had sustained at Shumy most certainly accentuated this. He began to become morose, suspicious, and evasive. "Whenever his close friends approached him desiring to learn his thoughts and opinions about a person or topic," observed one contemporary, "Kutuzov, as soon as he understood their intentions, would switch the subject of conversation; occasionally he would even tell them, 'What business do we have for others?' before adding that famous proverb, 'Nothing is better than to know thyself!' "[31] The formerly cheerful and sociable Kutuzov henceforth rarely revealed his emotions. "Kutuzov may seem accessible to everybody," observed one senior Russian officer, "but his heart is closed to them all."[32]

A great deal happened while Kutuzov was traveling in Europe. The Russo-Ottoman War ended with the Treaty of Küçük Kaynarca, signed on July 21, 1774. "This most glorious peace ever concluded by the Russians," as one British periodical proclaimed it, marked a Russian triumph, both military and political, with long-lasting effects on Ottoman rule.[33] In the wake of continued Russian military victories, Sultan Abdulhamid I recognized the independence of the Crimean khanate, which would pave the way for Russia to annex it just nine years later. It was the first time that an Ottoman ruler had surrendered a territory largely populated by Muslims. The Ottomans retained Moldavia and Wallachia but recognized Russia's special position in the region, a concession that would have major repercussions just a generation later. The sultan also gave Russian merchants commercial privileges throughout the empire and agreed to pay a heavy war indemnity.

The most consequential articles of the treaty, however, dealt with Russia's role inside the Ottoman Empire. The sultan granted the Russian empress the right to open consulates within the Ottoman Empire and to establish a Russian Orthodox Church in the Galata district of Istanbul. The treaty's Article 7 gave Russia the right to represent (and protect) the church and its personnel. These provisions proved to be highly controversial. Disagreements over their interpretation quickly emerged between St. Petersburg and Istanbul. Russia interpreted them as granting it the status of the protector of Ottoman Orthodox Christians, which allowed it to actively interfere in Ottoman domestic affairs. The treaty was crucial in the development of the "Eastern Question" and contributed to the outbreak of several more Russo-Ottoman wars over the next eight decades.[34]

Even as the war was under way, Empress Catherine faced a new challenge to her authority. In 1773, a Don Cossack named Emel'yan Pugachev claimed to be the dead emperor Peter III and launched a revolt in the eastern provinces of the empire. Promising political and social transformations, including emancipation of serfs from their gentry masters, Pugachev mobilized tens of thousands of serfs, Cossacks, and various minorities, who attacked noble estates, plundering, burning, and murdering as they went. The Russian imperial authorities rushed to negotiate a treaty with the Ottomans, partly to make battle-hardened troops available for domestic duty. The arrival of these units turned the tide of the rebellion in the government's favor. In early fall of 1774, just as Kutuzov was making his first steps toward recovery, the Russian army crushed the insurgents at Chernyi Yar and launched bloody reprisals. Pugachev was captured and transported by Lieutenant General Alexander Suvorov in a metal cage to Moscow, where in January 1775 he was beheaded and then quartered.[35] The Pugachev Rebellion had a long-lasting effect on the Russian Empire, halting many of reforms that Catherine had previously attempted and facilitating consolidation of the institution of serfdom.

During Kutuzov's convalescence, the Moscow Legion, in which he commanded a grenadier battalion, was disbanded and its units used to form new infantry regiments. Thus, in the spring of 1775 Lieutenant Colonel Kutuzov was formally transferred to the Tulskii Infantry Regiment, which was created from two battalions of the Moscow Legion. Two years later, as part of ongoing military restructuring, Kutuzov was struck from the list of officers of that regiment and assigned to the staff of Gregory Potemkin, who returned to St. Petersburg as a war hero and the empress's new lover. The letters Catherine and Potemkin sent each other reveal that their affair was one of "laughter, sex, mutually admired intelligence, and power."[36] Potemkin rapidly rose in political stature, becoming the governor-general of Novorossiya, a member of the State Council, vice president of the War College, and commander of the Russian light and irregular cavalry. Pleased to hear of Kutuzov's recovery, Potemkin decided to employ his knowledge and experience in organizing new hussar and lancer regiments. Consequently, he appointed him to command the Luganskii Pikineer (Lancer) Regiment and supported his promotion to colonel, which Catherine II approved in July 1777.[37]

With his career back on track, Kutuzov made one of the biggest decisions of his life: he proposed marriage to Catherine (Ekaterina Ilyinichna) Bibikova. He and Catherine had known each other for many years. She was the youngest daughter of Ilya Aleksandrovich Bibikov (1698–1784), an engineer lieutenant general who had distinguished himself during the Seven Years' War and later directed the famed Russian arms manufacturing plant in Tula. Their families knew each other well and had, in fact, recently bonded— Kutuzov's uncle, Admiral Ivan Loginovich Golenischev-Kutuzov, married Avdotya Bibikova, the eldest daughter of General Ilya Bibikov. Kutuzov first met Catherine when she was just an adolescent. After the death of her mother, she had moved with her elder sister into Admiral Golenischev-Kutuzov's house, which, as noted, Kutuzov frequented.[38] They would have spent time together on various occasions, though it is doubtful that this young officer would have paid much attention to a shy girl who was seven years younger than him. Over the years their relationship slowly evolved from acquaintance to friendship and then romance, though frequently interrupted by the young man's deployments. Kutuzov must have been surprised to see the girl blossoming into a woman of striking appearance, with dark brown wavy hair and gleaming brown eyes, great wit, and fun-loving personality. Spirited and enthusiastic, Catherine loved literature, adored theater, and delighted the society in which she sparkled and flashed with her wit and humor. He could not but notice her. Their parents did the rest.

With the imperatives of inheritance and lineage on their minds, families naturally hoped for a judicious blend of the practical and affective when arranging their children's marriages. Kutuzov's marriage seemed to achieve both. The Bibikovs were a well-known noble family that descended from the Tatar princes. Like the Golenischev-Kutuzovs, they produced generations of military and government officials in the service of the Muscovite rulers. After his brush with death, Kutuzov thought it was time to settle down and raise a family, though he doubtless felt a bit anxious in requesting Catherine's hand in marriage. What would this young, intelligent, eye-catching, and sociable woman make of the prospect of marrying a man who had never been particularly handsome and had now suffered such a disfiguring injury? His appearance notwithstanding, Kutuzov was a natural charmer, known for his way with words. "He did not just speak," observed one contemporary fawningly, "but rather played with his tongue like another Mozart or Rossini, enchanting listeners."[39] Describing his former superior, General Alexander Langeron made many critical comments about Kutuzov. Nonetheless, he also conceded that Kutuzov possessed an "extraordinary memory, excellent education, compassionate attitude [and] ability to maintain stimulating conversation."[40] For her part, Catherine must have found him attractive, intelligent, and gallant, and had no qualms about accepting his marriage proposal. The couple wed at the Church of St. Isaac of Dalmatia in St. Petersburg on April 27/May 8, 1778.[41]

They remained together for thirty-five years and throughout remained close and caring. Catherine paid no heed to her husband's flirtations, and Kutuzov closed his eyes to her extravagance and prodigality. Their letters are full of warmth and expressions of fondness and regard. After the wedding, Catherine embraced the challenges of being an officer's wife and accompanied her husband on his deployments, as evidenced by the steady births of their six children: daughters Praskovya in 1779, Anna in 1782, Elisabeth in 1783, Catherine in 1787, and Darya in 1789 (1788 under the Julian calendar) and son Nicholas in 1790. Throughout these years Kutuzov remained deployed in the southwestern provinces of the Russian Empire and traveled home only on a handful of occasions, including after the death of his father in the summer of 1784.[42] In later years, as the children required constancy and security, Catherine had to stay at home, which meant enduring long separations from her husband. "I have not seen Mikhailo Larionovich in eight months," she complained to a friend in December 1790. This would be a constant refrain in their relationship.[43]

Kutuzov remained with the Luganskii Pikineer Regiment, based in the southwestern regions of the Russian Empire, for almost a decade.[44] The regiment was part of the Russian effort to consolidate control over the newly acquired territories and to lay the ground for further expansion into the Crimean khanate. For Kutuzov, these were years of continuous military training and deployments against a population that had little desire to find itself under a new imperial rule.

After the end of the Russo-Ottoman War, the Crimean khanate, populated largely by Crimean Tatars but with a large community of Greeks and Armenians, had become virtually independent. As noted, the sultan recognized the khan's political independence but continued to exercise his leadership of the faithful as a caliph, the leader of the entire Muslim community. In the postwar turmoil, Devlet Giray, known for his anti-Russian sentiments, claimed the leadership of the khanate and refused to abide by the Russo-Ottoman peace treaty. Although she recognized Devlet as the Crimean khan, Catherine also began grooming the more pliant Şahin Giray, who resided at the Russian court, as his successor. Şahin soon moved to seize power in the Crimea with the Russian help; on Catherine's orders, the Russian army supported his claim, invaded the Crimea in the fall of 1776, and overthrew Devlet. "Şahin Giray is a tool," observed Sultan Abdul Hamid I upon receiving the news. "The aim of the Russians is to take Crimea."[45] He was right; under the cover of Crimean "independence," Catherine had successfully installed a puppet regime. Şahin Giray remained in power for less than seven years, during which he tried to consolidate his authority in the peninsula but faced continued resistance from the Crimean Tatars, who opposed these efforts to centralize governing structures and were incensed by gradual Russian encroachment on their lands. Between 1778 and 1782 the Tatars launched several revolts against the khan but were unable to remove him from power due to the timely interventions of Russian forces. After the final invasion, Catherine decided the time was ripe for resolving the Crimean question once and for all, and in April 1783 she issued a formal proclamation annexing the peninsula to the Russian Empire.[46]

Kutuzov's biographers traditionally claimed that he developed close relations with General Alexander Suvorov during this period. In the words of Filip Sinel'nikov, Suvorov "employed him in the most important missions and entrusted to him only those tasks that required particular exactitude and extreme prudence."[47] Echoing Soviet propaganda, Roger Parkinson claimed that Kutuzov had served for six years under Suvorov's direct command and that he was promoted to brigadier general in July 1782 "largely owing to Suvorov's influence."[48] Yet archival documents show that none of it is actually true.[49] In reality the two officers never crossed paths during these years. While Suvorov commanded a separate corps and fought in the Crimea and the Kuban region, Kutuzov's Luganskii Pikineer Regiment remained deployed in the Novorossiya Governorate under Potemkin's direct command. Thus, claims that Kutuzov went through the "Suvorovian school of training and educating troops," imbibing Suvorov's tactics and strategy and becoming "Suvorov's best disciple," are farfetched.[50]

Equally fanciful are suggestions that Suvorov played any role in Kutuzov's promotions to brigadier and major general. The former occurred at the recommendation of Lieutenant General Count Antoine de Balmain, who commanded Russian forces in the Novorossiya Governorate and who praised Kutuzov for his hard work in training and managing the regiment; after examining the Luganskii Pikineers, Balmain reported that he found the regiment "in all its elements, whether internal or external, as well as in its military drill, to be such excellent condition as one can only wish to find in cavalry regiments."[51] Kutuzov was not involved in the Russian interventions in the Crimea, though his unit—reorganized into the Mariupolskii Light Horse Regiment—was sent to suppress resistance in the peninsula in the aftermath of the Russian annexation.[52] It is because of his "most enterprising involvement in all directives and endeavors to subdue the rebels and restore peace and tranquility," as one biographer put it fulsomely, that Kutuzov was promoted to the rank of major general on December 5, 1784.[53] Rather than Suvorov, it was Potemkin who supported Kutuzov's promotion to a general's rank and then signed the order appointing him to lead the Bug Jäger Corps, a new light infantry unit that was to be formed.[54]

This appointment is significant for what it tells us about Kutuzov's military career. Since graduating as an engineer from a military school, he had been employed successively as a staff officer, quartermaster officer, and commander of musketeer, grenadier, pikineer, light cavalry, and now light infantry units. The diversity of his employments is striking; few officers in any country could boast such a range. Time and again his superiors turned to him to get things done. And he consistently rose to the occasion. He had survived a demotion that would have destroyed most careers, and a wound that would have killed most people. Kutuzov had shown that, in Pushkin's expression, he was becoming part of "that lofty flock of Catherine's eagles."[55]

CHAPTER 4 | "An Eagle from the Lofty Flock," 1786–1789

THE CONCEPT OF LIGHT-MOVING combat infantry was developed in the seventeenth century but came to a full fruition a century later. During the 1740s, Prussia and other German states experimented with recruiting gamekeepers and foresters for specialized units of jägers, or huntsmen, exploiting their familiarity and experience with true rifles, rather than smooth-bore muskets. In France, Jean-Chrétien Fischer formed the *Compagnie des Chasseurs*, one of the first of the French light infantry units, in 1743. The Seven Years' War proved the worth of these light infantry units, especially in North America, where they performed well amid the wooded and rugged terrain. The jägers were not employed in the traditional sense of a regular infantry, meaning deployed in a linear battle array; instead, they were intended to skirmish ahead of the main infantry to harass and disrupt the enemy's advance.

The first Russian light infantry units were established during the Seven Years' War as the Russians encountered Prussian jägers on battlefields. Realizing their great utility, the Russians soon adopted them, and by the end of the war twenty-five Russian regiments already had light infantry companies. In 1777, the Russian light infantry went through its first major round of restructuring as six jäger battalions were formed. Seven years later, Gregory Potemkin initiated yet another reform with an objective of forming ten jäger corps (*egerskiye korpusa*). One of these new four-battalion units was the Bug Jäger Corps (Bugskii Egerskii Korpus), which incorporated soldiers from the 4th Kharkovskii and 2nd Byelorusskii Field Battalions as well as the 1st and 2nd Jäger Battalions.[1]

As he assumed command of the Bug Jäger Corps, Kutuzov knew that he faced a long road before the corps could go from concept to reality. His immediate task was to find soldiers "suitable for the jäger service."[2] His instructions specified that the candidates had to be of short stature—so that they could pose a smaller target for the enemy and easily navigate mountainous or wooded terrain—while demonstrating outstanding agility, fortitude, and marksmanship. Once selected, these soldiers had to be educated and trained in light infantry tactics, something not yet fully familiar to the Russian military of the time. Over the next several months Kutuzov threw himself into the work. Surviving documents testify to his multifaceted and scrupulous efforts to organize and train a corps of some 4,000 men.[3] Kutuzov demonstrated not only his administrative talents but also the breadth of his military thinking, producing a military treatise, *Remarks on Infantry Service in General and That of the Jägers in Particular.*[4]

The tract, which Kutuzov completed in June 1786, was conceived as a concise and accessible manual on how to train and employ light infantry. It is a unique document. Unlike other Russian military treatises that dealt with an established branch of service (line infantry or cavalry), Kutuzov grappled with a subject that had been little explored and that required fresh and comprehensive consideration. The final work reflected central themes of the Military Enlightenment, as one modern historian aptly defined it—an attempt to incorporate the ideas of the Enlightenment philosophes into the military profession. Warfare was perceived a fundamental facet of human existence and a crucial instrument of sovereign states. It had to be studied, rationalized, shaped, and modernized. The "military philosophes" hoped to make a "good war" in a couple of ways. First, by waging it only for just causes, and doing so effectively and efficiently to spare precious resources of the fiscal-military state, especially manpower. Second, they wanted to see the military profession show more compassion, rationality, and dignity.[5] The goal was to wage enlightened warfare.

Kutuzov shared these ideals. His treatise opened with a section entitled "On the Maintenance of a Soldier" that reflected concern for soldiers' health and well-being. "The good care of a soldier being the utmost reason for the high quality and strength of any military unit," reads the opening line, "I therefore designate this issue to be the most important of subjects and the foremost concern of the battalion commanders." An officer's day-to-day responsibility was not only to uphold strict discipline in his unit; it was also to ensure the welfare of the soldiers. Soldiering was a unique calling, one that required a person to commit wholeheartedly to the service; a soldier could not be "left unprepared for his duty and cannot feel anything but faithfulness and readiness to carry out service required from him." But such readiness and devotion could be guaranteed only if he was provided with all the necessary sustenance—provisions, uniforms, equipment, and money. Otherwise, he would, as Kutuzov put it, "experience deficiencies that can undermine his health and, on some occasions, even endanger his life, and consequently cause an irreparable harm to military service." Thus, any mistreatment of soldiers by officers constituted a violation of military order. He was particularly attentive to soldiers' health and instructed officers to take the utmost care to "protect healthy soldiers from any illnesses," including by issuing proper uniforms, paying salaries on time, and organizing suitable training regimens; if a soldier became unwell, the officer was required to closely observe and facilitate his recovery. While demanding strict discipline, Kutuzov also cautioned his officers against excessive severity. Problems in the units, he noted in one of his orders, "are largely the result of poor care on the part of colonels; if the soldiers are cared for as needed, there would be few, if any, wanting to flee."[6] His attention to every human detail meant that the Bug Jäger Corps consistently showed the lowest rates of sick and missing soldiers, causing Potemkin to write admiringly that "there is not a single case of desertion in this corps while other corps have [plenty of] them." The Bug Jäger Corps also demonstrated better rates of convalescence—in 1788, only 9.1 percent of its rank and file were unavailable for service, compared to 15 percent in the Taurida Jäger Corps and 24.4 percent in the Ekaterinoslav Corps.[7]

The second and third parts of the treatise deal with the requirements of the "infantry service in general" and light infantry training in particular. Kutuzov's primary goal was to form a regiment of infantry capable of combining the discipline of the regular trained soldier with the qualities of the scout and skirmisher. Such training, he hoped, would ensure close interoperability between regular and light infantry units on the battlefield. He therefore initially drilled his men in the "ABCs of any and all soldiering"—that is, how to dress in a soldier-like manner, how to walk and march, how to disperse and regroup on given signals, and how to form, advance, and wheel in formation so they could effectively engage the enemy. As with the regular infantry, the jägers were required to learn three types of marching speeds: the ordinary pace (*obyknovennyi shag*), of up to 70 steps a minute; the fast pace (*skoryi shag*), of up to 120 steps a minute; and the rapid pace (*rezvyi shag*)— broadly defined as "running at a speed that humans can maintain without exhausting themselves"—which to Kutuzov's thinking was "the only movement appropriate for jägers," though he was careful to note that it should be employed only for short bursts of "up to 400 paces."[8] Kutuzov believed that on march and on fields of battle, jägers were to provide a vital support for the troops of the line by operating in defiles, brush, wooded areas, and other difficult terrain that would be hard to access for their heavier-footed brethren. Equipped with shorter-barreled rifles and lighter uniforms, they were better suited to exploit terrain to scatter in front of the line infantry, get closer to the enemy lines, and target enemy officers and soldiers, thus disrupting the chain of command and spreading confusion and fear in the enemy ranks.

Kutuzov was convinced that accurate fire was the very essence of light infantry service. Unlike the line infantry's volleys, the jägers were to maintain orderly and directed gunfire that could inflict heavy losses on the enemy. To achieve the necessary high level of marksmanship, Kutuzov insisted that as soon as a recruit learned "basic notions of maintaining his position in formations," he should "without delay" be trained in target practice. He emphasized personalized, individual instruction so that each soldier could understand what was asked of him.[9] Training had to be practical and comprehensible to the largely illiterate recruits, who were to be taught "in the simplest and most accessible manner." Soldiers were educated in the basics of firing trajectories, shown how to load and fire standing, kneeling, or lying down, and taught how to adjust the elevation of their weapons based on the distance to the target. Good marksmanship could be only achieved through constant practice, so Kutuzov devised special firing ranges that featured eight-foot wooden boards with human silhouettes painted in black on them; these were placed in front of an earthen barrier, which made it easier to recover spent bullets. Jägers were required to shoot at these targets from various ranges and positions, starting at 100 paces and gradually increasing to 300 paces; 150 paces was optimal for aimed firing. Soldiers were expected to practice with their own weapons so that they could become familiar with their properties. Kutuzov wanted his officers to observe soldiers and approach them after each shot to explain what they did right or wrong.[10]

Kutuzov's treatise represented the first comprehensive attempt to introduce light infantry service in the Russian army, offering a clear explanation of the goals and types of jäger combat training and a discussion of various ways light infantry could be employed in battle. His dream was to produce an eager and self-reliant skirmisher who would also be able to fit in with the regular infantry's shoulder-to-shoulder movement of line and column. The Kutuzovian system of training was thus designed to address practical needs—it offered nothing about reviews and parade grounds. Rather than teaching them how to shine buckles and powder wigs, it offered recruits pragmatic advice and encouraged common sense and fighting spirit.

How much Kutuzov, working in the relative isolation of southern Ukraine, knew about the ongoing light infantry experimentations in other European armies—especially the efforts by Frederick the Great in Prussia, Jeffery Amherst and Henry Bouquet in North America, and George Howe at the Salisbury camp in Britain—is not clear. The evidence is limited and there is nothing that establishes that Kutuzov was exposed to western European theory and practice of light infantry warfare.[11] But we may assume that a well-educated officer, one who spoke foreign languages and had traveled abroad, had been exposed to these lines of thinking. He might have learned about them during his voyage to Europe in the 1770s or read some of the light infantry treatises that appeared in print during this period.[12] Kutuzov did demonstrate a thorough understanding of new developments in tactical doctrines and shared the belief of one French military theorist who in 1782 wrote about the ideal qualities that a light infantry commander must have, in both theory and practice: "stern without being harsh, firm and constant in his endeavors without being stubborn, industrious in expeditions, courageous, bold and prudent."[13] Looking at Kutuzov's treatise and what he had accomplished at the Bug Jäger Corps, it is evident that his ideas and methods represented some of the approaches that were being pioneered elsewhere. In Russia, they were the foundation for jäger training—the "Kutuzovian jäger maneuvers," as they were known by 1810—and tactical employment for many years to come.[14]

In addition to forming an entire jäger corps, Kutuzov received additional assignments from Potemkin, who clearly appreciated the general's ability to multitask. Throughout late 1785 and early 1786, whenever he experienced the need for new companies and battalions, Potemkin turned to Kutuzov for help. The Russian army had but four grenadier regiments, which were considered elite assault units and staffed with the most able fighters—those who could lead a decisive assault that might sway the tide of battle. By late 1785, the Russian high command decided to double the number of grenadier regiments, and they entrusted this crucial task to Kutuzov. In February 1786 he was instructed to create, equip, and train five new grenadier units, an assignment that was kept secret due to its sensitive nature, particularly as relations between Russia and the Ottoman Empire were deteriorating. Kutuzov excelled at these tasks. Relying on his previous experience of forming various types of units, he delivered grenadier battalions—all well trained and equipped—a mere five months later and then continued to supervise the jäger corps training for the rest of the year.[15]

In the spring of 1787 Kutuzov learned that Empress Catherine, joined by the Austrian emperor Joseph II and accompanied by foreign diplomats, had embarked on a whirlwind tour through Ukraine and the Crimea. Potemkin spared no effort or expense in commemorating the twenty-fifth anniversary of the empress's reign and showcasing his success in consolidating Russian power in southern territories. His critics levied baseless accusations that he had constructed phony portable settlements (the notorious "Potemkin villages") along the banks of the Dnieper River to impress the empress, but the tales of such elaborate sham villages, with glowing fires designed to amuse the monarch and her entourage as they surveyed the barren territory at night, are fictional. Potemkin did, however, organize grand festivities—salutes, illuminations, and various celebrations—to entertain Catherine. He had also arranged for large-scale military maneuvers to be conducted at Kremenchug on May 11 and at Poltava on July 19. Kutuzov's jägers were stars in both events. At Kremenchug, Catherine was greeted with a massive artillery cannonade that started as soon as the imperial cortege, sailing down the river, approached the town, which was festooned and decorated; passing through the specially built triumphal gates, the empress traveled down the town's main thoroughfare, which was lined with thousands of troops, including the entire Bug Jäger Corps.[16] The court journal makes no mention of military maneuvers that, according to eyewitness accounts, left Catherine and her companion enthralled. However, Louis-Philippe de Ségur, the French ambassador to Russia, witnessed the Kremenchug maneuvers and was impressed by "the spectacle of a grand review of forty-five squadrons of cavalry and a numerous body of infantry," which had proven so effective in the war against the Ottomans: "I have seldom seen finer men or better equipment." During the maneuvers the Russian infantry, which included not only the jägers but also the Mariupolskii Light Horse Regiment that Kutuzov had formed earlier, advanced in several columns with a "screen of skirmishers" preceding them. Pretending that they had encountered an enemy force, soldiers quickly deployed into square formations with the cavalry staying in between them so that "the entire battle line presented the appearance of four bastions." After a few rounds of "very lively fire," as de Ségur noted, the squares moved against their imaginary opponent, Kutuzov's jägers scattering as skirmishers in front of them and the Cossacks, "lances in hand and loudly hollering," pursued the vanquished enemy.[17] For Kutuzov, the Kremenchug maneuvers were a doubly pleasing experience, for he could witness the success of his efforts to organize both light cavalry and light infantry units. Impressed by the martial display, the empress noted in one of her letters that "the troops here are such that even foreigners are honestly extolling them," and praised the light cavalry, which she deemed "magnificent" and "such as never before existed."[18]

A month later, the Bug Jäger Corps, as well as the four grenadier battalions that Kutuzov had formed and trained, took part in the commemoration of Peter the Great's victory over the Swedes at Poltava. On July 19, several thousand Russian troops gathered on the field outside the town, where, before the empress, they conducted a mock battle, "demonstrating exemplary order and praiseworthy swiftness of action."[19] Impressed by the performance of Kutuzov's light infantry, Catherine asked to meet him. "I shall henceforth consider you among the most capable people and the best of the generals," she told him. Then she admonished him for riding a high-spirited horse: "I shall not let you go until you change this horse, for I shall never forgive you if you got hurt riding it." Kutuzov gratefully complied.[20]

Empress Catherine's 1787 procession through the southern provinces took place during a moment of volatility. The Ottoman government had long complained about Russian infringements of the Treaty of Küçük Kaynarca and encroachments into the Ottoman sphere of influence. The fall of the Crimean khanate in April 1783 was just one component in this multifaceted imperial power struggle. That same year, Catherine approved the Treaty of Georgievsk with the Georgian kingdom of Kartli Kakheti, extending Russian authority across the mighty Caucasus Mountains. The Russo-Georgian treaty was of major importance. Not only did it challenge Iranian and Ottoman influences in the Caucasus, but it also served notice to rival European powers, most notably France, that the balance of power in the Near East was shifting. The Russo-Austrian alliance of 1781 also proved essential in Russia's continued expansionist policy in the Balkans. In agreeing to this alliance, Austria was forced to deal with the fundamental problem of its foreign policy: that of reconciling its need for Russia's support against Prussia with its fundamental opposition to further Russian expansion in southeastern Europe. By joining with Russia, Austria hoped both to strengthen its hand vis-à-vis Prussia and to limit Catherine's gains in the Ottoman domains. Catherine's triumphal procession through Ukraine and the newly annexed Crimea, however, caused new concerns about Russian intentions and exacerbated tensions between the Ottoman Empire and Russia. In late August 1787, Sultan Abdulhamid I, influenced by pro-war political factions and the ulama (religious leaders), as well as by the French and British prodding, once again imprisoned the Russian ambassador and declared war on Russia in an effort to reclaim territories lost in preceding conflicts.

Catherine welcomed this new conflict. With France mired in a financial crisis and unable to support its Ottoman ally, the Russian empress had an opportunity to take on the Ottomans, with an eye toward turning the Black Sea into a "Russian lake" and possibly fulfilling her cherished "Greek Project"—reestablishing a Byzantine state on Ottoman territory with Istanbul as its capital.[21] The Ottomans were ill-prepared for a new conflict. Although their empire contained Austrians in the Banat (parts of present-day Romania, Serbia, and Hungary), the Ottomans were unable to stem the Russian attack.

Even before war was formally declared, Potemkin had prepared for such an eventuality. On his orders the Russian units that participated in the Poltava celebrations were sent southward to beef up the Russian military presence along the border. On August 12, 1787, Kutuzov got secret orders to redeploy his entire jäger corps to a new camp south of the Dnieper River and closer to the Ottoman borders. Relocating more than 4,000 men was not an easy endeavor—the campsite had to be dismantled, ailing soldiers taken care of, and arrangements made along the route to ensure orderly relocation of units and equipment. Kutuzov's orders reveal his attention to detail as well as his continued care for the welfare of his men, who had to march some ninety miles, cross the Dnieper River, and concentrate near the border town of Ol'viopol.[22]

By late September, Kutuzov received news of the start of the war—Empress Catherine issued a declaration and appointed Potemkin to command the main Russian force, the Army of Ekaterinoslav, consisting of over 80,000 men and 180 cannon. Kutuzov was formally assigned to the corps of Général-en-chef Yuri Dolgorukov, where he commanded a special contingent—the Bug Jäger Corps and the Elisavetgradskii, Khersonskii, and Aleksandriiskii Light Horse Regiments, with twelve cannon—deployed along the Southern Bug River, which marked the boundary between the empires. He implemented extensive patrols to keep the imperial border under constant observation and, finding the fortress of Ol'viopol "not in the best condition," as he wrote to Potemkin, diverted resources to repair and fortify it.[23] On September 27, as the Ottomans appeared in force near the Kinburn (Kilburun) peninsula in the western part of the Crimea, Kutuzov received orders to move his men south and cover approaches to Kherson, the strategically important fortress at the estuary of the Dnieper River, where the Russian Black Sea fleet was based. He arrived there a week later, taking up positions near the mouth of the Bug River and coming under direct authority of his former superior, General Alexander Suvorov, who commanded forces in the Crimea.[24]

Suvorov's first major decision was to organize the defense of the Russian fortress at Kinburn, on the western end of the long and narrow Kinburn peninsula, which extended into the Black Sea on the western side of the Crimea and protected the approaches to Kherson. He ordered Kutuzov to send two light horse regiments to Kinburn and to use the remaining forces to protect the estuary of the Bug River. The Ottomans knew well how crucial Kinburn was to the success of their operations and dispatched a sizable expedition to claim it. On October 12, after a three-day naval bombardment, the Turks landed several thousand troops on the Kinburn Spit and tried to storm the fortress. As Suvorov gave the order to counterattack, a fierce fight raged for several hours. Finally, at day's end, the Russians prevailed and swept the Turks back into the sea.[25] As significant as the victory at Kinburn was, the Russian positions in the northwestern part of the Crimea were still directly threatened by the continued presence of the powerful Ottoman garrison at Ochakov (Özi), on the opposite side of the bay. With winter fast approaching, both sides chose to halt their campaigning season and wait for the spring. Aside from occasional Ottoman patrols appearing in the borderland, this was a peaceful time for Kutuzov; "the whole line is quiet and not a single person could be seen on the opposite side," he reported to Potemkin in early March 1788.[26] He spent the winter months organizing Cossack patrols, conducting reconnaissance along the frozen eastern bank of the Bug River, repairing a nearby fortress at Nikolaevka, and keeping winter quarters for the troops.[27] He routinely examined battalions' campgrounds and hospitals and was pleased to note in his order of May 15 that he found the 2nd Battalion's field infirmary in "such exemplary state that I cannot fully express my praise: cleanliness and abundance of linen, beds and blankets, clean tableware . . . and everything else in such faultlessness as to exemplify gentle care and humanity."[28] Winter offered Kutuzov the perfect opportunity to continue training his men and implement tactical improvements. Seeking to disprove "that old misconception that a Russian soldier cannot be taught on-target fire," he made his men—both the rank and file and the "indolent and untaught officers"—brave the cold weather for regular training that focused on target fire, skirmishing in open order, forming squares, and, after each jäger battalion received two guns, close coordination between infantry and artillery. Having spent eighteen years fighting the Turks, Kutuzov knew the Ottoman calvary was their greatest weapon, and he emphasized the threat it posed to the Russian infantry. "Square is an indispensable formation when facing our enemy," he stressed in one of the orders. "We must therefore teach troops how to form it rapidly from any type of a column . . . and to practice moving while in square formation in any direction" at all types of marching speeds. Kutuzov's orders were lengthy and thorough, neglecting no detail to ensure effective preparation of the rank and file.[29] They emphasized, of course, that mobility and target practice were key to success on the battlefield. Therefore, all exercises were deliberately designed for small groups of soldiers so that "each jäger can be thoroughly shown what he needs to do." Kutuzov kept track of individual records of jägers' performance, so that he could identify the "20 or 30 best marksmen from each company" who could be given distinct tactical assignments during a battle.[30]

In early June 1788 Kutuzov received fresh orders to march south. Potemkin had been alarmed by the appearance of the Ottoman squadron under Kapudan Pasha Cezayirli Gazi Hasan Pasha, the Georgian-born renegade who had earned a fearsome reputation commanding Ottoman fleets in the Mediterranean. Instantly recognizable by his fine white beard and the pet lion that accompanied him everywhere, Hasan Pasha had come to Ochakov because of the news that Potemkin had been building a heavily armed flotilla of several dozen ships at Kherson. The Russian naval threat had to be neutralized. However, this required the Ottomans to force their way into the Liman, the long narrow bay formed by the estuary of the Dnieper-Bug. The inlet was about eight miles across at the widest point but only two miles across at its mouth, where a strait separated the Ottoman-held fortress of Ochakov from the Kinburn Spit, which was controlled by Suvorov's forces. The Ottoman fortress had been one of the primary Russian targets since the start of the war. It was the easternmost outpost in the strategic line that stretched from the Balkans to the Crimea. Well protected from land, it could not be captured as long as the Ottomans controlled the sea and continued to supply it with men and resources. Hence Potemkin was determined to build up the Liman Fleet, as the Russian flotilla at Kherson was sometimes referred to, win naval control of the bay, and then besiege Ochakov, whose capture was of crucial importance to consolidating Russian power in the Crimea and southern Ukraine as a whole. As the Kapudan Pasha gathered his fleet of some thirty-one warships, twenty-one gunboats, and six galleys, Potemkin ordered his army to converge on Ochakov; Kutuzov's Bug Jäger Corps was instructed to leave its quarters and proceed south to participate in the forthcoming siege.[31]

By mid-June 1788, Kutuzov's jägers had reached the coastline near Kherson, where they could see the forest of masts of the Ottoman fleet in the Liman off Ochakov. On June 18, the Kapudan Pasha sent his rowing flotilla into the Liman to engage the Russian forces, which were commanded by French-born Prince Charles Heinrich von Nassau-Siegen and the American John Paul Jones—later hero of the War of 1812—who ordered their respective flotillas to give chase. The ensuing naval battle was an impressive sight, with dozens of ships maneuvering in the close confines of the Liman. The first engagement ended in a stalemate. Ten days later the Kapudan Pasha engaged in a much larger offensive, bringing his entire fleet into the Liman. "Nothing could present a more formidable front that this line [of Ottoman warships] extending from shore to shore," wrote a British eyewitness. "So thick that an interval could scarcely be perceived between their sails."[32] Undaunted, the Russian fleet counterattacked and, after fierce combat, inflicted heavy losses on the Ottomans. As the Kapudan Pasha, commanding from the shore after his ship was severely damaged, pulled his fleet out of the Liman, Suvorov ordered his land batteries to open fire at the enemy warships passing through the narrow mouth, causing additional losses. In the end, the second Battle of the Liman was a complete victory for the Russians, who not only protected their naval base and fleet but routed the Ottoman fleet, which lost more than a dozen warships and more than 3,500 casualties. This victory allowed a jubilant Potemkin to start the siege of Ochakov, which Kutuzov's corps joined in late July.

As the Russian army took up positions in an arc around the fortress, everyone expected the storming to begin immediately. But to minimize Russian casualties, Potemkin opted for a more methodical reduction of the enemy fortress, first cutting off the defenders' supply of food and ammunition and then bombarding the city. Suvorov was vocal about his disapproval of this approach, sending a short rhyming couplet: "I am sitting on a rock / and at Ochakov I still look." The monotony of military camp life under the most trying circumstances wore down the Russian army. "We live from day to day and apparently no arrangements are being made for victualing the army," complained one participant. "The discipline, that good mother of the

Russian armies, is already relaxing."[33] Roman Tsebrikov, the newly assigned clerk to Gregory Potemkin, was aghast at the conditions that soldiers lived in during this "long Ochakov sitting" (*ochakovskoe sidenie*). "As I walked around the campsite at sunset," he noted in his diary on July 19, "I saw some soldiers starting to dig graves for their fallen comrades, others already burying them and still others done with this sepulchral task. Most of the army suffers from diarrhea and dreadful fevers. All along the shoreline one can see corpses of the men who perished in the last three battles. . . . Furthermore, the horses and cattle are dying because of the lack of forage, and after all the edible parts are consumed, what is left of them is simply discarded either inside the camp or on the shoreline. The resulting stench is unbearable . . . especially when the sun is up, and the wind is blowing.[34]

Despite tedium and lack of sanitation, the Russian camp was a remarkable place because it was here that Kutuzov not only encountered foreign officers Prince Nassau-Zigen, Charles de Ligne, Roger de Damas, John Paul Jones, Victor Amadeus Anhalt, and others but also met many junior officers—most notably Levin Bennigsen, Peter Bagration, Mikhail Barclay de Tolly, and Matvei Platov—who later served under his command. Ochakov, in effect, served as a rite of passage for a whole new generation of Russian military leaders who went on to have stellar careers during the Napoleonic Wars.

Throughout the summer of 1788 the Ottoman garrison of Ochakov resisted steadfastly, launching numerous sorties under cover of cannon fire. One of them almost claimed Suvorov's life when he rushed, in defiance of Potemkin's orders, with reinforcements to contain an Ottoman charge on August 7; shot in the neck, he was forced to leave the field of battle. Potemkin angrily reprimanded him that "soldiers are not so cheap that one can sacrifice them so easily."[35] Three weeks later, on August 29, the Ottomans made another incursion, sending troops against the two artillery batteries that Potemkin had constructed on the left wing of his army. This position was defended by the jäger battalions, who fought resolutely, with Kutuzov commanding his men from one of the forward entrenchments. Next to him was Prince Charles-Joseph de Ligne, the Austrian soldier and diplomat who was then in the Russian camp. Watching the fighting through an embrasure, de Ligne asked Kutuzov to approach him so he could point out the Turks who had "skirted the sea and climbed the escarpment to fire rifle shots at the battery."[36] Just as Kutuzov looked out, a musket ball struck him in the head.

For quite some time, it was claimed that this second wound was identical to the one he had sustained fifteen years earlier. In 1813, Filip Sinel'nikov claimed—and subsequent generations of historians repeated—that a musket ball had once again torn a path through Kutuzov's skull and exited on the opposite side.[37] The odds of a person surviving two such traumatic injuries are too slim to be believable. More importantly, there is plenty of evidence to the contrary. Kutuzov was looking out of the embrasure when the bullet struck him, so the injury would have been to the front of his skull, not his temple. Further details can be gleaned from Potemkin's letter to Catherine, who was shaken by the news of Kutuzov's new injury and demanded constant updates about his health.[38] The dispatch contains a note by the surgeon general of the Russian army, French physician Jean Massot, explaining that "General Kutuzov has been wounded by a musket ball that *penetrated his left cheek all the way to the back side of his neck* [my emphasis]; part of the internal angle of the jaw has been shattered. The nature of injury, so close to the organs essential for life, has made the general's condition very serious."[39]

"Yesterday Kutuzov got shot in the head yet again," wrote the stunned Prince de Ligne to Emperor Joseph. "I suppose he will die today or to-morrow."[40] Against all odds, Kutuzov survived. The physician Massot performed a successful surgery and supervised his recovery. A week later, to everyone's amazement, the general showed signs of recovery. His wound was once again the talk of the Russian army and society; in her letters to Potemkin, the empress made frequent inquiries about his health. Himself surprised by his patient's rapid recovery, Massot supposedly remarked, "Providence seems to be preparing General Kutuzov for something extraor-dinary because he survived two wounds that, by the rules of medical science, should have been fatal."[41]

Less than six months after being shot, Kutuzov was ready to return to ac-tive duty. By then, the Russians had taken Ochakov in a bloody assault that claimed more than 12,000 Ottomans (among them more than 8,000 killed) and some 2,800 Russian casualties.[42] The jägers and grenadiers trained by Kutuzov formed one of the attack columns and played an important role in securing the fortress. Although Kutuzov no longer commanded the Bug Jäger Corps, he continued to serve as the chef of the corps, a role similar to proprietor or *inhaber* in other European armies. More importantly, he was able to spend time with his family and become father again—his fifth daughter, Darya, was born on January 2, 1789 (December 22, 1788, under the Julian calendar) and baptized at the Vladimir Orthodox Church in Elisavetgrad ten days later.

⟶⊶⊶⊷⊷⟵

As the New Year and baptismal celebrations abated, Kutuzov returned to the army, accepting Potemkin's offer to take charge of the Russian forces deployed on the Bug River that marked the Russo-Polish-Ottoman borderlands. The new assignment entailed assuming control of two out of six jäger corps (those of the Bug and Ekaterinoslav) and five other regiments, and ensuring their "advantageous deployment, preparation for the future campaign, equip-ping recruits and training men in musket fire and everything else needed for service."[43] In the spring of 1789 Kutuzov set up his headquarters at

Elisavetgrad, where for the next twelve months he remained preoccupied with regimental administration, equipping and training his regiments, and making numerous trips to the imperial borderlands. Aside from occasional minor border incidents,[44] this was a largely peaceful time in his life—"all quiet in the borderlands," he reported[45]—allowing him to fully recover his strength and focus on family and military affairs. He would have rejoiced to see his wife and five daughters—the eldest of whom, Praskovya, was already twelve years old, while the youngest, Darya, was just a few months old. This was a time, short as it was, when Kutuzov and his wife reconnected and enjoyed each other's company.

The New Year brought awards and recognition. In May Kutuzov received the Order of St. Anna (first class), the award established as a Holstein ducal order of chivalry by Duke Karl Friedrich of Holstein-Gottorp, the father of the future emperor Peter III, in honor of his wife, Anna Petrovna, the daughter of Peter the Great. Although not yet a formal Russian imperial order—it was recognized as such in 1797—the order was highly coveted and served as a token of the sovereign's recognition of a person's distinguished service and military valor. A month later, just as he was embarking on a new campaign, Kutuzov received the eight-cornered star of the Order of St. Vladimir (second class) in recognition of his "devoted service, zeal and outstanding assiduity in fulfilling the tasks."[46]

The summer of 1789 marked the resumption of military operations against the Turks. In late May, Kutuzov bid farewell to his wife and children and led his Bug Jäger Corps southwest, first to Ol'viopol, where he supervised transportation of the Ottoman prisoners of war, and then to the approaches to the Ottoman fortress of Bender.[47] On the last day of June, Kutuzov's troops encountered some 3,000 Ottoman troops ten miles from the fortress and engaged in a "resolute battle" that lasted five hours before "the enemy was routed and pursued all the way to the fortress, suffering great losses."[48] Heartened by this success, Kutuzov conducted a series of smaller operations against the Turks. Once again he demonstrated his versatility, both commanding the Bug Jäger Corps and taking charge of the reconnaissance cavalry (*peredovaya konnitsa*) in the *corps volant* (flying detachment) of Lieutenant General Pavel Potemkin, Potemkin's nephew.[49] One of the core objectives was to capture the Ottoman fortresses of Bendery and Akkerman. To cut Ottoman supply and communication lines, Gregory Potemkin, who of course exercised overall command of the Russian forces, ordered his nephew to secure Căuşeni (Kaushany). On September 13, as they approached the town, the Russians encountered stiff Ottoman resistance there. A timely charge by Kutuzov's cavalry, supported by Cossacks, achieved a decisive breakthrough and forced the enemy to flee; the Russians captured not only the town but the enemy camp as well. After the fall of Căuşeni, it was the turn of Hacıbey (Khadjibey, modern Odessa) and

Akkerman, where Kutuzov took part in the blockade and capture of the fortress in October. He ended the year celebrating the fall of the fortress of Bender.[50] Significant as these successes were, they were soon eclipsed by the victories General Suvorov had scored at Focşani and on the Rymnik River, where the sultan's armies were routed. The Ottomans were on the ropes and peace was within reach.

| "The Gutters Dyed with Blood," 1790

A FTER MONTHS OF DIPLOMATIC negotiations, however, the war did not end; peace remained elusive. Through the winter of 1790 Kutuzov enjoyed a brief respite, recovering his health, getting his units in order, and spending some time with his wife; one such visit resulted in Catherine's pregnancy, and the couple's sixth child and only son, Nicholas, was born later that spring and baptized on June 11 at the Vladimir Orthodox Church in Elisavetgrad. All in all, Kutuzov's life seemed fulfilled—his marriage was happy, his career was advancing, and now that an heir ensured the continuation of his family name, the future looked bright.

As it became clear that the Ottomans were committed to fighting on, Potemkin began planning a new campaign. The strategic situation in Europe was rapidly shifting. Russia's manpower and material resources were stretched thin between wars against the Ottomans and the Swedes, with neither conflict showing signs of nearing conclusion. In fact, the Swedes scored a decisive victory over the Russian fleet near Svensksund (Ruotsinsalmi) in July 1790 that threatened Russian control of the Baltic Sea. No less alarming was the news of a formal alliance signed between the Ottoman Empire and Prussia, posing a direct threat to Russia's sole ally, Austria, which had already lost the support of the French monarchy, mired in the revolutionary turmoil that had erupted the previous year. To make matters even worse, a revolution broke out in the Austrian Netherlands, and in February 1790 Austrian emperor Joseph II died. With his death, all vigor on the part of Austria in prosecuting the war in the Balkans expired. Joseph's successor, Leopold, was far less enthusiastic about the prospect of confronting Prussians in the north and Ottomans in the south, particularly as the revolution in France threatened his sister Queen Marie Antoinette.

The summer of 1790 marked a turning point for the Austrians. In June Austrian field marshal Frederick Josias of Saxe-Coburg-Saalfeld suffered an unexpected defeat at the hand of the Turks at Giurgiu; Potemkin fulminated that the "dimwitted" Austrian general had "rushed in like a fool and been thrashed like a whore."[1] He had reason to be dismayed. The defeat hardened Emperor Leopold's decision to abandon his predecessor's aspirations of gaining Ottoman territory. In July the court of Vienna negotiated a separate agreement with Prussia at Reichenbach, the conditions being the renunciation of the alliance with Russia and acceptance of armistice with the Ottomans, who had managed to reclaim the territory they had lost to the Austrians. Thus, Russia found itself deserted and left to continue the contest against the Turks singlehanded.

Potemkin knew that he had a small window of opportunity to end the war against the Turks before the international situation further adversely affected Russian geopolitical interests elsewhere. Relations with Prussia and the Polish-Lithuanian Commonwealth were already turning hostile. He threw himself into action. In March, he appointed Rear Admiral Fedor Ushakov to command the Black Sea Fleet and ordered him to sea to confront the enemy. Leaving one corps to protect Ochakov and another in the Caucasus, Potemkin readied two corps, under the command of Alexander Suvorov and Ivan Möller (Möller-Zakomelskii), respectively, for an invasion of the Danubian Principalities. To plan a new campaign, Potemkin needed fresh and reliable intelligence on the Ottoman forces and resources. Kutuzov seemed the right man for the job. On April 20, Mikhail Illarionovich, whose Bug Jäger Corps was formally assigned to Möller's corps, received an unexpected message from the army commander, informing him to leave at once for Akkerman and "take a command there." The vagueness of this order suggested the sensitive nature of the assignment he was to undertake.

Over the following several weeks Kutuzov set up an intelligence-gathering operation that covered a wide area of territory, from Akkerman to the Ottoman fortresses of Kilya and Izmail, some hundred miles to the south. Authorized to draw upon the "extraordinary funds" to recruit and dispatch scouts and agents, Kutuzov was advised to take the necessary precautions in enemy territory and report his findings.[2] Surviving documents testify to the success of his endeavors. He recruited agents and formed small mobile squads of Cossacks that crossed into Ottoman territory, gathered the necessary information, and evaded attempts to capture them. By May 13, Kutuzov reported about the success of one such reconnaissance mission. His agent had successfully infiltrated into Ottoman territory, made it to a village just ten miles from Kilya, and gathered information about enemy forces in the area as well as about troop movements farther inland. Two months later Kutuzov, hungry and tired from his travels, reported that he had personally observed the arrival of the Ottoman fleet in the Dniester estuary. Throughout the summer months, he supplied a steady stream of reconnaissance reports about Ottoman army and navy movements, as well as conditions in the borderland villages, towns, and fortresses, all of which informed and facilitated Russian war planning.[3]

Exhausted by the war and saddled with ever-increasing debt, Sweden abruptly ended the war against Russia and accepted the peace treaty of Värälä in mid-August. This meant that the Russian government could focus its attention on the Danubian region. On September 18, Kutuzov received secret orders to start preparing for a new offensive against the Turks.

The primary aim of the Russian army was to secure the fortress of Izmail, the Ottoman stronghold that was essential to their military and naval operations on the lower Danube and prevented any deeper incursions into the Ottoman realm. This was, in the opinion of Catherine, "the most important objective at this moment: [Izmail] will either bring us peace or prolong the war."[4] Rear Admiral Ushakov's naval victories had already secured a Russian presence in the western portion of the Black Sea, and Potemkin now needed to secure smaller fortresses on the lower Danube—especially those of Kilya, Tulcea, and Isaccea (Isakçi)—before leading an assault on the main prize.[5]

On October 9, Potemkin ordered Kutuzov to march south with his Bug Jäger Corps, reinforced with additional units, and "to resolve the Kilya matter as soon as possible . . . if the garrison surrender—so be it; if not, seeking the Lord's for help, you must try to take the fortress as soon as it would be possible."[6] By the end of October, Kutuzov had taken his forces southward, acquiring fresh intelligence from the prisoners of war that Kilya's garrison was undermanned and could not resist for "more than three days," as Kutuzov wrote in his report.[7] He assisted General Ivan Möller (and, after his death, Lieutenant General Ivan Gudovich) in besieging the fortress, cutting the Ottoman communication lines to deny the garrison any opportunity of alerting their brethren at Izmail. Kilya duly fell on October 29. Soon thereafter, with the arrival of the Russian flotilla and the capture of Tulcea and Isaccea, the entire lower Danube from the estuary to Galatz was under Russian control. All that remained was the fortress of Izmail, to which Kutuzov was ordered to proceed.[8]

In November, some 25,000 Russians (almost half of them irregulars), under Lieutenant Generals Gudovich, Pavel Potemkin, and Alexander Samoilov, supported by the flotilla led by Major General Osip (José) de Ribas, converged on the Ottoman fortress. Izmail was located in a "natural amphitheater" overlooking a wide bend formed by the Danube about sixty miles from its estuary.[9] An extensive valley stretched through the city from north to south, dividing it into two halves. The larger, western side formed the "old fortress," and the smaller housed the "new fortress." Conquered by the Ottomans in the fifteenth century, Izmail was located where the main roads from across the entire lower Danube region converged. In 1770, the Russian forces under Nikolai Repnin took advantage of Izmail's weakened defenses to capture the fortress, but the end of the war saw it return to the Ottomans. Having lost it once, the Ottomans were determined to avoid losing the fortress again, and they spent the next two decades improving its defenses. With the help of French and German engineers, Izmail was transformed into a formidable stronghold, with some 200 cannon, more than half a dozen bastions, a number of batteries, and battlements that stretched, by one estimate, nearly 3,000 *toises*, or almost 6,400 yards, on the northern side of the river.[10] British Major General E. Renouard James, who visited the fortress during the Crimean War shortly before it was demolished in 1856, kept a detailed journal in which he described the stronghold as shaped like "an irregular polygon, built on ground at its highest level 200 to 300 feet above the river, with a command in all directions except towards the north, on which side there was a gentle rise towards the country."[11] Roger de Damas, a Frenchman who took part in the assault on Izmail, recalled that the fortress's outworks were indeed "very high and well designed . . . the surface of the fortifications being made of earth, it was impossible to make a breach."[12] But the fortress did have weaknesses. Some of the construction works were only partially completed, and a network of palisades and earthworks proposed by a French engineer had not been finished. The fortress's broad base on the riverside was covered by a simple indented parapet, and the small number of gun batteries, offering only meager protection from a riverine assault, was, in the words of a contemporary, the result of the Ottoman refusal to "believe that the Russians could ever possess a flotilla on the Danube."[13]

The fortress was defended by a large garrison under the command of the experienced Ottoman *seraskir* (commander) Aydoslu Mehmed Pasha. Still, its size has traditionally been overstated. The widely cited number of 35,000 to 40,000 Ottoman troops reflects later Russian propaganda.[14] Throughout the summer and fall of 1790, as he supervised reconnaissance operations between Akkerman, Kilya, and Izmail, Kutuzov had obtained invaluable information that has been largely ignored by those keen to extol the Russian triumph at Izmail. Interrogating prisoners of war, defectors, and local inhabitants, he consistently reported that the Ottomans had between 10,000 and 15,000 men at the fortress and that the enemy garrison suffered from diminished supplies, low morale, and high desertion rates.[15] Probably the most valuable information was delivered by a Ottoman defector who fled from Izmail just three days before the assault and provided a detailed breakdown of the Ottoman forces and how they were distributed around the fortress perimeter. He revealed that the garrison included "up to 10,000 Janissaries under command of *yeniçeri ağası* . . . 3,000 Anatolian troops led by Ali Bey and his son Mahmud Bey . . . 2,000 infantry and 300 mounted Tatars . . . led by Sultan Aslan Girey"; in addition, there were about 2,900 armed local inhabitants. Just a quarter of these forces were in "good condition," while the rest were "penurious and unclothed."[16] The Ottoman forces defending Izmail therefore barely matched the size of the Russian army. They did, however, enjoy the immense advantage of being behind the imposing battlements.

The Russian army took up positions around Izmail, with de Ribas positioning his flotilla to blockade the fortress from the river and the army deploying in a semicircular position around the fortress to isolate it from the land. Kutuzov's corps put up its tents in groves on the left wing of the Russian army, a few miles away from the fortress, to sustain the blockade and to prevent any Ottoman relief efforts. The next few days saw no major combat, but in his personal file, Kutuzov later noted that he was involved in "numerous skirmishes with the enemy cavalry."[17]

By December, the situation had reached an impasse. The Ottoman garrison was determined to defend the fortress, hoping for a relief effort to be sent by the grand vizier.[18] Offered the chance to surrender, the Ottoman commander scornfully responded that "he could see nothing that makes him worried."[19] The Russian artillery bombardment produced meager results. In the words of a Russian general, "the guns merely crumbled the soil, and the damage was repaired during the night; thus, no progress could be made."[20] The Russian troops, suffering from cold weather and low supplies, continued to construct batteries and dig earthworks around Izmail, but the season was late for a protracted siege, and storming the fortress seemed an impossible task.

Moreover, discord reigned among the Russian generals, who, in the absence of a single commander in chief, bickered over strategy and seniority. Among three lieutenant generals, Samoilov, Pavel Potemkin, and de Ribas, the last of these was the most conspicuous and outspoken. Born José Pascual Domingo de Ribas y Boyons, the son of the Spanish consul in Naples, de Ribas served in the Neapolitan army before emigrating to Russia, where over the next two decades he made a stellar career, rising to the rank of general. "I cannot praise Major General Ribas enough," Potemkin wrote to his empress. "Along with his excellent bravery, he is filled with indescribable fervor."[21] Such praise appears frequently in Potemkin's descriptions of the Neapolitan, who received an excellent education and spoke seven languages.[22] Not everyone was a fan, however. De Ribas "possesses, in a supreme degree, all the vices with which Italians are reproached, and some of the pleasantry of their disposition in society, without having any of their good qualities," a contemporary remarked, arguing that there was no one "more supple, more artful, more jesuitical, more mean, more vile, more crafty, more watchful, more deceitful, and more hypocritical."[23] Accurate or exaggerated, the portrait contains kernels of truth about de Ribas, who was eager for glory and awards. It also points to the challenge of ensuring cooperation between officers who were proud, brave, strong-willed, and desirous of being independent commanders, especially when, as historian Nikolai Orlov put it, "there was no unity of command, or any general guidance, and every general operated autonomously."[24]

By December, the morale in the Russian camp had fallen to its lowest point. "The start of the campaign has been most unfortunate," wrote Gregory Chernyshev, who volunteered to fight at Izmail, in early December. "Everyone is feeling downcast, and nobody knows what to do. In the meantime, the Turks are celebrating." Chernyshev attributes this to a lack of cohesion among the generals. Potemkin, Kutuzov, and de Ribas "do not even want to assist each other; meanwhile, [General] Lvov is laughing at them all, and not without a reason." Chernyshev's criticism of Kutuzov seems misplaced, given that he was subordinate to Samoilov and Potemkin. Interestingly, in other letters Chernyshev laments that while most of the army remained idle, Kutuzov's men had daily skirmishes with the Turks. He expressed the desire "to transfer under command of Kutuzov, where there is far more action, especially for volunteers," and who "makes the Turks tremble while the rest of us [the Russian army] quivers out fear."[25]

The Russian generals held a council of war to discuss what to do next. They agreed that with winter imminent and supplies running low, the army should move back to its winter quarters, where it could regroup and return to besiege the fortress in the spring. On December 6, the Russian army opened a massive artillery fire and feigned preparations for assault in the hopes of intimidating the Turks to surrender. The ploy did not work. On that same day the troops were ordered to break camp and depart amid windy and snowy weather. "The comedy has ended . . . everything is over," wrote a disgusted officer to a friend. "We will not get Izmail, nor the laurels of victory."[26]

He wrote too soon.[27] Potemkin, acting on his own and eager to end the year with a major victory, had turned to the one man he believed was capable of taking the city—Alexander Suvorov. It was not a surprising choice. Suvorov was enjoying a streak of victories that brought him fame and recognition; after gaining a victory over the Turks on the Rymnik River in late September 1789, he was made a count of both the Russian Empire and the Holy Roman Empire. Count Suvorov-Rymnikskii, as he now styled himself, was a strong proponent of a mobile and aggressive style of warfare, urging his soldiers to train hard, move fast, and attack vigorously. Discerning, intelligent, and never one to shy away from combat, Suvorov seemed to be the kind of general Potemkin needed to resolve the Izmail quandary. "My only hope is in the Lord and your courage," he wrote to Suvorov in late November. "With God's help, take this place!" In a separate note he added, "There are a lot of generals there of equal rank and so it has turned into a sort of indecisive parliament [sejm]. Ribas will help you in everything and you will be pleased with Kutuzov too." This quick remark is noteworthy because Potemkin made no mention of his own relatives—Lieutenant Generals Potemkin and Samoilov—or other senior officers who were also at Izmail, and instead refers to Kutuzov as the person Suvorov should rely on. It testifies to Kutuzov's hard-earned reputation as a military professional.[28]

Departing from Galatz on December 11, Suvorov covered seventy miles in two days and arrived at Izmail just in time to countermand the orders of the council of war and instruct the army to return to its earlier positions.[29] Suvorov's arrival rejuvenated the army's spirits. He seemed far taller than his five feet six inches and knew precisely how to strike the imagination of the rank and file. Both officers and soldiers admired this "singular man," as the Duc de Richelieu put it, "who looks more like a leader of Cossacks or Tartars than a general of a European army." They loved his affability and good nature, his "uncommon intrepidity and boldness," and the kind of valor "that made him neglect all the rules of war."[30] Over the next few days Suvorov's confidence and vigor stood in stark contrast with the tentativeness of other generals. While the council of war expressed grave concerns about launching an assault, Suvorov was convinced that immediate attack, however bloody it might be, was the quickest means to secure the strategically important fortress.[31]

Suvorov immediately proceeded with preparations for an assault, regrouping the army, drafting dispositions, starting construction of artillery batteries, and personally devising drills for assault.[32] The British poet Lord Byron's epic poem *Don Juan* was inspired by the events at Izmail. His description of Suvorov seems apt: "Surveying, drilling, ordering, jesting, pondering; / For the man was, we safely may assert, / A thing to wonder at beyond most wondering."[33]

Suvorov perplexed some—"the count continues to fool around [*durachitsya*] and puts on exercises for the rehearsal of the impending assault," grumbled one participant—but his eccentric behavior belied his astute assessment of the situation and effective use of available resources to fulfill the task.[34] While some saw him as "now Mars, now Momus / and when bent to storm a fortress, Harlequin in uniform,"[35] Suvorov rolled up his sleeves and led through example, showing how to make numerous fascines to fill in the Ottoman ditches and ladders to climb the walls and directing the feverish training on specially built mock-ups of the fortress walls.[36] Kutuzov was actively involved in these preparations, commanding troops on the Russian left flank and engaged in frequent skirmishers with the enemy. The Duc de Richelieu, who was in the Russian camp at Izmail, noted in his journal that Kutuzov's corps was deployed so close to the fortress that "the enemy's cannonballs reached even his camp" and that on one occasion an Ottoman cannonball, ricocheting off the ground, struck a tent where more than a dozen officers were dining, "smashing the legs of seven chairs on which half of the guests were seated." Amazingly, no one was injured, which "excited a great joy of everyone in that company."[37]

On December 19, after almost a week of preparations, Suvorov sent a messenger to Izmail, demanding the garrison's surrender to avoid senseless shedding of "the innocent blood of women and children." If the Turks resisted, warned Suvorov, death awaited everyone inside the fortress.[38] The garrison responded defiantly, with one of the Ottoman pashas proclaiming that "the Danube will stop its course and the heavens will fall to earth before Ismail surrenders."[39]The following morning, on December 20, Suvorov summoned a new military council.[40] This decision was partly occasioned by Peter the Great's military statute requiring that "a commander should not, of his own volition, make any major undertakings without first convening a military council of all general officers where other generals can share their advice." Suvorov's primary motivation was not so much to seek the generals' advice as it was to raise the spirits of the men who, just a week earlier, had thought that storming Izmail was imprudent; in the words of Russian historians, Suvorov needed this meeting "to facilitate a moral transformation" in his generals, to "make his view as their view, his conviction as their convictions."[41]

Surrounded by Kutuzov and twelve other senior officers, Suvorov gave an impassioned speech, begging them to put aside "animosity and personal bickering" and reminding them of the glorious Russian exploits and of the importance of capturing this fortress.[42] "Twice have the Russians approached Izmail, and twice have they retreated. Now, the third time, all we can do is either take the city or die trying. . . . We are strong and confident. . . . If we conquer Izmail, who will dare to stand in our way?" Suvorov's words—especially his pledge to "take the fortress or die under its walls"—had a profound effect on the generals, who now stared at the blank sheet of paper that the commander in chief had laid in front of them asking for their votes and signatures on whether to attack or retreat. Brigadier General Matvei Platov, who, as the junior commander at the council, had the first say, stood up and bellowed, "Assault!," prompting Suvorov to embrace him. Others agreed in turn that the time of siege was over and that retreat was "dishonorable." They signed the council's judgment "to approach Izmail and, according to the disposition, to launch an immediate assault so to deny the enemy an opportunity to strengthen himself." Kutuzov was the eleventh to vote and sign the document.[43]

During these preparations for the assault, Kutuzov demonstrated the shrewdness for which he became famous. The flotilla commander, de Ribas, became concerned that Suvorov would receive the lion's share of acclaim for capturing Izmail. He sought to preempt this by ensuring that he would be the first to enter the fortress. He therefore asked Suvorov for additional troops "to ensure proper coordination between the flotilla and land forces." While making this request, he supposedly employed "such subtle turns of phrase and crafty expressions" that Suvorov "paid little attention to what was being asked and thus did not notice de Ribas's trickery." The soldiers were transferred, and the admiral began removing heavy cannon from his flotilla ships so that when the time came, he could lead an amphibious assault. Meanwhile, Suvorov solicited the advice of his generals on the proposed plan of attack and dispatched his nephew Lieutenant Fedor Shiryaev with a copy of the plan to Kutuzov, who, so the story goes, immediately noticed de Ribas's intention to lead the attack.[44] Reluctant to jeopardize his relations with the admiral or to demean Suvorov by pointing out his mistake, Kutuzov chose an indirect approach. As he bid farewell to the lieutenant, he casually mentioned to Shiryaev that "his uncle was about to be cheated out of victory" and wished that somebody would warn him about it. Stunned by such a remark, Shiryaev begged for an explanation. Kutuzov refused to tell him until the young officer pledged not to reveal the source of this information to Suvorov—a request Kutuzov must have known the lieutenant could not keep. He then explained de Ribas's design. Upon returning to the headquarters, Shiryaev conveyed this information to Suvorov. "How can this be true?" shouted the surprised commander in chief. "Who told you this? Tell me at once!" Shiryaev divulged the source, and Suvorov rushed to see everything for himself. He realized that Kutuzov was correct and immediately ordered de Ribas to disembark the troops and move all the heavy cannon back onto the ships. The whole business was kept secret until years later, when Suvorov was asked at a private dinner party who was the smartest general in the Russian army. Some suggested Kutuzov, to which Suvorov quietly observed, "Oh, he is crafty, very crafty. Even de Ribas cannot deceive him!" This remark circulated widely and eventually became a catchphrase, though few understood what Suvorov actually meant. Many tried to parse its meaning, but neither general was willing to divulge details; Suvorov kept referring to Kutuzov, who in turn pointed to him. This continued until Kutuzov finally told the whole story; upon hearing about this, Suvorov supposedly laughed. "Bravo! Kutuzov saw it, Kutuzov tied it up, and Kutuzov untied it!" Whether real or embellished, the story relies on the tired xenophobic trope of a foreigner trying to undercut a native-born Russian even as it tells us something about Kutuzov's character. For contemporaries, it served as an example of sagacity and good sense. But it also underscores Kutuzov's growing reputation for craftiness and double-dealing. Suvorov understood this well, commenting: "I do not bow to Kutuzov—he may bow once but will deceive you ten times."[45]

Suvorov proceeded with his plan for assault. Each column would advance in sections, with one throwing the fascines across the moat, another placing the scaling ladders in position, and a third charging across while others remained in reserve and covered with fire. Detailed instructions were given as to what was to be done when the troops made their way onto the top of the ramparts, including how to find the powder magazines and safeguard them against being blown up. Suvorov's "severe discipline made it certain that his arrangements would be carried out to the letter," observed one participant. The troops received a general benediction on the evening before the storming.[46] Hardly anyone slept; "anxiety, anticipation, and impatience were in everyone's mind . . . there was a deep silence—a dispiriting, oppressive silence," as a survivor described it.[47] We do not know what Kutuzov felt or thought that evening; his letters did not survive, and the participants are silent about this as well. But it seems likely he would have spent that night walking among his anxious men, encouraging them, checking their equipment, and, shortly after midnight, announcing to them the commander in chief's order of the day: "We must either conquer or die a glorious death." Under customary laws of war, the "law of sack" gave license for a besieging army to pillage a city if it failed to surrender once its walls were deemed to have a practicable breach; if victorious, Suvorov promised his men, they could have their way in the city for three days. Nonetheless, they were to spare the lives of Christians, women, and children.[48]

Kutuzov knew death well.[49] He had just received news that a smallpox epidemic had struck in parts of western Russia, claiming many lives. His wife, Catherine, did her best to care for the children but, as she revealed in a letter of December 8, "this misfortune befell us so quickly that I had no time to move out little Nicholas, who had succumbed to this evil ailment, which claimed him in just one day." Just several months old, the baby was buried on a cold November morning in Elisavetgrad.[50] Kutuzov's despair

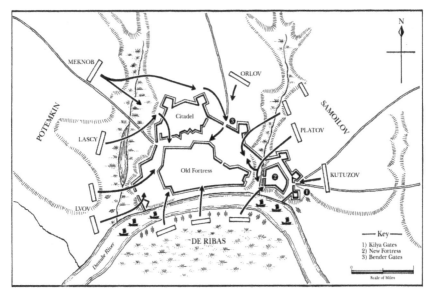

MAP 4 Storming of Izmail

upon learning of the death of his only heir can only be imagined. And he still had to worry about the rest of his family, for all of his children had fallen seriously ill and suffered greatly. Catherine herself had succumbed to a severe illness and "was without any hope for recovery for four days." She was "bled, given a few *Spanish flies* and somehow saved."[51] Grief-stricken after the loss of her son and concerned for the survival of her other children who were still very sick, Catherine was worried about her husband at Izmail. "I think they will capture that fortress soon," she wrote a friend, though the letter betrays her deep anxiety as well. "No one knows whose turn it would be suffer the blows of misfortune next and I am afraid that I would be the one to experience the loss of Mikhailo Larionovich. This thought has all but consumed my whole being."[52]

Around half past five, two hours before the sun rose on the cold morning of December 22, Russian soldiers—"eager, impatient and hearts pounding hard"—watched as the flare signaling the start of the assault arched slowly into the dark and cloudy sky. Some 25,000 men advanced under the cover of a pre dawn smog that cloaked the riverbank. They soon discovered that despite the almost daylong artillery bombardment that preceded the assault— "one of the most terrible cannonades in the annals of military history," in the words of an eyewitness—the enemy's battlements were largely intact.[53] In a moment, the fortress transformed into a "genuine volcano spewing flames and destructive elements . . . the heaven and the earth seemed to have caught on fire."[54]

Suvorov grouped the army in three wings. Major General de Ribas commanded some 9,000 men who were supposed to cross the river and attack Izmail's most vulnerable southern side. On the right wing, 7,500 men, led by Lieutenant General Pavel Potemkin, attacked the western, older side of the fortress, while the left wing—about 12,000 men under Lieutenant General Alexander Samoilov—was tasked with taking Izmail's eastern side. Each of these three commanders had his forces subdivided into three assault columns, with Kutuzov, who was assigned to Samoilov's left wing, taking charge of the sixth and leftmost column, which comprised three battalions of the Bug Jäger Corps spearheading the attack and two battalions of the Khersonskii Grenadier Regiment, a handful of volunteers, and 1,000 dismounted Cossacks armed with pikes in reserve.[55]

As soon as the flare shot up into the sky, Kutuzov gave the order to move forward. His men faced the unenviable task of assaulting Izmail's recently renovated "new fortress" with its wide moat, three large bastions, and wide and commanding ramparts. Trying his best to coordinate their advance with the neighboring assault columns in darkness, Kutuzov had skirmishers leading the way, followed by workers with entrenching tools, jägers, and dismounted Cossacks carrying hundreds of fascines and a handful of ladders that they had constructed in the previous few days; the Khersonskii grenadiers stayed behind in reserve.[56]

The sixth column's target was the Kilya Gates on the southeastern side of Izmail. Canister fire greeted it from the adjoining bastions, causing considerable losses even before the column had reached the ramparts. "Standing near the edge of the moat in darkness, the skirmishers made the most of the flashes of artillery fire that illuminated the area, to shoot at the heads of the defenders standing on top of the ramparts."[57] Despite having trained for days by scaling the mocked-up earthworks, the Russian troops, marching in the smog that enveloped the ground that night, were still staggered by Izmail's impressive moat—some twenty feet deep and forty feet wide—and high earthen slopes (glacis) rising behind it. "It is impossible, without actually seeing it for yourself, to form an idea of the great height of the battlements that these men had to climb," wrote the Duc de Richelieu in his journal upon examining the area that Kutuzov's troops had stormed.[58] The Ottoman fire took a murderous toll on the Russians as they hunched together in the dark around the moat and in "kill zones" between the bastions. Kutuzov ran to and fro, rallying his men, urging them to move forward, and witnessing the death of many of his comrades. One of the first casualties was his own brother-in-law, Brigadier Ivan (Jean-François) Ribeaupierre, whose death caused a momentary confusion among the troops.[59] Kutuzov rushed forward to rally his men. "Placing himself at their head," Suvorov later wrote Potemkin, Kutuzov "crossed himself three times, called upon his soldiers to follow him, and was first to jump into the ditch."[60] The soldiers threw down fascines to fill in the moat and, despite standing in water that was waist-deep in places, clambered across toward the glacis, which rose some forty feet above the bottom of the moat.[61]

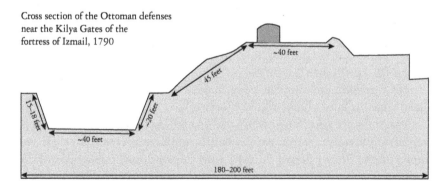

Cross section of the Ottoman defenses near the Kilya Gates of the fortress of Izmail, 1790

~40 feet

45 feet

15–18 feet

~20 feet

~40 feet

180–200 feet

Yards away from Kutuzov was Major Sherbakov of the 3rd Jäger Battalion of the Bug Jäger Corps. He later described how, upon reaching the bottom of the moat, his men discovered that the moat's depth and the height of the glacis had been miscalculated, and the ladders that the jägers had brought were, in fact, too short. The battalion, already unnerved by the intense enemy fire, "lay down in the moat" and, despite the battalion commander's "cajoling and threats, the men refused to advance."[62] Kutuzov and his officers were forced to improvise under a hail of musket balls and canister.[63] Some soldiers used bayonets to climb the earthen slopes, while others began to tie ladders together to increase their length. Kutuzov was among the first to scale the ladders, with his soldiers, weighed down by their waterlogged uniforms, following him up to the top. Pushing the Ottoman defenders back, they dismantled a palisade and rushed forward to secure the bastion, which they had almost accomplished when the Turks counterattacked with reinforcements and concentrated fire. Twice Kutuzov charged with his men onto the Ottoman bastion, and twice he was beaten and thrown back into the moat, where bodies of the fallen Russian soldiers began to form heaps.[64]

The battle hung in the balance as the Russian columns struggled to make headway against such a tenacious Ottoman defense. The fourth and fifth columns stumbled in their assaults, too, and suffered such casualties that Kutuzov had to divert one jäger battalion to assist them, further weakening his own column. Equally muddled was the situation on the right wing, where the first and second columns had seen their assaults grind to a halt while the third column, moving in darkness, veered off from the designated path and suffered grievously storming the key northern bastion. Much more successful—ironically enough—was de Ribas's attack from the river, where his flotilla was able to approach and storm the less strongly defended side of the Ottoman fortress.[65]

One story offers insights into Suvorov's peculiar style of command as well as his appreciation of Kutuzov's character. Just as his column was beaten back for the second time, Kutuzov apparently received a message from Suvorov, who was closely following events on the battlefield.[66] The commander in chief congratulated Kutuzov on "taking Izmail" and being appointed its commandant, and ended the message with the following comment: "The courtier is already on his way to deliver to the empress the news that the fortress has been taken." Confused at first, Kutuzov then understood what Suvorov was asking of him. Shouting "God is with us!," he led a new assault against the Turks and broke into the fortress.[67]

Or so the story goes. Suvorov may have sought to inspire his subordinates, but this story is also instructive of what the public expected from these two commanders. Writer Sergei Glinka, who collected and published various stories of Russian military exploits, recorded accounts that he had heard circulating in society of Kutuzov and Suvorov's first meeting after the assault ended; one of them was the story told by historian Friedrich von Smitt's relatives, who took part in this campaign and claimed to have heard it directly from Kutuzov. After Izmail was taken, the story went, Kutuzov met with Suvorov and asked what had prompted him to send such an unusual and premature message. Suvorov responded, "I know Kutuzov, and Kutuzov knows me. I knew that Kutuzov would take Izmail at all costs. And that if Izmail is not taken, I would die by its wall and so would Kutuzov."[68] If nothing else, this anecdotal conversation illuminates the ethos and values of the military culture that the Russian army (and Russian society) sought to cultivate at the start of the nineteenth century. Suvorov and Kutuzov exemplified the virtues of "fearlessness, generosity, noble rivalry, and foresight," as one contemporary observed, and they served as paragons of officers who led through example and were prepared to sacrifice themselves for the sake of honor and victory.[69] In this sense, Izmail was used to exalt certain values for future generations of Russian (and later Soviet) military leaders. Contrary to Soviet historians' claims of close collaboration between Kutuzov and Suvorov, the two men were never "firm friends" nor even close to each other.[70] In fact, contemporaries thought that Suvorov perceived Kutuzov as his rival. "Primacy is the essence of martial competitiveness," observed one contemporary. "Would Suvorov want to see anyone match him in matters of glory? Certainly not."[71] Yet even this competition between two distinguished generals served didactic purposes. Suvorov was praised for appreciating Kutuzov's talents and treating him fairly. Discussing events at Izmail, Glinka thus eulogized that "heroes must do justice to other heroes. They must be delighted to have rivals. The noble martial competition overcomes all challenges on the path to honor and glory!"[72]

Inspiring as such accounts might be, the reality was more muddled. In the confusion of the battle, his ears ringing, his face blackened by smoke and dirt, and his uniform covered in mud and blood, Kutuzov would have needed no encouragement from Suvorov to know what was expected of him. He knew that every second counted and that he would need to improvise fast to get his men out of the death trap in the moat. Calling up the remaining reserves of the Khersonskii grenadiers and the Cossacks, he rallied and regrouped his battered battalions for a new assault. This attack coincided with the renewed attacks by other columns that were, in Suvorov's words, "carried out daringly, courageously, and with a remarkable vigor."[73] The Ottoman garrison—already depleted and facing coordinated attacks around the perimeter and from across the river—was unable to halt the Russian onslaught. As the sun rose above the smoke-filled fortress, Kutuzov's soldiers clawed their way to the top of the Ottoman ramparts, secured the bastion, and then charged along the wall to claim the neighboring one before bursting into Izmail with, as the Duc de Richelieu put it, "the violence of a torrent that breaches the dam and floods the countryside."[74]

By late morning "the most horrible carnage" unfolded inside the fortress. The fighting turned into a series of isolated engagements in the small alleys and tight-set buildings, where the Ottomans, as one British periodical described based on dispatches from Izmail, "defended themselves with a gallantry scarce ever equaled," contesting every square and street corner.[75] The Russian advance was time and again held up by the "internal fortresses," the large stone buildings in which the Ottomans barricaded themselves and that the Russians had to storm every time. Ordered to clear one such building, Kutuzov personally led a jäger battalion, "climbing ladders to the top of the building and, despite the enemy's furious resistance, forcing the Turks to surrender."[76] He then advanced deeper into the city, leading two jäger battalions and saving an isolated group of Cossacks that were about to be slaughtered by the Janissaries. It was already early afternoon when, at one of the town's central squares, he encountered the Crimean Tatar prince Kaplan Giray, the proud descendant of Genghis Khan who had managed to rally about 2,000 soldiers and was desperately trying to fight his way out of the doomed city. Kutuzov immediately asked General Lascy, whose grenadiers were advancing from the Bender gates, to send reinforcements, and then led a charge on the Crimean Tatars. The hand-to-hand combat lasted almost an hour before all but 400 Crimean Tatars had been slain; Kaplan Giray made his last stand surrounded by the bodies of his five sons.[77] Meanwhile, the Ottoman *seraskir* Aydoslu Mehmed Pasha and some 3,000 men continued to resist inside one of the fortified buildings near the Khotin gates until most of the defenders were killed. Several hundred survivors, including the *seraskir* himself, surrendered. As they were being led out of the building, a Russian soldier—participants speak of either "a certain jäger" or "an English naval officer" in the Russian service—tried to claim a bejeweled dagger hanging on the *seraskir*'s belt and was attacked by a Janissary trying to defend the dignity of his commander. Enraged by this, the Russians charged and slaughtered the capitulating Ottomans.

The fighting inside the city raged throughout the afternoon and turned into a bloodbath. "It is no exaggeration to say that the gutters of the town were dyed with blood," one stunned officer wrote of the carnage that took place in Izmail. "Even women and children fell victims to the rage . . . [it was] the most unequalled butchery."[78] The furious soldiery, "not listening to the voice of its officers, blood-crazed and breathing of nothing but carnage," went on a rampage across the city. Contrary to Suvorov's orders not to harm the Christians and the defenseless, "neither the cries of the women, nor the complaints of the children, or anything else" was capable of softening soldiers' hearts. "I will not attempt to paint the horror that froze all my senses," wrote the Duc de Richelieu in his journal. "The image of death and desolation presented itself everywhere I looked."[79]

Izmail was an affluent town before the war, and its standing as a commercial hub had grown when it became a place to which merchant stores from other Ottoman cities and towns threatened by the Russians were relocated; in the words of one eyewitness, "never a city containing so much of wealth had fallen into the hands of the Russians."[80] A wholesale pillage of the town continued well into the evening as soldiers ravaged the stores and homes,

stripped their victims of clothing before killing them, and continued marauding draped in a jumble of looted outfits and filling everything they had
with coins, jewels, and possessions of various kind. Suvorov later admitted
that the value of the loot exceeded 1 million rubles, a colossal sum that
could pay for the annual pay of some 100,000 Russian soldiers.[81] "If one
million was officially taken, how much more would have been despoiled and
destroyed," wondered one Russian historian, pointing out that some Russian
officers took "an unknown number of captives of both gender and all ages."
Some soldiers were later seen paying fistfuls of pearls for a cup of wine.[82] The
plunder included thousands of horses and stallions, for which the Ottoman
cavalry was traditionally renowned.

As he assumed the responsibilities of the commandant of Izmail, Kutuzov
was said to have done his best to rein in the pillaging and restore order in the
fortress. He set up outposts at all gates and town squares, secured gunpowder
and supply stores, and sent jägers to protect local churches and mosques,
where survivors were seeking protection. "Despite the strongest indiscretion
that reigned among the Russian troops that day," the Duc de Richelieu jotted
down in his journal, "that same evening order was restored as five battalions
under General Kutuzov garrisoned the city." This seems to be an understatement. Other eyewitnesses suggest that, despite Kutuzov's efforts, the killing
and plundering went for at least another day.[83] As the night descended on
Izmail, wrote Byron in *Don Juan*,

> The crescent's silver bow
> Sunk, and the crimson cross glared o'ver the field,
> But red with no redeeming gore: the glow
> Of burning streets, like moonlight on the water
> Was imaged back in blood, the sea of slaughter.[84]

Thus was conquered one of the "keys" to the Ottoman Empire.[85] "We have
gained a complete victory," reported an overjoyed Suvorov. "The fortress of
Izmail, so well fortified, so vast and seemingly impregnable, has been taken
by the frightful force of the Russian bayonets." In his lengthy and carefully
constructed narrative of the assault, Suvorov sought to conceal the fact that
the Russian army in fact outnumbered the enemy. He claimed that the victory had been gained "in spite of the steadfast resistance of the enemy garrison
whose strength was rumored to have reached 42,000 men but which, now that
it has been destroyed, can be assumed to have counted 35,000 men."[86] Edited
and published in official newspapers, Suvorov's report laid the foundation
for the official narrative of the capture of Izmail that shaped public imagination for generations. In this version of events, a small but resolute Russian
army stormed an impregnable fortress defended by the vast Ottoman horde.

Empress Catherine herself enthused that "the scaling of Izmail and its fortress with a corps *half the size* [my emphasis] of the Turkish garrison is something that has rarely been attempted in history and bestows great honor on the undaunted Russian warriors."[87] She ordered a special church service and various festivities to commemorate this event. These celebrations elevated the capture of Izmail to one of the greatest Russian military accomplishments and solidified its place in the national consciousness through numerous prints, poems, hymns, and artistic productions. The Russian poet Gavrila Derzhavin and the composer Osip Kozlovsky commemorated the Russian victory with a special song, "Grom pobedy, razdavaysya!" (Let the thunder of victory sound) that was first performed in May 1791 and served as an unofficial Russian national anthem for decades.

This victory, however, came at a tremendous price, and the sheer scale of the carnage would be remembered for generations. "One can venture on a storming like the one at Izmail only once in a lifetime," commented Suvorov, who reported that some 26,000 Ottomans were killed and over 9,000 captured (many of whom perished). This number most certainly includes civilian losses, since in addition to the 15,000-man-strong Ottoman garrison, thousands of townsfolk perished in the bloodbath. Among the Russian trophies were more than 300 flags and pennants, 265 cannon, and vast supplies of ammunition.[88] The losses on the Russian side were staggering as well. Although official reports indicated that almost 4,600 had been killed and wounded, more than one participant suggested the total losses probably reached 10,000, including some 400 officers (out of 650). Alexander Langeron bewailed that "almost all of the assault columns lost a third of their men; one lost two-thirds," and that in his own battalion casualties included 7 out of 10 officers and 187 out of 540 men.[89] Kutuzov confided to his wife that he could not "even get my corps together because there are almost no officers left alive . . . Ivan [Ribeaupierre] and Glebov, who shared quarters with me, have both been killed; whoever I inquire about in the camp is either dead or dying. My heart is bleeding, and my eyes are full of tears."[90]

"The singular strength of [Izmail] must always make its reduction memorable in history," observed a British newspaper in February 1791. "The particulars of the assault will ever render it an interesting, though lamentable event."[91] Indeed, the storming of Izmail came to represent both a martial achievement to be celebrated and a stark example of horror and atrocity that customary laws of war still allowed in the Age of Reason. Despite the spread of Enlightenment ideas emphasizing rationality and humanity, extreme violence and gratuitous cruelty were endemic in wartime across Europe, and rape, pillaging, and summary killings were committed regularly. Kutuzov and many officers shared the ethos of the Military Enlightenment but also believed that such violence was in accordance with human nature and customary laws of war. "The notions of humanity and *sensibilité* had devastating limits," rightly points out one modern historian. These words echo the lament of the storming participant that "we must be careful not to believe that enlightenment and reason can do more on the minds of men than discipline and subordination."[92] Thousands of soldiers participated in the pillaging of Izmail, with officers tacitly, and in some cases actively, complicit in it. Participants expressed revulsion and shock at what happened in the fortress, as well as compassion and shame, and some described having intervened.[93] "Catherine, my dear friend . . . with the Lord's help, I am well," Kutuzov reassured his wife a few hours after the storming. He then confided to her that "I will not see another such [horrendous] affair again if I live another hundred years. My hair stands on its end just remembering it. Yesterday evening I felt cheerful because I was still alive, and this dreadful city was in our hands. But returning to my quarters at night was like venturing into the wasteland . . . I spent the whole night alone, grieving."[94]

The storming of Izmail played a central role in Kutuzov's life and career. This victory conferred an aura of martial glory that followed him for the rest of his life. "This brave soldier combined intrepidity with a great deal of acquired knowledge," enthused one contemporary. "He walked on the battlefield with the same gaiety that he showed in going to a fete."[95] Kutuzov emerged with an embellished reputation—that of a gifted officer who knew how to handle troops and be tenacious in combat. "Some officers need direct orders, others require explanations," observed Suvorov. "But there is no need to say anything to Kutuzov—he understands everything himself."[96] In his official report, Suvorov heaped praise on the general, mentioning him first when describing the exploits of the nine assault column commanders. "When the enemy, in superior numbers, compelled him to halt, [Kutuzov], leading through example, gallantly held his ground, defeated the powerful enemy, gained a foothold in the fortress and continued to inflict blows upon the enemy." Suvorov then added, in his own hand, a telling sentence: "He was posted on my left wing, but he was my right hand."[97] Like Suvorov, Potemkin appreciated Kutuzov's contribution and outstanding service, scribbling on the margins of the report, "[Award him] the Order of St. George of the third class" and nominating him for promotion to the rank of lieutenant general, which Empress Catherine confirmed in the spring.[98]

CHAPTER 6 | "The Glorious Hero of Măcin,"
1791–1792

T HE LOSS OF IZMAIL caused great consternation among the Ottomans.
Their dispirited army retired south while the grand vizier struggled to
mobilize fresh forces, contain the quickly spreading military mutinies, and
deal with the perennial logistical problems.[1] There seemed nothing standing
between the Russian army and Istanbul apart from the difficult passes
through the Balkan Mountains. Potemkin and Suvorov both knew that their
troops were fatigued and overstrained, however, and that it was not the time
to launch a new offensive, particularly not during a cold and harsh winter in
a war-depleted region. The Russian army pulled back to its winter quarters
between the Seret and Dniester Rivers. Kutuzov remained at Izmail with a
large garrison to maintain a forward observation post and to take care of the
sick and wounded.[2]

The first few weeks of what proved to be a six-month appointment
must have been extremely difficult for Mikhail Illarionovich. He was utterly drained. Memories of the horrific assault weighed heavily on his
mind as he visited the wounded at the hastily constructed hospitals and
tended to the needs of the indigent. He had lost his only son, brother-in-
law, and so many comrades-in-arms. To quote his contemporary William
Wordsworth, "solemn and sublime he might have seemed, but that in
all he said there was a strange half-absence."[3] This "half-absence" can
be deduced from a letter that his wife wrote upon receiving the news of
the fall of the Ottoman fortress and the survival of her husband. "He is
not only alive but healthy too," wrote Catherine, but "he is not yet returning home, even though all returning generals have told me that he
was allowed to leave."[4]

"Everything is well here," Kutuzov stated in an official report in January 1791. He was not entirely truthful, for he privately confided to Catherine that "there are so many things to tend to that I cannot even take care of [our own] wounded."[5] It took many long days to restore Izmail to some sense of normalcy. It had been so thoroughly devastated that there were few resources available to help the survivors during the winter weather. "There could not be any discussion of saving the wounded [enemies]," matter-of-factly noted one participant. "Almost all of them were pitilessly finished off; there were prisoners, who upon seeing such terrible slaughter, died of fear."[6] The most immediate and pressing task was to remove and bury the tens of thousands of corpses that filled the moat, earthworks, streets, and squares. Kutuzov employed some of the surviving Ottoman prisoners to do the gruesome job, though as late as March 1791, his superiors reminded him to hasten the burial of the cadavers before the spring thaw could spread the "stench and wicked consequences."[7] The Russians did their best to give their own dead a proper burial—in the 3rd Battalion of the Bug Jägers, private Nikifor Tikhonov built a coffin with his own hands for Captain Nikita Levshin, who had been mortally wounded while rallying his men on top of the bastion.[8]

The spring of 1791 saw Kutuzov saddled with an array of responsibilities. The Russian army had been regrouped into three corps. General Kakhovskii's Taurida Corps held positions in the Crimea, while General Gudovich's Caucasus corps defended the Russian interests in the North Caucasus and the Kuban region. The third contingent, the Danubian corps, was placed under command of General Nikolai Repnin after Potemkin returned to St. Petersburg in February, and it remained deployed on the Lower Danube, with the headquarters at Galatz. A third of this corps—scattered as it was north of the Danube and between the Prut and the Dniester—was under Kutuzov, who in addition to being the commandant of Izmail, also oversaw other captured Ottoman fortresses on the lower Danube.[9] Mikhail Illarionovich spent weeks preoccupied with communicating with the Ottoman officials about the prisoners of war, setting up new hospitals to nurse the Russian wounded (many of whom were still too weak to be moved), and tending to the needs of the local populace, which was in dire straits due to the war. As at Akkerman, he devoted considerable time and resources to setting up a network of flying detachments to gather intelligence about enemy forces and their movements, which provided him with a steady stream of information throughout the spring.[10]

In late February, Kutuzov received Repnin's order to start preparing for an "early campaign" should the sultan refuse to negotiate. The new instructions required him to raze Izmail's fortifications, fill in the moat, and search for as many of the cannonballs that the Russian army had fired at the fortress during the storming as possible. "There is a great need for them," stressed Repnin. Due to a lack of ammunition in the army that lasted through the spring, Kutuzov was also told to strip the roofs of the local mosque and residences and melt them down to make cartridges.[11] This was an order that he could not comply with, at least not fully. He knew that local Muslims would be enraged to see a mosque defiled and their homes left roofless; as late as mid-May, Repnin kept reminding him to carry out his instructions.[12] Kutuzov understood that to demolish a fortress of such vast size would require a gargantuan effort. He explained to Repnin that it would take at least 1,700 men and more than three months of unceasing work to accomplish it. Repnin advised him to force local inhabitants to do the grueling work of tearing down the bastions, demolishing ramparts, and moving the mounds of soil to fill up ditches. Kutuzov demurred, pointing out that there were not enough survivors—"barely 500 people"—who could undertake such physically demanding labor. Furthermore, with spring not far away, Kutuzov knew that most were focusing on providing food for their families. He countered that they "must be allowed to cultivate soil and tend to their vineyard, for otherwise they would simply starve to death."[13]

By March it was clear that peace was not forthcoming. Sultan Selim III, dismayed as he was by the fall of Izmail and despite pressing domestic issues, was disinclined to negotiate with the Russians in light of the fast-evolving international situation. Britain and Prussia were concerned by Catherine's successes and sought to foil Russian aggrandizement in southeast Europe. British prime minister William Pitt, fresh off the Nootka Sound Crisis, which pitted British and Spanish imperial interests in the northeast Pacific, turned his attention to the Crimea and the Danubian region, throwing the Turks a lifeline in what became known as the "Ochakov Crisis." With Prussian support, the British sought to force Catherine to end her war with the sultan on the basis of the *status quo ante bellum,* which would have compelled her to relinquish the Russian conquests made in the last three years of fighting. In the spring of 1791, the allies went so far as to threaten a military confrontation: if Russia refused to sit at the negotiating table, it would be attacked by the Royal Navy at sea and by Prussia on land. Sultan Selim III thus remained hopeful that the new campaign would turn the tide of war in his favor. He had the grand vizier executed for his failures and replaced him with the more capable and hawkish Koca Yusuf Pasha, yet another Georgian renegade.

The new grand vizier spent the first few months of the new year hurriedly moving freshly raised forces from Rumelia and Anatolia to the Danubian region. However, these reinforcements brought new problems with them. The Ottoman regular cavalry (*sipahis*) had been all but destroyed; in the words of Ottoman eyewitness Ahmed Cevdet, "the state of the cavalrymen in the ranks was to be pitied."[14] Their replacements were nothing but the "rebel bands from Sivas and other areas of Anatolia," as one historian put it, who were unruly, were more keen on plundering than fighting, and maintained stronger allegiance to their local leaders than to Ottoman military officials.

They arrived weary and petulant, quarreling with officers who attempted to bring some order to their ranks.[15] Despite these challenges, Grand Vizier Koca Yusuf Pasha was eager to concentrate his main forces north of Silistra, a key town on the lower Danube, where he could threaten Russian forces on the northern bank of the river and intercept their southward incursions.

—+—·≡·≡·—+—

The Ottoman arrangements did not escape Kutuzov, whose flying detachments provided him with a wealth of information. He reported that Seraskir Osman Pasha and five hundred men were occupying the village of Monastyrische, south of Tulcea, while a larger force held positions in the town of Babadag; furthermore, one pasha was stationed in the village of Văcăreni and two pashas were in Măcin, but Russian scouts could not determine the size of their forces. Rumor had it that the grand vizier himself was soon expected to arrive at Măcin with the main Ottoman army, estimated at some 80,000 men.[16]

In light of this information, Repnin decided to forestall the grand vizier's plans by launching the first trans-Danubian Russian incursion of the war. Kutuzov was an obvious choice for such a bold mission. In late March Repnin finalized his plan of operation, which called for Lieutenant General Prince Sergei Golitsyn, with about 3,000 men, to be conveyed by de Ribas's flotilla from Galatz to Isaccea for a raid in the direction of Măcin. Expecting that some enemy forces would flee the Russian advance to the southeast, Repnin asked Kutuzov to depart from Izmail with a large detachment, cross the Danube to Tulcea, and then conduct a reconnaissance in force as far as Babadag, thus intercepting any Ottomans fleeing from Isaccea. Once this was accomplished, Kutuzov could join Golitsyn for a joint offensive on Măcin.[17]

Selecting some 3,000 infantrymen and 1,300 Cossacks, Kutuzov crossed the Danube River on April 5 and 6,[18] brushed aside a sizable Ottoman outpost, and, as described in the official *Journal of Military Operations*, spent the following day "marching through the difficult defiles until midnight" to reach the outskirts of the town of Babadag, where he had a skirmish with an Ottoman force.[19] On April 7, knowing that time was of essence and unwilling to assault Babadag, Kutuzov turned northwest and proceeded on the road to Măcin, seeking out and destroying any enemy detachments he came upon, removing local inhabitants, and burning settlements, including the large village of Monastyrishe, to deny the Ottomans any shelter or sustenance in the region. Upon reaching Isaccea, Kutuzov united with Golitsyn; as junior in rank—he would learn of his promotion to lieutenant general only in June—he remained second-in-command. The Russian corps now advanced toward Măcin, but the road was difficult and, according to the official *Journal of Military Operations*, the soldiers had to navigate the rugged and mountainous terrain, which in places turned into "a narrow defile that compelled troops to deploy into a single column."[20] Near the village of Luncavița, about ten miles from Isaccea, Kutuzov and Golitsyn stumbled upon an Ottoman force under Gurju Ibrahim Deli Pasha holding positions in the narrow valley. Kutuzov led the assault, coordinating infantry attacks with Cossack charges and routing the enemy, which fled for six miles to the village of Văcăreni, where, despite receiving reinforcements, it was trounced once more. In hot pursuit of the fleeing enemy, the Russians approached Măcin, where they were greeted with artillery fire and a cavalry charge. They nonetheless pressed on with their assault, forcing the garrison to abandon the town and escape by boat. Golitsyn instructed his men to strip the newly taken town of all supplies, demolish most of its fortifications, and relocate its population to the northern bank of the Danube.[21]

The ease with which Măcin was taken encouraged Golitsyn and Kutuzov to pursue an even bigger prize. Just ten miles west of Măcin lay the Ottoman fortress of Brăila, which served as a logistical hub for the Ottoman army and a harbor for the Ottoman flotilla on the Danube. Located opposite of the peninsula formed by the innumerable estuaries of the great river, the town lay on the edges of a valley that rises abruptly above the Danube and was protected by an enceinte consisting of five bastions (three of them overlooking the river). Moreover, ditches, palisades earthworks, and two separate redoubts guarded the approaches from Măcin on the opposite bank. On April 8, the Russian forces approached the fortress, with de Ribas's flotilla sailing on the Danube, while Kutuzov and Golitsyn led their men along the main road from Măcin to Brăila. De Ribas drove the Ottoman flotilla farther upstream but could not get too close to the fortress, whose batteries posed a threat to his ships. Examining the layout, Golitsyn and Kutuzov agreed that their immediate task should be to secure the redoubts on the eastern bank. The Ottoman fortification on the marshy Kuncephan peninsula, formed by a sharp bend in the river, was stormed the same day, allowing de Ribas to ferry Russian infantry to the second, stronger redoubt, located on the island in the middle of the Danube. The Turks tried to prevent this assault by assembling a large battery in front of Brăila and involving their gunboats; the Russians nonetheless pushed ahead with the Vitebskii and Dneprovskii regiments, storming the redoubt on April 11.[22]

This allowed Golitsyn to set up dozens of cannon inside the redoubt and to bombard the Ottoman fortress while keeping Kutuzov's infantry safely out of the enemy's reach. The Russian barrage caused significant damage inside Brăila but could not break the garrison's resolve to defend it. Consequently, on April 12, Golitsyn ordered his entire corps to board the flotilla and sail away. Kutuzov returned to Izmail. Overall, this weeklong campaign proved to be fairly successful for Kutuzov and his men, who marched over 100 miles from Izmail to Babadag to Brăila, inflicted heavy losses (estimated at 4,000 men) on the Ottoman forces, and, by burning the stores, taking supplies, and removing the local population, caused further damage to the already hampered Ottoman logistical system.[23]

The raid stirred to action Grand Vizier Koca Yusuf Pasha, who began moving additional forces toward Brăila, with the goal of reclaiming Măcin and launching a counteroffensive against the Russian positions on the northern bank of the Danube. Throughout April and May, the Russians received a steady flow of reports about enemy forces concentrating in the environs of Măcin and Babadag. This made Repnin anxious, and he began to plan another trans-Danubian incursion to disrupt the enemy plans.[24] He urged Kutuzov to make all the necessary arrangements to secure the fortresses of Izmail and Kilya, to gather sufficient supplies and ammunition, and "to have the troops ready to depart at the first order."[25] In early June it was decided that the time was ripe for a coordinated attack on the Ottoman positions; Kutuzov would strike at the enemy forces gathering at Babadag, and once they were scattered, he would rush to support the main Russian offensive toward Măcin.[26]

During the night of June 14, Kutuzov crossed the Danube for the second time, taking with him some 12,000 men.[27] The following morning, he formed his corps into a single long column and left Tulcea, with the intention of marching to Babadag, over twenty miles away. In the afternoon his scouts reported that large masses of the Ottoman cavalry had been observed near Babadag. Kutuzov later estimated that some 15,000 Ottomans, commanded by Seraskir Ahmed Pasha, were positioned in front of the town, while up to 8,000 Tatars and Cossacks had taken up positions behind a mount, threatening his right flank.[28] Already familiar with the area from the earlier incursion, Kutuzov took full advantage of the local terrain, which was hilly and intersected by various streams, constraining cavalry operations. He deployed his corps into seven large squares—with regular cavalry interspersed and Cossacks on the wings and in the front—and steadily moved forward, crossing the Cataloi Rivulet and bivouacking about two miles outside Babadag.[29]

The following morning, June 15, the Ottomans sent out an advance guard to reconnoiter the enemy positions. Kutuzov drove it back and then advanced with his infantry squares directly on Babadag, diverting part of his corps to prevent the Tatar cavalry from making any flanking maneuvers. The fighting lasted only a few hours—the Ottomans were unable to break Kutuzov's squares and suffered hundreds of killed and wounded from their unremitting fire. They chose to abandon their camp, leaving behind eight cannon, several banners, and large supplies of provisions and gunpowder. Kutuzov estimated that "the enemy undoubtedly lost up to 1,500 men" and noted that the Cossacks showed no mercy to the wounded—"only thirty men could be rescued from the fury of the victors, and only three of them are lightly wounded." The Russians lost just sixteen killed and ninety-five wounded.[30]

Kutuzov remained at Babadag for another two days, sending out detachments to scour the countryside for miles around and implementing a scorched-earth policy in the region. His men carried off as many victuals as they could and "destroyed many dwellings" and whatever else could be of use to the Ottomans. At Babadag, which the Russians found abandoned by its inhabitants, Kutuzov found plenty of supplies, including a large gunpowder depot and large stores with biscuits and wheat flour. All of it was set on fire, which "inevitably spread into the rest of the settlement," as Kutuzov put it, largely destroying the town.

The battle at Babadag was the first major engagement that Kutuzov had fought independently. It proved that he could size up a situation with a *coup d'oeil*, make effective use of the terrain, and delegate authority to his officers. "I whole-heartedly congratulate you on this success," wrote Repnin. "I am thrilled for you, for me and for all of us."[31] The victory was reported across Europe, and even the *Sheffield Register*, a small newspaper published in South Yorkshire, England, ran a front-page story about it.[32] The news was welcomed in the Russian imperial capital, where Potemkin asked for Kutuzov to be given the Order of St. Alexander of Neva, and Catherine granted it.[33]

⊷—⊠⊹⊠—⊶

After returning to Izmail on June 17, Kutuzov was resting his men for two weeks when new orders arrived from Repnin. The Russian reconnaissance reports, some of them submitted by Kutuzov, had revealed that the Ottoman grand vizier, with at least 30,000 men, was on his way to Măcin, where the Ottomans were expected to concentrate about 70,000 men—twice the size of the Russian army—supported by a flotilla of almost fifty vessels anchored at Brăila. Everything pointed to a major offensive. Believing that the best defense was a good offense and unwilling to wait for the arrival of Potemkin, who could have claimed the glory of defeating the Ottomans, Repnin decided to strike at Măcin. In early July, he had two bridges constructed over the Danube and concentrated his forces around Galatz, instructing Kutuzov to leave a garrison at Izmail and come at once with the Bug Jäger Corps and some 500 Cossacks for the imminent offensive.[34] Repnin then organized three attack columns—Lieutenant General Golitsyn took charge of the right wing, Lieutenant General Prince Gregory Volkonskii assumed command of the center, and Kutuzov was given the left wing—and the reserves under Major General Spet. de Ribas's flotilla was nearby to provide logistical and artillery support.[35]

On July 7, leaving behind heavy equipment and the sick in the main camps, Repnin moved some 30,000 men across the Danube about two miles from Galatz and bivouacked on the Kuncephan peninsula, formed by the mighty river as it meandered through the Wallachian plains. "In daytime our soldiers remained hidden amidst the tall reeds of this marshland while at

night we were not allowed to ignite bonfires in order to keep the Turks unaware of our crossing," observed a participant.[36] While Quartermaster General
Yakov Pistor reconnoitered the area and cut reeds to make pathways for the
troops, Russian scouts scattered across the peninsula. They soon reported

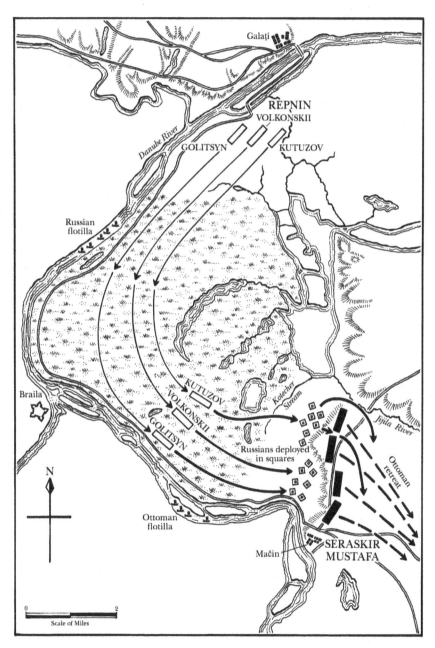

MAP 5 Battle of Măcin

observing the whole of the Ottoman army—commanded by Seraskir Mustafa of Rumelia, with the grand vizier a short distance away—encamped in front of Măcin, whose heights were covered with numerous tents. The enemy left flank was anchored on the river, while the right wing was protected by the heights that extended from Măcin to Baba Lake (present-day Jijila Lake). Repnin's battle plan was to launch a frontal attack on the Ottoman main camp with his right wing and the center (led by Golitsyn and Volkonskii), which would pin down the enemy and allow Kutuzov, with about 13,000 men, to turn the Ottoman flank and deliver a crushing blow from the left.[37]

On July 8, the Russian army broke up its camp at about six o'clock in the evening. It was a moonless night and, in the words of one participant, "the extreme darkness facilitated our furtive marching" through the tall reeds—"the grass was so tall and thick that a person could be barely seen in it"—toward the enemy positions.[38] General Golitsyn led his men along the edge of the marshland near the river, while Volkonskii marched with his column farther east, across the marshland. Knowing that the Ottomans enjoyed a considerable advantage in cavalry, Repnin instructed his commanders, as soon as they came out of the reeds, to form large infantry squares in checkered formation, with the cavalry dispersed in between.

As the sun cast its first rays upon the wetlands, the Ottomans were startled to find the enemy just a couple of miles away from their positions, and they hurriedly prepared for battle. Their cavalry—"with their usual blood-curdling howls of 'Allah! Allah!'"—charged at the Russians.[39] They were met with canister shots and rolling volleys but pressed on nonetheless, reaching the Russian squares. Some even managed to get inside one of them only to be immediately bayoneted. The ferocity of the Ottoman charges halted the Russian advance, and for the next several hours Repnin's attacks stalled, churned forward, and stalled again. His only hope was Kutuzov's flanking maneuver.[40]

As the fighting raged near Măcin, Kutuzov was leading his column about four miles northwest of the town, toward the valley of the Jijila River, where he intended to turn east, climb the steep mountain slopes, and turn the enemy's right flank. His movement was delayed by the difficult terrain, however, including streams and rivulets that had to be crossed. Ottoman scouts had observed Kutuzov's troops at first daylight and warned the main camp, which dispatched forces to reinforce the flank. As the column crossed the Kotecher Stream, Kutuzov sent ahead 200 Cossacks and prepared his battalions to scale the heights. But even before they could approach the slopes, Kutuzov's men came under sustained attack from the Ottoman infantry and cavalry, and endured intense fire from the enemy artillery. "Uncertainty of being in such closed confines, the enemy's numerical superiority, and his forceful attacks," as stated in the official report, forced Kutuzov to halt his advance. During these precious minutes, the Ottomans launched such fierce assaults on the

Russian squares that Kutuzov had "to resort to each and every means at our disposal to repulse them." Assisted by a group of officers, including Major General Alexander Tormasov, the future hero of 1812, and Quartermaster General Yakov Pistor, Kutuzov was able to keep his units steady and coordinate the infantry volleys with cavalry countercharges.

Throughout that morning, Repnin awaited Kutuzov's breakthrough but received no news. Noticing the opening that formed between the Russian main forces and the left wing, Seraskir Mustafa had moved some of his forces into the gap, effectively isolating Kutuzov in the narrow valley. "We could hear a fierce cannonade from behind the heights," remembered Lev Engel'hardt, who served in the Svyato-Nikolaevskii Grenadier Regiment, assigned to General Volkonskii's column. Repnin had sent his aide-de-camp to Kutuzov to find out why he was not ascending the mountain to move against the Ottoman flank. But this required traveling around the chain of foothills held by the Turks, a time-consuming enterprise. Meanwhile, "as the wind began to blow toward us, it seemed as if the gunfire [on the left wing] was moving further away from us."[41] Repnin was anxious. Why was the gunfire becoming so distant on the left flank? Was Kutuzov withdrawing? Worse would be if Ottoman forces had surrounded his column, allowing the enemy to move into the Russian rear, meaning the army would be effectively surrounded, pressed against the river, and destroyed. News arrived that some 10,000 Ottoman soldiers, under the protection of the Ottoman flotilla, were crossing the river from Brăila and trying to secure a bridgehead. From there they could threaten the Russian right flank and rear.

With his right wing under attack and the fate of Kutuzov's left wing unknown, Repnin contemplated pulling back his army before it was too late. He had crossed the Danube in direct contravention of instructions from Potemkin, who, eager to appropriate the impending victory, was already (literally) galloping from St. Petersburg to the front line. Repnin urgently needed a victory and wanted to secure it before the arrival of the empress's darling, whose custom it was to take credit for everything. "Repnin's trepidation only increased after Kutuzov's messenger informed him that the Russian left wing was struggling to make headway. Repnin was about to order the retreat when his son-in-law, Prince Volkonskii, convinced him otherwise. Instead, he moved the reserves to counter the threat from Brăila and to prevent the Ottoman landing on the right flank. This also allowed Volkonskii to send two grenadier regiments to secure the heights that separated Kutuzov's left wing from the rest of the army. Lev Engel'hardt, who led the assault of the Svyato-Nikolaevskii grenadiers, described how he took "the reserves of our regiment from within the square, dismounted my horse, and shouted, 'Lads, charge with bayonets! Hurrah!'" Supported by the Malorossiiskii Grenadier Regiment, Engel'hardt's men climbed the mountain slopes and forced the Ottomans to divert their forces. This eased pressure on Kutuzov's jägers and grenadiers, who were fighting on the other side of the ridge.[42]

This was the decisive moment of the battle. Kutuzov exploited the Ottoman confusion, caused by the attack of Volkonskii's grenadiers, by ordering a general advance up the mountainside, bearing down on all opposition "with canister, musket fire, and occasionally even bayonets." When he reached the top of the heights, Kutuzov formed his battalions into five squares, with the carabineer and hussar squadrons scattered in between them for support.[43] The Ottomans launched repeated assaults and at one point almost managed to break the square of the two Kyivskii grenadier battalions, but they were repelled.[44] Kutuzov then ordered a general advance with all of his forces, pressing so hard upon the enemy that the Ottoman troops on this flank fled in disorder. He then brought forward his cavalry, which pursued the fleeing enemy and threatened to cut off the rest of the Ottoman army's line of retreat, leaving Seraskir Mustafa no choice but to beat a retreat. The grand vizier, who was rushing with about 20,000 men from Hîrşova, could not reach the battlefield in time to prevent the Russian victory, which cost the Ottomans some 4,000 killed and wounded, 35 cannon, and almost the entire encampment, with numerous wagons; Repnin claimed to have lost just 131 killed and about 300 wounded.[45]

Măcin was the last major land battle of the Russo-Ottoman War. The Russian victory left the sultan's army "dispersed and in the greatest consternation," according to an eyewitness's letter published in Scotland, while Selim III was forced to sue for peace.[46] Just weeks later, the preliminaries were signed at Galatz and, in January of the following year, a final peace treaty was concluded at Jassy. The new agreement confirmed the provisions of the Treaty of Küçük Kaynarca (1774) but also established the Dniester River as the new imperial boundary. Though he recovered Moldavia and Bessarabia (including the fortresses of Izmail, Bender, Kilya, and Akkerman), Selim III was compelled to recognize the Russian takeover of the Crimean peninsula and most of the northern Black Sea coast.

Kutuzov had played a major role in the Russian triumph at Măcin and was widely praised for it.[47] "His efficiency and quick-wittedness are beyond praise," Repnin wrote in a letter to Empress Catherine.[48] The battle demonstrated how much Kutuzov had learned over the previous two decades of fighting the Turks. His tactical decisions—moving in columns, then deploying in squares and ensuring close coordination between infantry, cavalry, and artillery—reflect the lessons he had learned from observing Peter Rumyantsev and Alexander Suvorov. They testify to his ability to read the terrain and use it to his advantage, assess the battle situation, and react swiftly to changes. He led with courage and intelligence, and always from the front, even as he also cautioned against reckless bravery. "Rushing and getting injured is easy," he is said to have remarked. "But in the military service, it is fulfilling your tasks well that matters the most."[49] His rapport with the troops was renowned, and well founded.[50]

The Russo-Ottoman Wars elevated Kutuzov to the forefront of Russian military commanders. Catherine praised him for "the diligent service and gallant and valiant exploits with which you distinguished yourself" and bestowed upon him the Order of St. George (second class) for military valor.[51] As he left the Danubian region in the spring of 1792, Mikhail Illarionovich was no longer the wide-eyed inexperienced young officer who had arrived more than two decades earlier.[52] He had become "the glorious hero of Măcin," as contemporaries referred to him, the six-time decorated war hero with a reputation of being one of the most capable senior officers in the Russian army.[53] The question was how he would apply what he had learned fighting the Turks in a whole new theater.

PART II

CHAPTER 7 | The Envoy of Her Imperial Majesty, 1793

Kutuzov spent almost a full year, 1792 to 1793, in the Polish-Lithuanian borderlands while the Polish-Lithuanian Commonwealth experienced yet another political convulsion. The First Polish Partition had demonstrated the dangers a weak Polish state was facing and helped nurture public opinion favorable to the reform movement. Enlightenment ideals were in the air, as were prospects of structural reforms to strengthen the Polish monarchy and remove the Cardinal Laws (Prawa Kardynalne)—restrictive laws that were imposed on the Polish-Lithuanian Commonwealth by Russia, ostensibly to guarantee the traditional rights and liberties of the Polish-Lithuanian nobility. In the spring of 1791, the Great Sejm (the ruling body) saw an opportunity to enact an ambitious package of reforms while Poland's neighbors were preoccupied—Catherine was busy fighting the Swedes and the Ottomans, while Austria and Prussia were nervously following the revolutionary turmoil in France. On May 3, the Sejm produced Europe's first national codified constitution, which created a more effective constitutional monarchy and took steps toward reviving the Polish-Lithuanian state. "All power in civil society should be derived from the will of the people," proclaimed Article V. Other constitutional provisions redressed existing problems and strengthened state institutions. Among the reforms was the abolition of the *liberum veto*, which allowed a single member of the assembly to block any legislation, whether pushed by his conscience or by a bribe from a foreign state.

All this prompted an aggressive response on the part of Poland's neighbors, who felt threatened by the new ideals of its constitution and the prospects of a revitalizing state. "The worst possible news has arrived from Warsaw: the Polish king has become almost sovereign," lamented one of Catherine's chief foreign policy advisors, Alexander Bezborodko. In late April 1792, the conservative Polish and Lithuanian magnates gathered in St. Petersburg to condemn the new constitution and challenge the legitimacy of the Sejm. They formed what was called the Confederation of Targowica and appealed to the Russian empress to intervene into Polish affairs. Before long, Russian forces, some 100,000 men in total, crossed the border and the so-called War in Defense of the Constitution commenced. The Polish confederates' high hopes of restoring their ancient traditions and privileges with Russian help were about to be dashed on the rocks of Russian expansionism.

Lieutenant General Kutuzov was among the Russian troops sent to Poland. In April 1792 he assumed command of the First Section of the Army of Ukraine (Pervaya Chast' Ukrainskoi Armii), the largest force he had yet commanded, comprising more than 23,000 men grouped in four musketeer regiments, two grenadier regiments, two carabineer regiments, one horsejäger regiment, three hussar regiments, and five Cossack regiments, and reinforced by the Ekaterinoslavskii Jäger Corps and sixty cannon. He was given the task of invading Poland from the southeast and turning the right flank of the Polish army. After marching some 350 miles from the Dniester River to Winnica (Vinnytsia) in Poland-Lithuania, his men were weary and pining for rest, so Kutuzov spent most of the month of May gathering supplies and preparing for the campaign before military operations commenced in earnest in June. He was involved in a few minor skirmishes against the Polish forces of Józef Antoni Poniatowski (the future hero of the Napoleonic Wars and a Marshal of France) and Tadeusz Kościuszko (already famous for his part in the American Revolution), pursuing the retreating Polish forces to Warsaw. The campaign effectively ended late that summer.[1] The Second Partition, which started the war, further reduced the Polish state's territory. Russia gained the vast area of Byelorussia and Volhynia, including Minsk, Zytomier, and Kamieniec, while Prussia received an area nearly twice the size of its earlier gains. Austria, now preoccupied with its war with France, was excluded from this partition. Thus, Poland was reduced to a rump state dominated by its neighbors and destined to be destroyed just three years later in the third and final partitioning.

Kutuzov did not get to witness the conclusion of this historic event. In mid-November 1792, he received the news that Empress Catherine had selected him for an unexpected assignment—Russia's ambassadorship to the Ottoman Empire.[2] With the war against the sultan over, the empress was eager to consolidate peace on her southern borders so she could revive an economy sapped by the long war and, more crucially, deal with more pressing international matters, especially in Poland. Like the Russian czarina, Sultan Selim III was determined to exploit the end of the war to carry forward his program of domestic reform and engagement with the outside world. His predecessors, riding high on the wave of imperial expansion and convinced of their own cultural superiority, never troubled themselves with establishing permanent diplomatic missions in Europe; they expected the Europeans to come suppliant to them. As late as the 1780s, as contemporary historians have put it, "the world of Islam was still the world" to the Ottomans.[3] This mindset changed with the accession of Sultan Selim III in 1789. The new Ottoman leader had developed a fondness for the culture of western Europe, and particularly its military institutions and practices. He had corresponded with King Louis XVI of France concerning statecraft, social institutions, and the military arts. Selim III ushered in the "Europeanization of Ottoman diplomacy" by appointing the first permanent Ottoman embassies to London, Vienna, and Paris, and seeking to hone the political tools of modern diplomacy.[4]

Article 10 of the Treaty of Jassy specified that the two sides would restore diplomatic relations and exchange ambassadors "to guarantee the auspicious peace and sincere friendship between the two empires."[5] In late 1792 Selim III had named his envoy to Russia, forcing Catherine to hasten her selection. The post of ambassador in Istanbul was regarded as being among the most challenging in the Russian diplomatic service, both because of the crucial place the "Ottoman question" held in Russian foreign policy and because of the convergence here of the varied interests of other European powers. The Ottoman propensity for imprisoning Russian envoys did not make the job any easier. Catherine needed a shrewd, capable, and dependable individual who could settle relations with the Turks, defend Russian interests across the Ottoman realm, and maintain peace along the empire's southern borders for the foreseeable future. She initially considered sending the late Potemkin's nephew Count Alexander Samoilov (Kutuzov's former comrade-in-arms) but soon changed her mind, since skilled men like him were also needed closer to home. Samoilov was thus appointed to one of the highest imperial offices, that of general-procurator of the Senate.[6] After carefully considering other candidates, the empress decided to eschew professional diplomats in favor of battle-tested military professionals. On November 6, she publicly announced the appointment of Kutuzov as the new Russian ambassador plenipotentiary to the Sublime Porte.[7] His appointment startled many in Russian society. "No one expected such a pick," admitted one Russian diplomat. "Although he is a man of wit and a good general, Kutuzov has never been employed in any political matters."[8] Semen Vorontsov, the veteran Russian envoy who had spent decades at the Court of St. James, was also surprised by the choice but looked on it approvingly: "Kutuzov is a man of wit and prudent judgment; although he does not have the experience of [other ambassadors], I am convinced that, if given good instructions, he will do well."[9]

The decision to select a general over a diplomat may at first look puzzling, but there were good reasons for it. Catherine was aware of Kutuzov's abilities and accomplishments—especially during the last war against the Ottomans—and by choosing a man who had just recently trounced the Turks on the fields of battle, she was sending a clear message to the sultan: toe the line or risk a new war and fresh humiliations. She had already done this once before—Général-en-chef Nikolay Repnin, who had successfully commanded troops in the previous war against the Turks in 1768–1774, was sent as an ambassador to the Porte upon the conclusion of that war.

There were other considerations too. In addition to the customary political issues, the new ambassador would need to deal with practical matters relating to the recent war, including the fate of prisoners of war. He would also provide a steady stream of reports on the Ottoman military potential, assessing the extent to which the Turks would be able to threaten Russian interests in the near future. Who better to do this than a decorated war veteran who had spent years fighting the Turks? Catherine's instructions to Kutuzov made this reasoning explicit when she referred to his "skills in the art of war" and advised him to record "the location of places, roads, population, fortifications, troop dispositions, ammunition reserves, and everything else that relates to the land and naval forces."[10]

On November 23, Catherine signed an order formally recalling Kutuzov to St. Petersburg, where the general arrived by the end of the year.[11] The empress and the general met at the imperial palace. Thirty years had elapsed since she first laid eyes on him. Then he had been a young officer eager to distinguish himself. Now he was a middle-aged veteran. Catherine discussed political and diplomatic matters with Kutuzov, noticing, as one contemporary put it, "the subtleness of his thinking, the maturity of his reasoning on various diplomatic issues, and the prudence that he had demonstrated in all of his conversations and actions."[12]

With the imperial interviews completed, Kutuzov started preparing for the long journey to the Ottoman capital. He was a frequent visitor to the newly renovated neoclassical building on the English Embankment that housed the Collegium of Foreign Affairs, where he examined his instructions, discussed Ottoman affairs, and supervised staffing. The Russian legation quickly ballooned in size, taking on not just diplomats but also dozens of military officers, engineers, and naval officials, not to mention hundreds of servants and support personnel. Kutuzov was actively involved in selecting his staff members, some of whom were veterans of the Bug Jäger Corps and grenadier regiments that Kutuzov had previously commanded. The troops and officers selected for this mission were still with their units, scattered in various provinces. To expedite the preparations, they received orders to travel directly to the town of Elisavetgrad in southwestern Ukraine, where Kutuzov intended to assemble his entire legation before proceeding to the Porte.[13]

"It has not been yet determined when the ambassador will begin his journey," wrote Heinrich Christoph von Reimers, the young German nobleman who was appointed as one of Kutuzov's secretaries, to a friend in mid-March. "My future chief seems to be an amiable and excellent man," he added. "In addition to his mother tongue, he speaks fluent French and a very good German, and seems to love Germans and their language too."[14] Kutuzov could also converse in at least three other languages, including Turkish.

On March 30, Kutuzov received his passport and soon thereafter, accompanied by his family, left for Istanbul.[15] By now, the diplomatic train of his embassy included more than 600 individuals, among them eight interpreters, forty-nine musicians, twenty-four singers, twelve carpenters, six blacksmiths, ten tailors, five cobblers, dozens of cuirassiers, carabineers, grenadiers, and hussars, and numerous lackeys and domestics.[16] Transporting and sustaining this vast legation was a daunting enterprise. To help defray the costs, the imperial Treasury provided Kutuzov with 299,689 rubles and 962 kopecks, an unusually precise sum that prompted one of his companions to wonder whether "the fact that even the kopecks have been precisely recorded" was "the indication of a very high degree of punctuality and conscientiousness" expected from Kutuzov's mission.

In addition, Mikhail Illarionovich carried numerous sumptuous gifts and cash for the sultan. The presents included a dazzling aigrette valued at 40,000 rubles (equaling the annual pay of 4,000 Russian soldiers) and black fox furs priced at 65,000 rubles, which could have purchased 10,000 soldier's uniforms.[17] The embassy also carried diverse fabrics, diamonds and other precious gems, jewelry, watches, snuffboxes, and luxury items for the Ottoman viziers, ministers, and various dignitaries whom Kutuzov was expected to encounter on his way.[18] All of these offerings were packed into dozens of large carriages that were under constant protection. Coordinating the movement of so many carriages and transports was a logistical challenge. Kutuzov and his suite alone required 170 horses at each post station, which some post-masters simply could not manage. On some days, the embassy could pass through just two or three post stations before being forced to halt due to deep snow or a lack of horses. The heavily laden transports naturally slowed down the progress. Kutuzov left them behind and pressed on in clear weather and on roads that were "still frozen hard."[19]

The farther he got from St. Petersburg, the more slowly his voyage progressed along what one of his companions described as "the long and barren road."[20] The countryside was still covered in deep snow, while the quality of roads outside major towns left much to be desired. In some places the terrain was so rugged that the embassy members were obliged "to harness ourselves to the carriage to draw it along," complained Johann Christian von Struve, the newly appointed legation secretary.[21] "This whole region, formerly part of Poland but within Russia since 1772, bears the stamp of poverty," wrote Reimers, Kutuzov's other diplomatic secretary. "People are unhappy and miserable here; the scarcity of food is so great here that the peasants have to eat bread made from hemp seeds and often starve to death for the lack of it. One cannot ascribe the guilt so much to the government as to the local landlords, who bleed the poor peasants white and squander their income far from here." He noted that "these unfortunate people" were none-theless forced to pay for the horses' upkeep at the stations and were "dragged from one post to another following the carriage bearing sumptuous presents for a foreign country." At each station Kutuzov's carriage was surrounded by people begging for money or bread. "Their ragged clothes and haggard, gaunt faces spoke clearly of their misery. The charity, which was warmly dis-tributed, was greeted with loud shouts of thanks."[22]

After ferrying across the mighty Dnieper River, Kutuzov traveled on some "very bad and tiresome roads," as his companions described, amid snow-cov-ered fields that provided bare sustenance for the miserable inhabitants, whose "eyes reflected anguish and misery." The conditions were significantly better in Chernigov province, where people had a "healthier countenance and the horses got better from station to station." Kutuzov must have marveled at the local inhabitants' distinctive lifestyle; instead of Russian blockhouses, he saw "farmhouses made of plaited shrub and plastered with clay, with thatched roofs; they were heated with straw for lack of wood." The locals' inimitable vernacular—they spoke Ukrainian—would have also caught his ear, as they referred to him as *hospodin heneral* (lord general).[23] Kutuzov was fortunate that the Desna River, which flows through Chernigov, was still frozen and the locals could guide him across the river; if the ice had broken, it would have delayed his journey by weeks. By the time he reached the central Ukrainian provinces, "there was no longer any trace of winter and the eyes lingered longingly on the fresh green of the grass" of the immense Ukrainian plains that stretched all the way to the Ottoman border. "The roads were everywhere dry, the sky pure and serene, and the air mild."[24]

On April 24, 1793, Kutuzov arrived at Elisavetgrad, a small town of barely 3,000 inhabitants on the edge of the Russian Empire where his family had already lived before and where his son was buried. Founded in 1754 as a military stronghold against the Turks, the town, if one could even call it that, remained underdeveloped; its unpaved streets turned into mire even in a drizzling rain.[25] Nonetheless, a group of Cossacks, carrying their long pikes, ceremonially advanced through the settlement, escorting Kutuzov on a solemn entry into the fortress that was built on the small hill overlooking the plains. After a casual meeting with local officials—"our good ambassador is not a fan of rigid etiquette," observed a member of the Russian legation—Mikhail Illarionovich settled with his family at a house that the town mayor had prepared for him.[26] He soon learned that the Ottoman plenipotentiary Mustafa Rasih Pasha was about 250 miles south, at the town of Bender on the Dniester River, which served as the new boundary between the Ottoman and Russian domains.[27] However, the Russian legation was not yet ready for the meeting, as most of its transports were delayed by poor roads and ice breaking on the rivers. The start of the Muslim holy month of Ramadan on April 12 delayed the exchange of diplomatic missions even further, as the Ottomans spent the next thirty days fasting, praying, and reflecting.

Kutuzov welcomed this long layover because it allowed his embassy to assemble while he could relax with the family. "Many an evening passed in interesting conversations in small circles," confided Reimers in a letter to a friend. The governor general of the Byelorussian viceroyalty (*namestnichestvo*), Peter von Passek, who was designated as the Russian commissar at the ambassadorial meeting, regaled Kutuzov and his companions with delicious breakfasts, dinners, and balls to celebrate Easter.[28] The fine May weather offered an opportunity for Kutuzov and his family to enjoy time together, whether delighting in the panoramas of boundless plains surrounding the fortress or spending quiet time in a small garden "laid out in the English fashion," where they could sit "in the shade on the slope of the hill, watching the Ingul River flow through the valley and listening to the nightingales."[29]

The five weeks Kutuzov spent in Elisavetgrad gave him an opportunity to get better acquainted with the situation inside the Ottoman Empire. He solicited more information on the state of affairs in the sultan's domains and read numerous dispatches from various officials.[30] The unexpected arrival of former French ambassador Marie-Gabriel-Florent-Auguste de Choiseul from Istanbul was a godsend for Kutuzov. Hailing from a distinguished French noble family, Choiseul was a renowned scholar of ancient Greece who had served as a French envoy to the sultan's court since 1784. However, the recent events in France had changed the course of his life. In August 1792, the French monarchy was overthrown, and a republic was proclaimed in France; Choiseul refused to support the new government. After months of standoff, he was finally forced to leave Istanbul when the new envoy of the French Republic arrived at the sultan's court. Unable to return home for fear of being prosecuted, Choiseul chose to enter Russian service and was on his way to St. Petersburg when he encountered the Russian embassy in late May.[31] Kutuzov heartily welcomed the distinguished guest, assigning him a guard of honor and treating him to a sumptuous dinner. He gleaned a great deal from the experienced diplomat. Among other things, Choiseul mentioned that a French engineer, whom the Turks had recruited to supervise the construction and repair of fortresses in the Danubian principalities, was dissatisfied with his pay. Kutuzov made a note of this information.

Throughout May, the Russian and Ottoman sides continued to negotiate the details of the forthcoming official ceremony of exchanging ambassadors.

They agreed that the ceremony protocol would be the same as the one used in 1775 after the end of the last Russo-Ottoman War. In her instructions, Catherine reminded her new ambassador to emulate his predecessor and provided Kutuzov with copies of Repnin's reports so that he could get a better understanding of the challenges he was about to face. Among the examples the empress cited was Repnin's refusal to allow an Ottoman representative to hold him by his right hand during the exchange, which could be interpreted as acknowledging Ottoman superiority. Her advice was to follow everything to the letter: "You must ensure that the ceremony is carried out precisely as agreed upon and without any, even minor, omissions."[32]

Having diligently studied the documents, Kutuzov came prepared for the negotiations with the Ottomans. When they suggested holding the ceremony for the exchange of embassies in the Ottoman-held town of Bender, Kutuzov rejected their offer and instead insisted on the meeting taking place near Dubossary, a small border town on the left bank of the Dniester River. Dubossary had been recently incorporated into the Russian Empire and was a symbol of Russian imperial accomplishment. He did agree, though, that the exchange could take place on an Ottoman-built raft in the middle of the river. As for the date, the Russian side initially proposed June 14, but since it was a Friday, and thus the day of obligatory public prayer for Muslims, it was agreed that the ceremony would take place the following day, Saturday, June 15, 1793, or Zilkade 6, 1207, under the Muslim calendar.[33]

In late May, Kutuzov bade farewell to most of his family and gave the order to depart Elisavetgrad, knowing well that it would take his large deputation days to cover the 200 miles to Dubossary. The dozens of heavy transports and carriages were ferried across the Ingul River and slowly moved westward across the meadows that, like "a green carpet," stretched as far as the eye could see, Reimers remembered.[34] The journey was excruciatingly slow. "It took us hours to move just ten miles," lamented a Russian diplomat.[35] Many slept in the carriages. The area separating Elisavetgrad and Dubossary was sparsely populated, and the legation members struggled to find proper shelter, food, and water. The settlements were fewer and farther in between, the hovels smaller and lower; their windows, instead of being glazed, now were covered with stretched and dried ox bladders.[36] The sudden appearance of a huge cavalcade would have been a sight to behold, and the road was indeed lined with spectators, but few were welcoming the visitors, who required vast quantities of food. "We comprised a veritable small army advancing gaily and easily," remembered von Struve, who traveled with Kutuzov's suite and was pleased to see that the embassy was "abundantly provided with everything" because "our purveyors always went before us."[37]

On the evening of June 2, Kutuzov reached Dubossary, where he and his wife settled in a house arranged for them.[38] He ordered a large tent to be set up on a nearby meadow and provided food and drinks to the sixty or seventy officers of his entourage, who dined in style. This being the Moldovan countryside, good wine flowed freely at the dinner.[39]

It took another two weeks to finish preparations for the ambassadorial meeting. Both sides struggled to prepare for the event: the Russian transports were delayed by the spring inundations in Ukraine, while the Ottomans were confronted with significant logistical challenges in transporting all the necessaries from Istanbul to a town on the edge of their empire.[40] Finally, on June 15, in meticulously arranged choreography, the entourages of Kutuzov and Mustafa Rasih Pasha slowly moved toward the river. "The procession, favored by the finest weather," one eyewitness described it, "moved in such perfect order as to present a most striking and gratifying view."[41] A detachment of cavalry and infantry, followed by a troop of mounted Cossacks, opened the procession. These were followed by a file of elaborate carriages containing a portion of the civil officers of the embassy. Then came Kutuzov himself, surrounded by a cavalry detail and principal officers of his suite. They were succeeded by a considerable number of carriages bearing civil officers and domestics, all of them wearing yellow and blue liveries to represent the colors of Kutuzov's coat of arms. Behind them came another detachment of troops. The entire procession extended over a mile.[42]

Unwilling to let the other side outshine it, the Turks arrived amid dazzling pomp. "Nothing could be more strikingly contrasted than the appearance of these two embassies," observed Johann Christian von Struve. "The [Ottoman side] was seen covered with wealth, gold, silver, and costly ornaments, while the [Russian embassy] exhibited simplicity as well as a most martial and impressive appearance."[43] His colleague Heinrich Christoph von Reimers, who had traveled widely in earlier years, marveled at the splendor and magnificence. He had witnessed several historic events—the Betrothal of the Doge of Venice to the Adriatic Sea in 1788, the papal address to tens of thousands of believers at St. Peter's Square in Vatican the same year, and the opening session of the Estates-General in Versailles on May 5, 1789, to name just a few—but the exchange of the Ottoman and Russian embassies on the banks of the Dniester River surpassed them all. He marveled at the variety of costumes and countenances: *bostanjis*, the Ottoman imperial guardsmen, strutting in their red robes and long drooping caps; the water carriers in leather skirts sewn with bells; mules carrying the palanquins covered with rich fabric; the Moldovan boyars and their ornately costumed wives.[44]

As the ambassadors approached the river, cannon were fired from the Russian bank and immediately answered from the Ottoman side, creating a deafening rumble. On either side of the Dniester flat boats specially refurbished for this occasion would bear the parties. At the agreed hour, Kutuzov and Mustafa Rasih Pasha, accompanied by the exchange commissars, dignitaries, and interpreters, took off from opposite banks of the river.[45] They disembarked at the large raft that the Turks had constructed in the very middle of the Dniester, the border separating the two empires.[46] Kutuzov and Mustafa Rasih Pasha sat in armchairs on opposite ends of the raft and studied each other. They could not have been more different in personal background and upbringing—a war veteran and a consummate Ottoman administrator. Mustafa Rasih Pasha, slightly older than Kutuzov, had spent his career in the chancery of the grand vizier. Marriage to the daughter of a senior bureaucrat had boosted his career, which now culminated in his selection for an ambassadorial post.[47] He belonged to the narrow circle of trusted advisors who supported Selim III's reformist agenda.[48]

The ambassadors welcomed each other through the interpreters.[49] After a brief formal conversation, the two men stood. The exchange commissioners held the ambassadors by their right hands and, "with the reverence befitting their rank" and accompanied "with greetings and accolades," handed them over to the commissioners of the opposite side, who then seated the envoys in chairs on the right side of the boats. More cannon thundered on the riverbanks; troops fired their muskets three times. As the sound of gunfire echoed through the valley, the two ambassadors sailed in opposite directions and were greeted with yet another round of cannonade.[50]

Reaching the Ottoman side, Kutuzov was first led to a grand tent that the pasha of Bender had pitched not far from the river's edge. He was treated to Turkish coffee and presented with various gifts, including a beautiful stallion with a richly adorned caparison. To show his appreciation of the pasha's gift, Kutuzov mounted the steed and rode him along the bank, where he was greeted by the Ottoman troops drawn up in a parade formation. Later the same evening the Russians were taken to the nearby village, where "a grand celebration" was held and Kutuzov and his wife entertained his hosts with "delicious desserts and ice cream."[51]

It took another ten exhausting days—"not a single day passed that was not distinguished by some new rejoicing, be it fireworks, illuminations, feasts, balls, dances, and every other kind of merrymaking," in the words of an observer—for the ambassadorial trains to cross the river.[52] On June 25 Kutuzov bid farewell to the Dniester River and traveled in the direction of Istanbul, which still lay over 600 miles away.[53] Provided with the necessary pack animals and amenities (including "1,000 pairs of oxen and 500 horses"), the legation traveled for two days and rested on the third.[54] "Such is the custom of the Turks to travel so comfortably, and the good old Muslims must be thanked for keeping such a wonderful custom," effused one Russian diplomat.[55] Kutuzov instituted a laissez-faire approach, not insisting on strict adherence to ceremony.[56] After traveling most of the day, the embassy staff relaxed in the evening. The Russian diplomats marveled at the Moldavian countryside, with thatched homes painted in distinctive blue and white, and were impressed by the warmth of the "good-natured residents," who welcomed the guests into rooms decorated "with branches of wild cherry trees that were full of fruit." But not everything was idyllic—bedbugs remained omnipresent, even "in the seemingly clean peasant homes."[57]

On June 27, Kutuzov reached the town of Chişinău and reported to the empress that the Ottomans were treating him "with all respect and honors befitting" a Russian ambassador.[58] From here he ventured to the town of Jassy (Iaşi). Along the way, Kutuzov reached the spot where his great benefactor, Prince Potemkin, had died a year and a half earlier. While visiting the region in the fall of 1791, Potemkin fell ill of an epidemic that was raging at that time. His fever gaining ground, he tried returning to Russia, but it was too late. He was taken out of his carriage and laid down on the grass by the side of the road, where he expired on October 16. He had been just fifty-two years old. Kutuzov contemplated the spot where the man who had played a crucial role in his career breathed his last. "A humble pyramid of bricks covered with emblematic figures of stucco marks the spot," noted his companion. "The whole thing looks very ephemeral, just like the great man's reign!"[59]

The principality's new hospodar (ruler), Mihai Draco Suţu (Soutzos), arranged a reception for the Russian ambassador. Crowds gathered in the narrow streets of Jassy, and the bells of local churches and monasteries pealed in celebration. Kutuzov, riding a stallion that the hospodar had presented to him, paraded to the town center, where he was welcomed by the Arnaut troops, who fired several volleys in salutation.[60]

Kutuzov's ten-day stay in Jassy reflected its symbolic importance. First, this was the town where the Russo-Ottoman peace treaty had been negotiated more than a year earlier. Kutuzov thought it a fitting place to celebrate the twenty-first anniversary of Catherine's accession to power with a lavish fête.[61] He used his time there to cultivate relations with the Moldavian prince, who was clearly very eager to attain Russian support; the diplomatic briefing he had received had already informed him of Suţu's pro-Russian sentiments, and he praised the hospodar for "always demonstrating goodwill toward the affairs of our subjects." To ensure the prince's commitment to the Russian cause, Kutuzov assured Suţu and various nobles of Russian support and gave them generous presents (perhaps too generous, for he soon had to request additional funds from St. Petersburg to compensate for what he described as unexpectedly higher expenses he had encountered in Moldavia).[62] Nonetheless, the ambassador's gifts did accomplish their goal, as subsequent reports show that Suţu and Moldavian nobles provided him with a steady flow of secret information.

The time in Moldavia was fruitful for another reason. "As I traveled across the region and stayed at Jassy," Kutuzov reported, "I endeavored to gather intelligence on the condition of the Turkish border fortresses."[63] Remembering French envoy Choiseul's brief mention of a disgruntled French engineer in the Ottomans' employ, Kutuzov secretly made contact with the engineer, a certain "Kaufer," whom he described as "a rather adroit individual who can gain even greater confidence among the Turks and be very useful to us in the future." Kaufer agreed to enter the Russians' employ and provided crucial information on the extent of repair works, the size of Ottoman garrisons throughout Moldavia, and the shortcomings in artillery armament. Understanding the immense value of this information, Kutuzov told his superiors that "it is highly desirable to limit the number of people privy to the secret of our correspondence with [Kaufer], both out of concerns for his safety and for our own [continued] benefit."[64]

As it made its epic trek to Istanbul, the Russian mission crossed into the Wallachian principality ruled by the hospodar Alexander Mouruzi.[65] A scion of a prominent Phanariot (Ottoman Christian elite) family, Mouruzi was a talented Ottoman administrator who had mastered six languages and risen to the position of grand dragoman, the de facto deputy foreign minister. His involvement in the conclusion of the Treaty of Jassy was rewarded with the governorship of Moldavia in 1792, though a year later he was transferred to the Wallachian capital, Bucharest, where he welcomed Kutuzov on August 8.[66]

Unlike Draco Suţu, Mouruzi, whose family held senior positions at the sultan's court, was less inclined to seek closer relations with Russia. Like many Phanariotes, he was also a Francophile who embraced the spirit of the Enlightenment. The ferment occasioned by the French Revolution had already reached the Balkan peninsula and created hopes for the regeneration of Wallachia (and other Balkan principalities). Yet any attempts at government reform and more secular education were bitterly opposed by the Wallachian nobility, which loathed the hospodars' centralization efforts, and the Orthodox Church, which regarded itself as the guardian of the traditional way of life.[67] They also antagonized Empress Catherine, whose instructions to Kutuzov were explicit in condemning Mouruzi as a dangerous proponent of anti-Russian policies in the region. The court of St. Petersburg could not forgive him for the detention and expulsion of Gavril Bănulescu-Bodoni, whom the Russians had installed as the metropolitan of Moldavia.[68] Kutuzov was thus instructed to give a cold shoulder to Mouruzi, who "does not deserve," Catherine reminded him, "to be treated with any distinction."

The road to Bucharest ran through Focşani and Rymnik, the sites of the bloody battles in which Suvorov had routed the Ottoman forces just four years earlier. The scars of war were still clearly visible everywhere.[69] Meeting the Wallachian hospodar in Bucharest, Kutuzov was pleased to observe that Mouruzi was keen on mollifying the Russians and had spared no expense to welcome the legation. Yet Kutuzov nonetheless found him smug and suspect: "Despite his efforts to conceal it, [Mouruzi] still could not hide his affection for [French] Jacobinism and his futile hope of reviving the Ottoman Porte with the help of these [French] villains." Even junior Russian diplomats noticed a subtle but telltale difference between the receptions in Moldavia and Wallachia. "Courtesy, trustworthiness, and cordiality shone there; friendship, feigned by politeness, could be seen here," Reimers confided to a friend.[70] Kutuzov followed the empress's advice to "express to Mouruzi bluntly the obscenity of his behavior against the fellow Christian state . . . and that we consider him a true Turk who only appears to be a Christian." The ambassador suggested that there would be repercussions should the hospodar continue to flout Russian interests.[71]

After departing from Bucharest in late August, the Russian legation visited Giurgiu, Razgrad, Adrianople, San Stefano, and other locations as it slowly journeyed across the eastern Balkans.[72] "Everywhere I went, I was treated with great honor and respect and I am very pleased with this," Kutuzov reported. "These experiences encourage me to think that during the rest of my journey to Istanbul the Turks would extend similar hospitality and affection."[73] The oppressive summer heat was less hospitable, tormenting the Russian legation. "Many of my men are sick but, thank God, none are seriously," reported Kutuzov, who himself felt unwell and occasionally struggled to mount his horse.[74] But even illness had its advantages, giving him an excuse to avoid the never-ending ceremonies.[75] The slow progress was a boon to Russian intelligence-gathering efforts. In total, the Russian embassy had spent 114 days traveling the 650 miles from Dubossary to Istanbul and made more than fifty stopovers.[76] The military experts, engineers, topographers, and draftsmen Kutuzov brought with him exploited the snail's pace to study local topography, drawing maps, assessing available resources, and outlining possible military operations in case of a future war. One such report described in detail the area between Ruse and Istanbul, pinpointing the most advantageous routes of military advance and identifying the means of sustaining a 40,000-man-strong army in the area; the report remained a valuable source of information for nearly a century, publicized only in the wake of Russia's war with the Ottomans in 1878.[77] Kutuzov used the time to cultivate relations with Moldavian, Wallachian, and Bulgarian elites, many of whom were given munificent presents and assured of "continued Russian benevolence."[78] He observed the state of affairs in the Ottoman Empire's western dominions firsthand and became better apprised of the continued turmoil in the Rumelian (Balkan) countryside, where the sultan struggled to fully assert his authority.

Kutuzov, who celebrated his forty-sixth birthday near Adrianople on September 16, kept a close eye on the events in Europe and beyond, corresponding with Russia's envoys and consuls scattered everywhere, from Vienna to Alexandria.[79] With the help of the Russian envoy to the Habsburg court, he closely followed the War of the First Coalition. Thus he remained well apprised of the Austro-Prussian siege of the French fortress of Valenciennes, and of the British capture of Toulon, France's key naval base, with its entire Mediterranean squadron.[80] He was particularly interested in the news from Poland-Lithuania. Russia had finalized the Second Polish Partition by convening the last meeting of the Sejm at the town of Grodno and, through bribery and coercion, forcing it to ratify the agreement carving up the commonwealth. Kutuzov was elated by this news; "I cannot express with what pleasure and gratitude I read your letter [about the partition]," he wrote the Russian ambassador in Warsaw.[81] Eager not to miss out on any rewards—land would be given away as a result—he was not shy about reminding Catherine and her court of his devoted service and accomplishments. While still at Bucharest, he wrote a slightly fawning letter, extolling the Russian success in Poland and seeking some recompense "for my labors and ceaseless commanding of considerable number of troops that resulted in more than one accomplishment." As venerable as being an ambassador to the Porte was, Kutuzov was concerned that by being away from the court he might be overlooked in the empress's looming munificence.[82]

He need not have worried. In September Catherine signed a decree granting him the honorary title of governor-general of Kazan and Vyatka and gifting him "in perpetuity and hereditary ownership" two thousand "souls" residing in several estates that had been confiscated from Polish nobles who resisted the Russian invasion. Moreover, the governor of Ekaterinoslav province was authorized to transfer into Kutuzov's ownership 9,000 *desyatinas* of land (some 24,300 acres) "in the regions newly acquired from the Ottoman Porte."[83] Kutuzov thus became one of the wealthiest landowners in the Russian Empire. Nonetheless, he continued to worry about finances. His wife, Catherine, who had returned home, was profligate in her spending. But despite sharp exchanges, mainly over money and spending, the couple remained devoted to each other. "How sweet you are when you are not scolding me," Kutuzov wrote her in late August. He had tried sending gifts and souvenirs from Wallachia, but "there was nothing in Bucharest." "Please send me a list of anything you need at home, and I will dispatch items by sea. As for my needs, send me something that conveys your lovely self, when you are not quarreling with me. This would be the best sustenance I can hope for. . . . I kiss you in every possible way."[84]

The greater threat to Kutuzov's welfare was posed by French agents, who, it seemed, lurked everywhere, waiting for an opportune moment to strike, spreading revolutionary ideology and chaos. His anxieties, exaggerated as they were, were reinforced by the reports he had received from other Russian diplomats about suspected French activities and intrigues. Count Andrei Razumovskii, Russia's ambassador to Vienna, informed him of the Austrian arrest of the French envoys Charles Louis Huguet de Sémonville and Hugues-Bernard Maret, who were sent on a mission to Naples but whom

Razumovskii suspected of being agents and conspirators. The ambassador bemoaned the Austrian failure to nab "the main weapon" of the French espionage, Franz Angeli, who previously had been employed in Russia but had been expelled. Kutuzov knew Angeli well, having served with him in Bauer's First Army during the Russo-Ottoman War in 1770. "This man combines a cunning mind of an intriguer with a base and craven soul," he described Angeli in one of his letters. "Having been banished from Russia, he certainly bears malice toward us."[85] Throughout August and September 1793, Kutuzov spent considerable time trailing the movements of these French agents. Early reports suggested that Angeli was traveling in disguise to the Crimea to incite anti-Russian sentiments there. Kutuzov shared this information with the relevant Russian authorities but also noted that rumors of the threat the French agents posed seemed to be exaggerated. Angeli "mangles the Russian language so badly that as a [secret] emissary he can hardly pose any threat to us," thought Kutuzov.[86] The most the Frenchman could hope to achieve was to establish contact with the Circassian mountaineers in the northwest Caucasus.

Even more troublesome were the rumors regarding Ottoman intentions. In late August Kutuzov was startled to hear that Colonel Ivan Barrozzi, the military attaché in the Russian embassy in Istanbul, had been sending out reports alleging an imminent rupture in Russo-Ottoman relations. Citing intelligence he had procured with the help of a dragoman in the Prussian embassy, the colonel contended that the Turks were upset about Russian intransigence in the matters of commerce (and especially tariffs), were keen on reclaiming the lost territories, and had already started moving forces to resume hostilities. "You will find it hard to believe but even as we ventured into Bulgaria, there was growing talk that the embassy would have to turn back," wrote a jittery Russian diplomat on August 27. "It is suspected there that an inevitable break would take place between Russia and the Porte and there would be a new war between the two powers."[87]

Kutuzov was irked by Barrozzi's actions. He found his claims unsubstantiated and improbable. "It is reckless to speak of the Ottomans attempting a new war in light of the general situation in Europe and especially due to their domestic difficulties," he explained. "Barrozzi is either mistaken or is being misled by individuals who are sharper than him."[88] In a stream of letters to St. Petersburg Kutuzov did his best to dispel hearsay. He argued that the Ottoman fleet and army movements that the reports alleged were part of war preparations were in fact routine redeployments. Relying on his personal observations and intelligence he had gathered through his agents, Kutuzov pointed out that the Ottomans were militarily unprepared, that their fortresses, including the strategically important ones at Bender and Ismail, were still in the midst of repair works that would last months, and that the garrisons in Moldavia and Wallachia were woefully inadequate.

While crossing the Danube, Kutuzov personally examined the fortresses of Giurgiu and Ruse and managed to make his way into supply barns, where he could see the shortage of ammunition and supplies. Kutuzov was a veteran of one kind of warfare. The fight to control information and suppress rumors was a challenge of a different sort, though it was one he would have to learn to wage.[89]

CHAPTER 8 | At the Court of the Sultan, 1794

O N OCTOBER 3, 1793, Kutuzov approached the Ottoman capital.[1] Perched at the very tip of Europe and gazing across at the shores of Asia, Istanbul conveyed imperial grandeur like no other city, save for Rome, its long-standing rival. Founded by the Greeks and turned into "New Rome" by Emperor Constantine in the fourth century, the city's location at the crossroads of commerce and cultures blessed it as a cosmopolitan center for over a millennium but also made it a target of conquests and imperial ambitions. After Ottoman Sultan Mehmed II conquered it in 1453, Istanbul experienced a period of renaissance, growing in size, prospering, and turning into an incomparable multicultural metropolis. Approaching its famed double Theodosian walls, built by the eponymous Byzantine emperor some 1,300 years earlier, Kutuzov, a good student of antiquity, would have been enthralled by the grand panorama of history that the city presented.

On the orders of Sultan Selim III, dozens of opulent and fully furnished tents were put up on the outskirts of the capital to welcome the Russian embassy. "Many of these tents were extraordinarily beautiful," commented an eyewitness. The most splendid of them was for the ambassador and was valued at a small fortune.[2] Yet Kutuzov chose instead to spend the next few nights in his more modest ambassadorial tent. He insisted that every minutia of diplomatic protocol be precisely observed as he prepared for the entry into the city.[3] After Ottoman grand vizier Damat Melek Mehmed Pasha was formally informed of the Russian ambassador's arrival, Ottoman officials ventured out to welcome the foreign dignitary; they were joined by foreign diplomats, including Austrian, Prussia, and Neapolitan ambassadors, who also came out to greet the new envoy and take in the spectacle of the Russian troop parade in the field outside the city walls.

On October 7, Kutuzov made a solemn entry into the Ottoman capital. "The Turks made no fuss over the ceremony," he wrote his wife. "The Ottoman government's outward politeness toward me and my suite has exceeded all my expectations," he wrote in his more formal letter to the czarina.[4] The Russian procession drew numerous onlookers, including the Orthodox monk Meletij, who was on his way to the Holy Land. "That was a boisterous day," he jotted down in his journal. "Russia's envoy entered Istanbul today. The Turks forbade their subjects to observe his entry and prohibited the boatmen from ferrying anyone to Fener [a historic quarter midway up the Golden Horn] or carry anyone in the bay." The Russian priest was excited to see the Russian cuirassiers, "with their chest plates and backs decorated with two-headed eagles," at the helm of the Russian ambassadorial procession marching down the streets of Istanbul. They were followed by musicians whose "voluble and delightful music shook the narrow streets and excited the crowd." The well-ordered lines of the Russian infantry preceded the gilded carriage of the new Russian Orthodox archimandrite and the large group of "various legation officials and Greek and Russian merchants who happened to be in Istanbul."

Finally came Kutuzov himself, on horseback, surrounded by the officers of the delegation and a squad of imposing cavalrymen in full regalia, "holding their guns at their knees."[5] Ottoman authorities tried to prevent crowds from gathering. "The Janissaries beat people with sticks and pushed them away. The Turkish homes, which the embassy passed by, remained closed and in complete silence; the Jews were furtively looking from behind the gates and slightly opened windows, while all Greek homes were overflowing with spectators. Many women cried for joy seeing the fellow Orthodox Christian warriors in the streets."[6]

It took several hours for the procession to file through the narrow streets and reach its destination in Pera (modern-day Beyoğlu), the suburb of Istanbul that had long been the home of the European community.[7] Even though it was well after midnight, "numerous throngs of people accompanied it," noted an eyewitness.[8] Tired but overjoyed by the reception, Kutuzov boasted to his wife that "the [Ottoman] ministers had people inform me that [the sultan] likes me and wants to show me greater courtesy than was bestowed on Repnin." He was pleased to hear that the sultan had approved 600 piastres for the embassy's daily upkeep—a considerable sum, because the arrival of the large Russian embassy caused a massive hike in prices.[9] "In general, staying in Pera has not been cheap before, but now that the embassy is here, everything has become much more expensive," lamented a Russian diplomat.[10] The day after the arrival, the first dragoman of the Porte visited Kutuzov and, on behalf of the grand vizier, welcomed him to the capital, presenting him with precious gifts, including sumptuous textiles, a diamond-encrusted snuffbox, and a coffee cup decorated with diamonds and rubies, "of very exquisite craftsmanship." "All these gifts are valued at some 10,000 piastres,"

Mikhail Illarionovich wrote his wife. "There are rumors that the sultan is preparing even more lavish presents."[11]

Kutuzov marveled at the size and cultural complexity of this ancient city. "Traveling through various Ottoman towns, you may think you have an idea of what Constantinople would be like. But you will be mistaken!" he told his wife. "They build here so smartly and amusingly that it exceeds one's imagination." Some used a style he had never seen before, "homes that are so tall, with numerous windows and balconies that converge on the upper floors." He noted that his home had a "belvedere" from which he could take in the panorama of the entire city: "seraglio, an immense harbor that is perpetually packed with boats and ships . . . the rest of the city, with the beautiful [Cathedral of] Hagia Sophia, Süleymaniye [Mosque], Fener district, Galata, Pera, the delightful Constantinople strait that the ancients called Bosporus . . . and numerous other places. Seeing all these wondrous places is so moving that you not only smile but also cry from a surge of emotions sweeping over you."[12]

More than a month passed before Kutuzov got a formal audience at the Sublime Porte. This long delay was occasioned both by the Ottoman willingness to let the Russian ambassador rest and acclimate after a long journey as well as by Kutuzov's unwillingness to submit to all the Ottoman formalities.[13] The machinery of Ottoman diplomacy was elaborate and exacting. No foreign envoy could appear at the sultan's court without offering suitably plush gifts, a reflection of the Ottoman belief that a foreigner was privileged to be allowed into the sultan's presence. The grand vizier and other Ottoman ministers also expected gifts each time an audience was granted as well as on holidays and special occasions. The sultan granted audiences only when the Imperial Council sat, and a request for an audience with him had to be first made with the grand vizier, which involved a separate ceremony. The grand vizier conveyed the request to the sultan, who, if he deigned to do so, issued a special decree granting the audience. All ceremonies, but especially one with the sultan, involved strict etiquette and protocol. Kutuzov balked at some of them. For example, when a foreign dignitary arrived for the audience, Ottoman tradition required him to stand while palace functionaries dressed him in a robe of honor before he entered the presence of the Ottoman grand vizier or sultan. Kutuzov refused to allow this, arguing that it was beneath the dignity of the ambassador of the Russian Empire. He was fine with getting robed but insisted on doing so while seated. At one point he conceded that he was "willing to put on the robe myself while standing, but the vizier should be standing next to me as I do it." This was no trifling matter and negotiations continued for weeks. As late as October 31, the ambassador admitted that "this issue has not been resolved yet."[14]

Kutuzov made the best use of the free time he had to explore the city and to make the necessary connections. He ventured out on a boat into the Golden Horn and Bosporus, visiting various parts of Istanbul. More importantly, he paid courtesy visits to the ambassadors of the European powers, starting with the Austrian internuncio, Baron Peter Phillip von Herbert Rathkeal, and the British ambassador, Sir Robert Ainsley, underscoring their countries' importance to Russian interests. Then came visits to the Venetian, Spanish, Prussian, Swedish, Neapolitan, and Danish envoys, who were invited to grand fêtes that Kutuzov hosted at the embassy.[15] Meeting his diplomatic colleagues was useful and enlightening for the diplomatic novice. Kutuzov managed to establish close relations with the Prussian and Austrian envoys, who agreed to share some of their confidential information and to coordinate their remonstrances to the Ottoman court. The French mission was unmistakably absent from the list of embassies to which Kutuzov paid his respects, but this is hardly surprising. He had already met the French king's envoy at Elisavetgrad and had no intention of meeting with the French Republic's envoy, who had yet to be formally recognized by the Ottomans.

The date of the formal conference with Grand Vizier Damat Melek Mehmed Pasha was set for November 9. "At eight o'clock in the morning, wearing our best clothing, we all assembled at the ambassador's residence," remembered one of Kutuzov's secretaries. Soon afterward the grand vizier's officials, "wearing large white turbans," arrived to escort the envoy.[16] The procession turned into another parade as Kutuzov, carried in a *portechaise*, was accompanied by the finely dressed Russian embassy members as well as a company of Janissaries and Ottoman officials.[17] They navigated the streets to the Galata, where dozens of sloops—some splendidly decorated, "that for the ambassador being fitted up with blue silk"—awaited them. After crossing the Golden Horn to the old city, Kutuzov was taken to the chamber of the Kireçci Başi, where he was welcomed by an Ottoman official (the Çavuş Başi), served refreshments, and provided with horses before proceeding to the grand vizier's residence. By now the procession had grown and counted hundreds of individuals, both Ottoman and Russian, who lined up in two files, with Kutuzov moving in the middle and accompanied by senior embassy officials and twenty-two Russian soldiers.[18]

At the grand vizier's residence, recalled the Russian diplomat, the embassy encountered "so many people in the fine vestibules and rooms that we could barely push through."[19] Kutuzov was pleased to note that no sooner did he put his foot on the threshold of the door of the audience-chamber than the grand vizier entered by an opposite door. The two men saluted each other and, in another carefully choreographed move, came to their seats at the same time. Kutuzov presented his credentials to the vizier and explained the purpose of his embassy.[20] After a brief exchange of pleasantries, Mehmed Pasha ordered dried fruit, coffee, sherbet, and rose water to be served, as well as a water pipe with flavored tobacco, which Kutuzov offered to the officers of his suite after first sampling it himself. At the end of the meeting, the vizier ordered the distribution of lavish gifts, including magnificent robes that the guests were expected to wear. This part of the ceremony was what Kutuzov had been negotiating for the past two weeks. He remained seated as he received the "sable fur robe" but, because the armchair would not allow it, he had to briefly stand up to put on the robe, thus pleasing his hosts but also maintaining Russian dignity.[21] He was delighted to hear that the sultan had agreed to meet him just three days later.

On November 12, the Russian embassy woke up well before sunrise. "At four o'clock in the morning we assembled at the ambassador's place," remembered a participant. "At daybreak we advanced, as on the previous occasion, with equal order and magnificence, on the horse that had been equipped for the purpose," toward the Topkapi Palace.[22] Crossing the Golden Horn on seventy boats, Kutuzov and his companion soon arrived at the high gate, the eponymous Sublime Porte, of the sprawling imperial complex, where they were welcomed by Janissaries dressed in their splendid uniforms and standing in two ranks, between which the visitors had to advance. As foreign dignitaries approached the gate, they were required to undergo a series of ceremonies, and it was customary for the Ottomans to make them wait for some time, thus cultivating and projecting an aura of sovereignty, imperial grandeur, and political legitimacy.[23] Because even the slightest change of details in the ceremony could mean the loss or gain of prestige for the states whose representatives were involved in the encounter, long discussions and exchanges of letters often preceded the actual reception of an envoy. In his letters Kutuzov described how it took "rather lengthy negotiations" to review every ceremonial detail, as the Ottomans insisted on formalities and showed him "a protocol register and various other documents" indicating how things were ordinarily done.[24] However, on the day of the reception, Kutuzov was thrilled to see that the Turks did their best "to avoid anything that might be degrading to my standing" and that unlike his predecessors, who had had to wait in front of the gates, he was greeted by the grand vizier as soon as he arrived at the Porte.

The palace gates opened, and the Russians entered the inner court, preceded by the Çavuş Başi, who announced the visitors' arrival with the steady clinking of his silver cane on the pavement.[25] "The sultan's palace, its court, the clothing of the palace officials, various buildings, and the furnishing of rooms were all so sophisticated and unusual," Kutuzov later wrote to his wife. "Some ceremonies may seem silly, but everything looks imposing, grand, magnificent, and reverential. It felt as if I was in Shakespeare's tragedy, Milton's epic, or Homer's Odyssey."[26] As he walked through the inner courtyard, "several thousand Janissaries, who stood on the right side of the walkway, suddenly rushed to start eating food that was catered to them, while on the left side, stablemen held forty-eight horses that were richly adorned, including with ornate caparisons with precious stones."[27]

The next stage of the reception ceremony usually caused much grumbling among foreign envoys to the Ottoman court. They found it humiliating to wait in the antechambers, often a considerable time, sitting on a simple wooden bench—the "detested bench of the scullions," as Kutuzov put it—that was purposely made lower and less comfortable than the sofas of the Ottoman officials.[28] Nor were they happy with the practice of being held by the arms by palace officials when entering the imperial presence. In the days leading up to the audience, Kutuzov had quibbled over many such obligations and refused to submit to some of them. The dispute was, once again, no trifling matter; the Ottoman officials were even compelled to inform the sultan, who, however, instructed them to put an end to the disputations and forbade them to cause any further issues in this matter. "He is trusting that I will conduct myself as required," Kutuzov wrote in a letter. "He has sent me a message saying that he reckons a man of my upbringing and refinement would not disrespect him."[29]

Kutuzov indeed understood the importance of tact and subtlety. While insisting on due deference to be shown to Russian prestige, "I conduct myself in such a way that [the sultan] could be also pleased," he admitted. Upon entering the antechamber to the meeting room of the Ottoman Imperial Council (Dîvân-ı Hümâyûn), Kutuzov noted that it was "newly remodeled and very nicely furnished," a clear sign that the Ottomans were keen to placate the Russians. After a quick conversation with the viziers, the ambassador was invited to partake of some refreshments. It was already noon, and the famished diplomats did not have to be asked twice. After the lunch, Kutuzov was led to the gates into the innermost part of the palace, where the sultan's imperial hall was located. Knowing of the "ancient custom" of keeping envoys seated on "the scullions' bench" before entering the hall, Kutuzov was pleasantly surprised to discover that a special stool decorated with gold cloth was placed not far from the bench. "The interpreter told me that this has been done out of the sultan's goodwill to me, and contrary to what was done on earlier occasions," Kutuzov reported to St. Petersburg. Thanking the sultan for the honor, he sat down on the stool before allowing the Ottomans to put on him a new robe of sable furs and gold-cloth lining.[30]

Fifteen minutes later the grand vizier led him into one of the most magnificent rooms in the entire palace. The spacious domed room was splendidly and intricately furnished with carpets and tapestries, blue and white tiles, and exquisite ornaments. The upper balcony was reserved for harem ladies and female musicians, while men sat on the lower floor beside the sultan's throne. As Kutuzov entered the room, palace officials tried to take him by the arms, as was the custom, but Kutuzov refused to allow it, instead proudly stepping inside.[31] Casting a quick glance, Kutuzov found the room "a bit dim" but was taken aback by the opulence of the throne, which, he thought, was easily valued at 3 million rubles. Sitting on it was Selim III, the twenty-eighth ruler of the Ottoman Empire, only thirty-two years old. Western visitors found him "handsome and impressive . . . affable and possessing much speculative genius."[32] Kutuzov agreed, describing the sultan as "a gentle and intelligent man" who was "handsome, the most impressive-looking man in this entire gathering, dressed simply but in fine cloth; in his turban glistened a huge diamond solitaire, while the robe had diamond-encrusted buttons." After bowing three times, Kutuzov presented a letter from Catherine II and explained the motives of the Russian embassy. The sultan received the envoy "with a kind demeanor" and "listened attentively," frequently nodding. "At the end of my speech, as I addressed him with compliments, he slightly nodded with such an expression of his face as if to tell me, 'I am very pleased to hear your words and I like you very much; I am very sorry that I cannot talk to you directly.' "[33]

The next few weeks were an unending succession of receptions and balls, organized by various Ottoman officials and European diplomatic missions. "All ministers live outside the city," Kutuzov told his wife. "They all live very well here." Following the ceremony at the Topkapi Palace, he attended the galas organized in his honor by various Ottoman dignitaries, including the grand vizier on November 18, the Kapudan Pasha ten days later, the Kâhya Bey (minister for home affairs) on December 3, the Yeniçeri Ağası (commander in chief of the Janissary corps) on December 9, the Defterdar (minister of finance) five days later, and the Reis-ül-Küttab (minister for foreign affairs) on December 26.[34] Kutuzov hosted receptions that were designed to underscore the might and grandeur of the Russian Empire, the most impressive of them taking place on St. Catherine's Day (the feast day of the patron saint of the Russian empress) on December 5. Attended by Western diplomats and the Ottoman dignitaries alike, the fête was the talk of the town because Kutuzov spared no expenses to impress friend and foe alike. "I gave a magnificent lunch for 70 people," he told his wife. "Then there were fireworks attended by 500 people, followed by a sumptuous dinner for two hundred persons."[35] In March, he organized a "magnificent" masquerade celebration before the fasting and religious obligations associated with the penitential season of Lent.[36]

Kutuzov proved a quick study in the art of diplomacy. "The diplomatic profession, full of duplicity as it might be, is not as complicated as the military one if one performs it conscientiously," he told his wife.[37] While it remains unclear if he ever came across François de Callières's famous handbook for diplomats, Kutuzov intuitively practiced many of its suggestions. "A wise and able envoy," wrote the veteran French diplomat, "ought to be just and modest in all his actions; respectful toward princes; complaisant toward his equals; obliging toward his inferiors; gracious, civil, and courteous to everybody. . . . He ought to accommodate himself to the manners and customs of the country where he is, without showing any aversion to them, or despising them, as many ministers do, who are constantly praising the ways of living in their own country, that they may have occasion to find fault with those of others."[38]

Throughout his stay in Istanbul, Kutuzov tried to apply these principles, displaying a combination of persistence, firmness, charm, and finesse. This was a moment when his refinement of manners shone, causing his contemporaries to later describe him as "the smartest, the most refined, the most enlightened, and the most amiable of men," and to enthuse about his wide-ranging knowledge, wit, and silver-tongued conversations.[39] "He perfected the art of oratory and spoke with such enchanting mastery," commented one contemporary writer who got to know Kutuzov well. "Each time his listeners wondered whether anyone could be more enthralling than him."[40] His fluency in Turkish and raconteurship—fueled by an unending supply of old tales and bons mots—charmed many at the sultan's court; it was said that even an elderly Ottoman foreign minister (reis-efendi) who was rarely seen smiling could not resist laughing out loud when conversing with the Russian ambassador.

Kutuzov understood that an ambassador's two essential functions were to do everything that might help him attain the ends that his government had set for him, and to discover those of the host nation and rival diplomatic missions. The way to succeed was to gain the confidence of the senior figures in the Ottoman government. Kutuzov recognized that gifts and offerings were key to this complex system. The first thing he did upon returning from the imperial audience was to send gifts to the sultan's mother, Mihrişah Sultan, known for her political savvy as well as for her influence over her son. The gesture was readily appreciated at the palace—"the sultan cordially received the news of me paying respects to his mother," Kutuzov was pleased to note in another letter.[41] Furthermore, the "Georgian Beauty," as Mihrişah Sultan was known, responded in kind and sent a harem official to inquire about the Russian envoy's health and to deliver presents, including scarves and handkerchiefs, sumptuous textiles, and a delicate coffee cup embedded with precious stones. "Such a thing is unheard of here," Kutuzov boasted in a letter to his wife.[42]

This connection with the sultan's mother has churned out a number of myths and apocrypha, none more so persistent than the stories of the Russian ambassador managing to sneak into the inner sanctuary of the Ottoman imperial palace. One such story claimed that Kutuzov, out sightseeing one day, decided to make his way into the secluded gardens of the sultan's palace. A sentry supposedly tried to warn him that anyone who stepped through would face dire consequences and that Kutuzov brushed him aside, saying, "I know, I know." As he heeled his horse into the garden, the "head of the sultan's guard" rushed to him, demanding to know his identity. Kutuzov proudly retorted, "I am the envoy of a monarch before whom nothing withers and everything flowers—Catherine the Great, Empress of All the Russias, who now grants eternal peace to thee!" The guard commander and his men then fell to their knees and Kutuzov rode serenely through the forbidden garden and returned to his residence. Another involved Kutuzov sneaking into the seraglio for a clandestine assignation with the sultan's mother. Setting aside the complete ludicrousness of such claims—let alone the lack of evidence—these latter-day inventions were clearly intended as Russian imperial propaganda.[43]

Before departing from St. Petersburg, Kutuzov had received two sets of confidential instructions. The first offered a broad overview of what was expected of the ambassador in Istanbul and discussed technical aspects of the embassy. The second, lengthier document was about political matters. Kutuzov was tasked with consolidating peace with the Porte and preventing any possibility of Ottoman entrance into any anti-Russian alliance.[44] The Russian government was well aware of the reform movement that Selim III had recently initiated and was keenly interested in marshaling information about the combat capability of the Ottoman army and the progress of its military reorganization. Kutuzov was therefore ordered to gather political, military, and economic intelligence that could benefit Russia when—for it was never a question of if—a new war erupted between the two empires. Catherine admitted that she was not "particularly concerned" by the prospect of these reforms succeeding since the Ottomans' "earlier attempts had produced such meager results," but she needed to determine whether this was yet another half-measure or something more serious and "impelled by the ministers of other [European] powers." She stressed to Kutuzov that his military background should help him in achieving this task: "As your military talents are well known to us, you should be able to clearly discern the extent of these reorganizations in the [Ottoman] naval and land forces."[45]

Kutuzov was also to counter the influence of any foreign courts that might be trying to sway the Ottomans against Russia. The Russian empress was still primarily concerned about France, the traditional ally of the Ottoman Empire. The revolutionary "fiends" who had "usurped the power and callously murdered their sovereign" seemed determined "to sweet-talk or force the Ottomans to make common cause" with them against Russia and threaten Russian interests in the Black Sea.[46] Preposterous as such fears may seem in hindsight, Catherine was convinced that the French would not miss an opportunity to intervene in Ottoman affairs to Russia's detriment.

The next section of the instructions dealt with the potential for Ottoman interference into what Russia now considered its sphere of influence in eastern Europe. The ambassador was explicitly instructed not to mention the Polish issue at all, unless the Ottoman side itself initiated a conversation on this subject, in which case Kutuzov was told to pretend that he had no knowledge of it; if the Ottomans persisted in discussing the Polish matter, the Russian embassy was authorized to resort to veiled threats against Ottoman interests and, acting secretly through agents, to suggest to Ottoman officials that interfering with Russian interests would be dangerous.

Central to this was identifying and cultivating pro-Russian sympathizers in the Ottoman elite, and surreptitiously inciting anti-Ottoman sentiment among the sultan's Christian subjects, who were to be reassured of Russia's commitment to their safety and well-being. Drawing parallels to the history of the Muscovite Principality, Empress Catherine wanted Kutuzov to nurture the sympathies of the Ottoman Orthodox subjects while calling upon them to emulate Moscow's own struggle against the Mongols. The best way to end the Ottoman hegemony—"the barbarian yoke" (*igo varvarskoe*) or "the Hagarian bondage" (*igo agarianskoie*), as Catherine described it—was through the Ottoman Christians' demonstrating "the goodwill and determination" to fight and, when the time came, rising in an insurrection that would be then supported by Russian arms. Needless to say, Kutuzov was expected to conduct all these activities "with extreme caution" and in complete secrecy.[47]

After settling in at his newly remodeled residence in Pera, Kutuzov embarked on implementing his multifarious directives.[48] "I have so many matters to tend to that I barely keep up," he confessed to his wife. "Yesterday and today I have been writing incessantly. Among my secretaries only Stakheev is here and even he is barely alive."[49] His day-to-day responsibilities included managing the embassy's internal affairs, handling the repatriation of Russian prisoners, aiding efforts to locate Ottoman subjects who had gone missing during the war, and tending to the problems Russian merchants encountered in Istanbul or that the Ottomans experienced in the Russian realm. One of the most pressing issues involved the customs tariff on import and export duties for Russian merchants trading with the Ottoman Empire. The tariff had been set at 3 percent by the Ottoman-Russian commercial treaty of 1783, and the Ottomans were now keen to revisit this issue.[50] Kutuzov was convinced that foreign involvement was behind this. As far as the Russians were concerned, the issue had been settled a decade earlier. He believed that the British ambassador, Sir Robert Ainslie, had encouraged the Turks to renegotiate the tariff as a way to safeguard British commercial interests in the Ottoman realm.[51] This "restless man," as Kutuzov described Ainslie, seemed "incapable of existing without intriguing, either with the Porte or with other foreign envoys."[52] Moreover, Kutuzov further suspected that the British minister deliberately misled Russian military attaché Barrozzi about Ottoman intentions and thus contributed to the growing tensions between Istanbul and St. Petersburg.

In response Kutuzov was determined to maintain composure and resolve these issues; in a series of assessments to St. Petersburg, he argued that the tariff matter, important as it might be for the Ottomans, would not by itself make the sultan endanger the advantages of peace. He politely rebuffed Ottoman approaches and reminded them that they were legally bound to follow the provisions of the treaties they had signed and ratified. When the Turks persisted, Kutuzov submitted diplomatic notes of protest, negotiated a common position with the Austrian and Prussian envoys, and even confronted the British envoy. Ultimately, the Ottomans were forced to back down and reconcile with the status quo.

An ambassador must "labor always to be well instructed and to have the earliest intelligence of whatever passed," a veteran French diplomat recommended.[53] Kutuzov shared this view wholeheartedly and set out to create and manage a robust intelligence-gathering operation. Hosting receptions, offering gifts and other enticements, and exerting his persuasive charm, he was able to develop relations with many senior Ottoman officials as well as to recruit informants among their support staff and domestics. By late November, he alluded to "various channels" that shared with him court gossip, matters of business, and even confidential information about Ottoman government deliberations, its military, and its economy.[54] In November, upon hearing of the arrival of a delegation from the new Persian shah, Agha Muhammed Qajar, Kutuzov was able to infiltrate it with an agent—a Russian ensign who spoke Farsi and could pass as a Persian—and gained details about the Ottoman diplomatic proposals to the shah, including the pledge to recognize Persian claims to eastern Georgia, Russia's ally.[55]

As the embassy settled in, Kutuzov allowed his staff members to explore the Ottoman capital and beyond. Cultural enrichment was not the primary purpose of these activities. Russian officers, engineers, and artists scattered to various parts of the city and traveled up and down the Bosporus, taking detailed notes and drawings of the places, their strong and weak points. Kaufer, the French engineer whom, as we had seen, Kutuzov recruited in Moldavia, proved to be a particularly valuable asset, providing the blueprints of the Ottoman fortresses in the Danubian principalities. The draftsmen Kutuzov had brought along, meanwhile, prepared maps and sketches of Istanbul and other locations.[56] The embassy's secretary, Struve, noted in his journal that on one occasion Kutuzov dispatched several embassy officials with gifts to the Ottoman commander at Silivri (an area close to Istanbul, on the coastline of the Sea of Marmara), ostensibly to thank him for assistance he had provided the Russian ambassadorial train. The real point of it was "to scout the fortress and prepare a plan of it."[57] The final result of these excursions and voyages was a detailed map of Istanbul and the Bosporus that would figure prominently in Russian political and strategic considerations throughout the nineteenth century.[58] Kutuzov was also engaged in counterintelligence efforts, tracking foreign agents who could harm Russian interests. He remained informed of the whereabouts of Angeli, the French agent who had earlier caused so much anxiety, and informed Russian authorities of any Ottoman espionage. In January 1794, for example, he was able to learn the identity of a spy whom the Turks dispatched to Kherson to scout out Russian naval facilities.[59]

Kutuzov produced balanced assessments of the ongoing reorganization of the Ottoman military. Sultan Selim III hoped to revitalize the Ottoman navy, restructure the artillery and supply branches, bring greater order and subordination among the Janissaries, and train and equip regular infantry. Selim III was attempting a transformation of the Ottoman military from the top down, the main idea being to establish a European-style infantry corps and later use it as a core around which to form a modern army. Kutuzov applauded the changes when Selim III brought foreign (though largely French) instructors to serve as military advisors, and sanctioned translation and publication of the latest military literature. But the ambassador was unconvinced that the effort would succeed. He noted strong resistance among local elites, religious leaders, and the Janissaries. In one of the reports, Kutuzov describes the enormous challenge the Ottoman government faced in assembling just 5,000 new recruits for the artillery branch—"they only gathered about 1,000 men and this number is not expected to increase because for every new recruit, another deserts." He underscored that there was little enthusiasm among the Janissaries, "none of whom joined the new units despite all the enticements that the Porte is offering them." The prospects of the reform movements succeeding were, in Kutuzov's words, "doubtful."[60] All in all, Kutuzov's intelligence-gathering supplied a wealth of information that would help Russian military planners for years to come.

Far more challenging was navigating international politics. The war against revolutionary France was in its second year and expanding in scale and intensity. On February 1, 1793, eight days after the execution of King Louis XVI, France, already fighting against Austria and Prussia, declared war on Britain and the Dutch Republic. This was soon followed by a declaration against Spain, Portugal, Naples, and Sardinia as well. In short, the new French Republic was now at war with almost all of Europe. Yet the war proceeded disastrously at first. The revolutionary government struggled to contain counterrevolutionary revolts raging inside France. During the summer of 1793, the coalition of European powers won significant victories, the most famous of them being the capture of Toulon along with almost the entire French Mediterranean fleet. The French revolutionaries responded to these challenges by launching an unprecedented war effort, one that harnessed the explosive forces of modern nationalism, revolutionary terror, centralized economy, and national military mobilization. These radical measures soon delivered results. The revolutionary armies defeated the invading coalition forces in the Pyrenees and northern France and recaptured Toulon. At the same time, France reinvigorated diplomatic efforts to weaken or splinter the coalition, with the Ottoman Empire prominently featuring in these designs.

Kutuzov's arrival in Istanbul coincided with that of the French Republic's new envoy, Marie Louis Henri Descorches. Born the Marquis de Saint-Croix, Descorches was of noble pedigree and had served in the suite of the Comte d'Artois before embarking on a diplomatic career.[61] He had been France's ambassador to Poland during the turbulent period in 1791–1792. Suspected by the Russians of fomenting revolutionary turmoil, he was forced to leave Warsaw during the Second Polish Partition and was sent to Istanbul, where his arrival once again raised Russian concerns that he would spread revolutionary contagion and seek to incite the sultan to launch another war against them. This was no idle worry. The sultan's Francophile sentiments were well known, and a good number of senior Ottoman officials showed pro-French sympathies and welcomed France's support of the Ottoman modernization. France was, after all, the Ottoman Empire's long-standing ally. This became especially important in light of the challenges both powers faced. France's position in European power politics, like the Porte's, weakened in the late eighteenth century. Its public debt increasingly hampered the French state's ability to defend its interests within Europe, as evidenced by the Prussian intervention in the Dutch Republic in 1787. The French Revolution added a powerful ideological element to the war that broke out in 1792, but it did not simply erase geopolitical issues that stemmed from earlier rivalries. Threats to the Ottoman Empire were still considered threats to French interests, given that France continued to maintain considerable economic links with the Ottoman Empire and profited from the lucrative Levantine trade.[62] Under these circumstances, revolutionary France was keenly interested in maintaining Ottoman territorial integrity. Any dismemberment of it—as happened in Poland—would leave France on the outs and incapable of protecting its interests. Furthermore, the French Revolutionary Wars increased the value of the Ottomans as allies, for they could be France's strategic partner against the European powers that were forming the counterrevolutionary First Coalition. The detailed instructions Descorches received upon his departure from Paris testify to the importance that the French government attached to an alliance with the sultan. The new envoy had to initiate discussion for defensive and offensive cooperation; a prospective Franco-Ottoman alliance was envisioned as the basis for a future quadrilateral agreement with Sweden and Poland to confront Russian aspirations across all of eastern Europe, from the Baltic Sea to the Balkan Peninsula. Beset as it was on all sides by hostile powers, France pledged to help the Ottomans to recover the land lost to Russia since 1774 and promised not to make a separate peace until the Russians withdrew from the Crimea. To add weight to these

offers and underscore France's commitment to the cause, the French government promised to provide its ambassador with ample funding. Further, it
authorized him to inform the Turks that the French Mediterranean squadron
would conduct joint operations with the Ottomans as soon as the alliance
was formalized.[63]

Arriving in Istanbul four months before Kutuzov, Descorches made some
headway in fulfilling his objectives. With the help of Mouradgea d'Ohsson,
the Armenian dragoman of the Swedish embassy, he gained access to some
of the most senior Ottoman officials—among them the foreign minister,
the minister of finance, and members of the Imperial Council—who lent
a willing ear to his entreaties. In September the French envoy was pleased
to report that "French republicans enjoy support [at the sultan's court] that
they have hitherto not enjoyed amongst any other people, not excepting the
United States."[64] Kutuzov soon discovered how closely aligned the French
and Ottoman interests were. "You can always precisely judge the affairs of
this country by looking at the affairs of France," he told a fellow diplomat.
"The Ottoman Empire seems to be destined to serve as France's windvane."[65]
Discussing the activities of the French agents in Istanbul, the Russian ambassador had to acknowledge that Descorches and Mouradgea successfully
lobbied French interests and "misled" members of the Imperial Council
into believing that France could "survive another two campaigns" and that
"the coalition powers would soon get bored with the war and recognize the
Republic." He complained that the French were deliberately spreading false
news and "utterly ridiculous stories" to shape public sentiment and sway
the Ottoman government. In October, he noted that they had publicly celebrated the recapture of Toulon and defeat of the king of Prussia, "who, they
allege, has been wounded in battle." Two months later, the French representative was assuring the Ottomans, wrote Kutuzov, that "100,000 Polish
troops were ready to launch a diversion" as soon as the Turks moved against
Russia. "These and other similar absurdities force me to spend considerable
time compiling facts from the Allied bulletins to enlighten the blinded
[Ottoman] ministers."[66]

The "fake news" spread far and wide, reaching St. Petersburg as well, in
part because Ivan Severin, Russia's consul general in Moldavia, Wallachia,
and Bessarabia, eagerly reported any and every bit of hearsay as fact. There
was a growing fear in the Russian capital that a new war with the Ottomans
loomed. Kutuzov's early reports helped dissipate some of these apprehensions,
though Catherine and her foreign policy advisors remained concerned about
the French diplomatic outreach to the sultan, as well as about a possible
adverse Ottoman reaction to the Polish Partition. The latter could, in their
opinion, prompt Selim III to side with revolutionary France and endanger
relations with Russia. They received (probably embellished) reports that
Descorches, who maintained active contact with the Polish opposition, was

close to convincing the Ottoman government to intervene into Polish affairs. The viziers were supposedly told that "the spirit of insurrection has reached its zenith in Poland and that the entire Polish realm is ready to rebel" against the Russian overlordship should the sultan chose to intervene. Such reports heightened Russian worries to such an extent that by the end of the year Catherine approved preparations for a new confrontation with the Turks. She insisted on expediting construction of new warships for the Russian fleet in the Black Sea and, in January 1794, ordered Général-en-chef Yuri Dolgorukov to start mobilizing a 70,000-man-strong army "to prevent a sudden [Ottoman] attack and protect our imperial borderlands." Kutuzov was expected to lead one of the corps.[67]

Kutuzov found all of this very frustrating. His primary mission was to assure the Ottomans of Russia's peaceful intentions, and yet his own government, putting stock in unverified reports, was taking steps that undermined it all. The Ottomans, naturally, noticed the Russian military preparations and demanded explanations from Kutuzov, who struggled to dispel their doubts. Assuring the Ottomans of Russia's peaceful intent while its army was mobilizing along imperial borders was no easy task. He had to set the Ottomans' mind at rest while also trying to reassure Empress Catherine that the prospects of war had been exaggerated. He acknowledged the Porte was hopeful that the Russian actions in Poland would "incite jealousy among the neighboring states" and that the Turks "would not miss an opportunity to incite discord" among the European powers. However, he also stressed that "any suggestion that the Porte is intending to declare war within three months is nothing but a fairy tale." He lambasted Russian officials for spreading unverified information. "Based on available evidence and circumstances it seems to me that the news you have disseminated about impending war is exaggerated and too emphatic," he brusquely told the Russian consul who had sent frantic reports to St. Petersburg. "I am in the capital city and observe none of that."[68]

Kutuzov's memorandums demonstrate a solid grasp of facts and judicious analysis of the situation. He was well informed of the wider issues in the Ottoman realm, which allowed him to set the unfounded rumors of Ottoman saber-rattling within a broader context. He pointed out that the Turks' military had not recovered from the last war and that neither the army nor the navy was ready for action; out of twenty-six ships-of-the-line, two were too decrepit to sail, ten were still being constructed, and only fourteen were ready for service, though they were also showing their age.[69] He stressed that none of "their dilapidated border fortresses" had been repaired, resupplied, or fully garrisoned. Knowing that money was the sinew of war-making, he drew attention to Selim III's continued financial woes.[70] Revenue collection was in arrears, which forced the sultan to proclaim a state monopoly on the sale of bread and to rescind grants of life-term tax farms (*malikanes*).[71] These measures somewhat increased monthly revenue but also caused widespread disgruntlement. The Porte was struggling to assert central authority in its provinces and, as Kutuzov put it, "its internal affairs are in disarray." He pointed to the rebellions in Arabia, Albania, and Trapezund (Trabzon) in the eastern part of the empire, and spoke of "frequent highway robberies" on the road from Adrianople to Istanbul and rampant criminality in Rumelia, where he had seen people hanging on gallows and impaled on stakes. "Unruliness reigns almost everywhere, while rebellions rage in many parts," he wrote. Kutuzov was correct in his assessment: it would be absolute folly to start a war under such conditions. The Ottoman government therefore was determined to remain neutral and avoid conflict with any of the warring states in Europe. The French attempt to draw the Ottoman state into a new war against Russia—for the third time in the three decades—stood very little chance of success. Kutuzov predicted that the Ottomans would not hazard to fight Russians for years to come. As it turned out, the number was thirteen. In 1806 a new Russo-Ottoman War erupted. Kutuzov would play a decisive role in ending it.[72]

Kutuzov exploited the perennial factionalism of the Ottoman court. He supported Kapudan Pasha Küçük Hüseyin Pasha, the sultan's brother-in-law and confidant, who was locked in a bitter power struggle against the members of the Imperial Council, many of whom were Francophiles. Kapudan Pasha was trying to push his loyalists into key positions "to rein in his rivals in the Council," Kutuzov reported, but his foes were equally adept at intrigue and were seeking to elevate their own man to the position of Grand Vizier.[73] By cultivating close relations with Kapudan Pasha and other senior figures Kutuzov was able to get a good grasp of internal Ottoman deliberations, learn of Ottoman negotiations with other European powers, and even obtain highly sensitive and confidential documents. For example, he procured a copy of the secret French memorandum offering the Turks a joint alliance against Russia, and later reported on the French efforts to form a "Quintuple Alliance," consisting of France, the Ottoman Empire, Denmark, Sweden, and Poland, to contain Russian ambitions in eastern Europe.[74]

In his reports and letters to Catherine II, Kutuzov demonstrated independence of mind. He went against the prevailing opinion that the Ottomans were preparing for a new war. Selim III, beset with internal problems, would not be able to act on his Francophile sentiments and accept an alliance with France. This did not mean that the Ottomans would not try to exploit the rapidly shifting international environment. Kutuzov had already learned that the Porte had approved a sizable loan for the repair and maintenance of French warships, which would target the Russian merchant marine and bring lucrative prizes to the Ottoman ports, where they could be sold.[75] Kutuzov anticipated that as the tide of the First Coalition War turned in favor of the French, France could gain greater sway at the Ottoman court.

The news of the French revolutionary army—in which young Napoleon Bonaparte commanded the artillery—recapturing the port of Toulon and driving out the Anglo-Spanish forces delighted the French ambassador, while Kutuzov regretted that the French victory "would raise the Jacobin stock" at the Ottoman court and "would elicit no good consequences" for Russia. In February 1794, he talked of "arrogant Jacobins" parading down the streets and engaging in "fights with the soldiers."[76] He was thus eager to learn the extent of the French success at Toulon. "If the news that I received from Vienna about the survival of twenty five ships of various size is confirmed," he observed, "it will create a rather perilous situation in which the Porte might be lured into accepting offers that the French have been long extending it."[77] Further reports proved to be disheartening indeed—while the allies destroyed or captured thirteen French ships-of-the-line and more than a dozen smaller vessels, most of the French fleet, including fifteen ships-of-the line, had survived.

To counter the French threat, Kutuzov solicited and received support from the Austrian and Prussian missions, which agreed to prepare joint démarches against the French, lobby each other's positions at the Ottoman court, and share confidential information.[78] Kutuzov complained that the Ottomans turned a blind eye to "the vessels under nefarious flag of anarchy [revolutionary tricolor]" that were wreaking havoc on the Russian merchant marine, and demanded an immediate end to it. Should the Turks fail to act, Russia would be forced to intervene, which might include, he hinted, the dispatch of a squadron to the Aegean Islands. This was a calculated warning, and it sent shivers through the Ottoman government. Kutuzov knew that "the Porte would agree to anything apart from the Russian presence in the archipelago; they consider it as hallowed a place as their seraglio."[79] All this caused furious debates in the Ottoman Imperial Council, as Kutuzov knew through his agents.[80] He also knew that it involved complex matters of imperial rivalries, economic interests, and internal Ottoman court intrigues. He was further aware that the Kapudan Pasha was keen to exploit this opportunity to weaken his Francophile rivals inside the Imperial Council.

By maintaining pressure on the Ottoman authorities, denouncing French radicalism, threatening Russian response, and playing upon Ottoman internal divisions, Kutuzov was able to achieve several key objectives, including forcing the Turks to reaffirm their commitments under the Treaty of Jassy, put an end to the freebooting activities of the French and the Barbary pirates against the Russian merchants, and pledge to compensate Russia for any losses its merchants had suffered. Furthermore, by claiming that the French piracy had caused grievous harm to Russian commerce, Kutuzov urged the Ottoman authorities to rescind the prohibition against transporting Russian goods on Ottoman ships. On January 16, 1794, he informed Catherine II,

"Yesterday I received an official notification that the sultan had revoked the prohibition but asked [the foreign minister] to maintain confidentiality in this matter and quietly reveal the news to the merchants, without publicizing it among the foreigners."[81]

The task of limiting French influence was greatly facilitated by French infighting in Istanbul. Observers may have found Descorches to be "a frenzied Jacobin" and "an intriguer plucked from the revolutionary mire," but he was not as radical as he was made out to be.[82] In fact, he was himself the target of continued attacks and denunciations from the more radical members of the French community in the Porte, who complained that the envoy was not militant enough and collaborated with counterrevolutionaries. "His conduct is a series of small treasons to the common cause, until his own interest brings him to openly betray his country," read an address sent from the Club of Constantinople in September 1793.[83] This squabbling intensified after the arrival of Étienne-Félix Hénin, the newly appointed chargé d'affaires, who represented the Jacobin faction. He questioned the allegiance of Descorches and other French residents of Istanbul and founded the Republican Society of Liberty and Equality as a way to purge the French community of suspected royalists and counterrevolutionaries.[84] Kutuzov was pleased to observe the French rivalries, which he expected to increase with the arrival of new revolutionary emissaries in the spring of 1794. Not only would they further reduce Descorches's influence with the Ottomans, but their arrival would mean that the French representatives would not pose a united front and thus "would be far less dangerous than Descorches himself." The Jacobin activities—their radical rhetoric and noisy gatherings—played into the hand of Kutuzov, who urged the Ottomans to curtail them.[85]

⊷⊶ ⚜ ⊷⊶

The start of 1794 proved to be hectic for Kutuzov. "I have so many matters to attend to," he told his wife. "When I have to send mail [to St. Petersburg], I spend three days drafting a single letter. The content of these documents is such that every single word matters."[86] Just four months after arriving in Istanbul, he received an order from the Collegium of Foreign Affairs recalling him home.[87] The primary reason for the recall was the mounting problems with Mustafa Rasih Efendi's Ottoman embassy in St. Petersburg. The Russian officials complained about the boisterous behavior of the Ottoman diplomats, while the ambassador protested against Russian intransigence on the crucial issue of Ottoman subjects held in virtual slavery in Russia.[88] It was clear that Rasih Efendi's mission was at an impasse and the envoy was keen to return home. In contrast, Kutuzov's composed and steady leadership played a key role in normalizing relations and averting new confrontations between the two empires. His belief that the Ottomans "would create numerous hurdles in minor issues" but avoid war proved to be correct.[89] With the primary objectives of his mission achieved, it was time for career diplomats to step in and build upon its legacy.

The new ambassador extraordinary and plenipotentiary was Viktor Kochubey, who had already served in Sweden, Britain, and France.[90] One of Kutuzov's diplomatic secretaries described the new envoy, who arrived in early 1794, as "a nice, young, well-educated man of about 26–27 years of age [Kochubey was twenty-five] who was brought up mostly in France and then spent a few years in England."[91] The young man's rapid rise in Russian diplomatic circles owed much to his uncle, Count Alexander Bezborodko, one of Catherine II's most influential foreign policy advisors. At the age of sixteen, Kochubey had been assigned to the Russian embassy to Sweden and then embarked on an extended voyage through Europe, studying in London and Paris, before returning home. Kochubey was impatient to throw himself into the world of high diplomacy and geopolitical intrigues. A few months later his prayer was answered when Catherine named him to the Ottoman court.

Kutuzov welcomed his replacement, but beneath the customary niceties lurked mutual aloofness that would eventually devolve into hostility. In July 1793, Kochubey had quietly derided Kutuzov for the "inconceivable slowness" of his voyage to Istanbul, jeopardizing the young diplomat's own career aspirations. He called Kutuzov someone whom "a few individuals can make hateful or ill-disposed toward a person who has never done him any harm." The irony of levying such an accusation based on nothing but hearsay seems to have escaped the diplomat.[92] Kutuzov might have had his own misgivings about the youthfulness and inexperience of his successor, who had gotten the position largely due to nepotism. But he helped Kochubey get started, arranging his official visits to the grand vizier and the sultan in early March, and ensuring the successful start of a political career that would last for decades.[93] Still, the relations between them remained chilly, and when given an opportunity, Kochubey tried to sabotage Kutuzov's career.

Kutuzov was glad to return home. As much as he had enjoyed Istanbul, he longed to see his wife and daughters, and he was getting tired of the maneuverings and deceptions. Even inside the embassy, the relations between the diplomatic staff had frayed; "Khvostov, Pizanni, and Barrozzi are mad at each other and each is undermining the other," he complained about the senior officials of the Russian diplomatic staff.[94] Kutuzov spent much of January and February 1794 arranging everything for the arrival of the new ambassador, preparing a detailed accounting of his activities and expenses (down to the kopeck), and bidding farewell to the Ottoman officials.[95] On March 11, Kutuzov attended a farewell audience with Selim III, who praised the Russian envoy's "inborn sagacity and farsightedness" as well as his "diligent service and devotion" to his sovereign's cause.[96]

After receiving the sultan's permission to depart, Kutuzov wrote lengthy memos for his successor, bringing him up to date on principal matters and personalities. In late March 1794, he set out on the long journey back home.[97] The highlight of this otherwise uneventful voyage was the exchange ceremony with the Ottoman embassy of Mustafa Rasih, which was also returning from St. Petersburg, on June 5. Five weeks later, Kutuzov was in St. Petersburg.

| Military Philosophe and Courtier, 1794–1797

O N SEPTEMBER 26, 1794, St. Petersburg woke up to the startling news that Kutuzov, who had barely had time to recover from his long journey from the Porte, had been appointed as the director general of the Land Noble Cadet Corps (Sukhoputnyi Shlyakhetskii Kadetskii Korpus).[1] The news surprised everyone. The Land Noble Cadet Corps was one of the premier institutions of military education in Russia and its leadership was usually entrusted to an imperial grandee, such as Count Burkhard Christoph von Münnich (who directed it from 1731–1741), Prince Ludwig Wilhelm of Hesse-Homburg (1741–1745), Prince Boris Grigoryevich Yusupov (1750–1759), or Count Friedrich (Fedor Astafyevich) von Anhalt, whose tenure ended with his death in June 1794.[2] Contemporaries were thus puzzled by Kutuzov's selection, though the general's career had seen many such unexpected twists and turns and the new assignment reflected his growing reputation as a problem-solver.

Originally established by the decree of Empress Anna Ioannovna in 1731, the Land Noble Cadet Corps was to train future generations of military leaders.[3] Over the next six decades, the school grounds—located on Vasilievskii Island, in the opulent palace of Alexander Menshikov, the once-powerful courtier who had died disgraced and penurious in Siberian exile—had raised a generation of Russian commanders, including Peter Rumyantsev, Alexander Prozorovskii, Mikhail Kamenskii, Peter Melissino, and Mikhail Kakhovskii. However, the school's purpose evolved and gradually lost its military specialization, instead providing training in a wide variety of subjects. The cadets spent much of their time learning foreign languages, rhetoric, drawing, dancing, music, and fine arts; the Cadet Corps hosted a Russian theater group as well as the Society for the Lovers of Russian

Literature, at meetings of which cadets read out and discussed their own compositions. This transformation was the result of the great reorganization launched by school reformer Ivan Betskoi, who sought to establish a more unified system of public education.[4] His reforms represented one of the manifestations of the Military Enlightenment in Russia.

As noted earlier, throughout the mid-eighteenth century there were concerted efforts across Europe to engage with the science of war. Statesmen, philosophers, and educators explored the relationship between the military and civilian spheres; they debated what techniques they needed to instill to achieve their goals.[5] The Military Enlightenment embraced rationalism and professionalism, promoting greater proficiency in military matters, especially in military education.[6]

Betskoi's treatise on the education of youth of both sexes cited a good number of Enlightenment philosophes, including John Locke and Jean-Jacques Rousseau, as it proposed a grand vision of a restructured educational system to create "a new type of people": cadets who could do everything from leading a cavalry unit to composing a letter, who had "acquired a solid knowledge of geography, politics, ethics, arithmetic, geometry, and other mathematical sciences; gained understanding of history and nurtured the desire to read books about the deeds of famous military commanders, about how to keep records of revenues and expenses in their regiment or their corps." Everything needed to be taught—how to construct a pontoon bridge, how to pick the best site for an encampment—and it should be taught by example "rather than from reading books." Only if all of this were covered was their education to be deemed "sufficient."[7]

Betskoi was an ardent proponent of broad education.[8] He reorganized the Land Noble Cadet Corps, abolishing the military-style classification of putting cadets into companies and introducing five age-based grades. Children as young as five could be enrolled in the Cadet Corps and receive a well-rounded education for the next fifteen years.[9] In junior grades they were looked after by governesses; as they got older, officer instructors, noncommissioned officer assistants, and various other staff members tended to their needs.[10] Some 600 young people attended the academy, absorbing history, architecture, art, rhetoric, and theater, practicing their dance moves, putting on plays, and polishing their Latin, German, and French. The new educational process emphasized the importance of scientific knowledge, moral virtues, and philosophical ideals. Personal accomplishments counted for more than pedigree and status, and most important was "the light of reason."[11]

The Cadet Corps played a vital role in the institutionalization of the Enlightenment in Russia as well as the continued westernization of the Russian military. Its graduates shaped military culture for years to come and transmitted Enlightenment ideas they had absorbed during their schooling. As historian Eugene Miakinkov correctly points out, "the impulse for national education extended to the military as well, where officers took the cue from their empress and began to create a 'new type of officer' and to lay the foundations for the nineteenth-century military professional."[12] Count Anhalt, Kutuzov's predecessor at the Cadet Corps, became renowned for his innovative approach to the educational process. He deemphasized rote memorization, prohibited corporal punishment, and sought to create a nurturing environment for the cadets to thrive in. "May the desire to be honest and uphold your good name be at the root of all actions," the old count counseled his students, who extolled "his unbounded attention and, one could even say, fatherly care."[13] Among Anhalt's innovations was the "Talking Wall"—the walls of the school garden were decorated with diverse educational murals so that cadets could continue to learn even when outdoors. Anhalt required students to write their thoughts about weekly readings on special blackboards and had public discussions of these scribblings at the end of the week. Cadets found this a useful exercise because, as Sergei Glinka put it, "even those pupils who were less disposed toward learning than others still unwittingly gained some knowledge."[14]

However, educational reforms encountered setbacks. There were of course indolent students, as well as teachers who resorted to punishments to motivate then.[15] More importantly, while it worked on a philosophical level, the "encyclopedic character" of the education resulted in a lack of focus.[16] As exciting as the lofty rhetoric of the Enlightenment and the vision of creating a new society was, it clashed with the Russian army's desperate need for well-trained professional military officers. Behind the walls of Menshikov's palace, Betskoi and his successors, especially Count Anhalt, sought to protect the cadets from the corrupting influences of the world. The restriction of contact between the future officers and the world was designed to cultivate a certain chasteness of habits, thoughts, and nature among the cadets, who were destined to become "a new type of people." But it hardly prepared them for the grim realities of military service, not to mention the blood and gore of the battlefield. The cadets finished their training wholly unprepared for the rigid discipline of a military unit. Graduating cadets, who were commissioned as lieutenants, reached their units having very little if any experience of drills, firing weapons, deploying and maneuvering tactical units, or organizing marches. This disconnect caused some contemporaries to observe that those educated according to Betskoi's reforms "could perform comedies and write poetry, in short, they knew everything except what an officer should have known."[17] A change was needed, one that would maintain the Enlightenment spirit of Betskoi's reforms but reorient the educational process back to its military essentials.

Kutuzov's nomination thus was not as arbitrary as it might seem at first. The selection of a professional military man with few connections at the imperial court underscored the depth of Empress Catherine's concern for the well-being of Russia's premier institution of military education and her desire to fix it. Kutuzov was well acquainted with the ideals of the Military Enlightenment and practiced them. His reputation as a military leader was almost unmatched.[18] He thus personified what the Cadet Corps envisioned when it specified that the director general be a person who was "well experienced in both military and civilian matters" and who demonstrated "prudence," "impartiality of opinion," and an ability not only to resolve problems rapidly but also to understand their root causes.[19]

The appointment of the new director caused great excitement at the Cadet Corps, where students rushed to see the person who was about to replace the beloved Anhalt.[20] "Uncertainty and anticipation" excited their minds, as one of the eyewitnesses described. They knew about Kutuzov's battlefield prowess—the memories of Izmail, Măcin, and Ochakov were still fresh—but were more concerned about what kind of man he was.[21]

On September 27, the Cadet Corps gathered at Menshikov's palace and prepared to welcome its new leader.[22] Kutuzov still cut a striking figure, carrying himself with his customary dignity and poise. His face, scarred as it was with wounds and marked with deep furrows, exuded martial charisma, while his graying hair fell loosely from his brow. One of the cadets, the future writer and memoirist Sergei Glinka, watched as, "upon entering the hall, Kutuzov halted by the tall statue of Mars, whose base bore on one of its sides a phrase from Frederick the Great's oeuvre on tactics, 'Be like Fabius in the camp, and Hannibal in the field!' On the other side of the sculpture stood the bust of Julius Caesar."[23] There was a moment of awkward silence as the cadets stared at the seasoned commander in front of them. "Kutuzov had a stern appearance," remembered Ivan Zhirkevich, then a cadet. "Not frightening but appealing. I still vividly remember him standing there in a blue overcoat, with three stars—two on the left side of the chest, one on the right, and with a hat on his head."[24] Glinka broke the tension by stepping forward and giving an impromptu speech: "Your Excellency! With the passing of Count Anhalt, we have lost a tender father figure but hope that you will also embrace us with the same paternal affection. Count Anhalt lived and breathed for us; our hearts are forever etched with gratitude for his work. You have earned the laurels of glory on the fields of battle but here your loving care would instill us with the same appreciation that we felt toward our former paterfamilias."

Kutuzov must have been moved by the young cadet's words, but his outward expression remained stern and taciturn. Casting a "menacing look" at the cadets, he retorted, "Count Anhalt treated you like children. I shall treat you like soldiers." Everyone was stunned. "Dead silence was our only response to his words," remarked a cadet.[25] A chill air of change blew through the doors of the institution, which had been accustomed to Anhalt's laissez-faire approach.

Kutuzov threw himself into the work with his usual determination. A close examination of the inner workings of the Cadet Corps revealed a number of deficiencies. Kutuzov's predecessors, as laudable as they were in their commitment to Enlightenment ideals, had failed to deal with administrative and fiscal matters, leaving behind administrative problems and financial mismanagement. Kutuzov thus discovered that the corps was in fact deep in debt, owing "a not inconsiderable sum of money."[26] Staff members were disheartened by a lack of promotions and awards. Teachers complained of the cadets' inattention and indolence, while the students grumbled about the staff's and teachers' incompetence.[27] The new director therefore began his tenure by insisting on accountability and discipline in the corps. Cadets were expected to show up on time to their lectures and drills, look sharp, and perform to the best of their abilities. Instructors were required to provide regular updates on their students' progress. Cadets who failed to maintain academic standing or showed signs of "idleness" were given one month to improve their grades or suffer consequences. Kutuzov prohibited corporal or excessive punishment; cadets were usually punished with the loss of free time or by being confined to their rooms.[28] The corps officials, both instructors and the supporting staff, were also held accountable. Kutuzov stressed that "the poor performance of the cadets" could be ascribed in large part to the "carelessness" and ineffectiveness of their instructors and caretakers.[29] Conscientious officials were rewarded and promoted, while those found to be ineffectual or involved in inappropriate behavior were punished. Hence Cannonier Ivan Davydov was promoted for "diligence in performing his responsibilities and good behavior," while Kaptenarmus Ivan Bykov was cashiered for "incessant intemperance and unauthorized absences."[30] Kutuzov's emphasis on discipline and order did not mean that he was a martinet. He went out of his way to win over the hearts and minds of both staff and cadets, meeting them in person, addressing their questions, and soliciting their input on existing problems with the corps. Some of his first decisions involved reviewing cases of staff promotions that had gotten lost in the bureaucracy, some for as long as ten years. He thanked staff members for their meritorious service, nominated them for awards, extended support to the grieving families of recently deceased instructors, and insisted on smallpox inoculations.[31]

Kutuzov commissioned a thorough review of the corps's spending, announced a freeze on any capital refurbishments, and drastically cut down the size of the staff, abolishing redundant positions.[32] The Cadet Corps received a generous annual endowment of some 200,000 rubles—enough to cover the annual pay of 20,000 soldiers—but constantly experienced financial problems. Kutuzov went over the expenditures with a fine-toothed comb, paying attention to every detail. While reviewing textbook acquisitions, for example, he noticed that the Academy of Sciences was charging the Cadet Corps one ruble and fifty-six kopecks for each copy of a new mechanics textbook when that same book was selling for just thirty kopecks in the Academy's own store; the order of 300 textbooks was therefore cancelled.[33] To balance the budget, Kutuzov sold off land and properties that, as he put it, "brought no benefit to the corps,"[34] and he made arrangements to pay down the debt "with existing monies, without burdening the imperial treasury."[35] He demanded accountability from corps officials, instituted monthly reports on available funds, and insisted on "daily reports" on what the cadets ate and a monthly accounting of their basic necessities such as powder, pomade, ribbons, combs, and so on.[36] Requisitioning no longer involved writing haphazard orders on "scraps of paper," as Kutuzov put it derisively, but instead became a formalized process, requiring documentation and proof, and with a strict deadline at the start of each month. The same applied for any contractual agreements the Cadet Corps entered into for capital refurbishments. When hiring contractors, the Cadet Corps officials had to bear in mind the costs of any proposed works and were obliged "to conclude agreements that were advantageous to the Corps."[37] Overall, Kutuzov's reforms markedly improved the financial well-being of the institution, doing away with waste and misappropriation.

Kutuzov's biggest reform involved revising the Cadet Corps curriculum, which he found too theoretical and detached. He sought to reorient it to the corps's original objective—that of training a new generation of military officers. Over the next three years, Kutuzov supervised the introduction of the new educational program, which centered on practical military matters rather than on nonmilitary subjects. The cadets now spent more time learning military tactics, land navigation, weapons handling, and the basics of drill instruction, marching, field fortification, and artillery. Kutuzov took a keen interest in the curriculum and personally gave lectures on military history and battle tactics, drawing upon his experiences. He solicited and reviewed reports from each instructor on the academic performance of the pupils. Upon discovering that several cadets in the upper age groups struggled with mathematics, he instructed that they be offered additional help and training so that they could successfully complete their courses. The best students were praised and recognized with various awards. Kutuzov took note of the brightest students. Among these was Count Karl Wilhelm von Toll. Upon Toll's graduation in 1796, Kutuzov proposed that he stay on to further his education; Toll would go on to become one of the most distinguished Cadet Corps graduates, serving as the quartermaster general of the Russian armies and playing a central role in Kutuzov's last campaign in 1812.

To better prepare the cadets for military service, Kutuzov set up five companies (one grenadier and four musketeer) and a separate section for younger pupils. Each musketeer company comprised 96 privates and 10 NCOs, while the grenadier company included 96 privates, 9 army NCOs, and 4 artillery NCOs. In total, the new companies listed 480 privates and 53 NCOs, with another 110 cadets listed in the youth section.[38] Cadets were now required to participate in summer military exercises; they built campsites, slept in tents, and practiced tactical exercises.[39] Kutuzov was determined to prepare cadets for the realities of army life. For this purpose, he purchased hundreds of muskets, "composite grenades," and other military equipment, and acquired new maps and drawing supplies.[40] He also obtained years' worth of subscriptions to foreign newspapers, so that students could remain abreast of the newest developments in Europe.[41] Instead of graduating cadets every three years, as had been done under his predecessors, Kutuzov expedited the process and established an annual review and promotion based on "a thorough evaluation of each cadet's accomplishments, behavior, and academic performance."[42] In January 1795, he reported that his review had identified 111 cadets who were prepared to start military service at once. There were two army captains, seventy-seven lieutenants, and seventeen sub-lieutenants.[43] Kutuzov helped train a new generation of officers who went on to serve with great distinction during the Napoleonic Wars.

Kutuzov's success was soon noticed and duly rewarded—with new responsibilities. In March 1795, while remaining the director of the Cadet Corps, he was appointed the commander in chief of the Russian forces in Finland.[44] This was despite the fact that the Statute of the Cadet Corps prohibited the director from holding other positions or from being absent from the institution. Yet the empress wished it, and so it became a reality.

"Everyone in the city talks about the impending war with Sweden," Alexander Protasov confided to Semen Vorontsov, the Russian ambassador in London. "There are no overt indications except for the preparation of the fleets, the recall of the officers to their posts and the sudden departure of Kutuzov to Finland."[45] The war, which seemed imminent, did not materialize. Nonetheless, Kutuzov found himself stuck with the onerous duty of commanding more than 10,000 men in the former Finnish provinces, which Sweden had been forced to surrender in the previous Russo-Swedish Wars (1741–1743 and 1788–1790).[46] In addition to leading these forces, Kutuzov was tasked with preparing new maps of the entire region and completing the construction of projects designed to defend approaches to the Russian imperial capital.

Over the course of the next twelve months Kutuzov inspected the Russo-Swedish borderland and supervised the construction of fortresses, bastions, military hospitals, and other infrastructure at Ruotsinsalmen (Kotka), Nyslott (Savonlinna), Villmanstrand (Lappeenranta), and other locations. He was constantly on the move, directing the Cadet Corps in St. Petersburg, traveling to construction sites along the Finnish border, accompanying grand dukes and other dignitaries on their visits to the border (making arrangements for the arrival of the new Swedish king Gustav IV Adolf in August 1796),[47] overseeing the cartographic work that resulted in the creation of a new map of southeastern Finland, and dealing with a myriad of administrative problems that the Russian forces in Finland—perpetually lacking proper uniforms, ammunition, and equipment—had experienced.[48] Amid all of this, he still found time to spend with his wife and growing daughters.

<hr />

The reforms Kutuzov introduced in such a short period of time elicited diverse reactions at the Cadet Corps. Many found the pace of the changes too rapid and the academic demands too daunting. One cadet recalled that Kutuzov's arrival at the cadet school ushered in such a profound change from the re-laxed environment that Anhalt had cultivated that some cadets struggled to adjust.[49] Peter Poletika, who would be Russia's second ambassador to the United States, echoed this sentiment. After Kutuzov's arrival, "the longing for freedom, that is, graduating from the Corps, became so intense that it consumed all my thoughts and aspirations." One of his classmates was denied graduation due to his poor academic performance and committed suicide.[50] Such tragic incidents were the exception. Most cadets seemed to have thrived, even if their feelings toward Kutuzov never matched their adoration of his predecessor. Some historians suggest that the older cadets, who had been "molded" by Count Anhalt, tended to treat Kutuzov "reticently, even hos-tilely," while younger and more malleable cadets seemed to have been more receptive to the changes.[51]

There is a certain truth to this. Ivan Zhirkevich, who was in the junior cadet grades in the mid-1790s, remembered only good things from Kutuzov's tenure at the Cadet Corps. "Kutuzov treated us kindly and demanded a similar treatment for us from the corps's officers as well. He often appeared among us during our games or at recess, and each time we all crowded around him and sought some show of his love and affection, with which he was not parsimonious."[52] Meanwhile, Sergei Glinka, who had spent most of his cadet years under Anhalt (whom he admired) but graduated from the Cadet Corps during Kutuzov's tenure, offers a more circumspect assess-ment. He acknowledged that there was "a certain implicit distrust" between the senior cadets and the new director but rejected claims that Kutuzov treated cadets too harshly. Instead, he painted a nuanced portrait of a dir-ector who demanded much from others as well as from himself, and whose opinions were firmly held and often emphatically delivered. But Kutuzov was not simply another bureaucrat in charge of an educational facility. He found himself immersed in high society, with its elaborate rituals, mores, and rules—which in their way were no less involved than what he had seen in the sultan's court in Istanbul.

In St. Petersburg, winter was the high season, with dinner parties, receptions, and balls occurring in rapid succession before the start of Lent. Aristocrats visited one another, engaged in affairs, discussed the latest news, and arranged marriages. This was a close-knit society in which almost everyone had at least a nodding acquaintance with everyone else and many were interrelated. Kutuzov required little introduction to this society and quickly mastered any rituals and conventions he had been unaware of, ably navigating its cliques and coteries. Most of all, he had access to the empress. Almost every day she "invited him to join her private companionship that included only most trusted individuals," commented one of his earliest biographers.[53]

Russian high society was at that time "a reflection of the Court," observed a keen-eyed contemporary. "It might be compared to the vestibule of a temple, where no one has eyes or ears for anything but the divinity within."[54] The struggle between those who were "in" and enjoyed power and prestige and those who were "out" was unrelenting, bolstered by Empress Catherine's own penchant for lovers and favorites, each of whom developed a coterie of sycophants and followers and effectively maintain their own small courts. The latest of them was Platon Zubov, a capricious and arrogant young man who turned twenty-eight years old in 1795, "with a good figure and an agreeable countenance; his dark hair was curled and brushed up into a tuft; his voice was soft and clear."[55] Contemporaries left contrasting portrayals of him, though they agreed that he was supercilious and condescending, with a penchant for reciting memorized passages from books and passing them off as his own opinions. Alexander Suvorov, whose family was related to the Zubovs, could not stand the "Dupe," as he referred to young Platon, and neither could Alexander Khrapovitskii, Catherine's cabinet secretary, who in his private diary kept referring to "foolish [*duraleyushka*] Zubov."[56] "Count Zubov is everything here," grumbled Feodor Rostopchin, then an ambitious officer whose career path would cross with Kutuzov's in 1812. "There is no other will but his. His power is greater than that of Potemkin. He is as reckless and incapable as before, although the empress keeps repeating that he is the greatest genius the history of Russia has known."[57] Rostopchin thought Catherine's last favorite a mediocrity, "dimwitted by nature," whose "chatter is sometimes clever, occasionally mysterious, filled with technical terms that add weight and importance to what he says."[58] And yet the empress adored him and relied on his advice even in the most trivial matters. Crowds of petitioners thronged around the all-powerful favorite and tried desperately to attract his attention and support. Contemporaries were aghast by the almost royal manners and rituals in which Zubov indulged. Every morning at about eleven o'clock he held a levee, where, in the words of an eyewitness, "an immense crowd of petitioners and courtiers of all ranks hastened to assist at his toilet." The street was "full of carriages with four or six horses, exactly as at the theater. Sometimes, after a long period of waiting, the crowd was informed that the Count would not see them on that day, and they then dispersed to come again on the morrow." If Zubov was inclined to receive supplicants, the doors were opened and mobs of noblemen, generals, "high civil functionaries," and "merchants with long beards" crowded into the room, awkwardly rubbing shoulders with each other as they waited for the powerful favorite to wake up. "Each suitor showed in his face what he wanted. Some expressed grief and a simple desire to defend their property, their honor, and their existence; others betrayed a design to seize somebody else's property, or to keep it if they had already obtained it." Some were motivated by greed, others by some misfortune. A crowd of officials, generals, and various dignitaries of the empire, who "placed everybody in their districts under tribute and inspired universal fear," came humbly to kowtow in front of the omnipotent favorite. And yet they "either went away without obtaining a look from him, or stood waiting like messengers while he changed his dress reclining on a sofa."[59]

After three decades on active duty on the periphery of the empire, Kutuzov found himself thrust into a world of fawning, patronage, and intrigue. He survived by absorbing Jean de La Bruyère's tenets, which he had practiced in Istanbul: "An accomplished courtier is master of his gestures, his eyes, his face; he is deep and impenetrable; he can conceal an ill turn, smile on his enemies, restrain his temper, disguise his passions, act contrary to his feelings, speak and act against his convictions."[60] Kutuzov was just the courtier the French moralist had in mind. Describing his personality, Sergei Mayevskii who came to know him well in later years, observed that "no one could match his ability to induce a person to talk or make someone feel special; and no one was as subtle as Kutuzov in sweet-talking and hoodwinking a person whom he chose to deceive or enchant. One second you could see him in a blissful excitement, shedding tears of affection or compassion, but moments later—all was in the past. He possessed the craftiest political mind."[61] General Louis Alexandre Andrault de Langeron, who had served under Kutuzov's command on several occasions, acknowledged his shrewdness, "extraordinary memory," and keen intellect but also stressed his egoism, dangerous "free-thinking," ruthlessness, and brusqueness toward people of lower social standing. "His obsequiousness bordered on slavishness when dealing with persons of greater stature."[62]

The Frenchman was correct about Kutuzov's sycophancy and willingness to debase himself at the court. In 1795–1796, Kutuzov was a regular feature at the imperial court and in the palaces of Russian grandees. Amid the "contemptible crowd," as one contemporary put it, that crowded Zubov's residence, he went out of his way to ingratiate himself to the all-powerful favorite and to make sure that he was not overlooked in the imperial lar-gesse.[63] Kutuzov had followed Zubov's rapid ascent to power and thought to curry favor early on. Letters to Zubov written as early as 1793 were sup-plicatory. It was to Zubov that he wrote about getting land grants. As we have seen, his exertions were not overlooked, and in 1793 he was gifted two thousand "souls" from the lands appropriated from Polish "rebel" nobles. Two years later, on the third anniversary of the end of the Russo-Ottoman War, Catherine granted him additional former Polish *folwarks* (estates) with 2,667 "souls" in the newly acquired Volhynia.[64] In St. Petersburg, Kutuzov continued to play up to the all-powerful favorite. One cadet who happened to be at Count Zubov's was surprised to see Kutuzov meekly sitting in the waiting room for hours to see the favorite. "[Just as I entered the waiting room], a chamberlain came out of the count's bedroom carrying a tray and an empty coffee cup. Kutuzov hastened to approach him and asked in French, 'How soon will the count come out?' 'Probably in two hours,' the chamberlain responded pretentiously. Kutuzov, the man who breached the walls of Ochakov and Izmail, then timidly retreated to his spot. My youthful heart burned with rage," concluded the cadet.[65]

Such obsequiousness toward Zubov appalled contemporaries. "Passek and Kutuzov are the humblest servants of Count Zubov," scornfully wrote one.[66] Returning to St. Petersburg after a yearlong absence, Fedor Rostopchin dis-covered that "everything got worse" at the court. "Would you believe what Lieutenant General Kutuzov, the one who has served as the ambassador to Constantinople, is currently doing? Every morning he comes an hour before Count Zubov wakes up and prepares for him [Turkish] coffee, for which he claims to have a special talent. In front of a large crowd of people, he pours the drink into a cup and carries it to the impudent favorite, who is still in his bed."[67]

The sight of a distinguished general and grizzled war veteran preparing coffee and then serving it to the empress's paramour, who frequently appeared "with scarcely any underclothing," was disgraceful.[68] For many contemporaries, "Kutuzov's coffeepot" thus became a symbol of the debase-ment of the once-dignified Russian nobility, the manifestation of its fawning essence and unctuousness. "We have witnessed how [Empress] Catherine degraded the spirit of the nobility, and her favorites zealously assisted her in this," lamented Pushkin. "It is sufficient for us to recall . . . Kutuzov's coffeepot."[69]

Kutuzov's biographers have long struggled to deal with this unbecoming side of the general. Soviet historians chose to obfuscate it by focusing on the failings of Emperor Paul; Kutuzov's only English-language biography followed that trend and spoke of him being "on excellent terms with Zubov" without offering details.[70] Some modern Russian scholars have attempted justifications for his behavior. The truth is that Kutuzov was a product of his time and culture, reflecting all the virtues and vices of his social class. He was a gifted battlefield commander, a skilled diplomat, and a good manager of men. He was also a fawning courtier who was keenly attuned to societal undercurrents. He was both commanding toward subordinates and submissive to his superiors, sometimes excessively and even painfully so.

The cadets—many of whom Anhalt instilled with quixotic sentiments of righteousness, candor, and honor—found Kutuzov's behavior repugnant, and on at least one occasion they expressed their disillusionment. As the graduation date approached, the corps director attended examinations, listened to the cadets' answers, and quizzed their knowledge of history, literature, rhetoric, and military sciences. For the world history examination, some 120 cadets had gathered in a large auditorium to write essays and respond to examiners' questions. "Soon it was eight o'clock in the evening," remembered cadet Sergei Glinka. "Kutuzov got up and left the room. We all followed him. We knew that every evening Kutuzov visited that timeserver [Zubov]."[71] As soon as the director got into the carriage, the cadets confronted him and began to shout at him, "You are a scoundrel! You are Zubov's boob [*khvost Zubova*]!" As exciting as it was to give the director a piece of their mind, the cadets quickly grasped the gravity of their actions. Kutuzov held their fate in his hands, for he would inform the empress of the status of graduating cadets and recommend them for military service. Glinka and his comrades worried that their recklessness might cost them dearly.

Kutuzov bore no grudge for their escapade, perhaps remembering his own indiscretion of years before. The following morning, he delivered his report to the empress, who asked him how the cadets were doing. "They are fine, Your Majesty," replied Kutuzov, before adding, "They are well educated but lack military discipline." He recommended commissioning six of them not as lieutenants, as was the rule, but as captains. One can imagine the astonishment of the cadets when the director invited them for a meeting and, instead of castigating them for their impudence, broke the news of their promotion. Standing among the students, Kutuzov told them, "I know you scorn me ever since I told you that I would treat you as soldiers. But do you know what it means to be a soldier? I lack neither ranks nor awards or wounds, but I still consider it as the highest accolade when somebody says about me, 'He is a true Russian soldier!' Gentlemen, wherever you might find yourself, you will always find in me a person who sincerely wishes you all the best and who considers your glory, your honor, and your enduring love for the Fatherland as his greatest reward."

The cadets were genuinely moved. "There and then Kutuzov garnered laurels that he could not gain neither on the heights of Măcin, nor at the walls of Izmail or the fields of Borodino. At that moment he had conquered himself," remarked Glinka, pointing to a crucial trait of Kutuzov's character: flawed as he was, the general was self-aware, acknowledging and accepting his contradictions. Knowing that some of the graduating cadets were experiencing financial difficulties and could not afford new uniforms, he discreetly made arrangements to equip them. Commenting that "our young men are too proud to accept anything from me," he ordered his officials to take measurements of the cadets while they were asleep at night and prepare complete sets of uniforms that were then presented to the cadets as gifts from their families.[72] Kutuzov may have been no Anhalt, but he cared deeply about the cadets' future and wanted them to be ready for what lay ahead.

CHAPTER 10

The Wrathful Czar, 1796–1801

O N NOVEMBER 13, 1796, Empress Catherine, who had struggled with her health in preceding months, surprised her courtiers by organizing a grand luncheon, attended by Kutuzov and others. Pleading fatigue, she then retired earlier than usual. A few days later, she rose as always and settled down to work in her private apartments. On the morning of November 16, she dismissed her chamberlain, telling him to wait in the antechamber, and she would call upon him if she needed him. After waiting for over an hour and hearing no noise, the man grew uneasy and entered the room. He found the empress stretched out on the floor, the victim of a stroke. Catherine never regained consciousness and drew her last breath at 9:45 p.m. on November 17, in the sixty-eighth year of her life and the thirty-fifth year of her reign.[1]

The empress had not even been pronounced dead when her son Paul was declared the new "Emperor and Autocrat of All the Russias." Paul was forty-two years old, headstrong and capricious. The son of Catherine and Emperor Peter III, he had been old enough in July 1762 to be aware of what happened to his hapless father, whose overthrow and suspicious death paved the way for his mother's decades-long reign. Afterward, the relations between mother and son had remained tense, to put it mildly. Paul's eccentricity and his resemblance to his father never failed to irritate the empress, who sequestered him at a rural estate at Gatchina; in the last years of her reign, Catherine seriously considered omitting him from the succession in favor of her grandson.[2] Paul was no less contemptuous of his mother. At Gatchina, he established a ducal court that was worlds apart from the freewheeling imperial one. There, ignored and isolated, he kept the memory of his father alive, and with it a spirit of austerity, pedantry, oppressiveness, and militarism. He shared his father's admiration for all things Prussian and keenly cultivated

"Prussomania" at his court and especially in the Gatchina Troops, whom he equipped, clothed, and assiduously drilled in the Prussian manner.[3]

For over thirty years Paul patiently waited for his moment. He felt like a stranger in his own country, disliked at Catherine's court and disapproving of her famously lascivious life, in addition to the reforms that he fundamentally disagreed with. He was not the "Mad Czar" of black legend, a mentally deranged brute on the prowl. To the contrary, recent scholarship has revealed a number of positive attributes to Paul's reign, including his emphasis on accountability and efficiency as well as a willingness to confront shortcomings in the military and bureaucracy. He genuinely believed that a strong dose of order was needed to eradicate the corruption, inconsistencies, and laxness that his mother had tolerated for so long. Those who knew him well thought that "Paul was sincerely pious, really benevolent, generous, a lover of truth and hater of falsehood, ever anxious to promote justice," as Guards officer Colonel Nikolai Sablukov put it. They spoke of his "very romantic disposition" and his delight in "everything chevaleresque." His defense of traditional principles was unbending and yet he was, according to his admirers, capable of changing direction when he could see that something was not working. But even his supporters admitted that he was impatient and ill-tempered, and that he expected blind obedience.[4] His imperial high-handedness appalled Russian nobles, who had come to enjoy the freedoms that his father had granted them and who resented the new emperor's repeated infringements of their privileges, as well as his fondness for Prussian ways.[5]

The first sign of just how radically the situation would change came at the late empress's funeral in December. After praying at her coffin, Paul ordered a special requiem for his father, whose corpse was, in fact, exhumed for the reburial; the coffin was opened and the royal family and the courtiers, including those implicated in the 1762 conspiracy, were required to kiss the skeletal remains of the former emperor. In an act of ultimate retribution, Paul insisted that Catherine and Peter, who loathed each other in life, be reunited in death. He personally accompanied the two coffins in the vast public procession—"a dreadful sight," in the words of an eyewitness—through the streets of the imperial capital city and made Count Alexis Orlov, the aging leader of the conspirators, carry the crown of the man whose death he had caused.[6] Throngs of people, Kutuzov among them of course, attended the double funeral that winter day and could see and sense the dramatic changes unfolding everywhere. They marveled at the Gatchina Troops as they marched—goose-stepping in perfect alignment, and wearing the old-fashioned Prussian uniforms—down the main thoroughfares of St. Petersburg. "What officers! What strange-looking faces! What manners!" commented one nobleman. "In spite of our grief for the empress, we split our sides laughing at their [Prussian] uniforms."[7] Others were far less amused by the pace and extent of

Paul's alterations: "The change was so great, that it looked like nothing other than an enemy invasion . . . there were armed soldiers everywhere."[8]

The emperor dismissed his mother's appointees, reformed institutions, revived old manners, and established new rules and regulations. Russian courtiers and foreign ambassadors alike lamented the permeation of the "Prussian spirit" all around. "Everything is now military, and that most minutely," commented the British ambassador. "Every hour is marked with a new ukase, and frequently on the most frivolous pretexts, and for the purpose of introducing a change in some established custom. A most severe and exact discipline is introduced into every department, both civil and military, and this with such a degree of rigor, as has even absolutely changed the face of Society."[9]

Paul dismissed hundreds of officers, eliminated special privileges and loopholes that nobles had exploited, and struck down the patronage networks that had taken advantage of the military system. No longer could officers enjoy prolonged leaves or avoid actual service under various excuses. He emphasized the value of military professionalism.[10] These were laudable initiatives that reflected concerns of many of the reformers and military theorists of Catherine's period. However, Paul went about achieving them by fiat, and imperial decrees, proclamations, and rulings came fast and furious.[11] Public anxiety increased as it became clear that the emperor could be arbitrary and erratic, prone to impulsive decisions, and determined to eradicate what he perceived as "ills" affecting the Russian military and society. His micromanagement of the army meant a flood of reprimands and punishments for the slightest transgressions, which bred resentment and opposition. Regiments were no longer named after geographical regions and instead bore the names of their commanding officers. Even more troublesome was Paul's abandonment of the uniforms that Potemkin had introduced a decade earlier, which were practical and appropriate to the climate; Russian soldiers now had to wear tight and impractical Prussian-style costumes, with uncomfortable shoes, gaiters, heavy caps and hats, copious amounts of hair powder, and, of course, pigtails. The new uniforms were almost unanimously hated.

The magnitude and tempo of changes in the military that Paul initiated—new uniforms, new regimental names, new codes of service, and structural reorganizations—were staggering, sweeping aside customs that had been carefully nurtured for many years. The result was inevitable. Merely one month after Paul's accession "half the officers in the guards [had] already voluntarily resigned," reported the Habsburg ambassador Ludwig von Cobenzl.[12]

The changes soon extended to public life. Paul issued decrees full of minute provisions, forbidding fashionable attire and authorizing officials to use scissors to cut the tails off the "revolutionary" French frock coats; round hats, waistcoats, high collars, large neckties, and any other clothing that savored of "Jacobinism" were banned. He made censorship of the theater and the press more rigorous than ever. "Never was there any change of scene at a theatre so sudden and so complete as the change of affairs at the accession of Paul," recalled Adam Czartoryski, the Polish nobleman who was brought as a hostage to the Russian court after the Polish partitions. "In less than a day, costumes, manners, occupations, all were altered. . . . The military parade became the chief occupation of each day."[13] At the sight of the emperor or simply when passing a palace, "all those seated inside carriages [now] had to step out and make their bow," recalled Guard officer Sablukov. St. Petersburg, "the smartest, most elegant, and most fashionable metropolis in Europe, Paris and London perhaps excepted . . . ceased to look like a modern city, having become much more like a German one of two or three centuries back."[14]

Living in St. Petersburg, Kutuzov found himself at the epicenter of Pauline transformations. He left no record of his personal reaction to the death of the empress who had been so benevolent to him, but he must have been alarmed by the new emperor's intentions. Being a member of Catherine's "lofty flock of eagles" was a liability now. Paul was expunging his mother's loyalists and anyone expressing reservation about the reforms. The purge involved 7 field marshals, more than 330 generals, and more than 2,000 officers. Among them was Alexander Suvorov, who decried the introduction of the Prussian-inspired uniforms and drills.[15] "Sire, wig powder is not gunpowder; curls are not cannon; a pigtail is not a saber; I am not a Prussian, but a pure-blooded Russian," he bluntly told the emperor, who did not appreciate criticism.[16] Suvorov's exile to a rural estate had a chilling effect on the rest of the officer corps.

Soviet historiography has exalted Kutuzov for standing up to Paul's policies and "courageously defending progressive ideas during the dark years of the Pauline regime," as one historian put it.[17] Yet there is no evidence that Kutuzov ever publicly expressed his criticism of the military shakeup or questioned the emperor's initiatives. This is hardly surprising. He was no longer prone to rash or imprudent actions. He understood the importance of keeping his head low, adhering to imperial diktats, and concentrating on his responsibilities as the Cadet Corps director and the commander in chief of the Russian forces in Finland. Moreover, Paul's drive for reforms offered Kutuzov an opportunity to tackle some of the problems he himself had been complaining about, including in regimental provisioning, logistics, and practical training for the cadets. The czar inspected the Cadet Corps, approved of the changes Kutuzov had made there, and sought his involvement in military maneuvers that were held at Gatchina in the fall of 1797.[18] It was during these encounters that Paul came to appreciate Kutuzov's abilities and did not hesitate to use them.

On November 16, 1797, King Frederick William II of Prussia died unexpectedly at the age of fifty-three and was succeeded by his son Frederick William III. News of the transition in Prussia reached St. Petersburg days later when Prussian lieutenant general Franz Kasimir von Kleist delivered an official note to the Russian imperial court. The Russian sovereign was expected to convey his condolences on the passing of the king and congratulate the new sovereign on his accession to power. *Le roi est mort, vive le roi!*

This may seem a simple enough task, but in the world of international politics such things are rarely that simple, and certainly not at that crucial historical juncture. Europe was in the throes of the French Revolutionary Wars, which had begun in April 1792, when the French revolutionary government declared war against Austria and Prussia. The conflict rapidly expanded to embroil almost the entire continent—the First Coalition assembled against the French included Britain, the Dutch Republic, the Holy Roman Empire, Naples, Portugal, Piedmont-Sardinia, and Spain. The hopes of a quick ending to the war soon dissipated. Threatened on all sides, the French revolutionaries fought valiantly and ruthlessly, instituting the system of domestic terror and mobilizing the resources of the entire nation. Despite occasional setbacks, the revolutionary armies repelled the invading coalition forces and advanced beyond France's borders into neighboring territories. France also gained diplomatic victories, forcing Spain and Prussia to sue for peace in 1795. And the French conquests did not stop there. In Italy, Napoleon Bonaparte won a string of remarkable victories that compelled Austria to sue for peace in 1797. The subsequent Treaty of Campo Formio all but ended the war on the continent. The First Coalition imploded and France emerged triumphant, consolidating its positions in northern Italy, Rhineland, the Austrian Netherlands, and the Dutch Republic.

Such rapid French aggrandizement alarmed Russian authorities, who until then were preoccupied with their own enlargement in eastern Europe. To contain the French threat, Russia needed allies, the closest of which seemed Prussia. However, confronted by the French occupation of the Rhineland and Russian expansion into Poland, the Prussians chose the former, the lesser of two evils, and negotiated the Treaty of Basel (April 1795), recognizing French control of the west bank of the Rhine in exchange for the promise to indemnify Prussia with land on the right bank. The peace treaty was a major diplomatic victory for France and created a major rupture between the coalition partners. The relations between Austria and Prussia—already strained in light of earlier conflicts—worsened. For Prussia, Basel offered the dual advantages of increasing its influence in southwestern Germany while freeing its hands for involvement in the Third Partition of Poland.

Prussia's behavior, however, exasperated Russian diplomats, who were keen to contain the French menace. The private correspondence between Vice Chancellor Alexander Kurakin and Nikita Petrovich Panin, the Russian ambassador in Berlin (and soon-to-be regicide), reveals the power struggle that was unfolding at the Hohenzollern court as various factions and powers vied to influence the Prussian monarch. The Russians were annoyed at the continued influence of Christian August Heinrich Kurt Graf von Haugwitz, the Prussian foreign minister, who preferred to maintain Prussian neutrality and was one of the architects of the Treaty of Basel. Senior Russian officials suspected Haugwitz of clandestine communications with the French envoy Antoine Bernard Caillard and of seeking to use France's recent military victories to undermine Austria's positions in central Europe, thereby further aggrandizing Prussia.[19]

The death of King Frederick William II thus offered an opportunity to sway the new Prussian ruler to align himself more closely with Russia and to take a more determined stand against French expansion. The Russian ambassador was adamant that "the young king must clarify his position and make a choice between Russia and France." Panin complained that "current matters" could not be successfully resolved because of the challenges posed by the rigid Prussian court etiquette and the difficulty of getting the young monarch to "seek an understanding" with the Russian court.[20] The ambassador needed "a trusted individual" who "by the very nature of his pedigree and rank would be able to attend all court functions" and could thus gain access to the king and plant the seeds of Prusso-Russian rapprochement.[21] However, appointing a new emissary would inevitably raise questions, and the true objective of any such mission had to be concealed behind "some respectable cause." Panin pointed out that the death of Frederick William II offered such a cause, for the late king was the recipient of the Order of St. Andrew the First Called—the highest of the Russian imperial awards—and now the award had to be returned to Russia. Why not use this inconspicuous motive to further a political goal? Panin wrote Kurakin that it seemed a way of getting around the rule that prevented "members of the foreign diplomatic corps from being in the company of the king and the royal family.[22] Vice Chancellor Kurakin concurred with the ambassador and noted that finding an individual capable of such a delicate task was daunting, given the requirements of experience, character, rank, and status. "The decision has not yet been made," he ruefully told the ambassador.

Actually, the decision had already been made. Emperor Paul, in consultation with senior members of the Collegium of Foreign Affairs, decided to entrust this important mission to Kutuzov, who seemed to have thus far successfully dissociated himself from Catherine's "eagles" to become a trusted figure in the new regime. "Considering his intellect and abilities, we are certain that he would act reasonably and diligently and would deftly exploit the king's goodwill to our advantage," observed Kurakin.[23] On December 25, 1797, Paul ordered Kutuzov to embark on a special diplomatic mission to Berlin.[24] Publicly the envoy was to convey the czar's personal and formal congratulations to the

Prussian king and to reclaim the dead king's Russian imperial order for safe-keeping at the Order Capitulum, which administered Russian imperial awards and decorations. The instructions made no mention of the political aspect of this visit; in fact, article 5 advised Kutuzov to "avoid any discussion of political matters." In a letter to Panin, however, Kurakin acknowledged that the overt assignment would act as cover for "the actual secret goal of this mission," which was to sway Prussia to join Russia against France.[25]

Receiving his passport on December 27, Kutuzov departed from St. Petersburg and traveled across the Russian western provinces toward Berlin.[26] He was still en route when messengers were sent to apprise him of two important pieces of news. Emperor Paul had appointed him as the inspector of the Finland Inspectorate (a military administrative district) and the chef proprietor of the Ryazanskii Musketeer Regiment. The news would have been a great surprise for Kutuzov, for it meant that his tenure at the Cadet Corps had come to an abrupt end. The new appointments required him to depart from the imperial capital and reside in the small town of Vyborg (Finnish Viipuri), about eight miles northwest of St. Petersburg. Moreover, just eleven days later Kutuzov received news that he was being promoted to the rank of general of infantry, a rank that Paul had just recently revived to replace the more French-sounding général-en-chef. This was a clear sign of the emperor's trust. After more than thirty-five years of dedicated military service, Kutuzov had now almost reached the pinnacle of military service. The Table of Ranks—the official listing of positions and ranks in the military, government, and court—showed general of the infantry as the second-highest rank, superseded only by the rank of general field marshal.[27]

On January 18, 1798, Kutuzov arrived at the Prussian capital city and visited the Russian embassy. Panin immediately contacted the Prussian authorities and, explaining the reason for Kutuzov's visit, requested an audience with the king.[28] Just five days later, the Russian diplomats were received at the royal palace. The reception Frederick William III gave Kutuzov exceeded Russian expectations. Panin raved to Emperor Paul about the "signs of personal attention and respect" that the king had shown to Kutuzov: "neither his accomplishments nor military talents or wounds have been overlooked and everything has been praised in the pleasantest of expressions." Throughout the reception and subsequent dinner, Kutuzov put his fluency in German to good use. He delighted the Prussian nobles with stories of his military campaigns and ambassadorship in Istanbul, charmed Queen Louise, and had "a rather long conversation" with the king himself. Panin was so pleased with the outcome that he urged his superiors in St. Petersburg to let Kutuzov stay in Berlin. "I must admit I prefer him to anyone else," he wrote on January 24.[29]

Over the next few weeks Kutuzov seems to have captivated the Berlinese upper society, earning him invitations to dinners, fêtes, and receptions. "He is enjoying a remarkable success in Berlin," marveled Panin, pleading again with his superiors not to recall the general. "We would have to wait for a long time before we get to enjoy another welcome similar to the one given to Kutuzov," he advised.[30] Indeed, the hospitable reception that Kutuzov received meant that he could keep company with the grandees of the realm, senior royal officials, and officers, sounding them out on various issues, carefully soliciting information, overhearing conversations, and absorbing inadvertently revealed insider information. After each social event Kutuzov prepared a long report containing newly acquired information and insights, which was then conveyed to St. Petersburg. At another dinner, hosted by Princess Wilhelmina Caroline, the wife of Landgrave Wilhelm IX of Hesse-Kassel, Kutuzov had a long conversation with the Prussian king's adjutant general, who shared insights into the king's mindset and attitudes, including his conviction that "the salvation of Europe depends on the will of the Russian autocrat, who alone is capable of uniting the imperial powers" to curtail the growing power of France.[31]

Panin pushed hard to negotiate a Russo-Prussian alliance.[32] When the negotiations stalled, he asked Kutuzov to inquire into the causes of the delay. At a reception, Kutuzov broached this subject with Prussian field marshal Wichard Joachim Heinrich von Möllendorf, who shared valuable details. Shortly after the audience with Kutuzov, Frederick William had fallen ill with measles (which was blamed on the Austrian envoy) and remained in isolation until March.[33] Upon his recovery, the negotiations resumed, but despite their best efforts, Panin and Kutuzov were unable to achieve their goal that year. In mid-March, Kutuzov learned from his contacts that while the Prussian cabinet had submitted a memorandum, the king refused to approve it until he had read it in full, which he kept postponing because of his weak health. Meanwhile, Kutuzov's mission was coming to an end. Having spent over a month at the Prussian court, he could no longer delay his return. Panin was told in no uncertain terms that the general had to return home. Keeping a senior military figure like him without a clear diplomatic mission in Berlin would be highly "inappropriate" and inevitably raise questions. Besides, the general had two new responsibilities in Finland that he had to tend to.[34]

On March 13, Kutuzov visited the Prussian king to request his permission to depart. Frederick William received him munificently, giving him among other things a snuffbox bearing the royal portrait and a porcelain set. He invited him for a tour of the royal palace at Potsdam, where the Russian general was "properly fêted."[35] On March 18, two months after arriving, Kutuzov left the Prussian court. He would not return until fifteen years later, at the helm of a vast Russian army, seeking to support Frederick William III in his struggle against Napoleon.

In late April 1798, Kutuzov assumed the position of inspector of infantry for the Finland Inspectorate and the chef proprietor of the Ryazanskii Musketeer Regiment. One of Emperor Paul's earliest military reforms involved a military-administrative restructuring that created twelve new administrative units—"inspectorates" or "divisions"—that were designed to streamline command and control and centralize authority in the hands of division chiefs or inspectors for each military branch (infantry, cavalry, and artillery). The Finland Inspectorate was among the first administrative units formed and encompassed territory northwest of St. Petersburg.

Stationed at the town of Vyborg, Kutuzov found himself, as before, neck-deep in an administrative slog: tedious daily routines involving the never-ending cycle of inspecting units; requisitioning new uniforms, equipment, and ammunition; tending to the daily needs of his troops; containing the spread of summer pestilences that threatened people and cattle alike; and combatting those eternal army problems, alcohol and desertion.[36] When Grand Duke Constantine, Emperor Paul's younger son, came to visit, Kutuzov showed him around and entertained him with mock "naval battles and burning of the ships" at Ruotsinsalmi (Svenksund).[37] The general was constantly on the move, from Vyborg to Friedrikshamn (Hamina) and all along the Russo-Swedish border. "The weather got colder here but I still have to spend all day outside and will not return to Vyborg for another eight days," he wrote in a quick message from the imperial borderland. The cold of the north did not suit him well, leaving him unwell for weeks on end. "I still cannot get fully back on my feet," he mentioned in passing in a letter home in June 1799.[38]

The monotony was exacerbated by prolonged separation from his family. His eldest daughter, the twenty-year-old Praskovya, was already married to Matvey Fedorovich Tolstoy, a scion of a distinguished noble family. The couple had celebrated the birth of their first son, Illarion—Kutuzov's first grandson, named after his father—in June 1798 and welcomed their second son, Fedor, just a year later. The third baby, Pavel, was already on his way; he would become the heir to his illustrious grandfather's name and titles. Kutuzov was overjoyed to learn that Emperor Paul himself had agreed to become the new baby's godfather.[39] His other daughters were already reaching maturity— Anna, the second-eldest, was seventeen, Elisabeth sixteen, Catherine twelve, and Darya eleven—and all were ready to be introduced into high society. "I am impatient to learn how the children were presented," he wrote in January 1799, begging his wife for more details.[40] He was thrilled to hear that his younger daughters were well received at the imperial court and had been granted the titles of fräuleins, or maids of honor, to the grand duchesses of the imperial family.

Still, his letters remained full of melancholy. He was worried about the health of his wife and children, and there seemed to be never-ending money woes. Above all, he longed for the comforts of home. "I cannot describe how dreary it is to be here, without a family, finding not a moment to rest," reads one of his many letters.[41] A small border town like Vyborg had very little to offer in terms of entertainment, whether theatrical, musical, or culinary. On the rare occasions when his wife paid him a quick visit (usually for a day or two), Kutuzov always implored her to bring food. "I am sending you a list of what to bring, otherwise you will starve here," he wrote her on one occasion, asking in particular for fruit that was hard to come by.[42] The family reunions in Vyborg were special occasions for the entire town. In August 1798, Baroness Johanna (Margaret) von Nicolay (née Poggenpohl), whose husband owned the estate of Monrepos on the shores of Vyborg Bay on the Gulf of Finland, welcomed the Kutuzovs. "The general's wife is a witty woman, very courteous and friendly," the baroness commented in a letter. "She arrived here with five daughters. . . . They all love to dance and enjoy doing it, so the governor, the commandant, and his brother all arranged balls for them."[43]

But such distractions were few and far in between. The emperor demanded a thorough accounting of what was transpiring in the army, so Kutuzov worked late into the night every night.[44] After traveling the sixty miles separating Vyborg from Friedrikshamn in June 1799, he jotted down a quick dispatch home: "Returned before dawn today, thoroughly exhausted and having had barely any sleep; yet I must stay awake and write plenty of reports with respect to the assignments that His Majesty has given me."[45] Remarkably, Kutuzov still managed to indulge himself with reading, asking his wife to send new titles from the capital. "I am returning *Le danger des intrigues* but cannot find the second volume of *Valville*. I will send back *Journal du nord* sometime next week," he told his wife, asking her to "search for more novels" that might brighten his lonely existence in Vyborg.[46]

Kutuzov's hard work was nonetheless paying off. Emperor Paul praised his work and continued to rely on him for various tasks, including reviewing a tentative plan that he had prepared for a possible war against Sweden.[47] Mistrustful of his European neighbors, the emperor predicted that France would incite a war against Russia and recruit "the Prussians, Swedes, and Turks" to do its bidding. To forestall his enemies, Paul proposed to wage a preventive war, starting with Sweden, whose domains would be invaded by four Russian corps, including one under Kutuzov's command. Pleased with the operational plan that he had devised, the emperor sent it to Kutuzov for comment on the parts involving his corps. A quick glance sufficed for Kutuzov to see glaring problems. He responded with a lengthy commentary that not only examined the operations of his own corps but also suggested revising the entire plan and outlined an alternative strategy for the future conflict. Kutuzov identified possible logistical challenges and pinpointed individual routes and locations that Russian units could take in Finland to maximize the speed of movement and sustain the advance momentum.[48] Impressive as it was, the proposal was an implicit critique of the emperor's plan. This was an uncharacteristic misstep for a man known for his astuteness and subtlety and who should have known better when dealing with Paul's mercurial character. Some of his recent biographers suggested that "too much diligence and military aptitude" got the better of Kutuzov, who, as a true military professional, felt it was his responsibility to point out flaws and share his concerns with the emperor.[49] Paul did not appreciate the gesture. He bluntly told the general to mind his own business and "to execute what has been previously ordered."

The incident with the plan exemplifies Kutuzov's relations with Paul for the next three years. The general often found himself caught between imperial benevolence and disgrace, not knowing what to expect next. Paul was a micromanager with a mania for military minutiae and prone to outbursts. He disparaged the general for even trivial transgressions of his rigid military regulations—in early 1799, for example, Kutuzov was scolded for dispatching an officer on regimental business to St. Petersburg without first informing the emperor.[50] Kutuzov was then castigated for allowing a courier to carry a letter from the Comte de Provence (the future King Louis XVIII of France) across the Russian border. On the other hand, Paul also commended Kutuzov for his diligent work and generously rewarded him, including with the grand cross of the Order of St. John of Jerusalem in October 1799. The czar clearly appreciated his martial and diplomatic talents as well as his thoroughness and subtlety. Thus, while Suvorov remained in exile, Kutuzov continued to work assiduously at the Finland Inspectorate.

Mikhail Illarionovich was occasionally asked to dust off his diplomatic credentials. In July 1798, Paul instructed him to represent the Russian side in the Russo-Swedish negotiations on the delimitation of the border in Finland. The Treaty of Värälä (Wereloe) that had ended the last Russo-Swedish War in 1790 confirmed the *status quo ante bellum* with respect to the borders and required appointment of special commissars to complete the demarcation. Now, eight years later, both sides were finally ready to attempt it. Kutuzov's knowledge of the region and his involvement in cartographic projects in Russian-controlled eastern Finland came in handy as he wrangled with the Swedish representative, Count Wilhelm Mauritz Klingspor. Paul, though now notorious for his micromanagement, had faith in Kutuzov, allowing the general the latitude "to personally demarcate all locations" and, "having conditionally agreed on everything," to submit the agreement for the emperor's approval.[51] Embarking on his new mission, Kutuzov studied earlier Russo-Swedish conflicts, sought the necessary documents about the previous demarcation efforts, and surrounded himself with a group of knowledgeable and experienced men, including Major General Faddei (Fabian Gotthard) von Steinheil, who had been involved in Kutuzov's ongoing cartographic efforts in Vyborg province. On Kutuzov's orders, additional topographic surveys were conducted and special maps of the border areas prepared.

The negotiations began in earnest in January 1799 at Abborfors (present-day Ahvenkoski) and continued for several weeks. Both sides debated issues and disagreed, sometimes in spirited fashion, on specific details. Kutuzov demonstrated a willingness to listen and consider the Swedish demands. In February, he submitted a detailed memorandum outlining a tentative agreement that could be reached with Sweden on the Finnish borders. He suggested resolving one of the problematic areas of the borderline by exchanging the area of Mäntyharju, northwest of Lake Saimaa, for an equal territory near Lakes Puruvesi and Pyhäjärvi.[52] This was a sensible approach. However, Emperor Paul rejected the draft agreement, insisting on greater Swedish concessions. The Swedes, predictably, refused, and the negotiations collapsed in April.[53]

Kutuzov watched the events in Europe with growing alarm. A new war was looming. France had extended its authority far beyond its traditional sphere of influence, controlling much of Italy, Switzerland, the Austrian Netherlands, Holland, and the Rhineland, and was now launching expeditions overseas. It was clear that the victory in the War of the First Coalition had not satiated the French thirst for expansion, and that military convenience and opportunism, ideological conviction, and the political and economic advantages of continued conquests encouraged further aggression. To confront the French menace, the Second Coalition against the French began to form in early 1798, ultimately comprising not only the now-customary Britain, Austria, and Naples but also Sweden, Portugal, the Ottoman Empire, and Russia. Emperor Paul became an eager member of this new coalition and made major commitments to the allied cause, pledging to dispatch the bulk of the Russian forces to support the Austrian war efforts in Switzerland and Italy while a separate expeditionary corps would take part in a joint Anglo-Russian expedition to Holland.

The war began in earnest in the spring of 1799, just as Kutuzov was concluding negotiations with the Swedes. Any hopes he might have had of exchanging the peaceful but unexciting northern frontier for military action in Europe were quickly dashed when the imperial decrees revealed the lists of units and generals committed to various campaigns. The Russian expeditionary corps destined for Holland was placed under the command of General Ivan von Hermann von Fersen, and the one heading for Switzerland was given to Alexander Rimskii-Korsakov, while, at the request of his allies, Emperor Paul recalled Suvorov, the great victor of Focşani, Rymnik, and Izmail, from his bucolic exile and appointed him to lead the Austro-Russian forces in northern Italy. It remains unclear why Emperor Paul chose to overlook Kutuzov, but the fact remains that when the war broke out, Mikhail Illarionovich was still on the Finnish border. If he was disappointed, his letters did not betray this. He watched from afar as the Russian forces left their cantonments for distant lands and remained apprised of their progress through his wife's letters. "Please write me about Suvorov and if he has committed any more of his eccentricities," he urged his wife, before adding: "And tell me more about the Archduke [Charles]."[54]

There was much to tell, for the allies mounted a strong offensive against the French. Archduke Charles's Austrian army scored victories at Ostrach and Stokach in southwestern Germany in March and then drove the French from most of Switzerland. The Anglo-Russians, allied with the banditti of the charismatic cleric Fabrizio Ruffo and the brigand Michele Pezza (whom the people called "Fra Diavolo"—Brother Devil) challenged French control of southern Italy, while Russian and British navies achieved considerable success in the Mediterranean, capturing the Ionian Islands and besieging Malta.[55] More crucially, the Russo-Austrian forces, led by Suvorov, invaded northern Italy, while Anglo-Russian troops landed in Holland, seeking to incite a popular uprising and challenge French control of the Low Countries.[56]

These two Russian campaigns could not have been more different. Arriving in Lombardy in early April, Suvorov launched a dazzling campaign, defeating the French at Cassano, at Marengo, and on the Trebbia River; in just five months, he reclaimed virtually everything that the French had conquered in two years of fighting. Kutuzov was delighted to hear about his former commander's success. "Thank you, my dear, for the great news about Suvorov," he wrote his wife after learning about the Russian victories in Italy. "May the Lord assist him." Two months later he celebrated the "trouncing" of French general Jean Moreau at Novi. "Such news entertains me amid the dreariness of my existence here."[57]

The Anglo-Russian expedition to Holland, meanwhile, turned out to be a disaster. There were logistical challenges from the outset, and the difficulties only mounted as the campaign progressed. The lack of good leadership was one reason. The British commander, Frederick Augustus, Duke of York and Albany, had a mixed record of military success, having suffered defeats at the hands of the French in 1794–1795; the Russian commander, General Hermann, was an experienced but unimaginative commander who proved unable to cope with the worsening situation. The Allied troops landed in Holland in late August 1799 and, after initial success, suffered a disastrous defeat at Bergen in September, with the Russian contingent alone losing some 3,000 men, including Hermann, who was captured.

Fuming, Emperor Paul turned to Kutuzov for help, ordering him to depart at once and sort out the mess in Holland.[58] Mikhail Illarionovich must have been elated by this opportunity to get back into action. So were the British, as Russian ambassador Semen Vorontsov assured them that the new commander was "a skillful and shrewd man" who would be able to restore order among the Russian troops.[59] In early October, Kutuzov hastily embarked on the long journey to Hamburg, where the troops were to board ships destined for Dutch shores. The weather was wet and cold; the 600-mile journey from Vyborg to Königsberg turned out to be dreadful. "My dear, I barely managed to get here late last night," Kutuzov wrote Catherine from Königsberg on October 30; he complained about bad weather, broken carriages, and the constant challenge of finding post horses. "It is hard to convey just how terrible the road is here."[60] In Königsberg he did a little bit of sightseeing and bought some keepsakes for his kids. "My dear children, how are you? I am in Königsberg, sitting by the window, looking out into the main street, and observing German women walking to a ball, all dressed up and wearing headscarves that make their heads look huge," read his brief letter home.[61]

As he traveled west, Kutuzov followed newspaper reports about the campaigns in Europe. He was frustrated that the Allies seemed to be wasting precious time in internal bickering, giving the French an opportunity to regroup. In late September, French general André Masséna routed the Austro-Russian forces at Zurich and then pounced on Suvorov's expeditionary corps as it was crossing the Alps to Switzerland. The relations between the Russians and Austrians quickly deteriorated; Suvorov and his officers complained that their Austrian allies had neglected to gather a sufficient number of supplies and mules for the passage through the mountains, which forced them to lose precious days. Suvorov reached St. Gotthard Pass, which his men crossed despite immense difficulties, scaling steep cliffs, crossing chasms, and clashing with the French forces. He then plunged down narrow Alpine valleys enclosed between mountains so precipitous in places that the pathway ran along the edge of cliffs. "In this kingdom of terrors," Suvorov wrote in a dispatch, "abysses open beside us at every step, like tombs awaiting our arrival. Nights spent among the clouds, thunder that never ceases, rain, fog, the noise of cataracts, the crashing of avalanches, enormous masses of rocks and ice which fall from the heights, torrents which sometimes carry men and horses down the precipices. Words fail to describe the horrors we have seen, and in the midst of which Providence has preserved us." Suvorov's forces survived the harrowing crossing of the Alps, but the Russo-Austrian alliance did not. Imperial tensions turned into a public rupture as Emperor Paul accused Austria of betraying the alliance and contributing to the Russian defeats in Switzerland. A minor incident in Italy only increased Russia's sense of Austrian perfidy. A joint Russo-Austrian-Ottoman expedition to capture the port of Ancona turned into a diplomatic scandal after the Austrian general secretly concluded a capitulation with the French, stipulating that his troops alone should be admitted into the fortress. As a result, the Russian and Ottoman flags that had been fixed on the ramparts beside his own were removed. This was the last straw for Emperor Paul, who broke away from the coalition and recalled the Russian forces. On November 23, just hours after arriving at Hamburg and still recovering from the backbreaking 1,200-mile journey on "the most terrible roads," Kutuzov received the order to return home with all his troops.[62]

The expedition to Holland was therefore cancelled. Kutuzov never got a chance to take part in the War of the Second Coalition, which brought Suvorov to the pinnacle of his military success and made the careers of so many other Russian officers. That same day Kutuzov received the news that Emperor Paul had appointed him head of the Pskovskii Musketeer Regiment and the new military governor of Lithuania and inspector of infantry for the Lithuanian and Smolensk Inspectorates.[63] The Pskovskii Musketeer Regiment was one of the oldest and most distinguished Russian regiments, established by Peter the Great in 1700. It had served with distinction in the wars against Sweden, Prussia, and the Ottoman Empire. Becoming its chef proprietor (*shef*) was a singular honor. The new gubernatorial responsibility, meanwhile, conferred a great deal of authority and status. The Lithuanian Governorate had been formed three years earlier as part of Emperor Paul's new administrative restructuring of the Russian Empire. It encompassed the vast territory from the Baltic shores to the Bug River, the once Polish-Lithuanian lands that Russia had seized during the Third Partition of Poland four years earlier. The governor was required to spend half the year at Vilna and the other half at Grodno, once a hub of Polish-Lithuanian trade, commerce, and culture, and now a Russian border town and administrative center.

As gratifying as these appointments were, Kutuzov was still unsatisfied. "I will have to depart at once and travel directly to Grodno," he confided to his wife, who was still in St. Petersburg. "I cannot act otherwise, for I cannot return to St. Petersburg without permission. Admittedly, I am not keen on living in Grodno, where life would be as boring and unbearable as in Vyborg." His letters reveal a deep loneliness. "I dream of all of you every night," he wrote forlornly. "I am sending my blessings for the children."[64] Bad weather kept him at Hamburg for three more days, but on November 26, 1799, he was on the road heading for Lithuania.

Kutuzov arrived at Grodno on the eve of the New Year and the new century and remained in Lithuania for the next year and a half. His authority soon extended beyond military affairs. Starting in January 1800, he wielded supreme authority over both civil and military administrations and exercised extensive powers in matters of tax collection, law and order, and social welfare.[65] He shuttled between Vilna and Grodno. "I arrived at Vilna three days ago and found the town in the grip of a flu epidemic," he told Catherine. "I felt its symptoms but was so busy I could not afford to even lie down."[66]

His life got only more frenzied as the months went by. Emperor Paul frequently conjured up threats and conspiracies, which meant more work for his governors and army commanders. With the War of the Second Coalition still raging in Europe, the emperor became convinced that war with Prussia or some other European power was impending, and he considered forming four armies for a new forceful intervention into European affairs in order "to end the stream of French military success and to protect the Holy Roman Empire and Italy from certain destruction" as well as "to constrain the Viennese court's aspirations to claim half of Italy." Suvorov was to spearhead the Russian return to Italy, supported by a powerful reserve line of three armies under the command of Kutuzov, Ivan Gudovich, and Jean-François de Beaumont d'Autichamp. Kutuzov thus spent much of his time in Lithuania dealing with military matters, closely observing the imperial border with Prussia, billeting and provisioning the regiments stationed in the province, mobilizing hundreds of recruits, hunting down deserters, reviewing units, and setting up supply depots.[67] He was frequently on the move. "I am on my way to the inspectorate, will be gone for two weeks," he told Catherine on June 5. Two weeks later, he was on his way back to Vilna but "only for two-three days, before I head out again to examine regiments."[68] The amount of administrative work was overwhelming, causing him to complain that "there are too many papers to deal with, far more than what I had in Finland."[69] Just three months into the job, he was already exhausted and unwell. "My eyes are so overworked that I do not know what will happen to my sight," he admitted in March. "I get not a single free minute before lunch and have to work late into evening as well."[70]

Aside from his administrative and military responsibilities, there were also numerous social engagements that he had to tend to in his capacity as governor-general. He took no pleasure in any of it. "Just yesterday I had to attend a theater play," he wrote in a letter, "then a small ball at a private residence; but even a 'small ball' here involves 100 people, dancing *mazurka, kazachka, allemande, la périgordane, valse étrusque.* So I had to dance till my head hurt." His evening was not over yet, for he had to go to another performance attended by some 700 people. Only afterward, much to his delight, was he able get back home. He could not get used to the "exuberance" of life in Vilna. "I prefer spending time in small company so I can leave at six in the evening and be in bed by ten. Instead, I am forced to attend dinners because the public gets offended if I do not come. . . . And so I endure, unwell and unhappy."[71]

The War of the Second Coalition produced profound fissures in Russia's relations with European powers. Infuriated by military setbacks in Holland and Switzerland, Paul became convinced that Russia's sacrifices had been for naught. He had fought for the reestablishment of legitimate governments in Italy and France and of the old status quo in Europe. The only result had been the aggrandizement of Austria and Britain, with which he had far more reason to be concerned than with France. The coalition partners could no longer be trusted, a sentiment that Kutuzov would witness in Russian military and political circles throughout the Napoleonic Wars. The czar thus began to gravitate away from his former allies, expelling Austrian and British envoys, recalling his own ambassador from London (he refused to leave), and sidelining his Anglophile ministers.

Paul's foreign policy has nonetheless long been misrepresented. Though grandiose, it was not inconsistent.[72] His overarching goals remained the same as those of his predecessors—to protect Russian interests in central Europe and expand them in the Baltic, the Balkans, and the Caucasus. Despite being hostile to the ideas behind the French Revolution, Paul saw Napoleon Bonaparte, who had come to power in France in November 1799, as a statesman, someone who could stabilize France and serve as a potential partner in pacifying Europe and confronting Britain.[73] Bonaparte seized upon this favorable moment to seek rapprochement with Russia. Already in the early summer of 1800, he insisted that "it is necessary to give Paul some proof of our esteem, to let him know that we want to negotiate with him."[74] The French knew about Paul's penchant for quixotic ideals and chivalric gestures. European newspapers had recently published his article suggesting resolving international disputes through a knightly tournament of European heads of state and their seconds (Paul named Kutuzov as his second), where they could settle their grievances in feats of strength.[75] The idea—made in drunken jest and never meant seriously—was widely ridiculed. Still, the French were canny enough to play upon the czar's romantic sentiments. While the British refused to redeem the Russians who had been made prisoners while in their service, by exchanging them for an equal number of French, Bonaparte set some 6,000 Russian prisoners free without either exchange or ransom, instead providing them with new clothing and arms, and writing an effusive letter praising the gallantry of the Russian warrior. When the British refused to consider the Russian position on the future of the Order of the Maltese Knights—Paul was the grand master of the order—and suggested that they intended to keep Malta for themselves, Bonaparte presented the czar with the sword of Jean Parisot La Valette, the grand master who had defended the island from the Ottoman Turks in the sixteenth century.[76]

The bait was cast and swallowed. Paul was touched by what he regarded as acts of true chivalry on the part of the French leader and responded to them. The two sides were soon busy negotiating a broader agreement to check British ambitions in Europe and beyond. Paul began to limit British trade in Russian ports and recalled troops from Guernsey, where the Russian expeditionary corps was bivouacked after the failed invasion of Holland. He then launched his most significant foreign policy initiative—a union of neutral powers opposing the right alleged by Britain, when at war, to subject the

ships of all neutral powers to search.[77] This initiative offered Paul an opportunity to challenge British interests in the Baltic, burnishing his credentials
as a protector of the weak powers and as the leader of a general alliance of the
European powers.

As Anglo-Russian relations rapidly deteriorated, Emperor Paul ordered
the mobilization of 120,000 soldiers "for the protection of the shores of the
Baltic Sea and for operations against England."[78] In September, he decided
to test the battle-readiness of his forces by conducting extensive military
maneuvers around his estate at Gatchina. Kutuzov and Pahlen were tasked
with planning a mock campaign and leading their respective forces. Kutuzov
was thrilled by the opportunity to leave Vilna and visit the capital, even if
for a short period of time. "I will arrive just before the maneuvers," he wrote
to his wife; "I cannot come earlier, for the Emperor would be displeased."[79]
The prospect of seeing his family both excited and worried him; the children
must have grown up so much, he noted, and wondered, "Will they kiss me
like they used to do?"[80]

At the grand maneuvers at Gatchina, Kutuzov devised a solid plan and
outmaneuvered his opponent. What is more, he managed to get the best of
the emperor himself. As the maneuvers were under way, Paul accompanied
Pahlen and watchfully examined the field of battle through a spyglass. He
was startled to see Kutuzov standing away from the main body of his troops
and attended by just a handful of staff officers. The general had clearly made
a mistake and left himself vulnerable. "I will surely take him captive!" Paul
shouted excitedly; taking command of a squadron of hussars, he led them
furtively along the winding road through the woods. Reaching the edge of
the forest, Paul reconnoitered once more the "enemy" position and observed
Kutuzov, still standing with a few aides-de-camp, exposed and unprotected.
"Still marveling at Kutuzov's blunder," the emperor rushed forward with the
hussars. But just as he made his move, Kutuzov sprang his trap—dozens of
his troops appeared on the opposite side, quickly scattered, and surrounded
the hapless czar. Paul, who just moments earlier could taste the victory, was
dumbfounded but impressed. He went to congratulate the general: "Very
well done! I thought I could take you captive but, it turns out, I am now your
prisoner." Witnesses noted that "despite his approving and kind comments,
Paul could not conceal his vexation and went glum and dispirited back to
Pahlen's troops."[81] Happily, the czar did not hold a grudge for long, and after
the maneuvers were over he praised Kutuzov for demonstrating such mastery
of command, granting him the Order of St. Andrew the First Called, the
highest Russian imperial award, and rewarding his troops with money and
extra rations of liquor and beef.

Despite occasional stumbles, Kutuzov continued to enjoy the confidence
of the emperor, who kept him at Gatchina and entrusted him with new
responsibilities and commands. In late 1800 he assumed command of the

Inspectorates of Ukraine, Brest, and the Dniester—which, in fact, comprised almost all of the southwestern Russian provinces—and became closely involved in the preparations for a new campaign that Paul planned to launch should Britain dare to threaten Russia or its allies. In addition, Kutuzov was tasked with the repatriation of the Russian prisoners of war whom Bonaparte had released. As if his schedule was not sufficiently demanding, the general soon received instructions to return to the Finnish borderland for a conference with King Gustav IV Adolf of Sweden, who had secretly been invited to St. Petersburg for direct negotiations with the Russian czar. Serving as a Russian representative to the king required discretion (he was traveling incognito), a trait for which Kutuzov was now renowned.[82] In early December, Mikhail Illarionovich welcomed Gustav IV Adolf to Friedrikshamn, where he had seen him four years earlier. He then accompanied the king to St. Petersburg, where he attended him during the subsequent diplomatic negotiations and numerous social engagements.[83] Everything went off without a hitch. A week later Paul and Gustav signed an agreement uniting their efforts to protect the Baltic from the British. Kutuzov thus made his contribution to the creation of the League of Armed Neutrality, which comprised Russia, Prussia, Sweden, and Denmark and, embracing the principle of "free ships, free goods," sought to remove the British presence from the Baltic Sea and ensure free navigation in the region.[84]

The combined effects of French and Russian policies produced a virtual continental blockade that placed almost the entire coastline of Europe, from the arctic shorelines of Norway to the ports of Naples, beyond the reach of British commerce. Britain responded to these threats with a mixture of vigorous diplomacy and brute force. In January 1801, the British cabinet approved measures targeting the Russian, Danish, and Swedish merchant marine and sanctioned a naval expedition to the Baltic. Meanwhile, Russia geared up for war as Paul signed a new decree creating three armies along the western borders of the empire. He entrusted the command of the Army of Volhynia to Kutuzov.[85] The Anglo-Russian confrontation seemed imminent.

The war was averted by the assassination of Emperor Paul in a palace coup. The weight of the czar's authority, often capriciously applied, pressed hard upon many Russian nobles. They lamented his unpredictable behavior, decried reforms that fostered Prussian influences, and were anxious over their own future.[86] "The emperor is literally not in his senses," the British ambassador, Charles Whitworth, wrote to London. Many Russian nobles would have concurred; Czartoryski spoke of a "reign of terror," as "all who belonged to the court or came before the Emperor were in a state of continual fear. In going to bed, it was quite uncertain whether during the night some policeman would not come with a kibitka [wagon] to drive you off at once to Siberia."[87] Even the czar's own children, as Sablukov saw it, had "a terror of their father. If he looked in the least angry, they would tremble like aspen leaves." In this atmosphere of fear and suspicion, some Russian nobles concluded that the time had come to attempt a change in the supreme leadership. The conspiracy against the czar was months in the making and involved such leading Russian military and political figures as Peter von der Pahlen, Count Nikita Panin, Counts Platon and Nikolai Zubov, and Generals Levin Bennigsen and Vladimir Yashvil (Iashvili), with the alleged financial support of the British ambassador, whose mistress, Olga Zherebtsova, the Zubovs' sister, channeled the funds and provided a safe space at her house.[88] Even Paul's son, Grand Duke Alexander, has been implicated—aware of the plotting, he said nothing to his father and instead tacitly consented to his overthrow, though he had not supposed that this would be carried out by means of assassination.[89] The conspiracy involved at least sixty and maybe as many as two hundred individuals, quite a number of whom were Kutuzov's comrades, friends, acquaintances, and former colleagues.[90] And yet there is no evidence that he was involved in any of it. General Alexander Langeron, who conversed with many conspirators, categorically said that "Kutuzov was not complicit in the conspiracy."[91] But why?

Contrary to the traditional narrative of Kutuzov "steadfastly" defending the Russian "national way of war," as one Soviet historian proclaimed, and being harassed and harangued for it by the "reactionary" Prussophile emperor, he and the emperor got along well.[92] "Yesterday I was with His Majesty discussing various matters. He asked me to stay for dinner and then told me to regularly have lunch and dinner with him," Kutuzov told his wife in early 1801.[93] The palace *kammerfurier* journal, the official court ledger, reveals that from January through March 1801, Kutuzov visited the royal residences and attended royal eight-person luncheons and twenty-person dinners nearly every day.[94] Paul clearly enjoyed the general's company, talked to him on various matters, and even allowed him to borrow books from his own personal library so "we can discuss them in the evenings," as Kutuzov put it.[95] Moreover, the emperor came to rely on the general to such a degree that when a short time later the new czar, Alexander, and his friends in the "Unofficial Committee" mulled over the dangers of having "all-powerful individuals" in the government, they cited just two prime historical examples: Potemkin under Emperor Catherine and "Kutuzov during the last reign."[96]

Were the claims of Kutuzov valiantly standing up to the despotic ruler correct, he should have been a prime target for the conspirators to recruit. Yet there is no evidence that anyone even considered approaching him. Pahlen, the Zubovs, Panin, and others who were at the center of the plotting must have been apprehensive about involving a man with an inscrutable and manipulative character, "wise as Fabius and shrewd as Philip of Macedon," as one contemporary described him.[97] Peter von der Pahlen, the governor-general of St. Petersburg, who was at the heart of the conspiracy, was already concerned that aside from the ringleaders, the majority of plotters were "young, frivolous, inexperienced," a veritable "throng of featherbrains [*cette tourbe de freluquets*]" who railed against Paul's reforms but had to be plied with alcohol to gather "their still untested courage."[98] In short, Kutuzov was too close to Paul to be fully trusted; involving him in the conspiracy undoubtedly would have raised fears that he would turn against them.

This brings up the question of whether Kutuzov was oblivious to the assassination plot. His Soviet and Russian imperial biographers have skirted the subject, instead focusing on Paul's alleged ill-treatment of Kutuzov and describing the March events without implicating the general in any way.[99] Others have argued that he was in the thick and had played a leading role, both directly and through his wife and daughters, who were socially connected with a number of the conspirators.[100] More recently, historians adopted a more nuanced (but unflattering) view, acknowledging that Kutuzov must have known about the conspiracy but did nothing about it.[101] Considering the number and type of people involved in this conspiracy and the fact that rumors of it had reached even the emperor's ears, Kutuzov must have seen or heard something; his wife, well connected and socially active as she was, must have overheard something. That spring one officer had noticed unusual gatherings at dinner parties hosted by Pahlen, the Zubovs, and others; "there was no general conversation but everywhere *des apartes* [isolated groups] of people, who immediately dispersed if anyone new came to them."[102] The Kutuzovs must also have spotted such groups too or overheard rumors percolating through the salons of St. Petersburg. Nonetheless, there is no hard evidence to back this up. Even if Mikhail Illarionovich had misgivings about a czar who could invite him for a jovial conversation one evening and deride him for levying "too lenient punishments" the very next day, he had enjoyed a successful career during Paul's turbulent reign.[103] He had little reason to take action against the Lord's anointed representative on earth.[104]

Paul had always feared he might end up like his father, and he never felt safe at the Winter Palace. That is why in mid-February 1801, he abandoned that magnificent residence in favor of St. Michael's Castle (Mikhailovskii Zamok), the newly constructed and barely furnished royal complex about a mile away. He could relax behind the imposing walls, wide moats, and drawbridges.[105] The czar was aware of his unpopularity and certainly had a suspicion of impending danger. More than once he remarked about his intention to preempt any threat to his power by carrying out his own "grand coup d'état," even to the point of imprisoning his own sons. His gravest mistake, however, had been to entrust the governor-generalship of St. Petersburg to Count Pahlen, the man at the very heart of the conspiracy. Pahlen tailored what he told Paul as he saw fit, sharing rumors about the conspiracy while also assuring the czar that he was in control of the situation and was working to determine the extent of the plotting. Pahlen extracted from the emperor documents targeting his son, Grand Duke Alexander, and then showed them to the impressionable young man to secure his support for the plot.

The assassination took place on March 23. Paul hosted a dinner reception, as customary. Kutuzov was the only general among the nineteen officials and courtiers invited to the gathering and sat seventh on the right side of the czar.[106] He later noted that "the emperor was in a very good mood and joked around with my eldest daughter [Praskovya], who was present in her capacity of a lady-in-waiting and sat opposite the emperor." The dinner ended late in the wintry evening. As the guests were departing, Paul asked Kutuzov to stay to discuss some matters. "As I responded to his questions, the emperor suddenly glanced into the mirror, which had a defect and distorted the image. He laughed out loud and told me, 'Just look at this weird mirror. It shows me with my neck wrung.'"[107]

Shortly after midnight, as Paul retired to his private apartments, a group of about sixty accomplices, led by Pahlen, Bennigsen, and the Zubov brothers, quietly entered Mikhailovskii Castle. The men—fortified with alcohol to overcome their trepidations—overpowered the guards and rushed into the imperial bedroom, which they found empty. A momentary panic set in; some conspirators began to wail that the emperor had escaped and was probably already rallying the guards to arrest them. But Bennigsen and a few others kept their composure. "The wine is poured and must be drunk," Bennigsen was overheard saying. They searched the room and saw the czar's bare feet beneath a screen in a corner of the room. They dragged Paul out and demanded that he sign an abdication document. He refused and in the ensuing scuffle was badly beaten. It took several man to break him, some banging his head on the floor while others threw a sash around his neck and strangled him; not content with killing the czar, the conspirators kicked and mangled his body.[108]

The grisly deed done, Count Nikolai Zubov and Pahlen went downstairs to break the news to Grand Duke Alexander. "It is all over," Zubov shouted, his face flushed with wine and the excitement of the murder. Alexander was stunned and petrified by what had transpired. Just two hours earlier he had dined genially with his father, for whom he had retained affection despite everything. Now his father lay dead, beaten and strangled, so that he could take possession of a vast empire. "People will say I am my father's murderer," he meekly said before starting to sob. Pahlen roughly brought him to his senses: "That's enough childishness! Go and start your reign!"[109]

CHAPTER II | Walking the Tightrope, 1801–1804

D ESPITE THE SPECTER OF patricide hovering over it, Alexander's ascension was greeted with elation in Russian society, which hoped to leave behind memories of his father's reign. The new monarch was just twenty-three years of age and handsome, though he did have a receding hairline and displayed early signs of shortsightedness. He was intelligent and wanted to please, though behind "the regularity and delicacy of his features and the bright freshness of his complexion," as Sophie de Tisenhaus, comtesse de Choiseul-Gouffier, put it, lurked contradictions.[1] He remained torn between the liberal views impressed upon him by his republican tutor Frédéric-César de La Harpe and the hard reality of being the autocrat of a vast and conservative empire. The familial drama reinforced this duality. Alexander had sought to navigate the contrasting worlds of his father and grandmother. From an early age he became a master of dissembling and secrecy, publicly one thing and privately someone quite different. The manner in which he came to power left deep scars on him, and he was haunted by feelings of guilt. His father's murder loomed over him "like a vulture," commented Adam Czartoryski, his close companion. In a way reminiscent of King Claudius in *Hamlet*, his close friend said, the czar frequently "saw in imagination Paul's mutilated and bloodstained body on the steps of the throne" that he now occupied.[2]

"The fine beginning of Alexander's reign," as Pushkin once put it, was shaped by the March coup.[3] The czar had a mortal dread of the men who had raised him to the throne over his father's dead body. He feared that if he didn't measure up he would meet the same fate as his father.[4] Pahlen thus became a dominant figure in the new regime, controlling the sinews of state power and taking charge of the foreign ministry as he tried to forestall a British attack on Russian shores. According to well-informed eyewitnesses, all government proclamations were signed by him and issued at his direction.

He was not shy about reprimanding the young emperor when he did not do as Pahlen recommended.[5] Alexander, nudged and pushed by Pahlen, pledged to rule "according to the laws and in the spirit of my august grandmother Catherine the Great."[6] He introduced reforms of broadly liberal character, including the abolition of torture and the secret chancellery, the release of thousands of prisoners, a right of return for exiles Paul had condemned without trial, and confirmation of the Charter to the Nobility of 1785 that restated the rights and privileges bestowed upon the Russian nobility.[7] Moreover, the new czar even pledged to grant greater authority to the Senate and to consider a "Charter of the Russian People" that would have introduced constitutional reforms, though their extent still remains a subject of debate. These changes reflected discussions Alexander had had with his confidants about the need for, as it were, a revolution from above, one that would introduce reforms in a managed fashion and give the nation a constitutional government.[8] But the manner in which he was compelled to introduce these reforms—prodded and pressured as he was by the powerful courtiers—resulted in Alexander refusing to carry out the more substantive constitutional designs. He loathed the position he had found himself in, stained with the crime of regicide and dependent on the very men who made no effort to conceal their condescension for him and who, in the words of a Bavarian diplomat, openly called him "an insignificant person, ungrateful, and without character."[9]

Russian high society soon came to rue this situation, as many saw how much power the ringleaders now wielded and the magnitude of the changes they were intending to introduce. The more historically minded of them could look back to and draw parallels with the events of 1730, when a group of grandees compelled Empress Anna Ioanovna to accept conditions on her authority. Such an arrangement had provoked an outcry among the gentry, who denounced what was called "the conspiracy of privy councilors" and pleaded with the empress to retain her autocratic power; it was better to have "one autocrat" than the tyranny of several despotic and powerful families, these noblemen proclaimed. In the end Anna took heed and tore up the conditions; the ringleaders were banished. Seven decades later Emperor Alexander faced a similar challenge to his power from families like the Pahlens, Panins, and Zubovs, all of whom were keen on seeing the Russian autocrat's power curtailed. Their efforts once again evoked public fears of domination by powerful families. The Bavarian diplomat Johann Franz Anton von Olry reported that "the general cry against those guilty of the crime of March [23] 1801 was raised not because the affair was cruel in conception and execution but because the leaders of the conspiracy put to Alexander as a condition *sine qua non* the limitation of the supreme power, and they rather freely pronounced the word 'constitution.'"[10]

Kutuzov was in the middle of these rancorous power struggles, where, in a foreign diplomat's words, "too many undercurrents converged and clashed."[11]

He seems to have found a way of straddling the camps while not overtly supporting either one. The diplomatic mission to Berlin had acquainted him with Panin, who, as we have seen, admired Kutuzov's abilities. He also knew Pahlen, Bennigsen, and other officers from his decades-long military service. And then there was Platon Zubov, to whom he had served morning coffee. Kutuzov, still formally serving as the governor of Lithuania, watched from the sidelines as the conspirators nudged and pushed the czar toward reform, then quarreled and splintered, offering Alexander an opening to move decisively against them. On June 29, Pahlen was summoned to the Winter Palace, where upon his arrival he was handed a decree banishing him from the imperial capital; he meekly submitted to his fate and departed that same night. The very next day, Alexander signed a decree appointing Kutuzov as the military governor of St. Petersburg.

The appointment thus must be considered within the wider political wrangling at the court. Despite his liberal inclinations, the emperor understood the tight restraints of the larger social and political system and came to realize that the autocracy of his predecessors ran deeper in his blood than the liberalism of his education. The only way to impose his vision, liberal or otherwise, was through despotism. The emperor needed reliable people to consolidate control over vital positions in the imperial government. He surrounded himself with a group of young associates—Count Pavel Stroganov, Prince Adam Jerzy Czartoryski, Count Viktor Kochubey, and Count Nikolay Novosiltsev—who formed the Unofficial Committee, a consultative body that informally discussed governmental undertakings and reform plans.[12] Czartoryski recalled that he and the others met two or three times a week, usually after dinner, when the czar would quietly retire and the four liberals joined him to discuss some grand reform—a constitution, abolition of serfdom, and so on. Such counsel was invaluable to the czar, but what he really needed was someone who knew how to run the state machinery.

The emperor knew Kutuzov relatively well, having met him at his father's dinners. He had never really liked the general, finding him too evasive, his manners too old-fashioned, his speech and letters too flowery. He seemed a relic of bygone times. Nonetheless, Alexander was well aware that Kutuzov possessed considerable administrative experience, and, perhaps most crucially, that he was not implicated in the conspiracy.

Kutuzov therefore took charge of St. Petersburg on June 30, 1801. The czar's confidence in him was underscored by the fact that three weeks later he was given command over the Finland Inspectorate and then made the civil governor of St. Petersburg and Vyborg provinces.[13] As if this was not enough responsibility, Kutuzov was also appointed to the military commission that Alexander established in July to review fundamental challenges confronting the Russian military in the wake of a decade of wars and conflicts. Chaired by Grand Duke Constantine, this nine-member commission studied the challenges facing the army—its costs and upkeep, as well as necessary improvements in equipment and uniforms. The result was a series of broad memorandums with proposals for structural and organizational changes.[14]

The commission laid down new rules for the billeting and welfare of units, proposed new musketeer, cuirassier, and dragoon regiments, outlined a major restructuring of the supply depot system, and identified ways of keeping costs under control. The surviving documents show commission members engaged in lively debates on the reforms needed to modernize Russian forces. Particularly sharp disagreements arose over the issue of soldier uniforms. Grand Duke Constantine insisted on keeping the tricorn hats, braids, powder, and hair pomade that his father had introduced. Most members of the commission, including Kutuzov, spoke in favor of adopting more practical uniforms and getting rid of the Pauline innovations, which were impractical and expensive. "They prevent soldiers from doing their jobs and force them to get up early in the morning, without getting enough sleep, to curl each other's braids and apply powder and grease," observed Kutuzov. Drawing upon the principles of the Military Enlightenment, he and the others wanted to create an environment that, as their memorandum stated, "does not deprive soldiers of sleep, strengthens their bodies, and encourages them to patiently endure various labors and assignments inherent to the military service." The call for reforms produced mixed results—Alexander I approved most of the commission's recommendations but sided with his brother's conservative stand on uniforms and equipment.[15]

In the fall of 1802, Kutuzov was relieved of all of his commands. The standard narrative claims that Kutuzov had worked diligently and competently for more than a year when, in the words of historian Paul Zhilin, he was "unexpectedly subjected to Alexander's wrath" and dismissed.[16] Soviet historians were obdurate in insisting that Kutuzov was disgraced without any grounds for it, arguing that his removal reflected the deep-seated resentment that the czar felt toward a distinguished commander who was a constant reminder of his moral failings.[17] Both Alexander and Kutuzov had attended that last fateful dinner at St. Michael's Castle, conversing and laughing with the emperor Paul shortly before his murder. Alexander was supposedly never entirely convinced Kutuzov knew nothing about the conspiracy. "Though tact might ensure silence, memory imposed a barrier between the two men," concluded British historian Alan Palmer, one of many Western historians who echoed tenets of the Soviet historiography. Leontii Rakovskii went as far as to claim that Alexander never looked at Kutuzov directly but made a point of staring at his nonfunctioning eye to escape the general's penetrating glare.[18] A guilt-ridden Alexander evidently spent months fretting over what

Kutuzov thought of him, and the weight of this anxiety finally made him decide to rid himself of this painful reminder of the past.

Such claims are preposterous. Where was the czar's angst when he was choosing whom to entrust such important positions to, just three months after his father's death? Why would the "Autocrat of All the Russias" care about what one of his generals thought of him? More crucially, why would he disgrace Kutuzov over unsubstantiated claims but continue to employ actual participants of the conspiracy? Bennigsen, who continued to serve as the governor-general of Lithuania from 1801 to 1806, apparently elicited no such anguished memories in the czar. Some historians have argued that Kutuzov's appointment as the governor of St. Petersburg was part of Alexander's attempt to make the general "more dependent on the monarchical largesse and thereby to silence him" about the events at St. Michael's Castle.[19] This daft reasoning ignores the fact that Paul's murder was a loosely kept secret in Russian high society.

A careful reading of documents reveals a more complicated picture. There is no doubt that Kutuzov worked assiduously in his multiple posts. Every morning he navigated the usual route to the military governor's mansion on the Moika, between the Krasnyi and Sinii bridges, where he spent the day slogging through the never-ending administrative morass. As the military governor of the imperial capital and governor of two neighboring provinces, he exercised immense authority, managing a vast bureaucracy, maintaining law and order, and tending to the welfare of hundreds of thousands of residents. He was responsible for commanding the troops in and around the capital; ensuring that the imperial capital was adequately supplied with provisions; examining an unending stream of public complaints, appeals, and supplications; supervising the gathering of the harvest in the provinces; managing local charities, hospitals, and orphanages; and supervising theater groups.[20] The list was endless. To rein in rampant gambling in the capital, Kutuzov required officials to visit each residence and warn residents of severe punishments for hosting any gambling events or tolerating them on their property.[21] His readiness to uphold the law was demonstrated in August 1801 when he investigated an aristocrat for abusing her power and mistreating her serfs. Based on his findings, the czar deprived the landowner of the estate and approved prosecuting her "for her cruelty that is contrary to the laws and humanity."[22]

Despite his prior gubernatorial experience, however, Kutuzov was having trouble keeping up. In 1801, he turned fifty-four years old; four decades of military and diplomatic service had left his health fragile. He regularly complained of ailments that prevented him from carrying out his responsibilities. He was absent for days; his grasp of details slipped occasionally. Despite his efforts, criminal activity continued unabated in the capital and soon garnered public attention. In early 1802 a carriage struck and seriously injured a visiting foreigner in broad daylight on one of the central squares of St. Petersburg. A group of assailants roughed up a grandee near St. Michael's Castle. "His Majesty was very displeased with the activities of the St. Petersburg police," observed Evgraf Komarovskii. "Neither of these incidents had been solved."[23] These occurrences raised questions about Kutuzov's ability to ensure safety and order.[24] However, it would be a mistake to suppose that these minor issues were the sole cause of Kutuzov's dismissal. The emperor himself was partly responsible for having assigned so many tasks to a single individual.

We do not know what Kutuzov, who was always circumspect about his inner thoughts, really thought of the new emperor. In official correspondence and in public discussions, he was, of course, deferential to the czar. But the documents show that Kutuzov was worried about the direction in which the Russian monarchy was heading. In a letter written in April 1801, for example, Kutuzov took issue with the czar's decision to pardon the Polish nobles who had taken up arms against Russia during the Second Polish Partition in 1794. He was particularly worried by Alexander's pledge to recompense these individuals and pointed out that the property of these "rebels" had been already confiscated and given to Russian nobles.[25] Kutuzov was among these beneficiaries and was clearly alarmed by the prospect of his ownership being questioned. He had grown conservative, always expressing his disgust at the revolutionary changes unfolding in France and Poland and stressing the dangers that resulted from demolishing traditional institutions in the name of abstract concepts of liberty and rights.[26] The prospect of constitutional reforms, which Alexander's companions advocated, alarmed him. The new regime had inaugurated a generational conflict between Catherine's old guard and the young sovereign and his cohort of likeminded companions. Philip Weigel (Vigel'), whose memoirs provide insight into this period, pointed out that under Empress Catherine, "the aristocracy consisted of everyone who . . . could maintain pleasant conversations and be well-mannered." Alexander surrounded himself with a "coterie" of youthful companions who "cared not for a high rank, ancient princely name, or court position."[27] These younger people ridiculed the outdated looks and manners of the old-timers, with their constant bowing, ornate compliments, and endless deference. In a thousand little ways Kutuzov revealed his age and his preference for the golden years of Catherine the Great. Old expressions salted his speech, and his bearing and manners were judged to be out of vogue. Kutuzov was still an instinctive sycophant to power. "The emperor dislikes him for his excessive submissiveness," the Sardinian envoy later observed about Kutuzov's comportment.

Kutuzov struggled to adjust to this new reality, especially as the *novi homines* did their best to sideline the old hands. The lengthy memorandum that the Bavarian chargé d'affaires in St. Petersburg prepared in August 1802

contains a telling detail in this regard. It speaks about the tug-of-war between the proponents and opponents of constitutional changes and mentions
that "at this time people holding the highest position came under increased
attacks, especially Procurator General Bekleshov [and] Governor Kutuzov."[28]
Kutuzov was deeply embedded in the patronage culture. For him, power
was ingrained in personal connections; those seeking it had to abide by established norms for polite discourse, manners, and interaction. Even while
he was absent from the court for extended periods, Kutuzov was constantly
jostling for patronage, nurturing old relations and cultivating new ones. As
the governor of St. Petersburg, he found himself maintaining a delicate equilibrium between upholding the authority of the new emperor, who was keen
on introducing changes, and not burning bridges with the patronage network that had served him well.

Alexander remained deeply concerned about the potential threat the disgraced conspirators might pose to him. This apprehension only increased
when he received Kutuzov's reports about the reconciliation between Panin
and the Zubovs; the old conspirators had begun meeting and talking again.
He instructed Kutuzov to monitor these noblemen. This was a very delicate
task, which the governor, a patrician through and through, found disagreeable, if not outright humiliating. Kutuzov had to balance political factions.
"By his very nature, he could not belong to the conspirators or get involved
in some sort of group scheme," Oleg Mikhailov, the author of a historical
novel about the general, aptly observed. "All of his life he was a plotter for a
faction, but one that consisted of just himself."[29] The first year of Alexander's
reign accentuated this side of the general's personality. Kutuzov was adept at
navigating court politics, where his eloquence and "extraordinary cunning"
served him well.[30] But even the most consummate of courtiers eventually
overplay their hands. Kutuzov's turn came in the spring of 1802.

When Alexander ordered him to start monitoring the conspirators, Kutuzov
did it on his own terms. His police agents trailed the former conspirators,
as the emperor desired, but in such a way that these grandees became fully
aware of it. Through the winter of 1802, the Unofficial Committee discussed
more than once the "circumstances of the surveillance of Zubov and Panin,"
as stated in its meeting minutes, and complained about the fact that the
police showed incredible "ineptitude" and "lack of discernment" in their
operations. The situation became so absurd, complained the committee
members, that Zubov's footmen were seen making fun of the police agents
following behind them in an open carriage. Such blatant snooping enraged
Valerian Zubov, brother of Platon and Nikolai, who complained about it
to the emperor, who had to pretend that he was completely unaware of it
and promised to take measures to end police shadowing.[31] The committee

clearly understood that this was not simply a matter of the incompetence of individual agents. They noted that the military governor's own secret police was undermining the work of regular law enforcement, which was also involved in surveillance operations; it was even caught passing false information.[32]

Kutuzov's attempt to ride two horses at once was becoming a political liability, especially because he enjoyed considerable authority in the capital (like Pahlen did in the final days of Paul's reign) and cultivated close relations with the chief of the secret police, Fedor Aegerström, who, the Unofficial Committee believed, was doing the governor's bidding.[33] The members of the committee may have thought it time to rein in the governor, who was becoming too crafty for his own good.

In the matter of Kutuzov's sacking, no previous study has consulted the meeting minutes of the Unofficial Committee. Reviewing these transcripts, however, it becomes clear that the governor's dismissal was the culmination of a long process of discussion and debate, one in which Emperor Alexander and committee members engaged for months. Just six months after Kutuzov had assumed his responsibilities, the Unofficial Committee was already considering ways to remove him from power. During the January 15, 1802, meeting, Count Kochubey, who had replaced Kutuzov as the ambassador to the Ottoman Empire eight years earlier, spoke of the urgent need to dismiss the governor and, according to the meeting minutes, characterized him in "a very unfavorable manner." Why had Alexander appointed this general to such an important position? the Committee members wondered. The answer lay in the fact that there had been six coups since 1725, and the Russian czar was desperate to avoid any further challenges. Kutuzov was, if nothing else, a believer in the status quo. Fedor Rostopchin, who otherwise loathed the general, admired his ability to "never complain and, through intriguing and courting, to ensure that he was always employed at the very moment when everyone discounted him."[34] Alexander himself admitted as much when he told the Unofficial Committee that he agreed with them that the governor had to go but could not bring himself to fire him because he had no one better to put in his place, and that in the current political climate he could not afford to lose an experienced administrator like Kutuzov.[35] Just three days later, underscoring the urgency of this matter, the committee once again discussed removing Kutuzov from power and even considered several candidates as his replacement. Ultimately it deemed none of them reliable enough to manage the situation, which, as far as Emperor Alexander was concerned, was so unpredictable that "he could not vouch for what would happen within twenty-four hours" if a lesser man replaced Kutuzov at the helm of the imperial capital. This was a startling statement, accentuating the depth of anxiety that prevailed at the top of the Russian government in the months after Paul's murder.

The Unofficial Committee's efforts to remove Kutuzov stalled in March 1802 when St. Petersburg was shocked by the news of the brutal rape and murder of Madame Aurajo, the wife of a successful Portuguese merchant. She was renowned for her exquisite beauty almost as much as she was for her prodigal lifestyle.[36] Araujo had been having a passionate affair with Lieutenant General Karl Fedorovich Baur, who was known for being a rake but who was also a close friend of Grand Duke Constantine Pavlovich.[37] At one of the parties, the grand duke saw Madame Aurajo and was smitten by her beauty. Baur, scoundrel that he was, agreed to yield his mistress to him, but Aurajo herself would have none of it. The grand duke, enraged, plotted revenge.[38] On March 22, Aurajo received a message from her lover to join him for an assignation. When she arrived the grand duke was there with a dozen or so horse guards, who proceeded to assault her. Beaten and repeatedly raped, Aurajo suffered such severe injuries that she died later that day. "This was an unheard-of atrocity," wrote an appalled contemporary. "Everywhere in the city one could hear people discussing this incident and expressing their profound indignation."[39]

Stunned by his brother's behavior and the extent of the public uproar, Alexander rushed to cover up the crime and, in the words of Countess Edling, "managed to appease the victim's family."[40] The public was harder to mollify. The czar was forced to issue a special proclamation promising to conduct a thorough investigation. The municipal police were under the overall supervision of Kutuzov, who seems to have been unwilling to cover up the grand duke's crime. This raised the prospects of a public relations disaster for the imperial family. To forestall it, Alexander declared that the Aurajo case was too important to be entrusted to the municipal police (and thus to Kutuzov) and created a special investigative commission, which concluded that Araujo died of natural causes.[41] To conciliate the public, General Baur was dismissed from the service for tarnishing the uniform, but once the public interest died down he was reinstated. Just a week after the event, the Unofficial Committee discussed Kutuzov's "public confrontation with the grand duke," as it was called, and was concerned that removing him from the position was no longer possible, for it would be construed as an attempt to cover up royal misconduct. They had to wait for a more opportune moment.[42]

One arrived only weeks later. St. Petersburg was full of young officers who spent much of their free time pursuing vice. One of them was Lieutenant A. Shubin of the Life Guard Semeyonovskii Regiment, a swaggering junior officer who found himself deep in gambling debts and came up with what he thought was an easy scheme for settling them, and more. One summer evening, after a gunshot was heard at the Summer Garden, the police soon found Shubin, bleeding from a wounded hand and claiming that he had uncovered a conspiracy against Emperor Alexander. The authorities rushed to warn the czar, who had just returned from the coronation ceremony in

Moscow. Alexander had been fretting about his safety for months and was now confronted with what seemed to be tangible proof. He was infuriated by the police's failure to detect this potentially serious threat and demanded to see the governor. Kutuzov knew too well how dangerous it was to see an irate autocrat, and so he "pretended to be unwell," suggesting they meet in the morning.[43] Alexander was fuming. He appointed a special commission, led by Field Marshal General Count Mikhail Kamenski, to investigate the incident, and ordered Adjutant General Evgraf Komarovskii to take charge of the St. Petersburg police and root out abuses and malfeasance.

The following morning Kutuzov realized the gravity of the mistake he had committed. In vain did he argue that this entire incident was nothing but a "phantom"—under interrogation Shubin admitted that he had made everything up, hoping to get a reward from the emperor.[44] Komarovskii's inquiry revealed glaring deficiencies in police administration, including understaffed police outposts and officials who turned a blind eye to gambling and dueling. The new police chief made quick and decisive changes and, much to Kutuzov's embarrassment, solved a number of crimes. Reading Komarovskii's reports, Alexander declared this was unacceptable.[45] He must have been relieved. Not only was the conspiracy a false alarm, but it provided him with the public cover he needed to fire the governor.

On September 1, 1802, Kutuzov received an order to step down from his position. Just days later, the emperor signed additional orders removing him from his remaining posts as provincial governor and inspector.[46] The imperial disgrace was thus swift and complete.

Kutuzov chose to leave the imperial capital and travel to his estates in northwestern Ukraine; his family remained in St. Petersburg to plead for his cause at the court. Though he formally requested a one-year leave from active duty, he ultimately spent three times that in exile, devoting himself to the management of the estates. In the wake of the Polish Partitions, as we have seen, Catherine had confiscated properties of the "rebel" Polish nobles to reward her stalwarts. The repossessed *folwarks* or serfdom-based farms and agricultural enterprises could be of vast size, and Kutuzov was among those who had been handsomely rewarded for his service to the Russian crown. He had received nine *folwarks* and the township of Raigorodok, in the historical regions of Polesye and Volhynia.[47] The total number of serfs that Kutuzov owned on his estates probably exceeded 15,000.

Yet Kutuzov always seemed short on money. Raising a family as large as his involved considerable expenses, and his finances were constantly sapped by the extravagant lifestyle expected of them in St. Petersburg. While his older daughter was married and by this point had five children (and would go on to produce more offspring over the next decade, creating the largest branch of

Kutuzov's descendants), his four other daughters were of marriageable age, or close to it; beautiful, graceful, and well connected, they drew ample numbers of suitors.[48] In 1802 and 1803, two of them accepted offers of marriage: first, Kutuzov's beloved "Lizanka," Elisabeth, fell in love with Berend Gregor Ferdinand von Tiesenhausen, a young officer of His Imperial Majesty's Suite. Then Anna was betrothed to Nikolai Zakharovich Khitrovo, a guard officer who also served as one of the imperial adjutants. Their weddings were lavishly celebrated and drew a cross section of the Russian elite; despite his issues with Kutuzov, the czar himself attended them, as did the czarina and the grand duchesses. The rapid succession of new grandchildren (five were born in 1799–1803) and extravagant nuptial celebrations meant new debts for the family. Kutuzov's letters are replete with references to financial woes.

Kutuzov's situation was not unique. Étienne Dumont, a Frenchman who visited Russia about this time, was struck by the penury of the Russian nobles. He suggested that one reason for their impoverishment was that they rarely took the trouble to visit and properly manage their rural estates. Had they followed the example of their European brethren, he argued, they could easily have increased their income, improving both their own situation and that of their hapless serfs.[49] Kutuzov's exile thus had a silver lining, offering him an opportunity to visit estates that he had formally owned for years but on which he never actually stepped foot. He could examine how they were run and see if more revenue could be gained from them.

Kutuzov was startled to discover the extent to which his estates were mismanaged. Left to their own devices for years, estate managers ran amok, abusing power and embezzling revenue. The magnitude of their negligence and corruption stunned him: "I think my current illness is caused by my realization of how godlessly they have been stealing from me [all these years]." He had "numerous disagreements and quarrels" with managers, most of whom he had to fire and replace with more experienced and, he hoped, more honest ones. Then there were the "frequent troubles" with neighbors and renters over land ownership rights, payments, and other issues.[50] He was clearly interested in agricultural modernization and was willing to extend a helping hand to his peasants, but at no point did he ever consider emancipating serfs. Instead, he tried all sorts of ways to raise additional revenues from his estates—introducing new crops, building breweries, launching saltpeter manufacturing, and selling timber to the navy. Few of them proved to be as successful as Kutuzov hoped they would be.[51] He did manage to increase revenue from the estates and, in the years to come, regularly sent large sums to support his family in St. Petersburg. "I am sending you a thousand rubles, my dear, and will send you more as soon as I can afford it," reads one of his many missives to his wife. Yet there were hurdles and challenges too. Turnover was small, and access to the market uneven. Kutuzov frequently complained about bad weather and poor harvests, the disease killing cattle and peasants lacking essentials, including straw, hay, and grain. "A lot of money is needed to fix all of this," he observed dolefully in the spring of 1804.[52] He worked doggedly, but every time he made progress, a setback followed. After concluding a lucrative deal on the sale of potash, he discovered that one of his laborers had managed to sneak inside the manorial house and steal 2,200 gold coins—an enormous sum—before heading across the border into the Hapsburg domains. "I am despondent," he told his wife. "Why did I deserve such a misfortune!?"[53] A year later, a massive fire ravaged the township of Raigorodok, which Kutuzov had been expanding into a commercial hub. The conflagration claimed "forty-five Jewish taverns [korchma]" and dozens of stalls and shops. "This is a huge adversity for the local economy," the general wrote to his family. "Instead of growing it, as I planned to, I will now have to rebuild all that got destroyed."[54]

Kutuzov's repeated requests to be reinstated in the army were all rebuffed. He tried to manipulate his patronage network to secure a new appointment, telling his wife, "If you happen to see [Peter] Volkonskii or [Fedor] Uvarov, do mention this to them."[55] But even his associates could not convince the emperor to reinstate Kutuzov, though they did manage to include him in the list of senior officers invited to participate in the military maneuvers near St. Petersburg in the summer of 1804. Kutuzov must have been overjoyed. Rushing to the capital, he performed with his customary skill and even earned a commendation from his leadership. And yet the trip also made it clear that the czar was still wary of him; no appointment materialized, and Kutuzov was forced to return to his estates.[56]

The monotony and seclusion of life in a remote village deeply affected him. He suffered spells of depression, sinking into melancholia. His letters reveal a sense of weariness, disgust with the constant rush of affairs, and a feeling of having sacrificed so many things that made life pleasant. And for what? "It is a dull business trying to put the estate back on its feet when everything is in such utter ruin," he lamented. "Upon my word, sometimes I feel like throwing up everything in despair and resigning myself to the will of God."[57] A visit to his younger brother Semen only made things worse—he found him frail, confused, even delirious, constantly talking about an imaginary pipe. "I got mad at him and told him there was no such thing," wrote Kutuzov, who must have pondered his own old age as he confronted his brother's senility.[58] Old wounds bothered him more than ever before. His legs, ravaged by rheumatism, could hardly bear his expanding girth. His head constantly throbbed, leaving him unable to function. The eye that the Ottoman bullet had damaged began to react painfully to light. Local doctors had tried various treatments, but the side effects proved to be worse than the condition.

Suffering from loneliness and poor health, Kutuzov sank into anguish, dredging up memories of his old comrades in arms, reminiscing about past military exploits, and gloomily contemplating the future. He was worried about ending his days in a forgotten village, disgraced and abandoned. "I am haunted by the fear of spending my old age in penury and want, and of having labored for so long, encountered so much danger, and suffered such wounds, all in vain. This wretched thought keeps distracting me from everything and often leaves me petrified he wrote to his wife."[59] As he marked his fifty-seventh birthday in September 1804, he must have wished for a glimmer of a better future. The new year would grant his wish.

PART III

| Confronting Napoleon, 1805

After seizing power in a coup in November 1799, Napoleon moved quickly to consolidate his power in France and to strengthen French positions in western Europe. The Treaty of Lunéville, which ended the war between France and Austria in 1801, had extended the French frontiers to the Rhine River, resulting in the removal of numerous German imperial knights and the start of the Imperial Recess, which reshaped the future of Germany. Dozens of German polities disappeared; some 3 million people saw their allegiances switch from one ruler to another. Bavaria, Baden, Württemberg, and Prussia gained considerable land and power, while France vastly increased its sway in central Europe. Building upon his success in Germany, Napoleon helped reorganize the Swiss Confederation, where he assumed the title of "mediator," and then consolidated his positions in Italy, annexing parts of northern Italy. Facing the growth of the French imperial presence in Europe and a challenge to Russia's interests, Emperor Alexander moved to negotiate treaties with Prussia and Denmark to secure the status quo in northwestern Europe.[1] Relations between Russia and France remained tense.

The spring of 1804 marked the turning point. The discovery of a royalist conspiracy against Napoleon led to the arrest of Louis-Antoine-Henri de Bourbon-Condé, Duc d'Enghien, a prince of the Bourbon royal house who resided in the neighboring Principality of Baden. Despite the lack of evidence or of any witnesses, d'Enghien was found guilty and shot shortly after midnight on March 21. In the words of one keen observer, the d'Enghien affair was worse than a "crime," it was a "blunder."[2] Emperor Alexander was infuriated by the execution of a prince of royal blood but even more so by the flagrant violation by the French of the sovereignty of Baden, whose ruler was, in fact, the Russian emperor's grandfather-in-law.[3] A Russian diplomat noted that it "produced a general feeling of shock and indignation which those who did not witness it could not easily realize."[4] This was not a minor incident to be disregarded, and it did not occur in isolation. For Russia, it was yet another manifestation of the French readiness to willfully break existing international rules and norms, and it demonstrated a lack of respect for Russian interests in Europe. It was time to make a public stand against Napoleon.

The Russian court responded by going into mourning for the unfortunate duke and sending protests to Paris and to the Imperial Diet, the general assembly of the Imperial Estates of the Holy Roman Empire, of which Baden was part. The latter caused considerable consternation among the German states, which could not entirely ignore the Russian sovereign's demands yet did not want to alienate their powerful French neighbor. Ultimately, the German states reached a compromise, by which the elector of Baden claimed that the French had given him satisfactory explanations for their actions and asked that the matter be dropped in light of possible repercussions; the Diet quickly approved this request. Russia was naturally displeased by the feebleness of the German response, and its anger turned into outright fury upon receiving the French response to its note of protest. Napoleon advised Alexander to mind his own business. "The complaint which Russia presents today leads one to ask," the French emperor declared, "whether if, when England was planning the assassination of Paul I, one had known that the authors of the plot were to be found within a few leagues of the frontier, one would not have hastened to seize them."[5]

This was an astonishingly blunt answer. Its allusion, in public, to Emperor Alexander's supposed involvement in the murder of his father was impossible for the proud sovereign of "All the Russias" to ignore. In the words of a Russian court historian, this was "impertinence" that could not be ignored. In April 1804, Emperor Alexander raised, for the first time, the possibility of a war against France at the meeting of the Council of State and made Austria a secret offer of alliance to join forces against France. The Austrian government showed interest, though it also expressed reservations about the Russian offer, fearing that once it had committed to the alliance, Russia might make an advantageous deal with France, leaving Vienna in the lurch.[6] Alexander was a bit more successful in his overtures to Prussia, entering into an understanding with King Frederick William on preserving north German neutrality in case of continued French aggrandizement. Yet in what one historian has described as a policy of "the hedgehog and the possum," Prussia remained uncertain of how assertive it should be with regard to France. Thus, what Russians considered a defensive alliance aimed at France was anything but that for the Prussians.[7]

Russian efforts to challenge Napoleon were heartily welcomed in Britain, where Prime Minister William Pitt, well known for his hawkish stance toward France, returned to office in the spring of 1804. Unlike his predecessor,

Pitt pursued a more assertive policy on the continent and could not but rejoice upon receiving the news of the French ambassador's departure from St. Petersburg, marking an effective rupture in Franco-Russian relations and opening a door for a possible European alliance against France. The proclamation of the French Empire in May and the subsequent coronation of Napoleon in December 1804 only further deepened the ongoing diplomatic crisis, as the European powers were compelled to adjust to the new political reality in Europe. Napoleon's decision to assume an imperial title seemed to reveal a grand design for the revival of the empire of Charlemagne, which had covered much of western and central Europe. This naturally caused great consternation across Europe, but especially in St. Petersburg and Vienna. For Emperor Alexander, already embittered by the d'Enghien affair, the proclamation elevated the impudent French upstart while threatening to further undermine Russian interests in Germany. For Austria, the threat was especially acute because Napoleon was clearly challenging its standing not only within the Holy Roman Empire but also on the Italian peninsula, where Napoleon was proclaimed a king in early 1805.

Yet neither power acted. Holy Roman Emperor (Kaiser) Francis felt compelled to recognize Napoleon in this new capacity, though only after receiving assurances from France that he would be recognized as hereditary emperor of Austria and that his imperial title would take precedence over the French one.[8] Austria's decision once again to compromise with France greatly annoyed Russia, whose ruler perceived Napoleon's new title as a "new usurpation" that demonstrated his "boundless ambition to extend his domination still further beyond its current limits."[9] Alexander, joined by the king of Sweden, refused to recognize the new emperor, pressuring the Ottoman Empire to do likewise.

Throughout the fall of 1804 and the spring of 1805, diplomats from various European powers shuttled back and forth to forge a new alliance against France. Building an anti-French coalition was a challenging process, with the principal powers—Britain, Russia, Austria, Sweden—distrusting one another's ambitions, and some expressing reservations about the practicality of forming a new coalition when France had so soundly beaten the previous ones. The Austrians and Russians were still smarting from the experiences of the Second Coalition War in 1799, when the two countries repeatedly quarreled and failed to strike a decisive blow against the French. Archduke Charles, one of the senior Austrian commanders and the younger brother of Francis II, was not convinced of the practicality of relying on Russian help in the light of events in Italy and Switzerland six years earlier. He was particularly critical of the lack of overall command over the coalition forces and was worried that the allies would repeat the same mistakes in the new war. He gloomily warned, "In this land war, England can lose money, Russia people, but Austria stands to lose both, and even entire provinces."[10]

Despite their mutual concerns and suspicions, Russia and Austria signed a treaty of cooperation in St. Petersburg on November 6, 1804, with Alexander promising to deploy more than 100,000 men to support Austria against France.[11] Five months later Russia signed an agreement with Britain to remove the French presence in Holland, Switzerland, Italy, and parts of Germany, and to "reestablish the peace and equilibrium in Europe."[12] The Russian diplomats successfully negotiated treaties of cooperation with Sweden, Naples, and the Ottoman Empire but were unable to convince Prussian king Frederick Wilhelm III to break his policy of nonalignment and join the coalition. Prussia's monarchy continued to waver vis-à-vis France and pursued a steady policy of neutrality.[13]

The coalition identified several objectives that it hoped to achieve. Many of these dealt with reversing territorial changes France had made over the previous decade. The coalition wanted to push the French out of Hanover and northern Germany, the reestablishment of Swiss and Dutch independence, restoration of Piedmont-Sardinia, and complete removal of French forces from Italy. These were ambitious goals, and the allies did not stop there. They also sought "the establishment of an order of things in Europe that effectively guarantees the security and independence of the different states and presents a solid barrier against future usurpations."[14] Indeed, the treaty contained many references to "tranquility," "peace," "security," and other high-minded concepts that the powers believed were needed to set up a "federative system" that would maintain peace and stability in Europe.

The coalition plans for the campaign called for unprecedented Europe-wide coordination of operations. At the start of the summer of 1805, Emperor Alexander dispatched Adjutant-General Ferdinand Karl Friedrich Wintzingerode to Vienna to discuss logistical and operational details for the impending campaign. On July 16, the allies signed a comprehensive agreement outlining what needed to be done for the war.[15] They agreed to mobilize well over half a million soldiers across four major theaters of war, with Russia committing more than 180,000 soldiers to support Austria, and another 100,000 men stationed in garrisons close to the imperial borders.[16] In the southeast, General Alexander Tormasov's corps of 20,000 men was stationed to keep an eye on the Ottomans, who could exploit Russian preoccupation with Napoleon to attempt to regain some of the lost territories. Russian General Boris (Maurice) de Lacy was on his way to take charge of the 20,000 men for an Anglo-Russian expedition to Naples.

Hundreds of miles away in the north, General Peter Tolstoy was to lead a corps of more than 15,000 men to Stralsund, where he expected to meet up with the Swedish army for a joint campaign to Hanover. More crucially, two Russian armies were formed in the western borderlands. General Ivan Mikhelson was given the task of supervising the largest of these forces—some 90,000 men—designed both to exert pressure on Prussia and to conduct operations against France. This army group comprised General Levin Bennigsen's Army of the North (almost 50,000 men), which was stationed between Taurrogen and Grodno in an effort to nudge the Prussians out of their neutrality (forcibly if need be), and Friedrich Wilhelm Buxhöwden's Army of Volhynia (40,000 men), deployed around Brest-Litovsk and preparing for a campaign through Bohemia or Saxony.[17] During negotiations in July 1805, the Russian and Austrian sides agreed that at least 50,000 Russian troops—alternatively identified as the "First Army" (Pervaya Armiya) or the "Army of Podolia" (Podol'skaya Armiya)—would be sent to Bavaria to support Austrians in their campaign against Napoleon in southern Germany.[18] The Austrians intended to threaten Bavaria, whose ruler, Maximilian Joseph, remained closely aligned with Napoleon, and hoped that other German states, including Württemberg and Baden, would also peel away from France.

The coalition strategy faced a number of problems. Probably the biggest was its grandiose nature—undertaking to challenge France across the entire European continent. Coordinating operations over such vast distances was impossible, condemning allies to isolated actions that depended on local factors. The plan also greatly underestimated how quickly the French army would be able to react and march from its current encampments on the Atlantic coast to south-central Europe. Moreover, the coalition diplomacy had failed to secure the support of the German states, many of which, in fact, hoped to acquire territory and enhance their standing by siding against the Habsburgs, rather than joining them. Nor could the coalition hope to gain the advantage of surprise. Military preparations on such a grand scale could not escape the keen eyes and ears of Napoleon's spies.[19]

The Austrian leadership remained divided about the army's readiness for war and the strategy to be employed. Expecting Napoleon to go on the offensive in northern Italy, they tasked Austria's largest army under its most capable commander—Archduke Charles, with some 95,000 men—with reclaiming Austrian positions in Italy, while a smaller army was kept in southern Germany. The Austrian choice of the two commanders to lead the latter force proved to be unfortunate. Archduke Ferdinand Karl Joseph of Austria-Este, the twenty-four-year-old grandson of Empress Maria Theresa, was a recent graduate of the military academy in Wiener Neustadt and had neither combat experience nor practice in leading a multinational force. For this reason the more experienced Karl Freiherr Mack von Leiberich was appointed as chief of the quartermaster general staff and aide to the archduke, wielding effective command over the Austrian forces in southern Germany. The fifty-three-year-old Mack had been born in Bavaria to a lower-middle-class family and had steadily worked his way up through the ranks. He had served in the Austrian military since 1769 and seen action in several wars. However, his performance during the French Revolutionary Wars had left much to be desired; he was taken into French captivity in 1799, causing

British admiral Horatio Nelson, who had seen his performance (or lack thereof) in southern Italy, to go as far as to caution senior members of the British government, "Let not General Mack be employed, for I knew him at Naples to be a Rascal, a Scoundrel, and a Coward."[20] This was rather unfair. Mack was no less courageous than other Austrian leaders and had tried improving the Austrian military, though his reforms were ill-conceived and failed to bring about the desired improvements. Mack's persuasiveness, lively imagination, and self-assurance served him well, as he outmaneuvered his rival, Archduke Charles, perhaps the most talented Austrian commander and the leader of the Austrian peace party. This allowed Mack to cultivate connections with the senior members of the Habsburg court, including Foreign Minister Johann Ludwig Joseph Graf von Cobenzl, who continued to delegate important tasks to him. None of the general's commissions was more important than the command of the Austrian army in Germany, a task for which he proved unprepared.[21]

⚊ ⚎⚎⚎ ⚊

In late summer 1805, Kutuzov received the news that Emperor Alexander had selected him to command "the First Army" in the looming war against France.[22] He seemed a surprising choice. The memory of their past discords and frictions was still fresh. Kutuzov was not Alexander's first choice; the emperor would have preferred Jean Moreau, the brilliant French general and Napoleon's rival who lived in exile in the United States. But the offer letter sent to Moreau took months to be delivered, and the choice of commander in chief could not wait.[23] Kutuzov's name would have stood out in the list of readily available candidates. He was one of the most senior officers in the Russian military—in the seniority lists, he was ranked eighth among twenty-eight full generals in 1805—with a distinguished military record that could not be ignored even if the emperor were still personally ill-disposed toward him. In the public's eye he commanded respect—despite his having been sacked—and he had considerable diplomatic experience, a crucial attribute and one that Alexander needed to have in a commander leading the army that would conduct operations alongside other allied forces.[24] The last coalition war had revealed major problems in Austro-Russian relations, confounded by the fact that Suvorov, a brilliant military commander, lacked diplomatic finesse and indeed seemed to enjoy rubbing the allies the wrong way. Both sides were, therefore, keen to avoid past mistakes. The Russian emperor wanted to make sure that his commander possessed sufficient practical experience, acute military judgment, and keen understanding of diplomatic subtleties. Kutuzov was the only Russian general who satisfied such requirements. Whatever personal qualms he may have had, Alexander was a pragmatic man who overcame his personal feelings and selected Kutuzov because of, as he noted in a letter, "your prudence and zeal, as well as your talents, combined with your gallantry and recognized commitment to the glory of our Fatherland."

In August 1805, therefore, Kutuzov left his estate and hurried to St. Petersburg. He met the emperor and visited the Military Field Chancellery to receive briefings on the military and diplomatic situation. Among the numerous documents he examined were the lengthy imperial instructions—some two dozen handwritten pages—that outlined the mission he was to undertake in the new conflict. This document demonstrates Emperor Alexander's preoccupation with diplomacy and coalition matters and the emphasis he placed on Kutuzov's judgment. The guidelines contained twenty-three articles that first provided a synopsis of the situation in Europe, where "political tranquility is being threatened with each passing day because of the gradual collapse of the balance of power between various powers." France had become too dominant. French expansion had to be contained by force since "neither suggestions nor concessions or threats" had proved to be effective in restraining Napoleon. Alexander briefly explained the strategic plan that the coalition had drafted and noted that one of the immediate tasks was to force the Prussian monarchy out of its neutrality either peacefully or forcibly, should the Hohenzollern king refuse to grant the Russians the right of passage through his realm. The Russian emperor understood that close cooperation with the Austrians was the key to success in the war against France.

The second article of the instructions specified that Kutuzov would be subordinate to "the [Holy] Roman Emperor, Archduke Charles, or one of the princes of the blood" and was to follow their orders "faithfully" even if the Austrians decided to divert the Russian forces away from Germany to another theater of war. This is an important provision because it not only underscores Alexander's commitment to the unity of command in order to achieve the coalition's key goals but also challenges the long-standing claim by Russian historians that the Austrians appointed Archduke Ferdinand in a deliberate effort to deny Kutuzov seniority of rank over General Mack and limit his freedom of action. There was nothing sinister about the Austrian decision. Kaiser Francis exercised nominal command over all Austrian armies, while the archdukes represented the imperial authority. Since Archduke Charles was in Italy, Archduke Ferdinand was a natural choice for the German theater. The Russian side was fully aware of it. In fact, Alexander agreed to subordinate his army to the Austrian command only if the Austrian emperor or an archduke commanded an army, and advised Kutuzov to subordinate himself to the archduke and follow the Austro-Russian agreement precisely because "I approved all of its provisions."[25]

While campaigning, Kutuzov was to make clear wherever he went that Russia had no territorial ambitions in Europe; that the Russian emperor was fighting "not the French nation but only its current ruler," whose "personal ambition and pernicious system [of supremacy] roused all the calamities that

Europe currently suffers from"; and that the Russian government was ready to accept revolutionary transformations in Europe: "we do not intend to forcibly restore the rights or privileges of various families or privileged estates." Emperor Alexander was adamant that he was not seeking regime change in France or elsewhere and that "the choice of a new government must be completely free and reflecting the nation's interests."

The second half of the instructions dealt with diplomatic, operational, and logistical issues that Kutuzov might confront during the war. They emphasized the need for diplomatic subtlety. Kutuzov was expected to deal not only with Austrians but also with the numerous German princes and "imperial knights" in whose territories the allies expected to wage the war. He was directed to bring into the coalition as many German princes as possible but always in coordination with the Austrian court. "Keep your decision in complete secrecy and maintain extreme vigilance," Alexander advised the general.

In the twelfth article, the emperor seemingly anticipated an eventuality Kutuzov would face during the war. "Whenever they are hard-pressed," wrote Alexander, "the French generals skillfully conceal their difficulties and instead offer truce negotiations under various fair-faced pretexts . . . that in reality are designed to win them more time to get reinforcements or to secure an advantageous position from where they can attack their enemy." Kutuzov was therefore to avoid negotiations. Any French officers and soldiers willing to defect to the Russian side had to be welcomed and immediately conveyed to Russia, while Kutuzov was encouraged to recruit foreigners (but not Austrians) to fill the regimental rosters. Kutuzov's troops were to take only two days' worth of provisions because the Habsburg court took responsibility for fully supplying the Russian army as soon as it crossed into Austrian territory. He concluded the memo by hoping that Kutuzov would fulfill these responsibilities and that "the army you lead will gain glory and contribute to the restoration of peace and general tranquility in Europe."[26]

In late August, while Kutuzov was still in St. Petersburg, the Army of Podolia prepared to leave its encampments in the western Russian borderlands.[27] Contrary to the enduring myth that in drafting their plans the allies had failed to account for the twelve-day difference in their respective calendars (Gregorian vs. Julian), the Austro-Russian agreement was, in fact, prepared under the Gregorian calendar, while the Russian documents were frequently dated in both calendars. The agreement contained a detailed breakdown of the route that the Russian army had to follow to Bavaria and the daily marches it was to undertake. Departing from its quarters on August 16, the Army of Podolia was expected to follow a clearly defined route through Galicia, Moravia, and Upper Austria and to average three or four "postal miles" (14 to 19 miles) per day in order to arrive at Braunau am Inn, the small town on the border with Bavaria, by October 16, 1805.[28]

In Kutuzov's absence, Emperor Alexander's adjutant general, Baron Ferdinand Wintzingerode, assumed the responsibilities of acting army commander and began making arrangements for the long march westward. The army, organized into the vanguard and two corps, marched in six columns toward the Austrian border.[29] There was a sense of anxiety and excitement in the air. Lieutenant Colonel Alexey Yermolov, who commanded a horse artillery company, remembered that Wintzingerode's appointment provoked disgruntlement among senior officers, who were not too happy to find themselves subordinated to a thirty-five-year-old imperial aide-de-camp with barely any combat experience. Wintzingerode's "haughtiness and arrogant demeanor" only made matters worse.[30] The troops grumbled about the orders to leave their *artel* wagons behind and sell all their surplus possessions.[31] "Everything was sold for a penny and without any regard for soldiers."[32] As the army approached the imperial border, Fedor Glinka, the nineteen-year-old aide-de-camp of General Mikhail Miloradovich, felt nostalgic as he heard soldiers singing "forlorn and heartrending songs, as if the melancholy, imbedded deep inside the hearts of these heroes, was now pouring out. This was their farewell to their Fatherland."[33] Despite the orders prohibiting women from accompanying the troops, a number of senior officers' wives stayed with the army.[34] Wintzingerode occasionally reviewed the troops on the march. At one such review near the town of Brody, Major General Gregor von Berg, who commanded the Malorosiiskii Grenadier Regiment, was pleased to hear Wintzingerode express his delight at seeing his troops so well ordered. He promised to report about this to the emperor himself. But just as the last of his men marched by, Berg's wife appeared in a carriage with other officers' wives. "I thought it has been prohibited for officers to take women with them," Wintzingerode commented. Berg had the presence of mind to retort that the emperor had not prohibited traveling abroad and that his wife simply happened to be on the same route as the army as she journeyed to Austria. "Ah, yes, indeed," muttered Wintzingerode. "If you put it that way, I cannot object."[35]

Kutuzov left St. Petersburg in early September, slowly making his way southward to join the Army of Podolia, which was already marching through the Austrian countryside.[36] Autumn was setting in, bringing rains that turned the journey south into a grueling one. At Mogilev, 500 miles south of St. Petersburg, he was able to scribble a quick note for his wife about the "torrential" rain that turned "every sandy spot into a mud bog."[37] Russia was (and remains) notorious for its rough roads, and even the main highway from St. Petersburg to Moscow, which was considered the best in the empire, could be rather challenging to travel on. "The dirt, which covered the road and made it smooth in dry weather, turned it into a muddy bog under the softening rains, making it impassable," complained Russian writer Alexander Radischev on his journey from the new capital to the old one in 1790. Forty years later, another traveler lamented on the same route that "the tenure of adhesion between [his] soul and body" had been tested for 200 miles because the corduroy road was made "of trunks of trees laid transversely, bound down by long poles or beams fastened into the ground with wooden pegs, covered with layers of boughs, and the whole strewed over with sand and earth." Rain regularly washed away the top cover, while elements and lack of care decayed the trunks, so traveling on such roads meant undergoing a severe trial of physical endurance. For this reason, the log roads obtained the name of "spine crushers."[38] Kutuzov must have suffered greatly as he traveled on these wretched roads, trying to stay in the middle of the path and avoid falling into one ditch or the other, intermittently stopping to rest his weary body or get out of the carriage to walk on foot, as other travelers had done.[39] "I only just reached the border," he wrote to his wife on September 12, after days of arduous travel on "the most atrocious" roads. "Still, I feel suitably well."[40]

As he was crossing the Ukrainian countryside, Kutuzov did his best to tend to army matters. He made arrangements to set up an army hospital at Dubno, one large enough to accommodate the potentially high number of sick and wounded during the campaign. He specified that three large buildings had to be prepared and proofed against "water leaks, humidity, and cold," and instructed the commissary to acquire all the necessary medication, bedding, and other essentials.[41] More worrisome were the reports of possible resumption of hostilities with the Ottomans, whom, the Russian government feared, Napoleon was inciting to confront their old nemesis. The prospect of a new war with the sultan, inflated as it was, caused considerable alarm in the Russian government. It deemed General Tormasov's corps, which protected the Russian border on the Dniester River, too weak to contain an Ottoman offensive while most Russian forces were committed elsewhere in Europe. Therefore, Kutuzov was instructed to detach the sixth column, commanded by Lieutenant General Baron Ivan Rosen, to reinforce the Russian forces in the south. Yet this meant weakening the Russian war effort in Bavaria by more than 7,000 men, which understandably displeased the Austrian Hofkriegsrat (the central military administrative authority of the Habsburg monarchy). Emperor Francis personally wrote to his Russian counterpart urging him to reconsider this decision and to uphold commitments he had made in the July agreement. It took more than two weeks for the Russian emperor to consider the wider ramifications of Rosen's redeployment. In the end, he countermanded his earlier directive and Rosen was instructed to march back to Kutuzov, though his column would join the army only in November.[42]

The strategic situation soon changed. On September 10, with Kutuzov's army still hundreds of miles away and not expected to arrive for at least four more weeks, the Austrian army under General Mack invaded Bavaria, hoping to coerce the Bavarians (and other German states) into an alliance or neutrality before the French arrived. Not expecting the French to attack until November, the Austrian command thought it could restrain Bavaria easily and calculated that Kutuzov would have ample time to reach them.[43]

These were miscalculations of enormous consequences. First, the Austrian decision to start their operations while the Russian army was still hundreds of miles away from the theater of war made it much harder for the allies to cooperate in case of a French counterattack in Germany. Second, the Bavarians rejected the Austrian gambit and threw their support firmly behind the French, while Austrian aggression against Bavaria provided Napoleon with both a *casus belli* and a suitable target to engage. Mack's advance had increased the distance separating the Austrian and Russian forces and offered Napoleon an opportunity to engage enemy forces before they could unite. By late September, the emperor of the French already had developed a daring strategy that took advantage of the enemy's mistakes as well as the mobility of the corps system that the French had experimented with in previous years. Leaving Marshal André Masséna to defend Italy and pin down the main Austrian army, Napoleon decided to move his Grande Armée in a broad enveloping maneuver from the Atlantic coastline of France to the shores of the Danube River in Bavaria, where it would cut the enemy's communication lines and effectively surround the Austrian army, which was taking positions near the Bavarian town of Ulm.

On September 14, four days after the Austrian army invaded Bavaria, Kutuzov crossed the Russian imperial border at Radziwiłłów (Radyvyliv); more than 900 miles separated him from the Austrian army at Ulm. At the town of Brody, he had a rendezvous with Major General Gottfried von Strauch, an experienced officer who had been assigned as an Austrian liaison responsible for providing the Russian army with provisions and other essentials. On September 21, Kutuzov caught up with the army at Myslenice, reviewing the troops and revoking some of Wintzingerode's previous orders concerning soldiers' possessions. "It is impossible to describe the joy experienced by the troops on this occasion!" observed a Russian officer.[44] Among the officers who welcomed Kutuzov to the army was his son-in-law Ferdinand Tiesenhausen, the twenty-three-year-old flügel-adjutant of His Imperial Majesty's Suite, who was assigned to the Army of Podolia. Kutuzov adored this young man: "If I had a son, I would not wish him to be any different from Ferdinand."[45]

The Army of Podolia was already running behind the schedule agreed by the Austrian and Russian negotiators in July. It departed nine days late, on August 25, and saw its movement further delayed by the heavy rains that inundated waterways and turned the roads into rivers of mud, exhausting both men and animals. "This incessant rain had ruined the road so badly that people and horses suffered very much from it," lamented a Russian general. "I was extremely worried as I watched my beautiful regimental horses come down in ever increasing numbers."[46] At times the pace of movement was agonizingly slow—twelve miles in three days. But as the weather improved, the army picked up the pace, covering an impressive 350 miles between Radziwiłłów and Teschen (Cieszyn) in three weeks.[47] Unaware of the situation in Bavaria, the Russian officers took advantage of the resting days (every fourth day) to spend time in various diversions, visiting the famed salt mines at Vieliczka (on the outskirts of Krakow) and sightseeing in the country-side. At Lauscul, the army paraded in front of Adam Kazimierz Czartoryski, Austrian field marshal and one of the powerful Polish magnates.[48] After resting near Kalwaria (southwest of Krakow), the Army of Podolia proceeded toward Teschen (Cieszyn) amid the picturesque dales of Galicia and Upper Silesia, which captivated the Russian officers. They admired local paved roads and gazed at "the green valleys speckled with various colors," and, forgetting about the war, they listened to "the languorous flow of creeks" and pondered "the silvery ripples in the streams as they flowed . . . amidst the greenery of the flowering fields."[49] Alas, the weather soon worsened once more and "the unrelenting rains" caused much hardship and killed many of the horses.[50]

Meanwhile, events unfolded rapidly to the west. On September 24, Napoleon left Paris to rejoin the Grande Armée as it was racing toward the Rhine River, taking advantage of the superior mobility of its corps and the billets and supplies arranged by local authorities. Despite its large size, the army's movement was smooth and rapid, averaging about twenty miles per day. To thrust his troops behind the enemy, Napoleon pushed two of his corps through the Prussian territory of Ansbach, flagrantly violating its neutrality. This advance took the Austrians by surprise, as they had received assurances that Prussia would oppose any such moves and were, therefore, convinced of the security of their right wing. Napoleon's gamble paid off. The Prussian court protested vociferously but made no effort to confront the French, choosing to remain neutral and effectively allowing Napoleon to converge his forces on the isolated Austrian army. As the last days of September expired, the French crossed the Rhine at various locations and advanced in "seven torrents," forming a wide arc around to the north and east of the Austrian position at Ulm. On September 30, Mack, realizing that he was in danger of being encircled, tried to clear a line of retreat toward Vienna. However, his failure to fully assess the situation, conduct proper reconnaissance, and draw careful dispositions resulted in continued setbacks that doomed the Austrian army.

Kutuzov remained unaware of these momentous developments. The Hofkriegsrat provided the Russian commander with no details on the situation in Bavaria and instead sent ever more urgent letters imploring him to move faster so that he could get to the Austrian army in Bavaria in time. To assist the Russians, the Austrian authorities had prepared dozens of wagons to transport Russian troops the remaining 360 miles from Teschen to the Bavarian border through the Bohemian-Moravian Highlands.[51] Yet this was no easy task. Kutuzov found himself in the difficult position of trying to satisfy the demands of an allied power while doing his best to care for and protect his soldiers. "The forced marches that the Austrian court demands from us cannot but be harmful for our army," he wrote to the Russian ambassador in Vienna. "Our soldiers are already extremely fatigued and suffering." He also pointed out that, having marched for twenty miles a day, soldiers got barely any rest before they were required to move again. Furthermore, despite his "sincere desire" to comply with the requests of the Austrian court, he found it impossible to move artillery and cavalry "as fast as the infantry." Horses were so fatigued that even double forage rations could not keep them moving forward. "It would do our cause no good to see this important branch of the army so exhausted en route that upon arriving at its destination it is no longer capable of being effective," argued Kutuzov.[52]

Nevertheless, understanding that every minute was precious and that the Austrians were in a need of military succor, Kutuzov did his best to accommodate the coalition partner. He sought to reassure his Austrian counterparts that though the Russian army did not have the promised 50,000 men, reinforcements were on the way. He stressed that "it is not the quantity of troops but rather their gallantry, zeal, and reinvigorating spirit that largely determine the successful outcome of battle. And the Russian army possesses them in abundance."[53] Kutuzov ordered his army to leave all heavy transports and the field hospital behind in an effort to move as lightly as possible toward Bavaria.[54] The Army of Podolia was reorganized into two sections, each subdivided into five columns, whose commanders were instructed to move their men and equipment as fast as they could. One of the enduring problems was the continued presence of female companions and wives, who, despite repeated prohibitions, were still present in large numbers. Kutuzov issued a new order banning them. "No exceptions will be made, and I will hold commanders personally responsible," he warned. All the remaining women and sutlers had to proceed with the supply train to Brunn, which was designated as a logistical hub.[55]

Over the next three weeks, the Russian army made a wild dash through Upper Austria's valleys and hills, and the swiftness of its movement rivaled that of the Grande Armée's movement from Boulogne to the Rhine that has become so widely lauded. Kutuzov told Emperor Alexander that in order to get to Bavaria in time, the vast majority of marches had to be "between 45 and 60 *verstas* [30–40 miles] long."[56] To fully appreciate such mobility, it should be noted that 4,000 infantry on the march took up some two and a half miles of road, while sixty cannon with their caissons required close to three miles of roadway. The length of these marching columns made it man-datory to move the army along several roads, maintaining constant lateral communications. The last leg of the Russian advance was, thus, an unre-lenting and draining exercise. Each morning between four and five o'clock, the soldiers broke their camp, formed columns, and began marching, with little or no respite, until early evening, when they were given a few hours of rest. Seeing his grenadiers marching some thirty miles a day, General Berg underscored "how arduous" it was, since "each regiment got only eighty or ninety wagons [leiterwagen], each harnessed with two horses, so they could not carry the whole unit, with all of its ammunition, at once; soldiers had to take turns, some walking on foot alongside the cart." Marching from dawn till late evening was extremely strenuous, especially since every so often horses and wagons had to be replaced.[57] Ivan Butovskii, a twenty-one-year-old portupei-junker in the Moskovskii Musketeer Regiment, recalled that the travel arrangements for these wagons were precisely established—twelve men, with their weapons and ammunition, sat in the wagon, which also carried the ammunition and backpacks of another twelve soldiers, who walked beside it. Every ten verstas (6.6 miles) they changed places.[58] The fre-netic tempo of the Russian advance can be gleaned from Major General Peter Bagration's reports, which describe how the men of his first column made an "almost twenty-four-hour-long" trek on September 27 and, after a short respite, marched for "another twenty-four hours" the following day. After a day of rest at Wischau, Bagration departed with his men at four o'clock in the morning on September 30 and covered another forty miles to reach Pohrlitz (Pohorelice) at six o'clock in the evening. After just a few hours of sleep, the soldiers left their bivouac at five o'clock in the morning on October 1 and, after covering twenty-five more miles, arrived late that afternoon at Znaim, where they stayed until midnight, when Bagration ordered them to depart. Proceeding by forced marches of thirty miles on each of the following two days, the dog-tired Russians finally reached Krems at two o'clock in the afternoon on October 3.[59]

Yet as far as the Austrians were concerned, even this pace was not fast enough. On October 1, the Hofkriegsrat, alarmed by Napoleon's rapid ad-vance toward Ulm, urged Kutuzov to hasten his movement even more; it went as far as to suggest resting Russian soldiers only once every five days. Startled by such demands, Kutuzov wrote a lengthy response explaining why he could not consent to them. The Russo-Austrian agreement specified that the Russian army should not be marching more than "three and half German miles" a day and should be rested once every four days.[60] Kutuzov reminded his Austrian counterpart of this provision and pointed out that, to show Russian goodwill and commitment to the allied cause, he had ignored this stipulation and complied with earlier Austrian requests for longer marches. But how much faster did the Austrians expect the Russians to move? Kutuzov felt that he had already done as much as he could to accommodate their part-ners, while his men paid a heavy toll with their health. The number of un-well soldiers had doubled, while the healthy ones were "so spent that they could barely move," complained Kutuzov. Because of "the incessant rains and dreadful mud," hundreds of soldiers—as many as half of the men in the Bryanskii, Vyatskii, and Yaroslavskii Musketeer Regiments—had completely worn out their boots and were "compelled to walk barefooted, injuring their feet on the sharp-edged stones of the paved chaussée to such a degree that they can no longer remain in ranks."[61] He further noted that the Austrians made such demands while not upholding their own end of the bargain—they failed to provide a sufficient amount of alcohol for his men and "cooked meat in plain water, rather than with vegetables as it was agreed upon."

More crucially, the Austrians had not provided enough carriages to transport the troops, and Kutuzov was still waiting for the promised three regiments of light cavalry, almost 200 pack horses for the officers, and am-munition for infantry and artillery. The last issue was particularly important because the Austrian authorities informed Kutuzov that he would receive ammunition supplies only after their own needs were fully met. "I am highly concerned by the Austrian government's notice," Kutuzov told the Russian emperor. "It is probable that military operations will start sooner than we expect . . . and that the first major battle would consume two-thirds of my ammunition supplies at the very moment when it is difficult—one may even say impossible—to ensure timely delivery of ammunition from Russia."[62]

Realizing how important it was to ensure allied cooperation, Kutuzov reached out to the Russian embassy in Vienna, soliciting their help in communicating to the Austrian authorities the stark realities the Russian army was confronting in Upper Austria. He warned that accepting the Austrians' new demands would mean that "instead of bringing an army cap-able of fighting, I would arrive with a handful of battalions that would be incapable of undertaking anything for another month, which is how long it would take for the soldiers to fully recover their health and get themselves in order."[63] To make matters worse, Kutuzov lacked proper maps of Upper Austria and Bavaria, a crucial lapse in the allied strategic planning that was now causing problems on the operational level. Russian staff officers were unfamiliar with the region and lacked even basic maps to navigate. "Kutuzov beseeched Razumovskii to get him detailed regional maps of Austria and southern German states. Yet even the Russian ambassador could do no better than to send a few general maps, complaining that 'it is impossible to find detailed maps of Germany and Swabia in Vienna; I asked the vendor to order them from abroad.' "[64]

In light of so many thorny issues arising in Russo-Austrian relations, Kutuzov decided to travel to Vienna to meet personally with senior Austrian statesmen and military leaders.[65] Establishing friendly, personal rapport with

the Austrian leadership could go a long way in sustaining the special relationship between the two countries and helping develop a clearer view of
what was needed.[66] He arrived at the Austrian imperial capital on October
6. Some thirty years had elapsed since his last visit. Back then he had been an
obscure officer better known for his survival of a ghastly head wound than for
any military accomplishments. Now Kutuzov was in effect representing one
of the greatest European powers. The following day, he went, accompanied
by his aide-de-camp Tiesenhausen and Ambassador Razumovskii, to the
Schönbrunn Palace for the audience and dinner with Emperor Francis and
his ministers.

The Habsburg court received him respectfully but, in the words of a
contemporary, "not with the same enthusiasm as was shown to [Alexander
Vasilevich] Suvorov six years earlier," when the Russian expeditionary force
was marching to fight the French in Italy.[67] Kaiser Francis expressed deep
gratitude for the Russians' support, noting that "without the support of
[Emperor Alexander], none of the measures taken to contain the recent
successes of the French government would have been as imposing or well
arranged."[68] He thanked Kutuzov for his hard work and dedication as well
as for the orderly nature of the Russian advance and, as a token of his appreciation, granted him a generous sum of 60,000 silver guldens to cover the
Russian officers' daily necessities.[69]

Among the people Kutuzov met at the royal palace was his old acquaintance Ludwig Graf von Cobenzl, who had once been the Austrian ambassador
in St. Petersburg and now served as the vice chancellor and foreign minister.
The two men had a lengthy discussion of current matters and news. Startled
to hear from the Austrian chancellor about the French violation of Prussian
neutrality, Kutuzov hurried to inform the Russian foreign ministry, noting
that "the court of Berlin might find it beneficial to delay the delivery of
this news to Our Imperial Court." Another pressing issue that Kutuzov and
Cobenzl discussed involved appointing a Russian representative to handle
the reception of and payment for the supplies that the Austrian authorities
were providing to the Russian army.[70] Cobenzl introduced the Russian commander to the members of the Hofkriegsrat. "At first, these members were
afraid that they would find Kutuzov as stubborn and persistent as Suvorov
had been on the way to Italy," commented a well-informed contemporary.
"But from the first meeting they saw in Kutuzov a readiness to agree with
them on everything and even to be guided by their opinions."[71]

One of the core problems that Kutuzov had faced was the holdup of the
artillery, which could not match the pace of the Russian infantry and cavalry.
His earlier requests that the Austrians provide additional horses had been
rejected. Now he was able to raise this issue at the highest levels of the Austrian
government; both the kaiser and the president of the Hofkriegsrat pledged
to supply horses and double forage, as he requested.[72] The Hofkriegsrat also

agreed to provide topographic maps from its stocks and to dispatch staff officers and physicians to assist the Russian army with its most pressing problems. Among these officers was Johann Heinrich von Schmitt, whom Kutuzov welcomed as the new quartermaster-general of the Army of Podolia.

—·—⟩⊰✦⊱⟨—·—

As productive as this trip was, Kutuzov left Vienna unaware of the critical situation unfolding in Bavaria, where the French advance proceeded apace and led to a series of Austrian setbacks. First, on October 8, French marshals Joachim Murat and Jean Lannes mauled the Austrians under Franz Xaver von Auffenberg at Wertingen. Then, as the Grande Armée made good progress to Landsberg, Dachau, and Munich, the French scored a victory at Günzburg on October 9. Two days later, a mistake by Marshal Murat gave the Austrians an opportunity to defeat their enemy and break out of the rapidly tightening loop at Ulm. General Mack probed eastward along the northern bank of the Danube, hoping to find a weak spot to cut the French communications. He found one near the villages of Jungingen and Haslach, where Murat, misunderstanding Napoleon's missives and ignoring the protests of Marshal Michel Ney, had left only General Pierre Dupont's small division, thus opening the door for the Austrian escape. Yet, in a fierce and bloody battle, Dupont's 4,000 French troops withstood the onslaught of some 25,000 Austrians and secured a victory. Mack had a remarkable opportunity to evade Napoleon's enveloping maneuver and march out of Ulm, and then to effect the much-desired rendezvous with Kutuzov. Instead, the Battle of Jungingen-Haslach pushed him back into Ulm, where he postponed further attacks and allowed Napoleon to consolidate his positions. The French had scored another victory at Elchingen (October 14) and placed two corps in the vicinity of Munich, some eighty miles east of Ulm, severing the Austrian line of communication and closing the few remaining escape routes.[73]

As he journeyed from Vienna to Braunau, Kutuzov was thus deep in the fog of war, lacking precise information about what was happening in Bavaria and still convinced of his impending junction with Mack. The Austrians had shared with him only the reassuring news from Ulm, in which Mack proclaimed that "never has an army been posted in a manner more suited to ensuring its superiority over the enemy" and that he had "only one regret, that of not seeing the emperor being an eyewitness to the impending triumph of his armies."[74] The Austrian defeat at Wertingen was rationalized as an inconsequential incident caused by the failings of a local commander. "No doubt that General Auffenberg is the sole cause of this setback," observed the Russian ambassador.[75]

On October 13, after covering almost 700 miles in forty-seven days, the Russian army entered Braunau. To mark the occasion, regiments marched through the city in full parade, their shouts of "hurrah" thundering through the air. "Everyone was amazed at how beautiful my regiment was," boasted Major General Berg about his Malorosiiskii Grenadier Regiment. "Even after such an arduous march, it still looked dazzling."[76] Kutuzov could not share Berg's optimism, knowing full well the extent of the problems that the Army of Podolia faced. The army was utterly exhausted by long marches in stormy weather and had lost some 6,000 men to sickness and exhaustion. Out of the original six columns, only three had concentrated in Braunau, while two more columns, artillery, and heavy transports were still en route; the sixth column, led by Rosen, was hundreds of miles away, making its way through Galicia. The overall strength of the five Russian columns was no more than 35,000 men, though Kutuzov drew solace from the arrival of Maximilian Count von Merveldt, to whom Emperor Francis entrusted the command of the Austrian troops outside Ulm.[77] This meant that, once his army concentrated, Kutuzov could rally some 53,000–55,000 men under arms. Knowing that time was short, he urged his column commanders to move as quickly as possible. As the troops arrived, he reorganized them into new battle formations. Bagration was tasked with leading the vanguard of the army, deploying outposts on the Inn River and gathering intelligence on the French whereabouts; the remaining forces were rearranged into two ad hoc divisions (each composed of two brigades) commanded by Lieutenant General Dokhturov and Major General Miloradovich. Kutuzov also issued a special order to the army outlining the tactics that the troops were expected to employ against their French foes. He encouraged the use of bayonet charges as "intrinsic to the gallantry of the Russian soldiers" and stressed the need to employ skirmishers and "battalion columns," which could manage the difficult terrain. Since his men were in an unfamiliar territory, Kutuzov demanded that special signs be set up on the roads between Braunau and Enns to avoid any confusion on which routes to follow, "especially at nighttime." On his orders, a new "wagenburg" or supply train was formed to better manage logistical challenges and to coordinate evacuation of the sick and infirm to Linz.

Provisioning the army remained a challenge. Kutuzov was hounded by the debate over how many supplies Austrians were to provide under the coalition agreement and how much and when the Russians had to pay for it all.[78] In the meantime, Russian soldiers and officers marveled at the German way of life. "We were received as welcomed guests all over Austria," remembered a Russian general. One innkeeper "took in sixty or seventy of our men and entertained them in the best possible way." Yet he found the reception a bit chillier in the vicinity of Braunau, the borderland area where Austrian and Bavarian claims intersected. At Sankt Martin, property of a Bavarian count, "people were very afraid of the Russian troops since the Bavarians had united with the French and were therefore our enemies."[79] On the other hand, soldiers had enjoyed the first few days of welcome in and around

Braunau. "The Germans received us very well" at Braunau, remembered Ilya Popadichev of the Butyrskii Musketeer Regiment. "We were fed soup and white bread, treated to vodka and beer. The locals were very surprised to see us drinking vodka in beer pints and kept saying, 'Krank, krank,' meaning that we would get sick." They did not.[80]

Soon after his arrival at Braunau, Kutuzov received a letter from Archduke Ferdinand, under whose overall command he was now entering. The archduke mentioned that Napoleon's advance through Ansbach had temporarily cut the Austrian communication line and that "our union with the Russian Imperial Army should be postponed for the moment." However, he also assured Kutuzov that the Austrians still enjoyed "the important advantage of being masters of the Iller, Ulm, and Memmingen," had some 70,000 well-provisioned soldiers, and could hold out for a considerable time. The archduke stressed that "we cannot lose the advantage of remaining masters of both banks of the Danube" and urged Kutuzov to march forward and confront Napoleon. "We will fearlessly wait for the time when the Imperial Russian Army will arrive and then together we will easily find the opportunity to prepare that fate for the enemy which they deserve." This was a perplexing letter, for it was littered with vague descriptions that further muddled Kutuzov's understanding of what was happening at Ulm.[81] The archduke seemed both on the offensive and on the defensive.

Furthermore, just days later Kutuzov received the news of the victory that Mack and Ferdinand had claimed at Haslach. According to the Austrian account, Marshal Ney's entire corps had attacked "with great ferocity" but the Austrians routed it, "annihilating two enemy cavalry and two infantry regiments," killing 1,500 soldiers, and capturing "some nine hundred prisoners, 11 cannons and 20 ammunition caissons, a large number of wagons and baggage." Delighted by this report, Kutuzov issued a special proclamation to the army announcing the great victory and held a special religious service "to thank the Almighty for his blessing of our alliance, granting us ultimate victory and strengthening our resolve."[82] Rumors swirling in Braunau claimed that the Prussians, Hessians, and Swedes had joined the coalition and the war was about to end with the crushing defeat of the French. "This good news caused an indescribable joy in our army," recalled one participant.[83]

And yet amid this joy, "our old Kutuzov had become very thoughtful," remarked a Russian general.[84] Kutuzov was too observant not to notice that things were not what they seemed. That initial letter from Archduke Ferdinand was followed by a prolonged period of silence during which Kutuzov received no news from the Austrian commander. As days passed with no word from Ulm, he began actively to worry about the Austrian situation and made every effort he could to get in contact with the archduke, dispatching couriers "in various disguises."[85] These efforts proved futile. As late as October 22, Kutuzov reported that he still had had no direct intelligence from the Austrian army. Meanwhile, the rumors filtering into the Russian headquarters painted a confusing picture of the situation at the front line. Even as the Austrians assured him that the situation around Ulm was under control, the Russian envoy to Bavaria he met with informed him of the French capture of Munich, only seventy-five miles away. It was clear that the French had managed to turn the Austrian right wing and were now astride Kutuzov's route to Ulm. The junction with the Austrians suddenly became a distant prospect, and Russian confidence in the veracity of the Austrian reports was thoroughly shaken. "It must be said among us," wrote the Russian ambassador, "that the affair of October 11 [at Haslach] was not as great a success as [Austrians] want to make us believe. . . . Mack's victory is more a conjecture than a reality."[86] Increasingly Kutuzov came to the same conclusion. He believed that the Austrian army, though beaten, remained in the field and was retreating, either to Tyrol or toward his position along the left bank of the Danube.[87]

In this confused and fast-evolving environment, Kutuzov chose to act cautiously and remained at Braunau, sending messengers to Vienna seeking clarification from the Austrian emperor. Austrian officers urged him to move forward, storm Munich, and relieve the Austrian army trapped at Ulm, but the methodical Kutuzov could not accept such a rash proposition.[88] His army was worn out and had not fully concentrated yet; advancing toward the Bavarian capital would mean extending lines of communication even more and exposing them to a flanking strike from a resourceful opponent who had already outmarched and outfought one allied army. This was no time for impulsive decisions. Writing to both the Russian and Austrian emperors before he learned of the magnitude of the Austrian debacle, Kutuzov described his army as "Vienna's last line of defense" and laid out the unenviable options he faced: "If I advance, I could be cut off by an enemy that is three times stronger than me; and remaining here, I would equally expect to be attacked, and might easily find myself forced to retire to Vienna itself." Unaware of the desperate situation at Ulm, Kutuzov believed he could remain at Braunau for another week to get a better understanding of the strategic situation and in order to rest and reorganize the army.[89]

The truth of what had happened at Ulm was revealed in all its terrifying bleakness on October 23 when the Russian officers watched in bewilderment as an Austrian officer in a greatcoat and a bandage round his head arrived at Kutuzov's headquarters in Braunau. Leo Tolstoy paints the scene of Kutuzov coming out to greet Mack in *War and Peace*:

> The door of the private room opened and Kutuzov appeared in the doorway. The general with the bandaged head bent forward as though

running away from some danger, and, making long, quick strides with his thin legs, went up to Kutúzov. "Vous voyez le malheureux Mack [You see the unfortunate Mack]," he uttered in a broken voice. Kutuzov's face as he stood in the open doorway remained perfectly immobile for a few moments. Then wrinkles ran over his face like a wave and his forehead became smooth again, he bowed his head respectfully, closed his eyes, silently let Mack enter his room before him, and closed the door himself behind him.

The news was devastating. On October 20, the Austrian army had surrendered, leaving tens of thousands of men, dozens of cannon, and vast quantities of ammunition and matériel in French hands. On October 21, Napoleon's 9th Bulletin triumphantly announced the capture of 33,000 prisoners and 3,000 wounded, along with 60 cannon and 50 flags. Though the actual number of the Austrian prisoners was closer to 23,000, such details hardly mattered in the wider context. The Austrian army of Germany was gone. Kutuzov grieved that of the 70,000-man-strong army that had gone with Archduke Ferdinand to Bohemia, only a few battalions and squadrons had been saved. The rest "has all gone to the enemy."[90] In the words of a Russian diplomat, "Mack's madness or betrayal" had profoundly changed the allied campaign.[91]

Devastating as this news was, Kutuzov kept his composure and invited the Austrian general to lunch, during which he tried to learn as much as he could about the situation on the front lines. Mack told him that Napoleon was concentrating almost 140,000 men near Munich and advised not to advance forward, as had been previously agreed.[92] Although attacking such a powerful enemy force had never crossed his mind, Kutuzov nodded in agreement and then solicited advice from the Austrians as to what to do next. General Merveldt suggested withdrawing to Linz, where the allies could cross to the northern bank of the Danube and join Buxhöwden's corps, which had been advancing toward Bohemia. Kutuzov did not know where Buxhöwden's corps currently was and was unwilling to risk venturing into an unfamiliar region with no certainty of finding a friendly force there.[93] Furthermore, he pointed out to the Austrians, moving north meant exposing Vienna, which he could not do without the kaiser's permission. Ever mindful of the political dimensions of the war, Kutuzov explained in a letter to the Russian foreign minister that such a maneuver would "dishearten [*obeskurazhit'*] the Viennese court" and make it more susceptible to French diplomatic overtures.[94]

Meanwhile, the Habsburg court was alarmed by the news that a Russian withdrawal to Bohemia was actually being considered. As late as October 24, Emperor Francis and his ministers, still unaware of the scale of the calamity that had befallen their army, assured their Russian allies that "while the misfortunes of the Austrian army are undoubtedly very regrettable," the French had doubtless exaggerated them to sway public opinion.

The Austrians acknowledged that Archduke Ferdinand had suffered some "setbacks" but also assured their allies that the archduke was still in command of a sizable force. Ambassador Razumovskii told Kutuzov that, in spite of the rumors of the calamity at Ulm, the Habsburg court still wanted him to continue moving forward. Kutuzov disagreed. He knew that any forward movement risked destroying the Russian army. Consequently, he made the decision to ignore the Austrian appeals; instead, he destroyed bridges on the Inn River and moved the army to Lambach, where it would still protect the main road to Vienna while having the option of moving to Linz if the allies decided on it.[95]

At that lunch Kutuzov plied Mack with food and drink and encouraged him to speak unreservedly. And speak he did. Even as Merveldt tried to caution his colleague—and, in Kutuzov's words, "inconvenienced us a great deal"—Mack recounted in detail the long conversations he had had with Napoleon, who had offered peace to the Austrians and was prepared "to make sacrifices, even major concessions, to restore peace in Europe." Mack admitted that he had told the French emperor that the kaiser would be willing to consider "a peace on firm foundation," and agreed to deliver Napoleon's peace proposals to Vienna. Startled by this revelation, Kutuzov did his best to learn more, but the Austrian, realizing he had spoken too much, and with Merveldt "openly expressing dissatisfaction at his candor," shied away from further discussion. In any case, Kutuzov had heard enough, and he was convinced that Mack was concealing crucial details. As soon as the Austrian departed, he wrote a lengthy report to the Russian foreign minister, warning him that the Austrians might be negotiating secretly with the enemy and that Napoleon was evidently trying to splinter the coalition by offering "advantageous terms."[96]

The Habsburg court, realizing Mack's indiscretion, belatedly did its best to allay the Russians' fears. Austrian foreign minister Cobenzl assured the Russian ambassador that the kaiser would never act independently of "his august ally, the Emperor of Russia."[97] To underscore the Austrian refusal to consider the French overtures, Mack was forbidden from entering the capital and escorted to Brünn, where he was court-martialed. Emperor Francis decided to personally travel to meet with Kutuzov in order to assess the situation on the ground and develop a new plan of actions. He implored the Russian general to defend the common cause and stand firm: "I count on yours and on your goodwill, while you may also count on my eternal gratitude," the kaiser concluded his letter to Kutuzov.[98] Nonetheless, the first seeds of distrust between the coalition partners had been sown. The Austrians were disheartened by the state of the Russian soldiers, wearied as they were by long marches; their clothes and boots were worn to shreds. Ignoring the logistical challenges confronting Kutuzov, senior Austrian officers complained that he and the other generals could have done more to help them, and they were dismissive of Russian leadership.[99] In a letter designated as "top secret," Ambassador Razumovskii informed the Russian foreign minister that while they thought Kutuzov "a worthy and respectable man," the Austrians suspected him of acting "a little too timid in this affair."[100] Correspondence between Austrian officials was more plainspoken, claiming that the Russian generals "have no understanding of this war." General Merveldt seems to have been divided in his assessment of the Russian commander in chief. On the one hand, he found Kutuzov "the most forthright and righteous thinking man [der rechtlichste und rechtschaffen denkendste Mann]," yet was frustrated with his unwillingness to rush blindly to the rescue of the Austrian forces at Ulm. Merveldt complained to the Hofkriegsrat that Kutuzov showed "the greatest anxiety [die grösste Ängstlichkeit]" for his troops and that this had all but precluded the Russian army from moving forward.[101] Such criticism would have struck the Russians as insultingly dismissive of the efforts (and sacrifice) they had made on behalf of their allies. The Austrians had been consistently defeated by Napoleon in the past nine years and were hardly in a position to lecture about understanding the art of war. Indeed, many Russians were starting to loathe their allies for mismanaging the current war effort so badly, for promising yet failing to provide sufficient provisions and transports, and for being unable to clarify the situation at the front. "The consternation and confusion are so great here," complained the Russian ambassador. "All the reports are incomplete, conflicting, and bear traces of the confusion that marked the last days of Mack's army."[102]

After Mack's departure, Kutuzov assembled his officers and aides-de-camp at his headquarters. "As soon as we gathered," recalled one of them, "Kutuzov came out of the room, visibly upset. I will never forget the moment when he spoke to us." Kutuzov shared the terrible news and explained in broad strokes the danger the army was now facing. Some senior officers, who had fought against the French under Suvorov, seemed undaunted and suggested marching forward to confront the French. Kutuzov knew this would amount to self-annihilation. Still, he commended them on such bravery: "I expected no other response from the Russian heroes. Your gallantry impels you to attack, but my prudence commands me to retreat."[103] As he was about to dismiss the meeting, Kutuzov apparently grew quiet, as if carefully choosing the words that he was about to say. "Twirling a snuffbox in his hand, he told us plainly, 'The Imperials [Austrians] did not wait for us. They have now been routed. The few courageous ones are rushing to join us, but the rest of these cowards [trusy] have laid their arms at the enemy's feet. Our duty is to support and protect the wretched remnants of their scattered army.'"[104]

CHAPTER 13 | "The Glorious Retreat"

N APOLEON'S VICTORY AT ULM was a remarkable achievement. In just two months, he had transported an army of 190,000 men from the Atlantic coastline to the heartland of Bavaria, outsmarted his opponents, and destroyed one hostile army, and he was about to chase the second one into the heart of the Habsburg Empire. It was this success, conceived on the strategic level, brilliantly executed at the operational level, and then secured on the tactical level, that led French soldiers to jest that Napoleon had found a new way of making war: with their legs rather than their firearms. The Austrian defeat was a disaster for the allied cause, dramatically changing the strategic situation and placing the coalition on the defensive. The news of this setback was greeted with a mixture of shock and outrage in many parts of Europe. William Wyndham Grenville, soon to be the British prime minister, expressed the opinion of many when he observed that the army that had been considered the best in Europe was totally destroyed in a matter of three weeks and had capitulated "on a bare statement of the positions occupied by their enemy." The result "really confound[ed] one's imagination." He predicted darkly that it was "only the beginning of our misfortunes."[1]

The first to feel the consequences of Napoleon's triumph was Kutuzov, whose army was less than eighty miles from Munich. Yet he was still fortunate. Having incomplete knowledge of the strength, movement, and position of the Russian forces, Napoleon had chosen to halt his forces between Ulm and Munich. Had the French emperor ordered his army to proceed to the Inn River anytime between October 21 and 25, he would have found at Braunau a fatigued and rather dispersed Russian army that, without a doubt, would have been easy prey. Napoleon's decision to postpone his advance until after October 25 meant that Kutuzov was given an opportunity to carefully assess the situation, weigh different options, choose a course of action, and start to execute it. Skill would be required to extricate the army from this danger, but Kutuzov was up to the task.

MAP 6 The Campaign of 1805 on the Danube

His immediate objective was to avoid battle and safeguard the Russian army in the face of the French juggernaut, which had departed from Munich in the last days of October and, despite the incessant cold rain and sleet, was making rapid progress eastward. On October 25, informed that enemy forces were advancing on the western bank of the Inn River, Kutuzov began preparations to leave Braunau. He evacuated the sick, sent heavy transports to the rear, and marched the army via Reid and Lambach to Wels. The Austrian general Kienmayer withdrew from Salzburg, keeping level with the Russians and covering their left flank, while Johann Nepomuk von Nostitz-Rieneck led his troops from Passau to Linz, covering the Russian right flank. To ensure a safe and orderly withdrawal, Kutuzov decided, in the apt expression of one historian, to "keep a sting in his tail" and appointed Major General Bagration to command the rear guard.[2] Eighteen years younger than Kutuzov, Bagration was his complete opposite in appearance and temperament. A scion of the Georgian royal family, "Prince Peter," as Suvorov warmly called him, was famous for his tempestuous character and reckless gallantry. He enjoyed the reputation of a talented tactical commander who had honed his skills fighting the French in Italy and Switzerland in 1799. His "spirited presence, skill, courage, and good fortune," as Suvorov once put it, would serve Kutuzov well during this campaign.[3]

The last days of October 1805 were dispiriting, chilly, and wet. The "unremittingly rainy weather" muddied all roads and made the marching "very difficult," remembered one Russian general. Kutuzov lamented that he could not afford "to leave the paved road, which meant they all had to use the same route.[4] Poor weather wrought havoc in the allied logistical system, and just two days into the withdrawal, the Russian troops had "nothing but their dry biscuits to eat."[5] These were the first portents of the difficulties to come. On October 28, traveling ahead of the army, Kutuzov arrived at Wels for a meeting with Emperor Francis, who summoned a quick council of war to review the strategic challenges and come up with a possible plan of action. According to those who were there, the kaiser could not believe that the whole army under Mack had been destroyed and argued that those who had survived could be rallied under protection of the Russian troops at Wels.[6] Count Maximilian Latour, the president of the Hofkriegsrat, pointed out that the allies still had close to 300,000 men in the field and that despite the defeat in Bavaria, the coalition was still capable of fighting the war.[7] It was an overly optimistic assessment, for the coalition's forces were scattered across a vast area—Archduke Ferdinand was recovering in Bohemia, Archdukes Charles and John were still in Italy and Tyrol, and Buxhöwden's corps was on the march from Troppau to Olmütz, while Bennigsen was near Warsaw, over 500 miles northeast from Wels. Kutuzov's army could barely hope for any succor in the near future, and the allies had to find a way of holding off Napoleon's advance in Upper Austria with the forces they had at hand.

The allies drew some solace from the advantages that the local topography offered them. The valley of the Danube River between Ratisbon, where the river takes a turn to the southeast, and Passau is spacious, with a hundred miles of rolling plains separating the river from the Tyrolese Alps. But it gradually narrows to the east, forming a natural funnel that at its narrowest section between Linz and Krems an der Donau is slightly over a dozen miles wide. Marching upon a wide front down the valley, the Grande Armée would find itself gradually hemmed in. Furthermore, the Danubian valley is fed by a succession of rivers, including the Inn, Traun, Enns, and Ybbs, which offered several sound rear-guard positions (especially if the bridges were destroyed) for an army retreating eastward. At the meeting at Wels, the Austrians insisted on holding the line on one of these rivers until reinforcements could arrive. In a letter to Kutuzov, Emperor Francis exhorted him to avoid engaging in battle with Napoleon but to "challenge him at every turn, gaining time for Archdukes Charles and John to reach the theater of war, and the corps underway from Russia."[8]

Kutuzov agreed to comply with the imperial command, but he was not convinced of the expediency of the strategy the Austrians advocated. Rather than object openly, Kutuzov listened, nodded, and quietly devised his own plans. Whereas the Austrian priority was positional warfare and the defense of their capital, Kutuzov's was the preservation of his army now that the Austrian army had been routed. The coalition needed to gain time to regroup and rethink its approach to war. He knew that Emperor Alexander was on his way to Berlin and expected that the Prussians would be convinced to break their neutrality. The consequent arrival of more than 150,000 Prussian troops would tip the scales of war in the allies' favor. Hence Kutuzov was in no rush to confront Napoleon, certainly not with the forces he then had in the positions he then occupied.

He knew full well the insurmountable logistical challenges the army faced. The hungry and weary Russians marched along roads that icy rain and sleet had turned into quagmires, with many soldiers falling sick under such conditions. In a letter to Emperor Alexander, Kutuzov noted that "since we left Braunau, our troops have had to camp in the open, without tents, and receive provisions for one day at a time; some days they do not get any food at all." Because of the bad weather and relentless marching, the soldiers' uniforms and overcoats had become tattered, and the troops desperately needed new ones.[9] Yet it was impossible to get any clothing or equipment since the allied commissary service had broken down under the immense weight of its responsibilities. Austrian commissars were so overwhelmed, Kutuzov reported, that "even when they have sufficient provisions and forage in their stores, they are unable to process requests and, thus, leave our regiments without any supplies." The Russian commissary was equally hamstrung since some commissaries were sick and others were young and inexperienced. "There are not enough commissary officials to ensure uninterrupted furnishing for all of the men and horses," explained Kutuzov to the czar.[10]

Russian reports, letters, and memoirs paint a picture of widespread misery. Time and again, revictualing had failed, causing the troops to suffer. Kutuzov had to cut the daily rations for officers and was actively exploring opportunities to buy supplies from as far away as Hungary or Galicia since authorities in Upper Austria clearly could not satisfy the army's needs.[11] The first Russian units arriving at Wels found there some "fresh bread, meat and potatoes," but the latecomers were left famished.[12] Predictably, there were reports from local inhabitants involving "various abuses and devastation," reports that were widespread enough to reach the ears of the kaiser himself. Just as he was leading the army to Lambach, Kutuzov received Francis's letter complaining about "persistent excesses" committed by the troops.[13] Colonel Yermolov, commanding a horse artillery company, saw "many stragglers, whom we called 'marauders,' our first borrowing from the French." At one point a group of them were even ready to attack a squadron of hussars sent to prevent pillaging.[14] Harsh measures had to be taken to censure and punish soldiers who, in Kutuzov's words, "out of laziness and indulgence stayed behind in large groups by the side of the road with the sole purpose of robbing and plundering the nearby villages."[15] But even those soldiers who remained in the ranks and followed orders were exasperated by their experiences. They had been marching for days on end and all the inhabitants they came across had turned sour to their presence. They were clearly no longer welcome. The local women no longer gave them "sweet glances" and instead "greeted us with squinted eyes and pursed lips."[16] "It was here for the first time in my military career that I learned what retreating actually meant and may the Almighty protect you from ever experiencing it," recalled Ilya Popadichev of the Butyrskii Musketeer Regiment.[17] Standing near the crossing site on the

Traun River near Ebelsberg, some Russian troops got so frustrated waiting for the slow movement of the transports that they decided to spread the rumor of an enemy attack, which caused mayhem in the allied columns. "Suddenly everything fell into confusion," recalled an eyewitness. "The carriages were quickly abandoned, many fell off the bridge, and musket fire broke out in the camp, although not a single enemy soul was on our side of the river. . . . The agitators were never found."[18]

Austro-Russian relations had never been the friendliest; the events of late October only worsened them. Upset as they were about the Austrian failures at Ulm, the Russians were more incensed by what they considered to be the Austrians' haughty demeanor, foot-dragging, and mismanagement. Kutuzov and his officers certainly shared the sentiments of Archduke Charles, who felt that the kaiser was surrounded by "idiots or scoundrels."[19] The Russians were upset by reports that the Austrians had refused to provide sufficient care for the Russian sick in Linz, where the sole hospital quickly exceeded its capacity, housing some 700 patients when being intended for 250. "Hospital rooms are entirely unfurnished," a Russian army physician told Kutuzov. "There are no beds, bunks, or anything else."[20] Forced to choose between leaving the sick outside in the chilly autumn weather or sheltering them inside these bare rooms, the Russian physicians unsurprisingly picked the latter, though the Austrian authorities were refusing to assist them even with such basics as bandages and medication.[21]

Kutuzov issued orders to destroy all crossings on the Inn River, a tributary of the Danube, and moved the army to Enns, a small Austrian town on the banks of the eponymous river, where the allies agreed to make a stand. Kutuzov, knowing that he had little time, was keen to send on his heavy transports and thus to make the army more mobile. He ordered that the regiments get rid of personal carriages and move the wounded and sick to the town of Krems, meaning that only essential caissons and supply wagons remained.[22]

Such was the chaotic situation at the allied camp while Napoleon repaired the bridges over the Inn River. The French emperor thought that Kutuzov would not leave the southern bank of the Danube, assuming, correctly, that the allies would above all endeavor to unite Kutuzov's army with the Archduke Charles and try to protect Vienna. Napoleon placed little importance on military preparations in Prussia, knowing full well that even should the Prussians join the coalition, it would take many weeks for them to be ready for military operations. To complete the destruction of the coalition forces, he had to move quickly, so the Grande Armée charged forward. On October 31, Murat's cavalry caught up with the allied rear guard near Lambach, where the Austrian battalions of General Merveldt came under heavy attack and appealed for help to Kutuzov, who responded by sending some Russian jägers and hussars.[23] The French made several attacks on the allied positions on the outskirts of the town but were unable to break through, as the allied rear guard, led by Bagration, contested every inch of the ground until darkness descended; it then disengaged, burned the bridge over the Traun River, and followed the main army toward Enns.[24]

This first combat augured well for the allies, who had demonstrated that despite evident frictions they could successfully cooperate at the tactical level. The same could not be said of strategy. Kutuzov's thinking was clearly evolving in those last days of October. On October 24 he was worried about exposing Vienna and consequently "disheartening the Viennese court." A week later he was suggesting that the Austrians be prepared to sacrifice it to preserve their field army, a suggestion he would make on the outskirts of Moscow seven years later. He came to believe that it was beyond the power of the small Russian force to defeat the Grande Armée and certainly not in the tight confines of the Danubian valley. It would take Russian and Austrian reinforcements three or four weeks to arrive—and Napoleon's fierce war machine was rapidly converging on the Enns. However, avoiding battle with an opponent such as Napoleon while constantly challenging him, as the kaiser had suggested, was easier said than done. "If I confront him at every turn, I will have to endure his attacks," Kutuzov pointed out. "When some of my troops go into action, there will be a need to support them, from which a general battle may ensue, with a possibility of defeat."[25] Kutuzov argued in favor of a staggered withdrawal, one that would involve holding defensive positions on the rivers, then crossing over to the northern bank of the Danube to inhibit Napoleon's pursuit, and eventually linking up with the disparate parts of the allied forces. The Russians and Austrians could then attempt a new campaign against Napoleon, whose forces would by that time have lost their earlier advantage. However, the Austrians demurred, and in the end a compromise was reached. The Hofkriegsrat prepared a new memorandum on military operations on November 4–5, sending instructions to Kutuzov, Archduke Charles, and other commanders. The new plan called for Kutuzov to remain on the southern bank of the Danube "as long as possible" and hold a position as far to the west of Vienna as possible. If "extreme circumstances" forced him to retreat, Kutuzov would withdraw—"as slowly as possible"—to the bridgehead fortifications that the Austrians promised to construct at Krems. Here the Russians would hold a defensive position to gain enough time for reinforcements to arrive.[26]

Kutuzov had many misgivings about this Austrian plan of operations, which was, in any case, obsolete by the time it reached him. He foresaw "great difficulties" in carrying out these instructions, not the least of them being stranded in a fortified camp that the enemy could encircle. However, mindful of Emperor Alexander's orders to maintain amity and concord with the coalition partner, he did not openly express his disagreement and instead pledged to do his best. Once at Enns, he deployed the army near the river's confluence with the Danube and began constructing earthworks on the eastern bank, where he could hold a defensive line just as the Austrians had insisted. His correspondence reveals that Kutuzov, though hoping for the best, prepared for the worst. He understood that Napoleon would exploit his superior numbers to turn the allied left flank. Though Lieutenant General Merveldt held Steyr with his 15,000 men, Kutuzov was increasingly concerned that the French would be able to break through and envelop the Russian army from the south.[27] Thus, while assuring the emperors of his intention to hold the line on the Enns "as long as I can," Kutuzov was also making preparations for further withdrawal, ordering General Dokhturov to move part of the army to Amstetten, more than twenty miles east of Enns, and repeatedly emphasizing the need to closely "observe the road from Steyr."[28]

Napoleon had already seen the weakness of the allied position and resorted to his favorite *manoeuvre sur les derrières* (attacking the rear). He concentrated most of his army in the direction of Enns and dispatched Marshal Davout's corps to Steyr. Davout attacked the Austrians, pushing them back and capturing the crossing on the Enns River. This was a minor but important victory. With the Grande Armée advancing on Enns and Davout marching from Steyr, Napoleon hoped to pin Kutuzov and the Army of Podolia down in the cul-de-sac formed by the Enns and the Danube. As soon as he heard the news from Steyr, Kutuzov knew that holding a defensive line on the Enns was no longer tenable, especially since Merveldt had decided to leave the Russians and withdraw via Mariazell and Annaberg toward Vienna. There remains some debate as to what prompted the Austrian to do this. The Russian officers and imperial historians believed that Merveldt acted on orders from Vienna, yet Emperor Francis's letters, as well as the instructions from the Hofkriegsrat, clearly indicate that the Austrian high command expected Merveldt to be with Kutuzov in person and act as the quartermaster general of the allied armies.

Throughout the first week of November the Hofkriegsrat remained unaware of Merveldt's decision to abandon the Russians, developing its new plan of operations based on the assumption that Merveldt's corps would be providing direct and close support to Kutuzov. As it was, Merveldt's decision to march southeast instead of northeast served as a further example to the Russians that their coalition partners were unreliable. Operationally, it meant that the allied force was now split into two unequal parts and that the Russian army had lost the support of thousands of Austrian troops.[29] Left with just his own forces (and a handful of Austrian troops), Kutuzov had no choice but to abandon the position at Enns and fall back to Amstetten, where he expected to take a new position on the Ybbs River, as the kaiser had previously instructed him. "Our retreat from Enns proved terrible for the local inhabitants," remembered General Berg. "Our men were without bread and provisions and had to survive through robbery and pillage. For several days, my officers and I had nothing to eat but potatoes and cabbages that the locals used to feed their animals. All the villages were empty because the residents had fled and took away all their cattle and as many provisions as they could. And since most of the army had gone before us, anything of value had already been stripped."[30]

Unwilling to allow the enemy to escape, Napoleon attempted a double envelopment maneuver. As the Grande Armée pursued Kutuzov along the main route to Vienna, Napoleon instructed Marshal Adolphe Édouard Casimir Joseph Mortier to cross the Danube at Linz and advance along its northern bank, threatening the Russian right flank. Marshal Davout, meanwhile, marched from Steyr to Annaberg, driving Merveldt farther southeast and positioning himself on the Russian left flank. On November 3–4, Murat's cavalry crossed the Traun River and rushed toward Enns, where it arrived just as the last units of Bagration's rear guard were moving across the river. The French tried securing the crossing and storming the town but, in a combat memorably depicted in *War and Peace*, they were pushed back. In Tolstoy's apt description, someone standing on the shore of the river could see "equally uniform living waves of soldiers, shoulder straps, covered shakos, knapsacks, bayonets, long muskets, and, under the shakos, faces with broad cheekbones, sunken cheeks, and listless tired expressions, and feet that moved through the sticky mud that covered the planks of the bridge." A detachment of the Pavlogradskii hussars, led by Colonel Count Joseph O'Rourke, dismounted and, despite the hail of musket balls and canister, rushed to set fire to the bridge, which had been covered in advance with incendiary materials.[31] Some contemporaries believed that Kutuzov himself observed the fighting and, seeing the French rushing to extinguish the fire, sent in jägers, shouting to them, "You are Russians! So act as befits Russians!"[32]

The Russian rear guard held its position on the eastern bank, exchanging cannon and small-arms fire with the French while the main army struggled off along the road to Amstetten. "The ground shook, the neighboring mountains quivered, and a distressed echo in the depths of the valleys seemed to express the groans of nature itself," wrote a Russian eyewitness. "Kutuzov arrived at the riverbank and, at his sign, suddenly a few gallant jägers rushed forward, despite the enemy's canister fire, and drove the French back and set fire to the bridge. . . . The burning bridge increased the conflagration. The sky turned crimson while the raging waters of the Enns River seemed to turn into a fiery firmament. The exploding shells and grenades sent streams of shimmering sparks through the air. And if we add to this the terrible beating of drums, the intense musket fire . . . and the yells of the fighting men, one will have a sense of just what that nocturnal fighting on the Enns River was like."[33]

The weather was damp and cold, and there was seemingly unending grid-lock. "The pontoon wagons, heavy artillery, and other transports continued to block the roads, "so almost everything came to a standstill."[34] Kutuzov tried to resolve this problem by forming small squads whose only task was to move ahead of the units and clear the road of any superfluous transports and private carriages. Any wagons—even imperial transports—were to be pushed off the road.[35] To gauge the mood in the army, Kutuzov mingled with the soldiers, listening to their conversations and chatting with them on various subjects. On at least one occasion, as he stopped by a bonfire where some young officers were seeking warmth from the chilly weather, Kutuzov heard complaints about the continual retreat. "Everyone was unanimous in their desire to fight," a contemporary remembered. Kutuzov countered this by arguing that confronting the Grande Armée might sound heroic but was also foolish and self-defeating.[36] The Russian army had to live to fight an-other day. And so the retreat resumed, with the Russians destroying any bridges they could lay their hands on. "We found not a single bridge that we had not to rebuild entirely," complained one of Napoleon's staff officers. "The Russians burned them in a manner that was till then unknown to us."[37]

On November 5, the French repaired one of the bridges on the Enns River and resumed their pursuit of Kutuzov's army. The road from Enns ran through some wooded hills with a few clearings where the troops might be deployed. Bagration, the Russian rear-guard commander, took advantage of the terrain to organize a fighting retreat, halting intermittently to contain the advance of Marshal Murat's cavalry and General Charles Oudinot's in-fantry (from Marshal Lannes's corps). He first made a stand at Altenhofen, then slowly retreated to Strengberg, where he counterattacked with the support of Count Nostitz's Austrian troops. French numerical superiority soon forced him to fall back to Oed, where he repulsed fresh French attacks before approaching Amstetten itself. After four hours of fighting, the al-lied rear guard had suffered considerable casualties while snow hindered its movement.[38]

"It was a cold day," remembered a French staff officer. "The ground and trees in the Amstetten forest were alike covered with masses of snow, which produced a very remarkable effect on those of us who came from the south of Europe and had never before realized how beautiful nature can be in the winter." Everything seemed robed in a white, gleaming attire, creating "frozen vaults." Then, the officer remembered, they came upon an "unex-pected sight" of a very different sort.[39]

The unexpected sight was that of the new rear guard, which Kutuzov had deployed on the narrow road at the entrance to Amstetten. Receiving Bagration's urgent appeals for help, he sent reinforcements under Major

General Miloradovich, who was instructed to hold the ground at all costs.[40] By afternoon the Russian infantry had taken up positions on both sides of the road, protected by the woods and with the Austrian cavalry forming a screen.[41] Miloradovich let Bagration's weary men pass through his lines and then prepared to engage the enemy. Colonel Yermolov, who commanded a horse artillery company in this battle, observed as Miloradovich maneuvered against the enemy, who clearly underestimated the threat. Showing his customary impetuosity, Marshal Murat charged into the woods without regrouping his men. Seeing the enemy's disjointed attack, Miloradovich responded with a swift cavalry counterattack. "Our men were swept down, many were taken prisoner," remembered Murat's staff officer. A French artillery officer had the presence of mind to set two cannon in the road and fire a salvo at the Russians. The canister killed and maimed many Russian hussars, including their commanders, while the artillery also brought down "masses of snow" on the attacking Russians, who struggled to regroup amid "a dense hail of snow, shot and large icicles."[42]

The timely arrival of reinforcements allowed Murat to regroup. Observing a new French attack, the grenadier battalions of the Apsheronskii Musketeer Regiment counterattacked with bayonets leveled.[43] The fighting was unrestrained, as "the Russian bayonet showed itself worthy of the reputation it had acquired," a Russian contemporary proudly observed.[44] Stunned by the ferocity of the Russian soldiers, a French participant marveled that "none of them surrendered willingly. After they had been wounded, disarmed, and thrown to the ground, they still put up a fight and kept attacking. The only way we could assemble prisoners was to prod them with bayonets, like a poorly tamed herd of beasts, and belabor them with our musket butts."[45]

As the sun set over Amstetten, the Russian rear guard disengaged and marched in the wake of the main forces that were retreating through Melk to Sankt Pölten.[46] Both sides claimed victory and exaggerated their performances in the Battle of Amstetten—Murat embellished his account by claiming he had defeated "the entire Russian army" and captured 1,500 prisoners, while Kutuzov went as far as to assert that his rear guard had chased the enemy for miles, a claim that was repeated in more than one Russian biography of the general.[47] Both commanders knew that such claims were not true. If anything, Amstetten made one thing clear—it showed the French that defeating the Russians would not be an easy task. "Never have both sides fought with greater determination," observed Murat in a report to Napoleon.[48]

Advancing deeper into Austria proper, Napoleon faced a strategic quandary. His army was becoming progressively weaker through attrition and strategic consumption. Aside from the casualties, which were mounting by the day, the French had to detach troops to protect their ever-lengthening line of communication back to France and to engage the remaining Austrian forces; by mid-November, the Grande Armée was stretched over eighty miles between Sankt Pölten, where Murat's advance guard was located, and Linz, where the French emperor's headquarters was located. Controlling an army over such a vast area was becoming ever more difficult. Despite his victory at Ulm, Napoleon was unable to bring the war to a quick conclusion and had to decide what to do next. The bitter rear-guard actions at Lambach and Amstetten convinced him that Kutuzov was preparing to make a stand at Sankt Pölten.[49] This belief was further reinforced by reports of Archduke Charles retreating from northern Italy and of another Russian force northeast of Krems. The latter was the sixth column that Kutuzov had been forced to divert to the Ottoman border at the start of the campaign and which was now returning to the Army of Podolia.[50] Mistaking it for Buxhöwden's Army of Volhynia, Napoleon concluded that the Austrians would urge their Russian allies to defend the approaches to their imperial capital and that Kutuzov would probably await his reinforcements near Sankt Pölten. Based on these assumptions, the French emperor developed a new operational plan to destroy the Russo-Austrian army. Marshals Lannes, Murat, and Soult were to assault the town and pin down the Russian army while Marshal Bernadotte approached from the northwest and Davout turned the allied left wing, cutting Kutuzov off from Vienna. Napoleon assigned Marshal Mortier the task of crossing the river at Linz and hurrying to Krems to prevent Kutuzov from escaping to the left bank of the Danube.

Napoleon had misread Kutuzov's intentions. As his forces concentrated at Sankt Pölten, he had determined against making a stand and waiting for his army to be surrounded, as Mack had done at Ulm. The Austrian inability—or reluctance, as some Russians saw it—to accommodate the Russian wounded and its failure to provide sufficient provisions were causes for skepticism. However, it was the Austrian performance on the battlefield that truly alienated the Russians. Kutuzov was frustrated with the Hofkriegsrat's continued insistence on holding defensive lines as far south as possible in order to facilitate joint operations with the surviving Austrian forces. It was clearly impossible to do this with the meager resources he had at his disposal and in the face of the Grande Armée, which could maneuver around any position he took. Positional warfare meant little to him; retreating to the safety of northern Moravia or even Galicia, where he could reunite with the oncoming reinforcements, seemed far preferable.

In addition, there was the suspicion that the Austrians were engaged in behind-the-scenes discussions with the French. Mack's unfiltered conversation had sown the seeds of this distrust. On November 5, Kutuzov received yet more evidence of what he perceived as Austrian duplicity. At about three o'clock in the afternoon, at the monastery of Melk, Kutuzov was discussing matters with the Russian and Austrian officers when an orderly informed him of the arrival of a French messenger with a package addressed to Count Merveldt, who, as we have seen, had become separated from the main body. Kutuzov was surprised to hear of this unexpected guest and "hesitated for a moment before opening the package, but since the Austrian generals were all of the opinion that in the current circumstances it was important for me to read the dispatch, I decided to break the seal," wrote Kutuzov in a letter to the Russian foreign ministry. The letter, written by French marshal Alexander Berthier to Merveldt, discussed the earlier Franco-Austrian talks and asked Merveldt to convey Napoleon's personal letter to the kaiser.[51] Kutuzov must have been stunned. Merveldt had assured him earlier that his communications with the French involved a simple matter of delivering "a few letters" to the prisoners of war. "Now I have every reason to believe that there are secret negotiations under way between Austria and France," concluded Kutuzov.[52]

If "war is the continuation of politics by other means," as Clausewitz later observed, politics were playing an important role at this stage of the War of the Third Coalition. Kutuzov's suspicions that the Austrians were seeking a unilateral peace with Napoleon were confirmed when he learned that the French and Austrian emperors were indeed negotiating with the help of Count Ignac Gyulai, whom the kaiser had sent to Napoleon, in order to gain time until the Prussians made their decision on whether to join the coalition. A steady stream of messengers came and went from Vienna to Linz. "The emperor of Germany has written me many letters," Napoleon told his foreign minister, advising him that the Austrians might be willing to compromise. "There was hardly a day when messengers or negotiators did not arrive," remembered a French negotiator.[53] Murat sent a steady stream of reports suggesting that a truce, if not a peace, with the Austrians was imminent. Just two days later, November 7, Murat informed the emperor that "our outposts have received a messenger who declared, on behalf of the Austrians, that he has the imperial order not to fight anymore."[54]

Russian officers felt deeply betrayed. Fights and disagreements abounded. "There is a great degree of squabbling between the Russians and the Austrians," a French marshal joyfully reported. "They accuse each other of cowardice." The Austrian officers who dined at the monastery of Melk asked the monks not to serve food to them alongside the Russian "cowards" who were abandoning them "without a fight." Such sentiments were mutual and only worsened as days went by. A senior Russian officer confided to his wife that it was a "misfortune" to be in an alliance with these Austrian "scoundrels [*negodiai*]." "If this terrible campaign has taught us anything, it is that we should not count on the Austrians, who are our greater enemies than the French."[55]

To make matters worse, Kutuzov found himself dealing with two emperors whose instructions or suggestions often conflicted with the facts on the ground. As late as the first week of November, the kaiser was still urging Kutuzov to "defend my capital from misfortunes that would befall it if you [retreat]," while Emperor Alexander interjected himself into military operations to tell Kutuzov that he had "the supreme responsibility of protecting Vienna." Furthermore, Alexander reminded Kutuzov that he "must always bear in mind that you are commanding the Russian army." When he encountered the French he should attack, not simply hold a position, and thus "preserve the honor of my arms."[56] The Russian emperor was clearly misreading the situation in Austria, and his insistence on offensive warfare would have been catastrophic for the Russian army in the actual circumstances. Kutuzov refused to blindly follow such imperial dictates. His letters to both emperors were courteous, but his actions clearly indicated independence of mind. He knew that he could neither defeat nor contain the French army, and he did not have the desire to shed Russian blood for an ally that was actively seeking an understanding with the enemy. If the Austrians wanted to defend Vienna, then they should do it themselves.

Kutuzov believed that his primary mission was to extricate the Army of Podolia from the danger it faced and to ensure its survival and safety. As soon as he learned that a French corps had been observed on the northern bank of the Danube, he realized that Napoleon was setting up his trap around Sankt Pölten and that the Russian army would be caught between the anvil of Mortier's corps at Krems and the hammer of the Grande Armée striking from the south. Despite two sovereigns telling him to hold his position, he chose to evade Napoleon's enveloping maneuvers and retreat to the northern bank of the Danube, from where he could proceed to Brünn, there to unite with the reinforcements racing to meet him. Vienna could wait for another savior.

On November 8, the Army of Podolia was told to prepare to cross the Danube.[57]

Shortly after midnight, the Russians broke camp and marched northward, quickly covering the fifteen miles separating Sankt Pölten from Krems. Kutuzov was not pleased with what he had seen on this march. A good number of officers were absent from their units; when told that they were sick, he demanded they report for examination. Some units moved haphazardly, with the cavalry far ahead of the infantry. There were stragglers and absentees, which Kutuzov blamed on commanders who had failed to instill adequate discipline. "Such disorders must end at once," he demanded in a general order to the army, reminding his regimental commanders that "there must be a perimeter around each regiment; take a daily roll call; and never allow a private to leave without an officer."[58]

Despite all this, the Russian army moved its transports and men across the river and burned the twenty-eight-span wooden bridge in its wake.[59] By early evening, the allies were already in positions around Krems. As the sun was setting, Kutuzov rushed to examine the fortified camp that the Austrians had promised to construct here so that the Russians could hold out until the arrival of reinforcements. A quick visit revealed that the Austrians had, once more, failed to deliver on their promises; even the kaiser's assurance that "it would take a few more weeks to ready the fortification for a regular garrison" was clearly hyperbole.[60] Virtually nothing had been done at Krems. "We found no earthworks here," reported Kutuzov. "Just the foundation of a battery, and even there no one was in it." It was clear that this position could not be defended. Knowing that his departure from Krems would ruffle feathers in Vienna, Kutuzov wrote a letter to the kaiser, apologizing for being unable to comply with the imperial orders and explaining the reasons forcing him to withdraw: "The enemy's persistent pursuit of me in recent days has given me reason to think that he intended to attack us or have particular intentions from the left bank of the Danube. I was not mistaken." Captured prisoners of war testified that Napoleon intended to "catch [the Russians] between two fires." He stressed that he had done as much as he could but that circumstances now required him to fall even farther back.[61]

Kutuzov's decision to cross the Danube had major implications. It exposed Vienna to the French advance and forced the Austrian government to start its evacuation. Kutuzov had already been arguing for two weeks about the need to preserve a fighting force even if it meant sacrificing territory for it. Politically this was difficult. Militarily, the decision was justified because it deprived Napoleon of an opportunity to destroy the allied army on the southern bank of the Danube and led the French commanders into making a crucial mistake. The prospect of a defenseless Vienna lying just ahead proved too much for Murat to resist. The French marshal abandoned his pursuit of the retreating Russian army and dashed with his advance guard to the Austrian capital. Kutuzov was thus able to complete his withdrawal across the Danube. Once at Krems, he could take advantage of Napoleon's miscalculation, which left one French corps on the northern bank of the Danube.

The weather was overcast and cold; thick snow covered the hillsides around Krems. Almost as soon as he was across the river, Kutuzov ordered his men to reconnoiter the area. He already knew that part of the Grande Armée had crossed the Danube at Linz and was moving along the northern bank. Now he needed to know how close this enemy force was. It did not take long for Miloradovich's patrols to come across the French forward outposts and, after some skirmishing, capture a few soldiers. The prisoners confirmed that Marshal Mortier's corps was in the valley, with General Honoré Théodore Maxime Gazan de la Peyrière's division (5,800 men) already at Durrenstein (Dürnstein), while the division of General Pierre Dupont de l'Étang (4,200 men) was about eight miles behind it.[62] Kutuzov quickly

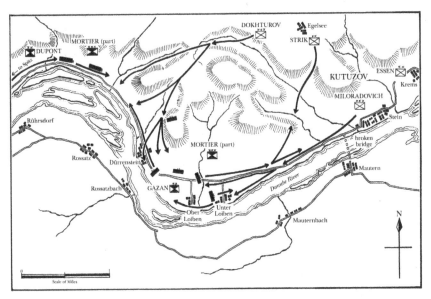

MAP 7 Battle of Krems-Durrenstein

grasped the importance of this intelligence. In his rush to Krems, Mortier had overextended his corps along the riverbank. With the wide and deep Danube separating it from the rest of the Grande Armée, Gazan's division was exposed and vulnerable, unable to receive any reinforcements or to escape to the opposite shore.[63]

On November 10, Kutuzov, assisted by the Austrian quartermaster general Johann Heinrich von Schmitt, a native of Krems, drafted a plan for the attack. The allies wanted to lure Mortier's forward division, led by Gazan, to advance through the narrow and flat valley just east of Durrenstein and below the ruins of the castle (in which Richard the Lionheart of England had been held for ransom more than 600 years earlier). At the end of the valley, Miloradovich's "left column"—five infantry battalions, supported by two squadrons of hussars—was to hold a position at Stein an der Donau with orders to engage the enemy face-on and pin him down, so that two other attack columns under Lieutenant Generals Dokhturov and Maltitz (who was replaced by Major General Fedor Strik) could launch an enveloping maneuver up and across the Weißkirchen gorge overlooking the river. Dokhturov, guided by Schmitt, was to reach the village of Scheibenhof and descend on the French rear near Durrenstein. Kutuzov thus hoped to surround and destroy the French troops on the promontory between Durrenstein and Krems.[64] Though only about five miles separated Krems from Scheibenhof, Kutuzov knew that his men would need plenty of time to make their way through this rugged terrain, where the snow was already clogging the passes over the mountains. The flanking columns were ordered to depart early on November

11 so that they could be in position to strike at the enemy; Schmitt assumed that Dokhturov's column would complete the movement by late morning.[65] To expedite the movement, Kutuzov ordered the troops "to leave knapsacks and raincoats [*plaschi*] behind under the guard of the sick soldiers." Well aware of the size of the Grande Armée and having been informed that Mortier's cavalry division was heading northeast, he was worried that Napoleon might concentrate his forces against the Russian position and strike the Army of Podolia in the rear or flank. He therefore left Bagration's entire "advance corps" (some 7,000 men) in the Imbach Valley with orders to observe the northern approach and the rear, and kept a reserve, under Lieutenant General Essen II, at Krems. Moreover, Kutuzov established artillery batteries along the riverbank to engage the French flotilla if it tried to come to Mortier's rescue.[66]

As the sun rose on that November morning, Miloradovich led his column from Stein to Rothenhof.[67] He soon encountered French skirmishers scattered across the vineyards and the hillsides. In the ensuing fight, Miloradovich sent out his own skirmishers and made a slow but steady advance, pushing the French back to Unter-Loiben. Mortier, receiving reports that the fighting involved a few isolated Russian units, decided to engage the enemy without sending out flanking patrols to reconnoiter the nearby valley and heights—which would have inexorably revealed the extent of the Russian movements.[68]

Gazan, having stayed overnight in Ober-Loiben and Unter-Loiben, set off along the riverbank toward Rothenhof. His infantry—about 1,500 men of the 4e Régiment d'Infanterie Légère and 2,000 men of the 100e Régiment d'Infanterie de Ligne, with artillery support—charged into the hamlet, where, in the words of Miloradovich, "relentless fighting ensued."[69] Mortier belatedly realized that instead of a weak rear guard he was actually facing a superior enemy force. He took advantage of the vineyards to organize a fighting retreat and sent urgent orders to Generals Dupont and Dumonceau to hasten to his rescue. The Russian troops pressed their advantage and, despite suffering heavy casualties, drove the French back to Unter-Loiben, where Mortier and Gazan did their best to rally their men, committed the 103e Régiment d'Infanterie de Ligne from the reserve, and held on to the position amid chaotic fighting.[70] The Russians launched several attacks on the villages, but each time they were repulsed.

Although remaining at Krems, Kutuzov was not a passive observer of the quickly evolving battle. Around noon he dispatched his aide-de-camp Count Tiesenhausen to Miloradovich with instructions to regroup and launch a new assault on the village.[71] At the same time, on Kutuzov's orders, Major General Strik's men, who had reached Egelsee, began to veer south and descend from the hills toward Loiben, striking Mortier's left flank and threatening to push the French into the river.[72] "Skirmishers from our regiment scattered in the woods," recalled Ilya Popadichev of the Butyrskii Musketeer Regiment. "We quickly approached the French, engaged them in a fierce firefight, and forced them to fall back."[73] "The ground was drenched in blood and strewn with dead and wounded," remembered a French officer. The village of Loiben was a scene of "carnage."[74] A Russian eyewitness wrote simply, "It was one of the most savage combats."[75]

The day was already slipping into the afternoon, but Dokhturov had not yet appeared to entrap the French. More than six hours after departing from Krems, the Russian flanking column had only managed to make it as far as the environs of Scheibenhof, five miles from Krems, and was already exhausted after having slogged up the "narrow defiles" and "very difficult valleys," in wind and snow, all night and morning.[76] And it still had to negotiate the steep, rocky, and winding trails down the hills to get behind Gazan's division. Hearing the muffled sound of cannon fire on his left, Dokhturov urged his men to move faster, left behind his artillery and cavalry, and pressed on with the infantry alone. Reaching the top of the heights, he ordered five infantry battalions and two hussar squadrons under the command of Major General Urusov to secure a position there to prevent the French from escaping across the gorge, and then rushed down the slopes with his remaining forces.[77] It was late in the afternoon when Dokhturov's vanguard—three infantry battalions led by Karl Ulanius—climbed down the hillside, reached the riverbank, and surprised the French outposts at Durrenstein, severing the line of retreat for Gazan's division. Dokhturov followed him with just four infantry battalions, keen to seal off the escape route for Mortier.

Yet by this point it was too late. As Dokhturov's men streamed down the hillside, they could see enemy reinforcements approaching from the west. This was Dupont's division, hurrying to rescue Mortier, who was horrified to see the Russians attacking his rear.[78] Dokhturov thus found himself caught between two fires, with Dupont pushing from the west and Mortier seeking to escape from the east. In the fast-encroaching darkness, the Russian general struggled to make sense of it all, finding himself without artillery or cavalry and deprived of the ability to discern the enemy's intentions or assert effective control over his own troops, split as they were between the valley and the hills. He further subdivided his forces, sending two musketeer battalions under Lieutenant Colonel Gvozdev to the west to contain Dupont's advance, while Dokhturov himself attacked Gazan's division.[79] "The confined nature of the place exacerbated the brutality of the fighting," observed a Russian historian who had interviewed the participants. "Round shot and canister, rumbling in the mountains, felled trees and crushed rocks. Men were struck with splinters and branches."[80] Owing to the high, steep rocks on one hand and the river on the other, it was impossible for either side to maneuver around. All that could be done was to attack in front and try to cut a way through. The French exploited their advantage in artillery to bring forward cannon, sending murderous canister fire on Dokhturov's battalions, caught in the narrow space between the bluffs and the river. The French charged. As they burst into Durrenstein, the men fought in the streets with bayonets and musket butts. Meanwhile, Gvozdev found himself hard pressed by Dupont's division, which attacked along the main road, the wooded hillsides, and the riverbank. "My battalions and I were surrounded and came under strong enemy fire from all directions," he reported. Repelling at least three enemy assaults and on the verge of being overwhelmed by the enemy, Gvozdev requested reinforcements. Observing the fighting from the top of the gorge, General Schmitt saw the Russian units faltering and tried to shore up the line by rushing down the slopes with a battalion of the Bryanskii Musketeer Regiment. He paid a heavy price for it—a French musket ball killed him on the spot—but the arrival of the Bryanskii musketeers helped Gvozdev's men to hold their ground.[81]

Hearing the sound of gunfire from Durrenstein, Kutuzov understood that Dokhturov had belatedly reached his destination, so he reinforced Miloradovich with a battalion of the Novgorodskii Musketeer Regiment and ordered him to advance to complete the French entrapment.[82] "The entire line rapidly charged forward, overwhelming the enemy everywhere," Miloradovich wrote in his after-action report. The next couple of hours saw some of the most brutal fighting of the entire war. Dokhturov was caught between two French forces at Durrenstein, while Mortier was surrounded at Unter-Loiben. "A ferocious fight was blazing from the banks of the Danube to the top of steep mountain slopes," recalled General Dupont. "Where the ground allowed, the troops threw themselves in with the bayonet. Both sides mixed in desperate close-quarter combat, spreading confusion among the participants."[83] As that November evening finally drew to its close, both sides disengaged, utterly exhausted. Miloradovich fell back to Stein, while Dokhturov, assailed both in front and at the rear, pulled his men back up into the mountains on the way to Krems. Amid cries of "France! France! You have saved us!," Mortier's exhausted grenadiers retook burning Durrenstein and threw themselves into the arms of their comrades from Dupont's division.[84] But so heavy were their losses that Gazan's division ceased to exist and Mortier was lucky to be able to clear his path with a few skeleton battalions.

Both sides claimed victory at the Battle of Krems-Durrenstein and blustered about their feats. Kutuzov reported that his army lost 2,000 casualties but had taken as many French prisoners, five guns, and two flags, to which Napoleon countered, in the 22nd Bulletin, that "more than 4,000 Russian were killed and wounded, and 1,300, among whom were two colonels, taken prisoner." Exaggerated as these claims were, there was no denying that the fighting was horrific. Each side lost over 3,000 men.[85] Napoleon summed up the ferocity of the fighting when he called it "a day of massacre."[86] He also drew solace from the dazzling gallantry and determination of the French soldiers. Despite being outnumbered and surrounded, the

French refused to give up and managed to fight their way out of a perilous position. Though Gazan's division suffered grievously and Mortier had to move the entire corps across the Danube, the battle was lauded as a shining example of French fearlessness.

Krems-Durrenstein, however, was hardly a French victory. Both Napoleon and Mortier had made mistakes that French military gallantry could not redeem. If the battle did not end with the complete destruction of the French division, the cause was partly in the fighting capability of the French soldiers but also in the mistakes the allies themselves had made. Kutuzov's ignorance of the area around Krems-Durrenstein meant that he was forced to rely on Austrian staff officers, who, in the words of a well-informed contemporary, "not only vouched for the feasibility of a flanking move but also took it upon themselves to lead Dokhturov behind enemy lines."[87] Schmitt was overconfident in his assessments, which led to the failure to get Dokhturov's entire force into position to entrap Gazan's division. Kutuzov's mistake was in acquiescing to such a complicated plan and trusting his Austrian colleagues that they could lead a flanking movement at night and in snow across the mountains. He should have known how precarious such an undertaking would be. Furthermore, his cautiousness meant that a significant part of the Russian force remained idle in the rear, while barely half of the army was involved in the fighting.

Krems-Durrenstein was no Ulm but it was, nevertheless, a victory for the allies. Thomas Robert Bugeaud, the future French marshal, who in 1805 was a young soldier serving in the Imperial Guard, liked to repeat an old saying: "'If you act as a sheep, you will be sheared.' So when retreating, you must become a lion. Once you give the enemy who gets too close three or four good punches, you will be respected."[88] Kutuzov had successfully evaded Napoleon's pursuit and delivered a powerful counterpunch that knocked Mortier's corps out of combat for the remainder of the campaign. The victory at Krems-Durrenstein gave a moral boost to the coalition partners, who were on a losing streak against Napoleon. After weeks of marching back and forth across Austria, the Russian troops had made a stand and not only held the field but defeated the French. News of the victory at Durrenstein caused much rejoicing in Vienna and St. Petersburg. Emperor Francis heartily congratulated Kutuzov on this success and granted him the Grand Cross of the Military Order of Maria Theresa (Militär-Maria Theresien-Orden). Founded to commemorate the Austrian victory over the Prussians at Kolin in 1757, the order was the highest award the Habsburg court could bestow for valor. The statute limited this order to officers in the Austrian armed forces, but on rare occasions the Habsburg rulers ignored this restriction in order to recognize the bravery or military competence of allied officers or rulers. Kutuzov became just the third Russian—after Grand Duke Constantine and Generalissimo Suvorov—to receive this award.[89]

The battle challenges the traditional image of a morose Kutuzov as a passive observer of historic events—a portrait that Tolstoy's writings has so deeply ingrained in popular imagination. If anything, Kutuzov might be criticized for undertaking an overly ambitious plan. Still, once he adopted it, he remained, as best he could in that rugged terrain, in close contact with subordinates and interjected himself (through aides-de-camp) into the flow of the battle. Emperor Alexander was pleased with Kutuzov's performance.[90] Krems-Durrenstein was not merely a tactical success, however. Kutuzov gained a vital operational advantage. By forcing Napoleon to pull Mortier back to the southern bank of the Danube, he won some breathing space for his wearied men, who for the first time in days were able to cook themselves a meal, then lie down to rest. He now had sufficient freedom of action on the northern side of the river and could afford to remain at Krems awaiting reinforcements or retreat farther north into Moravia. It could not, however, prepare him for what was ahead.

| The Tale of Two Ruses

VIENNA, THE MAGNIFICENT POLITICAL and cultural center of Mitteleuropa, lies among the last Alpine foothills before the Danube flows into the vast and rolling Hungarian plain. As the capital of the Habsburg Empire, the city had seen its share of triumphs and setbacks. Besieged twice by the Ottoman Turks, it succeeded in resisting on both occasions and prospered as the focal point of the rapidly expanding Habsburg domain. The city was famous for its baroque palaces, stately homes, ornate churches, and rich cultural heritage that made it the envy of the rest of Europe. It was the home of a remarkable generation of musicians and composers—Ludwig von Beethoven had just premiered his Third Symphony ("Eroica"), which he had originally dedicated to Napoleon for embodying revolutionary ideals. In November 1805, this resplendent city lay unprotected before the "the incarnation of the Revolution," as the Austrian statesman von Metternich described the French emperor.[1]

Napoleon was furious about the setback at Krems-Durrenstein, for which he held Murat responsible. The French marshal was supposed to be nipping at Kutuzov's heels, especially given that he had received reports that Kutuzov intended to retreat across the Danube at Krems.[2] Napoleon's grand design of enveloping the enemy and destroying him in another "battle of annihilation" was in jeopardy, and Murat should have pursued Kutuzov and prevented him from crossing the Danube just long enough for Mortier to secure the crossing site at Krems. Instead, Murat veered off to Vienna. The dazzling city beckoned him. Vienna had not been conquered in over 300 years, not since the Black Army of Hungarian king Matthias Corvinus had made a triumphal entry there in 1485, and the glory of being the first Frenchman to claim it was too enticing to resist. "Momentarily he was like a head-strong stallion that had ripped the bridle out of the grasp of its handler and bolted."[3]

Napoleon was not pleased. "I cannot approve of your way of advancing," he reprimanded his marshal. "You proceed like a scatterbrain [*étourdi*], and you pay no heed to the orders that I have sent to you. . . . You have thought only of the trifling glory of entering Vienna. There is no glory where there is no danger, and there is none in entering a capital that is undefended."[4] By then it was too late. Murat, with his advance guard and Lannes's corps, was already on the outskirts of the Austrian capital.

Located at the conflux of the Danube and Wien Rivers, Vienna was among the best-fortified metropolises in the region—it had strong ramparts, bastions, eleven "ravelins," and defensible outworks.[5] Yet the walls and moat had long been neglected, and the city's glacis was better-known for offering "a very agreeable walk round the walls of the town, planted with trees and commanding the neighboring suburbs," than for its defensive significance.[6] Capturing the city would not be a problem, but securing its bridges would be a far more challenging enterprise. Marcel de Serres, who visited the city in 1809, discovered that few places in Austria were so intersected with waters as Vienna, where "the Danube divides itself into a variety of channels."[7] In the absence of bridges, crossing the river would have posed a logistical nightmare. Thus the success of Napoleon's war efforts hinged on securing a crossing site, most notably a series of wooden bridges that spanned the Danube and were collectively known as the Tabor Bridge.[8] After the Russians had burned the crossing at Krems, the Tabor Bridge—some five hundred paces in length—represented the only permanent means of communication between the two banks of the Danube River west of Linz. It was therefore of immense strategic value.

To preserve the city intact, Emperor Francis ordered the imperial family and government evacuated, and entrusted the command of a garrison over 10,000 men in strength to Fürst Karl Joseph Franz von Auersperg, a veteran who was forced out of retirement. It had been over a decade since he had held a field commission, and the largely ceremonial responsibilities he performed at the Habsburg court hardly prepared him for the task at hand. Upon learning of the French approach, Auersperg chose to abandon the suburbs and took up positions guarding the Tabor Bridge. Left undefended, the citizens of Vienna sent a deputation to welcome the French into the city and pledging to supply all of their needs as long as order was maintained.

On November 13, Murat led his advance guard on a ceremonial entry into the Austrian capital. A crowd of curious onlookers gawked as the foreign troops marched down the boulevards. Murat was heartily relieved to hear that the Tabor Bridge was still intact. Taking a handful of soldiers, he and Marshal Lannes headed toward the riverfront. By then the Austrians had completed their preparations to destroy the valuable crossing and thoroughly laid the bridges with powder and fuses so that they could be set on fire at an instant's notice. Destruction of the Tabor Bridge would have had momentous consequences for the entire course of the war, as it would have denied Napoleon the means of getting across the Danube and brought his pursuit of the retreating allies to a standstill. Napoleon's own experiences just four years later indicate the extent to which the destruction of this bridge would have affected military operations.[9] As they observed the bridges from the shore, Marshals Murat and Lannes could see the Austrian troops posted on the opposite bank and understood that an overt attack would result in the immediate destruction of the bridge. Instead they resorted to a ruse that was as daring as it was outrageous.

Approaching an Austrian outpost, the marshals announced that peace negotiations between Emperor Napoleon and Kaiser Francis had resulted in an armistice and asked for the officer commanding at the bridge to be sent for. Startled to hear the news, the Austrian sentries rushed back to inform Auersperg, while the two French marshals and their companions, on foot with their hands behind their backs, strolled onto the bridge and jovially bantered with the Austrians, who tried vainly to stop them. How was it that they had not heard anything about the peace? the French generals disingenuously asked Auersperg and his officers. Did they not know that the kaiser had sent Count Gyulai to negotiate with Napoleon? Auersperg was baffled, for he was aware of ongoing Austrian diplomatic negotiations, and the French claims did not seem that far-fetched. As Murat and Lannes did their utmost to divert the Austrians' attention elsewhere, French grenadiers quietly moved onto the bridge and disarmed the Austrian sentries without fuss. Catching sight of these troops, one of the Austrian officers belatedly realized the French stratagem and tried to alert his men, but Lannes grabbed him by the collar and berated him for insubordination and endangering the truce, while other French officers shouted to drown out the Austrian's voice. Minutes later, it was all over. The grenadiers defused the incendiary devices on the bridge, and masses of French troops poured across the river. Instead of destroying the bridge, the hoodwinked Auersperg was allowed to withdraw his troops.[10]

Capturing Vienna with the Tabor Bridge intact was an extraordinary accomplishment. Napoleon, who just days earlier had derided Murat for his mishandling of the pursuit, promptly forgave the marshal and sought to make the best of the new situation. With the Habsburg capital and its bridges secured, the Grande Armée could advance northwest and intercept Kutuzov just as he was marching into Moravia.

One can only imagine the despair that the news from Vienna created in the Russian headquarters. "The failure to deny the bridge demonstrated the lack of will and intellect prevailing in the Austrian higher command in 1805," observed one eminent historian.[11] For Kutuzov and his officers, this incident only further underscored the treachery of their allies. Tolstoy brilliantly captures the essence of the fast-spreading anti-Austrian sentiment when he has Prince Andrei Bolkonskii wonder if "this may be a treason," while other Russian officers lamented that "it is not treachery, nor rascality nor stupidity." "We have been *Macked*!" Equally infuriating was the Austrian failure to alert their allies to what had transpired.[12] Interestingly, Kutuzov had anticipated that something like this might happen. Drawing upon his earlier experiences in the Danubian Principalities, he used the brief respite at Krems to solicit local help in intelligence gathering and offered inhabitants rewards for any information about the enemy movement. This quickly paid off, as late in the evening of November 13 one of the locals brought the news that the French had captured the Tabor Bridge earlier that day. Kutuzov understood immediately what this meant. "This unexpected event forced me to change my entire plan of action," he admitted later.[13] Archduke Charles was still hundreds of miles away, crossing the Isonzo River, while Buxhöwden was en route to Olmütz. The reports indicated that Murat intended to move toward Korneuburg and Wolkersdorf—the former direction meant that he would try reaching Hollabrunn in order to cut the Russian line of retreat to Znaim, while the French advance through Wolkersdorf was clearly aimed to anticipate the Russians at Brünn, should they be able to break through at Znaim.

A lack of maps once again seriously constrained Kutuzov's deliberations, as he was largely unfamiliar with the wider area; as a last resort, he sought the help of the kaiser, who belatedly sent him copies of maps of Moravia and Bohemia.[14] Kutuzov then considered several options. He could try the safer choice of marching northwest to Bohemia, which would take him away from Murat and Lannes and closer to Mikhelson's army group, which was supposed to be moving through Poland toward Saxony. But Kutuzov did not know the whereabouts of this force, nor was he certain that Prussia would break its neutrality and join the allies. The Bohemian scenario would have also moved him away from Archduke Charles and Buxhöwden, who could be attacked and destroyed piecemeal. Kutuzov opted in favor of a riskier alternative— heading northeast to Moravia. This route would take the army within striking distance of the French forces in Vienna but, if successful, would allow Kutuzov to seek the safety of the fortress of Olmutz, join Buxhöwden, and remain in touch with Archduke Charles.

Late on November 13 Kutuzov dispatched all heavy equipment ahead of the troops and ordered the army to depart from its campsite, leaving some 1,300 sick and wounded soldiers at Krems. Marching all night and day, he arrived at Ebersbrunn, fifteen miles away from Krems. "The unexpected appearance of such large [enemy] forces on this side of the Danube has placed the army in immense danger," he noted in a letter to Emperor Alexander. "Our men are shattered and yet I still have to march another [22 miles] to Jetzelsdorf to move beyond the roads that lead to my rear."[15] He could see that anything in the direction of Hollabrunn posed an immediate threat, given that the road from Vienna to Znaim was far better than the unpaved one the Russians had to take from Krems, putting them at a clear disadvantage compared to the fast-marching Frenchmen. He decided to send a small rear guard to intercept the French vanguard and hold it up until the army passed behind him as far as Jetzelsdorf on the road to Znaim. He knew full well how dangerous this mission was and what it would take to succeed. Prince Bagration seemed well suited for the task at hand.[16] Though his ill-shod and tired men had just finished the long march from Krems and had not yet had time to rest or eat a meal, Bagration hit the road at once. By nine o'clock in the morning on November 15, after marching some fifteen miles in darkness, on narrow paths across hills and through ravines and vineyards, the Russian rear guard—some 7,000 men, including a small Austrian brigade under Count Nostitz—reached the village of Hollabrunn.[17] The French were nowhere to be seen yet. Bagration found the terrain here unfavorable but decided to wage a defense in depth, forming three lines that would slow down the enemy advance and buy as much time as possible. Leaving Nostitz's brigade, with its Cossacks, to hold a forward position at Hollabrunn, he moved his remaining troops three miles north to the small village of Schöngrabern, where the terrain was better suited for defensive action: a large creek cut across the ground, while vast vineyards provided cover from enemy cavalry. The village of Grund (Guntersdorf), another mile to the rear, was hastily fortified and turned into the last line of defense. Determined to fight to the end, Bagration then summoned his senior officers to discuss the battle plan. Their meeting was interrupted by the news that the French had appeared in large numbers at Hollabrunn.

The Russian version of the events at Hollabrunn-Schöngrabern centers on the classic triad of the good (Bagration), the bad (Murat and Lannes), and the ugly (Nostitz). In this storyline it was late in the afternoon when Murat approached Hollabrunn and, after observing Bagration's rear guard standing across the road, felt distinctly anxious about attacking the Russians, fearing that the rest of Kutuzov's army might be close by. To allow the Grande Armée to catch up, he decided to resort to subterfuge. As soon as the skirmishing between the French and allied outposts had begun, Murat sent a messenger to Nostitz to announce that an armistice had been concluded between the French and Austrians, citing his unopposed crossing over the Tabor Bridge as the proof. Just as Auersperg had been, Nostitz was duped and agreed to withdraw from Hollabrunn, leaving the Russians to face the full might of the French vanguard's 35,000 men (as many as 60,000 in the more embellished Russian accounts).[18] "It seemed only a miracle could save our rear guard!" wrote Kutuzov.[19]

While some elements in this account are factual, they were heavily spun. Upon reaching Hollabrunn, Murat had only three cavalry divisions (approximately 10,000 men) available, though he knew that divisions of the IV Corps (Soult) and the V Corps (Lannes) were en route. This may partly explain why the marshal was wary of attacking that afternoon. The first hour of the encounter at Hollabrunn remains shrouded in uncertainty. The Austrians and Russians maintained that Murat had tried to fool them with an armistice offer; the Frenchman himself is silent on this issue.[20] We may assume that the allies were truthful in claiming that Nostitz received written assurance from Marshal Murat that an armistice had been concluded between Napoleon and Francis, and that he felt compelled to march his troops off the field until he received further clarification. Bagration tried in vain to convince the Austrian of the implausibility of such an armistice and warned him that the French assurances were a ruse. Nostitz remained unwavering, causing even some of his senior officers to defy him and keep their troops with Bagration.[21] Even thoroughly anti-Austrian Russian officers acknowledged that Prince Hohenlohe was incensed at the conduct of General Nostitz and that he ordered his men to rejoin the Russian rear guard and support its operations.[22]

Kutuzov had barely had any rest in the past two days but pushed his men onward through the night of November 14–15. He was near Jetzelsdorf when the news from Hollabrunn arrived. He was furious about Nostitz's actions and castigated him for "getting hoodwinked" by the French and for not committing his troops to fight. Nostitz's actions put the entire army in danger because they undermined any chance for a swift withdrawal, and the Russian soldiers were too exhausted for a battle.[23] Yet Kutuzov also grasped what a valuable opportunity Murat's ploy had presented him with, and he exploited it to repay the French in kind. With "a peculiarly Byzantine cunning," as one Austrian put it, Kutuzov dispatched his aide-de-camp Wintzingerode with instructions to engage and prolong negotiations for as long as possible.[24] Murat was about to discover that he was dealing with the wily "old fox of the North," as Napoleon later called Kutuzov.[25]

The draft agreement that Wintzingerode and Murat's chief of staff signed on the afternoon of November 15 has long been known, but its essence seems to have been misread. In fact, the published Russian translation of this document has been slightly distorted. Its title—"The Text of the Preliminary Armistice Between the Russian and French Forces"—does not reflect the nuance of the French original, which was "Capitulation Offered by the Russian Army."[26] Russian historians were naturally apprehensive about the word "capitulation" appearing in their narrative of valiant retreat. Still, the document itself is instructive for how Kutuzov handled the matter.[27] He knew that his sole chance for gaining time, giving exhausted troops some rest, and moving the transports and heavy convoys ahead lay in offering Murat something that made it worthwhile for him to halt in his tracks in the face of Napoleon's repeated orders to pursue. Therefore, what Kutuzov proposed was not a simple truce, as has been customarily observed. "When Wintzingerode was announced to me, I admitted him at once," reported Murat to Napoleon shortly after the meeting. "He asked to *capitulate* [il a demandé à capituler]."[28]

This short statement goes to the crux of the matter. The Russian offer, in effect, represented a request for what are called the honors of war, a privilege sometimes conferred by the winning side to the vanquished, permitting them to march out with their arms, baggage, and full honors.[29] Indeed, the draft agreement spelled out that the Russian army would leave "Germany" entirely and "return home along the same route along which it arrived." The opportunity of seeing the Russians knocked out of the war, leaving the Habsburg monarchy at the mercy of Napoleon, would have been too tantalizing for the marshal to pass up.[30] The deal was deliberately made to look advantageous to the French emperor, for it would signal an effective end to the war. "I thought it my duty to consent to this capitulation because it represents the preliminaries of peace that I know to be the object of your desires," Murat confided to the emperor.[31]

Kutuzov had no authority to do this. Caught in a desperate situation, he bluffed. "My intention was, above all, to gain time to seek the means to save the army and to have time to get away from the enemy," he explained to Emperor Alexander.[32] Both sides agreed that the accord would be sent for ratification to Napoleon and Kutuzov and that until they approved it the armies would remain in their positions; in the event the accord was rejected, both sides promised not to resume hostilities without first granting a four-hour notice.[33]

When the signed document reached him, Kutuzov must have been ecstatic. Murat had failed to see through the ruse and accepted a deal that the Russians considered in no way binding. "The good fortune presented here the means by which the army could be saved," Kutuzov wrote the emperor. "I held up an answer more than twenty hours, never thinking of accepting the agreement at all." Indeed, the twenty-four hours during which the French advance guard stood still were of decisive importance. Instead of remaining in his position, as specified in the agreement, Kutuzov kept marching his depleted army along the road to Znaim, denying it any rest and riding up and down the line to encourage the men. By the evening of November 16, he had thus managed to escape the French by a two-day march.[34] And fortune kept smiling on him. The news soon arrived that Bernadotte's corps, which Napoleon had sent in pursuit of the Russians on the north bank, was held up crossing the Danube by the bad weather and could not catch up in time.

To prevent Murat from realizing that he was being duped, however, Kutuzov had to leave behind his rear guard in full sight of the enemy.[35] He knew what it meant. "Although I saw the certainty of the annihilation of

Prince Bagration's corps," he admitted in a report to the czar, "I considered it nevertheless a necessitous sacrifice for the salvation of the army."[36]

The news of the armistice enraged Napoleon, who could not believe Murat's latest error of judgment. "It is impossible for me to find words to express my displeasure with you," he castigated his marshal. "You command only my advance guard, and have no right to conclude an armistice without my order. You made me lose the fruits of a campaign. Break the armistice at once, and march upon the enemy." Napoleon pointed out to Murat that the general who offered this "capitulation" had no authority to do so because only the emperor of Russia had that right. "The Austrians let themselves be duped over the [Tabor] bridge, but now you have been fooled by the Russians." He demanded that Murat press forward at once: "March and destroy the Russian army!"[37]

It was already late afternoon when Murat received the imperial reprimand. Stung by its harsh tone, he immediately prepared to fight, though the sun was expected to set in just a couple of hours on that short November day. Observing French movements, Bagration and his officers were dismayed by Murat's failure to provide the four-hour notice. Nostitz and Wintzingerode personally went to convey "displeasure at this unlawful violation of the agreement." Murat bluntly told them that Napoleon had rejected the armistice and ordered immediate resumption of hostilities; there would be no notice, period. Furthermore, Murat detained both officers. "We were not allowed to leave," complained Nostitz in a latter-day attempt to clear his name. "Instead, we were taken back to the French headquarters and held there for several days." The Russians refused to believe him, branding him a coward if not a traitor.[38]

The combat at Hollabrunn-Schöngrabern was among the most brutal of the entire war. As the autumnal darkness descended, Murat launched ferocious attacks with his cavalry and divisions of Soult's and Lannes's corps.[39] Soult advised Murat to postpone the attack until morning, warning that a nocturnal fight would impede the use of cavalry and play into the Russians' hands, causing heavy casualties among the assailing French troops. Furious both at having been swindled and at Napoleon's rebuke, Murat nonetheless insisted on attacking.[40] Soult's infantry tried to outflank the Russian left but was repulsed, while the divisions of Oudinot and Legrand suffered greatly as they pushed against the Russian center and right flank. Despite facing a far superior enemy, Bagration managed to hold out at Schöngrabern until sunset, when he rallied the remnants of his rear guard and slowly retreated to Grund.[41] Here he fought on with the stolid valor for which he remains legendary in Russia. The fighting inspired Tolstoy to write a stirring description of the heroism of common Russian soldiers so memorably exemplified by Captain Tushin and his men.[42] A French officer watched aghast as the villages of Schöngrabern and Grund were burned and recalled the sickening odor of roasted flesh and the desperate cries of the wounded unable to escape the flames. There was "terrible carnage" and "utter confusion" all around. "French battalions and squadrons were in the middle of the Russians, and the Russians in the middle of the French; our guns fired indiscriminately and Russian cannon did the same."[43]

It was well after midnight before the fighting died down. Murat inflicted heavy losses on Bagration but was unable to break his small force or prevent it from slipping away into the night. Almost half of the Russians had been killed, wounded, or captured.[44] However, they exacted a heavy price on the French as well.[45] The battlefield, littered with corpses and illuminated by the burning villages, presented a macabre sight. "We bivouacked on the battlefield that very cold night; it was barely six or seven degrees," recalled a French officer who watched in horror as his soldiers, trying to escape the cold, prepared a place to sleep by "dragging together a number of Russian corpses, put them face to the ground, and spread a layer of hay on top. I thus slept on this bizarre bed."[46]

The Russian rear guard's sacrifice accomplished what Kutuzov had asked of it. Through guile and pure grit, it had delayed the French advance for two entire days, allowing the main army to get away. There were wild celebrations when the news of Bagration's escape reached the Russian army. Officers and soldiers came out in droves to applaud the survivors as they arrived at Pohrlitz on November 18. Kutuzov personally greeted them, embracing Bagration and thanking him for what he had accomplished. "I shall not ask after your casualties," he quietly added. "You are alive and that is enough for me." The battle was exalted as the "Russian Thermopylae," and Bagration and his men became the latter-day Leonidas and his 300 Spartans. Soon it was said that Bagration fought not just a French advance guard but the entire Grande Armée and that Napoleon himself had been present at the battlefield. Reinforcing this Russian narrative was the presence of French prisoners whom Bagration had brought back. They were few in number, but their mere presence served as a tangible symbol of the Russian spirit and valor. In his letter to Grand Duke Constantine, Bagration could hardly contain his feelings: "Glory! Glory! Glory! Victory, honor, hurrah . . . we proved that 5,000 Russians can stand tall against 30,000 enemy troops, and save the army, honor, glory, and the sacred flags."[47] The Georgian was promoted to lieutenant general and received the Grand Cross of the Military Order of Maria Theresa, while his men were generously rewarded for their feats. "Five Against Thirty"—such was the proud motto that was henceforth displayed by the Russian regiments that had fought at Schöngrabern.

The war was not over yet. On November 17–18, Kutuzov led his army through Lechwitz (Lechovice) and Pohrlitz (Pohorelice) to reach Brünn.[48] The kaiser once again injected himself into the military operations. He stressed the imperative of uniting the Russian and Austrian forces and instructed Kutuzov to fall back to Brünn and Olmutz, where the Austrian forces of Feldmarschalleutnant Johann Joseph Fürst von und zu Liechtenstein could join the Army of Podolia. The kaiser also demanded that Kutuzov make a stand and fight. "It seems the most decisive moments of the war are upon us," the Habsburg ruler wrote. The kaiser expressed hope that Kutuzov would be able to defeat the French troops in detail, "similar to how Mortier was defeated by your skill and courage."[49]

Kutuzov must have chuckled reading these lines. The Russian army was in no position to contest the French. With his customary tact, Kutuzov conveyed the actual situation to the kaiser. He would "fulfill your command to the letter" if he had the means. "I dare not, however, conceal from Your Majesty that much as the opportunity has occurred to stake the fortune of war on a single battle, I dare not do so, for my troops, though imbued with zeal and an ardent desire to distinguish themselves, lack the strength." He pointed out that the forced marches had meant his troops had gone without food for days. They were weakened by hunger. Once they had joined Count Buxhöwden's detachments, there was a chance, after a few days' rest, that they could go on the offensive.[50] Kutuzov thus proceeded to Olmütz, where he arrived safely on November 20.[51]

The second phase of the campaign came to a close. After twenty-nine days of continuous retreat and six rear-guard actions, Kutuzov fulfilled his primary objective of denying Napoleon a chance to destroy the Russian army. This was partly the result of the French mistakes but partly due to the capable leadership Kutuzov had shown in evading the French envelopment maneuvers and leading his men to the safety of northeastern Moravia. Protected by the ramparts of Olmütz, the army could finally regroup.

The retreat from Braunau went a long way to redeem the allied missteps and helped save the Russian army. Kutuzov deserves the credit for this, though he was assisted in this by capable subordinates, most notably Miloradovich and Bagration, as well as by the rank and file, who demonstrated courage and resilience. Contemporaries remarked that despite stress and responsibilities, Kutuzov remained close to his troops. He knew the vital importance of morale and did his best to alleviate the unnecessary hardships that could degrade combat performance, though he also took measures to end looting and insubordination. Soldiers respected him for his stern but fair treatment. He personally visited companies and battalions to make sure that soldiers were well taken care of and oftentimes stopped by the bonfires to talk to them, to share their meager meals. He befriended a grenadier of the Yaroslavskii Musketeer Regiment by the name of Sergei Semenov and occasionally went to see him at a bivouac. "Get me some hay," he would tell Semenov, and then spend some time bantering with his comrades, smoking a pipe and enjoying dry biscuits. "Bread and water, such is our soldiers' feast," he joked. Before departing, he usually gave the men a few coins, saying, "Here, drink with your friends to this old man's health."[52]

The "Ulm-Olmütz March-Maneuver," as Kutuzov's retreat later became known, has long been extolled in Russia. "This glorious retreat will be forever remembered," wrote Count Buxhöwden as he congratulated Kutuzov on reaching Moravia.[53] "We went from worst to great," gushed Semen Bronevskii from Olmütz on November 20. "Kutuzov's withdrawal will be forever ranked among the most glorious exploits in the annals of military history."[54] Three decades later, writing the official history of the campaign, Alexander Mikhailovskii-Danilevskii was no less effusive: "Pursued and surrounded by a vast army led by a great commander, Kutuzov anticipated and forestalled enemy plans, defeated him at Krems, and carried out a withdrawal, regarded as one of the most exemplary in military history."[55] In the 1980s, the *Soviet Military Encyclopedia* proclaimed that, "expertly organized and brilliantly executed, this 400-km-long march-maneuver represents one of the most outstanding examples of military art of the 19th century," thus setting the official line that historians followed.[56] Such praise, however, concealed the muddled reality. The strategic retreat was hardly "expertly organized." The allies had made their share of mistakes throughout the campaign—they carried out the withdrawal in a haphazard manner, while a virtual collapse of the logistical system resulted in repeated incidents of ransacking. In the final days, hundreds of Russian soldiers, utterly exhausted, fell behind the army and were captured by the French advance.

Yet none of this should obscure Kutuzov's key achievement—the rescue of the Russian army. His insistence on retreating from Braunau to Olmutz reshaped the strategic situation. By late November, Napoleon's Grande Armée, with its lines of communication extended over hundreds of miles and its forces wearied and depleted, was deep in hostile territory, isolated and vulnerable. The allies, meanwhile, found their positions materially improved. The Russian and Austrian reinforcements were, at long last, converging. Buxhöwden was already at Olmutz; Archduke Ferdinand had rallied his forces in Bohemia, and Archduke Charles was marching from Italy. Prussia seemed to have awakened from its slumber and made up its mind to join the coalition. The allies may have lost a few battles but held to the hope of winning the war.

CHAPTER 15 | The Eclipse of Austerlitz

As THE MONTH OF November came to an end, the mood in allied head-quarters was jubilant. Newly arriving reports clearly indicated that the strategic situation was beginning to favor the allies. The Army of Podolia had survived and made it to Olmutz, where Russian and Austrian reinforcements were now assembling. Buxhöwden's corps and the Russian Imperial Guard, under Grand Duke Constantine, had already joined Kutuzov's veterans, while another 30,000 men, under Bennigsen and Essen, were expected to arrive by the end of the year. The Austrians did their best to rally their surviving forces. Archduke Ferdinand commanded some 10,000 men in Bohemia, just nine days' march away from Olmutz, while Archduke Charles, with a force as large as the combined allied army, had crossed the Julian Alps into Hungary, where he was replacing his losses and preparing to take up the offensive against Napoleon.

The arrival of both Russian and Austrian sovereigns promised to boost the allied war effort, for it seemed to ensure political and military unity. Moreover, the youthful Russian emperor—he was about to celebrate his twenty-eighth birthday on December 23—had arrived after a quick but memorable visit to the Prussian court in Berlin. Alexander was able to convince Prussian king Frederick Wilhelm III to sign the Treaty of Potsdam and promise to support the coalition if Napoleon did not accept Prussian mediation, which seemed all but certain, considering the steep concessions the allies expected from the French; within weeks, Prussia could commit more than 100,000 troops for the allied cause. The Anglo-Swedish army was, meanwhile, ready to march from Hanover into Holland, which was largely undefended, while an Anglo-Russian expedition was finishing its preparations for the invasion of Naples. The allies could thus hope to field more than a quarter million men for the next phase of the war.

Napoleon, threatened on all sides and with his army weakened—barely 50,000 men were in the vicinity of Brünn—seemed on the defensive and at the end of his logistical tether. The situation worried many French officers and soldiers. "In ten years of fighting," remembered a French general, "many of our officers had been risking their lives in one battle or another. The thought of making their wills had never occurred to them. Now they started to make them."[1] Rumors of anxiety in the ranks of the French army had reached the allied camp, reinforcing the growing belief in Napoleon's vulnerability. Some were convinced that the French emperor was about to be enclosed between converging allied forces and destroyed.

Such sentiments bred overconfidence. The allies, in the words of a modern historian, "began to think in terms of vast combinations of hundreds of thousands of troops acting in a coordinated fashion over hundreds of miles of separation."[2] Opinions as to what strategy to pursue were "very much divided," observed Major General Karl Wilhelm von Stutterheim, who commanded an Austrian cavalry brigade in 1805.[3] Alexander and Francis agreed to keep Kutuzov in charge of the combined allied army, which could muster some 68,000 Russian and 15,000 Austrian troops at Olmutz, but they disagreed with his strategic assessments. Kutuzov led a group of senior officers who urged not engaging the French in battle. To borrow Clausewitz's later phrase, he believed that "time allowed to pass unused accumulates to the credit of the defender who reaps where he did not sow."[4] It was in Napoleon's interest to fight, since the longer the Grande Armée remained far away from France, the weaker it would get. Kutuzov pointed out the advantages of remaining near Olmutz, where the army was bivouacked on an elevated position from where it was possible to survey the area for miles around. The front was covered by a river and marshes, while the allies could use the wide valleys behind them to conceal the reserves. Having seen French operational mobility in action, Kutuzov was concerned about Napoleon's ability to concentrate his forces and outmaneuver his opponents. Aware of the challenges of coalition warfare, he was worried that upon leaving the safety of the Olmutz ramparts, the allied army would be vulnerable to an enemy counterstrike. Hence, instead of giving battle, Kutuzov argued that a simple delay of the operations would in a very short time constrain Napoleon to withdraw due to the double necessity of concentrating his troops and preserving his supply and communication lines. It was crucial to gain a few more weeks, during which reinforcements would arrive and the Prussians would enter the war, tilting the scales decidedly in the allies' favor. The time thus gained would, by itself, equal to a decisive victory. And if Napoleon chose to attack the allies before then, Kutuzov was ready to fall back even farther east. "We could retreat farther into Galicia," he remarked. "For I intend to bury the French bones there."[5]

Neither Francis nor Alexander heeded Kutuzov's counsel. The kaiser, still reeling from the disaster at Ulm and the loss of Vienna, yearned for the calm of his palace, now occupied by the French, and hoped to bring the campaign to a quick and victorious conclusion; he was little inclined to listen to any advice that prolonged the occupation of his realm, particularly when the overall strategic picture seemed to favor the allies. Emperor Alexander was equally susceptible to such wishful thinking. This was his first war and he longed for the laurels of victory. Surrounding him was a group of young noblemen who lauded his talents as a military leader and urged him to lead the army against Napoleon. Few of them had experienced the grim realities of war before, and they remained oblivious to the hardship that the army had endured. "It has been twenty-six days since we left Braunau, yet we are still living in open air," a sullen General Dokhturov told his wife in late November. "Our poor officers and soldiers, without shoes and bread, are all in wretched condition. Looking at them is simply heartbreaking."[6] Another Russian officer remembered that "even our commanders were dressed in ill-assorted, even comic attire."[7] Observing the arrival of Alexander and his brilliant entourage, Langeron and other officers were "surprised by the deep silence and somber mood" of the fatigued troops as they dolefully greeted the emperor.[8]

Such details escaped the attention of the toadies who surrounded the czar. They relished the prospects of military glory and, despite knowing little about war and strategy, claimed to understand the military situation better than the military commanders. Among them was Aleksey Arakcheyev, a martinet renowned for his fondness for spit-and-polish marching and known for the severity with which he treated his subordinates. However, he had never taken part in a war; when offered the command of a column at Austerlitz, he refused it with the excuse that he had bad nerves.[9] The rest of the imperial suite was equally young and overconfident. Probably the most influential of them was Peter Dolgorukov, a scion of a distinguished Russian family of princes, born with a deep sense of power and privilege. He had been enrolled in the elite Life Guard Izmailovskii Regiment at the tender age of just three months and began actual service as a fifteen-year old captain, quickly rising through the ranks due to family connections. At twenty-one, he was already a major general and adjutant-general to Emperor Paul. His meteoric rise only accelerated after Alexander ascended the Russian throne in 1801. The young czar became very fond of Dolgorukov, who espoused hawkish views in foreign policy and wanted Russia to be more assertive in Europe. In 1804–1805, he was one of the architects of the Russian confrontation with Napoleon and carried out several diplomatic missions, including one to sway the Hohenzollern court to join the Third Coalition. Accompanying the czar to Olmutz, Dolgorukov extolled the rear-guard actions at Lambach, Amstetten, Durrenstein, and Hollabrunn as great Russian victories and spoke with profound contempt of the Austrians, who had allowed themselves to be defeated at Ulm. Any success Napoleon had achieved so far was, in his opinion, due to the imbecility of the Austrians.

Anti-Austrian sentiments remained high among the Russian officers, who continued to complain about logistical problems that the army experienced due to inadequate provisioning. Even the czar had to admit, in a letter to the Prussian king, that the allied camp at Olmutz was "neither well provisioned nor in an [adequate] state of defense."[10] The extent of allied difficulties can be gleaned from the progressively worsening relations between the Russian and Austrian officers, with accusations of cowardice and timidity flying back and forth. Russians alleged that some Austrian officers had been bribed by the French. Kutuzov went as far as to suspect at least one Austrian officer of outright spying for the enemy.[11]

Kutuzov's insistence on pragmatic retreat was too much for Alexander to swallow. He was the first Russian sovereign to command an army in battle since Peter the Great. He had no intentions of showing his back to Napoleon. Indeed, the czar was determined to march forward and confront the enemy. His advisors argued that the lack of movement by Napoleon indicated timidity and weakness; victory seemed within grasp. "In vain did Kutuzov, [Pavel] Suchtelen, Buxhöwden, Prince Karl zu Schwarzenberg, Prince Johann Lichtenstein, and other Austrian generals oppose such an absurd project," commented General Langeron. "Emperor Alexander desired a battle and so it was decided."[12]

Had Kutuzov been left to follow his own judgment, he would have adopted a Fabian approach to the war. But he could not exercise his authority freely. Alexander and Francis had formally appointed him commander in chief of the combined allied forces, but their very presence inexorably constrained the general, who also had to deal with a group of supercilious officers who—full of ardor, courage, and illusions—influenced the emperors and foretold glorious new conquests over the French. These men increasingly marginalized and ridiculed Kutuzov for his insistence on discretion. Here was an old man, clearly past his prime, almost blind in one eye, corpulent, and struggling to stay in the saddle; to them, he was more famous for his obsequious behavior at court and agility with a coffeepot than he was for three decades of military service. They called him "General Slowpoke" (Général Lambin) and spread rumors that Kutuzov had lost his mind during the retreat.[13] Emperor Alexander had little regard for old veterans like Kutuzov, observed General Langeron, who witnessed what transpired in the allied headquarters. "He received them rarely and spoke to them little. Instead, the emperor reserved all his favors for five or six young favorites who were his adjutants. He gave himself over to a familiarity with them that was humiliating for the old generals, who saw their bearing and manners ridiculed by all these children whose influence extended to everything."[14]

It has been long argued that Kutuzov was, once again, too obsequious to raise his voice in protest; that despite his intelligence and experience, he shied away from openly confronting Alexander and instead choose to acquiesce to his wishes, even when he knew they were wrong. "Kutuzov was far too good a courtier to assert his opinion seriously and emphatically," alleged one Russian officer; he "found it convenient to be silent," charged another officer, while still another thought that the commander, facing ridicule and "left without power and any consideration, should have quit but chose to stay."[15] Russian court historian Alexander Mikhailovskii-Danilevskii drew an unfavorable contrast between Kutuzov's acquiescence and the combativeness of Generalissimo Alexander Suvorov, who in 1799–1800 repeatedly clashed with the Hofkriegsrat over the planning and direction of the allied war efforts. Others spoke of not standing firm in his beliefs as a moral failing, of "the lack of sufficient civic courage to tell the whole truth" to the young czar.[16] Even a Soviet historian had to admit in his otherwise hagiographical biography of the field marshal that Kutuzov backed down too easily: "He lacked the courage to oppose his opinion to that of two emperors, their suites, the court of Vienna, and the Austrian generals. But this weakness was not evidence of Kutuzov's ambition or perfidy. It was an expression of his personal tragedy."[17]

There is some validity to the criticism. As we have seen, his contemporaries frequently remarked on Kutuzov's "timorous character and courtier-like habits" and commented that "one could not have more wit and less character" than him.[18] Throughout his life, Kutuzov operated within a deeply entrenched patronage culture, one that had shaped his character and manners; he had learned to fit himself within its received roles and expectations. Forcefully raising his voice of protest against the emperor, who held supreme military command, was simply unfeasible. Drawing parallels with Suvorov seems wrongheaded. Kutuzov faced a situation that was entirely different from the previous coalition war. In 1799, Suvorov had been the hero of Rymnik and Izmail, and his prestige had been much greater than Kutuzov's was in 1805; Suvorov had enjoyed a far greater degree of independence, and he could afford to quarrel with an Austrian military council that was hundreds of miles away. By contrast, Kutuzov had to contend with not just one but two emperors who were constantly breathing down his neck.

At the very heart of this matter lay Alexander's character. The czar was driven by the need to prove himself a great commander and to match the exploits of "the hero of the century," as Napoleon was being called.[19] But Alexander was also self-aware enough to know that it would not be prudent for him to assume direct command of the army. He did the next best thing: keeping the veteran around as a nominal commander but depriving him of actual decision-making authority. This arrangement gave the czar power over the army while also shielding him from any blowback. If a decisive victory over Napoleon was achieved, it would be attributed to the czar's sagacious leadership; in the event of a setback, Alexander could avoid personal responsibility by shifting the blame. Kutuzov thus found himself "without power and respect," aptly noted a Russian general.[20] Openly confronting an all-powerful sovereign would have changed nothing, and Kutuzov knew all too well what disagreeing with a ruler could entail in Russia. In spite of his brilliance and fame, even Suvorov had been hounded and disgraced. Nor was resigning an option, both because the czar could simply refuse to accept his resignation and because Kutuzov's own sense of duty and responsibility would not allow him simply to abandon the troops on the eve of the battle.

Yet as long as Alexander remained with the army, there was little Kutuzov could do to change plans or countermand orders. He was not the only one to grasp the gravity of the situation. Adam Czartoryski, the czar's influential advisor on all foreign matters, was equally exasperated to see that Alexander "would not believe what we continually repeated to him, that his presence would prevent Kutuzov from exercising any real authority over the movements of the army." Czartoryski acknowledged that Kutuzov was not admitted to the councils of war and that "his advice was certainly not listened to."[21]

Contrary to prevailing views, Kutuzov did try to convince the czar of the error of the strategy that he and the kaiser had approved. "I was young and inexperienced," Alexander later noted plaintively. "Kutuzov should have dissuaded me from undertaking the battle." This is a canard. Kutuzov repeatedly tried to warn him; Alexander simply would not listen to his advice. When the general asked to be involved in the planning, the emperor bluntly told him, "That is none of your business."[22] When Kutuzov pressed the matter and urged the czar to reconsider launching an offensive, Alexander explicitly called the general's courage into question; fighting the French was "not the same as trouncing those absconding Turks and Poles," he said, "and now your bravery is suddenly waning." This must have been maddening to Kutuzov, but he kept his calm. "Your Majesty, henceforth you should command the army as you please," he simply replied. "You know full well that I am no coward. I refuse to fight as a general and will instead serve as a soldier."[23] Therein lies the answer to Kutuzov's perceived reticence and indifference. Repeatedly mocked and humiliated, he was consigned to handling the mundane issues of supplies (and incompetent commissars), unit deployment, and discipline. He haplessly witnessed the unfolding of a planning disaster whose architects were men half his age and possessed little of his experience or foresight.[24]

Ignoring Kutuzov's advice, Emperor Alexander listened instead to his Austrian allies who, in the words of one diplomat, "took over the control of the war, did everything their way . . . and reserved the right to draft the plans."[25] The most influential of these was Franz von Weyrother, who had assumed the position of chief of staff of the Austro-Russian army.[26] A fortuitous series of events placed this fifty-year-old officer—"the very opposite of Kutuzov," as one Austrian historian described him—in such a powerful position.[27] Born in Vienna, Weyrother had served in the Austrian army for the better part of thirty years. After Austria became embroiled in the War of the First Coalition, he served as a staff officer first in the Rhineland and then in Italy, gradually advancing through the ranks but never really distinguishing himself, at least not in a positive way. His plan for the Austrian offensive against a young General Bonaparte led to a divided and disjointed advance of the Austrian army and a crushing defeat at Rivoli in January 1797. His fortunes somewhat recovered during Generalissimo Suvorov's campaign in Italy, which earned Weyrother promotion to colonel. However, many Russian officers, including Bagration and Miloradovich, were convinced that Weyrother's ineptitude and misconduct cost them dearly during the crossing of the Alps in the fall of 1799.[28] The new campaign against France in 1800 confirmed Weyrother's liabilities. Sent to the Rhineland, he drafted a convoluted plan for an offensive against the French that led to yet another Austrian debacle, this time at Hohenlinden, effectively ending Austria's involvement in the War of the Second Coalition.

Weyrother nonetheless continued to enjoy support and protection at the Habsburg court, which employed him during the War of the Third Coalition in 1805. Promoted to major general, he was assigned to the Army of Podolia, where he served as a quartermaster until the death of Johann Heinrich von Schmitt, Kutuzov's chief of staff, at the Battle of Krems-Durrenstein on November 11. Despite lacking Schmitt's talent and experience, Weyrother was appointed as his replacement. While his appointment might look baffling, given that so many Russian officers remembered his ineptitude, he clearly possessed the necessary people skills, convincing his superiors that his prior service with the Russians had actually made him better aware of how to work with them. Weyrother also gained Emperor Alexander's confidence in a short period of time.[29] "He won the Russians over by enduring their arrogance and flattering their vanity," scoffed a nineteenth-century German military historian. "In many respects he resembled Mack, being like him a learned *doctrinär* who came up with plans without the necessary consideration of real circumstances."[30] However, what mattered most was that the Austrian's call for an offensive appealed to Alexander, who, in the words of an eyewitness, "seemed to be confident of a victory that would place him one stroke above the man who as yet had no equal, if any rival, on the battlefield."[31]

On November 24, the allies made the decision to leave Olmutz and advance toward Brünn, where they intended to roll Napoleon's right flank, isolate him from Vienna and the logistical lines, and then push him into the mountains of Bohemia, where they would destroy him.[32] The allied sovereigns ordered the army to depart "as if on the parade grounds," with ranks and files lined up and marching in step.[33]

Napoleon understood perfectly well the dangerous situation he was in. Throughout the past three months of the campaign one of his most exasperating problems had been Kutuzov, whose strategy of avoiding pitched battles in favor of a war of attrition and indirection had again and again frustrated the French emperor. After destroying the Austrian army at Ulm, Napoleon clearly expected to defeat the Russians in a series of quick strikes and enveloping maneuvers, all of which Kutuzov had thwarted.

After establishing his headquarters at Brünn, Napoleon observed with growing anxiety the rapidly changing situation on the continent. Some 750 miles away from Paris, he was confronted with the myriad challenges of managing an empire and commanding an army scattered over a vast area in Germany and Italy. The Grande Armée was fatigued by the strenuous marches from the Atlantic coast to the heart of Moravia; strategic consumption and battles against the Austrians and Russians had significantly reduced its overall numbers, and now it had about a third of the army's original strength. Confounding these problems, he received news of the Battle of Trafalgar, where on October 21, 1805, the British Royal Navy destroyed much of the French fleet.[34]

Napoleon was conscious that a Russian force was threatening the electorate of Hanover, while a British expedition had landed at Stade in the Hanoverian dominion. The Swedes were ready to advance toward the Elbe, and the Prussians toward Franconia; additional Prussian forces were gathering in Silesia to bring immediate succor to the Austro-Russian army. The arrival of the Prussian envoy at French headquarters with the ultimatum from Prussia, as agreed on in the Treaty of Potsdam, underscored how fraught with danger the situation had become for the French. So long as the allies remained on the defensive, as Kutuzov had urged, Napoleon could not hope to obtain a quick military resolution to the war, and each passing day worsened his situation.[35]

Napoleon therefore avidly sought a diplomatic way out of this conundrum while he could still speak from a position of relative strength. "I wish to make peace promptly," he told his foreign minister, instructing him to offer moderate conditions to the Austrians. He then dispatched one of his trusted officers, General Anne-Jean-Marie-René Savary, to the allies, ostensibly to deliver a complimentary letter to Emperor Alexander but in reality "to take notice of what was going on around him" and to probe for any diplomatic openings.[36]

Informed of the arrival of the French envoy at the Cossack outposts, Kutuzov made sure Savary could not observe much by delaying his arrival until after sunset. "Kutuzov was lodged in the suburbs of Olmutz," Savary wrote Napoleon. "Everything was packing at his house and I saw plainly that he was preparing to follow the movement of his army." Kutuzov told the Frenchman that Emperor Alexander was sound asleep in the fortress of Olmutz and offered to personally deliver Napoleon's missive in due time.

However, the Frenchman declined, insisting that he had orders to deliver it himself. He thus waited for a considerable amount of time in an anteroom among a number of young Russian officers. Savary, a shrewd man who would soon become Napoleon's minister of police, took the opportunity to converse with these officers, whom he found ardently denouncing the ambition of the French emperor and full of confidence about their success in combat. He took note that "all the Russian youth of the highest quality were eager for battle. . . . They all made much the same kind of calculations as the maid with her pail of milk."

Around ten o'clock in the morning, a commotion in the street announced the Russian emperor's approach. Alexander stopped in front of Kutuzov's house and alighted to talk to the French envoy, who seemed smitten by the Russian ruler. "Nature had done much for him, and it would have been difficult to find a model so perfect and so graceful," Savary later observed. The czar—who spoke "the French language in all its purity, without foreign accent and always using its elegant academic expressions"—assured Savary of his goodwill toward France and his respect for Napoleon. "He has long been the object of my admiration," the emperor told him. "I have no wish to be his enemy, any more than that of France." And yet here they were in the fields of Moravia fighting a war. Alexander pointed out that it was Napoleon's growing imperial ambitions that had caused him to embark on this path. France was pursuing policies that gave European powers "a just cause of disquietude for their independence," he told Savary. "You are already a great and powerful nation, and by your uniformity of language, habits, and laws must always be formidable to your neighbors. What need have you of continual aggrandizement?"[37]

At the close of the conversation Alexander presented Savary with a written reply to Napoleon's letter—addressed not to the "emperor of the French" but to the "head of the French government"—and ordered him escorted back to the advance posts.[38] Savary was unable to achieve what Napoleon had wanted, but his mission was not a complete failure, as it produced a wealth of valuable information on the prevailing mood at the allied headquarters and the mindset of Emperor Alexander. Among other things, Napoleon learned that the prudent Kutuzov was being sidelined and that Alexander was "surrounded by twenty scamps" who were pushing him to attack. He greeted the news of the allied advance with great joy, confident that these scamps would bring about Alexander's downfall, particularly now that the Russians no longer had "a first-rate general" in charge. They would assume that the French supply and communication lines ran through Vienna and would therefore seek to disrupt them.[39] This was exactly what Napoleon hoped the allies would do. He now resolved to launch a decisive counterstroke.[40]

On November 27, the allied army left its encampment and marched in five columns southward.[41] Kutuzov must have been deeply frustrated, for he had voiced his objections at the councils of war on November 24 and 27 and had failed to convince the emperors to reconsider their strategy. Now the army was on the move, though the troops still lacked essential supplies despite his best efforts to secure at least two days' worth of provisions. Kutuzov lamented the fact that the army had "only half a day's worth of bread," which caused misery among his soldiers and delayed the start of the offensive by a whole day.[42]

Rarely had a commander in chief of an army wielded so little command as Kutuzov in November 1805. Once the allied offensive had commenced, he primarily dealt with matters of transport and supplies; none of his letters discuss planning or wider strategy, a clear sign of the extent to which he had been sidelined. The allied plan of operations was, in fact, the creation of Weyrother. It was complex and dense, with dispositions so puzzling that when the hour of advance came, many column commanders had not yet sufficiently understood their orders, a portent of the problems to come.[43] General Langeron, leading one of the columns, fumed that his men had to march "over very bad roads washed away by the autumnal rains . . . in very short days, with insufficient supplies and no way to distribute them." Weyrother kept sending out new orders that further complicated matters. A Russian officer bewailed the "incredible confusion that reigned everywhere, with daily changes that had no place and no reason, not even a pretext."[44]

General Bagration spearheaded the allied movement from Olmutz to Wischau, where his advance guard encountered French outposts on November 28.[45] Emperor Alexander accompanied the vanguard and received his baptism by fire that day. At first he found the sight of cavalry charges, the smell of gunpowder, and the din of battle exhilarating and cheered the allied victory over the small French rear guard. His mood changed when he toured the aftermath of the battle and saw firsthand the carnage of war, the dead corpses strewn on the plain and the wounded men bleeding and begging for help. The sight made him so sick that he retired to the rear and refused to eat for the rest of the day.[46] As the French pulled back to Raussnitz, where a strong reserve awaited them, Bagration launched a forceful pursuit, engaged the enemy, and took possession of the town. "Everything turned in favor of the arms of His Imperial Majesty," reported Bagration with a clear sense of bravado.[47]

The allied victories at Wischau and Raussnitz—partly orchestrated by Napoleon, who had intentionally deployed a small advance guard to bait the enemy—persuaded many at allied headquarters that the French were indeed weak. Alexey Yermolov remembered that "there was a rumor, which everyone believed, that the enemy was in full retreat."[48] The allies were increasingly convinced that Napoleon would not risk the fate of a battle in front of Brünn and would flee upon seeing the allied army approaching. After the action at Wischau, "this *hope* became the prevailing *opinion* at the headquarters," remarked General Stutterheim.[49] Like many of his comrades, Ivan Zhirkevich, a young artillery lieutenant, was euphoric after hearing the news of Bagration's victories: "It seemed to us that we were going straight to Paris!"[50] The allies thus resumed their advance in high spirits—and almost completely ignorant of their enemy's strength, location, or intentions.

In the last days of November Napoleon made another last-minute attempt to negotiate with Alexander. He instructed Savary to return to the Russian headquarters with an offer of an armistice and direct negotiations between emperors. On November 29, Alexander was pleasantly surprised to see Savary presenting himself once again. He welcomed the offer to negotiate, which he read as a clear sign that Napoleon was in a weak position. He declined a personal interview with the French leader, claiming a prior "appointment with the emperor of Germany," but sent his aide-de-camp Prince Dolgorukov to the French camp.[51]

Napoleon took care to not give the Russian envoy the same opportunity to make observations that Savary had had in the allied camp. He greeted the prince at the entrance to the French cantonments, where Dolgorukov was allowed to see only what Napoleon wanted him to witness: weary French troops falling back on all points, crowded, timid, and seemingly disheartened. The French emperor was annoyed that so young a man should be sent on such an important mission. And his irritation only grew when the Russian presented the terms. The czar would consider negotiating peace only if the French withdrew from all conquered territories, Dolgorukov haughtily declared. Napoleon was expected to give up Belgium, Holland, and Switzerland and surrender the "Iron Crown" of Lombardy (Italy). Taken aback by the sheer arrogance of such demands, Napoleon snapped that he would yield nothing, not even if the Russians were encamped on the heights of Montmartre. "The Emperor will never desert his allies," retorted Dolgorukov, to which Napoleon replied, according to Savary's memoirs, "Then we must fight."[52] The meeting ended in just fifteen minutes. Napoleon later confided to the elector of Wurttemberg that he had been annoyed by this Russian "coxcomb," who had spoken to him "as he would speak to a boyar whom he was about to send to Siberia." He said the young Dolgorukov "mistook my moderation for fear, an error that I encouraged for military reasons and which brought about the decisive battle."[53]

Dolgorukov returned to the allied headquarters convinced that the French army was in a pitiable state and that Napoleon was weak and easy to defeat. "He trembled with fear in front of me," Dolgorukov said of the Emperor. "Even our advance guard would be sufficient to defeat him."[54] Later that evening a council of war was convened. Dolgorukov reported on his meeting with Napoleon and urged attacking at once. Kutuzov objected. Time was on the side of the allies, he pointed out, and he advised the emperor to postpone the offensive and wait for reinforcements. Dolgorukov apparently sniggered upon hearing this. "What are you laughing at, young man?" Kutuzov snarled at him. "Maybe you think that I am a coward and fear a battle? My age and wounds speak for themselves." Witnesses recalled that he stormed out of the meeting.[55] Dolgorukov, noting that the czar seemed deep in thought, told him, "If Your Majesty retreats, Napoleon will consider all of us cowards." Alexander responded, "Cowards? Then it is better for us to die."[56] At midnight, the army was ordered to proceed to the small village of Austerlitz (Slavkov u Brna), fifteen miles east of Brünn. Underscoring the extent to which Kutuzov was detached from command, the new order did not even bear his signature.[57]

The meeting with the Russian envoy convinced Napoleon that he could not hope to reach an understanding with the czar. He shifted his focus to a military resolution, an eventuality for which he had been preparing for some time. He had carefully observed the enemy's movements. Marshals Murat, Lannes, and Soult received orders to fall back to Brünn while keeping a dense cavalry screen; Bernadotte was recalled from Bohemia, while Davout was told to come up with all imaginable haste from Vienna. Marshal Mortier was left behind with his corps—still recovering from the drubbing it had received at Durrenstein—to secure Vienna. In this way Napoleon could expect to have 56,000 men within twenty-four hours of the allied offensive, 70,000 within two days, 80,000 in three days, and 90,000 by the fourth day.[58] Time was clearly of the essence.

The allies showed no sense of urgency. Their movements were slow and vacillating, with the army taking two days to cover the fifteen miles separating Wischau from Austerlitz. General Stutterheim, not privy to the internal dynamics of the allied headquarters, blamed Kutuzov for giving confusing marching orders. He was right about the confounding movements on November 29–30 but wrong about the culprit—Kutuzov had no power to change the disposition, which had been drafted by Weyrother and approved by the czar and the kaiser. Carl Friedrich von Toll, serving in the Russian headquarters, had a much better view of the situation. He noted that "the very peculiar strategic maneuvers performed under Weyrother's direction" had squandered valuable time.[59] Instead of building on the success gained at Wischau and Raussnitz, the allies dithered, shifting their forces several miles to the left and reshuffling their columns.[60] "We made short marches," described a Russian officer, "but they were so confusing that we rarely completed them before ten o'clock in the evening or even midnight because the columns always crossed each other's path, in some cases as much as several times, and wasted time waiting for others."[61]

The mishandling of the advance gave Napoleon an opportunity. He spent the whole of these days on horseback, receiving a constant stream of reports about the enemy's movements. He grasped the significance of the allied sluggishness. Had they attacked on November 30 or even December 1, the battle would have turned out very differently, given that Napoleon's reinforcements would not have arrived in time. The delays gave him time to refine his plans. He increasingly focused his attention on the Pratzen plateau—an almost two-mile-long ridge that overlooked the wide, rolling plains between Austerlitz and Brünn. He decided to allow the allies to occupy this position in order to convince them of his weakness, and then lure them into attacking his right wing. He correctly assumed that in attempting such a maneuver the allies would shift most of their forces to the left, weakening their center to reinforce their main attack around the villages of Telnitz and Sokolnitz in the south. Two-thirds of the French army, meanwhile, would be in the north, concealed by the regular early morning fog and ready to break through the weakened allied right flank and center with a decisive assault, and conducting an envelopment to cut their line of retreat.[62] Napoleon had earlier told his generals that by holding the Pratzen heights he would be assured of "an ordinary battle," but that was not what he wanted. He chose to abandon the heights to the enemy and deliberately expose his right wing back. If the allies dared to descend from the heights in an attempt to envelop his flank, "they will surely be beaten, without a hope of success!"[63] As the month of December dawned, Napoleon, holding true to his dictum to "never interfere with an enemy while he was making a mistake," watched the dark and massy columns of the allied troops moving into position on the Pratzen plateau, clearly intending to turn his right flank. This was precisely what he had hoped for.[64]

On December 1, the Russians and Austrians—in large numbers but still lacking essential supplies—passed through the village of Austerlitz and climbed the slopes to the Pratzen plateau.[65] That the French had surrendered such crucial ground added to the impression of weakness that Napoleon so carefully cultivated. Many in the allied headquarters drew a contrast between his bold operations against the Austrians at the start of the war and the seemingly more subdued and defensive posturing now. By nightfall, some 80,000 Russian and Austrian troops had taken up their positions on the rolling plains west of Austerlitz. The first three columns—of Generals Dokhturov, Langeron, and Ignacy Przybyszewski—reached the Pratzen plateau. The fourth, under Austrian general Johann Karl von Kollowrath-Krakowsky, was behind them, while the main cavalry force, designated as the fifth column and commanded by Prince Liechtenstein, halted even farther to the rear. Bagration, still in charge of the advance guard, bivouacked his forces around Posoritz and formed the extreme right flank of the allied position. The Russian Imperial Guard was positioned in front of Austerlitz itself. Kutuzov and the army headquarters were lodged at the nearby village of Křižanovice.[66]

There was no moon the night of December 2, and the thick fog made movement difficult.[67] Around midnight Prince Peter Volkonskii summoned all column commanders to the council of war, held in the large drawing room of a local nobleman's house, where the allied headquarters was set up. Here gathered Kutuzov, Weyrother, and all but one of the column commanders—Bagration sent word that he could not arrive in time. Kutuzov welcomed the officers and curtly told them that they would attack the enemy positions at 7 a.m. the next morning.[68] Weyrother then took over the council. Because he had previously gone over the terrain on several occasions, he had already drafted a plan, which Emperor Alexander had approved, and now he presented it to the senior allied officers.[69] Reading rapidly and indistinctly, Weyrother ran through a litany of unfamiliar geographic names and maneuvers, but it was at least clear that he envisioned three columns—more than 40,000 men led by Generals Dokhturov, Langeron, and Przybyszewski, under overall command of Buxhöwden—descending from the Pratzen heights to launch a flanking maneuver across Goldbach Stream to overwhelm the weak French right flank and drive it northward, severing Napoleon's line of retreat to Vienna. As this attack was under way, additional forces—the fourth and fifth columns—would come down the plateau to support the left-wing columns, while Prince Bagration, in charge of the advance guard and forming the allied right flank, would serve as a pivot around which the rest of the army would swivel.[70]

Standing in front of a large and detailed map, Weyrother read "his dispositions in a loud tone and with a boasting air, which announced in him the intimate persuasion of his own merit and that of our incompetence," remembered a Russian participant. The Austrian "resembled a form-master in a high school reading a lesson to the young pupils," griped General Langeron.[71] The officers struggled to make sense of the complex dispositions; their confidence in Weyrother, as shaky as it already was, was further undercut when Austrian colonel Ferdinand Bubna von Littitz, upon hearing Weyrother bragging that he knew the terrain around Austerlitz very well because he had been on maneuverers there, remarked, "Let's hope you will not make the same mistakes as at last year's maneuvers."[72] Dokhturov (who days earlier in a letter to his wife had beseeched "the Almighty for only one thing—to get me out of here alive") remained taciturn throughout the meeting, stooping over the outspread map and diligently examining the dispositions.[73] According to Langeron, Buxhöwden seemed not to listen to or understand a word of what Weyrother was saying; Miloradovich, unusually somber and subdued, remained silent. Kutuzov sat quietly in a low armchair. He had already seen Weyrother's plan and disapproved of it. Some had overheard him yelling, "I cannot consent to this. This is Napoleon's plan!"[74] Others had heard him tell

1 The Golenischev-Kutuzov family coat of arms (State Archive of the Pskov Region, Russia)

2 Illarion Matveevich Golenischev-Kutuzov, the field marshal's father. A talented engineer, he was nicknamed "The Wise Book" for his deep knowledge and experience. (Portrait by V. Leschinskii, Military-Historical Museum of Artillery, Engineer and Signal Corps)

3 Twenty seven year old Kutuzov, wearing the uniform of the lieutenant colonel of the Luganskii Pikineer Regiment, in 1774. The portrait was painted before he suffered a grievous injury fighting the Ottomans in the Crimea.

4 Ivan Loginovich Golenischev-Kutuzov, intendant general of the Russian fleet and later the director of the Naval Cadet Corps. He had played the part of an older friend and advisor to young Kutuzov (portrait by Peter Bruks, State Hermitage Museum, Alamy Stock Photo)

5 Catherine Golenischeva-Kutuzova (née Bibikova). Elisabeth Louise Vigée-LeBrun's portrait (painted in 1795) conveys the striking beauty and vibrant character of the field marshal's wife. (The Uglich State Historical, Architectural and Art Museum).

6 Kutuzov's granddaughters Darya, the countess Ficquelmont and Catherine von Tiesenhausen in Naples. Both were renowned for their beauty. "To see Naples, the countess Ficquelmont, and die!," was a common refrain while Darya lived in Naples (painting by Alexander Brullov)

7 Anna Khitrovo, Kutuzov's second daughter. Her husband, Nikolai Khitrovo, caused much heartache to the family but the field marshal did his best to protect his daughter (miniature, c. 1802, Hermitage Museum).

8 Lizanka or Elisabeth, Kutuzov's favorite daughter. She was first married to Ferdinand von Tiesenhausen, who died at Austerlitz in 1805. Her second husband, Nikolai Khitrovo, also died early, leaving her deeply in debt. But she persevered and her daughters thrived. (Drawing by P.F. Sokolov).

9 Praskovya, Kutuzov's oldest daughter. She had eight sons and two daughters with her husband, Matvei Tolstoy. In 1859, Emperor Alexander II granted her son Pavel the right to inherit his grandfather's name and titles.

10 Emperor Paul of Russia wearing the imperial crown and the robe of the Grandmaster of the Maltese Knights. Contrary to the Soviety era claims, the czar did not maltreat Kutuzov but his behavior was erratic nonetheless (by Vladimir Borovikovskii, Museum of Fine Arts Academy, St. Petersburg)

11 Gregory Potemkin, Empress Catherine's favourite and Kutuzov's benefactor (19th century Russian engraving)

12   Generalissimo Alexander Suvorov, an outstanding military theorist and practitioner, continues to hold a unique place in the Russian military history. He was not Kutuzov's mentor, as it has long been alleged, but the two men did serve together, most notably at the storming of Izmail in 1790 (British engraving based on J. Kreutzinger's portrait, 1799)

13   Emperor Alexander at the start of his reign. Handsome and intelligent, the czar's relationship with Kutuzov was complicated. He disdained his personality but appreciated his martial talents (British engraving based on the portrait by Gerard Kügelgen, 1803).

14 Sultan Selim III on the arife throne, wearing his traditional robe and turban with a long aigrette. Kutuzov met the sultan during his embassy to Istanbul in 1793. (portrait by Joseph Warnia-Zarzecki, Pera Museum, Istanbul).

15 Russian assault on the Ottoman fortress of Ochakov in late 1788. Kutuzov was involved in the siege of the fortress but was shot in the head during an Ottoman sortie. Kutuzov would have witnessed the chaotic, bloody, and merciless fighting depicted on this Austrian engraving (1792, based on F. Cassanova's painting) at Izmail in 1790 and Braila in 1809.

16 Russian assault on the Ottoman fortress of Izmail in December 1790. Kutuzov commanded one of the assault columns and then served as the commandant of the fortress (Late eighteenth century German engraving, Russian Virtual Museum)

17 Color aquatint of the Ottoman encampment, showing honor guard flanking entrance to special pavilions. During his embassy to the sultan's court in 1792 and in subsequent campaigns against the Ottomans, Kutuzov would have seen many encampments like this one (Drawing by Luigi Mayer, 1809, Anne S.K. Brown Military Collection, Brown University Library)

18 Memorial nearly the village of Shumy (Crimea, Ukraine), where, in August 1774, Kutuzov was gravely injured when an Ottoman bullet struck his head. Remarkably, his brain was undamaged and, contrary to popular imagination, he did not lose an eye and never resorted to an eye-patch (photo courtesy of Boris Megorsky).

19 Napoleon and his generals while campaigning. Kutuzov witnessed the French emperor's military brilliance at Austerlitz and closely followed his subsequent campaigns, gaining a great deal of respect for the man he considered "the first Captain of the age." (early 19th century French print, author's collection)

Prince Peter Volkonskii that he did not want to fight and had been forced to sign off on the plan, though he was convinced that it "will not be to our benefit." He felt he had no choice except to comply.[75] Now he sat with his eyes closed, tired of voicing his opposition when "his advice was certainly not listened to," as Czartoryski ruefully observed.[76] Weyrother's droning lulled him into sleep. The sight, which was subsequently described in virtually every book written on Austerlitz—with various degrees of drama—reflected the depth of Kutuzov's misery and resignation.[77]

The basic idea of turning an enemy flank was simple and appropriate. Weyrother's strategy, however, was based on limited information, made too many false assumptions, and conveyed orders in such a convoluted manner that six weeks after the battle was over Kaiser Francis admitted to the Russian ambassador, "You might be surprised to hear that even at this time, I still do not yet comprehend this battle plan."[78] Weyrother treated Napoleon in a remarkably cavalier fashion, which prompted a contemporary Prussian military thinker to observe that "the allies adopted the plan of action against an enemy army they had not seen yet, assumed it was in the positions it never occupied, and expected it to remain as idle as the border posts."[79] The topography of the battlefield was not fully taken into account, and neither were the difficulties of the terrain, which was dotted with vineyards, ditches, garden walls, and other obstacles through which the Austro-Russian left wing had to move.[80] The reserve force, comprising the Russian Imperial Guard under Emperor Alexander's brother Grand Duke Constantine, was both inadequate and badly situated behind the Pratzen heights.[81] Weyrother, although in charge of an army numerically superior to Napoleon's, had divided the allied force into what were practically three disconnected sections, of which two— the right flank and center—were too weak to contain any offensive movement by the enemy. The possibility of counterattack was not even contemplated.

When Weyrother finished his peroration, Langeron, if we are to believe his own claims, was the only one to question the Austrian's assumptions. "All this sounds good," he supposedly asked, "but what will we do if the enemy attacks us?" Weyrother scoffed in response. Had he not just explained that Napoleon was weak and vulnerable? Why otherwise would he have abandoned the Pratzen heights? Given that the French had not already attacked, it was obvious that they were keen to avoid battle. The allies could not afford "allowing so good an opportunity to escape of destroying the French army and dealing Napoleon a decisive and fatal blow."[82] As the two officers began to debate, Kutuzov awakened from his slumber and cast a weary look at the assembled generals, reminding them of the lateness of the hour and urging them to get some rest before the battle.

The council ended around three o'clock in the morning. Kutuzov felt compelled to make a final effort to change Emperor Alexander's mind. Having previously been rebuffed and knowing that the czar would not listen to him, he went to Oberhofmarschall Nikolai Tolstoy, who enjoyed Alexander's confidence. "His Majesty intends to fight a battle, but you must dissuade him from it, because we are almost certain to lose the battle tomorrow," Kutuzov candidly told him, according to Toll. But "the hot-tempered" Tolstoy "got annoyed" at being awakened so late at night and snapped, "My function is to dabble with sauces and roasts, yours is war, so deal with it."[83] Kutuzov returned to the headquarters, where he watched as the adjutants made copies of the disposition, which ran for several closely written sheets. They struggled to make sense of the complicated German narrative, which many Russian regimental commanders could not read. In their rush to complete a translation, the officers misread or misinterpreted some passages; consequently, according to some, the Russian version was even more confusing.[84]

Not until around six o'clock in the morning—an hour before the scheduled attack—were the orders sent to the units scattered across the vast battlefield. There was hardly enough time for local commanders to read the documents and understand what was expected of them. The young artillery officer Alexei Yermolov recalled seeing "a disposition written on several sheets of paper, crowded with difficult names of villages, lakes, streams, and distances and heights. We were not permitted to make a copy because it had to be read by a good many other commanders and there were only a few copies available. I must confess that when I heard it read out, I understood very little of what was intended. The only thing I comprehended was that we were to attack in the morning."[85] Some commanders did not even receive orders and remained in total ignorance of the plan. When Alexander visited the fourth column shortly before sunrise, he discovered that some units were still resting. "Are your muskets loaded?" the czar asked General Berg, who commanded the Malorossiiskii Grenadier Regiment. Surprised by this question, Berg replied that they were not, as he had not yet received any instructions. Only after Alexander personally issued an order to him did Berg learn that the battle was about to commence. Three miles to the north, Prince Bagration was among the last to receive a copy of the disposition; according to Mikhailovskii-Danilevskii, after quickly perusing it he gloomily told his Austrian colleagues, "We will be defeated tomorrow."[86]

The night of December 2 was cold. The expected thick fog covered all the lower areas of ground and made it impossible to discern anything ten yards away. Rising before the sun's first rays and already chilled to the bone, the Russian and Austrian soldiers were lined up by their commanders, who were still struggling to make sense of the orders that they had received just moments before. Soon battalions began to move, every eye peering into the fog-covered plains to the west.

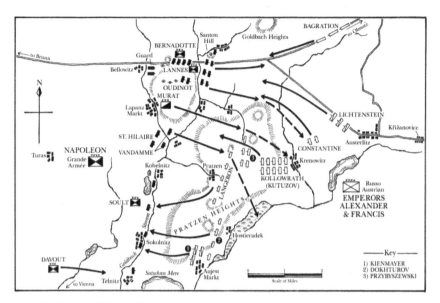

MAP 8 Battle of Austerlitz

"It was seven o'clock in the morning when we left our positions," Kutuzov reported. "I was in the center, accompanying the fourth column, while General Count Buxhöwden was on the left flank" supervising the columns of Dokhturov, Langeron, and Przybyszewski, which were supposed to march southwest from the Pratzen heights, force the passages of Goldbach Stream at three points between the villages of Telnitz and Sokolnitz, and sweep north through the French right flank.[87] The first column (Dokhturov's) proceeded as planned and soon found itself engaged in intense fighting on the banks of Goldbach Stream. The village of Telnitz, consisting of a few natural entrenchments, and whose vineyards were surrounded by a deep ditch, changed hands a few times before the allies succeeded in driving the French defenders back.[88] However, the column then found itself isolated and unsupported; Langeron's and Przybyszewski's units were nowhere to be seen. Their advance, so crucial for the success of the allied plan, had in fact been interrupted by the unexpected arrival of Prince Lichtenstein's fifth column. On receiving his orders that morning it became clear to the prince that his units were woefully out of place. They had been camped for the night behind the third column, east of the Pratzen heights, while Weyrother had assigned them a position on the left flank of Bagration's advance guard. Hastily breaking camp, Liechtenstein led his cavalry to the prescribed position only to discover the second and third columns in his way.[89] Owing to poor staff arrangement and the sudden and uncontemplated nature of the move, Lichtenstein thus crossed in front of Langeron's and Przybyszewski's columns, just at the point when they were launching a flanking maneuver and therefore needed to support Dokhturov's momentum at Telnitz. It seemed more proof that Weyrother had not been clear in his battle plan.[90] To make matters even worse, the cavalry's own path was itself crossed by Johann Karl von Kollowrath-Krakowsky's fourth column, accompanied by Kutuzov, which was supposed to advance toward the village of Kobelnitz, where it was expected to support the left flanking columns.

After an almost hour-long delay, Langeron and Przybyszewski were able to resume their march, but they struggled to navigate the steep slopes of the Pratzen heights and numerous ditches in thick fog. By nine o'clock in the morning, the columns had barely advanced two miles from their starting point. The consequence was that the allied left wing attacked the vulnerable passages of Goldbach Stream disjointedly, in succession instead of simultaneously, enabling the numerically inferior French to hold positions and bring up reinforcements. Soon the leading units of Marshal Davout's III Corps, which had covered a distance of over seventy miles in an astonishing forty-eight hours, began to arrive southwest of Telnitz. The "Iron Marshal" immediately sent his men into action, and the influx of this new (even if very fatigued) force revived the fighting in and around Telnitz.

As the last of Przybyszewski's men marched down the Pratzen heights, Kutuzov remained idle with the fourth column, numbering slightly over 13,000 men. This was probably the weakest of the allied columns, comprising the two Russian brigades that had suffered the most during the retreat from Braunau and an Austrian division (under Kollowrath-Krakowsky) that was largely made up of new and inexperienced recruits. After Lichtenstein's cavalry passed through, the fourth column was to descend from the Pratzen heights and proceed toward Goldbach Stream, to support the three left-flanking columns. Kutuzov delayed the advance. He instinctively felt that leaving the Pratzen heights would be a mistake and that it would weaken the allied center and expose it to a possible enemy counterattack. He therefore hung fire.

Emperor Alexander and his glittering entourage soon arrived on the heights to observe the fighting. Casting a cursory glance at the plateau, the czar was displeased to see the troops of the fourth column still standing there. Approaching the commander in chief, Alexander asked him, "Mikhail Larionovich, why are you not proceeding further?" Knowing that the czar was determined to fight, Kutuzov replied, according to Prince Peter Volkonskii's recollection, with his customary opaqueness: "I am waiting, Sire, for all the troops to assemble." The emperor, missing Kutuzov's allusion to not rushing with the attack, retorted, "But why? We are not at the Empress's Meadow, where one awaits the arrival of all the troops to begin the parade!" Kutuzov retorted, "Precisely, Sire. It is because we are not on a parade ground that I am not commencing the movement." Apparently Kutuzov then paused, realizing that he had perhaps gone too far, and eventually added, "However, if such be Your Majesty's order, we will advance."[91]

Alexander, failing to grasp the importance of holding on to the Pratzen heights, ordered the fourth column to move at once. Kutuzov bowed in his saddle and grudgingly complied, ordering two battalions of the Novgorodskii Musketeer Regiment and one battalion of the Apsheronskii Musketeer Regiment (with a handful of Austrian dragoons) under the command of General Miloradovich to move forward. Pleased to see the troops marching, Alexander turned to Kutuzov, saying, "Well, Count! What do you think, everything will be fine, right?" The old general replied with a clever repartee: "Who can doubt a victory under your leadership, Your Majesty?" This time the czar felt the veiled sarcasm and quickly countered, "No, Count, it is you who are in charge here, I am just a spectator." Kutuzov apparently reacted with a resigned nod. According to Major General Berg, who witnessed this exchange, when Alexander rode a little farther, Kutuzov turned to him and muttered in German, "Brilliant! He wants me to command and yet it was not me who ordered the attack. In fact, I did not want to fight this battle at all." Startled to hear this, Berg, who was about to lead his men down the Pratzen slopes, suddenly felt "a bad premonition," as he put it, of what was about to happen.[92]

Across the battlefield, Napoleon waited. The fog that had shrouded the Pratzen plateau began to clear at around eight o'clock and then, at last, the emperor could distinctly see the Russian and Austrian columns descending the plateau and disappearing in the mist that still hovered in the lowland on the French right flank. Napoleon observed the lack of concert and consistency in their movements, as well as the considerable intervals opening up between their marching columns. "The enemy behaved with an amount of ignorance and presumption difficult to conceive," he later commented.[93] Around nine o'clock in the morning, with Davout still holding positions in the south and the gunfire to the north confirming that Lannes was in action against Bagration, Napoleon ordered two divisions of Soult's IV Corps to assault the Pratzen plateau, which now seemed sufficiently bare of enemy troops. Previously obscured by the fog, these divisions now burst out into the open, taking the allies by surprise and threatening to cut their army in half.

Kutuzov at once realized the danger. "I could see that the enemy's intention was to seize the summit of the heights, cut off our line of retreat, and attack us from the rear," he later reported to Emperor Alexander. The outcome of the battle depended upon whoever was the master of the Pratzen.[94] Kutuzov instructed the fourth column units that were descending the slopes to halt and then moved forward an Austrian division "to contain the enemy's thrust." Furious fighting raged for the next twenty or so minutes. The allies desperately tried to stave off the French and suffered heavy losses; both Russian brigade commanders, Major Generals Repninskii and Berg, were wounded, along with many other officers, thus disrupting the chain of command. "There were confusion, questionable arrangements, and movements," described an eyewitness. "Precious minutes passed while disorder grew."[95] Just when it seemed that the initial French assault was contained, reported Miloradovich, "suddenly nine more enemy columns appeared; they deployed in chess formation, increased fire intensity, and launched new attacks, seeking to turn our flanks."[96] The Novgorodskii and Apsheronskii battalions that Kutuzov had sent forward at Emperor Alexander's insistence were overwhelmed and driven back in disarray.[97]

Kutuzov responded by deploying the Malorossiiskii Grenadier Regiments and the battalions of the Smolenskii and Apsheronskii regiments along the heights and then launching a new counterattack, which, in the words of Miloradovich, led to "the fiercest and most incredible combat." Twice the Russians charged, and twice they were rolled back; the Austrian troops could not bear the intense fighting, broke ranks, and fled, "completely exposing the flank of the column," Kutuzov wrote. "The enemy then hastened to regroup on our flank, received reinforcements, and made a most vigorous charge against our troops." Trying to halt the French momentum, Kutuzov ordered Major General Sergei Kamenskii, in charge of the Fanagoriiskii and Rizhskii regiments of the second column, to divert from his prescribed line of attack and secure the Pratzen heights. At the same time, Kutuzov's aides-de-camp rushed with orders to Grand Duke Constantine to bring up the Imperial Guard.[98]

For the next hour or so, the two sides contested the Pratzen plateau with fierce determination. The vigor and resolve seemed equal on both sides— battalion to battalion, man to man. The grim determination of the Russians, however, started to give way to the fervent intensity of the French, who benefited from numerical superiority as Napoleon committed additional forces in support of Soult's two divisions.[99] "My regiments inflicted heavy losses on the enemy but were forced to give way because of the enemy's superior numbers," noted Kutuzov, whose units climbed down the heights and deployed at the bottom.[100]

Just then the Russian Imperial Guard entered the fray, and the charge of its cavalry, storied in Russian military history, briefly turned the tide of battle—until Napoleon sent forth his own heavy Guard cavalry. The Russian cavalry and infantry gave way and were driven back in confusion, while the French columns consolidated their positions at the summit of the Pratzen plateau. Kutuzov, hurrying here and there and rallying the retreating troops, was injured when a bullet ripped through his cheek. He pressed the handkerchief to his bleeding wound and continued to shout out commands. Informed of the general's yet another head injury, the czar sent his personal physician to tend to the injury. Kutuzov refused the help: "Thank His Majesty on my behalf and assure him that my wound is not dangerous." Then, according to eyewitnesses, he pointed to the French columns on top of the Pratzen heights and said, "The mortal wound is actually over there."[101]

The struggle for the Pratzen heights decided the battle. The allied plans and chain of command were thrown into chaos. A number of senior officers were killed, wounded, or captured; some disappeared, only to reappear after the battle, and Kutuzov later spent hours investigating such cases and seeking strict punishment for cowardice.[102] According to Czartoryski's memoirs, Weyrother "wandered from point to point and by bravely exposing his life strove to remedy the evil of which he had been one of the chief causes."[103] The members of the imperial suites, once so arrogant and buoyant, fled. No one seemed to know the whereabouts of Emperor Alexander. Major von Toll ultimately found him sitting "on damp ground under a tree, his faced covered with a handkerchief, bitterly crying."[104]

Kutuzov remained at the center of activity for as long as he could. With the blood from his wound staining his uniform, he kept shouting orders, rallying troops, and dispatching messengers to various units. Amid the whistle of bullets, his beloved son-in-law Tiesenhausen, whom Kutuzov had sent to rally the retreating troops, seized the staff of the standard and, in a scene reminiscent of Prince Andrew Bolkonskii's valiant charge in Tolstoy's *War and Peace*, rushed forward, leading one of the Russian battalions, only to get shot through the chest by a musket ball. The French rushed to capture this splendidly dressed officer, but the Russians defended him fiercely; the wounded man was jostled around and smacked with musket butts, his decorations ripped away and his uniform torn to pieces. Miloradovich's men finally recovered the barely breathing Tiesenhausen. He survived for three agonizing days.[105]

By noon, Kutuzov knew that the battle was lost. His messengers galloped across the smoke-covered battlefield with orders for columns to fall back before the enemy converged onto them.[106] His commands were not promptly followed. Buxhöwden demonstrated no sense of the urgency of the situation, while the left-flanking column commanders fought disjointedly, with some refusing to believe that the battle had been irretrievably lost in the center and convinced that victory could be had by throwing back the French right wing.[107]

By two o'clock in the afternoon, it was too late. Napoleon, having completed the rout of the allied center and secured the Pratzen plateau, turned on the exposed allied columns in the south. Dokhturov, Langeron, and Przybyszewski found themselves attacked in front, flank, and rear, and, after a gallant resistance, were overwhelmed; Buxhöwden, with his hat missing and clothes in disorder, was seen among the retreating men, shouting forlornly, per Czartoryski, "They have abandoned me! They have sacrificed me!"[108] Dokhturov tried to get his men to safety by veering to the right and escaping through the network of neighboring ponds. Some troops ventured onto the ice of the vast Satschan Pond. A combination of French artillery fire and the weight of men and equipment caused the ice to break, dumping soldiers into the shallow but freezing cold water before they managed to escape across a causeway on the southern side of the pond. By six o'clock in the afternoon, the last allied troops had been swept from the battlefield and the battle was over. "It was impossible," gleefully concluded a French officer, "to put a better face on things."[109]

The cold darkness soon descended upon the battlefield and the fighting subsided. Kutuzov was with the Fanagoriiskii and Rizhskii regiments, determined to move the remnants of the army to Hungary, as had been agreed upon. He was unaware that Emperor Alexander, shocked and dejected, was with the survivors of Miloradovich's brigade near the village of Austerlitz, frantically searching for Kutuzov in order to get his advice on what to do next. "The shock of the defeat apparently had given the Russian emperor a newly-found respect for the opinion of the old general to whom he would not listen before the battle," aptly commented one modern historian.[110] After his aides were unable to find the general, the emperor decided to stick with the plan and proceed to Hodiegitz, a small Hungarian town that had been designated as the rallying spot for the army in case of a lost battle.

More crucially, the Russian and Austrian sovereigns met at Prince Kaunitz's castle in Austerlitz. They agreed it would be nearly impossible for them to recover from the devastating loss they had just suffered. Kaiser Francis suggested reaching out to Napoleon to end hostilities and begin negotiations. Alexander consented. Just two days after the battle, Francis met with Napoleon and arranged an armistice that ended the war for Austria. That same day, Kutuzov sent a message to Marshal Davout informing him of the suspension of hostilities and asking to negotiate.[111]

On December 6, the two sides signed the armistice agreement, which required the Russian army to vacate Austrian territory within thirty days.[112] After Emperor Alexander left later that day, Kutuzov shouldered the burden of leading the battered Russian regiments back home. It took him well over a month. There was so much to be done. Soldiers, scattered across the Moravian and Hungarian countryside in the wake of the battle, had to be located and assembled; the numerous wounded needed to be carefully evacuated; regimental rosters had to be closely examined and detailed reports on the army's losses prepared; marching routes had to be determined, and so on. The provisioning of the army remained, as ever, the most challenging task. In the aftermath of the battle, hundreds of transports had been lost and the Russian troops now subsisted on less than half rations. Many went unfed for days. Kutuzov complained that column commanders allowed "the lower ranks of various regiments to march not only in complete disorder but also without any supplies." Consequently, troops resorted to pillaging and committed "numerous rogueries [shalosti]," which Kutuzov did his best to suppress.[113]

He prohibited soldiers from leaving their units and set harsh punishments for anyone who violated the order; anyone caught pillaging or resisting apprehension was to be run twice through a thousand-men gauntlet, which was usually fatal. Officers were warned that they would be held accountable for any mistreatment of local inhabitants, even "the slightest looting" or "any damages or thefts."[114]

These exacting efforts soon produced results. Reaching the northeastern provinces of Hungary (modern-day Slovakia), the army was finally able to fully supply itself; writing from the town of Eperies (Prešov), Kutuzov was relieved to report the "assiduity with which the army is receiving supplies here." His insistence on strict discipline, payment for any and all provisions, and timely return of the requisitioned transports had borne fruits—the Austrian commissars praised Kutuzov for "severely punishing even the slightest transgressions" and maintaining tight discipline within the Russian army.[115] The "locals are so pleased with us," Kutuzov told the czar, "that in many towns the entire officer corps is regaled for free."[116] The Russian army was warmly welcomed in Hungarian villages and towns. "The locals greeted [Kutuzov] with great respect," remembered Yermolov. "Two celebrations were organized and, to our surprise, there were many who wished to entertain themselves after so shameful a defeat almost as though the enemy had lost and been destroyed."[117]

The strain of it all undermined Kutuzov's health. He complained to his wife that "every bone in my body" was aching and that he was "suffering bouts of infirmity that I never experienced before."[118] The psychological impact was even greater. He could not bring himself to reveal to his daughter Elisabeth von Tiesenhausen the news of her husband's death. She had accompanied her husband to Teschen and was eagerly awaiting his return. "I do not know what you will do with Lizinka [Elisabeth]," he wondered in a letter to his wife. "She is still unaware of Ferdinand's death. May the Lord give you and her the strength to bear it."[119] Melancholy and pain darkened those short winter days as he marched slowly back home. In late January 1806, the last of the Russian soldiers crossed the imperial border and left the Austrian domain. The war was over . . . at least for now.

Austerlitz—"the Battle of the Three Emperors," as it is sometimes grandly called—was a stunning victory for Napoleon—one gained, to great dramatic effect, on the first anniversary of his imperial coronation. The allied army was shattered. While the Grande Armée lost some 9,000 men, the allies suffered four times more: 6,000 killed, some 9,600 wounded, and another 20,000 taken prisoner, along with about 50 banners and more than 180 guns. The Russians bore the lion's share of these losses. Some regiments were almost entirely devastated. Amid the confusion of nocturnal retreat, Austrian guides chose the wrong path, and as a result the Russians were unable to move their heavy cannon and had to abandon them. All in all, the Russians lost 133 cannon, 100 caissons, and 106 transports.[120]

Military losses alone cannot adequately convey the significance of the French triumph. The Third Coalition was effectively destroyed, and so was the allies' will to continue the war. Austerlitz rekindled the bitterness that existed between the Russians and the Austrians. While acknowledging the courage of the Russian soldiers, the Austrians attributed the defeat to the slowness of their movements and the dullness of their leaders. The Russians were irate. Many openly spoke of the cruel snare that the Austrians had set for old Suvorov in the Alps and that the kaiser and his councilors had now pulled on Kutuzov—secretly negotiating with Napoleon for better terms for Austria by offering to lead the Russian forces to destruction. Such conversations became so widespread that Kutuzov was forced to issue a special order condemning "unsubstantiated and reckless assertions" and banning them on the pain of severe punishments.[121]

Nonetheless, senior Russian officers continued to accuse Austrians of folly, incompetence, and even treason. It was the Austrians, after all, who had sketched the plan of battle that was fought on terrain that they supposedly knew well from their parade maneuvers. They had wholly failed in the delivery of supplies, forage, and ammunition. The perfect understanding Napoleon displayed of the allies' intentions was soon attributed to the fact that the Austrians had divulged the allied plan to the enemy. Prince Dolgorukov was entirely convinced that the Russians had been duped and indeed directly told Alexander that the Austrians "steered the army of Your Majesty to deliver it to the enemy rather than to fight; and what puts the finishing touch to this infamy is that our dispositions were known to the enemy, a fact of which we have certain proof."[122] He never presented this proof, but it did not matter, for perceptions triumphed over the facts. Joseph de Maistre, the well-informed Sardinian envoy in St. Petersburg, reported that there was hardly anyone in St. Petersburg who doubted Austrian treachery.

Empress Consort Elisabeth Alexeyevna herself was convinced of it. She was enraged to learn of the Austrian treatment of her husband. After the battle he had passed the night in a wretched hut, on a bed of straw, accompanied by a handful of companions, including physician James Wylie. He reached the village in a feverish, depressed state, suffering from severe shivering and other symptoms of fever. Wylie, the empress told her mother, "became genuinely concerned whether the emperor would make it through the night." He went over to the Austrian headquarters to ask for a bottle of wine. To his utter surprise, he was told that as the kaiser was asleep, the members of his household could not take upon themselves to dispose of his stores. According to the empress, Wylie "begged on his knees," but it was all for naught. Only by bribing a servant was he able to procure half a bottle of "the vilest" red wine. "This is the way the Austrians treat their closest ally who has just sacrificed his entire army for their salvation!" fumed the empress. She was convinced that "not just for the Russians, but for anyone with a soul, the very word 'Austrian' should henceforth cause the feeling of revulsion."[123]

The thrashing at Austerlitz broke the Austrian determination to fight. With his treasury empty, prospects of Prussia joining the war against France evaporating, and the Russians keen on getting back home, the Habsburg ruler had no choice but to sign an armistice with the French emperor. The subsequent Treaty of Pressburg both humiliated Austria and contributed to a formidable growth of French power. The Habsburgs were forced to pay a huge financial indemnity, give up Venetia and Tyrol, and effectively surrender their influence in central Europe. Soon enough, the Neapolitan monarchy was dethroned, the kingdom of Italy expanded, and Germany reorganized in such a way that there was no longer a Russian clientele there. The sovereigns of Bavaria, Wurttemberg, and Baden, enriched by the spoils of Austria and decorated with the titles of king and grand duke, accepted Napoleon's dominion and joined, along with thirteen other German princes, the Confederation of the Rhine; that marked the death of the Holy Roman Empire, which had dominated Germany for almost a millennium.

Russian society was stunned by the news of what had transpired on the Moravian plains. Accustomed to victories over the Ottomans, Poles, and Swedes, the public genuinely believed in the superiority of Russian arms and yearned for a victory for Alexander, the first czar in decades to command the army in battle. The disastrous conclusion of the battle was a genuine shock. It had "paralyzed the entire empire," wrote Joseph de Maistre in a letter to Count de Fron.[124] After Austerlitz everything seemed lost; "it looked like the result of some kind of magic or witchcraft. . . . I cannot find words to describe it. . . . Never before has there been such a decisive and devastating catastrophe, and the consequences of Austerlitz are even more unfathomable than the battle itself."[125] Many shared Russian diplomat Semen Vorontsov's lament: "We did everything we could to lose the battle." It seemed as if "while other nations' armies advance and improve their tactics, ours forgets the basic principles of warfare . . . and remains constantly preoccupied with *wacht*-parades and poor Prussian imitations. The Russian army has lost its soul."[126]

"Here rises the Sun of Austerlitz," was Napoleon's famous greeting at dawn on December 2, a day he would always cherish and celebrate. For Kutuzov, the "Eclipse of Austerlitz" marked one of the worst moments of his life—one that overshadowed his long and successful career, leaving him in the gloom of imperial disgrace and awash in personal grief and disillusionment. He knew that, as commander in chief, he would be held responsible for the loss of a battle he had not wanted to fight.

His struggle for posterity, for how his involvement in the events at Austerlitz would be judged and remembered, began almost as soon as the battle had ended. In the morning of December 3, as he rode up to the Life Guard Izmailovskii Regiment and chatted with troops about what had gone wrong the day before, he was already proclaiming his innocence. "I wash my hands of it all," he told the officers.[127] Seeking to escape the winter chill at a bonfire, Kutuzov, "his face all gloomy," told soldiers that they were young and would still have a chance to settle scores with the French. "The vilification for Austerlitz would fall on my shoulders, even though I have done nothing wrong," he grumbled.[128] In a letter to Catherine, he wrote: "By now you must have heard about our misfortune. I can only console you by saying that I do not hold myself responsible for anything that has happened there, even though I am always very exacting of myself."[129]

In the days after the battle, Alexander instructed Kutuzov to produce two separate reports on what had transpired that dreadful December day—one designed to satisfy the public's curiosity and to combat Napoleon's propaganda efforts, and the other for private consideration.[130] The public version quickly received publicity around Europe, with at least half a dozen European newspapers printing it in the first week of April 1806. Kutuzov's public account seemed to be a straightforward recounting of events as he saw them, though it did carry a subtle but unambiguous censure of the Russian ruler and his advisors. The private version was more pointed. "As Your Majesty was present at the battle, I did not think it necessary to transmit to you any account of the leading circumstances of that affair," read the opening line of the private report. Kutuzov was telling the czar that he should know what had happened on those Moravian fields since he had been the one in charge there.[131] Furthermore, when the emperor ordered Kutuzov, in late December 1805, to divert one of his corps to Silesia to bolster Bennigsen's forces and support Prussia against France, the general wrote back an unusually sharp response. "The nine battalions that comprise this corps can hardly launch a diversion against [Napoleon] if he were to attack Prussia," he explained. "Who would be held responsible if Bonaparte, who acts without any constraints, dispatches a corps on the direct route to intercept and attack [the Russian forces]?" This was a not-too-subtle critique of the czar's blame-shifting at Austerlitz. Kutuzov concluded his letter with an acerbic note: "Assuming that Your Majesty already considered *all these particulars* [my emphasis] and decided to send to Bennigsen's army those troops that are [more readily available], I decided not to detach the corps and will instead lead all of my forces back home."[132]

In Kutuzov's telling, the primary responsibility for the debacle lay on the shoulders of Emperor Alexander, his suite members, and the Austrians. The czar could have listened to the general's advice but chose not to, instead siding with his youthful advisors and the Austrians, whose "meddling turned everything into a big mess," as Kutuzov put it.[133] Many in Russian society shared this view, though few dared to express it as forthrightly as Field Marshal Mikhail Kamenskii, who, in response to the czar's question about how the army performed at Austerlitz, plainly told him, "If Kutuzov had actually commanded the army that day, he would have been shot."[134] The intimation was clear: Alexander should look into mirror to see the man responsible for the defeat.

Be that as it may, Kutuzov knew that many would hold him accountable for not drawing upon his knowledge and experience to offer the czar better advice. Inaccurate as this judgment was, it became widespread enough to cause Kutuzov much pain and anguish. After returning home, the general was careful to avoid getting embroiled in any public debates about the Russian performance at Austerlitz, both because he wanted to remain "above the ambitiousness and intrigues of loafers," as he wrote to General Miloradovich, and because he felt "internally satisfied with my behavior" and "at peace with my conscience."[135]

Even so, in private moments, he must have felt the weight of responsibility for what had transpired. For when the time came, he spoke up about it. Seven years after Austerlitz, while pursuing Napoleon's disordered and disheveled army through the snow-covered Russian countryside, Mikhail Illarionovich halted near the town of Krasnyi, where his army had just fought a battle against the French. Soldiers presented him with a number of trophies, including a French flag bearing the gilded inscription "Austerlitz." He paused to examine the colors before addressing officers and soldiers. "Gentlemen," he told them, "you will outlive me and hear many stories about our wars. After everything we have witnessed, one more victory or defeat would make no difference to my legacy. But I want you to remember one thing: I am not to blame for the Battle of Austerlitz."[136]

PART IV

| The Wilderness Years, 1806–1808

"SOME OF MY REGIMENTS have already crossed the imperial border, while others are still [dozens of miles] from it," Kutuzov wrote Catherine on January 27, 1806. "I keep postponing crossing over myself, as if doing so would destroy me." Peering across the border and into Russia, he could foresee nothing but humiliation and disgrace. Early portents were not encouraging; unlike other senior officers who left the army to see their families, he was told to stay behind and supervise the army's cantonment and then to take charge of three divisions in the western borderlands. The order seemed to imply that Czar Alexander did not want to see him in St. Petersburg, at least not for now.[1] "I do not know how long this will last," Kutuzov confessed. "I will wait for a few more days and will then write a letter asking for permission to return to St. Petersburg."[2]

Days turned into weeks. He had hoped that the czar would request his presence in St. Petersburg—"this would be better for public perception"—but, realizing that a royal summons was not forthcoming, he felt compelled to write an appeal himself. He was ready to tug on his court connections, and his wife's.[3] More days were spent anxiously awaiting the czar's response. Kutuzov sought to channel the energies produced by his sense of injustice into his service to the army; he remained in western Ukraine, shuttling between Brest-Litovsk, Dubno, and Mozyr and handling a myriad of tasks that reorganizing a beaten army entailed. Regiments had to be replenished, equipment accounted for and refurbished, reports on losses finalized, men rewarded and disciplined. That spring proved to be the time of reckoning for many Russian officers whose performance during the campaign left much to be desired. Kutuzov investigated dozens of cases of senior officers who had mismanaged their units, embezzled funds, abandoned their men after the battle, and so forth. Some, even generals, were cashiered or expelled from service; others had their awards and promotions denied because of Kutuzov's inquiries.[4]

Perhaps more than he had ever done before, he saw to the needs of the rank and file. One of his first decisions upon returning to Russia was to gather information about the families of noncommissioned officers and soldiers who had died during the campaign so that they could receive assistance.[5] He knew firsthand how painful it was to lose a loved one, and his son-in-law's death weighed heavily on his mind as he made arrangements to transport the young man's remains to the Tiesenhausen family estate in Reval. His beloved daughter was of course utterly distraught by the death of her husband. "I know you will be shedding a lot of tears," he wrote to her in an effort to console her. "But let's make a deal—never cry without me, while together we can mourn him deeply."[6] Separated from his family, he felt helpless to comfort them or to share his own profound grief. "Greetings Lizanka, Dashenka, and my little Katenka, my dear friends," opens one of his many letters to his daughters. "I am so anguished to see you all so despondent. Is there anything I can do for you? It is an undeniable truth that children's love pales in comparison to the parents' affection for them.[7] He felt a growing sense of loneliness and disconnection.

Finally, in May 1806, word of the imperial recall reached him. The czar consented to see him in the capital, where the general arrived in the last days of the month.[8] Conventional accounts of this period make Kutuzov into a martyr, assuming that the czar's refusal to admit the general to the capital involved the general's being a reminder of what had happened at Austerlitz. Some contemporaries believed such claims. "Kutusoff is still in disgrace," commented a British newspaper in late 1806.[9] The reality, of course, was more byzantine. Alexander undoubtedly had misgivings about Kutuzov, but he also understood what had transpired in 1805, including his own part in the debacle. Mindful of public perceptions, if nothing else, he actually treated the general rather well. Kutuzov's youngest daughter, Darya, became a lady-in-waiting, while Mikhail Illarionovich himself received an imperial decree expressing the czar's thanks for his "exemplary courage and indefatigable enterprise" and "clever and prudent leadership" during the retreat from Braunau to Olmutz. In early March, Kutuzov was awarded the Order of St. Vladimir (first class), one of the highest Russian imperial awards.[10] Moreover, in a remarkable display of munificence—and perhaps as a way of atoning—the emperor inquired how many debts he owed. Catherine scrambled to provide an accounting of what proved to be a debt of almost a quarter million rubles (enough to provide annual pay for 25,000 soldiers).[11] "Much to my chagrin, I discovered that the debts, both yours and mine, are far greater than what I supposed," she admitted. As it was, Alexander paid 50,000 rubles' worth of arrears, an amount equivalent to ten years of a governor's or general's salary.[12] These were hardly the actions of a sovereign callously forsaking his general, as has long been claimed. Alexander continued to employ Kutuzov and appointed him to the imperial Council of War, the supreme advisory body of nine senior military figures that met through the summer of 1806 to discuss new plans, improve the army's preparedness, and, more broadly, consider and apply the lessons of 1805.[13] Of the thirteen newly formed divisions, Kutuzov, as "one of the foremost commanders," as he was described in the czar's letter, was given command of the 6th, 7th, and 8th.[14]

The scale and pace of Napoleon's conquests in 1805 left European powers dumbfounded and divided. The Anglo-Russian military and political alliance got badly strained, while relations between St. Petersburg and Vienna reached a new low, each side holding the other responsible for Austerlitz. Although Alexander did not openly blame the Austrians for "treachery and imbecility," to borrow one British statesman's expression, anti-Austrian sentiments continued to be rampant in the Russian army and in society at large.[15] The triumphs of 1805 seemed to have given Napoleon unchallenged mastery of Europe, where, through persuasion and pressure, he began to restructure the international order. The most far-reaching changes occurred in Germany, where, almost a thousand years after its inception, the Holy Roman Empire "died with a whimper" and was replaced by the French-dominated Confederation of the Rhine, which served as a marketplace for French products, a source of manpower, and a buffer against Prussia, Austria, and Russia; Russia's influence in central Europe had all but vanished.[16]

Emperor Alexander could not accept such drastic change, especially when it involved Russian interests in Germany. He thus rejected the draft of the Franco-Russian peace treaty that was signed in Paris in late July, and instead plunged ahead with the plans for a new anti-Napoleonic coalition, this time in concert with Prussia. By the end of September 1806, Kutuzov was receiving a steady stream of imperial instructions advising him to prepare for the new war; his three divisions, reinforced and refurbished, began moving toward the Russo-Prussian frontier.[17] Yet the flicker of hope that he might be given a chance to participate in the new war and acquit himself well was extinguished when a czar's decree instructed him to surrender his command and travel to Kyiv to assume the position of local military governor.[18]

Historians have long alleged that this was a new exile. "Kutuzov's appointment as the military governor of Kyiv is directly connected with the Austerlitz disaster," insisted Soviet historian Liubomir Beskrovnyi, who, like many others, believed that the czar held a deep grudge against the general.[19] The emperor's decision not to send Kutuzov to the army is, if nothing else, puzzling. The previous campaign had validated the general's judgment, and it would have been natural for the czar to select him to command a corps, if not the army, in a new war. Many thought that he should be given a second chance. Even British newspapers assumed this would be the case. "The French troops are naturally in a state of great alarm at the approach of the Russians, whose main body is commanded by General Kut-us-off," erroneously proclaimed one English periodical.[20] Alexander's reluctance to employ Kutuzov in the field army is all the more baffling given whom he nominated instead. Field Marshal Mikhail Kamenskii was known for his abrasive character and, at nearly seventy years old, had long been retired from active service. It seemed everyone except for the czar knew that he was both senile and in poor health. "I almost completely lost my vision and am unable to find any locations on the map," the field marshal admitted after arriving to the army. "I suffer from [excruciating] pains in the eyes and head and cannot mount the horse. . . . I am signing papers without even knowing what they prescribe."[21] Kamenskii's appointment raised eyebrows in Russian society. "If everything I hear from the army is true," wrote Kutuzov to Catherine, "he must have gone insane."[22]

Alexander's choice suggests lingering bitterness toward Kutuzov. But it might also reflect the czar's awareness that Kutuzov himself was not yet eager to get back to campaigning. His daughters needed his help, his family's finances required steadier hands, and he himself longed for a respite after a campaign that left him drained and disheartened. He shared his feelings in private letters to friends and acquaintances, one of whom noted how disgusted Kutuzov felt "with everything he witnessed at Austerlitz" and that he "prefers to accept any peace than to see war waged the way we are doing it now."[23] In conversations with Catherine, Kutuzov regularly spoke of the appeal of a quieter life and complained about missing out on family experiences. He noted that he would not have minded being posted as a governor to the Crimea or Ukraine; that would have put him conveniently close to his estates, which were in a dire state.[24] Little had changed over the previous three years in the family's finances. The Kutuzovs were still desperate for more income, and Mikhail Illarionovich was still convinced that his estate earnings were being embezzled in his absence. The czar's decision to send him to Kyiv may not have involved royal vindictiveness but probably was encouraged by Kutuzov so that he could focus his energies on rebuilding the family's fortunes and helping his newly married or widowed daughters.

Kyiv, the capital of the first great eastern Slavic state, is located on the steeply sloping banks of the Dnieper River, the meeting point of the pine forests of the north and the broadleaf woods of the south. The beginnings of this "mother of the towns of ancient Rus," as one medieval chronicle referred to it, remain obscure, but one popular tale credits three brothers and a sister who settled on the shores of the Dnieper at the end of the ninth century and built a town in honor of their eldest brother, Kyi. The city experienced some days of glory during the tenth to twelfth centuries when it became a prosperous trading emporium and the political center of the powerful Kyivan Rus, and then endured utter devastation from a Mongol invasion and Tatar raids. By the fifteenth century, it seemed to some European visitors a poor town whose residents scraped by, living in what had become the battleground between the Polish-Lithuanian Commonwealth and the rising Muscovite Rus.[25] In the late seventeenth century, the town fell under Muscovite control. It remained essentially a frontier town with a diverse population that reflected its checkered past. "From a distance the town conveys great beauty," wrote a Russian visitor in the 1780s. "The green and golden cupolas on the bluffs are particularly charming, but that charm disappears when you enter the wretched place."[26] Empress Catherine had a grand plan to revive the town. Though it was only partly implemented, it was sufficient to restore some sense of greatness to the beleaguered place. A visiting Russian dignitary found Kyiv "a great, well-built city with many tasteful homes . . . and more than ten fashionable shops, music, and bookstores."[27] On market days and religious holidays, especially during Lent, the town's population of about 20,000 residents almost doubled, and it was "overrun with pilgrims" or raucous Poles who transformed it into a veritable carnival.[28]

Having settled into Kyiv in the fall of 1806, Kutuzov busied himself with provincial affairs, which involved managing three massive provinces—Kyiv, Volhynia, and Podolia—and commanding divisions. As noted, it remains unclear whether he formally petitioned the czar for the position in Kyiv, but if he did, he might have regretted it, for he was soon facing an administrative morass. In the fall of 1806, Emperor Alexander called up new levies, and more than 600,000 men were recruited from Russia's thirty-one provinces.[29] These recruits had to be processed, equipped, trained, and prepared for war, tasks that fell to Kutuzov. "The arriving regiments bring only additional problems that keep me very preoccupied," he complained to his wife barely a month after arriving in Kyiv. Amid this frenzied work, he also had to keep responding to the family's persistent requests for more funds; even after the czar's generous gesture, the Kutuzovs could not keep up with their expenses and struggled financially to the point that the general considered selling some of his estates.[30] "I am expecting monies any day now," he wrote Catherine in December 1806. "But trust me, I am in a difficult position myself. Now is such a dead time that it is impossible to sell anything."[31] He scraped together 2,000 rubles, which was hardly enough. Three months later, on April 1, he wrote, "I was unable to get more monies in time for this mail dispatch. And no, this is not an April Fool's Day joke."[32]

Amid "so many woes," he again fell into a state of depression from overwork and a sense of helplessness.[33] "I am not happy here," he grumbled in December 1806. He pictured his family joining him in Kyiv but knew full well that it was just a dream.[34] He remained extremely concerned for his daughter Elizabeth, who could not cope with the death of her husband and was struggling to raise her two young daughters, three-year-old Ekaterina (Catherine) and two-year-old Darya (Dorothea). Elizabeth contemplated ending her life, and the news of this, revealed casually (as these things often are) in a letter to her father, stunned Kutuzov. His reply was upbraiding and stern (and self-centered): "Are you not concerned for your children? Have you given any thought what a calamity it would be for me in my old age?"[35] Days later he added, "How much longer are we supposed to live so separately? Our hearts can no longer endure such a painful existence."[36]

Meanwhile, the power struggles shaping the future of the continent distracted him from daily concerns. The news made its way slowly to Kyiv, so he learned belatedly that Prussian king Frederick William III, a man of good intentions but vacillating willpower, had blundered into a war against Napoleon before his Russian ally could support him. The ensuing Franco-Prussian war was brief and decisive. In just four weeks, Napoleon routed the Prussian army at the twin Battles of Jena-Auerstadt (October 14) and occupied the entire Prussian kingdom; on October 23, his Grande Armée paraded down the main boulevards of Berlin. The war not only destroyed Prussia's martial reputation but ended her claims to the status of a great power. The French emperor now felt free to take on Russia. "The unfortunate news . . . makes everyone here depressed," Kutuzov wrote to Catherine.[37]

When the new Franco-Russian conflict erupted in November 1806, confusion reigned in the Russian army. Count Kamenskii resigned his post just a few days after reaching the army headquarters. Generals Baron Levin Bennigsen and Friedrich Wilhelm Buxhöwden, who commanded separate corps, argued with each other, and their squabbles hampered Russian operations. Emperor Alexander lamented that he had "not a single general with the talent of the commander in chief."[38] The winter campaign in Poland proved a literal quagmire of snow and mud.[39] In December 1806, Napoleon led his Grande Armée into the snowy Polish countryside to confront the Russians and their hapless leaders.

His hopes for a quick and easy victory, however, soon vanished. The winter campaign began with bloody battles at Golymin and Pultusk, which, in the minds of many Russians at least, constituted victories that washed away the stains of Austerlitz. Kutuzov was delighted to receive news about them and attentively followed the army's movements in their aftermath. The battle at Preussisch-Eylau soon followed on February 7–8, 1807. This proved a bloodbath that left some 40,000 killed and wounded on the snowy fields around this Prussian town; one appalled eyewitness described it as "the most horrible butchery of men."[40] Ten days later the news of this "victory over Bonaparte," as Bennigsen claimed it, reached Kyiv, leaving Kutuzov elated. "Today I discovered that I am not a resentful person after all," he commented to his family members, though this admission does suggest his restlessness at being away from the action. Another week passed before he could learn the details about what had transpired at Eylau from the official battle account. He saw that the battle was not the victory that Bennigsen had alleged, and he noted that by moving toward Königsberg after the battle, the Russian commander had committed a crucial mistake and separated himself from the reinforcements led by Ivan (Magnus Gustav) von Essen I, thus giving an opportunity to "the enraged Bonaparte"—as Kutuzov referred to him—to destroy the isolated Russian force. He was relieved at least that his son-in-law Nikolai Khitrovo, married to his daughter Anna and assigned to Essen's corps, had come through it; the official reports praised him for bravery in battle, though the phrasing of it could have been better. "Tell Anna that she should not get angry about the expression 'reckless gallantry' in the report," he advised Catherine. "That just shows that [Nikolai's commanding] general does not know how to write properly."[41]

After Eylau, the French and Russian armies went to their winter quarters to recover, with the certain expectation of renewed fighting in the spring. Time passed unbearably slowly for Kutuzov, who counted the days between mail deliveries in eager anticipation of books, newspapers, and a fresh batch of gossip from St. Petersburg. He closely followed political developments in Europe and foresaw that the growing Russo-Swedish tensions would not be resolved amicably; he predicted a war over Finland a year before it broke out.[42] In his spare time, Kutuzov attended dinners hosted by the elderly Field Marshal Prince Alexander Prozorovskii, who lived in retirement nearby. Almost fifteen years older than Kutuzov, Prozorovskii had distinguished himself on the fields of Gross-Jägersdorf, Zorndorf, and Kunersdorf during the Seven Years' War and later shone in battles against the Poles and the Ottoman Turks. Leaving active service in the 1780s, he served as a senator, a governor of various provinces, and the commander in chief of Moscow before retiring to his estates in 1795. Kutuzov had known him for quite some time, and a recently discovered letter shows that he had long cultivated relations with the prince, whose estates were adjacent to the lands that Kutuzov received after the Polish partitions.[43] "[The field marshal] lives here quietly and has nothing to quarrel with me about," Kutuzov told Catherine in March 1807. "He speaks too much but, thank heaven, he does not make others talk as much because he is very hard of hearing."[44]

In late March 1807, Emperor Alexander visited the Russian troops in Poland, boosting their morale in expectation of a new campaign and bringing reinforcements, including the Russian Imperial Guard. Kutuzov, who was "impatiently" awaiting the good news from the army, was not asked to join.[45] Life in Kyiv went on. "I am getting rather fat," he admitted to Catherine, promising her that he would "force myself to start walking and riding as soon as the weather improves."[46] The dreary winter eventually gave way to spring. Delighting in watching flowers bloom and listening

to birds sing—"I have never heard so many nightingales in the garden"—
Kutuzov keenly followed events in Europe.[47] The war with France resumed
in late May, though the news was disheartening. Bennigsen's attempt to
destroy the seemingly isolated French corps had failed and instead played
into the hands of Napoleon, who launched a masterful counterstrike that
crushed the Russian army at Friedland on June 14. The battle was yet
another decisive military and diplomatic victory for the French emperor,
underscoring his ability to size up a situation and exploit the enemy's mistake, tailoring his tactics to circumstances. Having lost some 20,000 killed
and wounded, the Russians retreated toward the Niemen River, which
marked the boundary of the Russian Empire. On June 19, Bennigsen
offered an armistice. "After the torrents of blood which have lately flowed
in battles as sanguinary as frequent," read his message to Napoleon,
"[Russians] desire to assuage the evils of this destructive war, by proposing
an armistice before we enter upon a fresh war, perhaps more terrible than
the first." The offer was accepted.

On June 25, 1807, one of the most dramatic episodes of the Napoleonic Era
unfolded on the banks of the Niemen River. At a set hour Emperors Alexander
and Napoleon approached the river from opposite sides and boarded the
vessels that were to take them to a raft in the middle of the river. As the boats
reached the raft, the two emperors embraced each other. "I hate the English as
much as you do," Alexander supposedly told Napoleon, to which the French
emperor retorted, "In that case, the peace is made."[48] Over the next two
weeks, amid celebrations and military reviews, the two emperors conducted a
series of conferences and concluded an agreement (one to which secret articles
were later added). Signed on July 7, the Treaty of Tilsit proclaimed an alliance between the French and Russian Empires, effectively dividing Europe
into western and eastern spheres of influence. Alexander gave his formal recognition to the Confederation of the Rhine, firmly establishing Napoleon's
control in central Europe while greatly weakening Prussia, which lost large
territories and got saddled with a heavy war indemnity. In what constituted
one of most substantial concessions, the Russian sovereign agreed to mediate
between France and Britain. If this measure produced no positive results, he
pledged to declare war against Britain and to join French efforts to eliminate
their rival's commerce on the continent. In exchange, Napoleon agreed not
to impede Russian ambitions in Swedish-controlled Finland and offered to
mediate between Russia and the Ottoman Empire. Should the sultan refuse
to negotiate, Napoleon pledged to "make common cause with Russia against
the Ottoman Porte" and help Russia expand into the Danubian Principalities,
where a new Russo-Ottoman conflict had already been raging for almost a
year. In the provisions added later, Napoleon consented to the partitioning of

the Ottoman possessions in the Balkans, though he refused to acknowledge Russian claims to Istanbul.[49]

Much had changed since 1792, when the last war between the Russians and Ottomans had ended. The condition of the Ottoman Empire was so dire that some were predicting its dissolution. In the Caucasus, Russia seized the Georgian principalities, first annexing the eastern Georgian kingdom of Kartli-Kakheti and then extending its dominion to the Kingdom of Imereti and the Principalities of Megrelia and Guria, which the Ottomans traditionally claimed as spheres of interest. Elsewhere the sultan's authority was disregarded: Pasvanoglu Osman Pasha of Vidin was in open revolt, as was almost all of Serbia; Ali Pasha of Janina was obedient only when it suited his convenience; Djezzar Pasha enjoyed virtual independence in Syria, and Mehmed Ali was zealously consolidating his power in Egypt. The Wahhabi fundamentalists extended their influence across much of Arabia, while the hospodars of Moldavia and Wallachia showed clear affinities for self-rule. More crucially, Russo-Ottoman relations became strained in 1804–1805 when Napoleon approached Sultan Selim III with a proposal of possible alliance. The possibility of French presence in the Balkans and/or control of the strategic straits of the Dardanelles and Bosporus had concerned Alexander, who sympathized with the plight of the Slavic peoples under Ottoman domination and extended support to the Serbian insurgents who had been fighting the Ottomans since 1803. Caught between a rock (France) and a hard place (Russia), the Ottomans sought to remain neutral and avoid entanglement in European squabbles. In fact, the sultan was willing to negotiate with the Russians and accepted a new Russo-Ottoman treaty (September 1805) that confirmed friendship and amity between the two powers while also recognizing Russia's standing as the guardian of the Christian peoples of the Ottoman Empire.

The dramatic turn of events in Europe changed the Ottoman mind. After Austerlitz, Selim III decided to join the winning side, hoping to recover territories lost to Russia. He acknowledged Napoleon's imperial title, lent a willing ear to the talk of an alliance with France, and replaced the current pro-Russian hospodars of Moldavia and Wallachia with more pliant candidates. These initiatives threatened to overturn the existing state of affairs between Russia and the Ottoman Empire. Alexander and his advisors were quick to point out that the Ottoman actions had violated the articles of the Treaty of Jassy of 1792, which required joint agreement when it came to dismissing or appointing the hospodars. As negotiations reached a breaking point, both sides began concentrating their troops on their borders. In October 1806, just as he began preparing for the War of the Fourth Coalition, Alexander ordered the invasion and occupation of the Danubian Principalities. In a mere three months General Ivan Michelson, with some 40,000 men, had overrun these territories and driven the Turkish forces back to the Danube

River. As his army secured control of the region, Alexander reinstated the hospodars, extended financial and military support to the Serbian insurgents, and pledged protection for the Slav population across the Balkans.

The following year, the Russian campaign on the Danube was obstructed by the Franco-Russian war. Michelson received orders to detach part of his army to oppose the French in Poland. Nonetheless, General Mikhail Miloradovich managed to advance to Bucharest and defeated Ottoman forces at Turbat and Giurgiu in late March 1807. The Ottoman counterattack, led by Grand Vizier Ibrahim Hilmi Pasha, stumbled. In May, the Janissaries rebelled and overthrew Sultan Selim, which encumbered the Ottoman war effort. Then in June 1807, Miloradovich surprised the Turks at Obilesti and forced the Ottoman army to retreat beyond the Danube. On the Serbian front, the joint Russo-Serbian forces defeated the Turks at Malanica, paving the way for a formal agreement between the Russians and the Serbs (in July 1807) that officially recognized the Serbian aspirations for statehood.

The Russian victories in the Balkans were seemingly offset by the defeats in Poland, but the Treaty of Tilsit gave the Russians a chance to consolidate their positions in the Ottoman realm. Unaware of these momentous changes, General Ivan Meyendorff, who replaced Michelson as the commander of the Russian forces in the Danubian Principalities, signed an armistice with the Ottomans at Slobozia in September 1807. The agreement, negotiated without Emperor Alexander's sanction, called for Russian withdrawal from Moldavia and Wallachia while the Turks agreed to remain south of the Danube.[50]

Infuriated by the news of this armistice, Alexander replaced Meyendorff with Field Marshal Alexander Prozorovskii—the talkative retiree with whom Kutuzov had spent many evenings in Kyiv. This was, yet again, a startling choice. Like Kamenskii, Prozorovskii was a septuagenarian veteran of the Seven Years' War who had not experienced combat in over two decades. He was almost completely deaf. Upon arriving to take command of the army, the field marshal at first showed glimpses of his energetic self but soon felt overwhelmed with responsibilities. He may have regretted accepting the command, but he was unwilling to follow Kamenskii's example by simply giving up and returning home. Instead, he had the presence of mind to seek an assistant. He urged the czar to appoint Kutuzov as the second-in-command of the Russian forces in the Danubian Principalities. "I will employ him as my deputy, for he is my disciple and knows my methods very well," wrote the field marshal. In fact, Kutuzov was anything but his disciple and had a far greater grasp of military affairs. But Prozorovskii preferred his version of truth, and Kutuzov seems to have actively encouraged him in this.[51]

Prince Prozorovskii was convinced that taking on Kutuzov was a win-win situation for everyone. Kutuzov would get to escape from Kyiv, and Prozorovskii would acquire a capable officer who would do the heavy work of managing the army. The field marshal could claim the credit for any success that came out of it. He did note that the general had but one "defect": "He is not always very firm in character and especially in connection with court affairs." He also added that Kutuzov was "by nature lazy about putting pen to paper." These were minor drawbacks and, in the prince's mind, were more than compensated for by Kutuzov's strengths: he knew "all military affairs exceptionally well" and was "one of the best generals His Majesty currently has."[52] It never crossed the prince's mind, as one Russian general remarked, that Kutuzov, having commanded the Russian forces against Napoleon, would be uninterested in taking "a subordinate role in the army sent to fight the Turks."[53]

Be that as it may, Emperor Alexander approved the suggestion. On March 16, 1808, he ordered Kutuzov to hand over his gubernatorial duties to Major General Alexander Masse and, taking the 8th and 22nd Divisions, which had been cantoned in Kyiv province, join Prozorovskii in the Danubian Principalities.[54] "I am leaving Kyiv tomorrow," wrote Kutuzov to his daughters. The misery of his lonely existence and the tedium of daily chores suddenly faded in his memory. Looking back at the time he had spent in this town, he came to an unexpected conclusion: "Tyranny is a habit."[55] "I am departing this place with a heavy heart," he wrote his daughter Elisabeth, "for I have spent many serene months here: I went to sleep and woke up without fear and with a clear conscience."[56]

| The Carnage on the Danube, 1809

KUTUZOV ARRIVED AT JASSY in the last days of April 1808.[1] Prince Prozorovskii welcomed him with a warm embrace and made him second-in-command of the Army of Moldavia, as the Russian forces in the Danubian Principalities soon became known.[2] Kutuzov wasted not a moment in assessing the situation, which he found peaceful but perilous. The Armistice of Slobozia, which Meyendorff had negotiated six months earlier, was still technically in effect; the Russian and Ottoman armies were divided by the Danube River. The new commander in chief's first task was to inform the Ottomans that the armistice was void because his predecessor had had no authority to accept it. The Ottomans objected, and the two sides spent the rest of the year debating the legality of the agreement; neither wanted to rush into a resumption of hostilities before being fully prepared. Two years of military operations and the presence of tens of thousands of troops had taken a toll on the Danubian regions, which suffered from widespread looting; regular outbreaks of scurvy, plague, and other diseases; and the exodus of thousands of peasants, with the resultant drop in agricultural production. The Army of Moldavia, which had increased to some 80,000 men, suffered from a lack of supplies and adequate logistical support to conduct decisive military operations.[3] Kutuzov's first mission, therefore, was to ensure that the army was well supplied, trained, and prepared for war.

The army consisted of several corps. General Miloradovich led one on the right flank, near Bucharest, while the advance guard, under Cossack Ataman Matvei Platov, stood near Rymnik (present-day Râmnicu Sărat, Romania). On the left wing was Count Langeron's corps, supported by a special detachment that kept an eye on the Turks at Galati.[4] The army's central force, the so-called Main Corps, was placed under Kutuzov's command—a clear indication of Prozorovskii's trust and confidence. This was a sizable force of nineteen infantry battalions, thirty squadrons of cavalry, two heavy artillery companies, and one horse artillery company, supported by several hundred Cossacks and companies of pioneers and pontoniers. Moreover, during the summer of 1808, Kutuzov's corps was reinforced with thousands more troops from Peter von Essen III's 8th Division and General Zakhar Olsufyev III's 22nd Division.

Surviving documents in the Russian military archives testify to Kutuzov's diligence and industry in bolstering Russian military strength. Prozorovskii may have had the title of commander in chief, but Kutuzov handled day-to-day administration of the army, coordinated unit movements, managed logistics and recruitment, and supervised training exercises. Having a forgetful superior meant that he had to pay close attention to even small details. When Prozorovskii made a mistake in explaining steps soldiers had to follow during firing exercises, Kutuzov respectfully pointed it out and provided proper instruction for the soldiers; three months later, he noticed that some cooking kettles had lost their tin coating, which could have harmful effect on the soldiers' health, so he instructed regimental commanders to take measures to fix the problem.[5]

As always, logistics was the most pressing issue. During the earlier campaigns, Russian supplies had to be carried from the distant bases in the provinces, and transporting vast amounts of ammunition and provisions over such long distances was costly and time-consuming. To expedite the process, Kutuzov first undertook an inventory of supplies in the army and the neighboring Russian provinces. He established a central depot to which the Moldavian and Wallachian authorities were now expected to deliver supplies; smaller depots were set up in various towns and villages, and arrangements made to purchase food directly from the local population. Throughout the spring and summer of 1808, Kutuzov reorganized the field hospital system to accommodate sick soldiers, took measures to combat scurvy (which spread due to the lack of fresh supplies), and organized new medical facilities, including an officers' hospital in Jassy, a mobile infirmary, and a medical depot for soldiers. He made sure soldiers received new knapsacks, coats, and other equipment that had been recently modified.[6]

Almost as soon as he arrived at Jassy, Kutuzov helped set up training camps, where regiments could be regrouped, reinforced, and continually trained. The extent of his success can be judged by the fact that barely three weeks after arriving, the first ("chef's") and third ("commander's") battalions were fully equipped and ready to depart Jassy, while the second battalions were kept behind to train the new recruits and form a reserve corps. Later that summer and fall, Kutuzov continued to train the men at their new campsites, including the largest one, which was near the village of Călienii on the right bank of the Siret River.[7] The 8th and 22nd Divisions, which arrived in late summer, had thousands of inexperienced recruits that had to be properly trained before the campaign started.[8] Aware of the meager supplies and difficult conditions in the Danubian Principalities, Kutuzov insisted in his letters to the recruitment authorities in Kyiv province that "in selecting the recruits, particular attention should be paid to their healthy and strong constitution rather than their height and appearance."[9] Once these recruits arrived, they were distributed between the units to bring them all up to strength and then drilled alongside veteran soldiers.

As on many prior occasions, Kutuzov relied on his practical experience. Knowing that many of his officers had never fought the Ottomans before, he prepared a lengthy memorandum explaining the basics of Ottoman warfare. "The Turks employ no other maneuver except for charging with their numerous cavalry and seeking to surround an enemy force," he advised officers. Fending off that initial attack was crucial to success in battle, so Kutuzov exhorted his men to show "steadfastness, composure, determination, and firmness." He also expected them to act with restraint and not waste ammunition, for "in confronting their frenzied assaults, firing two or three [volley] rounds is usually sufficient to turn the Turks to flight." Like Rumyantsev and Suvorov before him, Kutuzov believed that the best way to negate the Ottoman superiority in cavalry was by employing the "moving redoubts" formation—infantry squares deployed in checkered formation (three in the front, two in the back), with cavalry and artillery kept in the intervals between the *carrés*. Every time the Main Corps redeployed, Kutuzov made sure the army practiced this formation, paying close attention to units' performance and coordination. He cautioned that any sign of disorder could cause "unfathomable consequences."[10] He set up special ranges where the troops could practice aimed musket firing. His improvement of the logistical system and insistence on sanitation and tidiness at the campsite meant that in August he was pleased to report that aside from a few cases of fever, not one of the officers was sick.[11]

Shortly after his arrival Kutuzov had an opportunity to demonstrate the value of his presence. In May, Horace François Bastien Sébastiani de La Porta, the French ambassador to the Ottoman Empire, who had helped organize Ottoman defenses against a British naval expedition to Istanbul the previous year, happened to be traveling across Wallachia on his way home. Prozorovskii welcomed him to Jassy but wisely decided to allow Kutuzov to handle the meeting. The former Russian ambassador thus met the current French envoy. Both men had years of experience in diplomatic and military matters. They greeted each other warmly, exchanged pleasantries, and discussed the recent news from the Ottoman capital, all the while keen to pick up any bit of useful intelligence. Kutuzov credited his "good-humored and frank attitude" for getting Sébastiani to relax his "formal ministerial antics" and "feigned military candor." He "half-jokingly and half-seriously" baited him with some questions. The ploy apparently worked, as Sébastiani freely shared his thoughts on the Eastern crisis; "I did not have to twist his arm," Kutuzov reported. In the Frenchman's opinion, the key to security in Europe was the survival of the Ottoman Empire. His assumptions were based on an older balance of power, one that no longer obtained given the fate of Germany, Italy, and Spain. He listened as Sébastiani described the sultan's realm as an "empire with a rotten core destined to fall apart," whose collapse would inexorably unleash a wave of wars. If Russia successfully fulfilled its eastern objectives, Sébastiani frankly told his counterpart, "you will impose a humiliating peace on the Ottomans, which would mean the downfall of the sultan. Everything would turn upside down and the consequences of that would be truly impossible to predict." Kutuzov listened attentively, "without making any direct objections to any of his statements," as the French diplomat touched upon the wider imperial policies across the Balkans and the Middle East. Kutuzov pointed out that while urging Russia to show restraint, Napoleon himself worked hard to consolidate his presence in the Ionian Islands, Dalmatia, and other parts of the Balkan peninsula. Sébastiani demurred, claiming France had modest aspirations in the region, and then switched the conversation to Russian aggrandizement in Georgia. Czar Alexander was waging a "war of vanity" against Iran, he charged. "It is a war of security," countered Kutuzov, pointing to the "commercial advantages" Russia hoped to gain in the greater Caspian region. The two generals-cum-diplomats spent some more time bantering about international politics, carefully prodding each other for clues and intimations. In the end, they agreed to disagree. "We are just generals," Sébastiani told his counterpart. "None of what we discussed would have any impact outside this room."[12]

Such were the first ten months of Kutuzov's service in Wallachia. Field Marshal Prozorovskii was extremely pleased with his choice of a second-in-command. When the news arrived of the impending war between France and Austria (it began in earnest on April 10, 1809) and the possibility of him leading an attack on the Hapsburg lands, Prozorovskii did not hesitate to recommend Kutuzov as his only viable successor because he was "equally well versed" in local affairs and "the finer points of the Ottoman politics." It would be "impossible to find anyone better suited," he wrote in a letter to the czar, adding, "He is one of the best generals His Majesty currently has."[13]

Kutuzov's reorganization of the Russian forces was made possible by the mayhem unfolding in the Ottoman Empire. Sultan Selim III was beset by too many problems to think about resuming hostilities and knew well that his empire could never reestablish its authority except through reforms. Yet the reforms that he advocated caused much grief among traditional power groups. In May 1807, the Janissaries erupted in a rebellion that forced the sultan to scale back his designs and disband the Nizam-i Cedid units, which had been trained and equipped in the European manner. But even such drastic concession could not save the sultan. It merely emboldened the rebels, who in late May 1807 dethroned and imprisoned Selim, ushering in a political crisis that hampered Ottoman military capabilities and forced the empire's armies, some of which were commanded by provincial notables engaged in power struggles, to seek a defensive posture on the Danube.

The new sultan, Mustafa IV, was young and inexperienced, a puppet in the hands of the religious clerics and Janissaries. Selim III's supporters found this intolerable. The most powerful of them was Bayraktar Mustafa Pasha of Ruse, who rallied other Ottoman provincial *ayans* (notables) under his leadership and marched on Istanbul in July 1808 to reinstate Selim. He arrived too late to save the former sultan, who was murdered by the rebels, but in time to depose Mustafa and install Mahmud II on the Ottoman throne in late July 1808. Like his predecessor, Mahmud II was politically impotent and depended for his survival on Bayraktar Mustafa Pasha, the first provincial notable ever to hold the position of grand vizier. Convinced that he had crushed the opposition, Bayraktar Mustafa Pasha began reviving the reforms of Selim III but underestimated the power of the religious clerics, Janissaries, and conservative elements of Ottoman society. Yet another revolt flared up in November 1808 in Istanbul, with the rebels killing the grand vizier and many of his supporters.

The Ottomans were keen on preserving the Armistice of Slobozia with Russia, but Emperor Alexander had little desire for peace at a moment when his opponent was in such disarray. "The Ottoman Empire is dead," the Russian foreign minister told the French ambassador, "so why should not Russia keep the spoils of war?"[14] The Russians increasingly thought in expansionist terms, seeking to compensate for what they had lost to Napoleon's aggrandizement elsewhere in Europe by taking territory in the Balkans. In October 1808, just as Kutuzov was busy reorganizing the Russian forces in Wallachia, the French and Russian emperors met once more at Erfurt with the goal of consolidating their alliance. In exchange for his support for France's war against Austria, Alexander extracted Napoleon's acceptance of the Russian presence in the Danubian Principalities.[15] A new war broke out between France and Austria in April 1809, putting the sincerity of the Russo-French alliance to a practical test. Alexander complied with the letter of his commitments to Napoleon by declaring war against the Austrians. But the Russian corps, sent to make a powerful diversion in Galicia, came so late into the field and moved so slowly that it was evident the Russians had no desire to contribute to the success of their ally. The War of the Fifth Coalition, as this conflict became known, revealed that there was no longer any cordiality between France and Russia, though both sides found it convenient—for the present—to preserve the appearance of mutual support.

With Napoleon promising not to interfere in Russian relations with the sultan, Emperor Alexander instructed Prozorovskii to offer new conditions to the Ottomans.[16] A new round of Russo-Ottoman negotiations took place in Jassy, with the Russians demanding the Ottoman surrender of Bessarabia, Moldavia, Wallachia, and eastern and western Georgian kingdoms and principalities, as well as Serbian independence under a joint Russo-Ottoman protectorate. The scale and breadth of Russian ambitions were striking, as was the firmness of the czar's demands. If the Porte refused, Prozorovskii was authorized to launch an offensive across the Danube with the goal of "achieving a glorious peace treaty that will define Russia's frontiers on the Danube," as Count Rumyantsev wrote in a letter to Prince Prozorovskii.[17] Needless to say, Sultan Mahmud II refused to yield any territories, prompting the Russians to withdraw from negotiations and resume military operations.[18] With Napoleon preoccupied with a war against Austria, Russia was keen to exploit an opportunity to consolidate its positions in southeastern Europe. "A swift crossing of the Danube is the only sure way to force the sultan to accept peace and surrender of Bessarabia, Moldavia, and Wallachia," Alexander told Prozorovskii.[19]

Prozorovskii had begun preparing for the new campaign without waiting for the official Ottoman rejection. He knew that the Ottomans had some 40,000 men under Grand Vizier Yusuf Pasha deployed between Adrianople and the Danube; continued disturbances in Istanbul hampered Ottoman logistics and mobilization efforts, with many local governors reluctant to provide additional troops. This meant, or so the Russian commander hoped, that the field army would be immobilized for some time. However, Russian intelligence also reported that the Turks had about 50,000 men scattered in garrisons along the Danube, with about 12,000 men at Brăila, 10,000 at Izmail, and thousands more defending Giurgiu, Ruse, Silistra, Turnu, Vidin, and other fortresses. Despite the czar's call for the Russian army to cross the Danube River, the field marshal was uneasy about leaving such strong garrisons in his rear. He declined, therefore, to conduct a rapid campaign to seek out and destroy the Ottoman field army and instead insisted on the systematic reduction of the enemy fortresses, starting with those of Giurgiu and Brăila. Once the Danube's northern bank was secured, the Russian army would cross the river and target the Ottomans in the Bulgarian uplands.[20]

The Army of Moldavia had spent the winter of 1809 in cantonments scattered across Wallachia. Miloradovich's right wing corps was near Bucharest, while General Langeron's corps held positions in front of Izmail on the left wing. Kutuzov's Main Corps was deployed in between them, holding a vast area, from Jassy to Focşani, with its headquarters at Jassy.[21] Kutuzov spent the months of March and April in preparations for the new campaign. His correspondence is littered with references to the urgent need for more provisions, more matériel, more men. As always, he paid close attention to details—receiving an endless stream of reports and rosters on how many men were present, what uniforms they wore, what equipment they had, what food they ate, how much back pay they were owed, what illnesses they suffered from, and so forth. He diligently went through each of them, identifying problems and seeking resolutions.[22] The Main Corps was soon ready for the campaign. "The war is upon us," Kutuzov wrote Catherine on April 5.[23]

When drafting the new operational plan, Prozorovskii had decided to first attack with his right wing, ordering Miloradovich to capture Giurgiu. In April, as the Russians approached this fortress, its Ottoman garrison proved to be well prepared. Miloradovich soon realized (as Kutuzov had at Izmail) that he had miscalculated the depth of the moat surrounding the fortress and that the Ottomans had improved their defenses. Precious time was lost as the Russian generals scrambled to regroup their attack columns. Under heavy enemy fire, casualties mounted so rapidly that the Russian commander had no choice but to beat a retreat, losing some 700 men in the process.[24] Stung as he was by this setback, Miloradovich took responsibility and wrote a straightforward account of what had transpired, blaming himself for the defeat.[25] Such candor served him well, and Emperor Alexander kept him in command of the corps.

Dismayed by the setback at Giurgiu, Prozorovskii now turned to the fortress of Brăila, an imposing castle overlooking the Danube on one of the river's last major bends before it empties into the Black Sea. Kutuzov was tasked with leading the Main Corps to the fortress.[26] He was familiar with the area, having fought here many years ago. Leading his men across the rolling hills toward the Danubian valley must have brought back many memories of the 1790–1791 campaign. His memory of it was exemplified in his decision to set up a "flying mail" system "following the example of the one employed by Count Alexander Vasilievich Suvorov," as he wrote General Ilovaiskii, and employing a long chain of outposts that could rapidly relay messages from and to the main headquarters.[27]

The Main Corps, some 35,000 strong, left Focşani on April 12 and marched toward the Danube, some sixty miles away.[28] The weather seemed to conspire against the Russians; cold, torrential rains hindered their advance.[29] Some units lost their way, forcing Kutuzov to halt the march for several days so he could rally his forces on the Buzau River, about twenty miles from Brăila. Drawing upon his prior experience fighting the Ottomans, Kutuzov deployed his forces in two lines, with General Sergey Kamenskii commanding the front one while the divisions of generals Yevgeny Markov and Olsufyev III formed the second line. In case of an Ottoman attack, the generals were to form squares and fight in the "moving redoubts" formation. Leaving a small rear guard and sending forth scouts to reconnoiter the area, Kutuzov led the Main Corps toward Brăila on April 20, brushing aside the Turkish outposts

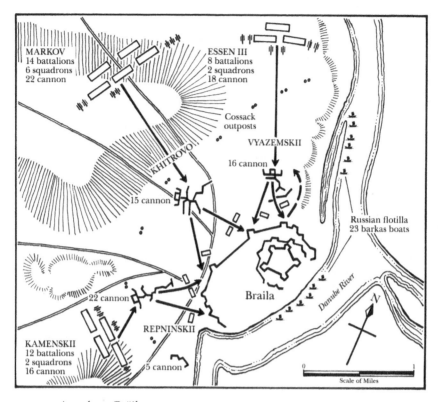

MAP 9 Assault on Brăila

and initiating the blockade of the fortress. The Russian corps deployed in a wide arch around the fortress, with General Sergey Kamenskii's division forming the right wing, Essen III's units on the left, and Yevgeny Markov's troops in the center.[30]

The fortress of Brăila was built around a former Orthodox monastery. The pentagon-shaped citadel had been overhauled in recent years, its stone walls repaired and its towers reinforced. Jutting from the walls were thirty-five-foot-tall diamond-shaped bastions that allowed the Ottomans supporting fields of fire. The bastions were further protected by an extensive moat. Nonetheless, most of the garrison's 12,000 men were stationed outside the citadel, protecting the *retrenchment*—a massive secondary line of defense consisting of a deep and wide ditch, with a steep counterscarp that the attacking units would have to descend before reaching the earthen ramparts with five bastions, which had been constructed within the range of the citadel's cannon. To capture the castle, the Russians would have to overcome these earthworks first.

Kutuzov commenced the siege works on April 19. Over the next few days, the Russian engineers, led by Engineer Major General Ivan Harting, constructed parallels that approached within half a mile from the *retrenchment*, as well as four large breaching batteries to target the Ottoman positions. The garrison made daily sorties but failed to interrupt the Russian preparations; instead, the Turks set the outer suburbs on fire to clear the view and to deny the enemy any cover.[31] On April 23, Russian heavy cannon arrived, along with a flotilla of nineteen gunboats from Galati. The artillery barrage silenced Ottoman artillery and caused significant damage in the Brăila suburbs.[32] By the end of April, Kutuzov's disciplined reduction of the fortress seemed to be working: Russian gunboats controlled the river, while the Main Corps effectively isolated the fortress on land.[33]

In early May, Field Marshal Prozorovskii arrived to assume the overall command of the corps. Now that Kutuzov had set up the blockade, the main question was whether to besiege the fortress or to expedite the process by a direct assault. Emboldened by the Russian artillery bombardment and the apparent feebleness of the Ottoman defenses, Prozorovskii thought the fortress would be an easy target, something to be taken, as he put it, "on the fly" (*mimokhodom*). He thus ordered the assault.[34]

Kutuzov disagreed. He was under no illusion that the fortress would fall easily, and pointed out that the Russian bombardment had not been strong enough to cause serious damage to the Ottoman defenses. Russian cannonballs could not shatter the thick earthen ramparts, and the Ottoman cannon had not been destroyed but, rather, were silent in expectation of the assault, while the garrison remained safe beneath the earthen ramparts.[35] Even more concerning was Prozorovskii's decision to commit only a small part of the Main Corps for the assault—just 8,000 men were to assail a fortress defended by almost 12,000 Ottomans. Prozorovskii argued that he only intended to capture the outside entrenchment. According to the rules of siege craft, if this was accomplished, the garrison would have to surrender.[36] Kutuzov was doubtful it would work and urged patience and systematic reduction of the fortress. A premature direct assault, especially with insufficient forces, risked heavy casualties and a defeat, he warned. His advice was ignored.

Russian historians almost unanimously accuse Prozorovskii of pigheadedness and incompetence; he contributed to the calamity that was about to unfold at Brăila in part by changing the timing of the attack from dawn (as Kutuzov apparently advocated) to late evening and reversing the sequence of assaults (as Kutuzov had envisioned them). But many of these claims are misleading, designed to exculpate Kutuzov. A careful examination of documents shows that Kutuzov and Harting (whom the soldiers nicknamed "the Coffinmaker" for his miscalculations), in consultation with Prozorovskii, drafted the disposition for the storming of the outer part (*retrenchement*) of the Ottoman defenses during the evening of April 30.[37] It was an unusual plan because it proposed a limited assault on the Ottoman fortress (upon which the commander in chief insisted) and contained a strict injunction for soldiers not to advance beyond the *retrenchment* or attempt storming the citadel itself. The disposition for attack specified that "the column commanders must closely observe and sternly remind their men that upon scaling the [outer] earthwork, nobody must venture forward for more than ten steps; any violators would be treated as traitors."[38] The plan called for three assault columns, under Major Generals Sergei Repninskii II, Nikolai Zakharovich Khitrovo (Kutuzov's son-in-law), and Vasilii Vyazemskii, to storm the Ottoman positions from multiple directions. Each column comprised three infantry battalions, preceded by sixty volunteers (*okhotniki*) who were to spearhead the assault, forty men with fascines and ladders to help in crossing the deep trench, and thirty engineers to defuse mines that the Russian scouts reported around the fortress. Infantry battalions and dragoon squadrons were deployed behind each column to serve as the reserves and sustain the momentum. Because the Ottoman outer defenses formed an irregular oval, with the left side being closest to the citadel and its cannon, Kutuzov and Harting decided to target the right side of the fortress, which was farthest from the castle. Vyazemskii's leftmost column, however, was designed as a partial diversion—upon approaching the enemy position, the column was to split into two, with one part supporting the central assault column while some 500 men would draw "along the Danube's bank" near the leftmost enemy position, shouting and firing muskets but not attempting to assault the enemy positions. Under cover of darkness, these men were to generate as much noise as possible to divert the garrison's attention (and draw away troops) while Repninskii (on the right) and Khitrovo (in the center) breached other sectors of the *retrenchment*.[39]

Prozorovskii, as the commander in chief, was indeed responsible for the assault. He insisted on it and he shaped it. "Storming this fortress was a long-standing dream of the old man," acknowledged General Langeron, who remembered the field marshal wishfully reciting examples of the celebrated Russian captures of Ochakov and Izmail—while making no mention of so many other assaults that had failed. "He told me about this in Jassy two months earlier, but I disagreed with him. The army did not approve of it either. Kutuzov dissented too, but [Prozorovskii] ordered it and everyone had to obey." In the wake of Suvorov's bloody but celebrated storming of Izmail, Prozorovskii might have been truly "yearning" to equal the great Russian generalissimo's exploit.[40] In his last order before the assault, the commander in chief exhorted column commanders to gallantly lead the assault and, "with the Lord's help," not only seize the Turkish entrenchment but to construct their own "in a few minutes." To reassure the no doubt disconcerted officers, Prozorovskii reminded them that he had served in the army for sixty years and had had a chance to witness "everything that might transpire in war and to have gained plenty of experience from it all."[41] The prince's arrogance, overconfidence, and obstinacy were on clear display.

Kutuzov's role in all of this remains ambiguous. Once again we see him as a Cassandra, a voice in the wilderness, warning of the catastrophe but ignored. The question is whether he could have been more forceful about conveying his opinion. Was Prozorovskii really so dim witted as to completely ignore the advice of his trusted second-in-command? The answer is that Kutuzov is not as blameless as he was long made out to be. He was directly involved in the drafting of the disposition, and the final plan bore the imprint of his thinking. He thus must be held accountable for the plan's flaws, including the poor choice of column commanders, the lack of coordination between attacking columns, and the insufficient number of ladders. He had fought against the Turks long enough to be fully cognizant of the challenges posed by assaults on a well-protected Ottoman fortress. Moreover, buried in the pile of historical evidence is testimony by Ivan Paskevich, who would later be a decorated field marshal and who in 1809 served as a staff officer in Prozorovskii's headquarters. Paskevich later wrote a detailed memoir of his experiences, only parts of which have been published.[42] It contains a scathing account of Kutuzov's actions at Brăila, accusing him of manipulating the old field marshal and (along with Chief Engineer Harting) egging him on to launch the assault that Kutuzov knew would fail. Kutuzov and Harting assured Prozorovskii that the Turkish artillery was running out of ammunition, that the Ottoman artillery had already been destroyed, that the moats were shallow, and that the *escarpes* were scalable. For two days, writes Paskevich, Kutuzov pressured the field marshal to sanction the attack.

These are startling claims, unsubstantiated by other participants and contrary to everything Kutuzov had done up to that moment. He might have had a penchant for court intrigues, but when it came to military service, Kutuzov had consistently shown himself to be clear-eyed and judicious. Gambling on an assault and imperiling thousands of soldiers' lives just so he could undermine his superior seems out of character. That a distinguished officer like Paskevich believed that this was possible is indicative of how differently contemporaries perceived Kutuzov's character. This allegation, doubtful as it may seem, is also worth mentioning because of Prozorovskii's own subsequent allegations of Kutuzov's meddling in the plans.[43]

At 2 a.m. on May 2, three Russian columns left their camps and advanced toward the Turkish position.[44] An hour later, the last flare signaled the start of the assault. Almost immediately, things went downhill.[45] The columns failed to coordinate their movements in the darkness. While Repninskii and Khitrovo were just starting to march, Vyazemskii's men moved through the *vorstadt* (outside suburb), where an engineer leading the column made a wrong turn, leading it toward a deep ravine that the Russians mistook for the ditch in front of the *retrenchment*. The troops charged, yelling, as per orders, "only to realize that it was just a gully," wrote Paskevich. "So we climbed out of it and ran forward" toward the Ottoman positions. By this point it was too late; the Turks had been forewarned. They waited until the leading Russian troops were crowded along the edge of the ditch before opening "a fierce canister and musket fire" almost point-blank, killing and wounding dozens and dampening the attack momentum.[46] Meanwhile, on the extreme left, Vyazemskii's *okhotniki* pushed on, climbing across the moat and reaching the top of the Ottoman ramparts. But amid the darkness and confusion, Vyazemskii—"very well educated and knowledgeable in military matters but rather careless and sluggish," in the words of a fellow general—could not comprehend what was happening, so he did not rush the rest of his men to build upon the initial success, allowing the Turks to counterattack and cut down most of the *okhotniki*.[47]

The feint assault on the left flank failed to distract the defenders, who opened "a vicious musket and artillery fire" on the main Russian assault columns. "The canister fire claimed many of the ladder-carriers and some ladders never made it to the moat," wrote General Sergei Kamenskii in his after-action report. Upon approaching the moat, some units discovered that instead of having been given seven ladders, there were just two or three, and even those had many rungs broken. The soldiers poured into the fifteen-foot-deep trench but could not climb out of it, while the Turks "mercilessly killed them with musket fire and hand grenades."[48] There was utter confusion; Paskevich, wounded in the head and crawling through the crowded ditch, remembered hearing soldiers shout that they had been betrayed and that ladders were missing. The groaning and moaning drowned out officers' orders, while the wounded soldiers scuttled in the ditch and tried to hide from the fire being directed at them from the top of the rampart.[49]

Standing on open ground on the left flank, Kutuzov must have had flashes of his own horrifying ordeal at Izmail as he observed—amid the bursts of gunfire that illuminated the smoke-filled battlefield—Russian soldiers descending into the ditch but struggling to get out of it. Time and time again, officers would collect a group of men in the ditch and try scaling the glacis; the few brave men would reach the summit of the *retrenchment*, only to be cut down by the Ottoman bullet or saber. Amid this mayhem, the soldiers hunkered down at the bottom of the ditch. They kept shooting their muskets "into the air and at each other, wasting ammunition and inanely shouting 'hurrah,' which only exacerbated disorder."[50] Major General Repninskii was slightly more successful in his attack on the right wing—some of his men penetrated the outer Ottoman defenses and even seized one of the bastions. But they were left unsupported and vulnerable to a counterattack. In the end they were driven into a deep moat, "from where they could not get out and where they died without being able to defend themselves."[51] Belatedly Prozorovskii rushed in reinforcements, but the Russian assault columns, bogged down, could not make any progress and were mowed down by what one eyewitness described as "the most ferocious enemy fire; one may even say, the canister fire rained down upon us as a hail of [lead]."[52]

The rising sun cast light on a gut-wrenching panorama of carnage and human folly. "The glacis and the moat were covered with numerous corpses," recalled an eyewitness.[53] Prince Prozorovskii spent that night on top of the hill on the right flank. He was confident of victory and kept sending out adjutants to learn what was going on in the columns. No one dared tell him that it was time to beat a retreat. When the wounded Paskevich managed to get to him and explain how dire the situation was, "the field marshal refused to believe my words," Paskevich remembered. Others thought that he was delirious from his wound. "Such comments enraged me and I unloaded my anger, explaining that the third column was not simply repulsed but rather annihilated." The doleful officer then lost consciousness and was carried away to the field hospital. While Prozorovskii equivocated, "the slaughter of our men continued in the *retrenchment*." Kutuzov, who had realized that the attack had failed, came in person to see the field marshal and told him flatly that it was time to retreat. The news threw the field marshal into despondency—he fell to his knees and began to cry and bewail the setback. Some remembered that Kutuzov stood by, calmly observing the old man's despondency, and then told him brusquely, "You need to get to grips with it, for worse things have happened. I lost the battle of Austerlitz that decided the fate of Europe, and still I did not cry."[54]

Around nine o'clock in the morning, Prozorovskii ordered the troops to fall back. The surviving Russian soldiers came to rue the daylight, for their retreating columns served as perfect targets for the Ottoman counterfire. In an incredible display of steadfastness and gallantry, the soldiers climbed out of the moat, straightened their lines despite the murderous fire that claimed so many of them, and then moved back while still being pummeled by the elated Turks.[55] The loss of life in this "accidental, so as not to say needless or even senseless, assault," as one participant put it, was startling.[56] Officially the attackers lost 2,229 killed and 2,550 wounded, though privately it was said that the number was almost twice as high.[57] The 13th Jäger Regiment went into action with 1,100 men; six hours later, all but 200 of them were gone.[58] "The splendid grenadier battalion of the Vyatskii Infantry Regiment was completely annihilated," mourned a Russian general. "All in all, two hundred officers were killed or mortally wounded."[59] According to General Langeron, the Ottoman commandant of Brăila sent "sacks filled with 8,000 Russian ears" to Istanbul.[60]

The debacle effectively ended the Russian spring offensive before it got fully under way. Stunned and dejected, Prozorovskii decided to launch a protracted blockade—as Kutuzov had suggested all along. For two weeks, the Main Corps stayed at Brăila, firing thousands of projectiles that devastated the town.[61] At last, the prince summoned the council of war, which included Kutuzov, Cossack leader Matvei Platov, Commander of Artillery Dmitrii Rezvyi, and Chief Engineer Harting. After some debate, the council agreed to lift the blockade on May 19 and take up new positions on the northern bank of the Danube.[62] "Before departing, Prince Prozorovskii decided to seek vengeance on the Brăila garrison," General Langeron observed. "He ordered all neighboring villages to be burned to the ground and destroyed. The unfortunate inhabitants were allowed to keep only a couple of bulls and a small wagon for a few items." In practice, the destruction of villages involved large-scale looting, with senior officers "shamelessly" participating in the plundering. According to Langeron, Prozorovskii remained blissfully ignorant of their involvement because "no one around him dared to report it, while the generals did not want to squeal on each other."[63]

The setback at Brăila sapped whatever was left of Prozorovskii's initiative and made him unwilling to undertake any further operations. Full of doubts and anxiety, the field marshal spent the next few weeks at the campsite, imagining threats and obstacles that, he argued, prevented him from engaging the Turks. One day it was a joint Anglo-Turkish expedition that he thought was about to target the Russian Black Sea coast; the next he argued that Austria was about to defeat Napoleon in the ongoing War of the Fifth Coalition and would then threaten Russia's western provinces. These were wild claims, unsupported by any facts, and reflective of the depth of the prince's paranoia. Even when the Serbs sent him frantic calls for help against the invading Ottoman army, Prozorovskii refused to provide any succor, effectively abandoning Russia's allies to Turkish vengeance. Nor did he comply with Emperor Alexander's repeated orders to cross the Danube and coerce the sultan to accept the peace terms. "Morally devastated and physically unable, [Prozorovskii] seemed afraid of Austria, Hungary, weather, in short, of everything," wrote a nineteenth-century Russian military historian.[64]

By now, the news of the bloody setback at Brăila had reached St. Petersburg, causing an uproar. The czar had expected news of a triumphant Russian crossing of the Danube, rather than of a rout with thousands of casualties less than one month into the campaign. Prozorovskii rushed to justify his actions, and in doing so, he did his best to shift the responsibility onto the shoulders of his subordinates, whom he accused of incompetence, insubordination, and cowardice. His lengthy letter to Emperor Alexander contained a litany of complaints and accusations against everyone and everything except the field marshal himself.[65] The target of his most vehement attacks was Kutuzov, with whom, he wrote, he had clashed on strategy and tactics.

The relations between Prozorovskii and his second-in-command rapidly deteriorated. They disagreed over administration, strategy, and tactics and "spent more time in intrigues against each other than pondering military operations," complained one officer.[66] Kutuzov criticized the prince's system of "methodical" warfare and favored a more mobile warfare with deep offensive thrusts into Ottoman territory; he believed that the Army of Moldavia was strong enough to blockade key Ottoman fortresses and to conduct a forceful campaign across the Danube, one that would force the sultan to the negotiating table. The prince refused to listen, but neither did he offer any plan of his own. Kutuzov thus had plenty of reason for concern about the future. And he was not the only one. When Prince Peter Bagration arrived at the Army of Moldavia's encampment at Bucharest, he was stunned to discover the extent to which Prince Prozorovskii ignored the planning side of the war. "Upon my arrival, the prince talked to me only about trivial matters, and even then he remained ambiguous and never offered any details. I thus remain unaware of any strategy that he adopted or pursued."[67] Similarly, in response to his inquiries, General Aleksei Arakcheyev was told that no one knew of any of Prozorovskii's plans, nor even whether they existed.[68]

Kutuzov would have found this situation unbearable. "Even my great forbearance is not sufficient to endure these intolerable circumstances," he confided to his wife in late May. "The field marshal does everything based on somebody else's advice but as soon as things go bad, he gets angry with me, as if I counseled him to do it."[69] Kutuzov was not sure what would happen, and he urged Catherine to "keep it quiet" and not talk or write about anything he shared with her. Resolution came sooner than he expected when a month later he realized how profoundly his standing had changed. "It seems St. Petersburg has sown the seeds of the quarrel between the prince and me," he admitted belatedly. "[People] must have said something and the word had reached him."[70]

As it turns out, it was his own son-in-law who brought about his downfall. Colonel Nikolai Zakharovich Khitrovo, married to Kutuzov's daughter Anna, was a well-mannered and good-looking officer who carried himself with a certain panache and arrogance, though there was little substance behind his bravura.[71] "This was the most ungrateful creature imaginable," commented a Russian general. "Fatuous, gossipmonger, inconstant, pusillanimous, capable of any misdeed."[72] Kutuzov was aware of his son-in-law's shortcomings, admonishing him at times and, on at least one occasion, as he put it, "reading him a genuine homily" on how to behave.[73] But his concerns for the welfare of his daughter and her three sons overrode any qualms he had about the son-in-law's character, so he continued to back Khitrovo's career, even entrusting him—as we've seen—with the command of an assault column at Brăila. Blood was thicker than water, but it also carried a huge liability. Khitrovo was an ambitious man whose abilities did not match his aspirations. Prozorovskii belatedly realized this and had him removed from the headquarters; incensed by this slight, according to Langeron, Khitrovo "began spreading the most besmirching slanders about him and weaving webs of intrigues."[74] He wrote derogatory letters to St. Petersburg and went so far as to send a complaint directly to senior officials at the Ministry of War denouncing the commander in chief and calling for his removal. The content of the letter became known in the wider society and then looped back to Prozorovskii; to crown it all, the ministry sent him a copy of Khitrovo's letter.

One can only imagine the depth of the prince's fury upon reading it. He was convinced that the colonel would not have dared to act without the encouragement of his father-in-law. The long-simmering feelings of jealousy, resentfulness, and distrust boiled over. The prince had come to resent Kutuzov's popularity in the ranks and envied his jovial good humor. "Kutuzov was always surrounded by a veritable harem and his house was invariably full of joy and merrymaking, where everyone felt very free," remembered an eyewitness. Officers loved to gather at his place; by contrast, they stayed away from Prozorovskii, "who was always in a bad mood, endlessly grumbling, and castigating the entire world and everyone in it."[75] No amount of reasoning and explanation could convince the prince that his deputy was not part of a deliberate effort to get him ousted from the command.

In June, Prozorovskii wrote to Emperor Alexander accusing Kutuzov of undermining his standing in the army and of "becoming a pest, rather than an assistant."[76] Alleging a variety of transgressions but providing no evidence, he implored the czar to have the general removed from the army. Alexander, as we've seen, harbored no goodwill for Kutuzov and readily agreed to Prozorovskii's request, sending him two sets of orders—one transferring Kutuzov to command a reserve corps in the Danubian backcountry and the other nominating him as the governor-general of Lithuania; Prozorovskii was allowed to choose one at his own discretion.[77]

The field marshal responded with a remarkable memo that reveals the degree of spitefulness and suspicion he harbored regarding the man whom just a year earlier he had described as his trusted disciple and "one of the best Russian generals." He declined to accept Kutuzov's appointment to the reserve corps because the general would still have, as he wrote in reply, "a wide field for all his intrigues against me." He went as far as to allege a treasonous streak in Kutuzov, one capable of endangering the entire campaign. If the Russian army crossed the Danube while Kutuzov commanded a reserve corps, the field marshal asserted, the general would use his "cunning" to get the Turks to attack and then blame the resulting disaster on "some honest general who would suffer for it while he himself would emerge blameless and true."[78] These were stunning allegations, dishonoring both the man who made them and the man who paid heed to them. Langeron's memoirs contain a telling comment about how Alexander handled this matter: "The Emperor did not even disguise his disgrace with some face-saving excuse or consolatory phrases. He never felt any compunctions in his relations [with

Kutuzov], knowing that the general lacked the moral backbone to take umbrage at any such affronts."[79]

On June 27, Prozorovskii presented Kutuzov with an imperial decree appointing him the governor-general of Lithuania. "He was bewildered to receive the package and after reading the decree went into his room and closed the door," the field marshal wrote jubilantly. There was much for Kutuzov to ponder. He knew he had made a mistake in supporting his son-in-law's career. "The old man [Prozorovskii] was right," he admitted two years later in a frank conversation with a fellow general. "I was indeed the main culprit in that affair because I put up with my bizarre son-in-law."[80] He also understood that no amount of explanation would mollify the field marshal. The die was cast. Just one year after being recalled, a new exile beckoned him; the winter of his life was upon him. He felt deeply wronged. "Prozorovskii blatantly lied about me," he wrote his family. "I have the whole army as a witness and everyone, except for the most wretched intriguers, is supportive of me." Nevertheless, he never revealed to them that it was Khitrovo's fault. He was concerned about the impact this new assignment would have on his already strained family finances, since he was expected to cover the relocation expenses. But he had no choice but obey the imperial rescript. "First, I need to comply with the order and get to my post; then we can contemplate if it is even worth remaining in the service," he told his wife as he prepared to depart.[81]

| Call to Arms, 1810–1811

Kutuzov assumed his responsibilities as governor-general of Lithuania on August 12, 1809.[1] Formed fifteen years earlier, the Governorate-General of Lithuania encompassed an immense territory that Russia had acquired in the wake of the last Polish partition. Kutuzov's life now revolved around the familiar routine of managing this huge province and handling the never-ending stream of supplications and administrative affairs. "The title of governor is more important than that of minister," commented a contemporary. One would very rarely see the czar or deal with the imperial minister; by comparison, the governor was directly responsible for the well-being of the people. "The governor was the czar's trusted representative, and his simple gesture could affect a million people."[2] The governors of the Russian provinces could be notoriously corrupt and self-serving, abusing their vast powers to enrich themselves. Those of the provinces of Kursk, Orel, Nizhegorodsk, Irkutsk, Novgorod, Smolensk, and Byelorussia, to name just a few, were all implicated in schemes, selling justice to the highest bidder and forcing officials and merchants to pay kickbacks amounting to tens of thousands of rubles. Rarely did these well-connected and powerful individuals face consequences for their misdeeds. When a whistleblower revealed that the governor of Grodno was allowing a huge contraband trade, the governor had him murdered. Unable to convince a town mayor to go along with his crooked schemes, the governor of Kharkov bribed local physicians to declare the mayor insane, promptly shipped him off to an asylum, and helped elect a more pliant town leader. In Kaluga province, Governor Dmitrii Lopukhin extracted 75,000 rubles to cover up a nobleman's murder and borrowed 30,000 rubles from a local merchant, whom he then targeted with unsubstantiated criminal proceedings until the merchant agreed to forgive the loan. Despite a thorough investigation that revealed the depth of depravity he was engaged in, the governor was ultimately acquitted by his peers in the Senate and continued to govern as if nothing had happened.[3]

Kutuzov differed from these men in nearly every respect. He came into the position already possessing considerable administrative experience and having served as governor-general almost a decade earlier. He took his responsibilities seriously, and there is no evidence that he ever abused power or enriched himself; he came to this post drowning in debt, and that's how he left it two years later. Powerful as they were, Russian governors often found themselves at the center of local power struggles and incessant squabbles among the haughty, boisterous, petulant, and hot-tempered nobles who surrounded them. "I rarely interact with the local nobles," observed a visitor to Novgorod. "They are all divided into discordant factions that constantly fight each other and keep denouncing the unfortunate governor. . . . Here, the nobles are arrayed against the governor, the governor is against them, and the merchants are against all of them."[4] The situation in Lithuania would have been no less complicated, or maybe even more so, considering that not even a generation earlier this region had formed the heartland of the Polish-Lithuanian Commonwealth. Just seven months before Kutuzov assumed his post, the election of local marshals descended into a boisterous and raucous affair as the Polish gentry disrupted the proceedings and incited violence that required direct intervention by the governor and later resulted in imperial decrees targeting the vestiges of the former "Polish diets or popular congregations."[5] Kutuzov thus had to navigate a labyrinth of local politics and cultivate relations with various factions without appearing to side with any of them. His official correspondence shows him involved in military administration of the units deployed in the borderland province, as well as in a diverse set of issues ranging from opening new textile manufacturing facilities and promoting trade and commerce to taking measures to curb poverty, prevent fires, support the establishment of a new medical journal, improve prisoners' daily rations, and investigate cases of peasant mistreatment.[6]

The most exciting event of his two-year-long stay in Vilna was undoubtedly the marriage of his daughter Ekaterina to Nikolai Kudashev, a young officer of aristocratic origins who had advanced through the ranks to become the aide-de-camp to Grand Duke Constantine. The wedding was sumptuously celebrated and the couple welcomed their first child, Ekaterina (Catherine), the following year. Two years later, Kudashev would be mortally wounded during the Battle of Leipzig, the second of Kutuzov's sons-in-law to perish in the struggle against Napoleon.[7]

The family finances remained at the top of the list of problems with which Kutuzov grappled. Chronic indebtedness was, as we have seen, a permanent feature of his life, just as it was of the Russian nobility as a whole. The Golenischev-Kutuzovs were perpetually in debt. Life in St. Petersburg and Vilna necessitated high accommodation and entertainment costs; the family spent a fortune on every conceivable luxury, including tapestries, carpets, porcelain, and works of art to adorn their home, in which they entertained. Patronage and influence greased the wheels of ancien régime societies, and to enjoy proximity to the royal person, keep up appearances, and cultivate a network of social connections, Kutuzov, like many others, had to spend huge sums.[8] "It is simply ruinous to live here," he complained about living in Vilna. "The costs of living are incredibly high."[9] As the governor, he was expected to attend numerous social dinners, carnivals, balls, and fêtes, all of which required new garments and accoutrements. Yet revenues from his rural estates could not keep up with his fast-accumulating debts. "I am troubled by money woes every day and night," Kutuzov wrote Catherine in early 1810. "At times I feel rather despondent thinking about our circumstances."[10] Catherine urged her husband to sell some of their estates, a solution that he thought too radical. "I have always been reluctant to sell estates because once they are sold, we would spend the monies and find ourselves with neither the monies nor the estates." Yet something had to give. "If the sale terms are as advantageous as you say," he finally conceded, "send me the details so I can consider." He found them "dreadful" but with clenched teeth agreed to part with some of the property.[11] Scrambling to find more money, he sought new loans, agreeing to use his home in St. Petersburg as collateral, and negotiated deals with local merchants.[12] In February 1810, fortune smiled on him, as he was able to find a buyer for a large shipment of potash from one of his estates. "I am sending you thirty thousand rubles' worth of pearls that I got for potash," he excitedly wrote Catherine, instructing her not to sell them "for a song." This was a princely sum, and Kutuzov urged Catherine to be more judicious in her spending. "With all these expenses, only the Lord knows how I will survive."[13]

The next twelve months were taxing and frustrating, his letters containing a litany of financial woes. "I am very hard pressed for the money; God knows how I will cope," reads one. "I might get about 2,000 rubles in wages but that's just pocket change; I have no choice but to live in debt." Two weeks later he was forced to pawn a gold snuffbox for 3,000 rubles. The news from the estates made him see red, for revenue was dwindling and mismanagement was rife; even many of the new estate managers he had hired earlier proved to be underhanded or inept, some failing to abide by the terms of sales that Kutuzov had negotiated, others becoming involved in needless and expensive legal disputes. He suspected estate managers were siphoning off cash; one of them, a certain Vedernikov, flat out refused to provide any accounting of his estate and bluntly told Kutuzov to mind his own business and "to stop asking for money."[14] "I have made a huge mistake with Vedernikov," Kutuzov admitted. In December 1810, he took a furlough and visited his estates once again, examining estate ledgers, firing and hiring estate managers, and trying to increase revenue flow. "I am about to return to Vilna," he wrote his daughter Elisabeth from Volhynia. "I had to spend several days at the estate settling essential matters."[15]

‹—·—·▄·▄▄·▄▄·—·—›

Of course, Kutuzov still closely followed events in Wallachia. Field Marshal Prozorovskii, exhausted and demoralized, died in August 1809, less than two months after Kutuzov left. The czar, eager to bring a quick conclusion to the protracted war, dispatched Prince Peter Bagration to lead the Army of Moldavia. The Georgian took advantage of the logistical base that Kutuzov had left behind to launch an immediate offensive across the Danube, capturing the fortresses of Măcin, Hirsova, and Constanta, with Izmail and Brăila falling soon thereafter. On September 16, he defeated the Ottomans at Rassevat (Rasova) and then laid siege to Silistra, one of the most fearsome Ottoman strongholds in the Danube valley. The Russian victories forced Ottoman grand vizier Yussuf to halt his invasion of Serbia and direct some 50,000 men to the lower Danube. Bagration met the vizier's advance head-on, fighting a numerically superior Ottoman army to a draw at Tataritsa in October.

These thrilling Russian victories raised prospects of a quick end to the war. However, the perennial logistical challenge of sustaining an army so far from its bases forced the Russian commander to lift the siege of Silistra, abandon the recent conquests, and return to the left bank of the Danube. Though Bagration accomplished more in three months than Prozorovskii had in over a year, the czar was displeased with his decision to return from Bulgaria. Ignoring the facts on the ground, Alexander insisted on a more forceful prosecution of the war. In the ensuing quarrel with the czar, Bagration resigned his command in March 1810. He was replaced by General Nikolay Kamenskii, still young (thirty-three) though less headstrong and impetuous than he used to be. Kamenskii commenced a new incursion into Bulgaria. The Russians again captured the Ottoman fortresses of Silistra, Razgrad, and Bazargic and even encircled the grand vizier's army at the fortified camp at Şumnu (Shumen/Shumla). The outcome of the war hung in the balance. The sultan rushed in reinforcements to rescue the grand vizier, but Kamenskii intercepted and routed them at Batin on September 7 and 8, 1810. This was a stunning success, one of the brightest victories Russian had gained over their Ottoman foes, which paved the way for the Russian capture of Ruse, Turnu, Pleven, Lovech, and Selvi. Yet even after these resounding victories, Kamenskii, like his predecessor, could not sustain his army south of the Danube and was forced to withdraw to winter quarters on the left bank. There he fell seriously ill with fever.

Emperor Alexander thus faced the unenviable task of selecting a fourth commander in chief in only two years and the sixth since the start of the war. He was impatient to end the conflict, which was entering its fifth year.

Relations between Russia and Napoleonic France were steadily worsening, and the czar was anxious to avoid confronting the French emperor while still engaged in a war against the sultan. Enormous challenges lay ahead. The recent victories may have allowed the Russians to establish a foothold on the Danube River, but they failed to destroy the Ottoman army or to break its spirit; in fact, Sultan Mahmud was so confident about winning the war with French backing that he rejected Russian diplomatic overtures that offered to end the war in exchange for the surrender of the Danubian Principalities. Instead, the Ottoman ruler insisted on Russia accepting the Dniester River as the imperial border, which would have meant returning to pre-war borders and forsaking five years' worth of Russian conquests. Alexander was not prepared to make such a sacrifice, though neither could he foresee a quick victory over the Turks just as Russia was facing the prospect of a two-front war. At this crucial moment, the czar decided to turn to the man he had scorned for so long.

In March 1811, Kutuzov received the news that he had been nominated to lead the Russian forces in Wallachia.[16] Though not surprised—rumors of his appointment had reached him days in advance—he was reluctant to head back to active service. War was no longer the romantic adventure it once was, and he had already seen more than enough bloodletting to last a lifetime. Notwithstanding his constant complaints about life in Vilna, he had clearly reconciled himself to the thought of finishing his career there. "Lizanka, my dear friend, I just received the news from St. Petersburg," he wrote to his daughter in mid-March. "It seems I would be appointed to command the army against the Turks. This possibility does not excite me at all; in fact, I am rather disheartened by it. At my age, it is difficult to bid goodbye to friends and give up one's habits and leisure!"[17] He could have mentioned money as well. Each new appointment entailed significant costs related to travel and accommodation. "All these assignments cost me dearly," he lamented. "This is the third time I am given just 10,000 rubles to relocate, but that is barely enough to even get started."[18]

Nor would he have been pleased to hear the czar's rationale for his appointment. Writing to Kamenskii in January 1811, Alexander described the profound threat Russia was facing from Napoleonic France and lamented the fact that the war with the Turks had not produced the decisive results he was seeking. "There is nothing else left for us but to change the type of war we are conducting [against the Turks]. Instead of offensive [nastupatel'naya] war, we must wage a defensive [oboronitel'naya] one."[19] The czar was convinced that Russia must scale down its military commitments in the Danubian Principalities to reinforce its forces against Napoleon. He needed young, competent, and spirited commanders in the western borderlands and expected Kamenskii, still gravely ill, to lead a new army against Napoleon.[20] In fact, Alexander was relieved that the general was unwell—he knew that relocating Kamenskii from Wallachia would have been an overt signal to the French that Russia was preparing for war, and he wanted to avoid a diplomatic scuffle. "This is why your illness has offered me such a good opportunity to [reassign you] without drawing any unwanted attention to it," he wrote Kamenskii. "I have ordered General Kutuzov to hasten to Bucharest and take command of the Army of Moldavia, while you should, under the pretense of poor health after a draining illness, hurry to Zhitomir, where you would receive my order to take charge of the Second Army."[21]

Such an arrangement could hardly have placated Kutuzov. While Kamenskii's "brilliant talents" were to be employed in "the most important assignment" against Napoleon, he was being asked to go to a secondary theater, take charge of an enfeebled army, and hold a defensive line against a resurgent opponent.[22] Drawing down the Army of Moldavia carried an obvious risk of ceding the initiative to the Turks and possibly losing positions in the region. The czar brushed aside such concerns and expected the new commander to win the war triumphantly. Among the documents Kutuzov received was the emperor's letter outlining the main Russian demand: "I do not find it necessary or respectable to accept anything less than an [imperial] border that runs on the Danube," read the instructions. This implied Russian acquisition of Bessarabia, Moldavia, and Greater and Lesser Wallachia. Quite a task for a man whom Alexander personally loathed, deriding his "advanced age" and questioning his character.[23] Kutuzov knew all of this, just as he understood the enormousness of the mission that was thrust upon him. How would he accomplish it with a much-reduced army? How well would he himself endure the hardships of a new campaign? "If only you knew how much I long for peace and quiet," he confided to his daughter Elisabeth.[24] His rheumatism had increased in recent months; headaches and sharp pain in his eyes had become regular occurrences. "In my younger days I could have been far more useful," he told minister of war Barclay de Tolly. "My only hope is that my spirit will be sufficiently matched by my corporeal strength."[25]

Despite many misgivings, Kutuzov did not decline his commission. On April 12, 1811, he arrived at Bucharest and assumed command of the Army of Moldavia.[26] Forty-one years had passed since he first caught a glimpse of the Wallachian meadows. Back then he had been a youthful captain, eager to distinguish himself. Now he was in the twilight of his career, weary of wars and service, longing for peace and family comforts. Deep in his heart he must have expected this to be his last and most challenging command.

⇠—⊰⊹⊱—⇢

Bucharest was a bustling city of at least 80,000 people and, as the British consul described it, "three hundred sixty-six churches, twenty monasteries and thirty large caravanserais."[27] European visitors marveled at its wood-paved streets, abundant shops "supplied with all kinds of wares," and the elegantly built houses of nobles with their charming gardens. But they also bewailed the lack of sanitation and the general poverty of the population, most of whom lived in houses little better than huts.[28] Kutuzov was surprised by the warm reception he received in Wallachia. "It is hard to convey the sense of jubilation," he wrote his family. "All the *boiers* [nobles] came out to welcome my carriage."[29] He admired the Wallachian women, dressed in their richly ornamented wraparound *fotă* skirts and delicate *maramă* head coverings, greeting him with smiles and flower garlands. "Bucharest is a major city, the like of which you will not find in Russia, save for two capitals. There are countless people but few women know what courtly society is; there are quite a few attractive and amusing young women, a handful of Russian madams who are supercilious and pretentious, and a multitude of Greeks, all of whom are passionate for dances."[30]

The emphasis on women is hard to miss in this letter. "Old age did not prevent Kutuzov from adoring and philandering with women," remarked one contemporary.[31] He loved female company, witty and flirtatious conversations, courtly pastimes, dancing, and theater. Complaining about solitude and separation from his wife and daughters, he sought out the company of women. The nature and degree of his attention seemed to run the gamut. His private correspondence reflects—and speaks to—his deep emotional bond with his wife and daughters; hence the extent of his physical involvement with other women remains unclear. He doubtless had affairs, particularly with women of lower social standing. Nikolai Muravyev, for example, makes a passing mention of Kutuzov "having a Jewish woman [*zhidovka*] as a concubine [*nalozhninatsa*]" at one time. And during Napoleon's invasion of Russia, senior officers, including Bennigsen, noted that Kutuzov was accompanied by a woman dressed in a Cossack uniform. "Bennigsen was mistaken—there were two of them," acerbically remarked young staff officer Alexander Scherbinin.[32] Kutuzov's relations with women of his own class seemed different. His private letters habitually mention women he flirted with, but they also reveal a dispassionate, almost clinical attitude toward them, which he freely shared with his family. While in Kyiv, he described enjoying the company of Madame Zubkova, "a lovely but shallow [*vetrenaia*] woman" who "rants and raves, quarrels with the whole world, and pounces on other women; it is all just good old fun for me." He found her "very pretty" but also "a chatterbox, erratic, with a strong desire to be liked."[33] In Vilna, his passion for theater led to a rapport with "Madame Franc, the famed singer," who, in his words, "amuses me very much by believing that I am actually feeling an unrestrained passion for her. But she does sing like an angel!"[34] As he departed from Vilna, General Bennigsen's wife followed him into the snow-covered street, where she embraced him and, as Kutuzov told his daughter, "bathed me in her tears." Learning about his departure, another woman, Madame Fischer, rode a horse for over fifty miles so she could say goodbye to him one last time.[35] Whether or not these relationships were ever consummated, they did earn him a reputation as a womanizer, and the events in Bucharest only reinforced it.

Kutuzov found the Wallachian nobility deeply divided between the feuding factions of Constantine Varlaam and Constantine Filipescu (Philipescu), who represented pro-Russian and pro-French interests, respectively. With the start of the Russo-Ottoman War, both leaders cultivated relations with the Russian military commanders to undermine their rivals. Filipescu—"the most daring scoundrel in all of Wallachia," as Langeron described him—had long been suspected of anti-Russian intrigues, but he knew that it was important to keep one's enemies closer than one's friends. Following this principle, he nurtured a relationship between his young daughter and General Mikhail Miloradovich, who commanded a Russian division in Bucharest. The woman not only kept the smitten general entertained—Miloradovich soon owed tens of thousands of rubles to local merchants—but also supplied her father with the sensitive information that the Russian general inadvertently revealed to her. For three years Miloradovich practically lived in the Wallachian *boier*'s house, complained one Russian officer. Filipescu thus "heard and knew every-thing" about the Russian military and political affairs, and he shared it all with the French consul and the Turks.[36] So concerned was Prince Bagration by Miloradovich's actions that he sent urgent letters to St. Petersburg saying, "An otherwise kind man has turned into a genuine Wallachian intriguer. It is hard to recognize him anymore." He ultimately arranged for Miloradovich's recall from the army, which was a heavy blow to Filipescu's ambitions and an opportunity for his rivals.[37]

Upon the arrival of the new Russian commander in chief, Varlaam arranged for Kutuzov to meet his fourteen-year-old niece Luxandra, clearly hoping that the general would take a liking to her. Despite her tender age, Luxandra had already been married to *boier* Nicolae Guliano for two years, and now she found herself as a pawn in her relatives' political intrigues. General Langeron's memoirs remain our chief source on the events in Bucharest, and they are highly critical, even disparaging, of Kutuzov. Discerning and courageous, Langeron was also self-centered and patronizing, considering himself the smartest person in the room and sneering at almost every Russian comrade-in-arms. His relationship with Kutuzov, therefore, was complex. He acknowledged his quick wit, "extraordinary memory," "thorough education," eloquence, "shrewdness," and other "true talents," but also lambasted him for obsequiousness and "incredible immorality." The Guliano affair was the Frenchman's favorite topic to bring up when speaking about his former commander. According to Langeron, Kutuzov met Luxandra Guliano the day of his arrival to Bucharest and liked her so much that he ordered the girl delivered to his quarters that same day. This "one-eyed, fat, and ugly" old man just "could not exist without being surrounded by at least three or four women,"

Langeron remarked, before proceeding to describe their affair in sordid detail. "Guliano became Kutuzov's favorite and visited him every evening. In front of everyone he treated her with such informality that it transcended every boundary of decency." Whenever a local noble invited Kutuzov to a dinner, he invariably came accompanied by Guliano. "After lunch he usually retired with her into his secluded room." This "little shameless girl" was often seen in the old man's lap, "playing with his aiguillettes and allowing him to kiss her, which made her laugh and giggle." The girl's mother was always close at hand to "secretly instruct her daughter on how to excite feelings in the general." In fact, according to Langeron, Kutuzov was dissolute enough to engage in a three-way relationship with the mother and daughter.[38]

These salacious claims are impossible to verify; we lack any corroborating account by another eyewitness. Considering the nature of the allegations, Soviet and Russian historians, unsurprisingly, avoided the subject altogether.[39] Langeron's story leaves many questions unanswered; his claims feel contrived and caricatured. Why would Varlaam choose such a young and barely literate girl to woo a man so burdened with years and experience? Kutuzov would have been astute enough to understand the intention and to use the girl to his own advantage, confiding to her only the information he wanted others to know. There is no evidence that he ever allowed anyone with whom he was involved to intervene in the affairs of state. We can only speculate on the interest a sixty-four-year-old man of the world would find in a relationship with a "very naive but pleasant girl," as he described her, who lacked the sophistication of the aristocratic women of St. Petersburg and Vilna.[40] It seems unlikely that Kutuzov would have invited his beloved daughter Elisabeth to visit him in Bucharest and promised to introduce her to Guliano were his relations with the young girl, who was the same age as his own granddaughters, that sordid.

Kutuzov, like many of his generation, cherished an active social life. In St. Petersburg and Vilna, whether attending the theater, masquerade balls, celebrations, or other social events, he thrived when surrounded by women. As even his rivals admitted, his wit and manners "made him very popular among the fair sex," and he remained so to the end of his days. At a ball in Kalisz in early 1813, Alexander Mikhailovskii-Danilevskii, the future Russian imperial historian, had left the dance hall to catch his breath when he heard loud laughter coming from one of the neighboring rooms. "I peeked in and was surprised to see our elderly field marshal bent down and tying ribbons around the shoes of the beautiful sixteen-year-old Polish noblewoman."[41] Even in the last weeks of his life (he had barely a month left to live at that point) Kutuzov could not resist the temptation to flirt. But there is no hard evidence that these dalliances ever led to any romances or infidelities. The relations he cultivated with women were never so serious that he could not mention them in letters sent home. Langeron's outrage notwithstanding, it is striking how few other contemporaries cared about or noted them—even when Kutuzov was observed in the company of a cross-dressed woman in the fall of 1812. Responding to the reports of Kutuzov's waywardness, one general flippantly observed, "What's the issue here?" For men of Kutuzov's generation, female companionship was not necessarily about sexual conquest but about entertainment, keeping up appearances, and projecting masculine appeal. The Russian ambassador to Paris, Prince Alexander Kurakin, insisted on having his carriage wait for "two hours" in front of the house of his alleged mistress every day, although, as a contemporary noted, "he had never actually seen her."[42] Ataman Matvei Platov returned from his trip to Britain with a young English woman, and when asked why he did that, he simply replied, "I did it not for carnal needs but for morality [*ne dlya fiziki, a dlya morali*]," thereby underscoring social attitudes toward manliness.[43]

Men were not the only ones to engage in this kind of flirtatious behavior. Kutuzov's wife, Catherine, was fairly coquettish, and her behavior occasionally became the talk of the imperial capital. "La maréchale Koutouzoff was a woman of infinite wit," remarked the future Major General Waldemar de Löwenstern, who knew her well. "In her youth, she would have cut a very flamboyant figure, but she struggled to adjust to the fact that she had aged."[44] Georg von Bradke, who stayed with the Golenischev-Kutuzovs in 1811, when he was fifteen, was amazed to see "the old lady Kutuzov, almost seventy years old, still dressing like a young and adventurous woman" and entertaining "people of dubious reputation," by which the young provincial meant artists, singers, and musicians. "Members of the French theater troupe frequented her house, which, back then, was not yet permissible at any respectable home."[45] While Kutuzov delighted in the company of Guliano in Bucharest, Catherine led a carefree life in St. Petersburg, giving at least the pretense of having young and virile lovers. "I do not know why she came up with such a crazy idea, but she told her intimate circle of friends that I was her lover," complained Löwenstern, who one day found himself being ogled by Golenischeva-Kutuzova's elderly friends. "I did not like that at all since such rumors could have ruined my reputation in the eyes of young women. So, I was determined to thwart her plans at once and did so in a rather brusque manner, I am afraid." Catherine nonetheless continued to invite him to her dinner parties.[46]

There is no doubt that Kutuzov enjoyed the idea of being surrounded by women, but it would have been out of character for him to consummate the relationship with Guliano, on account of her youth and *boier* status and because of the political implications. Moreover, this relationship should be seen within the wider context of his experiences in Bucharest. His private letters constantly spoke of old age, loneliness, and infirmity, and meditated on the meaning of life and the essence of happiness, which he believed resided only in family. Was his willingness to spend time with Guliano an expression of that longing for his own daughters and grandchildren? It seems more probable that Kutuzov's interaction with Guliano had nothing to do with sexual lust and depravity, despite what Langeron alleges, and far more to do with Wallachian factional power struggles, which Kutuzov was keen to exploit to bolster Russian interests in the region. Be that as it may, this relationship came at great cost to his personal reputation, for stories about his lechery circulated. By the spring of 1812, the Sardinian ambassador in St. Petersburg believed that "Kutuzov has been bewitched by a Wallachian woman . . . [who] is widely acknowledged as being in the Ottomans' pay."[47] Even Tolstoy acknowledges the "affair" in his epic novel. Kutuzov himself was aware of the nature of his indiscretions. "The company of women that I seek out is nothing but a passing caprice," he told his daughter.[48]

If we are to believe his critics, Kutuzov did little but sleep, drink, fornicate, and entertain. Surviving archival documents paint a different picture. The new commander in chief took his responsibilities seriously, and in the first days after his arrival he evaluated the situation in the Danubian principalities. The outlook was gloomy. While the Ottomans were busy mobilizing fresh forces for a new campaign, the Army of Moldavia had been weakened by the departure of five of its divisions (the 9th, 11th, 12th, 15th, and 18th), which were sent to Galicia to form an army against Napoleon. Only two days after arriving at Bucharest, Kutuzov had been forced to divert additional forces, including more than half a dozen Cossack regiments, one horse artillery company, and two pontonier companies.[49] Thousands of soldiers were sick and regiments were woefully undermanned; the Yaroslavskii Infantry Regiment listed just 560 men, while only 522 soldiers remained in the Kurskii Infantry Regiment.

In total, Kutuzov had 44,632 men in Wallachia, half as large an army as his predecessors had commanded over the previous two years.[50] This slimmer force was also stretched across a vast area. "Our defensive line extends for one thousand *verstas* [662 miles] . . . from the outskirts of Belgrade to the Dniester," complained Kutuzov.[51] Lieutenant Generals Langeron and Essen III were in charge of a corps deployed between Bucharest, Giurgiu, and Ruse. On the Russian right wing, Lieutenant General Andrey Zass was at Craiova, commanding a division that defended Little Wallachia and maintaining contact with the rebels in neighboring Serbia. On the left wing, Lieutenant General Alexander Voinov held positions on the lower Danube, while Major General Sergei Tuchkov II supervised garrisons in the key fortresses of Brăila, Kiliya, Izmail, Bender, and Akkerman.[52]

Kutuzov found his predecessor, Nikolay Kamenskii, on his deathbed. For over a week Kutuzov's arrival was kept secret from the general, who was in a

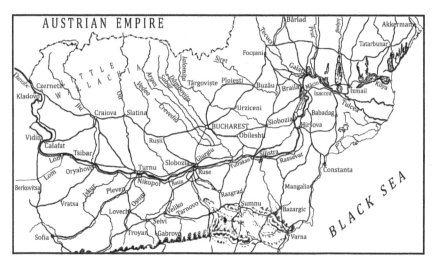

MAP 10 The Danubian Principalities

delirious state and struggled to hear and talk. On April 24, with the general's condition slightly improved, Kutuzov, who himself was feeling unwell, finally met him, pretending that he had just arrived. "He was delighted to see me and we both cried," he described in a letter to Catherine. "He is very frail and his memory is so feeble that he forgets almost immediately what he has said, keeps asking the same question."[53] A week later, Kamenskii, "in very poor health," was placed into a coach and taken to Odessa. "I hope he will make it," Kutuzov noted. He did not. On May 16, the general drew his last breath. His death shocked Kutuzov, who mourned the passing of a promising young man—Kamenskii was just thirty-four years old—who used to call him "uncle."[54] Contemporaries thought highly of Kamenskii, despite his temper and occasional callousness. They praised his devotion and valor, as well as his ability to seek out and destroy the enemy. But there were some who, in hindsight, thought his death was in fact providential. "The death of this brilliant young commander distressed all of Russia," remembered journalist Nikolay Gretsch in his memoirs. "Yet one cannot but feel God's benevolence in this tragic event. If Kamenskii had successfully ended the war with the Turks, he would have certainly been appointed the commander in chief of the army against the French, and he would have rejected the wait-and-see approach and would have gone straight on to confront Napoleon; he would have been defeated without fail, and the whole history of Russia, and Europe, would have taken a different turn."[55]

Kamenskii's death was not the only heartbreak Kutuzov experienced in the spring of 1811. In late April he received news of a tragic incident that had claimed the life of Arkadii Suvorov, the great Suvorov's only son. Kutuzov knew the young man well, having followed his rapid rise through the ranks.

The twenty-seven-year-old Lieutenant General Suvorov commanded the 9th Infantry Division, which was detached from the Army of Moldavia. On his way from Bucharest to Jassy, he came to the Rymnik River, the site of his father's great victory over the Turks. "His companions urged him not to ford the river, but he stubbornly refused to listen to them," Kutuzov described in a letter. "There was a sudden flash flood which overturned his carriage; three people survived but he did not."[56]

Barely one month into his command, Kutuzov was already finalizing a new war plan, one based on a solid understanding of local topography and careful analysis of prior campaigns.[57] Reading it, one can discern its author's keen judgment and adroitness. Kutuzov had no intention of repeating the mistakes of his predecessors, who had wasted men and matériel on storming Ottoman fortresses. Indeed, his core disagreement with Prozorovskii was rooted in differing strategic conceptions—he opposed the prince's system of "methodical" warfare and favored more flexible operations. Now that he was the commander in chief, Kutuzov could act on his strategic vision. He believed that the main object of warfare was the destruction of the enemy's field army, not the occupation of a geographical position. Traditionally castigated as cautious, Kutuzov was in fact offensive-minded when circumstances allowed it. Nonetheless, he did understand the crucial importance of careful planning. "My planning was not so much bold as it was thorough," he later observed about this campaign.[58] He thrived on developing scenarios of the possible actions his adversary could take, and whatever course of action he adopted was never final; rather, it simply reflected the facts on the ground, and it evolved as the situation changed. In his attitudes and beliefs, Kutuzov echoed the French military theorist Pierre de Bourcet's teachings that stressed the need for "a plan of many branches"—the commander should devise a master strategy with various attacks and maneuvers but also be ready to adjust his dispositions to anything unexpected.[59]

The new plan was based on principles of coordination, flexibility, maneuver, surprise, and counterattack. Having absorbed the lessons of the 1770–1771 campaigns that he had been involved in, Kutuzov refused to remain passive and simply hold the defensive line on the Danube. "It is hopeless to attempt to defend this vast area, especially when there are not enough troops available," he explained in a memorandum. "While our already diminished troops are scattered over such a large territory, the very first strong enemy attack would easily break through them."[60] Consequently, soon after his arrival Kutuzov recalled isolated garrisons even if this meant abandoning important fortresses, such as Silistra and Nikopol; their fortifications were blown up and local inhabitants relocated to the Russian-controlled territory on the left bank.[61] This was a crucial decision, for it highlighted the core element of Kutuzov's strategy, which was to hold a central position between Giurgiu and Bucharest that would allow him to control the main river crossings and to counteract Ottoman threats as they materialized; if the Turks attempted to break through on the Lower Danube, he wanted his main forces to "immediately shift to the left and act according to circumstances."[62] Kutuzov knew that it would be senseless for him to advance to Şumnu, where the grand vizier's army was still camped; assaulting these fortified positions would be "too costly and wasteful," while a move too far south could expose the Army of Moldavia to an Ottoman counterstrike. Instead, Kutuzov wanted to pursue a nimbler strategy, one that considered political, geographical, and psychological factors. He knew that Sultan Mahmud, encouraged by deteriorating Franco-Russian relations, was insisting on a more vigorous prosecution of the war from his commanders. The sultan had already replaced the elderly grand vizier Kör Yusuf Pasha with Laz Ahmed Pasha, a younger and more offensive-minded man who seemed more willing to take risks. After five years on the defensive, the Ottomans were eager to seize the initiative and turn the tide of war. Russian agents reported extensive Ottoman mobilization for the new campaign, with some 50,000 men expected around Şumnu and additional forces marching to the Danube. Ismail Bey, with more than 20,000 men, was already proceeding to Vidin, one of the largest towns on the Danube, with a population upward of 20,000. In the field, the Ottomans would outnumber their foes, probably by as much as three to one.

Kutuzov seemed undaunted. He had confidence in the discipline and training of the Russian troops, which, in his mind, could make up for inferiority of numbers. "Warfare against the Turks differs from the one against European forces," he told his officers in a special memorandum that drew upon his long experience of serving in the region. "We do not have to operate with the whole mass of forces all at once." Casting a broad historical look at the Russo-Ottoman wars, he pointed out how the Turks had failed to learn from their earlier defeats and were still unable to coordinate their operations on land and sea; as an example, if they had coordinated an amphibious landing near the estuary of the Danube with the main army's attack between Nikopol and Ruse, the Russian army would have been in great jeopardy. And yet Kutuzov remained confident that such an operation was beyond his opponent's ability. Instead, he wanted to seize the initiative in the war and conduct deep thrusts into Ottoman territory. If the czar deigned to return the five divisions he had detached, Kutuzov promised to end the war within a year. "As a rule, in wars against the Turks, victory is less dependent on numerical superiority than it is on the inventiveness and vigilance of the commanding general," he observed.[63] Kutuzov envisioned three corps, each acting independently of one another, launching a deep trans-Danubian incursion. The first corps would secure the Bulgarian countryside and pin down the main Ottoman army near Şumnu. The second corps would intercept the main routes to prevent any reinforcements from reaching the grand vizier. The third corps, meanwhile, would advance along the Black Sea coast, cross the Balkan Mountains, and head directly for Adrianople, which, in Kutuzov's opinion, would force the Turks to sue for peace. In its scale and ambition, the plan was unlike any previously considered during this war. The czar refused to grant the forces needed for such an operation, so the plan was never carried out. It would be another two decades before Kutuzov's ideas would be put into action, with great success, during a new Russo-Ottoman war.

<hr />

Soon after his arrival at Bucharest, Kutuzov received a letter from Grand Vizier Ahmed Pasha inquiring into the whereabouts of Ottoman prisoners whom Russians had captured the previous year. Kutuzov remembered the vizier well, having met him during the embassy to Istanbul in 1793–1794. He wrote a friendly response to Ahmed Pasha, congratulating him on his recent elevation to grand vizier and reminding him of "our long friendship."[64] Although he did not overtly mention the subject of negotiation, Kutuzov clearly intended for this letter to open communications with the Ottomans.[65] His hunch proved correct—Ahmed Pasha understood the intent and responded with an equally effusive letter, offering to negotiate; soon enough, the Ottoman envoy Abdul Hamid Effendi was on his way to Bucharest, where negotiations soon began in earnest. The Russian side was represented by Count Andrei Italinskii, the former Russian ambassador to the Porte, and Kutuzov, who received authorization to conduct peace talks.[66] It quickly became clear that the two sides had irreconcilable differences. The Russians insisted that the Ottomans withdraw from the Danubian Principalities, while Abdul Hamid Effendi stated that the sultan would negotiate peace only on the basis of the *status quo ante bellum*, which would have removed the Russian presence from the entire region.

Kutuzov urged moderation. In a lengthy letter to the Russian foreign minister, he argued that Russian demands were impossible for the sultan to accept. "The baseline of the peace that we are offering to the Porte entails the loss of four provinces: Little Wallachia, Greater Wallachia, Moldavia, and Bessarabia," he pointed out. It would be difficult for Sultan Mahmud— "whose stubbornness is attested by all of his subjects as well as foreigners acquainted with the Porte"—to accede to such a drastic demand. Moreover, "the crux of the matter is not so much in the scale of the territory involved or the quality of the land, but rather in the self-interests of the very people who are administering the Ottoman affairs." He drew attention to the great influence wielded by the Phanariot Greeks, who had vested interests in the Danubian Principalities, as well as other Ottoman officials who expected "abundant annual payments" for their support of claimants to the position of hospodar. Kutuzov believed Russia would gain far more by moderating its demands, which should be limited to Bessarabia, parts of Moldavia, and the payment of war indemnities.[67]

However, the czar's intervention left no diplomatic wiggle room—Alexander instructed Kutuzov to break off negotiations should the Ottomans refuse to relinquish all the principalities at once; Russia had conquered these territories and intended to keep them. "The Turkish ministers claim the Sultan is resolute in his rejection of our demands," the Russian foreign minister told Kutuzov. "So ask them why do they think the Russian Emperor would be any less determined in pursuing his intentions or be more willing to sacrifice his achievements to simply please the sultan?"[68] Diplomacy would have to wait a bit longer for its turn. Kutuzov had to find a way to end this war quickly.

In preparing for a new campaign, Kutuzov created and maintained an extensive network of "confidants" who kept him supplied with information. "We were aware of all the enemy movements," wrote Langeron "The best spies were the locals, Bulgarians."[69] Kutuzov made good use of this steady flow of information not only to adjust his unit positions but also to cultivate close relations with the Moldavian and Wallachian notables. He regularly issued orders prohibiting Russian military officials from mistreating the local population with inordinate demands and, as he put it, "intervening into the local affairs that remain the purview of the [Wallachian] civilian authorities."[70] He paid close attention to events in neighboring Serbia, where the anti-Ottoman insurrection had entered its eighth year. Russia had initially embraced the revolt and provided support for it, but the apparent inability of the Serbians to achieve military success without external assistance had caused disillusionment in the Russian government; for the czar and his advisors, the revolt, weakened by internal power struggles between Serbian leader Karadjordje and his political rivals, had lost its vitality and was increasingly regarded as a useful bargaining chip in the larger plans to redraw the map of southeastern Europe. Indeed, in the fall of 1810 and then again in the spring of 1811, Emperor Alexander had reiterated his offer to the Ottomans to sever his connections with the Serbs in return for the sultan's surrender of Wallachia and Moldavia. Kutuzov, however, believed that continued success of the Serbian uprising offered, as he wrote to one of his generals, "too many advantages to count" for the Russians in the region and he was keen to bolster and exploit it.[71] Just three days after arriving, he was already busy writing letters to the Serbian leaders, reassuring them of Russian support; as tangible proof of his commitment, he sent a large monetary gift to replenish their exhausted war chest, along with almost a million cartridges and ten cannon to bolster their military capacity. Furthermore, Kutuzov made secret arrangements with merchants in Temesvar, the Habsburg-controlled Banat region, to furnish the Serbs with much-needed provisions, and offered closer military cooperation between the Russian detachments and the Serbian forces, sending some 2,000 men under the command of Joseph O'Rourke to reinforce the rebel defenses.[72]

Knowing that both of his flanks would be vulnerable to an Ottoman attack, Kutuzov took measures to mitigate this threat. On the "weakly defended" left wing, he began repairing and improving existing fortresses, especially that of Brăila, to block the Ottoman advance; the presence of the Russian flotilla also bolstered defenses in this sector. To observe movements on the middle portion of the Danube, Kutuzov ordered the construction of a large artillery battery on the promontory where the Jiu River joined the Danube. It was harder to secure the right flank. The Russians did not control major fortresses, while the Ottomans held the town of Vidin. Were the Ottomans to invade Little Wallachia from the west, Kutuzov instructed his units to resort to defense-in-depth; Zass was to hold defensive positions behind the Danube's tributaries, most notably "the swift and wide Olt River," and slow the Ottoman offensive to a halt.[73] More crucially, the Russian commander in chief was determined to deny his opponent any means of crossing the Danube. The Russian flotilla was instructed to scour ports, villages, and riverbanks for any boats or rafts that could ferry troops across the river and its tributaries. "From the Danube's estuary to Ruse we left not a single vessel that the enemy can use, while our flotilla can now operate along the entire stretch of the Lower Danube," Kutuzov soon reported.[74]

There was, however, danger upstream. Russian scouts discovered almost 400 boats and vessels of all types gathered at Vidin, with which the Turks could move a sizable force across the river and launch an attack against the Russian right wing. Kutuzov hatched a scheme to negate this threat. He knew that the governor of Vidin, Mulla Pasha, had strained relations with the grand vizier and other provincial governors, and was concerned about his very survival. Kutuzov instructed Zass to open secret communications with the Ottoman governor and inform him that Russian agents had learned of the Ottoman imperial council's decision to have him killed.[75] The intelligence was plausible enough to alarm the governor. Kutuzov then wrote directly to the pasha, calling him "eminent and magnificent" and offering protection and employment, but only on condition that he transfer ships to Russian control as a pledge of his loyalty.[76] Otherwise Kutuzov would be unable to ensure either his personal safety or his access to the free trade that the Russians allowed in the region. Concerned about his well-being and the vast profits he derived from trade, Mulla Pasha agreed to cooperate. He assured Kutuzov that he would do his best to prevent Ismail Bey from crossing the Danube, and, as a token of his loyalty to Russia, he revealed the details of the operational plan that the last grand vizier had sent him. Kutuzov could see that the Ottomans had planned a multipronged offensive, with the grand vizier intending to feign an attack on Ruse while the main forces moved southwest and crossed the Danube unopposed somewhere between Lom and Nikopol. Once on the Wallachian side, the vizier would be supported by Ismail Bey, who was tasked with crossing the river at Vidin and rolling the Russian right flank from the west.

As thrilling as having these operational details was, Kutuzov needed those boats more. Mulla Pasha agreed to help the Russians secure the flotilla, but there was one major impediment—he could not simply transfer boats to the Russians because most of them belonged to local residents. He could, however, convince them to sell for the princely sum of 50,000 gold coins, which could be reduced by half as a bargain. Exorbitant as even this reduced sum was, Kutuzov was willing to pay it. "I will never second-guess spending this money because this deal would for a long time deprive the enemy of means to cross the river," he told the minister of war.[77] He just needed time to complete the deal.

In early June, news arrived that the Ottoman army was on the move. Kutuzov urged Zass to complete the purchase of the vessels at Vidin so as to deny Ismail Bey any opportunity to move across the Danube. Yet Mulla Pasha balked; he was concerned that such a mass purchase would raise suspicions among the Janissaries and endanger his life. Meanwhile, Russian spies confirmed that the grand vizier had already bivouacked his army at Razgrad, where the Turks had begun building a fortified camp.[78] The situation was becoming precarious, as Kutuzov was in danger of being caught in a vise between Ismail Bey, invading Wallachia from the west, and the grand vizier, striking from the south; they would collectively have over 80,000 men, when the Russians could barely muster 20,000 men in the field.[79]

Kutuzov broke off negotiations in Bucharest and, taking Langeron's corps, rushed to Giurgiu. He arrived there just as the grand vizier was resting his freshly reinforced army, now almost 60,000 strong, between Razgrad and Pisanetz, barely fifteen miles from Ruse.[80] Letters and orders reveal his keen awareness of the precariousness of the situation. The fact that the grand vizier had gathered all his forces in this direction caused Kutuzov to doubt the veracity of the information supplied by Mulla Pasha. Was the leaked information part of an Ottoman ruse to mislead him? He ultimately concluded that the new grand vizier had adopted a fresh plan of action. Though its primary objective eluded him, Kutuzov was determined to dictate the terms of engagement. Like Napoleon on the eve of Austerlitz, he strove to foster the illusion of Russian weakness by every means in his power, hoping that it would draw the enemy into a position where he could decisively defeat it. He thus kept Langeron's corps concealed behind the Danube and left Ruse, with its small garrison, deceptively weak and exposed. Kutuzov, in essence, wagered that the grand vizier would be tempted to grab this low-hanging fruit. "Through my cautious behavior [skromnym povedeniem] I hope to encourage the vizier to advance toward Ruse," he explained. "If it happens, I will take all the forces at my disposal and go out to confront him in a battle." But if the grand vizier refused to take the bait and attempted to cross the river west of Ruse, Kutuzov anticipated that the best crossing spot would be at the estuary of the Jiu River, which he was already protecting with a battery. If the Ottomans indeed moved in this direction, he intended to leave twelve battalions to cover Ruse and hasten with the rest of his army to Turnu (about eighty miles from Ruse), where he could be reinforced by Zass's division from Craiova.[81] This was a cogent and well-reasoned operational plan that was based on speed and maneuverability. Even the normally caustic Langeron admired it: "This was a brilliant plan."[82]

Throughout June the Ottomans showed none of the vigor that was needed to win the war. For days their forces idled away at Vidin and Razgrad; neither did the Turks attempt to dispatch the Ottoman fleet, which remained anchored at the entrance into the Bosporus, to the estuary of the Danube, where the appearance of an enemy landing force would have spelled disaster for the Russians.[83] Only at the end of June, just as Kutuzov expected, did the Ottoman army move from Razgrad to Kadikoy, a small town a few miles from Ruse, where its advance parties clashed with the Cossack patrols. One such scuffle, on July 1, quickly escalated into a much larger engagement; exploiting the dense fog swathing the area that morning, some 5,000 Turks surprised the Cossack outposts on the plains south of Ruse and pushed them back to the town. Realizing this was not a regular scouting party, Voinov, whom Kutuzov had put in charge of the advance guard, rushed forward ten lancer squadrons and five squadrons of hussars to contain the attack. A brief but intense cavalry melee unfolded across the Bulgarian lowland before the arrival of four Russian infantry battalions forced the Turks to withdraw.[84]

Kutuzov was now convinced that his ploy had worked and the grand vizier was on his way to Ruse. He moved Langeron's corps across the river and, leaving six infantry battalions under General Dmitry Rezvyj in Ruse, led the rest of his force—about 15,000 men with more than 100 cannon—south of the town.[85] The area in the immediate vicinity of Ruse was covered with orchards that were well watered by a great number of streams flowing down to the Danube. This made the terrain too rugged to arrange a large force. But just three miles away the landscape gradually turned to a wide-open plain suitable for a battle. "It was a mediocre position, but the only acceptable one in the area," Kutuzov confided to a friend. "From the front, the position was rather exposed, but both of the flanks could be anchored on the gullies, orchards, and vineyards, in short, precisely what is needed when dealing with the Turks."[86] He formed nine "moving redoubts" there—five squares in the first line and four in the second, with the cavalry arranged in the rear. This checkerboard formation, so effectively applied by Rumyantsev and Suvorov in previous campaigns, maximized Russian firepower, so any Ottoman riders who mustered the courage to attack would find themselves caught in a withering crossfire from the infantry squares, while those who managed to slip past them would be cut down by the cavalry in the back.

July 3 passed uneventfully as both sides prepared for the showdown. As a token of his respect for the vizier, Kutuzov conveyed six pounds of tea to

Ahmed Pasha, who returned the favor by sending lemons and oranges to his rival. "We are very courteous and frequently check on each other's health," Kutuzov told Catherine.[87]

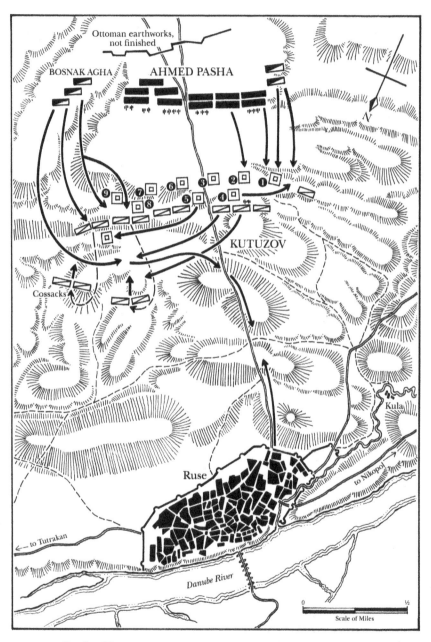

MAP 11 Battle of Ruse

At dawn on July 4, almost 60,000 Ottoman troops, looking picturesque in their diverse and colorful uniforms and carrying flags and pennants, approached the Russian positions. The large size of the enemy army startled Kutuzov, who confessed that "my eye is not accustomed to seeing such vast numbers [of the Turks]."[88] The grand vizier was keen on exploiting his numerical superiority. He intended to first attack with his left wing and center and then, once the Russians were pinned down, to launch a flanking maneuver from the right that would smash through the Russian left flank and cut Kutuzov's line of retreat. "The enemy movements were so well conceived and carried out that they would have done honor to even the most skilled general," Kutuzov admitted in a letter to the czar. "The [grand vizier's] forays against our flanks could have been very dangerous to us but, considering the terrain, it was easy to anticipate that he would try such maneuvers and I took all the necessary precautions against them."[89]

Observing the dense square formation of the Russian infantry, the grand vizier first ordered his seventy-eight cannon to bombard them.[90] "The high number of our men who have been killed by cannonballs bears witness to the fact that the enemy artillery performed very strongly [that day]," Kutuzov admitted after the battle. "I must do justice to the enemy who had done everything possible to deny us a victory; they waged intense artillery fire all along their line and then attacked our right flank."[91] And yet the Ottoman attack failed in this direction. The Russian right wing was protected by the steep slopes of the Lom River, forcing the Turks to launch frontal attacks on the enemy squares. Superior Russian discipline and firepower prevailed.[92] Some Ottoman units tried to scale the slopes in an attempt to get behind the Russian position, but Kutuzov ordered the 37th Jäger Regiment (forming in a square in the second line) to the edge of his right flank, where the light infantrymen scattered in an open order in the brush and orchards. Supported by Cossacks and the Liflandskii dragoons, they repelled Ottoman flanking attempts and secured the flank.

Around nine o'clock in the morning, Ahmed Pasha gave a signal to Bosnak Agha to lead a flanking charge against the Russian left wing.[93] More than 10,000 riders of "the famed Anatolian cavalry," as Kutuzov described them, hurled themselves across the plains, swirling around the infantry squares and charging them at least five times.[94] Despite the devastating crossfire, the Turks, acting with remarkable zeal and determination, galloped between the squares and attacked the Russian cavalry behind them. The Byelorussian hussars and the Kinburnskii dragoons, stationed to protect the extreme Russian flank, were surprised and so badly mauled that they broke and fled, exposing the road to Ruse. A nearby horse artillery company was also overrun and lost one of its cannon.[95] "The enemy cavalry acted with such arrogance that I have never witnessed among the Ottoman troops in all the years I have served against them," Kutuzov confessed. The Turks fought their way to the outskirts of Ruse but paid a heavy price for such "audacious arrogance."[96] Rezvyj's battalions defended the town, while Kutuzov redirected the Olivipolskii hussars, Chuguevskii uhlans, and St. Peterburgskii dragoons to shore up his left wing.

For the next couple of hours, a fierce battle raged there. Unable to seize the town, Bosnak Agha moved his men to a gently rising hummock half a mile from the Russian left wing, where they regrouped for a new charge. Kutuzov had anticipated this; on his orders, the 7th Jäger Regiment's square moved from its position in the second line toward the knoll where, supported by cavalry and artillery, it opened devastating volleys at the enemy. Hundreds of the Ottoman riders were cut down—"the ground was covered with their corpses," Kutuzov claimed in his after-action report—until their commander ordered them to withdraw.[97]

This was the turning moment of the battle. The momentum now shifted, quickly and decisively, to the Russians. Noting the growing confusion in the Ottoman ranks, Kutuzov put the whole line of "moving redoubts" in motion, carefully coordinating his cavalry and infantry movements. The sounds of drums beating and thousands of soldiers shouting "hurrah!" filled the air as the Russian army pressed forward. Around two o'clock in the afternoon, Ahmed Pasha, frustrated at being unable to make any headway, ordered his men to disengage and retreat to Kadikoy.[98] The elated Russian generals urged Kutuzov to pursue the fleeing enemy, but he demurred. His cavalry was not sufficiently strong to conduct a close pursuit. Moreover, he knew that the Ottomans were withdrawing toward their fortified camps. "If we pursue the Turks any further, we might even get as far as Şumnu," he told his officers, according to one participant. "But then what? We would have to turn back as we did in prior years and the grand vizier would claim victory. It will be better to encourage my friend Ahmed Pasha to regroup so he can come after us soon enough."[99]

Refusing to be carried away by his victory, Kutuzov stuck to his original plan of maintaining a central position and dictating the pace of the campaign. With the last rays of the setting sun, he moved the army back to Ruse.[100] "The almighty God has granted me a victory," he wrote jubilantly to his family. "I am well but so tired that I can barely hold the quill. I am very pleased with the generals and the soldiers' devotion. For five hours they fought, and did so very well at all points."[101] He was unaware that some of these generals were disparaging him behind his back—or at least one of them: Langeron deplored his "cowardice, old age, and obesity," which "made him incapable of not only acting but even thinking straight."[102]

Thus ended the largest battle of the entire Russo-Ottoman War. Kutuzov's success at anticipating enemy moves, together with the gallantry of his soldiers, ensured the Russian victory at Ruse. Russian casualties were light, while the Ottomans had lost over 3,000 men and more than a dozen pennants and flags belonging to various Ottoman units and commanders.[103] The news quickly spread across Europe, upsetting the French and delighting their opponents; British newspapers enthused about "the signal victory" and expressed hope that the war in the Danubian Principalities might end soon in the Russians' favor.[104] Emperor Alexander rewarded Kutuzov with a bejeweled miniature portrait that the general wore on his chest on special occasions.[105] "We gave the Turks a glorious thrashing," the writer Alexander Turgenev noted in a letter to his brother. "Kutuzov has reminded us of the glorious old days."[106]

The question of what to do next weighed heavily on Kutuzov's mind. Sustaining an army south of the Danube remained a serious logistical challenge and prevented him from carrying the war deep into the Bulgarian countryside. Despite the defeat at Ruse, the Ottoman army was still intact. Kutuzov knew that the Turks could exploit their numerical superiority to split their forces and attack him from multiple directions. "They could leave one part of their troops at Ruse and move the rest to Tutrukan, Silistra, or Nikopol, where they would cross the Danube and invade Wallachia," he supposed. "I would be thus forced to return to the left bank to confront the enemy." He came to the conclusion that abandoning Ruse would be far more expedient than staying in Bulgaria and defending it. The town's fortifications required at least eighteen infantry battalions to fully man them, but detaching such a force would have left Kutuzov with just eleven battalions in the field.[107] This would be clearly insufficient to face up to the grand vizier's army. "Even if our troops had retained Ruse and advanced as far as the Balkan Mountains, we would have still been not much closer to peace," he explained in a lengthy letter to Barclay de Tolly, the minister of war. Kamenskii's 1810 campaign had accomplished nothing after capturing half a dozen towns south of the Danube. He had been forced to return to Wallachia "without even nudging the Porte to think of peace."[108]

There was another reason Kutuzov wanted to abandon Ruse. Leaving would play into the Ottoman belief about his weakness. He could foresee the reaction news of his withdrawal would cause in the Ottoman camp—the grand vizier, smarting from the recent defeat, would be eager to capture the town to claim a win; encouraged by this success, the Turks would be more willing to cross to the Wallachian side in search of a decisive victory. There, closer to his reinforcements and supplies, Kutuzov would be able to concentrate his forces and to exploit any mistakes his opponent might commit. "Immediately after the victory over the grand vizier, I decided to retire from Ruse," he informed his superiors in St. Petersburg.[109] His order commanding the Army of Moldavia to evacuate Ruse and destroy all fortifications stunned many; senior officers asked for a meeting and tried changing his mind, pointing out the advantages of keeping a Russian garrison at Ruse. Kutuzov rejected all such arguments. "Ruse is not important to us," he told them. "We must entice the grand vizier to the left bank. Learning about our departure, he will unquestionably follow us."[110]

The evacuation of the Russian army and local inhabitants (more than 630 Bulgarian households) was soon completed. Everything portable was removed, fortifications were mined and blown up, and the entire city was set on fire. "We witnessed a hellish sight, astounding and terrifying at once; the waters of the Danube reflected the raging flames of the conflagration, whose glare eclipsed that of the waning moon," he wrote in a letter.[111] He knew that abandoning Ruse without a fight would cause public criticism. He mentions in one of the letters that it might even bring "personal dishonor." Nonetheless, he was convinced that this was the right course of action. Even those who, in the words of Langeron, "fiercely criticized him" later admitted that abandoning Ruse was a "very smart" decision.[112]

Grand Vizier Ahmed Pasha, who was regrouping at Kadikoy and building new entrenchments in expectation of a Russian attack, was incredulous that Kutuzov had left Ruse. Interpreting it as a clear sign of Russian weakness, he rushed to seize what was left of the burned-out town. He constructed two massive camps on its outskirts and wrote a glowing report about his accomplishments, asserting that the Battle of Ruse was an Ottoman victory and the Russian army was so depleted that it could not even hold on to its last stronghold in Bulgaria. The Ottoman conquest was celebrated in Istanbul and beyond, reaching even Napoleon's ears. "It is stated with greater confidence than ever that the Turks have defeated the Russians in Wallachia and forced them to abandon that province. The Turkish armies appear to be everywhere in a state of activity," reported more than one British newspaper.[113] Sultan Mahmud bestowed robes of honor on the vizier and his commanders and urged them to bring the war to a quick and victorious conclusion.

CHAPTER 19 | The Master of War, 1811

T HE ARMIES SPENT THE rest of the summer divided by the Danube, which was half a mile wide near Ruse. The Turks settled on the limestone bluffs on the Bulgarian side, while the Russians remained camped out on the Wallachian plain, its shoreline covered with rank grass, tall reeds, and scrubby bushes. "We suffered from the dreadful heat wave," remembered Langeron. "In fact, I struggle to recall another such summer in all the time I served in Moldavia." He credited the fact that the army was in good shape to Kutuzov, who had made sure the troops were provisioned and trained and were not made to perform "pointless exercise and drills." Compared to previous years, there were fewer sick soldiers. Despite himself, Langeron admitted that the army "genuinely appreciated Kutuzov's good care and become ever more strongly attached to him."[1]

The Russian inactivity caused concerns in St. Petersburg, as the czar expected quick and decisive results. Kutuzov's rivals accused him of sluggishness and ineptitude. "His Majesty was very unhappy to hear of his return from beyond the Danube, to the point of regretting his haste in sending the general his miniature portrait," reported the Austrian envoy, who had a private conversation with the czar.[2] In late August Alexander and his advisors decided to send a special representative to the Army of Moldavia. Kutuzov had known Ivan Barrozzi since his embassy days but despite valuing his talents—Kutuzov considered him a "very cunning and adroit" man—did not trust him. While in Istanbul, Kutuzov had tested Barrozzi by sharing with him intentionally false information which he then discovered had reached the ears of some Ottoman officials. "His indiscretions were not of the nature that one could consider treacherous," Kutuzov noted at the time, but they were serious enough to warrant Barrozzi's recall from the Ottoman capital. When their paths crossed once more seventeen years later, Kutuzov was instinctively mistrustful of the man whose official mission was to facilitate talks with the Turks but whom he suspected of having been sent to spy on him. Barrozzi indeed supplied a steady stream of reports that portrayed the commander in chief in an unflattering light and increased the czar's vexation with him.

Nonetheless, Kutuzov refused to commit to hasty actions and urged waiting for an opportune moment to strike. Responding to continued demands from St. Petersburg to reach a peace with the Porte, he underscored that the Turks had little incentive to negotiate since they were certain that the rupture between Napoleon and Alexander was imminent, and expected to force Russia to "accept the peace that they themselves desired." He pointed out that Alexander's continued demand for the secession of all the Danubian Principalities was "so terrifying" to the Turks that it was hardly surprising they were lending an attentive ear to the "gratifying" offers from France. Despite all their misgivings about Napoleon's assurances, the Turks "find French promises so genuine that they remain determined to continue this war."[3] Russia needed something to happen that might force the Ottomans to sit at the negotiating table.

Across the river, meanwhile, Ahmed Pasha also "remained very tranquil," in the words of a British newspaper, resting his men, receiving reinforcements, and, most crucially, waiting for the news about the Ottoman incursion from Vidin.[4] Ismail Bey was supposed to cross the Danube, brush aside Zass's small detachment, and force his way into Little Wallachia. Yet, despite having vastly superior numbers, the Ottoman commander was unable to make any headway, thwarted by the difficult terrain and capable Russian leadership. "In the kind of war that we are currently waging everything depends on the speed of action," Kutuzov told the czar.[5] After defeating the Turks at Ruse, he rushed to redeploy his forces, precisely to confront any incursions from Vidin, located almost 200 miles to the west. On his orders, several infantry battalions marched 125 miles to Craiova to join Zass, who then led his men another sixty miles to Calafat, just across the river from Vidin, where Kutuzov wanted to see redoubts constructed to foil Ismail Bey's incursion. Lieutenant General Essen, with eight infantry battalions and ten squadrons of cavalry, was sent to the Olt River, where he would be close enough to help Zass in case of an enemy attack. Langeron's corps, meanwhile, took up a central position between the Olt River and Giurgiu, allowing Kutuzov to be within striking distance in whichever direction the Ottoman attack first materialized. He was still concerned about the large fleet of boats that remained at Vidin. Despite the earlier agreement with Mulla Pasha, these vessels were still intact and in Ottoman hands; in fact, many of them had been moved downstream to Lom, suggesting an Ottoman intention to open a new front between Vidin and Ruse. This meant a border of some 250 miles on which Kutuzov now had to keep a close eye. To prevent these vessels sailing farther downstream and possibly assisting the grand vizier at Ruse,

Kutuzov reinforced the battery he had constructed at the estuary of the Jiu River and deployed a small flotilla of eighteen gunboats there.[6]

These preparations soon paid off. Zass, with thirteen battalions of infantry and sixteen cavalry squadrons, arrived at Calafat just as Ismail Bey was starting to cross the Danube.[7] The site of the Ottoman crossing, however, was poorly selected—the left riverbank was lined with a wide band of swamps and thick growths of reeds that extended for "over five miles in length and one and a half miles in depth."[8] Just three narrow paths cut through this morass. In this difficult terrain, the advantage was strongly on the side of the defender, who could harass and slow the attackers as they navigated the narrow passages through the marshland. The Russians dug in on the edge of the swamp and waited for the successive waves of Ottoman troops trudging through water, mud, and tall grass. As soon as they emerged onto the open ground, Russian canister and musket fire wreaked havoc on them. The Turks fought with great valor, but they lacked competent leadership that could have exploited their numerical superiority.[9] Throughout August, Ismail Bey moved most of his force (more than 15,000 men) to the small islands dotting the riverbank opposite Vidin.[10] Instead of maneuvering around the Russian defense, however, he chose to dig in on the muddy shores of the Danube.[11]

"My mind is in a constant state of agitation," Kutuzov scribbled in a short note to his family.[12] He was right to be worried; the situation was becoming perilous. The Army of Moldavia seemed caught between Ismail Bey, bearing down from the west, and Ahmed Pasha's 60,000 men, advancing from the south. Still, his eyes remained firmly set on the main prize, which was the Ottoman main army. "Difficult times call for any and all measures," he told his generals.[13] He urgently needed more fighting men. An earlier effort to raise a Bulgarian militia had produced just 1,000 untrained men.[14] He required properly trained and equipped soldiers, disciplined and capable of tactical maneuvers against the Ottoman cavalry. The only way to get them was by recalling the divisions that the czar had earlier detached from the Army of Moldavia. Kutuzov knew that this action would contravene the sovereign's will and that he did not have direct authorization to do so.[15] But he was willing to take responsibility for whatever came next. He had become convinced that Napoleon was not yet in position to threaten Russia and that the czar's fears were overblown; war would not start anytime soon, and the detached divisions would be simply idling away, just when they could help win the war against the Turks in Wallachia. Consequently, without waiting for the czar's formal response to his request, Kutuzov ordered the 9th and 15th Infantry Divisions to leave their camps at once and rush down to Bucharest.[16] In a subsequent report to the czar, he meekly noted that he "took the liberty" of moving these troops.[17] As it turned out, his decision was perfectly timed.

Ahmed Pasha had spent all of August constructing rafts and other vessels that could ferry his men across the Danube. He was encouraged by the news from Vidin, which suggested that his plan was steadily being implemented; it would be just a matter of days before Ismail Bey would be pushing across Little Wallachia and turning the right wing of the Russian army. The time was therefore ripe for the main Ottoman army to get across the Danube and pin down its opponent.

During the night of September 7–8, Ahmed Pasha ordered his men to cross the Danube. "The river still preserves its usual character, expanding itself over an enormous width, divided into many branches and forming a multitude of islands small and large," a visiting Englishman observed of the vicinity of Ruse.[18] Crossing the wide and powerful river here would have posed an immense challenge. So Turkish scouts scoured the vicinity of the town, searching for more favorable spots, which they found up- and downstream. The grand vizier then organized what Kutuzov admiringly called "deft feigned crossings" downstream, while the actual crossing took place about four miles upstream, where the Danube was narrower and its strong current was slowed by the presence of Gol Island.[19] The higher Bulgarian shore gave the Turks an excellent vantage point on which to deploy artillery, while tall reeds growing along the shoreline concealed their movements.[20] The crossing by thousands of troops was so well organized and implemented that Kutuzov later admitted that he learned of the crossing only after it was completed. Protected by strong artillery batteries that the vizier had set up on the nearby hills, some 6,000 Janissaries spearheaded the crossing, first securing Gol and then moving to the Wallachian shore near the village of Slobozia, where they immediately began digging earthworks. Major General Mikhail Bulatov, who commanded the local outpost, rushed to contain the Ottoman attack. He attacked three times, trying to push the enemy into the river, and each time he failed; the Janissaries fought back ferociously, while the tightly packed masses of the Russian infantry squares were easy targets for the Ottoman cannon firing from the opposite bank.[21]

As the reports poured into the Russian headquarters at Giurgiu, Kutuzov ordered Bulatov to disengage and pull back to defensive positions.[22] The first skirmish thus did not augur well for the Russians, who lost some 200 killed and 800 wounded, along with a flag and a cannon, which the elated grand vizier sent to Istanbul as trophies.[23] Langeron, echoing the opinion of other senior officers, thought the commander in chief had made a mistake by not anticipating the enemy crossing and failing to drive the Turks into the river.[24] Kutuzov's private letters suggest otherwise. "My dear friend, I am doing well and do not even care that much for the vizier," he wrote Catherine. "With the Lord's help, I will not yield even an inch to [the Turks]. . . . Trust me, we are all very calm here."[25]

The reason for Kutuzov's calm lay partly in his intimate understanding of his opponent. He anticipated that the grand vizier, instead of pushing forward and exploiting his vast numbers, would dig in like his predecessors and wait for Ismail Bey, who, Kutuzov was convinced, would never arrive. His earlier efforts to shore up the Russian defenses at Calafat thus assumed outsized importance—so long as the right flank held, the main Russian army had a fighting chance against the grand vizier. Moreover, Kutuzov knew that the preparations he had made two weeks earlier would pay off. The Army of Moldavia might not have been strong enough to prevent the crossing, but the 9th and 15th Divisions were just days away and would bolster its combat capacity.[26]

On September 9, just one day after the Ottoman crossing and while Langeron and other officers bemoaned his apparent "sleepiness, laziness, and effeminacy [*iznezhenost'*]" and spoke of the looming Russian defeat, Kutuzov confided to one of his senior generals that he intended to let the Turks cross the river and then "crush them in the decisive battle."[27] Four days later, as the 9th Division reached him, he assured the minister of war, Barclay de Tolly, that the situation was under control. "I can now calmly await the enemy attack in my current position and if, to my great delight, [the Turks] decide to enter upon the plains that separate us, I will attack and defeat them."[28]

For the next two weeks, the Russians watched as more and more Ottoman units crossed the Danube. The grand vizier soon had more than half of his army in a bridgehead camp on the Wallachian shore, while the other half remained at the encampment on the Bulgarian side. And then, just as Kutuzov had expected, he waited. The crossing had given the Ottomans an advantage, and with a suitable operational plan and some determination, the grand vizier could have accomplished much. Yet the Ottomans had no such drive or direction. A brave warrior, Ahmed Pasha failed to demonstrate the *coup d'œil*, that innate ability to see a military situation clearly, to assess the advantages and disadvantages of his situation. Once he had taken his forces across the river, he showed unusual complacency, remaining at his new position for days on end while waiting for word about Ismail Bey's attack on the Russian right flank. It took him a week to attempt a reconnaissance in force. That gave Kutuzov that most precious of commodities—time. Time to assess the situation, analyze possible developments, and come up with a response.

Kutuzov made the most of this respite, reinforcing his positions with earthworks that encircled the enemy camp and concentrating all available forces to contain the Ottomans if they tried to break out; the arrival of the two fresh divisions allowed him to bolster his forces and deploy detachments to observe the area between Ruse and Silistra in case the grand vizier attempted another flanking maneuver.[29] In mid-September, when his scouts reported that a large number of Ottoman boats had been moved from Vidin to Lom—supposedly to ferry part of Ismail Bey's force to circumvent Zass's defenses at Calafat—Kutuzov responded promptly and robustly; on his orders, some 800 men, supported by Russian gunboats, proceeded to Lom, where they stormed the Ottoman stronghold and destroyed boats, thus neutralizing this threat.[30]

Kutuzov still did not attack Ahmed Pasha's army. Not yet. He knew that the more the Turks settled in comfortably at their camp, the more they were contributing to his new plan. His caution would diminish the Turks' sense of urgency and make them passive and complacent. His forty years of experience fighting this opponent had convinced him that he would eventually be able to accomplish this. But the rest of the army did not see it that way. His generals, eager to fight, lambasted him for inactivity and languor. "For an entire day he sits inside his tent, wasting three hours on his lunch and then resting his eyes for another two hours," seethed Langeron.[31] But unbeknownst to him, Kutuzov had already settled on a scheme to end the war with one decisive blow.[32] Instead of attacking the Ottoman army head-on, he decided to entrap it by sending part of his army across the Danube, routing the enemy force on the right bank of the river and cutting the grand vizier's supply and communication lines. He anticipated that a surprise attack on the grand vizier's main camp would deprive the enemy of its leadership, and the Ottoman army could then be surrounded from both sides of the river.

This was an audacious idea, reminiscent of the *manoeuvre sur les derrières* (attack on the enemy's rear) that Napoleon had employed with such devastating efficacy. If successful, it could end the war. But it was a risky endeavor too, contingent on many factors, including the swiftness and secrecy of the flanking movement, close coordination between Russian units, and the inaction of the numerically superior enemy. Logistically, the plan posed challenges as well. To cross the river, the Russians would have to construct and gather rafts undetected. "It took me considerable time to concentrate the necessary manpower and resources so I could send sufficiently strong forces across the river," Kutuzov wrote. Huge effort was expended to avoid exposure, since as Kutuzov noted, the area was "infested with spies and foreign agents." He was concerned that the secret would be revealed.[33]

Kutuzov chose Yevgenii Markov for the trans-Danubian flanking maneuver. This general was well suited for this mission. Markov had enlisted as a private in an infantry regiment and risen steadily through the ranks, garnering praise for bravery, judgment, and "innate intelligence."[34] He earned his major general's epaulettes during the expedition to the Caspian Sea in 1796–1797 and later took part in the ill-fated Russian campaign in Switzerland (1799). Kutuzov got to know him after Markov was appointed commander of the Pskovskii Infantry Regiment, whose regimental colonel proprietor was Kutuzov himself; they fought together during the War of the Third Coalition, with Markov distinguishing himself at Krems-Durrenstein

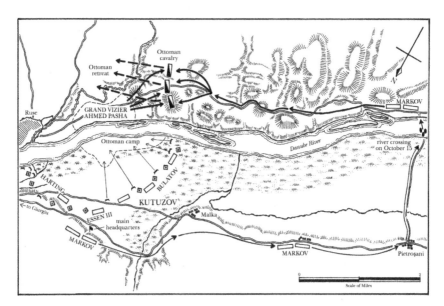

MAP 12 The Ruse-Slobozia Operation

and Austerlitz. His gallantry at Eylau earned him an award for bravery, while the exploits at Friedland led to promotion to a lieutenant general. In 1808 he met Kutuzov once more when both were assigned to the Army of Moldavia. Although Kutuzov left the army soon thereafter, he continued to follow Markov's career. It was no surprise, then, that when Kutuzov needed an officer to execute a daring plan, he did not hesitate to select Markov.[35]

To create an anvil for Markov's hammer, Kutuzov ordered nine redoubts and a deep trench to be constructed around the Ottoman campsite on the left bank.[36] "I have surrounded the enemy with the [strong] redoubts," he soon reported to St. Petersburg. "If the Turks try to break out, they would have to contend with these bulwarks and the troops behind them." Both Russian flanks were now firmly anchored on the river, so "the enemy cannot get around them to cause any mischief in our rear."[37]

Russian preparations were completed by mid-October. Several large rafts were gathered on the Olt River, away from the prying eyes of enemy scouts, so they could be floated down to the rendezvous point on the Danube. On the cool and "moonless" night of October 13, under the faint glow of the Great Comet of 1811, Markov's men—5,000 infantry, 2,500 cavalry, and 38 cannon—quietly departed from their campsites, leaving bonfires burning by their tents.[38] Marching ten miles upstream to evade enemy patrols, they reached the village of Pietroşani, where the rafts were supposed to have linked up with them, but there were no signs of the rafts. After anxiously waiting for them for several hours, Markov decided to improvise. His men scoured the area for timber and fashioned two small rafts that allowed the Cossacks to get across the river; to Markov's delight, the other rafts and boats arrived later that night, so he spent all of the next day ferrying the rest of his men and cannon. As the sun rose on October 15, the Russian detachment was ready to march downstream to the Ottoman camp near Ruse.[39]

"I awaited that morning with trepidation," Kutuzov admitted in a private letter. He knew that his plan was risky and would require a good deal of *bonne chance*. He was amazed that the grand vizier, who had spent that night in the camp on the left side of the Danube, did not have even a single outpost at the place where Markov crossed the river. Disbelieving that the enemy would be so careless, Kutuzov spent the night convinced that the Turks would detect his flanking march. "They could have dug several redoubts in the Ruse camp and then our enterprise would have been doomed. And yet none of that happened." With the first rays of the sun, Kutuzov rushed out of his tent to examine the opposite riverbank. There was no sign of the Turks gearing for battle. He was overjoyed.[40]

About three miles away as the crow flies, Markov cautiously marched forward. It took him twice as long to cross the river as planned, and in his rush to surprise the enemy he had moved the mounted troops ahead of his infantry. The Ottoman sentries were surprised to discover an isolated enemy cavalry unit and alerted the pashas at the Ruse camp, who mistook it for a simple raiding party and dispatched some troops to ride them down.[41] Squinting from across the river, Kutuzov struggled to follow the ensuing cavalry melee. What he saw was not encouraging. The Cossacks were pushed back. But then, around nine o'clock in the morning, Markov's "moving redoubts" appeared. "We felt indescribable delight in observing these five infantry squares, advancing proudly and in a superb order toward the enemy camp," described Kutuzov. The Russian attack routed the Ottoman cavalry and caused utter shock and terror among the still somnolent Turks at the main camp. "The thunderous roar of our cannon woke up the careless enemy, who did not even try to fight but rather fled at once toward the fortress [Ruse]," remembered Yakov Otroschenko, whose 14th Jägers spearheaded the assault.[42] As they fled in wild confusion on the roads to Ruse and Razgrad, the Turks left behind their entire camp, with numerous tents, carriages, stores, artillery, horses, and camels, along with twenty-two banners, the army treasury, and a prodigious quantity of spoils.[43] "We captured abundant supplies of rose water," remembered a Russian general. "There was so much of it that our entire camp soon smelled of roses and soldiers even poured the rose water into their soups."[44]

This was just an opening act. Watching Markov's attack from the opposite bank, Kutuzov remained on edge until he saw a Russian flag hoisted over the Ottoman camp. Only then did he smile and wave his hat while the air resounded with the Russian soldiers' celebratory chants. "Our entire army witnessed the panic and terror spreading in the Ottoman camp," he later reported.[45] Immediately turning the captured enemy guns, Markov opened fire on the rear of the grand vizier's army while Kutuzov's batteries bombarded it from the front. The Ottomans thus found themselves in desperate circumstances. The superior Russian artillery suppressed their batteries, while in their attempts to break out the Turks stumbled into the formidable semicircle of redoubts that Kutuzov had constructed around the enemy camp. That same evening, several hundred men from Markov's detachment crossed over to Gol Island and captured it after a fierce battle with the Ottoman garrison there. "This position was very important because it exposed the riverside part of the enemy camp to direct canister fire," Kutuzov noted in the official *Journal of Military Operations*.[46] The close-range Russian fire was destruction incarnate, sweeping everything within its range and mowing down soldier after soldier. To make matters even worse for the Turks, the Russian flotilla soon joined in on the action, bombarding the camp and capturing vessels, precluding any possibility of the Ottomans escaping across the water. "The Vizier must be deeply regretting crossing the Danube," wrote an elated Kutuzov to Catherine. "I must admit, this day gave me immense pleasure!"[47]

The Slobozia-Ruse operation is justly celebrated as Kutuzov's operational and tactical masterpiece. The plan—based on speed, concentration, flexibility, and audacity—reflected his grasp of the psychology of his opponent. It also militated against the prevailing stereotype (perpetrated by Langeron in particular) of him as a defensive-minded general. His decision to recall divisions without the czar's approval was decisive, providing the manpower needed to defeat the enemy. While contemplating a defense-in-depth strategy, Kutuzov demonstrated the hallmarks of what many now recognize as Napoleonic combat leadership—holding the central position, emphasizing speed and maneuverability, organizing a mobile reserve, ensuring close coordination between units, and bluffing as often as bludgeoning the enemy. In recognition of his great accomplishment, the czar bestowed on him the title of count of the Russian Empire.[48]

Realizing the gravity of his situation, the grand vizier soon reached out with an offer of armistice. Kutuzov initially refused, understanding that he had an opportunity to end the war; he insisted on first seeing proof of Ottoman willingness to accept major concessions.[49] That night there was a torrential downpour. Ahmed Pasha took advantage of it to escape. As the rain came down in sheets, he boarded a small boat and braved the windswept waters of the Danube, somehow making it across to Ruse. "I do not know how he did not drown that night," wrote Kutuzov, who must have been disappointed to hear about the vizier's escape.[50]

Kutuzov nonetheless still held all the cards. The core of the Ottoman army was trapped, and with each passing day the Russian position on the Danube was strengthening. Russian detachments swept along the river, hunting down the dispirited enemy troops and taking Ottoman bases at Turtukai and Silistra by surprise.[51] The news of what had transpired at Ruse spread far and wide, causing panic across the entire region. "It is hard to describe the mayhem that unfolded among the Turks," remembered Langeron. "Numerous inhabitants fled from their villages, Sumnu was left undefended, and the fugitives turned back transports and troops that were on their way to the vizier's camp."[52] To deprive the grand vizier of any hope of receiving reinforcement from Ismail Bey, Kutuzov ordered Zass to carry out a *manoeuvre sur la derrière* similar to the one he had implemented at Ruse. On October 19–21, Major General Mikhail Vorontsov led an attack that turned Ismail Bey's left flank and threatened to cut him off from Vidin. After a daylong fight, the Ottoman commander offered an armistice and pledged to withdraw his troops from Little Wallachia. Having consolidated his right wing, Kutuzov told Zass to capture the town of Lom to prevent Ismail Bey from marching unhindered along the Bulgarian shore to Ruse; his orders were successfully carried out on November 16–18, further demoralizing Ismail Bey and his men, many of whom gave up on the campaign and absconded.[53]

In light of these victories, Kutuzov expected that the grand vizier would be compelled to negotiate soon enough. To help him make up his mind, he ordered the Russian artillery to pummel the Ottoman camp relentlessly. On October 17 the grand vizier, who had earlier insisted on negotiating on the basis of the *status quo ante bellum*, offered territorial concessions, such as the fortress of Khotin with its environs. He also suggested that Russia might be compensated for its war costs.[54] But he still refused to discuss these matters any further until the Russians accepted an armistice and his army was safeguarded.

Kutuzov was pleased by the shift in the Ottoman negotiating position. Writing to the Russian foreign minister, he explained that the grand vizier would not have dared to even mention these propositions without the sultan knowing about it. Although the grand vizier would not admit to it, Kutuzov was convinced that the Ottomans were prepared for more meaningful concessions than a meager plot of land in northern Bessarabia. But he urged the czar and his advisors to moderate their demands and to show prudence and pragmatism. "Yesterday the Ottoman officials already offered me the border on the Prut River, which I think would be very advantageous to us," he told the minister of war, Barclay de Tolly. He was worried that insisting on the surrender of Moldavia and Wallachia would end discussions. "Our demand for Jassy has already caused all the Greeks, who accompany the grand vizier, to protest vocally against it," he noted.[55] The Turkish resolve to keep

Moldavia and Wallachia was due not so much to the sultan or his ministers as to the resolve of the Phanariote Greeks, who "own and control the most profitable places in these principalities and who do not want to lose their revenues." If the czar did not insist on Russian aggrandizement, Kutuzov wrote, he could secure "a timely end to the war."[56]

As the discussions entered their second week, life in the encircled Ottoman camp had become misery itself. "The Turks are already eating horsemeat and have no bread or salt," Kutuzov confided to Catherine in late October.[57] Two weeks later he sent a poignant letter to a friend, describing the devastation that Russian bombardment caused in the Turkish camp. The Russian flotilla, with its twenty-four-pounder cannon, fired deep into the encampment, wreaking havoc among the tightly packed enemy troops. Many Russian officers were astonished by the forbearance of the Ottoman soldiers, who stood on that Danubian shore like dim purgatorial apparitions awaiting disposition. "You would be surprised by the fortitude of these poor souls," commented Kutuzov. "They no longer scatter at every shot; some have dug holes to escape our shelling."[58] But these tomb-like shelters could not shield the men from the hail of lead and fire raining down upon them. Standing on the opposite bank, Major Otroschenko could see that "even inside these holes the Turks could not get away from the shrapnel shells that we fired using their own mortars from the Bulgarian side."[59]

Kutuzov's hope that the grand vizier would soon give in did not materialize. Ahmed Pasha rejected any diplomatic talks until the Russians accepted a full armistice and "released" his army.[60] Negotiations thus dragged on for days while the situation at the Ottoman camp became ever more desperate; tents were burned for fuel, and all the horses were eaten. Thousands of Turkish soldiers ate what they could find or lay despondently on the open ground, already strewn with the corpses of men and animals that "filled the air with the most rotten of stenches."[61] Fever, dysentery, and diarrhea flourished in this filth, and the unfortunate men had no access to physicians or medication. By the end of October, more than a third of the 36,000 soldiers who had crossed the river a month earlier was dead. "The intrepidity and strength with which these soldiers endured the suffering is worthy of utmost admiration," acknowledged a Russian general. Kutuzov agreed, commenting that "there is no other nation that could have endured such disasters. The patience of these men deserves to be extolled by historian's quill."[62] Yet even with their main army wasting away from hunger, the Ottoman diplomats were determined to make the best of their situation, well aware that the prospects of a Russo-French collision were rapidly increasing, as was Austria's opposition to Russian expansion to the Danube.[63] They might have lost this campaign, but there was still a chance to salvage the outcome of the entire war.

As pragmatic as ever, Kutuzov believed that one of the sides had to compromise to get the negotiations under way. If the Turks were unwilling to take the first step, the Russians should do it before it was too late. To ensure the survival of the Ottoman army, his key bartering chip, Kutuzov agreed to a five-day ceasefire and provided fresh water, bread, and meat to the Turks.[64] "As much as I loathed the idea of suspending military operations, I had to do it because otherwise the vizier would not have engaged in any negotiations with us," he explained to his superiors in St. Petersburg. He reiterated that if the entire Ottoman army died, the vizier would not feel any urgency to negotiate.[65]

This carrot-and-stick approach helped facilitate negotiations. With a temporary armistice in place, the grand vizier agreed to open negotiations, and the first formal meeting of "the congress," as Kutuzov called the Russo-Ottoman discussions, took place at Giurgiu on October 31, 1811.[66] At first there were encouraging signs that a Russo-Ottoman accord could be achieved. Emperor Alexander had finally listened to Kutuzov's earlier suggestion and moderated his demands. The czar's new instructions no longer insisted on having the border on the Danube. Instead, he was willing to end the war based on four core conditions: a new border along the Sereth River, thereby giving Russia all of Bessarabia and most of Moldavia; a large indemnity for leaving Wallachia, while the Porte would confirm all privileges formerly enjoyed by the inhabitants of that principality; Serbian autonomy; and an end to hostilities on the basis of *uti possidetis*, enabling Russia to claim vast territories in western Georgia that it had acquired during the war.[67]

Kutuzov presented these revised terms, but his expectations of a quick peace were still premature. The Ottoman delegates were willing to accept the loss of Bessarabia and parts of Moldavia but balked at the Russian demands in Serbia and Georgia as well as the immense war indemnity that the czar demanded.[68] More worrisome was the fact that these delegates still lacked official credentials from the sultan, raising the prospect that the Ottoman ruler might reject whatever agreement his diplomats had signed. Kutuzov repeatedly asked for a show of proof that Sultan Mahmud had authorized these negotiations and would abide by the settlement reached there.[69] The grand vizier's assurances that the sultan's envoy bearing the necessary authorization was already on his way to Giurgiu rang hollow to him. In November he turned to his agents to get a better sense of the situation in Constantinople. The news was discouraging. A well-placed source at the Ottoman court revealed that Mahmud, expecting a Franco-Russian confrontation, had refused to consider Russian demands and was willing to make only partial territorial concessions in Bessarabia.[70]

Kutuzov felt frustrated. He knew that the czar would be incensed by the sultan's response and insist on immediate resumption of hostilities. Yet the onset of cold weather meant that breaking off negotiations and resuming military operations was no longer an option. The Ottoman army was unlikely to make it through the winter, which would deprive the Russians of an important bargaining chip. So in an effort to resolve this challenge, Kutuzov made an unexpected offer to the grand vizier: why not conclude a permanent armistice on the condition of transferring the Ottoman army to Russian "safekeeping" (*na sokhranenie*) for the winter months? This would not be considered a formal capitulation because the Turkish soldiers would not be counted as prisoners of war; they would be instead treated as *musafirs* or "guests" of their benevolent captors, who would provide supplies, shelter, and medical care; weapons would be kept under joint control. This was a shrewd move on Kutuzov's part. First, such a deal would mean that the Russian army would no longer have to spend the winter months on the frozen and windy shores of the Danube but would be able to rest and recuperate at their winter cantonments. Second, the deal would ensure the survival of the enemy troops, so the Russians could continue to use this "phantom army" as a key bargaining chip in negotiations. Finally, Kutuzov hoped that this arrangement would allow the grand vizier to remain in power for a bit longer, as the news from Istanbul suggested that Ahmed Pasha might soon be dismissed.[71] Kutuzov knew him well and had developed close relations with him, so he naturally preferred dealing with him rather than with a new grand vizier. "He is a rare type of man among the Turks," Kutuzov admitted.[72] He hoped that the deal would help the vizier save face and allow him to continue negotiations, which with a bit of luck could lead to an agreement in the springtime.

On December 5, "my noble and distinguished friend," as Kutuzov referred to Ahmed Pasha, accepted this unusual deal.[73] A formal armistice was declared. Some 12,000 emaciated Turkish soldiers staggered out of the camp that, in the words of the contemporary Russian historian, looked like "the most dreadful of cemeteries." The Ottoman surrender was a remarkable accomplishment. Just eight months after taking command of the Army of Moldavia, Kutuzov had annihilated the main Ottoman army and achieved a breakthrough that had eluded all of his predecessors in this five-year-long conflict. His military victory could not have come at a better time for Russia, as it was gearing up for war with France. Napoleon was stunned and infuriated by the news from Bucharest. "Turks are dogs and scoundrels [*ces chiens, ces gredins*] who have a talent for getting themselves beaten in such a fashion," he fulminated in a private conversation that a Russian envoy reported to St. Petersburg.[74] The French emperor feared that with the loss of the main army, the Ottomans would have to negotiate a peace that would have been contrary to his "policies and interests." Time was of the essence for both sides. While Napoleon was dictating new letters and dispatching messengers on a mad dash to Istanbul, Kutuzov ordered his army to move to winter quarters, made arrangements for his Ottoman "guests," and turned to the crucial task of concluding a lasting peace agreement.[75]

| Between War and Peace,
January–June 1812

I N THE FINAL DAYS of December 1811, Kutuzov made a triumphant return
to Bucharest, "to the sound of thundering cannon and ringing bells."[1] For
the next several days "the city [was] illuminated with fireworks," he told
Catherine on December 25. "The streets are filled with placards emblazoned
with Greek inscriptions, some very beautiful indeed, and many [comparing
me] to Themistocles himself."

Even amid this revelry and the daily bustle—"I am on the go between war
and peace"—Kutuzov felt also profoundly discouraged.[2] The seven-month-
long campaign had left him feeling drained. "I have aged quite a bit in recent months," he confided in his wife. He complained about recurring bouts
of fevers, severe headaches, and "hemorrhoidal coughs" that laid him down
for days. Looking in the mirror, he saw an elderly man with a face wrinkled
from worries and concerns, his honey-brown eyes tired and full of melancholy.[3]
Loneliness and unhappiness permeate his letters. "I am getting sick when I reflect on how long I have been away from home," he wrote to his family. "I do not
even know what many of my grandchildren look like."[4] His daughter Elisabeth,
whom he had consoled so much after the tragic death of her husband and urged
to seek happiness with another man, finally heeded his advice and married for
the second time. Kutuzov was delighted to hear that his new son-in-law was
the czar's aide-de-camp Major General Nikolai Feodorovich Khitrovo, whom
he remembered as "a clever young man, a bit scrawny, but with an intelligent
and honest soul." The news also deepened his disaffection; he was upset about
missing the wedding festivities, not seeing his family, and being unable to play
with his grandkids. "I feel distraught that I still have to live God knows where
and that in the twilight of my life I cannot see any of my loved ones."[5]

The family was, he repeatedly declared, the only thing keeping him interested in this life, even if these relatives caused him considerable heartache. His son-in-law Nikolai Zakharovich Khitrovo—whose reckless behavior, as we have seen, had already caused so much anguish to Kutuzov and provoked a rupture with Prozorovskii in 1809—had managed to get himself involved in an even bigger scandal. He had irresponsibly engaged in a secret correspondence with the French ambassador and shared information that was sensitive enough for the Russian secret police to intervene; "there were rumors that he shared confidential intelligence, and not for nothing," commented one contemporary.[6] The government's response was swift and exacting. Khitrovo was arrested and exiled to the Vyatka region, a thousand miles east of St. Petersburg. The news stunned Kutuzov, who felt anguished to see his daughter's misfortune and feared her family would break up. "Mercifully, Anna is not the harshest of wives," he commented upon learning that his daughter had forgiven her husband and decided to join him in exile. But he remained anxious about her (and her children's) future. "They say each age has its passions," he wrote. "Presently, mine is to be devoted to my loved ones." He contemplated the passing nature of fame. "I cannot but laugh when I ponder my circumstances, all the honors I have been conferred, or the vast authority I have been given. I often think what it all means when I am getting compared to [ancient Greek warrior king] Agamemnon. Was he ever truly happy?" Fame, he noted, was "just a puff of smoke."[7]

He wished to sign a peace with the Turks so that he could return to his family and the quiet life. Yet negotiations kept getting prolonged week after week. The main obstacle remained the fact that "Russia found the pretensions of the Porte as exaggerated as those of Russia had appeared to the Porte."[8] The czar expected major Ottoman territorial cessions east and west of the Black Sea and autonomy for the Serbian rebels. The sultan's envoys did, in a departure from their earlier position, agree to a modification of the Russo-Ottoman boundary in Moldavia, but they were unwilling to accept the line proposed by their opponents.[9] The sultan's attitude toward territorial settlement in the Caucasus was even less accommodating, as it called for the reestablishment of the prewar territorial status quo and Russian withdrawal from western Georgia and neighboring territories. Nor were the Ottomans willing to provide any guarantees of autonomy for the Serbians, for it was rightly assumed in Istanbul that an autonomous Serbia would become a Russian "Trojan horse" and seriously impair the sultan's ability to control other Christian subjects.[10]

Ottoman intransigence was not the sole problem. Emperor Alexander was angered by the December armistice, which, in his mind, had treated the Ottomans too leniently. He argued that instead of accepting the enemy army for "safekeeping," Kutuzov should have attacked and forced it to "surrender at once." The czar was concerned that the Ottomans' refusal to accept Russian demands was damaging Russia's standing in Europe, and he preferred to wage war than to accept a peace "unworthy of Russia's honor." Therefore, he commanded Kutuzov to demand emphatically that the Ottoman delegates assent to Russian conditions at once; if they prevaricated, the general was to renounce the armistice, then declare the Ottoman soldiers prisoners of war and convey them to Russia.[11]

Kutuzov did not share the czar's belligerent ethos. He pointed out that his earlier instructions had explicitly stated that "His Majesty's primary objective is not to terminate current negotiations but to expedite the conclusion of peace."[12] The armistice worked to that purpose by both preserving the Ottoman army and maintaining a pretense of it still being in the field; no less important, in Kutuzov's mind, was the need to avoid unnecessary loss of Russian lives—hundreds of soldiers would have been needlessly killed or wounded, perhaps maimed for life, if he had tried to force the Ottoman army to surrender as the czar desired. Neither could he understand how resuming hostilities would bring a quick conclusion to the war when "cold season," "virtually unpassable roads," and the "impossibility of provisioning troops with basic essentials" prevented the Russian army from attempting any trans-Danubian operations.[13] Kutuzov did not share the czar's confidence that an offensive would necessarily break the Ottoman determination to fight. "The campaign of 1810 has shown that operations across the Danube fail to impress the enemy," he gently reminded him.[14]

Despite the general's appeal for diplomacy to be given another chance, the emperor's will prevailed. At the start of the new year, Kutuzov informed the Ottoman plenipotentiaries that the armistice was void and that the Ottoman troops were henceforth prisoners of war.[15] In a sign that he still hoped to reach a deal, he allowed the Ottoman plenipotentiaries to remain at Bucharest for the time being so that negotiations could continue. In February, he formed four mobile detachments for quick incursions across the Danube that were designed both to appease the czar and to increase pressure on the Turks. On February 14, while snow still covered the countryside, the first of these units crossed the river at Zimnicea and raided the towns of Svishtov, Nikopol, and Gulyantsi. Two days later, another detachment marched from Călăraşi to Silistra, despoiling the countryside. On February 17, it was the turn of the third and fourth detachments to foray into the area between Măcin, Babadag, and Tulcea, Kutuzov's old stomping grounds, where they captured almost a thousand Ottoman troops.[16]

"The future situation of the Continent seems to depend much on the question of peace or war between Russia and Turkey," declared a British newspaper on January 3, 1812.[17] There was a kernel of truth in the hyperbole. Napoleon's vast preparations and the rapid concentration of the Grande Armée in

East Prussia left no doubts that Russia and France, the two most powerful continental powers, were on the brink of war. This prospect caused considerable uneasiness in Russian court circles, and anxious officials in St. Petersburg implored the czar to moderate his stance in the ongoing negotiations with the Ottomans in an effort to secure the southern front before the new war broke out in the west. Minister of war Barclay de Tolly argued that a quick solution to the Russo-Turkish conflict might possibly avert a French attack altogether since it would free tens of thousands of troops and put Russia in a more advantageous defensive posture.[18] Nonetheless, Alexander mulishly resisted the advice of his counselors; in fact, in February he went as far as to contemplate a coordinated naval and land assault upon Istanbul to force the sultan to capitulate.[19] Kutuzov must have chuckled upon hearing this reckless idea. He knew how impractical it would be to attempt a campaign of such magnitude on the eve of war with the French Empire. He made no effort to implement it, confident that soon enough the czar would realize that in the current circumstances Russia simply could not afford to prolong this war any further.

In the spring of 1812 Napoleon launched a diplomatic offensive and concluded anti-Russian pacts with Prussia (February) and Austria (March). He then did his utmost to encourage Sultan Mahmud to end negotiations with the czar and accept an anti-Russian alliance with France. The French chargé d'affaires in Istanbul, Just-Pons-Florimond de Faÿ de La Tour Maubourg, did his best to assure the sultan of Napoleon's commitments and his readiness to defend the territorial integrity of the Ottoman Empire. Moreover, if the Turks were to renew the hostilities on the Danube, Napoleon promised to help the sultan recover not only Wallachia and Moldavia but the whole of the Crimean Peninsula as well. This was a rather enticing proposal. Show some fortitude and determination and the victory would be yours, the French told the Turks. Of course, a new army in the field would not hurt either.

For a time, it seemed that the Turks were willing to listen to the French entreaties. Negotiations in Bucharest had been prolonged while mobilization was under way in the eastern provinces of the empire. Citing letters and reports from Istanbul, Bucharest, Vidin, Belgrade, Semlin (Zemun), Pressburg, and Vienna, the French, German, and British newspapers informed their readers that the sultan had ordered his provincial governors to furnish "more numerous contingents" of troops. The French paper *Le Moniteur Universel* insisted that there was no outlook for a termination of hostilities between Russia and the Porte.[20]

However, Napoleon's "war-breathing message" to the sultan elicited a crucial change in the czar's attitudes.[21] As the winter cold gave way to the spring thaw, Alexander received a constant stream of ominous reports about French military and diplomatic preparations. Kutuzov provided his share of them. Based on the account supplied by the Sardinian envoy to the Porte, he described conversations the French diplomats had had at the Ottoman court. "Monsieur La Tour Maubourg recently told the [Imperial] Diwan that Napoleon intends . . . to annihilate the Russian Empire and has no doubt about the success of this endeavor because he is certain of the Prussian and Swedish support." Russia cannot "waste a minute," the Sardinian warned. "She is about to suffer a terrible blow."[22] By April, Alexander was sufficiently alarmed to seek peace with the sultan at all costs; he admitted to an Austrian envoy that he had been mistaken and now wanted to rectify this.[23] In his new instructions to Kutuzov, he no longer insisted on retaining the whole of Wallachia and Moldavia and consented to the imperial border on the Pruth River; he was even prepared to drop his territorial claims in the Caucasus. "International circumstances assume greater importance with each passing hour," he told Kutuzov on April 3. "By hastening to conclude peace with the Porte, you will render the greatest service to Russia. You will have an ever-lasting fame."[24]

For the next few weeks, Kutuzov engaged in frantic negotiations with the Ottoman plenipotentiaries. The process was long and challenging; at least twice the negotiations came close to breaking down. Nonetheless, Kutuzov held numerous meetings with Ottoman envoys in private, talking to them at length about the situation in Europe and explaining the advantages of accepting the deal with Russia. To prevent any outside interference, he insisted on discussions being conducted in absolute secrecy and restricted the flow of information so efficiently that the French and Austrian consuls could not report anything new to their respective governments; as late as May 27 they were unaware that the peace agreement had been reached. Even as Napoleon began his invasion of Russia on June 23, he remained confident that there would be no Russo-Ottoman accord. "The Turks are well aware of what is being prepared and, clumsy as they might be in politics, they are certainly not blind in questions of such great importance," the French emperor assured his ambassador to Russia.[25]

Napoleon was profoundly mistaken. The Russian representatives in Bucharest zealously promoted pacification between the czar and the sultan. In meetings with his Ottoman counterparts, Kutuzov reminded them that the Ottoman Empire had already suffered severely from the long and diffi- cult war and that its economic and military resources had been desperately strained. The Arabs, Serbs, Albanians, Greeks, Kurds, and Syrians were in open revolt. There were disquieting reports of riots among the Janissaries, who were tired of fighting and urged the sultan to end the war. This rising discontent served as an unsettling reminder that these volatile troops had, on so many other occasions, presided over the deposition of sultans who had incurred their displeasure. Kutuzov warned that even with a war against France looming, Russia was still capable of conducting operations against the Turks, a threat he underscored with an announcement that the Army of Moldavia had started preparations for the summer campaign.

More crucially, Kutuzov told the Ottoman plenipotentiary that a French victory in Europe was not in the Ottomans' best interests. Napoleon had long been considering partitioning the Ottoman Empire and had in fact offered Russia a chance to do that. As proof, he revealed Napoleon's letter urging Alexander to avoid the war by reconfirming earlier Franco-Russian agreements, including ones dealing with the dismemberment of Ottoman territory.[26] Moreover, he shared news of the arrival of Napoleon's aide-de-camp Louis Narbonne in Vilna. Although the Frenchman's actual mission was to see if Russia was ready for war, Kutuzov portrayed it as Napoleon's effort to a reach a compromise with the czar, which would inescapably involve the Ottoman matters. The specter of another Tilsit-like agreement, he hoped, would make the Turks more agreeable.

These revelations helped widen the Franco-Ottoman divide. "[Napoleon] pretends to be nice to our faces," observed the exasperated Ottoman diplomat, "but he is actually conspiring to apportion our realm behind our backs."[27] The Ottoman plenipotentiaries understood that in this volatile international environment their empire could not afford to wage war while coping with burgeoning internal revolts. There were no guarantees that Napoleon would not sacrifice the sultan's friendship, just as he had done on multiple occasions in earlier years. Besides, an open alliance with France would have entailed a direct confrontation with Britain, which the Turks were keen to avoid.

———·——

As Russia's international position became more and more difficult, Emperor Alexander, conveniently forgetting about his own refusal to moderate his demands until recently, began to grow impatient with Kutuzov's management of the seven-month-long negotiations. "Peace with Turkey is not moving forward fast enough, while the excesses committed by our troops have exasperated the inhabitants in Moldavia and Wallachia," the czar told one of his confidants. "Indolence and intrigues reign everywhere [in the Army of Moldavia]." He believed that Kutuzov was the reason for this and was not capable "of showing either energy, good intentions or celerity in his undertakings. . . . Time is running out."[28]

The confidant in question was Admiral Paul Chichagov. The son of an admiral, Chichagov had graduated from the Naval Corps and begun military service in 1779. Over the next decade, he distinguished himself fighting the Swedes in the Baltic, then resided in Britain for two years and, upon returning home, commanded various ships. The death of Catherine II was a turning point in Chichagov's career. He was among the many officers who were dismissed in Emperor Paul's purges, and he spent two years in disgrace; the czar soon changed his mind, recalling him to active service and promoting him to rear admiral before changing his mind a second time and imprisoning him, only to forgive and reinstate him once more.[29] Chichagov's career prospects improved under Alexander, and he became a vice admiral and the minister of the navy and spearheaded reforms to modernize the Russian navy. Contemporaries were deeply divided over this man, whose candor and honesty earned him many enemies. The admiral expressed his opinions bluntly, even when dealing with sovereigns.[30] Some found him "a strange man" full of "arrogance" and "pretentiousness" but also praised his "determination, firmness, strength of conviction and independence of spirit."[31] Count Fedor Tolstoy, who served under Chichagov and knew him quite well, thought that the admiral was "a very intelligent and educated man, of upright character," who loathed "the court sycophants" and was, in turn, "hated by virtually the entire court and all the empty-headed but haughty nobility."[32] Few appreciated Chichagov's constant criticism of the Russian aristocracy and his desire to see the Russian state and society reformed. He was denounced as a "Jacobin" and "liberal." Even de Maistre, who was otherwise effusive in his praise of the admiral, had to admit that "his excellent character traits" were overshadowed by two "grave flaws": indifference toward religion and "loathing, even a profound hatred, toward every principle established in [Russia], where he only sees feeblemindedness, ignorance, misbehavior, and despotism."[33] The fact that Chichagov had once expressed admiration for Napoleon—even displaying a bust of him in the Navy Ministry's office—was certainly not lost on his many critics.[34] Yet despite this constant tittle-tattle and denigration, Alexander was convinced that the admiral was just the person he needed to replace Kutuzov and bring an end to the war.[35]

The news of Chichagov's appointment to the Army of Moldavia came as a thunderbolt. "What a strange idea it is to entrust a land force to an admiral," quipped a visiting Swedish general.[36] Sardinian envoy Joseph de Maistre believed it was Chancellor Nikolai Rumyantsev, Chichagov's archenemy, who leaked the news to Kutuzov even before it was made public and warned him that "unless he signed the peace treaty at once, it would be done by the admiral."[37]

Kutuzov must have been infuriated. After months of hard campaigning, military victories, and protracted diplomatic talks, he was now being unceremoniously cast aside so that an upstart admiral, lacking soldiering or diplomatic experience, could reap all the acclaim for ending the war. All his talk of fleeting glory notwithstanding, Kutuzov was not averse to recognition and desired respect. Knowledge that his replacement was just days away from Bucharest impelled him to push hard to wrap up negotiations. "Sparing neither energy nor skills," as he later put it, he prodded and nudged the grand vizier and his envoys until they finally accepted a compromise and put their signatures to paper. And just in time. The Russian admiral arrived at the

Wallachian capital on May 18 only to discover that the preliminaries had been signed just the day before.[38] The admiral had no choice but to hand the general an imperial rescript praising his "distinguished accomplishments" and recalling him to St. Petersburg.[39]

Chichagov and Kutuzov both felt slighted by all this: the former was robbed of a chance to shape the peace, while the latter scorned the upstart who almost deprived him of his laurels. The admiral further strained his relations with the general when he began filing reports about alleged mismanagement and abuses committed under Kutuzov's supervision. At the heart of this matter was the very nature of the Russian presence in Wallachia and Moldavia. The Russians may have come promising to liberate the principalities from the Turks in the fall of 1806, but five years on, the prospects of freedom and a brighter future waned amid the grim realities of war and conquest, exploitation and repression. Like the French revolutionaries (a comparison he would have certainly found distasteful), Kutuzov believed the "liberated" peoples had to defray the costs of liberating and developing them. In August 1811, for example, he was disappointed to hear that the residents of Bucharest were complaining about extra dues he expected them to pay to repair the city's streets and sidewalks; local customs did not require inhabitants to pay any such taxes if their homes did not have gateways leading to the street. Kutuzov pointed to "the common well-being of all residents" and insisted that the monies be collected.[40] But he also expected the locals to bear the cost of the war. His correspondence shows clearly that he did his best to uphold the authority of the Wallachian governing council (*diwan*) but expected it to be fully compliant with Russian interests and pay for the needs of the army.

The arrival of the Russian troops brought little freedom to the common people, whether rural or urban, but a whole lot of control, increased taxation, requisitioning of supplies, and policing. When praising Major General Sergei Tuchkov for administering fortresses in southern Bessarabia, Kutuzov pointed out that the general had found less than 10,000 rubles in the local treasury upon his arrival but in just two years increased the annual revenue to over 250,000 rubles, which allowed him to undertake major renovations at Izmail and Kilia, while "Brăila has been almost entirely rebuilt."[41] He was very pleased with this improvement, but local residents would have certainly felt differently. Many found Russian demands exorbitant. "I am extremely displeased to learn that the Bucharest merchants are refusing to pay the annual tax that has been levied on their stalls to cover the needs of the Russian Imperial troops," ranted Kutuzov in August 1811. He had "ringleaders" arrested and transported to Russia for imprisonment, while other merchants were compelled to comply.[42]

The Ottoman practice of granting commercial concessions to foreign merchants only further complicated matters, since many Wallachian notables claimed that they were French or Austrian subjects and therefore not subject to taxes. This was a serious issue. When the governing council surveyed the merchants of Bucharest, it discovered, for example, that one in five claimed foreign citizenship and thus avoided taxes.[43] Small as this group might seem, it controlled a significant share of local trade and, if taxes were equally applied, would be expected to pay almost half of all taxes. Even members of the Diwan argued that the Ottoman concessions had to be revised, otherwise "the Wallachian merchants themselves would start avoiding payments."[44] Citing "natural law," Kutuzov could not see "any compelling reasons" for maintaining such a system and instead suggested that equality of taxation might be more appropriate and worthwhile.[45] Starting in the summer of 1811, he had worked with the members of the Diwan to revise the capitulatory system and create a uniform annual tax that the entire merchant estate of Wallachia, irrespective of citizenship, was liable to pay. Merchants were required to submit to new regulations or face harsh consequences: "If any merchant resists newly levied taxes, their stalls must be shut down and sealed and their rights to commerce restricted; they must be placed under strict police surveillance to ensure that they are not trading in secret."[46]

Relentless tax levies, requisitioning, and heavy-handed administration naturally bred plenty of resentment against the Russian authority in general and Kutuzov in particular. Upon arriving at Bucharest, Chichagov made the most of it all, alleging Kutuzov's incompetence and mismanagement. "Should one be surprised to see this when General Kutuzov, solely concerned about his personal pleasures, had no qualms about kidnapping and exiling a member of the Governing Council of Wallachia, who happened to be the husband of one of his mistresses [Guliano]?" Chichagov scathingly remarked.[47] The admiral was disingenuous. There is no denying that the occupation caused severe suffering and misery to the mass of the people in Wallachia. However, Kutuzov's correspondence offers plenty of examples of him trying to resolve issues caused by quartering troops with civilians or by the Russian officers "willfully changing billeting assignments, confiscating transports, and maltreating the inhabitants." Each time, he demanded that the culprits be held accountable, and he threatened to hold "divisional commanders and regimental chefs" responsible for any further incidents.[48]

Chichagov also touched off a bitter debate with Kutuzov by insisting that the preliminary agreement with the Turks must be revised and that the final settlement should be made contingent upon Ottoman consent to a military alliance with Russia.[49] In vain did Kutuzov protest that this was a futile endeavor that would waste precious time and undermine the whole process.[50] He pointed out that the sultan would never allow the arming and recruitment of his Christian subjects, as the czar expected, nor would he consent to ally himself with an enemy country. A quick agreement with the Ottomans would be more profitable to the Russians. "The peace treaty would inevitably draw Napoleon's displeasure and ire onto the Porte," he reasoned. "The more the French emperor threatens the Porte, the more the sultan would be inclined to consider our side of the matter, for an alliance with us would then become the means of ensuring his own safety."[51] Convinced that Russian interests would be ill served by any further demands, he insisted on signing the final treaty over Chichagov's protests and left it up to him to negotiate a separate treaty of alliance.[52] As subsequent events showed, the admiral spent weeks negotiating such an agreement but was unable to induce the Ottomans to agree to it, just as Kutuzov expected.

In any event, on May 28, 1812, the treaty ending the longest war between the Russian and Ottoman Empires was formally signed at a humble inn in Bucharest. It reflected both the Ottoman dexterity in exploiting Russia's international predicaments to gain very favorable terms and the Russian sense of urgency and pragmatism. The signatories agreed that there would "forever be peace, friendship, and harmony" between the two empires, and a general amnesty and pardon were given to subjects on both sides. By the Treaty of Bucharest, the Pruth River was established as the "perpetual" boundary separating the two states, from the point where it enters Moldavia to its confluence with the Danube. This meant that after almost six years of fighting, the czar was able to snatch Bessarabia from the Turks, but that the great prize of the Danubian Principalities was denied to him; the Russian troops had to evacuate all Moldavia to the right of the Pruth, as well as the whole of Wallachia. Though a far cry from the czar's original demands, the Russian territorial acquisition was sizable nevertheless.[53] The Ottomans pledged to restore all former privileges and immunities in Moldavia and Wallachia and to exempt local inhabitants from all taxes for two years, so that they might recover from the ravages of the war. All prisoners captured during the war were to be exchanged. The Ottomans agreed to make reparations for any losses suffered by the Russian merchant marine in the Mediterranean and promised to employ their good offices to mediate in the ongoing conflict between Russia and Persia.[54] One of the crucial diplomatic issues at Bucharest involved the future of Serbia, where for the last eight years Russia had sustained the flames of the rebellion. Article 8 of the treaty dashed any hopes the Serbs nurtured of independence, as it required them to restore to the Turks all fortifications and to resume the payment of tribute to the sultan; in return, the Ottomans granted the rebels a full amnesty and conferred upon the Belgrade pashalik an autonomous status like that of the Ionian Islands. But this was hardly enough to satisfy Karadjordje and his supporters, who were bound to be disappointed and heartbroken;

after eight years of fighting, they were now told to welcome the Turks back, knowing well that the returning Ottoman forces would not be inclined to be merciful.

The Treaty of Bucharest left much to be desired on both sides. Sultan Mahmud II was, in fact, so displeased with the outcome of the negotiations that he dismissed the grand vizier and had one of the lead Ottoman negotiators beheaded. The initial Russian reaction, though not as violent, was still quite critical of the treaty, which frittered away five years' worth of conquests. Russian foreign minister Rumyantsev expressed deep concern over the deleterious effects the treaty would have upon Russian prestige in the Balkans.[55] Kutuzov understood what the foreign minister did not—that a flawed peace was better than remaining at war at a time when Russia was confronting an unprecedented threat. The czar agreed. On June 23, just as Napoleon commanded his army to cross the Niemen River and commenced his invasion, Alexander approved the Treaty of Bucharest. This was, in his words, "a god-given peace," for it came at a crucial moment for Russia—it secured the southwestern frontiers, denied Napoleon a vital ally, and freed up tens of thousands of Russian troops to menace the French flank and lines of communication. "Which of us in the French army can ever forget his aston-ishment on hearing the news of the fateful treaty in the midst of the Russian plains," remembered a French participant. "How anxiously our looks turned toward our right uncovered flank."[56]

Thus ended yet another page in Kutuzov's life. He handed over military and diplomatic affairs to Chichagov and departed from Bucharest. Once more he was leaving with a heavy heart, unsure how the czar would react to the peace treaty he had negotiated. Instead of going to St. Petersburg, he first headed to his family estate at Goroshki to wait and see. Before leaving the army, he addressed his soldiers with a special proclamation, bidding them farewell and praising them for their gallantry, dedication, and perseverance. He reminded them of "the feats so gloriously performed each and every day during the campaign of 1811. What have you not gone through, the great warriors of the Danube!?" After listing the victories at Ruse, Slobozia, Silistra, Turtukai, Vidin, and other places, he concluded, "The memory of your deeds will remain forever engraved in the hearts of the patriots of our beloved country . . . and will serve as a reminder of the best hours of my life."[57]

PART V

| The Fateful Year

S TANDING ON THE HILL overlooking the Nieman River, which marked the
boundary of the Russian Empire, Emperor Napoleon watched as tens of
thousands of troops from his Grande Armée marched across pontoon bridges.
It was June 24, 1812, a clear summer morning. "Soldiers, Russia is swept
away by her fate," Napoleon exhorted his troops in a proclamation. "She
places us between dishonour and war: the choice cannot be in doubt. Let us,
then, march forward!"[1]

Kutuzov was still at his estate in northern Ukraine when he received the
news of the invasion. Over the previous two years he had followed Napoleon's
massive military preparations. Despite having more than a quarter million
troops tied down in Spain, the French emperor drew upon the resources of his
vast empire and raised close to 600,000 men (not counting a veritable army
of political officials, servants, and attendant women) for a new war in the east.
Of these, just half were French; the rest were Poles, Italians, Swiss, Bavarians,
Badenese, Württembergians, Hessians, Westphalians, Saxons, Croats, Danes,
Spaniards, and Portuguese, supported by two large contingents of Austrians
and Prussians. The task of equipping, provisioning, and moving such a
multitude was colossal, requiring patience, money, and organizational skill,
all of which Napoleon amply possessed.

By the late spring of 1812, the Grande Armée had assembled along Russia's
western frontier in three groups. Napoleon gathered his main force between
Warsaw, Königsberg, and Tilsit. Marshal Jacques-Étienne Macdonald's X
Corps, with Prussian units, guarded the northern flank of the Grande Armée
and had the task of advancing into Russia's Baltic provinces. Austrian corps
under General Karl Philip Schwarzenberg, supported by Franco-Saxon
troops, covered the southern flank, and threatened the Volhynian provinces
of Russia. On May 28, just as Kutuzov finalized the peace treaty with the

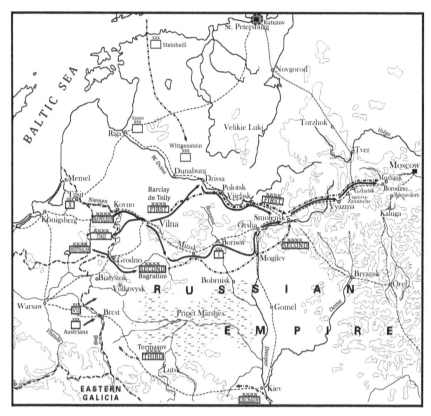

MAP 13 Napoleon's Invasion of Russia

Ottomans, Napoleon set out from the Saxon capital, Dresden, to join his army. A month later he was on the shores of the Niemen, near Kovno (now Kaunas), reconnoitering the area and supervising the construction of large pontoon bridges across the river. The die was cast.

Emperor Alexander was then attending a ball at General Bennigsen's country manor near Vilna, less than sixty miles southeast of Kovno, when his minister of police whispered in his ear that the war had commenced. He was not surprised by the news; Russian intelligence had given him ample warning. He had just 250,000 Russian soldiers to confront the Napoleonic juggernaut, and even these troops were scattered among three major armies and a handful of separate corps that had been mobilized. The 1st Western Army, commanded by general and minister of war Mikhail Barclay de Tolly, held positions in the Lithuanian countryside surrounding Vilna. Farther south was the 2nd Western Army, under Peter Bagration, whose units were spread out in the area between Volkovysk and Belostock (Białystok). General Alexander Tormasov commanded the 3rd Reserve Army of Observation, which was gathered at Lutsk and covered Ukrainian provinces. In addition to these three armies, Lieutenant General Baron Faddei von Steinheil Finland Corps in the north and Admiral Chichagov's newly renamed Army of the Danube in the south covered the extreme flanks of the Russian army.

Alexander took the news of the French crossing the Niemen in stride, keeping it to himself until the dinner festivities were over. Returning to his headquarters, he issued a proclamation condemning Napoleon's aggression and urging his men to resist. "We are left with no other choice but to turn to arms and appeal to the Almighty, the Witness and the Defender of the truth," declared the Russian sovereign. "The ancient blood of the valiant Slavs flows in your veins. Warriors! You must defend your Faith, your Country, and your Liberty!"[2]

Behind the defiant rhetoric, however, the reality was grim. The Russian armies were no match for the assault that Napoleon unleashed against them. More worrisome than the inferiority in numbers was the nebulousness of Russian military strategy. Valuable time had been wasted in drafting and discussing various options—more than thirty, by one count—all of which considerably underestimated the enemy's strength and consequently were ineffectual. Ultimately the czar lent a willing ear to Prussian general Karl Ludwig August Friedrich von Pfuel (Phull), whose strategy required the 1st Army to fall back to the Drissa fortified camp on the Western Dvina River while the 2nd Army turned the French flank and line of communication. Sound as the plan looked on paper, it ignored facts on the ground, for the Russians were outnumbered by at least two to one and Bagration's small army was in no position to attempt a diversion. Barclay de Tolly and a small group of officers who surrounded him understood that neither of the Russian armies could stand and fight. They examined recent British operations in Spain and were struck by the Duke of Wellington's defensive campaign, which had convinced them that the only way to prevail over Napoleon in Russia was through a similarly protracted and defensive war; the Prussian general and military reformer Gerhard von Scharnhorst urged the czar to "wage a defensive war like Wellington [does]." Even those French officers who had secretly met with a Russian spy resident in Paris in early 1812 advised the Russians to avoid decisive battles.[3]

Retreat was, therefore, the only sensible strategy, but it was never formally adopted or clearly communicated to army and corps commanders, who were exasperated by conflicting orders and the insistence on surrendering western Russian provinces. Arsenii Zakrevskii, the head of Barclay de Tolly's "special chancellery" (i.e., military intelligence), expressed the frustration felt by many. "We have meandered around speedily," he wrote General Mikhail Vorontsov in early July, "and then retreated even faster to that unfortunate Drissa position, which, it seems, would lead us straight to destruction." He thought that Pfuel should be shot.[4]

Kutuzov was not involved in any of these deliberations. He had been away from the capital for too long and had never been close enough to the czar to offer him advice on strategy and policy. Had he been able to, he would have counseled caution. Upon learning of the French invasion, he rushed from his estates to St. Petersburg, where the public welcomed him. "Count Kutuzov arrived here yesterday," wrote one St. Petersburgian on July 9. "His loved ones carry him in their arms while others . . . are all excited that he will live among us."[5] For the next few days he rested and entertained a long queue of visitors, all eager to know his opinion on current affairs. "Numerous people go to see him, pestering him with questions as if he is some sort of a prophet," remarked one contemporary.[6] Others were puzzled by the czar's silence on Kutuzov's recent successes. Despite winning the Russo-Ottoman war and bringing about peace with the Porte, the victorious general received none of the formal receptions or recognitions that were usually granted on such occasions. The czar effectively snubbed him. "Kutuzov has been treated just like another officer in spite of his accomplishments in the last war," commented Nikolai Longinov, the empress consort's secretary. "The czar did not even utter a single word about any of it." Whatever his feelings, Kutuzov did not complain, instead delighting in seeing his family after months of separation. He longed for a respite. "I found a garden where I can indulge in daydreaming," he told Elisabeth.[7]

On July 24, the Committee of Ministers, composed of the senior figures of the imperial government, held an emergency meeting to discuss the news from the front lines. The Russian armies had fallen back more than 300 miles in the searing summer heat and heavy rains, consuming, destroying, or carting away all usable provisions, leaving little for the invaders to pilfer. Realizing the pointlessness of Pfuel's strategy, Barclay de Tolly abandoned Drissa and withdrew in the direction of Smolensk, leaving General Peter Wittgenstein with some 20,000 men to cover the approaches to St. Petersburg, to which the czar had repaired. In the south, Bagration, frustrated by the vague and contradictory orders he was receiving from headquarters, decided to march first to Minsk and then to Smolensk, eluding Napoleon's enveloping maneuvers and gaining minor victories along the way. More worrisome was the news from the Baltic provinces. Franco-Prussian forces had steadily advanced into the Lithuanian countryside, defeating the Russians at Eckau on July 19 and approaching Riga. Although the enemy was still some 450 miles from St. Petersburg, the Committee of Ministers was sufficiently alarmed to start preparations to defend the imperial capital. They agreed unanimously that Kutuzov was the best candidate at hand and offered him the position.[8] Emperor Alexander accepted the committee's recommendation, signing the decree appointing him commander of Russian forces in St. Petersburg and the neighboring Finland province. "Our current circumstances necessitate the establishment of a corps to defend St. Petersburg," he wrote Kutuzov.

"Your military talents and long experience give me full confidence to expect that you will fully validate my trust."[9] We do not know how Kutuzov reacted to this new assignment. His surviving letters are silent on this subject. Considering his persistent complaints of old age, fatigue, and separation from family, he might not have been thrilled about returning to active service so soon after an arduous campaign—one that the czar had not even acknowledged. But he understood the critical importance of the moment. The fatherland was in danger, and everyone had to do their share. "We might lack sufficient numbers," enthused one resident of St. Petersburg. "But the hero Kutuzov is with us!"[10]

Kutuzov accepted the position. His first decision was to establish the Narva Corps, consisting of 8,000 men, by recalling troops from Finland and mobilizing forces in St. Petersburg.[11] On July 29, before he could proceed any further, he learned that the Assembly of the Nobility of St. Petersburg had held an emergency meeting to discuss ways it could support the Russian war effort. After some discussion, the assembly decided to raise a militia force (*opolchenye*) and unanimously voted to nominate Kutuzov as its leader.[12] A delegation was sent to invite the general to the assembly. Eyewitnesses testified to Kutuzov being "deeply moved" by this nomination and humbly accepting the command in response to the nobility's petition. But he was also blindsided by the turn of events and, as Ivan Odenthal noted in a letter to a friend, "he naturally could not decline it."[13] On his way to receive the czar's confirmation, he was stunned to hear that the nobility of Moscow had also elected him commander of the local militia.[14] Evgraf Komarovskii—the man whose police investigations had contributed to Kutuzov's dismissal ten years earlier—broke the news to the general. "I hear the nobility of *both capitals* had named you as their and the Fatherland's defender," he blurted out, assuming the general already knew about the vote. Kutuzov was overcome with emotion, declaring that "this is the best reward of my life!"[15] He could not, however, accept both nominations and had to choose. Ultimately he declined the leadership of the Moscow militia and stayed in St. Petersburg, close to his family and the court. He assumed command of the St. Petersburg militia and told the delegates of the Assembly of the Nobility, "There are so many things I want to tell you but will only say this—with this honor, you have exalted my entire career."[16]

For the next three weeks Kutuzov worked to organize the defenses of the Russian imperial capital. He corresponded with the commander in chief of St. Petersburg (General S. Vyazmitinov), members of the Imperial State Council, and the leaders of the local nobility, who rallied around the patriotic cause and pledged contributions to it. He supported the creation of five volunteer Cossack regiments, formed a river flotilla, examined the fortifications around St. Petersburg, and drew up plans to repair and enhance them.[17] All the while he worked to raise militia forces in St. Petersburg and neighboring

Novgorod, personally supervising the recruitment process and drafting the statute that outlined the militia's structure, ranks, equipment, training, pay, and provisioning. On August 4, he reported to the czar that the St. Petersburg nobility had agreed to a levy of one serf for every twenty-five they owned, resulting in the mobilization of thousands of militia. They were allowed to wear their peasant clothing but had to be trained and equipped. Kutuzov drafted simplified training exercises to prepare these recruits for the rigors of combat. "The first step in this training process," he wrote in his instructions, "is to educate the warrior about his place in the rank and file, so that he knows the person who stands in front and behind him as well to the right and the left." Kutuzov wanted to impress on the raw recruits the importance of unit cohesion, coordination, and group action. The alternative was "unorganized throngs."[18] Alexander Mikhailovskii-Danilevskii, the future historian, then a fresh graduate of the University of Göttingen, was appointed as an aide-de-camp to Kutuzov. He was impressed to see how much energy the old man put into every detail of his work: "He committed himself to it with all his heart, attending recruit receptions, supervising their outfitting, and giving advice and instruction to individual recruits."[19] In just four weeks, the St. Petersburg militia recruited, trained, and equipped 29,420 men, who were soon on their way to the front lines.

Emperor Alexander set additional tasks for Kutuzov. On August 11, he was instructed to establish two large camps on the outskirts of St. Petersburg, where recruits could undergo proper training before proceeding to the armies.[20] A day later the czar appointed him the commander of all land and naval forces in St. Petersburg, Kronstadt, and Finland so that he could better coordinate efforts to protect the imperial capital.[21] The man whom critics derided for "insurmountable idleness and apathy that extended to everything" (as Langeron had put it) was repeatedly entrusted with multiple responsibilities. As if in recognition, the czar finally publicly acknowledged Kutuzov's "diligent service and zealous work" to defeat the Ottomans and negotiate the Peace of Bucharest; a special service was held at the Kazan Cathedral, where the future American president John Quincy Adams, serving as ambassador to Russia, first saw Kutuzov amid a large crowd of people.[22] Judging from surviving evidence, Alexander did not do this of his own volition. Nikolai Longinov, who served at the court and was well informed of what had transpired there, confided to a friend that after not hearing anything from the czar, Kutuzov and his supporters had "pressed for the Emperor's opinion." The general was told to choose between a princely title and some reward for his wife.[23] He chose the former, and the imperial decree of August 10 elevated him to the ranks of the princes of the Russian Empire. It must have been a bittersweet moment for the boy from Pskov province, who had now entered the rarified ranks of the Russian aristocracy—a moment of triumph but also of anxiety over the czar's continued antipathy toward him.[24]

Kutuzov's supporters were not content. "Kutuzov has been made a prince," commented a contemporary four days after the announcement. "But even this honor cannot add sufficient radiance to his great deeds. The public desires to see him with the title of generalissimo!"[25]

The newly minted prince had been anxiously following events in the war zone. The previous five weeks had been dark ones for the Russians, as news arrived of their armies retreating and abandoning vast provinces in the west. The war was still hundreds of miles away from St. Petersburg, but everyone could feel its destructive nature. Dozens of noble families lost their entire estates. "The Sollogubs are completely ruined since all of their estates were in Byelorussia," wrote the dowager empress's lady-in-waiting Maria Volkova in August. She lamented that Matvei Tolstoy, who was married to Kutuzov's eldest daughter, Praskovya, had "only three hundred souls left out of 6,000 that he owns" after his Byelorussian estates were occupied by the French. "No matter how much you try to raise your spirits," commented Volkova, "you cannot but get disheartened hearing the news of deaths and devastations every day, from dawn till dusk."[26]

There were, however, encouraging signs too. By early August, as the two Russian armies united at Smolensk, Napoleon's hopes for a quick victory were dashed. Despite their best efforts, the French and their allies had failed to engage the main Russian army and were now hundreds of miles inland, suffering from attrition and disease. The sheer size of the Grande Armée sapped it. Napoleon raged about dilatory movements and lax leadership; just eight days after starting the invasion, he complained in a letter to Berthier that "nothing gets done."[27] Indeed, internal reports and correspondence reveal the deep sense of uncertainty at the French headquarters. Napoleon remained poorly informed of the enemy's positions and knew nothing of their intentions, not to mention local terrain and routes. "Our maps are so deficient that they are practically unusable," he had bemoaned to Berthier on June 25.[28] Three weeks later the Grande Armée was so far ahead of its supply trains that Napoleon was compelled to halt at Vitebsk to allow reinforcements and supplies to reach him. He spent two precious weeks here, mulling his next steps and considering if it might be better to remain in the Russian borderland instead of pursuing the elusive enemy farther to the east. In the end, he decided to press on, convinced that the Russians would make a stand soon enough and that he had still plenty of time before the snows came.

The Russian armies, meanwhile, faced a profound crisis. Their retreat had caused great consternation; there were loud murmurs about the Russian military leadership and questions about military strategy. What was the point of this constant retreating? Why were so many towns and villages simply abandoned to the enemy? The word "treason" began to be used more frequently.

Such grievances were exacerbated by sharp discord among the Russian aristocratic officers and the "foreigners" who had gained influence at court and in the army. Non-Russians had always been a significant element in the Russian military; now Napoleon's victories had driven numerous foreign-born officers to Russia, with the German states furnishing the largest number of them. Their arrival caused friction with the native officers, who complained about the foreigners getting preferential treatment and usurping senior posts in headquarters. "One hears nothing but German spoken at our headquarters," complained one Russian court official in a letter.[29]

At the 1st Western Army, Barclay de Tolly was surrounded by a group of foreign-born officers who advocated defensive strategy. Avoiding decisive battles, waging a war of attrition, targeting the enemy's lines of supply and communication, and staying resolute in prosecuting the war—such was the essence of the strategy they promoted.[30] Barclay de Tolly happened to share these sentiments and insisted on retreating, despite enormous public pressure to do otherwise. He could not boast ancient nobility, titles, serfs, or wealth; as one contemporary put it, "without his salary, he would have died penniless on a pile of excrement because he possessed nothing."[31] Barclay de Tolly's Scottish ancestors had settled in Livonia, on the eastern shores of the Baltic Sea, in the seventeenth century and loyally served the dukes of Courland and Semigallia and, by the late eighteenth century, the Russian sovereigns as well. Born in Riga, Barclay de Tolly grew up in St. Petersburg and had served in the Russian army since his youth, distinguishing himself in the storming of Ochakov (where Kutuzov was wounded) in 1788. Unlike many of his colleagues, he had not served under Kutuzov during the Austerlitz campaign, but he fought with distinction in the subsequent wars against Napoleon, earning accolades for his performance at Pultusk and Eylau. After Russia's war against Sweden in 1808–1809, he became the first governor-general of newly annexed Finland.[32]

His rise from humble beginnings to the pinnacle of his profession, however, caused envy among fellow officers who deplored the fact that Barclay de Tolly had been promoted to full general in contravention of the traditional seniority system.[33] Their animosity only increased after the czar appointed him to the post of minister of war in February 1810. Barclay de Tolly's administrative and structural reforms of the Russian armed forces, though timely and well conceived, earned him even more detractors. In the summer of 1812, exasperated by the Russian continuous retreats and ignorant of the full scope of challenges confronting the army, these officers undermined confidence in the commander in chief. They even taught the rank and file to call him by the nickname "Boltai da i Tolko"—"All Bark and No Bite." Every new stage of the retreat intensified the rumors about turncoats selling out Russia and leading the army to its destruction. Barclay de Tolly struggled to parry such criticisms. He never fully embraced Russian culture, always preferring to speak

German. His aloof demeanor earned him few friends; even those who praised his honesty and dedication spoke of him as a "heavy German character" and "a German soul" who "blended conceit with brusqueness."[34] Such perceptions were exacerbated by the fact that Barclay de Tolly surrounded himself with German officers, whom a Russian officer, speaking for many, compared to "fat poisonous spiders" quietly weaving their webs of intrigue and betrayal.[35]

All this was a stark contrast to Peter Bagration, Barclay de Tolly's counterpart, who, though also of foreign descent, had embraced Russian identity with the zeal of a religious convert. A scion of the royal dynasty of Georgia, the prince lacked formal education but was a gifted soldier. His assault on the French-held St. Gotthard Pass in the Alps in September 1799 was valiant, and the stand at Hollabrunn that saved the Russian army six years later was truly heroic. At Austerlitz, he was the only commander who came out with his reputation intact, and he was lionized at the English Club, the focal point of the Russian aristocracy in Moscow. And then there was his daring crossing of the frozen Gulf of Bothnia to threaten the Swedish capital in March 1809. Striking in appearance—dark complexion, large aquiline nose, arched brows, keen and quick eyes—Bagration seemed to radiate martial glory and prowess. The army and the public adored his impetuosity, combative instincts, and fiery temperament. To some, he was on a par with the Homeric heroes. Russian poet Gregory Derzhavin thought Bagration was no less than "Bog-rati-on," or "the God of the Army," a sobriquet that soon enough was on everyone's lips.[36] The prince's temperament made him the antithesis of the calm and orderly Barclay de Tolly. He could not bring himself to accept defensive strategy. "We must seize our destiny," he wrote Barclay de Tolly. "The entire army—nay, all of Russia—demands attacking!"[37]

Barclay de Tolly, as the minister of war, could claim authority, but Bagration held seniority in rank; given his stellar fighting record, he might, with some justice, consider that he had the better claim to the title of commander in chief. The impending meeting of the two commanders on August 2 was therefore eagerly awaited. To everyone's surprise, both generals displayed unusual tact, realizing the importance of unity and collaboration. When Bagration arrived accompanied by his generals and aides-de-camp, Barclay de Tolly met him wearing his parade uniform complete with medals and sash, plumed bicorn in hand. The two men then had a private conversation, each apologizing for any injustice he might have caused. Bagration praised his colleague's withdrawal from Vilna, while Barclay de Tolly complimented the Georgian on eluding Napoleon's entrapments. Pleased with the meeting, the prince, though senior in rank, agreed to subordinate himself to Barclay de Tolly. For the moment, good relations were established and the unity of command seemed to have been achieved.

As the Russian armies concentrated at Smolensk, everyone wondered about the next step to take. Should the armies continue retreating? How far? Was it time to take a stand and fight the enemy? On August 6, as the Russian generals gathered at the council of war, there was naturally considerable divergence of opinion. Recent intelligence reports suggested that Napoleon's forces were scattered over a wide area to the west and that a quick and vigorous counterstrike might surprise them. After a vociferous debate, the hawks prevailed; the council voted to drive the attack home with the full force of both armies. Barclay de Tolly, skeptical about the outcome of such a counterattack, agreed to the new plan only with a strict proviso that the armies would not go beyond a three-day march distance from Smolensk. The plan, thus confined, was but a half-measure.

The following day, August 7, the Russian armies advanced westward along a twenty-mile front. Yet just hours into the operation, Bagration and Barclay de Tolly had a falling-out. The latter received urgent news, later proved to be false, that the enemy had appeared north of Smolensk; it seemed Napoleon was attempting an enveloping maneuver to sever the Russian line of communication. Not waiting for further confirmation, Barclay de Tolly halted his entire army and moved it northeast, in contravention of the operational plan that the council of war had approved. Bagration was furious. For a counterattack to succeed, speed and time were of the essence. Unlike his colleague, the Georgian prince anticipated Napoleon's action in the south and pressed Barclay de Tolly to ignore the news and march as fast as possible westward to catch any unsuspecting French corps. These appeals had no effect. The 1st Western Army remained in the north, wasting precious hours awaiting new intelligence. Barclay de Tolly's orders recalling his advance guard arrived too late to prevent combat near Inkovo (Molevo Boloto), where Ataman Matvei Platov overwhelmed a French light cavalry brigade. The victory, minor as it was, seemingly confirmed what Bagration and the hawks had been saying all along—that the French were not to be feared and a spirited attack could deliver a victory for Russia. Be that as it may, it was now too late to build on this success. For five days Barclay de Tolly dithered, shifting direction from north to west and back, while his troops crisscrossed the area on what they resentfully called "dumbfounding" (oshelomelye) maneuvers. This vacillation and uncertainty exasperated everyone. "Mere rumors should not be affecting our operations, especially when each minute is so precious," thundered Bagration. Conspiracy theories flourished, all claiming that the main headquarters was full of enemy spies and traitors.

Russian indecision gave Napoleon an opportunity to adjust his plans. His first reaction to the news of the enemy counterattack was to suspend his forward movement and observe. As days passed and Russian armies dithered, he became convinced that the offensive presented no significant threat. To the contrary, it offered him a remarkable opportunity to outmaneuver the Russians and deliver a decisive blow to end the war. Napoleon concentrated his forces on a narrow front between Orsha and Rosasna and, under cover of a heavy cavalry screen, unleashed a massive flanking maneuver that moved around the left wing of the Russian armies and almost captured Smolensk in their rear. Almost. The elaborate plan was thwarted by a small and isolated Russian detachment under General Dmitry Neverovskii, whom Bagration sent to the village of Krasnyi to watch for French movements in the south. On August 14, as the Grande Armée crossed the Dnieper and rushed to Smolensk, Neverovskii's division, barely 5,000 men, fought to contain the enemy advance guard. "Retreating like lions," as one French eyewitness described it, the Russians delayed Napoleon's arrival at Smolensk for an entire day. Neverovskii's exploit enthralled the Russian army. The future partisan leader Denis Davydov could remember the sense of awe and excitement as he saw this battered but unbroken division proudly returning to Smolensk, "each of its bayonets glistening with an immortal glory."[38] Stunned by Napoleon's maneuver, the Russian armies hurried back to Smolensk, where a ferocious battle raged on August 15–18. The city was almost entirely destroyed, and thousands of soldiers died assaulting or defending its seventeenth-century red-brick bastions. In the end, Barclay de Tolly decided to pull back his forces and the Russian armies withdrew.

The surrender of Smolensk provoked an outcry. Sir Robert Wilson, who had been attached as British commissioner to the Russian army in 1806–1807 and was serving in the same capacity again, saw that "the spirit of the army was affected by a sense of mortification and all ranks loudly and boldly complained." The removal of Barclay de Tolly had become an almost universal demand. The abandonment of the recently incorporated Polish-Lithuanian provinces, though far from popular, had been reluctantly accepted in view of the enemy's numerical superiority and the general agreement that the Russian armies would fight once they united at Smolensk. But now the war was blighting ancient Russian soil and Smolensk itself lay in ruins. "Drowned in our sorrows, we were abandoning our provinces and their inhabitants to the enemy depredation," wrote a Russian officer. Thoughts of further retreat became intolerable. "Soldiers were eager, even demanding, to fight!" remembered Fedor Glinka, an aspiring poet and aide-de-camp to General Miloradovich. "At Smolensk, they kept shouting, 'We already see the beards of our fathers.'" Lieutenant Simanskii, like many of his comrades, was stunned by the scenes of destruction at Smolensk and could not but wonder what the future held for his own family, whom he had left behind. Like him, Ensign Konshin felt "a sense of heavy bleakness," while still another officer scoffed that "we are running away like hares. Panic has seized everyone. . . . Our marches look like a funeral procession."[39]

Most Russian generals and officers opposed the surrender of Smolensk and pleaded to fight on. Barclay de Tolly demurred, pointing out that the position at that city was no longer tenable and that Napoleon could flank and encircle the Russian armies. "Let everyone mind his own business and I shall mind mine," was his curt response to his critics.[40] That only further inflamed their feelings. One of the generals sniped back that Barclay de Tolly was unfit to lead the armies. "I cannot ascribe our minister's aloofness and indifference to anything but treason," charged Zakrevskii, head of Russian military intelligence. "When was there a time in our past when we simply abandoned our ancient cities?"[41] At one of the villages Barclay de Tolly and Bagration got into a shouting match. "You are a German and do not care for anything Russian," the Georgian yelled. "You are a fool and do not even comprehend why you call yourself a Russian," retorted the Livonian.[42] In Dorogobuzh, a group of officers openly slandered Barclay de Tolly, with Grand Duke Constantine confronting him in public: "You are German, a *schmerz* [filthy sausage-maker], traitor, scoundrel! You are selling out Russia!"[43] Cossack Ataman Matvei Platon went as far as to suggest that he could arrange matters so that the foreign-born staff officers "could never see the light of day again."[44] General Count Shuvalov, the czar's close advisor, painted a devastating picture of a demoralized and poorly managed army, blaming Barclay de Tolly for indecision and mismanagement. "The army is disgruntled. The soldiers are grumbling and have not the least confidence in [Barclay de Tolly]," he told the czar. "A new commander is necessary, one with authority over both armies, and Your Majesty should appoint him immediately. Otherwise, Russia is lost."[45]

This decision was not easy. Alexander liked Barclay de Tolly and valued his diligence, candor, and fortitude. But he admitted that the minister of war had committed, as he told his sister, Grand Duchess Catherine, "one foolishness after another" at Smolensk.[46] Visiting both imperial capitals, he could see that public opinion clamored for Barclay de Tolly's dismissal and the appointment of a "full-blooded" Russian.[47] The czar understood that the armies' continued retreat and the rancorous dispute between the generals had aggravated sentiments to such an extent that Barclay de Tolly had to be sacrificed to public opinion.

On August 17, still unaware of the tragedy unfolding at the walls of Smolensk, Alexander convened an Extraordinary Committee to ponder the question of whom to name. The committee consisted of some of the most senior imperial officials—the chairman of the State Council, Count Nikolai Saltykov; the commander in chief of St. Petersburg, General Sergei Vyazmitinov; the head of the Department of Laws of the State Council, Prince Peter Lopukhin; the head of the Department of Economy of the State Council (and former interior minister), Count Victor Kochubey; the minister of police, Alexander Balashev; and General Alexei Arakacheyev. The six men gathered at Saltykov's mansion in St. Petersburg and spent hours deliberating the question of who should be entrusted with the supreme military command at this crucial moment in their nation's history. The committee agreed to consider only the most senior officers but excluded two field marshals on the grounds of age and health. The military seniority register featured the names of thirty-two full generals. The council discussed the merits of many of them, including Bagration (ranked twenty-first in the seniority register), Bennigsen (fifteenth), Tormasov (twelfth), and Dokhturov (twenty-sixth); they even considered the still-disgraced Peter von der Pahlen, who was not even on the list of active generals. Senior or not, each possessed a unique set of shortcomings and faults, and each was rejected.[48]

Kutuzov's candidacy was a delicate issue, since the committee members knew how little the emperor cared for this general. They debated whether the sixty-five-year-old commander still possessed the physical and mental stamina to endure the rigors of a war on a scale different from any he had experienced. The effects of age had become more evident after the last campaign—Kutuzov had grown stouter, walked more slowly, and was often out of breath; he had difficulty riding a horse, preferring a carriage; and he had become prone to dozing off. The committee members must have had heard rumors that he had lost mental acuity and that he delegated most tasks.[49]

The committee also knew that Kutuzov remained a formidable military thinker, and that his reputation for craftiness was undiminished. He was living history—the last eagle from Catherine's "lofty flock." In the seniority register, he was listed sixth. The five more senior generals all either were too old and frail to command or lacked sufficient experience; none could claim to have won a major war.[50] Kutuzov was a true Russian from a well-known aristocratic family (newly elevated to the princely rank), which was a vital factor, considering prevailing xenophobic sentiments. He possessed ample charisma, which Barclay de Tolly lacked, and enjoyed good standing among his peers, so many of whom had voted for him at the recent noble assemblies. The clergy also looked upon him approvingly as a respectful son of the Russian Orthodox Church.[51] He thus appeared better able to incarnate the patriotic spirit that was permeating Russian society. Only a general with public support and unassailable patriotic credentials could overcome the restlessness and division in the army, and Kutuzov seemed to have it all. Even the czar admitted that Kutuzov was "in great favor with the public." Just days earlier he had received a letter from Governor Rostopchin, who assured him that "all of Moscow desires that Kutuzov should lead all the armies." Sentiment was just as strong in the imperial capital.[52] One week before the czar convened the Extraordinary Committee meeting, Ivan Odenthal, who worked at the St. Petersburg post office, confided to his friend that the public was confident that it was simply a matter of time before Kutuzov was called to take charge of the armies: "Everyone here is convinced that *when* [my emphasis] he takes charge of the army, any position would become suitable for a Russian soldier to fight."[53]

It was well after ten o'clock in the evening when the committee members voted unanimously in favor of Kutuzov's candidacy.[54] They prepared a letter to the czar, taking time to construct the arguments to convince him of the rightness of their pick. Prince Alexei Gorchakov, the acting minister of war, was tasked with delivering the committee's recommendation to the czar. He was rather anxious. "I have a terrible task to perform," he told the czar's aide-de-camp Komarovskii in front of the emperor's cabinet. Komarovskii was indeed troubled that the committee had endorsed Kutuzov's candidacy. This was that "rare occasion" when an official was supposed "to compel the Sovereign to change his mind" and replace a commander in chief he liked—Barclay de Tolly—with one he did not. The conversation between the czar and the minister was long and heated. When Gorchakov finally emerged from the emperor's officer, Komarovskii could see that "his face was red as if on fire." Catching his breath, the minister divulged that he had succeeded in convincing the czar to sign the document. "Just think of the audaciousness of what we have done he said. "I dared to flat out tell His Majesty that all of Russia wanted Kutuzov's appointment and that it seems only appropriate to have a genuine Russian commander lead armies in what will be a patriotic war."[55]

Alexander stewed over the outcome of these deliberations. He was reminded of the fiasco after the appointment of Field Marshal General Mikhail Kamenskii, whom, in the words of a contemporary, "the public supported as universally in 1806 as it did Kutuzov six years later."[56] The czar had conceded to the public's demands then, and it proved a huge mistake, given that the old and frail Kamenskii was woefully unprepared for the task. Would Kutuzov fare any better against Napoleon? In general, Alexander had a low opinion of his generals, especially older ones, finding most of them incompetent and "equally incapable of serving as a commander in chief," as he wrote Grand Duchess Catherine.[57] He had, as we have seen, long preferred foreigners to them, and he had earlier tried offering the command of the Russian army to French general Jean Moreau (then in exile in the United States); British general Arthur Wellesley, the Duke of Wellington; and even the Swedish crown prince (and former French marshal), Jean Baptiste Bernadotte. Nothing came of these efforts. Alexander's letters to his sister show how little enthusiasm he had for Kutuzov's candidacy. Although he had conferred a princely title on him, given him a seat on the State Council, and appointed him to command land and naval forces in the imperial capital, deep in his heart the czar clearly "cared very little" for him, as one diplomat put it.[58] "Knowing this man, I was rather reluctant to appoint him to lead the armies," the czar frankly told his sister. But in the end, Alexander could see no other way out, certainly not one that the Russian public would approve and embrace. "Everyone was decisively in favor of appointing the old Kutuzov," he conceded. "I could do nothing but to give in to this universal desire."[59] He had no choice but "to impose silence on my feelings," as he later told Barclay de Tolly.[60]

On August 19, Alexander summoned Kutuzov to his imperial residence on Kamennyi Island, where he announced his appointment as the supreme commander of Russia's armed forces.[61] The two men then spent about an hour conversing privately, and though the details of their conversation remain unknown, military matters would have been paramount. Letters, journals, and memoirs offer us glimpses of what Kutuzov told his friends and relatives and what he probably said inside the emperor's cabinet. This was the first time he had had an opportunity to discuss strategy with the czar, who, in the words of the court official Nikolai Longinov, "had not previously even broached the subject of war with him." Kutuzov was very critical of Pfuel's "most thoughtless" plan, which deployed the armies as if they were to "cordon off the plague" rather than wage a war against a gifted opponent.[62] He promised to take more forceful action against Napoleon and to prevent him from reaching "the lands of Russia proper." His acquaintances recall Kutuzov vowing that "the enemy would enter Moscow only over his dead body,"[63] though he was quick to qualify this by adding, "*if* I find our troops still at Smolensk."[64] Neither he nor the czar knew that Smolensk had already fallen and that the war had reached the Russian heartland. Alexander, in turn, gave the general carte blanche to command field armies and conduct military affairs. However, he strictly prohibited Kutuzov from entering into any negotiations with Napoleon.

Just as he was about to leave the czar's office, Kutuzov stopped near the door, remembering one crucial matter—he was, he told Alexander, so deeply in debt that he could not even afford to travel to the army. Alexander knew of the general's debts, so he was probably not too surprised by this confession. He ordered that Kutuzov be given 10,000 rubles for expenses. The exchange undoubtedly gave him one more reason to dislike this encounter.[65] The czar accompanied his new commander out of room and paid him the usual compliments, but afterward turned around and stonily told his aide-de-camp: "The public wanted his appointment, so I appointed him. As for myself, I wash my hands of it all."[66]

Russian society rejoiced upon hearing the news of Kutuzov's appointment. "This choice revived everyone's spirits," wrote Roxandra Stourdza, Countess Edling. Madame de Staël, the French writer who passionately hated Napoleon and who happened to be visiting St. Petersburg at the time, noted that the street where Kutuzov's house was located was jammed with carriages of well-wishers who came to congratulate him. Madame de Staël was among those eager to meet the new commander in chief and was surprised to discover that he was "an old man with the most graceful manners and animated expression." Looking at him, she wondered whether he would be equal to the struggle against "the strong and ruthless men who were swooping down upon Russia from every corner of Europe." As she bid farewell to Kutuzov, de Staël was unsure if she was embracing the future "conqueror or martyr," but she could see that Kutuzov understood "all the greatness of the cause" for which he was now responsible.[67]

Kutuzov spent the last two evenings before his departure with his family. His relative Login Ivanovich Golenischev-Kutuzov organized a farewell dinner for him, and the guests entertained the general by singing and reading poems by young and aspiring poets. Kutuzov was "very jovial" and demonstrated "incredible courtesy and quick wit," recalled artist Fedor Tolstoy, who attended the dinner and sculpted the general's portrait. As he was about to leave, Kutuzov looked at the relatives and friends who gathered around him, smiled, and said with a glint in his eye, "There is nothing I desire more than to outsmart [obmanut'] Napoleon!"[68]

On August 23, Kutuzov's preparations to depart from the imperial capital turned, in the words of an eyewitness, into "a majestic and touching procession."[69] That morning, vast crowds gathered along the Palace Embankment and the canals of the Moyka River to bid him farewell. Streets were so jammed that Kutuzov could not travel in his carriage and instead walked, to universal acclaim and cheers, to a special prayer service held at the newly consecrated Cathedral of Our Lady of Kazan. Styled after Gian Lorenzo Bernini's colonnades at St. Peter's Square in Rome, the cathedral features a vast courtyard in front of the church, and that day it was packed with throngs of worshipers. Kutuzov prayed in front of the Holy and Miraculous Icon of Our Lady of Kazan, which had a tradition of granting victories. It was an emotional scene, as the general kneeled and "with him, everyone else genuflected," wrote an eyewitness in a private letter. "The entire church was weeping with him." As the ceremony ended, people carried Kutuzov out. Everyone tried to touch his clothes. "Save us! Defeat this cruel enemy, crush the serpent!" they implored him.[70] "What an incredible moment this was for a mortal being!" observed Madame de Staël.

Kutuzov left St. Petersburg later that the same day. Hurrying southward, still unaware that Smolensk had fallen four days earlier, he expected to cover the 500 miles separating the imperial capital from that city in several days.[71] However, while the horses were being changed at the first relay post, a messenger found the commander-in-chief and gave him the latest reports from the front. Napoleon was already at Smolensk. "The key to Moscow has been given away," Kutuzov tersely remarked.

CHAPTER 22

The Road to Borodino

A S THE MONTH OF August neared its end, the Russian armies halted on the
outskirts of the village of Tsarevo-Zaimische, fifteen miles from Gzhatsk,
where their commanders were determined to give battle. Barclay de Tolly
had been "anything but satisfied with the results of his efforts at Smolensk,"
commented a staff officer with considerable understatement. Having retreated
without attempting to halt the enemy in a general engagement weighed
heavily upon him. His staff felt the urgency of such a battle even more keenly.[1]

The region of Tsarevo-Zaimische had several features to recommend
it as a place to give battle. Located at the edge of a wide plain, it was
dominated by gently rising ground, which provided the Russians with
vantage points for observing enemy movements and for deploying their
artillery batteries. Beyond the ridge the main road from Smolensk to
Moscow stretched eastward, offering an avenue of withdrawal. But the
area had flaws too—both flanks could be easily turned, while a river with
marshy banks flowed behind the Russian lines.[2] Despite reservations about
its suitability of this position, Barclay de Tolly was determined to fight
here and put soldiers to work digging ditches and building ramparts.
Hardly had the construction begun when the news spread that a new commander in chief was about to arrive.[3]

Kutuzov's journey from St. Petersburg had turned into a procession. At
every stop the townsfolk and villagers came out to greet him with ecstatic
cheers. At Novgorod, he attended another prayer service at the Cathedral
of St. Sophia and was surprised to receive some belated farewell gifts from
the Ottoman sultan, which Kutuzov regretfully described as insufficiently
opulent.[4] At Torzhok, he encountered Bennigsen and British commissioner
Wilson. The former followed the general to the army, while the latter gave
him a lengthy account of what had been going on and "of the temper in

which he would find the army," as he put it.[5] On August 29, after rains had slightly delayed his journey, Kutuzov reached Gzhatsk.

"The day was cloudy but our hearts filled with light," noted Alexander Scherbinin, serving in the quartermaster service, on Kutuzov's arrival at the army. The news spread like "an electric charge through the army," remembered artillery officer Ilya Radozhitskii. "Everyone who could rushed to meet the venerable commander, looking to him for the salvation of Russia."[6] Kutuzov quickly appreciated what the situation required. "Shrewdness and prudence are qualities that do not leave people even in old age, and Kutuzov certainly retained them," rightly observed Carl von Clausewitz in his study of the war in Russia, based on his experience as a participant and eyewitness. Kutuzov was, in his words, "a dashing warrior in his youth who, in old age, combined agility of mind with cunning and adroitness."[7] The supreme commander sought to ease the discontent in the army. He wore his simplest old uniform—entirely lacking in sashes, feathered bicorn, and ostentatious decorations. He looked authentically Russian. As messengers cantered ahead to spread the news of his arrival, Kutuzov spent his time trying to lift spirits. "Who could ever have convinced me that our enemy dared to fight with such excellent lads as you, my brethren!" he told soldiers at one point.[8] His "brethren" erupted in loud cheers and joyous songs, hurrahs resounding from regiment to regiment. "Everyone celebrated and praised him, while others breathlessly thanked the Almighty for sending this savior of the Fatherland," described an eyewitness.[9] Soldiers lined the road to watch him pass; veterans told stories of their time serving under Kutuzov and recounted his exploits from past campaigns. "For many, these were fresh memories," noted one of the eyewitnesses. These stories further increased the army's confidence in their new commander, who had "a Russian name, a Russian mind, and a Russian heart" and was well known for his accomplishments.[10]

At Tsarevo-Zaimische, Kutuzov greeted Barclay de Tolly, Bagration, and other generals and then inspected the soldiers who had been drawn up to welcome him. After weeks of retreating and fighting, they must have looked weary and scruffy; nonetheless, as he passed in front of them, he muttered, "How can one keep on retreating with fine fellows like these?"[11] The comment was on everyone's lips within hours, and "Kutuzov has arrived to let us thrash the French" became a common refrain among the soldiers.[12] Throughout that day he addressed the men directly, casually, and in their own language, reminding them of their past glories and urging them to gather their strength and persevere. "With astonishing assurance, he proclaimed himself the conqueror, announced everywhere the approaching destruction of the enemy army . . . and suffered no device of boasting to escape him," wrote Clausewitz. It was all a calculated act, designed to reanimate soldiers disillusioned by prolonged retreat and disgruntled at their leaders. The fact that he was Russian made anything he said appealing. Kutuzov "knew the Russians well and understood how to handle them," remembered an officer. "He flattered the vanity of the army and people and sought by proclamation and religious observances to work on the public mind."[13] Captain Pavel Puschin and his comrades in the Life Guard Semeyonovskii Regiment were all delighted to see the new supreme commander walking through the campsite and talking to the troops. "This visit brought us an immense pleasure. Called upon to lead the army by *the will of the people and against the will of the emperor* [my emphasis], Kutuzov enjoys universal trust in the army," Puschin jotted in his diary on August 31.[14] Young ensign Nikolai Muravyev remembered that day slightly differently. He found the new supreme commander "of short stature, fat, ugly, with a crooked eye," but at least approved of his "not flaunting his clothes." More crucially, the soldiers "genuinely loved" him because he knew very well how "to handle them."[15]

Knowing that some questioned his appointment because of his infirmities and age, Kutuzov quietly instructed a Cossack detachment to scout the woods about a mile from the main road. He then suggested going on a reconnaissance accompanied by a "suite of staff officers and generals who were all curious to see him," Nikolai Muravyev, one of the staff officers, remembered. Riding along the road, Kutuzov suddenly halted his horse, pointed out horsemen in the distance, and asked who they were. No one was able to distinguish the riders' uniforms, and some members of his suite anxiously suggested it was an enemy advance guard and urged the general to turn back. Kutuzov apparently gazed for a while at the men and then calmly reassured everyone that they were Cossacks. He then spurred his horse forward. Several orderlies rushed ahead to investigate and reported that they were indeed Cossacks. A simple ruse had worked—the entourage was impressed, and everyone marveled at the old man's sharp eyesight and self-confidence.[16] "Kutuzov's arrival stirred fresh confidence in the army," Clausewitz summed it up. "A true Russian, a new Suvorov," had arrived to exorcise "the evil genius of the foreigners."[17]

The Russian generals reacted more tepidly toward the new supreme commander. Some were outright dismissive of him. General Mikhail Miloradovich, for example, thought that Kutuzov lacked "any military talents" and was "a person of duplicitous disposition and a wretched courtier." General Nikolay Rayevskii dismissed him as a mediocrity and lamented that replacing Barclay de Tolly had been a mistake.[18] Barclay de Tolly was, unsurprisingly, annoyed at being supplanted by a man whose military talent he thought little of. "Only the Lord knows if we have made the right decision," he told his wife upon hearing about Kutuzov's appointment.[19] To further complicate matters, the czar had failed to clarify Barclay de Tolly's status in the army. Kutuzov asked him to remain in charge of the 1st Western Army, to which the general consented, thereby subordinating himself to the supreme commander. He also remained the minister of war—despite the Extraordinary Committee's precise recommendation to remove him from the ministerial position to avoid any conflict of authority, a fact the czar made no mention of in his letter to Barclay de Tolly, thereby leaving him nominally superior to Kutuzov. Barclay de Tolly immediately grasped the implications of this: "As an army commander I am subordinated to Kutuzov—I know my responsibilities and will fulfill them precisely," he told the czar. "But I am unsure what our relations would be like in my capacity as the Minister of War."[20] In vain he begged the czar to be relieved of command. Even more disappointed was Bagration, who derided the new supreme commander as a "fine goose" and a "swindler who is capable of selling us out for money"; he complained that Kutuzov "had a particular talent to fight unsuccessfully" and warned that he would lead Napoleon straight to Moscow.[21]

Kutuzov asked Barclay de Tolly and Bagration to remain in charge of their respective armies, a decision designed to appease them and their supporters, take full advantage of their talents, and overcome the many practical challenges that confronted the new commander in chief as he was getting acquainted with his command. He also retained the services of the two army chiefs of staff, Alexis Yermolov of the 1st Western Army, and Emmanuel St. Priest of the 2nd Western Army, though the former had actively worked to undermine Barclay de Tolly. Yermolov—"the modern sphinx," as Russian poet Alexander Griboedov described him for his cleverness—played a dangerous game of intrigue at Russian headquarters, undercutting his immediate superior (Barclay de Tolly), inciting others (namely Bagration) to insubordination, and writing private letters to the czar urging a change of leadership.[22] He was not particularly pleased with Kutuzov's appointment either.

The presence of several prominent generals with no clear assignments presented a problem. Kutuzov resolved it by creating an ad hoc *corps de bataille*—formations that these senior officers could lead without exercising tangible command authority. General Miloradovich was given command of one *corps de bataille*, comprising the 2nd and 4th Infantry Corps; Prince Andrei Gorchakov would lead another one. Lieutenant General Peter Konovnitsyn was put in charge of the reinforced rear guard and given the unenviable task of slowing down the advance of the Grande Armée. Kutuzov then appointed Major General Mikhail Vistitskii as the quartermaster general of the armies and named Bennigsen as the acting chief of staff of both armies.[23]

The last of these decisions seems especially noteworthy. Kutuzov encountered Bennigsen while he was en route from St. Petersburg to the army and conveyed to him the czar's order to join the army.[24] The two men had known each other for decades. Born into a Hanoverian noble family, Bennigsen was two years older than Kutuzov and had served with him in the Russo-Ottoman and Russo-Polish Wars. His involvement in the assassination of Emperor Paul darkened his reputation, but he continued to serve during the wars against the French; in 1807, he commanded the Russian army against Napoleon, whom he fought to a bloody stalemate at Eylau before suffering a defeat at Friedland. His command strengths were, however, offset by an inflated ego that made him question everyone else's accomplishments. Barclay de Tolly remarked that Bennigsen was "envious and spiteful" and that his pride made him believe he was the only one truly capable of commanding armies in battles; his presence in the army was "a veritable plague."[25] Kutuzov knew "all of this very well," Barclay de Tolly pointed out, and had discussed Bennigsen's failings on many occasions. He was too worldly-wise not to know that Bennigsen coveted supreme command and that he would complicate matters. But the czar thought Bennigsen might have valuable insights on how to fight Napoleon and insisted on his being employed; he had, in fact, offered him the supreme command but Bennigsen astutely declined it on the grounds that he could not accept it knowing that there was someone more deserving of it and, more crucially, that "the Russian army," as Bennigsen wrote, "must have a Russian commander."[26]

Such a magnanimous gesture did not mean that Bennigsen ruled out future possibilities. In a letter to General Alexander Fock, he admitted that "because of my ambition and pride, which every military man must possess, I found it distasteful to serve under another general after I had commanded armies against Napoleon and the very best of his marshals."[27] It is all but certain that the czar assigned him to the army in case Kutuzov's health deteriorated or he experienced a breakdown like Kamenski had five years earlier. Kutuzov had little choice but to comply with the emperor's wish. He brought Bennigsen back to the army and gave him a position appropriate to his senior rank and experience, but he never trusted him.

Amid this atmosphere of intrigue and backbiting at the headquarters, Kutuzov made sure to surround himself with people he could trust. Among them were his son-in-law Nikolai Kudashev and longtime confidant Paisii Kaisarov, who assumed the roles of his duty officers. Colonel Karl von Toll, whose youthful drive, sharp intellect, and competence had attracted Kutuzov's attention years ago at the Cadet Corps, became his right-hand man.[28] Logical as this was, it caused some to complain of the commander in chief's insularity. "Soon after his arrival the prince was surrounded by a crowd of useless people, many of whom I had previously removed from the army," complained Barclay de Tolly, who had earlier quarreled with Toll and who complained about the busybody Kaisarov, who "thought that, being both confidant and pimp [svodnik], he had no less right to command the army." He felt that Bennigsen, Kudashev, Kaisarov, and Toll sought to influence "the weak and elderly Prince" and issued orders without notifying him.[29] Alexander Scherbinin noted that although Vistitskii had assumed the mantle of quartermaster general of the united Russian armies, Colonel Toll wielded real influence and officers all flocked to him, while Vistitskii, a tall and lean old man, rode alone like the Commendatore in *Don Juan*.[30]

Kutuzov knew what he was up against. The war against Napoleon would be "a mammoth and extremely difficult endeavor," he admitted in a conversation.[31] He had witnessed the emperor's military brilliance at Austerlitz and closely followed his subsequent campaigns, gaining a great deal of respect for the man he considered "the first Captain of the age"; a family member remembered him admitting that he was "an enthusiastic admirer of Napoleon's military genius" and, he admitted, occasionally dreamed of his rival.[32] Whenever somebody criticized Napoleon, he often came to his defense. "Carried away by my youthful bashfulness, I once allowed myself to utter a few derogatory remarks about Napoleon," remembered Alexander Mikhailovskii-Danilevskii. "Kutuzov curtly interrupted me, 'Young man, what right do you have to mock one of the greatest commanders in history? Stop these unseemly insults at once!'"[33] As Kutuzov was leaving for the army that late August day in 1812, he confided to his family that he "felt overpowered by the magnitude of the responsibility he was taking upon himself."[34] He knew that despite losses sustained in the two months of campaigning, Napoleon's Grande Armée remained a powerful force, whose strength the Russian military intelligence estimated at over 165,000 men.[35] By contrast, the combined strength of the 1st and 2nd Western Armies was roughly 100,000 men.[36] Among the Russian troops, the continual retreat, agitation over suspected treason, supply problems, and emotional strains of the war had produced, in the words of Barclay de Tolly, "disorders, abuses, and thieving that increased with each passing day and nudged the army closer to ruin." Kutuzov needed to restore order. Just hours after arriving, he issued directives to combat "marauding that has spread in the army and reached such a scale that I am worried about maintaining order and peace in [Moscow] and its environs."[37] The following day the military police detained almost 2,000 "itinerant soldiers" caught ransacking nearby settlements. He offered pardons for the detained soldiers but threatened to shoot anyone caught in the future. Senior officers were expected to comply—on September 2, he threatened Major General Mikhail Levitskii, the chief of military police, with a court-martial unless he immediately took measures to combat marauding among the troops.[38]

Attacking with a weakened army both was unrealistic and went against Kutuzov's very being. In all his prior campaigns he had relied on careful assessment of the situation and preference for maneuver until all advantages were firmly on his side. There was no reason to expect him to behave any differently that August, and certainly not when facing a brilliant opponent like Napoleon. A year earlier, Kutuzov had been willing to confront a numerically superior Ottoman army; this time he was not ready for it yet. He grasped that further withdrawal would provide precious time for the Russians to mobilize manpower and resources to continue the war. He believed that the only way to prevail over Napoleon was not to confront him in a decisive battle but through careful strategy and a war of attrition. That is why he frequently spoke of not "defeating" Napoleon but "outsmarting" (*obmanut'*) him. As he left the capital, Kutuzov replied to all salutations, "I beseech the Lord to let me outsmart Napoleon."[39] After joining the army, he admitted in a candid conversation that Napoleon "might defeat me in a battle, but he would never outsmart me!"[40] Kutuzov prided himself on his ability to think long-term. He shared Emperor Alexander's perspective on the advantages Russia possessed. Napoleon may have conquered most of Europe, but those countries had "neither our climate nor our resources," the czar had stated in one conversation. "We shall not place ourselves in jeopardy. We have space and we shall preserve a well-organized army"; the Russian winter "will fight for us." Kutuzov agreed. Conversing with a French prisoner, he explained that as soon as the war commenced, he was determined to give away as much land as possible to "exhaust Napoleon's army, to spread it thin and to weaken it through fatigue and famine."[41]

Retreat thus was the only sensible option. Kutuzov was reaping the harvest that Barclay de Tolly had painstakingly sown over the preceding weeks. As the Russian armies withdrew deep into the interior, Napoleon's vast numerical superiority dissipated and the Grande Armée showed signs of fatigue and weakening. By late August, French, German, and Italian eyewitnesses drew a poignant picture of the suffering they and their comrades endured, walking day after day in the heat, hungry, thirsty, miserable, blinded and choked by the dust that they raised.[42] With each march, the Grande Armée was moving farther away from its depots and exposing itself to the scarcity of forage and provisions. Kutuzov did not intend to make any profound changes to the conduct of the war. The question of which was more critical to preserve, the army or territory, "still needs to be answered," he told Governor Fedor Rostopchin on August 29, but in his heart he could feel what the answer would be.[43]

Kutuzov's real advantage was that, unlike his predecessor, he possessed the trust and confidence of the army and society. He understood that to defeat Napoleon he needed to bide his time. This would not be a popular strategy—after all, Barclay de Tolly had been castigated for insisting on the same approach. But Kutuzov held supreme command and possessed greater credibility, charisma, and skills to manipulate circumstances to his advantage. "Barclay de Tolly [is] terrorized (if I may use the expression) by the reputation of his enemy," noted Sir Robert Wilson in a private letter to the British ambassador in St. Petersburg.[44] Another officer thought that Barclay de Tolly, though "a brave general, very capable and skilled in command," underperformed as a commander in chief because his "fear of responsibility dampened his abilities."[45]

Herein lay Kutuzov's strength. He may not have been the most brilliant general of his era, but his background, character, and experiences matched the circumstances. He respected Napoleon but was not overawed by him; nor did he feel threatened by any of the generals in his own army who had openly opposed Barclay de Tolly. Kutuzov could thus implement a military policy that his predecessor had been viciously upbraided for. He grasped that, as Wilson put it, the "struggle for the supreme command remains the inexorable cause of intrigues" at the Russian headquarters, but he was confident that he would eventually get the better of any of his opponents.[46] He knew that the challenges confronting the Russian army were immense, but he was determined to nurture what is now referred to as "positive illusions," meaning positive self-perception, a sense of control over events, and optimistic expectations of the future. Napoleon believed that in war, morale was three times more valuable than physical strength.[47] Kutuzov was of the same opinion, doing his utmost to improve morale and motivation. In private letters, which he knew would be publicized, he painted an image of army ready to fight. "Our army is strong in spirit, we have many good generals," he wrote his family just as he was taking measures to combat marauding. "I am very hopeful. . . . I think I shall retrieve the situation to the honor of Russia."[48]

The prevailing mood was against forsaking the native land without a fight. "When was it that we, Russians, simply abandoned our ancient cities and ran?" asked one officer.[49] Retreating was an unavoidable necessity, but to quench the public's and soldiers' "thirst for vengeance," as one participant put it, Kutuzov had to give them a battle even if he did not expect it to make a difference.[50] General Alexander Kutaisov told Eugene de Württemberg that "Kutuzov understands that the whole nation demands a battle. He must deliver it, even if at the risk of losing it."[51]

Such a battle, however, could not be fought at Tsarevo-Zaimische. Kutuzov did not abandon this position because it had been chosen by his predecessor and because he did not want to share the glory in case of victory, as some had alleged. There were heftier reasons for such a decision.[52] Before he could think of confronting Napoleon, Kutuzov had to assess the broader situation, examine the army rosters, and gather reinforcements. Lack of manpower was the most pressing issue. Even Bagration, who constantly complained about retreating, had to admit that "even if I get the command now, there are no means to [attack]."[53] After General Miloradovich brought 15,591 fresh but inexperienced recruits on August 31, the combined armies could muster only 111,323 men; there were almost 8,000 seriously sick and wounded soldiers who required care and whose transportation posed a major challenge.[54] In early September Irakli Markov, who took charge of the Moscow *opolchenye* after Kutuzov declined the offer to lead it, brought 7,000 militiamen—fewer than half of the promised 15,000—while Lieutenant General Nikolai Lebedev managed to raise only 3,000 militiamen in Smolensk province. These forces were made up of men ready to defend the Fatherland, but they were untrained, lacked battle experience, and were not even fully equipped. Seeking more manpower, weapons, and transports, Kutuzov sent urgent requests to Governor Rostopchin to start mobilizing local forces and to send tools and weapons from the Moscow arsenal. They were to gather 1,000 wagons at each relay post between Mozhaisk and Moscow. "If such preparations are not promptly made, military operations would be halted and lead to woeful consequences," he warned.[55] His instructions to the "recruitment depots of the second line" required that trained recruits be moved closer to Moscow, while General Dmitrii Lobanov-Rostovskii and Lieutenant General A. Kleinmichel were instructed to relocate their reserve regiments to the former capital so that they could reinforce the main army.[56] "If my regiments fully replenish their rosters, I will fear no one," Kutuzov remarked.

The decision to abandon the position at Tsarevo-Zaimische, therefore, was made in light of logistical challenges. "Do not be surprised to hear that I retreated a bit without a fight," Kutuzov forewarned his family members. "This needs to be done to reinforce the army."[57] He was determined to gain additional days to reinforce the army and was willing to take a chance on finding a better place to fight. At the same time, he wanted to use the opportunity to urge army and corps commanders to coordinate their operations: as the main army retreated inland and drew in the Grande Armée, Admiral Chichagov, General Tormasov, and General Wittgenstein were to converge on Napoleon's exposed lines of communication and threaten his right and left flanks, respectively.[58]

Late on August 31, Kutuzov commanded the army to pack up and move on eastward.[59] "That insufferable drum woke us up at three o'clock in the morning and we set off on the road to Moscow," wrote one weary Russian officer in his diary on September 1.[60] But he and others noticed an important change in the army. Instead of the usual grumbles and complaints, "we heard songs and music, which had not happened in quite some time. Despite the fact that we were retreating once more, we felt revitalized because we expected to confront the French very soon."[61]

There was one other important matter that required Kutuzov's attention. The war had affected his family, and he needed to make sure that his daughters and grandchildren were taken care of. His daughter Praskovya Tolstoy and eight grandchildren were still in Moscow. Kutuzov wrote to Governor Rostopchin asking him to take "good care" of them.[62] He was more worried about his second-eldest daughter, Anna Khitrovo, whose husband, despite being recently exiled on suspicion of selling secrets to the French, was causing problems once more. Kutuzov pulled strings to obtain a reprieve for the son-in-law. Khitrovo was soon recalled from distant Vyatka province and offered a quiet "retirement" at his rural estate southwest of Moscow. He had apparently learned nothing from his experiences. At his estate at Tarusa, in Kaluga province, he shocked the locals by "publicly rejoicing and celebrating Napoleon's victories, even displaying a [French] flag with his name on it," described his astounded neighbor Ivan Bezsonov. His friends begged him not to imperil himself and everyone else, for, as Bezsonov put it, "in those times such a behavior could have caused unrest among the serfs or led to a court-martial and execution."[63] Hearing of Khitrovo's behavior, Kutuzov had to intervene once more to mitigate the damage to the family. "My dear Annushka and the kids," he wrote just as the army prepared to break camp on August 31. "I am very worried about you remaining near Tarusa, where you can be easily exposed to danger; what can a lone woman with children do in wartime? That is why I urge you to get as far away as possible from the theater of war." He insisted that she leave at once, even if the local authorities detained her husband. "I will settle everything with the governor," he promised, and did eventually get his prodigal son-in-law transferred to Nizhegorod province. Kutuzov added a short note for his daughter: "Everything I just told you must be kept in utmost secrecy, for if this information is made public, it will cause me great troubles."[64] This brief sentence offers us a subtle clue to his inner world—while he was assuring the army and the public that he would stand and fight, he was privately urging his family to get as far away from Moscow as possible.

"Russia is very poor in defensive positions," observed Clausewitz, who had seen firsthand the vast Russian plains that the army marched through. The countryside was either too marshy or wooded for armies to take up positions. Where the forests were thinner, as between Smolensk and Moscow, the ground was too flat and the fields too open, which made flanking any position possible.[65] Throughout the first few days of September, Kutuzov kept searching for possible battle sites. "The present position is very good," he wrote to Governor Rostopchin about one of the locations he had examined. "But it is also too wide for the size of our army and could therefore expose one of our flanks."[66] On September 3, Bagration reflected the frustration of many Russian officers when he wrote, "As usual we have yet to make a decision where and when to give a battle—we are still selecting places and are finding each new one to be worse than the previous."[67] Later that night, however, a staff officer responsible for the maintaining the official *Journal of Military Operations* made a short entry in the log: "The army has set up its camp near the village of Borodino."

The new position, some seventy miles from Moscow and almost 200 miles from Smolensk, had been selected by Colonel Toll, reviewed by Bennigsen, and approved by Kutuzov late on September 3. It was a vast rolling plain intersected by several steep-banked streams and littered with woods and hamlets, stretching for over four miles from the confluence of the Moscow and Kolocha Rivers in the north to the village of Utitsa on the Old Smolensk road in the south. Its primary advantage lay in the fact that the Russian army could control both of the main routes from Smolensk to Moscow, the Old and New Smolensk roads, to the south and north respectively, which converged at Mozhaisk. The banks of the Kolocha River, flowing southwest to northeast across the Russian front, provided protection to Kutuzov's right flank against any flanking maneuvers. Several streams, including the Semeyonovskii and Kamenka, were too shallow to pose any serious obstacle to the French, but together they produced a kind of barrier, of varying tactical significance, that ran along almost the whole front of the Russian position. Robert Wilson noted that the whole position was "broken, billowy, and uneven," and even the plain in the southern part of it was intersected with ravines and brush, which "rendered approach difficult for compact bodies."[68] In the center of the Russian position, the gently rising slopes of Kurgan Hill overlooked the surrounding area and could serve as a site for a battery; behind it was the small village of Semeyonovskoe, whose wooden houses were largely dismantled by the Russian soldiers to reinforce their positions. At the southernmost edge was the hamlet of Utitsa, on the Old Smolensk road and surrounded by the extensive and dense Utitsa Forest, which protected the Russian left flank. Clausewitz commented that the terrain, comprised of "some hillocks with a gentle slope, and perhaps twenty feet high, together with strips of scrubby wood, formed so confused a whole, that it was difficult to pronounce which party would have the advantage of the ground."[69] Tolstoy's Pierre Bezukhov was not alone in trying to discover a proper, recognizable battlefield in this landscape.[70]

"The position at Borodino where I am currently halted is one of the best places one can find on plains. The weakest spot of this position is the left flank, but I will make up for it with [engineering] art," Kutuzov informed the czar on September 4.[71] The relative strengths and weaknesses of Borodino have long been debated. Many at the time criticized the commander in chief for blindly trusting Toll, who, as Bennigsen believed, "had taken over Kutuzov's mind."[72] Barclay de Tolly thought that the new position was "favorable" in the center and on the right flank. The left flank, on the other hand, was "completely exposed." Bagration, reconnoitering the southern portion of the position, also pointed out how exposed and vulnerable his troops would be on the left. Clausewitz argued that Borodino was "deceptive," for it promised "at first sight more than it delivers."[73] These were valid criticisms, especially given that Toll had made the crucial mistake of initially deploying the Russian armies parallel to the Kolocha River and thereby exposing them to a flanking attack on the left. In later years, he did his best to conceal these missteps by producing accounts that distorted the course of events at Borodino. But charges of Kutuzov's ignorance are misplaced. His greatest error was trying to cover up the mistakes that his favorite had committed in arranging the armies. He was not, however, oblivious to them. He reconnoitered the area late that day and saw firsthand that the army's position was far from perfect; he was "very displeased with it," remembered Mikhail Vistitskii, the quartermaster general of the combined armies.[74] After weighing the pros and cons, Kutuzov decided to stay in the area but took measures. Concerned about the threat of a flanking attack around his left wing, he told the czar, he had decided "to strengthen my wing by bending it back" to the village of Semeyonovskoe, where he ordered the construction of fortifications.[75]

Early in the morning of September 5, the sound of gunfire was heard from the direction of Kolotskii Monastery. By early afternoon the Russian rear guard came into view, hotly pursued by the Grande Armée. Napoleon had already learned about the appointment of the new Russian commander in chief, whom he had defeated at Austerlitz and whose later victories over the Ottomans he had dismissed. For him, and for the French army as a whole, Kutuzov was simply *le fuyard d'Austerlitz* (the fugitive of Austerlitz) and there was little doubt in their minds that he would be beaten again.[76] His army defeated and demoralized, the czar would then have no choice but to negotiate. The French scouts soon reported that the Russian army had halted on the banks of the Kolocha River and was building earthworks, including a large redoubt between the villages of Doronino and Shevardino.

Shaped like a pentagon and some sixty yards wide, the Shevardino Redoubt, as the fortification became known, was initially supposed to anchor the left flank of the Russian position. The construction works began on September 4, but hard ground delayed the progress. Lieutenant Dementii Bogdanov, who directed the construction, recalled that after seven hours of digging, his pioneers had barely managed to construct a foot-deep trench. By then it was too late, as Kutuzov pulled the 2nd Western Army back to Semeyonovskoe and the redoubt at Shevardino therefore lost its original function. Now its mission was, in Kutuzov's words, to prevent the enemy from approaching Russian positions "too soon."[77] A new *corps de bataille* under General Andrey Gorchakov was left behind to defend the redoubt and support the Russian rear guard if necessary. This proved a prudent decision, as during the fighting on September 5 the Russian rear guard could not withstand the pressure of the French attacks and withdrew too precipitously, resulting in the French advance guard appearing near Shevardino just as the 2nd Western Army was moving to new positions. "The changing of positions thus had to be conducted in front of the enemy, and, notwithstanding the speed with which it was made, [Napoleon] was given a chance to attack," remembered the chief of staff of the 1st Western Army. An otherwise useless redoubt now had to be defended in order to give Bagration's troops time to deploy on their new positions.[78]

As the French army approached Shevardino, Marshal Murat informed the emperor about the Russian redoubt. Napoleon soon arrived to conduct reconnaissance in person. Across the battlefield, General Ivan Paskevich could see "a cavalry group standing on the heights in front of us." He saw two generals leave the group, one of them in "a gray coat and three-corner hat." Paskevich said that the general "reconnoitered positions for about fifteen minutes and waved his hand to the right."[79] Napoleon grasped the importance of the redoubt's position and could tolerate no such hindrance to his army's advance, so that same evening he ordered Marshals Murat, Davout, and Poniatowski to assault it. The French outnumbered the Russian three to one, but the ensuing fighting was still long and ferocious. After an exchange of musket and artillery fire, the French stormed the entrenchment, only to be driven back by Russian grenadiers. A seesaw battle continued throughout the evening.

Both army commanders observed the fighting from afar. Napoleon spent most of the day in his tent near the village of Valuyevo, surrounded by his Imperial Guard. One participant saw him "walking to and fro on the edge of the ravine, his hands behind his back, now and then observing what was going on through his spyglass." His health was already weakened by the campaign, and his personal physician noted that the emperor "was very nervous."[80] Due to winds, rain, and nonstop horse riding, Napoleon suffered from a severe cold and high temperature. Summoning another physician, the emperor complained that his legs were swelling and he had difficulty urinating. A few miles away from him, in his headquarters northeast of Shevardino, Kutuzov also lamented the infirmities of old age before briefly traveling along the Russian lines. Second Lieutenant Nikolay Mitarevskii of the 12th Light Artillery Company recalled seeing Kutuzov approaching with his escort and setting up an observation post between the 7th and 24th Divisions from which he was able to observe the New Smolensk road and the fighting at Shevardino. "I have never seen Kutuzov before and now we all had a chance to observe him, although we could not dare to approach him too close," remembered Mitarevskii. "With his head bowed, Kutuzov sat in his frock coat without epaulettes, with a white forage cap on his head and a Cossack whip across his shoulder." Generals and staff officers of his suite stood around him, while messengers and Cossacks were behind him. Some of his young adjutants and messengers sat in a circle and were playing a card game. Kutuzov was briefed by arriving officers and remained "serious but calm" throughout the battle.[81]

As darkness approached, both sides were bloodied and exhausted. General Gorchakov later admitted that he "wanted nothing more than for the darkest night to fall and bring an end to the battle." The flames of burning villages lit some parts of the battlefield, which was largely obscured by the thick smoke of artillery cannonade. The chaotic fighting finally died down around 10:30 p.m., when Kutuzov was informed that the 2nd Western Army had taken its positions at Semeyonovskoe and that fresh French reinforcements were reaching the battlefield. There was no longer any point in defending the redoubt, so he recalled the troops. "We had an infernal battle," Kutuzov admitted in a letter to his wife. The Battle of Shevardino was indeed very costly for both sides, though Borodino was to claim so many officers responsible for submitting reports that the precise number of casualties remains difficult to establish. Napoleon lost somewhere around 4,000 men, while Russian casualties exceeded 5,000 men, along with several guns that were left behind in the redoubt. The extent of losses suffered by some Russian units can be gleaned from General Neverovskii's remark that "in this battle I lost almost all my brigade chefs, staff and junior officers. . . . I had some 6,000 in the ranks but left the battle with only 3,000."[82] Some Russian officers complained that Kutuzov defended the redoubt longer than necessary. A soldier of the 27th Division remembered that "as we were badly mauled, our battalion commander, in a fit of anger, griped, 'What a sham! First they [army leaders] cannot properly make any arrangements and then give us this nonsense to sort through!'"[83] However, Kutuzov believed that the defense of Shevardino had given the Russians time to continue constructing fortifications at new positions and to safely deploy the 2nd Western Army around the village of Semeyonovskoe. Just as the fighting ended, he wrote a special appeal to the troops in which he congratulated them on a victory gained and spoke of the captured enemy troops and cannon. Far from a setback, this combat restored, in his words, "the glory of the Russian host."[84]

The night of September 6 was damp; by morning, a mist covered the ground, presenting a peaceful and eerie scene. The Grande Armée bivouacked on the banks of the Kolocha River, though some of its patrols had moved as far east as the Moscow River, where they watered their horses. To impress his countrymen and convey a dramatic (but false) impression, Napoleon spoke of the approaching battle as *la bataille de la Moskowa* and, on the morning of the battle, inspired his men by telling them that they were fighting *sous les murs de Moscou* (under the walls of Moscow), though the city was still over sixty miles away. For the Russians, the battle would forever bear the name of Borodino, the small village where Kutuzov anchored his right flank.

Early in the morning, after attending to political and administrative affairs, Napoleon decided to reconnoiter the area where he hoped the "Old Fox of the North," as he referred to Kutuzov, would finally stand and give him the battle he had sought for so long. The emperor "rode all along the front lines, drawn up on high ground at right angles with the Moscow road and separated from us only by the winding stream of the [Kolocha], with its muddy banks," described Louis-François, Baron Lejeune, the talented painter who then served on Marshal Louis-Nicolas Davout's staff. "Everywhere our vedettes were barely a pistol-shot distance from those of the enemy, but neither fired on the other, both sides being probably too exhausted by the struggle of the evening before to feel any further irritation against each other."[85] Napoleon studied in great detail the vicinity of Borodino and the valleys of Kolocha and Voina before ordering "construction of several fortifications opposite them to divert enemy attention and establish a pivot for the rest of the army."[86] He then took advantage of a light haze to approach and examine the Russian positions near Kurgan Hill and the village of Semeyonovskoe. He could see that the Russians had thrown up several earthworks in this sector, but the mist prevented him from making out many details. Moving south, he reached the location of the 5th Polish Corps, where he ascended a hill and observed the area through a spyglass. Seeing the Old Smolensk road winding through thick woods, he told Poniatowski, "Tomorrow you will advance forward and sweep away anything you may encounter on your way." The Poles were then to turn left to flank the Russians and support the rest of the army.[87]

In the afternoon, the French emperor made the second reconnaissance of the day. The morning mist was long gone by now and he could better examine the enemy positions across the field.[88] Accompanied by his staff officers, he traveled along Voina Stream to reconnoiter the Russian right flank and then proceeded southward. As a result of his reconnaissance trips, Napoleon realized that the Russian right flank was difficult to assail, as it was located on the steep banks of the Kolocha River and was further reinforced by newly built batteries and earthworks. On the other hand, the left flank was far more exposed and provided an opportunity to launch a massive assault, and, if necessary, a flanking maneuver. However, Napoleon's observations were not complete since Russian jägers, as well as thick forest and brush, barred him from gaining a full grasp of the enemy position. He thus confused Kamenka Stream with the headwaters of Semeyonovskii Stream and believed that the Bagration flèches (arrowhead-shaped fortifications) and Rayevskii's Redoubt (known to the French as the Grande Redoute) were located on the same ridge and could be assaulted at the same time.

The Grande Armée had some 133,000 men and 587 cannon at Borodino, more than half of which Napoleon concentrated on the right wing. Poniatowski's 5th Corps was lined up between Shevardino and the old road to Utitsa on the edge of the French position. To the right, east of Shevardino, stood Davout's I Corps, with the cavalry corps of Nansouty, Montbrun, and Latour-Maubourg behind it. Ney's III Corps was on Davout's immediate left, with Junot's VIII Corps and the Imperial Guard behind it. Beauharnais's IV Corps, reinforced by two divisions of the I Corps, formed the left wing of the Grande Armée, which stood across the Kolocha River near Borodino, while General Ornano's cavalry covered the extreme left. Troops remained in their bivouacs for most of September 6 and began assuming their positions only during the night, preventing the Russians from determining the direction of their attack.[89] Napoleon opted for a simple strategy of a massive frontal assault on the Russian center with minor diversions on the flanks. This was perhaps the least imaginative and the costliest method of engagement. The plan displayed none of Napoleon's usual energy and mastery, prompting Kutuzov to admit that "it is difficult to recognize him because he is so unusually cautious."[90] Marshal Davout urged Napoleon to undertake a wide, sweeping maneuver with 40,000 men to turn Kutuzov's left flank and cut his line of retreat; if successful, this maneuver would have driven the Russians into the cul-de-sac formed by the Kolocha and Moscow Rivers, where they could be hammered into submission. And yet the emperor rejected this idea as "too dangerous."[91] He was reluctant to commit half of his infantry force to what he considered a perilous enterprise that would have to be done at night and, more importantly, might induce Kutuzov to retreat. Having pursued the enemy since late June, he was willing to sacrifice tactical advantages to have the Russians finally accept battle, so that he could put an end to the battle, the Russian army, and the war, all at the same time.[92]

In stark contrast to Napoleon, Kutuzov made little effort to personally reconnoiter the battlefield or supervise the final deployment, instead giving complete freedom of action to his senior subordinates to make the necessary arrangements. In his order to the armies, he stated that since he was "unable to be at all points during the battle," he would let the army commanders, Barclay de Tolly and Bagration, act "as best as they see fit in the circumstances to achieve the destruction of the enemy."[93] This was a wise decision, as it allowed these generals to display valuable initiative in combat, but, as Michael and Diana Josselson rightly pointed out, neither recognized the debt they owed to Kutuzov: they "could not appreciate the rare opportunity of fighting Napoleon without having to bear ultimate accountability for the outcome."[94] The Russian high command was thus effectively divided into three clusters, centering around Kutuzov, Barclay de Tolly, and Bagration.[95] The presence of three army commanders, three chiefs of staff, and their respective staff officers put the Russians at a disadvantage compared to the highly centralized system of the Grande Armée. Barclay de Tolly later complained that there were too many hands stirring the pot and "the troops kept receiving orders from Bennigsen, Kaisarov, Toll, and Kudashev." He forgot to mention himself, for he was both the army commander and the minister of war (the czar's order removing him had not arrived yet) and could command the units as he saw fit. Kutuzov's decisions to move the troops around the battlefield exasperated Barclay de Tolly, who had expected to be consulted and was routinely ignored. The overabundance of senior generals contributed to competing claims of authority: Miloradovich commanded a *corps de bataille* of the 2nd and 4th Corps, whose commanders were also subordinate to Barclay de Tolly, Bennigsen, and Kutuzov; Dokhturov was given command of the center but could not exercise his authority over Lieutenant General Rayevskii, whose 7th Corps defended the central redoubt but was formally under Bagration's command. Lieutenant General Dmitri Golitsyn joined the army shortly before the battle and expected to play a part in it even though there was no formal vacancy. Kutuzov's solution was to place him in charge of the 1st and 2nd Cuirassier Divisions even though they belonged to two separate armies. The high command was a minefield of competing egos, and Kutuzov had to tread carefully.[96]

The Russian commanders had contrasting views on how the battle should be fought, and we have already seen some of their arguments on the eve of the fighting at Shevardino. Soviet historians' attempts to depict Kutuzov as "the strategist of world significance" who predicted Napoleon's every move can safely be ignored.[97] The real picture of Russian battle planning is confusing. There was, as we have seen, the initial Russian deployment—parallel to the Kolocha River, with the right wing at Maslovo and the left moored at Shevardino—for which Colonel Toll was responsible. Kutuzov corrected it by pulling Bagration's army back to the village of Semeyonovskoe. This second position was anchored on the ridge running from Borodino in the north to the Utitsa woods in the south. This was a better and stronger position, which Kutuzov improved with the construction of multiple fortifications. Three flèches were constructed in front of Semeyonovskoe, ten fortifications on the right wing, and Rayevskii's Redoubt in the center.[98] The scale of these defensive preparations makes it clear that Kutuzov's intent was to dig in, wage a battle of attrition, and wear down his opponent—or, as he was overheard telling his companions, to let the enemy "break his teeth on us."[99] He was confident that the Russian army, positioned behind natural barriers and newly constructed battlements, would be able to withstand enemy frontal attacks that would, inherently, cost more for the attacking side. Even if Napoleon gained a victory, it would be a pyrrhic one. If the Russian army withstood the onslaught, Kutuzov intended, as he stated in the battle disposition, to counterattack the Grande Armée and promised to supply relevant instructions when the time came. And if Napoleon found the Russian position "too strong," as Kutuzov wrote the czar, and decided "to maneuver around it along the roads leading to Moscow," the Russian general was ready to abandon his position, fall back toward Moscow, and regroup at a different place.[100]

Contrary to Soviet claims, the Russian army actually enjoyed numerical superiority at Borodino, where it assembled some 150,000 men and 624 cannon. In this regard, Kutuzov's decision to retreat from Tsarevo-Zaimische was justified, given that it had allowed him to gain additional manpower. However, a full third of his troops were fresh recruits (almost 15,000) and irregular forces (8,000 Cossacks and 28,000 militiamen), thus giving Napoleon an advantage in veteran forces. Kutuzov deployed Barclay de Tolly's 1st Western Army in the north, forming the right flank, and Bagration's 2nd Western Army on the left wing.[101] Rayevskii's Redoubt anchored the center of the Russian position, defended by Lieutenant General Nikolai Rayevskii's 7th Corps, with the 4th Cavalry Corps in support behind it.[102]

The main flaw of the Russian battle deployment lay in the unbalanced distribution of forces. In his report of September 6, Kutuzov acknowledged that the "enemy's main thrust" would be on the left. Almost two-thirds of the Russian army was concentrated north of Semeyonovskoe, while the left wing remained relatively underdefended; some officers overheard Bagration loudly protesting this at the headquarters.[103] Bennigsen claimed in his memoirs that he had repeatedly tried to convince Kutuzov to shift more forces south and that the general had simply refused to follow his advice.[104] Other officers, from Barclay de Tolly and Yermolov to a certain Captain Alexander Figner, also bewailed the apparent weakness of the left wing.

But why did Kutuzov not share such concerns? With a five-mile front line, the Borodino battlefield was too large for the Russian army to defend, and Kutuzov could not afford to anchor his forces on the Moscow River in the north and the Utitsa woods in the south. Deploying forces over such a wide area would have made them too thin to withstand the enemy assault. He was worried for the safety of the New Smolensk road, which served as the main line of retreat for the Russian army, a fact even his detractors had to acknowledge.[105] Jean-Jacques Pelet, a French staff officer in Ney's III Corps and author of an insightful account of the Battle of Borodino, was convinced that Kutuzov (or staff officers who advised him) must have misjudged the Grande Armée's placement on September 5–6 and presumed that Napoleon would attempt a flanking diversion before smashing through the Russian center right, located between Gorki and Rayevskii's Redoubt, which would have split the Russian armies (just as had happened at Austerlitz), intercepted the New Smolensk road (the main line of retreat), and rolled the Russians back— with devastating results.[106] Neither could Kutuzov concentrate troops between the New and Old Smolensk roads, as some generals had suggested, because it would have exposed the army to flanking attacks on both wings.

The charges of Kutuzov ignoring suggestions to reinforce his left flank seem to be exaggerated, and a closer examination of documents challenges such a claim. He understood the need to shore up Bagration's forces, which is why, around five in the morning, before the battle commenced, Kutuzov ordered the entire guard infantry division to take up a new position behind the 2nd Western Army; half an hour later Bennigsen, probably at Kutuzov's instruction, commanded the Life Guard Preobrazhenskii, Semeyonovskii, and Finlyandskii Regiments to move closer to the first line of the 2nd Army.[107] Furthermore, Kutuzov deployed additional troops to the Old Smolensk road, which was, as he wrote to the czar, "concealed from us by the woods and where we anticipated Napoleon's intention to turn our left wing and, marching along the road, to cut us from Mozhaisk."[108] On September 6, he summoned Engineer Captain Folkner and instructed him to examine the terrain around the village of Utitsa to ascertain if it was possible to conceal any troops there. A staff officer listened as Kutuzov explained that after Napoleon had committed his last reserves against Bagration's left flank, he would attack with these troops into the Grande Armée's flank and rear. Folkner soon returned, reporting that the location was indeed well suited for such an endeavor. General Nikolai Tuchkov's 3rd Corps, supported by the Moscow and Smolensk *opolchenye*, was deployed there across the Old Smolensk route to guard against any flanking attacks.[109]

The exact nature of Tuchkov's mission has long been a subject of debate, one complicated by the fact that these arrangements were done in secrecy. Among those unaware of Tuchkov's deployment were Bennigsen and Barclay de Tolly; the latter recalled that after he had heard about Tuchkov's men moving, he could not determine "under whose command this corps should remain, to whom its commanders should report or receive orders from." He sent a message to Kutuzov about it and was told that "it was simply a mistake and that it would not be repeated in the future." It is unclear why Kutuzov chose to be so secretive about this element of his plan, but his failure to inform his own chief of staff is indeed striking and led to unintended consequences. Late at night, Bennigsen was examining the Russian left wing when he came across Russian jägers in the Utitsa woods. They told him that there was a considerable gap between Bagration's army at Semeyonovskoe and a Russian corps near Utitsa, between which the enemy could drive a wedge. Surprised to hear about troops so far to the south and clearly unaware of Kutuzov's plan, Bennigsen went to see Tuchkov and, upon examining the position, ordered him to leave his hidden position for open ground closer to Bagration. This proved to be a consequential decision. For the next 200 years, Bennigsen became a scapegoat for the failure of Kutuzov's counterattack. As years passed, participants and historians misinterpreted or exaggerated its very nature. Many were convinced that without Bennigsen's intervention, "the sudden appearance" of this hidden detachment would have been disastrous for the French.[110] Some believed that Tuchkov was supposed to turn the French right flank just as the Cossacks attacked the enemy's left wing, which would have caught Napoleon in a double-pincer movement and delivered the battle to the Russians.[111]

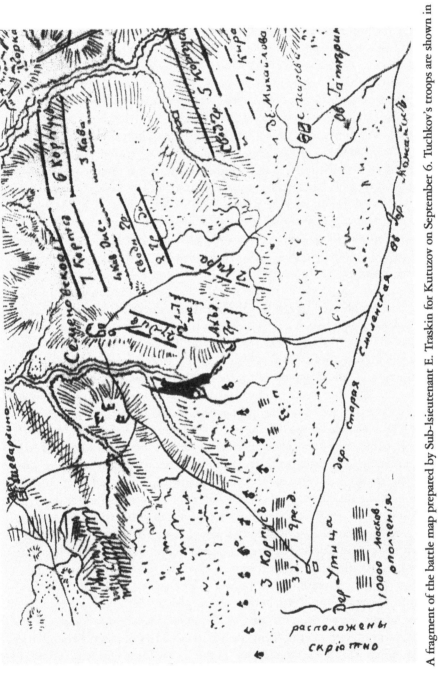

A fragment of the battle map prepared by Sub-lsieutenant E. Traskin for Kutuzov on September 6. Tuchkov's troops are shown in columns in the lower left corner, with a note, "deployed concealed," below them.

The debate over Tuchkov's mission centers on the original and subsequent positions of the 3rd Corps, which, some believe, hold the key to Kutuzov's intention. However, official documents offer no clarity as to whether Kutuzov wanted Tuchkov's troops deployed on the Old Smolensk road itself or south of it. The map prepared by a staff officer for Kutuzov shows the 3rd Corps deployed in columns (all other units on the map are in lines) on both sides of the road near Utitsa, with a note—"deployed concealed"—inscribed on the margin. This drawing generated much discussion regarding whether the position was indeed correctly shown and truly reflected Kutuzov's intent. How could these troops be effectively concealed on a major road? Soviet historians eschewed such difficult questions in favor of voluble castigation of Bennigsen. None of these historians offered any explanation as to why the chief of staff was kept out of the loop on such an important tactical decision or how a small corps, lacking sufficient artillery and cavalry support but accompanied by a ragtag militia, was supposed to confront two or more enemy corps that Napoleon could have sent on a flanking maneuver. Instead, Kutuzov's apologists railed that Bennigsen had spoiled Kutuzov's plan, and if this had no substantial effect on the battle, it was only because Kutuzov found creative ways of dealing with the tactical challenges he faced.[112] As one modern Russian scholar remarked, "The imagination of the Soviet 'historians' truly had no boundaries."[113]

Like their adversaries facing them from across the field, the Russian soldiers spent the day cleaning their muskets and uniforms, sharpening bayonets, preparing meals, and bantering around the campfires. The Russian army was, at long last, properly provisioned, in the words of an imperial historian, "due to the dedication of the good-hearted Russian people and the proximity to Moscow."[114] Yermolov issued over seventy pounds of pepper to each corps to spice up meals, while Bagration wanted his men to have a hot meal and a measure of wine before the battle; he did, however, instruct his corps commanders to prohibit setting fires in open places and advised that meals be prepared in "ravines and other concealed locations."[115]

Many of those who were there commented on an unusual calmness that descended on their camp the day before the battle. To lift the morale of his troops, Kutuzov had the Icon of the Black Virgin, rescued from burning Smolensk, paraded through the ranks of the army. The sight of this holy relic, carried by robed priests as they sang the Old Slavonic prayers, swung their smoking censers, and sprinkled holy water, had a profound effect on the soldiers. "It reminded us of our ancestors preparing for the Battle on Kulikovo Field," remembered Fedor Glinka, referring to the historic clash between Russian and Mongol forces on September 8, 1380; the Russians had won on that day, and history seemingly beckoned.[116] "Placing myself next to the icon, I observed the soldiers who waited in line behind me," remembered one soldier. "Looking at them, I felt certain that we would not give an inch to the enemy on that field of battle."[117]

Kutuzov, surrounded by his staff officers, also went to see the icon. According to some who were there, during the procession a bird of prey was seen circling in the sky above the general. Shouts of "Look, it is an eagle!" spread through the ranks as thousands of eyes followed the majestic bird gliding through the sky, a clear and auspicious sign of divine benevolence. Kutuzov took off his cap and bowed. "Victory for the Russian army!" he shouted. "The Lord himself has sent us this sign!"[118] Thunderous cheers spread through the army. Remembered Glinka: "The old commander standing with his bared head as the eagle was soaring in the sky, the Holy Mother's icon was held up, and one hundred thousand Russians shouting 'hurrah'—this was a singular scene indeed!"[119] Later that day, Kutuzov reviewed regiments, talking to and inspiring the men. Once more he was overheard muttering, "The French will break their teeth on us! It will be a pity if, having broken them, we will not finish them off." Then, stopping in front of another regiment, he told the rank and file, "Tomorrow, before the sun sets, you will have traced your faith and your allegiance to your Sovereign and country, in the blood of the aggressor and of his hosts."[120]

The night before a battle was a moment for contemplation and reflection. Several Russian officers commented about the almost spiritual manner in which the men readied themselves for the morrow. As darkness fell, Lieutenant Mitarevskii recalled that he had a hard time sleeping. He was convinced that "the forthcoming battle would be a terrible one." His mind was full of romantic notions about war acquired from history books and Homer's epic poems, so he remained "keen to experience a great battle, to live through all that there was and then to tell the tale."[121] Kutuzov spent the night quietly, making the final few arrangements and playing chess with Duke Alexander of Württemberg before going early to bed.[122] Officers took out their parade uniforms and soldiers dressed in the white shirts that were usually worn on such occasions. "Sacred silence reigned throughout our lines," remembered Glinka.[123] Officers and soldiers gathered around campfires, telling stories and sharing premonitions. Mitarevskii and his comrades knew that "tomorrow will bring a bloody resolution to our predicament, so everyone wanted to talk about it." One young lieutenant had seemingly acquiesced to his fate— he pointed to a bright star in the sky and said, "When I am killed, I want my soul to settle there."[124] Not far away from him, twenty-seven-year-old Captain Alexander Ogarev of the Life Guard Finlyandskii Regiment wrote what proved to be his last journal entry: "Our hearts are pure. Soldiers are putting on clean shirts. Everything is quiet now. [My friend] Mitkov and I stared for a long time up into the sky so full of twinkling stars."

CHAPTER 23

The Hollow Victory

MONDAY MORNING, SEPTEMBER 7, was cool and overcast. A thick fog cloaked the ground. Seeking to draw a comparison between Borodino and Austerlitz, Napoleon later claimed in his bulletin that "it was as cold as in Moravia in December. The army accepted the omen." Soldiers stood anxiously on opposite sides of the battlefield, counting down the minutes before the start of the battle. "The sun, hidden in the mist, maintained the deception of calm until 6:00 a.m.," remembered a Russian officer.[1] Across the field French veteran cuirassier Auguste Thirion de Metz thought how bizarre "modern battles" truly were: "Two armies slowly arrive at some piece of ground and place themselves symmetrically facing each other. . . . All these preliminaries are carried out with calm precision, as if on parade grounds. Commanders' sonorous voices can be heard from one army to the other while you observe as the mouths of the guns, which are about to kill you, take aim at you. A signal is given, the somber silence is interrupted by a terrible clash, the battle commences!"[2]

Kutuzov woke up in the village of Tatarinovo and before dawn traveled with his escort two miles to Gorki, where he established his command post. An orderly brought him his folding chair and Kutuzov sat down on it heavily, dressed in his usual frock coat and flat round white cap. Looking through a spyglass, he could make out the tall and lean figure of Barclay de Tolly—"in complete parade uniform, wearing all his decorations and a bicorn with a black feather," as his aide-de-camp Waldemar von Löwenstern remembered—standing with his staff several hundred yards away from Gorki, near the battery at the village of Borodino.[3] Barclay de Tolly had spent much of the previous day and night making final arrangements in the 1st Western Army. Almost two miles away (and outside Kutuzov's field of vision), Bagration, also dressed in his parade uniform and wearing his Order of

St. George cross (given for exceptional military valor), rallied his men around the newly constructed flèches; the last thing this dedicated tactician wanted was to be micromanaged. Kutuzov remained at Gorki throughout the battle and had a limited view of the unfolding events. Such a laissez-faire attitude has long puzzled historians. "This circumstance deprived our army of the much-needed unity of command and had a detrimental effect on the course of the battle," wrote the Russian historian Modest Bogdanovich.[4] Though Kutuzov was not entirely inactive and remained abreast of developments through messengers, Clausewitz, who saw him during the battle, thought that the commander in chief was "almost nullity in the individual scenes of this great act. He appeared destitute of inner activity, or any clear view of surrounding occurrences, of any liveliness of perception, of independence of action. He allowed his subordinates to take their own course, and appeared to be for the individual transactions of the day nothing but an abstract idea of a central authority."[5]

The image of a rotund man, as Tolstoy describes him in *War and Peace*, "with his gray nape sunk between his shoulders [and] his face wearing a strained look as if he found it difficult to master the fatigue of his old and feeble body," tranquilly observing the Battle of Borodino, "giving no orders and only assenting to or dissenting from what others suggested," would be forever engraved in the public imagination. The implied passivity is misleading, however. It reflected both the limited, defensive objectives Kutuzov had set himself in this battle and his conviction that with the presence of two superb army commanders and dozens of experienced and capable generals, he could afford to let his subordinates handle tactical matters.[6] On that day, at least, his mere presence was enough. "It was as though some kind of power emanated from the venerable commander, inspiring all those around him," Lieutenant Nikolai Mitarevskii later glowingly recalled. Fifteen-year-old Lieutenant Dushenkevich had been thrilled when the commander passed by the bivouac of his Simbirskii Infantry Regiment. "Boys," he remembered Kutuzov telling them, "today it will fall on you to defend your native land; you must serve faithfully and truly to the last drop of blood."

It was fortunate for the Russians that Napoleon was less dynamic at Borodino than he had been on previous occasions. The French emperor spent a restless night on September 7, regularly inquiring whether the Russian campfires were still burning. Would Kutuzov stay and fight? Or would he deny him the battle once more? "So many cares and intense and anxious expectations had worn him out," remembered an eyewitness. "The coldness of the atmosphere had made him ill; an irritating fever, a dry cough, and excessive thirst consumed him."[7] Napoleon continued to have difficulties urinating and, by the following morning, had begun to lose his voice. At night he was heard "meditating on the vanities of glory. 'What is war? A trade of barbarians, the whole art of which consists in being the strongest at a given point!'" He complained of the fickleness of fortune, which, he lamented, had begun to turn her back on him. Around five in the morning, one of the staff officers came to inform him that the Russians were still in position, and that the army was awaiting the order to attack. The emperor arose at once, summoned his officers, and went out, exclaiming, "We have them at last! Forward! Let us go and open the gates of Moscow!"[8]

Napoleon set up his observation point east of the Shevardino Redoubt, where his Imperial Guard was drawn up. From this point he could see the whole of the Russian center and the left wing, which he meant to attack in earnest. Surrounded by his entourage, he would remain here for the rest of the day, except for a brief excursion in the afternoon. Many participants, and later generations of scholars, commented about the emperor's unusual inertia, which was blamed on his age (he was all of forty-three), exhaustion, and poor health. More than one contemporary noted that they could not recognize the great leader of Austerlitz, Friedland, and Wagram.

At daybreak, as the Grande Armée got under arms and waited for the signal for action, Napoleon's special proclamation was read to the troops, exhorting them to victory, which would lead to glory and to a "prompt return to our native lands." He urged them to fight as they had at Austerlitz, Friedland, Vitebsk, and Smolensk. "May the most distant generations cite your conduct on this day with pride. Let it be said of you: *He was at that great battle under the walls of Moscow!*"[9] The statement, which was brief, produced a mixed response among the troops. "This short and bold proclamation galvanized the army," remembered Auguste Thirion, while others admired its "frankness, simplicity, and grandeur." The reference to Austerlitz was doubly important, both by alluding to the great triumph and by reminding soldiers who was in command of the Russian army—*le fuyard d'Austerlitz.* But others found the proclamation lacking. Georges de Chambray remembered the troops listening grimly to the words, whose "spirit did not dispose for enthusiasm."[10] Many of them instinctively felt that they must win or perish; defeat so deep in the hostile land would mean certain ruin. They might have drawn inspiration from the memories of Austerlitz and Friedland, but Vitebsk and Smolensk, against which repeated assaults had produced little effect except slaughter, reminded them of what lay ahead. As the sun broke through the morning mist, as it had on that glorious day seven years earlier, Napoleon smiled, turned to those around him, and exclaimed, "Voilà le soleil d'Austerlitz!"

The battle commenced with an intense artillery barrage.[11] Thick clouds of smoke from the hundreds of discharging guns mingled with the morning mist and curled upward, darkening the sun; as one eyewitness recalled, it "seemed to veil itself in a blood-red shroud."[12] The din was deafening. "I have never heard anything like it," remembered Roman Soltyk, one of Napoleon's

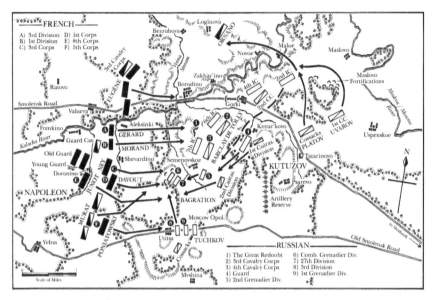

MAP 14 Battle of Borodino

staff officers. "The rumble was so staggering that at times it seemed more like steady discharge of broadsides by ships-of-the-line rather than an artillery engagement on land."[13] Across the field, Russian artillery officer Ilya Radozhitskii watched in astonishment as the rounds became so frequent that "there were no intervals between them and they all soon merged into one continuous roar like a frightful thunderstorm."[14] For Johann von Dreyling, Kutuzov's orderly, "the rumbling thunder of one thousand guns" made one's "conscience fade away, all feelings got numbed."[15]

Even before the artillery bombardment commenced, the Russian scouts reported enemy troops marching toward the village of Borodino, which, despite being on the opposite bank and somewhat isolated from the rest of the army, was still garrisoned by the Russian Life Guard Jäger Regiment and a small contingent of the Guard Equipage, a unit of marines that manned the imperial yachts and galleys in St. Petersburg.[16] Kutuzov, surrounded by his suite, was on the hill near Gorki. "Everyone's attention was directed toward the village of Borodino," wrote Pavel Grabbe, a staff officer present at the scene. "Barclay de Tolly insisted it was dangerous and futile to defend it and suggested recalling the jägers at once. Duke Alexander of Württemberg argued otherwise, Kutuzov silently listened to both of them."[17] Before the commander in chief could render his decision, the sound of gunfire was heard in the village. This was General Alexis Joseph Delzons's 13th Division (from Eugène de Beauharnais's IV Corps) attacking under the cover of thick fog that still covered the area. Kutuzov and the others were stunned by the speed of the French assault—"the enemy attack was carried out with incredible swiftness," acknowledged Kutuzov, while his bewildered staff officer noted that "the jägers were ejected from the village almost instantaneously."[18] The fighting could not have lasted more than twenty minutes. The French exploited the misty weather and their numerical superiority to surprise and overwhelm the Russian defenders, some of whom had spent the night drinking and enjoying bathhouses.[19]

Barclay de Tolly rushed his aide-de-camp Löwenstern to Borodino to re- call the troops, but it was too late. The haze was still covering the valley and concealed the French columns, which expertly advanced forward. "I had never been exposed to such an intense gunfire," Löwenstern recalled. In a matter of minutes, the jägers lost almost half of their men and two dozen officers.[20] Having achieved their objective of capturing Borodino, the French then got carried away and rushed beyond it, pursuing the Russians to the op- posite bank. This was a blunder, for they now came under fire from more than fifty cannon and were counterattacked by an entire Russian jäger brigade, which routed them and drove them back in disorder; General Louis-Auguste Plauzonne, desperately attempting to rally his men, was shot dead, the first of many French officers to lose his life that day. The Russians advanced as far as the village of Borodino, but Kutuzov and Barclay de Tolly, realizing how exposed the jägers would be at this position, ordered them to burn the bridge and return to the eastern bank of the Kolocha around eight o'clock in the morning.

The opening act of the battle thus ended in a stalemate—a portent of things to come. The short but bloody engagement claimed hundreds of casualties and had an impact on the Russian leadership. Contrary to the claims of Soviet historians that Kutuzov quickly grasped Napoleon's intent and correctly anticipated the main thrust of the Grande Armée, in fact he did neither.[21] The strength and speed of the French attack at Borodino alarmed him and caused him to suspect that Napoleon might try to pierce the Russian center right. The morning mist and gunsmoke prevented him from observing the French positions and determining the direction of Napoleon's main thrust, though many Russian officers were convinced it would be directed against the Russian left. At seven in the morning, Platov was surprised to report that he could not see any enemy troops moving against the extreme Russian flank and suggested a flanking attack across the Kolocha River. Kutuzov hesitated and initially made no changes in the battle disposition—the Russian army maintained its extended position and the majority of its troops remained on the right flank. Even when he received Bagration's urgent appeals for reinforcements on the left flank, the supreme commander delayed sending them until he was certain that there was no immediate threat to his right.

While Beauharnais's troops were storming Borodino, Marshal Davout moved forward to attack the left side of the Russian position near Semeyonovskoe. General Jean Dominique Compans's 5th Division spearheaded the assault on the Russian *redans* (flèches) but came under a hail of artillery fire and musketry. "Suddenly, from that peaceful plain and the silent hills, volumes of fire and smoke were seen spouting out, followed by a multitude of explosions, and the whistling of bullets tearing the air in every direction," a French spectator later wrote.[22] Bagration's men resisted stubbornly but were unable to stop the intrepid Frenchmen. Marching through the staggering volume of fire, the 5th Division lost many soldiers and officers—including General Compans (who was wounded) and Marshal Davout, who was bruised when his horse was shot beneath him—but pressed on with the attack and stormed the flèches. Impressed by the French gallantry, Bagration applauded them, shouting "Bravo, bravo!" before ordering a counterattack that drove the enemy out of the fortifications.[23]

The fighting at the blood-soaked flèches raged for the next two hours as the generals on either side threw in reinforcements and the earthworks were lost and retaken by successive charges. Amid incessant cannon and musketry fire, Russians, French, Germans, Portuguese, and Spaniards kept advancing and retreating, firing and reloading, colliding, tussling, falling, screaming, and dying. Dense gunsmoke shrouded the entire area, making it hard for either army commander to make out what was happening, though messengers and orderlies kept them constantly updated. Bagration, standing at his vantage point near Semeyonovskoe, could see vast enemy forces massing in front of him—more than half of the Grande Armée was in fact concentrated in this sector of the battlefield. Barely one hour after the start of the battle, he already feared being overpowered and kept sending urgent requests for help to Kutuzov, who, as noted, refused to commit any additional forces until the situation on the right flank clarified. Instead, he advised his commander to utilize the guard units that he had moved closer to the 2nd Army earlier that morning and to tap his army's reserves. Bagration complied, moving forward the 2nd Grenadier Division, along with the 1st and 2nd Cuirassier Divisions, and ordering all available cannon, including the eighty-gun-strong artillery reserve at Psarevo, to be redeployed to the front line to contain the enemy assaults. The Life Guard Izmailovskii and Litovskii Regiments were also moved to the ridge near the village of Semeyonovskoe.[24]

Neither Kutuzov nor Bennigsen took the trouble to inform Barclay de Tolly that the guard units had been committed. That morning, as cannonballs plowed the earth all around him, Barclay de Tolly rode southward to inspect the battle line and encountered the guard regiments from Lavrov's 5th Corps far ahead of the position he expected the reserve to be in.[25] Soldiers greeted him "calmly, with a true martial countenance," Löwenstern recalled. Despite cannonballs ripping through their ranks, the men remained steadfast, "standing with their muskets at the ready and quietly closing their ranks as soon as cannonballs claimed their victims."[26] Barclay de Tolly had earlier told Lavrov, according to Löwenstern, "not to detach any units of his corps under any pretense, intending to employ it around five or six o'clock in the evening, when this elite force could tilt victory in our favor by striking at the exhausted enemy."[27] Not realizing the extent of Bagration's predicament and upset to see the reserves moved forward so early in the battle, Barclay de Tolly sent Löwenstern to pull them back. The young officer found General Lavrov in "the most miserable condition, almost completely paralyzed, unable to walk or ride a horse. In a physical sense, he embodied powerlessness itself." Lavrov told him that he could not carry out Barclay de Tolly's order since Kutuzov had already ordered regiments to support Bagration and his men were already engaged in battle. Learning this, Barclay de Tolly "lost his usual impassiveness, his eyes burning with anger." He lambasted his superiors for wasting reserves at the start of the battle when he had planned to employ them later in the evening.[28] He then spurred his horse toward Gorki, where Kutuzov calmly followed the course of the battle through smoke and confusion. "Barclay de Tolly told him something in a passionate manner," remembered Löwenstern. "I could not hear what they discussed but it appeared that Kutuzov tried to calm down Barclay de Tolly. A few minutes later, the latter galloped back, telling me, 'At least now they will not waste the rest of the reserves.'"[29]

By now Kutuzov had realized that there was little likelihood of a major French attack on his right. Due to the reports from Bagration and other commanders, the weakness of the left wing became all too obvious to him; Bennigsen visited Semeyonovskoe that morning and, despite the early morning mist and gunsmoke, was able to observe large enemy formations storming the flèches. "I rushed back to Prince Kutuzov and told him, 'If you do not want to have your left wing routed . . . you need to hurry up with dispatching your troops from the right flank.'"[30] Kutuzov agreed.[31] He ordered the extreme right wing of the Russian army, composed of the 4th and 2nd Corps, to embark on a long march south, with the 4th Corps marching to the center while the 2nd Corps proceeded to reinforce the teetering left wing.[32] It would take an hour before any of these units arrived to help Bagration, giving the French enough time to prepare and launch another attack.

"The fighting [at the flèches] was so savage, desperate, and murderous that I can hardly find another to compare to it," Bagration, who had spent much of his life in war, later wrote. "Enemy corpses were piled up high in front of us and the flèches had become true graveyards for them. We suffered equally heavy casualties."[33] Repeated attacks from both sides increased the bloodshed. As one officer of the 27th Division described it, "Our division was annihilated. . . . I am simply incapable of conveying the horrors I witnessed that day and still shudder remembering it all." Only forty men survived from his entire regiment, while the rest of the division could rally only 700 men.[34] General Vorontsov, whose grenadier division defended the *redans*, wrote that resistance ended only "with the existence of my division." Just an hour after the fighting began, he and his division had lost 3,700 of its 4,000 men and all but three of its eighteen officers. "If I were asked the following day where my division was, I would have responded [by] pointing my finger at our position and proudly declaring, 'There it is.' "[35]

The struggle for Bagration's flèches soon devolved into a vicious cycle of charges and countercharges. Over the next three hours, these earthworks were stormed, captured, and retaken as both sides poured reinforcements into the fray. The new French assaults were spearheaded by Marshals Davout's and Ney's divisions, with General Andoche Junot's VIII Corps and Murat's cavalry in support—well over 35,000 men with nearly 300 cannon. Desperate for more men to defend the fortifications, Bagration begged Lieutenant General Tuchkov to divert some troops from his corps; Tuchkov complied and sent the 3rd Division to the flèches. These reinforcements, along with the units from the 4th Cavalry Corps, the guard infantry brigade, and the cuirassier divisions, proved vital, since Vorontsov's and Neverovskii's men were no longer able to bear the onslaught of the superior French numbers. The fighting was so intense that even battle-hardened men like General Jean Rapp, Napoleon's aide-de-camp, later admitted that they "had never seen such carnage before."[36]

Around nine in the morning, just as the French captured all three flèches, Bagration launched an all-out counterattack with all available forces to regain ground. "The battle descended into an individual struggle," wrote Glinka, "a private battle of man against man, warrior against warrior."[37] For Dmitrii Dushenkevich, this was not a battle but slaughter: "A previously flat plain now resembled a plowed field because of the crossfire from artillery batteries. Cannonballs, grenades, and canister ripped our columns to shreds and churned up the ground in front of us."[38] Bagration's counterattack resulted in the recapture of two fortifications and, though the French held the third, southern one, it gained the Russians precious time before other reinforcements could arrive. This time was bought at a terrible price, however. Thousands of soldiers were killed or wounded; the officer corps was devastated. The greatest loss was Prince Bagration himself. As the attack developed, he led his men from the front. A shell splinter suddenly smashed his shinbone; for a few moments he made a valiant effort to conceal his wound, but he bled profusely and, to the dismay of the soldiers who adored him, slipped from his horse and was carried away. What Bagration had most feared now occurred—"the rumor of his death instantly spread among the ranks and it became impossible to maintain order among the troops," remembered General Yermolov. "One feeling seized everyone—desperation!"[39] Apolinarii Butenev, a young diplomat assigned to Bagration's staff, remembered "the utter shock of the troops." Everyone had assumed Bagration was invulnerable because in twenty-five years of campaigns and battles he had rarely been wounded.[40] Bagration's injury meant that the cohesion and coordination of the Russian left flank vanished, and "each unit made its own arrangements whenever the enemy attacked it," admitted Quartermaster General Vistitskii.[41] Command of the sector passed to General Konovnitsyn before Kutuzov appointed General Dokhturov to lead, it but neither could match Bagration's charisma. After another round of desperate struggle, the French obtained final possession of the flèches around eleven o'clock in the morning. The Russian left flank was then drawn about a mile back and came to rest on the ridge before the village of Semeyonovskoe.[42] "There are no words to describe the depth of fury with which our soldiers threw themselves into the fray," remembered Captain Nikolai Lubenkov. "It was a fight between ferocious tigers, not men, and once both sides had determined to win or die where they stood, they did not stop fighting when their muskets broke, but carried on, using butts and swords in terrible hand-to-hand combat, and the killing went on."[43]

As the left flank teetered, the Russian center still held on at the Grande Redoute. General Nikolai Rayevskii's forces, however, were already weakened by having reinforced Bagration, who, as Rayevskii noted, "took my entire second line."[44] The initial French attack on the redoubt was mounted by General Charles Antoine Morand's 1st Division (from Davout's III Corps), of which the 30th Line rushed the earthworks and entered through the embrasures. The French infantry then spilled out into the area behind the redoubt. As Rayevskii pointed out, if Morand had been properly supported, the Russian center would have been shattered, bringing an end to the battle. But it was not. Rayevskii, despite being wounded in the thigh, rallied his 12th and 26th Divisions for a counterattack and was joined by elements of General Peter Likhachev's 24th Division (from the 6th Corps), directed by Löwenstern and Chief of Staff Yermolov, who happened to be in the area when the redoubt fell. Attacked from three sides, the 30th Line was decimated; eyewitnesses described the plain in front of the entrenchment as covered with the dead and wounded while riderless horses frantically galloped around.[45] There was a great exultation in the Russian ranks at the success of the counterattacks, and their joy only increased upon hearing the report that Marshal Murat himself had been captured during this assault. Exciting as this news was, Kutuzov remained reserved, even as his entire entourage broke out in cheers. "Let's wait for confirmation," he told his officers.[46] A French general, in "a frightfully battered state and reeling from side to side," was soon brought in front of him. It was not Murat, but General Charles-Auguste Bonnamy, commander of an infantry brigade that had stormed the redoubt and then been routed in the subsequent struggle. The general, wounded over twenty times, was "so badly injured," noted one Russian officer, "that one may say he was impaled on the points of our bayonets."[47] "Get him a physician!" Kutuzov shouted upon seeing this poor man; after exchanging a few words with him, Kutuzov had him carried away.[48]

The Russian success at the redoubt had cost many lives. "The ravine around the redoubt was full of corpses," wrote Staff Officer Nikolai Divov, who passed through the area as he was returning from a mission. Probably the most significant of the numerous Russian casualties was General Alexander Kutaisov, the commander of the Russian artillery—"a young hero, well known for his gallantry, good heart, and intelligence," as one Russian officer described him. An esteemed officer but perhaps too valiant for his own good, Kutaisov ignored Kutuzov's instructions to stay at the headquarters. Instead, he left his post to lead the counterattack at the redoubt. No one saw him alive again—his horse was later seen with its saddle "soaked in blood and splattered with pieces of human brain." It was never determined what had happened to him.[49] Many clung to the hope that Kutaisov might be still alive, probably grievously wounded and captured. (Kutuzov did not write Kutaisov's elderly father, whom he knew from the days of Emperor Paul, until a month later.) Kutaisov's loss was tragic, but its importance has long been exaggerated. Some went as far as to claim that after the general's death no one was directing the artillery and as a result the reserve park "stood idle all day."[50] This is untrue. As Ivan Liprandi pointed out, Kutaisov's entire staff and commanders were in place and every battery commander knew what to do. More crucially, the entire Russian reserve artillery took part in the battle, and of the artillery companies of the 1st Western Army, only three, deployed on the extreme right flank, did not participate in the battle.[51]

Around noon, the battle in the center was limited to cannonade while Napoleon sent reinforcements to Ney to penetrate the Russian left flank.[52] Preceded by a massive artillery bombardment, General Louis Friant's 2nd Division, with General Étienne-Marie Nansouty's I Cavalry Corps on its right and General Marie-Victor Latour-Maubourg's IV Cavalry Corps on its left, tried storming the village of Semeyonovskoe, where the remnants of the 2nd Western Army were entrenched. North of the village, Latour-Maubourg's Polish and Saxon cuirassiers assailed the Russian grenadiers as they were in the process of forming a square, rode them down, and went on to capture part of the village. Moments later they were countercharged by Sievers's dragoons and Borozdin's cuirassiers. Then the arrival of the Westphalian cuirassiers drove the Russians back, and Latour-Maubourg's men clung to the area north of the village. Meanwhile, Nansouty's ferocious *hommes de fer* assaulted the village from the south but stumbled upon Russian guard units that not only stood their ground but actually mounted a bayonet charge against the French cavalry and stabilized the situation in this sector.

Farther to the south, the Russian extreme left wing also found itself hard pressed. General Poniatowski began his flanking movement at daybreak, but it was only around eight in the morning, as the fighting raged around the flèches, that his V Polish Corps came into contact with Tuchkov's 3rd Corps, already weakened by the dispatch of a division to support Bagration. Poniatowski drove back the first line of the Russian defenses, which consisted of General Pavel Stroganov's 1st Grenadier Division. However, the arrival of Baggovut's 2nd Corps, which Kutuzov had sent on a long march from the extreme right flank, allowed the Russians to steady their battle line, although Tuchkov was mortally wounded leading one of the charges. Throughout the afternoon, Poniatowski contested the Utitsa mound, which offered a crucial vantage point, but was able to secure it only around four in the afternoon, when Junot's Westphalians came to support him. Baggovut, who assumed overall command of this sector after Tuchkov's death, rallied his men and gradually retreated toward Psareva, where he held position until nightfall.[53]

Throughout the afternoon Ney and Murat kept sending requests for reinforcements. Napoleon, seated on a chair and apparently in a state of lethargy, finally agreed to send in more forces but countermanded the order almost immediately because of the news from the extreme left wing of the Grande Armée. Earlier in the day, Cossack Ataman Matvei Platov had reconnoitered the northern edge of the battlefield and, as Clausewitz wrote, "was astonished where he had expected to find the entire left wing of the enemy to meet few or no troops."[54] The western bank of the Kolocha, northeast of Borodino, was virtually unguarded, with the French left flank protected by merely a cavalry screen from Beauharnais's corps. Sensing an opportunity, Platov dispatched Colonel Ernst Constantine Hesse-Philippsthal to Kutuzov to acquaint him with this discovery and to seek permission to fall on the exposed enemy flank. The colonel reached the Russian headquarters just as Toll was delivering a report that everything was going "favorably" on the left wing, where Bagration had repulsed attacks, and at the center, where the French attack had been repelled and "Marshal Murat" had been captured.[55] The actual situation was far from so favorable, but the truth was in the eye of the beholder and, as Clausewitz remarked, "enthusiasm blazed up like a lighted straw" when Toll and Hesse-Philippsthal presented the idea of attacking the French left flank. Some officers tried dampening this enthusiasm and cautioned against diverting forces that were needed elsewhere, but Kutuzov listened to Toll, nodded from time to time, and finally said, "Eh bien, prenez-le [Well, take it]!"[56]

All eyewitnesses agree that the proposal for launching a cavalry raid came from Platov, via Prince Hesse-Philippsthal and Toll, to Kutuzov. However, subsequent histories sought to mitigate the awkward fact that such an idea did not emanate from the commander in chief. The official history of the campaign therefore recast Kutuzov in the central role and described him going on a reconnaissance to observe the front line, which placed him in danger. "He ascended a nearby hill that was showered with enemy grenades and their fragments," wrote Mikhailovskii-Danilevskii, who had personally witnessed the scene but chose to misrepresent it. "The life of a man on whom Russia placed her hopes was hanging by a thread. In vain did his aides-de-camp try to convince him to come down from the hill; when no arguments could change his mind, they simply took the reins of his horse and led him out of the fire. After this reconnaissance, Kutuzov [instructed] Platov, with Cossacks, and Uvarov, with the 1st Cavalry Corps, to ford the Kolocha upstream from Borodino and attack the enemy left wing. With such a movement, Prince Kutuzov hoped to distract Napoleon's attention and divert some of his forces from our left wing."[57]

More than one participant found such an embellishment jarring and tried to put the record straight, but their voices were drowned in the sea of adulation that surrounded Kutuzov after his death. Soviet historians not only credited him with this idea but went as far as to suggest that he had planned it before the battle.[58] To bolster this version of history, state-sponsored paintings showed Kutuzov directing Platov (who was not even at Gorki) and Uvarov to launch the raid, while films such as *Kutuzov* (1943) portrayed him as diligently waiting for the right moment to launch the flanking attack to disrupt Napoleon's plans. The reality could not have been more different.

Around half past nine in the morning, Kutuzov assented to the flanking raid and committed not only Platov's 2,700 Cossacks but also 3,400 regulars from General Fedor Uvarov's I Cavalry Corps. Half an hour later Platov and Uvarov forded the Kolocha River and launched a wide outflanking maneuver to the north of Borodino village. They pushed aside cavalry outposts but were unable to break through Delzons's infantry, which formed a square on the shore of Voina Creek. The infantry repelled all Russian attacks, gaining precious time. Eugène de Beauharnais responded to the threat by sending in his Italian Guard and a light cavalry brigade, which was soon reinforced by the Polish lancers from the Imperial Guard, whom Napoleon diverted to shore up his flank. The sporadic fighting continued for almost three hours until Kutuzov ordered his commanders to fall back and return to their original positions.

The consequences of what became known as "the Platov-Uvarov Raid" have been debated for the past 200 years. Russian generals and staff officers were more disapproving of the whole enterprise than junior officers and the rank and file, and participants were, in general, more critical than later historians—especially those from the Soviet era. Barclay de Tolly was confident that had the attack been carried out "with greater determination, it could have produced splendid results."[59] Clausewitz questioned the entire undertaking, arguing that "a diversion attempted by 2,500 horsemen could not possibly decide the outcome of a battle involving 130,000 men on just one side; it could have, at best, put a spoke in the wheel of their plans for just a moment."[60] Still, many Russian participants believed the raid had potential for success and had been badly mismanaged by Platov and Uvarov, who were almost universally condemned for sluggish leadership. A. Golitsyn, who served as Kutuzov's orderly, remembered how coldly the commander in chief greeted the cavalry generals upon their return from their raid. "I know everything and may God forgive you for it!" were his words to Uvarov.[61] The fact that Platov and Uvarov were the only generals not nominated for rewards after the battle spoke volumes about Kutuzov's profound dissatisfaction. In December, he even explained to the czar that he could not recommend Uvarov for any rewards because he had failed to accomplish "anything of substance" and, along with Platov, "did not fight as such that day."[62] The report made no mention of Uvarov's incompetence or Platov's ineffectiveness and fondness for drink. "Both Barclay de Tolly and Bagration have been displeased with Platov for quite some time and have complained that he did not want to do anything," a Russian general told a friend in confidence.[63] Other participants admitted that Platov was "drunk and incapable of doing anything" on the day of the battle. Mikhailovskii-Danilevskii wrote in his private journal that Platov was so "utterly plastered" that the exasperated Kutuzov told a young officer, "This is the first time I have ever seen a full general so dead drunk in the middle of a crucial battle."[64] Unsurprisingly, when official histories of the battle were written, such awkward details were suppressed, and facts embellished. Despite knowing the truth, Mikhailovskii-Danilevskii extolled the raid in his official history of the campaign and portrayed it as successful and meeting "Prince Kutuzov's expectations."[65] In the end, Soviet historians depicted the raid as a brilliant example of Kutuzov's tactical genius that "dumbfounded" Napoleon, forced him to divert thousands of reinforcements to protect his flank, and, in the words of Nikolai Garnich, "completely paralyzed the enemy's main forces for two whole hours."[66]

For Napoleon, the Russian raid was only a temporary distraction, and his Grande Armée continued to assault the Russian positions on the left. He was informed about the capture of part of the village of Semeyonovskoe and contemplated a decisive blow against the Russian redoubt in the center. If successful, this attack would shatter the Russian defenses and bring him the decisive victory he was seeking. Then Napoleon received a new batch of complaints from Murat, mainly about his cavalry—deployed motionless within range of the Grande Redoute, suffering terrible losses to no purpose—and requesting permission for a new attack. Among the casualties was the talented commander of II Cavalry Corps, General Louis-Pierre Montbrun, killed by a shell splinter. To replace him Napoleon selected one of his own aides, General Auguste-Jean de Caulaincourt, younger brother of Napoleon's favorite diplomat and former ambassador to Russia, Armand-Augustin de Caulaincourt. The younger Caulaincourt had made a brilliant career during the Peninsular War. Before sending him on this new mission, Napoleon told him, "Do what you did at Arzobispo," referring to a daring attack that Caulaincourt had carried out in Spain in August 1809, when he forded the Tagus River with his dragoon troops and seized a fortified bridge. "You shall see me there presently, dead or alive," Caulaincourt was said to have replied.

Shrouded in dust and smoke and surrounded by hundreds of corpses, the Grande Redoute presented an almost surreal sight. One participant compared it to a "hellish concert," as the fortification was regularly illuminated by the "reddish, aurora-borealis glow" of its guns. After seven hours of fighting, the fortification was so badly damaged that its parapets were all but razed to the ground. Now, hundreds of cavalrymen—in gleaming cuirasses and dress uniforms, the feathers on their helmets billowing in the wind—massed in front of the redoubt. One eyewitness was mesmerized by this "mass of moving iron: the glitter of arms, and the rays of the sun, reflected from the helmets and cuirasses, mingled with the flames of the cannon that on every side vomited forth death, to give the appearance of a volcano in the midst of the army."[67] It was, in the eyes of the Russian artilleryman, "a dreadful yet sublime scene."[68]

Caulaincourt arrived at his new command to find Montbrun's officers in tears at their leader's death. "Do not weep for him, but come and avenge his death!" he told them. Just before three in the afternoon, another great attack was mounted on the redoubt. Caulaincourt led the first wave at the head of the 5th and 8th Cuirassiers, followed by Defrance's carabineer regiments; Eugène de Beauharnais's three infantry divisions attacked to his left, while Latour-Maubourg's IV Cavalry Corps charged from the south. Through the smoke and dust, the French troops could see as the cuirassiers "started to gallop, overthrowing everything in front of them, then turned toward the redoubt and rushed inside across the gorge and through places where the earth had rolled down into the ditch and made it easier of access."[69] The ensuing combat was horrifying, recalled Franz Ludwig von Meerheimb, who took part in the attack. "Men and horses, hit by murderous lead, fell down the slope and thrashed around among the dead and dying foe, each trying to tear the enemy with their weapons, bare hands, and teeth." The succeeding ranks of assaulting cavalry rode over the writhing mass of humans toward their ultimate target. "Masses upon masses of the enemy threw themselves furiously at the attackers, and scarcely had the first of them been smashed when the bayonets of fresh columns were already visible again."[70] "In the struggle," wrote an eyewitness, "the wind, which was blowing strongly, raised clouds of dust, which mingled with the smoke from the guns and whirled up in dense masses, enveloping and almost suffocating men and horses."[71] Caulaincourt was killed almost as soon as he reached the redoubt. "He has died as a brave man should," Napoleon later told his brother; "France lost one of her best officers." As the attack surged, hundreds of French, Saxon, and Polish cuirassiers overran the redoubt.

The capture of such a position by cavalry alone was a remarkable feat. Eugène de Beauharnais followed the cavalry with his infantry, which was, as described by a French spectator, "on the point of reaching the mouth of this volcano, when suddenly he saw its fires extinguished, its smoke disappear, and its summit glittering with the moveable and resplendent armor of our cuirassiers."[72] Entering the redoubt, they found a scene of carnage that was hard to convey in words. "The dead were heaped on one another, from among which the cries of the wounded were feebly heard."[73] The impetus of these hundreds of heavily armed cavalrymen carried the charge beyond the redoubt into the hollow behind it, where they encountered the Russian defenders. Barclay de Tolly was not prepared to accept the fall of the redoubt. Observing the vast numbers of enemy cavalry, he "already could foretell the terrible blow dealt to our destiny." Knowing that his own cavalry could not contain the enemy, he kept from committing it. He put his hope in the "courageous infantry and artillery, who made themselves immortal that day."[74] The Russian infantry contracted into squares whose volleys mowed down the successive waves of horsemen.[75] Their heroism gained Barclay de Tolly enough time to gather and feed in the remaining cavalry units—first the Life Guard Horse Regiment, followed by the Chevalier Guard Regiment and the rest of the 2nd and 3rd Cavalry Corps. Over the next two hours a protracted and confused cavalry melee unfolded around the redoubt as Napoleon's cavalry engaged the Russian cavalry and infantry but was unable to break the Russian central position. In the midst of this cauldron, as hundreds of men were killed or wounded, some still thought of seeking recognition. Seeing Barclay de Tolly standing intrepidly under fire, Miloradovich exclaimed, "He wants to top me!" and marched to a spot closer to the French lines, where he ordered that he be served lunch.[76] "There was a moment when the battlefield reminded me of one of the great military paintings," reminisced a Russian staff officer. "There were no precise lines or closed columns, but rather more or less numerous masses of men that kept colliding with one another. The men were fighting in the front and the rear, friends and foes all mixed up."[77]

By five in the afternoon, Napoleon's troops were firmly in control of the Grande Redoute. His cavalry, after being in the saddle for almost ten hours straight, fell back to its positions. The fighting around the redoubt, and elsewhere along the line, began to abate from the sheer exhaustion on both sides. "The grand spectacle of the Russian position, with troops arranged in

three lines and artillery in between them, was gone," recalled one participant. "The field of the battle was covered with the numerous corpses, the
ravines and brush were full of the moaning wounded asking for just one
thing, for someone to put them out of their misery."[78] At this final stage of
the battle, much depended on who could play one last trump card—the reserves. Kutuzov's had already been committed, but Napoleon still had his
vaunted Imperial Guard. His generals and marshals advised against sending
it into the battle. Marshal Jean Baptiste Bessières objected due to the lack of
any other reinforcements; the campaign was far from over and preservation of
the Imperial Guard was paramount. Others concurred, describing the Guard
as "a fortified town, under shelter of which the army might at all times have
rallied."[79] Napoleon declined to commit his reserve, one of his most controversial decisions as a commander, but one that was justified.

As the fighting subsided, the Russian army had been driven from its original positions on the left and in the center but still held a defensive line
that stretched from Gorki in the north to the Old Smolensk road in the
south. Kutuzov sent out staff officers and orderlies to examine the troops.
Clausewitz was one of them and found it "striking how the action gradually
reflected the weariness and exhaustion of the armies." Less than a third of the
original army was still in action. "The rest of the troops were dead, wounded,
engaged in carrying away the casualties, or rallying in the rear. Everywhere
there were wide gaps" in formations.[80] Major Mikhail Petrov, in charge of a
battalion of the 1st Jägers Regiment that held position on the Kolocha River,
welcomed the sunset that marked the end of the battle. "The moans of the
wounded could be heard among the piles of dead that covered the plains and
filled up ravines. To us, they represented the sacred shadows of our valiant
comrades, who bid us their last farewell after falling for the glory of their
Fatherland."[81]

Some on the Russian side could not understand why Napoleon did not
press his victory, for he had already gained possession of the principal points
of the battlefield.[82] Observing the situation at the front line, Barclay de
Tolly sent his aide-de-camp Wolzogen to Kutuzov to obtain further orders;
knowing the commander in chief's character, he instructed Wolzogen to
"get his reply in writing because one has to be very careful with Kutuzov."
Wolzogen found the commander on a hill near the New Smolensk road,
surrounded by an entourage of "rich young noblemen" who were, it seemed
to him, indulging "in all kinds of pleasures and had taken no part whatever in
the terrible and serious events of the day." Wolzogen reported with German
directness about the parlous state of the Russian army, noting that "all important posts had been lost" and "the regiments were all extremely tired and
shattered." He even mentioned encountering a Russian lieutenant and thirty
or forty men standing resolutely in the vicinity of the Russian line and said
that when he had ordered him to rejoin his regiment, the officer had replied,

"This *is* my regiment!" Such forthrightness infuriated Kutuzov, who shouted at Wolzogen for delivering an "absurd" report. "Where did you invent such nonsense?" he derided the staff officer. "You must have spent all day getting drunk with some filthy bitch of a sutler woman!" Ever aware of the power of public perceptions, Kutuzov moved quickly to limit the damage that testimony like this could have caused. He looked at the officers around him and proclaimed in a loud voice, "I know better than you do how the battle went! And I am telling you that the French attacks have been repulsed at every point, and tomorrow I shall place myself at the head of the army and we shall drive the enemy from the sacred soil of Russia." At this he glared menacingly at his stunned entourage, which could do nothing but applaud him.

Wolzogen quickly grasped that Kutuzov's "cunning, dishonest intention" was to shape the hearts and minds of the army and the public, to craft his own narrative of the battle even before the guns fell silent that day. The Russian commander in chief "knew very well what had happened," one Russian staff officer commented, but he could not allow any doubt and discouragement to spread in the army.[83] His men, and Russia as a whole, needed a victory. No matter the actual outcome, Kutuzov intended to claim a victory to shore up the will to fight. He anticipated that after twelve hours of fighting Napoleon's army would be exhausted and unable to make any further attacks. Consequently, the Russians would remain in control of the battlefield through the night, which would give them the grounds to claim a victory, at least in principle. Hence that was why he reprimanded Wolzogen and welcomed Rayevskii, who arrived moments later with a more sanguine report. Kutuzov, recalled Rayevskii, "received me more graciously than ever because just moments earlier somebody had reported our state of affairs in a negative light. He asked me, 'So you believe we should not retreat?' I responded that, on the contrary, we should attack the enemy the very next day since in such inconclusive battles the side that is most tenacious always wins."[84] Kutuzov applauded Rayevskii's attitude and then dictated the plan of the next day's attack, which was sent out to the army.[85]

The order was purely a ploy, designed to keep spirits up and to forestall a rout. The news of defeat could have had disastrous consequences, which is why Kutuzov reacted so vehemently to any suggestion of a setback. His orderly was certain that Kutuzov spoke of an attack "out of political considerations only."[86] But these were crucial considerations. The announcement of an impending attack would keep the units together and create the impression that the army was in better shape than it actually was. It was, undoubtedly, bluster. Nonetheless, as Clausewitz pointed out, "this impetuousness and mountebankism [*marktschreierei*] of the old fox was more useful at this moment than Barclay de Tolly's honesty." The army had lost more than 45,000 men, including twenty-seven generals; a high proportion of senior officers had been killed or wounded, which rendered some units inoperational.[87]

Vorontsov's Combined Grenadier Division had lost over 60 percent of its 4,000 men. Some regiments were reduced to just a few dozen men—in the Odesskii Infantry Regiment the most senior surviving officer was a lieutenant; in the Tarnopolskii Regiment it was a sergeant major. Kutuzov kept his entire officer corps in the dark because he needed them to believe that victory was tangible, even if that meant misleading them. Late that evening he met with Barclay de Tolly to discuss the next day's plans. He was pleased to hear that the 1st Western Army had been regrouped and that a new redoubt was being constructed near Gorki. "Kutuzov thanked me for these arrangements, all of which he approved, and then told me that he would join me at dawn to resume the battle," Barclay de Tolly recalled.[88]

Accompanied by his wounded and dog-tired aides-de-camp, Barclay de Tolly then rested at a hut near the Gorki knoll. He was drained and famished; a small glass of rum and a piece of bread constituted his first and only meal of that day. The battle had a remarkable effect on soldiers' perception of the man they had so virulently despised. Throughout the day Barclay de Tolly had been seen galloping on his horse and commanding troops in the thick of the action. "I searched for death and did not find it," he confided to another general. Three horses had been shot from under him, all but one of his aides-de-camp had been killed or wounded, yet still his life was spared. "My ardent wish to die on the field of battle did not come true," Barclay de Tolly commented. Inspecting the worn-out regiments that night, he must have drawn some solace from the spontaneous cheers from soldiers who had come to see him in a different light.

— ⊠⊠ —

Napoleon's bulletins claimed a triumph at Borodino. This was, of course, absurd, for the battle was far from conclusive. The Grande Armée lost some 35,000 men, one-quarter of its strength, and saw its officer corps decimated; one French general was captured, twelve were killed or mortally injured, and one marshal and thirty-eight generals were wounded; hundreds of other officers had become *hors de combat*. True, the Russian losses were higher, but the French had failed to achieve the outcome they desired. "This victory, so hardily pursued, so dearly bought, was incomplete," bemoaned Ségur. "The losses were immense and out of all proportion to the results."

Soviet historians proclaimed that Kutuzov had gained, as one put it, "a complete strategic and tactical victory" over Napoleon.[89] This is untrue, for Borodino was not a Russian victory. The Russian soldiers had, undeniably, fought with astonishing tenacity and courage, but Kutuzov's leadership requires a more nuanced assessment. He had relied heavily on his subordinates, especially Colonel Toll, which did result in mistakes. The initial Russian deployment was poor, necessitating a redeployment to a second position, where Kutuzov built too many fortifications and deployed too many troops on the right flank; if the fortifications on the left flank had received as much attention as was lavished on those in the north, Bagration might have had a better chance of holding out. Throughout the battle, as Napoleon held the initiative and dictated the course of events, Kutuzov remained absent from the thick of the action. This does not mean, however, that he was uninvolved in battle or had spent the day, in Tolstoy's memorable description, chewing on "a piece of roast chicken." He observed part of the battlefield from Gorki and remained attuned to the flow of battle elsewhere through his orderlies and aides-de-camp, who carried messages to and from unit commanders. On several occasions he instructed senior officers to proceed to threatened battle sectors. The long-standing criticism of him not doing enough to support Bagration is only marginally accurate. Before the first French attack commenced, Kutuzov did shift additional forces that helped to sustain the left wing throughout the morning. In fact, by afternoon, too many Russian troops had been hemmed in there along the narrow front. As one staff officer described it, "Our troops stood six ranks deep on the left flank, which is why the enemy found it so difficult to penetrate it."[90] Such dense deployment also offered a convenient target for artillery fire and resulted in heavier casualties. Meanwhile, the Platov-Uvarov Raid in the north, though interesting in concept, produced no results partly because Kutuzov chose not to support it with sufficient infantry force.

Such criticism notwithstanding, Kutuzov's central objectives of letting Napoleon "break his teeth on us" and satisfying the army's and public's thirst for a show of force (a vital psychological factor in itself) had been accomplished. Clausewitz was right to suggest that Kutuzov's value at Borodino was not as a tactical commander but as a leader whose "worth was more at the head of the whole," where his "cunning and prudence" allowed him "to survey his own position and that of his adversary" better than individual commanders with their limited perspective.[91] French officer Jean-Jacques Pelet, who witnessed the battle, also thought the Russian commander in chief deserved some praise. "Although Kutuzov initially deployed his forces poorly and did not grasp soon enough what he needed to do," the Frenchman commented, "he showed during the rest of the day that character that is one of the most essential traits for a good commander in chief. His tenacity offset and partly even upset [Napoleon's] grand designs."[92] These words echo Napoleon's own belief that one of the most important qualities of a general was having "a cool head," one that does not let itself be "dazzled, or carried away by good or bad news."[93]

The Russians' spirits on the evening after the battle remained high; the fact that they had stood up to Napoleon and held their ground gave the soldiers a sense of triumph. "Everyone was in such a rapturous state of mind that the thought of defeat, or even a partial letdown, would not even enter our minds," recalled Prince Vyazemskii, adding that nobody felt vanquished.

Yet the losses were horrendous. The night after the battle, as rain drizzled over thousands of corpses scattered on the battlefield, General Konovnitsyn struggled to come to grips with the horrors he had witnessed. "We have countless wounded and killed," he confided to his wife. "[Nikolai] Tuchkov is wounded in his chest, [his brother] Alexander is killed, the other brother, Pavel, was captured earlier; Ushakov's leg has been ripped off; Driezen is wounded, and so are Richter and Bagration. . . . My division no longer exists, for it has barely a thousand men."[94] Many other letters like this must have been written that night, but as shell-shocked, exhausted, and hungry as the Russians were, their will to fight was still as high as ever. "A fog soon covered the battlefield and a complete stillness descended," wrote a Russian officer. "Only now we were able to calmly ponder the events of this memorable day. Not a single one of us considered the battle lost."[95] The news of victory and the commander in chief's intent to attack the next day caused widespread rejoicing among the troops and officers, many of whom greeted Pavel Grabbe, the staff officer who delivered the news, with "joyful faces" and "utter delight."[96]

As the moon rose over the Borodino plains, Kutuzov was at his headquarters. "That evening we were still not aware of the huge losses we had suffered during the day," remembered Bennigsen. "We therefore considered, for a while, retaking our central battery during the night and continuing the battle on the morrow."[97] Kutuzov knew better and was simply waiting for a formal report that would reveal the extent of the losses before he announced his decision. Toll and his staff officers, sent to inspect the army, gave him what he needed. Their first reports began arriving around eleven at night, describing the frightfully parlous state of the army. Tens of thousands had been killed or wounded, entire regiments had been destroyed, and some divisions had been reduced to a few hundred men. By midnight, Kutuzov ordered the army to abandon its positions and retreat several miles to a new position behind Mozhaisk, where he could still control the key routes.

He weighed his options. Should the army head east to Moscow? North to St. Petersburg? Or maybe veer southward and withdraw toward Kaluga, closer to his supply bases, which would force the French to follow him and thereby spare the capital city? The last of these would have been a natural choice except that Kutuzov understood that the army needed breathing space to recover from the bloodshed. Marching south would have meant fighting an orderly retreat and facing Napoleon yet again. The Russian army was in no condition to give another major battle, and Kutuzov needed to find a way to distract Napoleon, to get him off his tail and gain precious time. Kutuzov resolved to sacrifice Moscow in order to save his army. It was the most consequential decision of the whole campaign. "It was very difficult for me to abandon Moscow," he reminisced two months later, "but I knew that fighting another battle might have led to the [defeat and the] end of the war, so I chose to forgo the city."[98] He knew that he was treading on perilous territory. The policy of retreat had brought down his predecessor just ten days earlier, and his decision to abandon the city could easily end his career. Ever aware of the power of propaganda, he claimed success at Borodino. The fact that Napoleon had ordered his troops to pull back to their original position played into his hands, fostering the illusion that the Russians had won the day. The battle was hardly over when Kutuzov wrote to Rostopchin. "Today was a fierce and bloody battle," he told the governor. "With the Lord's help, the Russian army refused to concede even a single step, even though the enemy was in far superior numbers. Placing my faith in the Lord and the Moscow saints, I hope to resume the battle with fresh forces tomorrow."[99]

Then came the first in a series of letters to the czar, in which Kutuzov was careful not to claim an outright victory—in fact, that word is not even mentioned in the first dispatch, and the closest he got to it was when he wrote, "The batteries changed hands over and over again, but in the end the enemy nowhere gained a step despite having superior forces." In St. Petersburg, this passage would be interpreted as describing a victory. Kutuzov instead described the course of the action, emphasized the bravery and tenacity of the Russian troops, and stressed the fact that the army had fought for an entire day and survived. "We remain the masters of the field of battle," Kutuzov underscored. His subsequent reports were more assertive about Russian success but also spoke of the heavy losses that compelled him to move the army to Mozhaisk, where he hoped to receive reinforcements and fight another day. He assured the czar that he was interested not in "the glory of merely winning the battles but rather in achieving the goal of annihilating the entire French army." The official army bulletin reiterated these points, claiming the French "were driven back at all points."[100]

Kutuzov saw Borodino as an important step toward Napoleon's defeat, for it had claimed so many of the best and brightest of the Grande Armée. He understood that as dreadful as the Russian losses were, they could be compensated for over time, since the army was deep in its native land and capable of tapping a wide network of supply magazines and recruitment depots. Napoleon, on the other hand, faced a far greater challenge in replenishing his losses (especially in cavalry), and without those who fell at Borodino he was substantially inferior in force. Knowing that even his private letters would become public, Kutuzov wrote Catherine, "I am well, my dear, and am unbeaten: I have won the battle over Bonaparte."[101]

Kutuzov's reports reached the Russian imperial capital during the night of September 11. Alexander did not publish the second dispatch, which spoke of the need to retreat, but had the first report properly edited and printed, thereby assisting Kutuzov in shaping public opinion. The following day,

Kutuzov's courier, with a revised report in his hand, was told to make an entry into St. Petersburg just as the public was celebrating the emperor's saint's day. The imperial family was attending a mass at the Alexander of Neva monastery. The report was read aloud after the liturgy and then released for publication in the newspapers.

The news of victory at Borodino was celebrated in cities and towns across Russia. "Kutuzov has turned St. Alexander's day into a new Christmas day," Ivan Odenthal wrote to a friend on September 15. "Everyone was congratulating each other with the victory, there were plenty of hugs and kisses. It is impossible to convey the depth of the joy and delight that shone on everyone's faces." Thousands filled up the streets, cheering the czar and reveling with such splendor and abandon as "has never been celebrated since the very founding of the city."[102] John Quincy Adams wrote that St. Petersburg was "illuminated," while the English traveler Ker Porter described how "with the victory being publicly declared, the Te Deum was again chanted, every voice united in the strain which gave glory to the God who had fought for Russia and covered her people with immortal honours."[103] In Moscow, Governor Fedor Rostopchin, who had been publishing patriotic proclamations for the past few weeks, issued more bulletins declaring that "the accursed one"—meaning Napoleon—would "perish through famine, fire, and sword." A Te Deum service was held at the Dormition Cathedral in Moscow, and the air over the city reverberated with singing and the constant pealing of church bells. The public devoured every last bit of news and any and all rumors from the army, no matter how outlandish. Joseph de Maistre informed the Sardinian foreign minister that he had heard stories that "by the end of the battle the French had completely run out of ammunition and were throwing stones." John Quincy Adams was exasperated by people giving "credit to all the stories" about the Russian victory at Borodino despite many of them being "without foundation."[104]

To celebrate the Russian victory, Emperor Alexander handed out numerous awards to generals and officers—the wounded Bagration received 50,000 rubles, Barclay de Tolly and Bennigsen–the Orders of St. George and St. Vladimir—and gave each soldier a gratuity of five rubles, amounting to half of their regular annual pay.[105] Kutuzov was the great beneficiary of this largesse. He received the field marshal's baton and 100,000 rubles, more than the combined annual salaries of one hundred infantry colonels; Catherine was elevated to the rank of stats-dame at the imperial court. "Please do not judge me for being overly delighted," she told Madame de Staël. "If one is meant to feel proud of anything, it is of having a husband like mine!"[106] The public applauded the victory at Borodino, extolled the supreme commander of the Russian armies, and awaited the imminent triumph over "the accursed one." Just days later arrived the news that Kutuzov had surrendered Moscow.

| The Torrent and the Sponge

A T DAWN ON SEPTEMBER 8, "deep silence" reigned at the village of Gorki as a Russian staff officer struggled to navigate his way through a hellish landscape—"countless corpses, abandoned carriages and caissons, cannonball craters, and groups of the wounded"—to a small peasant hut. This was Barclay de Tolly's humble quarters. With a candle in hand, he entered the dark parlor where the general was asleep on the ground, next to his aides-de-camp. The staff officer gently awakened him to share the news that the army had been ordered to leave the battlefield. Barclay de Tolly, remembered the officer, "leaped to his feet, and, probably for the first time in his life there burst from his lips, generally so mild and gentle, a torrent of the most bitter invective." He called for his horse, wanting to see Kutuzov to convince him to change his mind, but was told the troops were already moving back. "The only thing left for me was to obey with a heavy heart," Barclay de Tolly later wrote.[1]

About 70,000 Russian soldiers, accompanied by their guns and baggage, took up new positions near Mozhaisk. Barclay de Tolly later lamented the mass confusion that spread in the army during this movement and believed it was due to incompetent leadership. He certainly had an axe to grind against Bennigsen (who, he claimed, simply disappeared during this retreat) and against Kutuzov (whom he accused of duplicity and failure to make proper preparations).[2] The army would no doubt have suffered the effect of the bloody battle, but, as Bogdanovich pointed out, "had the widespread disorders described by Barclay de Tolly actually occurred, the Russian army, pursued by the resolute Murat, would have hardly been able to conduct an orderly retreat," which it did.[3] Clausewitz did not sense any "dissolution" in the army.

The Grande Armée remained bivouacked among the dead and the wounded. Although the Imperial Guard was intact, Davout's and Ney's corps as well as Murat's cavalry had suffered considerable losses. Having expended over 90,000 artillery rounds and about a million cartridges, Napoleon was anxious to replenish his ammunition supplies before waging another pitched battle. Most crucially, the fighting had left the Grande Armée numb and disheartened; gloomy silence reigned at its bivouacs. "Few battles won had produced such an extraordinary effect on the winners; they seemed to be stupefied," wrote Georges Chambray. Most were, as he put it, "more uncertain than ever how long this war would last and how it would end."[4] Borodino was a pyrrhic victory and, unlike the triumphs at Austerlitz, Jena, and Friedland, had exacted a terrible price yet brought no tangible results; the Russians had left the field and showed no desire to engage in negotiations. The Grande Armée would have to start the pursuit all over again. Napoleon himself had been worn out, according to one veteran, "his face sunburnt, his hair disheveled."[5] Still feeling ill and unable to talk, he rested until noon, when Murat's advance guard approached Mozhaisk and engaged the Russian rear guard under Ataman Platov. The Cossack had floundered at Borodino; by entrusting him with the rear guard, Kutuzov must have wanted to give him another chance to prove himself. It proved to be a mistake, for Platov bungled this assignment as well. "Instead of holding ground for as long as he could and fighting every inch of the way," as one participant wrote, the Cossack ataman retreated to Mozhaisk so precipitously that the army could not even finish its deployment before the French advance guard appeared at the outskirts of the town.[6] "Platov brought the enemy straight to our camp!" fumed Kutuzov as he relieved the Cossack ataman of his command.[7] The new Russian rear-guard commander, Miloradovich, did what was expect of him, digging in and contesting ground throughout that evening. Trifling as this combat was, it showed that the Russian army was far from broken.

Fedor Rostopchin, the governor of Moscow, had enjoyed an illustrious if brief career under Emperor Paul, when he directed Russian foreign policy and dreamed up grand imperial designs. The untimely death of his benefactor left him languishing in disgrace for over a decade before launching a comeback. In the summer of 1812, he became the governor of Russia's historic capital. Rostopchin was a complex character, full of contrasts, contradictions, and oddities. Empress Catherine nicknamed him "Fedor the Mad." A close companion of Emperor Paul, as noted, he quarreled with Alexander, whom he held responsible for the decline of Russia's standing in Europe. In 1807 he published a pamphlet that denounced the prevalence of French culture in the Russian aristocracy and called for the revival of traditional Russian culture. The booklet enjoyed considerable success and elevated its author's public profile.[8] Among his supporters was Grand Duchess Catherine, who lobbied her brother to appoint Rostopchin as the governor of Moscow.[9] The czar granted her wish in June 1812. Rostopchin threw himself wholeheartedly into the job, presiding over an unending series of balls, banquets, dinners, and festivities.[10] He assured everyone that any war against Napoleon would be quick and decisive in Russia's favor.

Despite the rumors and ominous news, the report of the Grande Armée's crossing the Niemen surprised Rostopchin. He saw it as his primary duty to root out subversion and to keep up the people's morale by, as he put it, "working on the minds of the people, arousing them and preparing them for any sacrifice for the salvation of the Fatherland." Yet, in his understanding, "patriotism" entailed condemnation of everything foreign and exaltation of everything Russian. He launched a media blitz, publishing his *afishy* (broadsheets), which mixed nationalism, xenophobia, and populism to produce a fresh and potent brew of propaganda.[11] The broadsheets were deliberately trivial and written in what he believed to be racy but popular Russian language to allow for quick comprehension by the masses. To ensure their effectiveness, Rostopchin recruited agents who were tasked with spreading rumors, maintaining "patriotic enthusiasm," and "diminishing the disagreeable impression made by bad news." He was infuriated when Muscovites did not display sufficiently patriotic fervor during a quick visit the czar made to the former capital. The governor was astonished to hear that some "cowards and malcontents," as he called them, were in fact very critical of the government's failure "to avoid a third war with the enemy who has already twice defeated Russian armies."[12] He suspected foreign influences—Illuminati, Freemasons, Martinists, Jacobins, freethinkers—of seeking to poison Russian minds and undermine traditional mores. "A firm supporter of serfdom and a reactionary by conviction," as one Russian historian observed, "Rostopchin was fanatically hostile to France as the source of revolutionary ideals and to Napoleon as the product of that revolution."[13] In his privy a shelf was built over a bronze bust of Napoleon to hold up the chamber pot.[14]

War offered Rostopchin a chance to settle old scores and to rid Muscovite society of what he saw as pernicious foreign influences. But it also brought foreboding. As the Russian armies retreated beyond Smolensk and refugees and the wounded poured into Moscow, Rostopchin began to suspect that Moscow itself was in danger; even while assuring the public that the capital was safe, he began evacuating key state institutions from the city.[15] The movement of hundreds of transports could hardly escape the eyes of a nervous populace. By the first week of September, most affluent Muscovites had ignored the governor's proclamations, packed their belongings, and left the city. Madame Louise Fusil, a French actress and singer who had been living in Russia for six years, recalled how after the fall of Smolensk, "a continuous procession of vehicles, carts, furniture, pictures, belongings of all sorts" began to leave the city.[16] Rostopchin was still confident, at least publicly, that the Russian army would make a stand and protect Moscow. Kutuzov's appointment as the supreme commander emboldened this thinking, for he

was confident that a true-blue Russian nobleman like him would not tolerate the loss of a great symbol of Russian glory. Indeed, Kutuzov assured
Rostopchin that he would do his best to defend the capital, noting that "I
believe that the loss of Moscow would mean the loss of Russia." A few days
later, he reiterated that "all of my movements have been hitherto directed
to a single goal of saving the great city of Moscow."[17] When in late August
Rostopchin inquired about Kutuzov's intentions concerning the defense of
Moscow, the Russian commander reassured him that "our armies will go no
further than Mozhaisk and there, with Lord's help and relying on Russian
bravery, I shall give battle to the enemy."[18]

Rostopchin had been delighted to hear such assurances. There could be
no discussion as to whether it was better to save the army or Moscow, for
the answer was clear: "Every Russian justly considers Moscow as the nation's
bastion. With its fall, the fetter that binds together popular opinion and
strengthens the throne of our Sovereign would be broken."[19]

Rostopchin was, therefore, quite surprised by a letter from Kutuzov that
arrived on the eve of the Battle of Borodino. "I shall fight a battle in the
present position," the general wrote him, "If, however, the enemy tries to
flank me, I shall retreat . . . to Moscow."[20] The governor was alarmed by such
a prospect. "Moscow is in a rather perilous situation," he wrote to a friend
on September 5, revealing his first doubts about Kutuzov's pledge "to fight
a battle and pursue no other goal but to defend Moscow."[21] The governor
eagerly awaited the news from Borodino. Late in the afternoon of September
7, Kutuzov wrote him that the army was engaged in "the bloodiest of
battles" against an enemy with superior numbers but that so far everything
was "going well." Neither this nor subsequent letters made any mention
of the grave losses the army had suffered, but Kutuzov did request that "as
many reinforcements as possible" be sent from Moscow so that he could continue the fight.[22] Rostopchin later recalled that the courier who delivered
this letter also informed him of the capture of Marshal Murat (not the case, as
we have seen). The governor immediately prepared a bulletin to share these
great tidings with the Muscovites.[23] A special Te Deum service was held at
the Uspenskii Cathedral inside the Kremlin, while church bells throughout
the city pealed wildly.

The bells were probably still ringing when Rostopchin received new
missives that gradually revealed the true situation with the army. Kutuzov
first spoke about the heavy fighting at Borodino and then broke the hard
news: "Bearing in mind that we seek not glorious victories, but the destruction of the French army, I have decided, after spending the night on the
battlefield, to retreat from Mozhaisk."[24]

Kutuzov's decision to abandon Mozhaisk was prompted by a combination
of factors. As we have seen, he gradually became convinced that sacrificing
Moscow was the only way to contain Napoleon's offensive. Moreover, the

Russian army had suffered great losses and required reinforcements. Kutuzov had earlier instructed the "recruitment depots of the second line" to start sending their trained recruits into the vicinity of Moscow, where Generals Lobanov-Rostovskii and Kleinmichel were also to deliver their reserve regiments. Expecting to utilize these forces to replenish his army and thus regain a numerical edge over the Grande Armée, Kutuzov led the army to the village of Vyazemy. One can only imagine his exasperation when he received the czar's order forbidding the use of reserve forces, which, Alexander argued, were needed to train a new, 180,000-man-strong recruitment levy that he had announced. The czar then advised Kutuzov to make use of the "Moscow militia" of some 80,000 men that Rostopchin had been telling him about.[25] There was just one slight problem: that force did not exist. Despite the governor's boastful promises, the army received only 24,300 militiamen, barely enough to replenish half of the losses the army had sustained at Borodino.[26] Moreover, despite Kutuzov's repeated requests for transports to evacuate the wounded, the Moscow governor failed to provide a single one. Kutuzov was astounded by this and chided Rostopchin: "The extreme nature of circumstances makes me hopeful that Your Excellency would comply with my request at the very moment when the salvation of Moscow is at stake!"[27]

Kutuzov found himself in a delicate position. Realizing that he would not receive as many reinforcements or transports as he had expected, he felt compelled to move his army farther east. It seems plausible that at this stage he had already realized that Moscow could not be defended but remained uneasy about sharing this with anyone. The last person he would have confided his thoughts to would have been Rostopchin, a foolhardy man who, Kutuzov believed, could jeopardize military operations. Rostopchin had suggested leading tens of thousands of regular Muscovites to support the army, a proposal Kutuzov would have found utterly reckless and perilous. Therefore, during those crucial September days, as he was still deciding what to do next, Kutuzov effectively kept the governor in the dark, apparently reassuring him that the battle of Borodino was a Russian victory and that Moscow would be defended.[28] On September 11, he assured him that despite the heavy losses sustained at Borodino, "my troops remain sufficiently strong to not only confront the enemy but even prevail over him."[29] Letters like this perplexed Rostopchin, who later denounced them as "outright deceptions."[30]

Refusing to admit the possibility of Napoleon reaching Moscow, the governor continued to assure Muscovites that the city would be protected and called upon local landowners "to remain calm and not to take any precautions to protect their properties."[31] Rostopchin's anxious behavior during these days can be understood if we consider that he effectively staked his own reputation on Moscow not falling to the enemy. Surrendering the city without a fight would have been too much to bear, irrespective of the military rationale for it. He felt the ground slipping away from under his feet, and uncertainty about Kutuzov's intentions only further exasperated him. "My heart bleeds to even contemplate the unfortunate possibility of the enemy entering the capital," he lamented on September 10. The fall of Moscow "would bring dishonor upon Russia, which would be worse than death itself."[32] Until the last moment, Rostopchin refused to admit that Moscow might fall.

The Russian retreat produced, in the words of a Muscovite resident, a "terrible tumult." Wounded officers and soldiers streaming into Moscow were often accompanied by hundreds of tearful peasants, who told stories of the French ruthlessly plundering and burning villages. Rostopchin did his best to calm things. Searching for scapegoats, he vented his frustration on outsiders.[33] "The foreigners here cannot be restrained," he claimed in mid-September.[34] To reassure the populace, the governor kept producing ever more outlandish news in his proclamations. He claimed that the Russian army had passed though Mozhaisk only because it intended to join up with reinforcements before counterattacking, and he promised that if the French reached Moscow, he would call upon Muscovites to do their duty. "An axe or a hunting spear will do its work, but a three-pronged fork will be best of all: a Frenchman is no heavier than a sheaf of rye."[35] Such proclamations, however, were ineffective. Those who could began to flee from the city— "the scenes on the outskirts of Moscow can inspire an artist to paint the 'Exodus from Egypt,'" wrote Maria Volkova to her friend. "Every day thousands of coaches depart through all the gates, some traveling to Ryazan, others to Nizhnii Novgorod and Yaroslavl."[36] Desperate officials begged their superiors to let them leave the city and save their families.[37] "At every step we encountered poignant scenes," remembered a Russian officer. "Women, elders, and children crying and wailing, and not knowing where to go. Pale and frantic people bustled about without understanding what they should do. Everything they knew was about to be destroyed and it seemed the Antichrist himself was approaching and the Doomsday was about to start."[38] In some churches, priests called their parishioners to mass, telling them that Judgment Day had come.[39]

On September 12, Rostopchin urged people to rise up and arm themselves. They were to bring three days' worth of supplies and "assemble beneath the holy cross and banners at the Three Hills."[40] The following day a vast crowd of factory hands, house serfs, and peasants, with some officials, seminarists, and gentry mingled among them, assembled, brandishing pikes, scythes, pitchforks, axes, and clubs. "There were thousands of people gathered there," described an eyewitness. "The distance of two or three miles was so densely packed that even an apple could not fall to the ground."[41] Waiting for Rostopchin's appearance, the crowd worked itself up to a feverish pitch of patriotic excitement. Yet the governor never showed up. Having waited for him for most of the day, the throng became convinced that they had been forsaken and that Moscow would be abandoned. They dispersed throughout the city, spreading ominous news; some resorted to "murderous disorders" and ransacked taverns.[42]

But where was the governor? Rostopchin had decided to travel to the army, in order, as he put it, "to confer with Kutuzov and to adopt, in conjunction with him, such measures that will lead to extermination of our enemies." His rhetoric, at least, had turned up a notch: "We shall rip the living breath out of them and send them all to the devil."[43]

Publicly, Kutuzov always professed—to Rostopchin and others—his intent to fight a battle on the outskirts of Moscow. The search for a suitable battlefield began shortly after he departed from Borodino, and he soon settled on a site near Poklonnaya Gora (Mount of Salutation), a few miles from the Russian capital. As with Borodino, Kutuzov was not involved in selecting it; Bennigsen, accompanied by Colonels Toll, Alexander Michaud, and Jean Baptiste de Crossard, examined the location on September 12. Poklonnaya Gora was located on the western bank of the Moscow River, straddling the heights between the villages of Vorobyevskoye and Fili and protecting the capital's Dragomilovskii suburb. It was immediately obvious to the colonels that it was not suitable for battle, but Bennigsen ignored their arguments. Making the sign of the cross, he declared that "he hoped to fight three more times before Moscow falls."[44]

It was there, at Poklonnaya Gora, that Rostopchin found the army. He saw disheveled soldiers digging entrenchments on top of the heights while officers argued ill-temperedly among themselves. There was an atmosphere of "great disorderliness," he remarked.[45] Seeing the Moscow governor, "the accursed Kutuzov," as Rostopchin was now privately describing him, welcomed him with the usual compliments.[46] The two men then conversed for quite some time, and this conversation, Rostopchin claimed in hindsight, "showed the baseness, timidity, and indecision of the man who was named the Savior of Russia even though he did nothing to deserve it." But at the time the governor was glad to see the commander in chief, who agreed with him on the importance of defending the city and declared that "here was where they would fight." Kutuzov even assured the governor that if it came to it they would keep on fighting "in the streets of Moscow" and asked the governor to return with the archbishop of Moscow and the icons of the Holy Virgin to inspire the soldiers.[47]

Golitsyn, Kutuzov's orderly, who was present at this conversation, could hear the two men discussing "the defense of Moscow" and how they agreed they would fight and die at the walls. Kutuzov was evidently not telling the truth, for by now he certainly must have made up his mind not to defend Moscow. Rostopchin's arguments would have made no difference to him. In fact, the governor's talk of organizing popular resistance or possibly destroying the city would only have alarmed him. He looked at the city as a piece on his strategic board. In Kutuzov's words, Napoleon's Grande Armée was like "a stormy torrent" that was hard to contain by conventional means. Moscow, however, could turn into "the sponge" that would absorb it and reduce it to nothing. Entering the Russian capital, Kutuzov reasoned, Napoleon would halt there, since he would undoubtedly seek a political resolution to the conflict. This would be a mistake, for the Russians had no intention of negotiating. Once inside Moscow, Napoleon would be absorbed, unable to squeeze himself out of this "sponge.[48] Meanwhile, the Russian army would gain time to regroup, replenish, and fight on.

Kutuzov would have rejected any suggestion that could jeopardize such a design. He could not afford to reveal to Rostopchin his intent to abandon Moscow, particularly when the governor spoke about destroying the city before the enemy entered it. Such a move would jeopardize the army. Kutuzov thus tried, in the words of one Russian historian, to "obfuscate and mislead Rostopchin over his actual intentions," assuring the governor that the city would be defended when he actually intended to leave it.[49] Golitsyn recalled that Rostopchin left the meeting "thrilled and delighted." He seemed not to notice the "surreptitious implications" of Kutuzov's assurances.[50]

Golitsyn seems to be wrong about Rostopchin's gullibility—the governor's own writings suggest that he left the meeting greatly disappointed. General Yermolov believed that the governor was "the last man who would have believed" Kutuzov. Rostopchin never had a high opinion of the field marshal's character, and his memories of Kutuzov's unctuous behavior at the court in the days of Paul would still have been fresh. The sight of the army also could not have been encouraging, nor the conversations the governor had with officers. As he was leaving, Rostopchin met Yermolov and took him aside for a private conversation. According to the general, the governor did not hide his suspicion that Kutuzov might be planning to abandon Moscow, and his parting words seemed ominous: "If you surrender Moscow without a battle, you would soon see it burning in flames behind you!"[51] Similarly, Prince Eugene of Württemberg remembered Rostopchin telling him, "If I were asked what to do, I would say, 'Destroy the city before you surrender it to the enemy.'" Rostopchin added that that was his opinion "as a private individual." Given that he was responsible for the welfare of the city, he would not give such an order.[52]

With Rostopchin on his way to Moscow, Kutuzov turned to his generals. Telling them that he was abandoning Moscow was fraught with danger; he was keen to avoid being the first to voice such an idea. To lay the grounds for the decision, he instructed them to better acquaint themselves with the terrain while he casually enjoyed lunch on a small bench set up on the crest of Poklonnaya Gora. General Dokhturov, clearly reluctant to spend the day out in the field and "apparently discovering a touch of the courtier inside him," shared a meal with the commander in chief. Their little picnic idyll was interrupted by the dour Barclay de Tolly, who "never held in high regard small comforts of life" and who, upon seeing Dokhturov staying behind, dispatched his aide-de-camp to fetch Dokhturov, "even if his mouth is still stuffed with food." Kutuzov apparently enjoyed seeing Dokhturov's disappointment at being summoned. "You must not keep the general waiting," he said with a glint in his eye, according to Löwenstern. "I shall manage very well by myself," he added, and proceeded with his meal.[53]

The generals spent much of the afternoon studying the position. They were surprised how meager its advantages were. The western slopes, where enemy attacks were expected, consisted of gentle rolling plains, while the eastern ones, to which the Russian army would have to retreat in case of need, were intersected with ravines. The reserves could not be deployed effectively behind the main position because of cliffs and the proximity of the Moscow River. Barclay de Tolly, worn out by fatigue and feverish, was the first to declare categorically that the position was so bad that "in the case of a forced retreat, the entire army would be annihilated down to the very last man."[54] Another general concurred that it was "utterly dreadful."[55]

Returning to Poklonnaya Gora, Barclay de Tolly found Kutuzov still sitting on a campstool, surrounded by the usual crowd of officers, who were arguing about the relative merits and weaknesses of the position. Barclay de Tolly pulled no punches in his criticism of Bennigsen, whom he confronted with his customary bluntness: "Have you decided to bury the entire army in this place?"[56] Bennigsen kept his cool, declaring that he would immediately inspect the position again. Barclay de Tolly then conversed with Kutuzov in private, pointing out major deficiencies in the position and urging him to make a decision before it was too late. Kutuzov, he wrote, appeared genuinely surprised, even "aghast."[57] Still, Count Ferdinand von Wintzingerode watched the old man "hesitate to make a decision," so discussions continued for quite some time.[58] Kutuzov asked Toll for his opinion. The colonel replied that the position was the worst imaginable and that he would never have placed the army in such a perilous position. Kutuzov then turned to Yermolov, Barclay de Tolly's chief of staff and former adversary (who changed his opinion of his boss at Borodino). The general agreed with the earlier assessments and condemned the position with such fervor that Kutuzov grabbed him by the wrist, checked his pulse, and inquired if he was feeling all right. This was, of course, part of a deliberate act. As Yermolov correctly noted, everyone knew that Kutuzov had no need for their opinions. He needed simply to show "his resolve in defending Moscow when in reality he never even considered it." And so the farce continued. Kutuzov solicited the opinion of Colonel Jean Baptiste de Crossard, a French émigré officer who had served in the Spanish and Austrian armies. The Frenchman was equally categorical, writing in his memoirs that he had responded, "Never has a position been better suited for the destruction of an army."[59]

It was already afternoon. Kutuzov was contemplating his next step when the silence was suddenly broken by the sound of gunfire, announcing the French attack on the Russian rear guard. With the enemy so close, the urgency became clear to everyone. Prince Eugene of Württemberg approached Kutuzov and whispered in his ear, "You must decide at once; irresolution is the worst thing you can do." Turning his gaze to the young general, Kutuzov snapped at him, "In this matter, for better or for worse, I must rely solely on myself," and departed from the crest to the village of Fili, where he set up his headquarters in a small peasant hut.[60] He must have already decided to surrender Moscow but, remaining mindful of the enormous responsibility it would place on his shoulders, was waiting for an opportunity that could serve as a foil for it. For that purpose, he summoned the army generals to a council of war later that evening.[61]

<hr />

The council of war was supposed to meet at four in the afternoon but was delayed for two hours by the late arrivals of some generals. Despite the Committee of Ministers' explicit requirements, the council of war did not keep any minutes of this meeting, so what we know about it comes from memoirs and letters written by the participants. Much remains unclear; even the number of people huddling inside Kutuzov's little hut varies from seven to twelve depending on the source. Candles illuminated the faces of Kutuzov, his aides Toll and Kaisarov, Generals Barclay de Tolly and Dmitri Dokhturov, Lieutenant Generals Fedor Uvarov, Alexander Osterman-Tolstoy, and Peter Konovnitsyn, and Major General Yermolov; Bennigsen, Ataman Platov, and Lieutenant General Nikolai Rayevskii came after the meeting had started, while Miloradovich could not attend because he had to remain with the rear guard.[62]

Despite arriving late, Bennigsen went straight to the crux of the matter, urging the council to vote in favor of another battle. He expressed his doubts about Kutuzov's conviction that the Russian army was not yet ready to fight and reminded the participants how often they had fought valiantly in the past. Kutuzov interrupted him, arguing that these were "useless and crude questions." What the council needed first to do was discuss the general state of affairs and then expound all the relevant factors. For at stake was not just the future of an army or a city but rather the very survival of the Russian Empire.[63] This was a clever move—by encouraging the council of war to debate first and vote second, Kutuzov in essence sought to shift the responsibility for this momentous decision from himself to the generals who were assembled there. Speaking with marked seriousness, he broadly described the situation they were facing and posed the question in different terms than had Bennigsen: "Should we wait to be attacked in this disadvantageous position or cede Moscow to the enemy?"[64]

Barclay de Tolly was first to respond, delivering a withering criticism of Bennigsen, deriding his choice of position and his insistence on fighting another battle so soon after Borodino. The loss of one city was a small price to pay to win a war: "By saving Moscow, Russia will not avoid this brutal, ruinous war; but having preserved our army, the hopes of our Fatherland would be preserved, and the war would be continued on better terms." Kutuzov must have been very pleased to hear this, for Barclay de Tolly expressed precisely what he himself desired. He remained quiet and let other generals respond. Osterman-Tolstoy and Rayevskii voiced their support for abandoning the city, both declaring, "Moscow is not the whole of Russia and our goal is not to defend Moscow, but all of the Fatherland."[65]

Bennigsen was not ready to give up yet. He argued that Russians could not give up their capital following the "victory" at Borodino; such an action would devastate the morale of the army and the nation at large; the public would doubt that Borodino had been a victory "if it would have no other consequence but the surrender of Moscow." He enumerated other reasons the city should not be surrendered, including the dangers of moving the army through the city with the enemy at one's heels and the shame of abandoning the great city. He proposed gathering all forces toward the left wing and launching a preemptive strike at Napoleon's center at dawn.[66] Some who were there thought the proposal was not seriously meant and that the general was aiming at something else. Bennigsen understood that Kutuzov had already made his decision to abandon Moscow and could very well be removed from command because of this momentous decision; Bennigsen would stand to benefit as the voice of experience and wisdom counseling against leaving the capital to the enemy without a fight. Barclay de Tolly found the proposal preposterous and derided Bennigsen for even suggesting it. He pointed out that it was too late to prepare the army for such an attack, particularly given that it did not "maneuver sufficiently well," a point that Kutuzov would echo in the weeks to come. The field marshal agreed with Barclay de Tolly and drew some measure of satisfaction in reminding Bennigsen of what had happened when he attempted a preemptive attack at Friedland five years earlier.[67] He then listened as Barclay de Tolly discussed the advantages of retreating to various parts of the empire: Vladimir, where they could maintain direct communications with St. Petersburg; or Tula, where the army could make use of foundries and armament factories. Yermolov, meanwhile, sensing the true meaning behind Kutuzov's silence but, as a junior general, unwilling to vote for the surrender of the capital, tacked in the other direction and urged an all-out attack against the French. Kutuzov scolded him for proposing such an idea and proceeded to listen to other generals. The majority of them—Dokhturov, Platov, Uvarov, Konovnitsyn, and, in the end, Yermolov—supported Bennigsen's idea of fighting another battle and defending the city, while only three generals (Barclay de Tolly, Osterman-Tolstoy, and Rayevskii) recommended retreating. The debate turned acrimonious until Kutuzov abruptly ended the meeting by declaring that the loss of Moscow did not mean the loss of Russia. After a pause, he looked at the generals and stated solemnly, "I am aware of the responsibility I am assuming, but I am willing to sacrifice myself for the welfare of my country. I hereby order the retreat."[68]

The generals left the hut and dispersed to their respective corps. They were staggered by the gravity of what had just transpired. "We were ashamed to look at each other," admitted one.[69] Moscow was no simple city. No other place could rival its historical, political, and cultural importance to the Russian state and Russian society.[70] "Moscow . . . how many strains are fusing in that one sound, for Russian hearts! What store of riches it imparts!" declared Pushkin. His fellow poet Konstantin Batyushkov thought the city was a "sight worthy of the greatest capital in the world, built by the greatest nation ever." In the eyes of many Russians, Moscow was the "sacred city" and "the true capital of Russia," as Alexander Herzen put it.[71] Surrendering it without a fight could be seen as tantamount to treason. "Our hair stood on end as we pondered the decision," remembered Konovnitsyn after the council of Fili, while Dokhturov was unsparing in his indictment of "the small-minded people" who had made the decision. He wrote to his wife that evening, "I am now convinced that all is lost."[72]

Kutuzov remained behind in the hut. "He walked backed and forth in the room," remembered an eyewitness. He was fully cognizant that his decision affected the lives of tens of thousands of people, not to mention his own future. He wondered how the czar and the public would react to the news. He must have asked himself when the abandonment of Moscow had become inevitable. Was it the fall of Smolensk that determined this decision? Borodino? He leaned toward the former, writing to the czar that the surrender of Moscow was "inherently connected with the loss of Smolensk and the complete state of disorganization in which I found the army." Contemporaries thought he was merely shifting the blame from his shoulders to those of Barclay de Tolly. Joseph de Maistre was among them. He condemned Kutuzov's "baseness and vileness" and was adamant that "we must call things by their real name, for there are few crimes as heinous as one openly attributing the horror of Moscow's destruction to General Barclay de Tolly, who is not Russian and who does not have anyone to protect him."[73]

Kutuzov's accusation of army disorganization was unfair, but his emphasis on the loss of Smolensk was appropriate. He did not ascribe timidity or treason to Barclay de Tolly's decision to leave the city, which Kutuzov knew was not at all suitable for defense, but was rather stating the fact that the fall of Smolensk was of strategic importance. Even before leaving St. Petersburg, he emphasized the importance of holding on to what he considered "the keys to Moscow." Others shared his opinion. When the news of the French capture of Smolensk reached the distant town of Kharkov, Mikhail Marakuev, a local merchant, was surprised to hear local officers "firmly stating that Moscow would inevitably fall since after Smolensk, there was no other position that was strong enough to stop the enemy."[74] Nikolai Longinov, private secretary to the czar's wife, was of the same opinion, writing to a friend: "As for Moscow, those who know this area and the army maintain that, having surrendered Smolensk, it would be ill-advised for us to defend Moscow."[75] Even Napoleon thought that Smolensk was "the key to old Russia" and railed against Barclay de Tolly for yielding it without battle.[76]

In hindsight, abandoning Moscow was the correct decision, though Kutuzov's responsibility remains in the fact that he had assured the czar, the governor, and everyone else that his foremost intent was to protect the city, even when he must have known that it was no longer feasible. He had refused to confide his thoughts, thereby blindsiding thousands of Muscovites who had to scramble to evacuate on a moment's notice. This in turn could have imperiled the army's withdrawal through the city. Kutuzov understood all these dangers and he knew how critical and consequential his decision was. He spent a restless night after the council; eyewitnesses remembered hearing low, suppressed sobs coming from his room.[77] He must have felt genuinely anguished. We get a hint of his reaction from the testimony of his longtime aide-de-camp Colonel Schneider, who tried to reassure the field marshal that everything would be fine before naively asking where the Russian retreat would end. Kutuzov, as if stung by the question, got up and approached the table, "angrily striking" it with his fist and yelling, "That is my business to know. But I am going to see to it, as I did last year with the Turks, that the French end up eating horse flesh!"[78]

Late that night a messenger brought Rostopchin a brief note announcing the retreat. "Difficult circumstances compel me, in great grief, to abandon Moscow," Kutuzov wrote. He requested Rostopchin to dispatch "as many police officers as possible" to guide the army by different byroads through Moscow to the main road leading to Ryazan.[79] Rostopchin must have realized by then that Moscow, a city of some 275,000 inhabitants, was doomed, but he was still incensed by the news. "Was not [Kutuzov] swearing just yesterday that Moscow would not be surrendered without a fight?" he angrily asked the courier, who apparently replied, "War is full of unexpected and unpleasant developments, to which we all must yield."[80] Coming in the form of a short note just before the army's passage through the city, the letter was particularly humiliating for the governor, who had been given assurances to the contrary earlier that same day; he must have felt foolish for visiting Archbishop Augustine to convey Kutuzov's request to conduct the religious service before the battle.[81] "My blood boils in my veins," he wrote to his wife that night. "I think I shall die of this grief."[82]

His first instinct was to dash off a letter to Emperor Alexander: "Your Majesty! [Kutuzov's] decision has decided the fate of your empire. People will foam with rage when they learn that the city, reflecting the grandeur of Russia and where the ashes of your ancestors reside, will be handed over to the enemy."[83] A month later he told everyone who would listen that "Kutuzov not only lied to me but also deceived the entire Fatherland and the Emperor himself."[84]

At eleven that evening, the Russian artillery began to move though the city, and at three in the morning on September 14, the infantry columns set off. Outside the town there was still a multitude of vehicles of all kinds. "Imagine the difficulties attending this march through a city that is about six miles wide, with countless narrow streets and with nearly all the inhabitants trying to depart," Bennigsen wrote in his memoirs. "Even a small incident with a single team of horses halted the entire column in the street!"[85] Barclay de Tolly, assisted by Jacob de Sanglen and his military police, supervised the army's passage through the city and did his best to anticipate possible disorder.[86] His orders demanded strict discipline and prohibited "even a single officer or soldier from leaving the ranks; whoever is found away from their units would be executed [velet' zakolot'] at once."[87] Barclay de Tolly requested that Rostopchin deploy the remaining police officials in the streets through which the army would pass so as to ensure that "no army officials, and especially the rank and file, enter any houses or leave their ranks for whatever reason.[88] Löwenstern was among those who were stationed to maintain order. "We each had a Cossack escort to turn soldiers out of taverns and to prevent them from entering houses. Anyone found with brandy or liqueurs was to be arrested on the spot and bottles broken."[89]

Such precautions, however, did not deter the rowdiness and plunder that occurred that night and in the following days. The governor paid little heed to Kutuzov and Barclay de Tolly's requests for policemen and guides, the result of his negligence being that "there were no guides posted for the troops," and those who were supposed to be repairing roads and bridges were mostly just blocking the way.[90]

As their regiments marched down the city's main thoroughfares, officers gathered to discuss what was happening, remembered an artillery officer. Left to their own devices, the rank and file, under the pretext of fetching water, "slipped into nearby shops, houses, and cellars that were left open as if to treat the passersby—and while there, they bid goodbye in their own manner to Mother Moscow."[91] The much-reduced police force was unable to prevent these incursions into wine cellars and taverns, and the surviving police reports describe a veritable bacchanalia. "The soldiers no longer form an army, but rather a horde of brigands who rob and plunder in front of their superiors," Rostopchin complained to the czar.[92] Muscovite resident Andrei Karfachevskii could not believe as he watched Russian soldiers "smashing up taverns and shops in the market," while Alexander Bulgakov, who entered Moscow late in the afternoon, was appalled to see soldiers murdering a shop-keeper and "plundering everything."[93] Tussles and shouts of drunken men only further disquieted the already anxious townsfolk; one of them kept hearing loud drunken brawls and shouts of "The French are coming!" throughout that night.[94] Some of these "Bacchus devotees" ran in the streets "armed with knives, axes, knob-sticks, clubs, and other weapons" and shouted "Beat, stab, cut, and murder the damned Frenchmen! Show no mercy to the accursed foreigners!"[95] They were joined by soldiers. "Our troops go pillaging under the very noses of their generals," Rostopchin wrote in a letter to his wife. "I saw them break down the door of a house and remove all of its contents. . . . I believe the inhabitants are less afraid of the enemy than they are of their own protectors."[96] The last day before the city's abandonment was "genuinely horrifying," recalled longtime Moscow resident Fedor Lubyanovskii, who for years after the event could not speak of it without "horror and trepidation."[97]

On September 14, young staff officer Nikolai Muravyev found Moscow in a woeful state; there was widespread panic. He and other eyewitnesses noted that the poor threw stones at the carriages of the affluent.[98] Some blamed Rostopchin's jingoistic broadsheets for this popular anger. By claiming that Moscow would be defended and the enemy vanquished, these broadsheets had instilled confidence among destitute Muscovites, who were naturally infuriated by what they perceived as a cowardly exodus of the nobility and merchants just as the enemy appeared.[99] While the rich fled, quipped one resident, "the poor were forced to stay and breathe air with the French fiends [izvergi]."[100] The sight of long lines of coaches and carriages leaving the city angered the common people.[101] Taking his mother out of Moscow, Dmitri Mertvago was startled by the hostility of the commoners he had encounters with, as they "impudently grumbled against the nobles."[102] Decades after the war, Dmitri Sverbeyev still remembered "the fear and anger" that he experienced as his family's carriage went through the streets. The crowd called them "gutless runaways." "My father just sat in the carriage, without uttering a word and with his head lowered."[103]

The Russian army reacted to the news of the abandonment of Moscow with a mixture of anger and disbelief. Nikolai Golitsyn, who joined Kutuzov's suite at the outskirts of the city, recalled that they rode through Moscow in a "melancholy silence." "This solemn and silent march, of which no one except Kutuzov knew either the destination or the duration, had a sinister air about it."[104] Rayevskii wrote that the troops were demoralized and griping openly about abandoning Moscow. Some tore their uniforms in protest.[105] General Borozdin denounced Kutuzov's order as "outright treasonous." On hearing the news, Prince Bagration, forgetting about his shattered leg, jumped from his bed, only to fall to the floor and exacerbate his condition; a night of agony ensued. "I am dying not of my wound, but of one in my heart caused by the surrender of Moscow," he proclaimed in a letter to Rostopchin.[106] The march of the army resembled "a funeral procession more than a military progress," noted Buturlin, who had participated in the war. "Officers and soldiers wept from rage and despair." General Dokhturov conveyed the raw emotion of the moment: "I am seething with rage but what can I do about it?" he wrote to his wife on September 15. "What a shame it is to abandon one's native cradle without a fight, without a single shot! I have no choice but to obey because it seems God is sending his punishment upon us. I cannot think of anything else."[107]

With the night sky already aglow from the fires that were breaking out in the city, Kutuzov maintained an imperturbable silence as he watched an endless stream of wagons, carriages, soldiers, and civilians passing by. The evacuation was proceeding chaotically and with little supervision, which resulted in vast supplies of ammunition being left behind, including more than 150 cannon, 141 caissons, almost 75,000 muskets, 2,500 carbines, 40,000 sabers, 18,000 cannonballs, and 3,500 explosive shells.[108] Kutuzov knew that some 22,000 wounded had been brought to Moscow after the Battle of Borodino.[109] Thousands of them had already been evacuated. Lightly wounded men simply followed in the wake of the army, but several thousand of the more seriously injured soldiers had to be left behind due to the lack of transportation. On Kutuzov's orders, his duty officer, Paisii Kaisarov, sent a brief message to Napoleon's chief of staff stating that "the wounded are entrusted to the humanity of the French troops."[110] Few of them survived the next few days. "The laments of the wounded being abandoned to the enemy tore at my soul," remembered Yermolov. "The troops were outraged by this whole affair."[111] They blamed Kutuzov. "For the first time, the soldiers did not shout 'hurrah' upon seeing him," observed an eyewitness.[112]

Kutuzov was not the only general who believed that abandoning Moscow was the right decision. He was, however, the only one who could make this decision and remain at the helm of the army. No other general in the Russian army would have survived such a momentous decision. Had Barclay de Tolly given such an order, he likely would have been strung up. Russian artillery officer Ilya Radozhitskii was correct when he commented that only Kutuzov, "the true son of Russia who was suckled with her breastmilk [vskormlennyi eye sostsami]," could give up Moscow without a fight. Such a great sacrifice seemed acceptable only "if it was offered by the chosen and foremost defender of the Fatherland."[113] Yet it was a heavy burden to bear. Kutuzov—rattled, angry, and frustrated by everything that had transpired—had instructed his staff officers to make arrangements for him to pass through Moscow as quickly as possible. Traveling alone inside the carriage, he was left to his own thoughts, sullenly watching the tragedy unfolding all around him. At the bridge over the Yauza River, amid what an eyewitness described as "indescribable confusion," he stumbled upon Rostopchin. "The meeting was glacial," remembered Golitsyn, Kutuzov's orderly. Rostopchin began to talk, but the field marshal refused to answer and simply ordered that the bridge be cleared so that the troops could march on. An officer rode up to him and broke the news of the French troops entering Moscow. "With the Lord's help," replied Kutuzov, "this will be their last triumph."[114]

The Grande Armée longed for rest. Its soldiers looked forward to a sojourn in Moscow, where they expected to rest, eat good food, and enjoy the city's comforts, just as they had in so many other European capitals. "The weather was warm and clear that day," recalled an eyewitness.[115] Reaching the top of Poklonnaya Gora, the soldiers stood awestruck by the magnificent panorama of Moscow, which, according to Ségur, "surpassed by far everything that our imagination had been able to conjure in terms of Asiatic splendor." Even Napoleon's marshals, still in shock after the bloodbath at Borodino, "forgot their grievances [and] pressed around the emperor, paying homage to his good fortune." Everything about this city looked different, strange, and exotic.[116] Napoleon himself is said to have gazed long and eagerly upon the city in the bright sunlight. Struck with the beauty of the sight, soldiers around him kept shouting, "Moscow! Moscow!" and clapping their hands, "just as sailors shout 'Land! Land!' at the conclusion of a long and toilsome voyage."[117]

Their hopes were dashed almost as soon as they entered the city. Like many of his comrades, Lieutenant Albert von Muralt of the Bavarian light cavalry was stunned to see that the streets were deserted and abandoned. "This deathly silence and desolation struck me as rather worrying, as it certainly did many others."[118] All but a few thousand of the city's quarter million residents had left, making it impossible to prevent pillaging. Fires soon appeared. Fanned by strong winds, they consumed markets, stalls, and stores, and spread with astonishing speed to the rest of the city, leaving eyewitnesses astounded by the ferocity of the conflagration, which reminded many of an immense volcano that kept disgorging torrents of flame and smoke. Napoleon's secretary Agathon-Jean-François Fain thought it was as if "the earth itself split open and ignited all the fires." Driven by the strong wind, the fire spread everywhere, even into the suburbs, "engulfing that unfortunate town in a sea of flames!"[119]

The origin of this devastating conflagration has long been disputed, but it is certain that it was not the outcome of any deliberate planning. Despite accusations that he burned the city, Napoleon had every motive to preserve it. Moreover, the fires were already beginning when the Russian army was still withdrawing through the city, and no Russian leader would have deliberately sanctioned it. Arthur Wellesley, the Duke of Wellington, pointed out in his 1825 memorandum on the war in Russia that "in a town abandoned by its inhabitants, doomed by its native governor to be destroyed by fire," the powder magazines would have been the primary target.[120]

The conflagration was caused by a combination of factors. The general evacuation of Moscow was an unprecedented move on the part of the Russian authorities, since no other European city—neither Berlin, Vienna, Rome, Venice, Naples, Milan, Madrid, Lisbon, nor Warsaw—had been completely evacuated upon the arrival of the French army. Instead, each of these cities retained functioning municipal authorities, sent out deputations, and negotiated surrender. In Moscow, none of that happened; instead, municipal authorities were evacuated and almost all of the residents left. There can be no doubt that Governor Rostopchin preferred to see the city destroyed rather than surrendered. Although he did not personally order it, he had in his way facilitated the fiery destruction of the city. His orders to remove police and fire brigades left the wooden city entirely vulnerable. The departure of municipal authorities encouraged disreputable elements in the remaining populace to take their chances on making a profit out of the fall of the city. And we cannot discount actions by patriotic Muscovites, who, whether under the influence of Rostopchin's broadsheets or because of their own conviction, chose to set their property on fire. Napoleon, who had every political and military reason to protect the city, had never had to deal with a situation like this, and he exacerbated matters by failing to maintain discipline. Plundering commenced almost as soon as his troops reached the city, and with soldiers, camp followers, beggars, and criminals all looting indiscriminately, there was every opportunity for a fire to break out.[121] As one knowledgeable contemporary pointed out, an act of despoliation would require light, which was generally procured by "flashing off a firelock, and setting fire to the oil rag with which the musket is commonly kept clean." After serving its purpose, the rag was thrown to the ground, igniting whatever it landed on. Plundered and abandoned houses thus quickly caught fire.[122]

Kutuzov contributed to the conflagration too. Upon abandoning the city, he had ordered any remaining supply and ammunition depots to be destroyed. A subsequent official investigation established that several ammunition-laden barges that could not be removed were set on fire.[123] Numerous eyewitnesses testified to seeing a colossal explosion—"a globe of fire"—in the area east of the Kremlin in the evening of September 14.[124] These were ammunition supplies exploding. The force of explosion and the wind would have scattered this flammable wreckage among the wooden buildings, setting them on fire just as firefighting equipment was being hurriedly removed from the city.

For five days the fires raged unabated, reaching their fullest intensity on September 17–18, when much of the city was destroyed in "a sea of flames that flooded the entire city," in the words of Abbe Surrugues, a Catholic priest residing in the northeastern part of Moscow. Napoleon had to flee to the safety of the suburbs, from where he watched in awe and terror as Moscow went up in flames. "This was a beautiful city," he ruefully wrote in a letter on September 18. "I say it *was* because today more than half of it has been destroyed."[125]

As the conflagration subsided, there was no longer any trace of the resplendent Moscow that had greeted the Grande Armée just four days earlier. The city offered "a scene of indescribable horror and utter desolation," remembered a Muscovite as he surveyed a blackened landscape of collapsed houses, ruined buildings, and burnt trees.[126] Out of over 9,000 homes, more than 6,300 had burned down. Blackened human corpses and animal carcasses, broken crockery, furniture, and debris of various kinds obstructed movement in the streets. Acrid smoke and putrid smells overwhelmed the senses. The historian Nikolai Karamzin wrote to a friend, "For seven centuries, Moscow was growing and maturing! What remarkable times we live in! Everything seems like a dream."[127] For many Russians, the world was seemingly coming to an end. "The last day of Russia" had dawned, Lieutenant Aleksandr Chicherin jotted in his notebook. He simply could not comprehend any strategic arguments that justified abandoning the city. "Wrapping myself in my greatcoat," he wrote, "I spent the whole day in an unthinking torpor, doing nothing, unsuccessfully trying to repress the waves of indignation that surged over me again and again."[128]

| "The Old Fox of the North"

A S THE RUSSIAN ARMY was filing through the streets of Moscow, Kutuzov was contemplating his next step. He did not have a precise plan of action, as mindful as ever that everything in war is relative. With Moscow receding behind him, Kutuzov faced a choice. He could lead the army east to Vladimir, to draw upon the resources of the western provinces and to protect the routes leading to the imperial capital. Had the Grande Armée continued to pursue him, Kutuzov most certainly would have chosen this route. Alternatively, he could take a more southerly path, to Kaluga, which would allow the Russians to protect the resources-rich provinces and threaten the enemy lines of communication. The latter offered greater strategic and operational advantages. It was also more dangerous, since it would require the Russian army to make a turn in front of the Grande Armée and thus expose itself to a potentially devastating flanking attack.

Kutuzov first consulted with his intendant general about the availability of supplies. The news was mixed. There were few supply depots readily accessible so far to the east, though arrangements had already been made to transport provisions to Vladimir. At the same time, the intendancy revealed that plentiful provisions could be had in Kaluga and Tula, southwest of Moscow. Kutuzov's solution was to keep open both possibilities and wait to see what circumstances allowed. He ordered the army to march southeast along the Ryazan road. This route allowed him to turn left and proceed to Vladimir should Napoleon choose to pursue him, or, should the Grande Armée show no sign of movement, to turn right and head to the Tula and Old Kaluga roads in the southwest.[1]

As the army marched on the road to Ryazan, Kutuzov anxiously awaited intelligence reports as to whether the French were still pursuing him beyond Moscow or whether the "sponge" had indeed soaked up the "torrent."[2] A staff officer, delivering a dispatch from Miloradovich, was surprised to find him inside a humble hut by the side of the Ryazan road—"he was all alone, looking crestfallen, with his head slumped."[3] On September 16, having marked his sixty-fifth birthday, Kutuzov learned that the Grande Armée's main forces had stayed in the city; Napoleon had sent forward only the advance guard. He thus felt confident enough to attempt the maneuver to Kaluga. Later that day he sat down and wrote a lengthy letter to Alexander, which he sent via the emperor's aide-de-camp Colonel Alexandre Michaud de Beauretour. That he waited for two days before sending word of the loss of Moscow underscores his deep sense of apprehension. He needed something to offset the grave news he was about to share with the czar. The flanking maneuver provided him with such a foil. He opened his letter with a description of the perilous state of the army as it retreated from Borodino. "After the battle, which though victorious for our cause was also rather bloody, I was obliged to abandon the position near Borodino." He explained that the army was in a "weakened state" as it approached Moscow, and being constantly harassed by the French vanguard. Offering battle would have had "disastrous results." Having described the challenges confronting the army, Kutuzov broke the news: "In this extremely critical situation I decided to leave the enemy free to enter Moscow." Having made this devastating statement, he hastened to add, "The loss of Moscow does not mean the loss of Russia." Indeed, his intended maneuver to Kaluga province was a promising sign. It meant that the Russian army was still in the field and maneuvering into a position that would allow it to regroup and strike back at the enemy.[4]

The news of Moscow's fall shocked Russian society. "How can one even convey the impression produced by this news?" Countess Edling, a lady-in-waiting to the Russian empress, wrote in her memoirs. She was stunned by the "violent murmurs" that filled the imperial capital; she and other Russian aristocrats feared popular disturbances and rioting. "The nobility loudly blamed Alexander for the state's misfortunes, and in conversations it was a rare person who tried to defend and justify him."[5] The depth of the popular rancor was visible on September 27, the anniversary of the czar's coronation. When the imperial procession arrived at the Kazan Cathedral, it was greeted there by "an immense crowd whose gloomy silence and angry faces contrasted with the festive occasion." Countess Edling would never forget the moment the czar and his companions ascended the steps of the cathedral amid this eerie silence. "We could hear the sound of our footsteps and I never doubted that a little spark would have sufficed at that moment to produce a general conflagration. I felt my knees trembling." The ceremony went on without a hitch, but concern over the public mood remained. Kutuzov's report, therefore, arrived just in time to dispel the clouds of popular discontent. It offered "satisfactory explanations of what had happened" and "gave us hopes for the future," the countess noted.[6] The loss of Moscow was, John Quincy Adams

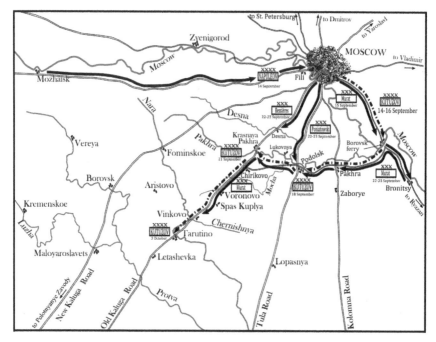

MAP 15 The Tarutino Maneuver

recorded in his diary upon reading the published version of Kutuzov's report on September 29, "attenuated into a circumstance of trifling importance as to the ultimate issue of the war."[7]

On September 17, the Russian army reached the Borovsk ferry, where the Pakhra River merges with the Moscow River, which, after flowing eastward, makes a sharp turn to the southeast. Kutuzov thought this would be a good place to attempt a flanking maneuver since the confluence of rivers would help conceal the true direction of his movement. Leaving a Cossack force to guard the crossing on the Ryazan road and to distract Napoleon's advance guard, Kutuzov ordered the rest of his army to make a sharp turn to the west.[8] The Russian soldiers then proceeded by forced marches along the Pakhra River's southern bank, hoping to reach the road to Tula before the French realized what was happening.[9] The crossing of the Moscow River at the Borovsk ferry, recalled General Yermolov, was accomplished with "great difficulty and in incredible confusion because of the countless vehicles belonging to the fleeing residents of Moscow." They could hear gunfire behind them in the rear, but the French did not seem to be pressing the attack.[10] General Horace Sebastiani, whom Kutuzov had met four years earlier in Bucharest and who was now leading the Grande Armée's advance guard, felt no urgency in pursuing the enemy, who seemed to be dolefully retreating eastward after the fall of Moscow. The French general sluggishly moved his forces to the Moscow River, where he found the bridge burned; it took him three days to realize that Kutuzov was no longer in front of him. Realizing the potential consequences of this development, Sebastiani sent an urgent missive to Napoleon, indicating that he did not know where the Russian army actually was.

Kutuzov's "flanking maneuver" earned the admiration of even his harshest critics. "This movement was the most important and most appropriate decision [Kutuzov] had made since his arrival," admitted Barclay de Tolly, while Bennigsen thought "the maneuver was boldly conceived" and, unsurprisingly, claimed that it had been his idea.[11] The westward march radically shifted the Russian line of operations and allowed the army to take up a strategically valuable position. The road to Kaluga offered many advantages. Once there, the army would be well supplied, since it would have behind it the untouched provinces of southeastern Russia, with its abundant resources and vast pool of recruits. No less important was the fact it enabled Kutuzov to protect the arms and munitions manufactories at Tula and the smelting works at Bryansk that sustained the Russian war effort. The new position also placed the army within striking distance of the enemy's line of communication and enabled it to coordinate its operations with Admiral Chichagov's Army of the Danube, which was making its way through Ukraine. Excoriated for abandoning Moscow, Kutuzov's defensive cautiousness was not due to lack of resolution; it stemmed from his conviction that he needed to stay nimble and flexible. Above all else was the need to gain time and space in which to muster additional resources. The "Tarutino maneuver"—as it came to be called—gave him all that. "Kutuzov did what he ought to have done," Napoleon remarked upon learning about it. "[His] measures were judicious."[12] A year and half later, with the benefit of hindsight, he told a captured Russian general, "Your wily Kutuzov pulled a good one on me with that flanking march."[13]

Late on September 18, "despite appalling weather and the most dreadful country roads," as Yermolov recalled, the Russian army reached the town of Podolsk, where it spent two days resting.[14] As it became clear that his gambit was successful and that the French scouts had failed to detect his movement, Kutuzov revisited his original intent and decided to push farther west. His new objective was to take up a position closer to the New Kaluga road, which would have brought the army even closer to Napoleon's line of communication.[15] On September 21, after another short march, Kutuzov stopped at the village of Krasnaya Pakhra, where his position was protected by the marshy banks of the Pakhra River. He deployed two strong advance guards to observe roads from Moscow: Miloradovich, with the 8th Corps and the 1st Cavalry Corps, was at Desna, just ten miles from Moscow, while Rayevskii, with the 7th Corps and the 4th Cavalry Corps, camped at the village of Lukovnya, protecting the Russian right flank and guarding the approaches from Podolsk.[16] Some urged Kutuzov to march farther eastward to the Old Smolensk road, where the Russians would be able to cut Napoleon's supply lines. But this was exactly what Kutuzov wanted to avoid doing. Such an attack would have provoked the French emperor to leave Moscow and confront him. He was convinced that his army needed time to recuperate, to train and equip the newly raised recruits, and to regroup before reengaging the enemy. The position on the Old Kaluga road gave him both the ability to control routes leading to the southern provinces and a base of operations across a wide area around the capital city. Kutuzov could continue to sustain himself with the vast supplies from the south while starving the enemy in Moscow. "Presently our main concern is to replenish the troops," he informed Alexander on September 23.[17] Since departing from Moscow, he kept sending out instructions on mobilizing supplies and recruits and instructed flying detachments of hussars, dragoons, and Cossacks to spread out around the capital to harass the enemy and deny him any supplies.[18]

On receiving Sebastiani's initial report on the "disappearance" of the Russian army, Napoleon was furious at the general's failure to conduct a proper pursuit. He was particularly upset about the news of tacit cease-fires that seemed to have developed between the French and Russian outposts, and his anger only increased after reading letters in which Murat spoke of meeting Russian officers and Cossacks who assured him of their goodwill and even spoke of their readiness to desert and serve under his leadership. To Napoleon, it was evident that the Russians were simply flattering Murat's ego and trying to pull the wool over his eyes. "Murat, the king of the Cossacks! Such a folly!" the emperor scoffed before sending a sternly worded letter to his brother-in-law, informing him that he was once again being duped by Russian promises of cease-fire, and that while some Cossacks had been "befriending" the French on the Ryazan road, others were busy killing them elsewhere around Moscow. "The emperor decrees the penalty of death for any officer who shall talk under the flag of truce with the enemy's outposts without authority to do so," the marshals were warned.[19]

For several days, the French remained unaware of the whereabouts of the Russian army. However, an increase in Russian raiding south of Moscow led the emperor to correctly surmise that Kutuzov might be executing a flanking movement, though he was not sure of the extent of it. The suggestion that Kutuzov might threaten his supply lines on the Old Smolensk road appeared to Napoleon as "nothing more than bluster" on the Russians' part, his chief of staff, Alexander Berthier, informed the marshals. "A victorious army would not deem itself to be in a proper condition to attempt such an undertaking;

how can it be believed that such a movement should really be contemplated by a vanquished army that has just abandoned its finest city?"[20] Napoleon then advised Murat to investigate the area southeast of Moscow, while Poniatowski and Bessières did the same directly south of the city.[21]

On September 22, the search for Kutuzov commenced. Murat advanced along the Ryazan road, Poniatowski moved south on the Tula road, and Bessières marched to the west of Poniatowski on the Old Kaluga road. Since the Russians had burned the bridge at the Borovsk ferry, Murat forded the river and proceeded as far as the town of Bronitsy until, finding no evidence of any Russian presence in this direction, he turned toward Podolsk, where the Poles were expected to arrive soon. His scouts ascertained that Kutuzov's army was moving to the west. Learning of the Russian presence south of Moscow, Napoleon envisioned a double-enveloping maneuver, with Bessières pinning Kutuzov's army down while Murat struck the Russian right flank.[22] Over the next two days the French and Polish troops marched in miserable weather, one of them complaining that "never in my life have I seen a muddier place nor a stickier mud."[23]

Receiving reports about the French movement, Kutuzov understood Napoleon's intent and sought to avoid direct confrontation by ordering his advance guards to fall back. Bessières soon occupied Desna, while Murat joined Poniatowski at Podolsk.[24] As Kutuzov considered his next move, Bennigsen urged him to conduct a reconnaissance in force by sending Miloradovich to confront Bessières while Rayevskii would "undertake a feint attack on [Murat] in order to distract him."[25] Kutuzov was not so certain, especially after reports revealed the large size of the enemy forces.[26] He argued that a major battle so close to Moscow was not in the Russians' interests—the army's current condition could scarcely be expected to deliver a success, while recent reports suggested that Napoleon, with the Grande Armée, could be upon them in no time. The Russians stood to gain more if they avoided combat, for time was on their side. Every passing day would ensure the steady increase of their numbers and the weakening of the opponent. "I am expecting large reinforcements and want to gain enough time so we can get fresh forces and then engage the enemy in a general battle," Kutuzov advised his advance guard commander. "That is why you must avoid a pitched battle."[27] He countermanded Bennigsen's orders and advised Miloradovich's advance guard to hold position and fight only if the French threatened it.[28] He then instructed General Alexander Osterman-Tolstoy to take command of a new *corps de bataille* (consisting of the 4th Corps and 2nd Cavalry Corps) and move forward to support Miloradovich's vanguard in case the enemy attacked in force.

Napoleon was keen to engage the Russian army and either defeat it in a decisive battle or, at the least, to drive it away from Moscow and his lines of communication. He instructed Murat and Bessières to probe the Russian defenses; if Kutuzov chose to stand his ground, Napoleon was ready to lead the rest of the Grande Armée out of Moscow and confront him in a new battle.[29] If a more offensive-minded general had been commanding the Russians, it is likely that he would have accepted this challenge. Considering the difficulties the army was experiencing, this might well have resulted in a French victory, profoundly affecting the outcome of the campaign. But Kutuzov understood that this was not the moment to give Napoleon what he wanted. The wounds of Borodino had barely healed. His reaction to the news of the French offensive was to order a withdrawal to the village of Tarutino.

The announcement of yet another round of retreats caused voluble grumbling among both officers and the rank and file. The news, observed one of Kutuzov's orderlies, "greatly upset Bennigsen," who sent letters full of grievances to St. Petersburg in the hope of seeing the commander in chief replaced. Sir Robert Wilson, who took it upon himself to be the czar's eyes and ears at the army, was among those who could find few redeeming traits in Kutuzov but appreciated his overall aptitudes and the fact that he was as "polished, courteous, shrewd as a Greek, naturally intelligent as an Asiatic, and well-instructed as a European." His letters depicted an utterly lazy and incompetent man who was physically frail and "unequal to much exertion in society."[30] Rostopchin could not hide his utter disdain. "What is maddening," he wrote to his wife, "is that our troops have gained the upper hand everywhere, but the general to actually lead them is still missing. . . . Kutuzov never shows himself; he just eats and sleeps alone, drags around with him a young girl dressed as a Cossack, and lets two scoundrels carry out all the responsibilities he is supposed to be doing." The governor's constant criticism annoyed even Kutuzov's detractors, one of whom groused that Rostopchin prevented all sleep by his bitter complaints about Kutuzov not giving him the "covenanted notice" and having deprived "the authorities and inhabitants" of Moscow of "an occasion to display not Roman, but more than Roman, *Russian* dignity."[31]

On October 3, the Russian army retreated to Tarutino while Miloradovich fought a series of rear-guard actions at Chirikovo, Spas Kuplya, and Voronovo—where Rostopchin had burned his magnificent estate to show what he would have done in Moscow if not for Kutuzov's perfidy—and held firm on the bank of the Chernishnya River, north of Tarutino. By now Murat's offensive had exhausted itself, and the French had no choice but to halt near the village of Vinkovo.[32]

"That's it—henceforth, not a step back!" Kutuzov supposedly said once he examined the new positions at Tarutino.[33] Located on the Nara River about fifty miles from Moscow, the area was not as deficient as Kutuzov's critics later claimed. The campsite was protected by the river's marshy banks in the north, while the rear and sides were reinforced with more than a dozen entrenchments and earthworks; abatis and other obstacles were constructed inside the wooded area on both flanks, which were constantly watched by special patrols. Kutuzov deployed the army in deep defensive formation: two infantry corps in the front line, followed by four infantry and one cavalry corps in the second, one cavalry and one infantry corps in the third, and the heavy cavalry and reserve artillery in the fourth lines. The Tarutino camp was sprawling—almost two miles deep and two and a half miles wide—and thus offered the weary soldiers the first real opportunity to rest and recuperate. "Our army currently enjoys many advantages," Sergei Marin, duty officer in the 2nd Western Army, wrote in mid-October. "We hold a position that is, by nature, advantageous and has been reinforced so much that the enemy will not dare to attack us." It was then that the rank and file came to appreciate what they assumed had been Kutuzov's plan all along. "So that is why we surrendered Moscow to the French! We were actually luring them into a trap!" Nikolai Mitarevskii remembered overhearing his comrades say. "That wily old man, Kutuzov! A tough cookie [*tertyi kalach*]! A shrewd old bird!"[34]

Over the next three weeks, both sides maintained an informal cease-fire. Kutuzov took advantage of this respite to begin reorganizing his army in the safety of the fortified camp. In the preceding months of campaigning and especially at Smolensk and Borodino, Russian regiments had been grievously weakened; some were effectively wrecked. Kutuzov's immediate task, therefore, was to rebuild these units and to instill discipline among the troops who had behaved so appallingly in Moscow. Most regiments were replenished with new recruits. Veterans of the combined grenadier battalions were split up and distributed into other units to help better integrate fresh recruits who brought the regiments up to strength.[35] Since horsemen could not be trained as readily as infantry, the Russian cavalry received fewer reinforcements and many of its regiments remained greatly reduced.

The time spent at Tarutino had a profound effect on the Russian army. By late October its strength increased from 75,000 men to over 120,000 men, with an artillery train of more than 620 cannon amply provisioned and horsed. The number of available infantry leapt from 35,000 in late September to over 60,000 in mid-October; more than two dozen Cossack regiments, each 500 men strong, had been raised, equipped, and delivered to Tarutino, increasing the size of their force to over 15,000 men. To make sure the fresh recruits came prepared, Kutuzov emphasized simplicity and accessibility in their training exercises. "Teach them the basics . . . how to march as a front, by companies and sections," he advised. "Do not look for any kind of beauty," as the rest would be acquired through practice.[36]

Kutuzov's constant care for "the benefit and contentment" of his soldiers, recalled one participant, "instilled an ardent spirit of bravery in the army and made it adore him with abandon."[37] The reality, however, was far removed from such romantic notions, as maintaining order and discipline remained one of the most crucial challenges. The number of soldiers leaving their regiments dramatically increased after the fall of Moscow. Mikhailovskii-Danilevskii recorded in his journal that "entire bands of marauders were wandering around in the woods and villages; thousands of them flooded the [local] roads."[38] Kutuzov responded with heavy-handed measures, demanding enforcement of strict discipline in the units, soliciting the support of civilian authorities in neighboring provinces in apprehending the marauding troops, and dispatching military police to round up the runaways. "We caught four thousand of them in just one day," commented Mikhailovskii-Danilevskii in early October.[39] The czar, apprised of the scale of the problem, had demanded results; hence Kutuzov dealt with these looters and deserters sternly, not shying away from "the harshest corporal punishments" and executions.[40] His correspondence is replete with examples of some of the sentences soldiers were subjected to, including running through thousand-man gauntlets.[41] Such measures did restore order in the army. Nonetheless, Kutuzov also understood that the best way to prevent plunder and marauding was an efficient supply system. He therefore made sure that food deliveries remained steady and plentiful and that the troops experienced few privations. By late October, he was pleased to report that "this evil of marauding has almost completely disappeared."[42]

"With the autumn fast approaching," Kutuzov told one of his generals, "marching with the main army would become progressively more difficult." He therefore remained determined to avoid a major battle and instead to wage a "small war" (*malaya voina*).[43] The main objective of this asymmetrical warfare was to hinder or prevent movement of enemy reserves, interrupt supply deliveries, attack isolated enemy forces, conduct diversionary attacks, and, in general, reduce the effectiveness of enemy operations. Flying detachments (or partisan detachments, as the Russians called them) already existed in the Russian army—Barclay de Tolly had formed one under Wintzingerode's command, while Bagration had created another, led by Denis Davydov. These were small mobile units of regular troops—Davydov's counted just fifty hussars and eighty Cossacks—whose mission it was to gather information concerning the enemy, intercept communications, and target isolated enemy soldiers. Kutuzov, however, envisioned a far more comprehensive approach. For him, "small war" was an integral part of the overall war effort. On his orders, a dozen flying detachments, commanded by Vasilii Orlov-Denisov, Alexander Figner, Alexander Seslavin, Otto von Stackelberg, Nikolai Kudashev (Kutuzov's son-in-law), Stepan Balyabin, Ivan Vadbolskii, Adam Ozharovskii, and others, fanned out across the countryside and effectively encircled Moscow. Their goal was not just to observe the enemy but also to wage a war of attrition. Kutuzov's instructions to one of these commanders are particularly interesting for what they reveal about his conception of partisan warfare. Its aim was "to inflict the greatest possible losses upon the enemy."[44] Upon learning that Ivan Dorokhov's men had allowed the French to surround them and barely managed to break out, Kutuzov explained to the unit commander that "a partisan should never find himself in such position." The flying detachments must be constantly on the move and "should remain in one spot only for as long as it takes to feed men and horses." Marching must be done at night and "covertly along remote tracks"; during the day, the men should "remain hidden in the woods or low-lying places." Upon arriving at a village, the commander must keep its inhabitants inside so that no one could spread the news. In short, "a partisan must be decisive, swift, and tireless" in pursuing his objectives.[45]

Dispersed in the forests around Moscow, the flying detachments patrolled the major roads leading out of the city and relentlessly harassed the French lines of communication. "Barely a day passes without us fighting the enemy, and we are enjoying an upper hand everywhere," Kutuzov wrote Catherine. "We are capturing prisoners without even breaking a sweat."[46] He appreciated the steady stream of intelligence reports that the flying detachments provided, allowing him to assess the situation and respond to operational challenges. "I am waging the small war with great advantages," he wrote his daughter in mid-October.[47] Flying detachment commanders were advised to act at their own discretion, but on some occasions Kutuzov set them specific objectives.[48] Learning about Russian prisoners of war being held at Mozhaisk, he tasked Vadbolskii with freeing them; when a report arrived that the French were seeking to secure a position at Vereya, Kutuzov reinforced Dorokhov and ordered him to storm the town, which was accomplished on October 10. Throughout October, Kutuzov's flying detachments acted with impunity, intercepting Napoleon's supply shipments and inflicting considerable losses in men and matériel. If we are to trust official Russian reports, by mid-October they had killed more than 4,000 enemy soldiers and captured almost 20,000. These detachments drew support from the second ring of defenses formed around Moscow by provincial militia forces in the provinces of Moscow, Vladimir, Kaluga, Ryazan, Smolensk, Tula, Tver, and Yaroslavl, where over 125,000 men were mobilized for war in the fall of 1812.[49]

Moreover, Kutuzov was keen to tap into the rising popular hatred of the French. He urged his subordinates to give captured weapons to the peasants and to inspire them by "reciting to them examples of the heroism displayed in other places."[50] In a letter to the czar, he explained that unlike many Russian aristocrats who feared that arming the serfs was dangerous, he was in favor of it. The leadership needed to tap into the peasants' "general zeal to inflict harm on the enemy everywhere."[51] Kutuzov did his best to encourage it. Dozens of peasant groups, some ad hoc and others assisted by the regular troops, were soon scattered across the countryside and wrought havoc on Napoleon's supply and communication lines. Controlling or coordinating such a mass movement was, of course, an impossible task, and inciting popular war was fraught with danger. Kutuzov understood this but remained convinced that the benefits of mobilizing the peasantry outweighed any fears of a popular revolt. Whenever landowners were threatened by unruly peasants, he felt no qualms about using the full might of the regular army to suppress unrest and ruthlessly punished the perpetrators.[52] But at the same time, inciting and harnessing popular fury offered vast operational advantages against the enemy, who, despite having been confronted by a guerrilla war in the Iberian Peninsula, clearly did not anticipate it in Russia. Upon reaching Moscow, Napoleon "took up the suitable fencing pose," in Tolstoy's apt expression, only to discover that instead of a rapier, his opponent was wielding "a peasant's cudgel." The French repeatedly complained that such a war went contrary to the established rules. Kutuzov paid no heed to these protestations and remained determined to employ guerrillas to maximum benefit.

The armed peasants, Cossacks, and flying detachments checked French foraging operations and caused considerable hardship for the troops inside Moscow. And yet Napoleon remained ensconced in the city for thirty-five days. As one Russian historian has aptly noted, this sojourn served as "a complete opposite" to his stay at Dresden in May 1812, when Napoleon was at the height of his powers—"the conqueror of Europe, surrounded by servile rulers and high court officials."[53] In Dresden the French emperor had been at the center of a carefully choreographed display of imperial power, fawned over by numerous German dukes and princes, ministers, and diplomats. He was "the God of Dresden," wrote French clergyman and diplomat Dominique Dufour de Pradt, one of the eyewitnesses. "It was, without a doubt, the highest point of his glory."[54] Now, just four short months later, Napoleon found himself trapped amid the ruins of Moscow, presiding over an increasingly disorderly army and anxiously trying to find a way to end the war. The only reason for prolonging his stay in the ruined capital was his expectation of a "speedy conclusion of peace," recalled a French general.[55] Abandoning Moscow and retreating would have been, in Napoleon's mind, tantamount to acknowledging defeat. And so he stayed amid the smoldering debris of the ancient Russian capital, hoping against hope to find an end to the war. Despite all the evidence to the contrary, he remained convinced that the czar would not hesitate to negotiate a peace. Twice he reached out to Alexander; each time he received no response.

Napoleon's letters and his conversations with the emissaries he dispatched to Alexander reveal how profoundly he misunderstood his circumstances, the czar's mindset, and, more broadly, the Russian attitude toward war. He dismissed the burning of Moscow as the irrational act of a lunatic governor and failed to comprehend that Russian society perceived it in a different light.

Russians saw the destruction of Moscow as the work of French "barbarians" and "monsters" who could no longer be shown any quarter. The city's smoke-begrimed ruins served as a powerful and unifying symbol. In the words of one contemporary, they were determined "to drown Napoleon in the sea of tears that he has created."[56]

Like many of his contemporaries, Napoleon misread Alexander's character. British historian Dominic Lieven has pointed out that many of his contemporaries, Russian and European, "shared some of the doubts on Alexander's strength of will."[57] Remembering Tilsit and Erfurt, the French emperor had hoped that Francophiles at the Russian court would push Alexander in a similar direction. He thus failed to perceive how profoundly their relationship had changed in recent years. "The further Napoleon advances the less he should believe that any peace would be possible," Empress Consort Elisabeth confided to her mother. "We are prepared for everything except for negotiations. Each step [Napoleon] advances in this immense Russia brings him closer to the abyss. Let us see how he copes with the winter."[58] Shortly after Colonel Michaud de Beauretour had delivered to him Kutuzov's report on the fall of Moscow, the czar instructed the colonel to transmit a special statement to the army. "I shall use up every last re-source of my empire; it possesses even more than my enemies yet think," he proclaimed, and spoke of his willingness to grow a beard and retreat into "the farthest confines of Siberia" rather than sign a peace that would humiliate him. "Napoleon or me, me or him, for we cannot both rule at the same time. I have learned to understand him and he will not deceive me again."[59]

Alexander was profoundly affected by the fall of Moscow. He later confided to Baroness Barbara Juliane von Krüdener, who introduced the czar to reli-gious mysticism, that "the burning of Moscow has illuminated my soul" and strengthened his commitment to confront Napoleon. "Be assured that my resolution to fight is more steadfast than ever," Alexander told his sister. "I would rather cease to be what I am than come to terms with the monster who is causing the world's misfortune."

Admittedly, Alexander had no other viable alternative. He was well aware of the prevailing displeasure with him and his rule; like Countess Edling, he understood what that ominous silence at his coronation anniver-sary meant. "A spirit of patriotism erupted spontaneously and without any particular efforts on the part of the government," remarked one contem-porary some years later. Hatred of the French ran deep, and "everyone wanted to avenge Austerlitz, Friedland, and other setbacks from previous wars that had humiliated us so much."[60] Prince Sergei Volkonskii remembered how Emperor Alexander's "meekness" with regard to Napoleon "left deep wounds" in Russian society. "Vengeance—and vengeance once more—was the unshakable feeling with which each and every heart was burning."[61] Such sentiments only further intensified in the wake of the continual withdrawal of the Russian armies and loss of Russian provinces. Just days after the fall of Moscow, Grand Duchess Catherine informed her brother, "You are openly accused of having brought disaster upon your empire. . . . If such news reaches me, you can imagine the rest. I leave it to you to judge the state of affairs in a country whose leader is so despised."[62]

Even if he desired it, Alexander could not afford to compromise with Napoleon. Public opinion was against it, and any sign of weakness on his part might have had severe consequences. A second Tilsit likely would have sealed his fate. Alexander knew only too well what happened to unpopular monarchs in Russia. Over the course of the decades there had been several palace coups and the assassination of two reigning sovereigns, including Alexander's own father. The bon mot about Russia's monarchy that it represented "autocracy tempered by assassination" contained a kernel of truth.

As weeks passed with no Russian response to his peace offer, Napoleon grew dismayed. He briefly considered marching his army to St. Petersburg, but his marshals pointed out the lateness of the season, the scarcity of provisions, and the poor condition of the roads. Why go north when winter was already at the door? And what about Kutuzov and the Russian army? The time had come to end the campaign, not to prolong it. Another pointless battle victory was less critical than getting into winter quarters as quickly as possible so that they could win a war. Disappointed by their lack of enthusiasm, Napoleon ended the meeting abruptly. The marshals' obstinacy prompted him to pursue peace once more—Emperor Alexander must be convinced to take the hand that Napoleon had proffered so late in the game. For this third (and last) diplomatic overture, Napoleon chose General Jacques Alexandre Bernard Law, Marquis de Lauriston. The scion of a Scottish family that had settled in France in the early eighteenth century, Lauriston had had a successful military career during the Revolutionary Wars and become an aide-de-camp to Napoleon, who employed him in various diplomatic missions, including as the ambassador to St. Petersburg. The emperor resolved to send him to Kutuzov's headquarters in search of peace. "I want peace, I must have peace, I absolutely will have peace," he told the marquis. "Save my honor by any means you can!"[63]

On October 5, the emperor's words still ringing in his ears, Lauriston rode up to the Russian lines and asked the outposts to convey a message to their headquarters. Kutuzov received the news around ten in the morning. He was conferring with Peter Volkonskii, the czar's aide-de-camp, who had just arrived to ascertain what was happening at Tarutino.[64] Despite the czar's specifically instructing him not to engage in negotiations with the enemy, Kutuzov was intrigued by the French approach, especially because it had been entrusted to such a senior figure, and he wanted to evaluate its scope and terms. Napoleon was clearly desperate, and Kutuzov was keen to exploit it. He agreed to hold a meeting at the advance post later that same evening.[65]

The news of the French envoy's arrival and Kutuzov's willingness to meet him drew strong opposition from the Russian generals. Rumors flew and many erroneously believed that Kutuzov had already agreed to discuss the terms of a peace convention that would allow the Grande Armée to leave Moscow un-molested; some even claimed that Napoleon himself was expected at the inter-view. Considering this tantamount to treason, about a dozen generals were resolved to take any measure needed to prevent it, including keeping Kutuzov from resuming command once he had left for the meeting.[66]

These were stunning allegations. The fact that so many senior officers believed them and were ready to "dispossess the Field Marshal of his au-thority," as one of them observed, points to a fundamental problem from which the Russian army suffered throughout this war.[67] Russian headquar-ters was a hotbed of intrigue, as officers jostled for position and competed for access to information. The first two months of the war had revealed deep divisions in the highest levels of the Russian command, and having observed the vitriol that Barclay de Tolly had been subjected to by his own peers, Kutuzov felt understandably suspicious of his commanders. Such feelings only strengthened after he became involved in daily altercations with his subordinates, who had little respect for "the Old Flounder," as some called him.[68] There was a dichotomy of views about Kutuzov in the Russian army. Soldiers and junior officers continued to admire him and spoke glowingly of his capable leadership; the letters of Vasili Norov, an ensign in a guard regiment, routinely spoke of the field marshal's "wise arrangements.[69] Senior officers held a very different view and regularly sent letters to the czar blaming Kutuzov for all their problems. The czar compounded the damage by sending copies of these letters to Kutuzov, whose sense of cyni-cism and suspicion of the people around him only increased as he perused them. Their overall tenor was that he was an imbecile and a coward, too old-fashioned, "decrepit," "half-blind," and guarded; that he spent too much time in the privacy of his quarters, where, as Alexander Bulgakov assured everyone, he "reposed in complete idleness, slept all day long, and constrained everyone's hands."[70] There was the usual accusation that he consorted with "a young woman dressed as a Cossack."[71] Even Sergei Mayevskii, who admired Kutuzov and, as an auditor-general, had frequent interactions with him, was critical of his physical infirmity. "For Kutuzov, to write ten words was more difficult than for some people to produce one hundred pages. Severe case of chiragra, old age, and lack of exercise—such were the mortal enemies of his quill."[72] Yermolov agreed, and thought that Kutuzov was now "a very different man from the one I remembered from the celebrated retreat from Bavaria. Age, a serious [head] wound, and scores of insults significantly reduced his powers."[73]

Kutuzov's surviving correspondence and the private papers of his staff officers paint a different picture. While he had less stamina, he retained his sharpness of mind and was very much in command. In his personal journal Mikhailovskii-Danilevskii described Kutuzov contemplating military situations, dictating orders, and attentively listening to staff officers' reports. The field marshal was generous with his advice, and as a result, Mikhailovskii-Danilevskii noted, he had gained "knowledge that would have otherwise taken me years to accumulate."[74] Observing his daily interactions, Baron Jean Anstedt, the director of the Russian army's diplomatic chancellery, admitted to his admiration of "the great superiority the prince demonstrates in conversations."[75] A quick survey of Kutuzov's correspondence provides copious evidence against his alleged lassitude, as it covers a multitude of matters, including mobilization of reserves and militia forces; procurement of food supplies, ammunition, gunpowder, horses, forage, winter coats, axes, and other matériel; arrangement of hospitals; coordination of the military operations of more than dozen flying detachments; and so on. After the war Colonel Toll, who along with Mikhailovskii-Danilevskii and a handful of staff officers spent most of their time with the field marshal and had ample opportunity to observe him, fiercely rejected any suggestions that Kutuzov had been uninvolved. He had rejected micromanagement in favor of delegation of authority. Toll said that Kutuzov had formulated the "general plans of action" and "designated when and where these plans had to be fulfilled," then tasked staff officers "with developing his ideas and drafting detailed instructions that were needed for a military operation."[76]

Kutuzov could not, however, resolve a long-standing problem of the Russian army—the lack of a proper and efficient staff system. His decision to delegate meant that a handful of individuals accumulated considerable authority with insufficient oversight. "As an old-school general, Kutuzov did not study the Yellow Book, containing the army regulations, in sufficient detail," noted Alexander Scherbinin, who served on his staff.[77] In fact, Kutuzov studied the statutes well enough to understand what was needed to sideline individuals he mistrusted. His relations with Bagration, Barclay de Tolly, Bennigsen, and other generals remained tense. None of these generals recognized Kutuzov's abilities; instead, they dwelled critically on his supposed ineptitude and blunders, souring relations with the field marshal. Bennigsen continued to claim, in public and in private, that all the best ideas were his. "The whole army knows that all the operations that are currently being carried out and from which we expect the most brilliant consequences, are the results of my work," Bennigsen wrote his wife in late September.[78] Ten days after the fall of Moscow, Rostopchin told a friend that "Bennigsen hopes to become the commander in chief."[79]

Bagration's injury deprived Kutuzov of a capable commander but also removed a thorn in his side. Nor was he keen on retaining Barclay de Tolly, whose courage, forbearance, and aptitude Kutuzov respected but whom he found too difficult to manage. Of course, there was also a matter of pride. Mikhailovskii-Danilevskii, who in his official histories avoided criticism of Kutuzov, wrote in his private journal that "upon being called to lead the war, Kutuzov could not conceal his sense of triumph [over Barclay de Tolly] nor could he ignore the memory of humiliation that Barclay de Tolly was initially chosen over him."[80]

Kutuzov shied from open confrontation; he preferred oblique methods, as befitted, in the words of one observer, "the grandest of the courtiers."[81] Barclay de Tolly was thus slowly deprived of staff officers and shut out of the decision-making; the place assigned to his headquarters was often completely separated from the main headquarters, causing one of his staff officers to quip that "they kept him beyond the outposts in the hope he would be snatched up by the French."[82] Increasingly, Barclay de Tolly was not consulted in matters involving the 1st Western Army, which he was still formally commanding, though Kutuzov at times made it all appear as the handiwork of Bennigsen, prompting Barclay de Tolly to lash out at the general. He watched helplessly as the army regulations that he had created and implemented were now routinely ignored. "The only grace that I implore is to be delivered from here and I do not care in what way it happens," he wrote sorrowfully to his wife on September 23.[83]

The Georgian prince had, meanwhile, suffered grievously after being hurt at Borodino. His wound was not thoroughly examined, and the critical nature of his injury was not determined until two weeks after the battle. By then, it was already too late—his wound festered, and gangrene set in. On September 24, feverish and suffering from agonizing pain, Bagration drew his last breath. "Not fearing Death, he awaited her with the same composure as he did on the fields of battle," described one of his physicians.[84] The report of his passing, arriving in the wake of the news about the fall of Moscow, amplified the shock to Russian society.

Bagration's death offered Kutuzov an opportunity to restructure the armies and further constrain his rivals. Four days after the general's demise, he announced the merger of the 1st and 2nd Western Armies into a single army but left their titles to Barclay de Tolly and his chief of staff, Yermolov.[85] This was a clever ploy. Kutuzov deprived Barclay de Tolly of actual authority and reduced him to one of the generals, but by retaining the title of army commander, he prevented the general from having an overt excuse to complain that he had been removed from the command, which, in reality, remained firmly in the hands of Kutuzov. "I am clearly shunned, and much is concealed from me," Barclay de Tolly complained to his wife in late September.[86] He was deeply offended by such treatment and by the unwarranted and insulting attacks made upon him in the preceding weeks, especially by Kutuzov's insinuation that his failure to protect Smolensk had led to the fall of Moscow.[87]

Two days after the army reorganization, Barclay de Tolly asked for sick leave, and he left the army on October 4. "The field marshal does not want to share the glory of expelling the invader from the sacred soil of our Fatherland," he told a staff officer. This intrepid general deserved better treatment than that, for his determination and unwavering commitment to preserve the army had laid the cornerstone in the Russian victory over Napoleon. "I have pulled the wagon uphill," he told his aides-de-camp as he bid them farewell. "It can roll downhill by itself with only a little steering."[88] Kutuzov would not have appreciated this sentiment for making light of the vast challenges he was facing; nor would he have liked the tone of the letter Barclay de Tolly wrote to the czar castigating Kutuzov for supposed mismanagement of the army. Unsurprisingly, he quickly approved the general's request and informed the czar; he made no mention of the amalgamation and the sidelining of Barclay de Tolly, but simply stated that he had assumed the general's responsibilities "until such time as Your Imperial Majesty will graciously name a new commander of the First Army."[89]

Barclay de Tolly's departure was a great loss for the army and exacerbated tensions within the Russian headquarters. Kutuzov was now determined to restrain Bennigsen's ambitions. Russian military regulations specified that army headquarters should consist of four principal departments, the most important of which was the main staff, led by the chief of staff, who supervised both the quartermaster service and the duty officers. Alexander Scherbinin was correct: when it suited him, Kutuzov made no effort to follow the statute. To the contrary, he greatly expanded the authority of a duty general, who had previously been subordinate to the chief of staff but who now effectively usurped his functions. For this senior position, Kutuzov chose Lieutenant General Konovnitsyn, a gallant and hardworking officer who was nonetheless not well versed in staff work. Yermolov understood that the general's inexperience in military administration empowered Colonel Toll, whom Kutuzov implicitly trusted. "After the retreat from Moscow, Toll became an imposing figure and began to act independent of Konovnitsyn," remarked a staff officer.[90] Konovnitsyn was angry and disappointed. "I am alive but tormented by my position," he confided to his wife. "If this incessant paperwork would not kill me, it would certainly exhaust my mind. I am ready to expose myself to cannonballs, bullets, and canister just to escape this place."[91]

Kutuzov was fond of the saying "Even the pillow on which a commander sleeps should not be privy to his thoughts." Wise though that might be, such a creed was hardly conducive to collaboration and teamwork. Barclay de Tolly's departure meant that many of his staff officers left as well, depriving the army of knowledge and experience.[92] "We are like sheep without the shepherd," grumbled Colonel Marin, the acting duty general of the 2nd Western

Army. "No one knows anything here. . . . Detachments are reporting directly to Konovnitsyn and not a word is shared with the duty officers, as if we are in a foreign army."[93] A general complaint, as we have seen again and again, was that Kutuzov had surrounded himself with a handful of staff officers (Toll, Kaisarov, Kudashev, and others) who shielded him from outsiders and exercised considerable authority in the army. "No one sees Kutuzov anymore," complained Rostopchin in late September. "Kaisarov signs papers for him, while Kudashev manages everything."[94] Yermolov was exasperated by the new changes. As a chief of staff of the 1st Western Army, he used to submit reports directly to the field marshal and issue orders in his name, but in the wake of the staff restructuring, he now reported to Kutuzov only in "extraordinary cases" and was increasingly marginalized. He bemoaned "the swagger, hauteur, intrigue, and machinations" of the men surrounding the field marshal and begged Kutuzov to relieve him formally of his nonexistent responsibilities. "Even on my rare visits I managed to see that Konovnitsyn is an utter boob in his new position. There is a complete mess in all affairs, while the chancellery has been split into 555 sections."[95] Other generals shared such concerns. Dokhturov's heart ached at the sight of "everything being done topsy-turvy."[96]

Kutuzov's decision to meet with Lauriston thus offered his detractors an opportunity to undermine him. That afternoon Robert Wilson received an urgent message "to return instantly to headquarters" because the field marshal had "not merely proposed but actually agreed in a written note" to negotiate with Lauriston. The sender of the note, unsurprisingly, was Bennigsen.[97] Wilson listened to the aggrieved generals and agreed to present their concerns to the commander in chief. Kutuzov was at his quarters and greeted the British officer warmly, asking if he had brought any news from the advance guard. After a slight conversation, Wilson asked about "a mischievous report" circulating in the army about Franco-Russian negotiations. Kutuzov was surprised and angered by these allegations and the conversation quickly turned spirited, as Wilson wrote in *Narrative of Events During the Invasion of Russia*, his contemporaneous campaign history that was not published until 1860.[98] Kutuzov admitted that he had agreed to give Lauriston an interview that evening but pointed out that as the supreme commander, he "knew best what the interests confided to him required." The British commissioner in turn reminded Kutuzov of the czar's injunction against any negotiations with the enemy. He went as far as to accuse him of possible treason, since "a project of meeting an enemy's general and envoy beyond his own advanced posts at midnight was unheard of in the annals of war, except when illicit communication had been intended."[99] Kutuzov must have seen red at being threatened by a man whom other British officers regarded as "a very slippery fellow."[100] He knew that he had many critics (and enemies) among the officers; that his reputation had taken a hit in the wake of Borodino and particularly with the abandonment of Moscow; and that "there was a general suspicion," wrote an eyewitness, "that he did not wish to push the enemy to extremity and a corresponding vigilance was exercised over his transactions."[101] Kutuzov might have known about the grumblings, but this was the first time that he had been openly accused of perfidy. To drive home his point, Wilson brought in "reinforcements"—Duke Alexander of Württemberg (Emperor Alexander's uncle), the Duke of Oldenburg (the emperor's brother-in-law), and Prince Peter Volkonskii, who proceeded to pressure Kutuzov not to meet with the French envoy outside Russian headquarters. "After much controversy and an expression of dissent," wrote Mikhailovskii-Danilevskii, Kutuzov, no doubt exasperated and irate, refused to accede to their demands, insisting on meeting the Frenchman alone, though at Russian headquarters. He also agreed to allow the officers to remain within call.[102]

Around eleven in the evening Lauriston was taken through the Russian camp. Although Wilson claimed the French envoy was "blindfolded," other eyewitnesses disagree. Kutuzov would have wanted to make the most of this opportunity to impress the French envoy with the orderliness and strength of the Russian army. He had, in fact, ordered bonfires to be lit so that it seemed as though more than 200,000 men were encamped there. Soldiers were told to cook porridge, sing rousing songs, and create an impression of a festive atmosphere.[103] "Traveling in an open carriage, Lauriston arrived as the darkness descended," recalled Scherbinin. "It was then that we saw, for the first time, Kutuzov in full uniform, even wearing his feathered half-moon hat. Not pleased with the tarnished appearance of his epaulettes, he had to ask General Konovnitsyn to lend him his. Alas, Konovnitsyn was no dandy and it would have been better if he had asked Miloradovich, who was more fastidious about his appearance." Lauriston was ushered into the field marshal's quarters, where he found a small group of generals, Wilson and the czar's relatives among them; the significance of their presence did not escape him. After an exchange of pleasantries, the Russian officers withdrew, leaving Kutuzov and the envoy to converse.[104]

The two were career military men who had considerable political experience and were well accustomed to the subtleties of the diplomatic game. Lauriston first complained of the "barbarity" to which the French had been subjected, citing examples of Cossacks and peasants attacking isolated French detachments, massacring prisoners, and burning homes and supplies to deny the French any sustenance. Such a war must come to an end, Lauriston said. "But why?" retorted Kutuzov. "We are only just starting." He pointed out that "he could not in three months civilize a nation that regards the enemy as worse than a marauding force of the Mongols of Genghis Khan." "But there is at least some difference," objected Lauriston. "There might be," the field marshal told him, "but none in the eyes of the people; besides, I can only be responsible for the conduct of my troops."

Lauriston briefly spoke of the fire of Moscow, noting that it was not the French who burned the city down. He then came to the point. "Need this strange and unprecedented war drag on interminably?" he inquired. "The emperor, my master, has a sincere desire to end this dispute between two great and generous nations and to end it forever." Kutuzov replied that when he took up his appointment with Emperor Alexander, the czar had made no mention of peace and that he could not therefore comment on such matters. "I should be cursed by posterity if I were regarded as the prime mover behind any kind of accommodation, for such is the present mood of my nation." However, Kutuzov agreed to inform the czar of Napoleon's offer. "You must not think we wish it because our affairs are desperate," said Lauriston. "Our two armies are nearly equal in force. You are, it is true, nearer your supplies and reinforcements than we are, but we also received reinforcements." He tried to underplay the importance of the British victories in the Iberian Peninsula. "Perhaps you have heard that our affairs are not going well in Spain?" he inquired. "I have," replied Kutuzov, "from Sir Robert Wilson, whom you just saw leave me, and with whom I have daily interviews." Lauriston argued that things were not as bad as the British commissioner might have described them; he acknowledged setbacks in Spain but expected that an infusion of troops would settle the matter. Kutuzov must have smiled inwardly at hearing the French diplomat talk down the gravity of the challenges Napoleon was facing, for his very presence underscored the discomfiture that the French emperor was experiencing. The sponge of Moscow had soaked up the Napoleonic torrent, and the situation was bound to grow worse for the French with the arrival of the winter. At the end of the conversation, Lauriston asked for safe passage to St. Petersburg with a view toward possible negotiations. Kutuzov, however, refused to let him through and instead simply reiterated his readiness to present the matter to the czar.[105] After a conversation that could not have lasted more than half an hour, the French envoy departed.

The following morning Kutuzov wrote a lengthy account of this meeting and dispatched two couriers to St. Petersburg. The first messenger, carrying Kutuzov's condemnation of Cossack behavior and endorsement of diplomatic discussions, was instructed to travel close to the French patrols and "inadvertently" fall into their hands, so as to make Napoleon believe that the Russians were indeed considering his offer. The czar's aide-de-camp Peter Volkonskii, meanwhile, took a more circuitous route to the capital, carrying a copy of Napoleon's message and Kutuzov's report, which favored rejecting the French demands and urged the emperor to fight on.[106]

Although Kutuzov was clearly baiting Napoleon, the Russian emperor was rather displeased with the field marshal. "In the interview I had with you when I confided my armies to your command, I informed you of my firm desire to avoid all negotiations with the enemy, and all relations with him that tended to peace," he rebuked the field marshal. "Now, after what has transpired, I must repeat with the same resolution that I desire this principle to be observed by you to its fullest extent, and in the most rigorous and inflexible manner."[107] The Russian minister of police privately told his acquaintances that "the emperor had less confidence in Marshal Kutuzov than he had before."[108] Rumors of Kutuzov's apparent willingness to negotiate continued to circulate. In late October, Arsenii Zakrevskii, former director of Barclay de Tolly's chancellery, alleged that he had heard from the czar's own flügel-adjutant that Kutuzov, joined by Nikolai Rumyantsev (former chancellor of the Russian Empire) and Alexei Arakcheyev, the former minister of war who now advised the czar on military affairs, had tried to convince the czar to conclude peace with Napoleon. Zakrevskii was quick to point out that he found such claims hard to believe and that the young officer in question was very likely lying. But that did not stop him from spreading the rumor and claiming that "at his old age Kutuzov has achieved his goal [of becoming a field marshal] so he has nothing more to wish than peace."[109] The durability of such vile gossip reflects the low opinion in which Kutuzov was held by so many in Russian military circles. For weeks the British commissioner and Russian generals persisted in their suspicion that Kutuzov must be secretly negotiating with the French; on at least one other occasion they demanded he reveal whether or not he had been negotiating "a convention." Kutuzov, no doubt exasperated, did his best to assure everyone that there was no such agreement and that he had no power whatever to enter into any negotiations with the French.[110]

Nor did he have any interest. In deciding to meet with Lauriston, Kutuzov had been guided by military considerations. The French diplomat's visit underscored the Grande Armée's growing uneasiness in Moscow. Just one and a half months later, while conversing with the French commissary official Louis-Guillaume de Puibusque, who had been taken prisoner during the retreat from Smolensk, Kutuzov admitted that his decision to meet Lauriston had been driven by his desire to outsmart Napoleon by prolonging negotiations. "In politics, you do not miss an opportunity that spontaneously presents itself to you," he remarked. He agreed to send letters to St. Petersburg only because "the distance between St. Petersburg and Moscow required time," and time was precisely what Kutuzov needed to continue marshaling resources for the war, molding his raw recruits into fighting regiments, and draining the Grande Armée. He confessed to having studied "for some time" Napoleon's character and was convinced that he could be defeated only through a prolonged war that would "spread and exhaust his army and cause fatigue and famine" before "the harshness of the climate" would destroy it. Kutuzov was astonished, recalled Puibusque, "at the ease with which all the tricks he had employed to keep [the French] in Moscow had succeeded" and scoffed at Napoleon's "ridiculous expectation to negotiate peace" when he no longer had the necessary forces to wage war. "It was precisely because Napoleon clung so conspicuously to the idea of peace that it was impossible to ignore the fact that there remained for him no other hope of salvation," Kutuzov remarked.[111]

Kutuzov's conviction of growing French weakness only grew stronger when, on October 18, Napoleon dispatched yet another envoy, whom the field marshal met despite the czar's injunction.[112] He quietly listened as the French officer conveyed Napoleon's request to "make arrangements to give the war a character that would be more in conformity with the established rules and would avoid all the evils not indispensable for its conduct."[113] For the Russian commander, such a plea only underscored how much the Grande Armée had been affected by the Russian flying detachments and peasant guerrillas. He had no interest in abiding by "the established rules" of war and easing up on the enemy. In his letter to Napoleon, Kutuzov explained that he could not change the temper of the "embittered" people who had not "seen an invader on their soil for over three hundred years." The distinction between "ordinary war" and war that was not ordinary was lost on those who were "ready to immolate themselves for the Fatherland."[114]

Ivan Krylov's fable "The Wolf in the Kennel," written at this time, offers the story of a wolf that tries climbing into a sheep enclosure and instead falls into a dog kennel. As the dogs wake and begin barking at the grisly intruder, the kennel keeper shuts the gate and men come running with clubs and sticks; the wolf is found backed into a dark corner, gnashing its teeth, its fur bristling, and its eyes full of fear. Seeing that he has been caught, the scheming wolf offers to negotiate and promises never again to raid the farm. "Listen, lad," interrupts the kennel keeper. "Your fur might be gray, but I am gray-haired too. I have long known your kind, and my custom is to never make peace with wolves until I have flayed the skin off their backs." And with these words, he sets the pack of hounds on the wolf. Kutuzov was fond of this fable—Krylov sent him a personal copy—and was known to have recited it in public on an occasion. As he got to the part where the kennel master says, "Your fur might be gray, but I am gray-haired too," Kutuzov invariably raised his cap and proudly displayed his gray hair. This plain fable expressed his intentions well—something that the dozen or so well-educated officers who found it plausible that the commander in chief of the Russian army would commit treason could not see. The French wolf was backed into a corner, and Kutuzov needed to have his hounds ready.

CHAPTER 26 | The Turning Point

NAPOLEON FELT A HUGE sense of relief when he heard Lauriston's account of the meeting with Kutuzov. The diplomat assured him that the letter would be delivered directly to the Russian emperor and that a response should arrive within two weeks. Had Kutuzov refused to accept the letter, Napoleon might have been forced to consider other possibilities, including hastening his departure. The field marshal's promise to transmit the message to the czar revived Napoleon's hopes for peace and, as Kutuzov anticipated, confirmed his decision to stay in Moscow. The emperor was convinced that the Russians would sign a peace treaty within a month. "On receipt of my letter St. Petersburg will celebrate with bonfires," Ségur remembers him saying to the marshals. Napoleon paid little heed to warnings of the arrival of Russian reinforcements, which could threaten the security of the Grande Armée's rear. General Mathieu Dumas later wondered whether the emperor had been properly informed about the situation.[1]

Napoleon was also misled by the weather, which was unusually mild. Golden autumn days passed, one succeeding another. "The weather is so lovely for the time of year that one is tempted to believe God is with the Emperor," commented one participant.[2] Napoleon had often been told about the rigors of the Russian climate, but on his daily outings he frequently drew parallels between it and France's. "The weather here is beautiful, as warm as in Paris. We have just had those lovely Fontainebleau days," he wrote Marie Louise, his youthful wife, on October 4.[3] He brushed aside the concerns expressed by Caulaincourt, who, based on his experiences as an ambassador to St. Petersburg, warned of the cold winter coming: "So this is the terrible Russian winter that Monsieur de Caulaincourt frightens the children with."[4] Napoleon's complacency proved to be consequential since, as one French general lamented, the weather took his mind off anything "respecting the difficulties of a retreat."[5] Enjoying those "Fontainebleau days," the emperor relaxed, organized reviews, and waited for the czar's answer.

The relative tranquility of the front line was also deceptive. There were no major combats, but Russian flying detachments and Cossacks constantly prowled the countryside in search of isolated French troops or patrols. The Russian army's *Journal of Military Operations* reported that hundreds of enemy soldiers were seized and delivered to the Russian campsite on a daily basis.[6] "Every day we capture up to three hundred men," enthused Kutuzov in a private letter.[7] One would have had to be blind not to see the growing weakness of the enemy force in front of the Russians. The French advance guard suffered especially, as it was camped out in the open fields, with no shelter to protect the men from the wind, rain, and autumn chill. The shortage of food had a ruinous effect on the troops, who could neither travel regularly to Moscow for provisions nor forage freely in the vicinity. The once-resplendent cavalry now consisted of fatigued and malnourished horses and men. Visiting the 11th Hussars, Captain Hubert Biot was stunned to see "the men and horses dying of hunger, quite literally, because they never received any supply distributions."[8] Squadrons were down to two dozen, while some regiments were at barely half-strength. Lieutenant Adrien de Mailly, who had rejoined his 2nd Carabineers Regiment, was shocked to find that it was down to 100 men, for "we had left France 1,400 strong."[9] These men lacked essentials and were reduced to eating unground rye, plants, and occasional horse flesh; Kutuzov's grim promise was becoming a reality. The condition of the horses was even more dreadful. Murat was aware of these difficulties and tried explaining them to Napoleon: "I have the whole enemy army in front of me. Our advance guard is reduced to nothing. It is starving, and it is no longer possible to go foraging without the virtual certainty of capture."[10] But the emperor dismissed such warnings.

Kutuzov's forces grew in strength throughout October, while the Grande Armée was weakening by the day. Like the Roman statesman Quintus Fabius, whose delaying strategy against Hannibal had saved Rome during the Punic Wars, "Fabius Larionovich," as Field Marshal Repnin occasionally referred to Kutuzov, was determined to use time, space, and the climate as his allies.[11] The parallel with the strategy employed by Fabius against Hannibal is striking indeed. As part of his education, Kutuzov had studied Plutarch; in fact, he discussed the Roman-Carthaginian War with his wife, drawing comparison to his own decisions.[12] He was confident that his strategy of avoiding pitched battles and frontal assaults in favor of wearing down an opponent through attrition and asymmetrical warfare would soon pay off. "Having had the honor of attending the councils of war," Mikhailovskii-Danilevskii commented, "I could see how pleased Kutuzov was with the situation in which he had placed the French army." He did not want to induce Napoleon to action, thinking it far more useful to avoid battles and keep the French "lion fast asleep inside the Kremlin." The longer Napoleon stayed in Moscow, the more certain a Russian victory became, Kutuzov kept repeating.[13] Staff officer Golitsyn confirms that Kutuzov's goal was to keep Napoleon distracted for as long as possible: "Every device that contributed to this objective was preferable to the empty pursuit of glory in attacking an enemy advance guard."[14] Whether writing to the czar or to his family, Kutuzov assured everyone that "the small war," *la petite guerre*, was conferring "great advantages" and that winter would soon devastate the enemy.[15] On October 12, he was delighted to share the news of Napoleon's setbacks in Spain, where the British had routed the French at Salamanca and captured Madrid. "Our enemies are losing everywhere and, having invaded our borders, they will find their tombs in our native lands!" the field marshal assured his soldiers.[16] "Patience and time are my warriors, my champions," Kutuzov proclaims in Tolstoy's retelling of history.

Nonetheless, the Russian Fabius Cunctator found himself increasingly at odds with his generals, who had grown unhappy with his dilatory approach. They wanted to fight triumphant battles and hear the lamentations of their enemies. Lieutenant Alexander Chicherin of the Life Guard Semeyonovskii Regiment wrote in his diary on October 15, "What unreasonable expectations and senseless suggestions our continued inactivity induced. I have heard such diverse opinions and vague rumors that I no longer know who or what to believe."[17] Four days later, Chicherin wrote that he could not understand "why we are remaining so fearful of the enemy." Nikolai Mitarevskii, who earlier in the month had heard soldiers praising Kutuzov's flanking maneuver, now overheard their grumbles about the dullness of life at the camp: "Old man Kutuzov must have fallen fast asleep."[18] Neither Nikolai Muravyev nor his comrades had seen the commander in chief in days.[19] Nikolai Durnovo, an officer on Bennigsen's staff, expressed the frustration of the many when he complained that Kutuzov was "sitting in his den like a bear who does not want to come out" while the French were so vulnerable. "It is driving us all mad with rage."

Bennigsen emerged as the ringleader of the generals who attacked Kutuzov for the lack of activity. "As winter was drawing on, it was feared that the enemy would retire suddenly from Moscow," Wilson commented. The Russians seemed to be losing their moment to "cripple the enemy."[20] The field marshal refused to sanction such a strike; hence relations between him and the chief of staff progressively worsened. "Every time the matter of moving forward to confront the enemy comes up, I quarrel with him," Bennigsen confided to his wife. Wilson lamented that he was forced to act as "a pacificator between the Field Marshal and General Bennigsen but peace can only be temporary."[21]

By mid-October Bennigsen was convinced that the time was ripe to attack.[22] Accompanied by Colonel Toll and several officers, he spent days reconnoitering the area where the French advance guard was deployed. It was soon evident that Marshal Murat had placed his 26,000 men and 187 cannon in a rather weak position. He seems to have made no attempt to strengthen the campsite or to construct entrenchments; the French left flank rested on a wood that General Horace Sebastiani's cavalrymen failed to properly secure. There was a bottleneck six miles behind the French front line, where the Old Kaluga road passed through a narrow defile between two thick forests. Bennigsen and Toll reasoned that a well-coordinated attack could overwhelm the French left flank and intercept the enemy line of retreat, resulting in an encirclement and destruction of Murat's force. Late on October 15, they submitted their findings to Kutuzov and pressured him to approve a plan that called for a demonstration by one part of the Russian army against Murat's extended front, while three infantry corps, supported by a strong cavalry detachment, smashed through his left flank and intercepted the French line of retreat. Despite having deep misgivings, Kutuzov approved the plan to appease his impatient generals. He offered Bennigsen the chance to command the troops in the battle, which was scheduled for October 17.[23]

Planning a battle is one thing; properly executing it quite another. The plan, drafted by Toll and approved by Bennigsen, required the flanking troops to perform a nocturnal march to be in position to strike when the battle commenced.[24] Yet at five in the afternoon on September 16, as Kutuzov signed off on the official disposition and instructed his duty officer to deliver it to General Yermolov, who was supposed to start executing it at six, neither Yermolov nor many other senior officers could be located.[25] It turned out that Major General Dmitry Shepelev had decided to host a lavish banquet at his quarters in the village of Spasskoe. Dozens of officers and generals gathered on the shore of the Nara River to enjoy "the most resplendent and delicious feast imaginable." Dazzled by the extravagance of this event, one participant thought it was conjured by a "sorceress who poured out the best of wines and tossed the most sumptuous dishes and the rarest of fruits from her inexhaustible cornucopia." Participants were "very festive," drinking, singing, dancing, and forgetting about the impending battle.[26] Frantically searching for the chief of staff, Kutuzov's duty officer dashed to Spasskoe, but arrived there too late; Yermolov had already returned to his quarters. Another hour was wasted in searching for him, and it was only around nine in the evening that the disposition finally reached him. By then it was too late.

Kutuzov remained unaware of the feast. Around eight that evening he left his quarters to examine preparations for battle and was utterly stunned to discover that there was almost no sign of activity, except for artillery horses being taken to the river.[27] His outburst of rage and fury stunned even his longtime orderlies. "Who is the senior staff officer here?" Kutuzov roared.

A hapless lieutenant colonel stepped forward, but instantly regretted his decision, as he found himself under a barrage of invective. Just as he was unloading on the unfortunate officer, Kutuzov noticed a red-cheeked man, clad in a slovenly soldier's coat and a plain green cap, riding a small fat horse through the camp. "What kind of riffraff is that?" he growled, only to be informed that it was a senior staff officer from one of the corps. This enraged the commander in chief even more, and he volubly berated both officers in front of the stunned soldiers. Once his supply of abuse was exhausted, Kutuzov called off the attack and returned to his quarters, where he harangued Toll and other staff officers, some of whom he threatened to court-martial. "His Excellency was angry beyond himself that entire evening and no one dared to even approach him," Mikhailovskii-Danilevskii wrote in his journal that night. A subsequent investigation quickly determined who the culprit was. Kutuzov wanted to expel Yermolov (who, unsurprisingly, makes no mention of this entire incident in his memoirs) from the army but was ultimately talked out of it.

The attack on Murat's forces was not canceled altogether. Instead, Kutuzov postponed it for twenty-four hours as Bennigsen worked to ensure that this time around the army was ready for battle. Kutuzov's new Order to the Army specified the units designated for the attack. It was agreed that Miloradovich would lead the assault on the French center, while Bennigsen would command the decisive flanking attack on the right. Kutuzov, with the guard regiments, chose to remain about six miles behind the front line.[28]

The soldiers were excited about going back into action, though they did not expect to fight a general battle like at Borodino. They had estimated Murat's forces at no more than 40,000 men, which, remembered Mitarevskii, "we considered a pittance."[29] Late in the evening of October 17, Kutuzov personally reconnoitered the French positions on the Nara River. The weather was stormy; thunder rumbled in the distance and lightning streaked across the dark sky. Löwenstern recalled that a large eagle hovered over Kutuzov's head, which of course was taken as a good omen: "The news of this apparition soon spread from mouth to mouth through the entire army."[30] Eager to take charge, Bennigsen spent the night examining units and having "a long discussion" with General Miloradovich about the battle plans.[31]

At dawn on October 18, the Russians advanced in four major columns, surprising the enemy. On the right, the Russian cavalry swept aside the French and Polish horsemen, captured part of Murat's baggage and artillery, and threatened to cut the French line of retreat. Yet bad luck, petty squabbles, and poor staff work once again intervened. The distances that various columns had to travel were not properly correlated, and the movements were not coordinated; while some flanking units reached their destination before

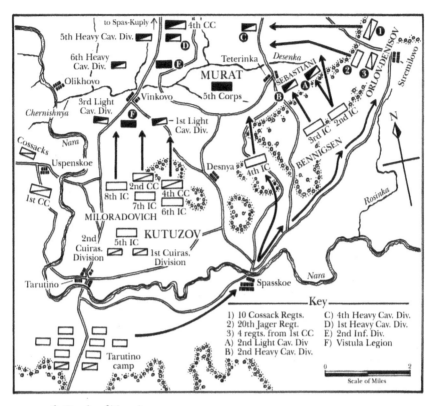

MAP 16 Battle of Tarutino

sunrise, others were still on march when the battle began and arrived too late to sustain the attack. "There was little communication between our forces," admitted Yermolov.[32] Bennigsen, despite demanding a battle for so long, was unable to provide effective leadership on the right flank. As a result, some units got lost in the woods, while others attacked disjointedly. As bad luck would have it, General Karl Gustav von Baggovut (Baggehufwudt), commanding the 2nd Infantry Corps, was killed at the very start of the attack, causing confusion among his men and delaying their attack.[33] Kutuzov then compounded the problem by refusing to sustain the assault. Bennigsen dispatched Wilson with a request for reinforcements, but Kutuzov "coldly checked this ardour," Wilson complained, and commanded some units to stand down; he also requested that Miloradovich come see him in person just as his troops were commencing the attack, which meant, as an eyewitness wrote, that "everything came to a standstill."[34]

These were unusual interventions on the part of the commander in chief, whom contemporaries had accused of an unwillingness to "share the glory."[35] Even his supporters, including Mikhailovskii-Danilevskii, struggled to explain Kutuzov's behavior. However, his actions appear more logical if one considers his state of mind. He was not convinced that confronting the enemy in a general battle was the right course of action, and he was still fuming about the staff officers' earlier misconduct, which, he feared, had already alerted Napoleon. During the battle, reports arrived (later proven erroneous) that sizable French reinforcements were approaching, and Kutuzov remained disinclined to wage a decisive battle against Napoleon at the current position.[36] Standing amid the guard units and surrounded by his entourage, he kept grumbling that while his generals were insisting they attack and devising plans, when it came time to do it, "nothing is ready while the forewarned enemy takes the necessary precautions." Miloradovich and Yermolov tried to reassure him that it was not too late. According to Löwenstern, Kutuzov snapped at them, "All you have on your minds is 'attack, attack'!" He added that he deeply regretted listening to Bennigsen's proposals. He bemoaned the poor staff work and the Russian failure to coordinate their attacks. "We are not yet ready for complex movements and maneuvers. Today's battle has confirmed this once more," he ruefully commented. "I deeply regret listening to General Bennigsen's proposals."[37] He dispatched Yermolov, Konovnitsyn, and other officers to examine the situation at the front; the bulk of the army otherwise remained "a passive spectator" of the battle.[38] Exploiting the uncoordinated nature of the Russian assaults, Murat and Poniatowski sprang into action, rallying their men and launching bold countercharges that drove the attackers back. By noon, the entire French advance guard had succeeded in evading the Russian envelopment and effected a retreat through the cleared pass at Spas Kuplya by late afternoon.[39]

What should have been a triumph thus turned into an "imperfect and unsatisfactory" (to use Wilson's terms) victory.[40] Despite enjoying two-to-one superiority, the Russian army was unable to destroy the French advance guard, which lost almost 3,000 men but was able to make an orderly retreat. Tensions were thus running high within the Russian command. Some senior officers felt ashamed of what had transpired and considered the battle "disgraceful to the Russian arms."[41] Wilson, almost beside himself with rage, asked to be recalled from the army if the field marshal remained in charge of the Russian armies.[42] Kutuzov, meanwhile, seethed over the poorly coordinated attacks, calling Bennigsen an "imbecile," "the red-headed fool," and a "coward."[43] Bennigsen felt the same way about the field marshal.

As darkness began to fall, Bennigsen reached the Russian headquarters, where he found the commander in chief sitting on a carpet that the Cossacks had laid down on the ground for him. The meeting was tense and if looks could kill there would have been a bloodbath. The two commanders glared at each other but remained courteous. "General, you have gained a glorious victory and I congratulate you," Kutuzov welcomed his rival.[44] Bennigsen coldly nodded in response and asked for permission to leave the army for a few days, ostensibly to recuperate from a contusion he had sustained during the battle. "I cannot get over it," he railed in a letter to his wife. "This beautiful and brilliant day could have had incalculable consequences if I had been supported. . . . Kutuzov will never end this war well."[45]

As he rode back to his quarters, Kutuzov was in a noticeably better mood, merrily conversing with Yermolov about the battle and what it had accomplished in terms of captured cannon and prisoners. The general grasped what the field marshal was attempting to do, however. If news represents the first draft of history, Kutuzov was determined to make it glorious. Notwithstanding the outcome, he proclaimed a decisive victory, doubled the size of the enemy force to 50,000 men, and praised his soldiers for acting with such perfection that it had seemed as though they were at "carefully rehearsed training maneuvers."[46] He announced the capture of thirty-eight cannon, which, as he and his followers pointed out, was the largest number of guns the Russians had captured since the start of the wars against Napoleon. Kutuzov wrote Catherine, "It was the first time that the French ran like hares."[47] The news thrilled St. Petersburg, which celebrated with gun salutes, religious services, and festivities. "The city was illuminated again in the evening," John Quincy Adams jotted in his diary on October 28.[48] "The news of your victory over Murat delighted me indescribably," the czar wrote the field marshal. "I remain hopeful that this is just the beginning [of the campaign] that will produce decisive results." Alexander presented Kutuzov with an exquisite ceremonial sword with gold laurels.[49]

Tarutino ratcheted up tensions at the Russian headquarters and left many officers disillusioned. Bennigsen kept writing letters claiming credit for the victory at Tarutino, and his supporters in St. Petersburg did their best to trump up his contributions. The American ambassador spoke of "Marshal Kutuzov's or rather General's Bennigsen's victory."[50] The day after the battle, General Rayevskii gloomily wrote to his wife, "I almost never visit the main headquarters anymore . . . there is nothing there but intrigues, jealousy, enmity, and above all extreme egotism."[51] Kutuzov anticipated that Bennigsen would complain to the czar. In his letter to Alexander, he made no mention of his rival's mistakes and instead extolled his leadership and courage, soliciting generous rewards for him. As the courier was departing, Bennigsen caught up with him and asked him to deliver his private letter to the czar. As Kutuzov had anticipated, it was replete with criticism and condemnation. Alexander thus read both dispatches at the same time. He approved the field marshal's recommendations, rewarded Bennigsen with 100,000 rubles and the diamond signs of the order of St. Andrew the First Called, and then sent Bennigsen's letter back to Kutuzov, who received it later that fall. The field marshal delighted in exacting a measure of vengeance on his opponent: Bennigsen and other senior officers were asked to gather at Kutuzov's quarters, where an orderly announced the czar's awards and loudly read Kutuzov's nomination letter, which praised Bennigsen as "a distinguished leader, who has been crowned with laurels of victory and is renowned for his great experience and enterprise. . . . He accomplished everything with gallantry and skill, his distinguishing character traits." Kutuzov then heartily congratulated the general, as did everyone else in the room. Next, as his rival was basking in glory, Kutuzov asked an orderly to read Bennigsen's letter to the czar. Everyone was stunned to hear the disparaging remarks the general wrote about the man who seemed so supportive of him. An eyewitness testified that Bennigsen "stood as if struck by lightning, alternatively blushing and blanching."[52]

Among the French prisoners of war delivered to Russian headquarters was General Pierre-Louis de Beauvollier, with whom the field marshal conversed for three hours. The Frenchman, who had been among the leaders of the royalist uprising in the Vendée before rallying to Napoleon's side, described the Russian commander in chief as "an old man . . . of ordinary height, with a pleasant countenance." "His white hair and his face," wrote Beauvollier in his memoirs, "furrowed as it was by several deep scars, inspired respect." He was surprised how fluently Kutuzov spoke French, and he praised the field marshal's "vast erudition." Conversing about recent history, Kutuzov told the Frenchman that he had read books about the war in the Vendée "with the keenest interest" and queried the general about "all the leaders of the heroic Vendean army." After quizzing the prisoner about the strength and condition of the French army, Kutuzov suddenly asked, "What opinion does Napoleon have of me?" "He is anxious about you," Beauvollier remembers replying. "He refers to you as the 'Old Fox of the North.'" "Good," the Russian field marshal retorted. "I intend to show that he is not mistaken."[53]

The Russian victory at Tarutino, incomplete as it was, marked a turning point in the war. It put an end to any hopes Napoleon might still have cherished for a peace with the Russians. He had already made some preparations for the abandonment of Moscow—as early as October 14, he had ordered the evacuation of hospitals and redirected columns of reinforcements back to Smolensk. The news of Murat's defeat prompted him to expedite his efforts for the departure. This setback made him rediscover "the fire of his earlier years," as Ségur observed. Marshals were instructed to start redeploying their forces to the Kaluga road at once and to be prepared to leave at daybreak for a hard day's marching. "We are going to withdraw to the frontiers of Poland," Napoleon confided to his trusted aide Jean Rapp. "I shall take good winter quarters and hope that [Emperor] Alexander will make peace."[54] He envisioned it as a strategic withdrawal, not a full-blown retreat, a point he underscored in later years.[55] The route from Moscow to Smolensk, via Gzhatsk, had been utterly devastated when the French fought their way to the Russian capital, so Napoleon's best option was to move his forces through the southwestern provinces of Russia, where supplies and magazines could allow him to sustain his army before resuming the war in the spring. Kutuzov, however, stood in his way.

I N THE PREDAWN HOURS of October 23, a messenger galloped into the village of Letashevka, where Kutuzov was bivouacked. He found everyone in the Russian camp asleep aside from the sentries and the duty general, Peter Konovnitsyn, who was still working. He welcomed the weary courier, Dmitrii Bolgovskii, captain of the Life Guard Izmailovskii Regiment, into his quarters. Bolgovskii carried a message of utmost importance: Napoleon had left Moscow four days earlier.[1]

The events at Tarutino had shaken Napoleon out of his complacency. On October 19, he gave the order to depart from Moscow. The Grande Armée had dwindled to 115,000 men, accompanied by a vast baggage train that counted thousands of wagons and carts, transporting food, the wounded, and refugees. Civilians who had thrown in their lot with the French and feared repercussions followed as well. Innumerable carriages and chaises were laden with booty—precious furs, articles of furniture, countless bejeweled icons, frames and jewelry melted into ingots of silvers and gold, and, more famously, the massive, gilded cross of the Bell Tower of Ivan the Great—followed cannon limbers and ammunition caissons, moving in parallel columns. Traffic on this scale not only slowed the army's movements but also distracted the troops, many of whom were more concerned about securing their portion of the loot than with following orders. Pierre-Armand Barrau and other French officers bemoaned the state of the army: "Anyone who did not see the French army leave Moscow can only have a very weak impression of what the armies of Greece and Rome must have looked like when they marched back from Troy and Carthage."[2]

"Moscow no longer exists and cannot serve as a military staging ground for future operations," Napoleon admitted in a letter to his foreign minister, Hugues-Bernard Maret, duc de Bassano. He had decided to proceed

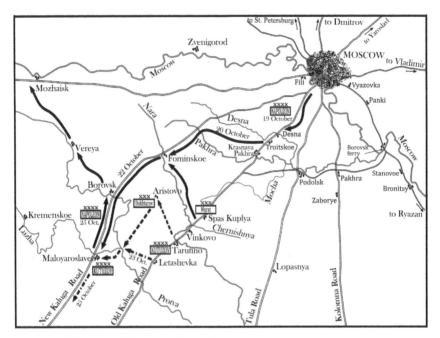

MAP 17 Napoleon's Departure from Moscow

southwest to Kaluga, where he could regroup and resupply, and from there either march to Tula and Bryansk, Russia's great armament centers, or move the army to winter quarters in Smolensk. Having revitalized his forces, he would, he hoped, be able "to go wherever [my] presence would be necessary."[3]

With so many Russian flying detachments around Moscow, leaving the city unnoticed seemed impossible, yet Napoleon once again demonstrated his operational brilliance. He dispatched Colonel Pierre Augustin Berthemy to Kutuzov, ostensibly to complain about the Russians' violation of "the established rules of war" (as we have already seen). In reality, Berthemy was to determine whether the Russian commander was aware of the ongoing French preparations for the departure from Moscow. All evidence pointed to the Russians being unaware of the French intentions, so Napoleon moved forward with his plans. Two roads led from Moscow to Kaluga. The western one, the New Kaluga road, went through the towns of Fominskoe, Borovsk, and Maloyaroslavets, while the eastern one, the Old Kaluga road, passed through Krasnaya Pakhra and Tarutino. The latter was shorter and more direct, but the Russian army held positions there. So Napoleon devised a maneuver that overcame this problem. On October 19, he ordered his troops to depart by the Old Kaluga road. Upon reaching the Pakhra River, the Grande Armée turned west and proceeded, behind a cavalry screen, along the shallow arc of a circle formed by the New Kaluga road. This allowed the

French to circumvent the Russian fortified camp at Tarutino, which lay some twenty miles to the east, and to reach Maloyaroslavets and Kaluga before the Russians even realized what was happening. The entire operation was very well conceived, and Napoleon managed to extricate tens of thousands of troops from the Russian capital with such efficiency that Kutuzov did not learn of their departure for those four days. Had this movement been carried out with greater haste, however, it might have achieved even more decisive results, for Maloyaroslavets was less than eighty miles from Moscow and could have been reached before the Russian headquarters reacted to the news. Yet the promising start of the Moscow-Kaluga maneuver was soon marred by a combination of factors. Burdened by so many transports, wounded soldiers, and civilians, the army slowly trudged forward, gridlocking when obliged to negotiate various streams and defiles. Its march ground to a virtual halt when interminable rains turned the roads into rivers of mud.

The Russian high command, meanwhile, remained unaware until late on October 22, as we have seen, when Kutuzov received reports about the arrival of enemy troops at Fominskoe, about twenty miles northwest from Tarutino. The Russian flying detachment of Major General Dorokhov was bivouacked near this village and had observed a long line of French infantry and cavalry moving steadily southwest.[4] These were the troops of the 14th Infantry Division of General Jean-Baptiste Broussier, spearheading Napoleon's movement to the town of Borovsk on the New Kaluga road. Dorokhov—"all but deaf and unable to hear the whistling of bullets, so he never suspected what danger he was exposing himself to," as one participant later described him—was unaware that the entire Grande Armée was nearby and instead informed Kutuzov about the presence of a sizable enemy foraging column, "about ten thousand strong," that seemed isolated and vulnerable to an attack.[5] The report caused considerable debate at the Russian headquarters, which was surprised by the size of this enemy detachment and questioned the veracity of Dorokhov's report. Some wondered whether it was conceivable that Napoleon would devote such a large force simply to protect his foragers.[6] Kutuzov also had his doubts, so he instructed General Dokhturov, with the entire 6th Corps, to support Dorokhov and probe the enemy forces.

Dokhturov, accompanied by Yermolov and Sir Robert Wilson, departed from Tarutino at dawn on October 22. After an arduous march over bad roads and in heavy rain, his men arrived at the village of Aristovo, near Borovsk, late in the day and prepared for the miserable bivouac—they were forbidden to set fires so as not to reveal their presence.[7] That evening Dokhturov convened a council of war to discuss the plan for the attack scheduled for the following morning. Just as the generals had finished their deliberations and prepared to catch a quick nap before the battle, Captain Seslavin careered into the Russian camp with a prisoner "across his saddle" and delivered some startling news.[8] The French prisoner had revealed that Moscow had been abandoned and that

Napoleon's entire army—not just a small detachment—was marching on Borovsk.[9] Seslavin said that he had personally climbed a tree to better observe the enemy units and claimed to have seen Napoleon himself, surrounded by his marshals and the Imperial Guard. "Had Seslavin failed to inform us in time," Yermolov later reminisced, "the 6th Corps would have suffered a serious defeat at Fominskoe, and Maloyaroslavets would have been captured without any difficulty." This would have permitted Napoleon to outflank the Russian army and reach the southern provinces before Kutuzov could react. Some argued that Seslavin's discovery had saved Russia.[10]

Stunned by the revelation, Dokhturov and his companions held an emergency council of war to consider what to do next. Yermolov urged the corps commander to make a dash for Maloyaroslavets and hold it against all odds in the hope that Kutuzov might reach them in time to block Napoleon's advance. Dokhturov, whom Denis Davydov, the famous partisan commander, described as "a gallant but not very perceptive general," hesitated. Kutuzov's orders specified holding positions around Fominskoe, and the general was unwilling to assume responsibility for defying them, especially when he might have to confront Napoleon himself.[11] And so he dithered until Yermolov, dismayed by such irresolution at a critical moment, wielded his trump—as a chief of staff, he represented the supreme commander and therefore could overrule the corps commander. On his orders, Captain Bolgovskii was sent to alert the main headquarters, while the men of the 6th Corps, who had barely gotten any rest from the previous march and were wet and hungry, embarked on a mad sprint through waterlogged and muddy countryside to Maloyaroslavets, a small town perched atop a curving ridge that ran along the steep right bank of the Luzha River.[12]

Kutuzov was asleep when Bolgovskii reached Tarutino. After a quick conversation with Konovnitsyn, the messenger was immediately ushered to the field marshal, whom he found "sitting on his bed, fully dressed in his coat and wearing decorations." Kutuzov asked if it was true that Napoleon had really left Moscow. Bolgovskii shared everything he knew and showed him the dispatch that Dokhturov and Yermolov had given him. The field marshal broke into tears—"not just cried, but wept," as Bolgovskii noted—as he understood the full magnitude of the news. He cast a look at the men gathered in his quarters and then turned to a holy icon hanging on the wall of his room and gave tearful thanks. "Henceforth Russia is saved," he said in a tremulous voice.[13] He asked for the map of the area, which he closely examined before sending an urgent order to Dokhturov "to march, nay, dash" to Maloyaroslavets, which he was supposed to defend at all costs to bar Napoleon's road to Kaluga—the gateway to the untouched fertile provinces in the Russian southwest. The Russian army began hastily to break camp; Platov's Cossacks were the first to get into the saddle and head off into the night.[14]

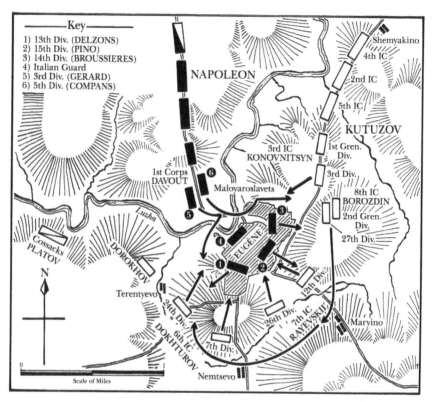

Key
1) 13th Div. (DELZONS)
2) 15th Div. (PINO)
3) 14th Div. (BROUSSIERES)
4) Italian Guard
5) 3rd Div. (GERARD)
6) 5th Div. (COMPANS)

NAPOLEON

1st Corps
DAVOUT

Maloyaroslavets

3rd IC
KONOVNITSYN

EUGÈNE

Luzha

Cossacks
PLATOV

DOROKHOV

Terentyevo

N

DOKHTUROV

24th Div.

6th IC

7th Div.

Nemtsevo

Scale of Miles
0   1

Shemyakino
4th IC

2nd IC

5th IC

KUTUZOV

1st Gren.
Div.

3rd Div.

8th IC
BOROZDIN
2nd Gren.
Div.

27th Div.

12th Div.

26th Div.

7th IC
RAYEVSKII

Maryino

MAP 18 Battle of Maloyaroslavets

Marching over execrable roads rendered nearly impassable by the pouring rain, Dokhturov's corps approached Maloyaroslavets late on October 23.[15] By then it was too late; several hours earlier, General Alexis-Joseph Delzons and the 13th Division, a part of Eugène de Beauharnais's advance guard, had occupied the town. Learning from locals that most of the French division was still on the other side of the Luzha River and that the town was held only by two battalions, Dokhturov ordered his exhausted troops to storm the town at dawn.[16] The fighting proved to be savage; the town changed hands several times, neither side gaining the upper hand. "Half of the day had passed," wrote Yermolov in his memoirs. He commanded troops on the Russian side. "Masses of enemy troops were approaching Maloyaroslavets and were deploying across the Luzha; enemy artillery fire increased, and their attacks became more and more persistent."[17]

Fortunately, the main Russian army soon approached the scene of action. Kutuzov halted about three miles from Maloyaroslavets to rest his troops and dispatched his staff officers to find out what was happening inside the town. The news was discouraging. Dokhturov's men, already fatigued from the long march, had been decimated in the house-to-house fighting inside

Maloyaroslavets. Yermolov kept sending urgent requests for reinforcements, warning that unless the main forces joined the battle at once, it would be lost. Kutuzov refused to commit them until he got a clearer sense of the situation. In a letter to the czar, he spoke of his uncertainty as to whether Napoleon had fully abandoned Moscow. He was concerned that the French emperor was moving part of his army as a diversionary attack while the rest of the Grande Armée was about to strike elsewhere. Lacking fresh and precise intelligence, he lambasted Platov for failing to provide any valuable information despite having twenty Cossack regiments at his disposal: "What have you done with your troops all day today?"[18] Now, as the battle raged at Maloyaroslavets, the field marshal wanted to keep his main army uncommitted out of precaution. Messengers kept arriving with what Kutuzov thought were overly dramatic dispatches from Maloyaroslavets. When yet another of Yermolov's couriers arrived asking for reinforcements, an exasperated Kutuzov spat so forcefully in frustration that the officer had to reach for his handkerchief, according to witnesses, for "his face was greatly in need of it."[19] After making sense of the situation, he finally agreed to send in troops and commanded Rayevskii's corps to join in the battle; the rest of the army took up position in a semicircle around the town and began constructing earthworks in case the French captured the town and attempted to advance beyond it.[20]

Over the next several hours tens of thousands of men fought for the possession of the smoldering heap of bloodstained ruins that had once been a quaint town. Rayevskii's men came just in time to shore up Dokhturov's weary divisions, and together they stormed Maloyaroslavets—"for the fifth time," Kutuzov noted in his report to the czar—and drove the French divisions back to their bridgehead.[21] Napoleon responded by sending General Jean Dominique Compans's 5th Division, along with Domenico Pino's 15th Italian Division and Maurice Étienne Gérard's 3rd Division, which bolstered Delzon's depleted units. The French and Italians beat back the oncoming Russians—"despite us spreading death amid their ranks," Kutuzov commented—and regained possession of the town.[22] It was now the Russians' turn to act. Kutuzov ordered Lieutenant General Mikhail Borozdin's 8th Corps, reinforced with the 3rd Infantry Division, to fight its way into the town.

Soldiers fought in close quarters amid burning buildings and a hail of musket and cannon fire. The wounded burned alive in the blazing houses or were crushed by the charging and countercharging soldiery. An eyewitness recalled "the crackling flames, the hissing ring of the grape as it flew from the cannon, the rattling of the musketry, the ignited shells traversing and crossing in the atmosphere, [and] the wild shouts of the combatants."[23] The French and Italians ultimately remained masters of the town, which had been almost entirely reduced to ashes (20 houses were left standing out of 2,000), but it was a pyrrhic victory, costing Napoleon over 6,000 casualties and without delivering the results he desired.[24] The following day, the French emperor—who arrived too late to directly command the battle—conducted a reconnaissance on the southern bank of the Lusha, barely escaping capture by the Cossacks. Returning to his quarters inside a miserable weaver's hut, Napoleon pondered his next move. Despite gaining a tactical victory at Maloyaroslavets, he realized that Kutuzov still held an operational advantage. The rejuvenated Russian army, despite losing over 7,000 men, held numerical superiority and occupied the higher ground, blocking the path forward. He knew his opponent was crafty—"the true Scythian," Ségur remembered Napoleon calling Kutuzov—and would be determined to avoid a full pitched battle until it suited him. In the dark hours of October, "in this crumbling hovel, in a dark and dirty chamber, divided into two by means of a cloth," to use the apt description of a French participant, "the fate of the army and of Europe was to be decided."[25] Napoleon reached his decision: the army must fall back to Mozhaisk and return to winter quarters via the Old Smolensk road.

This was a critical decision, for it forced the French to retrace their footsteps through the devastated provinces, where they could not hope to secure sufficient provisions. Kutuzov could thus be pleased with the results of that day. Maloyaroslavets was the third-largest engagement of the campaign (after Smolensk and Borodino) but surpassed the other battles in importance. "Losing the battle would have produced devastating consequences," Kutuzov noted in his letter to the czar, the most crucial of which would have been "opening the way to the bountiful [southern] provinces."[26] Just two days after the battle, he proudly declared that Kaluga, and therefore the southern provinces, was "completely safeguarded."[27] Given what was at stake, Napoleon should have taken direct control of the battle and attempted to envelop the Russian positions, as Kutuzov feared. As it was, Maloyaroslavets signaled a change in the campaign's character. What started as a strategic withdrawal from Moscow would henceforth morph into a full-blown retreat, as the Grande Armée ceased offensive operations and did its best to withdraw through the Russian provinces before it was too late.

Napoleon first directed his weary men to Mozhaisk, where the morale of the army, already undermined by the retreat from Maloyaroslavets, declined even more as the troops crossed the Borodino battlefield. It was still covered with numerous corpses, half-eaten by wolves and pecked at by carrion crows. To speed up the army's movement, Napoleon ordered all superfluous transports abandoned, while the wounded were to be evacuated on wagons and carriages. The soldiers who were forced to free up places in their carts were angered by the decision. Napoleon's master of the horse, Armand de Caulaincourt, watched "drivers deliberately driving their horses at speed over rough ground in order to rid themselves of the unfortunate [wounded men] with whom they had been burdened." Although the drivers knew that these poor men would be crushed by horses and wheels, "they would yet smile triumphantly when a jolt freed them of one of those wretches."[28]

Kutuzov's performance at Maloyaroslavets, eulogized by Soviet historians, provoked bitter criticism among the senior officers, who protested the lack of vigor and decisiveness in his decisions.[29] The main army should not have stopped three miles from the battlefield, they argued, but instead rushed directly to the town, where the arrival of over 90,000 troops and some 600 cannon would have brought a decisive victory.[30] They questioned Kutuzov's will to fight and went so far as to accuse of him cowardice. During the battle, the Duke of Oldenburg came across Robert Wilson and asked him if he had seen the field marshal. "He might be in that direction," the British officer responded, pointing to a distant tree. "No," replied the duke, "that cannot be true, for [it is too dangerous there] and I have just seen a cannonball pass there."[31] Disregarding such embarrassing testimonies, a good number of (again, mainly Soviet) historians argued that Kutuzov had demonstrated masterful leadership and "trounced Napoleon."[32] Following Stalin's latter-day command, they declared that the Russian field marshal used the triumph at Maloyaroslavets as the staging grounds for a "counteroffensive" that would shatter the French army by the end of the year.

Kutuzov's actions hardly constituted a "counteroffensive." At Maloyaroslavets, he had pursued the immediate and sensible goal of stopping the enemy's advance. Writing to the czar during the night of October 25, he stressed that "under no circumstances" would he let Napoleon reach Kaluga.[33] He claimed a victory in a battle that was, in his words, "one of the greatest during this ferocious war," but made no mention of Napoleon retaining control of the town and instead emphasized that the Russians had retained Maloyaroslavets and that the Grande Armée was forced to retreat. He knew full well what had happened that day but, like Napoleon, was willing to stretch the truth to shore up public support. Once the fighting had subsided, he summoned senior officers to his bivouac behind the town, congratulated them on a glorious victory, and thanked them for their bravery and dedication. He then announced that "he had made up his mind to resist the advance of Napoleon, and that he was prepared to decide the fate of the enemy by a general action." This surprised a good number of officers who had long complained of Kutuzov's idleness and did not expect him to show vim and vigor. Wilson, for one, went up to Kutuzov, heartily shook his hand, and "congratulated him upon the decision as one worthy of the Field Marshal's character, and the great cause confided to his charge." Kutuzov thanked him for the compliments and assured him that he was determined "to finish the war on that spot" by either winning or letting Napoleon pass over his dead body. "He expressed himself with a solemnity of devoted patriotism that would have become Leonidas at the pass of Thermopylae," Wilson noted.[34]

This seems to have been part of a well-played charade. Kutuzov had no intention of confronting Napoleon in a pitched battle. While Wilson was away, an entirely different scene unfolded at the Russian headquarters when Kutuzov revealed that he intended to pull the army back to Kaluga. He was concerned that Napoleon might send part of the Grande Armée to Medyn, where Russian scouts had already observed enemy units that, Kutuzov feared, might be trying to go around the Russian army's positions at Maloyaroslavets; once again he and other officers complained that Platov's failure to deliver intelligence was hampering their decision-making.[35] The choice to fall back toward Kaluga was therefore sensible in light of the uncertainty and reflected the operational challenges that the Russian army faced.

Of course, there were those who disagreed. In "a very lively discussion," Colonel Toll—whom Kutuzov greatly respected and always treated differently than other officers—questioned withdrawing the army when an all-out assault might bring a victory. Kutuzov patiently listened to the officer's arguments. He then told him to start drafting the orders to retreat. Frustrated, Toll replied "in a rather brusque manner," as Löwenstern commented, that he did not know what to write in the disposition because "there was only one correct decision to make, that of advancing and destroying the enemy army." Kutuzov calmly repeated his request: "My dear Toll, do not be so stubborn and for once, do what I want." To the utter astonishment of other officers who witnessed the scene, the colonel persisted in his refusal to follow the commander in chief's order.

Just as tempers flared, Bennigsen arrived from his reconnaissance trip and, with an air of self-importance, declared, "Monsieur Field Marshal, I congratulate you on the part two of the Battle of Eylau that Napoleon is about to serve you tomorrow." According to Löwenstern, he told Kutuzov that the French intended to maintain Maloyaroslavets at any cost and would therefore "confront you in battle tomorrow." Kutuzov could not have been more pleased with his rival's conceited and ill-timed announcement. "Well, well! What do you think about that?" he asked Toll with a sardonic smile. "Here is an eminent general announcing that the enemy will attack me tomorrow. You, meanwhile, expect me to charge ahead in a cavalier fashion. We must instead prepare for the enemy attack." Patting the colonel gently on the shoulders, he told him, "So now go and do as I told you." Toll had no choice but to comply, while Bennigsen remained standing, befuddled about what had happened.[36]

Kutuzov's announcement that the army would retreat toward Kaluga was "a thunderbolt that caused a momentary stupor" among the generals, commented the enraged Wilson, who lambasted the field marshal as affording "a memorable instance of incapacity in a chief, of an absence of any quality that ought to distinguish a commander."[37] The British commissioner's list of "heavy charges" against Kutuzov included those "for ignorance in the conduct of the troops, for sloth, for indecision of counsels, for panic operations and for a desire to let the enemy pass unmolested."[38] Wilson, along with others, confronted the field marshal over this decision. Sitting in the circle of officers, the field marshal calmly explained to them that he had received fresh intelligence of Napoleon's enveloping maneuver, inducing him to give up on his earlier intention of fighting for Maloyaroslavets and to retreat southward, in order to secure the road to Kaluga. When Wilson forcefully protested, Kutuzov snapped at him, "I don't care for your objections. I prefer giving my enemy a *pont d'or* [golden bridge], as you call it, to receiving a *coup de collier* [a strong shove]." He reiterated to them that he remained unconvinced that the "total destruction" of Napoleon would benefit anyone. It was clear to him that his succession "would not fall to Russia or any other continental power, but to that which already commands the sea, and whose domination would then be intolerable."[39]

This statement offers crucial insight into Kutuzov's decision-making throughout this campaign. Contemporary and scholarly opinion has long derided Kutuzov's comportment during these crucial months, with some suggesting that his age and poor health had clouded his judgment and that he feared confronting Napoleon. There is some truth to these claims. Kutuzov was indeed feebler than before, less active, more prone to somnolence. But he still retained his intellectual prowess, which was usually cloaked beneath silence and seeming torpor. Few figures in history have done more by appearing to do less. Unlike so many of his fellow generals, he looked beyond the confines of a battlefield to consider the wider repercussions of the conflict. War was always bound up with political considerations and had to reflect a clear policy—what is now called grand strategy—not the other way around. This was one of the cornerstones of his own strategy in the fall of 1812, when he became convinced that Napoleon could no longer prevail in the war against Russia. Had the French wished to carry their conquests farther than Moscow, Kutuzov told a captured French official, he would have "yielded another 500 *lieues*" and continued to fight.[40] He was certain that Russian geography, topography, climate, and asymmetrical warfare would defeat the enemy.

Now the tide of war had shifted, and Kutuzov was more concerned about the larger picture. Winning another battle might bring fame, but he was becoming preoccupied with the wider repercussions of Napoleon's defeat. What would happen when the Napoleonic empire crumbled? Would France remain the source of continued political turmoil in Europe? What about the balance of power, and what would be Russia's place and role? These were questions with no easy solutions. Kutuzov knew that in the byzantine world of European politics, providence usually favored those with big battalions, so he was keen on ensuring that Russia had its share of them by not losing soldiers unnecessarily. That is why he had told the captured French officer that he had no desire "to sacrifice a single soldier" to achieve the complete destruction of the Grande Armée. He would let flying detachments, guerrillas, starvation, exhaustion, and weather vanquish the enemy.[41] Moreover, Kutuzov's concern was that annihilating Napoleon's military capacity would not necessarily be in Russia's interests, as Britain would gain the most from the fall of its mighty continental foe. His response to Wilson was not simple invective aimed at a British officer. Kutuzov expressed such sentiments more than once. During yet another argument with Bennigsen, he reminded him of his Hanoverian origins: "We will never come to an agreement—you are thinking only of England's benefit, while to me, if that island sank to the bottom of the sea, I would not feel even the smallest regret."[42]

Kutuzov remained true to his word, sticking to the "small war" of attacking and harassing Napoleon but avoiding pitched battles that could result in unnecessary Russian sacrifices. Russia would need a strong army if it aspired to become a player in European political equilibrium in a post-Napoleonic world. This was an unpopular but sensible policy. Referring to the "golden bridge" approach with Napoleon, military historian John Lewis Gaddis writes that it "could serve as grand strategy's gold standard. For if ends are to fit within available means, then solvency and morality—practicality and principle—demand that they do so with the least possible expenditure of resources and lives."[43] Kutuzov would have agreed. Besides, there was also a deep sense of satisfaction in pursuing the "golden bridge" approach: he admitted to Catherine that driving before him "the best commander in the world" felt "rather sweet."[44]

CHAPTER 28 | The Chase

ON OCTOBER 31, NAPOLEON arrived at the town of Vyazma, a five-day march from Maloyaroslavets. His troops were exhausted. The weather had turned colder; the last few nights of October saw temperatures plunge to single digits. The Grande Armée was already experiencing an acute shortage of supplies, while lack of forage greatly weakened the horses. The march of tens of thousands of men and animals on unpaved roads soon created a muddy morass, causing further delays and exacerbating the suffering of the troops. "Our retreat had the semblance of a rout," lamented French officer Raymond Eymery de Montesquiou-Fezensac.[1] "Woe betide those who allowed themselves to be knocked over," recalled another French officer. Those who fell and could not get up were trodden underfoot, causing others to trip and fall on top of them. In places, small mounds of men and horses, dead and dying, blocked the way. But the mass kept moving—quarreling, pushing, and shoving—and the air was filled with "the cries of the unfortunates" crushed beneath the wheels of carriages.[2]

After a two-day rest, Napoleon led the army toward Smolensk, leaving behind Davout's I Corps to act as a rear guard. The retreating Grande Armée stretched for some fifty miles, and as the leading column was approaching Dorogobuzh, Davout's men were still in the rear, east of Vyazma, constantly harassed by the Cossacks. On November 3, the Russian advance guard approached Vyazma from the southeast.[3] While reconnoitering the vicinity of the town, Miloradovich noticed that a gap had formed between Davout, approaching the village of Fedorovskoye, east of Vyazma, and the troops of the IV Corps (Eugène de Beauharnais) and V Corps (Poniatowski), which were on the western side of the town. Recognizing an opportunity to intercept and destroy an enemy corps, the Russian general decided to attack at once. His men stormed the environs of Vyazma and intercepted the Old

Smolensk road just as Platov's Cossacks pushed Davout's beleaguered men from the east. Undaunted, the "Iron Marshal" charged forward and took advantage of the uncoordinated nature of the Russian attacks to clear his way to Vyazma, while Beauharnais, Ney, and Poniatowski halted their corps to assist their comrades-in-arms. Encouraged by their initial success, Miloradovich and Platov regrouped their forces and launched fresh assaults that led to the storming of Vyazma in the late afternoon. Cold, miserable, and exhausted, Davout and his men fought desperately to hold the Russians off while the rest of the army hastily evacuated the wounded and transports from the town. Eager to gain a decisive victory at Vyazma, Miloradovich urgently requested reinforcements from Kutuzov, who, although within earshot of the battle, sent only several thousand cavalrymen but otherwise refused to engage in the battle, which ended in a Russian victory but represented a missed opportunity to mangle the French army.[4]

Kutuzov's "golden bridge" strategy may have been rational and sensible, but it was not heroic, glorious, or exciting. After the fighting at Maloyaroslavets, he regrouped the army at Polotnyanye Zavody, known for

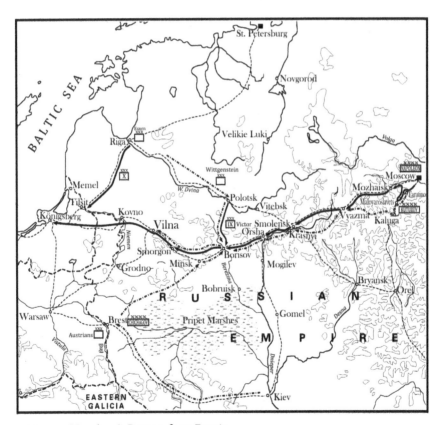

MAP 19 Napoleon's Retreat from Russia

being a cloth-manufacturing center.[5] His correspondence shows great concern for raising, training, and equipping the reserves that he thought would be crucial to winning the war in the long term. He also spent considerable time making arrangements to fix the problems with a supply system that was already struggling to keep up with the army; to set up hospitals to treat the increasing number of sick and infirm soldiers; to raise new levies of provincial militia recruits; to improve conditions for the French prisoners of war; to reinforce fortresses in Byelorussia, to which he expected the theater of war to transition in the forthcoming weeks; and to strengthen the flying detachments that would pursue the retreating enemy.

These were worthwhile endeavors, important to the health and success of Russian arms, but dispiriting to many officers at the Russian headquarters. Even Colonel Toll was upset about it, urging General Konovnitsyn to convince Kutuzov to go after Napoleon. "Peter Petrovich, if we do not push the field marshal, we might end up spending the whole winter here," he complained.[6] It seemed to him and so many others that the enemy was teetering and victory was tantalizingly close; pursuit offered many opportunities to garner laurels, to make a name or a career. Kutuzov consented to speed-up a pursuit, but caution still molded his actions. Even after receiving the czar's letter denouncing his "unnecessary and pernicious retreat" after the Battle of Maloyaroslavets and threatening to hold him personally responsible for any further setbacks, Kutuzov remained determined to follow his strategy. Instead of rushing in the wake of the retreating enemy, he insisted on a parallel march—he envisioned the flying detachments and advance guard relentlessly harassing Napoleon along the Old Smolensk road, while the main Russian army would maintain distance and proceed on a march parallel to the Grande Armée.[7] If the opportunity arose, he intended to engage isolated French corps, but otherwise he remained wary of confronting the bulk of the Grande Armée because the French would fight more fiercely to protect themselves (and their leader) and this would cost high casualties. Such a sacrifice would be senseless. Kutuzov believed that his approach offered three key advantages: by shadowing the enemy army, he could anticipate Napoleon's attempts to swerve into the fertile southern provinces, from which the Russian army continued to draw all its provisions; he could preserve the core of the Russian army and avoid losing men needlessly; and he could continue to harass the enemy through asymmetrical warfare.[8] In the instructions that he sent to one of the flying detachments, Kutuzov specified that the main objective was to destroy any provisions and forage along the road in order "to deprive the enemy cavalry and artillery of means to survive." He wanted his partisans to intercept enemy communications, demolish bridges, and target isolated units. "In short, take every means necessary to cause harm to the enemy."[9] He knew that time was against Napoleon and in his own favor.

Both the czar and senior Russian officers clamored for action. Even with the cannonade at Vyazma clearly audible and the officers demanding to fight, Kutuzov remained, in the words of one eyewitness, "a passive spectator of that day." Löwenstern could see that everyone at the main headquarters was "extremely impatient." The soldiers kept stomping their feet, while the generals and the officers grumbled. Löwenstern and his comrades awaited a signal to attack. None came. Kutuzov, as Löwenstern put it, "preferred to bear the burden of recriminations from the entire army rather than to exploit an occasion to pluck the finest laurels of victory."[10]

Kutuzov was of course well aware of the dissatisfaction with his approach. With dozens of officers volunteering to serve at the front line, he quipped that "the advance guard cannot fit the entire world."[11] Writing to his family, he admitted that chasing Napoleon was getting "tedious."[12] But he was convinced of the rightness of his policy. Even with the main army remaining uninvolved, events in Vyazma and elsewhere had a disruptive impact on Napoleon's forces. Wilson, who rarely missed an opportunity to carp at Kutuzov's dilatory strategy, was nevertheless overjoyed to see the roads and fields covered with the vestiges of the French army. "For many years the French have not seen such an unhappy day," he gleefully wrote two days after Vyazma, where the French lost at least 4,000 killed and wounded. (Kutuzov first reported 6,000, then increased the number to 7,000, and another 2,500 captured; the Russian casualties were supposedly less than 2,000 men.)[13] This defeat hastened the feeling of demoralization among French units, which their Russian opponents were quick to notice. While the Russians could still see "the skill of the French generals, the obedience of their subordinates, and their energy," as Yermolov noted, there was a change. Order and discipline had "disappeared" and the soldiers "seemed to have lost their last strength, each of them now a victim of hunger, exhaustion, and the cruelty of the weather."[14] The broader situation was also changing in Russia's favor. In mid-September, Admiral Chichagov had pushed the Austrian and Saxon forces beyond the Bug River and begun marching northward to intercept Napoleon's escape routes. Peter Wittgenstein, meanwhile, defeated Marshal Gouvion St. Cyr's corps at Polotsk. This was a major Russian victory, one that revealed how vulnerable the French wing was to attack and impelling Napoleon to speed up his retreat to Smolensk.

Kutuzov moved steadily forward with the bulk of his army. "I could pride myself on being the first general to put Napoleon to flight," he bragged to his family in late October. "He keeps running from place to place every night, but we are anticipating him everywhere. He is trying to get away somehow but won't be able to do it without heavy losses."[15] The main Russian army, therefore, continued to shadow the Grande Armée and prevent it from leaving the devastated countryside along the main road. "Everything here was burned down; one could not even find a cat to skin," remembered a Russian general.[16] There were wrenching scenes of human suffering and misery. "Yesterday two Frenchmen were found in the woods," Kutuzov wrote on November 8. "They were roasting and eating their third comrade. And one cannot but shudder watching what the peasants are doing to them."[17]

Witnessing the rapid dissolution of the enemy army—"they are running away in utter confusion," he commented on November 4—the field marshal felt justified in ignoring his many critics.[18] Describing events at Vyazma, Wilson charged that Kutuzov "fled, or rather was made to fly, from the enemy" and complained that his "preconcerted system" "deprived Russia of the glory, and the common cause of a success that would have terminated the war."[19] Staff officer Durnovo bemoaned "the turtle's pace" at which the army was advancing. "I am convinced that the field marshal requires rest, and the emperor should oblige by giving him a long furlough."[20] The more perceptive among them, however, grasped the logic of Kutuzov's indolence. "We have won—the enemy is perishing," Konovnitsyn acknowledged three days before reaching Smolensk.[21] Even those who earlier derided Kutuzov's caution now admitted that, as Löwenstern wrote, "the prince always followed the principle of leaving nothing to chance; he knew all along that everything had changed, and that the genius of Napoleon had dimmed. . . . The prudence that [Kutuzov] displayed was in contradiction to our ardor but was nonetheless commendable and his conduct later proved that it was in conformity with the interests of the Fatherland, even if not in harmony with the opinion of the army."[22]

The fact that Kutuzov had managed to survive such relentless criticism and disparagement and that he did not share Barclay de Tolly's fate points both to his ability to focus on the task at hand and to the support he received from his allies at the imperial court. He had long cultivated relations with Maria Naryshkina, the czar's mistress, celebrated as "Aspasia of the North." "Her beauty," wrote Wiegel, "is so perfect that it appears impossible, even supernatural." Kutuzov agreed. His letters underscore the degree to which he was fascinated by Naryshkina. "Please tell her that she is an angel," he asked his wife. "And that if I adore women, it is because she is of that gender and that if she were a man, I would become indifferent to all the women."[23] Naryshkina had the czar's ear. Kutuzov had other influential allies, too. Alexander Voyeikov, the Russian literary critic and scholar, remembered hearing from General Bogdan (Gotthard Johann) von Knorring that the czar had convened the privy council of war on several occasions to examine complaints against Kutuzov and to consider replacing him. In late October, the czar met with Barclay de Tolly's aide-de-camp Wolzogen, who delivered a detailed report on what had transpired at Borodino and its aftermath. It was scathingly critical of Kutuzov, causing the czar to angrily comment, "About all these details the scoundrel who at the present leads my army has written nothing to me. Instead, he told me lots of lies!" Wolzogen praised

Barclay de Tolly, reminding the czar of the many services that the general had rendered to the army and the nation. Alexander knew it well, too. "As a man, he towers above the depraved Kutuzov," he admitted. And yet, the czar went on to explain, he could not return Barclay de Tolly to the army. Even the Czar of All the Russias was afraid to confront public opinion, which derided Barclay de Tolly and extolled Kutuzov. He had to "subordinate his personal sentiments to imperative circumstances," he commented.[24] Most members of the privy council of war—Knorring, Prince Zubov (Kutuzov's old benefactor), Arakcheyev, Alexander Balashev (the minister of police), and Alexander Shishkov (the state secretary)—staunchly defended the field marshal. Once the council was presented with an allegation that Kutuzov was sleeping up to eighteen hours a day. "Thank God he is asleep; every day of his inaction is equal to a battle won," observed a council member, reminding everyone of the attrition that the Grande Armée was experiencing. And when the subject of Kutuzov's supposed Cossack-dressed consort arose yet again, Knorring curtly responded, "Rumyantsev used to have four of them with him. This is none of our business."[25] Thanks to these powerful guardians, Kutuzov remained at the helm of the Russian armies.

He soon gained another ally, too—"General Winter." The autumn of 1812 had been, as we've seen, warm, lulling Napoleon into a false sense of security.[26] But in the first days of November the weather became progressively colder and snow covered the ground. Napoleon later blamed an unusually cold winter for his defeat in Russia. In fact, the Grande Armée had been wrecked long before the cold set in; a thaw in the second half of November, when he reached the shores of the Berezina River, posed an even greater threat. Even a mild frost could pose a lethal danger to the wearied men, who wore inadequate clothing and slept in the open. "Snow fell heavily and severe cold immediately froze it, so the horses could move on the hard crust without sinking," recalled Westphalian officer Friedrich Klinkhardt in his memoirs. "It did not last for long, but I managed to freeze my nose, ears, hands, and feet and could move around and get on a carriage only with assistance."[27] The number of French prisoners rapidly increased as the Grande Armée's morale declined and discipline gave way to self-preservation. The horrors of the retreat multiplied with each passing day. Scenes of misery and death even shocked the Russian pursuers, one of whom described seeing "naked masses of dead and dying men," the mutilated carcasses of horses, and the splintered remains of countless carriages, caissons, and other equipment.[28] "It seems I am destined to see my enemies surviving on horsemeat and devoid of bread and salt," wrote Kutuzov to Catherine.[29]

He did his best to prepare his soldiers for the coming cold, sending repeated requests to provincial authorities for essential supplies and warm clothing. He also tried to inspire his men to fight on. His proclamation of October 31 reminded soldiers of the sacrifices they had already made in this war, and those to come: "The fire of Moscow must be put out with the blood of the enemy!"[30] Calling his soldiers the "Children of the North," he told them that their "iron hearts" should "fear neither the inclemency of the weather nor the wickedness" of the enemy. "You are the true bulwarks of the Fatherland."[31]

Napoleon reached Smolensk on November 9. The remnants of his army poured into the city over the next four days. The garrison was unable to restrain throngs of famished soldiers, stragglers, and civilians, many of whom had subsisted on horse flesh for almost a week, from storming the magazines and looting everything inside them. Supplies that should have lasted the army for quite some time were devoured at once, depriving the latecomers of warmth, food, and security. There were other factors forcing Napoleon to expedite his retreat. It was while at Smolensk that he received the news from France that a false report of his death had led to an attempted military coup d'état in Paris. News of the conspiracy stunned Napoleon, making him realize the urgency of quitting the army and hastening to Paris.

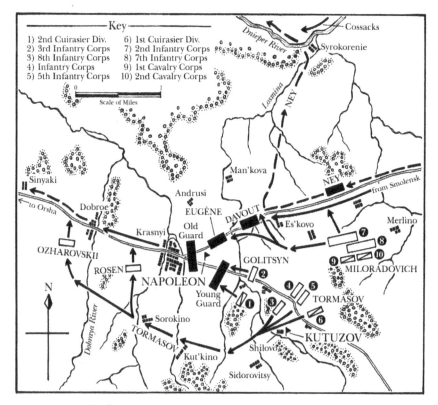

MAP 20 Battle of Krasnyi

Napoleon weighed his options. In the fourteen days since leaving Moscow, his army had lost almost half of its men; it was now reduced to barely 60,000 men. And with each passing day, the numbers diminished while those of the wounded, sick, and stragglers swelled. Remaining in Smolensk was pointless, since the stores were already exhausted. The wider strategic situation had also dramatically changed. Kutuzov's flying detachments, like the hounds of Krylov's fable, prowled the countryside, killing and capturing hundreds of soldiers every day; at Lyakhovo alone, they had captured an entire French brigade, which in Kutuzov's report to the czar was passed off as a whole corps. While the main Russian army was approaching Smolensk, Wittgenstein was closing in from the north, while Chichagov's Army of the Danube was nearing the Berezina River with the clear intent of intercepting the French line of retreat. The only viable option for Napoleon was to quit Smolensk, beat the converging enemy forces, and seek winter quarters in the Duchy of Warsaw.

On the morning of November 14, the emperor ordered his men to depart along the main road leading to Krasnyi and Orsha. Once again, the Grande Armée was stretched thin over thirty miles, which made it vulnerable to a flanking attack. Lack of cavalry made reconnaissance virtually impossible, and Napoleon remained largely unaware of the main Russian army's whereabouts. His four-day-long stay at Smolensk, in fact, had enabled Kutuzov to catch up to the Grande Armée and approach Smolensk from the southeast. Had the Russians been commanded by a leader looking to attack, Napoleon's fate might have been sealed. But they were not. It may well be, as Clausewitz remarked, that Kutuzov was concerned by the deteriorating condition of his own army, which was suffering from the cold and perishing in bivouac at an alarming rate—though, of course, less rapidly than the Grande Armée. A more impulsive general might have rushed to destroy the enemy before his own force weakened too much. Kutuzov, however, remained convinced that his Fabian strategy was working. He was also infirm, persistently complaining of various aches and a feeling of exhaustion. "Because of back pain, I cannot stand straight, and this, in turn, causes my headaches," he wrote Catherine.[32] He rarely appeared at the helm of the troops anymore, preferring to travel in a carriage or a sleigh. "There are, I admit, many delightful moments for me, but people rarely seem cheerful anymore," he confided to his daughter. "It is hard to relish any of it when you are sentimental."[33]

On November 14, after marching thirteen miles, Kutuzov halted the Russian main army—four infantry corps and two cuirassier divisions—at the village of Yurovo, twenty-four miles from Smolensk. Adam Ozharovskii's flying detachment entered Krasnyi, thereby intercepting Napoleon's line of retreat, and began to destroy the stores collected there. The French soon forced Ozharovskii's men out of the town and cleared the path for the Grande Armée, but it was a fleeting success. The following day, the renewed Russian assaults—from General Alexander Osterman-Tolstoy at Kobyzevich and from Miloradovich at Rzhavka—led to the capture of hundreds of prisoners and some thirty cannon, while three French corps found themselves cut off from the Grande Armée. An unexpected thaw brought little relief to the suffering of the worn-out troops (and equally numerous noncombatants), who kept marching through heavy snow; the Imperial Guard artillery, the best-preserved in the entire French army, took an entire day to cover twelve miles out of Smolensk. The small ravine east of Krasnyi proved to be the final resting place for dozens of cannon, wagons, and vehicles of every kind, which were all simply abandoned in heaps along the frozen road. "We walked on, thinking of all that had passed, stumbling over dead and dying men," remembered a French sergeant.[34]

On November 16, Kutuzov moved his main army to the village of Shilovo, closer to Krasnyi. He refused to commit his core units to the battle that was raging just a few miles away. He did, however, send the 2nd Reserve Corps to Merlino, where Miloradovich barred the road to the French. That afternoon Eugène de Beauharnais, leading what remained of the IV Corps, tried to fight his way through but was repulsed with heavy losses; he rejected with disdain Miloradovich's proposal of surrender—delivered by Kutuzov's son-in-law Kudashev—and waited until darkness had fallen to embark on a long and arduous flanking march. The French corps escaped, but not before losing more than 2,000 men and virtually all of its artillery and transports. Beauharnais's predicament stirred Napoleon to action. He turned back, leading no more than 18,000 men, but the Imperial Guard was among them, and it was ready to fight. A division of the Young Guard drove the Russians away from the main road, though it could not pursue this slight success because the Russian main army was nearby. Still, the heavy fighting of that day convinced Kutuzov—as well as a number of other Russian officers—that despite appearances, Napoleon's army was still formidably strong.

Kutuzov watchfully moved his men forward. Tormasov, with three infantry corps and a cavalry division, was told to move to the left and close off the Orsha road, barring Napoleon's routes of escape. Prince Dmitri Golitsyn, with the 3rd Corps and the 2nd Cuirassier Division, was instructed to attack Krasnyi directly, by way of a demonstration, while Miloradovich with the other two corps was to take up a position south of the Smolensk road, let Davout's I Corps pass, and then hold that road against Ney's III Corps. Not counting Platov's Cossacks north of the Dnieper and the various flying columns, Kutuzov had nearly 70,000 regulars with about 450 cannon. The plan was hardly inspiring, but had it been vigorously carried out, Napoleon's small available force would have been destroyed. Yet this golden chance to destroy at least one enemy corps was wasted. Throughout the fighting Kutuzov was apprehensive about committing his main forces. He personally interrogated a captured Bavarian officer and kept asking him who exactly was in command of the French forces at Krasnyi; he was clearly hoping to hear that Napoleon had already moved forward. The officer described a tall man leading the French (probably Marshal Adolphe Édouard Casimir Joseph Mortier, nicknamed "the Big Mortar" for his height), causing Kutuzov to exclaim with undisguised relief, "No, that is not *him*!" But just as he agreed to send in more troops, a local farmer delivered the news that he had seen enemy troops with bearskin hats—the unmistakable trademark of Napoleon's Imperial Guard. Kutuzov countermanded his decision. With Napoleon still near Krasnyi, he expected the French to fight more desperately, so he chose to pull back his men. Over the next two days, the Russians made uncoordinated attacks on the retreating French units, some of which were temporarily cut off, while Ney's corps was surrounded. None of the French corps laid down their arms. In one of the most spectacular feats of the entire Napoleonic Wars, Ney, outnumbered and outgunned, rejected calls to surrender—"a Marshal of France does not surrender," he proudly proclaimed—fought off the Russian assaults, and conducted a valiant retreat across the Dnieper River, which earned him the nickname "the Bravest of the Brave."

As to the question of who was the victor at Krasnyi, the answer remains in the eye of the beholder. "It was a conflict of heroes and even the vanquished have acquired honour," acknowledged Wilson. "The carnage was tremendous, the ground was covered with the dead and dying; the Russian bayonets were dripping with the crimson torrents."[35] Though Napoleon and the Imperial Guard had escaped unscathed, the rest of the Grande Armée paid a steep price, losing up to 10,000 killed or wounded and some 20,000 captured, along with more than 200 cannon.[36] The corps of Beauharnais and Davout were decimated, and Ney's corps simply ceased to exist; the army still nominally counted "corps" and "divisions," but these were skeleton units, some reduced to just a few hundred men. The total number of troops still under arms was 30,000 men. Nonetheless, the Russian victory at Krasnyi could have been far more decisive. As Philippe de Ségur later wrote, "The Russians had only to march forward, without maneuvers or even cannon fire; their mass would have sufficed, for they would have crushed Napoleon and his feeble troops." Instead of closing in with their infantry, the Russian commanders contented themselves with bombarding the enemy units with artillery, which took a heavy toll on the French units but was insufficient to destroy them.

Unsurprisingly, the senior Russian officers were deeply dissatisfied with the results of Krasnyi and complained of timidity and mismanagement. Kutuzov had indeed missed an opportunity to humble Napoleon. This was partly because of his own exhaustion and partly out of his wish to preserve the core of the army. Eugene de Württemberg later recalled how just as he was about to lead his division into attack, he received orders to stand down from

Miloradovich, who explained that the field marshal did not want to get too involved in a battle until he had determined Napoleon's whereabouts. "The old man's view is this: if we incite the enemy to desperation, it will cost us unnecessary losses. But if we let him run and give him a decent escort, he will destroy himself in the course of a few days."[37] Undercutting Kutuzov's credibility were the embellished reports that he submitted after the battle. *Mentir comme un bulletin*, to lie like a bulletin, was a familiar expression in Napoleon's army; the same could have been said about the field marshal's official reports, which consistently exaggerated and extolled, reflecting Winston Churchill's observation that in wartime truth is so precious that it needs to be defended by a bodyguard of lies. Describing events at Krasnyi, Kutuzov proclaimed to the army's generals and commanders that "such brilliant victories had never been scored in such short period of time." The Grande Armée was effectively destroyed: "The corps of Marshals Davout and Ney, along with the Italian viceroy [Beauharnais] and parts of the Imperial Guard, have been routed and dispersed. . . . The trounced enemy is running away so hastily that our army is barely keeping up with forced marches." Kutuzov spoke of the "countless" prisoners, the "complete destruction" of the IV Corps, and of Napoleon himself "galloping away with his entire suite and abandoning his troops for us to despoil."[38] Kutuzov's report to the czar was more measured, though he still claimed that the Grande Armée had been routed.

Some who were there argued that Krasnyi hardly even deserved the name "battle." "The action at Krasnyi, which some pompously refer to as a three-day battle, should instead be described as a three-day search for hungry, half-naked Frenchmen," Denis Davydov wrote in his memoirs. He admired the valor and resolve of the French Imperial Guard, which, with the emperor in their midst, "plowed through us like a 100-gun ship-of-the-line through fishing skiffs."[39] Yermolov was also critical of Kutuzov for his portrayal of the action; in his view, none of it "had been fought according to any general plan."[40] The fact that Kutuzov exploited the events to procure generous rewards for officers also disturbed many. They complained that the list of the nominated generals alone ran several pages. There were "incessant intrigues" to get promotions and awards, griped General Rimsky-Korsakov. "Some got their awards changed, others did not get enough."[41] In a letter to a friend, Rayevskii described how Miloradovich had been nominated for the Order of St. George (second class). However, "since the battle took place under his supposed leadership and he was rather displeased with the results, there was a concern that he might write to the Emperor, so he was upgraded to the Order of St. Vladimir of first class instead."[42]

Most crucially, officers were upset that a precious opportunity had been missed. Napoleon seemed cornered. "If Your Excellency brings the army to Krasnyi tomorrow, you will complete the routing of the enemy army," read Yermolov's urgent appeal to the field marshal on November 15. Kutuzov paid no heed to it, spending the next three days at a safe distance.[43] Colonel Alexander Euler, who commanded the Russian reserve artillery, thought much more could have been accomplished considering that "the French were driven back like a herd [of animals] and they were resisting only when their route was blocked; they kept abandoning wagons, carriages, and artillery without any struggle."[44] Wilson, meanwhile, was beside himself over Kutuzov's "dilatory and discursive marches" that reflected his "predetermination 'to make the victor weep, to see the vanquished fly'!" If not for the field marshal, the war could have ended at Krasnyi, the British commissioner told the czar.[45]

Kutuzov did not seem to care about such censures and hindsight moralizing. With "great finesse and tact," as Löwenstern put it, he maintained "a respectful distance" from his critics; he appeased some with rewards and made sure that others were never housed in the same village in which he stopped for the night, so that he could avoid "being continually besought by them."[46] The field marshal felt that Krasnyi was, in fact, a vindication of his strategy. The enemy had suffered grievous losses at a minimal cost in Russian lives. He spoke of the "indescribable horrors" that the French were experiencing: "I shed tears while observing the travails of the Ottoman prisoners [in 1811]," he wrote Catherine. "I do not cry for the French, but I detest the scenes I am witnessing."[47] He did, though, revel in the numerous French trophies. For the first time in weeks, he got out of the sleigh and, despite agonizing back pain, mounted his horse to examine the battlefield.[48] He was delighted to hear that among the captured items was Davout's marshal's baton. "This was the only occasion that I have seen him galloping on his white Mecklenburger steed," remembered his orderly. Equally pleasing was the review of the captured flags, some of which bore gilded inscriptions commemorating the French triumph at Austerlitz seven years earlier. As he visited the Life Guard Semeyonovskii Regiment, the field marshal's "face shone with happiness," described an eyewitness. "There is nothing that could compare to the universal joy that overwhelmed us at that moment and made us all tearful. The mighty 'hurrah' cheers rang out and moved our old general."[49]

Frustrated and disgruntled as they were, the senior Russian officers found in Kutuzov someone they could not coerce or intimidate with their accomplishments, connections, or ancestry. Regardless of what was said to or about him, he smiled, frowned, nodded, and still did it his way. The czar had warned him that "all misfortunes stemming from your actions would be your personal responsibility."[50] And still Kutuzov pursued his objectives with grim determination and consistency. His relations with Bennigsen devolved into outright animosity, undoubtedly facilitated by Toll's intrigues.[51] "I do not want to say anything about Bennigsen. He is a fatuous and evil man," Kutuzov told Catherine, who had known the general for decades and was friendly with his wife. "The fools around him have convinced him that he can besmirch me in front of the czar and then take over the command of the armies." At least one senior officer at the Russian headquarters suspected Bennigsen of being underhanded. "I do not pretend to say that Bennigsen, as commander-in-chief, would have followed his own counsels offered as second in command," Wilson aptly noted.[52] For once, Kutuzov agreed with the British commissioner. He expected Bennigsen to send a new batch of complaints to St. Petersburg and wanted to anticipate any damage they could cause him. "If you see the Prince [Volkonskii, the czar's aide-de-camp], do remind him of what Bennigsen was doing on those three days [at Tarutino]," reads a small note at the end of the letter that Kutuzov sent to his wife on November 9. Just two days later, he admitted, "I no longer allow Bennigsen to see me."[53] When the general pestered him with requests to press the attack at Krasnyi, Kutuzov glared at the last of Bennigsen's messengers: "Tell your general that I do not know him and I do not care to ever know him. And if he sends me another messenger, I will have him hanged." Kutuzov tolerated his former friend until late November, when he issued a concise but blunt order informing Bennigsen that because of "bouts of illness" he was to leave the army at once and proceed to Kaluga, there to await a new assignment from the czar.[54] Rid of one critic, Kutuzov dealt with others as well. Löwenstern watched as the field marshal curtly responded to Wilson's reproaches by reiterating his commitment "to guide the enemy over the golden bridge rather than compromise the army and the salvation of the empire."[55] Days later he told a captured French official that the war was all but over and that he did not wish to needlessly sacrifice a single Russian soldier. "That is how we, the northern barbarians, take care of our men."

Kutuzov's concern for his troops was well justified. The Russian army was under great strain. While the Grande Armée moved along the main (albeit devastated) road, the Russians proceeded down remote country roads, dragging cannon, caissons, and transports through deep snow and rough terrain. Kutuzov's headquarters did its best to supply the troops with fur coats and felt boots, but numerous problems remained due to logistical challenges, poor weather, the incompetence of local authorities, and corruption in the commissariat. Intendant General Egor Kankrin acknowledged that the supply trains oftentimes lagged far behind the main army, leaving the Russian troops with "very limited" provisions.[56] As late as November 28, Alexander Chicherin complained in his diary that "it has been already twelve days since the Guard received bread, while the army has not seen it for the past month."[57] With the war returning to the already devastated provinces, requisitioning became ever more challenging, and soldiers frequently resorted to extreme measures. "It is wrong to blame only the French for burning and looting everything along the road," admitted Nikolai Mitarevskii. "We did the same."[58]

In just four weeks, the Russian army, which had left the Tarutino camp with some 120,000 men, lost more than a third of its men from attrition. "Half of the troops in the army were sick," commented a Russian artillery officer.

"In my company, less than a third of the men listed on the roster were actually healthy."[59] Ilya Radozhitskii, another artilleryman, reminisced about the dreadful conditions he experienced after departing the Tarutino camp. For days he and his comrades could not find any shelter, as the wooden homes had all burned down and the few surviving structures were occupied by senior officers. Soldiers spent night after night in the snowy fields, barely warmed up by the meager fires that illuminated frozen ground. With their faces "blackened" and their bodies "wrapped in rags," some soldiers wore half-coats and others greatcoats. A few managed to lay their hands on special winter boots lined with fur; most could only dream of such luxuries. "I myself barely survived that winter wearing a sheepskin coat and double felt boots while my head was wrapped in a large scarf," remembered Radozhitskii. "Enduring such hardship, we could not but marvel how the French, who were deprived of any means of subsistence and protection from the elements, managed to survive at all."

Kutuzov did his best to provide for his men, and his correspondence is replete with orders for more sheepskin coats, warm footwear, bread, meat, and alcohol. But the supply columns could not keep up with the forces in their pursuit of the enemy. So on occasion the field marshal had to improvise. During one of his stops at the Life Guard Izmailovskii Regiment, he inquired if the soldiers had enough bread. "None, Your Excellency," was the guardsmen's response, which is indicative of the supply difficulties the army experienced. "How about wine?" "None," soldiers told him again. "And meat?" "None." With a furrowed brow, Kutuzov assured the troops that he would have "those commissariat officials hanged" and that they would receive their share of provisions the following day. As the soldiers cheered him, however, Kutuzov added, "But it must be said that while you wait, those [French] rogues would probably make good use of time and escape." A dull rumbling spread among the soldiers, who began to yell, "We do not need wine or biscuits, just let us pursue the enemy!" And so the pursuit continued.

Kutuzov knew of the hardship his men endured, and his decision to avoid battles was clearly shaped by his concern for the survival of the army. It also reflected his political considerations. Kutuzov, writes Clausewitz, saw his army "melting in his grasp" and anticipated the great "difficulty he would have in bringing any considerable portion of it to the frontier." He foresaw the total destruction of his enemy and kept repeating, "Tout cela se fondera sans moi" (It will all fall to pieces even without me) to those around him. The great Prussian theorist concluded, "Most commanders in his place would have reasoned the same way."[60] During the conversation with Prince Eugene de Württemberg, Kutuzov admitted that "our young hotheads are angry with me for restraining their frenzy." What they did not understand is that "our current circumstances are far more effective than our weapons." The war had been won, and Russia stood to gain much from it, so "we cannot afford reaching the frontiers like haggard tramps."[61]

| The Great Escape

To understand what happened on the frozen banks of the Berezina in the last days of November, we must look back to late summer, when Kutuzov assumed supreme command of the Russian forces. Among his earliest decisions was a set of new instructions to the 3rd Army of Observation (commanded by Tormasov), the Army of the Danube (led by Chichagov), and Peter Wittgenstein's corps, commanding them to intensify their attacks on Napoleon's flanks and rear. These orders, however, were soon superseded by a strategic plan that Emperor Alexander and his advisors had drafted upon receiving Kutuzov's (embellished) reports of the Russian victory at Borodino.[1]

The strategic considerations underpinning what became known as the "St. Petersburg Plan" had been circulating in the Russian high command since the start of the war. The czar's advisors pointed out that by steadily advancing deep into the Russian heartlands, the Grande Armée appeared as an arrow whose shaft (line of communication) was all too easy to snap off. The czar agreed. On September 12, the day after receiving Kutuzov's dispatch from Borodino, he signed off on a plan that called for three Russian armies, and as many separate corps, to converge behind Napoleon and cut off his escape routes. Wittgenstein's separate corps, reinforced by the St. Petersburg militia that Kutuzov had formed and supported by Count Faddei Steinheil's Finland Corps, was supposed to seize Polotsk, drive Marshal Gouvion St. Cyr's forces back to the Nieman, and then threaten the Grande Armée from the north. Chichagov's Army of the Danube—doubling in size after merging with the 3rd Army of Observation and drawing support from Friedrich Oertel's separate corps—could secure Byelorussian provinces and attack Napoleon from the south. The operational goal, in the words of the czar, was to drive "the Saxons into the Duchy of Warsaw, the Austrians into Galicia, the Prussians and Württembergers across the Nieman, while the

THE GREAT ESCAPE | 481

French must be annihilated to the last." While Napoleon waited in Moscow for a response to his peace overtures, Alexander envisioned concentrating more than 100,000 men on the defensive line along the Berezina River to serve as an "anvil" on which Kutuzov's "hammer" would shatter Napoleon's "arrowhead." If the plan was properly executed, the czar opined, "not even the smallest part of the main enemy army would escape our borders."[2]

The proposed strategy had strengths and weaknesses. Napoleon's line of communication was indeed stretched over a vast territory between the Nieman River and Moscow, and a setback on either flank would have dangerously exposed it. On paper, the plan assigned sufficient forces to execute the double-pincer operation and correctly designated an area between the Dvina and Berezina as the bottleneck, a place where Napoleon's line of operation could be easily intercepted. However, the plan made little accounting of the vast expanse of terrain that the Russian armies had to cross, with mud, snow, and cold. Nor did it fully consider the fact that Napoleon still had considerable forces in the rear, with no less than five full corps present in the area where Wittgenstein and Chichagov were supposed to operate. More crucially, effective communication and close coordination between the three Russian armies were essential elements of the plan, but ensuring them was virtually impossible, considering the vast distances involved; a failure to adhere to the agreed plan could allow Napoleon to engage and defeat each army separately.

Kutuzov received the St. Petersburg Plan in late September, just as he was completing the Tarutino maneuver. After consulting with Bennigsen, he fully endorsed the plan (a point Soviet historians tend to ignore) and communicated it to his subordinates, who began implementing it as Napoleon prepared to depart from Moscow.[3] In October, having received Steinheil's reinforcements, Wittgenstein went on the offensive, outmaneuvering and defeating Marshal St. Cyr's Franco-Bavarian forces at Polotsk (October 18–20) and shattering Napoleon's northern front line. Meanwhile, Chichagov left almost half of his forces to hold off the Austrians and Saxons in the south and marched the rest of the Army of the Danube to Byelorussia.[4] Just as the Grande Armée was battered at Krasnyi, the admiral captured Minsk, with its vast supply depots, and Borisov, with its all-important bridge over the Berezina River.

The destruction of the Grande Armée on the marshy banks of this river would have been possible had the Russian commanders worked toward a common goal. But it was quickly apparent that such concord did not exist. Poor weather and vast distances made effective communications impossible, and the Russian commanders remained inadequately informed of developments in other theaters of war. Logistical challenges were compounded by egotism and old rivalries. In late November, with his corps just one march away from Borisov, Wittgenstein hesitated to march forward—the proud general, who had been hailed (with some exaggeration) as the "Savior of St. Petersburg" for his victory at Polotsk, had no interest in subordinating himself to the admiral. Similarly, Lieutenant General Friedrich Oertel, who was supposed to join Chichagov with 15,000 men, found every possible excuse not to. The Prussian-born general earned notoriety for his "low and obsequious character," as Yermolov put it.[5] Later that winter, Armand Domergue, a theater stage manager who had fled from Moscow, watched as Oertel mistreated prisoners "in the cruelest manner." Not satisfied with insulting them with "the worst cursing imaginable," the general went as far as to punch men in the face.[6] The arrogant and brutish Oertel was also unwilling to subordinate himself to the admiral and refused to leave his headquarters using the flimsiest of pretenses.[7] His insubordination left Chichagov with about 30,000 men, a third of whom were cavalry, who could not fight in the swampy and wooded areas around Borisov. Chichagov was, understandably, furious. In a letter to the czar, he acidly noted that Oertel's misconduct testified to the fact that "insubordination is often left unpunished" in Russia. "Woe unto the armies that tolerate people like Oertel," he concluded before relieving the general of command and directing him to go to the main army to face a court-martial.[8]

What happened next offers a good example of the selfishness and division that plagued the Russian high command. Upon reaching the Russian headquarters, Oertel found there powerful allies who knew about Kutuzov's loathing of the admiral. Oertel himself seems to have been well aware of this and, according to Joseph de Maistre, disobeyed Chichagov to gain Kutuzov's approval.[9] Certain senior officers at the main headquarters, Yermolov tells us, "found a way to preclude Oertel from any responsibility for his insubordination."[10] Instead of being punished, Oertel was, in fact, welcomed at the headquarters and rewarded with a promotion to general police master of all Russian armies. It remains unclear whether Kutuzov was deliberately covering up Oertel's misdeeds or was misinformed by his savvy subordinates. His letters and reports suggest the latter. In mid-November, he was delighted to receive the admiral's dispatch informing him of the expected arrival at Minsk, which, he thought, "will have decisive consequences in present circumstances." He then informed Wittgenstein that Chichagov would soon reach the Berezina with "45,000 men," which implies that the field marshal was under the impression that the Army of the Danube had been already reinforced by Oertel's corps and was, therefore, sufficiently strong to block Napoleon's advance long enough for Wittgenstein to strike from the north.

The relations between the field marshal and the admiral had been strained since they met in the Danubian Principalities seven months earlier. They both remembered old insults and grudges. As early as October 18, Kutuzov complained that the admiral, despite having "a strong army," was acting "somewhat unassertively" and was not "reporting as to what he is doing."[11] Throughout the next four weeks this became a common refrain in the field marshal's correspondence. The admiral had similar complaints. George Carpenter, 3rd Earl of Tyrconnell, who served as an aide-de-camp to Robert Wilson but was attached to Chichagov, informed the British ambassador to Russia that "Kutuzov's communications to the Admiral are not only infrequent, but extremely brief: he informs [Chichagov] about his location but provides no details on the enemy forces, his intentions, etc." Just a day later, Tyrconnell received dispatches from Wilson describing the main army's movements, which he shared with Chichagov. The admiral was surprised by the details they contained and remained "extremely dissatisfied" that Kutuzov's letters "never contain any significant information on enemy intentions, about which we are so keen to learn at the moment."[12] Acting in a state of great uncertainty, the admiral compounded the problems with his share of mistakes. Instead of occupying the western bank of the Berezina, which offered stronger positions, he moved part of his army to the eastern side of the river and set up his headquarters at Borisov. He did not identify local crossing sites and made no effort to destroy the crucial wooden causeways, some half a mile long, that ran through the extensive Zembino marshlands on the western side of the Berezina. Moreover, he failed to properly reconnoiter the area and ignored warnings that Napoleon might be closer than he suspected; a Russian officer found, among the half-burnt French papers, a dispatch stating that the Grande Armée would probably reach Borisov by November 23. The news must have come as something of a shock to the admiral, since he remained poorly informed about the whereabouts of the Grande Armée. Yet he paid little heed to it and his subsequent decisions were misguided. He pushed forward a small advance guard, allowed most of his baggage trains to cross to the undefended town, and permitted most of his cavalry to disperse to forage.[13]

As soon as he heard that Minsk had fallen, Napoleon knew he had to hasten to the Berezina. "For the first time, the Emperor struck me as uneasy about the future," noted Caulaincourt. And well he might be, for he found himself in a highly perilous situation. He had with him only about 30,000 soldiers still capable of fighting, accompanied by a helpless mob of thousands of stragglers and noncombatants of both sexes, the majority of whom were in the last stages of misery and despair. The French army had scarcely any cavalry left; its artillery branch was decimated. An unexpected thaw had melted the ice on the rivers, yet the pontoon equipment, so crucial to any river crossing, had been abandoned during the retreat. With three Russian forces converging, the Grande Armée would be outnumbered three to one, and it seemed probable that Napoleon's whole empire might come crashing down on the marshy banks of this obscure river. This was the high point of the entire campaign for the Russians—the snare that the czar had envisioned two months earlier was set, and Napoleon seemed close to getting caught in it.

The emperor sprang into action. He diverted an entire corps under Marshal Nicolas Charles Oudinot to Borisov to secure the river crossing that would ensure safe passage to the Duchy of Warsaw. On November 23, Oudinot, who had been wounded more than two dozen times in battle, struck at the unsuspecting Russian advance guard, thrashing it and driving it helter-skelter down the road to Borisov. Chichagov, contentedly accommodated in the best house in the town, was about to dine with his officers when he saw Russian hussars galloping down the main street in mad panic and shouting "Frantzouzi! Frantzouzi!" The news spread like wildfire and caused pandemonium inside the town. "Our people—cavalry, infantry, gunners with their cannon—rushed pell-mell toward the [Borisov] bridge, pursued by the French, who were charging with terrifying yells," recalled General Langeron. "One cannot describe the confusion and disorder that reigned at headquarters, which was imprudently placed close to the outposts." Everyone seems to have lost his head and fled, "abandoning their carriages and dainty lunches."[14] As his troops hastily recrossed the river, the admiral, fearing that Napoleon would arrive at any moment, ordered the Borisov bridge to be destroyed.

This was a major setback. The Russians lost more than 300 wagons filled with supplies. "It seemed that Chichagov's officers took good care of themselves," crowed one French officer, "for never has such a profusion of hams, pâtés, smoked fish, meat, and wines of all kinds, not to mention biscuit, rice, cheese, etc., been seen in an army's supply train." More crucially, the defeat at Borisov shook Chichagov's confidence and made him more circumspect about his next actions. He was also more hamstrung—driven to the right bank of the river, he could no longer effectively coordinate operations with Wittgenstein and Kutuzov, who remained on the opposite side. Defending the long stretch of the river was a daunting challenge, requiring close support from other Russian forces, and none was forthcoming. As the Grande Armée approached Borisov, Wittgenstein was miles away from the Berezina, while Kutuzov, still near the Dnieper, had practically paused the pursuit. He sent forth the advance guard, along with various flying columns and Cossack detachments, but showed no intention of expediting the movement of the main army.

Such lassitude has long been the subject of fierce debate, and contemporaries were far more vocal about it than later generations of historians.[15] Emperor Alexander wrote more than one harshly worded letter to the field marshal condemning his dilatory strategy, which, in his words, "destroyed all the advantages." State secretary V. Marchenko confirms the depth of the czar's exasperation and notes that "the ambiguity of Kutuzov's intentions and the steady stream of unfavorable news about him almost convinced the Emperor to recall Barclay de Tolly."[16] Kutuzov tried to reassure the czar that the situation was under control and that neither Wittgenstein nor Chichagov was facing immediate threat. "The enemy army is no position to break away from me since I am constantly following on his heels," he claimed. This was not entirely true, as the main army was not keeping up with the fleeing Grande Armée; in fact, in letters sent to his subordinates, Kutuzov discussed the possibility of Napoleon rallying his forces and either attacking Wittgenstein or proceeding south to the Ukrainian plains.[17] Nevertheless, Yermolov could see that the field marshal was reluctant to push his men hard, believing that "the prolonged retreat, worsening winter weather, [and] raging hunger" would bring the French army to the verge of destruction without the involvement of the main army.[18] With the outcome of the campaign all but determined, Kutuzov remained more preoccupied with his army's immediate material needs and was unwilling to make the extra effort to obliterate the French emperor.

On November 24, Napoleon arrived ahead of the main army and personally reconnoitered the area around Borisov. He was thrilled to hear that a ford had been discovered at Studyanka, a hamlet north of Borisov, though he knew that Chichagov would contest any attempt to cross the river. The French needed to find a way to distract Russian attention long enough to construct a crossing and get most of the army across. Resorting to the simplest military stratagem, Napoleon feigned preparations to move across the Berezina south of Borisov while making preparations for an actual crossing in the north. Chichagov's failure to recognize this ploy has been sharply criticized by contemporaries and historians, though it must be said that the French diversion alone would not have worked had an inauspicious turn of events not resulted in the Russian commander's being misinformed. Throughout those tense days, Chichagov's greatest worry was that Napoleon might strike south of Borisov, which would have been strategically more advantageous for the French; the Grande Armée could then head for Minsk, where it could recapture the vast supply stores on which the Army of the Danube depended, or it could proceed to Bobruisk and sustain itself from the fertile Ukrainian provinces. Chichagov was not alone in dreading such a move; other senior Russian officers supposed that as well. Upon arriving at Wittgenstein's headquarters, Clausewitz found that "every man was possessed with the idea that the enemy would take the direction of Bobruisk."

More crucially, Kutuzov inadvertently came to Napoleon's rescue. In late November, he had written a series of letters that reflected his sense of uncertainty. Upon hearing about Chichagov's entry into Minsk, he warned Wittgenstein that Napoleon might be forced to leave the main road and veer northward to reach Vilna. Anxious about such a possibility, Wittgenstein halted his march, and his advance guard would only reach the village of Kolopenichi, just twenty-five miles from Studyanka, where Napoleon was hastily preparing to cross the river, on November 25. If not for the delay in this advance, Wittgenstein would have reached the Berezina in time to anticipate the French crossing. Kutuzov unintentionally misled Chichagov too. A week after sending his letter to Wittgenstein, the field marshal changed his opinion and warned the admiral that Napoleon might cross the Berezina downstream and move south to Bobruisk. The letter did not command the admiral to redeploy his army, but this information, coming from the commander in chief, did carry weight with the admiral, who, acting amid the fog of war, chose to believe the evidence that best fit his own assumptions. Kutuzov must have had a very good reason for sending such a dispatch, Chichagov reasoned. Napoleon's rumored southern movement must be true.

All Russian participants who served under Chichagov agree that Kutuzov's letter had a decisive influence on the admiral. "I wish this dispatch had never reached us," lamented Major General Sherbatov, while Tyrconnell explained that the arrival of this dispatch (along with similar letters from Wittgenstein) convinced Chichagov of the need to move south. According to General Yefim Czaplic, Chichagov hurried to follow Kutuzov's advice because it matched information he was receiving from Wittgenstein, who was also convinced that the Grande Armée was heading in a southerly direction. The admiral later complained that neither of his fellow commanders could tell him of Napoleon's precise location. He was naturally impressed by the concordance of the opinions of two commanders, who, he assumed, were better versed in ground operations than he was.

After the war, Russian officers pointed out that Kutuzov's letter did not specifically "order" Chichagov to move south but only "advised" him to consider the situation carefully; according to General Langeron, who had read these dispatches, Kutuzov counseled Chichagov "to act at his own discretion if these conjectures proved false."[19] General Ivan Sabaneyev and Langeron tried to dissuade the admiral from making what they believed was a grave mistake, the former apparently losing his temper and getting into a heated argument with his superior. But none of it worked. Chichagov argued that he could not "simply ignore" information provided by two experienced generals, one of whom was the supreme commander.[20] Fresh reconnaissance reports all suggested that Napoleon was retreating in the direction of Bobruisk. Austrian and Polish detachments had been seen probing the Minsk-Bobruisk road and their only goal, Chichagov assumed, was to facilitate the Grand Armée's crossing in the south. Any lingering doubts he might have had disappeared when French efforts to mislead the Russians through misinforming the local community—"that wretched ruse," as one Russian officer commented—paid off, as local peasants rushed to the Russian camp with the news that the French were preparing to cross the river near Ukholod'.[21]

On November 25, much to the delight of the French, who were looking on from the opposite riverbank, Chichagov led most of his army south, leaving just one division to protect Borisov. Napoleon rushed to build the bridges over the Berezina at Studyanka. Without pontoons and lacking the necessary equipment, the French, Polish, and Dutch pontonniers, under the capable leadership of General Jean Baptiste Eblé, braved the freezing waters. Standing chest-deep and warding off slabs of floating ice, they toiled for hours to build frames and supports. Dozens of them perished, but their sacrifice saved the day. By the late afternoon of November 26, three bridges were completed and the Grande Armée began crossing the Berezina. Chichagov had by now realized his mistake and rushed back to contest the crossing. With Wittgenstein's corps belatedly joining the action, the Russians launched simultaneous attacks on both sides of the river. Yet what little remained of Napoleon's once-glorious army fought exceptionally well, repelling attacks and allowing a confused mass of the wounded and stragglers—"a mob of tattered ghosts," as Philippe-Paul de Ségur memorably put it—to get to safety. All in all, Napoleon lost some 30,000 men (most of them stragglers) in the crossing, but he managed to salvage the bulk of his forces, a testament both to the tenacity and heroism of his troops and to the disunity and dysfunction that reigned on the Russian side.

Events on the Berezina came very close to marking a historical milestone. Had the Russians succeeded, history would have recorded a different "Waterloo," and its course might have gone in a different direction. One envisions Napoleon killing himself with the poison that he carried to avoid capture, or being captured and imprisoned in a dark cell at the Sts. Peter and Paul fortress in St. Petersburg. How would the Napoleonic legend have evolved without the dramatic events of Napoleon's return from exile in 1815 or his "martyrdom" on St. Helena? The counterfactual possibilities seem infinite, but none of them came to realization. The Russians had failed in their objective, and Napoleon eluded entrapment. "Oh Berezina! The fateful place where the misfortunes of mankind could have ended!" lamented one German participant, who saw it as a missed opportunity, for which Europe paid with hundreds of thousands of lives and two long years of devastation and war.[22] A British participant, while admiring the Russians' patriotism and valor, believed that the fact that Napoleon survived "will forever stain their achievements."[23]

Debate over who was responsible for Napoleon's escape began almost as soon as the battle on the Berezina ended. "At nightfall, everything calmed down," wrote Rafail Zotov, a soldier in Wittgenstein's corps. "Our entire corps gathered around bivouacs and, as bonfires ignited, reflections, debates, and speculations poured out at once." What did the events of the day mean? How and why was Napoleon allowed to cross? Why was he even allowed to build the bridges? Why had not Chichagov's army trampled him back into the river when the crossing began? Why did not Kutuzov follow on

Napoleon's heels to destroy him on the riverbank? "These thoughts kept us guessing all night long," Zotov commented. "We deplored Chichagov first, then Kutuzov, and finally even our own Wittgenstein. The whole Berezina affair seemed to us pathetic and suspicious."[24]

Kutuzov learned of Napoleon's escape en route to the Berezina. "He was very upset," remembered a staff officer. Trying to understand what had transpired there, he solicited documents and questioned various officers. Chichagov and Wittgenstein both committed their share of "grave mistakes," he concluded, conveniently forgetting that his own unenergetic pursuit, as one participant put it, "gave the French complete freedom to flee."[25] Chichagov should have gotten to Borisov earlier—Kutuzov had already criticized him for wasting time at Brest-Litovsk—and should have taken better precautions to guard against enemy diversions. The field marshal was particularly upset that, contrary to his earlier instructions, the wooden causeways through the Zembino marshes were not destroyed; had these had been burned or damaged, Napoleon might not have escaped so easily.[26] Wittgenstein was probably more culpable than the admiral. Despite the strength of his corps, the general made no attempt to press the enemy hard and proceeded so cautiously that he lost contact with the French rear guard. "We should not be surprised by his restraint," ruefully observed one Russian military historian, for Wittgenstein "did not want to imperil the fame he had acquired with earlier victories."[27] Receiving reports of the enemy crossing the river near Studyanka, the general ignored them and proceeded to Borisov instead, giving Napoleon additional time to save his army. Mikhailovskii-Danilevskii admitted that had Wittgenstein arrived even a day earlier, Napoleon's crossing would have turned disastrous.[28] Joseph de Maistre reflected what many in Russian society thought when he pointed out that Wittgenstein, in his subsequent report, spoke of "forcing" the enemy to cross the river, which meant that he was in fact undercutting Chichagov, whose mission was to prevent such a crossing in the first place.

Kutuzov was willing to overlook these transgressions. He pointed out that the admiral should be forgiven his mistakes because he was inexperienced in land warfare. This was a veiled criticism of the czar for entrusting such an important task to a man who, in the field marshal's words, was so "untried in the art of war."[29] One of the orderlies overheard Kutuzov commenting that Wittgenstein's actions "could not be justified" but they "could be forgiven because of his fame and for the sake of seeing the enemy out of Russia." Added the field marshal, "God would finish what certain Russian generals could not."[30]

The retreat from the Berezina to the Nieman River offers little of military interest. The Grande Armée ceased to exist and a mass of fugitives, trudging mechanically along the road, slowly made its way to Vilna. Participants described the corpses of men and horses, along with abandoned guns and vehicles, strewn as far as the eye could see. The burned-out remains of villages were scenes of human misery and death. "I have seen houses in which more than fifty corpses lay together, and among them three or four men were still alive, stripped to their shirts in fifteen degrees of frost," remembered Xavier de Maistre. The Russian troops suffered from weather as acutely as their enemies, struggling to find shelter and food in the devastated countryside. "The soldiers had no additional covering for the night bivouacs and to sleep longer than half an hour at a time was probable death," remembered Wilson, who bemoaned the fact that because of the continued marches, soldiers' trousers were becoming worn through "in the inner parts of the thighs," thus exposing the flesh to frost.

Napoleon considered his job as a military leader largely done. He decided to return to Paris to assume his mantle of political leader, which had been shaken by the recent coup attempt. On December 5, he left the army and returned to France to prepare for the new campaign. The unhappy victims of his overweening ambition plodded forward to Vilna, where they found only more desolation and death. Any meaningful sense of humanity had been extinguished as men fought for food, shelter, and warmth.

On December 12, Kutuzov reached Vilna, where he was welcomed by "the joyous cheers of the local inhabitants," as Lord Tyrconnell put it.[31] It was "as if an invisible force had transported me to the same house, the same room, the same bed where I lived just two years earlier," he told his family, before adding, "Even the same furniture and servants who came out to greet me."[32] He could not sleep that night, marveling that in August he had found the Russian army "fleeing from the enemy," while in December "the wretched remnants of the frozen enemy" barely made it across the border. "It is simply astonishing, isn't it?" he commented.[33] He could barely recognize the city where he had spent so many years as a governor. Like Wilson, he was appalled by the spectacle of the main road strewn with thousands of human carcasses, "frozen in the contortions of expiring agonies." The town entrance was "literally choked with dead bodies of men and horses, tumbrils, guns, carts, etc.," while the streets were inundated with the stragglers, wounded, and sick; all suitable buildings, even refectories of monasteries, had been transformed into hospitals that soon turned into mortuaries.[34] The severe cold now proved to be a blessing, for it prevented the decomposition of the bodies and the spread of contagion.

"The war has ended owing to the complete extermination of the enemy," Kutuzov reported. Three months after assuming the supreme command of the Russian forces, he was now presiding over the Russian triumph. The Grande Armée was almost entirely destroyed. The French invasion ultimately had involved almost 600,000 men. Just one-tenth of them recrossed the Niemen in

December. Equally catastrophic was the loss in matériel. Napoleon lost more than 900 cannon, while his cavalry was virtually wiped out, with the corpses of approximately 200,000 horses scattered in the Russian countryside. He never acknowledged his opponent's merits and contributions, instead laying all the blame on the weather. Kutuzov was more introspective regarding the man he called both "the modern-day Achilles" and "the scourge of humanity." He took an obvious pride in trouncing him and delighted in describing how Napoleon "ran away from me as a pupil does from his teacher."[35] Kutuzov admitted that he had spent a good deal of time thinking about Bonaparte, contemplating his remarkable career, accomplishments, and failures. The French emperor was both "a singular creature" who blended so many "vices and abominations" and the darling of Providence, but in the end he "proved unable or maybe unwilling to overcome his fate." Victory over such an opponent, Kutuzov understood, had ensured his place in the pantheon of historical figures. And yet even in his contemplative moments the field marshal retained his own foibles. Comparing Providence to "a capricious woman," he mused that she had gotten tired of Napoleon's "ingratitude" and imagined her choosing Kutuzov over her longtime favorite: "Here is an old man who adores and worships females, and who is always ready to please women. And so, to take a break from all the horrors of war, I have decided to join him, if only for just a little while."[36]

Late in the evening of December 23, Emperor Alexander arrived at Vilna. He had left the imperial capital just four days earlier and, accompanied by a handful of advisors, sprinted southward in an open sleigh; his dispatch riders raced ahead to warn of his approach.[37] Madame Choiseul-Gouffier noted that "to spare the emperor's feeling from the sight of the miseries caused by this cruel war, a new road had been made which kept him off the route which the armies had followed."[38] At the town gates enthusiastic soldiers unharnessed the horses from his carriage and dragged it up to the archepiscopal palace, where Kutuzov, dressed in his parade uniform, welcomed the czar. As the two men greeted each other, the czar warmly embraced his aging commander, listened to his report, and, holding his hand, entered the mansion. Kutuzov was delighted with the meeting. "The czar is very cheerful and inexpressibly kind with me," he wrote Catherine.

He should have known better. The two men did not see eye to eye on too many issues and the czar was far from satisfied with the outcome of the campaign. He reproached Kutuzov for his dilatory pursuit and for wasting precious time by retreating from Maloyaroslavets, for not destroying Napoleon at Krasnyi, and for letting him escape at the Berezina. "It is with extreme sadness that I realize that the hope of wiping away the dishonor of Moscow's loss by cutting off the enemy's retreat has been lost" thanks to Kutuzov's "inexplicable inactivity," wrote Alexander. He was frustrated that Kutuzov had emerged a public hero. And not just in Russia. The newspaper coverage of the field marshal in Britain was becoming progressively hagiographic. Though little known to the British public until late in his life, Kutuzov was now described as "an old and tried veteran, a true Russian patriot," who was beloved by all ranks of his countrymen and adored by the soldiers. Here was "the savior of Russia," "the worthy rival of our own Wellington," and "the most proper opponent for the able . . . tyrant of the Continent."[39]

Kutuzov, meanwhile, was busy crafting his own legend. He reviewed poems that had been devoted to him and quibbled over liberties some poets had taken in ascribing motives to his actions.[40] He also sought to preserve the Tarutino camp as a war memorial. Writing to Princess A. Naryshkina, on whose vast estate the Russian army was camped out in October, he envisioned future generations reciting the events at Tarutino alongside other great Russian victories. "The fortifications that put fear into the ranks of the enemy and proved a solid bastion at which the rushing torrent of the destroyers" had to be preserved for posterity. "Let them become the sacred monuments of the Russian valor; let our descendants, gazing upon them, become enflamed with the fire of emulation and say with rapture: this is the place on which the pride of the predators fell before the fearlessness of the sons of the Fatherland."[41]

Vilna was soon flooded with courtiers, nobles, and adventurers seeking favors. "While we had no hats, boots, or white pantaloons," complained one of Chichagov's officers, "these fashionably dressed heroes" kept arriving from St. Petersburg.[42] "Countless kamer-junkers, adjutants, and various adventurers, all seeking to benefit from the campaign, rushed to enlist in the army," remembered another officer. Politicking and exploiting their social connections, these newcomers solicited positions and rewards. Some "received medals for capturing half-frozen Frenchmen"; others got rewards for "capturing cannon that were already stuck in the snow." They strutted around showing off their new epaulettes and crosses and bragging, "We will show the French who the Russians truly are." Kutuzov became "the idol of the flatterers," as one participant noted, and was effusively praised for his leadership.[43] "It took Fabius a year to defeat Hannibal," wrote Egor Fuks, Suvorov's former adjutant and future historian. "But the new Colossus of Europe fell in just two months."[44] Kutuzov thus rested on his laurels and, in Yermolov's acerbic commentary, "nothing was allowed to reach his ears except the servile praise of flatterers."[45] When someone hazarded to remark about the disasters that had befallen Moscow because of Kutuzov's decision, the field marshal snapped, "What! The road from Moscow to Vilna is worth two Moscows!"[46]

Vilna was not only a place for flattery but also a vast charnel house. "Sickness has made a very serious progress in this city," wrote Wilson. Somewhere around 30,000 corpses were strewn in and around the city. In the monastery of St. Basil thousands of bodies were piled up against the walls and in the hallways. "All the broken windows and walls were stuffed with feet, legs, arms, hands, trunks, and heads to fit the apertures."[47] Survivors huddled in the surviving building, enduring hunger and cold. Amid this abject misery, Kutuzov was determined to welcome the czar, who turned thirty-five years old on December 23, with suitable pomp and celebration. On his orders, countless corpses were taken out of the town, some were burned, and others were thrown into ditches and covered with lime. The city was cleaned up and decorated, but, in the words of the German poet Ernst Moritz Arndt, it still looked like "some Tartar hell" as dense and acrid smoke from numerous bonfires smothered the streets.

Alexander initially refused to attend any festivities, arguing that in the current circumstances "dancing or even the sound of music could not be agreeable." He canceled one ball and suggested using the monies for the hospital needs. But Kutuzov insisted on proper celebration of victory, and as the czar admitted, he had "to give pleasure to this old fellow."[48] The emperor's birthday was therefore sumptuously celebrated. Alexander gathered generals and senior officers and congratulated them on victory. He was then treated to a military parade and a state banquet at which captured French flags were flung down on the floor in front of him. Despite the pungent smell and ghastly scenes, a Russian guard officer was enchanted by the beautiful illuminations even though they were clearly repurposed from the festivities arranged for Napoleon a few months earlier—one could still make out the outlines of a French eagle behind the double-headed Russian one. But few paid attention to such trivial things. "The joy was universal," remembered Pavel Puschin.[49]

Kutuzov enjoyed the celebrations, but it was the little luxuries of everyday life that he genuinely relished. He delighted in being able to take off his uniform, take a bath, and lie down in a clean bed for the first time in months. "I have spent the entire campaign sleeping dressed," he told Catherine, whom he thanked for warm socks and asked for more.[50] His relations with the czar, however, were far from blissful. Publicly and in his correspondence with the field marshal, Alexander spared no praise for Kutuzov, assuring him that he was "impatiently looking forward to see you, to tell you personally how greatly the new services you have rendered to your country and, we may add, to all Europe, have strengthened the respect I have always had for you." In private discussions, he denied Kutuzov's role in winning the war, commenting, "The old man must be thrilled, for the cold has served him well."[51] Sir Robert Wilson, exasperated by the anti-English sentiments of Kutuzov (that "sad old rogue"), recounted a conversation he had with Alexander just as the birthday celebrations were about to commence. The czar said that he had "a painful confession" to make, for he knew that "the field marshal has done nothing he ought to have done. All his successes have been forced upon him. He has been playing some of his old Turkish tricks."[52] But the czar also admitted that he could not dismiss the man whom the public regarded as the savior of the nation. "I have no choice. I must submit to a controlling necessity. The nobility supports him and insists on his presiding over the national glory of this war." He asked Wilson not to attend the award ceremony organized in Kutuzov's honor. "I should feel too much humiliated if you were there."[53]

Half an hour later, the czar, with his customary self-control and talent for saving appearances, stood in front of the large gathering praising Kutuzov and extolling his accomplishments. He announced that he had granted the field marshal the title of Prince of Smolensk (Knyaz Smolenskii) for his "memorable accomplishments" and "the stinging defeat" inflicted on Napoleon in the vicinity of that city, and decorated him with the Order of St. George (first class), the most prized of the military honors a Russian monarch could bestow.[54] Kutuzov thus became the first person to garner all four levels of this exalted order.[55] Moreover, he was also presented with a diamond-encrusted golden sword and a wreath of laurels with emeralds.[56] "There is nothing else left [for the czar] to confer on me," he noted, with a certain irony, in a letter to Catherine. "Now we will have to start getting awards for you." He already had a small gift for her; Countess Choiseul-Gouffier noticed on his table "a superb ministerial portfolio of black velvet," with the arms of France embroidered in gold on one side and Napoleon's crest on the other, ready to be mailed to Princess Kutuzov.[57] Attending the festivities, he could not but marvel how profoundly his life had changed. "If two or three years ago anyone had told me that fate would choose me to bring down Napoleon, the giant threatening the whole of Europe, I would have spat in his mug," he admitted.[58]

The royal munificence elicited jealousy and gossiping. Alexander himself fanned the flames as he privately complained that by decorating the field marshal with such a prestigious order, he had committed "a trespass on its institution" and, as he told Wilson, besmirched "the highest honor and hitherto the purest of the empire." Others were no less critical of Kutuzov; in the words of Grand Duchess Catherine, he "shines with splendor he does not deserve." General Rayevskii thought the field marshal "openly lied about our last victories" but then "claimed credit for it all and is now garnering the cross of St. George." Colonel Zakrevskii continued to call Kutuzov an "Old Flounder" who hardly deserved accolades. "He received St. George of 1st class, but do not ask me to explain what for," he commented. "Why was he ever promoted to field marshal general?" There was an outcry over the generousness with which the field marshal solicited awards and promotions that were not always impartial and did not reflect their recipients' actual accomplishments. The army headquarters had become a "morass of intrigues," bewailed General Rimsky-Korsakov. "Some are given too generous awards, and others do not get enough. General Rayevskii thought "too many awards" were given out, his criticism echoing in Colonel S. Marin's commentary that "for every decent officer, five wretched ones are getting promoted."[59]

Nor were such sentiments limited to the Russian officers alone. Austrian general Schwarzenberg spoke of "l'imbécile Kutuzov," who squandered precious opportunities, while the French marshals and generals, unsurprisingly, refused to give any credit to their adversaries.[60] "In every instance the Russians were beaten, and as soon as the army has had a little rest, they will see their victors again," Marshal Davout predicted in mid-December. John Quincy Adams captured the negative feelings toward Kutuzov when he recorded in his diary that it was "beyond all human calculation" that Napoleon's fame and glory vanished before an old man whose "own military reputation was a problem and whom many people have extolled very highly while as many others held in contempt."[61]

The czar's arrival fostered factionalism, behind-the-scenes machinations, and gossip-mongering to such an extent that, commented an eyewitness, it offered "an extensive field for intrigue," where Kutuzov proved "an invincible opponent."[62] Chichagov was the first to feel the consequences. His meeting with the field marshal was outwardly cordial. The two commanders, surrounded by a large suite of generals and officers, greeted each other with compliments interspersed with subtle jabs. Kutuzov told the admiral that the baggage and silverware that he had lost at Borisov had been retrieved for him; Chichagov replied with a sly smile.[63] "I want to congratulate Your Excellency on the victories you have gained over the enemy, and thank you for all your efforts," Kutuzov told the admiral, raising his voice so that the crowd of onlookers could hear him. "The glory and honor belong to you alone, Your Highness," replied the admiral, obviously trying to remind everyone that he was not the sole culprit for the events at the Berezina. "Everything was accomplished on your orders, and therefore all victories belong to you." Both sat quietly for a moment, carefully examining each other; tea was served and the conversation resumed for another half an hour.[64] Such displays of cordiality between old rivals left many puzzled, but sharp-eyed observers knew what lurked behind it all. As one of them noted, "whomever he suspected of sharing in his glory," Kutuzov "undermined so imperceptibly as a woodworm devouring his chosen piece of tree." Informed that Kutuzov was traveling to the Army of the Danube, Wilson could foresee nothing but "troubled waters" ahead for the admiral.[65]

He was right. With the army and the public demanding a scapegoat for Napoleon's escape, Kutuzov made no effort to defend Chichagov, still holding a grudge toward the admiral for having intended to deprive him of the glory of concluding peace with the Porte. Yermolov recalled a conversation he had with the field marshal in which he tried to justify Chichagov's decisions; the field marshal smiled and nodded, "pretending to be extremely satisfied to learn the truth," but his antipathy toward the admiral was palpable.[66] The admiral soon marched with his troops toward the border, giving Kutuzov an opportunity to exploit the growing public uproar. "It is impossible to describe the extent of public loathing aimed at Chichagov. Everyone suspects him of treason," wrote Weigel.[67] Kutuzov and Wittgenstein were unassailable public figures, eulogized as national heroes. The former was credited with saving the whole of Russia and extolled as "le vainqueur du vainqueur de la terre," the conqueror of the world conqueror; the latter was hailed as the savior of St. Petersburg.[68] It would have been impossible to assail them. Chichagov, on the other hand, lacked the gravitas of Kutuzov and the popularity of Wittgenstein; nor did he enjoy the support of the army or the nobility. His impetuosity and brash treatment of subordinates, an eyewitness commented, meant that his officers had no desire to stand up for a "commander who mistreats them, shows indecisiveness in planning, and always blames his mistakes on them."[69] Chichagov's earlier mockery of Russian society and military had earned him many opponents, who were keen to make the most of the situation. The entire nation was saturated with stories of his incompetence and bungling. "Our *admiral* [original emphasis] has scattered all our advantages to the winds," grumbled one general. Observed another general, "The public opinion holds the most prejudicial opinion of him. The military men cannot forgive him for letting Napoleon escape and there is not a single man who wishes him well."[70] The Sardinian ambassador could not find anyone who did not condemn Chichagov as "an abominable traitor."[71]

Kutuzov's family and friends piled on. On December 1, his son-in-law broke the news that "Napoleon has escaped" and charged Chichagov with "full responsibility for all the bloodshed that will come as the result of this." Catherine's comment that "my husband saved Russia, Wittgenstein—St. Petersburg, and Chichagov—Napoleon" was soon the talk of the capital.[72] Among the numerous caricatures that were produced that winter, there was one that represented Kutuzov holding one end of a long net while Napoleon, in the form of a hare, was slipping out at the other end, which was held by Chichagov, who was joyfully exclaiming, "I have saved him!" Gregory Derzhavin, the field marshal's old acquaintance, wrote a sharp-witted epigram praising Kutuzov for "tying up a deadly net around the French" and condemning the "amphibious general" for "slithering in to unravel it."[73] Hearing about the Berezina, Krylov the fabulist, another of Kutuzov's supporters, wrote a damning fable about the pike that pretends to be a cat and tries chasing the mouse, only to end up flailing helplessly on the shore.[74]

Ridiculed and ostracized, Chichagov soon requested a leave from the army for "health" reasons, but privately he confided that it was "due to Kutuzov's endless fault-finding [*pridirok*] against me." He complained that the field marshal was undermining him in everything. He endured the popular anger "with his usual dignity, honor, and firmness" (as de Maistre saw it), refusing to be drawn into a public confrontation with the field marshal. But behind the scenes he tried to justify his actions, speaking "with great contempt" of Kutuzov in a conversation with an American ambassador, who was surprised to hear the admiral say that for all their successes, the Russians were indebted to "Famine and Frost."[75] Chichagov tried to induce the emperor to defend him and give him due recognition, but Alexander refused to go against public opinion, especially if it required him to strike down "the nation's idol," Kutuzov.[76] "The crowd is blind," complained Chichagov. "It can be easily deceived and manipulated. But what should we think about those who, despite knowing the truth, still tolerate falsehoods and slander?" The admiral's friends urged him to defend himself and to confront Kutuzov's allegations; they advised him to insist on a meeting with the czar where, as one of them wrote, "Kutuzov would have been forced to defend you and admit, in the Emperor's presence, that you have done nothing wrong." Despite his protestations of innocence, Chichagov decided not to press for an inquiry into the events and was therefore relentlessly hounded by the public. He left Russia to escape this vitriol and spent the rest of his life in England, where he wrote his memoirs in an unsuccessful bid to clear his name. He outlived Kutuzov by almost four decades. These were years full of melancholy and frustration as he watched his great rival extolled and lionized while popular opinion still held him responsible for what had happened on the Berezina.

CHAPTER 30

The Last Campaign

THE NEWS OF WHAT had transpired in Russia sent shock waves through Europe, dramatically altering the balance of power and signaling an opportunity to cast off French hegemony. "What a career he has ruined!" remarked Czar Alexander to Countess de Choiseul-Gouffier as he reflected on Napoleon's defeat. "The spell is broken."

The Convention of Tauroggen, signed by Russian negotiators and Prussian general Johann von Yorck on December 30, 1812, marked the start of a new phase of the war. The Prussian general's decision to declare his Prussian contingent of the French army neutral was a clear act of defiance, both against his French superiors and against the Prussian king, Frederick William III, who had consistently discouraged the more patriotically minded Prussian officers and statesmen from openly opposing Napoleon. Although Frederick William initially disowned the convention, Yorck's decision altered the military situation, making it impossible for French forces to hold ground in East Prussia. Alexander was delighted to hear this news. Instead of letting his army rest in winter quarters during an exceptionally cold winter, he insisted on continuing the campaign beyond the Russian frontiers. This had become a personal, national, and religious mission for the czar, one that would prove decisive to European history. "You have saved not just Russia, but all of Europe," the czar told his officers at the banquet in Vilna, a clear indication of his intention to fight Napoleon for the future of the continent. "Time has never been as precious as in current circumstances," he wrote to Kutuzov, informing him that the army could not halt "even for the shortest time" in Vilna and had to press on across the imperial frontiers.[1]

Kutuzov saw matters differently. Liberating Europe was not a mission that he felt any desire to support. It was not Russia's responsibility to seek the destruction of the Napoleonic imperium; it should focus on the restoration of its own forces. The Russian army was utterly worn out—it had lost tens of thousands of soldiers and was so depleted that the main part counted fewer than 30,000 men in mid-December. This was a far cry from the some 120,000 men who had left the Tarutino camp just two months earlier; almost 50,000 soldiers were convalescing at hospitals.[2] Kutuzov wrote the czar to say that the Russian forces were in such a perilous state that a true picture of their condition had to be kept secret not only from the enemy but also from the army itself.[3] He had thought that with Napoleon expelled from Russia, the campaign was over and Russia could afford to rest on its laurels. Having marched almost 700 miles, the army needed rest—"for two weeks at the very least," he informed the czar.[4]

This did not mean, however, that he opposed *all* operations across the Nieman, as it is often alleged. His correspondence for the month of December shows that he was careful to distinguish between the main Russian army, which urgently required a respite, and the forces commanded by Wittgenstein, Chichagov, and Platov, which were fresher and capable of sustaining the offensive. Thus, he approved operational plans that had Platov's Cossacks pursue the retreating French forces and envisioned Chichagov and Wittgenstein coordinating to encircle Macdonald's isolated corps near Königsberg. Ever mindful of grand strategy, he sought clarification from the czar regarding how the Russian army should treat Napoleon's Prussian and Austrian allies. "There is a clear difference between waging war against one's actual enemy and against one that had been forced to participate in the war," he commented in a letter to the czar, urging him to initiate political outreach to Berlin and Vienna. He did his part too, instructing his forces not to engage the Austrians and facilitating secret negotiations with Austrian field marshal Schwarzenberg.[5] Kutuzov was also keen to see Russia invade and occupy the Duchy of Warsaw, thereby settling the Polish question once and for all. And then it should wait "until the time—which will certainly be soon—when the enemy reveals his intentions to us."[6] Regarding the broader situation in Europe, Kutuzov believed Russia should find common ground with Napoleon, who still retained vast resources at his disposal. It had been done once at Tilsit and could be done again, this time with the czar negotiating from a position of strength. Why should Russians shed any more blood for the liberty of other nations? And would Napoleon's downfall necessarily benefit Russia's interests?

The czar disagreed. He gave the army four weeks to rest, but his "mission" would not let him wait any longer. "The fire of Moscow lit up my soul and the judgment of the Lord which manifested itself on our frozen plains filled my heart with an ardent faith I had never felt before," he confided to a Lutheran bishop, portraying events of the past six months as biblical in scale. The crushing defeat of Napoleon signaled divine benevolence, and the czar increasingly looked at himself as a tool in the hands of the Almighty.

"It is the Lord who did everything; it is He who has changed everything so suddenly in our favor, by casting down on the head of Napoleon all the calamities which he had meant for us," Alexander told his sister Catherine.[7] Moreover, he saw a crucial political opportunity. Napoleon's prestige was waning, his forces shattered and in disarray. The best course of action was to invade central Europe, overrun as much imperial French territory as possible, and recast Russia's place and role in the international order. "You must place yourself, Sire, at the head of Europe's powers," Prussian reformer Heinrich Friedrich Karl vom und zum Stein wrote to the Russian emperor. "The exalted role of benefactor and restorer is yours to play." This sense of new power and pride animated the czar, just as it did many Russian officers eager for action. "Russia, if well governed, is destined to rule Europe," one of them told the American ambassador.[8]

State secretary Shishkov and others urged Kutuzov to confront the czar and insist on ending the war. "What harm can Napoleon cause us while sitting in Paris?" asked Shishkov, pointing out that Prussia was powerless and still under French control; Napoleon was married to the Austrian emperor's daughter, who was the mother of his son, so Austrian support was doubtful; and the king of Saxony remained loyal to the French court. Lacking allies, Russia should not be sacrificing its precious resources to liberate these nations when, in Shishkov's words, "we are leaving behind the burned-down Moscow, the devastated Smolensk, and the bloodied Russia, tending not to its wounds and instead demanded new expenditures."[9]

Kutuzov shared this assessment, of course, and worried that the czar might attempt "politically something that is not absolutely necessary."[10] By rushing forward, the czar might lead the Russian army to a military disaster that would negate all the advantages that had been gained so painfully and slowly. Unlike the czar, Russian junior officers and the rank and file appreciated the field marshal's cautiousness. "It was his prudence, not timidity, as so many accused him of," wrote one officer in his diary. "And it saved the lives of our brave men."[11]

Shishkov urged the field marshal to be more forceful in his discussions with the czar, but after several conversations with the czar, Kutuzov came to the conclusion that "the sovereign thinks differently" when it came to war and that his reasoning could not be "disregarded completely." The czar had also found a way to disarm the old field marshal: "when he cannot contest my arguments," Kutuzov told Shishkov, "he simply embraces and kisses me; then I start to weep and agree with him." The state secretary was not impressed, writing his journal that while Kutuzov was "clever and brave" when facing the enemy, he was timid and weak in front of the czar. "He would have gladly died for the Fatherland, but he would have never dared to do what [Duke of] Sully did to Henry IV [of France]," meaning stand up to a sovereign and make him do what was needed.[12]

Alexander's treatment of Kutuzov was part of a well-calculated act, for in his private correspondence he spoke matter-of-factly that it was "absolutely essential" to dispose of his bête noire and carry the war beyond the Nieman River.[13] In the waning days of 1812, the czar gradually sidelined the field marshal on the grounds that his "age, serious wounds, labors and anxiety of the last campaign" had weakened his faculties. Kutuzov's appointees were given furloughs and reassigned, their positions at the main headquarters taken by the czar's trusted men. Peter Volkonskii, Alexander's longtime aide-de-camp and confidant, became the new chief of staff of the Russian armies, while Colonel N. Selyavin replaced Peter Konovnitsyn as the duty general. "Wanting to give him some peace of mind," commented Yermolov, the czar let the field marshal retain the title of commander in chief and gave him "the external show of some authority," but there was no longer any doubt who actually commanded the armies.[14] Soon thereafter, Barclay de Tolly and Bennigsen received summonses to return. Kutuzov knew perfectly well what it all meant but acted his part.[15] The czar played along, insisting, as he told Wilson, on putting "an end to every appearance of ill will," showing Kutuzov "suitable courtesies," and "not refusing them when offered on his part."[16]

On January 13, 1813, Kutuzov attended a special religious service near the town of Merech (Merkine) on the banks of the Niemen River. "May this new year end as auspiciously as it is starting," he wrote Catherine.[17] The Russian army crossed the river, entered the Duchy of Warsaw, and thus commenced a new campaign against Napoleon. "Valiant and victorious soldiers," read Kutuzov's new proclamation. "At length you are on the borders of the Empire. Each of you is the savior of your Fatherland. Russia welcomes you by this name." Reminding soldiers of the suffering Russia had endured and of "the extraordinary challenges" they had surmounted, Kutuzov urged them to march farther and complete the defeat of Napoleon. "Let us not follow the example of our enemy in his cruelty and inhumanity," he reminded them. "Let us be generous and observe a difference between an enemy and peaceful inhabitants."

The continued withdrawal of the French forces had exposed much of the Polish duchy, so the Russian forces commenced a 400-mile march to the town of Kalisch, near the Prussian border. Kutuzov remained his cautious self. "Do not be afraid, we will not rush too far," he assured his family. "I am not getting any younger."[18] Nor was he getting healthier. His condition, worsened by the rigors of the winter campaign, continued to deteriorate, and he regularly complained about suffering from aches, cramps, and exhaustion; in late January, Wilson jotted down in his diary that the field marshal was "very unwell," and wondered whether he would live or die. "I was very sick for three days," Kutuzov wrote Catherine on January 22. But his condition improved, and upon arriving at Kalisch, he felt strong enough to attend social activities and flirt with young and loquacious "Warsaw beauties."[19]

The military situation seemed promising. "Everything is progressing well, both militarily and politically," Kutuzov wrote confidently home in late January.[20] He had reason to be pleased. The Russian troops had encountered virtually no resistance and captured large swaths of territory. Königsberg, Warsaw, and Berlin fell in quick succession. "This is the third capital we are occupying," he remarked about the Prussian capital. "As Bonaparte has said in Warsaw, 'from the sublime to the ridiculous in only a step.'"[21] The czar went out of his way to pay public respect to Kutuzov, embracing him in front of the army and leading the cheers in his honor. There was also good news for the family.[22] Kutuzov's persistent lobbying on behalf of his sons-in-law, relatives, and friends began to pay off.[23] On February 10 the czar told him, "You keep delivering great news every day, so it is now my turn to share good news with you." Mikhail Opochinin, the husband of Kutuzov's daughter Darya, was given the Order of St. Anna, while Nikolai Khitrovo, the scoundrel who had caused so many headaches for the family, was, in the czar's words, "completely forgiven"; he and wife could return to the imperial capital.[24] Further royal benevolence followed, as the czar elevated one of Kutuzov's granddaughters to the rank of lady-in-waiting.

The good news kept coming. Frederick William III, king of Prussia, had eluded the watchfulness of Napoleon's spies and made it to Breslau, the capital of Silesia, on the banks of the Oder River. This put him beyond the power of the French troops, so he could afford to publicly support the Convention of Tauroggen. Prussian emissaries traveled to the czar to arrange for military cooperation, resulting in a treaty that Kutuzov signed on February 27. Though largely overlooked in Napoleonic histories, the Treaty of Kalisch was of great consequence. It declared a cessation of hostilities between Russia and Prussia and established a military alliance, with both powers pledging to deploy tens of thousands of troops to fight against Napoleon. From the start, the Russians made it clear that they would be the senior partner in this alliance. The secret provisions of the treaty were particularly noteworthy because Russia pledged to restore Prussia to its "statistical, geographical, and financial" status as of 1806, but required the Prussian king to surrender territories he had gained in the Second and Third Partitions of Poland. In exchange, Alexander agreed to compensate Prussia for the loss of Polish territory with territories taken from German states allied to France.[25] "The treaty will gain us 100,000 [Prussian] soldiers," Kutuzov wrote ecstatically to Catherine.[26] He understood the wider strategic implications of this alliance. "Marching away from our borders does separate us from our reinforcements, but if we had remained east of the Vistula, we would have had to wage a war similar to the [Polish] campaign of 1807," he explained in a private letter. The advance was needed to consolidate relations with Prussia, for without the alliance with Berlin, "the entire the German realm, including Austria, would have been at the enemy's disposal." He was nonetheless worried about the future, and in particular the dangers of separating the army from its heartland and extending Russian lines of communication. "Our decision to move away from our borders, and the [logistical] means that we have there, might turn out to be improvident," Kutuzov wrote to his relative. "Just examine the distance from the Nieman to the Elbe and from the Rhine to the Elbe. Superior enemy forces might engage us before we receive reinforcement from Russia." Instead of rushing headlong to the west, Kutuzov suggested probing the enemy defenses with flying detachments and conducting gradual but systematic reduction of the French-occupied fortresses on the Vistula and the Oder to secure the rear; the Russian army also had to establish a strong logistical base and reserves to sustain the new campaign so far to the west.[27]

During the first three months of 1813 Kutuzov busied himself with replenishing regiments, organizing reserves, gathering supplies and forage, setting up field hospitals, and resolving logistical matters; he was soon pleased to report that the Russian army had grown to 129,101 men, with 743 cannon, while the Prussian contingent supplied 55,694 men.[28] With the Duchy of Warsaw under Russian control, Kutuzov created a statute (which the czar approved on March 13) that set up a provisional government to administer the Polish provinces until their future could be permanently decided.[29]

On March 15, Alexander and Frederick William III met at Breslau to coordinate measures for the prosecution of the war. To minimize the likelihood of national self-interest trumping coalition needs, the two monarchs decided that their armies would fight not as separate entities but as a single multinational force. Kutuzov was appointed the supreme commander of the Allied armies, Prussian Gebhard Leberecht von Blücher's Southern Army and Wittgenstein's Northern Army. Six days later, the Prussian king paid a visit to the Russian campsite at Kalisch. The entire army was deployed for a parade review. Kutuzov, despite feeling unwell and unable to sit on his horse, insisted on standing out in front to welcome the Prussian king.

Much had changed since their first meeting in Berlin fifteen long years earlier. Frederick William hailed the field marshal, "told me great compliments in front of the army," as Kutuzov put it, and conferred upon him the two highest Prussian awards, the Orders of the Black and Red Eagles. "The king granted no other awards, as he did not want to associate anyone with me," Kutuzov wrote Catherine.[30] He savored the triumph, delighting in hearing the public shouting, "Vivat Kutuzov! Vivat der Grosse Alte! Vivat unser großvater Kutuzov!" and meeting groups of Prussian men and women who came to thank him. "It is hard to describe the atmosphere," he wrote. Despite the effusive homages he had received in Russia, Kutuzov felt that they did not quite compare to what he had encountered in Prussia. "Enthusiasm like this would never be possible in Russia, for no prophet is accepted in his own country," he commented, clearly mindful of the criticism to which he had been subjected.[31] Throughout these weeks his thoughts kept revolving around his wife, daughters, and grandchildren, as he constantly inquired about their well-being—some of his grandchildren were sick with measles—and planned for their future. Passing through the Polish and Prussian towns, he made sure to pick out numerous gifts for the family. And as ever, his letters were replete with longing for the comforts of home and family. "I can only imagine how happy you are to be with them," he told his wife upon hearing of his daughter and grandson's arrival to St. Petersburg. "Meanwhile, here I am, wandering in the fleeting smoke that is glory."[32]

As March came to an end, Alexander ordered the general advance of the Prusso-Russian forces. Germany was the new battleground. Wittgenstein and Blücher formed the two wings, while Kutuzov and the main army marched along a front broad enough to support either of these generals.[33] The plan was to cross the Elbe River and invade Saxony, where the allies intended to facilitate a popular insurrection and confront Napoleon. As ever, Kutuzov was not convinced of the efficacy of the plan and worried about overextending his forces. "Is this advantage," he inquired about gaining territory west of Elbe and inciting popular unrest, "worth the danger that we will face by weakening ourselves through the extent of our separation, which only serves to reinforce the enemy?"[34] He urged restraint, as Napoleon was still strong and his plans unclear. "Crossing the Elbe is easy enough," Kutuzov grumbled. "But before long we might have to cross it again, with a bloodied nose." He was also becoming concerned about the Prussian aspirations, as General Blücher rushed to enter Saxony and issued a lengthy proclamation calling upon the Saxons to turn against the king and "raise the flag of resistance against the foreign oppressor" or face the prospect of despoliation.[35] Kutuzov was not amused. "Blücher acted politically irresponsibly when making his declaration," he wrote. "He committed a fatal error of not mentioning the czar of Russia. And by dismissing the Saxon authorities, he also acted against the wishes of his own court." The field marshal moved quickly to mitigate the damage. Blücher was reprimanded, the Saxons were assured of Russian goodwill, and a new proclamation was issued to the German nation. "The moment has come for you to take revenge for the humiliations you have suffered, and to raise yourself once more to the circle of free nations," read Kutuzov's appeal to the Germans.[36]

In April, the Russian advance guard entered Dresden, the Saxon capital. "This is our fourth capital," Kutuzov wrote Catherine.[37] It was also the last that he would hear about. Long miles of marching in cold, rainy, and windy spring weather were sapping his energy. "I long for rest," he wrote to his wife and daughter. "I am exhausted, for it has been a long time since I last had any respite. . . . This winter has aged me a lot."[38] Traveling in an open carriage in rainy weather, he felt unwell and suffered from a recurring cough. At Haynau (Chojnow), a small Silesian town, large crowds of people came out to greet Kutuzov with flowers and wreaths of laurels and oak leaves and proclaimed him their savior (*erlöser*). He was deeply touched by the sentiment and stopped to converse with them. It was a cold April day, Karl Montresor, Kutuzov's aide-de-camp, later recalled, and Kutuzov, after spending some time outside, felt unwell. "I am chilled to the bone," he told Montresor, and asked for a glass of alcohol to fortify himself. It did not help. On April 18, upon reaching the small town of Bunzlau (Bolesławiec) in Silesia, he was forced to take to bed at the house of a retired Prussian major at Nicolai und Schloss Strasse.[39] "The marshal has had a glimpse of the enemy and is taken ill very *opportunely*," Wilson sardonically wrote in his journal entry of April 25. "Perhaps it is a 'Kamenski' stratagem to get rid of the responsibility."

Too ill to follow the army, Kutuzov remained at Bunzlau for the next few days. He continued to read and sign documents even as his condition progressively worsened. "I am becoming anxious about this prolonged illness since I feel weaker with each passing day," he wrote to the czar on April 22.[40] The following day he was too weak to even hold a quill. "My dear friend, this is the first time I am sending you a letter written with somebody else's hand," read his last letter to Catherine. "It will, no doubt, surprise and even frighten you but, alas, my affliction has numbed my fingers." Realizing the end was near, he made arrangements to support his loved ones and sent whatever money he had to settle the family debts.[41]

Alerted to the field marshal's declining health, Alexander instructed his personal physician, James Wylie, to stay with Kutuzov, while the Prussian king sent Christoph Wilhelm Friedrich Hufeland, one of the most eminent German physicians, to examine him, but there was little they could do to alleviate his condition.[42] The Bunzlau inhabitants spread straw in front of the house to reduce the noise of military transports moving westward and create a sense of solitude for the dying field marshal. "The last days of his life were like a sunset at the end of a splendid day," reflected Mikhailovskii-Danilevskii. "It was impossible to observe without a sense of profound grief as our illustrious leader faded away."

Mikhail Illarionovich Golenischev-Kutuzov breathed his last at 9:35 p.m. on April 28, 1813.[43] He was sixty-five years old. Soviet historians were fond of reciting an old tale, first circulated by a man named Krupennikov who claimed to have been present in the room when the czar visited Kutuzov on his deathbed. "Mikhail Illarionovich, please forgive me," the czar supposedly said to the dying man. "I forgive you, Your Majesty," replied Kutuzov. "But Russia never will." The story is apocryphal. The czar had left Bunzlau days before Kutuzov's death, and even if he were in town, he would have been the last man to seek the field marshal's forgiveness.[44] More to the point, Kutuzov would not have dared insult the czar, knowing that the well-being of his family depended on the emperor's goodwill. Weeks earlier, when the Prussian king offered him Prussian nationality and a plush estate, Kutuzov declined both. "Emperor Alexander will never abandon me or my children in time of need," he said in the czar's presence.[45] He guessed right.

The news of the field marshal's death reached the Russian army on April 30, just as it was girding up for a battle with Napoleon's revitalized army. The information was kept secret for fear of the effect it might have on the soldiers' morale on the eve of battle; as late as mid-May, the Russian society was still unaware of the field marshal's passing.[46] Peter Wittgenstein was given the supreme command of the allied armies but, like Kutuzov before him, he found his hands tied because of the czar's presence. The subsequent battles, first at Lutzen (May 2) and then at Bautzen (May 20–21), were major defeats for the allies, forcing them back over the Elbe. Alexander got his nose bloodied, just as Kutuzov had feared.

The czar saw to it that Kutuzov received a regal funeral. The field marshal's body was carefully examined. The physicians were surprised by the large size of his heart and the abnormal shape of some of his organs, which caused some historians to suggest that he suffered from a chronic condition; the evidence, however, is inconclusive. After the autopsy, the body was embalmed. The heart was removed but, contrary to long-standing claims, it was not buried at Bunzlau.[47] Instead, it was embalmed, placed in a silver funerary vessel, and deposited inside the coffin for transportation to Russia. On the other hand, the bowels and other organs that were removed during the embalming process were entombed at the old cemetery of the village of Ober-Tillendorff on the outskirts of Bunzlau, where a local stonemason was recruited to construct a special memorial—a broken granite column with a wreath—that still survives.[48] On King Frederick William's orders, a sixty-ton cast-iron obelisk surrounded by four lions was later built in Kutuzov's honor in the main market square of Bunzlau. "To this spot, Prince Kutuzov of Smolensk led his victorious Russian troops," read the inscription on it. "Death put a stop to his glorious deeds. He saved his country and paved the way for the liberation of Europe. Blessed be the memory of this hero!"[49]

The funeral cortege left Bunzlau on May 9 and, traveling across the war-torn provinces, slowly made its way to the Russian imperial capital.[50] In town after town, the sight of the field marshal's casket provoked an outpouring of emotion as people lined up to pay their last respects. At Mittau and Narva, inhabitants stopped the hearse, unharnessed the horses, and took turns carrying it through the streets. The news of the field marshal's death reached St. Petersburg on May 14. The public was eagerly awaiting updates on Kutuzov's health and the lack of any news caused rumors circulating in the city. "For the past few days is no other preoccupation in the city than going from place to place, from dawn till dusk, and asking people if they have news about the prince's health," one contemporary remarked in a private letter on May 13. The following day, however, "it [was] all over." "The news [of Kutuzov's death] has just been shared with his wife and children. I visited them, saw his daughters but did not visit her [Catherine]. Children are all weeping, especially [Praskovya] Tolstoy. Oh Lord, what a remarkable life this was!"[51]

On June 5, the funeral procession approached St. Petersburg and halted at the Monastery of St. Sergius (Troitse-Sergieva Pustyn'), about twelve miles from the capital, where Catherine and other family members, along with vast throngs of people, were waiting. It was here that they welcomed back the remains of the man to whom they had so rapturously bid goodbye less than a year earlier.[52]

The cortege remained at the monastery for over two weeks, to allow time for the imperial authorities to make the necessary funeral preparations. State funerals remain exceptional occasions, for few individuals are deemed worthy of such an expression of national veneration. The most elaborate form of funerals, they are full of pageantry and symbology, designed to serve a singular purpose. Kutuzov's funeral was one of the largest public memorials of the nineteenth century, in scale and solemnity comparable to the return of Napoleon's ashes to Paris in 1841 and the Duke of Wellington's state funeral in 1852.

The funeral arrangements were almost unprecedented. The Russian treasury spent thousands of rubles to cover the expenses of transporting the casket to the capital, and tens of thousands more were needed for the final ceremony. In the end, the total cost of burying the field marshal rivaled what had been spent on his onetime benefactor, Emperor Paul. Financial issues aside, there was also the question of where "the savior of the nation" should rest. St. Petersburg had three sites suitable for such a burial: the Cathedral of Peter and Paul, the Holy Trinity Cathedral of the Alexander Nevskii Monastery, and the Kazan Cathedral. The first served as a royal sepulcher, where the remains of almost all the Russian emperors and empresses were laid to rest. The Alexander Nevskii Monastery could have been a fitting choice, since Generalissimo Suvorov was buried there, as was Kutuzov's uncle Ivan Loginovich Golenischev-Kutuzov; the family preferred to see the field marshal buried there.

The czar chose the newly consecrated Cathedral of Our Lady of Kazan. Reviewing the memorandum on the burial site selection, he inscribed on the margins, "It will be appropriate to lay Kutuzov to rest in the Kazan Cathedral adorned with the trophies he has taken."[53] This was a momentous decision. To be buried at the cathedral in the middle of the imperial capital was a singular honor. No other Russian figure, except for the czars, would ever be honored in this way. Alexander's choice transformed the Kazan Cathedral into the pantheon of Russian military glory and turned Kutuzov's grave into a shrine. A visiting foreigner soon marveled at the magnificence of the cathedral, with its "walls decked on every side with the trophies of Russian valour, the eagles and standard wrested from the French legions and the proud memorials" of Russian triumphs.[54] Henceforth, Kutuzov the man—foibles and all—would be erased by the historic figure whose actions had determined the course of history.

The imperial authorities recruited some of the best artists, architects, and artisans for the occasion. Commemorative plates and plaques, statues and prints of portraits and battles scenes, and fresh biographies of the field marshal all found a ready market. Foreign visitors marveled at the scale of preparations; the Russian capital "had not, for a long time, beheld so imposing a sight," noted one British newspaper. "Worthy of the Hero of the Nation."[55] Under the guidance of architect Andrei Voronikhin, the Kazan Cathedral was draped in black cloth and an underground crypt constructed in the northeastern part of the church. On Wednesday morning, June 23, Kutuzov's coffin left the Monastery of St. Sergius atop a gilded carriage, intricately decorated with laurels, crowns, and eagles and topped with an opulent canopy with ostrich feathers and a princely crown; atop the coffin lay an officer's sword. Dozens of officials accompanied it, carrying Kutuzov's coat of arms, insignia, and awards.[56]

As soon as the procession reached the city gates, St. Petersburgians rushed to unharness the horses and pulled the hearse through streets strewn with flowers and pine wreaths. The casket—preceded by two platoons of dragoons and the field marshal's riderless horse led by two grooms—moved slowly through the city along walkways packed with nobles, clergymen, ministers, senators, senior civil and military officials, and representatives of various social estates. "Everybody was weeping," Nikolai Turgenev wrote Mikhailovskii-Danilevskii. Another eyewitness marveled at people disregarding their ranks, titles, and distinctions. "Senior officials stood next to the poor and destitute, as they all tried to grab the ropes of the hearse and dragged it through the thick crowd of people toward the sacred edifice."[57]

An immense crowd gathered at the plaza in front of the cathedral to catch the last glimpse of the field marshal's remains. The empress's secretary, Nikolai Longinov, was one of these onlookers, and he admired "the deluge of people from across the city and the neighboring areas"; writing to Semen Vorontsov that same evening, he thought the display of popular admiration was more meaningful than "the splendor and pageantry" of the ceremony.[58]

Inside the Kazan Cathedral, the coffin was placed atop a ten-foot-tall arch-shaped dais that was illuminated with some 500 candles and decorated with more than 200 flags and trophies, celebrating Kutuzov's victories;

plaster models symbolizing Prudence, Fortitude, Courage, and Humanity—designed to convey the deceased's essential character traits—could not be finished on time, so a statue of Genius, a laurel crown in his hand, hovered over the coffin. A special lift was designed to raise the coffin, weighing almost a ton, to the top of the dais.[59]

The remains rested at the cathedral for another day to allow thousands of people to render their last homages. Dowager Empress Maria Feodorovna, Empress Consort Elisabeth Alekseyevna, Grand Dukes Nicholas (the future emperor) and Mikhail, and numerous court officials attended an evening religious service and conveyed their condolences to Catherine, who mourned her husband surrounded by her family members. On Friday, June 25, 1813, more than 600 invited guests gathered at the cathedral for the burial ceremony, which lasted nearly four hours. They stood solemnly as the sun shone through the dome to cast a final light on the coffin as it was lowered, to the thunderous sound of artillery salvoes, into the crypt.

Fame is the goddess who acquires common sense only with the passage of time; alas, even she fails to do that at times.

—*Voltaire to Catherine the Great, 1771[1]*

IN THE WORDS OF a contemporary, Kutuzov passed away "most opportunely for his fame."[2] He did not have to confront Napoleon and endure the allied setbacks in the spring and summer of 1813. He died, however, knowing that he had made a crucial contribution to the war and that Russia was safe and resurgent. Napoleon was, of course, defeated, first on the rolling plains of Leipzig, then at Waterloo, and the fate of his imperium and Europe was decided at the Congress of Vienna.

Alexander remained czar until 1825, the last years of his life full of disenchantment. In 1815 he was at the top of the world, the triumphant conqueror of Napoleon; a decade later, stirred by conflicting passions, he led a dismal existence in his palace. The victory over Napoleon had a tremendous effect on Russia, leaving a permanent imprint on the national psyche, and on the czar's mentality. He became enthralled by religious mysticism and sought to uphold conservative order and Christian ideals; such aspirations resulted in a harsh tyranny exemplified by the military colonies at home and the Holy Alliance, an instrument of repression against liberal tendencies, abroad. Everything that as a youth he loathed, Alexander now discovered in himself, justified and necessary. His prestige had fallen so low that people dared to criticize him openly in the salons. "The old men, the middle-aged, and above all the young—in a word, almost everyone—condemned his policies at every turn," recalled Alexander Koshelev, the son of the czar's advisor.[3] The czar's death in December 1825 sparked a revolution whose instigators were many young officers who had served under Kutuzov and went on to triumph over

Napoleon. In the process, they caught the fever of liberal ideas and returned home seeking to build a better world. Their Decembrist Revolt was short-lived, as a whiff of grapeshot shattered their dreams and aspirations.

The lives of men who served with Kutuzov followed divergent paths. Clausewitz returned to his native Berlin, where he wrote one of the most influential military treatises, *Vom Kriege* (*On War*), in which he proclaimed that "war is the continuation of politics by other means." Kutuzov would have heartily agreed. Kaisarov went on to become a general. Toll, Kutuzov's longtime favorite, also enjoyed a successful military career in the post-Napoleonic era, serving as chief of staff of the Russian armies; in 1839, three years before passing away, he returned to the Borodino battlefield, where he participated in the grand celebrations of the twenty-fifth anniversary of the battle. Among the generals, Dokhturov died just three years after Kutuzov, still feeling underappreciated for the service he performed silently and effectively. Miloradovich, probably the most colorful character in the Russian army, survived the carnage of the Napoleonic battlefields only to be shot dead by a Decembrist officer in view of his troops in the main square of the imperial capital. Barclay de Tolly was more fortunate—he led the Russian troops down the Champs-Élysées in Paris in March 1814 and returned home a hero; elevated to the rank of field marshal and a prince of the Russian empire, he was just the second person (after Kutuzov) to garner the complete set of St. George Crosses. Kutuzov's friend-turned-rival Bennigsen also celebrated victory over Napoleon before leaving Russian military service in 1818—the same year that Barclay de Tolly passed away from illness—and spending the last eight years of his life writing memoirs at his Hanoverian estate. Rostopchin outlived Kutuzov by thirteen years, vainly professing his innocence against the charge of the Moscow arson. Yermolov survived almost every one of his comrades, becoming the face of Russian imperialism in the Caucasus, where he proved himself a ruthless and effective ruler. He was a nationalist of the highest degree but not so blinded by his patriotic feeling that he could not admit Russian failings. In retirement, he had a large portrait of the French emperor hanging behind his cabinet desk because, as he told a friend, while alive Napoleon was "accustomed to seeing our absconding backs."

Despite his deep distaste for the man, Emperor Alexander treated Kutuzov's family with remarkable benevolence. "A great and painful loss has been caused not only to you but the whole Fatherland," Alexander consoled Catherine after the field marshal's passing. "I weep with you and all Russia weeps as well."[4] He granted the widow an annual pension in the full amount of her husband's wartime salary, which exceeded 85,000 rubles a year. Furthermore, once the war ended in 1814, the czar ordered the Ministry of Finance to pay the Kutuzov family debts. This drained the imperial treasury by some 400,000 rubles.[5] Finally debt-free, Kutuzov's family should have flourished, but they remained profligate and continued to grapple with financial difficulties for decades to come. Catherine outlived her husband by eleven years, cherishing his memory and indulging in her passion for theater. Even while the war was still raging she pushed hard for reopening of the French theater. "I am no less a patriot that anyone else but I do not comprehend how a French theater performance can interfere with the love of your Fatherland," she commented. The theater remained closed, but Kutuzov was able to secure the czar's permission for the private performances that his wife so adored.[6] Catherine passed away in St. Petersburg in July 1824; Alexander refused to grant her wish to be buried next to her husband at the Kazan Cathedral, and she was buried at the Holy Trinity Cathedral of the Alexander Nevskii Monastery.

Kutuzov had no surviving male offspring, so the main line of the Golenischev-Kutuzovs died with him. However, to ensure the preservation of the field marshal's name, in 1859 Emperor Alexander II granted Pavel Tolstoy, the son of Kutuzov's eldest daughter, Praskovya, and Matvey Tolstoy, the right to inherit his grandfather's name. His descendants, the Golenischev-Kutuzov-Tolstoys, thrived in the nineteenth century, but the last of them died in 1980. Kutuzov's other descendants, however, thrive to the present day.

The Golenischev-Kutuzov sisters went their own ways, but the shadow of their illustrious father followed them everywhere. Emperor Nicholas honored Kutuzov's memory by continuing to pay his field marshal's salary to his five daughters for the duration of their lives. Their offspring continued to play prominent roles in Russian society and the Russian state until the fall of the empire a century later.

Catherine, Kutuzov's second-youngest daughter, was still mourning her father's death when she received the news that her husband, Nikolai Kudashev, had been mortally wounded during the decisive battle at Leipzig on October 18, 1813. It was a heavy blow, but with time she recovered, later marrying a Russian general with whom she had four more children. One of her great-grandsons was Dmitri Horvat, a Russian lieutenant general who emerged as one of the leaders of the White movement during the Russian Civil War (1918–1921).

Darya Golenischeva-Kutuzova, the field marshal's youngest daughter, remained happily married to Fedor Opochinin and raised two sons and a daughter. Her eldest sister, Praskovya, whose marriage to Tolstoy produced nine children and laid the foundation for the largest branch of the field marshal's descendants, had one son, Ivan Tolstoy, who served as the minister of posts and telegraphs, and another, Feofil Tolstoy, who was a talented composer and music critic. Among the Tolstoy descendants of the field marshal was also his great-grandson Ivan Tolstoy, an eminent archeologist who served as the minister of education (1905–1906) and as governor of St. Petersburg during World War I; his incredible collection of coins still resides at the Hermitage Museum, which, incidentally, was directed by his brother Dmitri Tolstoy for almost a decade before the Bolshevik takeover in 1917.

Kutuzov's favorite daughter, Lizanka or Elisabeth, followed her second husband, Nikolai Fedorovich Khitrovo, on diplomatic assignments across Europe and became well known for her beauty and candor. Klemens von Metternich, Austrian chancellor and the architect of the post-Napoleonic reconstruction in Europe, was enamored of her and her daughters (from her first marriage, to Tiesenhausen), whom in the spring of 1818 he found the "prettiest" in all of Florence.[7] Elisabeth, however, could not escape the heartbreak of burying another husband: Nikolai Khitrovo died of illness in May 1819, leaving his family deeply in debt. Through guile, perseverance, and her father's pension, Elisabeth managed to get back on her feet; extremely proud of her father, she invariably signed her letters in French as "Elise Hitroff, née princesse Koutousoff-Smolensky," a title with which she had certainly not been born. Contemporaries thought there was something of the Wife of Bath in her character, as she flaunted her shoulders and *décolletage* as much as decency permitted at balls and festivities. "It is high time to draw a veil over the past," one society wit commented after seeing her in her later years. Others compared her to "a dreary huckster [*seryi torgash*]" for ceaselessly trying to gainfully marry off her daughters. The eldest of them, Catherine von Tiesenhausen, whom Kutuzov always lovingly inquired about in his letters, enjoyed a long and interesting life, serving as a lady-in-waiting for three empresses. She was at one point romantically linked to King Frederick Wilhelm III of Prussia, but this relationship failed, and the king married Auguste von Harrach instead. Elisabeth was disappointed for her daughter; she consoled herself by saying that "this would not have been an appropriate marriage for Kutuzov's granddaughter." As it was, Catherine von Tiesenhausen never married, though she did give birth to an illegitimate son whose father, contemporaries whispered, was King Frederick Wilhelm IV of Prussia himself. The boy was named Felix Elstone—rumor had it that the name derived from the mother's surprise, *elle s'etonne*, at being pregnant—and was raised by his grandmother; his grandson was Felix Yusupov, the man who murdered Gregory Rasputin.[8]

Kutuzov's other granddaughter, his "Dashenka" or Darya, was also celebrated for her beauty; "Vedere Napoli, la Ficquelmont e morire!" (To see Naples, the Countess Ficquelmont, and die!) was a common refrain while she lived in Naples.[9] At the age of seventeen, she married Karl Ludwig, Count of Ficquelmont, an Austrian diplomat who was twenty-seven years older than her and six years older than her mother. It proved to be a happy marriage. In July 1829, Ficquelmont became the Austrian ambassador to Russia, so Darya—or Dolly, as she was now called—spent years living in her grandfather's hometown, where she and her mother kept widely popular salons at which the cream of the St. Petersburg high society mingled; Elisabeth's "mornings (which in fact took place between one and four in the afternoon) and the evenings of her daughter, Countess Ficquelmont, are ineradicably engraved in the memory of those who had the good fortune to participate in them," Vyazemskii wrote in his memoirs. The whole of European and Russian political, literary, and social life was discussed in these two salons. Statesmen, diplomats, writers, and poets all frequented them. Both *salonnières* were great admirers and patrons of Pushkin. Elisabeth genuinely worshipped the poet, whose feelings for her were ambivalent—he quietly made fun of "bare Liza" among his friends but took her views on literature and politics seriously. Pushkin remained a close friend of Countess Ficquelmont, with whom he might have even had a fleeting affair.

Less fortunate was Kutuzov's second daughter, Anna. Her shiftless husband, Nikolai Zakharovich Khitrovo, upon receiving the czar's pardon, returned to his estate, where he devoted himself to helping peasants and promoting literacy through schools that he subsidized. Elected an honorary member of Moscow University, he died unexpectedly at the age of forty-eight in 1827. Anna squandered the fortune and, despite receiving her father's pension of over 17,000 rubles annually, found herself deep in debt. Her incessant solicitations for financial support incurred the wrath of Emperor Nicholas I, who barred her from court. She died at the age of sixty-four in 1846, leaving behind three sons.

The outpouring of grief at the news of Kutuzov's death, the unrestrained eulogies, and the superabundant imagery and over-the-top pomp that accompanied his funeral were the first steps in a process of mythologizing that continued for decades. "Now everyone praises [Kutuzov] to the heaven, but not so long ago almost everyone derided him," Lieutenant Chicherin wrote in his diary on May 16. Kutuzov's flaws and vices—the things that made him so fascinating and compelling, so central a figure in a tumultuous and defining period of Russian history—were soon forgotten. Just weeks after his death, Kutuzov's early biographer already described him as "the greatest Russian commander," "the lightning-like god Perun of the North," and a general who "accomplished more than Caesar, Hannibal, and Scipio combined."[10] Contemporary Russian writers and poets, whose works influenced public opinion, published numerous odes and pamphlets praising Kutuzov as "the Defender of the Half of the World" (G. Derzhavin), "the Hope of the Russians" (S. Marin), "The Savior of the Universe!" (A. Voeikov), and "The Demigod" (A. Izmailov).[11] Poet Peter Vyazemskii, who had witnessed the events of 1812, eulogized Kutuzov in his writings, including a poem that made the field marshal look almost like Napoleon of the romantic tradition. Here was the man who "in his thought soars high above the battlefield / his aquiline gaze moves the will and the power of human masses."[12] Pushkin, the greatest of the Russian poets, stood solemnly "with lowered head" in front of the "sacred sepulcher" at the Kazan Cathedral, amid "the throngs of granite pillars and their standards' pendent row," beneath which

> Sleeps that potentate,
> That idol of the northern hosts,
> The honored guardian of a sovereign land,
> Subduer of its enemies all,
> That relic of the lofty flock
> Of Catherine's eagles.[13]

Such exaltation has distorted Kutuzov's accomplishments, which, important as they were, must be viewed in a wider context. The victories over the Ottomans were the highlights of his military career; his triumph over Napoleon in 1812 came not through a victory in a decisive battle—the Battle of Borodino was, after all, a Russian defeat—but through a protracted and methodical campaign, the ground for which was laid by Kutuzov's predecessor, Barclay de Tolly, albeit it took the field marshal's leadership, persistence, and shrewdness to fully implement it. The truth is that Kutuzov, though revered in retrospect, was not well liked by his peers, who questioned not only his leadership but also his very character. For many he was a cold-blooded and devious man who, as Rostopchin put it, "could endure anything and sacrifice everything" to achieve his ambition.[14] Yermolov was equally scathing in his assessment: "History would eventually place him among great heroes while our national chronicles would acclaim him as the savior. But would any of my compatriots ever challenge this fantasy and reveal the truth?"[15]

Whether they did or not, it would have little effect. After his death, Kutuzov increasingly became Pushkin's portrayal—larger than life, a messianic figure who had saved Russia from the twin evils of the French Revolution and Napoleonic imperialism. As early as 1813, Filip Sinel'nikov published a six-part anthology of stories and events from Kutuzov's life and career that the author had collected over the years from the field marshal's family members and acquaintances. The anthology effectively laid another cornerstone in the Kutuzovian legend, as many of Sinel'nikov's stories were picked up in subsequent publications with little, if any, analysis or critique.[16] Major General Dmitry Akhsharumov's *Opisanie voiny 1812 goda*, published in 1819, was the first major attempt at a critical exploration of Napoleon's invasion of Russia; the author tried to avoid overpraising Kutuzov, who is described as *primus inter pares*, "first among equals."[17]

The tenth anniversary of Kutuzov's death was commemorated with several books and pamphlets, including Dmitry Buturlin's history of the 1812 campaign, widely considered one of the best nineteenth-century accounts of that war. Buturlin contributed to the development of the official view of Kutuzov's life and achievements, which, according to him, were "outstanding and could

1 Francois Vendramini's print remains one of the best contemporary portraits of the field marshal. It shows a scar in the temple area where an Ottoman musket ball struck Kutuzov, passing through his head and damaging his eye muscles.

2 Soviet actor Igor Ilyinskii as Kutuzov in Eldar Ryazanov's film "A Hussar Ballad" (1962). Kutuzov never wore an eye patch but it became an essential element of Soviet iconography of the field marshal.

3 Romanian poster for the Soviet film "Kutuzov," directed by V. Petrov in the midst of World War II in 1943. Kutuzov, ably portrayed by A. Dikii, was enlisted into the Soviet government's propaganda campaign that portrayed the field marshal as the brilliant strategist who had routed Napoleon with a brilliantly executed masterplan, ostensibly what Stalin himself did to the invading Nazi German armies (courtesy of Michael Creswell).

4 General Peter Bagration, the impetuous Georgian prince, nicknamed "the Lion of the Russian army." He served under Kutuzov in two campaigns but remained critical of his leadership (British engraving based on F. Vendramini's portrait, 1813).

5 General Mikhail Barclay de Tolly, courageous and prudent officer whose strategy of retreat was critical to the Russian victory over Napoleon in 1812. Kutuzov, however, received the lion's share of the public's acclaim (British engraving based on F. Vendramini's portrait, 1813).

6 General Levin Gottlieb Bennigsen, Kutuzov's one-time friend later turned into a rival. Born in Hanover, Bennigsen, despite being soundly beaten by Napoleon in 1807, believed he should be in command in 1812 and intrigued against Kutuzov (British engraving based on G. Dawe's portrait, 1823).

7   The "Bayard of the Russian army," General Mikhail Miloradovich, who had twice served under Kutuzov's leadership against Napoleon (portrait by G. Dawe, Hermitage Museum, St. Petersburg).

8   Kutuzov during the Battle of Borodino. S. Gerasimov's painting reflects the mythos that the Soviet government had carefully crafted around the field marshal.

9   Kutuzov praying in front of the Icon of the Black Virgin that had been rescued from the burning ruins of Smolensk. On the eve of the battle at Borodino, he organized a special religious ceremony to uplift the soldiers' morale. "I felt certain that we would not give an inch to the enemy on that field of battle," commented one of them. (painting by Evgenii Zaitsev, Central Artist's House, Alamy Stock Photo).

10   This nineteenth century print illustrates the famous incident with an eagle soaring above Kutuzov on the eve of the battle Borodino. Interpreted as a sign of impending victory, the incident laid the foundation for the subsequent mythologizing of the field marshal.

11   The Council of War at Fili before the retreat through Moscow in September 1812. Left to Right: Kaisarov, Kutuzov, Konovnitsyn, Rayevskii, Ostermann-Tolstoy, Bennigsen, Barclay de Tolly, Uvarov, Toll, Dokhturov and Yermolov (Painting by Aleksei Kivschenko, 1882, Alamy Stock Photo).

12   Kutuzov and Lauriston. Napoleon dispatched his trusted diplomat to seek peace with the Russians but Kutuzov saw a crucial opportunity to outsmart him. In war and politics, "you do not miss an opportunity that spontaneously presents itself," he commented. (painting by N. Ulyanov, Treatyakov Gallery, Alamy Stock Photo).

Michael Jlarionowitsch Golenischtschew Kutusow, Fürst Smolenskij.
Nach Stich von Bolt.

13 Kutuzov in the last year of his life, dressed in his usual frock-coat and flat round white cap (German print, early 19th century, James Smith Noel Collection)

Feld Marshal
PRINCE KOUTOUSOFF SMOLENSKY

14 Roman Volkov's portrait of Field Marshal Kutuzov, the last portrait drawn while he was alive, influenced how subsequent generations remembered him. Three-quarter length, standing in open air (with a battle scene in background) and leaning on a telescope on a table, on which also lies his hat, Kutuzov is shown as a strong and confident commander who had triumphed over Napoleon (author's collection).

15 Field Marshal Kutuzov as the triumphant Commander-in-Chief of the Russian Armies in 1812. This portrait, by Polish artists Józef Oleszkiewicz, clearly shows his sagging right eye, the result of the gunshot wound to the head. The field marshal is shown wrapped in the ermine mantle of the prince, wearing major imperial awards and the miniature portrait the czar had gifted him; a marshal's baton lays next to the bust of Emperor Alexander (State Hermitage Museum, Russia).

16 Kutuzov passed away at Bunzlau (Bolesławiec, Poland) on April 28, 1813. "The last days of his life was like a sunset at the end of a splendid day," commented one eyewitness (Drawing prepared by Kutuzov's aide-de-camp Colonel I. Yefimovich).

17 Early twentieth century photography of the house where Kutuzov passed away in Bunzlau (Bolesławiec).

18 Kutuzov's funeral procession approaching the grand Cathedral of Our Lady of Kazan in St. Petersburg. An immense crowd gathered at the plaza in front of the cathedral to catch the last glimpse of the field marshal's remains. Eyewitnesses marveled at "the deluge of people" and the splendor and pageantry of the ceremony. (Engraving by M. Vorobyev, 1814)

19 Kutuzov's coffin atop a ten-foot-tall dais in the middle of the Kazan Cathedral. It was illuminated with hundreds of candles and decorated with over two hundred flags and trophies, celebrating Kutuzov's victories; a statue of Genius, a laurel crown in his hand, hovered over the coffin.

20 On Prussian King Frederick William's orders, a sixty-tons obelisk surrounded by four lions was built in Kutuzov's honor in the main market square of Bunzlau(Bolesławiec). "To this spot, Prince Kutuzov of Smolensk led his victorious Russian troops," reads the inscription on it. "Death put a stop to his glorious deeds. He saved his country and paved the way for the liberation of Europe. Blessed be the memory of this hero!"

2 1 Kutuzov's statue in front of the Cathedral of Our Lady of Kazan in St. Petersburg. Emperor Alexander's decision to bury the field marshal in the middle of the imperial capital was a singular honor. No other Russian figure, except for the czars, would ever be honored in this way. The choice transformed the Kazan Cathedral into the pantheon of Russian military glory and turned Kutuzov's grave into a shrine.

2 2 Kutuzov as one of the prime architects (together with the Duke of Wellington and Prussian Field Marshal Gebhard Blücher) of Napoleon's defeat. The inscription reads: "What was begun by the Russian leader in 1812 was completed in 1815 by the victors at Belle-Alliance" (Early nineteenth century Russian miniature after S. Cardelli's engraving, Bukowskis Auction House)

withstand the most detailed scrutiny." He praised Kutuzov's military talents and argued that his Tarutino flanking maneuver and the strategy of parallel pursuit would "always serve as examples in military history." And he claimed that the country owed its deliverance from Napoleon to Kutuzov's "constant and profound wisdom."[18] In 1839, Alexander Mikhailovskii-Danilevskii, Kutuzov's youthful aide-de-camp who became the court historian, published his multivolume study of the Napoleonic Wars. These works were narrative histories of the campaigns, eschewing critical analysis that might have questioned Russian success. The books were read and edited by none other than Emperor Nicholas I, who removed entire sections of the works that contained even a hint of criticism of the Russian military. The narrative thus reflected imperial wishes and portrayed Kutuzov as "a radiant star that warmed up and enlivened everyone around," a man who "in four months achieved the most complete victory ever described in the chronicles, spread the glory of the Russian armies to the most distant corners of the world, and set the stage for the liberation of Europe."[19] In 1845, another Russian historian pronounced that only Kutuzov's "singular mind" and "inordinate military talents" could have accomplished three "mammoth deeds": saving the Russian army from Napoleon in the fall of 1805, destroying the Ottoman army in 1811, and triumphantly completing the Patriotic War of 1812.[20]

In the 1860s, Modest Bogdanovich, who taught at the St. Petersburg Military Academy, evaluated Kutuzov's role during the campaign of 1812. Although his multivolume campaign studies won several awards, Bogdanovich chose to ignore certain inconvenient truths to fit the officially approved interpretation of events; while admitting that the field marshal was a flawed man, the historian argued that "we honor Kutuzov as a commander who delivered Russia from the foreign invasion, and are not concerned by the questions whether it was possible to act better or accomplish more than Kutuzov."[21] To Bogdanovich's credit, he did attempt to critique some of Kutuzov's decisions, pointing to the field marshal's misleading report after the Battle of Borodino and his "sluggishness" during the Berezina operation that allowed Napoleon to escape.[22] Nonetheless, Bogdanovich's subsequent six-volume study of the reign of Emperor Alexander only reinforced the established vision of the field marshal as *primus inter pares*.

Such a view was only buttressed by Tolstoy's novel, whose historical backdrop overshadowed historical reality in cultural memory. *War and Peace* turned Kutuzov into a hero of the first magnitude, an unassailable national institution. The immediate response of Tolstoy's contemporaries was mixed, with veterans condemning the novel as a lampoon of actual history and deriding Tolstoy as the "killer of history" and contributor to "historical free-thinking and unbelief," as Peter Vyazemskii put it. The few who dared to oppose the Tolstoyan vision and question Kutuzov's accomplishments chose to do so quietly or anonymously. In the 1860s, an anonymous critic denounced

the "constant endeavor to portray Prince Kutuzov as superior to his contemporary generals." The same critic even challenged the view of Kutuzov
actually exercising command over the troops at Borodino and concluded that
"based on a close examination of official correspondence, Kutuzov's role in
deploying the army for battle is barely noticeable."[23]

Later imperial Russian historians chose to accept the official represen-
tation of Kutuzov, though perhaps less uncritically.[24] Lieutenant General
Vladimir Kharkevich, for example, challenged the prevailing views. In his
carefully researched 1893 study of the Battle on the Berezina River, he held
Kutuzov directly responsible for the Russian failures.[25] Nearly two decades
later, the centennial anniversary of the Patriotic War of 1812 caused a wave of
new studies, including the monumental seven-volume *The Patriotic War and
Russian Society*. The entire fourth volume was dedicated to Kutuzov; one of the
articles, by one S. Knyazkov, contained a rather forthright assessment of the
field marshal, who was described as a person with "exceptional intelligence,
enormous experience, and [who was] extremely cautious," who suffered from
"elderly immobility, illness, and fatigue that caused certain negative effects on
the [Russian] army in 1812." Knyazkov rejected previous representations of
Kutuzov and even questioned his moral integrity, noting that contemporaries
considered him "a true courtier," "a survivor," and a "courtesan."[26]

Emboldened by the revolutionary events of 1917, other historians began
to take a more confrontational approach. Mikhail Pokrovskii analyzed historical events through the prism of economic materialism, which minimized
the role played by individuals or ideologies inspired by individuals.[27] He
acknowledged Kutuzov's abilities as a military commander but noted that
by 1812 "he was too old for any decisive actions."[28] After Kutuzov's appointment, "the Russian army lost its central leadership for the rest of the
campaign and events unfolded without [Kutuzov's] active involvement."[29]
Furthermore, Pokrovskii disparaged Kutuzov's strategy of both retreating
and giving battle, which meant that his true nature "was revealed in his intention to catch two hares running in opposite directions." As the result, at
Borodino, the field marshal's only achievement was that "he was not routed
[*razbit nagolovu*]."[30] Pokrovskii eventually became one of the most influential Soviet historians, and his students, often referred to as disciples of the
"Pokrovskii School," published several insightful studies in the late 1920s
and early 1930s following the path set by their leader.[31]

Then, during the 1930s, the Soviet Communist Party instituted major
changes in official doctrine covering national history. Kutuzov's posthu-
mous reputation began to swing back to exaltation. Given an increasing
emphasis on a traditional interpretation of Russian history, Soviet historians
found themselves facing the dilemma of having to revise (and reject) their
own earlier works. In this perilous environment, no one could remain committed to impartial descriptions of the past. Eugene Tarle, one of the brightest

Russian historians who had written pioneering works on the Napoleonic Era, crafted a nuanced portrait of Kutuzov. On the brighter side, Kutuzov was a skillful commander who was unwilling to risk the lives of Russian soldiers and resisted the emperor's desires; he had given battle at Austerlitz only because "the czar refused to listen to his advice."[32] But Tarle also underscored the more sinister side of Kutuzov, the "adroit courtier, who played people against each other . . . [and] highly valued power, honors, luster, and success." On the whole, the historian concluded, he was "not the equal of Alexander Suvorov, let alone Napoleon."[33] Such opinions proved very costly to the Soviet historian, who was accused of having a "bourgeois worldview" and exiled to Central Asia.[34] Other historians were condemned for an anti-Marxist interpretation of history and the dissemination of bourgeois ideas. In the late 1930s, against the backdrop of Stalin's infamous purges and show trials, Pokrovskii's writings—the historian himself being already dead—were denounced as "sharing the views of the enemies of the nation and of the Trotsky-Bukharin counterrevolutionaries," and therefore preaching "national nihilism" and being "anti-patriotic," "anti-Marxist," "anti-Leninist," and "anti-scientific."[35] A new nationalist historical orthodoxy was established, centering on the cult of heroes and heroism, a boon for historical figures like Kutuzov.

Between June 1941, when Nazi Germany invaded the Soviet Union and launched the Great Patriotic War, and 1948, three years after the war ended, the number of publications on the Patriotic War of 1812 dramatically increased. Stalin wanted to draw parallels between the USSR's struggle against the Nazis and the Russian Empire's against the French.[36] Soviet historians bent over backward to show that the Russian retreat in 1812 was part of a thoughtful and premeditated strategy, foreshadowing the Soviets' "deliberate and planned" withdrawal in 1941. Kutuzov thus became a crucial figure in the new historical narrative that served political and ideological ends. It was no coincidence that when a new (and third-highest) Soviet military award was created in 1942, it was named after the field marshal; among its recipients were Soviet marshal Vasilii Sokolovskii (who received it three times), American general Omar Bradley, American admiral Henry Hewitt, and British air chief marshal Sir Trafford Leigh-Mallory.

After the war was over, Stalin moved to further exploit the historical memory of Kutuzov and the Patriotic War. In 1945, amid the Soviet Union's celebrations of its victory over Nazi Germany, Stalin commemorated the 200th anniversary of Kutuzov's birth with a special booklet that proclaimed the genius of the Russian general whose "military talents far surpassed those of Napoleon."[37] A year later, the Soviet autocrat personally responded to a certain Comrade Razin's seemingly innocent query about the Patriotic War. He placed it squarely within the context of Soviet operations against Nazi Germany and spoke of "close" parallels between the events. "I am of course speaking of the [strategy of retreat and] counteroffensive once an enemy invasion failed to yield decisive results. Our superbly gifted strategist, Kutuzov, who destroyed Napoleon and his army with the aid of a similar well-conceived and implemented counteroffensive, also grasped this strategy very well." Stalin extolled Kutuzov as the brightest and most talented Russian commander of the Napoleonic era. "[Friedrich] Engels once mentioned that General Barclay de Tolly was the only one of the Russian generals in 1812 worthy of commendation," Stalin commented. "Engels was, of course, wrong in this assessment. As a commander, Kutuzov was unquestionably two heads above Barclay de Tolly [*dvumia golovami vyshe*]."[38]

Stalin's words gave a clear sign regarding the direction historical research should follow. Historians heeded it faithfully. Studying at the famed Frunze Military Academy, Soviet historian Pavel Zhilin devoted his entire doctoral dissertation to "Kutuzov's counteroffensive in 1812," claiming that "Stalin followed Kutuzov's example when he lured the Nazis to Moscow, contrary to the assertions that the Germans forced our army to retreat to our capital."[39] Since the thesis coincided with the official canon, it was quickly approved and awarded the prestigious Stalin Prize. Encouraged by this success, Zhilin produced books and articles attacking the "evils of bourgeois historiography" that dared to criticize Kutuzov. No one was spared, including Clausewitz, who was branded as an "ardent falsifier" of history and his writings condemned as "forgery and libelous scribblings."[40] Zhilin refused to consider foreign sources because they represented corrupt bourgeois views, and he criticized others for consulting them.[41] Through his books, which the Soviet government printed in the thousands of copies, Zhilin created a new public perception of Kutuzov: a beloved leader of the Russian people and army, and a military genius who triumphed over Napoleon every time he confronted him.[42]

In his quest to sanctify Kutuzov, Zhilin was joined by two other historians, Liubomir Beskrovnyi and Nikolay Garnich, who took Zhilin's thesis even further. In their interpretations, the Battle of Borodino represented a masterpiece of Russian military strategy and tactics, and Kutuzov was its prime architect. Beskrovnyi believed that "Kutuzov prevented Napoleon from making any maneuvers or achieving any success" at Borodino, while according to Garnich the Russians won the battle so decisively that they pursued the fleeing French forces for miles.[43] The triumvirate of Zhilin, Beskrovnyi, and Garnich exercised considerable influence over Soviet historiography and made it all but impossible to challenge anything connected to Kutuzov.[44] Dissenters were condemned and persecuted. Even Tarle was forced to recant some of his earlier critical statements and revise his publications.[45] Once the renowned Soviet historian was forced to submit, other scholars quickly adhered to the "party line" and exerted themselves in glorifying Kutuzov. This sometimes resulted in farce. At one conference, a speaker was interrupted by a member of the audience who castigated him for not showing sufficient ardor in praising the great field marshal: "Comrade Stalin has showed us that Kutuzov was *two* heads above Barclay de Tolly, while your paper shows he was only *one* head above."[46]

The Kutuzovian myth continued to grow unabated after Stalin's death in 1953. For the next four decades, Soviet historians eulogized the field marshal, elevating him to a superhuman level with a glaring absence of human faults or limitations. Kutuzov's "military genius" was once more extolled as "superior" to Napoleon's, the defeat at Austerlitz was blamed on allies and foreigners, and Kutuzov was said to have achieved a "complete strategic and tactical victory" at Borodino.[47] The Battle of Tarutino, where the Russians defeated a French advance guard in October 1812, morphed into the crushing defeat of the Grande Armée itself, an event that for at least one historian rivaled the historic importance of the Battle on Kulikovo Field, where the Russians defeated the Mongols in September 1380.[48] Hyperbole thus distorted historical reality. The "elevation of the great commander to the ranks of the untouchables," lamented Russian historian V. Bezotosnyi, "has had a detrimental effect not only on the field of historical studies but also on the public perceptions of him."[49]

The collapse of the Soviet Union in 1991 ushered in a new era of Kutuzovian studies. Indeed, the last three decades have witnessed an upsurge in popular biographies of the field marshal, especially as Russia celebrated the bicentennial of Napoleon's defeat in 2012. These publications are of varying quality, many repeating the Soviet-era tropes and myths; "in all of world history I cannot find anything comparable to Kutuzov's thinking, his immense genius," gushed one recent author.[50] Fortunately, there are also works of serious academic revisionism. A new generation of historians—V. Totfalushin, V. Zemtsov, A. Popov, A. Vasiliev, V. Bezotosnyi, and A. Smirnov, to name just a few—has reassessed the events of the Patriotic War and Kutuzov's role in them. Perhaps the most vocal criticism of the field marshal came from Nikolai Troitskii, who persistently challenged long-held views about the field marshal.[51] Our understanding of Kutuzov's life has been greatly expanded by the scholarship of Yu. Gulyaev and V. Soglaev, L. Makeenko, and I. Tikhonov; Lidia Ivchenko has made important contributions to the field, and her book on Kutuzov, which was included in the prestigious *Lives of Remarkable People* series, has effectively become the standard Russian biography of the field marshal.[52]

A new generation of Russian historians will undoubtedly continue to enrich our understanding of this singular man. Yet Kutuzov seems destined to remain a Tolstoyan figure, so firmly has the novel shaped his image in the imagination. After a life in war and peace, he continues to lead a literary afterlife—part of history and yet beyond its reach.

Prologue

1. For example, Aleksandr Mikhailovskii-Danilevskii, *Vie du feld-maréchal Koutouzoff. . .* (Paris, 1860); M. Bragin, *Koutouzov* (Paris: R. Julliard, 1947); M. Bragin, *Field Marshal Kutuzov: A Short Biography* (Moscow: Foreign Languages Publishing House, 1944); E. Tarle, *How Mikhail Kutuzov Defeated Napoleon* (London: Soviet War News, 1943).

2. Roger Parkinson, *The Fox of the North: The Life of Kutuzov, General of War and Peace* (New York: D. McKay, 1976).

3. Serge Nabokoff and Sophie de Lastours, *Koutouzov: Le vainqueur de Napoléon* (Paris: Albin Michel, 1990).

4. Robert Wilson, *Private Diary of Travels, Personal Services, and Public Events During Mission and Employment with the European Armies in the Campaigns of 1812, 1813, 1814* (London: John Murray, 1861), I:203.

5. Dominic Lieven, *Russia Against Napoleon: The True Story of the Campaigns of War and Peace* (New York: Viking, 2010), 189–190, 251, 255. Also see Michael Adams, *Napoleon and Russia* (London: Bloomsbury Academic, 2006); Frederick W. Kagan, *The End of the Old Order, Napoleon and Europe, 1801–1805* (New York: Da Capo Press, 2006). To a lesser degree, Adam Zamoyski, *Moscow 1812: Napoleon's Fatal March* (London: HarperCollins, 2004).

6. See, for example, Michael V. Leggiere, *Blücher: Scourge of Napoleon* (Norman: University of Oklahoma Press, 2014); Charles Edward White, *Scharnhorst: The Formative Years, 1755–1801* (London: Helion, 2021); Rory Muir, *Wellington*, 2 vols. (New Haven, CT: Yale University Press, 2013–2015); Lee W. Eysturlid, *The Formative Influences, Theories, and Campaigns of the Archduke Carl of Austria* (Westport, CT: Greenwood Press, 2000). Napoleon has been the subject of a dozen new biographies in the last decade, including

Andrew Roberts's award-winning *Napoleon: A Life* (New York: Penguin, 2015), Adam Zamoyski's *Napoleon* (Basic Books, 2018), and multivolume sets by Philip Dwyer and Michael Broers. Among the new biographies of the French marshals and generals, see Franck Favier's *Berthier* (Paris: Perrin, 2015) and *Marmont* (Paris: Perrin, 2018), Antoine d'Arjuzon's *Caulaincourt* (Paris: Perrin, 2012), and Vincent Haegele's *Murat* (Paris: Perrin, 2015). Also see Ernst Rainer Gramm, *Karl Mack von Leiberich: Ein General gegen Napoleon* (Vienna: Böhlau, 2012); Herminio Lafoz Rabaza, *El general Palafox: Héroe de la guerra de independencia* (Zaragoza: Delsan, 2006)

7. The most recent biography of Alexander is Marie-Pierre Rey, *Alexander I: The Czar Who Defeated Napoleon* (DeKalb: Northern Illinois University Press, 2016). Most Russian generals of the Napoleonic Wars have not been deemed worthy of a biography. The sole exception is Barclay de Tolly, whose life and career have been explored in Michael Josselson and Diane Josselson, *The Commander: A Life of Barclay de Tolly* (Oxford: Oxford University Press, 1980).

8. Leo Tolstoy, *War and Peace*, translated by Louise and Aylmer Maude (Oxford: Oxford University Press, 2010), 799–800.

9. For interesting discussion, see Rick McPeak and Donna Tussing Orwin, eds., *Tolstoy on War: Narrative Art and Historical Truth in* War and Peace (Ithaca, NY: Cornell University Press, 2012), esp. chap. 6.

10. *Sovetskaya Rossia*, December 20, 2000, 5. Eight years later, another poll placed him among the top fifteen most distinguished historical individuals. See the survey "All-Time Most Distinguished Person from Around the World," August 31, 2008, Levada Center, https://www.levada.ru/2008/08/31/vydayus hhiesya-lyudi-vseh-vremen-i-narodov-v-rossijskom-obshhestvennom-mnenii/.

11. It is noteworthy that this poll showed Soviet dictator Joseph Stalin in the top spot. "Distinguished Historical Personalities," public opinion poll, June 26, 2017, Levada Center, https://www.levada.ru/2017/06/26/vydayushhie sya-lyudi/. A January 2016 poll of some 1,600 respondents, asked to name the greatest Russian military leaders, showed Kutuzov in the third spot, the highest-placed Napoleonic-era commander. Three other contemporary leaders appear in the list: Peter Bagration was number fourteen and Admiral Fedor Ushakov was number nineteen, while Mikhail Barclay de Tolly, who played a crucial role in crafting Russian strategy in 1812, has been all but forgotten, as he was ranked twenty-ninth. "The Most Distinguished Russian Commanders," February 18, 2016, Levada Center, https://www.levada.ru/2016/02/18/samye-vydayushhiesya-otechestvennye-voenachalniki/. In May 2021, the same "Distinguished Historical Personalities" poll showed Kutuzov at number seventeen, one spot ahead of Napoleon and three spots above Adolf Hitler. However, the percentage of people naming him among the "ten most distinguished people in history" has fallen precipitously from 11 percent of those polled in 1994–2008 to just 5 percent in 2021; Stalin, by contrast, gained support. "Distinguished Historical Personalities," public opinion poll,

June 21, 2021, Levada Center, https://www.levada.ru/2021/06/21/samye-vyd ayushhiesya-lichnosti-v-istorii/. Boris Nad, "Putin i strategiya Kutuzova," InoSMI March 20, 2017 <https://inosmi.ru/20170320/238906506.html> (accessed on April 17, 2022)

12. Leopold von Ranke, *The Theory and Practice of History*, edited by George G. Iggers, translated by Wilma Iggers (London: Routledge, 2011), 86.

Chapter 1

1. "Rod . . . proiskhodit ot vyekhavschago v Rossiyu . . . iz Nemets chestnago muzha imenem Gavriila." *Obschii gerbovnik dvoryanskikh rodov Rossiiskoi imperii*, part II, 31, accessible online at https://gerbovnik.ru/arms/181 .html. Also see the official genealogy tree of the Golenischev-Kutuzovs, prepared in 1802, at State Archive of the Pskov Region (Gosudarstvennyi arkhiv Pskovskoi oblasti; hereafter GAPO), f. 110, op. 1, d. 223, ll. 23b–24.

2. Filip Sinel'nikov, *Zhizn' chastnaya i kharakter Ego Svetlosti General-Fel'dmarshala Knyazya Mikhaila Larionovicha Golenischeva-Kutuzova Smolenskago* (St. Petersburg: Morskaya Tip., 1814), part VI, 3.

3. For an interesting discussion, see Serhii Plokhy, *The Origins of the Slavic Nations: Premodern Identities in Russia, Ukraine and Belarus* (Cambridge: Cambridge University Press, 2006).

4. For a broad overview, see Michael North, *The Baltic: A History* (Cambridge, MA: Harvard University Press, 2015), chaps. 1 and 2. The Golden Bull of Rimini in 1226 and the Papal Bull of Rieti in 1234 recognized the Teutonic control of Prussia.

5. See, for example, *Istoricheskie zapiski o zhizni i voinskikh podvigakh gen.-Fel'dmarshala svetleishego kn. M. I. Golenischeva-Kutuzova-Smolenskogo* (St. Petersburg, 1813), 7–8; Sinel'nikov, *Zhizn' chastnaya i kharakter*, 3. Many Soviet-era publications repeat this claim. For a critical analysis, see Yu. Gulyaev and V. Soglaev, *Fel'dmarshal Kutuzov. Istoriko-biograficheskii ocherk* (Moscow: Arkheograficheskii tsentr, 1995), 12–14; Lidia Ivchenko, *Kutuzov* (Moscow: Molodaya Gvardiya, 2012), 11–12, 17–18.

6. Nikolai Gogol, *Dead Souls*, translated by Donald Rayfield (New York: NYRB, 2012), 116.

7. The word "Kutuz" has long been interpreted by Kutuzov's biographers as meaning "a pillow." This explanation relies on Vladimir Dahl's famed *Tolkovyi slovar' zhivago velikorusskago yazyka* (Explanatory dictionary of the living great Russian language), which defines *kutuz* as "a pillow on which lace is woven." However, in his study of Russian family names of Turkic origin, Russian ethnologist and linguist Nikolai Baskakov has argued that the name "Kutuzov" is derived from the Turkic word *qutuz*, meaning "crazed" or "hot-tempered"; the word still survives in this meaning in Kyrgyz and other Turkic languages. It seems to me more probable that Gavriil's great-grandson was given his nickname because of his rowdy temperament, rather than any resemblance to a small cloth bag stuffed with feathers. A Turkic nickname would not

have been that unusual in fourteenth-century Russian society because of the Mongol yoke, which lasted until 1480. The *-ov* ending (*-ova* for females) is a surname possessive and is typical of many Russian last names. See *Tolkovyi slovar' zhivogo velikorusskogo yazyka*, online edition, http://v-dal.ru/word_s-44061.html; N. Baskakov, "Russkie familii tyurkskogo proiskhozhdeniya," *Sovetskaya etnografiya* 4 (1969): 19; N. Baskakov, *Russkie familii tyurkskogo proiskhozhdeniya* (Moscow: Nauka, 1979).

8. Official genealogy tree of the Golenischev-Kutuzovs, 1802, GAPO, f. 110, op. 1, d. 223, ll. 23b–24. For a detailed genealogy, see the famed Velvet Book, the official register of Russian nobility's genealogies, which contains genealogies of the Kutuzovs (no. 178) and the Golenischev-Kutuzovs (no. 179). Gavriil's grandson Alexander had three sons. Fedor Kutuz laid the foundation for the senior branch, which, however, died out by the seventeenth century. The offspring of Grigorii Gorbatyi ("The Hunchback") formed the middle branch, but it too became extinct. Ananiya's descendants initially formed a junior branch of the Kutuzov family, but after the two other branches waned, it became the main line, of which the Golenischev-Kutuzovs formed a cadet branch. *Rodoslovnaya kniga knyazey i dvoryan Rossiisikh i vyezzhykh* (Moscow: N. Novikov Tip., 1787) II, part XVIII, 1–13.

9. In the 1490s, three Kutuzovs served as Muscovite ambassadors to Lithuania and the Crimea. In 1554, Czar Ivan IV married Maria Golenischeva-Kutuzova to the last khan of Kazan, Yadegar Mohammad, who was captured by Muscovite troops in 1552, converted to Christianity, and assumed the name of Simeon Kasayevich. In the seventeenth century, many Kutuzovs served as *vojvodas* (military commanders) or middle-ranking palace officials (*okolnichii, stryapchii, stol'nik*). For an interesting discussion, see S. Veselovskii, *Issledovaniya po istorii klassa sluzhilykh zemlevladel'tsev* (Moscow: Nauka, 1969), 169, 430–432, 484–485; A. Zimin, *Formirovanie boyarskoi aristokratii v Rossii vo vtoroi polovine XV–pervoi treti XVI v.* (Moscow: Nauka, 1988).

10. It must be noted that the Kutuzov branch was the first to be listed in the Velvet Book in 1686 and some of its members refused to recognize their Golenischev-Kutuzov relatives. Only after a special investigation and genealogical research were the Golenischev-Kutuzovs recognized as a cadet branch of the Kutuzov family and listed in the Velvet Book in 1687. For details, see A. Antonov, *Rodoslovnye rospisi kontsa XVII veka* (Moscow: Arkheograficheskii Tsentr, 1996), 128–129.

11. Matvei Golenischev-Kutuzov's first wife was Natalya Chikhacheva, who gave birth to four children: Illarion, Ivan, Vasily, and Praskovya. After her passing in 1746, Matvei married Matrena Kutuzov, but he died less than a year later, on July 8/19, 1747. Lyudmila Makeenko, "Pskovskie predki fel'dmarshala," *Pskovskaya guberniya online*, no. 35/55 (September 2001), http://gubernia.media/number_55/8.php; Ivchenko, *Kutuzov*, 19.

12. There is still no separate biography of Illarion Kutuzov. It has been long claimed that he started military service under Peter the Great, but this would have been impossible since he was not even seven years old when Peter died in February 1725. Archival documents instead show that Illarion began military service in October 1733, when he was enrolled in the military engineering school at the age of fifteen. See *Russkii Biograficheskii slovar*, edited by A. Polovtsev (St. Petersburg: Tip. Glavnogo Upravleniya Udelov, 1903), IX:627; Gulyaev and Soglaev, *Fel'dmarshal Kutuzov*, 14–15; Yu. Yablochkin, "O vnov' vyyavlennykh dokumentakh k biografii M. I. Kutuzova," *Leningradskii dom uchenykh im. M. Gor'kogo. Sbornik dokladov voenno-istoricheskoi sektsii*, 1 (1957): 88.

13. Yablochkin, "O vnov' vyyavlennykh dokumentakh k biografii M. I. Kutuzova," 88–89; Ivchenko, *Kutuzov*, 19–21.

14. For details, see L. Makeenko, "Golenischevy-Kutuzovy na Pskovschine. M. I. Golenischev-Kutuzov," in *Materialy nauchnoi konferentsii M. I. Golenischev-Kutuzov* (St. Petersburg, 1993), 89.

15. *Istoricheskie zapiski o zhizni i voinskikh podvigakh gen.-Fel'dmarshala svetleishego kn. M. I. Golenischeva-Kutuzova-Smolenskogo*, 9.

16. Lyudmila Makeenko, *Golenischev-Kutuzov i ikh rodstvenniki* (Opochka: Opochetskaya Tip., 1997), online version at http://opochka.ru/content/ii-golenishchevy-kutuzovy-i-ih-rodstvenniki; Lyudmila Makeenko, "Pskovskie predki fel'dmarshala," *Pskovskaya guberniya online*, no. 35/55 (September 2001), http://gubernia.media/number_55/8.php; Yablochkin, "O vnov' vyyavlennykh dokumentakh k biografii M. I. Kutuzova," 86. Also see discussion in Ivchenko, *Kutuzov*, 24–25.

17. For differences, see *Kartina zhizni, voennykh i politicheskikh deyanii Ego Svetlosti kn. M. I. Golenischeva-Kutuzova-Smolenskogo* (Moscow, 1813), 13; *Zhizn' i voennye podvigi gen.-Fel'dmarshala svetleishego kn. M. I. Golenischeva-Kutuzova-Smolenskogo* (St. Petersburg, 1813), 10; *Zhizn' i voennye deyaniya gen.-Fel'dmarshala svetleishego kn. M. I. Golenischeva-Kutuzova-Smolenskogo* (St. Petersburg, 1813), 23; *Istoricheskie zapiski o zhizni i voinskikh podvigakh gen.-Fel'dmarshala svetleishego kn. M. I. Golenischeva-Kutuzova-Smolenskogo* (St. Petersburg, 1813), 10; "Arkhiv kn. M. I. Golenischeva-Kutuzova-Smolenskogo, nyne prinadlezhaischii pravnuku ego F. K. Opochininu," *Russkaya starina* 11 (1870): 499; *M. I. Kutuzov: Sbornik dokumentov* (Moscow: Voeniszdat, 1950), I:3; N. Munkov *M. I. Kutuzov—Diplomat* (Moscow, 1962), 12; I. Andrianova, *Spasitel' otechestva. Zhizneopisanie M. I. Golenischeva-Kutuzova* (Moscow, 1999); Gulyaev and Soglaev, *Fel'dmarshal Kutuzov*, 18–19; Nikolai Troitskii, *Fel'dmarshal Kutuzov: Mify i fakty* (Moscow: Tsentrpoligraf, 2002), 51–53; Ivchenko, *Kutuzov*, 27–28; Roger Parkinson, *The Fox of the North: The Life of Kutuzov, General of War and Peace* (New York: D. McKay, 1976), 4; Serge Nabokoff and Sophie de Lastours, *Koutouzov: Le vainqueur de Napoléon* (Paris: Albin Michel, 1990), 29. Soviet historian Mikhail Bragin incredibly claims that "much is unknown about

Kutuzov because, living in a complex and dangerous environment, the commander had to conceal his most intimate secret even from his acquaintances." *Kutuzov* (Moscow: Molodaya Gvardiya, 1970), 7–8.

18. For an excellent discussion, see Yu. Yablochkin, "O vnov' vyyavlennykh dokumentakh k biografii M. I. Kutuzova," 83–88. Yablochkin examined confessional books of St. Andrew's Cathedral in Kronstadt and the church at the Engineer Corps, which incongruously show Kutuzov as fifteen years old in 1758 and sixteen years old in 1761.

19. See *Vestnik evropy* 9/10 (1813): 139; *Syn otechestva* 20 (1813): 43; *Severnaya pochta* 50 (June 1813): 93; *Istoricheskii, statisticheskii i geograficheskii zhurnal* 2/1 (1813): 87. Filip Sinel'nikov, who published in 1813 a six-part biography of Kutuzov based on discussions with his relatives and friends, claimed in part I that the field marshal was born in 1743 but in part VI referred to September 1745 as his birthdate. Filip Sinel'nikov, *Zhizn', voennye i politicheskie deyaniya Ego Svetlosti General-Fel'dmarshala Knyazya Mikhaila Larionovicha Golenischeva-Kutuzova-Smolenskago* (St. Petersburg, 1813), I:2–3; VI:3.

20. *Istoricheskie zapiski o zhizni i voinskikh podvigakh general-fel'dmarshala, svetleishego knyazya M. L. Golenischeva-Kutuzova-Smolenskago* (St. Petersburg: Tip. Voennogo Ministerstva, 1813), 10.

21. Challenging the date of birth became harder once Kutuzov was shrouded in myth during the Soviet period, as discussed in the introduction. Starting in 1950, the Soviet Ministry of Defense published a multivolume anthology of Kutuzov's correspondence, gathering hundreds of letters and documents. The publication was supervised by eminent Soviet historian Liubomir Beskrovnyi, whose role in creating the Kutuzov myth we discuss in the epilogue. In the preface to volume I, Beskrovnyi reaffirmed the official date of birth, writing that Kutuzov was born "on 5/16 September 1745 in [St.] Petersburg." However, the volume editors—Lieutenant General A. Sukhomlin and Major General V. Styrov—had uncovered documents challenging this date. Unable to change the date in Beskrovnyi's preface, they included a brief footnote pointing out that "although it is accepted that M. I. Kutuzov's birthdate is 1745, information found in the records of service does not support such a date." Instead, they suggested 1747 as a possible date of Kutuzov's birth. *M. I. Kutuzov: Sbornik dokumentov*, I:viii, 3n1.

22. Lyubov Bogoslovskaya to the Governor of Pskov Province, March 18/30, 1911, GAPO, f. 366, op.1, d. 1066, ll. 133–133b. Bogoslovskaya was Anna Golenischeva-Kutuzova's great-granddaughter, and her letter is accompanied by a genealogical sketch of Illarion Golenischev-Kutuzov's family. It shows Anna's date of birth as August 20/31, 1746. Anna Illarionovna married a retired Guard officer, Osip Ushakov, in 1767.

23. *Formulyarnyi spisok*, January 12/23, 1791, Russian State Military Historical Archive (hereafter RGVIA), f. VUA, d. 2892, l. 75b. Other records of service point to 1747 as well. The *formulyarnyi spisok* prepared in February 1763

showed him as sixteen years old (he would have been fifteen years and five months if born in September 1747), and the list of officers nominated for promotion in 1772 shows him as twenty-five years old, while the list of officers of the Mariupolskii Light Horse Regiment prepared in August 1785 shows his age as thirty-seven (he would have turned thirty-eight one month later).

24. Yablochkin, "O vnov' vyyavlennykh dokumentakh k biografii M. I. Kutuzova," 84–86. Yablochkin's analysis shows that Kutuzov was most certainly born "during the period from 4[15] August 1747 to 11[22] January 1748."

25. One of the leading Russian biographers of Kutuzov, Lidia Ivchenko, suggests that Kutuzov might have been born in the village of Fedorovskoe, which his paternal grandfather owned. Ivchenko, *Kutuzov,* 27.

26. See, for example, Sinel'nikov, *Zhizn', voennye i politicheskie deyaniya . . .* , VI:9; Pavel Zhilin, *Kutuzov. Zhizn' i polkovodcheskaya deyatel'nost'* (Moscow: Voennoe Izdatel'stvo, 1978), 8; Vladimir Melentyev, *Kutuzov v Peterburge* (Leningrad: Lenizdat, 1986), 6.

27. Darya Illarionovna never married and spent most of her life in the village of Matyushkin, in the Opochetsk district, where she owned some property.

28. The Kholmskii district court's ruling on the incapacity of Semen Kutuzov, August 4/15, 1798, GAPO, f. 148. op. 1, d. 250, l. 11. Also see Ivchenko, *Kutuzov,* 21, 27.

29. Sinel'nikov, *Zhizn', voennye i politicheskie deyaniya,* VI:9–10.

30. See Ivan Turgenev, *A Nest of Gentlefolk and Other Stories* (Oxford: Oxford University Press, 1959).

31. Andrei Bolotov, *Zhizn' i priklucheniya Andreya Bolotova, opisannye samim im dlya svoikh potomkov* (Moscow: Terra, 1993), letter 15, http://az.lib.ru/b/bolotow_a_t/text_0080.shtml; I. Shestakov, "Vospominaniya I. A. Shestakova," *Russkii arkhiv* 3 (1873): 169.

32. Lev Engelhardt, *Zapiski Lva Nikolaevicha Engelhardta* (Moscow: Katkov, 1860), 4–5.

33. *The Poems of John Dryden,* edited by Paul Hammond and David Hopkins (London: Routledge, 2005), V:133n.

34. See Maurice Cranston, *The Noble Savage: Jean-Jacques Rousseau, 1754–1762* (Chicago: University of Chicago Press, 1991), chap. 7.

35. Sinel'nikov, *Zhizn', voennye i politicheskie deyaniya,* VI:10.

36. Mikhail Saltykov-Schedrin, "Melochi zhizni," in *Sobranie sochinenii,* edited by S. Makashin (Moscow: Khud. Literature, 1974), II:27. For an interesting contemporary assessment of the role of serf nurses and servants in noble children's upbringing, see V. Zinovyev, "Zhurnal puteshestvii po Germanii, Italii, Frantsii i Anglii, 1784–1788," *Russkaya starina* 10 (1878): 229.

37. This growth was partly a reflection of the expansion of the Russian Empire, which brought in Polish, German, Georgian, Ukrainian, and other nobles. By the mid-nineteenth century, the Russian nobility would nearly double in size,

528 | NOTES TO PAGES 9–11

with 918,000 individuals claiming noble descent. See N. Iakovkina, *Russkoe dvoriantsvo pervoi poloviny XIX veka. Byt i traditsii* (St. Petersburg, 2002), 8–9.

38. Étienne Dumont, "Dnevnik Etiena Diumona ob ego priezde v Rossiiu v 1803 g.," *Golos minuvschego* 3 (1913): 82.

39. Ivan Dubasov, "Iz Tambovskikh letopisei," *Istoricheskii vestnik* 9 (1880): 144n3. For an interesting discussion, see Jerome Blum, *Lord and Peasant in Russia from the Ninth to the Nineteenth Century* (Princeton, NJ: Princeton University Press, 1971), 367–385; Isabel de Madariaga, *Russia in the Age of Catherine the Great* (New Haven, CT: Yale University Press, 1981), 79–80; Tracy Dennison, *The Institutional Framework of Russian Serfdom* (Cambridge: Cambridge University Press, 2011); Elise Kimerling Wirtschafter, *Russia's Age of Serfdom, 1649–1861* (New York: Wiley, 2008).

40. Nikolai Turgenev, *Rossiia i russkie* (Moscow: Russkoe Tovarschiestvo, 1907), II:18. Also see Aleksei Tuchkov, "A. A. Tuchkov i ego dnevnik 1818 goda," *Vestnik evropy* 8 (1900): 690.

41. V. Semevskii, *Krestiane v czartsvovanie Imperatritsy Ekateriny II* (St. Petersburg: F. Sushinskii, 1881), I:30. This pattern continued well into the nineteenth century. See Blum, *Lord and Peasant in Russia*, 367–368.

42. D. Tselorungo, *Ofitsery Russkoi armii—uchastniki Borodinskogo srazheniya* (Moscow: Kalita, 2002), 100–103.

43. The surviving list of the officers and NCOs of the Corps of Engineers for the year 1760, when Kutuzov served there, does not specify the number of serfs he owned, instead noting that it is "unknown." Regimental records indicate that Kutuzov's father owned "600 souls" in 1763; eighteen years later, by which time he had already inherited his father's estates, Kutuzov's service files indicated that he owned "450 souls" in the Pskov and Ekaterinoslavl regions. See the Corps of Engineers' officer and NCO lists in RGVIA, f. 5, op. 2/73, d. 202, l. 247; *Formulyarnyi spisok*, February 1763, RGVIA, f. 53, op. 1/194, d. 11, ll. 336b-337; *Formulyarnyi spisok*, January 23, 1791, RGVIA, f. VUA, d. 2892, l. 75b. In Pskov province, Kutuzov's grandfather and father owned serfs in the villages of Fedorovskoe, Petrovskoe, Ignatovo, Knyshevo, Subotkino, Malofeevo, Trufanovo, Peschevitsy, Myskovo, Lutovo, Darnya, Gorki, and Pavlovo. See list of serfs owned by Illarion and Mikhail Kutuzov at GAPO, f. 39, op. 1, d. 1660; f. 39, op. 1, d. 2583; f. 55, op. 1, d. 36.

44. D. P. Troschchinski's memorandum cited in Sergei Korf, *Dvoryanstvo i ego soslovnoe upravlenie za stoletie, 1762–1855* (St. Petersburg: Trenke & Fusno, 1906), 351. Also see Aleksei Tuchkov, "A. A. Tuchkov i ego dnevnik 1818 goda," *Vestnik evropy* 8 (1900): 691–694.

45. For example, see Nikolai Shremetev's management of the estate at Kuskovo in Sergei Sheremetev, *Otgoloski XVIII veka. Vremya Imperatora Pavla, 1796–1800* (Moscow: Tip. Sytina, 1905), 124–125, 248–250.

46. See Priscilla Roosevelt, *Life on the Russian Country Estate: A Social and Cultural History* (New Haven, CT: Yale University Press, 1995); Mary W. Cavender,

Nests of the Gentry: Family, Estate and Local Loyalties in Provincial Russia (Newark: University of Delaware Press, 2007). For an old but still very useful study of the Russian provincial nobility, see Nikolai Chechulin, *Russkoe provintsialnoe obschestvo vo vtoroi polovine XVIII veka* (St. Petersburg: Tip. V. S. Balasheva, 1889)

47. For details see James Cracraft, *The Revolution of Peter the Great* (Cambridge, MA: Harvard University Press, 2006).

48. Janet M. Hartley, *A Social History of the Russian Empire, 1650–1825* (London: Longman, 1999), 16.

49. Cited in Lindsey Hughes, *Peter the Great: A Biography* (New Haven, CT: Yale University Press, 2002), 167.

50. V. Kliuchevskii, *A Course in Russian History: The Seventeenth Century*, translated by Natalie Duddington (Armonk, NY: M. E. Sharpe, 1994), 181.

51. Chechulin, *Russkoe provintsialnoe obschestvo vo vtoroi polovine XVIII veka,* 27–28.

52. See Yurii Lotman, Lidia Ginsburg, and Boris Uspenskii, *The Semiotics of Russian Cultural History: Essays*, translated and edited by Alexander Nakhomovskii and Alice Stone Nakhimovskii (Ithaca, NY: Cornell University Press, 1985). Also see Lotman's "Besedy o russkoi kul'ture," a series of video lectures presented in the 1980s, especially "Lyudi i chiny," "Gosudarstvennaya sluzhba," and "Formy obscheniya," KulturaLitvaCom channel, https://www.youtube.com/channel/UCwBTQSrgizKPb41dv5HzwvQ.

53. Filip Wigel (Vigel'), *Zapiski* (Moscow: Krug, 1928), I, part 2, 163.

54. Yakov Otroschenko, "Zapiski generala Otroschenko," *Russkii vestnik* 131/9 (1877): 126. He also notes, "My father soon became my teacher and he devoted himself wholeheartedly to raising his firstborn son, sparing neither himself nor the beautiful birch trees that overshadowed the front of our house [and provided a good source of rods]."

55. Sergei Tuchkov, *Zapiski Sergeya Alekseyevicha Tuchkova* (St. Petersburg, 1908), 4–6.

56. Sinel'nikov, *Zhizn', voennye i politicheskie deyaniya,* VI:12–13; Ivchenko, *Kutuzov,* 30–32.

57. *Obschii gerbovnik dvoryanskikh rodov Rossiiskoi imperii*, part II, 31, accessible online at https://gerbovnik.ru/arms/181.html.

58. Imperial decree of December 11/22, 1742 in *Polnoe sobranie zakonov Rossiiskoi imperii s 1649 goda* [hereafter cited as PSZ] (St. Petersburg: Tip. II Otd. Sobstv. Ego Imperat. Velichestva Kantselyarii, 1830), XI, no. 8,683, 737–740.

59. Russian State Archives of Ancient Documents (hereafter RGADA), f. 286, op. 1, d. 414, l. 610. This document was discovered and published by I. Tikhonov. See his "Pervyj smotr nedoroslya Mikhaila Kutuzova," *Otechestvennye arkhivy* 4 (1995): 89.

60. The report of this interview is at RGADA, f. 286, op. 1, d. 414, ll. 610–610b. Ivan Matveevich returned to the Herald's College on October 29, 1754, and signed a pledge to supervise his nephew's studies. See I. Tikhonov, "Pervyj

smotr nedoroslya Mikhaila Kutuzova," *Otechestvennye arkhivy* 4 (1995): 89. Also see Illarion Kutuzov to Peter Shuvalov, April 28, 1759, in *Fel'dmarshal Kutuzov: dokumenty, dnevniki, vospominaniya*, edited by A. Val'kovich and A. Kapitonov (Moscow: Arkheograficheskii tsentr, 1995), 13.

61. Sinel'nikov, *Zhizn', voennye i politicheskie deyaniya*, VI:11.

62. Ivan Loginovich Kutuzov was Illarion's sixth cousin. See genealogy tree of the Golenischev-Kutuzovs, 1818, GAPO, f. 110, op. 1. d. 222, l. 49.

63. Mikhail's younger brother, Semen Illarionovich, was also enrolled in the Artillery and Engineer Cadet Corps in 1766 and graduated two years later. After rising to the rank of major, he was forced to retire due to mental disability and spent the rest of his life at his estate at the village of Fedorovskoe in Velikoluksk district, where he died in 1834.

64. For an insightful overview, see Eugene Miakinkov, *War and Enlightenment in Russia: Military Culture in the Age of Catherine II* (Toronto: University of Toronto Press, 2020); Igor Fedyukin, *The Enterprisers: The Politics of School in Early Modern Russia* (Oxford: Oxford University Press, 2019).

65. See M. Lalaev, *Istoricheskii ocherk voennikh zavedenii, podvedomstvennikh Glavnomu ikh upravleniu* (St. Petersburg, 1880), 6–8. V. Krylov, *Kadetskie korpusa i Rossiiskie kadety* (St. Petersburg, 1998), 15–16. N. Zherve, *Istoricheskii ocherk 2-go Kadetskogo korpusa, 1712–1912* (St. Petersburg, 1912), I:2–9.

66. Marc Raeff, "Home, School, and Service in the Life of the 18th Century Russian Nobleman," *Slavonic and East European Review* 40, no. 95 (1962): 300–301.

67. Shuvalov's memorandum of 1758 is in K. Zherve and V. Stroev, *Istoricheskii ocherk Vtorogo Kadetskago Korpusa, 1712–1912* (St. Petersburg: Tip. Trenke, 1912), I:32–33

68. V. Benda, "K voprosu o deyatel'nosti Ob'edinennoi Artilleriiskoi i Inzhenernoi Shkoly v kontse 50–nachale 60x godov XVIII veka," *Izvestiya Rossiiskogo gosudarstvennogo pedagogicheskogo universiteta im. A. I. Gertsena* 92 (2009): 16–19; Zherve and Stroev, *Istoricheskii ocherk Vtorogo Kadetskago Korpusa*, I:33–35; N. Loman, *Istoricheskoe obozrenie 2-go kadetskago korpusa* (St. Petersburg: Obschestvennaya Polza, 1862), 96–99; Gulyaev and Soglaev, *Fel'dmarshal Kutuzov*, 22–25.

69. See Zhilin, *Kutuzov*, 9–10; A. Korch, *Mikhail Illarionovich Kutuzov* (Moscow: Vneshtorizdat, 1989), 2; Parkinson, *The Fox of the North*, 6.

70. N. Muravyev to Peter Shuvalov, April 8/19, 1759, in Yablochkin, "O vnov' vyyavlennykh dokumentakh k biografii M. I. Kutuzova," 88; Illarion Kutuzov to Peter Shuvalov, April 17/28, 1759, in *Fel'dmarshal Kutuzov: dokumenty, dnevniki, vospominaniya*, 13.

71. Order no. 1230, August 11, 1759, in *Fel'dmarshal Kutuzov: dokumenty, dnevniki, vospominaniya*, 13–14.

72. *Formulyarnyi spisok*, February 1763, RGVIA, f. 53, op. 1/194, d. 11, ll. 336b–337; *Formulyarnyi spisok*, January 23, 1791, RGVIA, f. VUA, d. 2892, l. 75b.

73. Shuvarlov's order of December 21, 1758, in *Fel'dmarshal Kutuzov: dokumenty, dnevniki, vospominaniya*, 14; Kutuzov's Record of Service (*Formulyarnyi spisok*) indicates that he was formally appointed as a *konduktor* on January 13, 1760. RGVIA, f. VUA, d. 2892, l. 75b. Also see details of the list of officers and NCOs of the Corps of Engineers for the year 1761, RGVIA, f. 5, op. 2/73, d. 202, l. 247; Gulyaev and Soglaev, *Fel'dmarshal Kutuzov*, 22–30; L. Punin, *Fel'dmarshal Kutuzov. Voenno-biograficheskii ocherk* (Moscow: Voennoe Izd., 1957), 13–14; Yablochkin, "O vnov' vyyavlennykh dokumentakh k biografii M. I. Kutuzova," 89–90; Sinel'nikov, *Zhizn', voennye i politicheskie deyaniya*, 2.

74. See V. Benda, "K voprosu o deyatel'nosti Ob'edinennoi Artilleriiskoi i Inzhenernoi Shkoly v kontse 50—nachale 60x godov XVIII veka," *Izvestiya Rossiiskogo gosudarstvennogo pedagogicheskogo universiteta im. A.I. Gertsena* 92 (2009): 16–19; Zhilin, *Kutuzov*, 11–13.

75. Loman, *Istoricheskoe obozrenie 2-go kadetskago korpusa*, 120; Gulyaev and Soglaev, *Fel'dmarshal Kutuzov*, 28.

76. The certificate, signed by Artillery Ober-Kriegs-Kommissar Mikhailo Mordvinov, is in *M. I. Kutuzov: Sbornik dokumentov*, V:593; *Fel'dmarshal Kutuzov: dokumenty, dnevniki, vospominaniya*, 15. The *Formulyarnyi spisok* of 1763 also notes that Kutuzov had mastered "one part of algebra, mechanics, fortifications and artillery [sciences]."

77. List of promotions in the Corps of Engineers, March 11, 1761, RGVIA, f. 5, op. 2/73, d. 202, ll. 194b–195; Major General Mikhail Dedenev's order of March 16, 1761, in *Fel'dmarshal Kutuzov: dokumenty, dnevniki, vospominaniya*, 14–15; 1761 certificate, *M. I. Kutuzov: Sbornik dokumentov*, V:593; list of officers and NCOs of the Corps of Engineers for the year 1761, RGVIA, f. 5, op. 2/73, d. 202, ll. 247, 311b, 312.

78. Kutuzov stayed at the JAENS until late July 1761, when Shuvalov formally assigned him to the Engineer Corps to fill in the vacancy created by the dispatch of another officer on a secret expedition to Siberia. *Spisok proizvdennym fo Inzhinernom korpuse i polku ober-ofitseram Fevralya 28 dnya 1761 goda*, in *M. I. Kutuzov: Sbornik dokumentov*, V:593.

79. Carol S. Leonard, *Reform and Regicide: The Reign of Peter III of Russia* (Bloomington: Indiana University Press, 1993), 40–72. Also see Marc Raeff, *Political Ideas and Institutions in Imperial Russia* (New York: Routledge, 2019), chap. 12.

80. For an interesting discussion, see Boris Mironov, *Sotsial'naia istoriia Rossii perioda imperii (XVIII–nachalo XX v.). Genezis lichnosti, demokraticheskoi sem'I, grazhdanskogo obschestva, i pravovogo gosudasrtva* (St. Petersburg: Bulanin, 1999), vol. 1; S. Ekshtut, *Na shluzhbe rossiiskomu Leviafanu. Istoricheskie opyty* (Moscow: Progress-Traditsiia, 1998), 23–116; Michael Confino, "The Nobility in Russia and Western Europe: Contrasts and Similarities," in *Russia Before the "Radiant Future": Essays in Modern History, Culture and Society* (New York: Berghahn Books, 2011), 119–140; Elise Kimerlin Wirtschafter,

Social Identity in Imperial Russia (DeKalb: Northern Illinois University Press, 1997); Patrick O'Meara, *The Russian Nobility in the Age of Alexander I* (London: Bloomsbury, 2019), 3–32.

81. Cited in D. Bantysh-Kamenskii, *Biografii rossiiskikh generalissimusov i general-feld'marshalov* (St. Petersburg: Tip. Tretyago Dept. Min. Gos. Imushestv, 1840), I:311.

82. Duke of Schleswig-Holstein-Sonderburg-Beck to the War College, no. 193, March 4, 1762; Journal of the War College, March 1/12, 1762, in *M. I. Kutuzov: Sbornik dokumentov*, V:594. Parkinson erroneously claims that Kutuzov became aide-de-camp to "Prince Golshtein-Bekckii" [*sic*] in late 1762 (*The Fox of the North*, 10).

83. *Anekdoty ili Dostopamyatnye skazaniya o ego svetlosti general fel'dmarshale knyaze Mikhaile Larionoviche Golenischeve-Kutuzove Smolenskom* (St. Petersburg: Morskaya Tip., 1814), I:1–2; Sinel'nikov, *Zhizn', voennye i politicheskie deyaniya*, I:3–4. Sinel'nikov records another story of an early encounter between Empress Catherine II and Kutuzov in Revel in 1764. When asked if he wanted to distinguish himself on the field of battle, Kutuzov responded with "heroic humbleness, 'With great pleasure,'" which earned him the empress's smile.

84. The Journal of the War College identifies Kutuzov among the "flügel-adjutants of a captain's rank." Journal of the War College, September 1, 1762, *M. I. Kutuzov: Sbornik dokumentov*, V:595.

85. Carol Scott Leonard, "A Study of the Reign of Peter III of Russia," Ph.D. dissertation, Indiana University, 1976, 270.

86. Journal of the War College, September 1, 1762, *M. I. Kutuzov: Sbornik dokumentov*, V:595.

87. Journal of the War College, September 1, 1762, *M. I. Kutuzov: Sbornik dokumentov*, V:595; *Formulyarnyi spisok*, February 1763, RGVIA, f. 53, op. 1/194, d. 11, ll. 336b–337. In his biography of Kutuzov, Roger Parkinson claims that "early in 1762 [Kutuzov] rode into the Volga delta and to the town of Astrakan where he would serve in the Astrakan infantry regiment." He then proceeds to allege that "soon after Kutuzov's arrival at Astrakhan the first reports arrived of the latest dramatic change-over in the Russian court. Catherine seized power from her husband in June" (*The Fox of the North*, 7, 9). This passage betrays the author's complete lack of knowledge of the Russian army. Kutuzov was appointed to the Astrakhanskii Infantry Regiment after the coup. He never traveled to Astrakhan, nor was the Astrakhanskii Infantry Regiment deployed in this town. Instead, the regiment was deployed at Novaya Ladoga, near the imperial capital, and was formally part of the garrison commanded by the commandant of St. Petersburg.

Chapter 2

1. Alexander Suvorov's autobiography, in *A. V. Suvorov. Sbornik dokumentov*, edited by G. Mescheryakov (Moscow: Voennoe Izdatel'stvo, 1949), I:32. Probably the

best Russian biographies of Suvorov remain A. Petrushevskii, *Generalisimus knyaz Suvorov* (St. Petersburg; Stasyulevich, 1884) and V. Lopatin, *Suvorov* (Moscow: Molodaya Gvardiya, 2012). Suvorov is still awaiting a decent English-language biography since the existing ones are some sixty years old. See Philip Longworth, *The Art of Victory: The Life and Achievements of Generalissimo Suvorov, 1729–1800* (London: Constable, 1965); K. Osipov, *Alexander Suvorov* (London: Hutchinson, 1941).

2. See "Polkovoe uchrezhdenie" in *A. V. Suvorov. Sbornik dokumentov*, I:75–152; *Nauka pobezhdat'*, www.elcocheingles.com/Memories/Texts/Suvorov/Nauka_ pobevdat.htm.

3. "Formulyarnyi spisok," in *A. V. Suvorov. Sbornik dokumentov*, I:6–7. Suvorov took command of the Astrakhanskii Infantry Regiment on September 11, 1762, and left on April 17, 1763.

4. For a contrary view, see Mikhail Bragin, *Kutuzov* (Moscow: Molodaya Gvardiya, 1970), 29–30.

5. "Formulyarnyi spisok," February 1763, RGVIA, f. 53, op. 1/194, d. 11, l. 337.

6. Sinel'nikov records a story of Kutuzov's meeting with Empress Catherine. During her visit to Revel in early 1764, Catherine examined the local garrison troops and encountered the seventeen-year-old Captain Kutuzov, who served as the local governor-general's adjutant. On her departure Catherine called Kutuzov to her and asked if he wished "to distinguish himself on the field of honor." He answered, "With great pleasure," which "elicited a smile" from the empress. The story is most probably apocryphal, since in 1764 Kutuzov was no longer the flügel-adjutant to Duke of Schleswig-Holstein-Sonderburg-Beck and instead commanded a company in the Astrakhanskii Infantry Regiment. Filip Sinel'nikov, *Zhizn', voennye i politicheskie deyaniya Ego Svetlosti General-Fel'dmarshala Knyazya Mikhaila Larionovicha Golenischeva-Kutuzova-Smolenskago* (St. Petersburg, 1813), I:3–5. Also see *Anekdoty ili dostopamyatnye skazaniya o ego svetlosti general fel'dmarshale knyaze Mikhaile Larionoviche Golenischeve-Kutuzove Smolenskom* (St. Petersburg: Morskaya Tip., 1814), I:2–3.

7. *Anekdoty ili dostopamyatnye skazaniya*, I:3–4.

8. "Formulyarnyi spisok," January 1791, RGVIA, f. VUA, d. 2892, ll. 75–76; *Anekdoty ili Dostopamyatnye skazaniya*, I:4. Sinel'nikov also records a story of Captain Kutuzov's involvement in another skirmish with Polish troops in 1765. Sinel'nikov, *Zhizn', voennye i politicheskie deyaniya*, 6–8. Parkinson erroneously claims that Kutuzov was "denied action" and remained in Revel in 1764–1768; Roger Parkinson, *The Fox of the North: The Life of Kutuzov, General of War and Peace* (New York: D. McKay, 1976), 11.

9. "Formulyarnyi spisok," January 1791, RGVIA, f. VUA, d. 2892, l. 76.

10. See the entry "Ivan longinnovich Golenischev-Kutuzov" in *Russkii biograficheskii Slovar'*, edited by Alexander Polovtsev, XII:626–627, http://rulex.ru/xPol/ index.htm?pages/12/626.htm; Lidia Ivchenko, *Kutuzov* (Moscow: Molodaya Gvardiya, 2012), 61.

11. Parkinson erroneously claims that Kutuzov returned to Revel and continued to serve as local military governor's aide "for three more years"; *The Fox of the North*, 11.

12. Kutuzov seems to have received a two-week furlough in September 1767 before assuming his new responsibilities. "Formulyarnyi spisok," January 1791, RGVIA, f. VUA, d. 2892, l. 76. He initially received an order to place himself at the disposal of Procurator General Prince Alexander Vyazemskii, the empress's right-hand man, who was tasked with supervising the work of the commission. He was then assigned to the working group. See Imperial Rescript, August 11, 1767, RGVIA, f. 2, op. 13, d. 58, l. 79; Adjutant General K. Razumovskii to Procurator General A. Vyazemskii, August 28, 1767, in *M. I. Kutuzov. Sbornik dokumentov* (Moscow: Voeniszdat, 1950), V:598.

13. "Imennoi spisok trebovannykh ot polkov gvardii I drugikh komand raznykh chinov ko ispravleniu pismennykh del u sochineniya proekt a novogo ulozheniya," August 18, 1767, in *M. I. Kutuzov. Sbornik dokumentov*, V:599.

14. Sinel'nikov, *Zhizn', voennye i politicheskie deyaniya*, VI:14.

15. Ismail Hakkı Uzunçarşılı, *Osmanlı Tarihi IV/I* (Ankara: Türkiye, 1988), 364.

16. Sinel'nikov, *Zhizn', voennye i politicheskie deyaniya*, I:9–13.

17. *Anekdoty ili dostopamyatnye skazaniya*, I:6–7.

18. See footnote 2 in *M. I. Kutuzov. Sbornik dokumentov*, I:3. Also see discussion in Ivchenko, *Kutuzov*, 92–93.

19. Cited in Andrei Petrov, "K biografii svetleishego knyazya Golenischeva-Kutuzova-Smolenskogo," *Voennyi sbornik* 3 (1900): 5.

20. A. Petrov, *Voina Rossii s Turtsiei i pol'skimi konfederatami c 1769–1774 god* (St. Petersburg: Weimeyer, 1866), I:65–73; Uzunçarşılı, *Osmanlı Tarihi IV/ I*, 368; Brian Davies, *The Russo-Turkish War, 1768–1774. Catherine II and the Ottoman Empire* (London: Bloomsbury, 2016), 12–13; Orville T. Murphy, *Charles Gravier, Comte de Vergennes: French Diplomacy in the Age of Revolution, 1719–1787* (Albany: State University of New York Press, 1982), 157–159; Albert Sorel, *The Eastern Question in the Eighteenth Century: The Partition of Poland and the Treaty of Kainardji* (London: Methuen, 1898), 26–27.

21. The Ottomans initially used the term "Moskov" or "Moskovlu" to refer to the Russian state that emerged under Moscow's leadership but switched to "Rusiya" at the end of the seventeenth century; it was only in 1741 that the sultan recognized the Russian rulers as the "Emperors of All the Russias."

22. Virginia H. Aksan, *Ottoman Wars, 1700–1870: An Empire Besieged* (New York: Pearson, 2007), 134–135. For an insightful discussion, see Stanford J. Shaw, *History of the Ottoman Empire and Modern Turkey* (Cambridge: Cambridge University Press, 1976), I:217–276; Brian Davies, *Empire and Military Revolution in Eastern Europe: Russia's Turkish Wars in the Eighteenth Century* (London: Continuum, 2011), esp. 180–284. For the Ottoman role in the Seven Years' War, see Virginia H. Aksan, "The Ottoman Absence from the

Battlefield of the Seven Years' War," in *The Seven Years' War: Global Views*, edited by Mark Danley and Patrick Speelman (Leiden: Brill, 2012), 165–190.

23. Petrov, *Voina Rossii s Turtsiei i pol'skimi konfederatami*, I:157–332; Davies, *The Russo-Turkish War*, 107–127. For details on the Russian siege of Khotin, see Cengiz Fedakar, *Hotin Kalesi'nin Sükutu (1768–1774 Osmanlı-Rus Savaşları'nda), Bozkırın Oğlu Ahmet Taşağıl'a Armağan* (Istanbul: Yeditepe, 2019), 450–478.

24. "Comte de Landeron's Journal de campagnes faites au service de Russie par comte Langeron, Général en Chef," Archives du Ministère des Affaires Etrangères, 20:14. For an interesting example of Rumyantsev's aloofness, see Charles François Philibert Masson, *Mémoires secrets sur la Russie, et particulièrement sur la fin du règne de Catherine II et le commencement de celui de Paul I* (Amsterdam: n.p., 1800), 302–303 (footnote).

25. Philip Weigel, *Vospominaniya Filippa Filippovicha Vigelya* (Moscow: Katkov, 1864), I, part 1, 80. Rumyantsev was a "great admirer of the Prussian army" and "was always free of the prejudices that weigh down lesser spirits," commented Semen Vorontsov. See his memorandum on the Russian army, prepared in 1802 for Emperor Alexander, in *Arkhiv knyazya Vorontsova* (Moscow: Tip. Gracheva, 1876), X:483.

26. Peter Rumyantsev to Nikita Panin, January 27/February 7, 1769, in *P. A. Rumyantsev. Sbornik dokumentov*, edited by P. Fortunatov (Moscow: Voennoe Izdatel'stvo, 1953), II:64.

27. Uzunçarşılı, *Osmanlı Tarihi IV/I*, 375; Cengiz Fedakar, *Bender Kalesi (1768–1774)* (Istanbul: Kitabevi, 2019), 47.

28. Five to six companies for infantry regiments, five squadrons for cuirassier regiments, and eight squadrons for carabineer regiments.

29. For example, the new Rites of Service set new rules concerning marching, setting and defending camps, conducting patrols, establishing field hospitals, supervising foraging and rations distributions, etc. See "Obryad sluzhby," March 1770, in *P. A. Rumyantsev. Sbornik dokumentov*, I:233–253.

30. Kutuzov is recorded third in the list of officers of the Smolenskii Infantry Regiment dated April 25/May 6, 1769. See discussion in footnote 1 in *M. I. Kutuzov. Sbornik dokumentov*, I:2.

31. War College to Rumyantsev, December 18/29, 1769, in *P. A. Rumyantsev. Sbornik dokumentov*, II:201–209; Yu. Gulyaev and V. Soglaev, *Fel'dmarshal Kutuzov. Istoriko-biograficheskii ocherk* (Moscow: Arkheograficheskii Tsentr, 1995), 57–58. Kutuzov's younger brother Semen, fresh out of the Cadet Corps, was also at the headquarters, serving as a flügel-adjutant to his father.

32. See entries for late May and early June 1770 in *Zhurnal voennykh deistvii armei Eya imperatorskago Velichestva 1770 goda* (hereafter cited as *The Journal of Military Operations in 1770*) (St. Petersburg: War College, 1771), 44–49.

33. Petrov, *Voina rossii s turtsiei i pol'skimi konfederatami*, II:82–83. The First Army had 38,818 men and 16,106 horses, but 2,122 men were on the sick list and

5,203 were noncombatants. Thus only 24,169 infantrymen and 7,328 cavalry could take part in combat operations.

34. Catherine II to P. Rumyantsev, December 10/21, 1769, in *P. A. Rumyantsev. Sbornik dokumentov*, II:196.

35. See Aksan, *Ottoman Wars, 1700–1870*, 143–151.

36. Rumiantsev and Général-en-chef Peter Olits in the center, Lieutenant General Peter Plemyannikov on the right flank, and Lieutenant General Yakov Bruce on the left—along two cavalry wings under command of Lieutenant Generals Ivan Saltykov and Nikolai Repnin. Order of Battle of the First Army, May 14/25, 1770, in *P. A. Rumyantsev. Sbornik dokumentov*, II:287–289.

37. *The Journal of Military Operations in 1770*, 53–54; Rumyantsev to Repnin, June 8/19–9/20, 1770; Rumyantsev to Catherine II, June 13/24, 1770, in *P. A. Rumyantsev. Sbornik dokumentov*, II:303–304, 309.

38. See Rumyantsev's reports in *P. A. Rumyantsev. Sbornik dokumentov*, II:312–319; Petrov, *Voina Rossii s Turtsiei i pol'skimi konfederatami*, II:99–101.

39. Rumyantsev's report has been published three times: first in a journal published by the University of Moscow in 1865, then as an excerpt in the great anthology of Kutuzov's documents published by the Soviet government in 1950, and finally in the anthology of Rumyantsev's documents published in 1953. The first two publications list Kutuzov among the officers: "Kapitanam Knoringu, Kutuzovu, Gandvikhu i Bergu." Remarkably, the 1953 publication omits Kutuzov's name and instead reads "Kapitanam Knoringu, Gaidvigu [*sic*] i Bergu." *Chteniya v Imperatorskom obschestve istorii i drevnostei rossiiskikh pri Moskovskom universitete* 2 (1865): 90; *M. I. Kutuzov. Sbornik dokumentov*, I:9; *P. A. Rumyantsev. Sbornik dokumentov*, II:310.

40. *The Journal of Military Operations in 1770*, 57–59; Petrov, *Voina rossii s turtsiei i pol'skimi konfederatami*, II:101–105.

41. Aksan, *An Ottoman Statesman in War and Peace*, 149.

42. *The Journal of Military Operations in 1770*, 62, 68–69, 72.

43. Filip Sinel'nikov recounts Kutuzov's exploits in some detail, noting that he "showed astonishing courage, standing with his men for a long time in close formation under enemy's heavy fire . . . whenever enemy riders approached, he rushed upon them himself with his troops and invariably pushed them back. During this combat, the enemy lost many men and after some of his best of riders had been killed, the enemy was forced to retreat." Yet this passage is an almost verbatim quote from the *Journal of Military Operations* and Rumyantsev's detailed report to the empress. Neither of them mentions Kutuzov's involvement; instead, the quoted passage describes the actions of Lieutenant Colonel Elchaninov, who commanded cavalry squadrons during this combat. It seems Sinel'nikov copied the passage but attributed the action to Kutuzov. Sinel'nikov, *Zhizn', voennye i politicheskie deyaniya*, I:17; Rumyantsev to Catherine II, July 12/23, 1770, in *P. A. Rumyantsev. Sbornik dokumentov*, II:331–332; *The Journal of Military Operations in 1770*, 75.

44. *The Journal of Military Operations in* 1770, 74.

45. Gregory Potemkin's conversation with Comte de Ségur, in Louis Philippe de Ségur, *Mémoires ou souvenirs et anecdotes* (Paris: Alexis Eymery, 1826), II:319.

46. Letter of August 1, 1788, in Charles Joseph Prince de Ligne, *Lettres et Pensées du Maréchal Prince de Ligne* (London: Cox, 1809), II:14.

47. For widespread problems in the Ottoman army during this campaign, see Virginia H. Aksan, *An Ottoman Statesman in War and Peace: Ahmed Resmi Efendi, 1700–1783* (Leiden: Brill, 1995), 117–162.

48. Disposition for Attack, July 6/17, 1770, in *P. A. Rumyantsev. Sbornik dokumentov*, II:322; *The Journal of Military Operations in* 1770, 77–78.

49. *The Journal of Military Operations in* 1770, 80.

50. *The Journal of Military Operations in* 1770, 82.

51. Aksan, *An Ottoman Statesman in War and Peace*, 150.

52. *The Journal of Military Operations in* 1770, 83; Rumyantsev to Catherine II, July 7/18, 1770; Rumyantsev to P. Panin, July 9/20, 1770; Rumyantsev to Catherine II (detailed report), July 12/23, 1770, in *P. A. Rumyantsev. Sbornik dokumentov*, II:323–338. For the Ottoman side, see Aksan, *An Ottoman Statesman in War and Peace*, 150–151.

53. *The Journal of Military Operations in* 1770, 86. According to Sinel'nikov, as Repnin's men stormed the main Ottoman camp, Bauer moved toward one of the enemy hilltop fortifications, as the grenadiers under Kutuzov's leadership rushed ahead and "with extraordinary bravery climbed the hill which the enemy did not expect and fled." Sinel'nikov, *Zhizn', voennye i politicheskie deyaniya*, I:18. Serge Nabokoff and Sophie de Lastours mistakenly claimed that Kutuzov was promoted to premier major and appointed "quartier-maitre principal" on July 1, 1770; *Koutouzov: Le vainqueur de Napoléon* (Paris: Albin Michel, 1990), 45.

54. Aksan, *An Ottoman Statesman in War and Peace*, 136–137.

55. *The Journal of Military Operations in* 1770, 91–92.

56. "Pravila general'nye . . . ," June 9/20, 1773, in *P. A. Rumyantsev. Sbornik dokumentov*, I:627. Also see *The Journal of Military Operations in* 1770, 93.

57. *The Journal of Military Operations in* 1770, 94–97; Davies, *The Russo-Turkish War*, 145–146.

58. Ahmed Resmi Efendi's journal, quoted in Aksan, *An Ottoman Statesman in War and Peace*, 153; *The Journal of Military Operations in* 1770, 100–101; Petrov, *Voina rossii s turtsiei i pol'skimi konfederatami*, II:141, 144–145.

59. In this regard the loss of Kilia, with its large gunpowder magazines, and of Brăila, with its food stores, was particularly painful for the Ottomans. See Işık Ertekin, "Kili Kalesi (1767–1792)," master's thesis, Institute of Social Sciences, Trakya University, Edirne, 2015, 51–56, 80; Hakan Engin, "1787–1792 Osmanlı-Rus Avusturya Harpleri sırasında İbrail Kalesi," master's thesis, Institute of Social Sciences, Trakya University, Edirne, 2013), 61. I am grateful to Prof. Cengiz Fedakar for bringing these studies to my attention.

60. Rumyantsev to Catherine II, August 18/29, 1770, in *P. A. Rumyantsev. Sbornik dokumentov*, II:372.

61. Fedakar, *Bender Kalesi*, 51–52.

62. Petrov, *Voina Rossii s Turtsiei i pol'skimi konfederatami*, II:330–337; Ivchenko, *Kutuzov*, 100; Gulyaev and Soglaev, *Fel'dmarshal Kutuzov*, 56. For the Ottoman perspective, see Fedakar, *Bender Kalesi*, 24–59.

63. Pavel Zhilin, *Kutuzov. Zhizn' i polkovodcheskaya deyatel'nost'* (Moscow: Voennoe Izdatel'stvo, 1978), 23; L. Punin, *Fel'dmarshal Kutuzov. Voenno-biograficheskii ocherk* (Moscow: Voennoe Izdatel'stvo, 1957), 18; Nabokoff and Lastours, *Koutouzov*, 47–48.

64. Gulyaev and Soglaev, *Fel'dmarshal Kutuzov*, 57. L. Ivchenko argues that Kutuzov preferred field service but remained as a staff officer out of his deference for his father, who served at the headquarters, and that once his father left the army, Kutuzov asked for a transfer; *Kutuzov*, 101.

65. *The Journal of the War College*, October 26/November 6, 1770; List of Officers Submitted for Promotion for the 1771 Campaign, in *M. I. Kutuzov. Sbornik dokumentov*, I:11–12.

66. For details see G. Grebenshikova, "Rossiiskie voenno-morskie sily v Egeiskom more v 1770–1774 gg.," *Voprosy istorii* 2 (2007): 117–129; A. Lebedev, "Strategicheskii i takticheskii obzor deyatel'nosti russkogo flota v Russko-Turetskoi voine 1768–1774 godov," *Gangut* 49 (2008): 16–30; 50 (2008): 40–70; 51 (2008): 32–58; 52 (2009): 32–48; 53 (2009): 51–54; Eugene Tarle, *Chesmenskii boi i pervaya russkaya ekspeditsiya v Arkhipelag* (Moscow: Soviet Academy of Sciences, 1945); Cengiz Fedakar, "Mora İsyanı," in *Abdülkadir Özcan'a Armagan* (Istanbul: Kronik Kitap, 2018), 587–604; Cengiz Fedakar, "Limni Müdafaası (1770)," *History Studies* 11, no. 5 (2019): 1563–1564; İsipek Ali Rıza and Aydemir Oğuz, *1770 Çeşme Deniz Savaşı: 1768–1774 Osmanlı-Rus Savaşları* (Istanbul: Denizler Kitabevi, 2006).

67. Davies, *The Russo-Turkish War*, 166.

68. To the west of the main army stood the so-called Wallachian Corps (under Général-en-chef Olitz, then N. Repnin), protecting the Russian right flank and covering Bucharest. Major General Otto-Adolf Weissman and the Third Division were east of the Prut River forming the left wing.

69. Saint-Priest to Duc d'Aiguillon, November 4, 1771, in *Documente privitóre la istoria românilor* (Bucharest: Romanian Ministry of Culture, 1886), I, supp. I, 854.

70. In Russian historiography, this engagement is known as the Battle of Popaşti/Popashty.

71. Sinel'nikov, *Zhizn', voennye i politicheskie deyaniya*, I:26.

72. Davies, *The Russo-Turkish War*, 170.

73. Sinel'nikov, *Zhizn', voennye i politicheskie deyaniya*, I:29.

74. Kutuzov's promotion was confirmed on December 8/19, 1771. "Formulyarnyi spisok," January 23, 1791, RGVIA, f. VUA, d. 2892, l. 75b;

"Iz spiska o prosyasikh za otlichnye postupki nagrazhdeniya voennymi ordenami," November 24/December 5, 1775, in A. Vlakovich and A. Kapitonov, eds., *Fel'dmarshal Kutuzov: Dokumenty, dnevniki, vospominaniya* (Moscow: Arkheograficheskii Tsentr, 1995), 20-21.

75. Cited in Andrei Petrov, "K biografii svetleishego knyazya Golenischeva-Kutuzova-Smolenskogo," *Voennyi sbornik* 3 (1900): 5.

Chapter 3

1. Filip Sinel'nikov, *Zhizn', voennye i politicheskie deyaniya Ego Svetlosti General-Fel'dmarshala Knyazya Mikhaila Larionovicha Golenischeva-Kutuzova-Smolenskago* (St. Petersburg, 1813), VI:15, 18.

2. It must be noted, however, that Rumyantsev did not bear the grudge for long and made no effort to hamper Kutuzov's career in the future.

3. Alan W. Fisher, *The Crimean Tatars* (Stanford, CA: Hoover Institution Press, 1978), 45-57; Baron Joseph von Hammer, *Geschichte des Osmanischen Reiches* (Pest: Hartleben, 1832), 8:386-390.

4. Sinel'nikov, *Zhizn', voennye i politicheskie deyaniya*, I:30-31.

5. Dolgorukov to Empress Catherine II, July 28/August 8, 1774, in *Chteniya v imperatorskom obschestve istorii i dvenostei rossiiskikh* [hereafter cited as CIOIDR], 1872, book 2, part II, 23; Dolgorukov's nomination of Kutuzov for the Order of St. George, November 24/December 5, 1775, in *M. I. Kutuzov. Sbornik dokumentov* (Moscow: Voeniszdat, 1950), I:17; Sinel'nikov, *Zhizn', voennye i politicheskie deyaniya*, I:31-32.

6. For details, see Alexander Andreyev, *Knyaz' Vasilii Mikhailovich Dolgorukov-Krymskii. Dokumental'noe zhizneopisanie. Istoricheskaya khronika XVIII veka* (Moscow: Mezh. Tsentr Otrasllevoi Informatiki Gosatomnadzora Rossii, 1997)

7. Dolgorukov to Empress Catherine II, July 28/August 8, 1774, in CIOIDR, 1872, book 2, part II, 22; Jacobi to Musin-Pushkin, July 27/August 7, 1774, in Alexander Prozorovskii, *Zapiski general-fel'dmarshala knyazya A. A. Prozorovskogo (1756–1776)* (Moscow: Rossiiskii Arkhiv, 2004), 597.

8. Dolgorukov to Empress Catherine II, July 28/August 8, 1774, CIOIDR, 1872, book 2, part II, 22.

9. Dolgorukov to Empress Catherine II, July 28/August 8, 1774, CIOIDR, 1872, book 2, part II, 22; Jacobi to Musin-Pushkin, July 27/August 7, 1774, in Prozorovskii, *Zapiski general-fel'dmarshala knyazya A. A. Prozorovskogo*, 597. See also results of the Ukrainian archeological excavations at the battlefield in V. Gerasimov and V. Tkachenko, "Razvedki v raione 'polya Shumskogo srazheniya 1774 goda' na teritorii Izobil'ninskogo sel'soveta Alushtinskogo gorsoveta," in *Terra Alustiana MMXI* (Simferopol, 2015), 200-232.

10. Plan of Attack Against the Turkish Troops Disembarked Near the Village of Alushta, July 24/August 4, 1774, RGVIA, f. 464, op. 1, d. 39, ll. 1-2.

11. Dolgorukov to Empress Catherine II, July 28/August 8, 1774, CIOIDR, 1872, book 2, part II, 22. Parkinson is mistaken when he dates this battle to 1773.

12. Jacobi to Musin-Pushkin, July 27/August 7, 1774, in Prozorovskii, *Zapiski general-fel'dmarshala knyazya A. A. Prozorovskogo*, 597.

13. Dolgorukov to Empress Catherine II, July 28/August 8, 1774, CIOIDR, 1872, book 2, part II, 22; Dolgorukov's nomination of Kutuzov for the Order of St. George, November 24/December 5, 1775, in *M. I. Kutuzov. Sbornik dokumentov*, I:17; Jacobi to Musin-Pushkin, July 27/August 7, 1774, in Prozorovskii, *Zapiski general-fel'dmarshala knyazya A. A. Prozorovskogo*, 599.

14. Jacobi to Musin-Pushkin, July 27/August 7, 1774, in Prozorovskii, *Zapiski general-fel'dmarshala knyazya A. A. Prozorovskogo*, 597; Sergei Glinka, *Ruskie anekdoty voennye, grazhdanskie i istoricheskie* (Moscow: University Tip., 1820), III:70–71. Parkinson falsely claims that the fighting was "amidst the ruins of Alushta" and, that upon seeing his men wavering, "Kutuzov seized the regimental standard and led the troops forward." Roger Parkinson, *The Fox of the North: The Life of Kutuzov, General of War and Peace* (New York: D. McKay, 1976), 17.

15. Dolgorukov to Empress Catherine II, July 28/August 8, 1774, CIOIDR, 1872, book 2, part II, 23; Sinel'nikov, *Zhizn', voennye i politicheskie deyaniya*, I:33, VI:23; *Anekdoty ili dostopamyatnye skazaniya ob ego svetlosti general-fel'dmarshale knyaze Mikhaile Illarionoviche Golenischeve-Kutuzove Smolenskom, nachinaya s pervykh let ego sluzhby do konchiny, s priobsheniem nekotoryh ego pisem, dostopamyatnyh ego rechei i prikazov* (St. Petersburg, 1814), I:6.

16. Glinka, *Ruskie anekdoty voennye, grazhdanskie i istoricheskie*, 71. In the 1830s a special fountain was built near the spot where Kutuzov was wounded to commemorate this incident. It was redesigned and expanded by the Soviet authorities in the 1950s. The memorial plate repeated the old myth of Kutuzov charging "at the head of the battalion, with a flag in hand." See Viktor Tkachenko and Alena Tkachenko, "Fontan Kutuzova. Istoriya mifa," http://wars175x.narod.ru/bgr_ktz5.html.

17. Archeological excavations by Ukrainian scholars produced many lead balls dating to the eighteenth century. These projectiles came in two calibers: 11–14 mm wide (weighing up to 17 grams) and 18 mm wide (weighing up to 35 grams). Gerasimov and Tkachenko, "Razvedki v raione 'polya Shumskogo srazheniya 1774 goda'," 202. Recently a group of medical experts who examined documents relating to Kutuzov's injury suggested that the projectile was fired from "a small-caliber hunting-type rifle"; however, such a weapon was not used in battle and no rifle bullets have been found on the battlefield. Sergiu Kushchayev, Evgenii Belykh, Yakiv Fishchenko, et al., "Two Bullets to the Head and an Early Winter: Fate Permits Kutuzov to Defeat Napoleon at Moscow," *Neurosurgical Focus* 39, no. 1 (2015), https://thejns.org/focus/view/journals/neurosurg-focus/39/1/article-pE3.xml.

18. For an interesting discussion of Kutuzov's injury, see A. Mefodovskii, "O raneniyakh M. I. Kutuzova," in *M. I. Golenischev-Kutuzov. Materialy nauchnoi konferentsii posvyaschennoi pamyati polkovodtsa* (St. Petersburg, 1993), 44–47; Mikhail Tyurin, "Pobeditel' frantsii. O raneniyakh M. I. Kutuzova," in *Kalashnikov. Oruzhie, boepripasy, snaryazhenie* 3 (2001): 66–68.

19. George James Guthrie, *Commentaries on the Surgery of the War in Portugal, Spain, France, and the Netherlands* (London: Henry Renshaw, 1855), 298. A similar observation was made by George Macleod, surgeon to the General Hospital at Sebastopol during the Crimean War. "Of all the accidents met with in field practice," he wrote, gunshots of the head "are, beyond doubt, the most serious, both directly and remotely, the most confusing in their manifestations, and least determined in their treatment." Macleod goes on to note that during the last year of the Crimean War there were sixty-seven cases of "wounds penetrating the cranium," and all led to fatal results: "Of 19 cases in which the skull was perforated, all died." *Notes on the Surgery of the War in the Crimea* (London: John Churchill, 1858), 175.

20. Guthrie, *Commentaries on the Surgery of the War,* 303.

21. Guthrie, *Commentaries on the Surgery of the War,* 303, 369–373; for a possible course of treatment that the physicians might have followed, see 304–309. For a quick overview of medical knowledge on head trauma, see F. A. Mettler and C. C. Mettler, "Historic Development of Knowledge Relating to Cranial Trauma," *Research Publications of Association for Research in Nervous and Mental Disease* 24 (1945): 1–47.

22. Sergei Glinka, *Korpusnye vospominaniya. Iz zapisok S. N. Glinki* (St. Petersburg: n.p., 1845), 25. Parkinson mistakenly claims that Kutuzov's father had "died during his absence"; in fact, Illarion Golenischev-Kutuzov died in 1784, ten years after Kutuzov's first injury. Parkinson also claims that Kutuzov lived with his uncle "I. N. Golenischev," but Kutuzov did not have a relative by that name. His uncle was Ivan Matveevich Golenischev-Kutuzov. Parkinson, *The Fox of the North,* 20.

23. Sinel'nikov, *Zhizn', voennye i politicheskie deyaniya,* VI:24.

24. P. Zavadovskii to A. Olsufiev, August 16/27, 1775, in *Arkhiv knyazya Vorontsova* (Moscow: M. Katkov, 1882), XXVI:9.

25. See the nomination documents in *M. I. Kutuzov. Sbornik dokumentov,* I:16–17. The Order of St. George was formally created in December 1769. See V. Shabanov, *Voennyi orden svyatogo velikomuchenika i pobedonostsa Georgiya* (Moscow: Russkii Mir, 2004).

26. Général-en-chef Gregory Potemkin's order of October 3/14, 1775; Catherine's decree to the War College, November 26/December 7, 1775, in *M. I. Kutuzov: Sbornik dokumentov,* I:14–15, 18.

27. Several nineteenth-century biographical dictionaries claimed that Kutuzov studied at the University of Strasbourg, where he "learned the French and German languages" and "acquired extensive knowledge in mathematics."

Alphone Rabbe, Claude Augustin Vieilh de Boisjolin, and Charles Claude Binet de Sainte Preuve, eds., *Biographie universelle et portative des contemporains* (Paris: Levrault, 1834), II:2250; Louis Gabriel Michaud, ed., *Biographie universelle ancienne et modern* (Paris: Delagrave, 1842), XXII:172; Marie Ludovic Lalanne, L. Renier, et al., eds., *Biographie portative universelle* (Paris: Garnier Frères, 1851), 849; Hugh James Rose, ed., *A New General Biographical Dictionary* (London: B. Fellowes, 1853), IX:143.

28. *Anekdoty ili dostopamyatnye skazaniya*, I:8; Alexander Langeron, "Zapiski grafa Lanzherona. Voina s Turtsiei 1806–1812 gg.," in *Russkaya starina* 9 (1907): 571.

29. "The memory is very often much impaired," one British surgeon noted while describing the impact of gunshot injuries to the head. "It is frequently defective as to things as well as to persons. The sign of one or both eyes may be impaired, or even lost. Ptosis or a falling of the upper lid, is not an uncommon, although a more curable defect. Speech is not only difficult but the power of uttering certain words is often lost; a language is occasionally for a time forgotten. . . . The more serious evils which befall these unfortunate sufferers are aberrations of mind, rendering some degree of restraint necessary, or a state of fatuity, which is not less distressing. These intellectual defects are often accompanied by various states of lameness or debility, from which there is but a little hope of recovery." Kutuzov was spared the worst of these effects. Guthrie, *Commentaries on the Surgery of the War*, 382.

30. Probably one of the most famous examples of personality changes as a result of a brain injury was that of Phineas Gage, a twenty-five-year-old construction foreman for a railroad company who, during a construction, prematurely denotated a charge that sent an iron rod through his skull. Gage survived the incident, but his personality transformed. Previously a well-mannered, respectable, and intelligent man, Gage reportedly became irresponsible, rude, careless, and aggressive. John Fleischman, *Phineas Gage: A Gruesome but True Story About Brain Science* (New York: Houghton Mifflin, 2002). Also see the case of photographer Edward Muybridge, who suffered brain damage in a stagecoach accident that changed his behavior and artistic expression. Sunil Manjila, Gagandeep Singh, Ayham Alkhachroum, and Ciro Ramos-Estebanez, "Understanding Edward Muybridge: Historical Review of Behavioral Alterations After a 19th-Century Head Injury and Their Multifactorial Influence on Human Life and Culture," *Neurosurgical Focus* 39, no. 1 (2015), https://thejns.org/focus/view/journals/neurosurg-focus/39/1/article-pE4.xml.

31. Sinel'nikov, *Zhizn', voennye i politicheskie deyaniya*, VI:28.

32. *Anekdoty ili Dostopamyatnye skazaniya*, I:83; V. Suvorov, *Svetleishii fel'dmarshal Mikhail Illarionovich Golenischev-Kutuzov i ego sovremenniki* (Moscow: I. Sytin, 1888), 17; Lidia Ivchenko, *Kutuzov* (Moscow: Molodaya Gvardiya, 2012), 105.

33. *Derby Mercury*, Friday, August 19, 1774, 2.

34. Roderic H. Davison, "Russian Skill and Turkish Imbecility: The Treaty of Kuchuk Kainardji Reconsidered," *Slavic Review* 3, no. 35 (1976): 364–483; Roderic H. Davison, "Treaty of Kuchuk Kainardji: A Note on Its Italian Text," *International History Review* 10 (1988): 611–620; Suraiya N. Faroqhi, ed., *The Cambridge History of Turkey*, volume 3, *The Later Ottoman Empire, 1603–1839* (Cambridge: Cambridge University Press, 2006), 57–58, 111–112.

35. See John T. Alexander, *Autocratic Politics in a National Crisis: The Imperial Russian Government and Pugachev's Revolt* (Bloomington: Indiana University Press, 1969).

36. Simon Sebag Montefiore, *Prince of Princes: The Life of Potemkin* (London: Weidenfeld & Nicolson, 2001), 111–114.

37. War College's order of April 3/14, 1777; War College's journal entry of April 28/May 9, 1777; Catherine's decree of June 28/July 9, 1777; War College's order of July 10/21, in *M. I. Kutuzov. Sbornik dokumentov*, I:18–19.

38. Sinel'nikov, *Zhizn', voennye i politicheskie deyaniya*, VI:25.

39. Sergei Mayevskii, "Moi vek ili istoriya Sergeya Ivanovicha Mayevskogo, 1779–1848," in *Russkaya starina* 8 (1873): 153.

40. Alexander Langeron, "Zapiski grafa Lanzherona. Voina s Turtsiei 1806–1812 gg.," *Russkaya starina* 9 (1907): 569–571.

41. Entry for April 27/May 8 in marriage records of St. Isaac of Dalmatia Church, Central State Historical Archive of Russia (hereafter cited as TSGIA), f. 19, op. 111, d. 84, l. 15. Also see Yu. Gulyaev and V. Soglaev, *Fel'dmarshal Kutuzov. Istoriko-biograficheskii ocherk* (Moscow: Arkheograficheskii Tsentr, 1995), 73–74; Ivchenko, *Kutuzov*, 114–115; Troitskii, *Fel'dmarshal Kutuzov*, 61–62; "Arkhiv knyazya M. I. Golenischeva-Kutuzova-Smolenskogo," in *Russkaya starina* 11 (1870): 499. Kutuzov was sent on a mission to St. Petersburg in March 1778, and he seems to have taken advantage of it to marry. He was later denied pay for six months during which he was gone. In 1779 he had to solicit the support of Lieutenant General V. Chertkov, the chef of the Luganskii Pikineer Regiment, and the all-powerful Gregory Potemkin to receive his back pay. See Chertkov to Potemkin, August 2/13, 1779, in *M. I. Kutuzov: Sbornik dokumentov*, I:20–21.

42. Kutuzov to V. Popov, September 1/12, 1784, in *M. I. Kutuzov: Sbornik dokumentov*, I:25.

43. Catherine Golenischeva-Kutuzova to Aleksey Kutuzov, January 6/17, 1791, in *M. I. Kutuzov: Sbornik dokumentov*, 76–77.

44. The regiment was deployed on the defensive line along the Dnieper River in the Novorossiya Governorate.

45. Cited in Fisher, *The Crimean Tatars*, 62.

46. See Alan W. Fisher, *The Russian Annexation of the Crimea, 1772–1783* (Cambridge: Cambridge University Press, 1970). On the Ottoman perspectives on Şahin Giray, who was ultimately executed on the sultan's orders, see Feridun M. Emecen, "Son Kırım Hânı Şahin Giray'ın İdamı Mes'elesi

ve Buna Dâir Vesikalar," *Tarih Dergisi* 34 (1984): 315–346; Cengiz Fedakar, "Son Kırım Hanı Şahin Giray'ın Muhallefatına Dair," in *İslam öncesinden çağdaş türk dünyasına Prof. Dr. Gülçin Çandarlıoğlu'na armağan* (İstanbul: Türk Dünyası Araştırmaları Vakfı, 2015), 385–408.

47. Sinel'nikov, *Zhizn', voennye i politicheskie deyaniya*, I:36–37.

48. Parkinson, *The Fox of the North*, 22–23. Also see Pavel Zhilin, *Kutuzov. Zhizn' i polkovodcheskaya deyatel'nost'* (Moscow: Voennoe Izdatel'stvo, 1978), 25; Mikhail Bragin, *Kutuzov* (Moscow: Molodaya Gvardiya, 1970), 39–40.

49. For an interesting discussion, see Gulyaev and Soglaev, *Fel'dmarshal Kutuzov*, 86–89.

50. See, for example, Bragin, *Kutuzov*, 40–41.

51. De Balmain to Gregory Potemkin, July 30/August 10, 1782, in *M. I. Kutuzov: Sbornik dokumentov*, I:24. Kutuzov was promoted to brigadier on June 28/July 9, 1782. See Catherine's decree in *M. I. Kutuzov: Sbornik dokumentov*, 23.

52. In 1783, Potemkin ordered restructuring of the pikineer regiments, and the Luganskii and Poltavskii Pikineers Regiments were merged to form the Mariupolskii Light Horse Regiment, which Kutuzov continued to command. See Kutuzov's receipt of delivery to Brigadier A. Levanidov, commander of the Poltavskii Pikineer Regiment, July 20/31, 1783, in *M. I. Kutuzov: Sbornik dokumentov*, I:24.

53. Catherine's decree of November 24/December 5, 1784, in *M. I. Kutuzov: Sbornik dokumentov*, I:26.

54. Potemkin to Kutuzov, May 23/June 3, 1785, in *M. I. Kutuzov: Sbornik dokumentov*, V:602–603. Kutuzov was first assigned to the 4th Military Division in July 1785 and then reassigned to the 3rd Military Division in September, remaining under Potemkin's overall command.

55. "Pered grobnitseyu svyatoi," in Alexander Pushkin, *Sobranie sochinenii. Stikhotvoreniya, 1823–1836* (Moscow: Gos. Izd. Khud. Lit., 1959), II:337.

Chapter 4

1. Potemkin to Kutuzov, May 23/June 3, 1785, in *M. I. Kutuzov. Sbornik dokumentov* (Moscow: Voeniszdat, 1950), V:602.

2. Potemkin to Kutuzov, May 23/June 3, 1785, in *M. I. Kutuzov. Sbornik dokumentov*, V:602.

3. By mid-July 1786, the Bug Jäger Corps had 3,949 men, the 1st Battalion 988 men, the 2nd Battalion 994 men, the 3rd Battalion 989 men, and the 4th Battalion 948 men. *M. I. Kutuzov. Sbornik dokumentov*, V:603.

4. Mikhail Kutuzov, *Primechaniya o pekhotnoi sluzhbe voobsche i o egerskoi osobenno* (Moscow: Voennoe Izdatel'stvo Ministerstva Oborony Soyuza SSR, 1955).

5. See Christy Pichichero, *The Military Enlightenment: War and Culture in the French Empire from Louis XIV to Napoleon* (Ithaca, NY: Cornell University Press, 2017). On the Military Enlightenment in Russia, see Eugene Miakinkov,

War and Enlightenment in Russia: Military Culture in the Age of Catherine II (Toronto: University of Toronto Press, 2020).

6. Cited in Kutuzov, *Primechaniya o pekhotnoi sluzhbe voobsche i o egerskoi osobenno*, 25.

7. Cited in Kutuzov, *Primechaniya o pekhotnoi sluzhbe voobsche i o egerskoi osobenno*, 26.

8. In the surviving copy of Kutuzov's treatise, a step is described as ¾ of an *arshin* (1.75 ft./0.5325 m). But it was probably closer to 1 arshin (2.3 ft./0.7 m), as it was defined in other contemporary regulations.

9. Kutuzov wanted his officers to be fully trained as well. "Not every officer is well informed of particular elements of the jäger training," he observed before specifying that such officers should receive appropriate guidance as well.

10. All citations are based on Kutuzov, *Primechaniya o pekhotnoi sluzhbe voobsche i o egerskoi osobenno* (1955). For a concise summary in English, see Alexander Zhmodikov and Yurii Zhmodikov, *Tactics of the Russian Army in the Napoleonic Wars* (West Chester, OH: Nafziger Collection, 2003), I:14–18.

11. For an interesting discussion of the Russian Military Enlightenment and its efforts to disseminate information, see Miakinkov, *War and Enlightenment in Russia* (2020). For comparison, on the knowledge of mobility in the British army, see Huw J. Davies, "Military Print Culture, Knowledge and Terrain: Knowledge Mobility and Eighteenth-Century Military Colonialism," in *Empire and Mobility in the Long Nineteenth Century,* edited by David Lambert and Peter Merriman (Manchester: Manchester University Press, 2020).

12. For example, Capitaine Grandmaison, *La petite guerre ou traite du service des troupes legeres en campagne* (Frankfurt: Knoch & Esslinger, 1758); George Sutton, *Standing Orders and Instructions to the Nottinghamshire Regiment of Marksmen* (Hull: J. Rawson, 1778); William Windham and George Townshend, *A Plan of Discipline for the Use of the Norfolk Militia* (London: J. Millan, 1768); Frederick the Great of Prussia, "Instruction für die Freiregimenter oder leichten Infanterie-Regimenter," in *Œuvres de Frédéric le Grand,* Digitale Ausgabe der Universitätsbibliothek Trier, http://friedrich.uni-trier.de/de/oeuvres/30/431.

13. *Traité sur la constitution des troupes légères, et sur leur emploi à la guerre* (Paris: Nyon, 1782), 3.

14. "Nachertanie o polevoi egerskoi sluzhbe," *Voennyi zhurnal* 9 (1810): 15. The periodical refers to the "Kutuzovian jäger maneuvers" without any explanation, implying that the term was already sufficiently well known.

15. Gregory Potemkin to Kutuzov, January 21/February 1, 1786; Lieutenant General Kh. Geikin to Gregory Potemkin, June 13/24 1786, in *M. I. Kutuzov. Sbornik dokumentov*, V:603–605; Kutuzov to Colonel A. Voevodskii, February 10/21, 1786, in *M. I. Kutuzov. Sbornik dokumentov*, I:29.

16. Entry for April 30/May 11, 1787, in *Kamer-fur'erskii tseremonial'nyi zhurnal 1787 goda* (St. Petersburg, 1886), 354.

17. Louis-Philippe de Ségur, *Mémoires, souvenirs et anecdotes* (Paris: Didot, 1859), II:42–43.

18. Catherine's letters to N. Saltykov and P. Eropkin are cited in V. Lopatin, *Potemkin i Suvorov* (Moscow: Nauka, 1992), 103. Also see V. Lopatin, *Svetleishii knyaz' Potemkin* (Moscow: Olma Press, 2005), 100.

19. Entry for July 8/19, 1787, *Kamer-fur'erskii tseremonial'nyi zhurnal 1787 goda*, 532–533.

20. *Anekdoty ili dostopamyatnye skazaniya ob ego svetlosti general-fel'dmarshale knyaze Mikhaile Illarionoviche Golenischeve-Kutuzove Smolenskom, nachinaya s pervykh let ego sluzhby do konchiny, s priobsheniem nekotoryh ego pisem, dostopamyatnyh ego rechei i prikazov* (St. Petersburg, 1814), I:51–52.

21. See Hugh Ragsdale, "Evaluating the Traditions of Russian Aggression: Catherine II and the Greek Project," *Slavonic and East European Review* 66, no. 1 (1988): 91–117; Virginia H. Aksan, *Ottoman Wars, 1700–1870: An Empire Besieged* (New York: Pearson, 2007), 160–161.

22. Kutuzov's Orders to the Bug Jäger Corps, August 1/12, 1787; Kutuzov to Général-en-chef Yu. Dolgorukov, August 12/23, 1787, in *M. I. Kutuzov. Sbornik dokumentov*, I:31; V:605.

23. Kutuzov to Potemkin, August 28/September 8, 1787; Kutuzov to Potemkin, September 2/13, 1787; Kutuzov to Yu. Dolgorukov, September 5/16, 1787, in *M. I. Kutuzov. Sbornik dokumentov*, I:36–40.

24. Potemkin to Yuri Dolgorukov, September 15/26, 1787; Dolgorukov to Potemkin, September 16/27, 1787; Kutuzov to Colonel I. Neplyuev, September 18/29, 1787; Dolgorukov to Potemkin, September 27/October 8, 1787; Suvorov to Potemkin, September 29/October 10, 1787, in *M. I. Kutuzov. Sbornik dokumentov*, I:42–44.

25. Suvorov's autobiography, in *A. V. Suvorov. Sbornik dokumentov*, edited by G. Mescheryakov (Moscow: Voennoe Izdatel'stvo, 1949), I:47. Also see Suvorov's correspondence with Potemkin in *A. V. Suvorov. Sbornik dokumentov*, II:307–344. For the Turkish perspective on Kilburun, see Cengiz Fedakar, "1787–1792 Osmanli-Rus harplerinde Kilburun, Özi Nehri ve Hocabey muharebeleri," in Proceedings of the Symposium "Uluslararası Türkiye-Ukrayna İlişkileri Kazak Dönemi (1500–1800)," Sakarya University, November 3–5, 2014, 120–126.

26. Kutuzov to Potemkin, February 19/March 1, 1788, in *M. I. Kutuzov. Sbornik dokumentov*, I:57. Also see a similar report dated March 12/23, 1788, in *M. I. Kutuzov. Sbornik dokumentov*, 59.

27. See reports by Kutuzov, Suvorov, and Dolgorukov from November 1787 to June 1788 in *M. I. Kutuzov. Sbornik dokumentov*, I:45–67.

28. Kutuzov's order to the Bug Jäger Corps, May 4/15, 1788, in *M. I. Kutuzov. Sbornik dokumentov*, I:65.

29. Kutuzov's order to the Bug Jäger Corps, February 19/March 1 and March 14/25, 1788, in *M. I. Kutuzov. Sbornik dokumentov*, I:57, 59–61.

30. Kutuzov's order to the Bug Jäger Corps, February 19/March 1 and May 5/16, 1788, in *M. I. Kutuzov. Sbornik dokumentov*, I:57, 66.

31. Potemkin to Général-en-chef Ivan Möller, May 21/June 1–May 24/June 4; Kutuzov to Potemkin, May 24/June 4–May 30/June 11, 1788, in *M. I. Kutuzov. Sbornik dokumentov*, I:68–71. Also see Galina Grebenschikova, *Chernomorskii flot v period pravlenya Ekateriny II* (St. Petersburg: Ostrov, 2012), II, chaps. 2 and 3; A. Lebedev, *"Esli zavtra voina . . ." O nekotorykh osobennostyakh sostoyaniya russkogo korabel'nogo flota v konfliktakh XVIII–pervoi poloviny XIX vv.* (St. Petersburg: Gangut, 2018).

32. General Fanshawe to General Conway, in Samuel Bentham, "Notes on the Naval Encounters of the Russians and Turks in 1788," in *The United Service Journal and Naval and Military Magazine*, 1829, part II, 335.

33. Prince de Ligne to Emperor Joseph, July 19, 1788, in *The Prince de Ligne: His Memoirs, Letters, and Miscellaneous Papers,* edited by Katharine Prescott Wormeley (Boston: Hardy, Pratt, 1902), II:78.

34. Roman Tsebrikov, "Vokrug Ochakova, 1788 god," *Russkaya starina* 9 (1895): 170. Prince de Ligne complained that, "owing to sickness, which prevails and inceases, we have only about 10,000 effective infantry, who are melting away under the filthiness of this camp," but he also observed that "as for the soldier himself, he is always a model of punctuality, cleanliness, patience, obedience, good-will, and good service, though no one takes care of him. I have never yet seen a drunken soldier, or a quarrelsome, argumentative, or negligent one. No one ever drills either the infantry or the light-horse. There is no forming in line; no standing motionless; but they keep their distances well. They march by fours in these vast plains; and the columns find means to intersect one another to enter camp." Prince de Ligne to Emperor Joseph, July 19, 1788, in *The Prince de Ligne: His Memoirs, Letters, and Miscellaneous Papers*, II:75–76.

35. Suvorov to Potemkin, July 28/August 8, 1788, in *A. V. Suvorov. Sbornik dokumentov*, II:434–435; Potemkin to Suvorov, July 27/August 8, 1788, in "Knyaz' Grigorii Aleksandrovich Potemkin-Tavricheskii, 1739–1791. Biograficheskii ocherk. Gl. VI. Ochakov i Suvorov," *Russkaya starina*, May 1875, 38. Also see Simon Sebag Montefiore, *Potemkin: Catherine the Great's Imperial Partner* (New York: Vintage Books, 2005), 404–406.

36. Prince de Ligne to Emperor Joseph, August 1788, in *Lettres et pensées du Maréchal Prince de Ligne*, 2nd ed. (Paris: J. J. Paschoud, 1809), 113–114.

37. Filip Sinel'nikov, *Zhizn', voennye i politicheskie deyaniya Ego Svetlosti General-Fel'dmarshala Knyazya Mikhaila Larionovicha Golenischeva-Kutuzova-Smolenskago* (St. Petersburg, 1813), I:50–51; Roger Parkinson, *The Fox of the North: The Life of Kutuzov, General of War and Peace* (New York: D. McKay, 1976), 26.

38. Potemkin informed the empress of Kutuzov's injury in a letter of September 3. Eight days later Catherine II asked Potemkin, "Write me how is Kutuzov and how was he wounded? And make sure to have someone see him regularly on my behalf." On September 29, she reminded Potemkin once more, "Have someone visit him regularly on my behalf, and report on how Major General

Kutuzov is doing. I am very sorry about his wound." More than a month later, on November 7, the empress again asked Potemkin to provide an update on "how General Kutuzov is doing." V. Lopatin, ed., *Ekaterina II i G. A. Potemkin. Lichnaya perepiska (1769–1771)* (Moscow: Nauka, 1997), http://az.lib.ru/e/ekaterina_w/text_0030.shtml; Potemkin to Catherine II, August 22/September 3, 1788, in *M. I. Kutuzov. Sbornik dokumentov*, I:75.

39. Massot's report and Potemkin to Catherine II, September 15/26, 1788, Arkhiv vneshnei politiki Rossiiskoi Imperii, f. 2, op. 2/8a, d. 21, ll. 97–98, printed in Lopatin, ed., *Ekaterina II i G. A. Potemkin*, http://az.lib.ru/e/ekaterina_w/text_0030.shtml. The nature of Kutuzov's injury was clearly known to some contemporaries because one of the earliest of the Kutuzov biographies, published just months after his death in 1813, noted that he was shot through the cheek. *Zhizn' i voennye dejania general-fel'dmarshala svetleishego knyazya Mikhaila Larionovicha Golenishcheva-Kutuzova Smolenskogo* (St. Petersburg, 1813), I:20. The same description is also given in V. Suvorov, *Svetleishii knjaz' Smolenskii, fel'dmarshal Mikhail Illarionovich Golenishchev-Kutuzov i ego sovremenniki: istoricheskii ocherk zhizni polkovodtsa i ego epokhi* (Moscow: I. D. Sytin, 1896), 47.

40. Prince de Ligne to Emperor Joseph, August 1788, in *Lettres et pensées du Maréchal Prince de Ligne*, 114. Kutuzov also made it to the pages of *Mercure de France*, which reported that "General Kutusof" was wounded during the fighting at Ochakov. *Mercure de France,* October 1788, 149.

41. Catherine II to Gregory Potemkin, September 18/29, 1788, *Russkaya starina* 8 (1876): 584; Nikolai Polevoi, *Russkie Polkovodtsy, ili zhizn' i podvigi Rossiiskikh polkovodtsev ot vremen Imperatora Petra Velikago to czarstvovaniya Imperatora Nikolaya I* (St. Petersburg: K. Zhernakov, 1845), 203; *Anekdoty ili dostopamyatnye skazaniya*, I:12–13. The type of injury Kutuzov suffered was quite common, and the sketches and drawings of the British and French physicians make it abundantly clear. See, for example, British physician John Thomson's line drawings in Michael Crumplin and Gather Glover, *Waterloo: After the Glory— Hospital Sketches and Reports on the Wounded After the Battle* (Warwick: Helion & Company, 2019), esp. 142–149.

42. A. Petrov, *Vtoraya turetskaya voina v tsarstvovanie Ekateriny II. 1787–1791* (St. Petersburg, 1880), I:202–203. For a Turkish view, see Fedakar, "1787–1792 Osmanli-Rus harplerinde Kilburun, Özi Nehri ve Hocabey muharebeleri," 127–129.

43. Potemkin to Kutuzov, January 21/February 1, 1789; Potemkin to Ivan Möller, January 21/February 1, 1789, in *M. I. Kutuzov. Sbornik dokumentov*, I:76. The five regiments were the Ekaterinoslavskii Grenadier Regiment, the Aleksandriiskii and Khersonskii Light Horse Regiments, and the Ol'viopolskii and Voronezhskii Hussar Regiments. See Potemkin's order of February 1 on winter quartering in *M. I. Kutuzov. Sbornik dokumentov*, I:77.

44. See Kutuzov's reports in *M. I. Kutuzov. Sbornik dokumentov*, I:78–83.

45. Kutuzov to Ivan Möller, April 7/18, 1789, in *M. I. Kutuzov. Sbornik dokumentov*, I:84.

46. Potemkin to Kutuzov, April 21/May 1 and June 11/22, 1789, in *M. I. Kutuzov. Sbornik dokumentov*, I:85, 89. Parkinson incorrectly claims Kutuzov received the Order of St. Vladimir for the Poltava maneuvers. *The Fox of the North*, 25.

47. Potemkin to Kutuzov, April 9/20, 1789; Kutuzov to Potemkin, April 24/May 5, 1789; Kutuzov to Potemkin, May 14/25, 1789, in *M. I. Kutuzov. Sbornik dokumentov*, I:85–87; entry for June 4/15, 1789, in *Zhurnal voennykh deistvii Soedinennoi armii* [Journal of Military Operations of the Combined Army], in N. Dubrovin, ed., *Bumagi knyazya Grigoriya Aleksandrovicha Potemkina-Tavricheskogo, 1788–1789 gg.* [hereafter cited as *The Potemkin Papers 1788–1789*] (St. Petersburg: Voen.-ucheb. Komitet glavn. Shtaba, 1894), 184.

48. Journal of Military Operations of the Combined Army, in *The Potemkin Papers 1788–1789*, 187.

49. Gregory Potemkin to Lieutenant General Pavel Potemkin, September 10/21, 1789, in *The Potemkin Papers 1788–1789*, 272.

50. *Formulyarnyi spisok . . .* , January 23, 1791, RGVIA, f. VUA, d. 2892, ll. 76–76b. Also see Yu. Gulyaev and V. Soglaev, *Fel'dmarshal Kutuzov. Istoriko-biograficheskii ocherk* (Moscow: Arkheograficheskii Tsentr, 1995), 108–109; Petrov, *Vtoraya turetskaya voina*, II:76–88.

Chapter 5

1. Potemkin to Empress Catherine II, June 19/30, 1790, in V. Lopatin, ed., *Ekaterina II i G. A. Potemkin. Lichnaya perepiska (1769–1771)* (Moscow: Nauka, 1997), http://az.lib.ru/e/ekaterina_w/text_0030.shtml; Modest Bogdanovich, *Pokhody Rumyantseva, Potemkina i Suvorova v Turtsii* (St. Petersburg: E. Weymar, 1852), 211; Alexander Petrushevskii, *Generalisimus Knyaz Suvorov* (St. Petersburg: M. Stasulevich, 1884), I:370–371.

2. Potemkin to Kutuzov, April 9/20, 1790, in *M. I. Kutuzov. Sbornik dokumentov* (Moscow: Voeniszdat, 1950), I:91–92.

3. Kutuzov to Ivan Möller, May 2/13, 1790; Kutuzov to Potemkin, July 12/23, 1790, in *M. I. Kutuzov. Sbornik dokumentov*, I:93, 96–97. Also see Kutuzov's other reports in *M. I. Kutuzov. Sbornik dokumentov*, 93–107.

4. Catherine to Potemkin, December 20/31, 1790, *Russkaya starina* 12 (1876): 644.

5. Nikolai Orlov, *Shturm Izmaila Suvorovym v 1790 godu* (St. Petersburg: Trenke & Fusno, 1890), 15–19; Friedrich von Smitt, *Suworow und Polens untergang* (Leipzig: C. F. Winter, 1858), I:505–507.

6. Potemkin to Ivan Möller, September 28–30/October 9–11, 1790, in *M. I. Kutuzov. Sbornik dokumentov*, I:110–111. Kutuzov commanded four battalions of the Bug Jäger Corps and two battalions of the Troitskii Infantry Regiment.

7. Kutuzov's report based on interrogation of Ottoman prisoners of war, September 28/October 9, 1790, in *M. I. Kutuzov. Sbornik dokumentov*, I:109.

8. Ivan Möller to Potemkin, October 2/13, 1790, in *M. I. Kutuzov. Sbornik dokumentov*, I:111–112; Orlov, *Shturm Izmaila Suvorovym*, 20–24; Bogdanovich, *Pokhody Rumyantseva, Potemkina i Suvorova*, 222–226. One of Kutuzov's early biographers claims that while marching to Izmail, Kutuzov's small detachment encountered a much larger Ottoman force under Ibrahim Osman Pasha but did not shy away from a confrontation. Demonstrating his familiarity with classic military tactics, Kutuzov employed a tactical maneuver favored by the Cossacks and the Mongols alike: he feigned a retreat and lured the enemy's cavalry into a narrow valley between two hills, behind which he had kept two Cossack regiments in an ambush. As the Ottomans pursued him into the dale, Cossacks suddenly charged them from the flanks while Kutuzov led a frontal assault with his jägers, routing the enemy and clearing his path to Izmail. It is unclear how much credence we can put into this account, since the author claims that Kutuzov garnered the Order of St. Alexander of Neva for this exploit, even though he received it for the battle of Babadag a year later. In his record of service (*formulyarnyi spisok*) Kutuzov does note, however, that on November 10/21, about six *verstas* from Izmail, he "routed enemy cavalry with light forces under my command." *Anekdoty ili dostopamyatnye skazaniya ob ego svetlosti general-fel'dmarshale knyaze Mikhaile Illarionoviche Golenischeve-Kutuzove Smolenskom, nachinaya s pervykh let ego sluzhby do konchiny, s priobsheniem nekotoryh ego pisem, dostopamyatnyh ego rechei i prikazov* (St. Petersburg, 1814), I:14–15; *Formulyarnyi spisok*, January 12/23, 1791, RGVIA, f. VUA, d. 2892, l. 76b.

9. Duc de Richelieu, "Journal de mon voyage en Allemagne," *SIRIO* 54 (1886): 152; Petrushevskii, *Generalisimus Knyaz Suvorov*, I:379–380.

10. Duc de Richelieu, "Journal de mon voyage en Allemagne," 152–153; Orlov, *Shturm Izmaila Suvorovym*, 30–33. Petrushevskii argues that the main rampart was six *verstas* or four miles long. Petrushevskii, *Generalisimus Knyaz Suvorov*, I:379. Gabriel de Castelnau, the author of a widely read apologia of the Russian expansionism, spoke highly of the improved Ottoman defenses at Izmail, with their "very massive walls" and guns in casemates, while around the fortress there was a deep trench, covered way, and glacis; on the right side stood "a cavalier some forty feet high, mounting twenty-two pieces of ordnance." Gabriel Marquis de Castelnau, *Essai sur l'histoire ancienne et moderne de la nouvelle Russie . . .* (Paris: Rey et Gravier, 1820), II:201–202. Also see Mikhail Presnukhin, "Vzytie Izmaila v 1770 godu," in *Flügel-Rota* https://fli gel-rota.ru/library/articles/vzyatie-izmaila-v-1770-godu/.

11. Major General E. Renouard James, "The Siege of Ismail, 1790," *Royal Engineers Journal* VI (1907): 12–14. Also see Smitt, *Suworow und Polens untergang*, I:508–509.

12. Roger de Damas, *Memoirs of the Comte Roger de Damas, 1787–1806*, edited and annotated by Jacques Rambaud (London: Chapman and Hall, 1913), 136–137.

13. Castelnau, *Essai sur l'histoire ancienne et moderne de la nouvelle Russie*, 202–203. Also see Duc de Richelieu, "Journal de mon voyage en Allemagne," 153.

14. Contemporary European newspapers offered varied information. The *Derby Mercury*, for example, specified in its coverage of the storming of Izmail that "the Grand Vizier had planted thirteen thousands of his best troops" at Izmail. On the other extreme, the *Cumberland Pacquet* repeated Russian claims that "the Turkish garrison consisted of forty-two thousand men." *Derby Mercury*, February 24, 1791, 3; *Cumberland Pacquet and Ware's Whitehaven Advertiser*, March 29, 1791, 4. Almost all Soviet-era publications embellish the size of the Ottoman garrison.

15. Kutuzov's report based on interrogation of the Ottoman prisoners of war, September 28/October 9, 1790; Kutuzov's interrogation of Cossack Osip Styagailo, October 20/31, 1790, in *M. I. Kutuzov. Sbornik dokumentov*, I:109, 112. Also see testimonies of defected Ottoman troops and local inhabitants—Janissary Akhmed Sale (June 20/July1), Mahmud Emir (July 28/August 8), Moldovan inhabitant Ivan Midazhi (September 18/29), Janissary Ismail (September 19/30), and others—all of whom reported 10,000 to 15,000 men in the Ottoman garrison of Izmail. Arkhiv Voenno-istoricheskogo muzeya Artillerii, Inzhenernykh voisk i voisk Svyazi, fond 2, opis' 'Shtab general-feldzugmeistera," delo 3246, published in A. Gladkii, "Razvedyvatel'naya deyatel'nost' M. I. Kutuzova pod Izmailom," in *M. I. Golenischev-Kutuzov: Materialy nauchnoi konferentsii posvyaschennoi pamyati polkovodtsa* (St. Petersburg, 1993), 30–31. Russian volunteer Gregory Chernyshev, who was in the Russian camp at Izmail, believed that the Ottoman garrison was about 20,000 strong, not counting the city's population. His estimation, however, progressively increased from 20,000 to 30,000 and then 40,000 as the day of the assault approached. Gregory Chernyshev to Sergei Golitsyn, November 21–27/December 2–9, 1790, in Gregory Chernyshev, "Pis'ma vo vremia osady Izmaila 1790 goda. Ot grafa G. I. Chernysheva k knyazyu S. F. Golitsynu," *Russkii arkhiv* 3 (1871): 388, 398, 401.

16. Testimony of Kalcehadar Ahmed, December 7/18, 1790, in Orlov, *Shturm Izmaila Suvorovym*, 135–138.

17. *Formulyarnyi spisok*, January 23, 1791, RGVIA, f. VUA, d. 2892, ll. 76–76b; Gregory Chernyshev to Sergei Golitsyn, November 21/December 2, 1790, *Russkii arkhiv* 3 (1871): 388; Duc de Richelieu, "Journal de mon voyage en Allemagne," 155–156.

18. Testimony of Kalcehadar Ahmed, December 7/18, 1790, in Orlov, *Shturm Izmaila Suvorovym*, 138.

19. Gregory Chernyshev to Sergei Golitsyn, November 21/December 2, 1790, *Russkii arkhiv* 3 (1871): 388

20. Damas, *Memoirs,* 137; Orlov, *Shturm Izmaila Suvorovym,* 25–30.

21. Potemkin to Catherine II, September 4/15, 1790, in Lopatin, ed., *Ekaterina II i G. A. Potemkin,* http://az.lib.ru/e/ekaterina_w/text_0030.shtml.

22. See also Bogdanovich, *Pokhody Rumyantseva, Potemkina i Suvorova,* 222.

23. Charles François Philibert Masson, *Mémoires secrets sur la Russie, et particulièrement sur la fin du règne de Catherine II et sur celui de Paul I* (Amsterdam: Vertrandet, 1802), III:378–379.

24. Orlov, *Shturm Izmaila Suvorovym,* 30.

25. Gregory Chernyshev to Sergei Golitsyn, November 21–24/December 2–5, 1790, *Russkii arkhiv* 3 (1871): 388, 395–396, 402.

26. Gregory Chernyshev to Sergei Golitsyn, November 27/December 9, 1790, *Russkii arkhiv* 3 (1871): 397, 399. For details on soldiers' privations, see Duc de Richelieu, "Journal de mon voyage en Allemagne," 162–164.

27. There is some evidence to suggest that de Ribas lobbied for Suvorov's appointment. Langeron and de Ribas's aide-de-camp both claimed that de Ribas had urged Potemkin to send Suvorov to Izmail. See *Journal des campagnes faites au service de la Russie, par le comte de Langeron,* Archives du Ministère des Affaires Étrangères, Mémoires et Documents, Russie 21; Bogdanovich, *Pokhody Rumyantseva, Potemkina i Suvorova,* 230.

28. Potemkin to Suvorov, November 25/December 6, 1790, *Russkii arkhiv* 10 (1877): 197; Suvorov to Potemkin, November 30/December 11, 1790, *A. V. Suvorov. Sbornik dokumentov,* edited by G. Mescheryakov (Moscow: Voennoe Izdatel'stvo, 1949), II:525. Also see Smitt, *Suworow und Polens untergang,* I:511–512; Petrushevskii, *Generalisimus Knyaz Suvorov,* I:381–382.

29. Suvorov to Potemkin, December 2–5/13–16, 1790, in *A. V. Suvorov. Sbornik dokumentov,* II:526–528.

30. Duc de Richelieu, "Journal de mon voyage en Allemagne," 168; Petrushevskii, *Generalisimus Knyaz Suvorov,* I:383.

31. He was convinced of the superiority of the Russian arms and discussed the battle plan with the generals, who only days earlier had supported the withdrawal. The state of the fortress and its outworks having been discussed in detail, the generals again argued that an assault was out of the question. According to General Damas, "General Suvorov rose from his seat and produced an order from the Empress to the effect that the place has to be taken, whatever the cost." Damas, *Memoirs,* 137.

32. Disposition for Attack, n.d. (ca. December 7/18, 1790); Addendum to the Disposition for Attack, December 1790, in *A. V. Suvorov. Sbornik dokumentov,* II:528–535; Bogdanovich, *Pokhody Rumyantseva, Potemkina i Suvorova,* 234–235; Orlov, *Shturm Izmaila Suvorovym,* 41–45; Duc de Richelieu, "Journal de mon voyage en Allemagne," 170–173; Petrushevskii, *Generalisimus Knyaz Suvorov,* I:384.

33. George Gordon Byron, *The Works of Lord Byron* (London: John Murray, 1833), XVI, 199.

34. Gregory Chernyshev to Sergei Golitsyn, November 27/December 9, 1790, *Russkii arkhiv* 3 (1871): 401–402.

35. Byron, *The Complete Works of Lord Byron,* 790. In Greek mythology, Momus was the personification of satire and mockery.

36. See *A. V. Suvorov. Sbornik dokumentov*, II:527–535; Orlov, *Shturm Izmaila Suvorovym*, 44.

37. Duc de Richelieu, "Journal de mon voyage en Allemagne," 168.

38. Suvorov to the Ottoman garrison, December 7/18, 1790; Suvorov to Potemkin, December 8/19, 1790; Suvorov to Potemkin, December 21, 1790/January 1, 1791, in *A. V. Suvorov. Sbornik dokumentov*, II:535–537, 544; Petrushevskii, *Generalisimus Knyaz Suvorov*, I:385.

39. Cited in Orlov, *Shturm Izmaila Suvorovym*, 45. Suvorov rejected an Ottoman request for a ten-day ceasefire and instead gave them twenty-four hours to consider. Suvorov to Seraskir Mehmet Pasha, December 9/20, 1790, in *A. V. Suvorov. Sbornik dokumentov*, II:539.

40. In his report Suvorov mentions the council taking place in the morning, but some sources suggested it was convened in the evening of December 20.

41. Orlov, *Shturm Izmaila Suvorovym*, 47; Petrushevskii, *Generalisimus Knyaz Suvorov*, I:386.

42. Duc de Richelieu, "Journal de mon voyage en Allemagne," 168. The council was attended by Brigadiers Matvei Platov, Vasilii Orlov, Fedor Westfalen, Major Generals Nikolai Arsenyev, Sergei Lvov, Osip de Ribas, Boris Lascy, Fedor Meknob, Boris Tischev, Duty Major General Ilya Bezborodko, Mikhail Kutuzov, and Lieutenant Generals Alexander Samoilov and Pavel Potemkin.

43. Kutuzov seems to have questioned the practicality of assaulting Izmail. In later years it was said that at the council of war he did not support it, "knowing that it would claim too many lives," but ultimately went along with Suvorov. *Anekdoty ili dostopamyatnye skazaniya*, I:82. Also see the Council of War's decree of December 9/20, 1790; Suvorov to Potemkin, December 21, 1790/January 1, 1791, in *A. V. Suvorov. Sbornik dokumentov*, II:537–538, 544; *M. I. Kutuzov. Sbornik dokumentov*, I:645; Bogdanovich, *Pokhody Rumyantseva, Potemkina i Suvorova*, 236; Smitt, *Suworow und Polens untergang*, I:518–520; Petrushevskii, *Generalisimus Knyaz Suvorov*, I:386. Parkinson erroneously claims that "Kutuzov made no answer [to Suvorov's question] because there seemed no need." Roger Parkinson, *The Fox of the North: The Life of Kutuzov, General of War and Peace* (New York: D. McKay, 1976), 27.

44. In the story, Shiryaev is identified as a colonel, but in 1790 he was a young lieutenant of the Byelorusskii Jäger Corps.

45. *Anekdoty ili dostopamyatnye skazaniya*, I:38–41; S. Glinka, *Ruskie anekdoty voennye, grazhdanskie i istoricheskie* (Moscow: University Tip., 1820), III:72; Lidia Ivchenko, *Kutuzov* (Moscow: Molodaya Gvardiya, 2012), 156–159; Yu. Gulyaev and V. Soglaev, *Fel'dmarshal Kutuzov. Istoriko-biograficheskii*

ocherk (Moscow: Arkheograficheskii Tsentr, 1995), 112; Nikolai Troitskii, *Fel'dmarshal Kutuzov: Mify i fakty* (Moscow, 2002), 68.

46. Damas, *Memoirs,* 138–139.

47. Smitt, *Suworow und Polens untergang,* I:525. In describing the atmosphere in the Russian camp, Smitt was undoubtedly relying on the recollections of his maternal uncle, who served under Suvorov.

48. Disposition for Attack, December 6/17, 1790, in *A. V. Suvorov. Sbornik dokumentov,* II:532; Orlov, *Shturm Izmaila Suvorovym,* 59, 78–79; A. Petrov, *Vtoraya turetskaya voina v tsarstvovanie Ekateriny II. 1787–1791* (St. Petersburg, 1880), II:179; Petrushevskii, *Generalisimus Knyaz Suvorov,* I:388.

49. It is unclear when Kutuzov learned about this tragedy. Catherine revealed the news of young Nicolas's death to a family friend in a letter written on December 8. She would have most certainly written to her husband prior to that, so Kutuzov should have received the news sometime in early to mid-December.

50. The entries on the baby Nicholas's baptism and burial can be found in the church ledger of the Vladimir Orthodox Church in Elisavetgrad, which are currently preserved in the fonds of the Kherson Consistory at the State Archives of the Odessa Region (Ukraine). For an interesting discussion see Sergei Reshetov, "Potomki i rodstvenniki M. I. Golenischeva-Kutuzova i Napoleona Bonaparta v Odesse," in *Almanach Deribasovskaya-Rishelevskaya* 51 (2012): 43–60. Parkinson mistakenly claims that the boy was "accidentally smothered by a nurse in his first year." *The Fox of the North,* 23.

51. The Spanish fly (*Lytta vesicatoria*) is an emerald-green beetle that was used in preparation of various traditional medicines.

52. Catherine Golenischeva-Kutuzova to Aleksey Kutuzov, November 27/December 8, 1790, in Yakov Barskov, *Perepiska moskovskikh masonov XVIII–go veka, 1780–1792 gg.* (Petrograd: Izd. Otd. Rus. yaz. i slovesnosti Imperatorskoi akad. Nauk, 1915), 45.

53. Duc de Richelieu, "Journal de mon voyage en Allemagne," 175; Suvorov to Potemkin, 21 December 21, 1790/1 January 1, 1791, in *A. V. Suvorov. Sbornik dokumentov,* II:545. Langeron states that the bombardment continued for twenty-one hours. The Duc de Richelieu's journal specifies that "forty cannon on the land side, one hundred on the island and at least one hundred and fifty from the various vessels of the flotilla maintained, without interruption, a terrible barrage for twenty-four hours." Alexandre-Louis Andrault, comte de Langeron, *Mémoire sur l'assaut et la prise d'Ismaël par les Russes le 21 décembre 1790,* Archives Nationales, 118AP/2 Fonds Langeron, Documents isolés.

54. Smitt, *Suworow und Polens untergang,* I:527. Also see Bogdanovich, *Pokhody Rumyantseva, Potemkina i Suvorova,* 244–245.

55. Suvorov to Potemkin, December 21, 1790/January 1, 1791, in *A. V. Suvorov. Sbornik dokumentov,* II:544–545. Also see the order of battle in Orlov, *Shturm*

Izmaila Suvorovym, 53; Smitt, *Suworow und Polens untergang*, I:520–521, 526–527; Petrov, *Vtoraya turetskaya voina*, II:179–180. One battalion of the Bug Jägers was assigned to the third riverside column, commanded by Guard Major Markov.

56. Marching in the darkness caused a certain amount of confusion in the Russian attack columns and "some of the soldiers had been killed by their own comrades," with officers overhearing "sounds of complaint and anxiety in the ranks on account of these mistakes." Damas, *Memoirs*, 140. At the council of war, de Ribas cautioned against attacking at night and suggested launching the assault just before sunrise; "the generals rejected this suggestion arguing that it was better to surprise the enemy in the dark and that the confusion that would necessarily arise among the Turks would weaken the resistance." Duc de Richelieu, "Journal de mon voyage en Allemagne," 176–178.

57. Filip Sinel'nikov, *Zhizn', voennye i politicheskie deyaniya Ego Svetlosti General-Fel'dmarshala Knyazya Mikhaila Larionovicha Golenischeva-Kutuzova-Smolenskago* (St. Petersburg, 1813), I:33.

58. Duc de Richelieu, "Journal de mon voyage en Allemagne," 188–189; Suvorov to Potemkin, December 21, 1790/January 1, 1791, in *A. V. Suvorov. Sbornik dokumentov*, II:563.

59. He was married to Agrafena Bibikova, the daughter of Catherine Golenischeva-Kutuzova's brother Alexander Bibikov. Ribeaupierre commanded the Bug Jägers at Izmail.

60. Suvorov to Potemkin, December 21, 1790/January 1, 1791, in *A. V. Suvorov. Sbornik dokumentov*, II:546. Also see Glinka, *Ruskie anekdoty voennye, grazhdanskie i istoricheskie*, III:75; *Anekdoty ili dostopamyatnye skazaniya*, I:16–17; Duc de Richelieu, "Journal de mon voyage en Allemagne," 189.

61. Glinka, *Ruskie anekdoty voennye, grazhdanskie i istoricheskie*, III:76; Sinel'nikov, *Zhizn', voennye i politicheskie deyaniya*, I:90–92.

62. Glinka, *Ruskie anekdoty voennye, grazhdanskie i istoricheskie*, I:199–201.

63. A list of officers who distinguished themselves is in Suvorov's report, Suvorov to Potemkin, December 21, 1790/January 1, 1791, in *A. V. Suvorov. Sbornik dokumentov*, II:564.

64. Glinka, *Ruskie anekdoty voennye, grazhdanskie i istoricheskie*, I:199–201; III:76–77; Bogdanovich, *Pokhody Rumyantseva, Potemkina i Suvorova*, 247.

65. Suvorov to Potemkin, December 21, 1790/January 1, 1791, in *A. V. Suvorov. Sbornik dokumentov*, II:545–546, 547–548; Sinel'nikov, *Zhizn', voennye i politicheskie deyaniya*, I:92–93; *Anekdoty ili dostopamyatnye skazaniya*, I:17; Glinka, *Ruskie anekdoty voennye, grazhdanskie i istoricheskie*, III:76; Orlov, *Shturm Izmaila Suvorovym*, 64–66; Petrov, *Vtoraya turetskaya voina*, II:182–183, 184–186. The Duc de Richelieu notes in his journal that in the first column officers had to plead with and threaten their soldiers to keep them moving forward instead of just firing their muskets. Soldiers did so only after they had almost completely exhausted their ammunition. At times the attacking Russian

soldiers, facing devastating enemy fire, turned back and fled, "bearing on their faces the imprint of fear and despair . . . it was easy to see that for a moment, they lost their heads." Duc de Richelieu, "Journal de mon voyage en Allemagne," 181.

66. One cannot but doubt how Suvorov observed the problem with Kutuzov's column amid the pre-dawn darkness and smoke, not to mention the general din and confusion of the battle. Some authors argue that Kutuzov sent a messenger requesting reinforcements, but I was unable to find any document confirming this. Historians Ivchenko, Gulyaev, and Soglaev note in passing that Kutuzov informed Suvorov that he was forced to retreat and asked for reinforcements, but they do not cite any sources containing such details. Russian historian Orlov, meanwhile, doubts that Kutuzov had sent any messages to Suvorov. Orlov, *Shturm Izmaila Suvorovym*, 67n1; Gulyaev and Soglaev, *Fel'dmarshal Kutuzov*, 113.

67. *Anekdoty ili dostopamyatnye skazaniya*, I:20; Glinka, *Ruskie anekdoty voennye, grazhdanskie i istoricheskie*, III:78; Bogdanovich, *Pokhody Rumyantseva, Potemkina i Suvorova*, 248.

68. Glinka, *Ruskie anekdoty voennye, grazhdanskie i istoricheskie*, III:78; *Anekdoty ili dostopamyatnye skazaniya*, I:20–21. Smitt offers a slightly different version of this conversation. In this telling, Suvorov responded by saying, "I know Kutuzov and Kutuzov knows Suvorov. If Ismail was not taken, we both would have died under its walls." Smitt, *Suworow und Polens untergang*, I:544.

69. Glinka, *Ruskie anekdoty voennye, grazhdanskie i istoricheskie*, III:74.

70. Parkinson, *The Fox of the North*, 22; L. Punin, *Fel'dmarshal Kutuzov. Voenno-biograficheskii ocherk* (Moscow: Voennoe izdatel'stvo, 1957), 5; Mikhail Bragin, *Kutuzov* (Moscow: Molodaya Gvardiya, 1970), 40–41. The Soviet-era publications all emphasize this "teacher-disciple" relationship between Suvorov and Kutuzov.

71. Glinka, *Ruskie anekdoty voennye, grazhdanskie i istoricheskie*, III:72.

72. *Anekdoty ili dostopamyatnye skazaniya*, I:21. Also see Glinka, *Ruskie anekdoty voennye, grazhdanskie i istoricheskie*, III:79.

73. Suvorov to Potemkin, December 21, 1790/January 1, 1791, in *A. V. Suvorov. Sbornik dokumentov*, II:546.

74. Duc de Richelieu, "Journal de mon voyage en Allemagne," 182–183. Also see Suvorov to Potemkin, December 21, 1790/January 1, 1791, in *A. V. Suvorov. Sbornik dokumentov*, II:546; Orlov, *Shturm Izmaila Suvorovym*, 66–75; Petrov, *Vtoraya turetskaya voina*, II:183; Castelnau, *Essai sur l'histoire ancienne et moderne de la nouvelle Russie*, 215–216.

75. *Derby Mercury*, February 24, 1791, 3. Also see *Scots Magazine*, January 1, 1791, 30; *European Magazine and London Review*, January–June 1791, XIX, 233.

76. Sinel'nikov, *Zhizn', voennye i politicheskie deyaniya*, I:95–96; *Anekdoty ili dostopamyatnye skazaniya*, I:17.

77. Orlov, *Shturm Izmaila Suvorovym*, 76; Sinel'nikov, *Zhizn', voennye i politicheskie deyaniya*, I:98; Bogdanovich, *Pokhody Rumyantseva, Potemkina i Suvorova*, 253.

78. Damas, *Memoirs*, 141.

79. Duc de Richelieu, "Journal de mon voyage en Allemagne," 183; Damas, *Memoirs*, 141; Orlov, *Shturm Izmaila Suvorovym*, 76–77, 145. Langeron notes that pillaging ended "the following day." Langeron, *Mémoire sur l'assaut et la prise d'Ismaël par les Russes le 21 décembre 1790*, Archives Nationales, 118AP/2.

80. Duc de Richelieu, "Journal de mon voyage en Allemagne," 183.

81. One contemporary thought that the Russians had taken 10 million piasters' worth of plunder in Izmail. Sinel'nikov, *Zhizn', voennye i politicheskie deyaniya*, I:103. A recent study of eighteenth-century Ottoman society and consumer culture shows that two-thirds of Damascus's inhabitants had estates valued at less than 500 piasters. James P. Grehan, *Everyday Life and Consumer Culture in Eighteenth-Century Damascus* (Portland, OR: Portland State University, 2007), 62–67.

82. Petrushevskii, *Generalisimus Knyaz Suvorov*, I:396; Petrov, *Vtoraya turetskaya voina*, II,188.

83. Duc de Richelieu, "Journal de mon voyage en Allemagne," 192; Sergei Mosolov, "Zapiski," *Russkii arkhiv* 1 (1905): 139; Sinel'nikov, *Zhizn', voennye i politicheskie deyaniya*, I:100–101; Petrov, *Vtoraya turetskaya voina*, II:188.

84. *The Works of Lord Byron*, XVI, 258.

85. Duc de Richelieu, "Journal de mon voyage en Allemagne," 192.

86. Suvorov to Potemkin, December 21, 1790/January 1, 1791, in *A. V. Suvorov. Sbornik dokumentov*, II:550.

87. Catherine II to Potemkin, January 3/14, 1791, in Lopatin, ed., *Ekaterina II i G. A. Potemkin*, http://az.lib.ru/e/ekaterina_w/text_0030.shtml.

88. Suvorov to Potemkin, December 21, 1790/January 1, 1791, in *A. V. Suvorov. Sbornik dokumentov*, II:550; Petrov, *Vtoraya turetskaya voina*, II:187; Petrushevskii, *Generalisimus Knyaz Suvorov*, I:395–396, 399; Petrov, *Vtoraya turetskaya voina*, II:187. The day after the storming Kutuzov believed that there were at least 15,000 Ottoman corpses that had to be removed. General Damas notes in his memoirs that "twenty-four thousand Turks, janissaries and other soldiers, were killed," while Richelieu thought that "30,860 or so Turks . . . among them at least 2,000 women and children," lost their lives. Sinel'nikov believed that 33,000 Ottoman troops were killed and about 1,000 captured; in addition, Russians captured 6,000 "wives and children," 2,000 Christians, and over 500 Jews. Damas, *Memoirs*, 141–142; Duc de Richelieu, "Journal de mon voyage en Allemagne," 187; Sinel'nikov, *Zhizn', voennye i politicheskie deyaniya*, I:102. For contemporary reporting, see *Scots Magazine*, January 1, 1791, 30; *Hereford Journal*, February 2, 1791, 3; *Cumberland Pacquet and Ware's Whitehaven Advertiser*, March 29, 1791, 4.

89. According to official reports, the Russian casualties included 64 officers and 1,815 soldiers killed, and 253 officers and 2,450 soldiers wounded. However,

the Duc de Richelieu, who participated in the assault, believed that 200 officers and 4,000 soldiers were killed, and about 5,000 officers and soldiers wounded in this assault. Another participant, Alexander Langeron, spoke of over 4,000 killed and another 6,000 wounded, more than half of whom later died of wounds. Russian historian Alexander Petrushevskii, who produced a massive three-volume biography of Suvorov, pointed out that the official report was written hastily and did not reflect the full scale of the Russian losses. "It has been said," he notes, "that the later, more reliable reports showed some 4,000 killed and 6,000 wounded, so a total of about 10,000, among them 400, out of 650, officers." He does concede that even these reports might not be accurate enough. The Russian losses given by Marquis de Castelnau—on the authority of a "général-en-chef" without naming who he was—were as follows: 2 generals, 33 lieutenants colonels and majors, 396 out of 650 officers, 4,000 soldiers killed, 4,000 wounded who later died of their injuries, and 2,000 wounded who survived. Petrushevskii, *Generalisimus Knyaz Suvorov,* I:396. See also Orlov, *Shturm Izmaila Suvorovym,* 81; Petrov, *Vtoraya turetskaya voina,* II:188; Duc de Richelieu, "Journal de mon voyage en Allemagne," 187; Langeron, *Mémoire sur l'assaut et la prise d'Ismaël par les Russes le 21 décembre 1790,* Archives Nationales, 118AP/2; Castelnau, *Essai sur l'histoire ancienne et moderne de la nouvelle Russie,* II:218.

90. Kutuzov to his wife, December 12/23, 1790, in "Arkhiv knyazya M. I. Golenischeva-Kutuzova-Smolenskago," *Russkaya starina* II (1870): 500–501 [hereafter cited as *The Kutuzov Papers*]. Also see Sergei Mosolov, "Zapiski," *Russkii arkhiv* I (1905): 138.

91. *Derby Mercury,* February 24, 1791, 3.

92. Christy Pichichero, *The Military Enlightenment: War and Culture in the French Empire from Louis XIV to Napoleon* (Ithaca, NY: Cornell University Press, 2017), chap. 3; Duc de Richelieu, "Journal de mon voyage en Allemagne," 189. For an interesting discussion, see Eugene Miakinkov, *War and Enlightenment in Russia: Military Culture in the Age of Catherine II* (Toronto: University of Toronto Press, 2020), 194–211. For a British perspective on the sackings during the Napoleonic Wars, see Gavin Daly, " 'The Sacking of a Town Is an Abomination': Siege, Sack and Violence to Civilians in British Officers' Writings on the Peninsular War. The Case of Badajoz," *Institute of Historical Research* 92, no. 255 (February 2019): 160–182.

93. See Duc de Richelieu, "Journal de mon voyage en Allemagne," 189–190.

94. Kutuzov to his wife, December 12/23, 1790, in *The Kutuzov Papers* 11 (1870): 500–501.

95. Castelnau, *Essai sur l'histoire ancienne et moderne de la nouvelle Russie,* 212.

96. Cited in Punin, *Kutuzov,* 27; Bragin, *Kutuzov,* 45.

97. Suvorov to Potemkin, December 21, 1790/January 1, 1791, in *A. V. Suvorov. Sbornik dokumentov,* II:551; *Anekdoty ili dostopamyatnye skazaniya,* I:19; Bogdanovich, *Pokhody Rumyantseva, Potemkina i Suvorova,* 258.

98. The list of officers nominated for promotion, January 12/23, 1791, is in *M. I. Kutuzov. Sbornik dokumentov*, I:122. Catherine II confirmed Kutuzov's promotion to lieutenant general and awarded him the Order of St. George, third class, on March 25/April 5, 1791. See imperial decrees in *The Kutuzov Papers* 1 (1870): 483; *M. I. Kutuzov. Sbornik dokumentov*, I:132–133.

Chapter 6

1. Virginia H. Aksan, *Ottoman Wars, 1700–1870: An Empire Besieged* (New York: Pearson, 2007), 167–169, 182–183. On the logistical issues the Ottomans faced, see Cengiz Fedakar, "1787–1792 Osmanlı-Avusturya Rus Savaşlarında Edirne Lojistiği," in *Prof. M. Tayyib Gökbilgin ve Edirne Sempozyumu bildiriler*, edited by Ibrahim Sezgin and Veysi Akin (Edirne: Trakya University, 2016), 151–160. Koca Yusuf Pasha was appointed grand vizier in February 1791, having previously held this position in 1786–1789.

2. Potemkin to Suvorov, December 24, 1790/January 4, 1791 (with an annex showing winter quarters assignments), in N. Dubrovin, ed., *Bumagi knyazya Grigoriya Aleksandrovicha Potemkina-Tavricheskogo, 1790–1793 gg.* [hereafter cited as *The Potemkin Papers 1790–1793*] (St. Petersburg: Voen.-Ucheb. Komitet Glavn. Shtaba, 1895), 200. Kutuzov was allowed to keep the Bug Jäger Corps, the Khersonskii Grenadier Regiment, the Polotskii Musketeer Regiment, a company of twelve cannon, and the Don Cossack regiments of Mashlykin, Sychov, and Semenov. Kutuzov to Potemkin, December 30, 1790/January 10, 1791, in *M. I. Kutuzov. Sbornik dokumentov* (Moscow: Voeniszdat, 1950), I:120; Modest Bogdanovich, *Pokhody Rumyantseva, Potemkina i Suvorova v Turtsii* (St. Petersburg: E. Weymar, 1852); A. Petrov, *Vtoraya turetskaya voina v tsarstvovanie Ekateriny II. 1787–1791* (St. Petersburg, 1880), II:189.

3. William Wordsworth, "The Prelude or, Growth of a Poet's Mind. An Autobiographical Poem," in *Complete Poetical Works* (Philadelphia: Troutman & Hayes, 1852), 496

4. Catherine Golenischeva-Kutuzova to Aleksey Kutuzov, January 6/17, 1791, in Yakov Barskov, ed., *Perepiska moskovskikh masonov XVIII-go veka, 1780–1792 gg.* (Petrograd: Izd. Otd. Rus. Yaz. i Slovesnosti Imperatorskoi Akad. Nauk, 1915), 76–77.

5. Kutuzov to Potemkin, January 10/21, 1791, in *M. I. Kutuzov. Sbornik dokumentov*, I:121; Kutuzov to his wife, December 12/23, 1790, in "Arkhiv knyazya M. I. Golenischeva-Kutuzova-Smolenskago," *Russkaya starina* II (1870) [hereafter cited as *The Kutuzov Papers*], 500–501.

6. Alexandre-Louis Andrault, comte de Langeron, *Mémoire sur l'assaut et la prise d'Ismaël par les Russes le 21 décembre 1790*, Archives Nationales, 118AP/2 Fonds Langeron, Documents Isolés. After the assault Kutuzov prepared a report on available provisions that showed 150 *chetvert'* (fourths, or 31,350 liters) of wheat in the three Ottoman storehouses and 25 *chetvert'* (5,225 liters) of wheat

and 17 *chetvert'* (3,553 liters) of barley hidden in various caverns. Kutuzov to Potemkin, December 1790, in *M. I. Kutuzov. Sbornik dokumentov*, I:119.

7. Repnin to Kutuzov, February 25/March 8, 1791, in Andrei Engel', *Opisanie del khryanyaschikhsya v archive Vilenskago general-gubernatorstva* (Vilna: Vilenskoe Gubern. Pravlenie, 1870) [hereafter cited as *The Repnin Papers*], vol. 1, part 2, 423.

8. S. Glinka, *Ruskie anekdoty voennye, grazhdanskie i istoricheskie* (Moscow: University Tip., 1820), I:200–201. Also see Filip Sinel'nikov, *Zhizn', voennye i politicheskie deyaniya Ego Svetlosti General-Fel'dmarshala Knyazya Mikhaila Larionovicha Golenischeva-Kutuzova-Smolenskago* (St. Petersburg, 1813), I:102–103.

9. The corps comprised 76 infantry battalions, 19 cavalry regiments, 160 cannons, and several thousand dismounted and mounted Cossacks.

10. Kutuzov to Potemkin, January 10/21, 1791, in *M. I. Kutuzov. Sbornik dokumentov*, I:121. For details on intelligence gathering, including testimonies of the Moldovan peasants captured by a flying detachment in March, see *M. I. Kutuzov. Sbornik dokumentov*, I:124–129. Also see Repnin to Kutuzov, February 11/22, 1791, in *The Repnin Papers*, vol. 1, part 2, 418–419. Engel's publication contains the journal of secret outgoing correspondence between Repnin and Kutuzov during the spring and summer of 1791.

11. Repnin to Kutuzov, March 11/22, 1791, *The Repnin Papers*, vol. 1, part 2, 425–426.

12. "While I was visiting Ismail I gave Your Excellency a verbal order to remove the lead roof from the Turkish mosque and the residence of the khan of Izmail," wrote an exasperated Repnin. "I then wrote about this in the letter of [May 5]. . . . I suggest Your Excellency to order immediately to remove these roofs and without waiting for any further instructions from me to send half of the lead to de Ribas [who desperately needed it to make more canister shots]." Repnin to Kutuzov, April 29/May 10, 1791, *The Repnin Papers*, vol. 1, part 2, 435.

13. Repnin to Kutuzov, February 11/22, 1791, *The Repnin Papers*, vol. 1, part 2, 418–419; Kutuzov to Repnin, February 23/March 6, 1791, in *M. I. Kutuzov. Sbornik dokumentov*, I:126. Two weeks later he apprised Repnin that he had identified almost 1,000 people at Izmail, 400 at Kilya, and some 500 at Akkerman who could be involved in the fortress demolition, but "the same factors that I reported before prevent me from employing them, for if they miss this moment and do not till the soil and take care of vineyards, they would wind up without provisions and thus a burden for the state treasure." Kutuzov to Repnin, March 11/22, 1791, in *M. I. Kutuzov. Sbornik dokumentov*, I:129.

14. Cited in Aksan, *Ottomans Wars*, 183.

15. Aksan, *Ottomans Wars*, 182.

16. Kutuzov to Repnin, with an annex containing testimonies of the captured Moldovan peasants, February 23/March 6, 1791; Kutuzov to Repnin, February 25/March 8, 1791, in *M. I. Kutuzov. Sbornik dokumentov*, I:126–127, 129.

17. Repnin to Kutuzov, March 13/24–20/31, 1791, *The Repnin Papers*, vol. 1, part 2, 427–429; Bogdanovich, *Pokhody Rumyantseva, Potemkina i Suvorova*, 263–264.

18. Kutuzov started his march by first moving his troops to the island of Sulin on March 25/April 5 and then crossing to the southern bank of the Danube near Tulcea on April 6.

19. Sinel'nikov, *Zhizn', voennye i politicheskie deyaniya*, I:115–116. Sinel'nikov claims the Ottomans had some 15,000 men at Babadag, but he might be confusing this combat with the battle that Kutuzov fought later that summer. The fact that he felt confident leaving Babadag behind him as he proceeded to join Golitsyn indicates that the Ottomans did not have a large force there.

20. Zhurnal voennykh deistvii soedinennoi armii [Journal of Military Operations of the Combined Army], in *The Potemkin Papers 1790–1793*, 230–231; Petrov, *Vtoraya turetskaya voina*, II:199–201; Sinel'nikov, *Zhizn', voennye i politicheskie deyaniya*, I:113–114.

21. Journal of Military Operations of the Combined Army, in *The Potemkin Papers 1790–1793*, 229–233; Sinel'nikov, *Zhizn', voennye i politicheskie deyaniya*, I:119–120. For the Ottoman side, see Aysel Yıldız, "Osmanlı tarihinde bir ordu boykotu: Maçin bozgunu (1791)," *Akabinde Yaşanan Tartışmalar, Cihannüma* II, no. 2 (Istanbul: Aralık, 2016), 134. I am grateful to Prof. Cengiz Fedakar for sharing this source with me.

22. Bogdanovich, *Pokhody Rumyantseva, Potemkina i Suvorova*, 264–265; Petrov, *Vtoraya turetskaya voina*, II:204–205.

23. The news of the Russian raid was reported even in small British newspapers, with one of them informing its readers that "Prince Galitsin" and "Major-General de Kutusow" "came unexpectedly upon the Ottoman troops [and] entirely defeated them." *Kentish Gazette*, May 13, 1791, 3. A more detailed account of the Russian attack on Brăila is given in *Leeds Intelligencer*, May 24, 1791, 4.

24. Kutuzov had a complex relationship with Repnin. The two were on friendly terms, and Repnin's letters are replete not just with the customary politeness expected between officers of noble birth but also with an affable demeanor that one hardly expects in orders sent from a commander in chief to a subordinate officer. "Amicably" was one of Repnin's common refrains. Before launching the campaign that led to the great victory at Măcin, Repnin implored Kutuzov for help. "I amicably and humble ask you to come here as soon as you can," he wrote on June 2. A week later, he entreated him, "I amicably beseech you, my dear Mikhail Larionovich, to tell me honestly if, having exhausted all possibilities, you can find the means to cross the Danube with twelve days' worth of supplies. . . . Knowing your diligence and zeal, I think that you will be able to find ways to implement the abovementioned [proposals], and such is my only hope for it all. Think of what you can do and let me know at once. . . . I eagerly await your response." However, Kutuzov did not reciprocate

the tone. Lidia Ivchenko suggests that Kutuzov might have been apprehensive since he knew that Repnin belonged to the faction of Grand Duke Paul that was hostile to Potemkin (whom Kutuzov considered as his benefactor) and supported pro-Prussian policies just as the all-powerful minister was confronting Prussia. She rightly points out that this complex relationship between Kutuzov and Repnin continued for years, and the former was twice (in 1793 and 1797) sent to deal with diplomatic issues caused by the latter. Repnin to Kutuzov, May 29/June 9, 1791, in A. Val'kovich, ed., *Fel'dmarshal Kutuzov. Dokumenty, dnevniki, vospominaniya* (Moscow: Arkheograficheskii tsentr, 1995), 30; Repnin to Kutuzov, May 18–29/May 29–June 9, 1791, in *M. I. Kutuzov. Sbornik dokumentov*, I:136–140; Lidia Ivchenko, *Kutuzov* (Moscow: Molodaya Gvardiya, 2012), 160–161.

25. Kutuzov faced several challenges. His troops still lacked ammunition; in early May, he complained that his forces had only nineteen *puds* (686 pounds) of lead remaining to create musket balls, not enough to last a prolonged campaign. More crucially, he struggled to deal with the Cossacks who served in the Ottoman army and constantly harassed the Russian outposts, which were manned by fellow Cossacks; fraternization often led to desertion. See correspondence in *The Repnin Papers*, vol. 1, part 2, 429–434, 440–452; *M. I. Kutuzov. Sbornik dokumentov*, I:128–129.

26. Repnin to Kutuzov, May 26–29/June 6–9, 1791, in *The Repnin Papers*, vol. 1, part 2, 443–446. "I am sending you two maps of our operations in 1771 and 1773 in the area where you now would have to operate," Repnin advised Kutuzov. "They will help you better understand the whereabouts of these places."

27. Kutuzov commanded the Bug Jäger Corps; the Khersonskii, Sibirskii, Dneprovskii, and Primorskii Nikolaevskii Grenadier Regiments; the Vitebskii, Ingermanlandskii, Uglitskii, Polotskii, and Aleksopolskii Musketeer Regiments; two carabineer (Glukhovskii and Kyivskii) regiments; several hundred Black Sea Cossaks (mounted and dismounted); and three Don Cossack units (of Ilovaiskii, Denisov, and Semenov). Kutuzov to Repnin, June 11/22, 1791, in *M. I. Kutuzov. Sbornik dokumentov*, I:144; Bogdanovich, *Pokhody Rumyantseva, Potemkina i Suvorova*, 268.

28. Kutuzov to Repnin, June 6/17 and June 11/22, 1791, in *M. I. Kutuzov. Sbornik dokumentov*, I,141–143. Kutuzov submitted two battle reports, one upon his return to Izmail and a second, more detailed account five days later.

29. The advance guard, under Colonel de Ribas, included two squares, the first formed by the Black Sea Cossacks (dismounted) and the second of two jäger battalions. The right wing, under Major General Spet, consisted of two squares, the first formed by the soldiers from the Vitebskii and Ingermanlandskii Infantry Regiments, the second by the Uglitskii Infantry Regiment. The left wing, led by Colonel Hagemeister, also included two squares—the first formed by the Polotskii Infantry Regiment, reinforced by a battalion of the

Aleksopolskii Regiment, the second by the Khersonskii Grenadier Regiment. Kutuzov reported that his middle square was the strongest and comprised the Sibirskii Grenadier Regiment (under Premier Major Rostein), with the carabineer regiments on both its sides. Two battalions of the Bug Jäger Corps were sent to secure the left wing against any flanking maneuvers. The field artillery was distributed between the squares. Kutuzov to Repnin, June 6/17, 1791, in *M. I. Kutuzov. Sbornik dokumentov*, I,144.

30. Kutuzov to Repnin, June 6/17, 1791, in *M. I. Kutuzov. Sbornik dokumentov*, I:141; Petrov, *Vtoraya turetskaya voina*, II:211–212.

31. Repnin to Kutuzov, June 7/18, 1791 in *The Repnin Papers*, vol. 1, part 1, 377.

32. The newspaper informed its readers that "near Bubada, Lieutenant General Kutusow's detachment attacked a body of 23,000 men, composed of Turks and Tartars, commanded by the Kan, three Seraskiers, and five Sultans— defeated it, killed 1,500 men, took possession of the camp." *Sheffield Register, Yorkshire, Derbyshire, & Nottinghamshire Universal Advertiser*, July 29, 1791. Also see *Caledonian Mercury*, July 23, 1791, 2.

33. Potemkin to Catherine II, June 24/July 5, 1791, in *M. I. Kutuzov. Sbornik dokumentov*, I:149. It is noteworthy that even though he did not have a detailed report about the battle and thus could not reward other officers, Potemkin went ahead and nominated only Kutuzov for the reward, a testament of his continued benevolence toward this general. Catherine approved the request on July 28/August 8.

34. Repnin to Kutuzov, June 5–18/16–29, 1791, *The Repnin Papers*, vol. 1, part 2, 449–451; Repnin to Kutuzov, June 18/29, 1791, in *M. I. Kutuzov. Sbornik dokumentov*, I:148; *Anekdoty ili dostopamyatnye skazaniya*, I:26.

35. Bogdanovich, *Pokhody Rumyantseva, Potemkina i Suvorova*, 269; Petrov, *Vtoraya turetskaya voina*, II:213–215.

36. Lev Engel'hardt, *Zapiski*, edited by I. Fedyukin (Moscow: Novoe literaturnoe obozrenie, 1997), 90.

37. Petrov, *Vtoraya turetskaya voina*, II:215–217; Bogdanovich, *Pokhody Rumyantseva, Potemkina i Suvorova*, 270–271. Kutuzov had four battalions of the Bug Jägers, two battalions of the Byelorussian Jägers, four battalions of the Sibirskii grenadiers, two battalions of the Kyivskii grenadiers, the Ol'viopol'skii and Voronezhskii Hussar Regiments, the Nezhinskii and Glukhovskii Carabineer Regiments, six Cossack regiments (of Orlov, Grekov, Ilovaiskii, Peter Denisov, Adrian Denisov, and Astakhov, under the overall command of Brigadier General Orlov), and several hundred *arnăuts* (locally recruited troops) under the command of Premier Major Muravyev. His field artillery consisted of twenty-four cannon.

38. Engel'hardt, *Zapiski*, 91.

39. Engel'hardt, *Zapiski*, 91.

40. Petrov, *Vtoraya turetskaya voina*, II:217–218.

41. Engel'hardt, *Zapiski*, 91.

42. Engel'hardt, *Zapiski*, 91–92; Sinel'nikov, *Zhizn', voennye i politicheskie deyaniya*, I:135–138.

43. Kutuzov reported that he formed five squares of two battalions each: of the Siberian Grenadier Regiment, 1st and 3rd Battalions of the Bug Jäger Corps, the Kyivskii Grenadier Regiment, the 1st and 4th Battalions of the Byelorussian Jäger Corps, and the 2nd and 4th Battalions of the Bug Jäger Corps. The Kyivskii grenadiers, supported by the Nezhinskii Carabineer Regiment, formed the left flank of Kutuzov's positions. The Glukhovskii Carabineer Regiment was kept in between the Bug Jäger and the Kyivskii Grenadier squares, and the Voronezhskii Hussar Regiment was next to the 1st and 3rd Bug Jäger battalions, while the Ol'viopol'skii Hussar Regiment was next to the Byelorussian Jäger Corps.

44. Kutuzov to Repnin, July 4/15, 1791, in *M. I. Kutuzov. Sbornik dokumentov*, I:149–150; Bogdanovich, *Pokhody Rumyantseva, Potemkina i Suvorova*, 271–272. Also see the submitted list of individuals who distinguished themselves in the Battle of Măcin, July 14/25, 1791, in *M. I. Kutuzov. Sbornik dokumentov*, I:150–151.

45. Engel'hardt, *Zapiski*, 92–93; Petrov, *Vtoraya turetskaya voina*, II:219–224; Bogdanovich, *Pokhody Rumyantseva, Potemkina i Suvorova*, 269–273. The contemporary British press discussed this battle in detail and, based on information delivered by "the Imperial Major Mr. Mallia" to the Russian embassy in Vienna, reported 4,000 Ottoman losses and "only 150 killed and 2 or 300 wounded" on the Russian side. *Chester Courant*, August 9, 1791, 3; *Bury and Norwich Post*, August 10, 1791, 4; *Hereford Journal*, August 10, 1791, 3; *Caledonian Mercury*, August 11, 1791, 2; *Derby Mercury*, August 11, 1791, 2; *Chester Chronicle*, August 12, 1791.

46. *The Scots Magazine* LIII (Edinburgh, 1791), 401. The journal based its account on "letters from Bucharest dated the 18th of July," which specified that after the battle "the Grand Vizier retired to Hirsova, and from thence to Schumla, where, by flight, he narrowly escaped being cut in pieces by his own people." Based on the same letters, another British newspaper reported that "immediately after the battle of Maczin, the Turkish Arnauts fell sword-in-hand on the corps of Janissaries, and, it is reported, killed more of them that were slain by the Russians." *Chester Courant*, August 23, 1791, 3. Also see *Cumberland Pacquet and Ware's Whitehaven Advertiser*, August 30, 1791, 2. It should be noted that the Ottomans did manage to recover from the defeat at Măcin and in the fall of 1791 their main army remained in the field, although it continued to suffer from mutinies and logistical difficulties. Admiral Fedor Ushakov's crushing victory over the Ottoman fleet near the Cape of Kaliakra, off the coast of northern Bulgaria, on August 11, 1791, also played a crucial role in the Ottoman decision to seek peace.

47. There is an interesting wrinkle in the story of the Battle of Măcin that underscores the byzantine nature of relations within the Russian officer corps

NOTES TO PAGE 91 | 565

and shows how some contemporaries perceived Kutuzov. At least one participant thought that Kutuzov deliberately delayed his flanking attack during the
battle. "He could have easily scaled those heights and he outright lied when he
reported facing superior forces," scoffed Engel'hardt, who, as we have seen, led
the assault from the other side of that ridge. "Quartermaster General Pistor,
who accompanied Kutuzov, even confronted him about this, rather insolently,
in front of the many witnesses." Engel'hardt observed that Kutuzov, a keen
judge of human character, had understood the army commander's cautious
and irresolute character and knew that if Repnin were to learn of the stalled
flanking maneuver, he would not "risk attacking strong enemy positions and
would call off his men. Kutuzov would have then [charged forward], climbed
the mountain, turned the enemy flank and defeated the [grand] vizier alone
[claiming all the glory]."

It is a startling allegation, but how much credence can we give to it?
No other participant expressed his concerns publicly or in writing; none of
the Russian imperial/Soviet/ historians discussed it, instead emphasizing
Kutuzov's good performance and the praise that Repnin heaped on him in the
aftermath of this battle. Modern Russian historians are also almost all silent
on this issue. The only historian who confronted this claim is Lidia Ivchenko,
who frames it within the context of wider intrigues and power struggles in
the Russian elite. Repnin was a Freemason of the Martinist sect and part of
Grand Duke Paul's Prussophile faction, which loathed and opposed Potemkin,
who, as we have seen, had been benevolent toward Kutuzov. By ignoring
Potemkin's instructions not to cross the Danube, argues Ivchenko, Repnin
placed Kutuzov in an awkward position of contributing to the success of his
benefactor's opponents. She also claims that Repnin was "rushing to conclude
peace with Turks on 'moderate conditions' that the Berlin court insisted on."
Yet the historian provides no evidence for such a close coordination between
the Hohenzollern court and the Russian commander, or of the latter's intent
to conclude a "moderate" peace. Repnin could, and did, negotiate an armistice, but it would have been impossible for him to conclude peace. Potemkin
had already secured a major diplomatic victory when, in July, he succeeded
in convincing his British and Prussian interlocutors to acknowledge Russian
control of the Crimea and pledge to mediate peace with the Ottomans on the
condition that the Dniester River would be recognized as the new imperial
border. Repnin could do little to stop this deal from happening, especially
since Potemkin was on his way to join him. In fact, Potemkin allowed Repnin
to negotiate the preliminaries, but he was infuriated to learn that the commander went as far as to sign the armistice, which led to a vocal confrontation
between the two men.

Equally suspect seems the suggestion that Kutuzov sought to claim greater
glory in this battle. Russian generals were indeed prone to jealousy, intrigue,
and scheming, but it is hard to envision them deliberately stalling the attack

and endangering the outcome of battle (and the lives of thousands of their men) for such personal motives. Kutuzov would certainly have known that if Repnin were to order a retreat, the Ottomans would have diverted additional forces to shore up their right wing and overwhelmed his column, as it was left unsupported and isolated in the Jijila valley. None of Repnin's reports or letters show Kutuzov's suspected noncompliance. To the contrary, Repnin profusely praised him and solicited rewards for him. Still, whether this incident is true or not, the fact that Engel'hardt thought Kutuzov capable of such cunning is notable by itself. It shows that some contemporaries perceived him as an unscrupulous man who manipulated people to his advantage. For an interesting discussion of Repnin, Potemkin, and relations between senior officers, see V. Lopatin, *Svetleishii knyaz' Potemkin* (Moscow: Olma Press, 2005), 238–239; Simon Sebag Montefiore, *Prince of Princes: The Life of Potemkin* (London: Weidenfeld & Nicolson, 2001), 480–481; Ivchenko, *Kutuzov*, 161–164.

48. "The Roll of Generals and Officers Nominated for Awards," in *M. I. Kutuzov. Sbornik dokumentov*, I:x, 152.

49. *Anekdoty ili Dostopamyatnye skazaniya*, I:23.

50. *Anekdoty ili Dostopamyatnye skazaniya*, I:23.

51. Kutuzov was worried that after the death of Potemkin, who had served as his benefactor for so many years, he might be left out of the list of officers nominated for awards and promotions. In late November he wrote a letter soliciting the help of Vasilii Popov, the head of Potemkin's chancellery. "I was certain that the late Prince would reward my endeavors at the end of the war but, having lost any hope for this after his passing, I trust that you, knowing well of my service, would not miss an opportunity to treat me fairly." Kutuzov seems to have worried needlessly, since in the roll of officers nominated for awards, Repnin mentioned Kutuzov's name several time, praising him for the battles of Măcin and Babadag, as well as highlighting his service on the Bug River, during the capture of Akkerman, and in the Russian advance to Bender. Kutuzov to Popov, November 12/23, 1791; Roll of Officers Nominated for Award, in *M. I. Kutuzov. Sbornik dokumentov*, I:155–156; Catherine II to Kutuzov, March 18/29, 1792, in *The Kutuzov Papers* 1 (1870): 484. Parkinson mistakenly claims that Kutuzov received the Order of St. George (second class) "for his campaign in Poland." He made no effort to examine the crucial battles of Babadag and Măcin, which are summed up in a single sentence in his book. Roger Parkinson, *The Fox of the North: The Life of Kutuzov, General of War and Peace* (New York: D. McKay, 1976), 30–31.

52. After the Battle of Măcin, the Russian army returned its positions on the Danube. Kutuzov spent the next few months at Izmail, once again supervising the fortresses on the Lower Danube. After Gregory Potemkin died in October 1791, Empress Catherine sent Général-en-chef Mikhail Kakhovskii (Kachowski) to assume command of the army. According to the army

disposition of November 10, 1791, Kutuzov was in charge of one-third of the Russian army forces in the Danubian principalities. The Cossack regiments were scattered at the winter quarters between the Prut and the Dniester Rivers. The infantry was deployed at the fortresses of Izmail and Kilya. *M. I. Kutuzov. Sbornik dokumentov*, I:154.

53. Order of St. George (fourth class) (1775), Order of St. Anna (first class) (1789), Order of St. Vladimir (second class) (1789), Order of of St. George (third class) (1791), Order of St. Alexander of Neva (1791), and Order of St. George (second class) (1792).

Chapter 7

1. See documents in *M. I. Kutuzov. Sbornik dokumentov* (Moscow: Voeniszdat, 1950), I:159–166; Filip Sinel'nikov, *Zhizn', voennye i politicheskie deyaniya Ego Svetlosti General-Fel'dmarshala Knyazya Mikhaila Larionovicha Golenischeva-Kutuzova-Smolenskago* (St. Petersburg, 1813), II:5–8.

2. Catherine II to Kutuzov, October 25/November 6, 1792, in N. Dubrovin, ed., *Bumagi knyazya Grigoriya Aleksandrovicha Potemkina-Tavricheskogo, 1790–1793 gg.* [hereafter cited as *The Potemkin Papers 1790–1793*] (St. Petersburg: Voen.-ucheb. Komitet Glavn. Shtaba, 1895), 335.

3. Norman Itzkowitz and Max Mote, *Mubadele: An Ottoman-Russian Exchange of Ambassadors* (Chicago: University of Chicago Press, 1970), 13.

4. For an interesting discussion, see Jacob Coleman Hurewitz, "The Europeanization of Ottoman Diplomacy: The Conversion from Unilateralism to Reciprocity in the Nineteenth Century," *Belleten* 25 (1961): 455–466; Thomas Naff, "Reform and the Conduct of Ottoman Diplomacy in the Reign of Selim III, 1789–1807," *Journal of the American Oriental Society* 83 (1963): 295–315; Carter V. Findley, "The Foundation of the Ottoman Foreign Ministry: The Beginnings of Bureaucratic Reform Under Selim III and Mahmud II," *International Journal of Middle East Studies* 3 (1972): 388–416; Fatma Müge Göçek, *East Encounters West: France and the Ottoman Empire in the Eighteenth Century* (New York: Oxford University Press, 1987). For a critical view of the westernization, see Berrak Burçak, "The Institution of the Ottoman Embassy and Eighteenth-Century Ottoman History: An Alternative to Göçek," *International Journal of Turkish Studies* 13 (2007): 147–151.

5. Treaty of Jassy, January 9, 1792, in Alexandre Louis Félix Alix, *Précis de l'histoire de l'empire ottoman: Notes et pièces justificatives* (Paris: Didot, 1824), III:638.

6. General-procurator was one of the highest offices in the central administration of imperial Russia, established by Peter the Great in January 1722. He had a seat in the Senate, acting there as the "czar's eye," to supervise all activities. This position should not be confused with ober-procurator, the head of the Most Holy Synod and effective leader of the Russian Orthodox Church.

7. Imperial Decree of October 26/November 6, 1792, in *M. I. Kutuzov. Sbornik dokumentov*, I:189–190.

8. Victor Kochubey to Semen Vorontsov, October 27/November 7, 1792, in *Arkhiv knyazya Vorontsova*, XVIII:66.

9. Semen Vorontsov to Alexander Vorontsov, December 4, 1792, in *Arkhiv knyazya Vorontsova* (Moscow: Tip. Gracheva, 1870–1895), IX:280.

10. Catherine to Kutuzov, with the secret instructions "On Political Matters," February 21/March 4, 1793, in *M. I. Kutuzov. Sbornik dokumentov*, I:199. In 1811, Kutuzov admitted that "Empress Catherine had planned to capture Istanbul and for that purpose she dispatched [me] in 1793 to reconnoiter roads in the entire region from Şumnu/Shumla and the Black Sea." See his 1811 plan of war against the Ottomans in RGVIA, f. VUA, d. 2952, ll. 180–184.

11. On December 31, 1792, Alexander Khrapovitskii noted in his diary that "Mikhail Larionovich Golenischev-Kutuzov is preparing to depart to Tsargrad [Istanbul] to replace Samoilov." *Dnevnik A. V. Khrapovitskogo, 1782–1793* (St. Petersburg: A. F. Bazunov, 1874), 417.

12. Sinel'nikov, *Zhizn', voennye i politicheskie deyaniya*, II:14.

13. In late March 1793 he wrote to Alexander Suvorov, who commanded troops in the Crimea and the Ekaterinoslav province and was one of the officials that Kutuzov was supposed to keep in direct communication with, asking him to convey soldiers who formerly served under his command for the diplomatic mission to Istanbul; Suvorov accommodated this request.

14. Heinrich Christoph von Reimers, *Reise der Russisch-Kaiserlichen Ausserordentlichen Gesandtschaft an die Othomanische Pforte im Jahr 1793* (St. Petersburg: Schnoorschen Buchdruckerei, 1803), I:5, 16.

15. Passport, signed by Empress Catherine II, in *M. I. Kutuzov. Sbornik dokumentov*, I:647. There is a discrepancy in dates in the published versions, with the heading dating it March 13/24 and the text itself referring to March 19/30. Also see Reimers, *Reise*, I:18.

16. See details in Reimers, *Reise*, I:7–12; I. M. El'terman, *Posol'stvo kutuzova v Turtsii v 1793–1794 g.g.* (Moscow: Moscow State University, 1945), 70.

17. Aigrette was a headdress consisting of a white egret's feather with various precious gems and decorations.

18. A brief register of items, dated February 23/March 6, 1793, is in *M. I. Kutuzov. Sbornik dokumentov*, I:646. For more details, see Reimers, *Reise*, I:13. The total value of gifts was estimated at over 650,000 rubles.

19. Reimers, *Reise*, I:19–20. Reimers notes that Kutuzov only traveled during the day.

20. Johann Christian von Struve, *Reise eines jungen Russen von Wien über Jassy in die Crimm und ausführliches Tagebuch der im Jahr 1793 von St. Petersburg nach Constantinopel* (Gotha: Ettinger, 1801), 60.

21. Struve, *Reise*, 62.

22. Reimers, *Reise*, I:22–25. See also Struve, *Reise*, 61. In the small town of Shklow, which had long served as a Jewish religious center in Poland-Lithuania and in 1772 had been incorporated into the Russian domains, Kutuzov spent the night at an inn owned by a local Jewish family. He was treated to a small

theatrical production and a ball at the estate of the local landlord, Semyon
Zorich (Zorić), who had served with Kutuzov during the Russo-Ottoman War
of 1768–1774 and fought at Kagul and Ryabaya Mogila. His next layover was
in Mogilev, a quiet town in eastern Byelorussia whose "charming and excellent
location" delighted the legation members in spite of cold and miserable weather. Struve, *Reise*, 63; Reimers, *Reise*, I:27–28.

23. Struve, *Reise*, 64; Reimers, *Reise*, I:30–32.
24. Reimers, *Reise*, I:33; Struve, *Reise*, 65.
25. Reimers, *Reise*, I:43. In a letter to Empress Catherine, Kutuzov complained
that "the extremely poor roads" had delayed him and he could not get to
Elisavetgrad before April 24. Kutuzov to Catherine II, April 20/May 1, 1793,
in *M. I. Kutuzov. Sbornik dokumentov*, I:204.
26. Reimers, *Reise*, I:38.
27. In a brief letter, the Ottoman envoy called Kutuzov "the mighty general,"
"our amiable, distinguished and noble friend," and "the adornment of the
company of men of penetrating intellect," and expressed hope to see him soon
enough. Reimers, *Reise*, I:42. The European press was paying close attention to
the events in this remote corner of southeast Europe, and even a small British
periodical reported that "the Turkish ambassador to Russia has commenced
his journey from Istanbul with great pomp, attended by a retinue of upwards
of 300 persons. He takes with him a great number of rich presents, consisting
of jewels and pearls." *Hereford Journal*, April 10, 1793.
28. Reimers, *Reise*, I:40. Orthodox Easter was on March 31/April 11.
29. Reimers, *Reise*, I:4. Also see Struve, *Reise*, 66.
30. Kutuzov instructed Ivan Severin, Russia's consul general in Moldavia,
Wallachia, and Bessarabia, to convey copies of all reports that he had sent
to St. Petersburg. Kutuzov to Severin, April 14/25, 1793, in *M. I. Kutuzov.
Sbornik dokumentov*, I:203. Among his immediate tasks was handling the
growing political crisis caused by a large number of Polish troops crossing
into Ottoman-controlled territory in an attempt to escape Russian forces.
Seeking to neutralize the Polish forces and deny them safe haven in the future,
Kutuzov argued to the Ottomans that it was demeaning to the honor of the
Ottoman Empire and insulting of its sovereignty. The Ottoman authorities
agreed, and the Poles were forced to leave the territory. Kutuzov to Catherine
II, April 20–27/May 1–8, 1793, in *M. I. Kutuzov. Sbornik dokumentov*, I:203–
204, 206. For Kutuzov's instructions to the embassy officials on how to handle
this crisis, see his letters to A. Khvostov, A. Bezborodko, and I. Severin, in *M.
I. Kutuzov. Sbornik dokumentov*, I:204–206.
31. Kutuzov to A. Bezborodko, May 12/24, 1793, in *M. I. Kutuzov. Sbornik
dokumentov*, I:209; Léonce Pingaud, *Choiseul-Gouffier, la France en Orient sous
Louis XVI* (Paris: Picard, 1887), II:251–258; Jean-Pierre Poussou, Anne
Mézin, and Yves Perret-Gentil, eds., *L'influence française en Russie au XVIIIe
siècle* (Paris: Presses de l'Université de Paris-Sorbonne, 2004), 414–415.

32. Catherine II to Kutuzov, February 21/March 4, 1793, in *M. I. Kutuzov. Sbornik dokumentov*, I:192.

33. "Zhurnal torzhestvennogo Rossiiskogo posol'stva v Konstantinopol'" [hereafter cited as *The Journal of the Russian Embassy to Constantinople*], in *M. I. Kutuzov. Sbornik dokumentov*, I:648; Kutuzov to Catherine II, April 27/May 8, May 10/21, June 1/12, and June 7/18, 1793; Kutuzov to I. Osterman, April 27/May 8, 1793, in *M. I. Kutuzov. Sbornik dokumentov*, I:207–209, 211–212. Also see Reimers, *Reise*, I:40–42, 57; Hayreddin Nedim, *Bir elçinin tarihçe-i sefareti* (Istanbul: Matbaa-i Orhaniye, 1917), 14–27; Ahmed Cevdet, Târih-i Cevdet (Istanbul: Matbaa-yı Amire, 1861), V:306; F. Clément-Simon, "Un ambassadeur extraordinaire russe à l'époque de Catherine II et de Sélim III," *Revue d'histoire diplomatique* 21 (1907): 25–39; Halil İnalcık, "Yaş muahedesinden sonra Osmanlı-Rus münasebetleri (Rasih Efendi ve Ceneral Kutuzof elçilikleri)," *Ankara Üniversitesi Dil ve Tarih Coğrafya Fakültesi Dergisi* 4 (1946): 195–203; N. P. Mun'kov, *Diplomaticheskaia deyatel'nost' M. I. Kutuzova (1792–1813 g.g.)* (Kazan: Kazan State University, 1958). Kutuzov blamed the Ottoman attempt to switch the location to Bender on the intrigues of the prince of Moldavia, who "wanted to avoid losses that he would suffer from the arrival of the pasha of Bender with his vast entourage to his principality." Kutuzov to Catherine II, May 10/21, 1793, in *M. I. Kutuzov. Sbornik dokumentov*, I:208. Also see Itzkowitz and Mote, *Mubadele*.

34. Reimers, *Reise*, I:53.

35. Reimers, *Reise*, I:46.

36. Reimers, *Reise*, I:47.

37. Approaching Dubossary, the Russian embassy's march assumed "a very different mode from what it had previously been. The most distinguished persons in the suite were in handsome carriages followed by a long file of vehicles filled with servants and luggage. The march was closed by a detachment of well-disciplined Russian troops." Struve, *Reise*, 67–68. However, his colleague von Reimers had a different view. "Our procession was very much like an army's supply train," he wrote to a friend. Upon seeing its approach, the locals frequently "rushed into their houses with great noise . . . They were probably shooing away young girls from homes. . . . Arriving at a village, we first went to the nicest-looking farmhouse and asked for milk and eggs to prepare our meager meals. . . . There was seldom anything better to find. It was common for the locals to ask the advance payment for the required items or even to deny them for fear of not receiving any payment. . . . It seemed to me that a trace of a certain distrust from the last war was still lurking in the hearts of these inhabitants." Reimers, *Reise*, I:48, 53–54.

38. *The Journal of the Russian Embassy to Constantinople*, in *M. I. Kutuzov. Sbornik dokumentov*, I:648.

39. Reimers, *Reise*, I:55–56.

40. See June 13–14 entries in *The Journal of the Russian Embassy to Constantinople*, in *M. I. Kutuzov. Sbornik dokumentov*, I:648–649.

41. *The Journal of the Russian Embassy to Constantinople*, in *M. I. Kutuzov. Sbornik dokumentov*, I:649; Struve, *Reise*, 72–73.

42. *The Journal of the Russian Embassy to Constantinople*, in *M. I. Kutuzov. Sbornik dokumentov*, I:649–650; Reimers, *Reise*, I:61–62; Struve, *Reise*, 73; Sinel'nikov, *Zhizn', voennye i politicheskie deyaniya*, II:17–21.

43. Struve, *Reise*, 73–74.

44. Reimers, *Reise*, I:58–59. Frédéric Clément-Simon's article "Un ambassadeur extraordinaire russe à l'époque de Catherine II et de Sélim III"—published in *Revue d'histoire diplomatique* 21 (1907) and then as a small booklet by Plon-Nourrit that same year—is largely based on Reimers's evidence. All citations are from the booklet edition.

45. Struve, *Reise*, 74–75.

46. *The Journal of the Russian Embassy to Constantinople*, in *M. I. Kutuzov. Sbornik dokumentov*, I:650. Also see Clément-Simon, *Un ambassadeur extraordinaire russe*, 7–8.

47. Mustafa Rasih Pasha previously served as *topçu kâtibi* (scribe in the artillery corps), *süratçi nâziri* (superintendent in the rapid-fire rifle corps), *tezkire-i sani* (second secretary of the grand vizier), *tezkire-i evvel* (first secretary of the grand vizier), and *rikâb-i hümâyûn kethüdasi* (chief attendant of the sultan's retinue), his last position before being appointed ambassador. He was married to the daughter of Âtifzade Ömer Vahid Efendi, who held, at different times, the posts of *tersane emini* (supervisor of the naval arsenal), *reis-ül-küttap* (director of foreign affairs), and *defterdar-i şikk-i evvel* (first treasurer). For details on the Ottoman ambassador, Mustafa Rasih Pasha, see Ahmed Resmî, *Halifetü'r-rüesâ, Sefinetü'r-rüesâ* (İstanbul: Takvimhane-i Âmire, 1853), 140–141; Mehmed Süreyyâ, *Sicill-i 'Osmânî yâhûd Tezkire-i meşâhir-i 'Osmâniyye* (Istanbul, 1894), II:347–348; Ahmed Cevdet, *Târih-i Cevdet* (Istanbul, 1862), V:274. For biographies of Ömer Vahid Efendi, see Süreyyâ, *Sicill-i 'Osmânî yâhûd Tezkire-i meşâhir-i 'Osmâniyye*, III:594–595; Resmî, *Halifetü'r-rüesâ, Sefinetü'r-rüesâ*, 116–118; İnalcık, "Yaş muahedesinden sonra Osmanlı-Rus münasebetleri," 195–203.

48. See Stephan Conermann, "Das Eigene und das Fremde: Der Bericht der Gesandtschaft Musafa Rasihs nach St. Petersburg 1792–1794," *Archivum Ottomanicum* 17 (1999): 249–263.

49. Kutuzov was accompanied by Oriental languages secretary Zanetti, secretary Prince Yurii Obolenskii, and two kamer-pages. His exchange commissar, Passek, was attended by his aide-de-camp Premier Major Czaplitz, Captain Peter Passek, and interpreter Duza. *The Journal of the Russian Embassy to Constantinople*, in *M. I. Kutuzov. Sbornik dokumentov*, I:650; Sinel'nikov, *Zhizn', voennye i politicheskie deyaniya*, II:21.

50. *The Journal of the Russian Embassy to Constantinople*, in M. I. Kutuzov. *Sbornik dokumentov*, I:650; Reimers, *Reise*, I:63–64.

51. Struve, *Reise*, 75; Reimers, *Reise*, I:66.

52. Struve, *Reise*, 76. For details on lavish dinners and other pastimes, see Reimers, *Reise*, I:66–67.

53. The bad weather delayed the departure as well. Reimers mentions heavy rains in the preceding days and "the still cloudy weather" on June 25, although "the sun soon broke through the thick clouds." *Reise*, I:79.

54. Reimers, *Reise*, I:79.

55. Reimers, *Reise*, I:77.

56. Reimers, *Reise*, I:82.

57. Reimers, *Reise*, I:82–84, 88.

58. Kutuzov to Catherine II, June 16/27, 1793, in M. I. Kutuzov. *Sbornik dokumentov*, I:213.

59. Reimers, *Reise*, I:87, 89–90.

60. Reimers, *Reise*, I:90–91. On Suţu's appointment, see French agent Constantin's report of February 20, 1793, in Vasile Urechiă, ed., *Istoria Romaniloru: Seria 1786–1800* (Bucharest: T. Basilescu, 1893), III:9.

61. Kutuzov to Catherine II, July 2/13, 1793, in M. I. Kutuzov. *Sbornik dokumentov*, I:215; Reimers, *Reise*, I:89–91, 94–95.

62. Kutuzov to I. Osterman, July 2/13, 1793, in M. I. Kutuzov. *Sbornik dokumentov*, I:215–216.

63. Kutuzov to P. Zubov, July 2/13, 1793, in M. I. Kutuzov. *Sbornik dokumentov*, I:216.

64. Kutuzov to P. Zubov, July 2/13, 1793, in M. I. Kutuzov. *Sbornik dokumentov*, I:216. Also see Kutuzov to Zubov, January 19/30, 1794, in M. I. Kutuzov. *Sbornik dokumentov*, I:296–297.

65. For excellent details of this journey, see Reimers, *Reise*, I:104–109.

66. Kutuzov to Catherine II, July 29/August 9, 1793, in M. I. Kutuzov. *Sbornik dokumentov*, I:217.

67. For an interesting discussion, see Pompilu Eliade, *De l'influence française sur l'esprit public en Roumanie* (Paris: Ernest Leroux, 1898), 81–114.

68. During the Russo-Ottoman War, the Russian presence in Moldavia-Wallachia resulted in the split of the Wallachian Orthodox Church as the Russian Holy Synod began appointing local clergymen, including Bănulescu-Bodoni, who was named the bishop of Cetatea Albă in 1791 and then metropolitan of Moldavia in 1792. However, Wallachia has been traditionally under the sway of the Patriarchate of Constantinople, which perceived the new appointments as the direct challenge of its authority. Patriarch Neophytus VII thus asked the sultan for help in removing the new pro-Russian metropolitan. Receiving the sultan's order, Mouruzi detained Bănulescu-Bodoni and sent him to Istanbul, where he was kept in detention until freed through Russian intervention.

69. Reimers, *Reise*, I:114–118.

70. Reimers, *Reise*, I:121.

71. Catherine II to Kutuzov, February 21/March 4, 1793; Kutuzov to Catherine II, August 9/20, 1793, in *M. I. Kutuzov. Sbornik dokumentov*, I:202, 219; Reimers, *Reise*, I:121–122.

72. For details see Reimers, *Reise*, I:140–181. The leisureliness of his advance raised concerns among some Russian diplomats. See Kochubey to Vorontsov, July 9/20, 1793, in *Arkhiv knyazya Vorontsova*, XIV:10.

73. Kutuzov to Khvostov, July 20/31, 1793, in *M. I. Kutuzov. Sbornik dokumentov*, I:217.

74. Kutuzov to Bezborodko and to A. Khvostov, n.d. [ca. early September 1793], in *M. I. Kutuzov. Sbornik dokumentov*, I:225, 227. "I have numerous sick men and officials," he told his wife. Kutuzov to his wife, August 12/23, 1793, in *The Kutuzov Papers* 11 (1870): 501.

75. Kutuzov to his wife, August 15/26, 1793, in *The Kutuzov Papers* 11 (1870): 502. Reimers noted in his journal that Kutuzov wanted to speed up the movement of the legation but could not because of the high number of ill persons. In late September, Reimers also acknowledged Kutuzov's "minor ailment," although it is unclear if it was real or a pretend one. As he approached Adrianople, Kutuzov was "unable to mount a horse because of his little indisposition and thus rode in his parade carriage in full ceremony." *Reise*, I:160, 169, 182.

76. For a list of locations, distances between them, and the time spent at each place, see Reimers, *Reise*, I:203–205.

77. "Podrobnoie opisanie puti chrezvychaynogo i polnomochnogo rossiiskago imperatorskogo posol'stva, posle Yasskago mira, ot Rushchuka chrez Shumlu v Konstantinopol', v 1793 godu. S voiennymi zamechaniyami o zemle, s pokazaniem sposoba provest' i prodovol'stvovat' ot 30-ti do 40-ka tysiach voiska," *Russkaya starina* 21 (1878): 100–124.

78. Catherine II to Kutuzov, February 21/March 4, 1793, in *M. I. Kutuzov. Sbornik dokumentov*, I:202.

79. Reimers, *Reise*, I:156, 167.

80. Kochubey to Kutuzov, July 22/August 2, 1793; Kutuzov to Catherine II, September 21/October 2, 1793, in *M. I. Kutuzov. Sbornik dokumentov*, I:227, 230.

81. Kutuzov to Sievers, August 12/23, 1793, in *M. I. Kutuzov. Sbornik dokumentov*, I:223.

82. Kutuzov to P. Zubov, August 9/20, 1793, in *M. I. Kutuzov. Sbornik dokumentov*, I:221.

83. Imperial Rescript of September 2/13, 1793, in *The Potemkin Papers, 1790–1793*, 352; Sinel'nikov, *Zhizn', voennye i politicheskie deyaniya*, II:32; Yu. Gulyaev and V. Soglaev, *Fel'dmarshal Kutuzov. Istoriko-biograficheskii ocherk* (Moscow: Arkheograficheskii Tsentr, 1995), 124.

84. Kutuzov to his wife, August 12/23, 1793, in *The Kutuzov Papers* 11 (1870): 501.

85. Kutuzov to Razumovskii, September 8/19, 1793; Kutuzov to Khvostov, August 6/17, 1793, in *M. I. Kutuzov. Sbornik dokumentov*, I:218, 228. Also see his letter to Khvostov of August 29/September 9, 1793, in *M. I. Kutuzov. Sbornik dokumentov*, I:226–227.

86. Kutuzov to Razumovskii, September 8/19, 1793, in *M. I. Kutuzov. Sbornik dokumentov*, I:228.

87. Reimers, *Reise*, I:136–137.

88. Kutuzov to Zubov, August 20/31, 1793, in *M. I. Kutuzov. Sbornik dokumentov*, I:224.

89. Kutuzov to Zubov, July 2/13, 1793; Kutuzov to Catherine II, August 21/September 1, 1793, in *M. I. Kutuzov. Sbornik dokumentov*, I:216, 226.

Chapter 8

1. "Tomorrow I will be at San Stefano, just ten *verstas* [6.6 miles] from Istanbul. Today is Wednesday. With the Lord's help, I will enter Istanbul on Monday." Kutuzov to his wife, August 15/26, 1793, in *The Kutuzov Papers* 11 (1870): 502

2. Heinrich Christoph von Reimers, *Reise der Russisch-Kaiserlichen Ausserordentlichen Gesandtschaft an die Othomanische Pforte im Jahr 1793* (St. Petersburg: Schnoorschen Buchdruckerei, 1803), I:200; F. Clément-Simon, "Un ambassadeur extraordinaire russe à l'époque de Catherine II et de Sélim III," *Revue d'histoire diplomatique* 21 (1907): 10–11. The tent was valued at 30,000 piastres.

3. Kutuzov to Khvostov, September 12/23, 1793; Kutuzov to Korf, September 22/October 4, 1793, in *M. I. Kutuzov. Sbornik dokumentov* (Moscow: Voeniszdat, 1950), I:229–230. Kutuzov was pleased to inform the empress that "currently there are no disputes with regards to the procedures." See his letter of September 21/October 2, 1793, in *M. I. Kutuzov. Sbornik dokumentov*, 230. Also see Reimers, *Reise*, I:207.

4. Kutuzov to his wife, October 4/15, 1793, in *The Kutuzov Papers* 11 (1870): 502; Kutuzov to Catherine II, October 5/16, 1793, in *M. I. Kutuzov. Sbornik dokumentov*, I:231–232.

5. Monk Meletij, *Puteshestvie vo Ierusalim Sarovskija Obshhezhitel'nyja Pustyni Ieromonaha Meletija v 1793 i 1794 godu* (Moscow: A. Reshetnikov, 1798), 17–18.

6. Meletij, *Puteshestvie*, 19. See the similar account in Reimers, *Reise*, I:214.

7. Reimers, *Reise*, I:212–214, 216–217.

8. Meletij, *Puteshestvie*, 19.

9. Contrary to some claims that this was a significant increase from the 400 piastres that were given to Repnin in 1775, Kutuzov noted in his report that the sum represented the same allotment as in 1775 but adjusted for inflation.

10. Reimers, *Reise*, I:218.

11. Kutuzov to his wife, October 4/15, 1793, in *The Kutuzov Papers* 11 (1870): 502.

12. Kutuzov to his wife, October 4/15, 1793, in *The Kutuzov Papers* 11 (1870): 503. Also see Reimers, *Reise*, I:218–220.

13. Writing to Catherine on October 16, Kutuzov admitted that he felt weak and could not yet start official visits to various embassies. *M. I. Kutuzov. Sbornik dokumentov*, I:233.

14. Kutuzov to Catherine II, October 20/31, 1793, in *M. I. Kutuzov. Sbornik dokumentov*, I:235. Also see Kutuzov to his wife, January 6/17, 1794, in *The Kutuzov Papers* 11 (1870): 506.

15. *The Journal of the Russian Embassy to Constantinople*, I:653–654; Reimers, *Reise*, II:19.

16. Entry for October 29/November 9 in *The Journal of the Russian Embassy to Constantinople*, I:654; Johann Christian von Struve, *Reise eines jungen Russen von Wien über Jassy in die Crimm und ausführliches Tagebuch der im Jahr 1793 von St. Petersburg nach Constantinopel* (Gotha: Ettinger, 1801), 173.

17. Entry for October 29/November 9, in *The Journal of the Russian Embassy to Constantinople*, I:654.

18. For a full list of participants, see entry for October 29/November 9 in *The Journal of the Russian Embassy to Constantinople*, I:654–656.

19. Struve, *Reise*, 173.

20. Entry for October 29/November 9, in *The Journal of the Russian Embassy to Constantinople*, I:656–657.

21. Kutuzov to Catherine II, November 5/16, 1793, in *M. I. Kutuzov. Sbornik dokumentov*, I:242; entry for October 29/November 9, in *The Journal of the Russian Embassy to Constantinople*, I:658; Struve, *Reise*, 176.

22. Struve, *Reise*, 176–177. The embassy journal states that Kutuzov left his residence at five o'clock in the morning. *The Journal of the Russian Embassy to Constantinople*, I:658.

23. For an excellent discussion, see Hakan T. Karateke, ed., *An Ottoman Protocol Register Containing Ceremonies from 1736 to 1808: BEO Sadaret Defterleri 250 in the Prime Ministry Ottoman State Archives* (London: Asiatic Society, 2007); Hakan T. Karateke, *Padisahim cok yasa! Osmanli devletinin son yuzyilinda merasimler* (Istanbul, 2004).

24. Kutuzov to Catherine II, November 5/16, 1793, in *M. I. Kutuzov. Sbornik dokumentov*, I:242.

25. *The Journal of the Russian Embassy to Istanbul*, I:659.

26. Kutuzov to his wife, November 5/16, 1793, in *The Kutuzov Papers* 11 (1870): 503.

27. *The Journal of the Russian Embassy to Istanbul*, I:659.

28. Kutuzov to Sievers, November 5/16, 1793, in *M. I. Kutuzov. Sbornik dokumentov*, I:249.

29. Kutuzov to Catherine II, November 5/16, 1793, in *M. I. Kutuzov. Sbornik dokumentov*, I:243; Kutuzov to his wife, November 5/16, 1793, in *The Kutuzov Papers* 11 (1870): 503–504.

30. Kutuzov to Catherine II and Kutuzov to Sievers, November 5/16, 1793, in *M. I. Kutuzov. Sbornik dokumentov*, I:243, 249. Also see *The Journal of the Russian Embassy to Istanbul*, I:660.

31. *The Journal of the Russian Embassy to Istanbul*, I:660; Kutuzov to Sievers, November 5/16, 1793, in *M. I. Kutuzov. Sbornik dokumentov*, I:250. He did allow other embassy members to be held, slightly, by the edges of their robes.

32. "Character of the Reigning Sultan Selim III," in *An Historical Miscellany of the Curiosities and Rarities in Nature and Art* IV (1793): 176.

33. Kutuzov to his wife, November 5/16, 1793, in *The Kutuzov Papers* 11 (1870): 504. Kutuzov's speech and Selim's response are included the embassy's journal. *The Journal of the Russian Embassy to Istanbul*, I:660–661. Also see Kutuzov to Catherine II and Kutuzov to Sievers, November 5/16, 1793, in *M. I. Kutuzov. Sbornik dokumentov*, I:243, 249–250.

34. For details, see Reimers, *Reise*, II:46–56, 65, 70–76, 84–92, 95–98, 102; I. M. El'terman, *Posol'stvo kutuzova v Turtsii v 1793–1794 gg* (Moscow, 1945), 72; Clément-Simon, *Un ambassadeur extraordinaire russe*, 12–15.

35. Kutuzov to his wife, December 7/18, 1793, in *The Kutuzov Papers* 11 (1870): 504–505.

36. Kutuzov to his wife, February 21/March 4, 1794, in *The Kutuzov Papers* 11 (1870): 506.

37. Kutuzov to his wife, December 18/29, 1793, in *The Kutuzov Papers* 11 (1870): 505.

38. François de Callières, *De la manière de négocier avec les souverains* (Amsterdam: La Compagnie, 1716), 173–176.

39. Denis Davydov, *Sochineniya Denisa Vasil'evicha Davydova* (St. Petersburg: Evg. Evdokimov, 1893), II:294.

40. Fedor Glinka, *Ocherki Borodinskogo srazheniya* (Moscow: N. Stepanov, 1839), I:27.

41. Kutuzov to Catherine II, November 5/16, 1793, in *M. I. Kutuzov. Sbornik dokumentov*, I:243; Kutuzov to his wife, November 5/16, 1793 in *The Kutuzov Papers* 11 (1870): 503.

42. Kutuzov to his wife, December 7/18, 1793, in *The Kutuzov Papers* 11 (1870): 504.

43. Kutuzov to Catherine II, November 5/16, 1793, in *M. I. Kutuzov. Sbornik dokumentov*, I:242; Kutuzov to his wife, December 7/18, 1793, in *The Kutuzov Papers* 11 (1870): 504–505; Dmitrii Bantysh-Kamenskii, *Biografii rossiiskikh generalissimusov i general-fel'dmarshalov* (St. Petersburg: Tip. Tret'ego dept. Min. Gos. Imuschestv, 1840), III:39–40. L. Rakovskii's popular novel *Kutuzov* may have contributed to the popularity of the seraglio story that endures to the present day. Implausible as such claims may sound, one Russian historian even claimed that it took him "twenty years to establish the names of women with whom Kutuzov conversed in the gardens of the seraglio." Yet none of Kutuzov's letters or other embassy

documents mention such a meeting ever taking place. Kutuzov simply mentions dispatching Pizzani with two other officials to deliver gifts to Mihrişah Sultan in the seraglio. For examples of the "seraglio visit myth," see Polovtsev, *Russkii biograficheskii slovar'*, IV:640 (e-version at http://rulex .ru/xPol/); Roger Parkinson, *The Fox of the North: The Life of Kutuzov, General of War and Peace* (New York: D. McKay, 1976), 34; L. Rakovskii, *Kutuzov* (Leningrad: Lenizdat, 1971); Vitalii Sheremet, "Kak Kutuzov v garem popal," *Nauka i religiya* 4 (1995): 20–23, e-version at https://litresp.com/ chitat/ru/%D0%9F/plugin-vladimir-aleksandrovich/razvedka-bila-vsegda/ 11; Vitalii Sheremet, *Voina i biznes: vlast' den'gi i oruzhie. Evropa i Blizhnii Vostok v novoe vremya* (Moscow: Techn. Shkola Biznesa, 1995), 120–121; Olga Dmitrieva, "Kutuzov v gareme," *Sovershenno sekretno*, November 1, 2010, https://www.sovsekretno.ru/articles/kutuzov-v-gareme_1/; Valerii Voskoboinikov, "Kutuzov v gareme turetskogo sultana," *Partner* 4, no. 223 (2016), https://www.partner-inform.de/partner/detail/2016/4/235/7920/ kutuzov-v-gareme-tureckogo-sultana?lang=ru; "Kak Kutuzov zaklyuchil sdelku v gareme," *Rambler novosti*, April 17, 2018, https://news.rambler.ru/ other/39636579-kak-kutuzov-zaklyuchil-sdelku-v-gareme/.

44. See Catherine II's instructions in *M. I. Kutuzov. Sbornik dokumentov*, I:195–203. "Our genuine desire is to maintain peace and good understanding with the Porte, which are needed for the respite after the hard toil and turmoil that our empire has experienced, and for the revival of the trade and the flourishing of our various regions and industries," stressed Empress Catherine. Catherine II to Kutuzov, February 21/March 4, 1793, in *M. I. Kutuzov. Sbornik dokumentov*, I:196.

45. Catherine II to Kutuzov, February 21/March 4, 1793, in *M. I. Kutuzov. Sbornik dokumentov*, I:196.

46. Catherine II to Kutuzov, February 21/March 4, 1793, in *M. I. Kutuzov. Sbornik dokumentov*, I:196–197.

47. Catherine II to Kutuzov, February 21/March 4, 1793, in *M. I. Kutuzov. Sbornik dokumentov*, I:198–199.

48. See his letter explaining high costs of remodeling his home in order to make it comparable to other ambassadorial residencies. Kutuzov to Catherine II, October 5/16, 1793, in *M. I. Kutuzov. Sbornik dokumentov*, I:234.

49. Kutuzov to his wife, October 20/31 and December 18/29, 1793, in *The Kutuzov Papers* 11 (1870): 503, 505.

50. *Polnoe sobranie zakonov Rossiiskoi Imperii*, XXI, no. 15757, cols. 939–956.

51. For context, see Michael Talbot, *British-Ottoman Relations, 1661–1807: Commerce and Diplomatic Practice in Eighteenth Century Istanbul* (Woodbridge, UK: Boydell Press, 2017).

52. Kutuzov to Kochubey, March 15/26, 1794, in *M. I. Kutuzov. Sbornik dokumentov*, I:326.

53. Callières, *De la manière de négocier avec les souverains*, 177.

54. Kutuzov to Catherine II, November 5/16, 1793, in *M. I. Kutuzov. Sbornik dokumentov*, I:245.

55. Kutuzov to Catherine II, November 5/16, 1793, in *M. I. Kutuzov. Sbornik dokumentov*, I:247.

56. Kutuzov to Zubov, January 19/30, 1794, in *M. I. Kutuzov. Sbornik dokumentov*, I:296–297.

57. Struve, *Reise*, 244.

58. For details, see Igor' Fomenko, *Diplomaticheskaia missiia M. I. Kutuzova. Karta Konstantinopolia 1794 goda* (Moscow: State Historical Museum, 2013).

59. Kutuzov to Mordvinov, January 5/16, 1794, in *M. I. Kutuzov. Sbornik dokumentov*, I:290.

60. Kutuzov to Empress Catherine, October 20/31, 1793, in *M. I. Kutuzov. Sbornik dokumentov*, I:237.

61. See his biography in Louis Gabriel Michaud, *Biographie universelle ancienne et modern* (Paris: Madame C. Desplaces, 1855), X:477.

62. For details, see Amaury Faivre d'Arcier, *Les oubliés de la liberté: Négociants, consuls et missionnaires français au Levant pendant la Révolution, 1784–1798* (Brussels, 2007); Orville T. Murphy, "Louis XVI and the Pattern and Costs of a Policy Dilemma: Russia and the Eastern Question, 1787–1788," *Proceedings of the Consortium on Revolutionary Europe 1750–1850* (1986): 264–274.

63. See "Memoire pour servir d'instructions à Marie Descorches allant à Constantinople en qualité d'envoyé extraordinaire de la République française, près la Porte ottomane," Centre des Archives Diplomatiques (Nantes), Constantinople, Ambassade, Série B3. For more historical context, see Pascal Firges, *French Revolutionaries in the Ottoman Empire: Diplomacy, Political Culture, and the Limiting of Universal Revolution, 1792–1798* (Oxford: Oxford University Press, 2017).

64. Descorches to French Foreign Minister, September 1, 1793, Archives du Ministère des Affaires Etrangères, Correspondance politique, Turquie 185, fol. 280.

65. Kutuzov to Sievers, December 5/16, 1793, in *M. I. Kutuzov. Sbornik dokumentov*, I:267. "The French affairs served as a political barometer of the Porte," Kutuzov wrote to the Russian ambassador in Vienna. Kutuzov to Razumovskii, November 14/25, 1793, in *M. I. Kutuzov. Sbornik dokumentov*, I:252.

66. Kutuzov to Empress Catherine, October 20/31, 1793; Kutuzov to Sievers December 5/16, 1793, in *M. I. Kutuzov. Sbornik dokumentov*, I:235, 267–268.

67. Catherine to Dolgorukov, January 14/25, 1794; Catherine's Decree on Contingency Disposition of the Army, January 16/27, 1794, in *M. I. Kutuzov. Sbornik dokumentov*, I:295–296.

68. Kutuzov to Catherine II, November 5/16, 1793; Kutuzov to Dolgorukov, January 5/16, 1794; Kutuzov to Severin, January 5/16, 1794, in *M. I. Kutuzov. Sbornik dokumentov*, I:244, 292.

69. Kutuzov to N. Mordvinov, January 5/16, 1794, in *M. I. Kutuzov. Sbornik dokumentov*, I:290–291.

70. As a well-read man, Kutuzov would have been aware of Marcus Tullius Cicero's Orationes Philippicae, where the Roman statesman famously states that "the sinews of war are infinite money" (Nervos belli, pecuniam infinitam).

71. The practice of *malikanes* was introduced in the latter part of the seventeenth century. The idea was that the holders of these life-term tax farms would have a long-term interest in protecting the sources of their revenues in order to ensure the longevity and stability of their investment. For details, see Dina Rizk Khoury, *State and Provincial Society in the Ottoman Empire* (Cambridge: Cambridge University Press, 1997), 102–103; Sevket Pamuk, *A Monetary History of the Ottoman Empire* (Cambridge: Cambridge University Press, 2000), 200–201.

72. Kutuzov to Empress Catherine, October 20/31, 1793; Kutuzov to Catherine II, December 20/31, 1793; Kutuzov to Suvorov, January 5/16, 1794, in *M. I. Kutuzov. Sbornik dokumentov*, I:237, 275–277, 289–290; Rimers, *Reise*, I:185–186.

73. Kutuzov to Catherine, October 20/31, 1793, in *M. I. Kutuzov. Sbornik dokumentov*, I:238.

74. Kutuzov to Catherine, November 20/December 1, 1793, and March 6/17, 1794, in *M. I. Kutuzov. Sbornik dokumentov*, I:252–253, 320.

75. Kutuzov to Razumovskii, October 31/November 11, 1793; Kutuzov to Catherine II, November 5/16, 1793, in *M. I. Kutuzov. Sbornik dokumentov*, I:242, 246. Also see Descorches's reports in Archives du Ministère des Affaires Etrangères, Correspondance politique, Turquie 186.

76. Kutuzov to Razumovskii, January 14/25, 1794, in *M. I. Kutuzov. Sbornik dokumentov*, I:294; Kutuzov to his wife, February 5/16, 1794, in *The Kutuzov Papers* 11 (1870): 506.

77. Kutuzov to Catherine II, January 20/31, 1794, in *M. I. Kutuzov. Sbornik dokumentov*, I:297–298.

78. When the Austrian agents secretly intercepted French diplomatic communications, the Austrian embassy shared details with Kutuzov, who then informed his superiors. Kutuzov also developed close relations with the Prussian ambassador, Friedrich Wilhelm Ernst von Knobelsdorff, who even shared the instructions he had received from King Frederick Wilhelm II authorizing him to coordinate activities with the Russian mission because "the interests of the Russian court coincide with ours." Kutuzov to Catherine II, November 5/16, 1793, in *M. I. Kutuzov. Sbornik dokumentov*, I:245. For an interesting discussion of the Austrian side, see Karl A. Roider, *Austria's Eastern Question, 1700–1790* (Princeton, NJ: Princeton University Press, 2016/1982); David Do Paço, "A Social History of Trans-Imperial Diplomacy in a Crisis Context: Herbert von Rathkeal's Circles of Belonging in Pera, 1779–1802," *The International History Review* 41, no. 5 (2019): 981–1002.

79. Kutuzov to Catherine II, December 5/16, 1793, in *M. I. Kutuzov. Sbornik dokumentov*, I:263.

80. In a letter to Catherine, Kutuzov elusively describes his agent as "an official who is employed by the Porte and who has supplied us with information during the Congress of Jassy." Kutuzov to Catherine II, December 5/16, 1793, in *M. I. Kutuzov. Sbornik dokumentov*, I:262.

81. Kutuzov to Catherine, 5/16 January 1794, in *M. I. Kutuzov. Sbornik dokumentov*, I:287.

82. Anton Boudewijn Gijsbert van baron Dedem van de Gelder, *Un général hollandais sous le premier empire: Mémoires du général Bon de Dedem de Gelder, 1774–1825* (Paris: L. Plon, 1900), 81. Dedem's father-in-law was the Prussian ambassador to the Porte.

83. Firges, *French Revolutionaries in the Ottoman Empire*, 169–172.

84. Frédéric Hitzel, "Étienne-Félix Hénin, un jacobin à Istanbul (1793–1795)," *Anatolia moderna. Yeni anadolu* 1 (1991): 35–46.

85. Kutuzov to Catherine II, January 5/16, 1794; Kutuzov to Kochubey, March 15/26, 1794, in *M. I. Kutuzov. Sbornik dokumentov*, I:288, 325.

86. Kutuzov to his wife, December 18/29, 1793, and January 20/31, 1794, in *The Kutuzov Papers* 2 (1870): 505–506.

87. Kutuzov to Catherine II, January 20/31, 1794, in *M. I. Kutuzov. Sbornik dokumentov*, I:300.

88. See discussion in Halil Inalcik, "Yaş muahedesinden sonra Osmanlı-Rus münasebetleri Rasih Efendi ve General Kutuzof Elçilikleri," *Ankara Üniversitesi dil ve Tarih-Coğrafya Fakültesi Dergisi* IV, no. 2 (1946): 195–203; Will Smiley, "Freeing 'The Enslaved People of Islam': The Changing Meaning of Ottoman Subjecthood for Captives in the Russian Empire," *Journal of the Ottoman and Turkish Studies Association* 3, no. 2 (2016): 235–254; Thomas Naff, "Reform and the Conduct of Ottoman Diplomacy in the Reign of Selim III, 1789–1807," *Journal of the American Oriental Society* 83, no. 3 (1963): 304; Stanford J. Shaw, *Between Old and New: The Ottoman Empire Under Sultan Selim III, 1789–1807* (Cambridge, MA: Harvard University Press, 1971), 189. Also see Valeriy Morkva, "Russia's Policy of Rapprochement with the Ottoman Empire in the Era of the French Revolutionary and Napoleonic Wars, 1792–1806," Ph.D. diss., Bilkent University, 2010.

89. Kutuzov to Catherine II, November 5/16, 1793; Kutuzov to Razumovskii, November 15/25, 1793, in *M. I. Kutuzov. Sbornik dokumentov*, I:247, 252.

90. Collegium of Foreign Affairs to Kutuzov, November 30/December 11 and December 9/20, 1793, in *M. I. Kutuzov. Sbornik dokumentov*, I:259, 271.

91. Reimers, *Reise*, II:188.

92. Kochubey to Semen Vorontsov, July 9/20, 1793, in *Arkhiv knyazya Vorontsova* (Moscow: Tip. Gracheva, 1870–1895), XIV:10. Also see Kochubey to Vorontsov, July 20/31, 1793, and November 19/30, 1793, in *Arkhiv knyazya Vorontsova*, XIV:12, 26.

93. As a close friend of Emperor Alexander I, Kochubey later became one of the most influential statesmen in the Russian Empire, serving as the president of the Collegium of Foreign Affairs in 1801–1802, minister of interior in 1802–1807 and 1819–1823, chair of the State Council in 1827–1834, chair of the Committee of Ministers in 1827–1832, and the chancellor of the Russian Empire in 1834.

94. Kutuzov to his wife, January 20/31, 1794, in *The Kutuzov Papers* 11 (1870): 506.

95. Kutuzov to Catherine II, December 20/31, 1793, in *M. I. Kutuzov. Sbornik dokumentov*, I:274–275.

96. Selim III to Catherine II, February 23/March 6, 1794; Kutuzov to Catherine II, March 6/17, 1794, in *M. I. Kutuzov. Sbornik dokumentov*, I:316, 320–321. Kutuzov was somewhat disappointed that he received no gifts from the sultan on his departure. He ruefully wrote his wife, "The sultan gave no gifts, but it is not a custom to do so." He was pleased with the gifts from the grand vizier and viziers. Kutuzov to his wife, January 6/17, 1794, in *The Kutuzov Papers* 11 (1870): 506.

97. Kutuzov to Catherine II, March 23/April 3, 1794, in *M. I. Kutuzov. Sbornik dokumentov*, I:329. Kutuzov departed from Istanbul on March 15/26, having spent six months in the Ottoman capital. Parkinson mistakenly claims that Kutuzov stayed there "for about twelve months." *The Fox of the North*, 34.

Chapter 9

1. The Senate confirmed his appointment a week later. Decree of the Senate, September 21/October 2, 1794, in *M. I. Kutuzov. Sbornik dokumentov* (Moscow: Voeniszdat, 1950), I:345–346.

2. Alexander Viskovatov, *Kratkaya istoriya pervago kadetskago korpusa* (St. Petersburg: Von. Tip. Glavnago Shtaba, 1832), 76–77.

3. Imperial Decree of June 29/July 10, 1791, in PSZ, VIII, no. 5811, 519. For the early history of the Cadet Corps, see Peter Luzanov, *Sukhoputnyi slyakhetskii kadetskii korpuss pri grafe Minikhe (s 1732 po 1741)* (St. Petersburg: Schmidt, 1907); A. Antonov, *Pervyj Kadetskii korpus* (St. Petersburg: Skoropechatnya Rashkova, 1906), 1–14; Viskovatov, *Kratkaya istoriya pervago kadetskago korpusa*, 1–72. On the cadet corps system in general, see N. Aurova, *Sistema voennogo obrazovaniya v Rossii: kadetskie korpusa vo vtoroi polovine XVIII—pervoi polovine XIX veka* (Moscow: Institut Rossiiskoi Istoriia RAN, 2003). For a broader look at the Russian educational system in the eighteenth century, see Igor Fedyukin, *The Enterprisers: The Politics of School in Early Modern Russia* (Oxford: Oxford University Press, 2019).

4. Fedyukin, *The Enterprisers*, 171–203; Thomas Barran, *Russia Reads Rousseau, 1762–1825* (Evanston, IL: Northwestern University Press, 2002), 58–62.

5. The best discussion of the Russian Military Enlightenment is in Eugene Miakinkov, *War and Enlightenment in Russia: Military Culture in the Age of Catherine II* (Toronto: University of Toronto Press, 2020). For a broader view

on the Enlightenment in Russia, see Emmanuel Waegemens, Hans van Koningsbrugge, and Marcus Levitt, *A Century Mad and Wise: Russia in the Age of the Enlightenment* (Groningen: Instituut voor Noord- en Oost-Europese Studies, 2015); Gary Hamburg, *Russia's Path Toward Enlightenment: Faith, Politics, and Reason, 1500–1801* (New Haven, CT: Yale University Press, 2016); Elena Marasinova, *Psikhologiia elity rossiiskogo dvorianstva poslednei treti XVIII veka: Po materialam perepiski* (Moscow: ROSSPEN, 1999); Anna Kuxhausen, *From the Womb to the Body Politic: Raising the Nation in Enlightenment Russia* (Madison: University of Wisconsin Press, 2013); Elise Wirtschafter, *Religion and Enlightenment in Catherinian Russia: The Teachings of Metropolitan Platon* (DeKalb: Northern Illinois University Press, 2013); Elise Wirtschafter, *From Serf to Russian Soldier* (Princeton, NJ: Princeton University Press, 1990).

6. For an interesting discussion, see Christy Pichichero, *The Military Enlightenment: War and Culture in the French Empire from Louis XIV to Napoleon* (Ithaca, NY: Cornell University Press, 2017), 65–150; Elisabeth Krimmer and Patricia Anne Simpson, eds., *Enlightened War: German Theories and Cultures of Warfare from Frederick the Great to Clausewitz* (Rochester, NY: Camden House, 2011), 1–20; Azar Gat, *A History of Military Thought: From the Enlightenment to the Cold War* (Oxford: Oxford University Press, 2001), 27–96.

7. The Statute of the Land Noble Cadet Corps, September 11/22, 1766, in PSZ, XVII, no. 12741, 976.

8. On Betskoi and his ideas, see P. Maikov, *Ivan Ivanovich Betskoi: Opyt ego biografii* (St. Petersburg: Tip. Tovarischestva Obschestvennaia pol'za, 1904); David L. Ransel, "Ivan Betskoi and the Institutionalization of the Enlightenment in Russia," *Canadian-American Slavic Studies* 14, no. 3 (1980): 327–338.

9. Chapter III of the Statute of the Land Noble Cadet Corps, September 11/22, 1766, in PSZ, XVII, no. 12741, 963.

10. See Chapters III and IV of the Statute of the Land Noble Cadet Corps, September 11/22, 1766, in PSZ, XVII, no. 12741, 964–986.

11. Sergei Glinka, *Zapiski Sergeya Nikolayevicha Glinki* (St. Petersburg: Russkaya starina, 1895), 65.

12. Miakinkov, *War and Enlightenment in Russia*, 18.

13. Glinka, *Zapiski*, 309. Also see V. Selivanov, "Iz davnykh vospominanii," *Russkii Arkhiv* 1 (1869): 162–163.

14. Glinka, *Zapiski*, 72–73; Peter Poletika, "Vospominaniya Petra Ivanovicha Poletiki," in *Russkii arkhiv* 11 (1885): 310; Sergei Glinka, *Korpusnye vospominaniya: Iz zapisok S. N. Glinki* (St. Petersburg: n.p., 1845), 14–19.

15. Peter Poletika, for example, recalled how he was enrolled in the Cadet Corps at the tender age of four years. He was so small that he could not "dress and undress myself and kept constantly losing laces on my shoes or handkerchiefs," for which he was punished with a rod. "Vospominaniya," *Russkii arkhiv* 11 (1885): 307–308.

16. Christopher Duffy, *Russia's Military Way to the West: Origins and Nature of Russian Military Power, 1700–1800* (London: Routledge & Kegan Paul, 1981), 144.

17. Semen Vorontsov to Alexander Vorontsov, June 8/19, 1789, in *Arkhiv knyazya Vorontsova* (Moscow: Tip. Gracheva, 1870–1895), IX:146.

18. Ivan Stakhov to Semen Vorontsov, October 10/21, 1794, in *Arkhiv knyazya Vorontsova*, XIV:477.

19. Article II of the Statute of the Land Noble Cadet Corps, September 11/22, 1766, in PSZ, XVII, no. 12741, 961–962.

20. Glinka, *Zapiski*, 108–111.

21. Glinka, *Zapiski*, 114.

22. Kutuzov formally assumed his authority on September 28, 1794. See his report to Catherine II, September 17/28, 1794, in *M. I. Kutuzov. Sbornik dokumentov*, I:345. Also see the interesting discussion in Vladimir Melentyev, *Kutuzov v Peterburge* (Leningrad: Lenizdat, 1986), 32–40.

23. Glinka, *Zapiski*, 114. Quintus Fabius Maximus was the Roman general who pursued a strategy of caution and delay to wear down the mighty forces of Hannibal during the Punic Wars. This earned him the nickname of "Cunctador," meaning "delayer."

24. Ivan Zhirkevich, "Zapiski 1789–1848 gg," *Russkaya starina* 2 (1874): 216.

25. Glinka, *Zapiski*, 114. Glinka notes that Kutuzov understood why the cadets had said these words and that they had been "uttered because of outside influence." But he does not elaborate what he meant by this.

26. Kutuzov to Catherine II, November 25/December 6, 1794, in *M. I. Kutuzov. Sbornik dokumentov*, I:348.

27. Melentyev, *Kutuzov v Peterburge*, 56.

28. Order to the Cadet Corps, February 13/24, 1797, in *M. I. Kutuzov. Sbornik dokumentov*, I:361. Also see Kutuzov's orders of May 7/18 and July 1/12, 1797, in *M. I. Kutuzov. Sbornik dokumentov*, I:367–368.

29. Order to the Cadet Corps, January 26/February 7, 1797, in *M. I. Kutuzov. Sbornik dokumentov*, I:361.

30. Order to the Cadet Corps, November 29/December 10, 1794; Order to the Cadet Corps, March 22/April 2, 1796; Order to the Corps, September 19/30, 1797, in *M. I. Kutuzov. Sbornik dokumentov*, I:349, 359, 370.

31. Kutuzov to the Senate, September 26/October 7, 1794; Kutuzov to the Military Collegium, October 2/13, 1794; Order to the Cadet Corps, November 29/December 10, 1794; Kutuzov to V. Ems, February 28/March 11, 1795, in *M. I. Kutuzov. Sbornik dokumentov*, I:346–349, 355.

32. Kutuzov to Catherine II, November 25/December 6, 1794; Kutuzov to V. Ems, December 31, 1794/January 11, 1795; Order to the Cadet Corps on the Accounting Review, January 27/February 7, 1795, in *M. I. Kutuzov. Sbornik dokumentov*, I:348, 350–352. In April 1797, Kutuzov reported the results of his staff reductions. The trimmed-down Cadet Corps now employed 414 officials, not counting instructors. See Kutuzov to Adjutant

General A. Nelidov, April 9/20, 1797, in *M. I. Kutuzov. Sbornik dokumentov*, I:362–365.

33. Kutuzov to the Academy of Sciences, June 6/17, 1795, in *M. I. Kutuzov. Sbornik dokumentov*, I:356.

34. Kutuzov to Catherine II, February 13/24, 1795, in *M. I. Kutuzov. Sbornik dokumentov*, I:353–354. Kutuzov's decision to sell off the Cadet Corps's property was exploited by his rivals, who accused him of profiting from this sale. Count Ivan Evstafevich Fersen, who became the new director of the Cadet Corps in late 1797, was an old rival of Kutuzov and sought to tarnish his reputation by accusing him of mismanagement and embezzlement. Evgraf Komarovskii, who handled the Cadet Corps's paperwork, remembered receiving "numerous documents from Count Fersen about Kutuzov's alleged profiteering in selling the unused land belonging to the corps." He was convinced that at the root of this accusation lay "the mutual animosity that these two generals felt toward each other" as well as "professional jealousy." Feeling uncomfortable at being asked to undercut Kutuzov and denounce him to the emperor, who was well known for his erratic behavior, Komarovskii decided to solicit the help of Grand Duke Constantine, who reviewed the submitted documentation, found no fault in Kutuzov's actions, and instructed Fersen to make no further accusations against him. "Count Fersen was highly displeased," observed Komarovskii. "When I later met General Kutuzov, who was probably fully aware of what had transpired, he thanked me profusely." Evgraf Komarovskii, *Zapiski grafa E. F. Komarovskogo* (St. Petersburg: Ogni, 1914), 65–66.

35. Kutuzov to Catherine II, November 25/December 6, 1794, in *M. I. Kutuzov. Sbornik dokumentov*, I:348.

36. Order to the Cadet Corps, January 27/February 7, 1795, Order to the Cadet Corps, May 1/13, 1797, in *M. I. Kutuzov. Sbornik dokumentov*, I:352, 366.

37. Order to the Cadet Corps, May 2/13, 1797, in *M. I. Kutuzov. Sbornik dokumentov*, I:366.

38. Kutuzov to Emperor Paul I, November 17/28, 1796, in *M. I. Kutuzov. Sbornik dokumentov*, I:360. Once the emperor approved the proposal, Kutuzov implemented it in January 1797. See Order to the Cadet Corps, January 16/27, 1797, in *M. I. Kutuzov. Sbornik dokumentov*, I:361. In 1796, the Cadet Corps received the remaining students from the newly abolished Corps of Foreigners of Co-Religionists (Korpus Chuzhestrannykh Edinovertsev), which trained Greek, Bulgarian, Serbian, and other foreign Orthodox refugee youths as part of the Russian "soft power" outreach to the Christians of the Ottoman Empire. Because many of these students could not prove nobility, they were listed as "gymnasists" and graduated as Class 14 civil service officials or as ensigns if they entered the Russian military service. See Kutuzov to Rostopchin, October 16/27, 1797, in *M. I. Kutuzov. Sbornik dokumentov*, I:371.

39. Order to the Cadet Corps, July 2/13, 1795, in *M. I. Kutuzov. Sbornik dokumentov*, I:356–358. Also see his decree of September 30 thanking the staff for the successful summer exercises, in *M. I. Kutuzov. Sbornik dokumentov*, I:358.

40. See Kutuzov's orders of September 7/18 and December 18/19 1795, in *M. I. Kutuzov. Sbornik dokumentov*, I:369.

41. Kutuzov to the Newspaper Expedition of the *St. Petersburg Mail*, October 12/23, 1794; Kutuzov to V. Ems, December 24, 1794/January 4, 1795; Kutuzov to V. Ems, April 20/May 1, 1795, in *M. I. Kutuzov. Sbornik dokumentov*, I:347, 350, 356.

42. Kutuzov to Catherine II, December 22, 1794/January 2, 1795, in *M. I. Kutuzov. Sbornik dokumentov*, I:349. Also see Order to the Cadet Corps, January 9/20, 1795, in *M. I. Kutuzov. Sbornik dokumentov*, I:350. Company commanders were required to maintain a special ledger where they registered individual cadets' behavior. "During graduation, this book would be considered more than any other documentation," stated Kutuzov in one of his orders. Order to the Cadet Corps, January 26/February 7, 1797, in *M. I. Kutuzov. Sbornik dokumentov*, I:361.

43. Of the remaining number, one became a lieutenant in the marine battalion and fourteen went into the artillery branch (four lieutenants and ten sub-lieutenants).

44. Statute of the Land Noble Cadet Corps, September 11/22, 1766, in PSZ, XVII, no. 12741, 962.

45. Protasov to Semen Vorontsov, March 9/20, 1795, in *Arkhiv knyazya Vorontsova*, XV:47.

46. According to the Treaties of Abo (1743) and Värälä (1790), Sweden ceded to Russia the areas east of the Kymi River with the fortress of Olavinlinna and the towns of Lappeenranta and Hamina, which meant Russia came to control the southern part of the Karelia region. Collegium of War's Decree of March 14/25, 1795; Roster of Units Deployed in Finland, June 12/23, 1795, in *M. I. Kutuzov. Sbornik dokumentov*, I:377, 381–382. In 1795, the Russian forces in Finland comprised six infantry regiments, the Finland Jäger Corps, two naval artillery battalions, and 200 Cossacks. As of November 1796, Kutuzov commanded four musketeer regiments—Ryazanskii (1,983 men), Nevskii (1,901 men), Velikolutskii (1,863 men) and Sofiiskii (1,792 men)—and the Finland Jäger Corps (3,234 men).

47. In August 1796, King Gustav IV Adolf and his uncle Regent Charles, duke of Södermanland, visited St. Petersburg to arrange a marriage between the young king and Grand Duchess Alexandra Pavlovna, the granddaughter of Catherine the Great. However, the arrangement foundered on Gustav's unwavering refusal to allow his intended bride liberty of worship according to the rites of the Russian Orthodox Church. Kutuzov welcomed the king onto Russian soil and accompanied him to St. Petersburg. The Soviet historiography, however, tends to exaggerate his role in this diplomatic event,

with some historians alleging that Kutuzov's "personal charm" was crucial to "smoothing over tensions and avoiding a diplomatic rupture between the two powers." L. Punin, *Fel'dmarshal Kutuzov. Voenno-biograficheskii ocherk* (Moscow: Voennoe izdatel'stvo, 1957), 38.

48. See Zubov's lengthy instructions to Kutuzov, dated May 3/14, 1795, in *M. I. Kutuzov. Sbornik dokumentov*, I:378–381. For Kutuzov's activities, see *M. I. Kutuzov. Sbornik dokumentov*, I:383–391.

49. Selivanov, "Iz davnykh vospominanii," in *Russkii Arkhiv* 1 (1869): 165. Selivanov states that two cadets committed suicide by jumping out of a window, but he did not witness it and relied on hearsay.

50. Poletika, "Vospominaniya," 311.

51. Lidia Ivchenko, *Kutuzov* (Moscow: Molodaya Gvardiya, 2012), 183.

52. Zhirkevich, "Zapiski," 2:216.

53. Dmitrii Bantysh-Kamenskii, *Biografii rossiiskikh generalissimusov i general-fel'dmarshalov* (St. Petersburg: Tip. Tretyago Dept. Min. Gos. Imushestv, 1840), III:41.

54. Adam Czartoryski, *Memoirs of Prince Adam Czartoryski and His Correspondence with Alexander I*, edited by Adam Gielgud (London: Remington, 1888), I:64.

55. Czartoryski, *Memoirs*, I:71.

56. See Alexander Khrapovitskii, *Dnevnik A. V. Khrapovitskogo, 1782–1793* (St. Petersburg: A. F. Bazunov, 1874), 378; also see 378–389, 394, 401–403, 408–418, 422, 425, 503–504.

57. Rostopchin to S. Vorontsov, August 20/31, 1795, in *Arkhiv knyazya Vorontsova*, VIII:105.

58. Rostopchin to S. Vorontsov, July 8/19, 1792, in *Arkhiv knyazya Vorontsova*, VIII:52.

59. Czartoryski, *Memoirs*, I:74–76.

60. Jean de La Bruyère, *Les caracteres de Theophraste, traduits du Grec: avec les caracteres ou les Mœurs de ce Siecle* (Lyon: T. Amaulry, 1689). This is the fourth edition of this book, but it appeared in more than a dozen other editions in the eighteenth century, and Kutuzov would have certainly been aware of it.

61. Sergei Mayevskii, "Moi vek ili istoriya generala M. I. Mayevskogo," *Russkaya starina* 8 (1873): 153.

62. Louis Alexandre Andrault de Langeron, "Zapiski grafa Lanzherona. Voina s Turtsiei, 1806–1812," *Russkaya starina* 9 (1907): 569–571.

63. Rostopchin to S. Vorontsov, July 8/19, 1792, in *Arkhiv knyazya Vorontsova*, VIII:52.

64. Catherine II's Decree to the Senate, August 18/29, 1795, in *M. I. Kutuzov. Sbornik dokumentov*, I:382. Also see Bezborodko to Semen Vorontsov, August 19/30, 1795, in *Arkhiv knyazya Vorontsova*, XIII:355.

65. Glinka, *Zapiski*, 125.

66. A. Bezborodko to Semen Vorontsov, October 18/29, 1794, in *Arkhiv knyazya Vorontsova*, XIII:315.

67. Rostopchin to S. Vorontsov, September 14/25, 1795, in *Arkhiv knyazya Vorontsova*, VIII:111.

68. Czartoryski, *Memoirs*, I:76.

69. Alexander Pushkin, "Zametki po russkoi istorii XVIII veka," in *A. S. Pushkin. Sobranie sochinenii*, 4th ed. (Leningrad: Nauka, 1978), VIII:91–92.

70. Roger Parkinson, *The Fox of the North: The Life of Kutuzov, General of War and Peace* (New York: D. McKay, 1976), 32.

71. Glinka does not specify the reason for Kutuzov's visit. Historian Lidia Ivchenko pointed out that the cadets, upset as they were about Kutuzov's servility, seem to have forgotten that as the commander in chief of the Russian forces in Finland, Kutuzov was required to regularly report to his immediate superior, Feldzeugmeister General Zubov.

72. Glinka, *Zapiski*, 120–121. Also see Kutuzov to Rostopchin, October 21/November 1 and November 20/December 1, 1797, in *M. I. Kutuzov. Sbornik dokumentov*, I:372–373.

Chapter 10

1. John T. Alexander, *Catherine the Great: Life and Legend* (Oxford: Oxford University Press, 1989), 324–326; Nikolai Shil'der, *Imperator Pavel Pervyj* (St. Petersburg: A. S. Suvorin, 1901), 274, 277–286; Dmitrii Bantysh-Kamenskii, *Biografii rossiiskikh generalissimusov i general-fel'dmarshalov* (St. Petersburg: Tip. Tretyago Dept. Min. Gos. Imushestv, 1840), III:41.

2. Shil'der, *Imperator Pavel Pervyj*, 269–274.

3. Roderick E. McGrew, *Paul I of Russia, 1754–1801* (Oxford: Clarendon Press, 1992), 135–136, 163–165, 177–179, 193–195; Isabel de Madariaga, *Russia in the Age of Catherine the Great* (London: Phoenix Press, 2003), 256–257, 569–570.

4. Nikolai Sablukov, "Reminiscences of the Court and Times of the Emperor Paul I of Russia up to the Period of His Death," *Fraser's Magazine for Town and Country* 72 (1865): 235–236. A scion of a prominent Russian noble family, Sablukov married an Englishwoman and later settled in Britain, where he died in 1848. He wrote his recollections in English, and they were first published in *Fraser's Magazine* in 1865; excerpts from his memoirs appeared in French in *Revue Moderne*, while the Russian translations appeared in 1869 and 1908. For the Russian edition, see *Czareubiistvo 11 marta 1801 goda. Zapiski uchastnikov i sovremennikov* (St. Petersburg: A. S. Suvorin, 1908). "Never was there a sovereign more terrible in his severity or more liberal when he was in generous mood," noted Czartoryski. "Amid all that was eccentric and ridiculous, there was an element of seriousness and justice. The Emperor wished to be just." Adam Czartoryski, *Memoirs of Prince Adam*

Czartoryski and His Correspondence with Alexander I, edited by Adam Gielgud (London: Remington, 1888), I:146.

5. On Paul's character, see Hugh Ragsdale, *Paul I: A Reassessment of His Life and Reign* (Pittsburgh: University of Pittsburgh Press, 1979), 17–30, 171–178; R. E. McGrew, "A Political Portrait of Paul I from the Austrian and English Diplomatic Archives," *Jahrbücher für Geschichte Östeuropas* 18 (1970): 503–529; Alain Blondy, *Paul Ier. La folie d'un czar* (Paris: Perrin, 2020); Aleksei Peskov, *Pavel I* (Moscow: Molodaya gvardiya, 2016); Gennadii Obolenskii, *Imperator Pavel I* (Moscow: Russkoe Slovo, 2000).

6. Alexander Shishkov, *Zapiski, mneniya i perepiska Admirala A. S. Shishkova*, edited by N. Kiselev and Yu. Samarin (Berlin: B. Behr's Buchhandlung, 1870), I:13.

7. Sablukov, "Reminiscences," 228.

8. Shishkov, *Zapiski*, I:9–10.

9. Whitworth to Grenville, December 5, 1795, cited in McGrew, "A Political Portrait of Paul I," 513–514.

10. For interesting details, see new military statues, including the Military Statute of 1796 (Voinskij ustav) and the Tactical Rules of 1797 (Takticheskie pravila ili nastavlenie voinskim evolutsiyam), in *Voinskii ustav gosudarya imperatora Pavla pervago o polevoj pekhotnoi sluzhbe* (St. Petersburg: Tip. Morskgogo schlyakhetnogo kadetskogo korpusa, 1797); D. Sckalon, ed., *Stoletie voennago ministerstva, 1802–1902. The General Staff: Part 1, Book 2, Section 3* (St. Petersburg: Berezhlivost', 1903).

11. For details, see John Keep, "Paul I and the Militarization of Government," *Canadian-American Slavic Studies* 7, no. 1 (1973): 1–14.

12. Cited in McGrew, *Paul I of Russia*, 212.

13. Czartoryski, *Memoirs*, I:140–141.

14. Sablukov, "Reminiscences," 230.

15. See Suvorov's letters to D. Khvostov, written in January 1797, in G. Mescheryakov, ed., *A. V. Suvorov. Sbornik dokumentov* (Moscow: Voennoe izdatel'stvo, 1949), III:566–575.

16. Suvorov to Paul, January 11/22, 1797; Imperial Decree of January 19/30, 1797; Rostopchin to Suvorov, February 14/25, 1797, in Mescheryakov, ed., *A. V. Suvorov. Sbornik dokumentov*, III:573, 579, 582.

17. Pavel Zhilin, *Kutuzov. Zhizn' i polkovodcheskaya deyatel'nost'* (Moscow: Voennoe Izdatel'stvo, 1978), 69.

18. His Imperial Majesty's Field Chancellery to Kutuzov, September 9/20, 1797, in *M. I. Kutuzov. Sbornik dokumentov* (Moscow: Voeniszdat, 1950), I:370.

19. Panin to Kurakin, December 13/24, 1797, *Russkaya starina* 8 (1873): 362. Also see Panin-Kurakin correspondence, *Russkaya starina* 10 (1874): 71–85.

20. Kurakin to Panin, December 29, 1797/January 9, 1798, *Russkaya starina* 8 (1873): 367.

21. Panin to Kurakin, December 13/24, 1797; Kurakin to Panin, December 29, 1797/January 9, 1798, *Russkaya starina* 8 (1873): 363, 367.

22. Panin to Kurakin, December 13/24, 1797, *Russkaya starina* 8 (1873): 363, 367.

23. Kurakin to Panin, December 29, 1797/January 9, 1798, *Russkaya starina* 8 (1873): 367.

24. Paul to the Collegium of Foreign Affairs, December 14/25, 1797; Collegium of Foreign Affairs to Kutuzov, December 16/27, 1797, in *M. I. Kutuzov. Sbornik dokumentov*, I:395–397. Parkinson mistakenly claims that Kutuzov was appointed Russian "ambassador in Berlin" and "removed from the post of Director of the Cadet School, possibly to prevent his influence on future officers." Roger Parkinson, *The Fox of the North: The Life of Kutuzov, General of War and Peace* (New York: D. McKay, 1976), 37.

25. Kurakin to Panin, December 29, 1797/January 9, 1798, *Russkaya starina* 8 (1873): 367.

26. On December 27, 1797, Kutuzov announced to the Cadet Corps that he was departing on a diplomatic mission to Berlin and leaving Lt. Colonel Andreevskii as acting Cadet Corps director. Order to the Cadet Corps, December 16/27, 1797, in *M. I. Kutuzov. Sbornik dokumentov*, I:374.

27. Imperial Decrees of December 24, 1797/January 4, 1798 and January 4/15, 1798, in *M. I. Kutuzov. Sbornik dokumentov*, I:398–399.

28. Panin complained of "losing all of yesterday [January 23] in numerous audiences, visits, and boring correspondences" needed to secure the audience. Panin to Kurakin, January 9/20, 1798, *Russkaya starina* 10 (1874): 73.

29. "He is smart, capable and I discovered that we have an affinity of views on many issues. . . . He enjoys a [great] success at the court and the society, both of which are far more accessible to an old warrior than anyone else and Kutuzov amplifies this advantage by yet another one, fluently speaking the German language, which is essential here." Panin to Emperor Paul I, January 13/24, 1798, in *M. I. Kutuzov. Sbornik dokumentov*, I:400–401; Panin to Kurakin, January 13/24, 1798, *Russkaya starina* 10 (1874): 74.

30. Panin to Kurakin, January 13/24, 1798, *Russkaya starina* 10 (1874): 78; Filip Sinel'nikov, *Zhizn', voennye i politicheskie deyaniya Ego Svetlosti General-Fel'dmarshala Knyazya Mikhaila Larionovicha Golenischeva-Kutuzova-Smolenskago* (St. Petersburg, 1813), II:63–68.

31. Panin to Emperor Paul I, January 26/February 6, 1798, in *M. I. Kutuzov. Sbornik dokumentov*, I:402–403. See also John Quincy Adams's reports and letters from Berlin in *Writings of John Quincy Adams*, edited by Worthington Chauncey Ford (New York: Macmillan, 1913), II:240–259.

32. For details see A. Briekner, ed., *Materialy dlya zhizneopisaniya Grafa Nikity Petrovicha Panina (1770–1837)* (St. Petersburg: Tip. Imp. Akademiis Nauk, 1890), III:1–12.

33. John Quincy Adams to John Adams, January 31, 1798, in *Writings of John Quincy Adams*, II:249.

34. Kurakin to Panin, January 26/February 6, 1798, *Russkaya starina* 10 (1874): 81.

35. Panin to Emperor Paul I, March 4/15, 1798, in *M. I. Kutuzov. Sbornik dokumentov*, I:405.

36. For select published documents, see *M. I. Kutuzov. Sbornik dokumentov*, I:409–488. Documents related to the Finland Inspectorate are preserved at RGVIA, fonds 26 and 14758. Also see Andrei Krasnov's excellent article "Kutuzov v Vyborge," *Neva* 10 (2015), online publication accessible at https://magazines .gorky.media/neva/2015/10/kutuzov-v-vyborge.html.

37. Kutuzov to his wife, May 11/22, 1799, in *The Kutuzov Papers* 11 (1870): 507.

38. Kutuzov to his wife, n.d. [1800], in *The Kutuzov Papers* 11 (1870): 509.

39. Kutuzov to his wife, n.d. [1800], in *The Kutuzov Papers* 11 (1870): 509.

40. Kutuzov to his wife, December 29, 1798/January 9, 1799, in *The Kutuzov Papers* 11 (1870): 508.

41. Kutuzov to his wife, April 11/22, 1799, in *The Kutuzov Papers* 11 (1870): 508.

42. Krasnov, "Kutuzov v Vyborge."

43. Cited in Nadezhda Rassakhatskaya, "Tot samyj Kutuzov," Museum-Preserve "Park Monrepos," online publication at http://www.parkmonrepos.org/novo sti/tot-samyy-kutuzov.

44. See, for example, detailed reports Kutuzov submitted on July 5/16, 1798, and July 12/23, 1799, in *M. I. Kutuzov. Sbornik dokumentov*, I:430–432, 484–486.

45. Kutuzov to his wife, June 15/26, 1799, in *The Kutuzov Papers* 11 (1870): 509.

46. Kutuzov to his wife, September 27/October 8 and October 19/30, 1798, in *The Kutuzov Papers* 11 (1870): 507. *Valville* probably refers to the popular novel *La Vie de Marianne*, by Pierre de Marivaux, which appeared in eleven parts between 1731 and 1742 and was subsequently reprinted in several editions. For an interesting discussion, see Vivienne Mylne, *The Eighteenth-Century French Novel: Techniques of Illusion* (Cambridge: Cambridge University Press, 1965), 104–124.

47. Emperor Paul to Kutuzov, July 14/25, 1799, in *M. I. Kutuzov. Sbornik dokumentov*, I:486.

48. Kutuzov to Emperor Paul I, n.d. [April 1798]; Kutuzov to Emperor Paul I (with a memorandum outlining the new strategy), April 27/May 8, 1798, in *M. I. Kutuzov. Sbornik dokumentov*, I:409–410, 412–422.

49. Yu. Gulyaev and V. Soglaev, *Fel'dmarshal Kutuzov. Istoriko-biograficheskii ocherk* (Moscow: Arkheograficheskii Tsentr, 1995), 178.

50. Emperor Paul I to Kutuzov, February 15/26, 1799, in *M. I. Kutuzov. Sbornik dokumentov*, I:458.

51. Emperor Paul to Kutuzov, October 7/18, 1798, in *M. I. Kutuzov. Sbornik dokumentov*, I:442.

52. For the full extent of discussions, see Kutuzov's memorandum, January 23/February 3, 1799, in *M. I. Kutuzov. Sbornik dokumentov*, I:453–457.

53. For Kutuzov's correspondence on the border demarcation, see *M. I. Kutuzov. Sbornik dokumentov*, I:443–475.

54. Kutuzov to his wife, April 11/22, 1799, in *The Kutuzov Papers* 11 (1870): 508.

55. See Eugene Tarle, *Admiral Ushakov na Sredizemnom more, 1798–1800* (Moscow: Voennoe Izdat. Ministerstva Oborony SSSR, 1948); Desmond Gregory, *Malta, Britain and the European Powers, 1793–1815* (Madison, NJ: Fairleigh Dickinson University Press, 1996); Michael Broers, *Napoleon's Other War: Bandits, Rebels and Their Pursuers in the Age of Revolutions* (Oxford: Peter Lang, 2017), 53–84.

56. See Dmitrii Miliutin, *Istoriya voiny Rossii s Frantsiei v czarstvovanie imperatora Pavla I v 1799 g.*, 5 vols. (St. Petersburg: Tip. Shtaba voenno-uchebnykh zavedenii, 1852–1857); Edouard Gachot, *Souvarow en Italie* (Paris: Perrin, 1903); Carl von Clausewitz, *La campagne de 1799 en Italie et en Suisse* (Paris: Champ Libre, 1979); Christopher Duffy, *Eagles over the Alps: Suvorov in Italy and Switzerland, 1799* (Chicago: Emperor's Press, 1999).

57. Kutuzov to his wife, June 11/23 and August 26/September 6, 1799, in *The Kutuzov Papers* 11 (1870): 509–510.

58. Emperor Paul to Kutuzov, September 27/October 8, 1799; Imperial Decree of September 27/October 8, 1799, in *M. I. Kutuzov. Sbornik dokumentov*, I:488, 491.

59. Semen Vorontsov to Alexander Vorontsov, October 19/30, 1799, in *Arkhiv knyazya Vorontsova* (Moscow: Tip. Gracheva, 1870–1895), X:65.

60. Kutuzov to his wife, October 16/27 and 19/30, 1799, in *M. I. Kutuzov. Sbornik dokumentov*, I:493.

61. Kutuzov to his wife, October 19/30, 1799, in *The Kutuzov Papers* 11 (1870): 509–510.

62. Emperor Paul to Kutuzov, October 26/November 6, 1799, in *M. I. Kutuzov. Sbornik dokumentov*, I:495; Emperor Paul to Kutuzov, October 23/November 3, 1799, in *The Kutuzov Papers* 4 (1870): 484; Kutuzov to his wife, November 12/23, 1799, in *The Kutuzov Papers* 11 (1870): 510.

63. Imperial Decree, October 26/November 6, 1799, in *M. I. Kutuzov. Sbornik dokumentov*, I:495.

64. Kutuzov to his wife, October 19/30 and November 12/23, 1799, in *The Kutuzov Papers* 11 (1870): 510–511. Interestingly, eleven years later, Kutuzov remembered this period of his life very differently. "If you write to Vyborg, send my best regards to our acquaintances. The time I spent in this town was the most serene moments in my entire life and I have never again enjoyed such tranquility." Kutuzov to his wife, October 7/19, 1812, in *The Kutuzov Papers* 4 (1872): 649.

65. Senate's Decree, January 23/February 3, 1800, Lithuanian State Historical Archives, f. 290, op. 2, D. 60, l. 1.

66. Kutuzov to his wife, January 23/February 3, 1800, in *The Kutuzov Papers* 11 (1870): 511.

67. Hundreds of documents related to Kutuzov's activities are still preserved at the Lithuanian State Historical Archives. Some of them were published in *M. I. Kutuzov. Sbornik dokumentov*, I:501–601.

68. Kutuzov to his wife, May 25/June 6 and June 5/16, 1800 in *The Kutuzov Papers* 11 (1870): 512–513.

69. Kutuzov to his wife, January 14/25, 1800 in *The Kutuzov Papers* 11 (1870): 511.

70. Kutuzov's letters to his wife, January 14/25 and March 5/16, 1800, in *The Kutuzov Papers* 11 (1870): 511–512.

71. Kutuzov to his wife [n.d., ca. spring 1800], in *The Kutuzov Papers* 11 (1870): 512.

72. One Russian historian, Aleksandr Kornilov, called Paul a "crowned psychopath" and characterized his reign as "a sudden incursion, an unexpected squall, which fell in from without, confused everything, turned everything topsy-turvy, but was unable for long to interrupt or to profoundly alter the natural course of the ongoing process." Aleksandr Kornilov, *Kurs istorii Rossii XIX veka* (The Hague: Mouton, 1969), 58. For more judicious and insightful discussion, see Ole Feldbaek, "The Foreign Policy of Czar Paul I, 1800–1801: An Interpretation," *Jahrbücher für Geschichte Osteuropas* 30 (1982): 16–36; Hugh Ragsdale, "The Origins of Bonaparte's Russian Policy," *Slavic Review* 27, no. 1 (March 1968): 85–90; Hugh Ragsdale, *Détente in the Napoleonic Era: Bonaparte and the Russians* (Lawrence: University of Kansas Press, 1980).

73. Robert Meynadier, "Un plan de l'Empereur Paul de Russie," *La Revue de Paris* 6 (November–December 1920): 193–194; Sergey Tatishchev, "Paul Ier et Bonaparte," *Nouvelle Revue* XLIX (1889): 260; Miliutin, *Istoriya voiny Rossii s Frantsiyeyu*, V:494.

74. Bonaparte to Talleyrand, June 4 and July 4, 1800, in *Correspondance Générale*, edited by. Michel Kerautret and Gabriel Madec (Paris: Fayard, 2004–215), III:280, 326.

75. For contemporary coverage, see *London Courtier and Evening Gazette*, January 29, 1801, 1; *Bury and Norwich Post*, February 4, 1801, 4; *Hull Advertiser and Exchange Gazette*, December 26, 1801, 4; *The Monthly Visitor*, January 1802, 11–15.

76. See Franco-Russian diplomatic correspondence in Alexander Trachevskii, "Diplomaticheskie snosheniya Frantsii i Rossii v epokhu Napoleona I, 1800–1802," in *SIRIO* 70:1–10; F. Martens, *Recueil des traités et conventions conclus par la Russie avec les puissances étrangères* (St. Petersburg: A. Böhnke, 1902), XIII:250–270.

77. Senior British statesmen believed that for Britain the right to search convoys was a "question of little less than its independence, affecting all its sources of greatness, and shaking the very foundations of its naval power." Cited in Piers Mackesy, *War Without Victory: The Downfall of Pitt, 1799–1802* (Oxford: Clarendon Press, 1984), 134.

78. Sinel'nikov, *Zhizn', voennye i politicheskie deyaniya*, II:83.

79. Kutuzov to his wife, [n.d.] June and July 29/August 9, 1800, in *The Kutuzov Papers* 11 (1870): 513.

80. Kutuzov to his wife, August 9/20, 1800, in *The Kutuzov Papers* 11 (1870): 513.

81. Pavel Karabanov, "Istoricheskie rasskazy i anekdoty zapisannye so slov imenitykh lyudei," *Russkaya starina* 11 (1874): 581–582.

82. Paul to Kutuzov, November 23/December 4, 1800; Kutuzov to Paul, November 24/December 5, 1800; Kutuzov to Christopher Lieven, November 24/December 5, 1800, in *M. I. Kutuzov. Sbornik dokumentov*, I:605.

83. Kutuzov to Paul I, November 26/December 7, 1800; Kutuzov to P. Obolyaninov, December 8/19, 1800, in *M. I. Kutuzov. Sbornik dokumentov*, I:606.

84. Originaltraktater med främmande makter (traktater), August 31, 1805, *Riksarkivet* (Swedish National Archives), SE/RA/25.3/2/39/A-B; Russian Imperial Declaration, August 27, 1800; Convention Between Russia, Sweden, and Denmark-Norway, December 16, 1800, Convention Between Russia and Prussia, December 18, 1800, in August James Brown Scott, ed., *The Armed Neutralities of 1780 and 1800: A Collection of Official Documents* (New York: Oxford University Press, 1918), 489–492, 531–549.

85. Imperial Decree of December 14/25, 1800, in *M. I. Kutuzov. Sbornik dokumentov*, I:607. Count Pahlen was given command of the forces at Brest-Litovsk, while Field Marshal General Count I. Saltykov led the troops gathered at Vitebsk.

86. Friedrich Bienemann Heyking, *Aus den Tagen Kaiser Pauls: Aufzeichnungen eines kurländischen Edelmanns* (Leipzig: Duncker & Humblot, 1886), 111–154, 211–240; Mikhail von Wiesen (Fonvisin), "Zapiski . . . ," *Russkaya starina* 4 (1884): 66. Also see various eyewitness accounts in *Czareubiistvo 11 marta 1801 goda: Zapiski uchastnikov i sovremennikov* (St. Petersburg: A. S. Suvorin, 1907).

87. Czartoryski, *Memoirs*, I:187.

88. Some Russian contemporaries believed that the British government was involved in the assassination and that English gold helped finance the conspiracy. For contemporary testimonies, see *Czareubiistvo 11 marta 1801 goda: Zapiski uchastnikov i sovremennikov* (St. Petersburg, 1907); *Arkhiv kniazya Vorontsova* (Moscow, 1870–1895), X:113–114, XIV:146–148. Also see James J. Kenney, "Lord Whitworth and the Conspiracy Against Czar Paul I: The New Evidence of the Kent Archive," *Slavic Review* 36, no. 2 (June 1977): 205–219.

89. Alexander Langeron, "La Mort de Paul Ier, d'après les mémoires inédits de Langeron," *Revue britannique* 7 (1895): 63–64. Also see Alexander Brückner, *Smert' Pavla I* (St. Petersburg: M. V. Pirozhkov, 1907), 19–93.

90. For a list of some prominent conspirator names, see Mikhail von Wiesen (Fonvisin), "Iz zapisok Fonvisina," in *Czareubiistvo 11 marta 1801 goda*, 201–202. Also see *Aus allen Zeiten und Landen* 10 (1882): 13–14.

91. Langeron, "La Mort de Paul Ier," 78.

92. Zhilin, *Kutuzov*, 69.

93. Kutuzov to his wife, n.d. [early 1801], in *The Kutuzov Papers* 11 (1870): 514.

94. See January–March entries in *Kamer-fur'yevskii tseremonial'nyj zhurnal* [The Palace Kammerfurier Journal], January–June 1801 (St. Petersburg, 1901), 12–16, 30, 32–35, 37, 39–41, 45–46, 48–49, 52, 54, 56–58, 60–62, 64, 66, 68–69, 71, 74–76, 78–79, 82, 87, 88, 90–91, 94–95, 97, 99–100, 103, 106, 108, 115, 123–124, 127, 140–142, 145–146, 148–149, 151–152, 154–155, 161–162, 165, 167–168, 170–171, 173–176, 178, 181, 184–188, 190, 193–194, 196–197, 200, 202–204, 208, 210.

95. Kutuzov to his wife, n.d. [early 1801], in *The Kutuzov Papers* 11 (1870): 514.

96. The Minutes of the Meeting of the Unofficial Committee, December 23, 1801/January 4, 1802, in Grand Duke Nikolai Mikhailovich, *Graf Pavel Aleksandrovich Stroganov (1774–1817). Istoricheskoe izsledovanie epokhi Imperatora Aleksandra I* (St. Petersburg: Eksp. Zagot. Gos. Bumag, 1903), II:150. The French edition was published as *Le Comte Paul Stroganov*, edited by Frédéric Masson (Paris: Imprimerie Nationale, 1905).

97. Dimitri Buturlin, *Istoriya nashestviya imperatora Napoleona na Rossiyu v 1812 g* (St. Petersburg: Voen. Tip. Glavnogo Shtaba, 1823), I:253.

98. Pahlen's testament in Langeron, "La Mort de Paul Ier," 62–63, 66.

99. A good example of this approach can be found in the works of P. Zhilin and L. Punin, who conveniently omit the events of March 1801. The former simply focuses on Paul's criticism of Kutuzov and notes that the "situation had not changed even after Alexander I ascended the throne." The latter is even pithier, only noting that "in 1801, Alexander inherited the throne." Zhilin, *Kutuzov*, 70; L. Punin, *Fel'dmarshal Kutuzov. Voenno-biograficheskii ocherk* (Moscow: Voennoe Izdatel'stvo, 1957), 42.

100. Some levied unsubstantiated accusations that Kutuzov was "a spiteful Freemason who played a leading role in the murder of Paul; he knew about the conspiracy and assisted the murderers, both personally and through his wife and daughter." Kutuzov was indeed a Freemason, having joined the order during his European voyage in 1777. However, there is no evidence that his Freemason connections ever played any role in his professional career. See V. Ivanov, *Russkaya intelligentsia i masonstvo. Ot Petra I do nashikh dnei* (Harbin, 1934; reprint, 2008); Aleksey Martynenko, *Tainaya missiya Kutuzov* (Moscow: Litres, 2011).

101. Lidia Ivchenko, *Kutuzov* (Moscow: Molodaya Gvardiya, 2012), 223–224; Nikolai Troitskii, *Fel'dmarshal Kutuzov: Mify i fakty* (Moscow, 2002), 89–93. See also Parkinson, *The Fox of the North*, 40.

102. Sablukov, "Reminiscences," 311; Theodor von Bernhardi, "Die Ermordung des Kaisers Paul I. von Russland am 23. März 1801 (Nach Graf Levin August Theophil von Bennigsen)," *Historische Zeitschrift* 3 (1860): 150–156; Langeron, "La Mort de Paul Ier," 67–68. Also see Brückner, *Smert' Pavla I*, 95–97.

103. Kutuzov to Paul, March 19/30, 1800 (with Paul's note reprimanding him); Imperial Decree, February 24/March 8, 1801, in *M. I. Kutuzov. Sbornik dokumentov*, I:536, 608.

104. Unlike Grand Duke Alexander, who seems to have been under the illusion that his father would just step down and live happily thereafter, the ringleaders knew better than to leave a deposed monarch alive. See Pahlen's testament in Langeron, "La Mort de Paul Ier," 64. Czartoryski, *Memoirs*, I:223–255, gives an account of the conspiracy's gestation based on what he later learned from Alexander, Bennigsen, and Valerian Zubov.

105. Shil'der, *Imperator Pavel pervyj*, 439–440.

106. Entry for March 11/23 in *Kamer-fur'yevskii tseremonial'nyj zhurnal*, 221–222. Kutuzov also attended a luncheon earlier that day.

107. Langeron, "La Mort de Paul Ier," 77–78. For a different account of the conversation between Paul and Kutuzov, see Matvei Muravyev-Apostol, *Vospominaniya i pis'ma . . .* (Petrograd: Byeloe, 1922), e-version at http://www.hrono.info/libris/lib_m/mu_ap_pav1.html. For a different version of Paul's comment, see Heyking, *Aus den Tagen Kaiser Pauls*, 218. For Paul's premonition of death, see Sablukov, "Reminiscences," 312–313.

108. Langeron, "La Mort de Paul Ier," 69–72; Heyking, *Aus den Tagen Kaiser Pauls*, 219–221; Bernhardi, "Die Ermordung des Kaisers Paul I," 159–161; *Aus allen Zeiten unda Landen* 10 (1882): 12–13; Sablukov, "Reminiscences," 315–320.

109. Pahlen's words were, "C'est assez faire l'enfant, allez régner." Langeron, "La Mort de Paul Ier," 76. See also "Zapiski Iakova Ivanovicha de-Sanglena," *Russkaya starina* 37 (1883): 4; Czartoryski, *Memoirs*, I:231–232.

Chapter 11

1. Sophie de Tisenhaus, comtesse de Choiseul-Gouffier, *Historical Memoirs of the Emperor Alexander I and the Court of Russia* (London: Kegan Paul, Trench, Trubner, 1904), 82

2. Adam Czartoryski, *Memoirs of Prince Adam Czartoryski and His Correspondence with Alexander I*, edited by Adam Gielgud (London: Remington, 1888), I:253. For recent biographies of Alexander, see Marie-Pierre Rey, *Alexander I: The Tsar Who Defeated Napoleon* (DeKalb: Northern Illinois University Press, 2012); Alexander Arkhangel'skii, *Aleksandr I* (Moscow: Molodaya gvardiya, 2012); Janet Hartley, *Alexander I* (London: Longman, 1998). For earlier works, see Henry Troyat, *Alexander of Russia: Napoleon's Conqueror* (London: New English Library, 1984); Alan Palmer, *Alexander I: Tsar of War and Peace* (London: Weidenfeld and Nicolson, 1974); Grand Duke Nicholas, *Imperator Aleksandr I. Opyt istoricheskago izsledovaniya* (Petrograd: Eksp. Zag. Gos. Bumag, 1914); Nikolai Shil'der, *Imperator Aleksandr pervyi. Ego zhizn' i tsarstvovanie*, 4 vols. (St. Petersburg: A. S. Suvorin, 1897–1898). For Alexander's early correspondence with his Swiss tutor Frédéric-César de La Harpe, see V. Mil'china and A. Andreev, eds., *Imperator Aleksandr I i Frederik-Tsezar Lagarp: Pis'ma, dokumenty* (Moscow: ROSSPEN, 2014), vol. 1.

3. Diary entry for April 2/14, 1834, in *A. S. Pushkin, Dnevniki, Zapiski*, edited by Ya. Levkovich (St. Petersburg: Nauka, 1995), 36.

4. Czartoryski, *Memoirs*, I:247.

5. Czartoryski, *Memoirs*, I:248–249; Duroc to Bonaparte, May 14/26, 1801, in *SIRIO* 70:155; Semen Vorontsov to Novosiltsev, May 6/18, 1801, in *Arkhiv knyzya Vorontsova* (Moscow: Tip. Gracheva, 1870–1895), XI:391–393.

6. Imperial Manifesto of March 12/24, 1801, PSZ XXVI, no. 19,779, 583–584.

7. Pahlen's role in these reforms is still debated. See Allen McConnell, "Alexander I's Hundred Days: The Politics of Paternalist Reformer," *Slavic Review* 28, no. 3 (1969): 373–393; Rey, *Alexander I*, 87–112.

8. Czartoryski, *Memoirs*, I:161–162; Alexander to La Harpe, September 27/October 8, 1797, in *Le gouverneur d'un prince. Frédéric César de Laharpe et Alexandre Ier de Russie d'après les manuscrits inédits de F. C. de La Harpe* (Lausanne: Georges Bridel, 1902), 331–334.

9. Bavarian chargé d'affaires Olry's report of September 18, 1802, *Istoricheskii vestnik* 147 (1917): 125.

10. Bavarian chargé d'affaires Olry's report of September 18, 1802, *Istoricheskii vestnik* 147 (1917): 115. Also see Grand Duke Nikolai Mikhailovich, ed., *Iz donesenii Bavarskago poverennago v delakh Olry v pervye gody tsarstvovaniya (1802–1806) Imperatora Aleksandra I* (Petrograd: Suvorin, 1917).

11. Bavarian chargé d'affaires Olry's report of September 18, 1802, *Istoricheskii vestnik* 147 (1917): 123.

12. Czartoryski, *Memoirs*, I:260.

13. See imperial rescripts of June 18/30 and July 10/22, 1801; Senate's Decree of July 22/August 3, 1801, in *M. I. Kutuzov. Sbornik dokumentov* (Moscow: Voeniszdat, 1950), I:615, 617, 620.

14. In addition to Kutuzov, the commission comprised Generals A. Prozorovskii, I. Lamb, N. Tatischev, and N. Svechin, Intendant General D. Volkonskii, and Lieutenant Generals A. Tormasov and S. Dolgorukov. Major General I. Rusanov served as the secretary. Imperial Decree of June 24/July 6, 1801, in *M. I. Kutuzov. Sbornik dokumentov*, I:666.

15. See memorandums in *M. I. Kutuzov. Sbornik dokumentov*, I:668–680.

16. Pavel Zhilin, *Kutuzov. Zhizn' i polkovodcheskaya deyatel'nost'* (Moscow: Voennoe Izdatel'stvo, 1978), 74.

17. Zhilin, *Kutuzov*, 74–75; Vladimir Melentyev, *Kutuzov v Peterburge* (Leningrad: Lenizdat, 1986), 107–108; Liubomir Beskrovnyi's editorial note in *M. I. Kutuzov. Sbornik dokumentov*, I:636–637.

18. Palmer, *Alexander I: Tsar of War and Peace*; Leontii Rakovskii, *Kutuzov* (Leningrad: Leinizdat, 1971), 373.

19. Yu. Gulyaev and V. Soglaev, *Fel'dmarshal Kutuzov. Istoriko-biograficheskii ocherk* (Moscow: Arkheograficheskii Tsentr, 1995), 188.

20. See documents in *M. I. Kutuzov. Sbornik dokumentov*, I:615–636.

21. *M. I. Kutuzov. Sbornik dokumentov*, I:618.

22. Alexander to Kutuzov, July 29/August 10, 1801, in *M. I. Kutuzov. Sbornik dokumentov*, I:620.

23. Evgraf Komarovskii, *Zapiski grafa E. F. Komarovskogo* (St. Petersburg: Ogni, 1914), 123–124.

24. Nikolai Troitskii, *Fel'dmarshal Kutuzov: Mify i fakty* (Moscow, 2002), 94–95; Gulyaev and Soglaev, *Fel'dmarshal Kutuzov*, 188–189; Aleksey Shishkov, *Kutuzov* (Moscow: Veche, 2012), 153–154. Also see Lidia Ivchenko, *Kutuzov* (Moscow: Molodaya Gvardiya, 2012), 233–235.

25. Kutuzov to Bekleshov, April 16/28, 1801, in *M. I. Kutuzov. Sbornik dokumentov*, I:608. Alexander Bekleshov was procurator general and presided over the Senate.

26. For an interesting discussion of Russian conservatism under Alexander I, see Alexander M. Martin, *Romantics, Reformers, Reactionaries: Russian Conservative Thought and Politics in the Reign of Alexander I* (DeKalb: Northern Illinois University Press, 1997); Paul Robinson, *Russian Conservatism* (Ithaca, NY: Cornell University Press, 2019), chap. 2.

27. Weigel, *Zapiski*, II:630.

28. Bavarian chargé d'affaires Olry's report of September 18, 1802, *Istoricheskii vestnik* 147 (1917): 121.

29. Oleg Mikhailov, *Kutuzov* (Moscow: Voenizdat, 1988, reprint 2010), I:236–237.

30. S. Glinka, *Ocherki Borodinskogo srazheniya (vospominaniya o 1812 g.)* (Moscow: Tip. N. Stepanova, 1839), 27. Online edition available at Project 1812, http://www.museum.ru/1812/Library/glinka/index.html.

31. Meeting Minutes of the Unofficial Committee, January 27/February 8, 1802, in Grand Duke Nikolai Mikhailovich, *Graf Pavel Aleksandrovich Stroganov (1774–1817). Istoricheskoe izsledovanie epokhi Imperatora Aleksandra I* (St. Petersburg: Eskp. Zagot. Gos. Bumag, 1903), II:172.

32. Meeting Minutes of the Unofficial Committee, January 27/February 8, 1802, in Grand Duke Nikolai Mikhailovich, *Graf Pavel Aleksandrovich Stroganov*, II:172. During the meeting on March 29, the committee heard that the chief of regular police, Nikolai Ovsov, was "completely perplexed" about what was happening and was complaining about numerous "disagreements with the military governor that made him absolutely unneeded; he was surprised that police officers were still listening to his orders." Grand Duke Nikolai Mikhailovich, *Graf Pavel Aleksandrovich Stroganov*, II:195.

33. Meeting Minutes of the Unofficial Committee, March 17/19, 1802, in Grand Duke Nikolai Mikhailovich, *Graf Pavel Aleksandrovich Stroganov*, II:172.

34. Fedor Rostopchin, "Zapiski," in *Pozhar Moskvy. Po vospominaniyam i perepiske sovremennikov* (Moscow: Obrazovanie, 1911), II:54.

35. Meeting Minutes of the Unofficial Committee, January 3/15, 1802, in Grand Duke Nikolai Mikhailovich, *Graf Pavel Aleksandrovich Stroganov*, II:162.

36. Nikolay Grech, *Zapiski o moej zhizni* (Moscow: Zakharov, 2002), 148.

37. Fedor Tolstoy, *Zapiski grafa Fedora Petrovicha Tolstogo* (Moscow: RGGU, 2001), 140.

38. Tolstoy, *Zapiski*, 140; Vladimir Steinheil, *Sochineniya i pis'ma. Tom 1. Zapiski i pis'ma* (Irkutsk: Vostochno-Sibirskoe knizhnoe izd., 1985), 154.

39. Tolstoy, *Zapiski*, 140; Steinheil, *Zapiski*, 154.

40. Roxandra Stourdza, Comtesse Edling, *Mémoires de la comtesse Edling, Demoiselle d'honneur de Sa Majesté l'Imperatrice Elisabeth Alexéevna* (Moscow: Holy Synod, 1888), 67–68.

41. Proclamation of March 30/April 12, 1802, in *Russkaya starina*, March 1875, 629–632; Steinheil, *Zapiski*, 152; E. Karnovich, *Tsesarevich Konstantin Pavlovich. Biograficheskii ocherk* (St. Petersburg: A. S. Suvorin, 1899), 274–277; Grech, *Zapiski*, 149.

42. Meeting Minutes of the Unofficial Committee, March 17/29, 1802, in Grand Duke Nikolai Mikhailovich, *Graf Pavel Aleksandrovich Stroganov*, II:195.

43. Komarovskii, *Zapiski*, 124. Contradicting Komarovskii, Bavarian diplomat Olry's report described Kutuzov sending a report about the incident to Alexander.

44. Bavarian chargé d'affaires Olry's report of September 18, 1802, in "Iz donesenii Bavarskago poverennago v delalkh Olry v pervye gody tsartsvovanya (1802–1806) Imperatora Aleksandra I," *Istoricheskii vestnik* 147 (1917): 116–117; Grech, *Zapiski*, 148.

45. Komarovskii, *Zapiski*, 124–127.

46. On September 5, 1802, Kutuzov sent a lengthy letter admitting that poor health had interfered with his responsibilities but also reminding the emperor of his four-decade-long honorable service and the sacrifices he had made. He tendered his resignation as the governor of St. Petersburg, which was accepted five days later. Alexander to Kutuzov, August 20/September 1, 1802; Kutuzov to Alexander, August 24/September 5, 1801; The Senate's Decree, August 28/September 8, 1801; Imperial Decree of August 29/September 10, 1801, *M. I. Kutuzov. Sbornik dokumentov*, I:636–638.

47. Catherine II's Decree to the Senate, August 18/29, 1795, in *M. I. Kutuzov. Sbornik dokumentov*, I:382. Also see Bezborodko to Semen Vorontsov, August 19/30, 1795, in *Arkhiv knyazya Vorontsova*, XIII:355. The *folwarks* were those of Zubovshinskii, Shershnevskii, Kropivsnyi, Volyanskii, Selyanschinskii, Skolobvskii, Kraevschinskii, Mogilyanskii, and Nemerovskii.

48. Praskovya had eight sons and two daughters with her husband, Matvei Tolstoy: Illarion (1798–1821), Fedor (1799–1818), Pavel (1800–1883), Nikolai (1802–1880), Gavriil (1803–1848), Ivan (1806–1867), Anna (1809–1897), Feofil (1810–1881), Ekaterina (1814), and Grigorii (1816–1870).

49. Étienne Dumont, "Dnevnik Etiena Diumona ob ego priezde v Rossiiu v 1803 g.," *Golos minuvschego* 3 (1913): 157.

50. Kutuzov to his wife, August 4/16 and December 7/19, 1803; January 7/19 and May 26/June 7, 1804, in *The Kutuzov Papers* 3 (1871): 50–53.

51. For the wider context of the challenges Kutuzov confronted, see Simon Dixon, *The Modernization of Russia, 1676–1825* (Cambridge: Cambridge University Press, 1999), esp. 239–255.

52. Kutuzov to his wife, January 1/13 and March 10/22, 1804, in *The Kutuzov Papers* 3 (1871): 52.

53. Kutuzov to his wife, September 23/October 5, 1803, in *The Kutuzov Papers* 3 (1871): 51.

54. Kutuzov to his wife, August 11/23, 1804, in *The Kutuzov Papers* 3 (1871): 52.

55. Kutuzov to his wife, October 20/November 1, 1803, in *The Kutuzov Papers* 3 (1871): 51.

56. See documents in M. I. Kutuzov. *Sbornik dokumentov*, I:640–641; A. Nikolai to Semen Vorontsov, September 11, 1804, in *Arkhiv knyazya Vorontsova*, XXII:193.

57. Kutuzov to his wife, November 17/29, 1804, in *The Kutuzov Papers* 3 (1871): 54.

58. Kutuzov to his wife, March 10/22, 1804, in *The Kutuzov Papers* 3 (1871): 52.

59. Kutuzov to his wife, November 17/29, 1804, in *The Kutuzov Papers* 3 (1871): 54.

Chapter 12

1. *Vneshnaya politika Rossii XIX i nachala XX veka: dokumenti Rossiiskogo Ministerstva Inostrannikh del* [hereafter cited as *VPR*] (Moscow, 1961), I:442–445, 463–466.

2. André François Miot de Mélito, *Memoirs of Count Miot de Mélito, Minister, Ambassador, Councillor of State and Member of the Institute of France, Between the Years 1788 and 1815*, edited by Wilhelm August Fleischmann (New York: Scribner, 1881), 311.

3. Alexander's wife, Elizabeth Alexeyevna, was born Louise of Baden, the daughter of Charles Louis, Hereditary Prince of Baden, and his wife, Landgravine Amalie of Hesse-Darmstadt. Her father never assumed power because he died in 1801, long before his father (and Elizabeth's grandfather), Charles Frederick, who served as the Grand Duke of Baden between 1738 and 1811.

4. Adam Czartoryski, *Memoirs of Prince Adam Czartoryski and His Correspondence with Alexander I,* edited by Adam Gielgud (London: Remington, 1888), II:14.

5. Czartoryski, *Memoirs*, II:15; Albert Sorel, *L'Europe et la Révolution française* (Paris: Plon Nourrit, 1903), VI:361.

6. For the Russian overtures to Austria, see *VPR*, I:216, 222–223, 236, 246, 251, and 295. For the Austrian side, see Adolf Beer, *Zehn Jahre österreichischer Politik, 1801–1810* (Leipzig: F. A. Brockhaus, 1877), 73–77.

7. The Berlin Declaration, May 24, 1804, in F. de Martens, *Recueil des traités et conventions conclus par la Russie avec les puissances étrangères* (St. Petersburg: A. Böhnke, 1895), VI:337–345. For a broad discussion, see Harold C. Deutsch, *The Genesis of Napoleonic Imperialism* (Cambridge, MA: Harvard University

Press, 1938), 160–171, 197–316; Frederick C. Schneid, *Napoleon's Conquest of Europe: The War of the Third Coalition* (Westport, CT: Praeger, 2005), 53–62; Paul Schroeder, *The Transformation of European Politics, 1763–1848* (New York: Oxford University Press, 1994), 253–255; Oleg Sokolov, *Bitva trekh imperatorov. Napoleon, Rossiya i Evropa, 1799–1805 gg.* (St. Petersburg: Piter, 2019), 5–162.

8. In July 1804, with Austria delaying the recognition, Napoleon threatened to take action. In July the Russian envoy reported a conversation Napoleon had with his aides-de-camp in which he threatened that "if [Austria] continued to prevaricate, he would fix a term for her to make a decision and then, if she let that term pass without sending new letters of accreditation to her ambassador, he would change the face of Europe." Oubril to Czartoryski, July 6, 1804, in *SIRIO* 77:659.

9. Czartoryski to Razumovskii, June 19, 1804, *VPR*, II, no. 31.

10. From Archduke Charles's Assessment of the Austrian War Plans, *Ausgewählte Schriften weiland seiner kaiserlichen Hoheit des Erzherzogs Carl von Oesterreich* (Vienna: Wilhelm Braumüller, 1894), VI:81.

11. *VPR*, II:36–38, 41–43, 174–179, 355–377.

12. For details, see the Russo-Swedish Convention, January 14, 1805; Russian Declaration of Guarantee of the Anglo-Swedish Convention, August 31, 1805, in Originaltraktater med främmande makter (traktater), Riksarkivet (Swedish National Archives), SE/RA/25.3/2/42/A-H; SE/RA/25.3/2/43/A-B. Also see Convention Between Russia and Kingdom of the Two Sicilies, September 10, 1805, *VPR*, II:570–577; Russo-Turkish Treaty, September 23, 1805, *VPR*, II:584–94; Article I, St. Petersburg Convention, April 11, 1805, *VPR*, II:356; *SIRIO* 77:547–563.

13. Berlin Declaration, May 24, 1804, in Martens, *Recueil des traités*, VI:337–345. For a broad discussion, see Deutsch, *The Genesis of Napoleonic Imperialism*, 160–171; Schneid, *Napoleon's Conquest of Europe*, 77–89.

14. Article 2, in Martens, *Recueil des traités*, II:435.

15. Baron de Wintzingerode negotiated with Prince de Schwarzenberg, Mack, and Baron de Collenbach, signing an agreement addressing various issues of Austro-Russian military cooperation in the forthcoming campaign. Protocole des Conférences, July 16, 1805, RGVIA, f. 341/1, d. 26, l. 50. An abridged version of this agreement was published under title "Extrait du Protocole des Conférences entre les Généraux Autrichiens et l'Aide-de-Camp Général de Wintzingerode," in *Campagnes de la Grande Armée et de l'Armée d'Italie en l'an XIV (1805)* (Paris: Librairie Economique, 1806), supplément, 58.

16. Official "Rosters of Armies" acknowledged 463,687 men in all Russian armies and reserves. RGVIA, f. 846, op. 16, d. 3158. For an interesting discussion, see Alexander Mikhailovskii-Danilevskii, *Opisanie pervoi voiny Imperatora Aleksandra s Napoleonom v 1805 godu* (St. Petersburg: Tip. Shtaba Otdel'nago Korpusa Vnutrennei Strazhi, 1844), 12–13, 19–21.

17. Deployment of the 1st or the Podolsk Army Under Command of General of Infantry Golenischev Kutuzov, RGVIA, f. 846, d. 16, ll. 1–4; Order of Battle of General Bennigsen's Corps, n.d., RGVIA, f. 846, op. 16. d. 3130, ll. 2–3; Order of Battle of Count Tolstoy's Corps, n.d., RGVIA, f. 846, op. 16. d. 3130, ll. 1–1b; Order of Battle of Count Buxhöwden's Corps, n.d., RGVIA, f. 846, op. 16. d. 3130, ll. 4–4b. Also see Article 12 in the Austro-Russian Protocole des Conférences, July 16, 1805, RGVIA, f. 341/1, d. 26, l. 50. There is a certain confusion regarding the designation of the forces commanded by Bennigsen and Essen, with some scholars referring to the "Army of Lithuania" under Essen I and the "Army of the North" led by Bennigsen. But both generals were part of the army group commanded by Ivan Mikhelson. See *M. I. Kutuzov: Sbornik dokumentov* (Moscow: Voeniszdat, 1950), II:v–vi; *VPR*, II:691; Mikhailovskii-Danilevskii, *Opisanie pervoi voiny*, 24–25.

18. In the Russo-Austrian agreement, the Army of Podolsk is referred to "the first Russian army designated to operate in Germany." Protocole des Conférences, July 16, 1805, RGVIA, f. 341/1, d.26, l.50.

19. Schneid, *Napoleon's Conquest of Europe*, 77–90; Frederick W. Kagan, *The End of the Old Order: Napoleon and Europe, 1801–1805* (New York: Da Capo, 2006), 229–282; Alfred Krauss, *Beilagen zu 1805 der Feldzug von Ulm* (Vienna: Seidel und Sohn, 1912), Beilage III:1–6; Moritz Edler von Angeli, "Ulm und Austerlitz. Studie auf Grund archivalischer Quellen über den Feldzug 1805 in Deutschland," *Mittheilungen des Kaiserlichen und Königlichen Kriegsarchivs* 2 (1877): 398–400; Paul Claude Alombert and Jean Lambert Alphonse Colin, *La campagne de 1805 en Allemagne* (Paris: R. Chapelot, 1902), I:39–69.

20. Cited in James Stanier Clarke and John M'Arthur, *The Life of Admiral Lord Nelson from His Manuscripts* (London: T. Caddel and W. Davies, 1809), II:421.

21. For the most recent biography of Mack, see Ernst Rainer Gramm, "'Der unglückliche Mack': Aufstieg und Fall des Karl Mack von Leiberich," Ph.D. diss. University of Vienna, 2008, 310–312, 336–349. I am grateful to John H. Gill for bringing this study to my attention. For Mack's relationship with Cobenzl and its impact on the Austrian preparations for the war, see Oskar Regele, "Karl Freiherr von Mack und Johann Ludwig Graf Cobenzl: Ihre Rolle im Kriegsjahr 1805," in *Mitteilungen des österreichischen Staatsarchivs* 21 (1968): 142–164. On Archduke Charles and his relations with Mack, see Gunther Rothenberg, *Napoleon's Great Adversaries: The Archduke Charles and Austrian Army, 1792–1814* (Bloomington: Indiana University Press, 1982); Lee W. Eysturlid, *The Formative Influences, Theories, and Campaigns of the Archduke Carl of Austria* (Westport CT: Greenwood, 2000), 31–38.

22. It is unclear precisely when Kutuzov received the imperial summons. He remained at his estate throughout July. The minister of war's secret letters to Kutuzov, dated from August 19, already discuss matters pertinent to the Army of Podolsk, so the appointment most certainly took place in early August.

23. Mikhailovskii-Danilevskii, *Opisanie pervoi voiny*, 22–23.

24. Even British newspapers praised Kutuzov as "a man of bravery, active, vigilant, and enterprising." *Morning Chronicle*, October 28, 1805, 2; *Saint James's Chronicle*, October 29, 1805, 3.

25. See, for example, Mikhailovskii-Danilevskii, *Opisanie pervoi voiny*, 25; Yu. Gulyaev and V. Soglaev, *Fel'dmarshal Kutuzov. Istoriko-biograficheskii ocherk* (Moscow: Arkheografcheskii Tsentr, 1995), 192; Lidia Ivchenko, *Kutuzov* (Moscow: Molodaya Gvardiya, 2012), 256. For Austrian internal deliberations, see Gramm, " 'Der unglückliche Mack,' " 310–312, 336–349.

26. Emperor Alexander to Kutuzov, RGVIA, f. VUA, d. 3117, part 2, ll. 24–41.

27. As of August 1805, the army was deployed between Dubno, Radziwiłłów, Kremenets', Vyshnivets, Staro-Konstantinov, and Husyatyn. For precise encampments, see Plan of Concentration of the Army of Podolsk in the Radziwiłłów-Husyatyn area, August 1805, RGVIA, f. VUA, d. 3118, ll. 1–2.

28. The most influential proponent of this "calendar myth" was British historian David Chandler, who claimed "a second error was the inexcusable failure of the Austrian staff to make proper allowance for the ten days' difference between their calendar and that of the Russians who still calculated dates after the ancient Julian system." His claim has been then repeated in many subsequent publications, despite the fact that it is not true. First, the difference between the two calendars had reached twelve days, not ten, by the start of the nineteenth century. Second, many Russian documents were dated in both calendars to avoid any confusion. Third, the Austro-Russian negotiators calculated the Russians' march according to the Gregorian calendar, and the final agreement shows dates only in the new style. The marching route of the Russian army contained a list of forty-seven locations; the army was expected to march for three days and then rest on the fourth. It was to depart from Brody on August 16, reach Lemberg five days later, then proceed through Przemyśl (Premissel) to Tarnow, Biala, Teschen, Wischau, Krems, Amstetten, and Lambach, and arrive at Braunau on October 16. Austria pledged to provide sufficient provisions and supplies to the Russian troops as soon as they crossed the border. See Protocole des Conférences, July 16, 1805, RGVIA, f. 341/1, d. 26, ll. 50–70; "Extrait du Protocole des Conférences entre les generaux autrichiens et l'Aide-de-Camp Général de Wintzingerode," in *Campagnes de la Grande Armée*, supplément, 67–68. David Chandler, *The Campaigns of Napoleon* (New York: Macmillan, 1966), 383. See also Christopher Duffy, *Austerlitz 1805* (London: Seeley Service, 1977), 29; Owen Connelly, *The War of the French Revolution and Napoleon, 1792–1815* (London: Routledge, 2006), 234n16.

29. As of late August, the vanguard was 12,879 men strong, the 1st Corps had 24,852 men, and the 2nd had 18,982, for a total of 56,713 men. The total number, however, includes noncombatants and camp followers. If we exclude them, the army had 48,536 soldiers—including 33,600 infantry, 2,616 jägers, 5,920 cavalry, and 3,000 Cossacks, with more than 300 guns.

Plan of Concentration of the Army of Podolsk in the Radziwiłłów-Husyatyn Area, August 1805, RGVIA, f. VUA, d. 3118, ll. 1–4; Order of Battle of the First Army of General of Infantry Golenischev Kutuzov Marching Abroad, RGVIA, f. 846, op. 16, d. 3157, ll. 11–12; Deployment of the Army of Podolsk, RGVIA, f. VUA, d. 3109, ll. 7b–8b; Roster of the Army of the Podolsk, August 26/September 7, 1805, RGVIA, f. VUA, d. 3108, ll. 60–61. On the march, the Army of Podolsk was organized as follows: first column, Major General Peter Bagration; second column, Lieutenant General Alexander Essen II; third column, Lieutenant General Dmitrii Dokhturov; fourth column, Lieutenant General Vasilii Shepelev; fifth column, Lieutenant General Baron Leontii Maltitz; sixth column, Lieutenant General Baron Ivan Rosen. Deployment of the Army of Podolsk for the Marching, August 1805, RGVIA, f. 846, op. 16, d. 3118, ll. 9–9b; Order of Battle of the First Army of General of Infantry Golenischev Kutuzov Marching Abroad, RGVIA, f. 846, op. 16, d. 3157, ll. 11–12.

30. Alexey Yermolov, *The Czar's General: The Memoirs of a Russian General in the Napoleonic Wars*, translated and edited by Alexander Mikaberidze (Welwyn Garden City: Ravenhall Books, 2005), 37.

31. Artels were soldiers' unions established by permission of regimental commanders. Artel members shared their possessions and provisions, helping each other to survive during campaign.

32. Order to the Army, August 13/25, 1805, Lithuanian State Historical Archives, Fond 378, Office of the Governor-General of Vilnius, Kaunas and Grodno, op. 13, d. 312, l. 13. Many documents from this fond have been printed in S. Salimov and B. Tungusov, eds., *Dokumenty shtaba M. I. Kutuzova, 1805–1806* (Vilnius: Gos. Izdatel'stvo Polit. i Nauchnoi literatury, 1951); Yermolov, *The Czar's General*, 38.

33. Fedor Glinka, *Pis'ma ruskago ofitsera o Pol'she, Avstriiskikh vladeniyakh i Vengrii, s podrobnym opisaniem pokhoda rossiyan protivu frantsuzov v 1805 i 1806 godakh, takzhe Otechestvennoi i Zagranichnoi voiny s 1812 po 1815 god* (Moscow: Tip. S. Selivanovskago, 1815), I:4–5. Glinka originally published his letters in 1808.

34. See Peter Bagration's Order to the First Column, August 12/24, 1805; Leontii Maltitz's Order to the Fifth Column, August 20/September 1, 1805, in *Dokumenty shtaba M. I. Kutuzova*, 31, 36.

35. Gregor von Berg, *Autobiographie des Generalen der Infanterie Gregor von Berg* (Dresden: E. Blochman, 1871), 170.

36. On August 25, Kutuzov sent a request to V. Kochubey to make arrangements, including providing twenty horses at stopovers, along the route from St. Petersburg to Radziwiłłów. Kutuzov to V. Kochubey, August 13/25, 1805, Lithuanian State Historical Archives, f. 378, op. 13, d. 312, l. 1. For a probable route that Kutuzov took, see *Post Guide Through Russia*, translated by J. Tournier (London: T. Denham, 1812), 5–8.

37. Kutuzov to his wife, August 21/September 2, 1805, in *M. I. Kutuzov: Sbornik dokumentov*, II:36. The day before arriving at Mogilev, Kutuzov stopped for the night at the estate of Alexander Prozorovskii, under whose command he served in the Danubian Principalities in 1809.

38. Other travelers also lamented that the Russian roads were "most abominable," seemingly constructed "to delight self-mortifying pilgrims, to break postilions' constitutions, horses' backs, and travelers' hearts." Adolph Erman, *Travels in Siberia* (London: Longman, Brown, Green, and Longmans, 1848), I:306; George Augustus Sala, *A Journey Due North, Being Notes of a Residence in Russia in the Summer of 1856* (London: Richard Bentley, 1859), 127; John G. Stephens, *Incidents of Travel in Greece, Turkey, Russia and Poland* (Dublin: William Curry, 1839), 374. Also see Charles Colville Frankland, *Narrative of a Visit to the Courts of Russia and Sweden* (London: Henry Colburn, 1832), 181–182; John Dundas Cochrane, *Narrative of a Pedestrian Journey Through Russia and Siberian Tartary* (London: Charles Knight, 1825), II:10, 186, 194, 199.

39. Alexander Radischev, *A Journey from St. Petersburg to Moscow*, translated by Leo Wiener, edited by Roderick Page Thaler (Cambridge, MA: Harvard University Press, 1958), 44, 46, 118. Also see Alexander Pushkin's "Puteshestvie iz Moskvy v Peterburg" [Journey from Moscow to St. Petersburg], an interesting polemic to Radischev's work that also touches upon the subject of the road conditions. See *A. S. Pushkin. Sobranie sochinenii*, 4th ed. (Leningrad: Nauka, 1978), VI:378–405.

40. Kutuzov to his wife, August 31/September 12, 1805, in *The Kutuzov Papers* 3 (1871), 54.

41. Kutuzov to Commissary Commissioner V. Montrésor, August 30/September 11, 1805, Lithuanian State Historical Archives, f. 378, op. 13, d. 312, l. 4.

42. Christian von Lieven to Kutuzov, August 22/September 3, 1805; Kutuzov to Rosen, August 28/September 8, 1805; Kutuzov to Grabovskii, September 3/15, 1805; Christopher von Liven to Kutuzov, September 9/21, 1805, Lithuanian State Historical Archives, f. 378, op. 13, d. 315, ll. 50–50b, 84; d. 312, ll. 2, 8–9; Kutuzov to Alexander I, August 28/September 9, 1805, in *M. I. Kutuzov: Sbornik dokumentov*, II:40; Mikhailovskii-Danilevskii, *Opisanie pervoi voiny*, 35. Kutuzov did not have a high opinion of Rosen's military capabilities and was worried about his return because he would have claimed the status of the most senior lieutenant general. In October 1805, as soon as he heard about the imperial order turning Rosen's column back, Kutuzov wrote a lengthy letter to Adam Czartoryski urging him to reassign the general. "Rosen does not possess traits needed for a military command," he noted, asking the influential minister to pull the necessary strings informally in order to get Rosen a different appointment. Kutuzov to Czartoryski, ca. October 5, 1805, in *M. I. Kutuzov: Sbornik dokumentov*, II:81–82.

43. Gramm, "'Der unglückliche Mack,'" 350–372; Schneid, *Napoleon's Conquest of Europe*, 77–89. Also see Beer, *Zehn Jahre österreichische Politik*, 140–141.

44. Order to the Army, September 9/21, 1805, Lithuanian State Historical Archives, f. 378, op. 13, d. 285, l. 1; Mikhailovskii-Danilevskii, *Opisanie pervoi voiny*, 35; Yermolov, *The Czar's General*, 38.

45. Kutuzov to Elisabeth von Tiesenhausen (née Golenischeva-Kutuzova), n.d. [1805], in *The Kutuzov Papers* 6 (1874): 339. Tiesenhausen left St. Petersburg after Kutuzov, who was hoping that they would be able to meet en route and travel together. However, it did not happen, and Kutuzov noted a few times in his letters that "Ferdinand has not caught up with me yet."

46. Berg, *Autobiographie*, 171.

47. Berg, *Autobiographie*, 171. The route, as set in the Austro-Russian agreement, was as follows: Radziwiłłów—Brody—Podhirtsi—Lemberg (Lvov)—Horodok—Sudova Vyshnya—Przemysl—Radymno—Rzeszow—Debica—Tarnow—Brzesko—Gdow—Myslenice—Andrychow—Biala—Teschen (Cieszyn). Protocole des Conférences, July 16, 1805, RGVIA, f. 341/1, d. 26, ll. 53–60. Berg notes that the army had marched "some 500 *verstas*" (about 330 miles) from the Russian border to Biala in twenty-one days. If we subtract days of rest, the Russian army averaged over twenty miles a day.

48. Berg, *Autobiographie*, 171, 173–174; Glinka, *Pis'ma ruskago ofitsera*, I:7–26.

49. Glinka, *Pis'ma ruskago ofitsera*, I:20, 193–194; for description of Russian perceptions of the local population, see 171–184, 189.

50. "My fine regiment suffered grievously on this march," complained General Berg. "I lost everything that I had painstakingly saved through good parsimony. . . . It cost me a lot of money to replace the missing horses and to keep all regimental wagons in good order." Berg, *Autobiographie*, 174.

51. According to the Russo-Austrian agreement, the Russian army had to take the following route: Teschen—Frydek—Bystrice—Kromeriz—Wischau (Vyskov)—Brunn (Brno)—Pohrlitz (Pohorelice)—Krems—St. Pölten—Melk—Amstetten—Wels—Ried—Braunau.

52. Kutuzov to Razumovskii, September 11/23, 1805, in *M. I. Kutuzov: Sbornik dokumentov*, II:53–54.

53. Kutuzov to Razumovskii, September 11/23, 1805, in *M. I. Kutuzov: Sbornik dokumentov*, II:54, 57.

54. Berg noted that "all officers had to leave all their equipages behind and only the generals were allowed to take light carriages with them." *Autobiographie*, 174.

55. Kutuzov's Orders to the Army, September 11–13/23–25, 1805, Lithuanian State Historical Archives, f. 378, op. 13, d. 285, ll. 3–4b, 9, 91–92b.

56. Kutuzov to Emperor Alexander, September 12/24, 1805, RGVIA, f. VUA, d. 3108, ll. 65–66.

57. Berg, *Autobiographie*, 175. Kutuzov advised his subordinates that "the first part of each column must always go ahead on the transports so that it can complete the first half of the march before the rearward part of column, which comes on the foot." Order on Accelerating the March, September 19/October 1, 1805, Lithuanian State Historical Archives, f. 378, op. 13, d. 311, l. 6.

58. I. Butovskii, *Fel'dmarshal knyaz Golenischev-Kutuzov pri kontse i nachale svoego boevogo poprishha. Pervaya voina imperatora Aleksandra s Napoleonom v 1805 g.* (St. Petersburg, 1858), 14.

59. Bagration to Kutuzov, September 21/October 3, 1805, Lithuanian State Historical Archives, f. 378, op. 13, d. 331, l. 7.

60. See Article 6 of the Protocole des Conférences, July 16, 1805, RGVIA, f. 341/1, d. 26, ll. 50–70.

61. Maltitz to Kutuzov, September 20/October 2, 1805, Lithuanian State Historical Archives, f. 378, op. 13, d. 331, l. 128.

62. Kutuzov to Major General Strauch, October 1, 1805; Kutuzov to Alexander, n.d. [ca. early October 1805], Kutuzov to Razumovskii, October 4, 1805, in *M. I. Kutuzov: Sbornik dokumentov*, II:68–70, 75–78. Austrian documents offer interesting insights into the Russian army on the march. On September 20, 1805, Austrian officials in the Korneuburg district (northwest of Vienna) announced the impending arrival of Russian columns, with the first column expected to rest at Jetzelsdorf on October 7, at Hohenwart on October 8, and at Krems on October 9. The local population was instructed to stock up sufficient supplies and to sell them at "an appropriately low price." On September 23, the district officials received details on the size of the Russian force so that they could prepare supplies accordingly. The five Russian columns were shown as having 8,440, 9,366, 6,980, 9,200, and 10,680 men, respectively. The local authorities delivered 300 horses and dozens of wagons to facilitate the Russian movement. And yet it still took the Russian army almost three weeks to pass through the Korneuburg district, with the last Russian cavalry units reaching Schöngrabern on October 17. Ernst von Kwiatkowski, *Die Kämpfe bei Schöngrabern und Oberhollabrunn 1805 und 1809* (Vienna, 1908), 30.

63. Kutuzov to Razumovskii, September 19/October 1, 1805, in *M. I. Kutuzov: Sbornik dokumentov*, II:65–66. Kutuzov also sent a separate letter to Emperor Alexander, explaining the current challenges and requesting additional funds to purchase boots. The emperor approved granting fifty kopecks for each soldier. Kutuzov to Alexander, September 22/October 4, 1805, in *M. I. Kutuzov: Sbornik dokumentov*, II:73–74.

64. Kutuzov to Razumovskii, September 11/23, 1805, in *M. I. Kutuzov: Sbornik dokumentov*, II:65–67. One Russian participant later complained that "we found small maps of the theater of war in almost every captured French soldier's knapsack while even our senior officers had no such maps." Butovskii, *Fel'dmarshal knyaz Golenischev-Kutuzov*, 65–66.

65. The timing was not accidental. "Until now urgent army matters gave me no occasion to attempt a trip to Vienna," he explained. "But now that the Emperor [Francis] is preparing to depart for Hungary, I have decided to go."

66. Kutuzov to Razumovskii, September 22/October 4, 1805, in *M. I. Kutuzov: Sbornik dokumentov*, II:79–80. During Kutuzov's absence, Lieutenant

General Essen II commanded the Russian infantry, Shepelev the cavalry, and Müller-Zakomelskii the artillery.

67. Mikhailovskii-Danilevskii, *Opisanie pervoi voiny*, 37.

68. Kutuzov to Adam Czartoryski, September 26/October 8, 1805, in *M. I. Kutuzov: Sbornik dokumentov*, II:79–80.

69. Kutuzov to Emperor Alexander, October 2/14, 1805, in *M. I. Kutuzov: Sbornik dokumentov*, II:88.

70. Kutuzov to Adam Czartoryski, September 26/October 8, 1805, in *M. I. Kutuzov: Sbornik dokumentov*, II:82–83.

71. Mikhailovskii-Danilevskii, *Opisanie pervoi voiny*, 37.

72. Kutuzov to Emperor Alexander, September 27/October 9, 1805; Baillet de Latour, president of the Hofkriegsrat, to Kutuzov, October 12, 1805, RGVIA, f. VUA, d. 3108, ll. 68, 123.

73. Gramm, "'Der unglückliche Mack,'" 401–429; Schneid, *Napoleon's Conquest of Europe*, 105–114; Kagan, *The End of the Old Order*, 331–432.

74. Razumovski to Czartoryski, October 8/20, 1805, in Alexander Vasil'chikov, *Les Razoumowski. Tome II. Le Comte André Razoumowski. Deuxième partie, 1801–1806* (Halle: Tausch & Grosse, 1893); Mikhailovskii-Danilevskii, *Opisanie pervoi voiny*, 39. For a wider Austrian context, see Gramm, "'Der unglückliche Mack,'" 398–400.

75. Razumovski to Czartoryski, October 8/20, 1805, in Vasil'chikov, *Les Razoumowski*, 266.

76. Glinka, *Pis'ma ruskago ofitsera*, I:58–59; Berg, *Autobiographie*, 177.

77. Baillet de Latour, president of the Hofkriegsrat, to Kutuzov, October 17, 1805, RGVIA, f. VUA, d. 3108, l. 125.

78. Kutuzov to Maltitz and other column commanders, October 2/14, 1805; Order to the Army, October 3/15, 1805; Order to the Army, October 6/18, 1805; Kutuzov to Stakelberg, October 7/19, 1805, Lithuanian State Historical Archives, f. 378, op. 13, d. 312, ll. 25, 37; f. 378, op. 13, d. 285, ll. 14–16b. For other documents, see *M. I. Kutuzov: Sbornik dokumentov*, II:98–111.

79. Berg, *Autobiographie*, 176–177.

80. Ilya Popadichev, *Vospominaniya suvorovskogo soldata*, edited by Major General D. Maslovskii (St. Petersburg: V. Berezovskii, 1899), electronic edition.

81. Cited in Beer, *Zehn Jahre österreichische Politik*, 148–149; Mikhailovskii-Danilevskii, *Opisanie pervoi voiny*, 40–41. Mikhailovskii-Danilevskii notes, for example, "speaking about the possibility of the French march on the Lech, should [Kutuzov] understand the movements of the French to be on the left bank of this river, or on the right? Mentioning his intention to cross to the left bank of the Danube, and then again switch to the right bank, 'downstream,' [Archduke Ferdinand] left in the unknown exactly where he would make this second crossing." Mikhailovskii-Danilevskii, *Opisanie pervoi voiny*, 42–43.

82. Mack's report is cited in Gramm, "'Der unglückliche Mack,'" 419–420. Kutuzov announced slightly different numbers: five captured cannon

and eight ammunition caissons. Kutuzov's Order to the Army, October 5/17, 1805, Lithuanian State Historical Archives, f. 378, op. 13, d. 285, l. 15. Also see General Dokhturov to his wife, October 7/19, 1805, *Russkii arkhiv* 1 (1874): 1090. General Berg recalled that his regiment held "several parades before the Austrian princes and generals." Berg, *Autobiographie,* 177.

83. Berg, *Autobiographie,* 178.

84. Berg, *Autobiographie,* 178.

85. Kutuzov to Emperor Alexander, October 7/19, 1805, in *M. I. Kutuzov: Sbornik dokumentov,* II:98.

86. Razumovski to Czartoryski, October 8/20, 1805, in Vasil'chikov, *Les Razoumowski,* 266.

87. Kutuzov to Czartoryski, October 7/19, 1805, in *M. I. Kutuzov: Sbornik dokumentov,* II:97. In a letter to Emperor Alexander, Kutuzov notes that Austrian general Michael von Kienmayer had received a letter from Bavarian general Karl Philipp von Wrede describing the Austrian defeat between Ulm and Memmingen. Kutuzov to Emperor Alexander, October 7/19, 1805, in *M. I. Kutuzov: Sbornik dokumentov,* II:97–98.

88. Kutuzov to Miloradovich, June 23/July 5, 1806, in *M. I. Kutuzov: Sbornik dokumentov,* II:349. This lengthy letter effectively constitutes Kutuzov's reminiscences of the campaign, written just six months after it ended. It was prompted by General Miloradovich's complaint that Kutuzov's official report did not properly acknowledge the general's contributions.

89. Kutuzov to Emperor Alexander, October 10/22, 1805, cited in Mikhailovskii-Danilevskii, *Opisanie pervoi voiny,* 56; Kutuzov to Czartoryski, October 7/19, 1805; Kutuzov to Razumovskii, October 9/21, 1805, in *M. I. Kutuzov: Sbornik dokumentov,* II:97, 109. It seems Kutuzov considered a forward movement sometime after October 23. He discussed the possibility of proceeding toward Erding and Munich, bypassing the vast forest around Ebersperg, and sending a small column through Landshut to threaten the flank of an enemy force that might be in the vicinity of Munich. Kutuzov's intentions are discussed in Merveldt's letter of October 14 to the Hofkriegsrat, cited in Moritz von Angeli, "Ulm und Austerlitz," 298–299.

90. 9e Bulletin de la Grande Armée, October 21, 1805, in *Correspondance de Napoleon Ier* (Paris: Henri Plon, 1863), XI:344. For the Austrian side, see Gramm, " 'Der unglückliche Mack,' " 453–476. Also see Kutuzov to Emperor Alexander, October 11/23, 1805, cited in Mikhailovskii-Danilevskii, *Opisanie pervoi voiny,* 57; Kutuzov to Czartoryski, October 12/24, 1805, in *M. I. Kutuzov: Sbornik dokumentov,* II:116–117.

91. Semen Vorontsov to Adam Czartoryski, February 6/18, 1806, in *Arkhiv knyazya Vorontsova* (Moscow: Tip. Gracheva, 1870–1895), XV:370. Also see Semen Vorontsov to Mikhail Vorontsov, November 21, 1805, in *Arkhiv knyazya Vorontsova,* XVII:117.

92. Kutuzov to Czartoryski, October 12/24, 1805, in *M. I. Kutuzov: Sbornik dokumentov*, II:117. The French captured some 27,000 men, while another 4,000 Austrians had been killed or wounded.

93. Kutuzov to Czartoryski, October 12/24, 1805, in *M. I. Kutuzov: Sbornik dokumentov*, II:118. In a separate letter to Czartoryski, Kutuzov asked for the whereabouts of Buxhöwden's corps, noting that his request had been prompted "by the frequent inquiries of the Austrian generals about this matter." Kutuzov to Czartoryski, October 12/24, 1805, in *M. I. Kutuzov: Sbornik dokumentov*, II:121.

94. Kutuzov to Czartoryski, October 12/24, 1805, in *M. I. Kutuzov: Sbornik dokumentov*, II:118.

95. Kutuzov to Emperor Francis; Kutuzov to Razumovskii, Razumovskii to Kutuzov, October 11–12/23–24, 1805, in *M. I. Kutuzov: Sbornik dokumentov*, II:112–113, 122–123.

96. Kutuzov to Czartoryski, October 12/24, 1805, in *M. I. Kutuzov: Sbornik dokumentov*, II:117–118; Kutuzov to Razumovskii, October 12/24, 1805, in *VPR*, II:611–612. Mack submitted a lengthy account of his meeting with Napoleon, "Précis de mon entretien avec l'Empereur des Français," which can be found in Gramm, " 'Der unglückliche Mack,' " 467–470.

97. Razumovski to Czartoryski, October 17/29, 1805, in Vasil'chikov, *Les Razoumowski*, 277.

98. Emperor Francis to Kutuzov, October 26, 1805, in *The Kutuzov Papers* 4 (1870): 490–491. Also see Razumovski to Emperor Alexander, October 14/26, 1805, in Vasil'chikov, *Les Razoumowski*, 274.

99. Austrian historian Moritz von Angeli, who had written an in-depth study of the Austrian war effort in 1805, also unfairly accuses Kutuzov of being "undecided himself" and "completely under the influence of his doubting generals." Angeli, "Ulm und Austerlitz," 299.

100. Razumovski to Czartoryski, October 14/26, 1805, in Vasil'chikov, *Les Razoumowski*, 275. Razumovski pointed out, "This is the opinion shared with me by [General] Merveldt."

101. Merveldt to Latour, October 18, 1805, cited in Angeli, "Ulm und Austerlitz," 299–301.

102. Razumovski to Czartoryski, October 17/29, 1805, in Vasil'chikov, *Les Razoumowski*, 276.

103. *Anekdoty ili dostopamyatnye skazaniya ob ego svetlosti general-fel'dmarshale knyaze Mikhaile Illarionoviche Golenischeve-Kutuzove Smolenskom, nachinaya s pervykh let ego sluzhby do konchiny, s priobsheniem nekotoryh ego pisem, dostopamyatnyh ego rechei i prikazov* (St. Petersburg, 1814), I:68.

104. Butovskii, *Fel'dmarshal knyaz Golenischev-Kutuzov*, 17.

Chapter 13

1. *Report on the Manuscripts of J. B. Fortescue Preserved at Dropmore* (London: Historical Manuscripts Commission, 1910), VIII:311–312.

2. Orders to the Army, October 12–16/24–28, 1805, Lithuanian State Historical Archives, f. 378, op. 13, d. 285, ll. 20–25. Other orders to the army, including orders to column commanders, are in d. 213, part 1, ll. 65–69. Also see *General Staff Study of 1805 Campaign*, RGVIA, f. 846, op. 16, d. 3124, l. 71; Moritz Edler von Angeli, "Ulm und Austerlitz. Studie auf Grund archivalischer Quellen über den Feldzug 1805 in Deutschland," *Mittheilungen des Kaiserlichen und Königlichen Kriegsarchivs* 2 (1877): 285–288; Christopher Duffy, *Austerlitz 1805* (London: Seeley Service, 1977), 55. Formally, Bagration was still listed as the "commander of advance guard." See Order to the Army, October 12/24, 1805, Lithuanian State Historical Archives, f. 378, op. 13, d. 285, l. 21.

3. Kiril Pigarev, *Soldat-Polkovodets: Ocherki o Suvorove* (Moscow, 1943), 35–36; G. Meerovich and F. Budanov, *Suvorov v Peterburge* (Leningrad, 1978), 277.

4. Kutuzov to Miloradovich, June 23/July 5, 1806, in *M. I. Kutuzov: Sbornik dokumentov* (Moscow: Voeniszdat, 1950), II:349; Gregor von Berg, *Autobiographie des Generalen der Infanterie Gregor von Berg* (Dresden: E. Blochman, 1871), 178.

5. Berg, *Autobiographie*, 178.

6. Berg, *Autobiographie*, 178.

7. Angeli, "Ulm und Austerlitz," 310.

8. Cited in A. Mikhailovskii-Danilevskii, *Polnoe sobranie sochinenii. Opisanie pervoi voiny imperatora Aleksandra s Napoleonom v 1805 godu. Opisanie vtoroj voiny imperatora Aleksandra s Napoleonom v 1806 i 1807 godah* (St. Petersburg, 1849), 84. Also see Emperor Francis to Kutuzov, October 29–30, 1805, in *The Kutuzov Papers* 4 (1870): 491–493.

9. Kutuzov to Alexander, October 23/November 4, 1805, in *M. I. Kutuzov: Sbornik dokumentov*, II:140; Kutuzov to Lieutenant General S. Dolgorukov II, October 21/November 2, 1805, Lithuanian State Historical Archives, f. 378, op. 13, d. 312, l. 51–52.

10. Kutuzov to Alexander I, October 23/November 4, 1805, in *M. I. Kutuzov: Sbornik dokumentov*, II:142.

11. Order to the Column Commanders, October 16/28, 1805, Lithuanian State Historical Archives, f. 378, op. 13, d. 311, l. 17b; Kutuzov to Commissioner Oreus, October 21/November 2, 1805, Lithuanian State Historical Archives, f. 378, op. 13, d. 312, l. 48; Kutuzov to Dokhturov, October 21/November 2, 1805, Lithuanian State Historical Archives, f. 378, op. 13, d. 213, part 1, l. 75.

12. Berg, *Autobiographie*, 178.

13. Emperor Francis to Kutuzov, October 30, 1805, in *The Kutuzov Papers* 4 (1870): 492.

14. Alexey Yermolov, *The Czar's General: The Memoirs of a Russian General in the Napoleonic Wars*, translated and edited by Alexander Mikaberidze (Welwyn Garden City: Ravenhall Books, 2005), 43.

15. Kutuzov singled out several units, including the Moskovskii and Podoliaii Infantry Regiments, for a lack of discipline, and held regimental and battalion commanders responsible for continued disorder. Orders to the Army, October

16–17/28–29, 1805, Lithuanian State Historical Archives, f. 378, op. 13, d. 213, part 1, l. 66; d. 285, l. 27.

16. I. Butovskii, *Fel'dmarshal knyaz Golenischev-Kutuzov pri kontse i nachale svoego boevogo poprishha. Pervaya voina imperatora Aleksandra s Napoleonom v 1805 g.* (St. Petersburg, 1858), 18.

17. Ilya Popadichev, *Vospominaniya suvorovskogo soldata*, edited by Major General D. Maslovskii (St. Petersburg: V. Berezovskii, 1899), electronic edition.

18. Yermolov, *The Czar's General*, 43. On November 2, Kutuzov ordered the arrest of Colonel Bibikov of the Vyatskii Musketeer Regiment after his soldiers got "agitated by a simple rumor" of enemy appearance, "loaded their muskets without an order, of their own volition, and then, in order to discharge them, fired them in the air." Kutuzov stressed that "one must be completely oblivious to military affairs to not realize how harmful and dangerous such behavior can be in wartime." Order to the Army, October 21/November 2, 1805, Lithuanian State Historical Archives, f. 378, op. 13, d. 285, l. 28.

19. Cited in Manfried Rauchensteiner, *Kaiser Franz und Erzherzog Karl. Dynastie und Heerwesen in Österreich 1796–1809* (Vienna: Verlag für Geschichte und Politik, 1972), 78.

20. Stackelberg to Kutuzov, October 26, 1805, Lithuanian State Historical Archives, f. 378, op. 13, d. 213, part 1, l. 483.

21. Physician Michelson to Chief Army Physician Johann Georg von Ruehl, October 14/26, 1805, Lithuanian State Historical Archives, f. 378, op. 13, d. 213, part 1, l. 725–726. "Our sick are experiencing extreme shortages of everything," complained one of the Russian physicians. "In the current cold weather soldiers desperately require such necessities as shoes, winter robes, and simply shirts since some do not even have those." By early November, Linz housed more than 1,000 sick soldiers, who had to be evacuated as the Russian army withdrew eastward. Kutuzov chose to move them to Znaim, but with the roads being "very bad" and the weather "very damp and cold," he and the army physicians struggled to make arrangements to ensure the safety of the ailing soldiers. "I asked the Austrian authorities for warm robes, blankets, and other essentials," reported Michelson. "But they are not giving me anything." Physician Michelson to von Ruehl, October 23/November 3, 1805, Lithuanian State Historical Archives, f. 378, op. 13, d. 213, part 1, l. 724.

22. Order to the Army, October 17–20/October 29–November 1, 1805, Lithuanian State Historical Archives, f. 378, op. 13, d. 213, part 1, ll. 70–73; Kutuzov to Miloradovich, June 23/July 5, 1806, in *M. I. Kutuzov: Sbornik dokumentov*, II:349.

23. Kutuzov committed two battalions of the 6th Jägers and two battalion of the 8th Jägers, supported by the Pavlogradskii hussars and a handful of horse artillery cannon.

24. Bagration to Kutuzov, October 20/November 1, 1805; Major General Ulanius to Bagration, October 20/November 1, 1805, Lithuanian State Historical

612 | NOTES TO PAGES 208–212

Archives, f. 378, op. 13, d. 213, part 1, ll. 153–157. Ulanius reported reported almost 100 killed, including Colonel Golovkin of the 8th Jäger Regiment, and about 50 wounded. See also Kutuzov to Alexander, October 23/November 4, 1805, in *M. I. Kutuzov: Sbornik dokumentov*, II:139–140.

25. Cited in Mikhailovskii-Danilevskii, *Opisanie pervoi voiny*, 84.

26. Emperor Francis to Kutuzov, October 30–November 4, 1805, in *The Kutuzov Papers* 4 (1870): 491–493; Mikhailovskii-Danilevskii, *Opisanie pervoi voiny*, 86; Angeli, "Ulm und Austerlitz," 286–288; Frederick W. Kagan, *The End of the Old Order: Napoleon and Europe 1801–1805* (New York: Da Capo, 2006), 455–458, 461–462.

27. The size of Merveldt's detachment remains unclear. See discussion in Kagan, *The End of the Old Order*, 456.

28. Kutuzov to Dokhturov, October 22–23/November 3–4, 1805, Lithuanian State Historical Archives, f. 378, op. 13, d. 213, part 1, ll. 81–82; Kutuzov to Emperor Alexander, October 23/November 4, 1805, in *M. I. Kutuzov: Sbornik dokumentov*, II:139. Kutuzov's order to Dokhturov specified that he was to take "the Bryanskii, Narvskii, Vyatskii, Moskovskii and Chernigovskii Musketeer Regiments, along with the St. Peterburgskii Dragoon Regiment and all the artillery attached to these units."

29. Kutuzov to Miloradovich, July 26/August 7, 1806, cited in Mikhailovskii-Danilevskii, *Opisanie pervoi voiny*, 90; Emperor Francis to Kutuzov, November 4–5, 1805, in *The Kutuzov Papers* 4 (1870): 493–495. Also see Angeli, "Ulm und Austerlitz," 287; Alois Moriggl, *Der Feldzug von Ulm und seine Folgen für Oesterreich überhaupt und fürTirolinsbesonders* (Innsbruck: Verlag der Wagner'schen Buchhandlung, 1861), 557; Kagan, *The End of the Old Order*, 457–458, 462–463.

30. Berg, *Autobiographie*, 179.

31. Bagration to Kutuzov, October 23/November 4, 1805, Lithuanian State Historical Archives, f. 378, op. 13, d. 213, part 1, l. 159; Mikhailovskii-Danilevskii, *Opisanie pervoi voiny*, 89.

32. *Anekdoty ili dostopamyatnye skazaniya ob ego svetlosti general-fel'dmarshale knyaze Mikhaile Illarionoviche Golenischeve-Kutuzove Smolenskom, nachinaya s pervykh let ego sluzhby do konchiny, s priobsheniem nekotoryh ego pisem, dostopamyatnyh ego rechei i prikazov* (St. Petersburg, 1814), I:69.

33. Fedor Glinka, *Pis'ma ruskago ofitsera o Pol'she, Avstriiskikh vladeniyakh i Vengrii, s podrobnym opisaniem pokhoda rossiyan protivu frantsuzov v 1805 i 1806 godakh, takzhe Otechestvennoi i Zagranichnoi voiny s 1812 po 1815 god* (Moscow: Tip. S. Selivanovskago, 1815), I:72–74.

34. Popadichev, *Vospominaniya suvorovskogo soldata*.

35. Orders to the Army, October 17/29 and October 23/November 4, 1805, Lithuanian State Historical Archives, f. 378, op. 13, d. 213, part 1, ll. 70, 83.

36. *Anekdoty ili dostopamyatnye skazaniya*, I:70.

37. Anne-Jean-Marie-René Savary, *Mémoires du duc de Rovigo écrits de sa main, pour servir à l'histoire de l'Empereur Napoleon* (Paris: Colburn, 1828), I:102.

38. Yermolov, *The Czar's General*, 44; Berg, *Autobiographie*, 182. Regrettably, Bagration's official report is just two pages long and rather vague, offering no insights into how the battle at Amstetten unfolded. Bagration to Kutuzov, October 25/November 6, 1805, Lithuanian State Historical Archives, f. 378, op. 13, d. 213, part 1, l. 161.

39. Louis-François Lejeune, *Souvenirs d'un officier de l'empire* (Toulouse: Impr. de Viguier, 1851), I:73–74.

40. Milarodovich brought the 8th Jäger Regiment, the Malorossiiski grenadiers, the Apsheronskii and Smolenskskii Musketeer Regiments, ten squadrons of the Mariupol Hussar Regiment, a horse artillery company under Lt. Col. Aleksey Yermolov, and a half company of battery artillery of the 5th Artillery Regiment. Miloradovich to Kutuzov, October 25/November 6, 1805, Lithuanian State Historical Archives, f. 378, op. 13, d. 213, part 1, ll. 167–168. See also Mikhailovskii-Danilevskii, *Opisanie pervoi voiny*, 91–92; Berg, *Autobiographie*, 179.

41. Fedor Glinka states it was "four o'clock in the afternoon" when the fighting began. Glinka, *Pis'ma ruskago ofitsera*, I:76. Also see Berg, *Autobiographie*, 182.

42. Lejeune, *Souvenirs d'un officier de l'empire*, 74–76; Octave Levasseur, *Souvenirs militaires . . . , 1802–1815* (Paris, 1914), 40. See also Paul Claude Alombert and Jean Lambert Alphonse Colin, *La campagne de 1805 en Allemagne* (Paris: R. Chapelot, 1902), IV:515, 517; Glinka, *Pis'ma ruskago ofitsera*, I:76–77.

43. Miloradovich to Kutuzov, October 25/November 6, 1805, Lithuanian State Historical Archives, f. 378, op. 13, d. 213, part 1, l. 168; Kutuzov to Emperor Alexander, October 25/November 6, 1805, in *M. I. Kutuzov: Sbornik dokumentov*, II:146–147; Glinka, *Pis'ma ruskago ofitsera*, I:77–78; Berg, *Autobiographie*, 182–183.

44. Ivan Golovin, *History of Alexander the First, Emperor of Russia* (London: Thomas Cautley Newby, 1858), 74. Bagration reported 232 killed, 174 missing, 130 heavily wounded who had to be left behind at Amstetten, and 241 wounded. In addition, he lost more than 170 horses. Miloradovich reported 43 killed, 47 missing, and 162 wounded. Bagration and Miloradovich to Kutuzov, October 25/November 6, 1805, Lithuanian State Historical Archives, f. 378, op. 13, d. 213, part 1, ll. 161, 168.

45. Philippe-Paul Comte de Ségur, *Histoire et memoires* (Paris: Didot Frères, 1873), II:429. A similar description is in Mathieu Dumas, *Précis des évènements militaires ou Essai historique sur les campagnes de 1799 à 1814* (Hamburg: Perthès et Besser, 1822), XIII:303–304.

46. Order to the Army, October 25/November 6, 1805, Lithuanian State Historical Archives, f. 378, op. 13, d. 213, part 1, l. 84.

47. Murat to Napoleon, November 5, 1805, in Alombert and Colin, *La campagne de 1805 en Allemagne*, IV:507; Kutuzov to Emperor Alexander, October 25/November 6, 1805, in *M. I. Kutuzov: Sbornik dokumentov*, II:146. In private correspondence Kutuzov was more circumspect. See Kutuzov to Miloradovich, June 26/July 8, 1806, cited in Mikhailovskii-Danilevskii, *Opisanie pervoi voiny*, 93. Yermolov makes no mention of chasing the enemy but rather speaks of the French "withdrawing" and the Russians spending the night on the battlefield; *The Czar's General*, 45. For the French side, see Alombert and Colin, *La campagne de 1805 en Allemagne*, IV:507, 515–518; Louis-Florimond Fantin des Odoards, *Journal du général Fantin des Odoards, étapes d'un officier de la Grande Armée, 1800–1830* (Paris, 1895), 56–57.

48. Murat to Napoleon, November 5, 1805, in Alombert and Colin, *La campagne de 1805 en Allemagne*, IV:507.

49. Dumas, *Précis des évènements militaires*, XIII:304.

50. It must be noted that Kutuzov got his way with regard to Lieutenant General Baron Rosen, whose reassignment he sought at the start of the campaign. On November 2, Kutuzov informed Rosen of his assignment to the Moldavian border and the transfer of his column to the command of Major General Voropaiskii. See Kutuzov to Rosen; Kutuzov to Voropaiskii, October 21/November 2, 1805, Lithuanian State Historical Archives, f. 378, op. 13, d. 312, l. 48.

51. Napoleon's letters to Francis have been published in *Correspondance générale*, edited by Michel Kerautret and Gabriel Madec (Paris: Fayard, 2008), V:830–831, 836–837. For Francis's letters, see Adolf Beer, *Zehn Jahre österreichischer Politik, 1801–1810* (Leipzig: Brodhaus, 1877), 454–455.

52. Kutuztov to Czartoryski, October 24/November 5, 1805, in *M. I. Kutuzov: Sbornik dokumentov*, II:143–144. It is noteworthy that Kutuzov made no mention of this incident in his letters to Emperor Alexander. As an experienced diplomat, he avoided being the bearer of bad news to the emperor and preferred to do it indirectly.

53. Napoleon to Talleyrand, November 9, 1805, in *Correspondance générale*, V:838; Auxonne-Marie-Théodose de Thiard, *Souvenirs diplomatiques et militaires du général Thiard* (Paris: Flammarion, 1900), 192.

54. Cited in Alombert and Colin, *La campagne de 1805 en Allemagne*, IV:128, 582.

55. Dokhturov to his wife, in *Russkii arkhiv* 12, no. 1 (1874): 1091–1092.

56. See also Emperor Francis to Kutuzov, November 4–5, 1805, in *The Kutuzov Papers* 4 (1870): 495; Emperor Alexander to Kutuzov, October 24/November 5, 1805, in Mikhailovskii-Danilevskii, *Opisanie pervoi voiny*, 76–77. On November 5, Kutuzov informed Emperor Alexander that he had "received the Roman Emperor's order to veer off the Vienna route, move from Sankt Pölten to Krems and, having crossed the river, take a first position there." *M. I. Kutuzov: Sbornik dokumentov*, II:143–144.

57. Kutuzov's Order to the Army and Duty General Inzov's Order to the Army, October 27/November 8, 1805, Lithuanian State Historical Archives, f. 378,

op. 13, d. 213, part 1, ll. 85, 92. That night the calm and unassuming Kutuzov, dressed in his customary plain tunic and cap, walked around the campsite and mingled with the men, enquiring about their well-being and needs. "What are you chatting about?" he asked a group of officers snuggled around a bonfire. "Hoping we will fight the French soon enough," came the response. Kutuzov must have grinned upon hearing this. "All Russian officers should respond thus," he assured them. "Just not now. If the enemy anticipates us even by an hour, we would be cut off and doomed. But if we get to Krems first, we will beat the enemy as well. Let us be ready for it!" *Anekdoty ili dostopamyatnye skazaniya*, I:66.

58. Order to the Army, October 28/November 9, 1805, Lithuanian State Historical Archives, f. 378, op. 13, d. 285, ll. 35–38.

59. Miloradovich's rear guard covered the army's withdrawal and skirmished with a French advance guard near Sankt Pölten, but the French did not press the attack. Miloradovich to Kutuzov, October 29/November 9, 1805, Lithuanian State Historical Archives, f. 378, op. 13, d. 213, part 1, ll. 317.

60. Emperor Francis to Kutuzov, November 5, 1805, in *The Kutuzov Papers* 4 (1870): 495.

61. Kutuzov to Emperor Francis, October 30/November 11, 1805, in Mikhailovskii-Danilevskii, *Opisanie pervoi voiny*, 96–97. Also see Möller-Zakomelskii to Kutuzov, October 27/November 8, 1805, Lithuanian State Historical Archives, f. 378, op. 13, d. 345, l. 296.

62. Kutuzov to Emperor Francis, October 30/November 11, 1805, in Mikhailovskii-Danilevskii, *Opisanie pervoi voiny*, 96–97; Paul Claude Alombert, *Campagne de l'an 14 (1805): Le corps d'armée aux ordres du maréchal Mortier. Combat de Dürrenstein* (Paris: Berger-Levrault, 1897), 28–48, 75–86; Dumas, *Précis des événements militaires*, XIV:8–10.

63. "The Danube at Melk is more than a quarter of a league wide; no boats or ferries could be seen on the banks," described General Édouard Colbert, then captain aide-de-camp to Berthier, who dispatched him on a mission to Mortier during the battle. Cited in Alombert, *Combat de Dürrenstein*, 88.

64. Kutuzov later noted that his intention was "to not just push back" Mortier's corps but "to annihilate it." Kutuzov to Miloradovich, June 23/July 5, 1806, in *M. I. Kutuzov: Sbornik dokumentov*, II:351.

65. Major General Ulanius speaks of receiving the order to "march in accordance with [Kutuzov's] disposition at 4 o'clock in the morning [*popolunochi v 4 chasa*] on October 30 [November 11]" and of "departing at nine o'clock following special instructions of His Excellency [Kutuzov]." Miloradovich describes leaving Stein "at 7 o'clock in the morning." Ulanius to Dokhturov, November 2/14, 1805; Miloradovich to Kutuzov, November 9/21, 1805, Lithuanian State Historical Archives, f. 378, op. 13, d. 213, part 1, ll. 171, 320.

66. Disposition to Attack at Weißkirchen, October 29/November 10, 1805, Lithuanian State Historical Archives, f. 378, op. 13, d. 213, part 1, ll.

201–218b. Also see Kutuzov to Dokhturov, October 29/November 10, 1805; Dokhturov to Kutuzov, November 8/20, Lithuanian State Historical Archives, f. 378, op. 13, d. 213, part 1, ll. 89, 279–280; Mikhailovskii-Danilevskii, *Opisanie pervoi voiny*, 101–102; Rainer Egger, *Das Gefecht bei Dürnstein-Loiben. 1805. Militärhistorische Schriftenreihe. H. 3.* (Vienna: Österreichischer Bundesverlag, 1986), 1–10; Wilhelm von Kotzebue, *Versuch einer Beschreibung der Schlacht bey Dürnstein am 11. November 1805* (Königsberg: [n.p.], 1807), i–vi. The allied plan was, broadly speaking, evocative of some battles of antiquity, notably the battle at Thermopylae in 480 BCE, where a small Greek force was similarly flanked and destroyed by the Persian army, and the Battle of Lake Trasimene in 217 BCE, when Carthaginian general Hannibal surprised and trapped a Roman army on the north shore of Lake Trasimene.

67. His column consisted of the Grenadier Battalion of the Apsheronskii Musketeer Regiment, the Grenadier Battalion of the Malorossiiskii Musketeer Regiment, the Grenadier and 3rd Battalions of the Smolenskii Musketeer Regiment, and the 3rd Battalion of the 8th Jägers, about 2,500 infantrymen in all. Disposition to Attack at Weißkirchen, October 29/November 10, 1805, Lithuanian State Historical Archives, f. 378, op. 13, d. 213, part 1, ll. 217–218.

68. Colonel Jean-Hilare Alexis Talandier, "Relation de la bataille de Diernstein," cited in Alombert, *Combat de Dürrenstein,* 91. Some Russian historians claim that Kutuzov was concerned that Mortier, learning of the early skirmishes at Krems, would try to avoid the battle and retreat from Durrenstein. Therefore, to lure him westward, Kutuzov spread rumors that the army was preparing for the retreat to Moravia and informed local officials that he was halting at Krems only for a few hours to get the necessary supplies. Mortier fell for the ruse and moved forward in pursuit of the fleeing Russians. Such claims are, however, spurious.

69. Alombert, *Combat de Dürrenstein,* 106–108, 338, 340; Miloradovich to Kutuzov, November 9/21, 1805, Lithuanian State Historical Archives, f. 378, op. 13, d. 213, part 1, ll. 320–321.

70. The French accounts (for example, Talandier) claim that the Russian soldiers were hindered by their thick overcoats. However, Kutuzov specifically ordered his men to drop packs and overcoats in order to fight more nimbly.

71. Miloradovich to Kutuzov, November 9/21, 1805, Lithuanian State Historical Archives, f. 378, op. 13, d. 213, part 1, ll. 321–322.

72. The written orders have not been preserved. But diverting such a large force from a flanking maneuver would not have occurred without Kutuzov's involvement. Most probably he sent an aide-de-camp with a verbal command to divert from the prescribed path. Soviet historians, and some modern Russian historians, argue that Kutuzov ordered Miloradovich to fall back as a tactical ruse to lure Mortier out of Loiben and expose his flank. However, Kutuzov's and Miloradovich's reports make no mention of this. Instead, Miloradovich

points out that it was lack of ammunition and fatigue that forced him to move his men back to Stein.

73. Popadichev, *Vospominaniya suvorovskogo soldata*, electronic edition. Popadichev mentions Kutuzov sending reinforcements to sustain the attack, but he does not provide any further details on this.

74. Talandier, "Relation de la bataille de Diernstein," cited in Alombert, *Combat de Dürrenstein*, 110.

75. Yermolov, *The Czar's General*, 49–50.

76. Ulanius to Dokhturov, November 2/14, 1805; Dokhturov to Kutuzov, November 8/20, 1805, Lithuanian State Historical Archives, f. 378, op. 13, d. 213, part 1, ll. 171–172, 279. Also see Egger, *Das Gefecht bei Dürnstein-Loiben*, 17; Dumas, *Précis des événements militaires*, 10–15.

77. Urusov to Dokhturov, November 4/16, 18015; Dokhturov to Kutuzov, November 8/20, Lithuanian State Historical Archives, f. 378, op. 13, d. 213, part 1, ll. 240, 279–280.

78. General Pierre Dupont de l'Étang, "Lettre sur la campagne de 1805," in *Journal des sciences militaires des armées de terre et de mer* (Paris: M. Corréard, 1826), V:171.

79. Dokhturov to Kutuzov, November 8/20, Lithuanian State Historical Archives, f. 378, op. 13, d. 213, part 1, ll. 89, 279–280.

80. Mikhailovskii-Danilevskii, *Opisanie pervoi voiny*, 106.

81. Gvozdev to Urusov, November 8/20, 1805, Lithuanian State Historical Archives, f. 378, op. 13, d. 213, part 1, ll. 89, 281.

82. Ulanius to Dokhturov, November 2/14, 1805; Essen II to Kutuzov, November 6/18, 1805; Dokhturov to Kutuzov, November 8/20, 1805, Lithuanian State Historical Archives, f. 378, op. 13, d. 213, part 1, ll. 171–172, 254, 279.

83. Dupont de l'Étang, "Lettre sur la campagne de 1805," 171–172. See also Semen Bronenovskii to G. Lomonosov, November 8/20, 1805, *Russkii arkhiv* 2 (1864): 1189.

84. Dumas, *Précis des événements militaires*, XIV:14–15; Louis-Pierre-Edouard Bignon, *Histoire de France* (Paris: Charles Béchet, 1830), IV:402–403.

85. The official reports show 2,534 casualties, including some 700 killed. However, these reports are partial and do not reflect the full array of losses. Miloradovich reported 14 officers, 13 NCOs, and more than 280 soldiers killed, while 1 general, 30 officers, 50 NCOs, and more than 780 soldiers were wounded. In addition, 5 officers, 15 NCOs, and more than 320 soldiers were "missing in action." His report showed only two (!) prisoners, "one staff officer and one junior officer." Lieutenant Colonel Gvozdev, who fought west of Durrenstein, reported losing 4 officers and more than 250 soldiers killed, while 7 officers were wounded; interestingly, he left the space for the number of wounded soldiers blank. Urusov, who defended the heights from the retreating French troops, reported 89 killed and 56 wounded, while Ulanius reported that his two battalions lost 8 killed, 76 wounded, and 30 missing. Strik's column lost 27 killed and 130 wounded, with

51 missing. Ulanius to Dokhturov, November 2/14, 1805; Strik to Kutuzov, November 3/15, 1805; Gvozdev to Urusov, November 8/20, 1805; Miloradovich to Kutuzov, November 9/21, 1805, Lithuanian State Historical Archives, f. 378, op. 13, d. 213, part 1, ll. 172, 174, 281, 321–322.

86. 22nd Bulletin, November 13, 1805, in J. David Markham, ed., *Imperial Glory: The Bulletins of Napoleon's Grande Armée, 1805–1814* (London: Greenhill Books, 2003), 37–38.

87. Mikhailovskii-Danilevskii, *Opisanie pervoi voiny*, 108–109.

88. Thomas Robert Bugeaud, *Œuvres militaires du maréchal Bugeaud, duc d'Isly* (Paris: L. Baudoin, 1883), 51.

89. See *Statuten des löblichen militärischen Maria Theresien-Ordens* (Vienna: Kaiserl. Königl. Hof- und Staats-Druckerey, 1811). Kutuzov wrote to Alexander for permission to accept the foreign award. The Habsburg emperor also asked Kutuzov to submit a list of Russian officers who had distinguished themselves at Krems-Durrenstein and pledged to reward the rank and file as well. Kutuzov to Alexander, November 7/19, 1805, Lithuanian State Historical Archives, f. 378, op. 13, d. 213, part 1, l. 268.

90. "The Battle of Krems is a new crown of glory for the Russian army, and for the man who led it. My words cannot suffice to express to you and to the whole corps under your command, the pleasure and appreciation that I feel from receiving this delightful news." Alexander to Kutuzov, November 5/17, 1805, Lithuanian State Historical Archives, f. 378, op. 13, d.285, l. 61.

Chapter 14

1. Klemens Wenzel Nepomuk Lothar von Metternich, *Memoirs . . .* (New York: Harper & Brothers, 1881), I:38.

2. Murat to Napoleon, November 7, 1805, in Paul Claude Alombert and Jean Lambert Alphonse Colin, *La campagne de 1805 en Allemagne* (Paris: R. Chapelot, 1902), IV:583.

3. Alistair Horne, *Napoleon, Master of Europe, 1805–1807* (New York: William Morrow, 1979), 120.

4. Napoleon to Murat, November 11, 1805, in *Correspondance générale*, edited by Michel Kerautret and Gabriel Madec (Paris: Fayard, 2008), V:839.

5. Charles Campbell, *The Traveller's Complete Guide Through Belgium, Holland and Germany* (London: Sherwood, Neely and Hones, 1815), 268.

6. *Picture of Vienna Containing a Historical Sketch of the Metropolis of Austria* (Vienna: V. Mösle, 1839), 57. For an interesting discussion, see Yair Mintzker, *The Defortification of the German City, 1689–1866* (Cambridge: Cambridge University Press, 2012), 220–223.

7. Marcel de Serres, *Voyage en Autriche, ou essai statistique et géographique sur cet empire* (Paris: A. Bertrand, 1814), II:110.

8. The Danube River had a few small islands that anchored three bridges. The first two bridges were known as the First and Second Tabor Bridges, while the

last one was the Spitz Bridge. However, the Viennese called them collectively the Tabor Bridge.

9. In 1809, with the bridges over the Danube destroyed, Napoleon was forced to move south of Vienna and cross the river via Lobau, one of the numerous islands that divided the river into minor channels. The Austrian army contested the crossing and defeated the French army at Aspern-Essling in May 1809.

10. See Frederic Louis Huidekoper, "The Surprise of the Tabor Bridge at Vienna by Prince Murat and Marshal Lannes, November 13, 1805," *Journal of the Military Service Institution of the United States*, January–February 1905, 275–293; May–June 1905, 513–530; Victor Bernard Derrécagaix, *Les états-majors de Napoléon: Le lieutenant-général comte Belliard, chef d'État-Major de Murat* (Paris: R. Chapelot, 1909), 328–330.

11. Gunther E. Rothenberg, *The Napoleonic Wars* (London: Cassell, 1999), 88.

12. Kutuzov received two letters from Emperor Francis dated November 14. The first one congratulated him on winning the battle of Krems and urged him to confront the French corps. The second one, written in Brünn and dated 11:30 p.m. on November 14, reached him days later. Emperor Francis to Kutuzov, November 2/14, 1805, in *The Kutuzov Papers* 4 (1870): 497–499.

13. Kutuzov to Miloradovich, June 23/July 5, 1806, in *M. I. Kutuzov: Shornik dokumentov* (Moscow: Voeniszdat, 1950), II:352.

14. Emperor Francis to Kutuzov, November 15, 1805, in *The Kutuzov Papers* 4 (1870): 500. The maps would have arrived on November 16–17.

15. Kutuzov to Emperor Alexander, November 2/14, 1805, RGVIA, f. VUA, d. 3108, ll. 70–71.

16. Order to the Army, November 2/14, 1805, Lithuanian State Historical Archives, f. 378, op. 13, d. 213, part 1, l. 206. The army was ordered to march from Ebersbrunn via Ziersdorf and Gross (Grossnondorf) to Jetzelsdorf.

17. For an in-depth discussion, see A. Vasiliev, "Boi pri Shengrabene," *Imperator* 9 (2006): 41–49. Nostitz's detachment included Husarenregimente Nr. 4 Friedrich Erbprinz von Hessen-Homburg and the remnants of the Peterwardeiner Infanterieregiment Nr. 9. Ernst von Kwiatkowski, *Die Kämpfe bei Schöngrabern und Oberhollabrunn 1805 und 1809* (Vienna, 1908), 13. Parkinson is mistaken in claiming that a third of Bagration's army fell behind on the march and that he had only 4,000 men; Roger Parkinson, *The Fox of the North: The Life of Kutuzov, General of War and Peace* (New York: D. McKay, 1976), 71.

18. The strength of French troops, a key element in the eventual glorification of the Russian exploits at Shongrabern, was variously estimated at 40,000–60,000 troops, though Bagration and Kutuzov were more modest in their estimates, putting the enemy force at about 30,000 men. Kutuzov to Alexander, November 19, 1805, RGVIA f. 846, op. 16, d. 3108, ll. 75–76b; Kutuzov to Miloradovich, June 23/July 5, 1806, in *M. I. Kutuzov: Shornik dokumentov*, II:352; Louis Alexandre Andrault de Langeron, *Journal inédit de la*

campagne de 1805 (Paris: La Vouivre, 1998), 21; Nikolai Troitskii, *Fel'dmarshal Kutuzov: mify i fakty* (Moscow, 2002), 104; L. Punin, *Fel'dmarshal Kutuzov. Voenno-biograficheskii ocherk* (Moscow: Voennoe Izdatel'stvo, 1957), 75; Pavel Zhilin, *Kutuzov. Zhizn' i polkovodcheskaya deyatel'nost'* (Moscow: Voennoe Izdatel'stvo, 1978), 102; G. Oksman, "Marsh-manevr M. I. Kutuzova v kampanii 1805 g.," in *Polkovodets Kutuzov: sbornik statei* (Moscow, 1951), 77; E. Mezentsev, *Voina Rossii s Napoleonovskoi Frantsiei v 1805 g.* (Moscow, 2008), 145.

19. Kutuzov to Miloradovich, June 23/July 5, 1806, in *M. I. Kutuzov: Sbornik dokumentov*, II:352.

20. Murat speaks of the Austrian general asking him not to attack since he intended "to separate from the Russians" and that the Russians then twice sent a messenger to negotiate. Murat to Napoleon, November 15, 1805, in *Lettres et documents pour servir à l'histoire de Joachim Murat, 1767–1815*, edited by Paul Le Brethon (Paris: Plon-Nourrit, 1910), IV:153.

21. Hohenlohe to Francis, November 18, 1805, in Kwiatkowski, *Die Kämpfe bei Schöngrabern und Oberhollabrunn*, 31; Langeron, *Journal inédit de la campagne de 1805*, 21. Prince Hohenlohe defied Nostitz's orders and remained with Bagration. Kwiatkowski, *Die Kämpfe bei Schöngrabern und Oberhollabrunn*, 12–14. Kutuzov reported that Nostitz was swayed by the French assurances and that when the skirmishing began, "General Murat sent a trumpeter to offer an armistice." Kutuzov to Alexander, November 7/19, 1805, RGVIA, f. 846, op. 16, d. 3108, l. 75; same letter at Lithuanian State Historical Archives, f. 378, op. 13, d. 213, part 1, l. 267.

22. Dolgorukov to *The Hamburg Paper*, February 5, 1806, published in the *London Sun*, February 26, 1806, 4.

23. Kutuzov to Alexander, November 3–7/15–19, 1805, RGVIA, f. 846, op. 16, d. 3108, ll. 73–76.

24. "I sent Adjutant Generals Wintzingerode and Prince Dolgorukov to the French to have talks so that after a few days of truce we may gain even a little time. I instructed them to make conditions, if possible, not binding us to anything, relying upon their discretion because we could not afford to waste even a single moment." Kutuzov to Alexander, November 3/15, 1805, RGVIA, f. 846, op. 16, d. 3108, l. 73b.

25. Alphonse de Beauchamp, *Mémoires secrets et inédits, pour servir à l'histoire contemporaine* (Paris: Vernarel et Tenon, 1825), II:64.

26. *M. I. Kutuzov: Sbornik dokumentov*, II:173. The document itself is at RGVIA, f. VUA, d. 3108, l. 77.

27. Oleg Sokolov credits Bagration with making the offer to Murat. Considering what was at stake, it is doubtful that Bagration, a major general in charge of a rear guard, would have made a decision of such import. On the other hand, Kutuzov, as the commander in chief and an experienced diplomat, could make it.

28. Murat to Napoleon, November 15, 1805, in *Lettres et documents pour servir à l'histoire de Joachim Murat*, IV:153. Reporting on the Austerlitz campaign to King Victor Emmanuel I of Sardinia, Sardinian envoy Joseph de Maistre also specified that Kutuzov dispatched an envoy "to sign capitulation, *sub spe rati* [in the hope of ratification], which was indeed done." See his letter of January 19/31, 1806, in *Russkii arkhiv* 6 (1871): 71.

29. For a contemporary understanding of the word "capitulation," see Alexandre-Toussaint de Gaigne, *Nouveau dictionnaire militaire* (Paris: Levacher, 1801), 80; La Chesnaye des Bois, *Dictionnaire militaire, portatif, contenant tous les termes propres à la guerre* (Paris: Duchesne, 1758), I:340–343.

30. It must be noted that the Russian ambassador to Vienna had discussed the possibility of armistice as well. Writing to Adam Czartoryski, Razumovskii described how upon "learning of Prince Auersperg's foolishness and fearing disastrous consequences," he discussed possible measures that might have to be taken if the French defeated Kutuzov. "We agreed to offer the French an armistice to gain time. The basis of the offer that we wished to make was a complete renunciation of everything that [the coalition agreement] obliged us to do in support of the house of Austria, and possibly adding a few other sacrifices." See Alexander Vasil'chikov, *Les Razoumowski. Tome II. Le Comte André Razoumowski. Deuxième partie, 1801–1806* (Halle: Tausch & Grosse, 1893), 288.

31. Murat to Napoleon, November 15, 1805, in *Lettres et documents pour servir à l'histoire de Joachim Murat*, IV:153. Murat also argued that he did not have all his forces in position and the Russian army "would have escaped from me during the night."

32. Kutuzov to Alexander, November 7/19, 1805, Lithuanian State Historical Archives, f. 378, op. 13, d. 213, part 1, l. 267. That same day, Kutuzov, well aware of the political repercussions that even rumors of Franco-Russian agreement might have, sent a report "with all relevant details" to Emperor Francis. "I was concerned that the enemy might exploit this opportunity to misrepresent this agreement to the Austrian court and, through devious insinuations, to turn it against Russia." Kutuzov to Alexander, November 7/19, 1805, Lithuanian State Historical Archives, f. 378, op. 13, d. 213, part 1, l. 268.

33. The text of the draft agreement is at RGVIA, f. VUA, d. 3108, l. 77, and at Service Historique de la Défense, Correspondance, mémoires et travaux divers, 2 C 7. It was published in French in *Mémorial du Dépôt Général de la Guerre* (Paris: Ch. Picquet, 1843), VIII:66–67. In 1951, an important compilation of Kutuzov's documents related to the 1805 campaign failed to reproduce this document because ostensibly the editors could not find it. However, that same year a separate anthology of Kutuzov's documents reproduced the copy that is preserved at the Russian State Military Historical Archive. See footnote 1 in *Dokumenty shtaba M. I. Kutuzova, 1805–1806. Sbornik* (Vilnius: Gos. Izd. Polit. i Nauch. Literatury, 1951), 163; *M. I. Kutuzov: Sbornik dokumentov*, II:173. The agreement, as written, reflected the prevailing sentiment of honorable

surrender as practiced in the late seventeenth and eighteenth centuries: just as a fortress garrison could honorably surrender and evacuate with arms and flags flying, so could the army, after a valorous fight, withdraw with its honor and arms intact. See John A. Lynn, "The Other Side of Victory: Honorable Surrender During the Wars of Louis XIV," in *The Projection and Limitations of Imperial Powers, 1618–1850*, edited by Frederick C. Schneid (Leiden: Brill, 2012), 51–67.

34. Kutuzov to Alexander, November 7/19, 1805, RGVIA, f. 846, op. 16, d. 3108, l. 75b.

35. Yermolov recalled that during the armistice Bagration wanted to withdraw his troops so that he would not be cut off from the main army by superior French troops. However, the French noticed the movement in the Russian positions and insisted that Bagration keep his troops as they were when the armistice was signed.

36. Kutuzov to Alexander, November 7/19, 1805, Lithuanian State Historical Archives, f. 378, op. 13, d. 213, part 1, l. 267. "Sending Prince Bagration to this glorious mission," eulogized a contemporary historian, "Kutuzov made the sign of the cross for him: the ultimate subject for the brush of a Russian artist—Kutuzov blessing Bagration!" A. Mikhailovskii-Danilevskii, *Polnoe sobranie sochinenii. Opisanie pervoi voiny imperatora Aleksandra s Napoleonom v 1805 godu. Opisanie vtoroj voiny imperatora Aleksandra s Napoleonom v 1806 i 1807 godah* (St. Petersburg, 1849), 127–128; Robert Ker Porter, *Travelling Sketches in Russia and Sweden: During the Years 1805, 1806, 1807, 1808* (London, 1809), 103.

37. Napoleon to Murat, November 16, 1805, in *Correspondance générale*, no. 11, 112, V:856.

38. Nostitz's report cited in Kwiatkowski, *Die Kämpfe bei Schöngrabern und Oberhollabrunn*, 13–14. Also see Hohenlohe to Francis, November 18, 1805, in Kwiatkowski, *Die Kämpfe bei Schöngrabern und Oberhollabrunn*, 31; Bagration to Kutuzov, November 5/17, 1805, Lithuanian State Historical Archives, f. 378, op. 13, d. 213, part 1, l. 241. After the war was over, Nostitz published an article in a Hamburg newspaper to justify his actions. Prince Peter Dolgorukov wrote a harsh response denouncing him. See Dolgorukov to the *Hamburg Paper*, February 5, 1806, *London Sun*, February 26, 1806, 4; "Iz donesenii Bavarskago poverennogo v delakh Olri v pervie godi tsartsvovania (1802–1806) imperatora Aleksandra I," *Istoricheskii Vestnik* 147 (1917): 436.

39. Although he had some 35,000 men at his disposal, only the divisions of Oudinot and Legrand, with a cavalry brigade, took active part in the battle. Probably no more than 15,000 French troops were actually engaged in the fighting.

40. Auguste Petiet, *Souvenirs historiques, militaires et particuliers, 1784–1815: Mémoires d'un hussard de l'Empire, aide de camp du maréchal Soult*, edited by Nicole Gotteri (Paris: S.P.M., 1996), 115–116.

41. Bagration to Kutuzov, November 5/17, 1805, Lithuanian State Historical Archives, f. 378, op. 13, d. 213, part 1, ll. 241–242.
42. Although Nostitz was not by Bagration's side, the Austrian troops were and they fought with "exceptional gallantry" that "earned them the satisfaction and praise of General Prince Bagration," reported an Austrian officer to the kaiser. Yet none of the Russian after-action reports acknowledged their contribution, meaning that the subsequent Russian accounts paid no heed to the Austrians. Kutuzov only briefly mentioned that Prince Hohenlohe had defied Nostitz and stayed with Bagration. Kutuzov to Alexander, November 3/15, 1805, RGVIA, f. 846, op. 16, d. 3108, l. 73; Hohenlohe to Francis, November 18, 1805, in Kwiatkowski, *Die Kämpfe bei Schöngrabern und Oberhollabrunn*, 31.
43. Jean Pierre Sibelet, "Mémoires . . . ," in *Aventures de guerre, 1792–1809: souvenirs et récits de soldats*, edited by Frédéric Masson (Paris: Boussod, Valadon, 1894), 109. Sibelet was a lieutenant of the 11th Chasseurs à Cheval.
44. As customary, the French exaggerated Russian losses, with some participants claiming as many as 6,900 Russian casualties. The 26th Bulletin declared that the Russians had lost 2,000 killed, 2,000 wounded, 12 cannon, and 100 wagons, but in his after-action report, Bagration acknowledged losing 2,410 men, of whom 1,479 men were killed or missing; 931 men were wounded, but only 194 men were evacuated, while the rest were left to the mercy of the French, and most probably perished. Among the casualties were 4 officers and 26 NCOs killed and 14 officers and 49 NCOs wounded. Bagration to Kutuzov, November 5/17, 1805, Lithuanian State Historical Archives, f. 378, op. 13, d. 213, part 1, l. 242.
45. The French probably lost some 1,200 men, mostly from Oudinot's division. Although their overall casualties were fewer in number, the French lost twice as many officers (54 French to 21 Russians), including 11 killed. Two generals (Oudinot and Fouche du Careil) were wounded.
46. François René Cailloux-Pouget, *Souvenirs de guerre du Général Baron Pouget* (Paris: Plon, 1895), 69. Also see Jean-Baptiste-Antoine-Marcelin, baron de Marbot, *Mémoires du général Baron de Marbot* (Paris: Plon, 1891), I:244. For the Austrian report of the devastation after the battle, see Kwiatkowski, *Die Kämpfe bei Schöngrabern und Oberhollabrunn*, 34.
47. Bagration to Constantine, RGVIA, f. VUA, fond 846, op. 16, d. 3117, ll. 40–40b. The letter is dated October 14 [26], 1805; however it is obviously a mistake, since there was no major fighting on October 26.
48. Orders to the Army, November 4–6/16–18, 1805, Lithuanian State Historical Archives, f. 378, op. 13, d. 285, ll. 58–63.
49. Emperor Francis to Kutuzov, November 14, 1805, in *The Kutuzov Papers* 4 (1870): 497–499. "You must take into consideration the strength of the enemy confronting you," the kaiser advised Kutuzov. "I leave operations to your discretion and prudence, knowing in advance that you . . . will take measures that are most advantageous for the common cause and glory of your army."

50. Kutuzov to Emperor Francis, November 6/18, 1805, in *M. I. Kutuzov: Sbornik dokumentov*, II:167–168.

51. Kutuzov's decision to abandon Brünn, with its well-fortified citadel and vast supplies of ammunition, is clearly indicative of his wish to avoid any dispersion of his forces, since he understood that a small garrison would not be able to hold out at Brünn for long, while the outcome of the campaign depended on success in the decisive battle. One may lament the abandonment of considerable resources, especially provisions, but even this decision is understandable considering the stark realities of the Russian withdrawal. See Anne-Jean-Marie-René Savary, *Mémoires du duc de Rovigo écrits de sa main, pour servir à l'histoire de l'Empereur Napoleon* (Paris: Colburn, 1828), I:110.

52. *Anekdoty ili dostopamyatnye skazaniya ob ego svetlosti general-fel'dmarshale knyaze Mikhaile Illarionoviche Golenischeve-Kutuzove Smolenskom, nachinaya s pervykh let ego sluzhby do konchiny, s priobsheniem nekotoryh ego pisem, dostopamyatnyh ego rechei i prikazov* (St. Petersburg, 1814), I:71–74.

53. Buxhöwden to Kutuzov, November 6/18, 1805, Lithuanian State Historical Archives, f. 378, op. 13, d. 347, l. 132.

54. Semen Bronenovskii to G. Lomonosov, November 8/20, 1805, *Russkii arkhiv* 2 (1864): 1188–1189.

55. Mikhailovskii-Danilevskii, *Opisanie pervoi voiny*, 133. See also Yermolov, *The Czar's General*, 54.

56. P. Matrosov and E. Ustinov, "The Ulm-Olmütz March-Maneuver," in *Sovetskaya voennaya entsiklopediya*, edited by A. Grechko et al. (Moscow: Voenizdat, 1980), VIII:190.

Chapter 15

1. Paul Thiébault, *Mémoires du général Baron Thiébault* (Paris: Plon, 1894), III:439.

2. For a judicious analysis, see Frederick W. Kagan, *The End of the Old Order: Napoleon and Europe, 1801–1805* (New York: Da Capo, 2006), 550–559.

3. Major General Karl von Stutterheim, *La bataille d'Austerlitz, par un militaire témoin de la journée du 2 décembre 1805* (Paris: Fain, 1806), 14.

4. Michael I. Handel, ed., *Clausewitz and Modern Strategy* (London: Frank Cass, 1986), 139.

5. I. Butovskii, *Fel'dmarshal knyaz Golenischev-Kutuzov pri kontse i nachale svoego boevogo poprishha. Pervaya voina imperatora Aleksandra s Napoleonom v 1805 g.* (St. Petersburg, 1858), 37.

6. General Dmitry Dokhturov to his wife, in *Russkii arkhiv* 1 (1874): 1904.

7. Alexey Yermolov, *The Czar's General: The Memoirs of a Russian General in the Napoleonic Wars*, translated and edited by Alexander Mikaberidze (Welwyn Garden City: Ravenhall Books, 2005), 50. On the problems with supplies, see Stutterheim, *La bataille d'Austerlitz*, 32–34.

8. Louis Alexandre Andrault de Langeron, *Journal inédit de la campagne de 1805* (Paris: La Vouivre, 1998), 24–25; Nikolai Shil'der, *Imperator Aleksandr pervyi. Ego zhizn' i tsarstvovanie* (St. Petersburg: A. S. Suvorin, 1897), II:133–134, 283. Bavarian diplomat Olry described Grand Duke Constantine demanding that his guard units move by parade marches from St. Petersburg to Olmütz. He estimated that the Guard Corps lost 2,000 men as a result. See Olry's correspondence in *Istoricheskii Vestnik* 147 (1917): 435.

9. Carl Friedrich von Toll, *Denkwürdigkeiten aus dem Leben des Kaiserl. russ. Generals von der der Infanterie Carl Friedrich Grafen von Toll*, edited by Theodor von Bernhardi (Leipzig: Otto Wigand, 1856), I:151; Shil'der, *Imperator Aleksandr pervyi*, II:138–139.

10. Alexander to Frederick Wilhelm of Prussia, November 19, 1805, in Paul Bailleu, ed., *Briefwechsel könig Friedrich Wilhelm's III und der königin Luise mit kaiser Alexander I* (Leipzig: S. Hirzel, 1900), 84. To alleviate food shortages, Kutuzov suggested spreading the army over the wider area and billeting units in the villages around Olmutz "in such a manner as to be able to reassemble the army within twenty-four hours." His advice, however, was not considered. Langeron, *Journal inédit de la campagne de 1805*, 27.

11. In his letter Kutuzov claimed that the Austrian "imperial-royal police has determined that *Rotmistr* de Winzell of the de Bussy Regiment is employed by the enemy to spy on the Russian army." Inzov to Dokhturov; Kutuzov to Prince Liechtenstein, November 12/24, 1805, Lithuanian State Historical Archives, f. 378, op. 13, d. 213, part 1, l. 196.

12. Alexander Langeron, "Mémoires du Comte de Langeron," in *Nouvelle Revue Rétrospective* (January–June 1895): 290.

13. Langeron, "Mémoires du Comte de Langeron," 290; Butovskii, *Pervaya voina imperatora Aleksandra I s Napoleonom I v 1805 godu*, 37.

14. Langeron, *Journal inédit de la campagne de 1805*, 26.

15. Toll, *Denkwürdigkeiten*, I:141–142; Langeron, *Journal inédit de la campagne de 1805*, 31.

16. I. Heisman's entry on Kutuzov in *Russkii biograficheskii slovar'*, IX:650 (e-version at http://rulex.ru/xPol/); Heinrich Leer, *Podrobnyi konspekt voiny 1805 goda. Austerlitskaya operatsiya* (St. Petersburg: Tip. V. Bezobrazova, 1888), 57–58.

17. Mikhail Bragin, *Polkovodets Kutuzov* (Moscow: Gospolitizdat, 1944), 86. A similar opinion is voiced in many other publications, most recently in Oleg Sokolov, *Bitva trekh imperatorov, 1805–1812* (St. Petersburg: Astrel, 2012), 426–427.

18. Adam Czartoryski, *Memoirs of Prince Adam Czartoryski and His Correspondence with Alexander I*, edited by Adam Gielgud (London: Remington, 1888), 103; Langeron, *Journal inédit de la campagne de 1805*, 8.

19. Toll, *Denkwürdigkeiten*, I:142.

20. Langeron, *Journal inédit de la campagne de 1805*, 31.

21. Czartoryski, *Memoirs*, II:103, 106.

22. A. Langeron, *Mémoires de Langeron: Général d'infanterie dans l'armée russe. Campagnes de 1812, 1813, 1814* (Paris: A. Picard, 1902), 290.

23. Lev Engelhardt, *Zapiski*, edited by I. Fedyukin (Moscow: Novoe Literaturnoe Obozrenie, 1997), 168–169.

24. Kutuzov's numerous letters and orders are at Lithuanian State Historical Archives, f. 378, op. 13, d. 213 (part 1), ll. 285 and 312. A handful of these documents have been published in *M. I. Kutuzov: Sbornik dokumentov* (Moscow: Voeniszdat, 1950), II:189–198.

25. Joseph de Maistre to King Victor Emmanuel I of Sardinia, January 19/31, 1806, in *Russkii arkhiv* 6 (1871): 73.

26. Toll, *Denkwürdigkeiten*, I:141.

27. Clemens d'Elpidio Janetschek, *Die Schlacht bei Austerlitz: 2. December 1805* (Brünn: Päpstliche Benedictiner-Buchdruckerei, 1898), 70.

28. For interesting details on Weyrother's role and the continued infighting between Austrian officers, see letters written by British master spy William Wickham in *The Correspondence of the Right Honourable William Wickham* (London: Richard Bentley, 1870), II:260, 270–271, 278, 306–308, 323, 391. For a critical discussion, see Otto Hartmann, *Der Antheil der Russen am Feldzug von 1799 in der Schweiz: Ein Beitrag zur Geschichte dieses Feldzugs und zyr Kritik seiner Geschichtschreiber* (Zurich: A. Munk, 1892), 84–88, 138, 161, 168.

29. Toll, *Denkwürdigkeiten*, I:141. In the eyes of Langeron, Weyrother was "callous, rude, insolent, convinced of his own merit, and carrying self-esteem to the most disturbing excess. He had all the faults of an upstart." Langeron, *Journal inédit de la campagne de 1805*, 28.

30. Wilhelm Rustow, *Der Krieg von 1805 in Deutschland und Italien* (Frauenfeld: Verlags-Comptoir, 1853), 325. "Weirother . . . was an officer of great bravery and military knowledge, but, like General Mack, he trusted too much in his combinations, which were often complicated, and did not admit that they might be foiled by the skill of the enemy." Czartoryski, *Memoirs*, II:102. A similar characteristic is in Toll, *Denkwürdigkeiten*, I:141.

31. Langeron, *Journal inédit de la campagne de 1805*, 28; *Austerlitz raconté par les témoins de la Bataille des Trois Empereurs* (Geneva, 1969), 147.

32. Rustow, *Der Krieg von 1805*, 336; Toll, *Denkwürdigkeiten*, I:144. Kutuzov made arrangements to supply the army with two days' worth of provisions—"at least 3 pounds of meat per soldier, and, similarly, an appropriate ration of bread"—on November 24–25 in preparation for the army's departure on the 26th. However, he was unable to get sufficient supplies and the departure was therefore postponed by a day. See Kutuzov's orders of November 24–26 in Lithuanian State Historical Archives, f. 378, op. 13, d. 285, l. 78, and d. 311, l. 272b; Kutuzov to Lieven, November 13/25, 1805, in *M. I. Kutuzov: Sbornik dokumentov*, II:199.

33. Toll, *Denkwürdigkeiten*, I:144–145.

34. Philippe-Paul, comte de Ségur, *Histoire et mémoires* (Paris: Firmin Didot Frères, 1873), II:445–446.

35. Rustow, *Der Krieg von 1805,* 345–346.

36. Claude-François Baron de Méneval, *Memoirs Illustrating the History of Napoleon from 1802 to 1815* (New York: D. Appleton, 1894), I:399.

37. Anne-Jean-Marie-René Savary, *Mémoires du duc de Rovigo écrits de sa main, pour servir à l'histoire de l'Empereur Napoleon* (Paris: Colburn, 1828), I, part 2, 113–123.

38. It is noteworthy that, in his letter, Napoleon deliberately tried to cultivate the allied perception of his weakness by addressing the czar as "Sire" rather than "Mon frère," as was customary for royal sovereigns and as he had been doing in correspondence with the rulers of Bavaria and Wurttemberg. He knew well that such details would not go unnoticed at the allied camp. See *Correspondance générale,* edited by Michel Kerautret and Gabriel Madec (Paris: Fayard, 2008), V:866, 874–875.

39. Note A on Kutuzov's report in *Campagnes de la Grande Armée et de l'Armée d'Italie en l'an XIV (1805)* (Paris: Librairie Economique, 1806), 96.

40. Napoleon to Frederick II, Elector of Wurttemberg, December 5, 1805, in *Correspondance Générale,* V:875; Ségur, *Histoire et mémoires,* II:446–447. Also see Jean Lambert Alphonse Colin, "Campagne de 1805 en Allemagne," *Revue d'histoire* 77 (1907): 65–68; Sokolov, *Bitva trekh imperatorov,* 422–423.

41. Kutuzov's Orders to the Army, November 14–15/26–27, 1805, Lithuanian State Historical Archives, f. 378, op. 13, d. 285, ll. 75, 82; Disposition for the Offensive Operations of the Allied Forces, November 14/26, 1805, Lithuanian State Historical Archives, f. 378, op. 13, d. 213, part 1, ll. 208–215. Also see a copy of the disposition at RGVIA, f. 846, op. 16, d. 3174, ll. 13–18b; General Uvarov's documents at RGVIA, f. 846, op. 16, d. 3154, ll. 1–1b; Langeron, *Journal inédit de la campagne de 1805,* 31; Rustow, *Der Krieg von 1805,* 348–349; A. Mikhailovskii-Danilevskii, *Polnoe sobranie sochinenii. Opisanie pervoi voiny imperatora Aleksandra s Napoleonom v 1805 godu. Opisanie vtoroj voiny imperatora Aleksandra s Napoleonom v 1806 i 1807 godah* (St. Petersburg, 1849), 159–161.

42. The offensive was planned for November 26 but was postponed because the army lacked sufficient supplies and additional time was needed to translate dispositions. Kutuzov to Lieven, November 13/25, 1805, in *M. I. Kutuzov: Sbornik dokumentov,* II:199. Also see Stutterheim, *La bataille d'Austerlitz,* 35.

43. Stutterheim, *La bataille d'Austerlitz,* 35.

44. Yermolov, *The Czar's General,* 56; Langeron, *Journal inédit de la campagne de 1805,* 31–32.

45. Disposition for Offensive Toward Wischau, n.d. [ca. November 28, 1805], RGVIA, f. 846, op. 16, d. 3174, ll. 3–5.

46. Mikhailovskii-Danilevskii, *Opisanie pervoi voiny,* 160–161; Shil'der, *Imperator Aleksandr pervyi,* II:135.

47. Bagration to Kutuzov, November 16/28, 1805, Lithuanian State Historical Archives, f. 378, op. 13, d. 213, part 1, ll. 491–492.

48. Yermolov, *The Czar's General*, 57.

49. Stutterheim, *La bataille d'Austerlitz*, 44. A well-informed participant later pointed out that "it was here that Emperor Alexander and his advisers were in fault. They imagined that Napoleon was in a dangerous position, and that he was on the point of retreating. The French outposts had an appearance of hesitation and timidity which nourished these illusions, and reports came at every moment from our outposts announcing an imminent movement of the French army to the rear." Czartoryski, *Memoirs*, II:104–105. See also Rustow, *Der Krieg von 1805*, 349–350.

50. Ivan Zhirkevich, "Zapiski Ivana Stepanovicha Zhirkevicha, 1789–1848," *Russkaya starina* 2 (1872): 218.

51. Savary, *Mémoires*, I, part 2, 110–124. Also see Modest Bogdanovich, *Istoriya tsarstvovaniya imperatora Aleksandra I i Rossii v ego vremya* (St. Petersburg: Tip. F. Sushinskogo, 1869), II:46–47, 50–52.

52. Savary, *Mémoires*, I, Part 2, 127–128; Ségur, *Histoire et mémoires*, II:448–449; Mikhailovskii-Danilevskii, *Opisanie pervoi voiny*, 163–165.

53. Napoleon to Frederick II, Elector of Wurttemberg, December 5, 1805, in *Correspondance Générale*, V:875.

54. Langeron, *Journal inédit de la campagne de 1805*, 30.

55. Sergey Glinka, *Zapiski Sergeya Nikolayevicha Glinki* (St. Petersburg: Russkaya Starina, 1895), 152.

56. Additional Bulletin, December 31, 1805, correspondence of Olry, in *Istoricheskii Vestnik* 147 (1917): 460–461. Olry mentions that Prince Bagration, who, in the words of one diplomat, "loved to fish in murky waters," was present at the meeting.

57. Disposition for the Offensive to Austerlitz, 12:00 a.m., November 18/30, 1805, Lithuanian State Historical Archives, f. 378, op. 13, d. 213, part 1, l. 200. The order was issued by Duty General Inzov.

58. Michel de Lombarès, "Devant Austerlitz, sur les traces de la pensée de l'Empereur," *Revue Historique de l'Armée* 3 (1947): 41–43.

59. Toll, *Denkwürdigkeiten*, I:148.

60. Langeron, *Journal inédit de la campagne de 1805*, 32.

61. Yermolov, *The Czar's General*, 56.

62. For a discussion of Napoleon's evolving plan of battle, see Colin, "La Campagne de 1805 en Allemagne," 303–309; Robert Goetz, *1805: Austerlitz. Napoleon and the Destruction of the Third Coalition* (London: Greenhill Books, 2005), 92–96, 106–110, 112–113, 117–118; Sokolov, *Bitva trekh imperatorov*, 446–449; Ian Castle, *Austerlitz: Napoleon and the Eagles of Europe* (Barnsley: Pen & Sword, 2005), chap. 13.

63. Ségur, *Histoire et memoires*, II:451–452.

64. Colin, "La Campagne de 1805 en Allemagne," 300–302.

65. "My men are suffering greatly, for it is already the second day that they do not have meat and only a little bread. Horses remain without forage," reported Bagration to Kutuzov on November 30. Lithuanian State Historical Archives, f. 378, op. 13, d. 213, part 1, l. 535.

66. Disposition for the Offensive to Austerlitz, n.d. [ca. November 30, 1805], RGVIA, f. 846, op. 16, d. 3174, ll. 48–49; Disposition for Offensive to Menin and Sokolnice, n.d. [ca. December 1, 1805], RGVIA, f. 846 op. 16, d. 3174, ll. 47–47b. Also see Mikhailovskii-Danilevskii, *Opisanie pervoi voiny*, 165–170; Rustow, *Der Krieg von 1805*, 356–359; Langeron, *Journal inédit de la campagne de 1805*, 41; Colin, "La Campagne de 1805 en Allemagne," 291; de Lombarès, "Devant Austerlitz," 47.

67. Jean-Baptiste-Antoine-Marcelin, baron de Marbot, *The Memoirs of Baron de Marbot, Late Lieutenant General in the French Army*, translated by Arthur J. Butler (New York: Longmans, 1903), I:160.

68. Mikhailovskii-Danilevskii, *Opisanie pervoi voiny*, 174.

69. Czartoryski, *Memoirs*, 106.

70. Disposition for Attack, n.d. [ca. December 2, 1805], RGVIA, f. 846, op. 16, d. 3117/1, ll. 50–53. Also see Disposition for Attack on the Enemy Position Behind Slapanitz and Sokolnitz on November 20 [December 2], 1805, RGVIA, f. 846, op. 16, d. 3113, ll. 1–3; Stutterheim, *La bataille d'Austerlitz*, 67–75.

71. Langeron, *Journal inédit de la campagne de 1805*, 33–34.

72. Mikhailovskii-Danilevskii, *Opisanie pervoi voiny*, 175.

73. General Dmitri Dokhturov to his wife, in *Russkii arkhiv* 1 (1874): 1904.

74. Glinka, *Zapiski*, 153.

75. A. Val'kovich and A. Kapitonov, eds., *Fel'dmarshal Kutuzov: dokumenty, dnevniki, vospominaniya* (Moscow: Arkheog. Tsentr, 1995), 316.

76. Czartoryski, *Memoirs*, 106.

77. French historian Claude Manceron imagined the following scene, almost all of it fictional: "There he was, lying rather than sitting in a huge portable armchair, hollowed out by his heavy frame, which accompanied him everywhere. . . . To his left, dispatches were piled on a great oak table, where he tolerated only one candlestick with three candles. He did not want it to be seen that he was asleep. He was drunk. He usually overcame his annoyance with some girls: he had three in his baggage-train and would undoubtedly have sent for them all together, in accordance with the habits attributed to him for ten years on great occasions, if his wagons had not remained near Olmutz. Fortunately, his personal berlin contained immediate relief: the armchair, the fur-lined coat for his knees, the icon of the Virgin of Kazan, and a supply of highly fortified Crimean wine, a sort of liqueur, two bottles of which had been poured out for him before supper. He reacted by giving sketchy salutes to the messengers who came to bring him news, and smiled and grunted without anyone knowing why or what he was trying to say." *Austerlitz: The Story of a Battle*, translated by George Unwin (London: George Allen & Unwin, 1966), 180.

78. Count Razumovskii's letter of January 11/23, 1806, cited in Mikhailovskii-Danilevskii, *Opisanie pervoi voiny*, 212.

79. Adam Dietrich Heinrich Bulow, *Der Feldzug von 1805 militärisch-politisch betrachtet von dem Verfasser des Geistes des neuern Kriegssystems* (Leipzig, 1806), II:65–66.

80. For an interesting discussion, see Toll, *Denkwürdigkeiten*, I:152–153.

81. For detailed criticism, see Rustow, *Der Krieg von 1805*, 360–363.

82. Langeron, *Journal inédit de la campagne de 1805*, 33–34; Czartoryski, *Memoirs*, 105. Czartoryski goes on to note that "everything in the French army seemed to announce a resolution to attempt a retreat. It was therefore decided to advance, in order to take advantage of this disposition of the enemy." Also see Toll, *Denkwürdigkeiten*, I:155–156.

83. Joseph de Maistre to Chevalier de Rossi, January 3, 1807, in Joseph de Maistre, *Oeuvres completes de J. de Maistre. Correspondance, 1806–1807* (Lyon: Librairie Générale Catholique, 1885), X:291. Also see *Russkii arkhiv* 6 (1871): 91.

84. Toll, *Denkwürdigkeiten*, I:156.

85. Yermolov, *The Czar's General*, 57; Langeron, *Journal inédit de la campagne de 1805*, 33–34; Colin, "Campagne de 1805 en Allemagne," 324–325; Mikhailovskii-Danilevskii, *Opisanie pervoi voiny*, 175; Shil'der, *Imperator Aleksandr pervyi*, II:138.

86. Mikhailovskii-Danilevskii, *Opisanie pervoi voiny*, 196. For Bagration's criticism of the plan, see Toll, *Denkwürdigkeiten*, I:157. Prince Czartoryski described an interesting incident: "Someone remarked that the following day [December 2] was Monday, a day regarded as unlucky in Russia. As the Emperor was passing over a grassy mound his horse slipped and fell, and he was thrown out of the saddle. Although the accident was not serious, it was regarded by some people as a bad omen." *Memoirs*, 106.

87. Kutuzov to Alexander, January 14/26, 1806, in *M. I. Kutuzov: Sbornik dokumentov*, II:255.

88. Stutterheim, *La bataille d'Austerlitz*, 81; Kutuzov to Alexander, January 14/26, 1806; Buxhöwden to Kutuzov, n.d. [ca. December 1805], in *M. I. Kutuzov: Sbornik dokumentov*, II:241–242, 256.

89. Langeron, *Journal inédit de la campagne de 1805*, 43; Stutterheim, *La bataille d'Austerlitz*, 89; Goetz, *1805: Austerlitz*, 136–139.

90. Toll, *Denkwürdigkeiten*, I:154–155.

91. From the recollections of Prince Peter Volkonskii, in Mikhailovskii-Danilevskii, *Opisanie pervoi voiny*, 181; Toll, *Denkwürdigkeiten*, I:161.

92. Gregor von Berg, *Autobiographie des Generalen der Infanterie Gregor von Berg* (Dresden: E. Blochman, 1871), 186.

93. Napoleon to Frederick II, Elector of Wurttemberg, December 5, 1805, in *Correspondance Générale*, V:875.

94. Kutuzov to Alexander, January 14/26, 1806, in *M. I. Kutuzov: Sbornik dokumentov*, II:257.

95. Toll, *Denkwürdigkeiten*, I:162.

96. Miloradovich to Kutuzov, December 3/15, 1805, Lithuanian State Historical Archives, f. 378, op. 13, d. 213, part 1, l. 794.

97. In a confidential report to Alexander, Kutuzov complained that "two battalions of the Novgorodskii Musketeer Regiment barely held ground before fleeing, which disheartened and disordered the rest of the [fourth] column." Kutuzov to Alexander, March 1/13, 1806, in *M. I. Kutuzov: Sbornik dokumentov*, II:265.

98. Kutuzov to Alexander I, January 14/26, 1806; Kutuzov to Alexander I, December 26, 1805/January 7, 1806, in *M. I. Kutuzov: Sbornik dokumentov*, II:240, 257–258.

99. Miloradovich to Kutuzov, December 3/15, 1805, Lithuanian State Historical Archives, f. 378, op. 13, d. 213, part 1, ll. 794–795.

100. Kutuzov to Alexander I, January 14/26, 1806, in *M. I. Kutuzov: Sbornik dokumentov*, II:258.

101. Mikhailovskii-Danilevskii, *Opisanie pervoi voiny*, 183–184.

102. See, for example, the case of Colonel D. Kudryavtsev, who abandoned his post as commander of an artillery battery and could not be seen anywhere. Kutuzov instructed Miloradovich to investigate and later reported the findings—that "Colonel Kudryavtsev and his officers fled"—to Emperor Alexander. See Lithuanian State Historical Archives, f. 378, op. 14, d. 225, l. 96. Captain Sukhotin, Staff Captain Khatov, and Lieutenant Frank were discharged from military service for claiming to be sick, even though physicians testified that there was nothing wrong with them. Kutuzov to Alexander, December 4/16, 1805, in *M. I. Kutuzov: Sbornik dokumentov*, II:232. In a confidential report to the emperor, Kutuzov complained that many individuals left their units and "ended up in the wagenburg, claiming that they have suffered concussions, while the cavalry troopers alleged that their horses had been killed. Such explanations cannot be accepted because if, after suffering concussion, these officers could walk to the wagenburg, they could have also stayed with the units; as for troopers who had lost horses, if they could not walk back to their units, they should have joined infantry regiments." Kutuzov thought it would be "fair" not to include these officers in the next round of promotions and not to give them any awards they had been nominated for. For the rank and file, he recommended the punishment of adding another five years of service. Kutuzov to Alexander, March 1/13, 1806, in *M. I. Kutuzov: Sbornik dokumentov*, II:265–266. Major General Ivan Loshakov, chef of the Galitskii Musketeer Regiment, had abandoned his regiment and traveled to Lemberg. Kutuzov ordered him to be conveyed to Kyiv, where the general was later court-martialed. Kutuzov to Alexander, January 10/22, 1806, in *M. I. Kutuzov: Sbornik dokumentov*, II:317–318.

103. Czartoryski, *Memoirs*, II:108–109.

104. Toll, *Denkwürdigkeiten*, I:167.

105. Glinka, *Pis'ma ruskago ofitsera*, 107–108; Mikhailovskii-Danilevskii, *Opisanie pervoi voiny*, 184.

106. Kutuzov to Alexander, January 14/26, 1806, in *M. I. Kutuzov: Sbornik dokumentov*, II:258. Buxhöwden stated that he received Kutuzov's order to retreat at two o'clock in the afternoon. Buxhöwden to Kutuzov, n.d. [ca. December 1805], in *M. I. Kutuzov: Sbornik dokumentov*, 242.

107. Kutuzov to Alexander, March 1/13, 1806, in *M. I. Kutuzov: Sbornik dokumentov*, II:265. Kutuzov believed that Przybyszewski had made a crucial mistake when he "advanced with his men to the village of Kobelnitz without taking any precautions and allowing the enemy to get behind his column, which led to the capture of most of his troops."

108. Czartoryski, *Memoirs*, II:110; Mikhailovskii-Danilevskii, *Opisanie pervoi voiny*, 182. See also Przybyszewski to Emperor Alexander, July 11/23, 1806, in *M. I. Kutuzov: Sbornik dokumentov*, II:269–270.

109. For a detailed discussion, see Goetz, *1805: Austerlitz*, 242–258.

110. Goetz, *1805: Austerlitz*, 273–274.

111. Kutuzov to Davout, December 4, 1805, in *Mémorial du dépôt général de la guerre. Tome VIII: Les Campagnes de 1805, 1806 et 7, 1809* (Paris: Picquet, 1843), Pièces Officielles, 108.

112. The agreement specified that the Russians had to leave Moravia and Hungary within fifteen days and evacuate Galicia within a month. Armistice of December 6, 1805, in Jean-Baptiste Honoré Raymond Capefigue, *L'Europe pendant le Consulat et l'Empire de Napoléon* (Paris: Pitois-Levrault, 1840), V:445–446.

113. Kutuzov to D. Esipov, December 2/14, 1805, Lithuanian State Historical Archives, f. 378, op. 13, d. 312, l. 72b.

114. Orders to the Army, November 26 and December 31, 1805/December 8, 1805, and January 12, 1806, Lithuanian State Historical Archives, f. 378, op. 13, d. 285, ll. 118–118b, 137. For Kutuzov's marching orders, see Lithuanian State Historical Archives, f. 378, op. 13, d. 213 (part 1), ll. 285, 311, and 312. Some of these documents have been published in *M. I. Kutuzov: Sbornik dokumentov*, II:279–290. For eyewitness account of the lack of supplies and disorders in the army, see Butovskii, *Pervaya voina imperatora Aleksandra I s Napoleonom I v 1805 godu*, 52–61. On the Russian perceptions of Hungary, see Glinka, *Pis'ma ruskago ofitsera*, I:112–171.

115. Josef Haller to Kutuzov, December 27, 1805/January 8, 1806, RGVIA, f. VUA, d. 3117, part 2, l. 147.

116. Kutuzov to Alexander I, December 27, 1805/January 8, 1806, in *M. I. Kutuzov: Sbornik dokumentov*, II:307–308. For Kutuzov's insistence on strict accountability and his criticism of the incompetence of Chief Supply Commissar Krok, see his letter to S. Dolgorukov, December 31, 1805/January 12, 1806, Lithuanian State Historical Archives, f. 378, op. 13, d. 312, ll. 88–90.

117. Yermolov, *The Czar's General*, 61.

118. Kutuzov to his wife, December 3/15, 1805, in *The Kutuzov Papers* 3 (1871): 55.

119. Kutuzov to his wife, December 25, 1805/January 6, 1806, in *The Kutuzov Papers* 3 (1871): 55.

120. The official report on losses that Kutuzov submitted on January 6, 1806, showed Russian losses as follows: 55 staff officers, 437 junior officers and 954 noncommissioned officers, 432 musicians, over 500 non combatants, and 17,493 rank and file. Kutuzov noted that 4,579 men who had previously been considered killed or missing reported back as the army retreated. However, his report did not discuss Russian artillery losses, which were later shown to include over 1,250 killed. See rosters of the killed and wounded in *M. I. Kutuzov: Sbornik dokumentov*, II:235–239. Also see Alexander Mikaberidze, "Russian Prisoners of War After the Battle of Austerlitz," in *Napoleonica. La Revue* 21, no. 3 (2014): 8–16.

121. Order to the Army, December 4/16, 1805, Lithuanian State Historical Archives, f. 378, op. 13, d. 85, l.129.

122. Dolgorukov to Emperor Alexander, December 6/18, 1805, in Mikhailovskii-Danilevskii, *Opisanie pervoi voiny*, 173. Also see Dolgorukov to Grand Duke Constantine, December 2/14, 1805, RGVIA, f. VUA, d. 3117, part 1, ll. 65–66.

123. Empress Consort Elizabeth Alexeyevna to Princess Amalie of Baden, December 11/23, 1806, in *Russkaya starina* 2 (1910): 317–318. The letter concluded, "It is hard to bear when one person commits such vileness, but it is impossible to convey the sense of exasperation when you see an entire nation that is so fatuous, loathsome, and capable of treachery, in short, possessing the most abominable traits one can imagine. Not words but facts testify the best to what kind of people Austrians really are: they starve to death those who come to shed blood for them and act towards their friends more wickedly than the enemies do. . . . If you know a word that fully describes the feeling that all these transgressions arouse, please let me know, for I cannot find it."

124. Joseph de Maistre to Count de Fron, January 4/16, 1806, in Joseph de Maistre, *Peterburgskie pisma, 1803–1817*, edited by D. Solovyev (St. Petersburg: Inapress, 1995), 60–61.

125. Joseph de Maistre to Chevalier de Rossi, January 19/31, 1806, in *Peterburgskie pisma, 1803–1817*, 61.

126. Semen Vorontsov to Mikhail Vorontsov, January 8, 1806, in *Arkhiv knyazya Vorontsova* (Moscow: Tip. Gracheva, 1870–1895), XVII:123–124. Vorontsov wondered, "Where were caution and circumspection? Would it not have been better to 'fall back to the borders of Hungary, the most plentiful region in the world, and then advance with the united forces capable of crushing the infamous Corsican,' just as Kutuzov advised? How could the Russian leadership ignore the enemy's strength? Why did we not have spies? With money and intelligence we could have known everything!"

127. General Khrapovitskii's testimony in Mikhailovskii-Danilevskii, *Opisanie pervoi voiny*, 212.

NOTES TO PAGES 258–264

128. Butovskii, *Pervaya voina imperatora Aleksandra I s Napoleonom I v 1805 godu*, 52.

129. Kutuzov to his wife, November 30/December 12, 1805, in *The Kutuzov Papers* 3 (1871): 54–55.

130. Alexander to Kutuzov, December 22, 1805/January 3, 1806, in *M. I. Kutuzov: Sbornik dokumentov*, II:234.

131. Kutuzov to Alexander, January 14/26, 1806, in *M. I. Kutuzov: Sbornik dokumentov*, II:254. Kutuzov's second report, submitted in March, was much shorter than the first one. "The position where I remained that day did not allow me to personally observe many other parts of the battle and therefore I had to gather testimonies from others. But because column guides and many regimental chefs have been captured or wounded, I was forced to question their subordinates, who undoubtedly backed each other and thus concealed truth in many matters. I am therefore compelled to report only that which I am certain of." Kutuzov to Alexander, March 1/13, 1806, in *M. I. Kutuzov: Sbornik dokumentov*, II:265.

132. Kutuzov to Alexander, December 26, 1805/January 7, 1806, RGVIA, f. VUA, d. 3108, ll. 80–81. See also Kutuzov to Bennigsen, December 30, 1805/January 11, 1806, Lithuanian State Historical Archives, f. 378, op. 13, d. 213, part 1, ll. 1111–1112b.

133. Butovskii, *Pervaya voina imperatora Aleksandra I s Napoleonom I v 1805 godu*, 52.

134. *Hereford Journal*, January 28, 1807, 1; *Bury and Norwich Post*, January 28, 1807, 4; *Norfolk Chronicle*, January 31, 1807, 4.

135. He did break his silence to write a long response to Miloradovich's complaint of not being shown due credit in Kutuzov's reports. Kutuzov to Miloradovich, June 23/July 5, 1806, in *M. I. Kutuzov: Sbornik dokumentov*, II:353.

136. Mikhailovskii-Danilevskii, *Opisanie pervoi voiny*, 212–213.

Chapter 16

1. Alexander to Kutuzov, February 5/17, 1806, in *M. I. Kutuzov: Sbornik dokumentov* (Moscow: Voeniszdat, 1950), II:357–358. Kutuzov was given command of the 5th, 6th, and 7th Divisions.

2. Kutuzov to his wife, January 15/27, 1806, in *The Kutuzov Papers* 3 (1871): 55–56.

3. Kutuzov to his wife, n.d. [January/February 1806], in *M. I. Kutuzov: Sbornik dokumentov*, II:329–330. The same letter is misdated as written in December 1806 in *The Kutuzov Papers* 3 (1871): 56.

4. For example, based on Kutuzov's report, Major General Ivan Loshakov, chef of the Galitskii Musketeer Regiment, was court-martialed for abandoning his regiment during the battle of Austerlitz. He was deprived of all ranks and sent, as a private, to the 7th Jäger Regiment. Loshakov went on to serve with distinction in the Army of Moldavia, where Kutuzov noticed his hard work, helped him get promoted to lieutenant, and then petitioned the czar for clemency. Loshakov was not restored in his military rank but was allowed to

retire as an active state councilor, a civil rank of the 4th class and equal to that of major general.

5. Kutuzov's Orders to the Army, February 9–12/21–24, 1806, Lithuanian State Historical Archives, Fond 378, Office of the Governor General of Vilnius, Kaunas and Grodno, op. 13, d. 213, part 2, ll. 1194–1195.

6. Kutuzov to Elisabeth von Tiesenhausen (née Golenischeva-Kutuzova), January 15/27, 1806, in *The Kutuzov Papers* 6 (1874): 339.

7. Kutuzov to Elisabeth von Tiesenhausen (née Golenscheva-Kutuzova), June 24/July 6, 1806, in *The Kutuzov Papers* 6 (1874): 339.

8. See Kutuzov to Vyazmitinov, May 19/31, 1806, in *M. I. Kutuzov: Sbornik dokumentov*, II:385–386.

9. *Hereford Journal*, December 10, 1806, 3.

10. Alexander to Kutuzov, February 24/March 8, 1806, RGVIA, f. VUA, d. 3112, ll. 4–5.

11. See "Zapiska o obshikh dolgakh generala ot infanterii Golenischeva-Kutuzova," in RGVIA, f. VUA, d. 337, part 4, l. 3. See also *M. I. Kutuzov: Sbornik dokumentov*, II:409.

12. Ekaterine Kutuzov to Mikhail Kutuzov, September 20/October 2, 1806, in RGVIA, f. VUA, d. 337, part 4, l. 9. The letter was also published in *M. I. Kutuzov: Sbornik dokumentov*, II:409. Remarkably, Kutuzov's wife was not fully pleased with the imperial largesse. She thought the emperor would pay "fifty thousand each [husband and wife]" and was "distraught to see that so little has been approved."

13. Minutes of the First and Second Meetings of the Council of War, June 29/July 11, 1806, and July 5/17, 1806, RGVIA, f. VUA, d. 386, ll. 1–3; d. 3158, ll. 5–9. These minutes have been also printed in *M. I. Kutuzov: Sbornik dokumentov*, II:396–399. Besides Kutuzov, the council included Count N. Saltykov, Field Marshal M. Kamenskii, General S. Vyazmitinov, General Lassi, Engineer General Sukhtelen, Lieutenant General Tolstoy, Vice Admiral P. Chichagov, and Adjutant General Count Kh. Lieven.

14. Alexander to Kutuzov, June 4/16, 1806; Kutuzov to Alexander, June 7/19, 1806, in *M. I. Kutuzov: Sbornik dokumentov*, II:390–391. Kutuzov also initiated a minor but important alteration in the design of musket stocks so the soldiers could aim and fire the weapons with greater ease. Kutuzov to Alexander, June 28/July 10, 1806, in *M. I. Kutuzov: Sbornik dokumentov*, II:394.

15. James Howard Harris, ed., *Diaries and Correspondence of James Harris First Earl of Malmesbury* (London: R. Bentley, 1845), IV:347.

16. Sam A. Mustafa, *Germany in the Modern World: A New History* (New York: Rowman & Littlefield, 2011), 94.

17. Kutuzov to Alexander, September 19/October 1, 1806, in *M. I. Kutuzov: Sbornik dokumentov*, II:406–409. In this letter Kutuzov also admitted that the 6th Division was the weakest of the three divisions because quite a few of its soldiers had contracted serious diseases earlier that summer and many of them

were still too weak to embark on the campaign. This earned him a rebuke from the emperor for not reporting this matter earlier.

18. Alexander to Kutuzov, September 28/October 10, 1806, in *Russkaya starina* 96 (1898): 586.

19. *M. I. Kutuzov: Sbornik dokumentov*, II:423.

20. *Morning Post*, October 20, 1806, 3.

21. Kamenskii to Alexander, December 22, 1806, cited in Alexander Mikhailovskii-Danilevskii, *Opisanie vtoroi voiny Imperatora Aleksandra s Napoleonom v 1806–1807 godakh* (St. Petersburg: Tip. Schtaba Otd. Korpusa Vnut. Strazhi, 1846), 76.

22. Kutuzov to his wife, January 10/22, 1807, in *The Kutuzov Papers* 3 (1871): 57.

23. Pavel Nikolai to Semen Vorontsov, September 19, 1806, in *Arkhiv knyazya Vorontsova* (Moscow: Tip. Gracheva, 1876), XXII:336.

24. Kutuzov to his wife, October 20/November 1, 1803, in *The Kutuzov Papers* 3 (1871): 51.

25. See, for example, Lord Stanley of Alderley, ed., *Travels to Tana and Persia by Josafa Barbaro and Ambrogio Contarini* (London: Hakluyt Society, 1873), 112–113.

26. Cited in Vladimir Ikonnikov, *Kyiv v 1654–1855 gg. Istoricheskii ocherk* (Kyiv: Tip. Imp. Un-ta. Sv. Vladimira, 1904), 58.

27. Cited in Ikonnikov, *Kyiv v 1654–1855 gg.*, 90–91.

28. Cited in Ikonnikov, *Kyiv v 1654–1855 gg.*, 92–93. Also see Michael F. Hamm, *Kiev: A Portrait, 1800–1917* (Princeton, NJ: Princeton University Press, 2014), 3–23. For the nineteenth-century description of Kyiv, see Edward Morton, *Travels in Russia and a Residence at St. Petersburg and Odessa in the Year 1827–1829* (London: Longman, Rees, Orme, Brown, and Green, 1830), 145; Robert Lyall, *Travels in Russia, the Krimea, the Caucasus and Georgia* (London: T. Cadell, 1825), I:103–115.

29. Mikhailovskii-Danilevskii, *Opisanie vtoroi voini Imperatora Aleksandra s Napoleonom v 1806–1807 godakh*, 47–53.

30. Kutuzov to his wife, n.d. [December 1806], in *The Kutuzov Papers* 3 (1871): 56.

31. Kutuzov to his wife, November 28/December 10, 1806, in *The Kutuzov Papers* 3 (1871): 56.

32. Kutuzov to his wife, April 1/13, 1806, in *The Kutuzov Papers* 3 (1871): 59.

33. Kutuzov to his wife, December 20, 1806/January 1, 1807, in *The Kutuzov Papers* 3 (1871): 57.

34. Kutuzov to his wife, December 6–13/18–25, 1806, in *The Kutuzov Papers* 3 (1871): 56–57; Kutuzov to Elisabeth von Tiesenhausen (née Golenischeva-Kutuzova), May 6/18, 1807, in *The Kutuzov Papers* 6 (1874): 340.

35. Kutuzov to Elisabeth von Tiesenhausen (née Golenischeva-Kutuzova), May 27/June 8, in *The Kutuzov Papers* 6 (1874): 342.

36. Kutuzov to Elisabeth von Tiesenhausen (née Golenischeva-Kutuzova), July 1/13, in *The Kutuzov Papers* 6 (1874): 342.

37. Kutuzov to his wife, December 20, 1806/January 1, 1807, in *The Kutuzov Papers* 3 (1871): 57.

38. Alexander to Tolstoy, n.d., in *The Kutuzov Papers* 3 (1871): 72–73.

39. For the Russian perspective on the war, see Alexander Mikaberidze, ed., *The Russian Eyewitness Accounts of the Campaign of 1807* (London: Pen & Sword, 2015), 27–108.

40. Jean-Baptiste Barrès, *Memoirs of a Napoleonic Officer* (New York: Dial Press, 1925), 101.

41. Kutuzov to his wife, February 11/23, 1807, in *The Kutuzov Papers* 3 (1871): 58.

42. Kutuzov to his wife, February 20/March 4, 1807, in *The Kutuzov Papers* 3 (1871): 58.

43. Kutuzov to Prozorovskii, October 13/24, 1795, published in A. Afanasyev, "Kutuzov M. I. Neizvestnoe pis'mo Prozorovskomu A. A.," *Rossiiskii arkhiv: Istoriya Otechestva v svidetel'stvakh i dokumentakh XVIII–XX vv.* 12 (2003): 27–28.

44. Kutuzov to his wife, March 18/30, 1807, in *The Kutuzov Papers* 3 (1871): 58.

45. Kutuzov to his wife, April 1/13, 1807, in *The Kutuzov Papers* 3 (1871): 59.

46. Kutuzov to his wife, March 25/April 6, 1807, in *The Kutuzov Papers* 3 (1871): 58–59.

47. Kutuzov to his wife, April 29/May 11, 1807, in *The Kutuzov Papers* 3 (1871): 59.

48. As overheard by one of British commissioner Robert Wilson's contacts. Michael Glover, *A Very Slippery Fellow: The Life of Sir Robert Wilson, 1777–1849* (Oxford: Oxford University Press, 1978), 40. For an alternative version, in which Alexander's first words were "I will be your second against England," see Napoleon to Alexander, July 1, 1812, in *Correspondance générale*, edited by Michel Kerautret and Gabriel Madec (Paris: Fayard, 2008), XII:787. Also see Louis Pierre Bignon, *Histoire de France depuis le 18 brumaire jusqu'à la Paix de Tilsit* (Paris: Charles Béchet, 1830), VI:316; Armand Lefebvre, *Histoire des cabinets de l'Europe pendant le Consulat et l'Empire* (Paris: Pagnerre, 1847), III:102.

49. During one of their meetings Napoleon and Alexander shut themselves up in a cabinet with numerous maps spread out in front of them. Napoleon, apparently in brisk conversation with Alexander, asked his secretary, Meneval, for the map of the Ottoman Empire, which the two rulers examined while conversing. Napoleon suddenly placed his finger on Constantinople and loudly stated several times, "Constantinople! Constantinople is the conquest of the world." The czar, however, pressed hard to have Constantinople. See Claude François de Meneval, *Memoirs to Serve for the History of Napoleon I from 1802 to 1815* (London: Hutchinson, 1895), II:92–93; Adolphe Thiers, *History of the Consulate and the Empire of France Under Napoleon* (Philadelphia: Claxton, Remsen & Haffelfinger, 1879), II:326.

50. For a wide context of the war, see A. Petrov, *Voina Rossii s Turtsiej 1806–1812 gg.* (St. Petersburg: V. S. Balashev, 1887), II:1–44; Alexander Mikhailosvkii-Danilevskii, *Polnoe sobranie sochinenii. Tom III: Opisanie Turetskoi voiny s 1806*

do 1812 goda (St. Petersburg: Tip. Shtaba Otd. Korpusal Vnutren. Strazhi., 1849), 1–82.

51. "Exploiting the old field marshal's weaknesses, he incessantly repeated in his presence that when it came to military affairs, he was nothing but his true apprentice. The student's humility thus soon completely beguiled the old master." Major General Prince Alexander Sherbatov, *General-fel'dmarshal Knyaz Paskevich, ego zhizn' i deyatel'nost* (St. Petersburg: V. A. Berezovskii, 1888), I:38.

52. Prozorovskii to Arakcheyev, December 9/21, 1808, RGVIA, f. VUA, d. 2911, l. 115b.

53. Langeron, "Zapiski grafa Lanzherona. Voina s Turtsiei 1806–1812 gg," *Russkaya starina* 6 (1908): 665.

54. Alexander to Kutuzov, March 4/16, 1808, in *M. I. Kutuzov: Sbornik dokumentov*, II:492–493.

55. Compare to Fedor Dostoyevsky's famous passage: "Tyranny is a habit; it may develop, and it does develop at last, into a disease. I maintain that the very best of men may be coarsened and hardened into a brute by habit." *The House of the Dead*, translated by Constance Garnett (New York: Macmillan, 1915), 186.

56. Kutuzov to Elisabeth von Tiesenhausen (née Golenischeva-Kutuzova), April 3/15, 1808, in *The Kutuzov Papers* 6 (1874): 344.

Chapter 17

1. Kutuzov to his wife, April 20/May 2, 1808, in *The Kutuzov Papers* 2 (1871): 201.

2. Order to the Army, April 20/May 2, 1808, RGVIA, f. VUA, d. 2876, l. 18b; Kutuzov to his wife, April 20/May 2 and May 2/14, 1808, in *The Kutuzov Papers* 2 (1871): 201–202. Also see Kutuzov to Prozorovskii and Kutuzov to Lieutenant Generals I. Gika and N. Rtischev and Lt. Colonel S. Leparskii, April 21/May 3, 1808, in *M. I. Kutuzov: Sbornik dokumentov* (Moscow: Voeniszdat, 1950), III:4–5.

3. For details, see Disposition of the Army of Moldavia, in *M. I. Kutuzov: Sbornik dokumentov*, III:20–29.

4. Disposition of the Army of Moldavia, in *M. I. Kutuzov: Sbornik dokumentov*, III:20–29.

5. Kutuzov's Order to the Army, May 17/29, 1808, RGVIA, f. VUA, d. 2916, l. 19; Kutuzov's Order to the Main Corps, September 13/25, 1808, in *M. I. Kutuzov: Sbornik dokumentov*, III:64. When a divisional commander rejected eighty-three recruits for a variety of reasons, Kutuzov reviewed each of them and argued that missing fingers on the left hand, missing "three or four teeth," or "weak constitution due to young age" were not sufficient grounds for rejecting recruits. See Kutuzov to Lieutenant General Evgeny Markov, May 29/June 10, 1808, in *M. I. Kutuzov: Sbornik dokumentov*, III:32.

6. Kutuzov to Minister of War A. Arakcheyev, April 25/May 7, 1808, in *M. I. Kutuzov: Sbornik dokumentov*, III:5–6. In addition, Kutuzov set up new

recruitment depots at Zhitomir and Akhtyrka to facilitate the process of receiving and processing new recruits. See Kutuzov to Essen III and to Olsufyev III, July 9/21, 1808, in *M. I. Kutuzov: Sbornik dokumentov*, III:42–44.

7. Kutuzov's Orders to the Army, May 10/22 and May 26/June 7, 1808, in *M. I. Kutuzov: Sbornik dokumentov*, III:14, 30–31.

8. Prozorovskii to Kutuzov, July 7/19, 1809; Kutuzov to Essen III and Olsufyev III, July 9/21, 1809, in *M. I. Kutuzov: Sbornik dokumentov*, III:40–42.

9. Kutuzov to Arakcheyev, April 29/May 10, 1808, in *M. I. Kutuzov: Sbornik dokumentov*, III:9–10. The two divisions arrived in late May, starting with the 8th Division, which reached its cantonment on May 21. See Kutuzov to Prozorovskii, May 9/21, 1808, in *M. I. Kutuzov: Sbornik dokumentov*, III:13.

10. Kutuzov's memorandum to Rtischev, Essen III, Olsufyev III, and Kamenskii, August 27/September 8, 1808, in *M. I. Kutuzov: Sbornik dokumentov*, III:59–61. For an example of Kutuzov's instructions on the training exercises at Tecuci in August, see *M. I. Kutuzov: Sbornik dokumentov*, III:49–51.

11. Kutuzov's Order to the Army, August 7/19, 1808, in *M. I. Kutuzov: Sbornik dokumentov*, III:55; Kutuzov to his wife, August 8/20, 1808, in *The Kutuzov Papers* 2 (1871): 202.

12. Kutuzov's Memorandum of April 27/May 9, 1808, RGVIA, f. VUA, d. 2910, ll. 44b–45. This document was also published in *M. I. Kutuzov: Sbornik dokumentov*, III:7–8. See also A. Petrov, *Voina Rossii s Turtsiej 1806–1812 gg.* (St. Petersburg, 1887), II:69–70.

13. "Kutuzov knows all these places, all local peoples, their customs and traditions," Prozorovskii commented. "He is more capable than anyone else." Prozorovskii to Arakcheyev, December 9/21, 1808, RGVIA, f. VUA, d. 2911, l. 115b. A month earlier Minister of War Arakcheyev had informed Prozorovskii of the possible war and mentioned that Emperor Alexander was considering assigning Kutuzov to lead the corps that Russia pledged to commit in support of France against Austria. Ultimately, the czar appointed Prince Sergey Golitsyn to lead it.

14. Savary to Napoleon, November 4, 1807, in *SIRIO* 83:180.

15. See Articles 8, 9, and 11 of the Erfurt Convention, http://www.napoleon-ser ies.org/research/government/diplomatic/c_erfurt.html.

16. These instructions were delivered through a series of letters from Rumyantsev to Prozorovskii. October 16 and December 6, 1808, *VPR*, IV:365–369.

17. Count Rumyantsev to Prince Prozorovskii, August 7 [19], 1808, and October 3 [15], 1808, Weimar, cited in Alexander Mikhailovskii-Danilevskii, *Polnoe sobranie sochinenii. Tom III: Opisanie Turetskoi voiny s 1806 do 1812 goda* (St. Petersburg: Tip. Shtaba Otd. Korpusal Vnutren. Strazhi., 1849), 88–89, 92–96.

18. See correspondence in *VPR*, IV:367–368, 439–440, 456–458.

19. Cited in Mikhailovskii-Danilevskii, *Opisanie Turetskoi voiny s 1806 do 1812 goda*, 104.

20. The eminent Russian military historian criticized Prozorovskii for approaching the planning of the new campaign with "the tactics of the 1769 campaign" still on his mind. A. Petrov, *Vlianie Turetskikh voin s polovini proshlogo stoletia na razvitie Russkago voennago iskusstva* (St. Petersburg, 1894), 227.

21. The main corps comprised five divisions: Essen III's 8th Division was at Byrlad (Bârlad), Olsufyev III's 22nd Division was at Bacâu, Rtischev's 16th Division was at Vaslui, Kamenskii's 12th Division was at Focşani, and Markov's 15th Division was at Roman. See Disposition of the Army of Moldavia, in *M. I. Kutuzov: Sbornik dokumentov*, III:76–80. The army entered the winter cantonments in late November. See Kutuzov to Prozorovskii, November 7/19, 1808, in *M. I. Kutuzov: Sbornik dokumentov*, III:82–84.

22. For example, though reports by the commander of the 16th Division showed that the Mingrelian Musketeer Regiment was fully equipped and supplied, Kutuzov took the time to go through the long monthly report to determine that 534 muskets had to be replaced because of wear and tear; he then made inquiries about the extent of the equipment problem in the regiment and ascertained that the regiment had already replaced 464 muskets the previous year and that one of the core problems was the fact that "muskets and other items in the company *zeughauses* [armories] were kept in great disorder, damaged and not properly cleaned, some missing locks, screws, ramrods, bayonets and with beat-up stocks." Kutuzov to Prozorovskii, March 7/19, 1809, in *M. I. Kutuzov: Sbornik dokumentov*, III:110–111.

23. Kutuzov to his wife, March 24/April 5, 1809, in *The Kutuzov Papers* 2 (1871): 203. Throughout that winter Kutuzov again suffered from acute angst at being separated from his family, and his deep sense of nostalgia spilled from the tip of the quill every time he wrote home. "The life that I am leading here is starting to exhaust me, despite my natural gaiety. For so long I have lived away from everyone I hold dear and yet as I age, I want to be surrounded by my loved ones. My little [granddaughter] Katenka is growing so fast but I see none of her." Kutuzov to his daughter E. Tiesenhausen, January 6/18, 1809, in *Russkaya starina* 6 (1874): 348.

24. Mikhailovskii-Danilevskii, *Opisanie Turetskoi voiny s 1806 do 1812 goda*, 106–107; Petrov, *Voina Rossii s Turtsiej 1806–1812 gg.*, II:206–215.

25. Cited in Petrov, *Voina Rossii s Turtsiej 1806–1812 gg.*, II:215.

26. Prozorovskii to Kutuzov, March 28/April 9, 1809, in *M. I. Kutuzov: Sbornik dokumentov*, III:118–120.

27. Kutuzov to Major General Ilovaiskii II, March 27/April 8, 1809, in *M. I. Kutuzov: Sbornik dokumentov*, III:117.

28. See Kutuzov's orders of April 10–12 and the marching disposition of April 11 in *M. I. Kutuzov: Sbornik dokumentov*, III:126–131.

29. Afanasii Krasovskii, "Iz zapisok general-adjutanta Krasovskago," in *Russkii Vestnik* 8 (1880): 502.

30. For details, see the Journal of Military Operations of the Main Corps in *M. I. Kutuzov: Sbornik dokumentov*, III:141–143, 150–151. Also see Kutuzov's Marching Disposition of 6/18, April 1809, in *M. I. Kutuzov: Sbornik dokumentov*, III:144–146.

31. Entries for April 19–21, in the Journal of Military Operations of the Main Corps in *M. I. Kutuzov: Sbornik dokumentov*, III:151–152.

32. See the Journal of Military Operations of the Main Corps and Kutuzov's orders in *M. I. Kutuzov: Sbornik dokumentov*, III:147–159; Langeron, "Zapiski grafa Lanzherona. Voina s Turtsiei 1806–1812 gg," *Russkaya starina* 4 (1908): 229–230.

33. "Trenches have been completed everywhere; the heavy and siege batteries have been constructed and the bombardment has commenced; the few remaining works are nearing completion," read the entry in the Journal of Military Operations of the Main Corps for April 28. *M. I. Kutuzov: Sbornik dokumentov*, III:166. Also see Prozorovskii to Emperor Alexander I, April 23/May 5, 1809, in *M. I. Kutuzov: Sbornik dokumentov*, III:182.

34. Prozorovskii to Rodofinikin, May 20/June 1, 1809; Prozorovskii to Emperor Alexander I, April 23/May 5, 1809, in *M. I. Kutuzov: Sbornik dokumentov*, III:166, 182–183.

35. Langeron mentions this issue several times in his memoirs, including while discussing the assault on Brăila. Langeron, "Zapiski," 226. Also see interesting details in Ivan Paskevich's memoirs in Sherbatov, *General-fel'dmarshal Knyaz Paskevich, ego zhizn' i deyatel'nost* (St. Petersburg: V. A. Berezovskii, 1888), 55–56.

36. Prozorovskii to Emperor Alexander I, April 23/May 5, 1809, in *M. I. Kutuzov: Sbornik dokumentov*, III:183.

37. Krasovskii, "Iz Zapisok," 503.

38. Disposition for the Storming of the Brăila Retrenchment, n.d. [probably April 30, 1809], RGVIA, f. VUA, d. 2929, ll. 108–108b. The disposition has also been published in *M. I. Kutuzov: Sbornik dokumentov*, III:172–174. On the feint attack, see Kutuzov to Essen III, April 19/May 1, 1809, in *M. I. Kutuzov: Sbornik dokumentov*, III:175. Also see Petrov, *Voina Rossii s Turtsiej 1806–1812 gg.*, II:220–223.

39. Disposition for the Storming of the Brăila Retrenchment, n.d. [probably April 30, 1809], RGVIA, f. VUA, d. 2929, ll. 108–108b.

40. Langeron, "Zapiski," 231–232. In his report to Emperor Alexander, Prozorovskii does state that Suvorov's success at Izmail encouraged him to assault Brăila. Prozorovskii to Emperor Alexander, April 23/May 5, 1809, in *M. I. Kutuzov: Sbornik dokumentov*, III:185.

41. Prozorovskii's order to the Army, April 19/May 1, 1809, cited in Petrov, *Voina Rossii s Turtsiej 1806–1812 gg.*, II:223.

42. Excerpts from Paskevich's memoirs appeared in print in Major General Prince Alexander Sherbatov's *General-fel'dmarshal Knyaz Paskevich* (1888), a

seven-volume magnum opus examining the war hero's career based on arch-ival sources and his unpublished private papers. Later, Paskevich's memoirs of 1812 appeared in print—V. Kharkevich, ed., *1812 god v dnevnikakh, zapiskakh i vospominaniyakh sovremennikov* (Vilna: Shtab. Vilen. Voen. Okr., 1900, I:82–111); A. Tartakovskii, ed., *1812 god v vospominaniyakh sovremennikov* (Moscow: Nauka, 1985, 75–105)—but his earlier writings are still unpub-lished and remain preserved at the Russian State Historical Archive, fond 1018, opis' 9.

43. Sherbatov, *General-fel'dmarshal Knyaz Paskevich,* I:59–60. Adjutant General Afanasii Krasovskii points the finger at Harting who, in Krasovskii's words, believed that the artillery had done its job in damaging the Ottoman defenses. Krasovskii, "Iz zapisok," 503.

44. Contrary to the long-standing claims that Kutuzov warned against launching a nighttime assault and Prozorovskii overruled him, archival documents show that the plan all along was to attack at night. The dispo-sition did not indicate when the assault would commence, simply stating that "the column commanders would be informed about the hour of attack." However, Kutuzov's orders to Essen III, Sergei Kamenskii, and D. Akimov, who commanded the flotilla, specified that the first signal flares would be fired at 2:45 a.m. and the second ones fifteen minutes later, "and these flares should serve as the signal for assault" at 3 a.m. The sun rises around 5:50 a.m. at Brăila in May, so the plan would have given the Russian columns about two hours of darkness to initiate the assault and the rest of the morning to complete it. Kamenskii's after-action report confirms that his troops left the camp at 2 a.m., gathered at the rallying points, and "upon the firing of the second flare" began the assault. See documents in *M. I. Kutuzov: Sbornik dokumentov,* III:175, 177–178.

45. "The soldiers advanced still carrying their knapsacks; no one remembered to tell them to leave them behind, for the absurd and lethal *caporalisme* that infected the entire Russian army made their immediate commanders fearful of ordering them to take off knapsacks since the regulations required soldiers to carry them." Langeron, "Zapiski," 233.

46. Sherbatov, *General-fel'dmarshal Knyaz Paskevich,* I:61; Kutuzov to Prozorovskii, May 1/13, 1809, in *M. I. Kutuzov: Sbornik dokumentov,* III:198.

47. Langeron, "Zapiski," 233. After the assault, Vyazemsky was investigated for his failure to support the *okhotniki* in time, but he was ultimately acquitted. Kutuzov to Markov, April 23/May 5, 1809; Markov to Kutuzov, April 28/ May 10, 1809, in *M. I. Kutuzov: Sbornik dokumentov,* III:181, 190–191.

48. Sergei Kamenskii to Kutuzov, April 22/May 4, 1809, in *M. I. Kutuzov: Sbornik dokumentov,* III:178.

49. Sherbatov, *General-fel'dmarshal Knyaz Paskevich,* I:61.

50. Langeron, "Zapiski," 235.

51. Langeron, "Zapiski," 235–236.

52. Sergei Kamenskii to Kutuzov, April 22/May 4, 1809, in *M. I. Kutuzov: Sbornik dokumentov*, III:178.

53. Sherbatov, *General-fel'dmarshal Knyaz Paskevich*, I:61.

54. Langeron, "Zapiski," 237. Langeron thought Kutuzov's comment was "rather frivolous." Also see Krasovskii, "Iz zapisok," 504; Mikhailovskii-Danilevskii, *Opisanie Turetskoi voiny s 1806 do 1812 goda*, 112; Petrov, *Voina Rossii s Turtsiej 1806–1812 gg.*, II:228.

55. Prozorovskii to Emperor Alexander, April 23/May 5, 1809, in *M. I. Kutuzov: Sbornik dokumentov*, III:184.

56. Langeron, "Zapiski," 232.

57. Petrov, *Voina Rossii s Turtsiej 1806–1812 gg.*, II:228.

58. Krasovskii, "Iz zapisok," 503.

59. Langeron, "Zapiski," 236.

60. Langeron, "Zapiski," 237.

61. Kutuzov wrote lengthy instructions on how to conduct the siege works. *M. I. Kutuzov: Sbornik dokumentov*, III:180–181. Also see the Journal of the Military Operations of the Main Corps, in *M. I. Kutuzov: Sbornik dokumentov*, III:187–189.

62. Prozorovskii to Emperor Alexander, April 30/May 12, 1809, in *M. I. Kutuzov: Sbornik dokumentov*, III:195.

63. Langeron, "Zapiski," 239–240. Langeron singles out Duty General Tyszkiewicz and his assistants, who, in his words, gained "scandalous fortunes" through plundering.

64. Petrov, *Voina Rossii s Turtsiej 1806–1812 gg.*, II:233–310.

65. He blamed the "inexperience of the generals that engendered indecision" and accused his officers of failing to "show sufficient courage and gallantry," while the troops did not "demonstrate sufficient subordination and confidence in their commanders." Prozorovskii to Emperor Alexander, April 23/May 5, 1809, in *M. I. Kutuzov: Sbornik dokumentov*, III:184; Petrov, *Voina Rossii s Turtsiej 1806–1812 gg.*, II:229.

66. Alexander Benckendorf, "Iz memuarov grafa A. Kh. Benckendorfa," in *Rossiisskii arkhiv* 18 (2009): 287, http://feb-web.ru/feb/rosarc/rai/rai-258-.htm.

67. Bagration to Alexander, August 19/31, 1809, in S. Golubov, ed., *General Bagration: Sbornik dokumentov i materialov* (Moscow, 1945), 61–62.

68. Trubetskoi to Arakacheyev, August 17/29, 1809, in *Voennyi sbornik* 10 (1864): 34.

69. Kutuzov to his wife, May 16/28, 1809, in *The Kutuzov Papers* 2 (1871): 203–204.

70. Kutuzov to his wife, June 3/15, 1809, in *The Kutuzov Papers* 2 (1871): 204.

71. See [I. Bezsonov], "Russkie dostopamyatnye lyudi," *Russkaya starina* 5 (1892): 234–235; V. Bessonov, "Nikolai Zakharovich Khitrovo. Materialy k biografii," in *Epokha Napoleonovskikh voin: lyudi, sobytiya, idei. Materialy VI Vserossiiskoi nauchnoi konferentsii* (Moscow, 2003), http://www.reenactor.ru/ARH/PDF/Bessonov_02.pdf.

72. Langeron, "Zapiski," 665.

73. Kutuzov to his wife, May 2/14, 1808, in *The Kutuzov Papers* 2 (1871): 201.

74. Langeron, "Zapiski," 665.

75. Langeron, "Zapiski," 666.

76. Cited in Petrov, *Voina Rossii s Turtsiej 1806–1812 gg.*, II:241.

77. Alexander to Prozorovskii, June 4/16, 1809, RGVIA, f. VUA, d. 2907, ll. 26–27. Also see Arakcheev to Prozorovskii, June 7/19, 1809, RGVIA, f. VUA, d. 2931, ll. 36–36b.

78. Prozorovskii to Alexander I, June 18/30, 1809, RGVIA f. VUA, d. 2929, ll. 229b–230b. The letter was printed in Sherbatov, *General-fel'dmarshal Knyaz Paskevich*, I, annex 2, 34–35; excerpts appeared in Petrov, *Voina Rossii s Turtsiej 1806–1812 gg.*, II:242.

79. Langeron, "Zapiski," 665.

80. Langeron, "Zapiski," 665–666.

81. Kutuzov to his wife, June 3–18/15–30, 1809, in *The Kutuzov Papers* 2 (1871): 204.

Chapter 18

1. On July 19, Emperor Alexander appointed Kutuzov the military governor of Lithuania. On August 5, he then announced that Kutuzov would also assume authority over civilian administration of the governorate-general. See imperial decrees of July 19 and August 5 in *M. I. Kutuzov. Sbornik dokumentov* (Moscow: Voeniszdat, 1950), III:223–224.

2. P. Sumarokov's memorandum cited in Nikolai Dubrovin, "Russkaya zhizn' v nachale XIX veka," *Russkaya starina* 6 (1899): 493.

3. See Dubrovin, "Russkaya zhizn' v nachale XIX veka," *Russkaya starina* 6 (1899): 498–508.

4. "Vyderzhki iz druzheskikh pisem Evgeniya (vposledstvii Mitropolita Kievskado) k Voronezhskomu priyatelyu ego Vasiliyu Ignatievichy Makedontsu," *Russkii arkhiv* 1 (1870): 837, 841.

5. "O dvoryanskikh vyborakh v Guberniyakh ot Pol'shi priobretennykh," March 3/15, 1809, in *PSZ* 30, no. 23513, 839–842.

6. Hundreds of documents related to Kutuzov's activities as the governor are preserved at the Lithuanian State Historical Archives, fond 378, opis' 17, 18, and 19. A handful of these documents appeared in *M. I. Kutuzov. Sbornik dokumentov*, III:226–287.

7. Ekaterina Golenischeva-Kutuzova later married Ilya Stepanovich Sarochinskii, with whom she had four sons (Fedor, Ilya, Mikhail, and Stepan). Her daughter, Ekaterina Kudasheva, first married Karl Magnus Pilar von Pilchau and then Napoleon Herman Christoff Hoyningen-Huene.

8. The quarter million rubles that he owed pales in comparison to the over 2 million rubles that Count N. Sheremetev owed in 1800 or Prince

I. Yusupov's debt of nearly 700,000 rubles in 1818. B. Kurakin, who owned more than 7,000 serfs and drew an annual income of 7,500 rubles, left over 207,000 rubles in debt upon his death in 1764. Langeron assures us that General Mikhail Miloradovich had debts amounting to 600,000 rubles in 1810. "The tone of society . . . is almost universally marked by an excess of expenses over income," John Quincy Adams, then serving as American ambassador to St. Petersburg, observed in a letter to his mother. "The public officers all live far beyond their salaries, many of them are notorious for never paying their debts, and still more for preserving the balance by means which in our country would be deemed dishonorable but which are here much less disreputable than economy." Jerome Blum, *Lord and Peasant in Russia from the Ninth to the Nineteenth Century* (Princeton, NJ: Princeton University Press, 1971), 379–382. See Adams's letter of February 8, 1810, in Worthington Chauncey Ford, ed., *Writings of John Quincy Adams* (New York: Macmillan, 1914), III:396.

9. Kutuzov to his wife, February 16/28, 1811, in *The Kutuzov Papers* 2 (1872): 261.

10. Kutuzov to his wife, February 4/16, 1810, in *The Kutuzov Papers* 2 (1872): 258.

11. "I put [the township of] Raigorodok up for sale but there are so many other sale notices that it might be a while before it actually sells." Kutuzov to his wife, February 4/16, 1810, in *The Kutuzov Papers* 2 (1872): 259.

12. The 40,000-ruble loan was approved by the Committee of Ministers in 1811. Kutuzov's home was valued at 52,278 rubles and the loan was for an eight-year period. See *Zhurnaly Komiteta ministrov, 1810–1812 gg.* [hereafter cited as *Proceedings of the Committee of Ministers*] (St. Petersburg: V. Bezobrazov, 1891), II:302.

13. Kutuzov to his wife, February 4/16, 1810, in *The Kutuzov Papers* 2 (1872): 259.

14. Kutuzov to his wife, April 12/24, April 23/May 5, May 8/20, 1810, in *The Kutuzov Papers* 2 (1872): 259–260.

15. Kutuzov to E. von Tiesenhausen, February 12/24, 1811, in *The Kutuzov Papers* 6 (1874): 355–356.

16. Contemporaries thought Aleksey Voyeikov, the emperor's flügel-adjutant, may have played a role in this selection. In 1811, he was dispatched to consult with Kamenskii on who the best replacement for him might be. He interviewed officers and gathered information that nudged the czar to select Kutuzov.

17. Kutuzov to Elisabeth von Tiesenhausen, February 27/March 11, 1811, in *The Kutuzov Papers* 6 (1874): 358.

18. Kutuzov to Elisabeth von Tiesenhausen, March 13/25, 1811, in *The Kutuzov Papers* 6 (1874): 359.

19. Alexander to Kamenskii, January 1811, RGVIA, f. VUA, d. 3684, l. 5.

20. "This illness is endangering his life," the minister of war confided to Kutuzov. Barclay de Tolly to Kutuzov, February 23/March 7, 1811, RGVIA, f. VUA, d. 2957, l. 57b.

21. Alexander to Kamenskii, March 7/19, 1811, RGVIA f. VUA, d. 3684, ll. 4–4b. Also see A. Petrov, *Voina Rossii s Turtsiej 1806–1812 gg.* (St. Petersburg, 1887), III:247–248.

22. Alexander to Kamenskii, March 7/19, 1811, RGVIA f. VUA, d. 3684, l. 4.

23. Pavel Chichagov, *Mémoires inédits de l'Amiral Tchitchagoff. Campagnes de la Russie en 1812 contre la Turquie, l'Autriche et la France* (Berlin: F. Schneider, 1855), 4.

24. Kutuzov to Elisabeth von Tiesenhausen, March 6/18, 1811, in *The Kutuzov Papers* 6 (1874): 359.

25. Kutuzov to Barclay de Tolly, March 1/13, 1811, RGVIA f. VUA, d. 2952, l. 95. "I am leaving Vilna with a heavy heart," he told his daughter. "I got rather used to living here." Kutuzov to Elisabeth von Tiesenhausen, March 13/25, 1811, in *The Kutuzov Papers* 6 (1874): 359–360.

26. Order to the Army, April 1/13, 1811; Kutuzov to Alexander, April 1/13, 1811, in *M. I. Kutuzov. Sbornik dokumentov*, III:295–296.

27. Order to the Army, April 1/13, 1811; Kutuzov to Alexander, April 1/13, 1811, in *M. I. Kutuzov. Sbornik dokumentov*, III:295–296; William Wilkinson, *An Account of the Principalities of Wallachia and Moldavia* (London: Longman, Hurst, Rees, Orme and Brown, 1820), 86. Wilkinson was a British consul resident at Bucharest.

28. Auguste de La Garde, *Journal of a Nobleman Comprising an Account of His Travels and a Narrative of His Residence at Vienna During the Congress* (London: Colburn and Bentley, 1831), I:271, 293. Also see Wilkinson, *An Account of the Principalities of Wallachia and Moldavia*, 86.

29. Kutuzov to Elisabeth von Tiesenhausen, March 27/April 8, 1811, in *The Kutuzov Papers* 6 (1874): 360.

30. Kutuzov to Elisabeth von Tiesenhausen, April 10/22, 1811, in *The Kutuzov Papers* 6 (1874): 361.

31. Nikolai Muravyev, "Zapiski Nikolaya Nikolayevicha Muravyeva," *Russkii arkhiv* 10 (1885): 245.

32. Muravyev, "Zapiski," 245; Alexander Scherbinin, "Zapiski . . . ," in V. Kharkevich, *1812 god v dnevinikakh, zapiskakh, i vospominaniyakh sovremennikov* (Vilna: Tip. Shtaba Vilen. Voen. Okruga, 1900), 43.

33. See his letters to Elisabeth von Tiesenhausen in *The Kutuzov Papers* 6 (1874): 342–343.

34. Kutuzov to Elisabeth von Tiesenhausen, August 22/September 3, 1809, in *The Kutuzov Papers* 6 (1874): 346.

35. Kutuzov to Elisabeth von Tiesenhausen, December 28, 1810/January 8, 1811, in *The Kutuzov Papers* 6 (1874): 352.

36. Alexander Langeron, "Zapiski," *Russkaya starina* 7 (1908): 175.

37. On Constantine Varlaam, see Gheorghe Bezviconi, *Călatori ruși în Moldova și Muntenia* (Bucharest: Institutul de Istorie Nationala din București, 1947), 214–215. For details on Filipescu and Miloradovich, see G. Bezviconi, *Contribuții la istoria relațiilor romîno-ruse* (Bucharest, 1962).

38. Langeron, "Zapiski," *Russkaya starina* 7 (1910): 168; 8 (1911): 257–258.
39. Romanian scholars largely repeat Langeron's account. See Dan A. Lăzărescu, *Imaginea poporului român în conștiința europeană: 1821–1834* (Bucharest: AGIR, 1999), 237; G. Filitti, B. Marinescu, et al., *Călători străini despre țările române în secolul al XIX–lea, vol. I, 1801–1821* (Bucharest: Academiei Române, 2004), 349–355. A recent Russian study pointed out that Langeron made false accusations against Kutuzov's right-hand men, Coronelli and Barrozzi. See E. Ivanov and G. Coronelli, *Kniga Coronello. Istoricheskie issledovaniia* (Moscow: Evgart, 2011), 101–108.
40. "Une femme mariée de 13 à 14, tres naïve et tres plaisante." Kutuzov to Elisabeth von Tiesenhausen, April 28/May 10, 1811, in *The Kutuzov Papers* 6 (1874): 361.
41. Alexander Mikhailovskii–Danilevskii, "Zhurnal 1813 goda," in A. Tartakovskii, ed., *1812 god . . . Voennye dnevniki* (Moscow: Sovetskaya Rossiya, 1990), 325.
42. Vladimir Sollogub, *Povesti. Vospominaniya* (Leningrad: Khud. Literatura, 1988), 370.
43. The subject of illegitimate relations or perceptions of masculinity in the Russian army has not been explored. But other European armies have benefitted from recent academic endeavors, including Jennine Hurl-Eamon, *Marriage and the British Army in the Long Eighteenth Century* (Oxford: Oxford University Press, 2014); Michael J. Hughes, *Forging Napoleon's Grande Armée: Motivation, Military Culture and Masculinity in the French Army, 1800–1808* (New York: New York University Press, 2012).
44. Waldermar de Löwenstern, *Mémoires du général-major russe Baron de Löwenstern (1776–1858)* (Paris: A. Fontemoing, 1903), I:170.
45. Yegor (Georg) von Bradke, "Avtobiograficheskie zapiski Yegora Fedorovicha Fon-Bradke," in *Russkii arkhiv* 1 (1875): 24.
46. Löwenstern, *Mémoires*, I:170–171.
47. Joseph de Maistre to Chevalier de Rossi, May 9, 1812, in de Maistre, *St. Peterburgskie pis'ma* (St. Petersburg, 1995), 206.
48. Kutuzov to E. von Tiesenhausen, January 19/31, 1812, in *The Kutuzov Papers* 6 (1874): 366. "La societe des femmes que je cherche, n'est qu'un goût."
49. Kutuzov to A. Suvorov, April 3/15, 1811, in *M. I. Kutuzov. Sbornik dokumentov*, III:296.
50. The Disposition of the Army of Moldavia, dated April 19, showed that the Army of Moldavia had 26,722 infantry, 8,836 cavalry, 4,917 irregular cavalry, and 4,157 artillery. *M. I. Kutuzov. Sbornik dokumentov*, III:306, 407. Also see General Langeron's memorandum on the challenges the Russian army faced in 1810–1811, in Langeron, "Zapiski," *Russkaya starina* 7 (1911): 139–140.
51. Kutuzov to Barclay de Tolly, April 7/19, 1811, RGVIA, f. VUA, d. 2952, l. 166.
52. Disposition of the Army of Moldavia, April 7/19, 1811, in *M. I. Kutuzov. Sbornik dokumentov*, III:306–310. Mikhailovskii-Danilevskii cites the following strengths for the Army of Moldavia:

Unit	Cavalry	Infantry	Artillery	Total	Cannon	Field Horse
8th Division	1,650	7,608	992	10,350	48	12
10th Division	2,141	5,469	464	8,074	12	24
16th Division	2,121	6,067	540	8,728	36	—
22nd Division	1,693	6,167	600	8,460	36	12
Cossacks				6,539		
Artillery and Pioneers				2,315		
The Danube Flotilla				1,774		
Total	7,605	25,311	2,596	46,240	132	48

53. Kutuzov to his wife, April 13/25, 1811, in *The Kutuzov Papers* 2 (1872): 262.

54. Kutuzov to his wife, April 13/25, 1811, in *The Kutuzov Papers* 2 (1872): 262.

55. Nikolai Gretsch, *Zapiski o moej zhizni* (Moscow: Zakharov, 2002), 230. See also Alexander's letter to Kamenskii's mother cited in Petrov, *Voina Rossii s Turtsiej 1806–1812 gg.* III:249.

56. Kutuzov to his wife, April 15/27, 1811, in *The Kutuzov Papers* 2 (1872): 262. Also see Langeron, "Zapiski," *Russkaya starina* 7 (1910): 168.

57. "Mysli generala Kutuzova zamechenny v razgovore s nim," n.d., RGVIA, f. VUA, d. 2952, ll. 180–184. The document was also printed in *M. I. Kutuzov. Sbornik dokumentov*, III:350–353. The date is missing, but a handwritten note indicates that it was sent to the minister of war and arrived in St. Petersburg on May 9/21, 1811.

58. Kutuzov to Barclay de Tolly, December 14/26, 1811, RGVIA, f. VUA, d. 2952, l. 406–406b.

59. Pierre de Bourcet, "Raisons du premier mouvement de l'armée d'offensive," in *Principes de la guerre de montagnes* (Paris, 1775), 148.

60. Kutuzov to Barclay de Tolly, April 7/19, 1811, RGVIA, f. VUA, d. 2952, ll. 166–167.

61. Kutuzov to St. Priest, April 15/27, 1811; Kutuzov to Barclay de Tolly, April 26/May 8, 1811, in *M. I. Kutuzov. Sbornik dokumentov*, III:324–325, 350.

62. "Mysli generala Kutuzova zamechenny v razgovore s nim," n.d., RGVIA, f. VUA, d. 2952, ll. 180–181.

63. "Mysli generala Kutuzova zamechenny v razgovore s nim," RGVIA, f. VUA, d. 2952, l. 184. Also see Petrov, *Voina Rossii s Turtsiej 1806–1812 gg.*, III:252–253, 255–256.

64. Kutusov to Ahmed Bey, April 20/May 2, 1811, in *M. I. Kutuzov. Sbornik dokumentov*, III:336.

65. Kutuzov to Rumyantsev, May 6/18, 1811, in *M. I. Kutuzov. Sbornik dokumentov*, III:368.

66. Kutuzov to Rumyantsev, April 26/May 8, 1811, in *M. I. Kutuzov. Sbornik dokumentov*, III:343–344.

67. Kutuzov to Rumyantsev, June 18/30, 1811, in *M. I. Kutuzov. Sbornik dokumentov*, III:452–454.

68. Rumyantsev to Kutusov, June 21/July 3, 1811, RGVIA, f. VUA, d. 2958, ll. 56b–60.

69. Langeron, "Zapiski," *Russkaya starina* 7 (1910): 178.

70. See, for example, Kutuzov to V. Krasnomilashevich, May 2/14, 1811; Kutuzov's order (June 16) prohibiting unwarranted requisition of firewood and hay, in *M. I. Kutuzov. Sbornik dokumentov*, III:364, 425.

71. Kututzov to Voinov, May 14/26, 1811, in *M. I. Kutuzov. Sbornik dokumentov*, III:372.

72. Kutuzov to Karadjordje, April 4/16, May 5/17, and September 15/27, 1811; Kutuzov to Voinov, May 14/26, 1811; Kutuzov to Rumyantsev, May 24/June 5 and October 2/14, 1811, in *M. I. Kutuzov. Sbornik dokumentov*, III:300–303, 372–374, 396–397, 607, 635–636.

73. Kutuzov to Zass, April 8/20 and June 9/21, 1811, in *M. I. Kutuzov. Sbornik dokumentov*, III:315–316, 429–430.

74. Kutuzov to Barclay de Tolly, April 7/19, 1811, RGVIA, f. VUA, d. 2952, ll. 167–168.

75. Kutuzov to Zass, April 13/25, 1811; Kutuzov to Barclay de Tolly, April 13/25, 1811, Kutuzov to Zass, May 8/20, 1811, in *M. I. Kutuzov. Sbornik dokumentov*, III:321–322, 370.

76. Kutuzov to Mullah Pasha, June 9/21, 1811, in *M. I. Kutuzov. Sbornik dokumentov*, III:432–433.

77. Kutuzov to Zass, June 9/21, 1811, and June 18/30, 1811, in *M. I. Kutuzov. Sbornik dokumentov*, III:429–432, 458–459. The quote is from Kutuzov to Barclay de Tolly, June 10/22, 1811, RGVIA, f. VUA, d. 2952, ll. 217–218.

78. Journal of Military Operations of the Army of Moldavia, RGVIA, f. VUA, d. 2953, ll. 2–4.

79. Kutuzov to Barclay de Tolly, May 3/15, 1811, RGVIA, f. VUA, d. 2952, l. 189. To make matters worse, regimental commanders were routinely late in submitting their monthly reports. "I still have not received last month's reports from some units," Kutuzov fulminated in July. "I will not name names this time around but if such waywardness continues, I will start disciplining without leniency." Reviewing the new regimental reports (for the month of April!), he was shocked to discover that some of his regiments lacked sufficient ammunition. "Just as His Majesty's army is about to wage war against the enemy, I am confronted with the fact that it is lacking cartridges!" he fumed in a general order to the army. He had reason to be upset. The Olonetskii Infantry Regiment was missing 22,607 rounds, the Moskovskii Grenaderskii 25,000, and the 38th Jägers-an astounding 32,251 cartridges; in some units, soldiers had just twelve to fifteen rounds each, instead of the required sixty. Kutuzov demanded a "thorough investigation" of this maladministration and frantically tried to deliver more ammunition from the

depots in Bucharest. But it was too late, and he had to make do with what he had. See documents in *M. I. Kutuzov. Sbornik dokumentov*, III:445, 473, 529–530, 558–559.

80. Journal of Military Operations of the Army of Moldavia, RGVIA, f. VUA, d. 2953, ll. 2–3; Kutuzov to Langeron, May 2/14, 1811, in Nikolai Shil'der, *Imperator Aleksandr pervyi. Ego zhizn' i tsarstvovanie* (St. Petersburg: A. S. Suvorin, 1897), III:104–105; Kutuzov to Zass, June 4/16, 1811, in *M. I. Kutuzov. Sbornik dokumentov*, III:425–426. On June 23, Kutuzov received a report from his Bulgarian agent who had passed through the Ottoman campsites and delivered precious details on the Ottoman forces. He claimed the grand vizier had 58,000 men. "This number might be exaggerated," Kutuzov acknowledged, "but I cannot simply ignore this intelligence." Kutuzov to Barclay de Tolly, June 11/23, 1811, RGVIA, f. VUA, d. 2952, ll. 224–225. A week later Kutuzov estimated the Ottoman force as having at least 50,000 men. See his letter to Barclay de Tolly, June 18/30, 1811, RGVIA, f. VUA, d. 2952, l. 241.

81. Kutuzov to Zass, June 2/14, 1811, in *M. I. Kutuzov. Sbornik dokumentov*, III:423.

82. Langeron, "Zapiski," *Russkaya starina* 7 (1910): 174–175.

83. Kutuzov to Barclay de Tolly, May 20/June 1, 1811, RGVIA, f. VUA, d. 2952, ll. 191–191b.

84. Kutuzov to Alexander, June 21/July 3, 1811, RGVIA, f. VUA, d. 2952, l. 243; Voinov to Kutuzov, June 24/July 6, 1811, in *M. I. Kutuzov. Sbornik dokumentov*, III:470–471. For a broader context, see Petrov, *Voina Rossii s Turtsiej 1806–1812 gg.*, III:266–267.

85. In the after-action report, Kutuzov states he had twenty-five battalions, thirty-nine squadrons, and three Cossack regiments. Kutuzov to Alexander, June 23/July 5, 1811, RGVIA, f. VUA, d. 2952, l. 246.

86. Kutuzov to unknown recipient, July 1811, in *M. I. Kutuzov. Sbornik dokumentov*, III:477. Some parts of this letter are used verbatim in Kutuzov's letter to Barclay de Tolly, July 3/15, 1811, RGVIA, f. VUA, d. 2952, ll. 254–255.

87. Kutuzov to his wife, June 23/July 5, 1811, in *The Kutuzov Papers* 5 (1872): 263–264.

88. Based on testimonies of the prisoners and local inhabitants, Kutuzov claimed that the Ottoman army was about 60,000 men strong. Kutuzov to Alexander, June 23/July 5, 1811, RGVIA, f. VUA, d. 2952, l. 246.

89. Kutuzov to Alexander, June 23/July 5, 1811, RGVIA, f. VUA, d. 2952, l. 245.

90. Petrov, *Voina Rossii s Turtsiej 1806–1812 gg.*, III:268. Langeron claims that he could see no more than thirty-two cannon on the Ottoman side. "Zapiski," *Russkaya starina* 7 (1910): 180.

91. Kutuzov to Alexander, June 23/July 5, 1811, RGVIA, f. VUA, d. 2952, l. 246; Kutuzov to unknown recipient, July 1811, in *M. I. Kutuzov. Sbornik dokumentov*, III:477. Langeron, who commanded the left flank, also complained

about "several enemy batteries that caused us a lot of harm." Langeron to Kutuzov, June 28/July 10, 1811, in *M. I. Kutuzov. Sbornik dokumentov*, III:472.

92. Essen to Kutuzov, June 30/July 12, 1811, in *M. I. Kutuzov. Sbornik dokumentov*, III:475.

93. Petrov argues that the grand vizier thought Kutuzov brought all available forces and left Ruse poorly defended. He therefore intended this flanking attack to "capture Ruse, destroy the bridge over the Danube and then entrap the Russian army on the riverbank." Petrov, *Voina Rossii s Turtsiej 1806–1812 gg.*, III:269.

94. Langeron to Kutuzov, June 28/July 10, 1811, in *M. I. Kutuzov. Sbornik dokumentov*, III:472.

95. The loss of the cannon was such a serious matter that Emperor Alexander himself demanded an accounting of circumstances. See Kutuzov to Barclay de Tolly, August 13/25, 1811, RGVIA, f. VUA, d. 2952, ll. 412–421b.

96. Voinov to Kutuzov, June 28/July 10, 1811, in *M. I. Kutuzov. Sbornik dokumentov*, III:471.

97. Kutuzov to Alexander, June 23/July 5, 1811; Kutuzov to Barclay de Tolly, July 3/15, 1811, RGVIA, f. VUA, d. 2952, ll. 245–246, 256–257. Also see Langeron to Kutuzov, June 28/July 10, 1811; Essen to Kutuzov, June 30/July 12, 1811, in *M. I. Kutuzov. Sbornik dokumentov*, III:472, 476; Petrov, *Voina Rossii s Turtsiej 1806–1812 gg.*, III:270–271.

98. Journal of Military Operations of the Army of Moldavia, RGVIA, f. VUA, d. 2953, ll. 3–4; Kutuzov to Alexander, June 21/July 3, 1811, RGVIA, f. VUA, d. 2952, l. 243.

99. Cited in Petrov, *Voina Rossii s Turtsiej 1806–1812 gg.*, III:273; Langeron, "Zapiski," *Russkaya starina* 8 (1910): 343.

100. Journal of Military Operations of the Army of Moldavia, RGVIA, f. VUA, d. 2953, l. 4.

101. Kutuzov to his wife, June 23/July 5, 1811, in *The Kutuzov Papers* 5 (1872): 263–264. As always, Langeron was highly critical of his colleagues, accusing them of "complete indolence" and "dishonoring themselves." He claimed Kutuzov was "too old, too pudgy, and too lazy" to direct the battle. See his "Zapiski," *Russkaya starina* 8 (1910): 341–343.

102. Langeron, "Zapiski," *Russkaya starina* 8 (1910): 343. Langeron alleges that if Kutuzov had advanced on the Ottoman camp, "the Turks would have been terrified and fled." But such an opinion flies in the face of the Russians' experiences in the previous two campaigns; just a year earlier, the grand vizier had held ground at Şumnu and Kamenskii was unable to do much against the fortified Ottoman positions.

103. Proclamation of June 24/July 6, 1811, in *M. I. Kutuzov. Sbornik dokumentov*, III:470; Kutuzov to Alexander and to Barclay de Tolly, June 23/July 5 and July 3/15, 1811, RGVIA, f. VUA, d. 2952, ll. 247–248, 256–257. Parts of

this proclamation were reused in Kutuzov's July 15 report to Barclay de Tolly, RGVIA, f. VUA, d. 2952, ll. 256–257.

104. *Chester Courant*, August 20, 1811, 4. Napoleon was rather displeased with the news. "I hear you had a clash [*échauffourée*] at Ruse," he remarked dismissively during a conversation with Alexander Chernyshev, the czar's special envoy in Paris. "This was not just a clash, but a regular battle and a rather lively one too. It ended marvelously for our arms," replied the gleeful Russian officer. Napoleon was clearly misinformed about the battle because he criticized Kutuzov for moving the army "too far" from the town. But Chernyshev pointed out that the Russian army was not that far from Ruse and the town garrison provided close support. Chernyshev to Chancellor Nikolai Rumyantsev, August 5/17, 1811, in *SIRIO* XXI: 235–236.

105. Alexander to Kutuzov, July 18/30, 1811, in *M. I. Kutuzov. Sbornik dokumentov*, III:502.

106. Alexander Turgenev to Sergei Turgenev, July 7/19, 1811, in *Arkhiv bratyev Turgenevykh* (St. Petersburg: Imperial Academy of Sciences, 1911), II:444.

107. In another letter Kutuzov explained that "the location of this cursed fortification [Ruse] is such that it cannot be simply left on its own, even with a strong garrison. I did a thorough assessment of it and concluded it would require nineteen battalions to hold it." Kutuzov to unknown recipient, July 1811, in *M. I. Kutuzov. Sbornik dokumentov*, III:478.

108. Kutuzov to Barclay de Tolly, November 29/December 11, 1811, in *Otechestvennaya voina 1812 goda. Materially Voenno-Uchebnogo Arkhiva Glavnogo Shtaba* [hereafter cited as *General Staff Archives*] (St. Petersburg: Voen.-Uchen. Kom. Gl. Shtaba, 1905), VI:345–346.

109. Kutuzov to Barclay de Tolly, July 2/14, 1811, RGVIA, f. VUA, 2952, ll. 251–252. "This evacuation could have been done only after a successful battle; otherwise, it would have been portrayed as a forced move. If we had suffered even the slightest setback in battle, we would have been compelled to put up with all the inconveniences and steadfastly defended Ruse to save the honor of our army."

110. Cited in Alexander Mikhailovskii-Danilevskii, *Opisanie Turtsekoi voiny s 1806 do 1812 goda. Polnoe sobranie sochinenii Aleksandra Ivanovicha Mikhaiovskago-Danilevskago* (St. Petersburg: Shtab Otdel. Korpusa Vnut. Strazhi, 1849), III:299.

111. Kutuzov to unknown recipient, July 1811, in *M. I. Kutuzov. Sbornik dokumentov*, III:478; Langeron, "Zapiski," *Russkaya starina* 8 (1910): 344–348.

112. Langeron, "Zapiski," *Russkaya starina* 8 (1910): 348–349.

113. *Leicester Journal*, October 4, 1811, 1; *Saint James's Chronicle*, October 1, 1811, 2 (based on "a letter from Vienna," dated August 28, 1811).

Chapter 19

1. Langeron, "Zapiski," *Russkaya starina* 8 (1910): 350.

2. Count St. Julien to Klemens von Metternich, August 13, 1811, in Grand Duke Nikolai Mikhailovich, *Imperator Aleksandr I. Opyt istoricheskago izsledovaniya* (St. Petersburg: Eksp. Zag. Gos. Bumag, 1912), I:437.

3. Kutuzov to Barclay de Tolly, August 20/September 1, 1811, RGVIA, f. VUA, d. 2952, ll. 306–307b. Emperor Alexander was well aware of the Ottoman intransigence. In a conversation with the Austrian envoy, he complained that "the Divan is influenced by France" and that the Turks, knowing of "the cooling" of Franco-Russian relations, were bidding for time. Count St. Julien's report to Austrian foreign minister Klemens von Metternich, August 13, 1811, in Grand Duke Nikolai Mikhailovich, *Imperator Aleksandr I*, I:436–437.

4. *Saunders's Newsletter and Daily Advertiser*, October 1, 1811, 1.

5. Kutuzov to Barclay de Tolly, July 29/August 10, 1811, RGVIA, f. VUA, d. 2952, ll. 279–280.

6. Mulla Pasha was able to deliver only twenty-nine boats to the Russians. Kutuzov to Barclay de Tolly, July 16/28, 1811, in RGVIA, f. VUA, d. 2952, ll. 263–264.

7. Kutuzov to Barclay de Tolly, July 29/August 10 and August 20/September 1, 1811, RGVIA, f. VUA, d. 2952, ll. 279–280, 310–311. Also see Journal of Military Operations of the Army of Moldavia, RGVIA, f. VUA, d. 2952, ll. 298–299.

8. Journal of Military Operations of the Army of Moldavia, RGVIA, f. VUA, d. 2952, ll. 298–299.

9. Petrov, *Voina Rossii s Turtsiej 1806–1812 gg.*, III:278–287.

10. Based on intelligence reports, Kutuzov and Zass consistently estimated 15,000–20,000 men under Ismail Bey's command. The Journal of Military Operations estimated that 10,000 Turks attacked Zass's positions. Kutuzov to Zass, July 18/30 and August 24/July 5, 1811, in *M. I. Kutuzov. Sbornik dokumentov* (Moscow: Voeniszdat, 1950), III:501–502, 513; Kutuzov to Barclay de Tolly, July 23/August 4, 1811, RGVIA, f. VUA, d. 2952, l. 265; Journal of Military Operations of the Army of Moldavia, RGVIA, f. VUA, d. 2952, l. 301.

11. Kutuzov to Barclay de Tolly, July 26/August 7, 1811, RGVIA, f. VUA, d. 2952, l. 274; Journal of Military Operations of the Army of Moldavia, RGVIA, f. VUA, d. 2952, ll. 298–301, 303–304. Also see Afanasii Krasovskii, "Iz zapisok general-adjutanta Krasovskago," *Russkii vestnik* 8 (1880): 515–519.

12. Kutuzov to E. von Tiesenhausen, July 23/August 4, 1811, in *The Kutuzov Papers* 6 (1874): 363.

13. Kutuzov to Zass, July 24/August 5, 1811, in *M. I. Kutuzov. Sbornik dokumentov*, III:514.

14. Kutuzov to Barclay de Tolly, July 31/August 12, 1811, in *M. I. Kutuzov. Sbornik dokumentov*, III:525–526.

15. In late July Kutuzov asked for permission to return the 9th and 15th Divisions to Wallachia. The minister of war replied that "His Majesty agrees to have 9th Division moved closer and the 15th Division to be ready to rejoin him [Kutuzov], but this division should not be recalled except for *a reason of utmost importance which {Kutuzov} must let us know well in advance* [my emphasis]."

Kutuzov to Barclay de Tolly, July 16/28, 1811, with Barclay de Tolly's hand-written note on it, RGVIA, f. VUA, d. 2952, ll. 262–262b.

16. Kutuzov to Lieutenant General Yevgenii Markov (commanded 15th Division) and Major General S. Yermolov (commanded 9th Division), August 2–16/14–28, 1811, in *M. I. Kutuzov. Sbornik dokumentov*, III:527–528, 551; Kutuzov to Barclay de Tolly, August 20/September 1, 1811, RGVIA, f. VUA, d. 2952, ll. 308–309.

17. Kutuzov to Alexander, September 8/20, 1811, RGVIA, f. VUA, d. 2952, ll. 327–328.

18. Charles Boileau Elliott, *Travels in the Three Great Empires of Austria, Russia and Turkey: A Voyage down the Danube* (London: Richard Bentley, 1838), I:184.

19. Kutuzov to unknown recipient, October 28/November 9, 1811, in *M. I. Kutuzov. Sbornik dokumentov*, III:681. Langeron was equally impressed, observing that "this was one of the most brilliant Ottoman operations that I have ever witnessed." Langeron, "Zapiski," *Russkaya starina* 8 (1910): 354.

20. Kutuzov to Alexander, September 1/13, 1811, RGVIA, f. VUA, d. 2952, l. 323.

21. Kutuzov to Barclay de Tolly, September 8/20, 1811, RGVIA, f. VUA, d. 2952, l. 329; Kutuzov to Alexander, September 1/13, 1811, RGVIA, f. VUA, d. 2952, l. 323; Mikhail Bulatov to Kutuzov, September 4/16, 1811, in *M. I. Kutuzov. Sbornik dokumentov*, III:579–582; Langeron, "Zapiski," *Russkaya starina* 8 (1910): 355–357.

22. Kutuzov criticized Bulatov for not stopping the attack after the first failed assault that led to needless loss of life. Bulatov's urgent appeals for help prompted Kutuzov to send him twelve infantry battalions. "By sunrise I only had six fresh battalions remaining, which is why I ordered Bulatov to disengage." Kutuzov to Barclay de Tolly, September 8/20, 1811, RGVIA, f. VUA, d. 2952, ll. 329–329b. Also see Kutuzov to unknown recipient, October 28/November 9, 1811, in *M. I. Kutuzov. Sbornik dokumentov*, III:681.

23. Kutuzov to Alexander, September 1/13, 1811, RGVIA, f. VUA, d. 2952, ll. 324–324b. The captured flag belonged to the battalion of the Staroingermanlandskii Regiment, which was later shamed for losing it. As with the cannon lost at Ruse, Kutuzov had to investigate the circumstances of the loss of this second piece of ordnance. See his report in Kutuzov to Alexander, September 8/20, 1811, RGVIA, f. VUA, d. 2952, ll. 327–328.

24. Langeron, "Zapiski," *Russkaya starina* 8 (1910): 355–356.

25. Kutuzov to his wife, September 7/19, 1811, in *The Kutuzov Papers* 5 (1872): 265.

26. On September 9, Kutuzov ordered these divisions to move by forced marches to join him. "You must march in the following manner," specified his order. "Four hours marching, two hours resting, three hours marching, three hours resting, three hours marching, followed by a respite of eight to ten hours; having cooked porridge, you must advance in the same manner the following

day." Kutuzov to S. Yermolov, August 28/September 9, 1811, in *M. I. Kutuzov. Sbornik dokumentov*, III:568.

27. Langeron, "Zapiski," *Russkaya starina* 8 (1910): 359; Kutuzov to Zass, August 28/September 9, 1811, in *M. I. Kutuzov. Sbornik dokumentov*, III:568.

28. Kutuzov to Barclay de Tolly, September 1/13, 1811, RGVIA, f. VUA, d. 2952, ll. 325–326.

29. Kutuzov to Zass, August 17/29, 1811, in *M. I. Kutuzov. Sbornik dokumentov*, III:553; Petrov, *Voina Rossii s Turtsiej 1806–1812 gg.*, III:295–297. He did launch a diversion from Turnu to the village of Museli (Muselievo) on the right bank, where the Ottomans had established a supply depot. Kutuzov to Barclay de Tolly, September 20/October 2, 1811, RGVIA, f. VUA, d. 2952, ll. 342–343b. Also, in early October, observing the ongoing Russian construction of redoubts, Grand Vizier Ahmed tried to interrupt them with a quick sortie, but the Russians repelled it. See Petrov, *Voina Rossii s Turtsiej 1806–1812 gg.*, III:297–299. The 15th Division reached Kutuzov on September 12, four days after the Ottomans crossed the river. Kutuzov deployed the 1st Brigade at Slobozia, the 2nd Brigade at Obilesti, and the 3rd at Buseo. Kutuzov to Markov, September 1/13, 1811, in *M. I. Kutuzov. Sbornik dokumentov*, III:572.

30. Kutuzov to Lieutenant Colonel A. Engelhardt, August 17/29, 1811, and August 23/September 4, 1811, in *M. I. Kutuzov. Sbornik dokumentov*, III:552–553, 562; Journal of Military Operations of the Army of Moldavia, RGVIA, f. VUA, d. 2952, ll. 350–353b.

31. Langeron, "Zapiski," *Russkaya starina* 9 (1910): 534.

32. The first mention of this plan is in Kutuzov's letter to Barclay de Tolly dated October 2. RGVIA, f. VUA, d. 2952, ll. 339–339b. Langeron claimed the plan was actually his and Markov's idea. Langeron, "Zapiski," *Russkaya starina* 9 (1910): 535.

33. Kutuzov to unknown recipient, October 28/November 9, 1811, in *M. I. Kutuzov. Sbornik dokumentov*, III:682.

34. Langeron, "Zapiski," *Russkaya starina* 8 (1910): 360. Langeron spent more time pointing out Markov's flaws: "He was rude, harsh, unfair to his subordinates, and envious of his comrades; prone to intrigues with superiors, always ready to undermine his immediate commander so he could gain some personal profit. He was despised and disliked by everyone."

35. Kutuzov to Markov, September 29/October 11, 1811, in *M. I. Kutuzov. Sbornik dokumentov*, III:627–628.

36. Journal of Military Operations of the Army of Moldavia, RGVIA, f. VUA, d. 2953, ll. 9–11b.

37. Kutuzov to Barclay de Tolly, September 20/October 2, 1811, RGVIA, f. VUA, d. 2952, ll. 339–339b.

38. Kutuzov to unknown recipient, October 28/November 9, 1811, in *M. I. Kutuzov. Sbornik dokumentov*, III:682. Markov's corps included the Nasheburgskii, Belostokskii, Vitebskii, and Kurinskii Infantry Regiments,

the 8th, 10th, 13th, 14th, and 38th Jäger Regiments, and the Oliovopolskii Hussars, with two Cossack *sotnyas*.

39. Yakov Otroschenko, *Zapiski generala Otroschenko (1800–1830)* (Moscow: Bratina, 2006), chap. 6; Langeron, "Zapiski," *Russkaya starina* 9 (1910): 536–537. The Journal of the Military Operations lists nine rafts (four large, three medium, and two small) and sixty-five boats utilized in the crossing. See RGVIA, f. VUA, d. 2953, ll. 15–15b. Markov states that the rafts and boats arrived at six o'clock in the morning of October 14. Markov to Kutuzov, October 3/15, 1811, in *M. I. Kutuzov. Sbornik dokumentov*, III:640.

40. Kutuzov to unknown recipient, October 28/November 9, 1811, in *M. I. Kutuzov. Sbornik dokumentov*, III:683.

41. Langeron, "Zapiski," *Russkaya starina* 9 (1910): 537.

42. Otroschenko, *Zapiski*.

43. The official report stated nine killed and forty wounded; one of Kutuzov's relatives, Major Bibikov of the Olviopolskii Hussar Regiment, was wounded and captured by the Turks, but the vizier later released him as a favor. Kutuzov to Barclay de Tolly, October 3/15, 1811, RGVIA, f. VUA, d. 2952, l. 354. Also see Kutuzov to Alexander, October 3/15, 1811, RGVIA, f. VUA, d. 2952, l. 356; Langeron, "Zapiski," *Russkaya starina* 9 (1910): 538–539; Petrov, *Voina Rossii s Turtsiej 1806–1812 gg.*, III:306–307.

44. Langeron, "Zapiski," *Russkaya starina* 9 (1910): 539. Also see Otroschenko, *Zapiski*.

45. Kutuzov to Barclay de Tolly, October 3/15, 1811, RGVIA, f. VUA, d. 2952, l. 354.

46. The Journal of Military Operations of the Army of Moldavia, RGVIA, f. VUA, d. 2934, l. 143.

47. Kutuzov to his wife, October 3/15, 1811, in *The Kutuzov Papers* 5 (1872): 265; Kutuzov to unknown recipient, October 28/November 9, 1811, in *M. I. Kutuzov. Sbornik dokumentov*, III:683.

48. Imperial Decree of October 29/November 10, 1811, in *M. I. Kutuzov. Sbornik dokumentov*, III:694.

49. Kutuzov to Ahmed Pasha, November 3/15, 1811, in *M. I. Kutuzov. Sbornik dokumentov*, III:644.

50. Kutuzov to unknown recipient, October 28/November 9, 1811, in *M. I. Kutuzov. Sbornik dokumentov*, III:683. There is a long-standing myth that the Russian scouts observed the grand vizier getting into the boat and informed Kutuzov that he intended to flee. "Let him go," Kutuzov supposedly responded, purportedly because an Ottoman "custom" forbade the vizier to negotiate while surrounded. Kutuzov's own letters, however, disprove this claim. On October 15, he wrote to the minister of war that "it is probable that despite the vigilance of our gunboats the vizier would try to escape to Ruse tonight. I will do my best to prevent him from absconding." On October 21, he lamented the fact that the vizier took advantage of "the heavy

rain and tempestuous weather to clandestinely escape to Ruse." Kutuzov to Barclay de Tolly, October 3/15, 1811, RGVIA, f. VUA, d. 2952, ll. 355–355b; Kutuzov to Rumyantsev, October 9/21, 1811, in *M. I. Kutuzov. Sbornik dokumentov*, III:650. Langeron claims that when he warned about the vizier's possible escape, Kutuzov told him, "I would actually welcome it since I would have somebody with whom to negotiate the peace that I desire so much." Langeron, "Zapiski," *Russkaya starina* 9 (1910): 541. Also see Petrov, *Voina Rossii s Turtsiej 1806–1812 gg.*, III:309–310.

51. Kutuzov to Alexander, October 16/28, 1811, RGVIA, f. VUA, d. 2952, ll. 369–370b. Also see Petrov, *Voina Rossii s Turtsiej 1806–1812 gg.*, III:310–311.

52. Langeron, "Zapiski," *Russkaya starina* 9 (1910): 542.

53. Petrov, *Voina Rossii s Turtsiej 1806–1812 gg.*, III:312–319.

54. Ahmed Pasha to Kutuzov, October 5/17, 1811, in *M. I. Kutuzov. Sbornik dokumentov*, III:651n1.

55. Kutuzov to Barclay de Tolly, October 10/22, 1811, in *M. I. Kutuzov. Sbornik dokumentov*, III:654–655.

56. Kutuzov to Rumyantsev, October 29/November 10, 1811, cited in Alexander Popov, *Otechestvennaia voina 1812 goda. Snoshenia Rossii s inostrannymi derzhavami pered voinoiu 1812 goda* (Moscow: Grossman & Wendelstein, 1905), I:338–339.

57. Kutuzov to his wife, October 10/22, 1811, in *The Kutuzov Papers* 5 (1872): 265.

58. Kutuzov to unknown recipient, October 28/November 9, 1811, in *M. I. Kutuzov. Sbornik dokumentov*, III:683.

59. Otroschenko, *Zapiski*; Langeron, "Zapiski," *Russkaya starina* 9 (1910): 544–545.

60. Kutuzov to Barclay de Tolly, October 10/22, 1811, in *M. I. Kutuzov. Sbornik dokumentov*, III:654.

61. Kutuzov to Barclay de Tolly, December 14/26, 1811, RGVIA, f. VUA, d. 2952, ll. 407–408; Langeron, "Zapiski," *Russkaya starina* 9 (1910): 544.

62. Langeron, "Zapiski," *Russkaya starina* 9 (1910): 543; Kutuzov to Barclay de Tolly, December 14/26, 1811, RGVIA, f. VUA, d. 2952, 407b.

63. In mid-November Kutuzov was reporting about the Austrian military mobilization along the frontier with Moldavia. Kutuzov to Rumyantsev, November 3/15, 1811, in *M. I. Kutuzov. Sbornik dokumentov*, III:695–696.

64. When allowing the sale of meat, he extended this profitable privilege only to the Russian sutlers. "Not a single Wallachian or Greek [merchant] should be involved in this," he stipulated. Kutuzov to Langeron, October 19/31, 1811, in *M. I. Kutuzov. Sbornik dokumentov*, III:674; Kutuzov to unknown recipient, October 28/November 9, 1811, in *M. I. Kutuzov. Sbornik dokumentov*, III:684.

65. Kutuzov to Barclay de Tolly and to Rumyantsev, October 18/30, 1811, in *M. I. Kutuzov. Sbornik dokumentov*, III:671–672.

66. Kutuzov to Rumyantsev, October 29/November 10, 1811, in *M. I. Kutuzov. Sbornik dokumentov*, III:684.

67. Rumyantsev to Kutuzov, September 30/October 12, 1811, in *M. I. Kutuzov. Sbornik dokumentov*, III:631–632. For Kutuzov's response, see his letter of October 18/30, 1811, in *M. I. Kutuzov. Sbornik dokumentov*, III:672–673.

68. See Kutuzov to Ahmed Pasha, October 28/November 9, 1811; Kutuzov to Barclay de Tolly, October 29/November 10, 1811, in *M. I. Kutuzov. Sbornik dokumentov*, III:686–688.

69. Kutuzov to Ahmed Pasha, November 3/15, 1811, in *M. I. Kutuzov. Sbornik dokumentov*, III:700–701. Kutuzov moved forward with talks partly because he knew that twenty years earlier, the peace negotiations that led to the conclusion of the Treaty of Jassy had also begun without the sultan's full authorization but still led to a diplomatic resolution.

70. Kutuzov to Rumyantsev, November 10/22, 1811, in *M. I. Kutuzov. Sbornik dokumentov*, III:699.

71. *Nottingham Journal*, January 25, 1812, 3. The journal cites "advices from Constantinople" dated November 25, 1811.

72. Kutuzov to his wife, October 29/November 10, 1811, in *The Kutuzov Papers*, 2 (1872): 266.

73. Armistice Agreement, November 23/December 5, 1811, in *The General Staff Archives*, VI:346–347. Langeron served as Kutuzov's intermediary and offers an interesting account of his discussions with the grand vizier. See his "Zapiski," *Russkaya starina* 7 (1911): 129–137.

74. Alexander Chernyshev to Nikolai Rumyantsev, December 6/18, 1811, in *SIRIO* XXI (1877): 266. Also see Vladimir Zemtsov, *Russkii posol v Parizhe knyaz' A. B. Kurakin. Khronika rokovykh let* (Moscow: ROSSPEN, 2019), 77–78.

75. Kutuzov to Alexander, November 26/December 8, 1811, RGVIA, f. VUA, d. 2952, l. 374; Kutuzov to Rumyantsev, November 26/December 8, 1811; Kutuzov to Langeron and Zass, November 27/December 9, 1811, in *M. I. Kutuzov. Sbornik dokumentov*, III:708–709, 711–713. Kutuzov instructed Langeron to escort the captive Ottoman soldiers to the designated areas more than thirty miles away from the Danube and "to always keep up the appearance that they are not prisoners of war, but rather our guests, willingly staying here." Kutuzov to Langeron, November 24/December 6, 1811, in *M. I. Kutuzov. Sbornik dokumentov*, III:707. For the Russian winter cantonment, see Disposition of the Army of Moldavia, November 27/December 9, 1811, in *M. I. Kutuzov. Sbornik dokumentov*, III:742–749. Kutuzov's report showed that at the end of the year the Army of Moldavia (including the 9th and 15th Divisions) had 52,296 men: 11,606 cavalry, 37,162 infantry, and 3,528 artillery, with 100 pontoons and 39 siege, 72 battery, 119 field, and 47 horse artillery cannon.

Chapter 20

1. *Public Ledger and Daily Advertiser*, January 29, 1812, 2. Also see *London Statesman*, February 18, 1812, based on letters from Bucharest dated December 24.

2. Kutuzov to his wife, October 17/29, 1811, in *The Kutuzov Papers* 2 (1872): 266. Also see his letter of March 6/18, in *The Kutuzov Papers* 4 (1872): 647.

3. Kutuzov to his wife, December 13/25, 1811, and February 12/24, 1812, in *The Kutuzov Papers* 2 (1872): 267–268. Also see his letter of December 22, 1811/ January 3, 1806, in *M. I. Kutuzov. Sbornik dokumentov* (Moscow: Voeniszdat, 1950), III:734n2.

4. Kutuzov to his wife, February 20/March 4, 1812, in *The Kutuzov Papers* 2 (1872): 268.

5. Kutuzov to his wife, January 19/31, 1812, in *The Kutuzov Papers* 2 (1872): 267.

6. [I. Bezsonov], "Russkie dostopamyatye lyudi," *Russkaya starina* 5 (1892): 234.

7. Kutuzov to E. von Tiesenhausen, January 19/31, 1812, in *The Kutuzov Papers* 6 (1874): 366.

8. *The London Sun*, March 3, 1812, 3.

9. Whereas the Russians evinced readiness to accept the frontier along the Sereth River, which would have given them Bessarabia and half of Moldavia, the Ottomans insisted on drawing the line almost 100 miles east, along the Pruth River and the northernmost Kiliya channel to the Black Sea, which would have forced the Russians to return the whole of the Danubian Principalities, save for Bessarabia.

10. In the words of Ottoman chief plenipotentiary Ghalib Efendi, "If autonomy is granted to the Serbs, who share the same faith as the Russians, other Orthodox Christians will seek to benefit from this measure by seeking similar concessions." Besides, as far as the Turks were concerned, events in Serbia represented an internal Ottoman problem, which the Russians had no right to interfere in. Cited in Stojan Novaković, *Vaskrs države srpske. Poltikicko-istorijcka studija o prvom Srpskom ustanku 1804–1813* (Begrade: S. B. Tsvijanov, 1914), 182.

11. Alexander to Kutuzov, December 12/24, 1811, in *M. I. Kutuzov. Sbornik dokumentov*, III:730–731. This was a matter of "his glory," the czar told the Austrian envoy. "One cannot expect that he would make a shameful peace [*paix honteuse*]." Count St. Julien's report to Austrian foreign minister Klemens von Metternich, September 28, 1811, in *Imperator Aleksandr I. Opyt istoricheskago izsledovaniya* (St. Petersburg: Eksp. Zag. Gos. Bumag, 1912), I:462.

12. Rumyantsev to Kutuzov, October 26/November 7, 1811, cited in Alexander Popov, *Otechestvennaia voina 1812 goda. Snoshenia Rossii s inostrannymi derzhavami pered voinoiu 1812 goda* (Moscow: Grossman & Wendelstein, 1905), I:340–341.

13. In addition, the two divisions he had "borrowed" earlier had to be sent back to Volhynia, further sapping Russian military resources in the region.

14. Kutuzov to Rumyantsev, December 13/25, 1811; Kutuzov to Barclay de Tolly, December 14/26, 1811, in *M. I. Kutuzov. Sbornik dokumentov*, III:733, 735; Kutuzov to Barclay de Tolly, December 14/26, 1811, RGVIA, f. VUA, d. 2952, ll. 409–411; Kutuzov to Barclay de Tolly, December 14/26, 1811, RGVIA, f. VUA, d. 2952, ll. 405–405b. Kutuzov also reminded the czar

that the Bulgarian countryside was utterly devastated. "The area south of the
Danube is almost entirely depopulated for the distance of one hundred *verstas*
[66 miles]. Our raiding parties have forced everyone to flee deep into the
Balkan mountains."

15. Kutuzov to Alexander, December 22, 1811/January 3, 1812, in *M. I. Kutuzov.
Sbornik dokumentov*, III:759–760. Also see Langeron, "Zapiski," *Russkaya
starina* 8 (1911): 249–250.

16. Documents related to these raids are in *M. I. Kutuzov. Sbornik dokumentov*,
III:784–789, 793–794, 799–801. For a critical view, see Langeron, "Zapiski,"
Russkaya starina 8 (1911): 254–256.

17. *The London Sun*, January 3, 1812, 2. A similar article also appeared in other
newspapers, including the *Kentish Gazette* (January 3) and *Northampton Mercury*
(January 4).

18. Of this same opinion were "certain" French political and military figures who
secretly met with the czar's special envoy Alexander Chernyshev in faraway
Paris. "They all tell me what a huge impression the new turn of events in the
Ottoman affairs has made it," read one of his reports. "At first the extent of
our success was minimized but once the miserable state of the grand vizier
became clear, it produced considerable anxiety and fear. . . . These individuals
want us to conclude peace with the Turks because they see in it the only means
to place us in such advantageous position that we never held before . . . and
to delay, at least for some length of time, those misfortunes and calamities
that a [Franco-Russian] war would bring." Alexander Chernyshev to Nikolai
Rumyantsev, September 7/19, 1811, in *SIRIO* XXI (1877): 259–260.

19. Alexander to Kutuzov, February 16/28, 1812, in *M. I. Kutuzov. Sbornik
dokumentov*, III:805.

20. *Morning Chronicle*, January 20, 1812, 2; *Public Ledger and Daily Advertiser*,
February 17, 1812, 2; *The London Star*, February 27 and March 3, 1812, 2;
The London Sun, March 3, 1812, 3. As late as mid-June the *Moniteur Universel*
was still anticipating the renewal of hostilities and was reporting about the
Ottoman forces moving toward the Danube. See sporadic coverage in January–
June issues of *Le Moniteur Universel* at https://fsu.digital.flvc.org/islandora/obj
ect/fsu%3A356296.

21. Walter Scott, *Life of Napoleon Bonaparte*, in *The Complete Works of Sir Walter Scott*
(New York: Conner & Cooke, 1833), VII:448.

22. Kutuzov to Barclay de Tolly, December 26, 1811/January 7, 1812; Kutuzov
to Rumyantsev, January 3/15, 1815, in *M. I. Kutuzov. Sbornik dokumentov*,
III:760–761, 764.

23. Count St. Julien's report to Austrian foreign minister Klemens von Metternich,
January 3, 1812, in Grand Duke Nikolai Mikhailovich, *Imperator Aleksandr
I*, I:476.

24. Alexander to Kutuzov, March 22/April 3, 1812, in *M. I. Kutuzov. Sbornik
dokumentov*, III:851.

25. Armand-Augustin-Louis, Marquis de Caulaincourt, *Mémoires du Général de Caulaincourt, duc de Vicence, grand écuyer de l'empereur* (Paris: Plon, 1933), I:327.

26. For details, see correspondence between the Russian ambassador to Paris, A. Kurakin, Emperor Alexander, and Chancellor Rumyantsev in *VPR*, VI:306–307, 719.

27. Minutes of Kutuzov's meeting with Ghalib Efendi, March 13/25, 1812, in *M. I. Kutuzov. Sbornik dokumentov*, III:846.

28. P. Chichagov, *Mémoires inédits de l'Amiral Tchitchagoff. Campagnes de la Russie en 1812 contre la Turquie, l'Autriche et la France* (Berlin: F. Schneider, 1855), 4.

29. For details on his early life, see Leonid Chichagov, "Admiral Pavel Vasilievich Chichagov. Zapiski o sobytiyakh ego zhisni (epokha imperatora Pavla)," *Russkaya starina* 38 (1883): 487–506. For a revisionist biography of Chichagov, see Vladimir Yulin, *Admiral P. V. Chichagov—istinnyi patriot otechestva: Novoye v traktovke ego roli v istorii Rossii* (Moscow, 2002).

30. Joseph de Maistre praised him as "one of the most remarkable men in Russia. Nowadays, there is no one here to . . . equal him in judgment, sharpness of intellect, strength of character, sense of justice, impartiality and even austerity of morals." In one of his letters, de Maistre also noted that "Chichagov is feared because he insists on order and is despised because he does not allow anyone to steal in his ministry." Maistre to King Victor Emmanuel I, June 2/14, 1813, in *Arkhiv knyazya Vorontsova* (Moscow: Tip. Gracheva, 1876), XV:491–492.

31. Karl Friedrich von Toll, *Denkwürdigkeiten aus dem Leben des Kaiserl. russ. Generals von der der Infanterie Carl Friedrich Grafen von Toll*, edited by Theodor von Bernhardi (Leipzig: Otto Wigand, 1856), II:353.

32. "Like no other minister, [Chichagov was] plain in his relations and conversations with the Emperor and the royal family. He knew well his superiority in sciences, education, as well as honesty and firmness of character, over the court sycophants, and treated them with great inattentiveness, oftentimes even carelessly, for which he was, naturally, hated virtually by the entire court and all the empty-headed but haughty nobility." Fedor Tolstoy, "Zapiski," *Russkaya starina* 1 (1873): 44–45. Also see *Arkhiv admirala P. V. Chichagova* (St. Petersburg, 1885), 29. Unsurprisingly, Langeron left one of the most critical portraits of Chichagov. See Alexander Langeron, *Mémoires de Langeron: Général d'infanterie dans l'armée russe. Campagnes de 1812, 1813, 1814* (Paris: A. Picard, 1902), 1–2.

33. Maistre to King Victor Emmanuel I, June 2/14, 1813, in *Arkhiv knyazya Vorontsova*, XV:492.

34. Contemporaries vilified him as "haughty, boastful of his imaginary merits, with an audacious tongue, and hateful of his own motherland" and wondered, "How could a man who expressed so much disgust for everything Russian enjoy such close relations with the Emperor?" Alexander Shishkov, *Zapiski, mneniya i perepiska Admirala A. S. Shishkova* (Berlin: B. Behr's Buchhandlung, 1870), I:111.

35. Alexander to Kutuzov, September 1/13, 1812, cited in Modest Bogdanovich, *Istoriya otechestvennoi voiny 1812 goda po dostovernym istochnikam* (St. Petersburg: S. Strugovshikov, 1859) II:613; Chichagov, *Mémoires inédits de l'Amiral Tchitchagoff*, 4–6.

36. Shishkov, *Zapiski,* 126.

37. Maistre to Rossi, May 9, 1812, *Correspondance diplomatique de Joseph de Maistre (1811–1817)* (Paris, 1860), I:100. Langeron claimed it was Kutuzov's wife who "told him about the rumors that began to circulate in high society." Langeron, "Zapiski," *Russkaya starina* 7 (1911): 129. Others thought that Kutuzov learned of his replacement from "his friends in St. Petersburg, probably sooner than the Emperor expected it." Toll, *Denkwürdigkeiten*, II:4. Varvara Bakunina, Kutuzov's cousin and the wife of the governor of St. Petersburg, commented that Kutuzov's "well-wishers swear that he would sign the peace before Chichagov's arrival, and it is highly desirable that it indeed happens so." See her "Zapiski," *Russkaya starina* 9 (1885): 396.

38. Kutuzov to Alexander, May 7/19, 1812, in *M. I. Kutuzov. Sbornik dokumentov*, III:897. The text of the preliminary agreement is in *M. I. Kutuzov. Sbornik dokumentov*, III:897–899. Kutuzov did not sign the treaty since he was not formally authorized to act as a Russian delegate. Instead, the treaty was signed by A. Italinskii, I. Sabaneev, and I. Fonton. Langeron describes meeting, in 1826, the Phanariote Greeks who claimed to have engineered the final compromise. See "Zapiski," *Russkaya starina* 8 (1911): 265–266.

39. Chichagov carried two copies of the imperial order. The first one, dated April 17, was couched in plain, if not brusque, terms, commanding Kutuzov to transfer command of the army to Chichagov and return to St. Petersburg to join the State Council, an assignment that carried no great weight. The second, dated April 21, was more fulsome and intended to be revealed only if Kutuzov had signed the peace treaty before Chichagov arrived at Bucharest. See both rescripts in *M. I. Kutuzov. Sbornik dokumentov*, III:867.

40. Kutuzov to I. Schteter, August 7/19, 1811, in *M. I. Kutuzov. Sbornik dokumentov*, III:531.

41. Kutuzov to Barclay de Tolly, May 11/23, 1812, in *M. I. Kutuzov. Sbornik dokumentov*, III:901.

42. Kutuzov to I. Schteter, August 8/20, 1811, in *M. I. Kutuzov. Sbornik dokumentov*, III:532–533.

43. Out of 2,981 merchant stalls, 2,215 belonged to Wallachian merchants, but the remaining stalls were kept by merchants claiming Russian (268), French (126), or Austrian (372) citizenship.

44. Kutuzov to Rumyantsev, June 1/13, 1811, in *M. I. Kutuzov. Sbornik dokumentov*, III:407–412. See, for example, the case of Peter Ignatiev, a local merchant who refused to pay taxes on his imported goods by claiming he was actually a subject of the French Empire. *M. I. Kutuzov. Sbornik dokumentov*, III:339.

NOTES TO PAGES 334–336 | 663

45. "The foreigners' ability to trade and compete with local merchants without bearing any [fiscal] burdens [is] contrary to the natural law," Kutuzov observed.

46. Kutuzov to Rumyantsev, June 1/13, 1811, in *M. I. Kutuzov. Sbornik dokumentov*, III:409.

47. Chichagov, *Mémoires inédits de l'Amiral Tchitchagoff*, 14–15.

48. See, for example, Order to the Army, May 14/26, 1811; Kutuzov to I. Schteter, August 7/19, 1811, in *M. I. Kutuzov. Sbornik dokumentov*, III:371, 530–531.

49. Kutuzov noted that Articles 7, 11, and 13 of the final agreement were "negotiated after Admiral Chichagov's arrival, at his insistence, and with his acquiescence." Kutuzov to Rumyantsev, May 16/28, 1812, in *M. I. Kutuzov. Sbornik dokumentov*, III:904.

50. Kutuzov to Rumyantsev, May 16/28, 1812, in *M. I. Kutuzov. Sbornik dokumentov*, III:904–905; Chichagov, *Mémoires inédits de l'Amiral Tchitchagoff*, 7–12.

51. Kutuzov to Rumyantsev, May 16/28, 1812, in *M. I. Kutuzov. Sbornik dokumentov*, III:905.

52. Kutuzov gave up command of the Army of Moldavia as soon as Chichagov handed him the imperial order. But he retained the status of a Russian plenipotentiary, which allowed him to complete the negotiations.

53. The contemporary Russian court historian pointed out that the land "extended for 40,000 square *verstas* [26,520 miles]" and included five major Ottoman fortresses: Ismail, Kilia, Bender, Khotin, and Akkerman. "It had numerous herds of cattle and horses, was endowed with fertile soil, extensive hayfields, aromatic and healing herbs, centuries-old oaks that are so useful in shipbuilding; the region was blessed with beekeeping, fishing, fruit gardens, mineral waters, deposits of coal, lime, and marble, as as well salt lakes."

54. In a separate and secret agreement, the Porte formally recognized Russian control of western Georgia and agreed to Russian use of the coastland on the Caucasian side of the Black Sea "to facilitate the transport of munitions and other war material" to Russian troops fighting the Persians in eastern Caucasus.

55. "What rights will we have in arousing the Slavic peoples to join us when they will have under their eyes such a striking and complete example of the weakness with which we abandon and betray those whose hopes rested on us and who were devoted to our empire? I confess that in my view, these preliminary articles will for a long time ruin our credit in the Orient among the Greek and Slavic peoples." Rumiantsev to Chichagov, May 26, 1812, quoted in Patricia K. Grimsted, *The Foreign Minister of Alexander I: Political Attitudes and the Conduct of Russian Diplomacy, 1801–1825* (Berkeley: University of California Press, 1969), 189–190.

56. Philippe-Paul de Ségur, *Histoire de Napoléon et de la grande-armée pendant l'année 1812* (Paris: Baudoin Frères, 1824), I:37.

57. Order to the Army, May 12/24, 1812, in *M. I. Kutuzov. Sbornik dokumentov*, III:903–904.

Chapter 21

1. 2nd Bulletin, June 22, 1812, *Imperial Glory: The Bulletins of Napoleon's Grande Armée, 1805–1814*, edited by J. David Markham (London, 2003), 246.
2. Order to the Armies, June 25, 1812, in *VPR*, VI:442–443.
3. Quoted in Gabriel Fabry, *Campagne de Russie, 1812. Operations militaires (24 juin–19 juillet)* (Paris: L. Gougy, 1900), I:i. Mathieu Dumas, who participated in the French campaign in 1812, passed down a story he had heard from Barthold Georg Niebuhr that sheds light on Barclay de Tolly's strategic thinking. As early as 1807 Barclay de Tolly had told Niebuhr that the Russian army—in case it ever again fought against France—should apply a "plan de retraites combinées." The idea was a coordinated retreat of all Russian armies in order to inflict on Napoleon's forces "un second Pultawa." Mathieu Dumas, *Souvenirs du lieutenant général comte Mathieu Dumas de 1770 à 1836* (Paris, 1839), 416–417. See also Michael Josselon and Diana Josselson, *The Commander: A Life of Barclay de Tolly* (Oxford: Oxford University Press, 1980), 89–90. "The system of war that we should follow in this impending conflict," wrote Colonel Alexander Chernyshev, who supervised Russian espionage operations in France, "is the one that Fabius [Cunctator] and Lord Wellington offer the best examples of." On February 20, 1812, Chernyshev described conversations that he had had with French "officers who are of great merit and knowledge and who have no affection for [Napoleon]. I have asked them about what strategy would be best in the coming war, taking into account the theater of operations, the strength and the character of our adversary." These officers all assured Chernyshev that Napoleon would seek a decisive battle at the start of the campaign and therefore the Russians should avoid giving him what he wanted. Chernyshev's reports to Alexander, Barclay de Tolly, and Rumyantsev have been published in *SIRIO* CXXI–CXXII (1905–1906). The quote is from Chernyshev to Barclay de Tolly, February 20, 1812, SIRIO CXXI (1906): 208.
4. A. Zakrevskii to Mikhail Vorontsov, n.d. [early July 1812], in *Arkhiv knyazya Vorontsova* (Moscow: Tip. Gracheva, 1876), XXXVII:229. Also see Nikolai Rumyantsev to A. Samoilov, June 28/July 10, 1812, in *Arkhiv Rayevskikh* (St. Petersburg, 1908), I:152.
5. Ivan Pukolov to Alexei Arakcheyev, June 27/July 9, 1812, in Nikolai Dubrovin, ed., *Pis'ma glavenishikh deyatelej v tsarstvovanie imperatora Aleksandra I, 1807–1829 godakh* (St. Petersburg, 1883), 60.
6. Ivan Odenthal to A. Bulgakov, July 2/14, 1812, in "Sto let nazad: pis'ma I.P. Odentalya k A. Ya. Bulgakovu o peterburgskikh novostyakh i slukhakh," *Russkaya starina* 7 (1912): 134.
7. Kutuzov to E. von Tiesenhausen, July 19/31, 1812, in *The Kutuzov Papers* 6 (1874): 368.

8. Minutes of the Emergency Meeting of the Committee of Ministers, July 12/ 24, 1812, in *Proceedings of the Committee of Ministers*, II:497–498.

9. Alexander to Kutuzov, July 15/27, 1812, RGVIA, f. VUA, d. 3645, l. 2.

10. Ivan Pukolov to Alexei Arakcheyev, July 17/29, 1812, in Nikolai Dubrovin, ed., *Otechestvennaya vojna v pismakh sovremennikov, 1812–1815 gg.* (St. Petersburg, 1882), 55. Despite his anxiety about the outcome of the war, Postmaster Ivan Odenthal consoled himself with the fact that the aged general was in St. Petersburg: "I keep repeating my prayer—may the Lord prolong [Kutuzov's] life and grant him good health!" Ivan Odenthal to A. Bulgakov, July 19/31, 1812, in *Russkaya starina* 7 (1912): 140.

11. Memorandum on the Troops Assigned to the Narva Corps, in *Proceedings of the Committee of Ministers*, II:707. Also see the minutes of the committee's meeting on July 31, which Kutuzov attended for the first time in his new capacity. *Proceedings of the Committee of Ministers*, II:501.

12. The Decree of the Assembly of the Nobility of Moscow, July 17/29, 1812, in A. Bobrinskii, ed., *Materialy dlya istorii dvoryanstva S.-Peterburgskoi gubernii* (St. Petersburg: Tip. Min. Vnut. Del, 1912), II:17–21.

13. Vladimir Steinheil, *Zapiski kasatel'no sostavleniya i samogo pokhoda sanktpeterburgskogo opolcheniya protiv vragov otechestva v 1812 i 1813 godakh* (St. Petersburg: V. Plavil'shikov, 1814), I:30–32; Ivan Odenthal to A. Bulgakov, July 19/31, 1812, in *Russkaya starina* 7 (1912): 140; Ivan Pukolov to Alexei, July 17/29, 1812, in Dubrovin, *Otechestvennaya vojna v pismakh sovremennikov*, 54–55.

14. The Degree of the Assembly of the Nobility of Moscow, July 16/28, 1812, in *M. I. Kutuzov. Sbornik dokumentov* (Moscow: Voeniszdat, 1950), IV:6–7. Kutuzov received 243 votes, Fedor Rostopchin 225, and Field Marshal General Ivan Gudovich 198; four other candidates shared the remaining votes.

15. Evgraf Komarovskii, *Zapiski grafa E. F. Komarovskogo* (St. Petersburg: Ogni, 1914), 197.

16. Vladimir Steinheil, *Sochineniya i pis'ma. Tom 1. Zapiski i pis'ma* (Irkutsk: Vostochno-Sibirskoe Knizhnoe Izd., 1985), I:30–32; Bobrinskii, *Materialy dlya istorii dvoryanstva S.-Peterburgskoi gubernii*, 18.

17. Minutes of the Committee of Ministers, August 6/18, 1812, in *Proceedings of the Committee of Ministers*, II:512–513.

18. Kutuzov to Alexander, July 23/August 4, 1812, in *M. I. Kutuzov. Sbornik dokumentov*, IV:26–28. Also see Statute of the St. Petersburg Opolchenye, which Kutuzov drafted in August, in *M. I. Kutuzov. Sbornik dokumentov*, IV:57–62. For an eyewitness account, see Steinheil, *Zapiski*, 39–42.

19. Alexander Mikhailovskii-Danilevskii, *Opisanie Otechestvennoi voiny v 1812 godu* (St. Petersburg, 1839), II:184.

20. Alexander to Kutuzov, July 30/August 11, 1812, in N. Dubrovin, ed., *Otechestvennaya voina v pis'makh sivremennikov, 1812–1815* (St. Petersburg, 1882), 35–36.

21. Alexander to Kutuzov, July 31/August 12, 1812, in Dubrovin, *Otechestvennaya voina v pis'makh sivremennikov,* 70.

22. John Quincy Adams, *Memoirs of John Quincy Adams Containing His Diary from 1795 to 1848,* edited by Charles Francis Adams (Philadelphia: Lippincott, 1874), II:393.

23. N. Longinov to S. Vorontsov, September 13/25, 1812, in *Arkhiv knyazya Vorontsova* XXIII:154.

24. Imperial Decree of July 29/August 10, 1812, in *M. I. Kutuzov. Sbornik dokumentov,* IV:47–48. Four days later Alexander appointed him to the State Council. *M. I. Kutuzov. Sbornik dokumentov,* IV:53.

25. Ivan Odenthal to A. Bulgakov, August 2/14, 1812, in "Sto let nazad: pis'ma I. P. Odentalya k A. Ya. Bulgakovu o peterburgskikh novostyakh i slukhakh," *Russkaya starina* 8 (1912): 165.

26. Maria Volkova to Varvara Lanskaya, August 5/17, 1812, in *Vestnik Evropy* 4 (1874): 588–589.

27. Napoleon to Berthier, July 2, 1812, in *Correspondance de Napoleon Ier, publ. par ordre de l'Empereur Napoléon III* (Paris: Henri Plon, 1863), XXIV:7.

28. Napoleon to Berthier, 5:00 a.m., June 25, 1812, in Gabriel Fabry, ed., *Campagne de Russie, 1812. Opérations militaires (24 juin–19 juillet)* (Paris: L. Gougy, 1900), I:9. Bordesoulle's report to Murat shows that complaints about cartographic deficiencies were not limited to senior command only. For example, at 8:00 a.m. on June 25, he laments, "I beseech you, Sire, to provide me with a map and have one or two Polish officers, who speak French or German, sent from the 9th Polish Regiment, since otherwise it is absolutely impossible to lead a vanguard. I grope about as if I am blind and it is rather detrimental to operate in such a manner." Murat's solution to the problem was to approach a local Jew, "who promised to provide me with accurate information while I promised him a lot of money." Murat to Napoleon, June 25, 1812, 4:00 p.m., in Fabry, *Campagne de Russie,* I:18.

29. N. Longinov to S. Vorontsov, September 13/25, 1812, in *Arkhiv knyazya Vorontsova* XXIII:152.

30. A good example of this line of thinking is Peter Chuikevich's memorandum "Patriotic Thoughts or Political and Military Considerations on the Upcoming War Between Russia and France and on Inciting an Insurrection in Germany by Means of a Military Expedition," translated by A. Mikaberidze, in The Napoleon Series, https://www.napoleon-series.org/military-info/organization/Russia/MilitaryThought/c_Chuikevich.html.

31. F. Rostopchin to S. Vorontsov, July 8/20, 1818, in *Arkhiv knyazya Vorontsova,* VIII:342.

32. The sole English-language biography remains Josselson and Josselon, *The Commander.* The Russian bibliography is more diverse, though the best works remain A. Tartakovskii, *Nerazgadannyj Barklai. Legendy i byl'* (Moscow,

1996); V. Totfalushin, *M. B. Barclay de Tolly v Otechestvennoi voine 1812 g.* (Saratov, 1991).

33. The seniority system determined who held the highest rank. It operated on two different levels. For officers of different ranks, seniority was simply determined by whoever held the highest rank. For officers in the same rank, seniority was determined by the dates on which they assumed their ranks. In 1809, when Barclay de Tolly was promoted to a full general, he was ranked forty-fifth in the list of fifty-nine lieutenant generals. His promotion, of course, would have embittered dozens of officers who held seniority over him. See the seniority rankings ("Spisok generaliteta po starshinstvu") as of January 18/30, 1808. I relied on the copy from the State Public Library of St. Petersburg containing annotations that updated it to February 28, 1809.

34. N. Longinov to S. Vorontsov, September 13/25, 1812, in *Arkhiv knyazya Vorontsova* XXIII:152; Carl von Clausewitz, *Der Feldzug von 1812 in Russland, der Feldzug von 1813 bis zum Waffenstillstand und der Feldzug von 1814 in Frankreich,* edited by Marie von Clausewitz (Berlin: Ferdinand Dümmler, 1835), 132. Also see Jacob de Sanglen, "Zapiski Yakova Ivanovicha de Sanglena (1776–1831)," *Russkaya starina* 37, no. 3 (1883): 546.

35. Clausewitz, *Der Feldzug von 1812 in Russland*, 131.

36. Sir Robert Ker Porter, *Traveling Sketches in Russia and Sweden: During the Years 1805, 1806, 1807, 1808* (London: Longman et al., 1809), 50; Robert Wilson, *Narrative of Events During the Invasion of Russia by Napoleon Bonaparte and the Retreat of the French Army* (London: John Murray, 1860), 156; Sergey Volkonskii, *Zapiski Sergia Grigorievicha Volkonskogo (Dekabrista)* (St. Petersburg, 1901), 38; Gregory Derzhavin, *Sochineniya* (St. Petersburg, 1868), II:579.

37. Bagration to Barclay de Tolly, August 3, 1812, no. 394, *General Staff Archives*, XIV:199.

38. Philippe-Paul de Ségur, *Histoire de Napoléon et de la grande-armée pendant l'année 1812* (Brussels: H. Tarlier, 1825), I:165; Denis Davydov, *Sochineniya* (Moscow: Gos. Izd. Khud. Lit., 1962), 23.

39. M. Konshin, "Iz Zapisok Konshina," *Istoricheskii vestnik* 8, no. 17 (1884): 283; Boris von Uxkull, *Arms and the Woman: The Diaries of Baron Boris von Uxkull, 1812–1819* (London, 1966), 74–75; A. Simanskii, *Pis'ma L. A. Simanskogo k materi ego i bratyam po vystuplenii ego v pokhod v byvshuyu s frantsuzami voinu 1812, 1813, 1814 i 1815 godov* (St. Petersburg, 1912), 159.

40. Pavel Grabbe, *Iz pamyatnykh zapisok grafa Pavla Khristoforovicha Grabbe* (Moscow: Katkov, 1873), II:57.

41. Zakrevskii to Vorontsov, August 17–18, 1812, in *Arkhiv knyazya Vorontsova*, XXXVII:229–230.

42. Ivan Zhirkevich, "Zapiski . . . ," *Russkaya starina* 8 (1874): 648.

43. Alexander Muravyev, *Sochineniya i pis'ma* (Irkutsk: Vostochno-Sibirsk. Knizh. Izd., 1986), 103.

44. Alexey Yermolov, *The Czar's General: The Memoirs of a Russian General in the Napoleonic Wars*, translated and edited by Alexander Mikaberidze (Welwyn Garden City: Ravenhall Books, 2005), 147.

45. Count Shuvalov to Emperor Alexander, July 31/August 12, 1812, in Dubrovin, *Otechestvennaya vojna v pismakh sovremennikov*, 71–72.

46. Emperor Alexander to Grand Duchess Catherine, September 18/30, 1812, in Grand Duke Nikolai Mikhailovich, ed., *Perepiska imperatora Aleksandra I s sestroj, velikoj knyaginej Ekaterinoj Pavlovnoj* (St. Petersburg: Eskp. Zag. Gos. Bumag, 1910), 87.

47. Emperor Alexander to Grand Duchess Catherine, August 8/20, 1812, in Grand Duke Nikolai Mikhailovich, ed., *Perepiska imperatora Aleksandra I s sestroj*, 82.

48. For generals' seniority ranks, see "Spisok generalitetu po starshinstvu po 24-e iunya 1812 goda," 2–14. For Alexander's views on some candidates, see his letter to Grand Duchess Catherine, September 18/30, 1812, in Grand Duke Nikolai Mikhailovich, ed., *Perepiska imperatora Aleksandra I s sestroj*, 87.

49. Langeron, "Zapiski," *Russkaya starina* 9 (1907): 570. Also see Joseph de Maistre to Comte de Front, September 2/14, 1812, in Joseph de Maistre, *Oeuvres complètes de J. de Maistre. Correspondance, 1806–1807* (Lyon: Librairie Générale Catholique, 1885), XII:201.

50. The five generals who superseded Kutuzov in seniority were Platov Zubov (still disgraced but formally in furlough), the seventy-year-old Prince Gregory Volkonskii (last commanded a division in 1796; military governor of Orenburg since 1803), Count Semen Vorontsov (Russia's long-standing ambassador to Britain who had last seen action, alongside Kutuzov, during the Russo-Ottoman War of 1767–1774), the seventy-three-year-old General Andrei Rosenberg (last saw action under Suvorov in Italy and Switzerland in 1799; in full retirement since 1805), and the seventy-three-year-old Count Nikolai Tatischev (who was in full retirement and had not seen action since the Russo-Swedish War of 1788). The two field marshal generals were the seventy-six-year-old Count Nikolai Saltykov I and the seventy-one-year-old Count Ivan Gudovich.

51. There is no evidence that Kutuzov's membership in the Masonic lodges had any influence in this process.

52. N. Longinov to Semen Vorontsov, September 13/25, 1812, in *Arkhiv knyazya Vorontsova*, XXIII:154.

53. Emperor Alexander to Grand Duchess Catherine, August 8/20, 1812, in Grand Duke Nikolai Mikhailovich, *Perepiska imperatora Aleksandra I s sestroj*, 82; Rostopchin to Alexander, August 5/17, 1812, in "Pis'ma grafa F. V. Rostopchina k imperatoru Aleksandru Pavlovichu," *Russkaya starina* 8 (1892): 443; Ivan Odenthal to A. Bulgakov, August 2/14, 1812, in *Russkaya starina* 8 (1912): 165. The British envoy to St. Petersburg, George Cathcart, summed up the reasons for Kutuzov's selection: "It was considered that his

long-standing in the army, his recent able conduct of the Turkish campaign, and his former military reputation would place him above rivalry, and that in consequence he might be a kind of head to unite all parties." Sir George Cathcart, *Commentaries on the War in Russia and Germany in 1812 and 1813* (London: John Murray, 1850), 62.

54. Decision of the Extraordinary Committee, August 5/17, 1812, in *M. I. Kutuzov. Sbornik dokumentov*, IV:71–73.

55. Komarovskii, *Zapiski*, 198.

56. A. Mikhailovskii-Danilevskii, *Polnoe sobranie sochinenii. Opisanie pervoi voiny imperatora Aleksandra s Napoleonom v 1805 godu. Opisanie vtoroj voiny imperatora Aleksandra s Napoleonom v 1806 i 1807 godah* (St. Petersburg, 1849), 74. "During the war of 1806, public opinion forced the Emperor to select Field Marshal Kamenskii, but you remembered only too well what happened next," Joseph de Maistre reminded his friend Comte de Front in October 1812. *Oeuvres complètes de J. de Maistre*, XII:256.

57. Emperor Alexander to Grand Duchess Catherine, September 18/30, 1812, in Grand Duke Nikolai Mikhailovich, *Perepiska imperatora Aleksandra I s sestroj*, 87.

58. Joseph de Maistre to Comte de Front, October 7/19, 1812, in *Oeuvres complètes de J. de Maistre*, XII:256.

59. Emperor Alexander to Grand Duchess Catherine, September 18/30, 1812, in Grand Duke Nikolai Mikhailovich, *Perepiska imperatora Aleksandra I s sestroj*, 87. He repeated the same explanation in the December 6 letter to Barclay de Tolly. See *M. I. Kutuzov: Sbornik dokumentov*, IV:475. Also see Nikolai Shil'der, *Imperator Aleksandr pervyi. Ego zhizn' i tsarstvovanie* (St. Petersburg: A.S. Suvorin, 1897–1898), III:97–98. Joseph de Maistre told his friend that "the [Russian] public opinion soon reached the point where even the Emperor could not resist it." Joseph de Maistre to Comte de Front, September 2/14, 1812, in *Oeuvres complètes de Joseph de Maistre*, XII:201–202.

60. Alexander to Barclay de Tolly, November 24, 1812, in Vladimir Kharkevich, ed., *Barklai-de-Tolli v Otechestvennuyu voinu posle soedineniya armii pod Smolenskom* (St. Petersburg: Tip. Gl. Upr. Udelov, 1904), 50.

61. The official decree was signed on August 20. Alexander to the Imperial Senate, August 8/20, 1812, in *M. I. Kutuzov. Sbornik dokumentov*, IV:75. Peter Vyazemskii claims that when the czar invited Kutuzov to the palace, the general did not arrive on time. "More than five minutes passed, and he was still nowhere to be seen. The Emperor even inquired several times, 'Has he arrived?' And yet Kutuzov was still missing. Messengers were sent to various parts of the city to find him. At long last, it was determined that Kutuzov was at the Kazanskii Cathedral, attending a prayer service." Peter Vyazemskii, "Staraya zapisnaya knizhka," in *Polnoe sobranie sochinenii Knyazya P. A. Vyazemskago* (St. Petersburg: M. Stasyulevich, 1883), VIII:122.

62. N. Longinov to Semen Vorontsov, September 13/25, 1812, in *Arkhiv knyazya Vorontsova*, XXIII:157.

63. N. Longinov to Semen Vorontsov, September 13/25, 1812, in *Arkhiv knyazya Vorontsova*, XXIII:155. Countess Edling also heard Kutuzov state this: "Le général Koutouzoff avait assuré l'Empereur, en le quittant, que l'ennemi n'arriverait à Moscou qu'en passant sur son corps (c'est l'expression dont il se servit)." Roxandra Stourdza, Comtess d'Edling, *Mémoires de la comtess Edling, demoiselle d'honneur de sa majesté l'imperatrice Elisabeth Alexéevna* (Moscow: Holy Synod, 1888), 74.

64. Fedor Tolstoy, "Zapiski Grafa F. P. Tolstago," *Russkaya starina* 2 (1873): 137.

65. Alexander to Kutuzov, August 8/20, 1812, in *M. I. Kutuzov. Sbornik dokumentov*, IV:74; Komarovskii, *Zapiski*, 198.

66. Vyazemskii, "Staraya zapisnaya knizhka," 122.

67. Comtess Edling, *Mémoires*, 73; Madame Anne Louise Germaine de Staël, *Dix années d'exil* (Paris, 1904), 369.

68. Tolstoy, "Zapiski Grafa F. P. Tolstago," 137.

69. Ivan Odenthal to A. Bulgakov, August 16/28, 1812, in *Russkaya starina* 8 (1912): 170.

70. Ivan Odenthal to A. Bulgakov, August 16/28, 1812, in *Russkaya starina* 8 (1912): 170.

71. Kutuzov to Prince Aleksey Gorchakov, Lieutenant General Ertel, and General Miloradovich, August 10–11/22–23, 1812, in *Podrobnyi zhurnal iskhodyashikh bumag Sobstvennoi kantselyarii Glavnokomandyushego Soedinennymi Armiyami General-Feldmarshala Knyazya Kutuzova-Smolenskago v 1812 godu* [hereafter cited as *Journal of the Outgoing Correspondence of the Commander in Chief*], edited by V. Nikolskii and N. Polikarpov, in *Trudy Moskovskago otdela imperatorskago Russkago Voenno-istoricheskago obschestva* (Moscow: Tip. Shtaba Moskov. Voen. Okruga, 1912), II:2, 4.

Chapter 22

1. Carl von Clausewitz, *Der Feldzug von 1812 in Russland, der Feldzug von 1813 bis zum Waffenstillstand und der Feldzug von 1814 in Frankreich*, edited by Marie von Clausewitz (Berlin: Ferdinand Dümmler, 1835), 126.

2. Barclay de Tolly to Kutuzov, August 16/28, 1812, RGVIA, f. VUA, d. 3502, l. 171; Alexander Scherbinin, "Zapiski Aleksandra Scherbinina," in V. Kharkevich, ed., *1812 god v dnevnikakh, zapiskakh i vospominaniyakh sovremennikov* (Vilna: Tip. Shtaba Vilen. Voen. Okruga, 1900), I:13.

3. Mikhail Barclay de Tolly, *Izobrazhenie voennykh deistvii 1-oi armii v 1812 godu* (St. Petersburg: P. Soikin, 1912), 20–21. Also see Order to the 1st Western Army, August 17/29, 1812, in *M. I. Kutuzov. Sbornik dokumentov* (Moscow: Voeniszdat, 1950), IV, part 1, 91; Kutuzov to Barclay de Tolly,

August 15–16/27–28, 1812, *General Staff Archives*, XVI:232. For an interesting discussion see V. Totfalushin, *Barclay de Tolly v Otechestennoi voine 1812 g.* (Saratov, 1991), 75–77.

4. Kutuzov to his wife, August 13/25, 1812, in *The Kutuzov Papers* 2 (1872): 268.

5. Robert Wilson, *Narrative of Events During the Invasion of Russia by Napoleon Bonaparte and the Retreat of the French Army, 1812* (London: John Murray, 1860), 115; Kutuzov to his wife, August 16/28, 1812, in *The Kutuzov Papers* 2 (1872): 268. Kutuzov encountered Bennigsen at the relay station at Vyshnyi Volochyok, about fifty miles from Torzhok. Levin von Bennigsen, "Zapiski grafa L. L. Bennigsen o kampanii 1812 goda," *Russkaya starina* 9 (1909): 491.

6. Ilya Radozhitskii, *Pokhodnye zapiski artillerista s 1812 po 1816 god* (Moscow: Instit. Vost. Yazyk., 1835), I:131. For an English translation, see *Campaign Memoirs of the Artilleryman. Part 1: 1812*, translated and annotated by Alexander Mikaberidze (Tbilisi: NSG, 2011).

7. Clausewitz, *Der Feldzug von 1812 in Russland*, 135.

8. Cited in Alexander Polovtsev, ed., *Russkii biograficheskii Slovar'*, XII:673, http://rulex.ru/xPol/index.htm?pages/12/673.htm.

9. Alexander Muravyev, *Sochineniya i pis'ma* (Irkutsk: Vostochno-Sibirsk. Knizh. Izd., 1986), 108.

10. Radozhitskii, *Pokhodnye zapiski artillerista*, I:132.

11. Modest Bogdanovich, *Istoriya otechestvennoi voiny 1812 goda po dostovernym istochnikam* (St. Petersburg: S. Strugovshikov, 1859), II:125; V. Voronovskii, *Otechestvennaya voina 1812 g. v predelakh Smolenskoi gubernii* (St. Petersburg: A. Suvorin, 1912), 168.

12. Radozhitskii, *Pokhodnye zapiski artillerista*, I:132.

13. Clausewitz, *Der Feldzug von 1812 in Russland*, 135–136.

14. Entry for August 19/31, 1812, in Pavel Puschin, *Dnevnik Pavla Puschina, 1812–1814* (Leningrad: Leningrad University Press, 1987) http://www.museum.ru/museum/1812/Library/Puschin/index.html. For an English translation, see Pavel Puschin, *Diaries of the 1812–1814 Campaigns*, translated and edited by A. Mikaberidze (Tbilisi: NSG, 2011), 44.

15. Nikolai Muravyev, "Zapiski N. N. Murav'eva-Karskogo," *Russkii arkhiv* 10 (1885): 244.

16. Muravyev, *Sochineniya i pis'ma*, 108.

17. Clausewitz, *Der Feldzug von 1812 in Russland*, 132–133.

18. Alexander Mikhailovskii-Danilevskii, "Iz vospominanii . . . ," *Russkaya starina* 6 (1897): 466–467; "Lichnye pos'ma gen. N. N. Raevskago," in *1812–1814: Relyatsii, pis'ma, dnevniki*, edited by A. Afanasyev (Moscow: Terra, 1992), 218.

19. Barclay de Tolly to his wife, August 16/28, 1812, in *Russkaya starina* 12 (1912): 633.

20. Barclay de Tolly to Emperor Alexander, August 16/28, 1812, RGVIA, f. VUA, d. 3502, l. 171. On September 5, Alexander belatedly realized his oversight and removed Barclay de Tolly from the ministerial position, but

the letter would arrive after the Battle of Borodino. Alexander to Barclay de Tolly, August 24/September 5, 1812, RGVIA, f. VUA, 3387, l. 3. Also see *Trudy imperatorskogo Russkogo voenno-istoricheskogo obschestva* [hereafter cited as *TIRVIO*] (St. Petersburg: Gr. Skachkov, 1912), V:261; *Sbornik istoricheskikh materialov izvlechennykh iz arkhiva sobstvennoi e.i.v. kantselyarii* (St. Petersburg, 1876), 68–69.

21. Fedor Rostopchin, "Tysyacha vosemsot dvenadtsatyi god v zapiskakh grafa F. V. Rostopchina," *Russkaya starina* 12 (1889): 693; Bagration to Rostopchin, August 16/28 and August 22/September 3, 1812, in N. Dubrovin, ed., *Otechestvennaya voina v pis'makh sovremennikov* (St. Petersburg, 1882), 101, 109; Bagration to Barclay de Tolly, September 14/26, 1811, in *General Staff Archives*, V:74.

22. See A. Pogodin, *Yermolov: Materialy dlya ego biografii* (Moscow, 1864), 445–446.

23. Bennigsen's position was dubious because it lacked legal base. As the minister of war, Barclay de Tolly helped draft and implement the Uchrezhdenie dlya Upravleniya Bolshoi Deistvuyushei Armii (Statute on Commanding a Large Active Army), which defined the organization, structure, and functions of the Russian military during the concluding years of the Napoleonic Wars. The statute contained no provisions for the position of a chief of staff of combined armies, which is why Kutuzov was careful to note in his order that "General of Cavalry Bennigsen would be assigned to me and serve in the same capacity as the chiefs of staff of separate army commanders." See Orders to the Armies, August 18–19/30–31, 1812, RGVIA, f. VUA, d. 3524, ll. 1–3. Also see *General Staff Archives*, XVI:81–84; Kutuzov to Konovnitsyn, August 19/31, 1812, in *M. I. Kutuzov. Sbornik dokumentov*, IV, part 1, 105.

24. Bennigsen, "Zapiski," 491–493.

25. Waldemar de Löwernstern, *Mémoires du général-major russe baron de Löwernstern* (Paris: A. Fontemoing, 1903), I:269–270. Also see Barclay de Tolly, *Izobrazhenie*, 22.

26. For an interesting discussion of Bennigsen's status in the army, see N. Longinov to S. Vorontsov, September 13/25, 1812, in *Arkhiv knyazya Vorontsova* (Moscow: Tip. Gracheva, 1876), XXIII:160–161.

27. Bennigsen to General Alexander Fock, September 8/20, 1812, in *Russkaya starina* 9 (1909): 492.

28. Order to the Armies, August 19/31, 1812, RGVIA, f. VUA, d. 3524, l. 2b.

29. Barclay de Tolly, *Izobrazhenie*, 22–24.

30. Scherbinin, "Zapiski," 19–20. Also see Karl Friedrich von Toll, *Denkwürdigkeiten aus dem Leben des Kaiserl. russ. Generals von der der Infanterie Carl Friedrich Grafen von Toll*, edited by Theodor von Bernhardi (Leipzig: Otto Wigand, 1856), II:175–176.

31. Kutuzov's quote in Evgraf Komarovskii, *Zapiski grafa E. F. Komarovskogo* (St. Petersburg: Ogni, 1914), 198.

32. John Quincy Adams, *Memoirs of John Quincy Adams Containing His Diary from 1795 to 1848*, edited by Charles Francis Adams (Philadelphia: Lippincott, 1874), 424. On December 3, Adams attended a dinner hosted by Count Rumyantsev, where he met "Admiral Koutouzof, a nephew of the Prince of Smolensk," who discussed his illustrious relative. The person in question must have been Login Ivanovich Golenischev-Kutuzov, who served in the Russian navy. In his November 22 letter, Kutuzov told his daughter Elisabeth that he saw Napoleon in his dreams. See *The Kutuzov Papers* 6 (1874): 372.

33. Alexander Mikhailovskii-Danilevskii, *Aleksandr I i ego spodvizhniki v 1812 g.* (St. Petersburg: Tip. K. Kraya, 1846), III:70.

34. Adams, *Memoirs of John Quincy Adams Containing His Diary*, 424.

35. Kutuzov to Alexander, August 19/31, 1812, in *M. I. Kutuzov. Sbornik dokumentov*, IV, part 1, 98–99. According to Georges de Chambray, the Grande Armée had 155,675 men as of mid-August and 133,819 men on September 2. See *Histoire de l'expédition de Russie* (Paris: Pillet Ainé, 1823), I:261–262, 274.

36. The rosters of August 29 showed 65,528 combatants in the 1st Western Army (81,838 if counting noncombatants) and 34,925 men in the 2nd Western Army. The former had 432 cannon and the latter 173. In *M. I. Kutuzov. Sbornik dokumentov*, IV, part 1, 98.

37. Kutuzov to Iraklii Markov, August 19/31, 1812, *Journal of the Outgoing Correspondence of the Commander in Chief*, 5. Also see *Russkaya starina* 12 (1896): 648.

38. Kutuzov complained that "such a high number of soldiers abandoning their units reveals remarkable loosening of discipline on the part of regimental commanders. This penchant for marauding, facilitated by the weakness of their superiors, had an effect on the soldier's morale and now almost evolved into his habit that must be eradicated through the strictest measures." Order to the Army, August 18/30, 1812, RGVIA, f. VUA, d. 3524, ll. 1b–2. Also see *General Staff Archives*, XVI:81–82; Kutuzov to Emperor Alexander, August 19/31, 1812, in *Proceedings of the Committee of Ministers*, II:541. These measures barely had any effect on the rank and file, forcing Kutuzov to repeat his order on September 2. Order to the 2nd Western Army, September 4, 1812, in *Borodino: dokumental'naya khronika*, edited by A. Valkovich and A. Kapitonov (Moscow, 2004), 74; Kutuzov to Levitskii, August 21/September 2, 1812, *Journal of the Outgoing Correspondence of the Commander in Chief*, 9.

39. Sergei Glinka, *Zapiski o 1812 gode* (St. Petersburg: Russian Imperial Academy, 1836), 35–36.

40. Alexander Mikhailovskii-Danilevskii, *Opisanie Otechestvennoi voiny v 1812 godu* (St. Petersburg: Voen. Tip., 1839), III:145.

41. Louis Guillaume de Puibusque, *Lettres sur la guerre en Russie en 1812* (Paris: Magimel, Anselin, et Pochard, 1817), 159.

42. Eugene Labaume, *The Crime of 1812 and Its Retribution*, translated by T. Dundas Pillans (London: A. Melrose, 1912), 58, 94, 99–100. Also see Heinrich von

Brandt, *In the Legions of Napoleon: The Memoirs of a Polish Officer in Spain and Russia, 1808–1813* (London, 1999), 215.

43. Kutuzov to Rostopchin, August 17/29, 1812, in *Fel'dmarshal Kutuzov: dokumenty, dnevniki, vospominaniya*, edited by A. Val'kovich and A. Kapitonov (Moscow: Arkheog. Tsentr., 1995), 168.

44. Robert Wilson to Earl Cathcart, August 27, 1812, in Wilson, *Narrative of Events During the Invasion of Russia by Napoleon Bonaparte and the Retreat of the French Army* (London: John Murray, 1860), 384.

45. George Carpenter, 3rd Earl of Tyrconnell, to the Duke of York, October 2, 1812, in Dubrovin, *Otechestvennaya voina v pis'makh sovremennikov*, 164. Tyrconnel served as an acting aide-de-camp to the British commissioner to the Russian army, Sir Robert Wilson.

46. Robert Wilson to Lord Cathcart, September 28, 1812, in N. Dubrovin, *Otechestvennaya voina v pis'makh sovremennikov*, 151.

47. See Dominic Johnson, *Overconfidence and War: The Havoc and Glory of Positive Illusions* (Cambridge, MA: Harvard University Press, 2004). On Napoleon's views, see Bruno Colson, *Napoleon on War* (Oxford: Oxford University Press, 2015), 124–131.

48. Kutuzov to Nikolai Saltykov, August 23/September 4, 1812, in *M. I. Kutuzov. Sbornik dokumentov*, IV, part 1, 133; Kutuzov to his wife, August 19/31, 1812, in *The Kutuzov Papers* 2 (1872): 268.

49. Arsenii Zakrevskii to Mikhail Vorontsov, August 6/18, 1812, in *Arkhiv knyazya Voronstova*, XXXVII:231.

50. Radozhitskii, *Pokhodnye zapiski artillerista*, I:133. "The prospect of giving away the [ancient] capital without a battle horrified each and every Russian," commented Colonel Toll. "The commander in chief therefore decided to confront the enemy in battle." Karl von Toll, *Opisanie srazheniya pri sele Borodine 24–26 avgusta 1812 goda . . .* (St. Petersburg, 1839), 48–49. Toll's lengthy account needs to be considered very carefully because it contains many deliberate inaccuracies and embellishments, all designed to extol and aggrandize Kutuzov and Toll.

51. Eugene von Württemberg, *Aus dem Leben des kaiserlich-russischen Generals der Infanterie Prinzen Eugen von Württemberg* (Berlin: Hempel, 1862), II:34.

52. Kutuzov at first considered making a stand at Tsarevo-Zaimische and, as Barclay de Tolly himself acknowledged, "he found the position advantageous and ordered the construction works to be expedited." However, once he saw the extent of the problems in the army, he felt compelled to fall back. Barclay de Tolly, *Izobrazhenie*, 22–23. Bennigsen agreed that the position was not sufficiently "advantageous." Bennigsen, "Zapiski," 492.

53. Bagration to Rostopchin, n.d. [late August 1812], in Dubrovin, *Otechestvennaya voina v pis'makh sovremennikov*, 99.

54. Barclay de Tolly to Kutuzov, August 16/28, 1812, RGVIA, f. VUA, d. 3502, l. 172; Miloradovich to Emperor Alexander, August 18/30, 1812, in *M.*

I. Kutuzov. Sbornik dokumentov, IV, part 1, 94; Kutuzov to Rostopchin, August 20/September 1, 1812, in *M. I. Kutuzov. Sbornik dokumentov*, 110; Bogdanovich, *Istoriya Otechestvennoi voiny 1812 goda*, II:126.

55. Kutuzov to Rostopchin, August 17/29 and August 23/September 4, 1812, in *M. I. Kutuzov. Sbornik dokumentov*, IV, part 1, 90, 133.

56. Kutuzov to Lobanov-Rostovskii and Kleinmichel, August 19/31, 1812, in *Journal of the Outgoing Correspondence of the Commander in Chief*, 4–5. The "recruitment depots of the second line" were located at Staraya Russa, Toropets, Vyazma, Roslavl, and Sumy. Lobanov-Rostovskii and Kleinmichel supervised the formation of reserve units in Kostroma, Vladimir, Ryazan, Tambov, Yaroslavl, and Voronezh. Kutuzov to Lobanov-Rostovskii, August 19/31, 1812, *Journal of the Outgoing Correspondence of the Commander in Chief*, 101. On September 5, Emperor Alexander prohibited Kutuzov from using reserve forces at the recruitment depots, arguing that these troops had not been properly trained yet. He then advised Kutuzov that 120,000 Russians should be able to confront and defeat 165,000 Frenchmen. Alexander to Kutuzov, August 24/September 5, 1812, in *Journal of the Outgoing Correspondence of the Commander in Chief*, 138.

57. Kutuzov to Anna Khitrovo, August 19/31, 1812, in *M. I. Kutuzov. Sbornik dokumentov*, IV, part 1, 109.

58. Kutuzov to Chichagov, August 14/26 and August 20/September 1, 1812, in *M. I. Kutuzov. Sbornik dokumentov*, IV, part 1, 83–84, 113; Kutuzov to Tormasov, August 14/26, 1812, in *General Staff Archives*, XVI:66–67; Kutuzov to Tormasov, August 20/September 1, 1812, *Journal of the Outgoing Correspondence of the Commander in Chief*, 7–8.

59. Kutuzov to Barclay de Tolly, August 19/31, 1812, RGVIA, f. VUA, d. 3540, l. 32; Journal of Military Operations of the 1st and 2nd Western Armies, RGVIA, f. VUA, d. 3485, l. 43; Kutuzov to Barclay de Tolly and Bagration, August 20/September 1, in *Journal of the Outgoing Correspondence of the Commander in Chief*, 5.

60. Entry for August 20/September 1, 1812, in Puschin, *Dnevnik*.

61. Radozhitskii, *Pokhodnye zapiski artillerista*, I:134.

62. Kutuzov to Rostopchin, August 20/September 1, 1812, in N. Dubrovin, "Moskva i Graf Rostopchin v 1812 godu," *Voennyj sbornik* XXXII (1863): 143.

63. I. Bezsonov, "Russkie dostopamyatye lyudi," *Russkaya starina* 5 (1892): 234–235.

64. Kutuzov to Anna Khitrovo, August 19/31, 1812, in *M. I. Kutuzov. Sbornik dokumentov*, IV, part 1, 109. Kutuzov dictated the letter to his son-in-law Kudashev because he was feeling unwell and complained of eye pain.

65. Clausewitz, *Der Feldzug von 1812 in Russland*, 141–142.

66. Kutuzov to Rostopchin, August 31, 1812, in *M. I. Kutuzov. Sbornik dokumentov*, IV, part 1, 118–120.

67. Bagration to Rostopchin, August 22/September 3, 1812, in Dubrovin, *Otechestvennaya voina v pis'makh sovremennikov*, 109.

68. Wilson, *Narrative of Events During the Invasion of Russia*, 134–136.

69. Clausewitz, *Der Feldzug von 1812 in Russland*, 143.

70. For a detailed description of the area in English, see E. R. Holmes, *Borodino, 1812* (London: Hippocrene Books, 1971), 32–36.

71. Kutuzov to Alexander, August 23/September 4, 1812, in *M. I. Kutuzov. Sbornik dokumentov*, IV, part 1, 129.

72. Bennigsen, "Zapiski," 494.

73. Barclay de Tolly, *Izobrazhenie*, 24; Mikhail Vistitskii, "Iz zapisok Vistitskago," in Kharkevich, ed., *1812 god v dnevnikakh*, I:186; Clausewitz, *Der Feldzug von 1812 in Russland*, 142. Clausewitz thought that "the ground taken up by the left wing presented no particular advantages. Some hillocks with a gentle slope, and perhaps twenty feet high, together with strips of shrubby wood, formed so confused a whole, that it was difficult to pronounce which party would have the advantage of the ground. Thus, the best side of the position, the right wing, could be of no avail to redeem the defects of the left. The whole position too strongly indicated the left flank to the French as the object of operation, to admit of their forces being attracted to the right."

74. Mikhail Vistitskii, "Iz zapisok Vistitskago," in Kharkevich, ed., *1812 god v dnevnikakh*, I:186.

75. Kutuzov to Alexander, August 25/September 6, 1812, in *M. I. Kutuzov. Sbornik dokumentov*, IV, part 1, 144. Also see Kutuzov to Alexander, n.d. [ca. September 8, 1812], RGVIA, f. VUA, d. 3561, l. 52.

76. Heinrich von Brandt, *Souvenirs d'un officier polonais* (Paris: G. Charpentier, 1877), 270; Jean Sarrazin, *Histoire de la guerre d'Espagne et de Portugal de 1807 à 1814* (Paris: J. G. Dentu, 1814), xiv.

77. Kutuzov to Alexander, August 25/September 6, 1812, in *M. I. Kutuzov. Sbornik dokumentov*, IV, part 1, 144–145; Württemberg, *Aus dem Leben*, II:32–33; Vistitskii, "Iz zapisok Vistitskago," 186. The Shevardino Redoubt's purpose was the subject of a long debate among Russian historians. Buturlin, citing official reports, repeated Kutuzov's opinion that "the redoubt was built only to determine the direction of the advance of the French column." However this claim seems to have been put forth by Colonel Toll himself as a way to conceal his original mistake in arranging the armies. Other historians identified two main objectives for the redoubt: to prevent the French from "observing the entire disposition of the Russian troops" and "to delay the enemy advance along the main road by acting against his flank." However, not everyone shared such an interpretation. Historians M. Dragomirov, A. Witmer, G. Ratch, M. Bogdanovich, N. Polikarpov, A. Skugarevskii, A. Gerua, B. Kolyubkyin, and V. Kharkevich could not see how the Shevardino Redoubt could threaten the flank of the French army advancing along the main road since the fortification was located beyond the effective artillery range. The Soviet historians, meanwhile, wrote history as they saw fit. N. Garnich claimed that the

Shevardino Redoubt was designed to threaten the French flank and claimed Russian cannon could bombard the enemy at a distance of one and a half miles.

78. Alexey Yermolov, *The Czar's General: The Memoirs of a Russian General in the Napoleonic Wars*, translated and edited by Alexander Mikaberidze (Welwyn Garden City: Ravenhall Books, 2005), 154. Also see Avraam Norov, "Iz vospominanii," in *Borodino v vospominaniyakh sovremennikov* (St. Petersburg, 2001), 190.

79. Ivan Paskevich, "Zapiski Paskevicha," in Kharkevich, ed., *1812 god v dnevnikakh, zapiskakh*, I:100. Writing to his wife, Kutuzov also remarked that Napoleon "has been observed wearing his great overcoat." Kutuzov to E. Golenischeva-Kutuzova, August 25/September 6, 1812, in *The Kutuzov Papers* 5 (1872): 647.

80. Attestations du Docteur Ywan, in Philippe-Paul, Comte de Ségur, *Histoire et mémoires* (Paris: Didot Frères, 1873), VI:15.

81. Nikolai Mitarevskii, *Vospominaniya o voine 1812 goda* (Moscow: A. Mamontov, 1871), 54–55.

82. D. Neverovskii, "Iz zapisok . . . ," in *Borodino: dokumenty, pis'ma, vospominaniya*, edited by Liubomir Beskrovnyi and G. Mescheryakov (Moscow, 1962), 379.

83. "Rasskaz Georgievskogo Kavalera iz divizii Neverovskogo," *Chtenia imperatorskogo obschestva istorii drevnostei* 1 (1872): 119. Barclay de Tolly was enraged about the whole affair since he had previously requested that the redoubt be abandoned, and blamed Bennigsen for this failure, since "[he] had chosen the position and did not want to lose his face. Consequently, Bennigsen sacrificed six or seven thousand valiant soldiers and three cannon on September 5."

84. Order to the Armies, August 25/September 6, 1812, RGVIA, f. VUA, d. 3524, l.7.

85. Louis-François, Baron Lejeune, *Memoirs of Baron Lejeune, Aide-de-Camp to Marshals Berthier, Davout, and Oudinot* (New York: Longmans, Green, 1897), II:176.

86. Jean-Jacques Pelet, "Bataille de la Moskwa," in *Le spectateur militaire* VIII (1829): 112–118.

87. Klemens Kołaczkowski, *Wspomnienia jenerała Klemensa Kołaczkowskiego* (Krakow: Spółka Wydawnicza Polska, 1898), I:119–120.

88. Jean Rapp, *Mémoires du général Rapp, premier aide-de-camp de Napoléon* (Paris: Bossange Frères, 1823), 199–200.

89. Karl Friedrich Emil von Suckow, *Fragments de ma vie* (Paris, 1901), 178; Charles Pierre Pajol, *Pajol, général en chef* (Paris, 1874), 41; Jean François Boulart, *Mémoires militaires du général baron Boulart sur les guerres de la république et de l'empire* (Paris, 1892), 252.

90. Kutuzov to E. Kutuzova, August 25/September 6, 1812, in *The Kutuzov Papers* 5 (1872): 648.

91. Ségur, *Histoire et mémoires*, IV:362; Louis-Nicolas Davout, *Mémoires et souvenirs* (Paris, 1898), II:95; Adolphe Thiers, *Histoire du Consulat et de l'Empire* (Paris, 1845), VIII:130.

92. Ordre, September 7, 1812, in *Correspondance de Napoleon Ier, publ. par ordre de l'Empereur Napoléon III* (Paris: Henri Plon, 1863), no. 19181. For an interesting discussion, see Mariel Kukiel, "Les Polonais à la Moskova," *Revue des études napoléoniennes* 28 (1929): 28. Russian historian Bogdanovich pointed out, "Considering that Marshal Davout's proposal required nocturnal march in forested and unfamiliar terrain, one cannot but doubt the success of such an enterprise, which promised to be much harder to execute than the failed flanking maneuver of Junot at the Battle of Valutino." Bogdanovich, *Istoriya Otechestvennoi voiny 1812 goda*, II:166.

93. Disposition of the 1st and 2nd Armies, August 24/September 5, 1812, in *M. I. Kutuzov. Shornik dokumentov*, IV, part 1, 142.

94. Michael Josselson and Diana Josselon, *The Commander: A Life of Barclay de Tolly* (Oxford: Oxford University Press, 1980), 136.

95. The three clusters consisted of:
    • Kutuzov's main headquarters (including Chief of Staff Bennigsen, Quartermaster General Vistitskii, Colonel Toll, and Artillery Chief Major General Kutaisov), which remained around Gorki but kept a close watch over the army through a regular dispatch of orderlies and staff officers.
    • Barclay de Tolly's headquarters (including Chief of Staff Major General Yermolov, Duty General Colonel P. Kikin, Chief of Artillery Major General O. Bucholtz, and Engineer General Major Ch. Trousson, assisted by a small staff of officers), who all managed and supervised the deployment of the 1st Western Army on the right flank and center of the Russian positions.
    • Bagration and his staff officers (led by Chief of Staff Emmanuel St. Priest, Duty General Sergei Mayevskii, Chief of Artillery Major General Karl von Löwernstern, and Engineer Major General E. Förster).

96. He did make a crucial mistake. When Bagration was wounded, Kutuzov first sent Duke Alexander of Württemberg to take command of the 2nd Western Army, but then he gave command to General Dokhturov, only to realize that Miloradovich was more senior in rank (both were generals but promoted at different dates) and expected to lead the army. "After the battle Kutuzov profusely apologized to me that he had to deprive me of command and give it to Miloradovich since he was more senior in rank," Dokhturov confided to his wife. See his letter of September 12/24, 1812, in *Russkii arkhiv* 5 (1874): 1101–1102.

97. N. Garnich, *1812 god* (Moscow: Gos. Izd. Kult.-Prosvet. Literaturym, 1956), 140–141, 147–148, 150–190.

98. On the right wing, Kutuzov constructed the Maslovskie flèches (a pentagon-shaped redoubt with two lunettes), the Kriushinskii redoubt, five earthworks along the Kolocha River, two batteries near the village of Gorki and a larger, eight-cannon battery in front of the village of Borodino. For

details see B. Kolyubyakin, "Borodinskoe srazhenie i podgotovka polya srazheniya v inzhenernom otnoshenii," *Inzhenernyi zhurnal* 8 (1912): 907–962; A. Vefedovich, "Ukrepleniya na Borodinskom pole srazheniya 1812 g.," *Inzhenernyi zhurnal* 8 (1912): 963–984; Emmanuel St. Priest, "Bumagi grafa St. Priest," in Kharkevich, ed., *1812 god v dnevnikakh, zapiskakh*, I:150; Barclay de Tolly, *Izobrazhenie*, 25.

99. Radozhitskii, *Pokhodnye zapiski artillerista*, I:140.

100. Kutuzov to Alexander, August 23/September 4, 1812, in *M. I. Kutuzov. Sbornik dokumentov*, IV, part 1, 129. See also Disposition of 1st and 2nd Western Armies, August 24/September 5, 1812, in *M. I. Kutuzov. Sbornik dokumentov*, 143–144.

101. The Russian command structure also included the so-called *corps de bataille*, an ad hoc formation that served as an intermediary layer between army and corps commanders and offered employment to many senior officer who otherwise would have held no command. General Miloradovich commanded the *corps de bataille* of the right flank, which included the 2nd and 4th Corps and the cavalry of Uvarov and Korff, while Lieutenant General Gorchakov led the *corps de bataille* of the left flank, consisting of the 7th Corps and the 27th Division. Lieutenant General Golitsyn I was given command of the 1st and 2nd Cuirassier Divisions, which were deployed behind the 5th Corps.

102. On the northern edge of the Russian positions were the 2nd and 4th Corps, with Ataman Matvei Platov's Separate Cossacks Corps and the 2nd Cavalry Corps behind them in the reserves. General Dokhturov assumed command of the right center, comprising the 6th Corps and Major General P. Pahlen's 3rd Cavalry Corps, which held the high ground between the village of Gorki and Raevskii's redoubt. The 5th (Guard) Corps, supported by the 1st Cuirassier Division and the 1st Combined Grenadier Division, formed the main reserve behind the village of Knyazkovo; nearby stood the main artillery reserve of 306 cannon commanded by Colonel A. Euler. Lieutenant General Mikhail Borozdin's 8th Corps held the flèches, while Major General Mikhail Vorontsov's 2nd Combined Grenadier Division and Major General I. Duka's 2nd Cuirassier Division formed the left wing's main reserves; the artillery reserve of 168 cannon, led by Major General Karl von Löwernstern, stood near the village of Semeyonovskoe. Disposition of the 1st and 2nd Armies, August 24/September 5, 1812, in *M. I. Kutuzov. Sbornik dokumentov*, IV, part 1, 140–144; Kutuzov to Emperor Alexander, n.d. [September 8, 1812], RGVIA, f. VUA, d. 3561, ll. 53–54. Kutuzov's disposition is interesting for the instructions he shared with his subordinates. They were to do their best to preserve the reserves since "the general who saves the reserves remains unbeaten." "In case of an offensive, all movements must be done in attacking columns, in which case soldiers should not waste time firing but act swiftly with their cold steel arms."

103. "Rasskaz o Borodinskom srazhenii otdelennogo Unter-Ofitsera Tikhonova," *Chtenia imperatorskogo obschestva istorii drevnostei* I (1872): 119.

104. As the battle at Shevardino progressed, Bennigsen traveled south to meet Bagration, who shared his opinion that Napoleon would inevitably target his flank. "I promised to convey his concerns about the dangers facing this part of the army to the commander in chief. Returning to the headquarters, I delivered a detailed report to Kutuzov and suggested, as I did the day before, to shorten our left flank. Yet [Kutuzov made no decision] and everything was left as before." Bennigsen, "Zapiski," 495–496.

105. Bennigsen, "Zapiski," 499.

106. Pelet, "Bataille de la Moskwa," 123.

107. Lavrov to Dokhturov, September 3/15, 1812, RGVIA, f. VUA, d. 3561, l.30. In his report, Colonel A. Kutuzov of the Life Guard Izmailovskii Regiment states that he was ordered to leave the reserves at six o'clock in the morning. Kutuzov describes his unit encountering "a fierce cannonade that caused us great harm." Kutuzov to Lavrov, September 1/13, 1812, RGVIA, f. VUA, d. 3561, l. 34.

108. Kutuzov to Emperor Alexander, n.d. [September 8, 1812], RGVIA, f. VUA, d. 3561, l. 52.

109. Scherbinin, "Zapiski," 14–15. Also see Journal of Military Operations of the 1st and 2nd Western Armies, RGVIA, f. VUA, op. 16, d. 3485, l. 43b; Barclay de Tolly to Kutuzov, October 8, 1812, RGVIA, f. VUA, op. 16, d. 3561, l. 8; Kutuzov to Emperor Alexander, n.d. [September 8, 1812], RGVIA, f. VUA, d. 3561, l. 52.

110. Scherbinin, "Zapiski," 15–18.

111. Dmitrii Bolgovskii, "Iz vospominanii D. N. Bolgovskogo," in Kharkevich, ed., *1812 god v dnevnikakh, zapiskakh*, I:229–230.

112. Garnich, *1812 god*, 151.

113. For an interesting discussion, see A. Popov, "'Zasadnyi otryad' N. A. Tuchkova (somneniya v ochevidnom ili apologia Bennigsena)," in *Otechestvennaya voina 1812 goda: istochniki, pamyatniki, problemy* (Borodino, 1998), 122–143.

114. Bogdanovich, *Istoriya Otechestvennoi voiny 1812 goda*, II:171.

115. Yermolov's Order to the 1st Western Army, August 24/September 5, 1812, in *Borodino: Documenty, pisma, vospominaniya*, 84; Bagration's Order to the 2nd Western Army, August 25/September 6, 1812, in *General Bagration. Sbornik dokumentov i materialov*, edited by S. Golubov (Moscow: OGIZ, 1945), 241–242.

116. Fedor Glinka, *Ocherki Borodinskogo srazheniya* (Moscow: N. Stepanov, 1839), I:39.

117. N. Sukhanin, "Iz zjurnala uchastnika voiny 1812 goda," *Russkaya starina* 2 (1912): 281.

118. Johann Reinhold von Dreyling, "Vospominaniya...," in *1812 god: Vospominaniya voinov russkoi armii* (Moscow: Mysl', 1991), 373; Nikolai Muravyev, "Zapiski

N. N. Muravyeva," *Russkii arkhiv* 10 (1885): 251. Muravyev dates this incident to September 5.

119. Glinka, *Ocherki Borodinskogo srazheniya*, I:39.

120. Wilson, *Narrative of Events During the Invasion of Russia*, 134; Radozhitskii, *Pokhodnye zapiski artillerista*, I:140; Dimitrii Dushenkevich, "Iz moikh vospominanii ot 1812 to 1815 goda," in *1812 god v vospominaniyakh sovremennikov*, edited by A. Tartakovskii (Moscow: Nauka, 1985), 114.

121. Mitarevskii, *Vospominaniya o voine*, 51.

122. Eugene von Württemberg, *Aus dem Leben*, II:35.

123. Glinka, *Ocherki Borodinskogo srazheniya*, I:41.

124. Mitarevskii, *Vospominaniya o voine*, 55–56.

Chapter 23

1. Alexey Yermolov, *The Czar's General: The Memoirs of a Russian General in the Napoleonic Wars*, translated and edited by Alexander Mikaberidze (Welwyn Garden City: Ravenhall Books, 2005), 155.

2. Auguste Thirion de Metz, *Souvenirs militaires* (Paris: Berger-Levrault, 1892), 182.

3. Waldermar de Löwenstern, "Zapiski generala V. I. Löwensterna," *Russkaya starina* 12 (1900): 573. Also see Michael Josselson and Diana Josselson, *The Commander: A Life of Barclay de Tolly* (Oxford: Oxford University Press, 1980), 137–138.

4. Modest Bogdanovich, *Istoriya otechestvennoi voiny 1812 goda po dostovernym istochnikam* (St. Petersburg: S. Strugovshikov, 1859), II:177.

5. Carl von Clausewitz, *Der Feldzug von 1812 in Russland, der Feldzug von 1813 bis zum Waffenstillstand und der Feldzug von 1814 in Frankreich*, edited by Marie von Clausewitz (Berlin: Ferdinand Dümmler, 1835), 135–136.

6. The Russian command structure at Borodino included an additional tier between corps and army commanders: on the right, General Mikhail Miloradovich commanded a *corps de bataille* that gave him jurisdiction over the corps of Baggovut (2nd) and Ostermann-Tolstoy (4th) and the cavalry of Uvarov (1st Cavalry Corps) and Korff (2nd Cavalry Corps). Similarly, Rayevskii's 7th Corps, Borozdin's 8th Corps, and Sievers's 4th Cavalry Corps came under the authority of Prince Andrei Gorchakov's *corps de bataille*; on the left, Dokhturov had authority over his own 6th Corps and Kreutz's 3rd Cavalry Corps cavalry. Grand Duke Constantine commanded the reserve.

7. Philippe-Paul, Comte de Ségur, *Histoire de Napoléon et de la Grande-Armée pendant l'année 1812* (Paris: Baudouin Frères, 1824), I:379–380.

8. Ségur, *Histoire de Napoléon et de la Grande-Armée*, I:381.

9. Proclamation of September 7, 1812, in *Correspondance de Napoleon Ier, publ. par ordre de l'Empereur Napoléon III* (Paris: Henri Plon, 1863), no. 19182, 207.

10. Cesare de Laugier, *Gl'italiani in Russia: memorie di un ufiziale italiano per servire alla storia della Russia, della Polonia, e dell'Italia nel 1812* (Florence: n.p.,

1826), III:49; Charles-Pierre-Lubin Griois, *Mémoires du Général Griois, 1792–1822* (Paris: Plon-Nourrit, 1909), II:33; Georges de Chambray, *Histoire de l'expédition de Russie* (Paris: Pillet Ainé, 1823), I:298.

11. There are many interesting studies on the Battle of Borodino, but I found most detailed and useful the recent Russian series of books by A. Popov, I. Vasil'ev, and V. Zemtsov: I. Vasil'ev, *Borodino: yuzhnyj flang* (Moscow: Kniga, 2009); V. Zemtsov and A. Popov, *Borodino: severnyj flang* (Moscow: Kniga, 2008); V. Zemtsov and A. Popov, *Borodino: tsentr* (Moscow: Kniga, 2009); V. Zemtsov and A. Popov, *Borodino: yuzhnyj flang* (Moscow: Kniga, 2010); V. Zemtsov, *Bitva pri Moskve-reke: armiya Napoleona v Borodinskom srazhenii* (Moscow, 2001).

12. Ilya Radozhitskii, *Pokhodnye zapiski artillerista s 1812 po 1816 god* (Moscow: Instit. Vost. Yazyk., 1835), I:143. Also see I. S. Tikhonov, "Ob ustanovlenii neizvestnogo avtora vospominanii 'Istoricheskie svedenia o Borodinskom srazhenii,'" in *Otechestvennaia voina 1812 goda. Rossia i Evropa* (Borodino, 1992), 16–20.

13. Roman Soltyk, *Napoléon en 1812. Mémoires historiques et militaires sur la campagne de Russie* (Paris: A. Bertrand, 1836), 218.

14. Radozhitskii, *Pokhodnye zapiski artillerista*, I:143.

15. Johann Reinhold von Dreyling, "Vospominaniya . . . ," in *1812 god: Vospominaniya voinov russkoi armii* (Moscow: Mysl', 1991), 375. Also see Alexander Mikhailovskii-Danilevskii, "Zapiski A. I. Mikhailovskago-Danilevskago," *Istoricheskii vestnik* 10 (1890): 144.

16. Kutuzov states that the French movement toward Borodino commenced at "four o'clock after midnight." Kutuzov to Emperor Alexander, n.d. [September 8, 1812], RGVIA, f. VUA, d. 3561, l. 52b. For a detailed discussion of events at Borodino, see A. Popov, *Borodino: severnyi flang* (Moscow, 2008), 6–28; Alexander Mikaberidze, *The Battle of Borodino: Napoleon Against Kutuzov* (Barnsley: Pen & Sword, 2010), 92–99.

17. Pavel Grabbe, *Iz pamyatnykh zapisok grafa Pavla Khristoforovicha Grabbe* (Moscow: Katkov, 1873), 73.

18. Kutuzov to Emperor Alexander, n.d. [September 8, 1812], RGVIA, f. VUA, d. 3561, l. 52b; Grabbe, *Iz pamyatnykh zapisok*, 75; Mikhail Barclay de Tolly, *Izobrazhenie voennykh deistvii 1-oi armii v 1812 godu* (St. Petersburg: P. Soikin, 1912), 27.

19. Russian participants derided Colonel Makarov, who commanded the jäger battalion at Borodino and allowed such carelessness. Staff officer Nikolai Durnovo lamented that "Makarov was in a state of such intoxication that it was simply unpardonable for a commander." Pavel Puschin of the Life Guard Semeyonovskii Regiment was also very critical of the leadership of the Life Guard Jäger Regiment that resulted in the loss of so many lives. "Our jägers, joining us in the morning, earned severe reprimand for their carelessness and inattentiveness on advance posts as a result of which the

NOTES TO PAGES 380–383 | 683

enemy inflicted such heavy casualties on them." In their reports, Kutuzov and other senior officers made no mention of the negligence at Borodino and avoided criticizing the Life Guard Jäger Regiment, one of the elite units of the Russian army; Makarov, who was accused of such gross ineptitude, was later awarded the Order of St. Vladimir (third class) and given command of another elite unit, the famous Pavlograd Grenadiers. The whole affair was largely suppressed in official histories but survived in personal memoirs and letters of participants. See Yermolov, *The Czar's General*, 157; N. Nikolai Durnovo, "Dnevnik 1812 g.," in *1812 god: voennye dnevniki* (Moscow, 1990), 107; Pavel Puschin, *Diaries of the 1812–1814 Campaigns*, translated and edited by A. Mikaberidze (Tbilisi: NSG, 2011), 45; M. Petrov, "Rasskazy sluzhivshego v 1-m egerskom polku polkovnika Mikhaila Petrova o voennoi sluzhbe i zhizni svoeji," in *1812 god: Vospominaniya voinov russkoi armii*, 181–182; I. Liprandi, "Zamechaniya na vtoroi tom," in *Voina 1812 goda: Zamechaniya na knigu 'Istoriya Otechestvennoi voiny 1812 goda po dostovernym istochnikam' soch. G.-M. Bogdanovicha* (Moscow: University Tip., 1869), 28–29. In 1812, Liprandi served as the ober-quartermaster of the 6th Corps.

20. Waldemar de Löwenstern, *Mémoires du général-major russe Baron de Löwenstern (1776–1858)* (Paris: A. Fontemoing, 1903), I:254–255. The Life Guard Jäger Regiment lost almost 40 percent of its roster that morning.

21. For the most egregious example, see Pavel Zhilin, *Borodino 1812* (Moscow: Mysl', 1987), 112–115.

22. Ségur, *Histoire de Napoléon et de la Grande Armée*, I:383.

23. Mikhail Orlov, "Capitulation of Paris in 1814: Razskaz M. F. Orlova," *Russkaya starina* 12 (1877): 647.

24. Kutuzov to Emperor Alexander, n.d. [September 8, 1812], RGVIA, f. VUA, d. 3561, l. 53; Lavrov to Dokhturov, September 3/15, 1812, RGVIA, f. VUA, d. 3561, l. 30; Udom to Lavrov, August 31/September 12, 1812, in *M. I. Kutuzov. Sbornik dokumentov* (Moscow: Voeniszdat, 1950), IV, part 1, 146–147.

25. Barclay de Tolly, *Izobrazhenie*, 28. These must have been the Life Guard Izmailovskii and Litovskii Regiments, reinforced by a combined grenadier brigade, that were detached from the reserves around 5:30 a.m. Lavrov to Dokhturov, September 3/15, 1812, RGVIA, f. VUA, d. 3561, l. 30.

26. Löwenstern, *Mémoires*, I:256.

27. Löwenstern, *Mémoires*, I:261.

28. Löwenstern, *Mémoires*, I:262–263.

29. Löwenstern, "Zapiski," 575.

30. Levin von Bennigsen, "Zapiski . . . ," *Russkaya starina* 9 (1909): 497.

31. Kutuzov to Emperor Alexander, [September 8, 1812], RGVIA, f. VUA, d. 3561, l. 54b. Vistitskii states that Kutuzov agreed to move troops from the right to the left after Bagration's third appeal. Mikhail Vistitskii, "Iz zapisok Vistitskago," in V. Kharkevich, ed., *1812 god v dnevnikakh, zapiskakh*

i vospominaniyakh sovremennikov (Vilna: Tip. Shtaba Vilen. Voen. Okruga, 1900), I:187.

32. Kutuzov to Emperor Alexander, n.d. [September 8, 1812], RGVIA, f. VUA, d. 3561, l. 52.

33. Bagration to Alexander, August 27/September 8, 1812, no. 488, in *Borodino: dokumenty, pis'ma, vospominaniya*, edited by Liubomir Beskrovnyi and G. Mescheryakov (Moscow, 1962), 110.

34. Nikolai Andreyev, "Iz vospominanii Nikolaya Ivanovicha Andreyeva," *Russkii arkhiv* 10 (1879): 192.

35. Vorontsov, "Iz vospominanii grava Vorontsova," in Kharkevich, ed., *1812 god v dnevnikakh*, I:204. The Combined Grenadier Division, which counted 4,059 men in its eleven battalions on the eve of the battle, sustained a staggering 62percent loss, with 526 killed, 1,224 wounded, and 750 missing; it tallied only 1,559 men (95 out of 243 NCOs), or 38percent of its fighting force, by September 18.

36. Jean Rapp, *Memoirs of General Count Rapp, First Aide-de-Camp to Napoleon* (London: H. Colburn, 1823), 205.

37. Fedor Glinka, *Ocherki Borodinskogo srazheniya* (Moscow: N. Stepanov, 1839), II:72.

38. Dimitrii Dushenkevich, "Iz moikh vospominanii ot 1812 to 1815 goda," in *1812 god v vospominaniyakh sovremennikov*, edited by A. Tartakovskii (Moscow: Nauka, 1985), 114.

39. Yermolov, *The Czar's General*, 158.

40. Apolinarii Butenev, *Diplomat pri armii knyazya Bagrationa: Vospominaniya A. P. Buteneva o 1812 gode* (Moscow: [n.p.], 1911), 41. Bagration was lightly wounded in 1799 and 1807.

41. Vistitskii, "Iz zapisok Vistitskago," 188. Also see Kutuzov to Emperor Alexander, n.d. [September 8, 1812], RGVIA, f. VUA, d. 3561, ll. 54b–55; Barclay de Tolly, *Izobrazhenie*, 28.

42. Kutuzov did praise Konovnitsyn for stabilizing the front line—Bagration's death "could have had the most ruinous effects if Konovnitsyn did not assume command under Dokhturov's arrival." Kutuzov to Emperor Alexander, n.d. [September 8, 1812], RGVIA, f. VUA, d. 3561, ll. 54b–55.

43. Nikolai Lubenkov, *Rasskaz artillerista o dele Borodinskom* (St. Petersburg: E. Pratz, 1837), 49–50.

44. Nikolai Rayevskii, "Iz zapisok N. N. Rayevskogo ob Otechestvennoi voine 1812 goda," in *Borodino: dokumenty, pis'ma, vospominaniya*, 380.

45. Griois, *Mémoires*, II:36.

46. Alexander Mikhailovskii-Danilevskii, *Opisanie Otechestvennoi voiny 1812 goda* (St. Petersburg, 1843), II:226–227; Clausewitz, *Der Feldzug von 1812 in Russland*, 152.

47. Bonnamy was captured by Feldfebel Zolotov of the 18th Jägers, who was promoted to sub-lieutenant after the battle. Kutuzov's Order to the Army, September 9, 1812, no. 11, RGVIA, f. VUA, d. 3524, l. 8; Kutuzov to

Alexander, n.d. [September 1812], RGVIA, f. VUA, d. 3561, l. 56. Meshetich and Radozhitskii claim a soldier "dragged" the French general to Kutuzov, who rewarded the soldier with the St. George Cross, but they might be confusing this incident with another involving a jäger who, according to Muravyev, captured a French staff officer at the village of Borodino and brought him to Kutuzov. Gavriil Meshetich, "Istoricheskie zapiski voiny rossiyan s frantsuzami i dvadtsatyu plemenami 1812, 1813, 1814 i 1815 godov," in *1812 god: vospominaniya voinov russkoi armii*, 48; Radozhitskii, *Pokhodnye zapiski artillerista*, I, 144–145; Muravyev, "Zapiski," *Russkii arkhiv* 10 (1885): 255.

48. General Yermolov arranged for Bonammy to be conveyed to his "family estate in Orel and asked my father to take particular care of him." Yermolov, *The Czar's General*, 160–161.

49. Grabbe, "Iz pamyatnykh zapisok," 78; Nikolai Divov, "Iz vospominaniii N. A. Divova," *Russkii arkhiv* 7 (1873): 01337–01338.

50. Adam Zamoyski, *1812: Napoleon's Fatal March on Moscow* (London: HarperCollins, 2004), 274.

51. For further discussion, see A. Larionov, "Ispol'zovanie artillerii v Borodinskom srazhenii," in *1812 god: sbornik statei* (Moscow, 1962), 130–131; Ivan Liprandi, *Materialy dlya Otechestvennoi voiny 1812 goda* (St. Petersburg, 1867), 112–114.

52. "It seemed Napoleon was trying to destroy us with his artillery," remarked Barclay de Tolly. See *Izobrazhenie*, 30.

53. For an excellent discussion, see V. Zemtsov and A. Popov, *Borodino: yuzhnyi flang* (Moscow: Kniga, 2009), 58–101.

54. Clausewitz, *Der Feldzug von 1812 in Russland*, 151.

55. Clausewitz, *Der Feldzug von 1812 in Russland*, 151–152.

56. Clausewitz, *Der Feldzug von 1812 in Russland*, 153.

57. Mikhailovskii-Danilevskii, *Opisanie Otechestvennoi voiny*, III:255.

58. N. Garnich, *1812 god* (Moscow: Gos. Izd. Kult.-Prosvet. Literaturym, 1956), 167.

59. Barclay de Tolly, *Izobrazhenie*, 32.

60. Clausewitz, *Der Feldzug von 1812 in Russland*, 154.

61. A. Golitsyn, "Iz vospominanii A. B. Golitsyna," in *Borodino: dokumenty, pis'ma, vospominaniya*, 343.

62. Kutuzov to Alexander, November 22/December 4, 1812, in *M. I. Kutuzov. Sbornik dokumentov*, IV, part 1, 219.

63. Vorontsov to Longinov, October 20/November 1, 1812, in N. Dubrovin, ed., *Otechestvennaya voina v pis'makh sovremennikov* (St. Petersburg, 1882), 264.

64. Muravyev, "Zapiski," 257; Mikhailovskii-Danilevskii, "Zapiski," 154. Also see Alexander Scherbinin, "Zapiski Aleksandra Scherbinina," in V. Kharkevich, ed., *1812 god v dnevnikakh, zapiskakh i vospominaniyakh sovremennikov* (Vilna: Tip. Shtaba Vilen. Voen. Okruga, 1900), I:22.

65. Mikhailovskii-Danilevskii, *Opisanie Otechestvennoi voiny*, III:257.

66. Garnich, *1812 god*, 167. Also see Pavel Zhilin, *Kutuzov. Zhizn' i polkovodcheskaya deyatel'nost'* (Moscow: Voennoe Izdatel'stvo, 1978), 180; *M. I. Kutuzov. Sbornik dokumentov*, IV, part 1, xvi.

67. Eugene Labaume, *A Circumstantial Narrative of the Campaign in Russia* (London: S. Leigh, 1815), 140.

68. Radozhitskii, *Pokhodnye zapiski artillerista*, I, 148.

69. Griois, *Mémoires*, II:37.

70. Franz Ludwig August Meerheimb and Richard von Meerheimb, *Erlebnisse eines Veteranen der grossen Armee wahrend des Feldzuges in Russland, 1812* (Dresden: Meinhold, 1860), 101.

71. Louis-François, Baron Lejeune, *Memoirs of Baron Lejeune, Aide-de-Camp to Marshals Berthier, Davout, and Oudinot* (New York: Longmans, Green, 1897), II:182.

72. Ségur, *Histoire de Napoléon et de la Grande-Armée*, I:402.

73. Labaume, *Circumstantial Narrative of the Campaign in Russia*, 141.

74. Barclay de Tolly, *Izobrazhenie*, 31.

75. Kutuzov to Alexander, n.d. [September 1812], RGVIA, f. VUA, d. 3561, ll. 56b–57; "Opisaniye srazheniya pri sele Borodine," *General Staff Archives*, XVI:117.

76. Mikhailovskii-Danilevskii, *Opisanie Otechestvennoi voiny*, III:261.

77. Löwerstern, "Zapiski," 578.

78. Meshetich, "Istoricheskie zapiski," 49.

79. Ségur, *Histoire et mémoires*, IV:395–396; Gaspard Gourgaud, *Napoleon and the Grand Army in Russia* (London: M. Bossange, 1825), 212.

80. Clausewitz, *Der Feldzug von 1812 in Russland*, 158.

81. Mikhail Petrov, "Rasskazy sluzhivshego v 1-m egerskom polku polkovnika Mikhail Petrova o voennoi sluzhbe," in *1812 god: vospominaniya voinov russkoi armii*, 185.

82. Ludwig Wolzogen und Neuhaus, *Memoiren des Königlich Preussischen Generals der Infanterie Ludwig Freiherrn von Wolzogen* (Leipzig, 1851), 145–146.

83. Golitsyn, "Iz vospominanii," 344.

84. Rayevskii, "Iz zapisok," 382.

85. "From all the movements of the enemy, I conclude that he has been weakened no less than us during this battle, and that is why I have decided this night to draw up the army in order, to supply the artillery with fresh ammunition, and in the morning to renew the battle with the enemy." Kutuzov to Barclay de Tolly and Dokhturov, September 7, 1812, in *Borodino: dokumenty, pisma, vospominanya*, 96–97.

86. Golitsyn, "Iz vospominanii," 344.

87. The 1st Western Army suffered the largest casualties (21,727 men), but the 2nd Western Army, with 16,845 killed and wounded, sustained a higher percentage of losses. Their combined casualties total 38,569 men, a figure that is often cited in Soviet studies. However, this number is misleading, since it does not account for casualties among officers, *opolchenye*, and Cossack forces.

Yet another dossier, containing reports on the Russian casualties for the 1812–1814 campaigns, includes a report on the actions of September 5–7 showing 6 generals and 166 officers killed, 23 generals and 438 officers wounded, and up to 45,000 soldiers dead or injured.

88. Barclay de Tolly, *Izobrazhenie*, 33.

89. *M. I. Kutuzov. Sbornik dokumentov*, IV, part 1, xvi.

90. Muravyev, "Zapiski," 250. Clausewitz pointed out the density of the Russian deployment: "They were disposed in two lines with a third and fourth line of cavalry behind, and a third besides of their whole force as reserve. If we reflect that the first position of the Russians occupied only some 8,000 paces in extent, that the five corps which formed the first line were 40,000 strong, thus 20,000 in each line, and if we consider also the great proportion of artillery (six pieces to 1,000 men), we shall see that the disposition was very deep. If we further consider that the corps of Baggowut and Ostermann, being found useless on the right wing, were subsequently removed thence and brought to the support of other points, and were in fact used as reserves." Clausewitz, *Der Feldzug von 1812 in Russland*, 145.

91. Clausewitz, *Der Feldzug von 1812 in Russland*, 135.

92. Jean-Jacques Pelet, "Bataille de la Moskwa," *Le spectateur militaire* VIII (1829): 146.

93. "Précis des guerres de Frédéric II," *Correspondance de Napoléon*, XXXII:231.

94. Konovnitsyn to his wife, August 27/September 8, 1812, in P. Schukin, ed., *Bumagi otnosyaschiyasya do Otechestvennoi voiny 1812 goda* (Moscow: A. Mamontov, 1904), VIII:109–110. "There is nothing to say about the events of [the Battle of Borodino]," observed General Peter Kaptsevich of the 7th Infantry Division. "This was a sheer hell that lasted fourteen hours." Kaptsevich to Arakcheyev, September 6/18, 1812, in Dubrovin, *Otechestvennaya voina v pis'makh sovremennikov*, 126.

95. Löwenstern, "Zapiski," 581.

96. Pavel Grabbe, "Iz pamyantnykh zapisok Grafa P. Kh. Grabbe: 1812 god," *Russkii arkhiv* 3 (1873): 464–465.

97. Bennigsen, "Zapiski," 499; Mikhailovskii-Danilevskii, *Opisanie Otechestvennoi voiny*, II:281–283.

98. Kutuzov to D. Troshinskii, October 28/November 9, 1812, in *M. I. Kutuzov. Sbornik dokumentov*, IV, part II, 225.

99. Kutuzov to Rostopchin, August 26/September 7, 1812, in *Borodino: dokumenty, pisma, vospominanya*, 97.

100. Kutuzov to Alexander, August 27/September 8, 1812, in *M. I. Kutuzov. Sbornik dokumentov*, IV, part 1, 154–155; Official News from the Army, September 1812, RGVIA, f. VUA, d. 3652, ll. 48–49. The Official News also alleged that Kutuzov had dispatched Platov to "chase the enemy and [the Cossacks] caught up with the [French] rear guard eleven *verstas* from Borodino," a claim that Soviet historians were only too eager to repeat and elaborate in later years.

101. Kutuzov to his wife, August 29/September 9, 1812, in *The Kutuzov Papers* 2 (1872): 269.

102. Ivan Odenthal to Alexander Bulgakov, September 3/15, 1812, in *Russkaya starina* 9 (1912): 289.

103. Robert Ker Porter, *A Narrative of the Campaign in Russia, During the Year 1812* (London: Longman, 1814), 152–153.

104. John Quincy Adams, *Memoirs of John Quincy Adams Containing His Diary from 1795 to 1848*, edited by Charles Francis Adams (Philadelphia: Lippincott, 1874), 411.

105. Soldiers received the payments in late September. See Kutuzov to Kankrin, September 9/21, 1812, in *Journal of the Outgoing Correspondence of the Commander in Chief*, 23.

106. Ekaterina Golenischeva-Kutuzova's letter to Madame de Staël, cited in Yu. Gulyaev and V. Soglaev, *Fel'dmarshal Kutuzov. Istoriko-biograficheskii ocherk* (Moscow: Arkheograficheskii Tsentr, 1995), 316.

Chapter 24

1. Pavel Grabbe, "Iz pamyantnykh zapisok Grafa P. Kh. Grabbe: 1812 god," *Russkii arkhiv* 3 (1873): 467–468; Mikhail Barclay de Tolly, *Izobrazhenie voennykh deistvii 1-oi armii v 1812 godu* (St. Petersburg: P. Soikin, 1912), 33–34.

2. He spoke of the "troops without guides oftentimes stopping for several hours upon encountering destroyed bridges or when passing through defiles and villages; oftentimes [engineers] tasked with repairing road instead created obstacles with their pontoons, wagons with instruments and the *opolchenye* carts . . . the troops, unaware where they should stop for the night, had to wander round until, exhausted, they threw themselves into the mud to spend the night." Barclay de Tolly, *Izobrazhenie*, 34.

3. Modest Bogdanovich, *Istoriya otechestvennoi voiny 1812 goda po dostovernym istochnikam* (St. Petersburg: S. Strugovshikov, 1859), II:236.

4. Georges de Chambray, *Histoire de l'expedition de Russie* (Paris: Pillet Ainé, 1823), II:82.

5. Louis-François Bausset-Roquefort, *Mémoires anecdotiques . . .* (Paris, 1829), II:110.

6. Vorontsov to Longinov, October 20/November 1, 1812, in N. Dubrovin, ed., *Otechestvennaya voina v pis'makh sovremennikov* (St. Petersburg, 1882), 265.

7. "I did not realize that Platov was such a shithead [*govnyuk*]," Kutuzov remarked. Alexander Mikhailovskii-Danilevskii, "Zapiski A. I. Mikhailovskago-Danilevskago," *Istoricheskii vestnik* 10 (1890): 146; Vorontsov to Longinov, October 20/November 1, 1812, in Dubrovin, *Otechestvennaya voina v pis'makh sovremennikov*, 264–265.

8. For an interesting discussion of Russian conservative circles, to which Rostopchin belonged, see Alexander Martin, *Romantics, Reformers, Reactionaries: Russian Conservative Thought and Politics in the Reign of Alexander I* (DeKalb: Northern Illinois University Press, 1997).

9. Alexander Bulgakov, *Vospominaniya A. Ya. Bulgakova o 1812 gode i vechernikh besedakh u grafa Fedora Vasilievicha Rostopchina* (St. Petersburg: M. Stasyulevich, 1904), 2–3. The emperor justified his initial refusals by noting that Rostopchin held a civil position, that of chief chamberlain, and thus could not be appointed to the position of governor of Moscow, which required the holder to wear a military uniform. "And this is the only insurmountable obstacle?" the grand duchess observed cannily. "This seems to be a simple task for a tailor."

10. M. Evreinov, "Pamyat' 1812 g," *Russkii arkhiv* 1 (1874): 95; Bulgakov, *Vospominaniya*, 98–135.

11. *Afishy 1812 goda, ili druzheskie poslaniya ot glavnokomanduyushego v Moskve k zhitelyam eye*, 1812 Internet Project, http://www.museum.ru/1812/Library/Rostopchin/index.html.

12. Fedor Rostopchin, "Tysyacha vosemsot dvenadtsatyi god v zapiskakh grafa F. V. Rostopchina," *Russkaya starina* 12 (1889): 655. Also see Fedor Rostopchin, *Okh, frantsuzy!*, edited by G. Ovchinnikov (Moscow: Sovetskaya Rossia, 1992), e-version http://az.lib.ru/r/rostopchin_f_w/text_0190.shtml.

13. S. Melgunov, "Rostopchin—Moskovskii glavnokomanduyushii," in *Otechestvennaya voina i Russkoe obschestvo* (Moscow, 1911), IV:36.

14. Bulgakov, *Vospominaniya*, 103. "Next to his cabinet there was a small dark room, where, as the French saying goes, even the king has to walk. Inside this privy room, there was a beautiful bronze bust of Napoleon. A slim plank nailed to the imperial head held a porcelain vessel that was so necessary for visitors seeking to relieve their natural needs." Rostopchin's wife, who had converted to Catholicism, tried her best to save Napoleon, a fellow Catholic, from this unsavory fate. But her argument that Napoleon was a crowned head blessed by the Pope himself had no impact on Rostopchin, who continued to use the bust for the abovementioned purpose.

15. Rostopchin, "Tysyacha vosemsot dvenadtsatyi god," 706–707.

16. Louise Fusil, *Souvenirs d'une actrice* (Paris: Dumont, 1841), II:269.

17. Kutuzov to Rostopchin, August 17/29, 1812, in *Fel'dmarshal Kutuzov: dokumenty, dnevniki, vospominaniya*, edited by A. Val'kovich and A. Kapitonov (Moscow: Arkheog. Tsentr., 1995), 168; Kutuzov to Rostopchin, n.d. [ca. September 1–2, 1812], in *Feldmarshal Kutuzov. Sbornik dokumentov i materialov* (Moscow, 1947), 156–157; Nikolai Dubrovin, "Moskva i Graf Rastopchin v 1812 godu," *Voennyi sbornik* 7 (1863): 148.

18. Kutuzov to Rostopchin, September 2, 1812, *Borodino: dokumenty, pis'ma, vospominaniya*, edited by Liubomir Beskrovnyi and G. Mescheryakov (Moscow, 1962), 54. On September 1, Kutuzov urged Chichagov to intensify his effort to threaten Napoleon's line of communications. "Upon joining the army, I found the enemy in the very heart of the ancient Russia, one may say, at the gates of Moscow. My current objective is to save Moscow and I do not think I need to explain that the task of saving a few remote Polish provinces cannot be compared in any way with the saving of the

ancient capital city and the heartlands." *Journal of the Outgoing Correspondence of the Commander in Chief*, 8.

19. Rostopchin to Kutuzov, August 31, 1812, in *Russkaya starina* II (1870): 305.

20. Kutuzov to Rostopchin, August 22/September 3, 1812, in Dubrovin, *Otechestvennaia voina v pis'makh sovremennikov*, 108.

21. Rostopchin to Peter Tolstoy, August 24/September 5, 1812, in *Pamyatniki novoi russkoi istorii* (St. Petersburg: Maikov, 1872), II:183.

22. Kutuzov to Rostopchin, August 26/September 7, 1812, in *Journal of the Outgoing Correspondence of the Commander in Chief*, 12, 14.

23. Rostopchin, "Tysyacha vosemsot dvenadtsatyi god," 706.

24. Kutuzov to Rostopchin, August 27/September 8, 1812, in *M. I. Kutuzov. Sbornik dokumentov* (Moscow: Voeniszdat, 1950), IV, part 1, 155–156; *Journal of the Outgoing Correspondence of the Commander in Chief*, 12–13. The governor later wrote that he would have remained unaware of the Russian retreat if not for "the courier's slip of the tongue when he accidentally mentioned that our troops were at Mozhaisk, that is, already ten *verstas* from the battlefield." However, Kutuzov's letter (no. 71) clearly informed him of the army redeployment to Mozhaisk. Rostopchin, "Tysyacha vosemsot dvenadtsatyi god," 706.

25. Kutuzov to Lobanov-Rostovskii, August 19/31, 1812; Alexander to Kutuzov, August 24/September 5, 1812, in *M. I. Kutuzov. Sbornik dokumentov*, IV, part 1, 101, 138.

26. Iraklii Markov to Peter Volkonskii, January 20/February 1, 1813, in *M. I. Kutuzov. Sbornik dokumentov*, IV, part 1, 461–463. This latter-day accounting of what had happened in September 1812 shows that 24,267 men of the "Moscow Force" joined the army after Borodino.

27. Kutuzov to Rostopchin, August 27/September 8, 1812, in *M. I. Kutuzov. Sbornik dokumentov*, IV, part 1, 158.

28. "Although the battle has been conclusively won [*sovershenno vyigrana*]," he wrote to Rostopchin, "my intention is . . . to gather as many reinforcements as possible and to confront the already defeated enemy in a decisive battle near Moscow." Kutuzov to Rostopchin, August 27/September 8, 1812, in *M. I. Kutuzov. Sbornik dokumentov*, IV, part 1, 158–159.

29. Kutuzov to Rostopchin, August 30/September 11, 1812, *Journal of the Outgoing Correspondence of the Commander-in-Chief*, 15.

30. Rostopchin, "Tysyacha vosemsot dvenadtsatyi god," 707. He complained that "Kutuzov had sent me ten letters providing to defend Moscow and that the future of Russia is innately intertwined with the fate of this city." Rostopchin to Peter Tolstoy, September 13/25, 1812, in *Pamyatniki novoi russkoi istorii*, II:184–185.

31. Dmitri Sverbeyev, *Zapiski* . . . (Moscow, 1899), I:438–439. "I cannot envision the enemy reaching Moscow," Rostopchin told Bagration on August 24. See his letter in *Russkii vestnik* 2 (1842): 257.

32. Rostopchin to Balashov, September 10, 1812, in *Borodino: dokumenty, pis'ma, vospominaniya*, 85.

33. "The foreigners here cannot be damped down," he reported on September 10. "Just yesterday one of them openly called for an uprising, describing various things that Bonaparte would do here, and berating His Majesty the Emperor. Because of the extraordinary circumstances, the people are angry and are not satisfied with my leniency toward the foreigners, thus the day after tomorrow I shall have that foreigner hanged with the help of a horse cart for the disturbance." Rostopchin to Balashov, September 10, 1812, in *Borodino: dokumenty, pis'ma, vospominaniya*, 85.

34. Rostopchin to Balashov, September 10, 1812, in *Borodino: dokumenty, pis'ma, vospominaniya*, 85.

35. Broadsheet no. 14, August 30/September 11, 1812, *Afishy 1812 goda*, 1812 Internet Project, http://www.museum.ru/1812/Library/Rostopchin/index.html.

36. *Pis'ma 1812 goda M. A. Volkovoi k V. A. Lanskoi* (Moscow, 1990), http://az.lib .ru/w/wolkowa_m_a/text_0010. shtml.

37. A. Bestuzhev-Ryumin, "Proizshestviya v stolitse Moskve do vtorzheniya v onuyu nepriyatelya," in *Chteniya v Imperatorskom Moskovskom obshestve istorii i drevnosti* 2 (1859), V:81, 84.

38. Ilya Radozhitskii, *Pokhodnye zapiski artillerista s 1812 po 1816 god* (Moscow: Instit. Vost. Yazyk., 1835), I:88–89.

39. Semen Klimych, "Moskovskii Novodevichii monastyr' v 1812 godu. Razskaz ochevidtsa—shtatnogo sluzhitelya Semena Klimycha," *Russkii arkhiv*, 1864, 417.

40. No. 15 Broadsheet, August 11, 1812, in *Afishy 1812 goda*, http://www.mus eum.ru/museum/1812/Library/rostopchin/.

41. Bestuzhev-Riumin, "Proizshestviya," 83.

42. Bestuzhev-Ryumin, "Proizshestviya," 82.

43. No. 16 Broadsheet, September 12, 1812, in *Afishy 1812 goda*, http://www.mus eum.ru/museum/1812/Library/rostopchin/.

44. Jean Baptiste de Crossard, *Mémoires militaires et historiques* (Paris, 1829), IV:361.

45. Fedor Rostopchin, *Oeuvres inédites* (Paris, 1894), 214–215.

46. Rostopchin to his wife, September 13, 1812, in *Russkii arkhiv* 8 (1901): 461.

47. Rostopchin, "Tysyacha vosemsot dvenadtsatyi god," 715; Natalie Narichkine-Rostopchine, *1812. Le Comte Rostopchine et son temps* (St. Petersburg, 1912), 161–162; Pierre de Ségur, "Rostopchin en 1812," *La revue de Paris* 7 (1902): 104.

48. Alexander Golitsyn, "Zapiska o voine 1812 goda . . . ," in Konstantin Voenskii, *Otechestvennaya voina 1812 goda v zapiskakh sovremennikov* (St. Petersburg: Tip. Glav. Uprv. Udelov, 1911), 70. "Vous craignez la retraite pas Moscou et moi je la considère comme une Providence car cela sauve l'armée. Napoléon

est comme un torrent que nous ne pouvons pas encore arrêter. Moscou sera l'éponge qui le recevra."

49. Andrei Tartakovskii, "Obmanutyi Gerostrat: Rostopchin i Pozhar Moskvy," *Rodina* 6, no. 7 (1992): 93.

50. Alexander Golitsyn, "Zapiska," 70.

51. "Razgovor s A. P. Yermolovym," *Russkii arkhiv*, 1863, 856–857; Grabbe, "Iz pamyantnykh zapisok," 470.

52. J. M. von Helldorff, *Aus dem Leben des kaiserlich-russischen Generals der Infanterie Prinzen Eugen von Württemberg* (Berlin, 1862), II:58–59.

53. Waldemar de Löwenstern, *Mémoires du général-major russe Baron de Löwenstern (1776–1858)* (Paris: A. Fontemoing, 1903), I:280.

54. Barclay de Tolly, *Izobrazhenie*, 35–36. "I was surprised how disadvantageous this position was," he later wrote. "The right wing was adjacent to the woods, which extended for several miles in the direction of the enemy, who thus had an opportunity to send out skirmishers, seize the woods, and turn our right flank. Behind the left wing there was a 20–30-meter-deep ravine with such steep banks that one could only climb them single file. The reserve of the right wing was so close to the front that any enemy artillery round could target all four of our lines. . . . The cavalry, deprived [by deep ravines] of any opportunity to participate in this battle, would have had to immediately leave the battlefield or remain idle as it was destroyed by the enemy artillery."

55. Winzegorode to Emperor Alexander I, September 13/25, 1812, in Dubrovin, *Otechestvennaya voina v pis'makh sovremennikov*, 138.

56. Barclay de Tolly, *Izobrazhenie*, 36.

57. Barclay de Tolly, *Izobrazhenie*, 36.

58. Wintzingerode to Emperor Alexander I, September 13/25, 1812, in Dubrovin, *Otechestvennaya voina v pis'makh sovremennikov*, 138.

59. Jean Baptiste Louis de Crossard, *Mémoires militaires et historiques* (Paris: Migneret, 1829), IV:363–365. Kutuzov, wanting to show that he had done everything possible to accept battle at the current position, then told officers to examine the position one more time. Alexey Yermolov, *The Czar's General: The Memoirs of a Russian General in the Napoleonic Wars*, translated and edited by Alexander Mikaberidze (Welwyn Garden City: Ravenhall Books, 2005), 168–169.

60. Helldorff, *Aus dem Leben*, II:58–59.

61. Yermolov, *The Czar's General*, 169–170.

62. Some sources also name Intendant-General V. Lanskoi (chief supply officer) and Kutuzov's duty officer, Colonel Paisii Kaisarov, as participants in this council. Kutuzov's orderly Alexander Golitsyn, however, clearly indicates that Lanskoi was not invited to the council but was summoned after the meeting. As for Kaisarov, there is no direct evidence for his participation and his inclusion is usually done in light of his position as a duty general at the headquarters. In his memoir, Konovnitsyn mentions that General Karl Baggovut had attended the council, but no other source confirms this information. For an interesting

discussion, see V. Totfalushin, *M. B. Barclay de Tolly v Otechestvennoi voine 1812 g.* (Saratov, 1991), 100–105; V. Totfalushin, "Voennyi sovet v Filyakh po romanu L. N. Tolstogo 'Voina i mir' i istoricheskaya deistvitel'nost,'" in *Sobytiya Otechestvennoi voiny 1812 g. na territorii Kaluzhskoi gubernii: Problemy izuchenia. Istochniki. Pamyatniki* (Maloyaroslavets, 1995), 86–91. On the identity of the owner of this historic hut, see M. Prokhorov, "Novye dokumenty o vladel'tsakh Kutuzovskoi izby," *Otechestvannaya voina 1812 goda. Istochniki. Pamyatniki. Problemy* (Borodino, 1997), http://www.museum.ru/museum/1812/Library/Borodino_conf/1997/Prohorov.pdf.

63. Levin von Bennigsen, "Zapiski," *Russkaya starina* 9 (1909): 501–502; Barclay de Tolly, *Izobrazhenie*, 36.

64. September 1/13, 1812, entry in the Journal of Military Operations, RGVIA, f. VUA, d. 3465, part 5, ll. 229–230.

65. Yermolov, *The Czar's General*, 170. Barclay de Tolly's account differs in some details of this speech; *Izobrazhenie*, 36–37.

66. Bennigsen, "Zapiski," 502; Karl Friedrich von Toll, *Denkwürdigkeiten aus dem Leben des Kaiserl. russ. Generals von der der Infanterie Carl Friedrich Grafen von Toll*, edited by Theodor von Bernhardi (Leipzig: Otto Wigand, 1856), II:140.

67. Barclay de Tolly, *Izobrazhenie*, 37.

68. September 1/13, 1812, entry in the Journal of Military Operations, RGVIA, f. VUA, d. 3465, part 5, ll. 229–230; Barclay de Tolly, *Izobrazhenie*, 37–38; Nikolai Rayevskii, "*Zapiski o 1812 gode*," in Denis Davydov, *Zamechaniya na nekrologiyu N. N. Rayevskogo s pribavleniem ego sobstvennykh zapisok na nekotorye sobytiya voiny 1812 goda v koikh on uchavstvoval* (Moscow, 1832), 72–74; Bennigsen, "Zapiski," 503; Waldemar de Löwenstern, "Zapiski generala V. I. Lewernsterna," *Russkaya starina* 105, nos. 1–2 (1900–1901). Kaisarov's opinion (if he indeed took part in the council) remains unknown. Toll, as a colonel, could not have wielded much authority among the generals. Challenges inherent to memoir literature become apparent when one considers Dokhturov's position. Writing to his wife just two days after the council, Dokhturov noted that he wanted to fight and "did everything I could to convince [the council] to advance against the enemy. Bennigsen was of the same opinion. . . . But this gallant idea had no effect on these pusillanimous men, so we retreated through the city." Yet Yermolov, in his memoirs, writes, "General Dokhturov said that it would be good to march against the enemy, however, because of the loss of so many commanders at Borodino, who had been replaced by less familiar officers, success in the ensuing battle could not be guaranteed; therefore, he proposed to retreat." Dokhturov to his wife, September 15, 1812, in *Russkii arkhiv* 1 (1874): 1098; Yermolov, *The Czar's General*, 171.

69. A. Mikhailovskii-Danilevskii, *Opisanie Otechestvennoi voiny 1812 goda* (St. Petersburg, 1839), II:329. Soviet historian Bragin cites the testimony of "Rayevskii's aide-de-camp" without providing the source: "I was riding close behind the corps commander, wondering why he, who was usually so polite,

had not replied to my enquiry as to what had happened at the council of war. Suddenly, in the silence of the night, I heard our beloved hero quietly sobbing. A terrible thought crossed my mind, 'Are they going to surrender Moscow?' There could now be no doubt about it."

70. For an excellent discussion, see Alexander Martin, *Enlightened Metropolis: Constructing Imperial Moscow, 1762–1855* (Oxford: Oxford University Press, 2013).

71. Friedrich von Schubert, *Unter dem Doppeladler (Erinnerungen eines Deutschen in russischem Offizieersdienst 1789–1814)* (Stuttgart: K. F. Koehler Verlag, 1962), 250; Alexander Herzen notes, "La nouvelle de son occupation et de son incendie avait fait tressaillir toute la Russie, car pour le peuple Moscou était la vraie capitale"; "Du développement des idées révolutionnaires en Russie," in *Sobranie sochinenii . . .* (Moscow: Academy of Sciences of USSR, 1956), VII:64.

72. Peter Konovnitsyn, "Vospominaniya," in V. Kharkevich, ed., *1812 god v dnevnikakh, zapiskakh, i vospominaniyakh sovremennikov* (Vilna: Tip. Shtaba Vilenskago Voen. Okruga, 1900), I:128; *Russkii arkhiv* 1 (1874): 1098–1099.

73. Joseph de Maistre to King Victor Emmanuel I of Piedmont, June 2/ 14, 1813, in *Russkii arkhiv* 1 (1912): 48. Also see Michael Josselson and Diana Josselson, *The Commander: A Life of Barclay de Tolly* (Oxford: Oxford University Press, 1980), 153–154.

74. Mikhail Marakuev, "Zapiski M. I. Marakueva," *Russkii arkhiv* 5 (1907): 115–116.

75. N. Longinov to S. Vorontsov, September 13/25, 1812, in *Arkhiv knyazya Vorontsova* (Moscow: Tip. Gracheva, 1876), XXIII:157.

76. Claude-François, Baron de Méneval, *Memoirs . . .* (New York: P. F. Collier and Son, 1910), III:851–852; Philippe-Paul de Ségur, *Histoire de Napoléon et de la grande-armée pendant l'année 1812* (Bruxelles: H. Tarlier, 1825), I:150, 152, 177–178.

77. Colonel Kaisarov's testimony in Mikhailovskii-Danilevskii, *Opisanie Otechestvennoi voiny 1812 goda*, II:332; Toll, *Denkwurdigkeiten*, II:143.

78. Colonel Schneider's testimony in Mikhailovskii-Danilevskii, *Opisanie Otechestvennoi voiny 1812 goda*, II:330.

79. Kutuzov to Rostopchin, September 13, 1812, in *Borodino: dokumenty, pis'ma, vospominaniya*, 143–144; Rostopchin, "Tysyacha vosemsot dvenadtsatyi god," 717; Rostopchin to his wife, September 13, 1812, in *Russkii arkhiv* 8 (1901): 461; Rostopchin to the Senate, August 9, 1814, in *Russkii arkhiv* 6 (1868): 884.

80. *Russkii invalid*, December 3, 1846, no. 279, 1077. "At 1 p.m. on [13] September [Kutuzov] assured me that the city would be defended," Rostopchin later complained to the Imperial Senate. "And yet, by midnight, he informed me that it would be abandoned." Rostopchin to the Senate, August 9, 1814, in *Russkii arkhiv* 6 (1868): 884.

81. Rostopchin, "Tysyacha vosemsot dvenadtsatyi god," 716–717.

82. Rostopchin to his wife, September 13, 1812, 11 p.m., in Narichkine-Rostopchine, *1812*, 164–165. Eugene of Württemberg and August of Oldenburg visited Rostopchin urging him to come with them for a last-minute attempt to compel Kutuzov to reverse his decision and fight at the gates of Moscow. Rostopchin declined, knowing well that the die was already cast. Rostopchin, "Tysyacha vosemsot dvenadtsatyi god," 719–720; "Zametki o 1812 gode," *Russkii arkhiv* 8 (1901): 503.

83. Rostopchin to Alexander, September 13, 1812, in *Russkii arkhiv* 8 (1892): 530–531. Also see Rostopchin to his wife, September 15, 1812, in Narichkine-Rostopchine, *1812*, 175; Rostopchin to his wife, September 25, 1812, in *Russkii arkhiv* 8 (1901): 474.

84. Rostopchin to Mikhail Vorontsov, October 30, 1812, in *Russkii arkhiv* 6 (1908): 270–271.

85. Levin von Bennigsen, *Mémoires du Général Bennigsen* (Paris, 1908), III:94–95.

86. Jacob de Sanglen, "Zapiski Yakova Ivanovicha de Sanglena, 1778–1831 gg.," *Russkaya starina* 3 (1883): 553.

87. *M. I. Kutuzov. Sbornik dokumentov*, IV, part 1, 225. A similar order was issued on September 12 and specified that any official or officer who left the ranks without permission should be hung or shot, while rank and file "should be bayoneted [*zakolot'*] on the spot." Journal of Incoming Correspondence, in *General Staff Archives*, XVII:192.

88. Barclay de Tolly to Rostopchin, September 13, 1812, in Dubrovin, *Otechestvennaya voina v pis'makh sovremennikov*, 118–119.

89. Löwenstern, *Mémoires*, I:283.

90. Barclay de Tolly, *Izobrazhenie*, 38.

91. Radozhitskii, *Pokhodnye zapiski artillerista*, I:89.

92. Rostopchin to Emperor Alexander, September 8/20, 1812, in *Russkii arkhiv* 8 (1892): 535.

93. Andrei Karfachevskii's memoirs in P. Schukin, ed., *Bumagi otnosyaschiyasya do Otechestvennoi voiny 1812 goda* (Moscow: A. Mamontov, 1904), V:165–167; Bennigsen, *Mémoires*, III:94–95; Alexander Bulgakov, "Zametka na pamyat," *Russkii arkhiv*, 1866, 701–702. To prevent the rabble and soldiery from getting drunk, the police received orders to start smashing barrels that contained wine or beer, but for a variety of reasons such instructions were not carried out everywhere. In some districts, "no orders prohibiting the sale of alcohol had been received and the police therefore took no action," reported one of the constables two years later. For police reports and other documents, see Dmitri Gorshkov, ed., *Moskva i Otechestvennaya voina 1812 goda* (Moscow: Glav. Arkhiv. Uprav., 2011), I:430–431, 530–540. Kutuzov was well aware of this marauding and tried to solicit support from the governors of Tula, Kaluga, Vladimir, Ryazan, and Tambov in restraining the troops and protecting the civilians. See his letters in *Journal of the Outgoing Correspondence of the Commander-in-Chief*, 19.

94. Fusil, *Souvenirs d'une Actrice*, II:274.

95. Alexander Ryazanov, *Vospominaniya ochevidtsa o prebyvanii Frantsuzov v Moskve v 1812 godu* (Moscow, 1862), 46.

96. Rostopchin to his wife, September 15, 1812, in Narichkine-Rostopchine, *1812*, 175–176. See also Ivan Yakovlev to E. Golokhvastova, November 13, 1812, in *Russkii arkhiv*, 1874, 1057; Bulgakov, "Zametka na pamyat," 701–702; G. Kozlovskii, "Moskva v 1812 godu, zanyataya frantsuzami. Vospominaniya ochevidtsa," *Russkaya starina* 1 (1890): 106; F. Rastkovskii, *Ob Otechetsvennoi voine 1812 g.: Rasskaz starika finlyandtsa* (St. Petersburg, 1900), 31; Elena Pokhorskaya's recollections, in T. Tolycheva, ed., *Razskazy ochevidtsev o Dvenadtsatom gode* (Moscow, 1912), 47–48.

97. Fedor Lubyanovskii, *Vospominaniya* (Moscow, 1872), 281.

98. Nikolai Muravyev, "Zapiski," *Russkii arkhiv* 11 (1885): 346.

99. "Rasskazy ochevidtsev o dvenadtsatom gode: Na Mokhovoi," *Moskovskie vedomosti*, March 1, 1872.

100. Peter Zhdanov, *Pamyatnik Frantsuzam, ili priklyucheniya Moskovskogo zhitelya P . . . Zh . . .* (St. Petersburg, 1813), 4.

101. Sergei Glinka, "Iz zapisok o 1812 gode," http://www.museum.ru/1812/libr ary/glinka1/glinka.html#p22.

102. Dmitri Mertvago, *Zapiski . . .* (Moscow, 1867), 316.

103. Sverbeyev, *Zapiski*, I:72. Also see "Rasskaz meshchanina Petra Kondratieva," *Russkii vestnik* 102 (1872): 275–276; Bestuzhev-Ryumin, "Proizshestviya," 79–80. Also see T. Tolycheva, *Rasskaz starushki o dvenadtsatom gode* (Moscow, 1878), 40–41.

104. N. Golitsyn, *Ofitserskie zapiski ili vospominaniya o pokhodakh 1812, 1813 i 1814 godov* (Moscow, 1836), 21.

105. Rostopchin to Emperor Alexander, September 8/20, 1812, in *Russkii arkhiv* 8 (1892): 535.

106. Cited in Rostopchin, *Okh, frantsuzy!*, 300. Denis Davydov also recalled Bagration exclaiming, "I am dying not of the obvious wound, but of the one in my heart. The enemy has pierced the heart of my Motherland." See "K stoletiu so dnia konchini kniazia P. I. Bagrationa," *Russkii invalid*, September 1912, no. 200, 4–6.

107. Dokhturov to his wife, September 15, 1812, in *Russkii arkhiv* 1 (1874): 1098–1099.

108. See the special report, prepared in September 1815, on the lost ammunition in RGVIA, f. VUA, d. 3465, part 5, ll. 396–397. This report was also published in *M. I. Kutuzov. Sbornik dokumentov*, IV, part 2, 715–716.

109. Rostopchin to his wife, September 13, 1812, in *Russkii arkhiv* 8 (1901): 461–462; Wyllie to Arakcheyev, September 24, 1812, in Dubrovin, *Otechestvennaya voina v pis'makh sovremennikov*, 133–136. According to Wyllie, 8,000 wounded were at the Golovinskie Kazarmy and another 5,000 at the Spasskie Kazarmy. Some 4,000 were lodged at the Alexandrov and Ekarinenskii Institutes, 3,000

at the Kudrinskii Institute, about 2,000 at the Western Palace, and some 500 were billeted at private apartments.

110. Jean-Jacques Pelet, "Bataille de la Moskwa," *Le spectateur militaire* VIII (1829): 144.

111. Yermolov, *The Czar's General*, 173. Napoleon later accused Kutuzov of "callousness for abandoning 10,000 wounded soldiers without food and care." Tutolmin to Dowager Empress Maria Fedorovna, November 23, 1812, in *Chteniya v Imperatorskom obschestve istorii i drevnostei rossiiskikh* 2 (1860): 168–169.

112. Anonymous eyewitness account found in the papers of Alexander Mikhailovskii-Danilevskii. See V. Kharkevich, ed., *1812 god v dnevnikakh, zapiskakh i vospominaniyakh sovremennikov* (Vilna: Tip. Shtaba Vilen. Voen. Okruga, 1900), II:192.

113. Radozhitskii, *Pokhodnye zapiski artillerista*, I:87–88.

114. Golitsyn, "Zapiska o voine 1812 goda," 70; Glinka, "Iz zapisok o 1812 gode," http://www.museum.ru/1812/library/glinka1/glinka.html#p40.

115. Peter Kicheev, *Iz nedavnei stariny. Razskazy i vospominaniya* (Moscow, 1870), 7.

116. Adrien-Jean-Baptiste François Bourgogne, *Mémoires du Sergent Bourgogne, 1812–1813* (Paris, 1910), 13; Louis Florimond Fantin des Odoards, *Journal du Général Fantin des Odoards. Étapes d'un officier de la Grande Armée* (Paris, 1895), 331–332.

117. Ségur, *Histoire de Napoléon et de la grande-armée pendant l'année 1812*, II:51–52.

118. Albrecht von Muralt, *Beresina: Erinnerungen aus dem Feldzug Napoleons I in Russland 1812* (Bern: Hallwag, 1940), 69.

119. Agathon Jean François Fain, *Manuscrit de mil huit cent douze* (Paris, 1827), II:88; Abbé Surrugues, *Lettres sur l'incendie de Moscou* (Paris: Plancher, 1823), 23.

120. Arthur Wellesley, Duke of Wellington, "Memorandum on the War in Russia in 1812," in George R. Cleig, ed., *Personal Reminiscences of the First Duke of Wellington* (New York: Charles Scribner's Sons, 1904), 387.

121. For recent studies of the Moscow fire, see V. Zemtsov, *1812 god: Pozhar Moskvy* (Moscow: Kniga, 2010); Alexander Mikaberidze, *Napoleon's Trial by Fire: The Burning of Moscow* (Barnsley: Pen & Sword, 2014).

122. Wellesley, "Memorandum on the War in Russia in 1812," 387–388.

123. *M. I. Kutuzov. Sbornik dokumentov*, IV, part 1, 473. Similarly, General P. Kaptsevich, who commanded the 7th Infantry Division, reported that two ammunition magazines were blown up on the orders of General Miloradovich, who would have been acting with Kutuzov's consent. Kaptsevich to Arakcheyev, September 6/18, 1812, in Dubrovin, *Otechestvennaya voina v pis'makh sovremennikov*, 124–125. Sergei Glinka concurs that the explosions, at least near the Simonov Monastery, were caused by the Russian efforts to destroy barges with commissariat supplies. This monastery alone contained over 8,500 *puds* of lead and almost 6,000 *puds* of gunpowder that could not be simply abandoned to the enemy.

124. Surrugues, *Lettres sur l'incendie de Moscou*, 17.

125. Napoleon to Cambacérès, September 18, 1812, in *Correspondance de Napoleon Ier, publ. par ordre de l'Empereur Napoléon III* (Paris: Henri Plon, 1863), XII:1100. Also see Napoleon to Marie Louise, September 18, 1812, in *Correspondance générale* (Paris: Fayard, 2004–2015), XII:1101.

126. F. Korbeletskii, *Kratkoe povestvovanie o vtorzhenii frantsuzov v Moskvu i o prebyvanii ikh v onoi* (St. Petersburg, 1813), 38.

127. Nikolai Karamzin to Ivan Dmitriev, October 11/23, 1812, in *Pis'ma M. M. Karamzina k I. I. Dmitrievu* (St. Petersburg, 1866), 165–166.

128. Alexader Chicherin, *Dnevnik . . .* (Moscow: Nauka, 1965), e-version at http://www.museum.ru/museum/1812/Library/Chicherin/chicherin_1812.html.fs.

Chapter 25

1. Entry for September 14, Journal of Military Operations, in *M. I. Kutuzov. Sbornik dokumentov* (Moscow: Voeniszdat, 1950), IV, part 1, 335.

2. The army rested on September 15. Journal of Military Operations, in *M. I. Kutuzov. Sbornik dokumentov*, IV, part 1, 335; Kutuzov to Miloradovich, September 3/15, 1812, in *Journal of the Outgoing Correspondence of the Commander in Chief*, 17. Kutuzov had initially intended to proceed to Ryazan and Vladimir, where, as early as September 10, he instructed reinforcements and supplies to be diverted. On September 14, some of the units were instructed to "proceed through Bogorodsk to Vladimir, where the army would turn from the Ryazan road." This indicates that Kutuzov's original intention was to make a flanking movement in a northeastern direction, but he quickly adjusted his plan in light of new intelligence he received on September 14–16. For details, see his orders to various generals in *Journal of the Outgoing Correspondence of the Commander in Chief*, 15–17; *M. I. Kutuzov. Sbornik dokumentov*, IV, part 1, 220–234.

3. Alexander Scherbinin, "Zapiski Aleksandra Scherbinina," in V. Kharkevich, ed., *1812 god v dnevnikakh, zapiskakh i vospominaniyakh sovremennikov* (Vilna: Tip. Shtaba Vilen. Voen. Okruga, 1900), I:29.

4. Kutuzov to Alexander, September 4/16, 1812, in *General Staff Archives*, XIX:377–378. The first clear indication of Kutuzov's plan to turn right and proceed to the Tula and Kaluga roads appears on September 15, when he sent instructions to Major General Ferdinand Winzegorode. See *M. I. Kutuzov. Sbornik dokumentov*, IV, part 1, 231, 233–234.

5. Roxandra Stourdza, Comtess d'Edling, *Mémoires de la comtess Edling, demoiselle d'honneur de sa majesté l'imperatrice Elisabeth Alexéevna* (Moscow: Holy Synod, 1888), 75. Also see John Quincy Adams, *Memoirs of John Quincy Adams Containing His Diary from 1795 to 1848*, edited by Charles Francis Adams (Philadelphia: Lippincott, 1874), 404–405. Adams mentioned Kutuzov reporting "a splendid victory" at Borodino but then sardonically noted that "the result of this great Russian victory was to put the French in possession of Moscow."

6. Edling, *Mémoires*, 75–81.

7. Adams, *Memoirs of John Quincy Adams Containing His Diary*, 408.

8. Kutuzov to Miloradovich, September 16–17, 1812, in *M. I. Kutuzov. Sbornik dokumentov*, IV, part 1, 236–237, 240–241. The Cossack forces were commanded by Colonel I. Efremov and consisted of Andrianov II's Cossack, Simferopolskii Horse Tatar, and 1st Bashkirskii Regiments. The first two regiments remained on the Ryazan road, while the Bashkirs moved to the road to Serpukhov.

9. For details, see Journal of Military Operations, RGVIA, f. VUA, d. 3465, part 5, ll. 229–231b; Disposition of the 1st and 2nd Western Armies, September 16, 1812; Kutuzov to Miloradovich, September 17, 1812; Kutuzov to Emperor Alexander, September 18, 1812, in *M. I. Kutuzov. Sbornik dokumentov*, IV, part I, 237–238, 241, 243; Order to the Armies, September 18, 1812, RGVIA, f. VUA, d. 3524, ll. 15–16b.

10. Alexey Yermolov, *The Czar's General: The Memoirs of a Russian General in the Napoleonic Wars*, translated and edited by Alexander Mikaberidze (Welwyn Garden City: Ravenhall Books, 2005), 174.

11. Mikhail Barclay de Tolly, *Izobrazhenie voennykh deistvii 1-oi armii v 1812 godu* (St. Petersburg: P. Soikin, 1912), 38; Levin von Bennigsen, "Zapiski," *Russkaya starina* 9 (1909): 507–508; Yermolov, *The Czar's General*, 174. Either Bennigsen or Toll suggested a move onto the Kaluga road at the council of war at Fili, but attempting this deployment at that moment would have been ineffective since Napoleon would have detected it at once and reacted accordingly.

12. Berthier to Bessières, September 27, 1812, in Gaspard Gourgaud, *Napoléon et la Grande Armée en Russie ou examen critique de l'ouvrage de M. Le Comte Ph. de Ségur* (Paris: Bossange, 1825), 528.

13. "Votre fin merle de Koutoùzof m'a joliment mis dedans avec sa marche de flanc." See "Conversation de l'Empereur Napoléon avec le Général Russe Constantin Poltoratzky en 1814, après la bataille de Champaubert," *Revue d'Alsace* VI (1855): 228.

14. Yermolov, *The Czar's General*, 174; Kutuzov to Miloradovich, September 18, 1812, in *M. I. Kutuzov. Sbornik dokumentov*, IV, part I, 248. Also see Kutuzov to Emperor Alexander, September 18, 1812, in *M. I. Kutuzov. Sbornik dokumentov*, IV, part 1, 243.

15. Kutuzov to Alexander I; Kutuzov to Chichagov; Kutuzov to Tormasov, September 18, 1812, in *M. I. Kutuzov. Sbornik dokumentov*, IV, part 1, 243–245.

16. Journal of Military Operations, RGVIA, f. VUA, d. 3465, part 5, ll. 231–231b; Disposition of the 1st and 2nd Armies for September 20, 1812; Kutuzov to Miloradovich, September 19, 1812, in *M. I. Kutuzov. Sbornik dokumentov*, IV, part I, 252–253; Miloradovich to Konovnitsyn, September 22, 1812, in *General Staff Archives*, XVIII:45–46.

17. Kutuzov to Alexander I, September 23, 1812, in *M. I. Kutuzov. Sbornik dokumentov*, IV, part I, 277–278.

18. Kutuzov to Lobanov-Rostovskii, Lanskoi, and Miloradovich, September 18–21, 1812, in *M. I. Kutuzov. Sbornik dokumentov*, IV, part 1, 247, 254, 261–262; Kutuzov to Dorokhov, September 20, 1812, RGVIA, f. VUA, d. 3463, l. 52.

19. Philippe-Paul de Ségur, *Histoire de Napoléon et de la grande armée pendant l'année 1812* (Brussels: H. Tarlier, 1825), I:56; Berthier to Murat, September 22, 1812, 4 p.m., in Agathon Jean-François, Baron de Fain, *Manuscrit de mil huit cent douze* (Paris: Delaunay, 1827), II:177.

20. Berthier to Bessières and Murat, September 22–27, 1812, in Gourgaud, *Napoléon et la Grande Armée en Russie*, 525–529.

21. Fain, *Manuscrit de mil huit cent douze*, II:109–111; Georges de Chambray, *Histoire de l'expedition de Russie* (Paris: Pillet Ainé, 1823), II:148–149. Bessières's force consisted of the 4th and 5th Guard Cavalry Brigades, the 3rd Cavalry Corps, the 1st Light Cavalry Brigade, and the 4th Division of the 1st Corps.

22. Berthier to Murat and Bessières, September 22–23, 1812, in Gourgaud, *Napoléon et la Grande Armée en Russie*, 525–527. Also see Journal of Military Operations, *M. I. Kutuzov. Sbornik dokumentov*, IV, part 1, 337.

23. Claude François Madeleine Le Roy, *Souvenirs de Leroy, major d'infanterie, vétéran des armées de la République et de l'Empire* (Dijon, 1914), 185–189.

24. Chambray, *Histoire de l'expedition de Russie*, II:149.

25. Bennigsen to Miloradovich, September 24, 1812, in *M. I. Kutuzov. Sbornik dokumentov*, IV, part I, 291–292.

26. Barclay de Tolly, *Izobrazhenie*, 40; Journal of Military Operations, in *M. I. Kutuzov. Sbornik dokumentov*, IV, part 1, 337–338.

27. Kutuzov to Miloradovich, September 24, 1812, 7 p.m., in *M. I. Kutuzov. Sbornik dokumentov*, IV, part I, 292–293.

28. This flurry of orders and counterorders from the commander in chief and his chief of staff confused Miloradovich so much that he required a separate explanation of what exactly was expected of him. Bennigsen to Miloradovich, September 24, 1812, 8 p.m.; Toll to Miloradovich, September 25, 1812, midnight, in *M. I. Kutuzov. Sbornik dokumentov*, IV, part 1, 293–294. Also see Disposition of the 1st and 2nd Armies for September 27, 1812, in *M. I. Kutuzov. Sbornik dokumentov*, IV, part I, 308–309; Bennigsen to Osterman-Tolstoy, September 27, 1812, RGVIA, f. VUA, d. 3463, l. 69.

29. Berthier to Bessières and Murat, September 26–28, 1812, in Gourgaud, *Napoléon et la Grande Armée en Russie*, 528–530; Chambray, *Histoire de l'expedition de Russie*, II:150.

30. Robert Wilson, *Private Diary of Travels, Personal Services, and Public Events* (London: J. Murray, 1861), I:175; Robert Wilson, *Narrative of Events During the Invasion of Russia by Napoleon Bonaparte and the Retreat of the French Army* (London: John Murray, 1860), 131.

31. Wilson, *Narrative of Events During the Invasion of Russia*, 178–179.

32. Miloradovich to Konovnitsyn, October 3, 1812, in *General Staff Archives*, XVIII:100–101; Journal of Military Operations, *M. I. Kutuzov. Sbornik dokumentov*, IV, part 1, 338–341. For a concise discussion of the rear-guard actions, see V. Bessonov, *Tarutinskoe srazhenie* (Moscow: Kniga, 2008), 16–52.

33. Alexander Mikhailovskii-Danilevskii, "Iz vospominanii . . . ," *Russkaya starina* 6 (1897): 480.

34. Sergei Marin to unknown, October 14, 1812, in P. Schukin, ed., *Bumagi otnosyaschiyasya do Otechestvennoi voiny 1812 goda* (Moscow: A. Mamontov, 1904), I:60–64; Nikolai Mitarevskii, *Vospominaniya o voine 1812 goda* (Moscow: A. Mamontov, 1871), 91. Such views spread far and wide within months. In the United States in June 1813, special celebrations were held in Washington, DC, to celebrate the Russian victories over Napoleon. At the event, attended by the American president and vice president and foreign ambassadors (including the Russian envoy), the keynote speaker, Robert Goodloe Harper, portrayed the abandonment of Moscow and subsequent flanking maneuver as part of Kutuzov's deliberate plan. *The Celebration of the Russian Victories in Georgetown, District of Columbia, on the 5th of June 1813* (Washington, DC: James B. Carter, 1813), 25–26.

35. This reorganization began as early as September 21, though Kutuzov did not fully implement it. See Kutuzov's instructions to Barclay de Tolly and Miloradovich in *Journal of the Outgoing Correspondence of the Commander in Chief*, 25–26, 31.

36. See his instructions on the training of St. Petersburg militia in *M. I. Kutuzov. Sbornik dokumentov*, IV, part I, 28.

37. Mitarevskii, *Vospominaniya*, 102.

38. Alexander Mikhailovskii-Danilevskii, "Zapiski A. I. Mikhailovskago-Danilevskago," *Istoricheskii vestnik* 10 (1890): 153.

39. Mikhailovskii-Danilevskii, "Zapiski," 153–154.

40. Order to the Army, September 25/October 7, 1812, RGVIA, f. VUA, d. 3524, l. 35. Also see Alexander to Kutuzov, October 8/20, 1812, in *M. I. Kutuzov. Sbornik dokumentov*, IV, part II, 52–53.

41. On October 21, Kutuzov announced that Ensign Timoshenko of the 6th Jäger Regiment and eighteen of his comrades had been convicted of "operating as a brigand gang, beating and robbing residents, and even killing some of them." Timoshenko was executed, while eleven of his comrades were sentenced to "undergo a thousand-man gauntlet three times each." Another fourteen jägers were accusing of failing to prevent their comrades' behavior and sentenced to "five-hundred-man gauntlets three times each." *Journal of the Outgoing Correspondence of the Commander in Chief*, 333–334.

42. Order to the Army, October 10/22, 1812, RGVIA, f. VUA, d. 3524, l. 53. Also see Kutuzov to Alexander, October 10/22, 1812, in *M. I. Kutuzov. Sbornik dokumentov*, IV, part II, 69–70.

43. Kutuzov to Wittgenstein, September 20/October 2, 1812, RGVIA, f. VUA, d. 3514, l. 410.

44. Kutuzov to Vadbolskii, September 15/27, 1812, RGVIA, f. VUA, d. 3463, l. 73.

45. Kutuzov to Dorokhov, September 13/25, 1812, RGVIA, f. VUA, d. 3463, l. 67. Dorokhov later complained that Kutuzov's response had tarnished his name and "caused an unfavorable opinion in the army." Kutuzov, therefore, had to reassure the anguished major general. See his letter of September 20/October 2, 1812, in *Journal of the Outgoing Correspondence of the Commander in Chief*, 47.

46. Kutuzov to his wife, October 1/13, 1812, in *The Kutuzov Papers* 4 (1872): 648. Some commanders did commit atrocities against the French, and Figner especially earned notoriety for massacring prisoners. But Kutuzov paid no attention to this savagery and continued to support him as a capable and valuable guerrilla commander whom he soon elevated to a lieutenant colonel. Kutuzov to Emperor Alexander, October 1/13, 1812, in *M. I. Kutuzov. Sbornik dokumentov*, IV, part 1, 419. "You will receive this letter from Figner," Kutuzov told his wife on November 12. "Take a good look at him, for he is an extraordinary person. I have never seen a soul so lofty as his; he is a fanatic when it comes to valor and patriotism, and only the Lord knows what he is capable of." *The Kutuzov Papers* 4 (1872): 653.

47. Kutuzov to Ekaterina Khitrovo, October 2/14, 1812, in *The Kutuzov Papers* 6 (1874): 368.

48. Kutuzov to Vadbolskii, September 15/27, 1812, RGVIA, f. VUA, d. 3463, l. 73.

49. For details see V. Babkin, *Narodnoe opolchenie v Otechestvennoi voine 1812 g.* (Moscow, 1962); V. Apukhtin, *Narodnaya voennaya sila. Dvoryanskie opolcheniya v Otechestvennuyu voinu* (Moscow, 1912), vol. 1; I. Lapina, *Zemskoe opolchenie Rossii 1812–1814 godov* (St. Petersburg, 2007).

50. Kutuzov to Seslavin, September 30/October 12, 1812, RGVIA f. VUA, d. 3521, l. 13. Also see *General Staff Archives*, XVIII:11.

51. Kutuzov to Alexander, November 22/December 4, 1812, in *General Staff Archives*, XXI:293.

52. Kutuzov to Zemskii ispranik of Borovsk, October 19/31, 1812, in *Journal of the Outgoing Correspondence of the Commander in Chief*, 132. Also see *General Staff Archives*, XIX:13–14, 125–126; Journal of Outgoing Correspondence of General Peter Konovnitsyn, in Schukin, *Bumagi*, VIII:314.

53. A. Popov, *Frantsuzy v Moskve v 1812 godu* (Moscow, 1876), 149.

54. D. Dufour de Pradt, *Histoire de l'ambassade dans le Grand Duché de Varsovie en 1812* (Paris, 1815), 52–54, 64–65.

55. Mathieu Dumas, *Souvenirs . . .* (Paris, 1839), III:454–455.

56. Sophie de Choiseul-Gouffier, *Historical Memoirs of the Emperor Alexander I and the Court of Russia* (London: Kegan Paul, 1904), 130. For an interesting contemporary assessment, see Colonel Peter Kikin's letter to his brother in Schukin, *Bumagi*, V:3–5.

57. Dominic Lieven, *Russia Against Napoleon* (London: Penguin, 2010), 251.

58. Empress Elisabeth to the Margravine of Baden, August 26/September 7, 1812, in Grand Duke Nikolai Mikhailovich, ed., *L'impératrice Elisabeth, épouse d'Alexandre Ier* (St. Petersburg, 1908), II:443.

59. Modest Bogdanovich, *Istoriya otechestvennoi voiny 1812 goda po dostovernym istochnikam* (St. Petersburg: S. Strugovshikov, 1859), II:288–289.

60. Alexander Muravyev, *Sochineniya i pis'ma* (Irkutsk: Vostochno-Sibirsk. Knizh. Izd., 1986), 83–84.

61. Sergei Volkonskii, *Zapiski Sergia Grigorievicha Volkonskogo (Dekabrista)* (St. Petersburg, 1902), 147.

62. Grand Duchess Catherine to Emperor Alexander, September 18, 1812, in Grand Duke Nikolai Mikhailovich, ed., *Correspondance de l'empereur Alexandre Ier avec sa soeur. Perepiska imperatora Aleksandra s sestroi velikoi knyaginei Ekaternoi Pavlovnoi* (St. Petersburg: Eksp. Zagot. Gos. Bumag, 1910), letter XXXIII, 83.

63. Ségur, *Histoire de Napoléon et de la grande-armée pendant l'année 1812*, I:53; Gourgaud, *Napoléon et la Grande Armée en Russie*, II:52.

64. Alexander Mikhailovskii-Danilevskii, *Opisanie Otechestvennoi voiny 1812 goda* (St. Petersburg, 1843), III:82.

65. During the conversation with Lauriston, Volkonskii agreed to arrange the meeting at a station several miles from the Russian outposts, but he needed to confirm this with Kutuzov. In French, he ordered his aide-de-camp to return to the headquarters for further instructions, but he then added a few words in Russian, telling him to gallop off for the first hundred yards until he was out of sight and then slow down to a walking pace. The French envoy's meeting with Kutuzov had to take place after dark. Mikhailovskii-Danilevskii, *Opisanie Otechestvennoi voiny 1812 g.*, III:83 (based on conversation with Volkonskii).

66. Wilson, *Narrative of Events During the Invasion of Russia*, 182–183.

67. Wilson, *Narrative of Events During the Invasion of Russia*, 183.

68. A. Zakrevskii to A. Bulgakov, December 16/28, 1812, in *Rossiiskii arkhiv* XII (2003), 35.

69. Vasilii Norov to his family, October 10/22, 1812, in *Russkii arkhiv* 2 (1900): 276. Norov was an ensign in the Life Guard Jäger Regiment.

70. Alexander Bulgakov to Konstantin Bulgakov, October 28, 1812, in *Russkii arkhiv* 5 (1900): 35. Also see Yermolov to Zakrevskii, n.d. [early October 1812], in *SIRIO* 73 (1890): 188.

71. Luka Simanskii, "Zhurnal uchastnika voiny 1812 g.," *Voenno-istoricheskii sbornik* 2 (1913): 162; Scherbinin, "Zapiski," 43.

72. Sergei Mayevskii, "Moi vek ili istoriya Sergeya Ivanovicha Mayevskogo, 1779–1848," *Russkaya starina* 8 (1873): 153.

73. Yermolov, *The Czar's General*, 178.

74. Mikhailovskii-Danilevskii, "Zapiski," 158.

75. Jean Anstedt to Nesselrode, October 11/23, 1812, in N. Dubrovin, ed., *Otechestvennaya voina v pis'makh sovremennikov* (St. Petersburg, 1882), 236.

76. See Toll's letter to Dimitri Buturlin, cited in Pavel Zhilin, *Kutuzov. Zhizn' i polkovodcheskaya deyatel'nost'* (Moscow: Voennoe Izdatel'stvo, 1978), 377–378.

77. Scherbinin, "Zapiski," 18–19.

78. Bennigsen to his wife, September 11/23, 1812, in Dubrovin, *Otechestvennaya voina v pis'makh sovremennikov*, 129.

79. Rostopchin to Peter Tolstoy, September 13/25, 1812, in *Pamyatniki novoi russkoi istorii* (St. Petersburg: Maikov, 1872), II:185.

80. Cited in Andrei Tartakovskii, *Nerazgadannyi Barclay: legendy i byl' 1812 goda* (Moscow: Arkheog. Tsentr, 1996), 143.

81. Mikhailovskii-Danilevskii, "Zapiski," 159.

82. Ludwig Wolzogen und Neuhaus, *Memoiren des Königlich Preussischen Generals der Infanterie Ludwig Freiherrn von Wolzogen* (Leipzig, 1851), 160.

83. Barclay de Tolly to his wife, September 11/23, 1812, in Dubrovin, *Otechestvennaya voina v pis'makh sovremennikov*, 129.

84. Dr. Ganhardt's testimony in *Syn Otechestva* 11 (1813): 28.

85. Order to the Armies, September 28, 1812, RGVIA, f. VUA, d. 3524, ll. 26b–28.

86. Barclay de Tolly to his wife, September 11/23, 1812, in Dubrovin, *Otechestvennaya voina v pis'makh sovremennikov*, 128.

87. See Barclay de Tolly's letters justifying his actions in Dubrovin, *Otechestvennaya voina v pis'makh sovremennikov*, 287–295.

88. Waldemar von Löwenstern, *Denkwürdigkeiten eines Livländers (Aus den Jahren 1790–1815)* (Leipzig: Winter, 1858), I:246–247. The Russian and French versions of his memoirs do not mention the wagon metaphor. Waldemar de Löwenstern, *Mémoires du général-major russe Baron de Löwenstern (1776–1858)* (Paris: A. Fontemoing, 1903), I:287.

89. Kutuzov to Alexander, September 19/October 1, 1812, in *M. I. Kutuzov. Sbornik dokumentov*, IV, part 1, 323–324.

90. Yermolov, *The Czar's General*, 178. Scherbinin, "Zapiski," 31; Sergei Mayevskii, "Moi vek," 161.

91. Konovnitsyn to his wife, October 4/16, 1812, in Schukin, *Bumagi*, VIII:111.

92. Löwenstern, *Mémoires*, I:297.

93. Marin to Mikhail Vorontsov, September 27/October 9, 1812, in *Arkhiv knyazya Vorontsova* (Moscow: Tip. Gracheva, 1876), XXXV:465.

94. Rostopchin to Peter Tolstoy, September 13/25, 1812, in *Pamyatniki novoi russkoi istorii*, II:185.

95. Yermolov to A. Zakrevskii, n.d. [early October 1812], *SIRIO* 73 (1890): 188; Yermolov, *The Czar's General*, 179.

96. Dokhturov to his wife, September 9/21, 1812, in *Russkii arkhiv* 5 (1874): 1100.

97. Wilson, *Narrative of Events During the Invasion of Russia*, 182. Also see Mikhailovskii-Danilevskii, *Opisanie Otechestvennoi voiny 1812 g.*, III:82–84.

98. For reasons, see Wilson, *Narrative of Events During the Invasion of Russia*, xiv–xvi.

99. Wilson, *Narrative of Events During the Invasion of Russia*, 185–186.

100. The quote is by the Duke of Wellington. On Wilson's career, see Michael Glover, *A Very Slippery Fellow: The Life of Sir Robert Wilson, 1777–1848* (Oxford: Oxford University Press, 1977).

101. Wilson, *Narrative of Events During the Invasion of Russia*, 182.

102. Mikhailovskii-Danilevskii, *Opisanie Otechestvennoi voiny 1812 g.*, III:84–85. In his classic *Histoire du Consulat et de l'Empire* (Paris, 1845), XIV:419–420, Adolphe Thiers included a different version of Lauriston's arrival at the Russian camp; his version can be found unchanged in the works of subsequent generations of historians. Thiers described how upon reaching Russian outposts, Lauriston was greeted by Prince Volkonskii, who intended to entertain the French envoy at Benningsen's quarters. But Lauriston, offended at this reception, refused to confer with Volkonskii and returned to Murat's headquarters, declaring that he would only speak to Kutuzov. "This sudden rupture of relations somewhat disturbed the Russian staff," writes Thiers. "For the vehement national hatred against the French began to subside amid the higher ranks of the army, and they were unwilling to render peace quite impossible. And even the persons opposed to peace regretted the manner in which M. de Lauriston had been treated, although for a different motive—their fear that this offensive treatment might induce the French army to advance against them full of anger and determination before the Russian army had been reinforced or reorganized." Consequently, Thiers argues, Russians agreed to receive Lauriston at the main headquarters.

103. Mikhailovskii-Danilevskii, *Opisanie Otechestvennoi voiny 1812 g.*, III:76–77.

104. Wilson recorded in his diary that Kutuzov required "the Duke of Wurttemberg and myself to be present when Lauriston entered, that he might let him see how he was entouré en conseil." This decision was probably equally aimed at reassuring the Russian officers. "After mutual salutations from the Marshal, that Lauriston might not be ignored who we were, we retired but waited very near and saw that the conversation was very animated on the part of the Marshal by his gesture." Wilson, *Private Diary of Travels*, 184. Also see Joseph de Maistre to King Victor Emmanuel, October 8/20, 1812, in *Oeuvres complètes de J. de Maistre. Correspondance, 1806–1807* (Lyon: Librairie Générale Catholique, 1885), XII:262.

105. Kutuzov to Alexander, October 5, 1812, RGVIA, f. VUA, d. 3697, l. 2; Wilson, *Narrative of Events During the Invasion of Russia*, 187–190; Also see *Vestnik Evropy*, nos. 21–22, November 1812, 155–158.

106. Alexander Muravyev, "*Zapiski,*" *Russkii arkhiv* 11 (1885): 363; Louis Guillaume de Puibusque, *Lettres sur la guerre en Russie en 1812* (Paris: Magimel, Anselin, et Pochard, 1817), 160.

107. Alexander to Kutuzov, October 16, 1812, in Wilson, *Narrative of Events During the Invasion of Russia*, 203–204.

108. Adams, *Memoirs of John Quincy Adams Containing His Diary*, 414.

109. Arsenii Zakrevskii to Mikhail Vorontsov, October 10/22, 1812, in *Arkhiv knyazya Vorontsova*, XXXVII:236–237.

110. Wilson, *Private Diary of Travels*, 187. Colonel Marin, on the other hand, was pleased with Kutuzov's responses to Lauriston, which, he thought, "bloodied the vile Bonaparte's nose." Marin to Mikhail Vorontsov, September 27/October 9, 1812, in *Arkhiv knyazya Vorontsova*, XXXV:466.

111. Puibusque, *Lettres sur la guerre en Russie en 1812*, 163. Also see Dmitri Buturlin, "Kutuzov v 1812 g.," *Russkaya starina* 11 (1894): 194–195.

112. Wilson promptly denounced Kutuzov in a letter to the czar. See Wilson to Emperor Alexander, October 13/25, 1812, in Dubrovin, *Otechestvennaya voina v pis'makh sovremennikov*, 238.

113. Berthier to Kutuzov, October 18, 1812, *Correspondance de Napoleon Ier, publ. par ordre de l'Empereur Napoléon III* (Paris: Henri Plon, 1863), XXIV:267, no. 19, 277.

114. The French original of Kutuzov's letter to Berthier is in Dubrovin, *Otechestvennaya voina v pis'makh sovremennikov*, 229–230. The Russian copy, slightly revised, is in *M. I. Kutuzov. Sbornik dokumentov*, IV, part 2, 38–39. Also see Wilson, *Private Diary of Travels*, 200–201; Wilson to Lord Cathcart, October 20, 1812, in Dubrovin, *Otechestvennaya voina v pis'makh sovremennikov*, 230–231.

Chapter 26

1. Mathieu Dumas, *Souvenirs* . . . (Paris, 1839), III:455.

2. Albrecht von Muralt, *Beresina: Erinnerungen aus dem Feldzug Napoleons I in Russland 1812* (Bern: Hallwag, 1940), 78.

3. Napoleon to Marie-Louise, October 4–6, 1812, in *Correspondance générale* (Paris: Fayard, 2004–2015), XII:1133, 1161. See Napoleon to Cambacérès; Napoleon to Marie-Louise, September 23–24, 1812, in *Correspondance générale*, XII:1109–1110, 1114.

4. When the grand equerry continued to raise his concerns about a protracted sojourn at Moscow and about the winter, Napoleon again ridiculed him, telling Berthier and Michel Duroc that "Caulaincourt is already half-frozen."

5. Dumas, *Souvenirs*, III:455. "The mild temperatures that lasted much longer than usual this year all contributed in lulling him," believed Caulaincourt. "Even in private so strongly did the Emperor express his convictions of remaining in Moscow now that those held in his closest confidence continued to believe him for quite some time." Armand-Augustin-Louis, Marquis de Caulaincourt, *Mémoires du Général de Caulaincourt, duc de Vicence, grand écuyer de l'Empereur* (Paris: Plon, 1933), II:25–26.

6. Journal of Military Operations, October 1812, in *M. I. Kutuzov. Sbornik dokumentov* (Moscow: Voeniszdat, 1950), IV, part I, 400–401, 408–410, 434–435.

7. Kutuzov to Praskovya and Matvey Tolstoy, October 1/13, 1812, in *The Kutuzov Papers* 5 (1872): 648.

8. Hubert François Biot, *Souvenirs anecdotiques et militaires . . .* (Paris, 1901), 49.

9. Adrien Augustin Amalric, Comte de Mailly, *Mon journal pendant la campagne de Russie . . .* (Paris: J.-B. Gros, 1841).

10. Murat to Belliard, October 10, 1812, in Augustin Daniel Belliard, *Mémoires du Comte Belliard* (Paris: Berquet, 1842), I:112.

11. D. Bantysh-Kamenskii, *Biografii Rossiiskikh generalissimusov i general-fel'dmarshalov* (St. Petersburg: Tip. 3-go Departamenta Min. Gos. imushestv, 1840), III:157.

12. Kutuzov would have been well aware of the following passage in the ancient Greek historian's magnum opus: "Fabius did not purpose to fight out the issue with Hannibal, but wished, having plenty of time, money, and men, to wear out and consume gradually his culminating vigour, his scanty resources, and his small army. Therefore, always pitching his camp in hilly regions so as to be out of reach of the enemy's cavalry, he hung threateningly over them. If they sat still, he too kept quiet; but if they moved, he would fetch a circuit down from the heights and show himself just far enough away to avoid being forced to fight against his will, and yet near enough to make his very delays inspire the enemy with the fear that he was going to give battle at last. But for merely consuming time in this way he was generally despised by his countrymen, and roundly abused even in his own camp." Plutarch, *The Parallel Lives* (Cambridge, MA: Loeb Classical Library, 1916), III:133, e-edition at https://penelope.uchicago.edu/Thayer/E/Roman/Texts/Plutarch/Lives/Fabius_Maximus*.html.

13. Alexander Mikhailovskii-Danilevskii, *Opisanie Otechestvennoi voiny 1812 goda* (St. Petersburg, 1843), III:220; Alexander Mikhailovskii-Danilevskii, "Zapiski," *Istoricheskii vestnik* 10 (1890): 158.

14. Alexander Golitsyn, "Zapiska o voine 1812 goda . . . ," in Konstantin Voenskii, *Otechestvennaya voina 1812 goda v zapiskakh sovremennikov* (St. Petersburg: Tip. Glav. Uprv. Udelov, 1911), 72.

15. Kutuzov to his wife, September 19/October 1, 1812; Kutuzov to the czar, October 1/13, 1812, in *M. I. Kutuzov. Sbornik dokumentov*, IV, part I, 325, 419; Kutuzov to his daughter, October 2/14, 1812, in *Russkaya starina* 6 (1874): 368.

16. News for the Army, September 30/October 12, 1812, in *M. I. Kutuzov. Sbornik dokumentov*, IV, part 1, 406.

17. Alexander Chicherin, *Dnevnik Aleksandra Chicherina, 1812–1813* (Moscow, 1966), 32.

18. Nikolai Mitarevskii, *Vospominaniya o voine 1812 goda* (Moscow: A. Mamontov, 1871), 118–119.

19. Alexander Muravyev, "Zapiski," *Russkaya starina* 11 (1885): 363. "The inaction of the Russian main army was becoming the subject of dissatisfaction"; Robert

Wilson, *Narrative of Events During the Invasion of Russia by Napoleon Bonaparte and the Retreat of the French Army* (London: John Murray, 1860), 205. "No one has seen Kutuzov," Rostopchin wrote a friend on September 25; *Pamyatniki novoi russkoi istorii* (St. Petersburg: Maikov, 1872), II:185.

20. Wilson, *Narrative of Events During the Invasion of Russia*, 205; Levin von Bennigsen, "Zapiski . . . ," *Russkaya starina* 9 (1909): 515–518.

21. Bennigsen to his wife, October 10/22, 1812, in N. Dubrovin, ed., *Otechestvennaya voina v pis'makh sovremennikov* (St. Petersburg, 1882), 235; Robert Wilson, *Private Diary of Travels, Personal Services, and Public Events* (London: J. Murray, 1861), 194.

22. Bennigsen, "Zapiski," 519.

23. Disposition for the Battle at Tarutino, October 3/15, 1812, in *M. I. Kutuzov. Sbornik dokumentov*, IV, part II, 3–7. Also see Mikhail Vistitskii, "Iz zapisok Vistitskago," in V. Kharkevich, ed., *1812 god v dnevnikakh, zapiskakh i vospominaniyakh sovremennikov* (Vilna: Tip. Shtaba Vilen. Voen. Okruga, 1900), I:189; Bennigsen, "Zapiski," 518; M. Evreinov, "Pamyat' o 1812 g.," *Russkii arkhiv* 2 (1874): 451. For discussion of the battle, see V. Bessonov, *Tarutinskoe srazhenie* (Moscow: Kniga, 2008), 49–52.

24. In his after-battle nominations, Kutuzov described Toll as an "outstanding" officer who "personally conducted reconnaissance of the enemy camp, prepared the plan of attack, and precisely fulfilled my instructions." *M. I. Kutuzov. Sbornik dokumentov*, IV, part II, 25.

25. Kutuzov to Yermolov, October 4/16, 1812, in *M. I. Kutuzov. Sbornik dokumentov*, IV, part II, 8–9.

26. E. Gersevanov, "Obyasnenie prichiny pochemu otlozheno bylo napadenie pri Tarutino: rasskaz veterana 1812 g. E. P. Gersevanova," *Zhurnal dlya chteniya vospitannikam voenno-uchebnykh zavedenii* 123 (1856): 242–244; Denis Davydov, *Sochineniya* (Moscow, 1962), 538; Golitsyn, "Zapiski," 74; Alexander Scherbinin, "Zapiski Aleksandra Scherbinina," in V. Kharkevich, ed., *1812 god v dnevnikakh, zapiskakh i vospominaniyakh sovremennikov* (Vilna: Tip. Shtaba Vilen. Voen. Okruga, 1900), 38. Glinka, who attended the banquet, states thirty generals were there. Letter of October 4/16, 1812, in Sergei Glinka, "Pis'ma russkago ofitsera," http:// militera.lib.ru/db/glinka1/01.html.

27. Kutuzov to Yermolov, October 5/17, 1812, in *M. I. Kutuzov. Sbornik dokumentov*, IV, part II, 12.

28. Order to the Army, October 4/16, 1812, in *M. I. Kutuzov. Sbornik dokumentov*, IV, part II, 10. Also see Kutuzov to Dorokhov, October 5/17, 1812, RGVIA, f. VUA, d. 3521, l. 18.

29. Nikolai Mitarevskii, *Vospominaniya o voine 1812 goda* (Moscow: Tip. A. I. Mamontova, 1871), 119.

30. Waldemar de Löwenstern, *Mémoires du général-major russe Baron de Löwenstern (1776–1858)* (Paris: A. Fontemoing, 1903), I:302.

31. Letter of October 7/19, 1812, in Glinka, "Pis'ma russkago ofitsera," http://militera.lib.ru/db/glinka1/01.html; Evreinov, "Pamyat' o 1812 g.," 451.

32. Alexey Yermolov, *The Czar's General: The Memoirs of a Russian General in the Napoleonic Wars*, translated and edited by Alexander Mikaberidze (Welwyn Garden City: Ravenhall Books, 2005), 180.

33. Bennigsen to Kutuzov, October 7/19, 1812, in *M. I. Kutuzov. Sbornik dokumentov*, IV, part II, 20.

34. Wilson, *Narrative of Events During the Invasion of Russia*, 209; Bennigsen, "Zapiski," 522; Pavel Grabbe, "Iz pamyantnykh zapisok Grafa P. Kh. Grabbe: 1812 god," *Russkii arkhiv* 3 (1873): 371.

35. Joseph de Maistre to Victor Emmanuel of Sardinia, June 14, 1813, in de Maistre, *Peterburgskie pis'ma* (St. Petersburg, 1995), 239. De Maistre also believed that Kutuzov did not want "to see two field marshals instead of one," i.e., to see his rival Bennigsen promoted in case of victory. Maistre noted that this was why Kutuzov declined to employ Filippo Paulucci delle Roncole, an Italian marquis who had served in the Sardinian army before making a stellar career in the Russian service. "Kutuzov would rather let Russia perish than receive help from a foreigner, especially a young and enterprising one, to whom the public opinion could attribute his successes, even if in part." Joseph de Maistre to Comte de Front, October 7/19, 1812, in *Oeuvres complètes de J. de Maistre. Correspondance, 1806–1807* (Lyon: Librairie Générale Catholique, 1885), XII:257. Exasperated by Kutuzov's actions, Wilson accused him of "suspending the offensive and changing it to a timid defensive, as if desirous of averting the catastrophe of his enemy; and his conduct in this affair would only be explicable by that suspicion, unless the relation of subsequent proceedings should prove that his motive was to be ascribed with more truth to a rival jealousy of his second in command." Wilson, *Narrative of Events During the Invasion of Russia*, 212.

36. Wilson, *Narrative of Events During the Invasion of Russia*, 211.

37. Davydov, *Sochineniya*, 538; Löwenstern, *Mémoires*, I:303–304; Mikhailovskii-Danilevskii, *Opisanie Otechestvennoi voiny 1812 g.*, III:228; Yermolov, *The Czar's General*, 180–181.

38. Löwenstern, *Mémoires*, I, 303.

39. The French lost some 2,800 men, of whom 1,150 were prisoners or missing; two generals were killed and two more wounded. The Russian losses amounted to 1,500 killed and wounded, but they captured thirty-eight cannon, a standard, and the bulk of the enemy baggage. For an in-depth study of the battle, see Bessonov, *Tarutinskoe srazhenie*, 69–103, as well as a series of articles by A. Ulyanov and A. Vasiliev: A. Ulyanov, "Tarutinskoe srazhenie: problemy izucheniya," in *Sobytiya Otechestvennoi voiny 1812 g. na territorii Kaluzhskoi gubernii* (Maloyaroslavets, 1993); A. Ulyanov, "Boi na reke Chernishne," in *Ot Tarutino do Maloyaroslavetsa. K 190-letiyu Maloyaroslavetskogo srazheniya. Sbornik statei* (Kaluga, 2002), http://www.museum.ru/museum/1812/Libr

ary/Mmnk/1994_4.html; A. Vasiliev, "Frantsuzskie karabinery v boyu pri Vinkovo 18 oktyabrya 1812 goda," in *Sobytiya Otechetsvennoi voiny 1812 g. na territorii Kaluzhskoi gubernii* (Maloyaroslavets, 1998), http://www.museum.ru/museum/1812/Library/Mmnk/1998_6.html.

40. Wilson, *Narrative of Events During the Invasion of Russia*, 212.

41. Scherbinin, "Zapiski," 42.

42. Wilson to Lord Cathcart, October 20, 1812, in Dubrovin, *Otechestvennaya voina v pis'makh sovremennikov*, 231.

43. Sergei Mayevskii, "Moi vek ili istoriya Sergeya Ivanovicha Mayevskogo, 1779–1848," *Russkaya starina* 8 (1873): 156–157.

44. Löwenstern, *Mémoires*, I:305.

45. "Before the eyes of the whole army, Kutuzov forbids sending even a single man to my aid, those are his own words. . . . His cowardice exceeds even the limits accepted for poltroons." Bennigsen to his wife, October 10/22, 1812, in Dubrovin, *Otechestvennaya voina v pis'makh sovremennikov*, 235.

46. Kutuzov to Alexander, October 7/19, 1812; Kutuzov to the Commanders of the Flying Detchments, October 8/20, 1812, in *M. I. Kutuzov. Sbornik dokumentov*, IV, part II, 19, 37.

47. Kutuzov to his wife, October 7/19, 1812, in *The Kutuzov Papers* 4 (1872): 649.

48. John Quincy Adams, *Memoirs of John Quincy Adams Containing His Diary from 1795 to 1848*, edited by Charles Francis Adams (Philadelphia: Lippincott, 1874), 418.

49. Alexander to Kutuzov, October 16–18/28–30, 1812, in RGVIA, f. VUA, d. 3645, ll. 4–6. Kutuzov nominated dozens of officers for rewards and promotions, which the czar approved in January 1813. For a list of the nominated senior officers, see *M. I. Kutuzov. Sbornik dokumentov*, IV, part II, 23–29.

50. Adams, *Memoirs of John Quincy Adams Containing His Diary*, 418.

51. "Lichnye pis'ma generala Raevskago," in *1812–1814* (Moscow: Terra, 1992), 228.

52. Testimony of Captain Skobelev, who read the dispatches, in Alexander Voyeikov, "General Graf Leontii Leontievich Bennigsen," *Russkii arkhiv* 11 (1868): 1858–1859.

53. Pierre-Louis de Beauvollier, "Mémoires sur l'expédition de Russie," in Alphonse de Beauchamp, *Mémoires secrets et inédits pour servir à l'histoire contemporaine* (Paris: Vernarel et Tenon, 1825), II:63–64.

54. Jean Rapp, *Mémoires du général Rapp, premier aide-de-camp de Napoléon* (Paris: Bossange Frères, 1823), 181.

55. Charles Tristan Montholon, *Mémoires pour servir à l'histoire de France sous Napoléon, écrits a Sainte-Hélène* (Paris, 1823), II:104.

Chapter 27

1. Dokhturov to Kutuzov, October 10/22, 1812, RGVIA, f. VUA, d. 3509, ll. 117–117b.

2. Jean-Pierre Barrau, "Jean-Pierre Armand Barrau, quartier-maître au IVe Corps de la Grande Armée, sur la campagne de Russie," *Rivista italiana di studi Napoleonici* 1 (1979): 91; Charles-Pierre-Lubin Griois, *Mémoires du Général Griois, 1792–1822* (Paris: Plon-Nourrit, 1909), II:82; Hauptmann K. G. F. Kurz, *Die Würtemberger in Rußland: Denkwürdigkeiten aus dem Jahre 1812. Von einem Würtembergischen Officier* (Esslingen: J. F. Schreiber, 1838), 125–126. Also see Adrien Mailly, *Mon journal pendant la campagne de Russie* (Paris, 1841), 72; Adrien-Jean-Baptiste François Bourgogne, *Mémoires du Sergent Bourgogne, 1812–1813* (Paris, 1910), 56.

3. Napoleon to Maret, October 16, 1812, *Correspondance de Napoleon Ier, publ. par ordre de l'Empereur Napoléon III* (Paris: Henri Plon, 1863), XXIV, no. 19, 275, 265.

4. See Dorokhov's reports of October 7–10/19–22 in RGVIA, f. VUA, d. 3509, ll. 85–87, 100–100b, 115–116. Also see *General Staff Archives*, XIX:23, 27–28.

5. Dorokhov to Konovnitsyn, October 9/21, 1812, in *M. I. Kutuzov. Sbornik Dokumentov* (Moscow: Voeniszdat, 1950), IV, part II, 57–58; Dmitrii Bolgovskii, "Iz vospominanii D. N. Bolgovskogo," in V. Kharkevich, ed., *1812 god v dnevnikakh, zapiskakh i vospominaniyakh sovremennikov* (Vilna: Tip. Shtaba Vilen. Voen. Okruga, 1900), I:239; Alexey Yermolov, *The Czar's General: The Memoirs of a Russian General in the Napoleonic Wars*, translated and edited by Alexander Mikaberidze (Welwyn Garden City: Ravenhall Books, 2005), 181–182; Waldemar de Löwenstern, *Mémoires du général-major russe Baron de Löwenstern (1776–1858)* (Paris: A. Fontemoing, 1903), I:308.

6. Bolgovskii, "Iz vozpominanii," 239.

7. Dokhturov to Kutuzov, October 10/22, 1812 (7 p.m.), RGVIA, f. VUA, d. 3509, ll. 117–117b.

8. Yermolov, *The Czar's General*, 181–182; Denis Davydov, "Dnevnik partizanskikh deistvii 1812 goda," in *Sochineniya* (Moscow, 1962), 303, 344–345; Bolgovskii, "Iz vozpominanii," 240–241.

9. Dokhturov to Kutuzov, October 10/22, 1812 (9:30 p.m.), RGVIA, f. VUA, d. 3509, ll. 117–117b. Also see Dokhturov to Kutuzov, October 14/26, 1812, RGVIA, f. VUA, d. 3509, l. 220.

10. Davydov, *Sochineniya*, 347–348.

11. Dokhturov to Kutuzov, October 10/22, 1812, RGVIA, f. VUA, d. 3509, l. 117b.

12. Dokhturov to Kutuzov, October 14/26, 1812, RGVIA, f. VUA, d. 3509, ll. 220–221; Davydov, *Sochineniya*, 345; Nikolai Mitarevskii, *Vospominaniya o voine 1812 goda* (Moscow: A. Mamontov, 1871), 125–126. Also see Nikolai Mitarevskii, *Nashestvie nepriyatelya na Rossiiu* (Moscow, 1878), 161.

13. Bolgovskii, "Iz vospominanii," 242–243. Löwenstern describes being sent by Kutuzov on a reconnaissance mission to confirm the reports of Napoleon's retreat from Moscow. *Mémoires*, I:309–310.

14. Disposition for Departing from the Tarutino Camp, October 11/23, 1812, in *M. I. Kutuzov. Sbornik dokumentov*, IV, part II, 83–84. Also see Kutuzov to Dokhturov, Platov, and Miloradovich, October 11/23, 1812, RGVIA, f. VUA, d. 3521, ll. 23–25. Dokhturov's 6th Corps was reinforced with the 1st Cavalry Reserve Corps, five Cossack regiments, 32nd Battery Company, 7th Horse Artillery Company, and the Guard Horse Artillery Company.

15. Yermolov, *The Czar's General*, 183; Davydov, "Dnevnik partizanskikh deistvii 1812 goda," 346.

16. Yermolov to Dokhturov, October 11/23, 1812, in *General Staff Archives*, XIX:35; Dokhturov to Kutuzov, October 14/26, 1812, RGVIA, f. VUA, d. 3509, ll. 220–221. Kutuzov told the czar the battle commenced at five o'clock in the morning. *M. I. Kutuzov. Sbornik dokumentov*, IV, part II, 97.

17. Yermolov, *The Czar's General*, 184.

18. Kutuzov to Platov, n.d. [ca. October 11–12/23–24, 1812], in *M. I. Kutuzov. Sbornik dokumentov*, IV, part II, 97.

19. Yermolov, *The Czar's General*, 184–187.

20. Davydov suggests that Kutuzov's order to construct "several redoubts" behind Maloyaroslavets reflected experiences he had gained fighting the Ottomans, who routinely resorted to such tactics. Davydov, "Dnevnik partizanskikh deistvii 1812 goda," 346; Yermolov, *The Czar's General*, 185.

21. Kutuzov to Alexander, February 9/21, 1813, in *M. I. Kutuzov. Sbornik dokumentov*, IV, part II, 109.

22. Kutuzov to Alexander, February 9/21, 1813, in *M. I. Kutuzov. Sbornik dokumentov*, IV, part II, 109.

23. Robert Wilson, *Narrative of Events During the Invasion of Russia by Napoleon Bonaparte and the Retreat of the French Army* (London: John Murray, 1860), 229. Also see Modest Bogdanovich, *Istoriya otechestvennoi voiny 1812 goda* (St. Petersburg: S. Strugovshikov, 1859), III:38–39.

24. See Ivan Bezsonov, *Bitva v Maloyaroslavtse* (Kaluga: Tip. Gubern. Pravlenia, 1912); A. Vasiliev, "Srazhenie za maloyaroslavets 12 oktyabrya 1812 goda," in *Ot Tarutino do Maloyaroslavtsa: k 190-letiyu Maloyaroslavetskago srazheniya* (Kaluga: Zolotaya Alleya, 2002), http://www.museum.ru/1812/Library/Mmnk/2002_9.html.

25. Philippe-Paul de Ségur, *Histoire de Napoléon et de la grande armée pendant l'année 1812* (Brussels: H. Tarlier, 1825), II:81–82.

26. Kutuzov to Alexander, February 9/21, 1813, in *M. I. Kutuzov. Sbornik dokumentov*, IV, part II, 110.

27. Kutuzov to P. Kaverin, October 15/27, 1812, RGVIA, f. VUA, d. 3521, l. 27.

28. Armand de Caulaincourt, *Mémoires du général de Caulaincourt, duc de Vicence, grand écuyer de l'Empereur* (Paris: Plon, 1933), II:111–112.

29. Löwenstern, far from being Kutuzov's admirer, noted that he had "never seen so much activity from the field marshal" as in those days. *Mémoires*, I:310.

30. On the size of the Russian army, see Sergei Shvedov, "O chislenosti i poteryakh Russkoi armii v srazhenii pri Maloyaroslavtse oktyabrya 1812 goda," in *M. I. Kutuzov i russkaya armiya na II etape Otchestvennoi voiny 1812 goda* (Maloyaroslavets, 1995), http://www.museum.ru/1812/Library/Mmnk/1995_9.html.

31. Wilson, *Narrative of Events*, 231.

32. N. Garnich, *1812 god* (Moscow: Gos. Izd. Kult.-Prosvet. Literaturym, 1956), 264. Also see Pavel Zhilin, *Otechestvennaya voina 1812 goda* (Moscow: Nauka, 1988), 289–290; L. Beskrovnyi, *Russkoe voennoe iskusstvo XIX v* (Moscow, 1974), 118.

33. *M. I. Kutuzov. Sbornik dokumentov*, IV, part II, 98.

34. Wilson, *Narrative of Events*, 232.

35. The day after the battle, Yermolov complained that Platov "failed to deliver intelligence about the enemy and did not determine which route the enemy retreated." See Yermolov to Kutuzov, October 15/27, RGVIA, f. VUA, d. 3509, l. 206. On October 27, Platov's short report simply stated that Napoleon was retreating along the Borovsk road. Platov to Konovnitsyn, October 15/27, 1812, RGVIA, f. VUA, d. 3509, l. 209.

36. Löwenstern, *Mémoires*, I:311. Events at Krasnyi in mid-November offer another example of the interesting relationship between Kutuzov and Toll. Late in the afternoon of November 16, Colonel Euler received Toll's order to immediately move his artillery companies to Krasnyi. He complied at once, marching through the night and passing by the main headquarters where everyone was asleep. The noise of dozens of artillery limbers and caissons passing by woke up Baron Karl von Löwenstern, the commander of the army artillery, who seemed unaware of the order and was "quite surprised by my movement, though, having read [Toll's] directive, he told me to proceed with it." Approaching Krasnyi, Euler discovered a chain of Cossack patrols marking the edge of the Russian positions; realizing that he no longer had any protection, he immediately stopped to seek clarity on his directive. At dawn, Kutuzov stumbled across this "dense artillery column" and was very "surprised" to see it there. "He asked to see me, but it seems he was forewarned that this was not my mistake, for he simply asked me, 'What are you doing all the way here, at the Cossack outposts,' and then proceeded to ask me about supplies." This incident suggests that either Toll made a mistake amid the fog of war or deliberately tried to circumvent Kutuzov's order and move troops closer to the scene of battle. The fact that the commander in chief and the artillery commander both were "surprised" by the reserve artillery deployment is telling. A. Euler, "Zapiski . . . ," *Russkii arkhiv* 2 (1880): 361.

37. Wilson, *Narrative of Events*, 234. "The retreat dismayed the entire army," commented Löwenstern. *Mémoires*, I:314.

38. Robert Wilson, *Private Diary of Travels, Personal Services, and Public Events* (London: J. Murray, 1861), 203.

39. Wilson, *Narrative of Events*, 234.

40. Louis Guillaume de Puibusque, *Lettres sur la guerre en Russie en 1812* (Paris: Magimel, Anselin, et Pochard, 1817), 169.

41. Puibusque, *Lettres sur la guerre de Russie en 1812*, 164–165.

42. Testimonies of Peter Konovnitsyn and Peter Kikin, in Alexander Voyeikov, "General Graf Leontii Leontievich Bennigsen," *Russkii arkhiv* 11 (1868): 1858.

43. John Lewis Gaddis, *On Grand Strategy* (New York: Penguin, 2018), ebook sec. 176.

44. Kutuzov to his wife, November 14/26, 1812, in *The Kutuzov Papers*, 5 (1872): 655.

Chapter 28

1. Raymond Eymery de Montesquiou-Fezensac, *A Journal of the Russian Campaign of 1812* (London: Parker, Furnivall, and Parker, 1852), 76.

2. François Dumonceau, *Mémoires du Général Comte François Dumonceau, 1812–1813* (Brussels: Editions Brepols, 1960), II:190–191.

3. After Maloyaroslavets, Kutuzov rested his army and them split it into three columns. The northernmost consisted of Cossacks and Paskevich's 26th Division, tasked with advancing along the Moscow-Smolensk high road. Miloradovich, leading the advance guard, formed the central column, while Kutuzov himself marched with the main body of the Russian army some distance to the south.

4. Waldemar de Löwenstern, *Mémoires du général-major russe Baron de Löwenstern (1776–1858)* (Paris: A. Fontemoing, 1903), I:314.

5. Kutuzov spent a couple of days regrouping his army before launching the pursuit. The main Russian army moved along the Kuzovo-Suleika-Bykovo route, while the advance guard, led by Miloradovich, operated between the main forces and the Old Smolensk road, and Ataman Matvei Ivanovich Platov's Cossacks (fifteen regiments, reinforced by the 26th Infantry Division of General Ivan Paskevich) pressed the enemy along the Old Smolensk road. In addition, the flying detachments were always at hand to harass the enemy.

6. Karl Friedrich von Toll, *Denkwürdigkeiten aus dem Leben des Kaiserl. russ. Generals von der der Infanterie Carl Friedrich Grafen von Toll*, edited by Theodor von Bernhardi (Leipzig: Otto Wigand, 1856), II:271–272.

7. Kutuzov to Alexander, October 16/28, 1812, *General Staff Archives*, XIX:135–136; Kutuzov to Wittgenstein, October 16/28, 1812, RGVIA, d. VUA, d. 3521, ll. 29b–30.

8. Kutuzov to Chichagov, October 23/November 4, 1812, RGVIA, f. VUA, d. 3518, part 2, l. 540.

9. Kutuzov to Major General Adam Ozharovskii, October 17/29, 1812, RGVIA, f. VUA, d. 3521, l. 33.

10. Löwenstern, *Mémoires*, I:317.

11. Löwenstern, *Mémoires*, I:319.

12. Kutuzov to Praskovya and Matvey Tolstoy, October 17/29, 1812, in *M. I. Kutuzov. Sbornik dokumentov* (Moscow: Voeniszdat, 1950), IV, part 2, 156.

13. Robert Wilson, *Private Diary of Travels, Personal Services, and Public Events* (London: J. Murray, 1861), 211.

14. Alexey Yermolov, *The Czar's General: The Memoirs of a Russian General in the Napoleonic Wars*, translated and edited by Alexander Mikaberidze (Welwyn Garden City: Ravenhall Books, 2005), 192.

15. Kutuzov to his wife, October 16/28 and October 20/November 1, 1812, in *The Kutuzov Papers* 4 (1872): 649–650.

16. Dmitrii Neverovskii, "Zapiska o sluzhbe svoei v 1812 g.," *CIOIDR* 1 (1859): 81.

17. Kutuzov to his wife, October 28/November 9, 1812, in *The Kutuzov Papers* 4 (1872): 651.

18. Kutuzov to his wife, October 23/November 4, 1812, in *The Kutuzov Papers* 4 (1872): 650.

19. Wilson, *Private Diary*, 218.

20. Nikolai Durnovo's diary in A. Tartakovskii, ed., *1812 god . . . voennye dnevniki* (Moscow: Sovetskaya Rossiya, 1990), 102.

21. Konovnitsyn to his wife, in P. Schukin, ed., *Bumagi otnosyaschiyasya do Otechestvennoi voiny 1812 goda* (Moscow: A. Mamontov, 1904), VIII:113.

22. Löwenstern, *Mémoires*, I:317–318.

23. Kutuzov to his wife, October 30/November 11, 1811, in *The Kutuzov Papers* 4 (1872): 652.

24. Ludwig Wolzogen und Neuhaus, *Memoiren des Königlich Preussischen Generals der Infanterie Ludwig Freiherrn von Wolzogen* (Leipzig, 1851), 162–163.

25. Testimonies of Bogan von Knorring and Alexander Balashov in Voyeikov, "Bennigsen," *Russkii arkhiv* 11 (1868): 1857.

26. The weather was warm enough for Kutuzov and his entire headquarters to sleep in the open air after the battle at Maloyaroslavets. "The evening was pleasant. The day was as hot as at the height of the summer." Löwenstern, *Mémoires*, I:310.

27. Friedrich Klinkhardt, *Feldzugs-Erinnerungen des Königlich Westfälischen Musikmeisters Friedrich Klinkhardt aus den Jahren 1812–1815* (Braunschweig, 1908), 61; Claude-François de Méneval, *Memoirs Illustrating the History of Napoleon I from 1802 to 1815* (New York, 1894), III:71.

28. Entry for November 13, 1812, in Wilson, *Private Diary*, 214.

29. Kutuzov to his wife, October 28/November 9, 1812, in *The Kutuzov Papers* 4 (1872): 651.

30. Order to the Army, October 19/31, 1812, in *M. I. Kutuzov. Sbornik dokumentov*, IV, part 2, 166.

31. Order to the Army, October 29/November 10, 1812, RGVIA, f. VUA, d. 3524, l. 61b.

32. Kutuzov to his wife, October 28/November 9, 1812, in *The Kutuzov Papers* 4 (1872): 651.

33. Kutuzov to Elisabeth Khitrovo, November 10/22, 1812, in *The Kutuzov Papers* 10 (1874): 372.

34. Adrien Jean Baptiste François Bourgogne, *Memoirs of Sergeant Bourgogne (1812–1813)* (London: W. Heinemann, 1899), 76.

35. Wilson, *Private Diary*, 225.

36. Kutuzov to Alexander, November 18, 1812, in *M. I. Kutuzov. Sbornik dokumentov*, IV, part 2, 308; Journal of Military Operations Between November 15 and 19, in *M. I. Kutuzov. Sbornik dokumentov*, IV, part 2, 318. On November 21, Kutuzov wrote that "the captured alone include 6 generals, 190 staff and junior officers, 19,170 rank and file, 97 guns in addition to 112 pieces that [the French] abandoned upon departure from Smolensk." In a letter to Wittgenstein, he repeated the same numbers but added that "6 flags and field marshal's baton, entire train and treasury" were also captured. Prince Kutuzov to General Kutuzov, November 21, 1812, no. 477; Kutuzov to Wittgenstein, November 22, 1812, no. 480, in V. Kharkevich, *1812 g. Berezina* (St. Petersburg, 1893), 29, 32–33.

37. Eugene de Württemberg, *Erinnerungen aus dem Feldzuge des Jahres 1812 in Rußland von dem Herzog Eugen von Württemberg* (Breslau, 1846), 154–155. Löwenstern also recalls how his request to attack was rebuffed by a Russian general who grumbled about Kutuzov's strategy of a "golden bridge." Löwenstern, *Mémoires*, I:349–350.

38. Kutuzov to Mikhail Komburley, November 10/22, 1812, RGVIA, f. VUA, d. 3521, l. 75b; Kutuzov to Wittgenstein, November 10/22, 1812, RGVIA f. VUA, d. 3514, l. 588; Kutuzov to Chichagov, November 6/18, 1812, no. 449, in Kharkevich, *1812 g. Berezina*, 1–2.

39. Denis Davydov, *Sochineniya* (Moscow, 1962), 371, 541–542.

40. Yermolov, *The Czar's General*, 202.

41. Rimsky-Korsakov to O. Kozodavlev, December 16/28, 1812, in N. Dubrovin, ed., *Otechestvennaya voina v pis'makh sovremennikov, 1812–1815 gg.* (St. Petersburg, 1882), 401.

42. N. Rayevskii to Count A. Samoilov, December 13/25, 1812, in *Arkhiv rayevskikh* (St. Petersburg, 1908), I:183.

43. Yermolov to Kutuzov, November 3/15, 1812, in *General Staff Archives*, XX:30. Kutuzov also rebuffed appeals by Konovnitsyn, Toll, and other officers to commit forces on the last day of the battle. See Alexander Scherbinin, "Zapiski Aleksandra Scherbinina," in V. Kharkevich, ed., *1812 god v dnevnikakh, zapiskakh i vospominaniyakh sovremennikov* (Vilna: Tip. Shtaba Vilen. Voen. Okruga, 1900), 47–48.

44. A. Euler, "Zapiski . . . ," *Russkii arkhiv* 2 (1880): 361.

45. Robert Wilson, *Narrative of Events During the Invasion of Russia by Napoleon Bonaparte and the Retreat of the French Army* (London: John Murray, 1860), 319;

Wilson to Alexander, November 19, 1812, in Dubrovin, *Otechestvennaya voina v pis'makh sovremennikov*, 326.

46. Löwenstern, *Mémoires*, I:324–325.

47. Kutuzov to his wife, October 28/November 9, 1812, in *The Kutuzov Papers* 4 (1872): 651.

48. Kutuzov to his wife, October 30/November 11, 1812, in *The Kutuzov Papers* 4 (1872): 652.

49. Pavel Puschin, *Dnevnik Pavla Puschina, 1812–1814* (Leningrad: Leningrad University Press, 1987), 60.

50. Alexander to Kutuzov, October 30/November 11, 1812, in Dubrovin, *Otechestvennaya voina v pis'makh sovremennikov*, 303.

51. Yermolov commented that "Toll took advantage of every chance to provoke disagreement between [Kutuzov and Bennigsen] and prudently sought to increase his influence over the frail" field marshal. *The Czar's General*, 217–218.

52. Robert Wilson to his wife, November 19/December 1, 1812, in Dubrovin, *Otechestvennaya voina v pismakh sovremennikov*, 364; Wilson, *Private Diary of Travels, Personal Services, and Public Events*, 232.

53. Kutuzov to his wife, October 28–30/November 9–11, 1812, in *The Kutuzov Papers* 4 (1872): 651–652.

54. Voyeikov, "Bennigsen," 1859. Also see Robert Wilson to his wife, November 19/December 1, 1812; Emperor Alexander to Bennigsen, November 21, 1812; Bennigsen to his wife, November 21, 1812, in Dubrovin, *Otechestvennaya voina v pismakh sovremennikov*, 364, 370–372.

55. Löwenstern, *Mémoires*, I:321.

56. "Otchet o deistviyakh intendantskogo upravleniya v voine protiv frantsuzov v 1812, 1813 i 1814 godakh," in *M. I. Kutuzov. Sbornik dokumentov*, IV, part 2, 703.

57. Alexander Chicherin, *Dnevnik Aleksandra Chicherina, 1812–1813* (Moscow, 1966), 63.

58. Mitarevskii, *Vospominaniya o voine 1812 goda*, 141–142, 148–149.

59. Aleksei Karpov, "Iz zapisok . . . ," in V. Kallash, ed., *Dvenadtsatii god v vospominanyakh i perepiske sovremennikov* (Moscow: I. Sytin, 1912), 222. Also see Boris von Uxküll, *Arms and the Woman: The Diaries of Baron Boris von Uxküll, 1812–1819* (New York: Macmillan, 1966), 100.

60. Carl von Clausewitz, *Der Feldzug von 1812 in Russland, der Feldzug von 1813 bis zum Waffenstillstand und der Feldzug von 1814 in Frankreich*. Edited by Marie von Clausewitz (Berlin: Ferdinand Dümmler, 1835), 203–204.

61. Eugene de Württemberg, *Erinnerungen aus dem Feldzuge des Jahres 1812 in Russland von dem Herzog Eugen von Württemberg* (Breslau, 1846), 171–172. Also see Eugene de Württemberg, "Vospominania o kampanii 1812 g v Rossii," *Voennii zhurnal* 3 (1849): 131.

Chapter 29

1. Emperor Alexander to Chichagov, September 13, 1812, RGVIA, d. 3546, ll. 6–9b; Alexander to Tormasov, Wittgenstein and Steinheil, September 13, 1812, in *General Staff Archive*, XVIII:210–212; Alexander to Kutuzov, September 13, 1812, in Modest Bogdanovich, *Istoriya otechestvennoi voiny 1812 goda* (St. Petersburg: S. Strugovshikov, 1859), II:344–345, 605–614.

2. Alexander to Chichagov, September 13, 1812, in Bogdanovich, *Istoriya otechestvennoi voiny 1812 goda*, II:607; *General Staff Archive*, XVIII:211; *M. I. Kutuzov. Sbornik dokumentov* (Moscow: Voeniszdat, 1950), IV:463–465. For an interesting discussion, see S. Shvedov, "Deistviya M. I. Kutuzova v Berezinskoi operatsii," in *Vrotoi etap Otechestvennoi voiny 1812 g.* (Maloyaroslavets, 1997), 77–81.

3. Soviet historians—P. Zhilin, B. Abalykhin, L. Beskrovnyi, etc.—did their best to denigrate the czar's role in the drafting of the plan and to assign all credit to Kutuzov, who, in their words, saw the weaknesses of the plan, formally accepted it, and then carried out his own plan.

4. See Chichagov's lengthy report to Kutuzov, dated October 3/15, 1812, which took almost two weeks to reach Kutuzov, who then forwarded it to the czar. *M. I. Kutuzov. Sbornik dokumentov*, IV, part 2, 140–143.

5. Alexey Yermolov, *The Czar's General: The Memoirs of a Russian General in the Napoleonic Wars*, translated and edited by Alexander Mikaberidze (Welwyn Garden City: Ravenhall Books, 2005), 208.

6. Armand Domergue, *La Russie pendant les guerres de l'empire (1805–1815): Souvenirs historiques* (Paris: A. Bertrand, 1835), II:282–283.

7. Earlier that fall Oertel had received orders from Kutuzov to gather supplies for the approaching main Russian army and prepare to engage the enemy, *if* he received no other instructions from his immediate superior, Chichagov. Despite this proviso, Oertel used these dispatches to justify his refusal to submit to the admiral. See Kutuzov to Oertel, October 28/November 9, 1812, in *M. I. Kutuzov. Sbornik dokumentov*, IV, part 2, 230–231; Kutuzov to Chichagov, October 28/November 9, 1812, in RGVIA, f. VUA, d. 3518, part 2, ll. 590–590b.

8. Chichagov to Ertel, November 11, 13, and 19, 1812, nos. 1091, 1095, 1103, and 1138, RGVIA, d. 3517, ll. 39b–40, 41–41b, 45, 55; Chichagov to Alexander, November 17, 1812, RGVIA, d. 3700, l. 314; Chichagov to Tuchkov and Ertel, November 19, 1812, RGVIA, d. 3517, ll. 53b, 55; Tuchkov to Chichagov, November 26, 1812, RGVIA, d. 3518/2, ll. 110–111. Chichagov replaced Oertel with Major General Sergei Tuchkov, who was later dismissed for plundering Prince Radziwill's estate.

9. Joseph de Maistre to the King of Sardinia, July 14, 1813, in *Russkii arkhiv* 1 (1912): 56.

10. Yermolov, *The Czar's General*, 208.

11. Kutuzov to D. Troshinskii, the Marshal of Nobility of Poltava Province, October 9/21, 1812, in *M. I. Kutuzov. Sbornik dokumentov*, IV, part 2, 56.

12. Tyrconnell to Cathcart, November 6/18, 1812, in N. Dubrovin, ed., *Otechestvennaya voina v pismakh sovremennikov, 1812–1815 gg.* (St. Petersburg, 1882), 322, 324.

13. For details, see Alexander Mikaberidze, *Napoleon's Great Escape: The Battle of the Berezina* (Barnsley: Pen & Sword, 2010), 53–69. Chichagov's "hasty intention of leading the entire army through the town and fighting the enemy on the opposite riverbank was, however, cancelled because of strong insistence of [Chichagov's] officers and, around 11:00 a.m., orders were issued to fortify [the] heights on the [right] bank and make arrangements for the burning of the bridge." Tyrconnell to Cathcart, November 30, 1812, in Dubrovin, *Otechestvennaya voina v pismakh sovremennikov*, 343.

14. Tyrconnell to Cathcart, November 30, 1812, in Dubrovin, *Otechestvennaya voina v pismakh sovremennikov*, 343; Louis-Alexandre de Langeron, *Mémoires de Langeron: général d'infanterie dans l'armée russe campagnes de 1812, 1813, 1814* (Paris: A. Picard, 1902), 53; Aleksey Martos, "Zapiski inzhenernogo ofitsera Martosa," *Russkii arkhiv* 8 (1893): 497; Louis-Victor-Léon de Rochechouart, *Memoirs of the Count de Rochechouart* (New York: E. P. Dutton, 1920), 168–170; Peter Fallenberg, "Iz zapisok P. I. Falenberga," *Russkii arkhiv* 10 (1877): 202–203; Silvestr Malinovskii, "Zapiski general-leitenanta S.S. Malinovskago o deistviyakh pri Berezine v 1812 godu," in Konstantin Voyenskii, ed., *Istoricheskiye ocherki i statii otnosyashiesya k 1812 godu* (St. Petersburg, 1912), 91; Yason Khrapovitskii, "Vospominaniya . . . ," in Voyenskii, ed., *Istoricheskiye ocherki i statii*, 114; Ivan Arnoldi, "Iz zapisok I.K. Arnoldi o 1812 gode," in Voyenskii, ed., *Istoricheskiye ocherki i statii*, 101–102.

15. Levin von Bennigsen, "Zapiski grafa L. L. Bennigsena o kampanii 1812 g.," *Russkaya starina* 11 (1909): 374; "Kutuzov v 1812 godu: Istoricheskaya kharakteristika D. P. Buturlina," *Russkaya starina* 12 (1894): 139, 146; Bogdanovich, *Istoriya otechestvennoi voiny 1812*, III:287; Dimitri Buturlin, *Istoriya nashestviya imperatora Napoleona na Rossiyu v 1812 g.* (St. Petersburg: Voen. Tip. Glavnogo Shtaba, 1823), II:238–239, 270.

16. Alexander to Kutuzov, November 12, 1812, RGVIA, d. 3572, ll. 35–35b; Alexander to Kutuzov, November 13, 1812, in *M. I. Kutuzov. Sbornik dokumentov*, IV, part 2, 322–333; "Avtobiograficheskaya zapiska," *Russkaya starina* 3 (1896): 103.

17. Kutuzov to Platov and Seslavin, November 19, 1812, nos. 455, 458, RGVIA, d. 3521, ll. 67b–68b.

18. Yermolov, *The Czar's General*, 205.

19. "This letter, which [Chichagov] made me read, was very simple, precise, and clearly written. Kutuzov did not irrevocably order the Admiral to move to his right but rather advised him to do it if the enemy were to move in that direction; he wrote that he could guess Napoleon's intentions and let Chichagov

act on his own discretion if these conjectures proved false; they indeed were such, but Chichagov was persuaded by Kutuzov's advice to make a movement much more absurd than that which he conceived on 11/23 [November]." Langeron, *Mémoires*, 55. Wilson went as far as to claim that Kutuzov had been deliberately duped by Napoleon, who "made the field marshal think that he would march on Igumen but instead built bridges at Studenka." He praised Napoleon for having demonstrated "great skill in carrying out this plan" and for undertaking "various ruses" that diverted the admiral's attention. Robert Wilson to Emperor Alexander, November 18/30, 1812, in Dubrovin, ed., *Otechestvennaya voina v pismakh sovremennikov*, 350–351.

20. "Having received information, directions and advice from his Commander in Chief, the Admiral was bound to follow the counsel of his superior," commented Rochechouart. Lord Tyrconnell believed that "the Admiral might be excused to a certain extent because Prince Kutuzov gave him reason to think that the enemy might try fighting across the river to the right side from us. It is most regrettable that he did not follow the advice of General Sabaneyev and other generals who urged him, if he decided to proceed to Shabashevichi, to wait for at least another day before marching." Rochechouart, *Memoirs*, 172; Lord Tyrconnell to Lord Cathcart, November 8–18/20–30, 1812, in Dubrovin, ed., *Otechestvennaya voina v pismakh sovremennikov*, 349. As one officer commented, "There was a deception, and a great deception indeed . . . but the Admiral was deceived not by the enemy, in opposition to whom he had taken every possible precaution . . . but by friends, against whose conduct he had not been sufficiently on his guard." These are anonymous notes added to Frédéric-François Guillaume de Vaudoncourt, *Critical Situation of Bonaparte in His Retreat out of Russia, or a Faithful Narrative of the Repassing of the Beresina by the French Army in 1812* (London, 1815), 51–52.

21. Khrapovitskii, "Vospominaniya . . . ," in Voyenskii, ed., *Istoricheskiye ocherki i statii*, 116.

22. Cited in Eugene Tarle, *Nashestvie Napoleona na Rossiyu, 1812 god* (Moscow: Voennoe Izd., 1992), 265.

23. Wilson to his wife, December 1, 1812, in Dubrovin, ed., *Otechestvennaya voina v pismakh sovremennikov*, 367.

24. Rafail Zotov, *Razskazy o pokhodakh 1812-go I 1813-go godov* (St. Petersburg: I. Glazunov, 1836), 86.

25. Kutuzov to Alexander, n.d. [probably December 1812], in *M. I. Kutuzov. Sbornik dokumentov*, IV, part 2, 421–422; Martos, "Zapiski," 496.

26. Kutuzov complained that in his earlier reports Chichagov implied that the Zembino causeway was already destroyed. Kutuzov to Chichagov, November 18/30, 1812, RGVIA, f. VUA, d. 3518, part 2, ll. 714–715. For broader correspondence, see Kutuzov to Alexander, November 14/26, 1812, RGVIA, f. VUA, d. 3521, ll. 80–80b; Kutuzov to Chichagov, November 13–17/25–29,

1812, RGVIA, f. VUA, d. 3518, part 2, ll. 614–614b, 712–713; Foerster's Memo, RGVIA, f. VUA, d. 3701, l. 2; Kutuzov to Alexander, October 23/ November 4, 1812, in *M. I. Kutuzov. Sbornik dokumentov*, IV, part 2, 189. Also see V. Kharkevich, *1812 g. Berezina* (St. Petersburg, 1893), 135–140.

27. Bogdanovich, *Istoriya otechestvennoi voiny 1812*, III:294.

28. A. Mikhailovskii-Danilevskii, *Opisanie Otechestvennoi voiny v 1812 godu* (St. Petersburg, 1839), IV:196.

29. Alexander Golitsyn, "Zapiska o voine 1812 goda . . . ," in Voyenskii, ed., *Istoricheskiye ocherki i statii*, 145. Others concurred with this point. Tyrconnell believed that "the government [i.e., the czar] must be held responsible for appointing an admiral, instead of a general, to handle such an important mission." Lord Tyrconnell to Duke of York, November 18/30, 1812, in Dubrovin, ed., *Otechestvennaya voina v pismakh sovremennikov*, 356.

30. Dmitri Buturlin, "Kutuzov v 1812 godu," *Russkaya starina* 12 (1894): 145; de Maistre to King Victor Emmanuel, June 14, 1813, in *Arkhiv knyazya Vorontsova* (Moscow: Tip. Gracheva, 1870–1895), XV:501; Golitsyn, "Zapiska," 146.

31. Lord Tyrconnell to Lord Cathcart, November 29/December 11, 1812, in Dubrovin, ed., *Otechestvennaya voina v pismakh sovremennikov*, 386.

32. Kutuzov to Praskovya and Matvey Tolstoy, December 15/27, 1812, in *M. I. Kutuzov. Sbornik dokumentov*, IV, part 2, 610; Kutuzov to Elisabeth Khitrovo, December 16/28, 1812, in *Russkaya starina* 6 (1874): 373–374.

33. Kutuzov to Elisabeth Khitrovo, December 16/28, 1812, and December 25, 1812/January 6, 1813, in *Russkaya starina* 6 (1874): 373–374.

34. Robert Wilson, *Private Diary of Travels, Personal Services, and Public Events* (London: J. Murray, 1861), 251–252.

35. Kutuzov to E. Khitrovo, October 29/November 10, 1812, in *Russkaya starina* 6 (1874): 370–371.

36. Kutuzov to his wife, October 30/November 12, 1812, in *The Kutuzov Papers* 4 (1872): 562.

37. Nikolai Shil'der, *Imperator Aleksandr pervyi. Ego zhizn' i tsarstvovanie* (St. Petersburg: A. S. Suvorin, 1897–1898), III:132. Alexander was accompanied by Oberhofmarschall Nikolai Tolstoy, Count Arakcheyev, State Secretary Shishkov, Adjutant General Peter Volkonskii, State Secretary Karl Nesselrode, and Acting State Councillor Marchenko.

38. Sophie de Tisenhaus, comtesse de Choiseul-Gouffier, *Mémoires historiques sur l'empereur Alexandre et la cour de Russie* (Paris, 1829), 142.

39. *The Pilot of London*, Tuesday, January 5, 1813, 1.

40. Kutuzov was upset about A. Bunina's poem "On the Destruction of the French Who Insolently Invaded the Russian Heartlands," which contained a passage describing Kutuzov holding a balance scale and placing "the lives of warriors" in one pan and Moscow in the other. "I did not balance Moscow against the warriors' lives, but rather against the survival of Russia, the salvation of St. Petersburg, and the freedom of Europe," the field marshal complained.

Kutuzov to his wife, December 13/25, 1812, and February 4/16, 1813, in *The Kutuzov Papers* 5 (1872): 658–659, 691–692.

41. Kutuzov to A. Naryshkina, n.d. [ca. December 1812], in *M. I. Kutuzov. Sbornik dokumentov*, IV, part 2, 650–651.

42. Martos, "Zapiski," 506.

43. Martos, "Zapiski," 507.

44. Fuks to Derzhavin, December 18/30, 1812, in J. Grott, ed. *Sochineniya Derzhavina* (St. Petersburg: Imperial Academy of Sciences, 1876), VI:288.

45. Yermolov, *The Czar's General*, 215.

46. Choiseul-Gouffier, *Mémoires historiques*, 130.

47. Robert Wilson, *Narrative of Events During the Invasion of Russia by Napoleon Bonaparte and the Retreat of the French Army* (London: John Murray, 1860), 354.

48. Rimsky-Korsakov to O. Kozodavlev, December 16/28, 1812, in Dubrovin, ed., *Otechestvennaya voina v pismakh sovremennikov*, 400; Choiseul-Gouffier, *Mémoires historiques*, 151, 155.

49. Pavel Puschin, *Dnevnik Pavla Puschina, 1812–1814* (Leningrad: Leningrad University Press, 1987), 67.

50. Kutuzov to his wife, December 13/25, 1812, in *The Kutuzov Papers* 5 (1872): 658–659.

51. Choiseul-Gouffier, *Mémoires historiques*, 155.

52. In a separate note Wilson states that "the emperor explained afterwards in private to what he alluded when he used the expression 'Turkish tricks.'" Sadly, Wilson did not elaborate on this matter. *Narrative of Events*, 357–358. Kutuzov "is a sad old rogue, hating English connection, and basely preferring to independent alliance with us a servitude to the canaille crew who govern France and her fiefs," Wilson raged in a letter written in mid-November. Robert Wilson, *Private Diary of Travels, Personal Services and Public Events* (London: J. Murray, 1861), I:221–222.

53. Wilson, *Narrative of Events*, 356–357. The czar frequently complained about the field marshal's enduring appeal and his frustration with public opinion. During the preceding reigns "nobody troubled himself with the affairs of state," he told Countess Choiseul-Gouffier shortly after his arrival. Yet now public opinion was voicing itself so forcefully. "This unfortunate campaign has cost me ten years of my life!" Choiseul-Gouffier, *Mémoires historiques*, 141–142.

54. Imperial Decree of December 6/18, 1812, in *M. I. Kutuzov. Sbornik dokumentov*, IV, part 2, 545.

55. Only three other individuals accomplished this feat: Barclay de Tolly in 1813 and Ivan Diebitsch and Ivan Paskevich in 1829.

56. The golden sword was valued at 25,120 rubles. Countess Choiseul-Gouffier claims that Kutuzov was not pleased with emerald-encrusted laurels, finding the stones too small. "He assured me that he would call the emperor's attention to it." Choiseul-Gouffier, *Mémoires historiques*, 156; Minister of Finance

D. Guryev to Oberhofmarschall Nikolai Tolstoy, December 15/27, 1812, in *M. I. Kutuzov. Sbornik dokumentov*, IV, part 2, 611.

57. Choiseul-Gouffier, *Mémoires historiques*, 130.

58. Yermolov's note in *Zapiski A. P. Yermolova, 1798–1826* (Moscow: Vysshaya Shkola, 1991), 258–259.

59. Arsenii Zakrevskii to Alexander Bulgakov, December 16/28, 1812, in *Rossiiskii arkhiv* XII (2003): 35; Arsenii Zakrevskii to Mikhail Vorontsov, September 20/October 1, 1812, in *Arkhiv knyazya Vorontsova*, XXXVII:234–235; Rayevskii to his wife, December 22, 1812, in *1812–1814: Lichnye pisma generala N. N. Rayevskogo* (Moscow, 1992), 236. Also see Rimsky-Korsakov to O. Kozodavlev, December 16/28, 1812, in Dubrovin, ed., *Otechestvennaya voina v pismakh sovremennikov*, 401; V. Bezotosnyi, *Rossiiskii generalitet epokhi 1812 goda: opyt izucheniya kollektivnoi biografii* (Moscow: ROSSPEN, 2018), 222.

60. Schwarzenberg to Metternich, December 24, 1812, cited in *Correspondance inédite de l'Empereur Alexandre et de Bernadotte pendant l'année 1812* (Paris: R. Chapelot, 1909), xxxii.

61. John Quincy Adams, *Memoirs of John Quincy Adams Containing His Diary from 1795 to 1848*, edited by Charles Francis Adams (Philadelphia: Lippincott, 1874), II:447.

62. Yermolov, *The Czar's General*, 215–216. A quick conversation was enough for him to properly assess Wittgenstein, whom he found a vainglorious and vacuous man who described his victories with such bluster that it seemed he alone defeated the mighty invader. "Even Kutuzov's finesse was not enough to hide his indignation," remarked Yermolov. But Wittgenstein, whom contemporaries accused of "not even bothering to think," posed little threat to the field marshal who focused his attention on the admiral.

63. Golitsyn, "Zapiska," 146.

64. Khrapovitskii, *Vospominaniya*, 120.

65. Sergei Mayevskii, "Moi vek ili istoriya Sergeya Ivanovicha Mayevskogo, 1779–1848," *Russkaya starina* 8 (1873): 154; Wilson to Cathcart, November 22/December 4, 1812, in Dubrovin, ed., *Otechestvennaya voina v pismakh sovremennikov*, 374–375.

66. Yermolov, *The Czar's General*, 211, 217.

67. Filip Weigel, *Zapiski . . .* (Moscow: Krug, 1928), II:28.

68. December 3 entry in Adams, *Memoirs of John Quincy Adams Containing His Diary*, 424. An Englishman present at the dinner where Kutuzov was extolled admitted that "Prince Koutouzof was destined to be a second Wellington." The field marshal's relatives were not amused, one of them responding that "if his uncle had done nothing more than Wellington, he would sink low indeed from the summit of his merited fame."

69. Tyrconnel to the Duke of York and to Cathcart, November 18/30, 1812, in Dubrovin, ed., *Otechestvennaya voina v pismakh sovremennikov*, 355–357.

70. Dokhturov to his wife, December 3, 1812, in *Russkii arkhiv* 1 (1874): 1107. Also see Wilson to Lord Cathcart, December 4, 1812; Rimsky-Korsakov to O. Kozodavlev, December 16/28, 1812, in Dubrovin, ed., *Otechestvennaya voina v pismakh sovremennikov*, 375, 400.

71. Maistre to King Victor Emmanuel, June 14, 1813, in *Arkhiv knyazya Vorontsova*, XV:500.

72. Kudashev to Ekaterina Kutuzova, December 1, 1812, in *M. I. Kutuzov. Sbornik dokumentov*, IV, part 2, 417; *Literaturnoye nasledstvo* (Moscow, 1982), 91:402.

73. Zhukovskii to A. Turgenev, April 9, 1813, in V. Zhukovskii, *Sobranie sochinenii* (Moscow, 1960), 490; Gregory Derzhavin, *Sochineniya . . .* (St. Petersburg, 1866), III:451.

74. For an English translation, see W. R. S. Ralston, ed., *Krilof and His Fables* (London: Strahan, 1871), 27–28. For an interesting discussion of the historical context, see M. Gordin, *Otechestvennaya voina 1812 goda na fone basen I. A. Krylova* (St. Petersburg, 2012).

75. Adams, *Memoirs of John Quincy Adams Containing His Diary*, II:472.

76. Maistre to King Victor Emmanuel, June 14, 1813, in *Arkhiv knyazya Vorontsova*, XV:502.

Chapter 30

1. Alexander to Kutuzov, December 2/14, 1812, in N. Dubrovin, ed., *Otechestvennaya voina v pismakh sovremennikov, 1812–1815 gg.* (St. Petersburg, 1882), 390.

2. The roster of December 7/19 shows the main Russian army with 141 staff officers, 1,103 ober-officers, and 26,220 soldiers, for a total of 27,464 men, with 200 cannon. Chichagov's army was just 17,454 men strong, but with the reserves its strength increased to 24,488 men. Wittgenstein commanded 34,493 men. In total, the December roster shows that the combined Russian forces consisted of 86,447 men and 273 cannon. See *M. I. Kutuzov. Sbornik dokumentov* (Moscow: Voeniszdat, 1950), IV, part 2, 552–553.

3. Kutuzov to Alexander, December 7/19, 1812, in *M. I. Kutuzov. Sbornik dokumentov*, IV, part 2, 551.

4. Kutuzov to Alexander, December 2/14, 1812, in *General Staff Archives*, XIX:223. He repeated the request on December 21, warning the czar that moving the army forward would result in "its complete destruction [*sovershennoe unichtozhenie*]." Also see the new operational plan that Kutuzov drafted in early December, in *General Staff Archives*, XIX:220–221.

5. On December 30, Kutuzov authorized I. Anstedt to open secret negotiations with Schwarzenberg. See his instructions in *M. I. Kutuzov. Sbornik dokumentov*, V:7–8.

6. Kutuzov to Wittgenstein, February 2, 1813, RGVIA, f. VUA, op. 16, d. 3921, ll. 24b–25b.

7. Alexander to Grand Duchess Catherine, November 8/20, 1812, in Grand Duke Nikolai Mikhailovich, ed., *Correspondance de l'empereur Alexandre 1er avec sa soeur. Perepiska imperatora Aleksandra s sestroi velikoi knyaginei Ekaternoi Pavlovnoi* (St. Petersburg: Eksp. Zagot. Gos. Bumag, 1910), 103.

8. "Monsieur, la Russie, bien gouvernée, est faite pour commander a l'Europe." John Quincy Adams, *Memoirs of John Quincy Adams Containing His Diary from 1795 to 1848*, edited by Charles Francis Adams (Philadelphia: Lippincott, 1874), II:426.

9. Alexander Shishkov, *Zapiski, mneniya i perepiska Admirala A. S. Shishkova*, edited by N. Kiselev and Yu. Samarin (Berlin: B. Behr's Buchhandlung, 1870), I:167.

10. Kutuzov to his wife, December 31, 1812/January 12, 1813, in *The Kutuzov Papers* 5(1872): 687–688.

11. May 16 entry in Chicherin, "Dnevnik," http://www.museum.ru/museum/1812/Library/Chicherin/chicherin_1813.html.

12. Shishkov, "Zapiski," I:168–169.

13. Alexander to Count Saltykov, December 16/28, 1812, cited in Nikolai Shil'der, *Imperator Aleksandr pervyi. Ego zhizn' i tsarstvovanie* (St. Petersburg: A. S. Suvorin, 1897–1898), III:137.

14. Alexey Yermolov, *The Czar's General: The Memoirs of a Russian General in the Napoleonic Wars*, translated and edited by Alexander Mikaberidze (Welwyn Garden City: Ravenhall Books, 2005), 216.

15. Hearing about Barclay de Tolly's return, Kutuzov told his wife, "I do not think the two of us will quarrel anymore, especially since we are not going to be staying together." Kutuzov to his wife, January 13/25, 1813, in *The Kutuzov Papers* 5 (1872): 689.

16. Robert Wilson, *Narrative of Events During the Invasion of Russia by Napoleon Bonaparte and the Retreat of the French Army* (London: John Murray, 1860), 357. Ivchenko argues that the relations between Alexander and Kutuzov improved after Vilna and that they both came to truly appreciate each other. However, there are many reasons to suspect the genuineness of the czar's treatment of the man he had derided for so long. See Lidia Ivchenko, *Kutuzov* (Moscow: Molodaya Gvardiya, 2012), 453–460.

17. Kutuzov to his wife, January 1/13, 1813, in *The Kutuzov Papers* 5 (1872): 688.

18. Kutuzov to his wife, January 10/22, 1813, in *The Kutuzov Papers* 5 (1872): 688.

19. Kutuzov to Elisabeth Khitrovo, February 1/12, 1813, in *The Kutuzov Papers* 6 (1874): 376.

20. Kutuzov to his wife, January 16/28, 1813, in *The Kutuzov Papers* 5 (1872): 689.

21. This is one of the earliest citations of Napoleon's famous expression. Kutuzov to his wife, February 2/14, 1813, in *The Kutuzov Papers* 5 (1872): 691.

22. *Anekdoty ili dostopamyatnye skazaniya ob ego svetlosti general-fel'dmarshale knyaze Mikhaile Illarionoviche Golenischeve-Kutuzove Smolenskom, nachinaya s pervykh let*

ego sluzhby do konchiny, s priobsheniem nekotoryh ego pisem, dostopamyatnyh ego rechei i prikazov (St. Petersburg, 1814), II:112–113.

23. Kutuzov's letters are replete with references to various individuals whose causes he lobbied with the czar. "I will find a way to get [the Order of St.] Vladimir for Albrecht, but it would be much harder to think of something for Nilov," reads his letter of February 25. This and other letters substantiate contemporary complaints that Kutuzov was too generous with promotions and awards. Kutuzov to his wife, February 13/25, 1813, in *The Kutuzov Papers* 5 (1872): 692.

24. Kutuzov to his wife, January 29/February 10, 1813, in *The Kutuzov Papers* 5 (1872): 690.

25. For an excellent discussion, see Michael V. Leggiere, *Napoleon and the Struggle for Germany, Volume 1: The War of Liberation, Spring 1813* (Cambridge: Cambridge University Press, 2015), 21–119.

26. Kutuzov to his wife, February 15/27, 1813, in *The Kutuzov Papers* 5 (1872): 692.

27. Mikhail Kutuzov to Login Ivanovichy Kutuzov, March 28/April 9 1813, in Dubrovin, ed., *Otechestvennaya voina v pismakh sovremennikov*, 469.

28. Ten-Day Roster of the Armies, April 3/15, 1813, in *M. I. Kutuzov. Sbornik dokumentov*, V:513–519. The Russian forces included 20,940 regular cavalry, 23,053 irregular cavalry, 66,951 infantry, and 6,542 militia; the regular artillery employed more than 9,800 men.

29. Statute on the Provisional Government of the Duchy of Warsaw, in *M. I. Kutuzov. Sbornik dokumentov*, V:329–334.

30. Kutuzov to his wife, March 22–25/April 3–6, 1813, in *The Kutuzov Papers* 5 (1872): 696.

31. Kutuzov to his wife, March 31/April 12, 1813, in *The Kutuzov Papers* 5 (1872): 697–698.

32. Kutuzov to his wife, February 22/March 6, 1813, in *The Kutuzov Papers* 5 (1872): 693. Kutuzov was able to secure a 2,000-ruble annual pension for his sister, Darya. Kutuzov to his wife, March 17/29, 1813, in *The Kutuzov Papers* 5 (1872): 695.

33. Leggiere, *Napoleon and the Struggle for Germany*, I:120–166.

34. Kutuzov to Wittgenstein, March 17/29, 1813, in *M. I. Kutuzov. Sbornik dokumentov*, V:427–428.

35. The English translation of the proclamation is in Leggiere, *Napoleon and the Struggle for Germany*, I:129.

36. For details, see *Listovki Otechestvennoi voiny 1812 goda. Sbornik dokumentov* (Moscow: Academy of Science of USSR, 1962), 97–98, 121, 124. For an English-language discussion, see Leggiere, *Napoleon and the Struggle for Germany*, I:131–133.

37. Kutuzov to his wife, March 20/April 1, 1813, in *The Kutuzov Papers* 5 (1872): 696.

38. Kutuzov to his wife, March 31/April 12, 1813, in *The Kutuzov Papers* 5 (1872): 697; Kutuzov to Elisabeth Khitrovo, December 16/28, 1812, in *Russkaya starina* 6 (1874): 377.

39. Karl Montresor's testimony in F. Nordman, "Pamyatniki kn. M. I. Golenischevu-Kutuzovu v Silezii," *Russkaya starina* 6 (1874): 380–381.

40. Kutuzov to Alexander, April 10/22, 1813, RGVIA, f. VUA, d. 3921, l. 172b.

41. Kutuzov to his wife, April 11/23, 1813, in *The Kutuzov Papers* 5 (1872): 698.

42. Kutuzov to his wife, April 11/23, 1813, in *The Kutuzov Papers* 5 (1872): 698.

43. Egor Fuks to Peter Volkonskii, April 16/28, 1813, in *M. I. Kutuzov. Sbornik dokumentov*, V:557.

44. Yu. Gulyaev and V. Soglaev, *Fel'dmarshal Kutuzov. Istoriko-biograficheskii ocherk* (Moscow: Arkheograficheskii Tsentr, 1995), 373–375.

45. Kutuzov to his wife, March 25/April 6, 1813, in *The Kutuzov Papers* 5 (1872): 697.

46. "Prince Mikhail Illarionovich's illness is frightening everyone. Neither his wife nor his children received any letters from him in quite some time. We hear some rumors but they all seem false. Still, the fact it is all kept secret makes me conclude that something bad has happened." Unknown to A. Shishkov, May 1/13, 1813 in Dubrovin, ed., *Otechestvennaya voina v pismakh sovremennikov*, 469.

47. This myth was persistent enough for the Russian Imperial Military Historical Society to convene a special meeting in 1913 to discuss ways to return it; World War I made it impossible. Yet, in 1933, Sergei Kirov, the famed Soviet politician and Bolshevik revolutionary, personally demanded an investigation of this matter. A special commission of scholars from the Soviet Academy of Sciences opened and examined Kutuzov's crypt at the Kazan Cathedral, which was then functioning as the Museum of History of Religion and Atheism. The commission's report specified that Kutuzov's remains lay inside two coffins: an outer tin coffin that was sealed with screws and an inner pinewood coffin that was covered with red velvet and gilded braid. Inside they found the field marshal's skeleton and a silver funeral vessel holding his embalmed heart. The commission found no jewelry or decorations, which would have been returned to the Order Capitulum, which administered Russian imperial awards and decorations. Despite these findings, Soviet historians (with a few exceptions) continued to repeat the claim for decades, and it was included in the 1953 edition of the *Great Soviet Encyclopedia*. For details, see Vladimir Melentyev, *Kutuzov v Peterburge* (Leningrad: Lenizdat, 1986), 195–196.

48. The monument was destroyed in the summer of 1813 when French troops occupied Bunzlau, but it was rebuilt in August 1814. Gulyaev and Soglaev, *Fel'dmarshal Kutuzov*, 376–377. Vice Admiral F. Nordman saw the monument in 1871 and complained that it was neglected and surrounded by a grove that had grown up since the end of the Napoleonic Wars and threatened

to consume the memorial. Nordman, "Pamyatniki kn. M. I. Golenischevu-Kutuzovu v Silezii," 382.

49. Nordman, "Pamyatniki kn. M. I. Golenischevu-Kutuzovu v Silezii," 381–382. Vice Admiral F. Nordman visited Bunzlau in 1871, examined monuments to Kutuzov, and prepared detailed descriptions and photographs of them. In 1893, the obelisk was moved closer to the house where Kutuzov passed away. It was damaged during World War II but restored on the orders of Marshal Ivan Konev in March 1945. A. Smirnov, "Pamyatnik bessmertnyj Russkoi slavy," Project 1812, http://www.museum.ru/museum/1812/Memorial/Smirn ov1/index.html.

50. Kutuzov's body was accompanied by a special escort comprising Colonels Ya. Schneider, I. Skobelev, I. Efimovich, and Salloggub, and Kutuzov's four aides-de-camp, Rotmistr K. Dzichkanetz, K. Montresor, Captain E. Zlotnitskii, and Lt. Colonel A. Kozhukhov.

51. Unknown to A. Shishkov, May 1/13, 1813 in Dubrovin, ed., *Otechestvennaya voina v pismakh sovremennikov*, 484–485.

52. Sergei Vyazmitinov to Count A. Arakcheyev, May 25/June 5, 1813, in Dubrovin, ed., *Otechestvennaya voina v pismakh sovremennikov*, 489. This monastery became the final resting place for many of Kutuzov's family members, including two daughters (Anna, who passed away in 1846) and Darya (d. 1854), son-in-law Fedor Opochinin (d. 1853), grandsons Konstantin Opochinin (d. 1848) and Pavel Golenischev-Kutuzov-Tolstoy (d. 1883), and great-grandchildren Natalya Tolstoy (d. 1839), Konstantino Tolstoy (d. 1852), and Darya de Beauharnais (d. 1870). Their gravesites were, however, destroyed during the Soviet period.

53. For a detailed and insightful discussion of Kutuzov's funeral, see E. Bochkov, "Tseremonial pogrebeniya M. I. Golenischeva-Kutuzova: Neizvestnye stranitsy," Museum Borodisnkoe Pole, https://www.borodino.ru/wp-content/uploads/2017/08/18_Bochkov_E.A.pdf.

54. John Thomas James, *Journal of a Tour in Germany, Sweden, Russia, Poland During the Years 1813 and 1814* (London: John Murray, 1817), II:88.

55. *Public Ledger and Daily Advertiser*, July 15, 1813, 3.

56. It is noteworthy that some of these items were not Kutuzov's actual possessions but were rented for the occasion from various private individuals. The sword that lay on top of the coffin was rented for sixty rubles from a Frenchman. The Prussian Orders of Red and Black Eagles had to be returned (as required by the statute) to Prussia within three months of the owner's passing. The Prussian decorations featured in the funeral procession were also rented from a Russian merchant for forty rubles. Bochkov, "Tseremonial pogrebeniya M. I. Golenischeva-Kutuzova," 234–235.

57. Cited in Bochkov, "Tseremonial pogrebeniya M. I. Golenischeva-Kutuzova," 232.

58. Nikolai Longinov to Semen Vorontsov, June 12/24, 1813, in *Arkhiv knyazya Vorontsova* (Moscow: Tip. Gracheva, 1870–1895), XXIII:266.

59. Bochkov, "Tseremonial pogrebeniya M. I. Golenischeva-Kutuzova," 239. On June 24, John Quincy Adams visited the Kazan Cathedral and made a detailed description of what he had seen: "The catafalque is in the centre of the church, immediately under the dome, a cubic basis, and about twelve feet high, with steps to ascend at the four corners. There is an arch in the middle of it, high enough for a man to pass through; the coffin is placed at the summit, on bars, over a cavity large enough to let it down by machinery. The coffin is said to weigh sixty poods, about a ton *avoirdupois*. It is surrounded by trophies—French eagles and standards, and [Ottoman] bashaws' horse-tails. All around the basis are rows of large tapers to be lighted. The whole fabric, which is of painted wood, appears to be rested on four fluted Corinthian pillars at the four corners. A figure of Fame or of an Angel, with a crown of laurel in one hand, hovers over the coffin, suspended by a rope from the summit of the dome. On the two sides of the catafalque are ranged stools, with velvet cushions, on each of which is placed some mark of dignity which he had acquired—the sword, the Marshal's truncheon, the orders of the Prussian Black and Red Eagles, the Austrian order of Maria Theresa, and the Russian orders of St. Andrew, St. Alexander Newsky, St. George of the first class, St. Ann, and St. Wladimir. The church was much crowded, but, by the civility of the Master of the Police, General Gorgoly, we saw everything." *Memoirs of John Quincy Adams Containing His Diary*, II:483.

Epilogue

1. "La renommée est une déesse qui n'acquiert le sens commun qu'avec le temps; encore même ne l'acquiert elle pas toujours." W. F. Reddaway, ed., *Document of Catherine the Great: The Correspondence with Voltaire* (Cambridge: Cambridge University Press, 1931), 145.

2. Robert Wilson, *Private Diary of Travels, Personal Services, and Public Events* (London: J. Murray, 1861), 356.

3. Alexander Koshelev, *Zapiski Aleksandra Ivanovicha Kosheleva (1812–1813)* (Moscow: Nauka, 2022), 15.

4. P. Schukin, ed., *Bumagi otnosyaschiyasya do Otechestvennoi voiny 1812 goda* (Moscow: A. Mamontov, 1904), VII:404.

5. Yu. Gulyaev and V. Soglaev, *Fel'dmarshal Kutuzov. Istoriko-biograficheskii ocherk* (Moscow: Arkheograficheskii Tsentr, 1995), 376.

6. Unknown to A. Shishkov, February 19/March 3, 1813, in N. Dubrovin, ed., *Otechestvennaya voina v pismakh sovremennikov, 1812–1815 gg.* (St. Petersburg, 1882), 464. Catherine's comments raised a few eyebrows in Russian society, especially when she remarked that the reopening of the French theater meant that she would have to sit with "muzhiks," common Russian men. Her own relative pointed out that "these very muzhiks contributed to the glory of her husband."

7. Metternich to the Countess de Lieven, March 22, 1818, in Jean Hanoteau, ed., *Lettres du prince de Metternich à la comtesse de Lieven, 1818–1819* (Paris: Plon-Nourrit, 1909), 261–262.

8. For an interesting discussion, see Nikolai Rayevskii, *Izbrannoe* (Moscow: Khud. Literature, 1978); Prince Felix Youssoupoff, *Lost Splendor: The Amazing Memoirs of the Man Who Killed Rasputin*, translated by Ann Green and Nicholas Katkoff (New York: Helen Marx Books, 2003), 29.

9. Alfred-Frédéric-Pierre, comte de Falloux du Coudray, *Memoirs . . .* (London: Chapman and Hall, 1888), I:125.

10. F. Sinel'nikov, *Zhizn, voennye i politicheskie deiania Ego svetlosti general feldmarshal kn. M.I. Golenisheva-Kutuzova-Smolenskogo* (St. Petersburg, 1813), I:1, II:47–49, IV:59. For other authors, see *Kartina zhizni, voennikh i politicheskikh deianii Ego svetlosti kn. M. I. Golenisheva-Kutuzova-Smolenskogo* (Moscow, 1813); *Zhizn i voennye podvigi gen.-feldmarshal svetleishego kn. M. I. Golenisheva-Kutuzova-Smolenskogo* (St. Petersburg, 1813); *Zhizn i voennye deyania gen.-feldm. Svetleishego kn. M. I. Golenisheva-Kutuzova-Smolenskogo* (St. Petersburg, 1813); *Istoricheskie zapiski o zhizni i voennikh podvigakh gen-feldm. Sveitleishego kn. M. I. Golenisheva-Kutuzova-Smolenskogo* (St. Petersburg, 1813).

11. A. Izmailov, *Sochinenia* (St. Petersburg, 1849), I:211.

12. Peter Vyazemskii, "Pominki po Borodinskoi bitve," *Pushkinskaya karta*, https://www.culture.ru/poems/41936/pominki-po-borodinskoi-bitve.

13. "Pered grobintseyu svyatoi," in A. S. Pushkin, *Sobranie sochinenii v 10 tomakh* (Moscow: GIKHL, 1959), II:337, https://rvb.ru/pushkin/01text/01versus/0423_36/1831/0563.htm.

14. Fedor Rostopchin, "Zapiski," in *Pozhar Moskvy. Po vospominaniyam i perepiske sovremennikov* (Moscow: Obrazovanie, 1911), II:54.

15. Aleksey Yermolov, "Kharakteristika polkovodtsev 1812 g.," *Rodina* 1 (1994): 57–58.

16. Filip Sinel'nikov, *Zhizn' chastnaya i kharakter Ego Svetlosti General-Fel'dmarshala Knyazya Mikhaila Larionovicha Golenischeva-Kutuzova Smolenskago* (St. Petersburg: Morskaya Tip., 1814).

17. D. Akhsharumov, *Opisanie voiny 1812 g.* (St. Petersburg, 1819), 293–294.

18. D. Buturlin, *Istoria nashestvia imperatora Napoleona na Rossiu v 1812 g.* (St. Petersburg, 1823), II:245.

19. A. Mikahilovskii-Danilevskii, *Opisanie otechestvennoi voini v 1812 godu* (St. Petersburg, 1839), I:13, III:142, IV:340, 347, 394.

20. N. Polyakov, *Russkie polkovodtsy ili zhizn' i podvigi russkikh polkovodtsev ot vremen imperatora Petra velikago do tsarstvovaniya imperatora Nikolaya I* (St. Petersburg: K. Zhernakov, 1845), 223–225.

21. Modest Bogdanovich, *Istoria Otechestvennoi voini 1812 g. po dostovernym istochnikam* (St. Petersburg, 1860), II:14–15.

22. Bogdanovich, *Istoria Otechestvennoi*, II:229–230.

23. A.B., "Istoria Otchestvennoi voini 1812 g.," *Voennyi sbornik* 6 (1860): 470, 481. Among the few critics was Major General Ivan Liprandi, who had taken part in the 1812–1814 campaigns and who, in 1869, wrote a critical review of Modest Bogdanovich's book and held Kutuzov responsible "for letting Napoleon and the remnants of his hordes escape from Russia." I. Liprandi, *Voina 1812 g. Zamechania na knigu "Istoria Otechestvennoi voini 1812 g. po dostovernym istochnikam" M. I. Bogdanovicha* (Moscow, 1869), 41–42.

24. For details see S. Soloveyev, *Imperator Aleksandr I. Politika, diplomatia, in Sochinenia* (Moscow, 1996), XVII:408–411; P. Heisman, "M. I. Golenishev-Kutuzov-Smolenskii," *Russkii biograficheskii slovar* (St. Petersburg, 1903), IX; G. Leer, *Voina 1805 g. Austerlitskaia operatsia* (St. Petersburg, 1888); A. Witmer, "Borodinskii boi," *Voenno-istoricheskii sbornik* 3 (1912).

25. V. Kharkevich, *1812 god. Berezina* (St. Petersburg, 1893), 207–208.

26. A. Dzhivelegov, S. P. Melgunov, et al., eds., *Otechestvennaia voina i russkoe obshestvo* (Moscow, 1912), IV:3–5.

27. For details on Pokrovskii, see C. E. Black, *History and Politics in the Soviet Union: Rewriting Russian History* (New York, 1956), 3–31; Rudolf Schlesinger, "Recent Soviet Historiography," *Soviet Studies* 4 (1950): 293–312. Also see "Pokrovskii, Mikhail Nikolaevich: Istorik, revolutsioner, obshestvennyi deyatel'," http://Pokrovsky.newgod.su.

28. Mikhail Pokrovskii, *Diplomatiya i voiny czarskoi Rossii* (Moscow, 1924), 54.

29. Pokrovskii, *Diplomatiya i voiny czarskoi Rossii*, 54.

30. Pokrovskii, *Diplomatiya i voiny czarskoi Rossii*, 55. Pokrovskii refers to a Russian proverb: "The man who endeavors to catch two hares would lose both of them."

31. A. Svechin, *Istoria voennogo iskusstva* (Moscow, 1923); M. Svechnikov, *Voina 1812 g. Borodino* (Moscow, 1937), N. Levitskii, *Voina 1812 g.* (Moscow, 1938), S. Borisov, *Kutuzov* (Moscow, 1938).

32. See Eugene Tarle, *Napoleon* (Moscow: Molodaya Gvardiya, 1936); Eugene Tarle, *Nashestvie Napoleona na Rossiu* (Moscow: OGIZ, 1938). Online edition available at http://www.museum.ru/museum/1812/Library/tarle1/index.html; English edition, *Napoleon's Invasion of Russia, 1812* (New York: Oxford University Press, 1942).

33. *Iz literaturnogo nasledia akd. E. V. Tarle* (Moscow, 1981), 241.

34. Joseph Stalin later brought the historian back from exile, gave him luxurious apartments in Moscow and Leningrad, and made him a member of the Academy of Science. But Tarle had to follow the official line when it came to history. For an interesting discussion of Tarle's career, see Ann K. Erickson, "E. V. Tarle: The Career of a Historian Under the Soviet Regime," *American Slavic and East European Review* 19, no. 2 (1960): 202–216.

35. For an interesting discussion, see David Brandenberger, "Politics Projected into the Past: What Precipitated the 1936 Campaign Against M. N.

Pokrovskii?," in I. D. Thatcher, ed., *Reinterpreting Revolutionary Russia: Essays in Honour of James D. White* (London: Macmillan, 2006), 202–214. Also see *Protiv istoricheskoi kontseptsii M. N. Pokrovskogo* (Moscow, 1939); *Protiv antimarksistskoi kontseptsii M. N. Pokrovskogo* (Moscow, 1940).

36. G. Pisarevskii, *M. I. Kutuzov* (Baku, 1942); K. Osipov, *Mikhail Kutuzov* (Molotov, 1942); N. Podorozhnyi, *Kutuzov*, (Moscow, 1942); M. Bragin, *Feldmarshal Kutuzov* (Moscow, 1942), V. Lebedev, *Velikii russkii polkovodets M. I. Kutuzov* (Saransk, 1942); M. Nechkina, *Mikhail Kutuzov* (Moscow, 1944); I. Berkhin, *Otechestvennaia voina 1812 g.* (Molotov, 1942); E. Berkov, *Bitva za Borodino* (Moscow, 1943).

37. *Mikhail Illarionovich Kutuzov: K 200-letnei godovshine so dnia rozhdenia* (Moscow, 1945), 32.

38. "Otvet tov. Stalina na pismo tov. Razina," *Bolshevik* 3 (1947): 7–8. The article also appeared in I. V. Stalin, *Sochineniya* (Moscow: Pisatel', 1997), XVI:21–24. Electronic version available at https://c21ch.newcastle.edu.au/stalin/t16/t16_03.htm.

39. P. Zhilin, *Kontrnastuplenie Kutuzova* (Moscow: Voenn. Izd-vo., 1950).

40. Zhilin, *Kontrnastuplenie Kutuzova*, 7–10, 28.

41. Zhilin, *Kontrnastuplenie Kutuzova*, 28.

42. Zhilin's biography was, without a doubt, the best-selling Soviet-era biography of Kutuzov, as it was printed in several editions. See *Kutuzov* (Moscow: Voenizdat, 1978, 1983); *Feldmarshal M. I. Kutuzov. Zhizn i polkovodcheskaia deiatelnost* (Moscow: Voenizdat, 1988).

43. L. Beskrovnyi, *Otechestvennaia voina 1812 g. i kontrnastuplenia Kutuzova* (Moscow, 1951), 66; N. Garnich, *1812 god* (Moscow, 1956), 181.

44. Zhilin became a member of the Academy of Sciences and a recipient of the Lenin Award before heading the prestigious Institute of Military History of the Ministry of Defense. His books went through multiple editions and are still in circulation in Russia.

45. For an attack on Tarle's views, see S. Kozhukhov, "K voprosu ob otsenke M. I. Kutuzova v Otechstvennoi voine 1812 g.," *Bolshevik* 15 (1951): 24. For the evolution of Tarle's views, compare various editions of his work.

46. V. Pugachev and V. Dinse, *Istoriki, izbravshie put' Galilea: Stati, Ocherki* (Saratov, 1995), 137.

47. O. Orlik, *Groza dvenadtsatogo goda . . .* (Moscow, 1987), 105; N. Ryazanov, "M. I. Kutuzov i ego pisma," in *Kutuzov M. I. Pisma, zapiski* (Moscow, 1989), 554. Also see V. Melentyev, *Kutuzov v Peterburge* (Leningrad, 1986); I. Rostunov, *Otechestvennaia voina 1812 g.* (Moscow, 1987).

48. Orlik, *Groza dvenadtsatogo goda*, 75.

49. "Spasitel Otechestva. Kutuzov—bez khrestomatiinogo glyantsa," *Rodina* 9 (1995): 60.

50. Petr Stanev, *Krepost Ruschuk. Repetitsia razgroma Napoleona* (Moscow: U Nikitskikh Vorot, 2019), 2. Among the bestselling books about Kutuzov is

NOTES TO PAGE 511 | 733

Oleg Mikhailov's two-volume biographical historical novel *Kutuzov*, which has been published in multiple editions. A. Shishov published at least three popular biographies of Kutuzov, but his publications show suspicious similarity to the works of other scholars. See his *Neizvestnyi Kutuzov* (Moscow: Olma-Press, 2001); *Kutuzov. Fel'dmarshal velikoi imperii* (Moscow: Olma Press, 2006); and *Kutuzov, Fel'dmarshal pobedy* (Moscow: Veche, 2012). Other notable popular works include Waldemar Balyazin, *Mikhail Kutuzov* (Moscow: Moskovskii Rabochii, 1991); Aleksey Martynenko, *Tainaya missiya Kutuzova* (Kirov: KOGUP, 2011); V. Scheremet, B. Nigmatulin, and I. Pestun, *Kutuzov: Zhizn', srrazheniya, pobedy* (Moscow: Nigma, 2012); V. Boyarintsev, *M. I. Kutuzov—pobeditel' Napoleona* (Moscow: Russkii Lad, 2013); V. Lapin and V. Goncharov, eds., *Kutuzov: Pro et Contra* (Moscow: Pal'mira, 2016); Yakov Nersesov, *Genii voiny Kutuzov* (Moscow: Eksmo, 2013); Yakov Nersesov, *"Svet i Teni" Kutuzova* (Moscow: Ridero, 2018), 2 vols.; V. Vladimirov, *Kak Kutuzov prognal frantsuzov i za chto Suvorov khvalil ego Ekaterine* (Moscow: Vako, 2016); Lyubov' Mel'nikova and Kirill Nikitin, *Kutuzov, Spasitel' Rossii* (Moscow: AST-Press, 2018).

51. N. Troitskii, *1812. Velikii god Rossii* (Moscow, 1988); N. Troitskii, *Feldmarshal Kutuzov: mify i fakty* (Moscow, 2002). More recently, Eugene Ponasenkov reiterated many of Troitskii's criticisms in his ambitiously titled book *Pervaya nauchnaya istoriia voiny 1812 goda* (Moscow: AST, 2017).

52. Lidia Ivchenko, *Kutuzov* (Moscow: Molodaya Gvardiya, 2012). The series Lives of Remarkable People (Zhizn' zamechatenykh lyudei) began under the leadership of Florentii Pavlenkov in 1890 and continued under editorial supervision of famed Russian writers, including Maxim Gorkii, during the Soviet era. It now includes more than 1,500 biographies of historical personalities, each blending scholarly rigor with accessible style to appeal to discerning Russian readers.

SELECT BIBLIOGRAPHY

Abbreviations

CIOIDR: *Chteniya v Imperatorskom Obschestve Istorii i Dvenostei Rossiiskikh*

General Staff Archives: *Otechestvennaya voina 1812 goda. Materialy Voenno-Uchebnogo Arkhiva Glavnogo Shtaba.* 21 volumes. St. Petersburg: Voen.-uchen. Kom. Gl. Shtaba, 1905–1914.

Journal of the Outgoing Correspondence of the Commander in Chief: *Podrobnyi zhurnal iskhodyashikh bumag Sobstvennoi kantselyarii Glavnokomandyushego Soedinennymi Armiyami General-Feldmarshala Knyazya Kutuzova-Smolenskago v 1812 godu*, edited by V. Nikolskii and N. Polikarpov. In *Trudy Moskovskago otdela imperatorskago Russkago Voenno-istoricheskago obschestva*, volume II (Moscow: Tip. Shtaba Moskov. Voen. Okruga, 1912).

The Kutuzov Papers: "Arkhiv knyazya M. I. Golenischeva-Kutuzova Smolenskogo 1745–1813 gg." In *Russkaya starina*, 1870–1872.

Proceedings of the Committee of Ministers: *Zhurnaly Komiteta ministrov, 1810–1812 gg.* St. Petersburg: V. Bezobrazov, 1891.

PSZ: *Polnoe sobranie zakonov Rossiiskoi imperii s 1649 goda.* 45 volumes. St. Petersburg: Tip. II Otd. Sobstv. Ego Imperat. Velichestva Kantselyarii, 1830.

RGADA: Russian State Archive of Ancient Documents, Moscow.

RGVIA: Russian State Military Historical Archives, Moscow.

SIRIO: *Sbornik Imperatorskago russkago istoricheskago obschestva.* 148 volumes. St. Petersburg, 1867–1916.

TIRVIO: *Trudy imperatorskogo Russkogo voenno-istoricheskogo obschestva.* 7 volumes. St. Petersburg: Gr. Skachkov, 1909–1912.

TSGIA: Central State Historical Archive of St. Petersburg.

VPR: *Vneshnaya politika Rossii XIX I nachala XX veka: dokumenti Rossiiskogo Ministerstva Inostrannikh del.* Series 1, 8 volumes. Moscow: Gos. izd. polit. lit., 1960–1995.

Institutions

Archives du Ministère des Affaires Etrangères
Archives Nationales, Paris
Boris Nikolayevich Yeltsin Presidential Library
Central State Historical Archive of St. Petersburg
Institute of the Russian Literature (Pushkinskii Dom) of the Russian Academy of
    Sciences
Lithuanian State Historical Archive
National Digital Library of the Ministry of Culture of the Russian Federation
Nekrasov Central Library of Moscow
Russian State Archive of Ancient Documents
Russian State Library
Russian State Military Historical Archive
State Archive of the Pskov Region, Russia
Vernadsky National Library of Ukraine

Periodicals

Gazette Nationale, ou Le Moniteur Universel
Istoricheskii vestnik
Istoricheskii, statisticheskii I geograficheskii zhurnal
Otechestvennye zapiski
Russkaya starina
Russkii arkhiv
Russkii invalid
Sankt-Peterburgskie vedomosti
Sbornik imperatorskogo russkogo istoricheskogo obshhestva
Severnaya pochta
Syn Otechestva
The Times (London)
Vestnik Evropy
Voenno-Istoricheskii vestnik
Voennyi sbornik

Kutuzov's Private Correspondence

"Arkhiv knyazya M. I. Golenischeva-Kutuzova Smolenskogo 1745–1813 gg."
    Russkaya starina 3 (1870): 249–258; 11 (1870): 498–514; 1 (1871): 49–60; 2
    (1871): 201–204; 2 (1872): 257–269; 5 (1872): 647–660, 698–705.
"Dva pis'ma general-majora Mikhaila Illarionovicha Golenischeva-Kutuzova
    Smolenskogo." *Zapiski imp. Odesskogo o-va istorii i drevnostei*, 1881, XXII, t. 12, 486.
Fel'dmarshal-general M.I. Kutuzov. Pis'ma, zapiski, eds. N.I. Ryazanov and N.
    Shakhmagonov (Moscow: Voen. Izd. 1989).
"Iz lichnoj perepiski (1811–1813 gg.)." *Znamya* 5 (1948): 89–120.

"Perepiska knyazya M. I. Kutuzova s rodnymi." *Zhurnal Ministerstva narodnogo prosveshheniya* 1 (1912): 1–36.

"Pis'ma avstriiskogo imperatora Frantsa I k M. I. Kutuzovu, 1805 g." *Russkaya starina* 4 (1870): 325–344.

"Pis'ma k docheri grafine E. M. Tiesengauzen 1803–1813 gg." *Russkaya starina* 6 (1874): 338–377.

"Pis'mo k zhene." *Russkaya starina* 2 (1870): 500–501; 4 (1874): 647.

Kutuzov's Military Correspondence

Dokumenty shtaba M. I. Kutuzova, 1805–1806. Edited by S. Salimov and B. Tungusov. Vilnius: Gos. Izdatel'stvo Polit. i Nauchnoi Literatury, 1951.

Fel'dmarshal Kutuzov: sbornik dokumentov i materialov. Edited by N. Korobkov. Moscow: Gospolitizdat, 1947.

Fel'dmarshal Kutuzov: dokumenty, dnevniki, vospominaniya. Edited by A. Val'kovich and A. Kapitonov. Moscow: Arkheog. Tsentr., 1995.

Kutuzov v dunaiskih knyazhestvah: sbornik dokumentov. Kishinev: Gos. Izd-vo Moldavii, 1948.

M. I. Kutuzov: Sbornik dokumentov. Edited by Liubomir Beskrovnyi. 5 volumes. Moscow: Voeniszdat, 1950–1956.

Materialy po Otechestvennoi voine. Podrobnyi zhurnal iskhodyashikh bumag sobstvennoi kantselyarii Glavnokomanduyushego soedinennymi armiyami general-fel'dmarshala Kutuzova Smolenskogo v 1812 g. 2 volumes. Edited by V. Nikol'skii. Moscow: Tip. Shtaba Moskov. Voen. Okruga, 1912.

Primechaniya o pekhotnoi sluzhbe voobshhe i o egerskoi osobenno. Edited by Liubomir Beskrovnyi. Moscow: Voenizdat, 1955.

Sources

1812–1814: relyatsii, pis'ma, dnevniki. Edited by A. Afanasyev. Moscow: Terra, 1992.

Adams, John Quincy. *Writings of John Quincy Adams.* Edited by Worthington Chauncey Ford. New York: Macmillan, 1913.

Adams, Michael. *Napoleon and Russia.* London: Bloomsbury Academic, 2006.

Aksan, Virginia H. *An Ottoman Statesman in War and Peace: Ahmed Resmi Efendi, 1700–1783.* Leiden: Brill, 1995.

Aksan, Virginia H. *Ottoman Wars, 1700–1870: An Empire Besieged.* New York: Pearson, 2007.

Alexander, John T. *Catherine the Great: Life and Legend.* Oxford: Oxford University Press, 1989.

Alombert, Paul Claude. *Campagne de l'an 14 (1805): Le corps d'armée aux ordres du maréchal Mortier. Combat de Dürrenstein.* Paris: Berger-Levrault, 1897.

Alombert, Paul Claude, and Jean Lambert Alphonse Colin. *La Campagne de 1805 en Allemagne.* Paris: R. Chapelot, 1902.

Altschuler, Roman. "Kutuzov kak voennyi pedagog—Direktor Kadetskogo Korpusa." In *Voprosy voennoi istorii Rossii XVIII i pervoi poloviny XIX veka,* 251–262. Moscow, 1969.

Andreyev, Alexander. *Knyaz' Vasilii Mikhailovich Dolgorukov-Krymskii. Dokumental'noe zhizneopisanie. Istoricheskaya khronika XVIII veka.* Moscow: Mezh. Tsentr otrasllevoi informatiki Gosatomnadzora Rossii, 1997.

Anekdoty ili dostopamyatnye skazaniya ob ego svetlosti general-fel'dmarshale knyaze Mikhaile Illarionoviche Golenischeve-Kutuzove Smolenskom, nachinaya s pervykh let ego sluzhby do konchiny, s priobsheniem nekotoryh ego pisem, dostopamyatnyh ego rechei i prikazov. 2 volumes. St. Petersburg, 1814.

Antonov, A. *Pervyi kadetskii korpus.* St. Petersburg: Skoropechatnya Rashkova, 1906.

Arkhangel'skii, Alexander. *Aleksandr I.* Moscow: Molodaya gvardiya, 2012.

Arkhiv bratyev Turgenevykh. St. Petersburg: Imperial Academy of Sciences, 1911.

Arkhiv knyazya Vorontsova. 40 volumes. Moscow: Tip. Gracheva, 1870–1895.

Austin, Paul Britten. *1812: Napoleon's Invasion of Russia.* Combined edition. London, 2000.

Bailleu, Paul, ed. *Briefwechsel könig Friedrich Wilhelm's III und der königin Luise mit kaiser Alexander I.* Leipzig: S. Hirzel, 1900.

Balyazin, Waldemar. *Fel'dmarshal M. B. Barclay de Tolly: zhizn' i polkovodcheskaya deyatel'nost'.* Moscow: Voenizdat, 1990.

Balyazin, Waldemar. *Mikhail Kutuzov.* Moscow: Moskovskii rabochii, 1991.

Bantysh-Kamenskii, Dmitrii. *Biografii rossiiskikh generalissimusov i general-feld'marshalov.* St. Petersburg: Tip. Tretyago Dept. Min. Gos. Imushestv, 1840.

Bantysh-Kamenskii, Dmitrii. *Slovar' dostopamyatnykh lyudei Russkoi zemli.* Volume 1. St. Petersburg, 1847.

Barclay de Tolly, Mikhail. *Izobrazhenie voennykh deistvii 1-oi armii v 1812 godu.* Moscow, 1859. Also *Chteniya v Imperatorskom Moskovskom obshestve istorii i drevnosti* 2 (1858): 1–32.

Barran, Thomas. *Russia Reads Rousseau, 1762–1825.* Evanston, IL: Northwestern University Press, 2002.

Barskov, Yakov, ed. *Perepiska moskovskikh masonov XVIII-go veka, 1780–1792 gg.* Petrograd: Izd. Otd. Rus. yaz. i slovesnosti Imperatorskoi akad. Nauk, 1915.

Bartenev, A. *Biografiya generalissimusov i general-fel'dmarshalov Rossiiskoi imperatorskoi armii.* St. Petersburg, 1912.

Bartenev, A. "Knyaz' Mikhail Illarionovich Golenischev-Kutuzov Smolenskii." *Voenno-istoricheskii sbornik* 3 (1912): 1–14.

Beer, Adolf. *Zehn Jahre Oesterreichischer Politik, 1801–1810.* Leipzig: Brodhaus, 1877.

Belloc, Hilaire. *Napoleon's Campaign of 1812 and the Retreat from Moscow.* New York, 1926.

Benckendorf, Alexander. "Iz memuarov grafa A. Kh. Benckendorfa." *Rossiiskii arkhiv* 18 (2009). http://feb-web.ru/feb/rosarc/rai/rai-258-.htm.

Bennigsen, Levin. *Mémoires du Général Bennigsen.* Edited by Eutrope Cazalas. 3 volumes. Paris, 1908.

Bennigsen, Levin. *Pis'ma o voine 1812 goda.* Translated and edited by P. Maikov. Kyiv, 1912.

Bennigsen, Levin. "Zapiski grafa L. L. Bennigsena o kampanii 1812 g." *Russkaya starina* 138, nos. 4, 6 (1909); vol. 139, nos. 7, 9 (1909); vol. 140, nos. 11–12 (1909).

Berg, Gregor von. *Autobiographie des Generalen der Infanterie Gregor von Berg.* Dresden: E. Blochman, 1871.

Beskrovnyi, L. *Otechestvennaia voina 1812 goda.* Moscow, 1968.

Beskrovnyi, L. *Otechestvennaya voina 1812 goda i kontrnastuplenie Kutuzova.* Moscow: Academy of Sciences of SSSR, 1951.

Beskrovnyi, L., and G. Mescheryakov. *Borodino: dokumenty, pis'ma, vospominaniya.* Moscow, 1962.

Bessonov, V. *Tarutinskoe srazhenie.* Moscow: Kniga, 2008.

Bestuzhev-Riumin, A. "Proizshestviya v stolitse Moskve do vtorzheniya v onuyu nepriyatelya." *Chteniya v Imperatorskom Moskovskom obshestve istorii i drevnosti* 2 (1859), V, 69–89.

Bezotosnyi, Viktor. *Donskoi generalitet i Ataman Platov v 1812 godu: Maloizvestnye i neizvestnye fakty na fone znamenitykh sobytii.* Moscow, 1999.

Bezotosnyi, Viktor. *Napoleonovskie voiny.* Moscow: Veche, 2010.

Bezotosnyi, Viktor, ed. *Otechestvennaia voina 1812 goda: Entsiklopedia.* Moscow, 2004.

Bezsonov, Ivan. *Bitva v Maloyaroslavtse.* Kaluga: Tip. Gubern. Pravlenia, 1912.

Blum, Jerome. *Lord and Peasant in Russia from the Ninth to the Nineteenth Century.* Princeton, NJ: Princeton University Press, 1971.

Bochkov, E. "Tseremonial pogrebeniya M. I. Golenischeva-Kutuzova: Neizvestnye stranitsy." Museum Borodisnkoe Pole. https://www.borodino.ru/wp-content/uploads/2017/08/18_Bochkov_E.A.pdf.

Bogdanovich, Modest. *Istoriya otechestvennoi voiny 1812 goda po dostovernym istochnikam.* St. Petersburg: S. Strugovshikov and Co., 1859.

Bogdanovich, Modest. *Istoriya tsarstvovaniya imp. Aleksandra I i Rossii v ego vremya.* 6 volumes. St. Petersburg, 1869–1871.

Bogdanovich, Modest. *Istoriya voiny 1813 goda za nezavisimost' Germanii oo dostovernym istochnikam.* St. Petersburg, 1863.

Bogdanovich, Modest. *Pokhody Rumyantseva, Potemkina i Suvorova v Turtsii.* St. Petersburg: E. Weymar, 1852.

Bogolyubov, A. *Polkovodcheskoe iskusstvo A. V. Suvorova.* Moscow: Voenizdat, 1939.

Borisov, S. *Kutuzov. Ocherk zhizni i deyatel'nosti velikogo russkogo polkovodtsa.* Moscow: Voenizdat, 1938.

Borodino v vospominaniyakh sovremennikov. St. Petersburg, 2001.

Boudon, Jacques-Olivier. *Napoléon et la campagne de Russie 1812.* Paris: Armand Colin, 2012.

Boyarintsev, V. *M. I. Kutuzov—pobeditel' Napoleona.* Moscow: Russkii Lad, 2013.

Bragin, Mikhail. *Polkovodets Kutuzov.* Moscow: Gospolitizdat, 1944. English edition: *Field Marshal Kutuzov: A Short Biography.* Moscow: Foreign Languages Pub. House, 1944. French edition: *M. Koutouzov.* Paris: R. Julliard, 1947.

Briekner, A., ed., *Materialy dlya zhizneopisaniya Grafa Nikity Petrovicha Panina (1770–1837).* St. Petersburg: Tip. Imp. Akademiis Nauk, 1890.

Brückner, Alexander. *Smert' Pavla I*. St. Petersburg: M. V. Pirozhkov, 1907.

Butovskii, I. *Fel'dmarshal knyaz Golenischev-Kutuzov pri kontse i nachale svoego boevogo poprishha. Pervaya voina imperatora Aleksandra s Napoleonom v 1805 g*. St. Petersburg, 1858.

Buturlin, Dimitri. *Istoriya nashestviya imperatora Napoleona na Rossiyu v 1812 g*. St. Petersburg: Voen. Tip. Glavnogo Shtaba, 1823.

Buturlin, Dmitri. "Kutuzov v 1812 godu." *Russkaya starina* 10 (1894): 201–220; 11 (1894): 193–213; 12 (1894): 133–154.

Capefigue, Jean-Baptiste Honoré Raymond. *L'Europe pendant le Consulat et l'Empire de Napoléon*. Paris: Pitois-Levrault, 1840.

Castle, Ian. *Austerlitz: Napoleon and the Eagles of Europe*. Barnsley: Pen & Sword, 2005.

Cate, Curtis. *The War of the Two Emperors. The Duel Between Napoleon and Alexander: Russia 1812*. New York, 1985.

Cathcart, George. *Commentaries on the War in Russia and Germany in 1812 and 1813*. London: John Murray, 1850.

Caulaincourt, Armand-Augustin-Louis, Marquis de. *Mémoires du Général de Caulaincourt, duc de Vicence, grand écuyer de l'empereur*. Paris: Plon, 1933.

Cavender, Mary W. *Nests of the Gentry: Family, Estate and Local Loyalties in Provincial Russia*. Newark: University of Delaware Press, 2007.

Chechulin, Nikolai. *Russkoe provintsialnoe obschestvo vo vtoroi polovine XVIII veka*. St. Petersburg: Tip. V. S. Balasheva, 1889.

Chichagov, Pavel. *Memoires inédits de l'Amiral Tchitchagoff. Campagnes de la Russie en 1812 contre la Turquie, l'Autriche et la France*. Berlin: F. Schneider, 1855.

Chichagov, Pavel. "Pis'ma admirala Chichagova k imperatoru Aleksandru I." *Sbornik imperatorskogo russkogo istoricheskogo obschestva* 6 (1871).

Choiseul-Gouffier, Sophie de. *Historical Memoirs of the Emperor Alexander I and the Court of Russia*. London: Kegan Paul, 1904.

Clausewitz, Carl von. *Der Feldzug von 1812 in Russland, der Feldzug von 1813 bis zum Waffenstillstand und der Feldzug von 1814 in Frankreich*. Edited by Marie von Clausewitz. Berlin: Ferdinand Dümmler, 1835.

Conermann, Stephan. "Das Eigene und das Fremde: der Bericht der Gesandtschaft Musafa Rasihs nach St. Petersburg 1792–1794." *Archivum Ottomanicum* 17 (1999): 249–263.

Crossard, Jean Baptiste Louis de. *Mémoires militaires et historiques*. Volume 4. Paris: Migneret, 1829.

Czartoryski, Adam. *Memoirs of Prince Adam Czartoryski and His Correspondence with Alexander I*. Edited by Adam Gielgud. 2 volumes. London: Remington, 1888.

Damas, Roger de. *Memoirs of the Comte Roger de Damas, 1787–1806*. Edited and annotated by Jacques Rambaud. London: Chapman and Hall, 1913.

Davies, B. *Empire and Military Revolution in Eastern Europe: Russia's Turkish Wars in the Eighteenth Century*. London: Continuum, 2011.

Davies, Brian. *The Russo-Turkish War, 1768–1774. Catherine II and the Ottoman Empire*. London: Bloomsbury, 2016.

Dennison, Tracy. *The Institutional Framework of Russian Serfdom*. Cambridge: Cambridge University Press, 2011.

Deyaniya rossiiskikh polkovodtsev i generalov, oznamenovavshikh sebya v dostopamyatnuyu voinu s Franciei v 1812, 1813, 1814 i 1815 gg. S kratkim nachertaniem vsei ikh sluzhby s samogo nachala vstupleniya v onuyu, I:1–115. St. Petersburg, 1822.

Dixon, Simon. *The Modernization of Russia, 1676–1825*. Cambridge: Cambridge University Press, 1999.

Djevegelov, A., and N. Makhnevich, eds. *Otechestvennaia voina i Russkoye obshestvo*. 7 volumes. Moscow, 1911–1912.

Documente privitóre la Istoria Romậnilor. Bucharest: Romanian Ministry of Culture, 1886.

Dubrovin, N., ed. *Bumagi knyazya Grigoriya Aleksandrovicha Potemkina-Tavricheskogo, 1788–1789 gg*. St. Petersburg: Voen.-Ucheb. Komitet Glavn. Shtaba, 1894.

Dubrovin, N., ed. *Bumagi knyazya Grigoriya Aleksandrovicha Potemkina-Tavricheskogo, 1790–1793 gg*. St. Petersburg: Voen.-Ucheb. Komitet Glavn. Shtaba, 1895.

Dubrovin, N. "Materialy dlya istorii tsarstvovaniya Aleksandra I. Turetskaya voina 1806–1812 gg." *Voennyi sbornik*, 1864, nos. 3–9, 11, 12; 1865, nos. 1–9.

Dubrovin, N. "Moskva i graf Rostopchin v 1812 godu. Materialy dlya istorii 1812 goda." *Voennyi sbornik* 7 (1863): 99–105; 8 (1863): 419–471.

Dubrovin, N., ed. *Otechestvennaya voina v pismakh sovremennikov, 1812–1815 gg*. St. Petersburg, 1882.

Dubrovin, N., ed. *Pis'ma glavenishikh deyatelej v tsarstvovanie imperatora Aleksandra I, 1807–1829 godakh*. St. Petersburg, 1883.

Dumas, Mathieu. *Précis des évènements militaires ou essai historique sur les campagnes de 1799 à 1814*. Hambourg: Perthès et Besser, 1822.

Edling, Roxandra Stourdza, Comtess. *Mémoires de la comtess Edling, demoiselle d'honneur de sa majesté l'imperatrice Elisabeth Alexéevna*. Moscow: Holy Synod, 1888.

Egger, Rainer. *Das Gefecht bei Dürnstein-Loiben*. 1805. Militärhistorische Schriftenreihe, H. 3. Vienna: Österreichischer Bundesverlag, 1986.

Elchaninov, A. "K 120-letiyu vzyatiya Suvorovym turetskoi kreposti Izmail 11 dekabrya 1790 g." *Russkii invalid*, 1910, no. 270.

El'terman, I. M. *Posol'stvo kutuzova v Turtsii v 1793–1794 g.g.* Moscow, 1945.

Engel', Andrei. *Opisanie del khryanyaschikhsya v archive Vilenskago general-gubernatorstva*. Vilna: Vilenskoe Gubern. Pravlenie, 1870.

Engelhardt, A. *Vzglyad na Dunaiskuuu kampaniyu 1811 goda*. St. Petersburg, 1813.

Engel'hardt, Lev. *Zapiski*. Edited by I. Fedyukin. Moscow: Novoe Literaturnoe Obozrenie, 1997.

Engin, Hakan. "1787–1792 Osmanlı-Rus Avusturya Harpleri sırasında İbrail Kalesi." Unpublished master's thesis, Trakya University, Institute of Social Sciences, Edirne, 2013.

Ertekin, Işık. "Kili Kalesi (1767–1792)." Unpublished master's thesis, Trakya University, Institute of Social Sciences, Edirne, 2015.

Fabry, G. *Campagne de 1812. Documents relatifs à l'aile droite. 20 août–4 décembre*. Paris, Chapelot, 1912.

Fabry, G. *Campagne de 1812. Documents relatifs à l'aile gauche 20 août–4 septembre. IIe, VIe et IXe corps*. Paris: Chapelot, 1912.

Fabry, G. *Campagne de 1812. Mémoires relatifs à l'aile droite. 20 août–4 septembre*. Paris, Chapelot, 1912.

Fabry, G. *Campagne de Russie, 1812*. 5 volumes. Paris: L. Gougy and Chapelot, 1900–1903.

Fedakar, Cengiz. *Bender Kalesi (1768–1774)*. Istanbul: Kitabevi, 2019.

Fedakar, Cengiz. *Hotin Kalesi'nin Sükutu (1768–1774 Osmanlı-Rus Savaşları'nda), Bozkırın Oğlu Ahmet Taşağıl'a Armağan*. Istanbul: Yeditepe, 2019.

Fedakar, Cengiz. "1787–1792 Osmanlı-Avusturya Rus Savaşlarında Edirne Lojistiği." In *Prof. M. Tayyib Gökbilgin ve Edirne Sempozyumu Bildiriler*, edited by Ibrahim Sezgin and Veysi Akin, 151–160. Edirne: Trakya University, 2016.

Fedyukin, Igor. *The Enterprisers: The Politics of School in Early Modern Russia*. Oxford: Oxford University Press, 2019.

Feldbaek, Ole. "The Foreign Policy of Czar Paul I, 1800–1801: An Interpretation." *Jahrbücher für Geschichte Östereuropas* XXX (1982): 16–36.

Firges, Pascal. *French Revolutionaries in the Ottoman Empire: Diplomacy, Political Culture, and the Limiting of Universal Revolution, 1792–1798*. Oxford: Oxford University Press, 2017.

Fisher, Alan W. *The Crimean Tatars*. Stanford, CA: Hoover Institution Press, 1978.

Fisher, Alan W. *The Russian Annexation of the Crimea, 1772–1783*. Cambridge: Cambridge University Press, 1970.

Fomenko, Igor. *Diplomaticheskaia missiia M. I. Kutuzova. Karta Konstantinopolia 1794 goda*. Moscow: State Historical Museum, 2013.

Foord, Edward. *Napoleon's Russian Campaign of 1812*. London, 1914.

Fortunatov, P., ed. *P. A. Rumyantsev. Sbornik dokumentov*. Moscow: Voennoe izdatel'stvo, 1953.

Fuks, E. "Suvorov i Kutuzov." *Sorevnovatel' prosvesheniya* VII (1819): 275–281.

Garnich, N. "Borodinskoe srazhenie." In *Polkovodets Kutuzov. Sbornik statei*, edited by L. Beskrovnyi, 177–256. Moscow: Gospolitizdat, 1955.

Garnich, Nikolai. *1812 god*. Moscow: Gos. Izd. Kult.-prosvet. Literatury, 1956.

Gendel', G. "M. I. Kutuzov i Bukharestskii mir." *Uchennye zapiski* (Gorkovskii University) 25 (1954): 93–105.

Gerua, A. *Borodino*. St. Petersburg, 1912.

Glinka, F. *Pis'ma ruskago ofitsera o Pol'she, Avstriiskikh vladeniyakh i Vengrii, s podrobnym opisaniem pokhoda rossiyan protivu frantsuzov v 1805 i 1806 godakh, takzhe Otechestvennoi i Zagranichnoi voiny s 1812 po 1815 god*. Moscow: Tip. S. Selivanovskago, 1815, 1870.

Glinka, F. *Pis'ma russkogo ofitsera o voennykh proisshestviyah 1812 g*. Moscow, 1821.

Glinka, S. *Zapiski o 1812 gode*. St. Petersburg, 1893.

Glinka, Sergei. *Zapiski Sergeya Nikolayevicha Glinki*. St. Petersburg: Russkaya starina, 1895.

Glinka, S. "Cherty iz zhizni grafa F. V. Rostopchina: Moskva i graf Rostopchin: 1812 god." In *Russkoe chtenie* I:237–248. St. Petersburg, 1845.

Glinka, S. *Iz zapisok o 1812 gode.* http://www.museum.ru/1812/library/ glinka1/ glinka.html.

Glinka, S. *Korpusnye vospominaniya. Iz zapisok S. N. Glinki.* St. Petersburg, 1845.

Glinka, S. *Ruskie anekdoty voennye, grazhdanskie i istoricheskie.* Moscow: University Tip., 1820.

Glover, Michael. *A Very Slippery Fellow: The Life of Sir Robert Wilson, 1777–1849.* Oxford: Oxford University Press, 1978.

Golitsyn, A. "Zapiski o voine 1812 goda." *Voennyi sbornik* 12 (1910).

Golitsyn, N. "Ocherki voennykh stsen 1812–1814 gg. Zapiski." *Russkii arkhiv* 4 (1884): 338–374.

Golitsyn, N. *Ofitserskie zapiski ili vospominaniya o pokhodakh 1812, 1813 i 1814 godov.* Moscow, 1836.

Gorchkoff, Dimitri, ed. *Moskva i Otechestvennaya voina 1812 goda.* 2 volumes. Moscow: Izdatelstvo Glavnogo Arkhivnogo Upravleniya Goroda Moskvy, 2011–2012.

Gourgaud, Gaspard. *Napoléon et la Grande Armée en Russie.* Paris, 1825.

Grabbe, Pavel. *Iz pamyatnykh zapisok grafa Pavla Khristoforovicha Grabbe.* Moscow: Katkov, 1873.

Grabbe, P. "Iz pamyantnykh zapisok." *Russkii arkhiv* 3 (1873): 416–418.

Grabbe, P. "Zapiski (Ot Vil'ny do ostavleniya Moskvy)." *Russkii arkhiv* 3 (1873): 416–480.

Gramm, Ernst Rainer. " 'Der unglückliche Mack': Aufstieg und Fall des Karl Mack von Leiberich." Unpublished Ph.D. dissertation, University of Vienna, 2008.

Grech, Nikolay. *Zapiski o moei zhizni.* Moscow: Zakharov, 2002.

Hamburg, Gary. *Russia's Path Toward Enlightenment: Faith, Politics, and Reason, 1500–1801.* New Haven, CT: Yale University Press, 2016.

Hartley, Janet M. *A Social History of the Russian Empire, 1650–1825.* London: Longman, 1999.

Horne, Alistair. *Napoleon, Master of Europe, 1805–1807.* New York: William Morrow, 1979.

Huidekoper, Frederic Louis. "The Surprise of the Tabor Bridge at Vienna by Prince Murat and Marshal Lannes, November 13, 1805." *Journal of the Military Service Institution of the United States,* January–February 1905, 275–293; May–June 1905, 513–530.

Iakovkina, N. *Russkoe dvoriantsvo pervoi poloviny XIX veka. Byt i traditsii.* St. Petersburg, 2002.

Istoricheskie zapiski o zhizni i voinskikh podvigakh general-fel'dmarshala svetleishego knyazya M. L. Golenischeva-Kutuzova Smolenskogo. St. Petersburg, 1813.

Ivchenko, Lidia. *Kutuzov.* Moscow: Molodaya gvardiya, 2012.

Ivchenko, Lidia. "M. I. Kutuzov v borodinskom srazhenii." *Bombardir* 3 (1995): 38–47.

Ivchenko, Lidia. "M. I. Kutuzov v sovremennoi istoriografii. Prigovor istorii ili proizvol istorikov?" In *Otechestvennaya voina 1812 goda. Istochniki. Pamyatniki.*

Problemy: Materialy XI Vserossiiskoi nauchnoi konferentsii. Edited by A. Gorbunov. Borodino, 2003. http://www.museum.ru/museum/1812/Library/Borodino_conf/ 2004/Ivchenko. pdf.

Ivchenko, Lidia. "Plany russkogo komandovaniya v Borodinskom srazhenii i ikh realizaciya." In *Borodinskoe pole. Istoriya, kul'tura, ekologiya: Sbornik.* Edited by A. Gorbunov. Borodino, 2000. http://www.museum.ru/museum/1812/Library/ Borodino _conf/2000a/Ivchenko.pdf.

Ivchenko, Lidia. "Toll i istoriografiya Borodinskogo srazheniya." In *Otechestvennaya voina 1812 goda. Rossiya i Evropa: Tezisy nauchnoi konferentsii.* Borodino, 1991. http://www.museum.ru/museum/1812/Library/Borodino_conf/1992/Ivche nko.pdf.

Janetschek, Clemens d'Elpidio. *Die Schlacht bei Austerlitz: 2. December 1805.* Brunn: Päpstliche Benedictiner-Buchdruckerei, 1898.

Josselson, Michael, and Diana Josselson. *The Commander: A Life of Barclay de Tolly.* Oxford: Oxford University Press, 1980.

Kagan, Frederick W. *The End of the Old Order: Napoleon and Europe, 1801–1805.* New York: Da Capo, 2006.

Kallash, V., ed. *Dvenadtsatyi god. V vospominaniyakh i perepiske sovremennikov. Sbornik.* Moscow, 1912.

Kamer-fur'yevskii tseremonial'nyj zhurnal. St. Petersburg, 1901.

Kartina zhizni, voennykh i politicheskikh deyanii ego svetlosti knyazya M. L. Golenischeva-Kutuzova Smolenskogo, pisannaya odnim rossiiskoi sluzhby ofitserom. Moscow, 1813.

Kazakov, N. "Iz istorii russko-bolgarskikh svyazei v period voiny Rossii s Turtsiei (1806–1812 gg.)." *Voprosy istorii* 6 (1955): 42–55.

Kazakov, N. "M. I. Kutuzov i natsional'no-osvoboditel'noe dvizhenie narodov Balkan v period russko-turetskoi voiny 1806–1812 gg." In *Polkovodets Kutuzov. Sbornik statei,* edited by L. Beskrovnyi, 141–176. Moscow: Gospolitizdat, 1955.

Kazakov, N. "Polkovodcheskaya deyatel'nost' M. I. Kutuzova v period russko-turetskoi voiny 1806–1812 gg. (kampaniya 1811 g.)." In *Polkovodets Kutuzov. Sbornik statei,* edited by L. Beskrovnyi, 86–140. Moscow: Gospolitizdat, 1955.

Kenney, James J. "Lord Whitworth and the Conspiracy Against Czar Paul I: The New Evidence of the Kent Archive." *Slavic Review* 36, no. 2 (June 1977): 205–219.

Kharkevich, V. *1812 g. Berezina.* St. Petersburg, 1893.

Kharkevich, V., ed. *1812 god v dnevnikakh, zapiskakh i vospominaniyakh sovremennikov. Materialy Voenno-uchenogo arkhiva Glavnogo shtaba.* 4 volumes. Vilna, 1900–1907.

Kharkevich, V. *Barklai-de-Tolli v Otechestvennuyu voinu posle soedineniya armii pod Smolenskom.* St. Petersburg: Tip. Gl. Upr. Udelov, 1904.

Kharkevich, V., ed. "Perepiska imperatora Aleksandra I i Barklaya de Tolli v Otechestvennuyu voinu posle ostavleniya gosudarem armii." *Voennyi sbornik* 11 (1903): 241–262; 12 (1903): 219–230; 1 (1904): 217–242; 3 (1906): 191–198; 4 (1906): 210–232; 5 (1906): 251–260; 6 (1906): 227–238; 7 (1906): 179–184; 8 (1906): 161–169; 9 (1906): 221–223.

Kharkevic, V. *Voina 1812 goda. Ot Nemana do Smolenska.* Vilna: Nikolaevsk, akad. gen. shtaba, 1901.

Khatov, A. "Opisanie turetskogo pokhoda rossian pod nachal'stvom generala Golenischeva-Kutuzova v 1811 godu." *Otechestvennye zapiski,* 1827, nos. 81, 82, 83, 96, 97.

Klimych, Semen. "Moskovskii Novodevichii monastyr' v 1812 godu. Razskaz ochevidtsa–shtatnogo sluzhitelya Semena Klimycha." *Russkii arkhiv,* 1864, 417.

Klokman, Yu. "M. I. Kutuzov v period russko-turetskih voin vtoroi poloviny XVIII v." In *Polkovodets Kutuzov. Sbornik statei,* edited by L. Beskrovnyi. Moscow: Gospolitizdat, 1955, 13–51.

Kolubyakin, B. "1812 g. Poslednie dni komandovaniya Barklaem 1-i i 2-i Zapadnymi armiyami. Period so vremeni okonchaniya boev pod Smolenskom 8 avgusta do pribytiya k armiyam Kutuzova 17 avgusta." *Russkaya starina* 6 (1912): 467–476.

Kolubyakin, B. "1812 god. Izbranie Kutuzova glavnokomanduyushhim nad vsemi armiyami, priezd ego v armiyu i pervye dni ego deyatel'nosti." *Russkaya starina* 7 (1912): 3–32.

Komarovskii, Evgraf. *Zapiski grafa E. F. Komarovskogo.* St. Petersburg: Ogni, 1914.

Korch, A. *Mikhail Illarionovich Kutuzov.* Moscow: Vneshtorizdat, 1989.

Korf, Sergei. *Dvoryanstvo i ego soslovnoe upravlenie za stoletie, 1762–1855.* St. Petersburg: Trenke & Fusno, 1906.

Korobkov, N. "Kutuzov i osvoboditel'nyi pokhod russkoi armii v 1813 g." In *Polkovodets Kutuzov. Sbornik statei,* edited by L. Beskrovnyi, 403–426. Moscow: Gospolitizdat, 1955.

Korobkov, N. "Kutuzov—strateg." *Istoricheskii zhurnal* 5 (1942): 38–52.

Korobkov, N. *Mikhail Kutuzov.* Moscow: Voenizdat, 1944.

Korobkov, N. *Mikhail Kutuzov, 1745–1945. Ocherk polkovodcheskoi deyatel'nosti.* Moscow: Voenizdat, 1945.

Korobkov, N. "Voennoe iskusstvo Kutuzova." *Voprosy istorii* 3, no. 4 (1945): 3–33.

Korobkov, N. "Vzyatie Izmaila (1790 god)." *Istoricheskii zhurnal* 4 (1941): 24–39.

Kotzebue, Wilhelm von. *Versuch einer Beschreibung der Schlacht bey Dürnstein am 11. November 1805.* Königsberg, 1807.

Krylov, V. *Kadetskie korpusa i Rossiiskie kadety.* St. Petersburg, 1998.

Kukiel, Marian. *Wojna 1812 roku.* Krakow, 1936.

Kwiatkowski, Ernst von. *Die Kämpfe bei Schöngrabern und Oberhollabrunn 1805 und 1809.* Vienna, 1908.

Langeron, A. *Mémoires de Langeron: général d'infanterie dans l'armée russe. Campagnes de 1812, 1813, 1814.* Paris: A. Picard, 1902.

Langeron, A. *Voina s Turtsiei 1806–1812 gg. Zapiski gr. Lanzherona.* Edited by E. Kamenskii. St. Petersburg, 1911.

Langeron, A. "Zapiski grafa Lanzherona. Voina s Turtsiei 1806–1812 gg." *Russkaya starina* 1907, nos. 5–11; 1908, nos. 2–4, 6–11; 1909, nos. 6–9; 1910, nos. 7–10; 1911, nos. 7–8.

Lapin, V., and V. Goncharov, eds., *Kutuzov: pro et contra*. Moscow: Pal'mira, 2016.

Leer, H. *Podrobnyi konspekt. Voina 1805 goda. Austerlitskaya operatsiya*. St. Petersburg, 1888.

Leer, H. *Podrobnyi konspekt. Voina 1805 goda. Ul'mskaya operatsiya*. St. Petersburg, 1887.

Leggiere, Michael V. *Napoleon and the Struggle for Germany. Volume 1: The War of Liberation, Spring 1813*. Cambridge: Cambridge University Press, 2015.

Lieven, Dominic. *Russia Against Napoleon: The True Story of the Campaigns of War and Peace*. New York: Viking, 2010.

Ligne, Charles Joseph Prince de. *Lettres et pensées du Maréchal Prince de Ligne*. London: Cox, 1809.

Liprandi, I. "Kratkoe obozrenie epizoda Otechestvennoi voiny (s pribytiya knyazya Smolenskogo k armii 17 avgusta do ostavleniya Moskvy 2 sentyabrya 1812 goda)." *Severnaya pchela*, 1858, nos. 151, 152, 154, and 155.

Liprandi, Ivan. *Materialy dlya Otechestvennoi Voiny 1812 goda*. St. Petersburg, 1867.

Longworth, Philip. *The Art of Victory: The Life and Achievements of Generalissimo Suvorov, 1729–1800*. London: Constable, 1965.

Lopatin, V., ed. *Ekaterina II i G. A. Potemkin. Lichnaya perepiska (1769–1771)*. Moscow: Nauka, 1997.

Lopatin, V. *Potemkin i Suvorov*. Moscow: Nauka, 1992.

Lopatin, V. *Suvorov*. Moscow: Molodaya Gvardiya, 2012.

Lopatin, V. *Svetleishii knyaz' Potemkin*. Moscow: Olma-Press, 2005.

Lubenkov, Nikolai. *Rasskaz artillerista o dele Borodinskom*. St. Petersburg: E. Pratz, 1837.

Luzanov, Peter. *Sukhoputnyi slyakhetskii kadetskii korpuss pri grafe Minikhe (s 1732 po 1741)*. St. Petersburg: Schmidt, 1907.

Löwenstern, Waldemar de. "1812 god v zapiskah generala Lewenshterna." *Russkaya starina* 11 (1900): 331–361; 12 (1900): 553–582; 1 (1901): 103–128; 2 (1901): 361–381; 4 (1901): 177–195; 5 (1901): 427–444; 6 (1901): 643–668; 7 (1901): 205–224.

Löwenstern, Waldemar de. *Denkwürdigkeiten eines Livländers (Aus den Jahren 1790–1815)*. Leipzig: Winter, 1858.

Löwenstern, Waldemar de. *Mémoires du général-major russe Baron de Löwenstern (1776–1858)*. Paris: A. Fontemoing, 1903.

Löwenstern, Waldemar de. "Zapiski generala V. I. Lewernsterna." *Russkaya starina* 1900–1901, vol. 103 (nos. 8–9), vol. 104 (nos. 10–12), vol. 105 (nos. 1–2).

Madariaga, Isabel de. *Russia in the Age of Catherine the Great*. London, 1981, 2003.

Maikov, P. *Ivan Ivanovich Betskoi: Opyt ego biografii*. St. Petersburg: Tip. Tovarischestva Obschestvennaia Pol'za, 1904.

Maistre, Joseph de. *Correspondence diplomatique de Joseph de Maistre (1811–1817)*. Paris, 1860.

Maistre, Joseph de. *Peterburgskie pis'ma*. St. Petersburg, 1995.

Marakuev, Mikhail. "Zapiski rostovtsa M. I. Marakueva." *Russkii arkhiv* 5 (1907): 107–129.

Marasinova, Elena. *Psikhologiia elity rossiiskogo dvorianstva poslednei treti XVIII veka: po materialam perepiski*. Moscow: ROSSPEN, 1999.

Martin, A. *Romantics, Reformers, Reactionaries: Russian Conservative Thought and Politics in the Reign of Alexander I*. DeKalb: Northern Illinois University Press, 1997.

Martin, Alexander M. *Enlightened Metropolis: Constructing Imperial Moscow, 1762–1855*. Oxford: Oxford University Press, 2013.

Martos, Aleksei. "Zapiski inzhenernogo ofitsera Martosa (o russko-turetskoi voine 1806–1812 gg. i Otechestvennoi voine 1812 g.)." *Russkii arkhiv* 7 (1893): 305–368; 8 (1893): 449–542.

Martynenko, Aleksey. *Tainaya missiya Kutuzova*. Kirov: KOGUP, 2011.

Mayevskii, Sergei. "Moi vek ili istoriya Sergeya Ivanovicha Mayevskogo, 1779–1848." *Russkaya starina* 8 (1873): 125–157; 9 (1873): 253–305.

McGrew, Roderick E. *Paul I of Russia, 1754–1801*. Oxford: Clarendon Press, 1992.

McPeak, Rick, and Donna Tussing Orwin, eds. *Tolstoy on War: Narrative Art and Historical Truth in* War and Peace. Ithaca, NY: Cornell University Press, 2012.

Melentyev, Vladimir. *Kutuzov v Peterburge*. Leningrad: Lenizdat, 1986.

Mel'nikova, Lyubov', and Kirill Nikitin. *Kutuzov, Spasitel' Rossii*. Moscow: AST-Press, 2018.

Mertvago, Dmitri. *Zapiski . . .* Moscow, 1867.

Mescheryakov, G., ed. *A. V. Suvorov: Sbornik dokumentov*. Moscow: Voennoe izdatel'stvo, 1949.

Metternich, Klemens von. *Memoirs . . .* New York: Harper & Brothers, 1881.

Miakinkov, Eugene. *War and Enlightenment in Russia: Military Culture in the Age of Catherine II*. Toronto: University of Toronto Press, 2020.

Mikaberidze, Alexander. *The Battle of Borodino: Napoleon Against Kutuzov*. Barnsley: Pen & Sword, 2007.

Mikaberidze, Alexander. *Napoleon's Great Escape: The Battle of the Berezina*. Barnsley: Pen & Sword, 2010.

Mikaberidze, Alexander. *Napoleon's Trial by Fire: The Burning of Moscow*. Barnsley: Pen & Sword, 2014.

Mikaberidze, Alexander, ed. *The Russian Eyewitness Accounts of the Campaign of 1807*. London: Pen & Sword, 2015.

Mikaberidze, Alexander, ed. *The Russian Eyewitness Accounts of the Campaign of 1812*. Barnsley: Pen & Sword, 2012.

Mikhailov, Oleg. *Kutuzov*. Moscow: Voenizdat, 1988; reprint, 2010.

Mikhailovskii-Danilevskii, A. "Iz vospominanii . . ." *Russkaya starina*, 1897, no. 6.

Mikhailovskii-Danilevskii, A. *Opisanie Otechestvennoi voiny v 1812 godu*. St. Petersburg, 1839.

Mikhailovskii-Danilevskii, A. *Polnoe sobranie sochinenii. Opisanie pervoi voiny imperatora Aleksandra s Napoleonom v 1805 godu. Opisanie vtoroj voiny imperatora Aleksandra s Napoleonom v 1806 i 1807 godah*. St. Petersburg, 1849.

Mikhailovskii-Danilevskii, A. *Polnoe sobranie sochinenii. Tom III: Opisanie Turetskoi voiny s 1806 do 1812 goda.* St. Petersburg: Tip. Shtaba Otd. Korpusal Vnutren. Strazhi., 1849.

Mikhailovskii-Danilevskii, A. *Vie du feld-maréchal Koutouzoff.* Paris, 1860.

Mikhailovskii-Danilevskii, A. "Zapiski . . ." *Russkaya starina*, 1893, no. 7.

Mikhailovskii-Danilevskii, A. "Zapiski A. I. Mikhailovskogo-Danilevskogo. 1812 god." *Istoricheskii vestnik*, 1890, no. 10.

Miloradovich, Mikhail. "O sdache Moskvy. Rasskaz zapisannyi v 1818 g. A. I. Mikhailovskim-Danilevskim." In *1812 god v vospominaniyakh sovremennikov*, 59–60. Moscow, 1995.

Milovidov, N. *Pamyati fel'dmarshala, svetleishego knyazya Mikhaila Illarionovicha Kutuzova Smolenskogo.* Moscow, 1912.

Mitarevskii, Nikolai. *Vospominaniya o voine 1812 goda.* Moscow: A. Mamontov, 1871.

Montefiore, Simon Sebag. *Prince of Princes: The Life of Potemkin.* London: Weidenfeld & Nicolson, 2001.

Munkov, N. *M. I. Kutuzov—Diplomat.* Moscow, 1962.

Muravyev, Alexander. *Sochineniya i pis'ma.* Irkutsk: Vostochno-Sibirsk. knizh. izd., 1986.

Muravyev, Alexander. "Zapiski." In *Dekabristy: Novye materialy*, 57–207. Moscow, 1955.

Muravyev, Nikolai. "Zapiski N. N. Murav'eva-Karskogo." *Russkii arkhiv* 9 (1885): 5–84; 10 (1885): 225–272; 11 (1885): 337–408.

Méneval, Claude-François Baron de. *Memoirs Illustrating the History of Napoleon from 1802 to 1815.* New York: D. Appleton and Company, 1894.

Nabokoff, Serge, and Sophie de Lastours. *Koutouzov: Le vainqueur de Napoléon.* Paris: Albin Michel, 1990.

Napoleon. *Correspondance de Napoleon Ier, publ. par ordre de l'Empereur Napoléon III.* 32 volumes. Paris: Henri Plon, 1863.

Napoleon. *Correspondance Générale.* 15 volumes. Paris: Fayard, 2004–2015.

Nechkina, M. *Mikhail Kutuzov.* Moscow: Voenizdat, 1944.

Nersesov, Yakov. *Genii voiny Kutuzov.* Moscow: Eksmo, 2013.

Nersesov, Yakov. *"Svet i Teni" Kutuzova.* 2 volumes. Moscow: Ridero, 2018.

Nicolson, Harold. *Napoleon 1812.* Cambridge, 1985.

Nikolai Mikhailovich, Grand Duke. *Graf Pavel Aleksandrovich Stroganov (1774–1817). Istoricheskoe izsledovanie epokhi Imperatora Aleksandra I.* St. Petersburg: Eskp. zagot. gos. bumag, 1903.

Nikolai Mikhailovich, Grand Duke. *Imperator Aleksandr I. Opyt istoricheskago izsledovaniya.* St. Petersburg: Eksp. zag. Gos. Bumag, 1912.

Nikolai Mikhailovich, Grand Duke, ed. *Imperator Aleksandr I. Opyt istoricheskago izsledovaniya.* Petrograd: Eksp. Zag. Gos. Bumag, 1914.

Nikolai Mikhailovich, Grand Duke, ed. *L'impératrice Elisabeth, épouse d'Alexandre Ier.* St. Petersburg, 1908.

Nikolai Mikhailovich, Grand Duke, ed. *Perepiska imperatora Aleksandra I s sestroi, velikoi knyaginei Ekaterinoj Pavlovnoi.* St. Petersburg: Eskp. Zag. Gos. Bumag, 1910.

Norov, Avraam. "Vospominaniya Avraama Sergeevicha Norova." *Russkii arkhiv* 3 (1881): 173–214.

Odenthal, Ivan. "Sto let nazad. Pis'ma I. P. Odentalya k A. Bulgakovu o peterburgskikh novostyah i slukhakh." *Russkaya starina* 5 (1912): 409–429; 6 (1912): 596–614; 7 (1912): 134–144; 8 (1912): 165–171; 9 (1912): 289–293; 10 (1912): 12–16; 11 (1912): 322–339; 12 (1912): 542–550; 5 (1913): 428–437.

Oksman, G. "Marsh-manevr M. I. Kutuzova v kampanii 1805 g." In *Polkovodets Kutuzov: sbornik statei,* edited by L. Beskrovnyi, 52–85. Moscow: Gospolitizdat, 1955.

Okunev, N. *Rassuzhdenie o bol'shikh voennykh deistviyakh, bitvakh i srazheniyakh, proiskhodivshikh pri vtorzhenii v Rossiyu v 1812 godu.* St. Petersburg, 1841.

Okunev, N. *Razbor glavnykh voennykh operatsii, bitv i srazhenii v Rossii v kampaniyu 1812 goda.* St. Petersburg, 1912.

O'Meara, Patrick. *The Russian Nobility in the Age of Alexander I.* London: Bloomsbury, 2019.

Orlov, Nikolai. *Shturm Izmaila Suvorovym v 1790 godu.* St. Petersburg: Trenke & Fusno, 1890.

Orlov, V. *M. I. Kutuzov.* Moscow: Goskinoizdat, 1942.

Otechestvennaya voina 1812 goda. Materially Voenno-Uchebnogo Arkhiva Glavnogo Shtaba. 21 volumes. St. Petersburg: Voen.-Uchen. Kom. Gl. Shtaba, 1905–1914.

Otroschenko, Yakov. *Zapiski generala Otroshenko (1800–1830).* Ebook. Moscow: Bratina, 2006.

Palmer, Alan. *Alexander I. Tsar of War and Peace.* London: Weidenfeld and Nicolson, 1974.

Palmer, Alan. *Napoleon in Russia.* London, 1967.

Panaev, V. *Istoricheskoe pokhval'noe slovo svetleishemu knyazyu Golenischevu-Kutuzovu Smolenskomu, chitannoe v S.-Peterburgskom voennom obshhestve lyubitelei slovesnosti. Dekabrya, 5 dnya 1821 goda.* St. Petersburg, 1823.

Parkinson, Roger. *The Fox of the North: The Life of Kutuzov, General of War and Peace.* New York: D. McKay, 1976.

Peskov, Aleksei. *Pavel I.* Moscow: Molodaya Gvardiya, 2016.

Petrov, A. "K biografii svetleishego knyazya Golenischeva-Kutuzova Smolenskogo." *Voennyi sbornik* 3 (1900): 1–13; 4 (1900): 231–244; 5 (1900): 96–103.

Petrov, A. *Vliyanie Turetskikh voin s poloviny proshlogo stoletiya na razvitie Russkago voennago iskusstva.* St. Petersburg, 1894.

Petrov, A. *Voina Rossii s Turtsiei 1806–1812 gg.* St. Petersburg: V. S. Balashev, 1887.

Petrov, A. *Voina Rossii s Turtsiei i pol'skimi konfederatami c 1769–1774 god.* St. Petersburg: Weimeyer, 1866.

Petrov, A. *Vtoraya turetskaya voina v tsarstvovanie Ekateriny II. 1787–1791.* 2 volumes. St. Petersburg, 1880.

Petrushevskii, A. *Generalisimus knyaz Suvorov.* St. Petersburg; Stasyulevich, 1884.

Pichichero, Christy. *The Military Enlightenment: War and Culture in the French Empire from Louis XIV to Napoleon.* Ithaca, NY: Cornell University Press, 2017.

Pis'ma 1812 goda M. A. Volkovoi k V. A. Lanskoi. Moscow, 1990.

Polevoi, N. *Russkie polkovodtsy ili zhizn' i podvigi rossiiskikh polkovodtsev ot vremeni imperatora Petra Velikogo do tsarstvovaniya imperatora Nikolaya I.* St. Petersburg: Zhernakov, 1845.

Polosin, I. "Kutuzov i pozhar Moskvy 1812 goda." *Istoricheskie zapiski* 34 (1950): 122–165.

Ponasenkov, Eugene. *Pervaya nauchnaya istoriya voiny 1812 goda.* Moscow: AST, 2017.

Popadichev, Ilya. *Vospominaniya suvorovskogo soldata*, edited by Major General D. Maslovskii. St. Petersburg: V. Berezovskii, 1899, electronic edition.

Popov, A. *Otechestvennaya voina 1812 goda. Ot Maloyaroslavtsa do Bereziny. Istoricheskoe issledovanie.* St. Petersburg, 1877. Also see Russkaya starina 1 (1877): 21–68; 2 (1877): 261–307; 3 (1877): 419–453; 4 (1877): 609–640; 6 (1877): 191–216; 9 (1877): 35–76; 10 (1877): 177–204; 11 (1877): 353–365.

Popov, Alexander. *Otechestvennaia voina 1812 goda. Snoshenia Rossii s inostrannymi derzhavami pered voinoiu 1812 goda.* Moscow: Grossman & Wendelstein, 1905.

Popov, Andrei. *Smolenskie bitvy.* 2 volumes. Moscow: Knizhnoe izdatelstvo, 2012.

Porter, Robert Ker. *Traveling Sketches in Russia and Sweden: During the Years 1805, 1806, 1807, 1808.* London, 1809.

Poussou, Jean-Pierre, Anne Mézin, and Yves Perret-Gentil, eds. *L'influence française en Russie au XVIIIe siècle.* Paris: Presses de L'université de Paris-Sorbonne, 2004.

Pozhar Moskvy. Po vospominaniyam i perepiske sovremennikov. 2 volumes. Moscow: Obrazovanie, 1911.

Protsenko, N. *Svetleishii knyaz Mikhail Larionovich Golenischev-Kutuzov Smolenskij, spasitel' Otechestva v 1812 godu ot polchisch Napoleona i s nim dvadtsati narodov.* Moscow, 1864.

Prozorovskii, Alexander. *Zapiski general-fel'dmarshala knyazya A. A. Prozorovskogo (1756–1776).* Moscow: Rossiiskii Arkhiv, 2004.

Puibusque, Louis Guillaume de. *Lettres sur la guerre en Russie en 1812.* Paris: Magimel, Anselin, et Pochard, 1817.

Punin, L. *Fel'dmarshal Kutuzov. Voenno-biograficheskii ocherk.* Moscow: Voennoe izdatel'stvo, 1957.

Puschin, Pavel. *Dnevnik Pavla Puschina, 1812–1814.* Leningrad: Leningrad University Press, 1987.

Radozhitskii, Ilya. *Pokhodnye zapiski artillerista s 1812 po 1816 god.* Moscow: Instit. Vost. Yazyk., 1835.

Ragsdale, Hugh. *Paul I: A Reassessment of His Life and Reign.* Pittsburgh: University of Pittsburgh Press, 1979.

Rayevskii, Nikolai. "Zapiski o 1812 gode." In Denis Davydov, *Zamechaniya na nekrologiyu N. N. Rayevskogo s pribavleniem ego sobstvennykh zapisok na nekotorye sobytiya voiny 1812 goda v koikh on uchavstvoval,* 33–89. Moscow, 1832.

Reimers, Heinrich Christoph von. *Reise der Russisch-Kaiserlichen Ausserordentlichen Gesandtschaft an die Othomanische Pforte im Jahr 1793.* St. Petersburg: Schnoorschen Buchdruckerei, 1803.

Remizov, S. *Osvoboditel' Moskvy M. I. Golenischev-Kutuzov Smolenskii.* St. Petersburg, 1867.

Rey, Marie-Pierre. *Alexander I: The Czar who Defeated Napoleon.* DeKalb: Northern Illinois University Press, 2016.

Rey, Marie-Pierre. 1812. *Histoire de la campagne de Russie.* Paris: Flammarion, 2021.

Rey, Marie-Pierre, and Thierry Lentz, ed. *1812. La Campagne de Russie: Histoire et postérités.* Paris: Perrin, 2012.

Riehn, Richard. *1812: Napoleon's Russian Campaign.* New York: McGraw-Hill, 1990.

Robinson, Paul. *Russian Conservatism.* Ithaca, NY: Cornell University Press, 2019.

Roosevelt, Priscilla. *Life on the Russian Country Estate: A Social and Cultural History.* New Haven, CT: Yale University Press, 1995.

Rostopchin, F. "Graf F. V. Rostopchin. Ego bumagi." *Russkii arkhiv* 1 (1909): 26–51.

Rostopchin, F. "Kratkoe opisanie proisshetviyam v Moskve v 1812 godu." *Russkii arkhiv* 7 (1896): 341–385.

Rostopchin, F. *Oeuvres inédites.* Paris, 1894.

Rostopchin, F. "Pisma grafa F. V. Rostopchina k Imperatoru Aleksandru Pavlovichu v 1812 godu." *Russkii arkhiv* 8 (1892): 419–446; 9 (1892): 519–565.

Rostopchin, F. "Pisma k svoei supruge v 1812 godu." *Russkii arkhiv* 8 (1901): 461–507.

Rostopchin, F. "Tysyacha vosemsot dvenadtsatyi god v zapiskakh grafa F. V. Rostopchina." *Russkaya starina* 12 (1889): 643–725.

Rostopchin, Fedor. *Okh, frantsuzy!* Edited by G. Ovchinnikov. Moscow: Sovetskaya Rossia, 1992.

Rothenberg, Gunther E. *The Napoleonic Wars.* London: Cassell, 1999.

Rustow, Wilhelm. *Der Krieg von 1805 in Deutschland und Italien.* Frauenfeld: Verlags-Comptoir, 1853.

Sablukov, Nikolai. "Reminiscences of the Court and Times of the Emperor Paul I of Russia up to the Period of His Death." *Fraser's Magazine for Town and Country* 72 (1865): 222–241, 302–327.

Scheremet, V., B. Nigmatulin, and I. Pestun. *Kutuzov: Zhizn', srrazheniya, pobedy.* Moscow: Nigma, 2012.

Schneid, Frederick C. *Napoleon's Conquest of Europe: The War of the Third Coalition.* Westport, CT: Praeger, 2005.

Schubert, Friedrich von. *Unter dem Doppeladler (Erinnerungen eines Deutschen in russischem Offzieersdienst 1789–1814).* Stuttgart: K. F. Koehler Verlag, 1962.

Ségur, Louis Philippe de. *Mémoires ou souvenirs et anecdotes.* Paris: Alexis Eymery, 1826, 1859.

Ségur, Philippe-Paul de. *Histoire de Napoléon et de la grande-armée pendant l'année 1812.* Paris: Baudoin Frères, 1824.

Ségur, Philippe-Paul. *Histoire et mémoires.* Paris: Didot Fréres, 1873.

Shaw, Stanford J. *History of the Ottoman Empire and Modern Turkey.* Cambridge: Cambridge University Press, 1976.

Shefskii, Harold K. "Tolstoy's Vindication of General Kutuzov as Subtext in *War and Peace.*" *Russian History* 22, no. 1 (1995): 79–90.

Sherbatov, Alexander. *General-fel'dmarshal Knyaz Paskevich, ego zhizn' i deyatel'nost.* St. Petersburg: V. A. Berezovskii, 1888.

Shil'der, Nikolai. *Imperator Aleksandr pervyi. Ego zhizn' i tsarstvovanie.* 4 volumes. St. Petersburg: A. S. Suvorin, 1897–1898.

Shil'der, Nikolai. *Imperator Pavel Pervyi.* St. Petersburg: A. S. Suvorin, 1901.

Shishkov, Aleksey. *Kutuzov.* Moscow: Veche, 2012.

Shishkov, Alexander. *Zapiski, mneniya i perepiska Admirala A. S. Shishkova.* Edited by N. Kiselev and Yu. Samarin. Berlin: B. Behr's Buchhandlung, 1870.

Shishkov, N. "Vospominaniya o knyaze Smolenskom M. I. Golenischeve-Kutuzove." *Russkii arkhiv* 3 (1866): 460–474.

Shishov, A. *Kutuzov, Fel'dmarshal pobedy.* Moscow: Veche, 2012.

Shishov, A. *Kutuzov. Fel'dmarshal velikoi imperii.* Moscow: Olma Press, 2006.

Shishov, A. *Neizvestnyi Kutuzov.* Moscow: Olma-Press, 2001.

Shvedov, Sergei. "Deistviya M. I. Kutuzova v Berezinskoi operatsii." http://www.reenactor.ru/ARH/PDF/Schvedov_02.pdf.

Simanskii, A. *Pis'ma L. A. Simanskogo k materi ego i bratyam po vystuplenii ego v pokhod v byvshuyu s frantsuzami voinu 1812, 1813, 1814 i 1815 godov.* St. Petersburg, 1912.

Sinel'nikov, Filip. *Zhizn', voennye i politicheskie deyaniya ego svetlosti general-fel'dmarshala knyazya Mikhaila Larionovicha Golenischeva-Kutuzova Smolenskogo s dostovernym opisaniem chastnoi ili domashnei ego zhizni . . . i s prisovokupleniem anekdotov, gde viden duh sego velikogo muzha.* 6 volumes. St. Petersburg, 1813–1814.

Smitt, Friedrich von. *Suworow und Polens untergang.* Leipzig: C. F. Winter, 1858.

Sokolov, O. *Austerlitz. Napoleon, Rossiya i Evropa, 1799–1805.* 2 volumes. Moscow: Imperia Istorii, 2006.

Sokolov, Oleg. *Bitva dvukh imperii, 1805–1812.* St. Petersburg: Astrel, 2012.

Stankevich, Afanasii. *Kriticheskii razbor kampanii 1809 goda. Voenno-istoricheskoe issledovanie.* St. Petersburg, 1861.

Steinheil, Vladimir. *Sochineniya i pis'ma. Tom 1. Zapiski i pis'ma.* Irkutsk: Vostochno-Sibirskoe knizhnoe izd., 1985.

Steinheil, Vladimir. *Zapiski kasatel'no sostavleniya i samogo pokhoda sanktpeterburgskogo opolcheniya protiv vragov otechestva v 1812 i 1813 godakh.* St. Petersburg: V. Plavil'shikov, 1814.

Struve, Johann Christian von. *Reise eines jungen Russen von Wien über Jassy in die Crimm und ausführliches Tagebuch der im Jahr 1793 von St. Petersburg nach Constantinopel.* Gotha: Ettinger, 1801.

Stutterheim, Karl von. *La Bataille d'Austerlitz, par un militaire témoin de la journée du 2 décembre 1805.* Paris: Fain, 1806.

Suvorov, V. *Svetleishii knyaz' Smolenskii, fel'dmarshal Mikhail Illarionovich Golenishchev-Kutuzov i ego sovremenniki: Istoricheskii ocherk zhizni polkovodtsa i ego epokhi.* Moscow: I. D. Sytin, 1896.

Tarle, E. *How Mikhail Kutuzov Defeated Napoleon*. London: Soviet War News, 1943.

Tarle, E. *Napoleon*. Moscow: Gospolitizdat, 1939, 1941, 1942.

Tarle, E. *Napoleon*. Moscow: Molodaya Gvardiya, 1936.

Tarle, E. *Nashestvie Napoleona na Rossiu*. Moscow: OGIZ, 1938; revised edition, 1943. English edition: *Napoleon's Invasion of Russia, 1812*. New York: Oxford University Press, 1942.

Tarle, Eugene. *Mikhail Kutuzov*. Moscow: Voenizdat, 1932.

Tartakovskii, A., ed., *1812 god . . . Voennye dnevniki*. Moscow: Sovetskaya Rossiya, 1990.

Tartakovskii, A. *Nerazgadannyj Barklai. Legendy i byl'*. Moscow, 1996.

Tartakovskii, Andrei, ed. *1812 god v vospominaniyakh sovremennikov*. Moscow: Nauka, 1985.

Thiard, Auxonne-Marie-Théodose de. *Souvenirs diplomatiques et militaires du général Thiard*. Paris: Flammarion, 1900.

Thiers, Adolphe. *History of the Consulate and the Empire of France Under Napoleon*. Philadelphia: Claxton, Remsen & Haffelfinger, 1879.

Toll, Karl Friedrich von. *Denkwürdigkeiten aus dem Leben des Kaiserl. russ. Generals von der der Infanterie Carl Friedrich Grafen von Toll*. Edited by Theodor von Bernhardi. 2 volumes. Leipzig: Otto Wigand, 1856.

Toll, Karl Friedrich von. "Opisanie bitvy pri sele Borodine, proiskhodivshei mezhdu rossiiskoyu imperatorskoyu armiei pod predvoditel'stvom general ot infanterii knyazya Golenishheva-Kutuzova i frantsuzskoyu soedinennoyu armieyu iz voisk vsekh derzhav Zapadnoi Evropy, sostavlennoyu pod lichnym predvoditel'stvom imperatora Napoleona." *Otechestvennye zapiski* 28 (1822): 145–193; 29 (1822): 309–354.

Tolstoy, Fedor. *Zapiski grafa Fedora Petrovicha Tolstogo*. Moscow: RGGU, 2001.

Tolstoy, Leo. *War and Peace*. Translated by Louise and Aylmer Maude. Oxford: Oxford University Press, 2010.

Totfalushin, V. "M. B. Barclay de Tolly v dvoryanskoi istoriografii Otechestvennoi voiny 1812 goda." *Istoriograficheskii sbornik* 14 (1989): 35–49.

Totfalushin, V. "M. B. Barclay de Tolly v otechestvennoi istoriografii 1861–1917 godov." *Istoriograficheskii sbornik* 17 (1998): 69–79.

Totfalushin, Viktor. *M. B. Barclay de Tolly v Otechestvennoi voine 1812 g.* Saratov: SGU, 1991.

Totfalushin, V. "Voennyi sovet v Filyah po romanu L. N. Tolstogo «Voina i mir» i istoricheskaya deistvitel'nost'" in *Sobytiya Otechestvennoi voiny 1812 goda na territorii Kaluzhskoi gubernii. Problemy izucheniya. Istochniki. Pamyatniki.* Maloyaroslavets: Maloyaroslavets. tip, 1995, 86–91.

Totfalushin, V. "Zhizn' i deyatel'nost' Kaisarova." In *Chetyre veka: sb. st., posvyashh. 400-letiyu Saratova*, 190–208. Saratov: SGU, 1991.

Tsareubiistvo 11 marta 1801 goda. Zapiski uchastnikov i sovremennikov. St. Petersburg: A. S. Suvorin, 1908.

Troitskii, Nikolai. *1812. Velikii god Rossii*. Moscow, 1988.

Troitskii, Nikolai. *Fel'dmarshal Kutuzov: mify i fakty*. Moscow, 2002.

Troyat, Henry. *Alexander of Russia: Napoleon's Conqueror*. London: New English Library, 1984.

Tselorungo, Dmitri. *Ofitsery Russkoi armii—uchastniki Borodinskogo srazheniya*. Moscow: Kalita, 2002.

Tuchkov, Sergei. *Zapiski Sergeya Alekseyevicha Tuchkova*. St. Petersburg, 1908.

Uxkull, Boris von. *Arms and the Woman: The Diaries of Baron Boris von Uxkull, 1812–1819*. London, 1966.

Val'kovich, A. *Zolotoi vek Rossiiskoi gvardii*. 2 volumes. Moscow, 2010.

Vandal, Albert. *Napoléon et Alexandre 1er: l'alliance russe sous le 1er Empire*. 3 volumes. Paris: Plon-Nourrit, 1894–1897.

Vasil'chikov, Alexander. *Les Razoumowski. Tome II. Le Comte André Razoumowski. Deuxième partie, 1801–1806*. Halle: Tausch & Grosse, 1893.

Vasiliev, A. "Boi pri Shengrabene." *Imperator* 9 (2006): 41–49.

Vasiliev, A. "Srazhenie za Maloyaroslavets 12 oktyabrya 1812 goda." In *Ot tarutino do Maloyaroslavtsa: k 190-letiyu Maloyaroslavetskago srazheniya*. Kaluga: Zolotaya Alleya, 2002. http://www.museum.ru/1812/Library/Mmnk/2002_9.html.

Viskovatov, A. *Kratkaya istoriya 1-go kadetskogo korpusa*. St. Petersburg, 1832.

Vladimirov, V. *Kak Kutuzov prognal frantsuzov i za chto Suvorov khvalil ego Ekaterine*. Moscow: Vako, 2016.

Voenskii, K. *Otechestvennaya voina 1812 g. v pis'makh sovremennikov. Materialy Voenno-uchenogo arkhiva*. St. Petersburg, 1911.

Voenskii, K. *Priezd Loristona k Kutuzovu v Tarutinskii lager' 23 sentyabrya 1812 g. Neizdannoe pis'mo ochevidtsa*. Petrograd, 1915.

Voina 1813 goda. Materialy voenno-uchenogo arkhiva. 3 volumes. St. Petersburg: Otd. general-kvartirmeistera Gl. upr. general'nogo shtaba, 1914–1917.

Volkonskii, Sergei. *Zapiski Sergia Grigorievicha Volkonskogo (Dekabrista)*. St. Petersburg, 1901.

Voronovskii, V. *Otechestvennaya voina 1812 g. v predelakh Smolenskoi gubernii*. St. Petersburg: A. Suvorin, 1912.

Vyazemskii, Peter. "Staraya zapisnaya knizhka." In *Polnoe sobranie sochinenii Knyazya P. A. Vyazemskago*, volume 8. St. Petersburg: M. Stasyulevich, 1883.

Weigel [Vigel'], Filip. *Zapiski . . .* 2 volumes. Moscow: Krug, 1928. Also see *Vospominaniya Filippa Filippovicha Vigelya*. Moscow: Katkov, 1864.

Wilson, Robert. *Narrative of Events during the Invasion of Russia by Napoleon Bonaparte and the Retreat of the French Army*. London: John Murray, 1860.

Wilson, Robert. *Private Diary of Travels, Personal Services, and Public Events during Mission and Employment with the European Armies in the Campaigns of 1812, 1813, 1814*. London: John Murray, 1861.

Wirtschafter, Elise Kimerling. *Russia's Age of Serfdom, 1649–1861*. New York: Wiley, 2008.

Wirtschafter, Elise Kimerling. *Social Identity in Imperial Russia*. DeKalb: Northern Illinois University Press, 1997.

Wolzogen und Neuhaus, Ludwig. *Memoiren des Königlich Preussischen Generals der Infanterie Ludwig Freiherrn von Wolzogen*. Leipzig, 1851.

Wormeley, Katharine Prescott, ed. *The Prince de Ligne: His Memoirs, Letters, and Miscellaneous Papers*. Boston: Hardy, Pratt and Company, 1902.

Württemberg, Eugen von. *Aus dem Leben des kaiserlich-russischen Generals der Infanterie Prinzen Eugen von Württemberg*. Berlin: Hempel, 1862.

Württemberg, Eugen von. *Erinnerungen aus dem Feldzuge des Jahres 1812 in Russland von dem Herzog Eugen von Württemberg*. Breslau, 1846.

Württemberg, Eugène de. *Journal des campagnes du prince de Wurtemberg, 1812–1814*. Edited by Gabriel Fabry. Paris: Chapelot, 1907.

Yermolov, Alexey. *The Czar's General: The Memoirs of a Russian General in the Napoleonic Wars*. Translated and edited by Alexander Mikaberidze. Welwyn Garden City: Ravenhall Books, 2005.

Zamoyski, Adam. *1812: Napoleon's Fatal March on Moscow*. London: Harper Collins, 2004.

Zemtsov, V. *Bitva pri Moskve-reke: armiya Napoleona v Borodinskom srazhenii*. Moscow, 2001.

Zemtsov, V. *Russkii posol v Parizhe knyaz' A. B. Kurakin: khronika rokovykh let*. Moscow: ROSSPEN, 2019.

Zemtsov, Vladimir. *1812 god: Pozhar Moskvy*. Moscow: Kniga, 2010.

Zemtsov, V., and A. Popov. *Borodino: severnyj flang*. Moscow: Kniga, 2008.

Zemtsov, V. and A. Popov. *Borodino: tsentr*. Moscow: Kniga, 2009.

Zemtsov, V. and A. Popov. *Borodino: yuzhnyi flang*. Moscow: Kniga, 2010.

Zherve, V. *Slavnyi vozhd' 1812 goda Kutuzov*. Moscow, 1912.

Zherve, K., and V. Stroev. *Istoricheskii ocherk Vtorogo Kadetskago Korpusa, 1712–1912*. St. Petersburg: Tip. Trenke, 1912.

Zhilin, P. *Kontrnastuplenie Kutuzova v 1812 godu*. Moscow: Voenizdat, 1950.

Zhilin, P. *Kontrnastuplenie russkoi armii v 1812 godu*. Moscow: Voenizdat, 1953.

Zhilin, P. *Kutuzov. Zhizn' i polkovodcheskaya deyatel'nost'*. Moscow: Voennoe Izdatel'stvo, 1978.

Zhilin, P. *Pazgrom turetskoi armii v 1811 godu*. Moscow: Voenizdat, 1952.

Zhirkevich, Ivan. "Zapiski 1789–1848 gg." *Russkaya starina* IX, no. 2 (1874): 207–244; X (1874): 633–666; XI (1874): 411–450, 642–664.

Zhizn' i voennye podvigi general-fel'dmarshala, svetleishego knyazya Mikhaila Illarionovicha Golenischeva-Kutuzova Smolenskogo. S opisaniem rodoslovnoj ego familii. St. Petersburg, 1813.

Zhmodikov, Alexander and Yurii Zhmodikov, *Tactics of the Russian Army in the Napoleonic Wars*. West Chester, OH: The Nafziger Collection, 2003.

Zhurnal voennykh deistvii armei Eya imperatorskago Velichestva 1770 goda. St. Petersburg: War College, 1771.

Zhurnaly Komiteta ministrov, 1810–1812 gg. St. Petersburg: V. Bezobrazov, 1891.

For the benefit of digital users, indexed terms that span two pages (e.g., 52–53) may, on occasion, appear on only one of those pages.

Note: Page references followed by a "*t*" indicate table; "*f*" indicate figure.